Auditing

*A Business
Risk Approach*

8e

Larry E. Rittenberg
University of Wisconsin–Madison

Karla M. Johnstone
University of Wisconsin–Madison

Audrey A. Gramling
Kennesaw State University

SOUTH-WESTERN
CENGAGE Learning

Australia • Brazil • Japan • Korea • Mexico • Singapore • Spain • United Kingdom • United States

SOUTH-WESTERN
CENGAGE Learning

Auditing: A Business Risk Approach, 8e

Larry E. Rittenberg, Karla M. Johnstone and Audrey A. Gramling

Vice President of Editorial, Business:
Jack W. Calhoun

Vice President/Editor-in-Chief: Rob Dewey

Senior Acquisitions Editor: Matt Filimonov

Senior Developmental Editor: Craig Avery

Editorial Assistant: Ann Mazzaro

Marketing Manager: Natalie Livingston

Marketing Coordinator: Libby Shipp

Content Project Management: PreMediaGlobal

Media Editor: Bryan England

Manufacturing Coordinator: Doug Wilke

Production Service: PreMediaGlobal

Copyeditor: PreMediaGlobal

Senior Art Director: Stacy Shirley

Cover Designer: Stuart Kunkler, triARTis Communications

Cover Image: iStock Photo/Shutterstock

For product information and technology assistance, contact us at
Cengage Learning Customer & Sales Support, 1-800-354-9706

For permission to use material from this text or product,
submit all requests online at **www.cengage.com/permissions**

Further permissions questions can be emailed to
permissionrequest@cengage.com

Library of Congress Control Number: 2011926004

ISBN-13: 978-0-538-47624-9

ISBN-10: 0-538-47624-9

South-Western

5191 Natorp Boulevard
Mason, OH 45040
USA

Cengage Learning products are represented in Canada by Nelson Education, Ltd.

For your course and learning solutions, visit **www.cengage.com.**

Purchase any of our products at your local college store or at our preferred online store **www.cengagebrain.com.**

Printed in the United States of America
1 2 3 4 5 6 7 15 14 13 12 11

Dedication

We dedicate this book to our families who encourage and support us through many hours of development, to our students who inspire us to always improve, to our mentors who guide us, to our professional friends who continue to educate us, and to our colleagues who challenge us.

Larry E. Rittenberg
Karla M. Johnstone
Audrey A. Gramling

Preface

The auditing environment continues its pattern of escalating change since we introduced the seventh edition just two years ago. Auditors continue to face a very high standard of responsibility to the public. The Public Company Accounting Oversight Board (PCAOB), the U.S. Securities and Exchange Commission (SEC), the American Institute of Public Accountants (AICPA) and the International Auditing and Assurance Standards Board (IAASB) have emerged as major players in regulating the profession both domestically and internationally. Audit firms are challenged to find efficient ways to integrate risk and control analysis into the design of audits of financial statements and internal control over financial reporting. In our various professional roles, we have been at the center of this change, and we have infused the eighth edition with our unique knowledge of risk, audit, and control as it relates to performing the integrated audit.

In the first edition, we raised two fundamental questions that ought to be asked of all textbooks:

- Does the textbook cover the fundamental elements that all students should know?
- Does the textbook facilitate learning?

Since then, we have come to increasingly emphasize two additional questions:

- Does the textbook encourage students to develop a judgment and decision-making process that facilitates their growth in an ever-changing audit and business environment?
- Does the textbook highlight the importance of ethical decision making and professional skepticism, and does it facilitate students' developments in those areas?

We encourage each potential adopter to evaluate this text, as well as others, on these dimensions. Users will find that the eighth edition continues to address these fundamental questions in a way that facilitates student learning and application of fundamental concepts. Since the first edition, we have believed that students must understand and develop frameworks for decision-making—and then apply judgment within those frameworks. Consequently, we have worked hard to focus on important conceptual frameworks, while designing end-of-chapter material to challenge students to think and apply such frameworks. A conceptual basis, reinforced with practical application, should provide students with skills for success in their professional careers.

Major Themes in the Eighth Edition

The eighth edition maintains the themes developed previously, with a commitment to update the text to reflect the evolving nature of the auditing profession and the environment in which it operates. The eighth edition:

1. **Emphasizes professional judgment, including professional skepticism and decision-making.** We recognize that students are entering a professional world in which they are expected, very early in their careers, to make complex judgments and decisions for which there are significant real-world consequences. As such, we include a *professional decision-making framework*, along with end-of-chapter materials that reinforce that framework throughout the entire text. Further, each chapter begins with a *Professional Judgment in Context* feature highlighting chapter-relevant professional judgments, along with questions that challenge students to apply those judgments as they read the chapter. In addition, the eighth edition adds new material on professional skepticism (Chapter 3), including a discussion of the role of professional skepticism in auditors' judgments and the relationship between auditor independence and professional skepticism. We reinforce this theme with end-of-chapter materials that emphasize the importance of professional skepticism.
2. **Includes a chapter (Chapter 18) on particularly complex auditing judgments including (1) materiality, (2) error correction, (3) evaluation of internal control deficiencies, (4) evaluating the quality of internal audit functions, (5) audits of fair value, and (6)** *new* **sustainability reporting.**

The sections on *auditing fair values* and *sustainability reporting*, along with end-of-chapter materials, are particularly relevant to the current financial crisis and recent developments in practice. The chapter integrates many of the concepts developed throughout the text and presents the theme that virtually all account balances are subject to realizability, estimation, or fair value considerations.

3. **Includes a comprehensive case in the end-of-chapter problems that illustrates chapter-relevant concepts within the context of two companies, Ford Motor Company and Toyota Motor Corporation.** Each chapter's section of the case requires students to access these companies' 10-Ks, 20-Fs, proxy statements, and 8-Ks so that students can gain an appreciation for the practical application of the concepts that are being emphasized throughout the textbook. Topics addressed include gaining an understanding of the auto industry, corporate governance elements, risk assessment, planning considerations, analytical procedures, and materiality judgments, among others.

4. **Incorporates continuing changes in the regulatory environment and standards-setting.** The regulatory environment continues to evolve, and we have revised the text to keep pace with associated changes. The text covers *new standards on risk assessment and audit planning*, the role of the PCAOB in setting standards and performing inspections of audit firms, and the important role of the AICPA's Auditing Standards Board in setting standards for nonpublic companies. The eighth edition includes a comparison of auditing standards from the AICPA, the PCAOB, and the IAASB, along with selected references to relevant professional guidance at the end of each chapter that highlight alternative sources of guidance on chapter-relevant topics. Importantly, we incorporate end-of-chapter materials relating to actual PCAOB inspection reports and enforcement actions and SEC AAERs for areas that demonstrate the need for careful analysis and reasoning. We have also integrated these audit quality related issues and recommendations into the text. Further, we have *expanded coverage to introduce international auditing standards where relevant*.

5. **Emphasizes the importance of corporate governance in relation to auditing.** Auditing is a critical element in the functioning of the capital market system as it is intended to serve the public interest. The eighth edition explores corporate governance as a foundation to better understand the unique role of the financial statement and internal control audit as an important component of corporate governance. As an example of serving the public interest, we have included excerpts from investor letters to the FASB that illustrate user needs to facilitate better understanding of materiality from a stakeholder perspective. Chapter 2 discusses the parties involved in corporate governance and their respective roles, and principles of effective corporate governance, and it describes events of the last decade that have had a significant effect on the evolution of corporate governance practices. In addition, Chapter 2 also provides details on the responsibilities of audit committees, along with principles of effective audit committees and required communications between the audit firm and the audit committee.

6. **Provides a framework and a demonstration of an integrated audit.** Building on changes made in the seventh edition, we illustrate how to conduct an integrated audit throughout chapters that describe specific transaction cycles, including *new material on cycle-specific relevant assertions, cycle-specific critical controls, and cycle-specific evidence based on results of inherent and control risk assessments*. Our discussion of integrated audit concepts emphasizes that the auditor's evidence decisions are based on the identified business and inherent risks, the effectiveness of the controls designed to mitigate those risks, and the assessment as to which assertions are most relevant for an account balance.

7. **Continues practice cases and ACL audit software.** Practice cases and the ACL software, along with exercises from the previous edition, are included in the current edition.

Major Changes to the Eighth Edition

Students entering the profession must find ways to demonstrate their excellence in professional judgment and decision-making processes, appropriate application of ethical standards and practices, and knowledge of controls and auditing to add value to their audit engagements. While this edition retains the basic structure of previous editions, there have been major changes, including the following:

1. **Substantially increased emphasis on integrated discussion of auditing standards from U.S. and international audit standard-setting bodies.** Chapters now feature *comparisons of standards issued by the AICPA, the PCAOB, and the IAASB*. Further, each chapter includes an indexed listing of auditing standards, U.S. and international, relevant to the topics in each chapter.

2. **Inclusion of an integrated practical case across most chapters in the book that relies on student analysis of the *2010 10-Ks, 20-Fs, proxy statements, and 8-Ks from Ford Motor Company and Toyota Motor Corporation*.** We built end-of-chapter homework for individual learners and groups that use these new, real-life corporate disclosures in order to expose students to the practical applications of the theoretical concepts from each chapter.

3. **Expanded discussion of corporate governance.** The eighth edition expands discussion of corporate governance and emphasizes it as a foundation for high-quality financial reporting and auditing. A *substantially revised Chapter 2* discusses the parties involved in corporate governance and their respective roles, along with principles of effective corporate governance, and it describes events of the last decade that have had a significant effect on the evolution of corporate governance practices. In addition, the revised Chapter 2 provides details on the responsibilities of audit committees, along with principles of effective audit committees and required communications between the audit firm and the audit committee.

4. **Updated to reflect new auditing standards.** The AICPA, the PCAOB, and the IAASB have all recently issued *new auditing standards*, and the eighth edition reflects all of those changes. For example, the eighth edition now includes discussion of AS No. 6 (*Evaluating Consistency of Financial Statements*), AS No. 7 (*Engagement Quality Review*), AS No. 8 (*Audit Risk*), AS No. 9 (*Audit Planning*), AS No. 10 (*Supervision of the Audit Engagement*), AS No. 11 (*Consideration of Materiality in Planning and Performing an Audit*), AS No. 12 (*Identifying and Assessing Risks of Material Misstatement*), AS No. 13 (*The Auditor's Responses to the Risks of Material Misstatement*), AS No. 14 (*Evaluating Audit Results*), and AS No. 15 (*Audit Evidence*). The eighth edition also *reflects changes relevant to the AICPA's and the IAASB's clarity project*.

5. *NEW* **end-of-chapter academic research cases.** Each chapter includes reference to a relevant academic research article in addition to suggestions on where to locate it. Based on that article, each academic research case requires the student to answer the following types of questions: (1) What is the issue being addressed in the paper? (2) Why is this issue important to practicing auditors? (3) What factors are identified as contributing to this issue? (4) What are the implications of these findings for audit quality or audit practice on the audit profession? (5) What research methodology is used to form the basis for the conclusions? (6) What are the limitations of the research? The authors have used many of these research articles in class discussions and find that the discussion broadens the learning experience of students and illustrates to them the potential relevance of academic research.

6. **Articulation of a decision-making framework that complements the existing discussion on ethical decision-making.** We supplement the existing end-of-chapter materials with *new cases* that require students to apply the decision-making framework. Further, we expand the number of existing cases that emphasize ethical decision-making presented in the text. Each chapter begins with a *current Professional Judgment in Context feature* that requires students to think about a real-life professional decision associated with that chapter. Practical examples that relate to the recent financial crisis are featured in most chapters. End-of-chapter homework items follow up on the questions initially addressed in the *Professional Judgment in Context* features.

7. **Addition of material on sustainability reporting in Chapter 18.** A *new section on sustainability reporting* defines "sustainability" and articulates the auditors' role in providing assurance on management sustainability reports. It describes information that organizations provide to external users about their sustainability efforts. It also discusses how organizations provide assurance that their sustainability disclosures are deemed credible and reliable by external users.

Featured Pedagogical Elements

The eighth edition features such pedagogical elements as:

1. *Professional Judgment in Context* **feature** that requires students to think about a current real-life professional decision associated with that chapter.
2. **New iconography** helps instructors to locate end-of-chapter problems that emphasize key elements by including graphic callouts aside problems featuring these important judgments, issues, and activities.

Professional Skepticism

Ethics

Fraud

International

Internet

Group Activity

3. **A chapter-opening** *Audit Opinion Formulation Process* **diagram** helps students identify the major steps in the audit process, and how those steps relate to specific chapters and the relationships among chapters within that process. Students viewing this process are able to see how each chapter fits into the overall context of the materials covered throughout the text. The process is depicted at the beginning of each chapter as follows:

I. Assessing Client Acceptance and Retention Decisions CHAPTER 4	II. Understanding the Client CHAPTERS 2, 4–6, and 9	III. Obtaining Evidence about Controls and Determining the Impact on the Financial Statement Audit CHAPTERS 5–14 and 18	IV. Obtaining Substantive Evidence about Account Assertions CHAPTERS 7–14 and 18	V. Wrapping Up the Audit and Making Reporting Decisions CHAPTERS 15 and 16

The Auditing Profession, Regulation, and Corporate Governance CHAPTERS 1 and 2	Decision-Making, Professional Conduct, and Ethics CHAPTER 3	Professional Liability CHAPTER 17

Through this process diagram, we illustrate *three fundamental environmental features* that affect the conduct of the audit process:

1. Principles and rules governing the auditing profession, the regulatory environment, and the role of corporate governance
2. The importance of decision making, professional conduct, and ethics
3. Professional liability

Within this general context, we present a *five-step audit opinion formulation process* that includes:

Step 1. Assessing client acceptance and retention decisions.
Step 2. Understanding the client.
Step 3. Obtaining evidence about controls.
Step 4. Obtaining substantive evidence about account balances.
Step 5. Completing the audit.

Organization of the Eighth Edition

The eighth edition is organized as follows:

Chapters 1–3: Understanding Auditor Responsibilities. *Chapters 1 and 2* discuss the importance of audit and assurance services in the context of corporate governance and the economic market place. *Chapter 3* introduces a professional decision-making framework and contains a discussion of ethical principles that goes beyond traditional "rules-based" definitions of ethics and instead explores theories of ethical decision-making. Professional skepticism is introduced in Chapter 3 and each subsequent chapter touches on this important topic and includes end-of-chapter materials designed to illustrate the concept and judgmental application of professional skepticism.

Chapters 4–6: Understanding the Risk Approach to Auditing and Understanding the Integral Role of Internal Controls. *Chapter 4* introduces risk concepts and links them to internal control. The auditor's understanding of risk facilitates the evaluation of internal controls, which is covered in *Chapter 5*. We extend the discussion of internal control in *Chapter 6* and demonstrate how the internal control evaluation extends into the performance of an audit.

Chapters 7–9: Understanding Audit Concepts and Tools. *Chapter 7* develops the concepts related to audit evidence, and includes the PCAOB standard on audit documentation. *Chapter 8* incorporates concepts involving various tools used to gather audit evidence, including audit sampling, computer audit techniques, and substantive analytical procedures. *Chapter 9* provides an understanding of factors that make fraud more likely to occur, going beyond a listing of the "red flags" literature to present the fraud risk model. Numerous illustrations from corporate frauds are used to illustrate fraud risks and audit approaches necessary to respond to those risks. Extensive discussion is included that reflects the recent economic crisis as it relates to fraud.

Chapters 10–14: Performing Audits Using the Transaction Cycle Approach. These chapters focus on the application of the concepts developed earlier for assessing risk, identifying, and testing controls designed to address those risks, and using substantive approaches to testing account balances. These chapters highlight the importance of fraud-related substantive procedures. Each chapter includes a step-by-step approach to conducting an integrated audit within each particular transaction cycle. Further, students are asked to develop audit programs that identify needed controls in these environments, given risks typical to those environments. The coverage is expanded to cover high-risk areas that have been overlooked on some audit engagements, including the need to review material journal entries. We also expand the coverage of subjective estimates via an in-depth discussion of auditing goodwill and fixed asset impairments. Further, we expand coverage of substantive analytical procedures relevant to each of the transaction cycles.

Chapters 15–16: Completing the Audit and Auditor Reporting. *Chapter 15* examines the various tasks that auditors need to complete prior to issuing the audit report, including topics such as going-concern judgments, management representation letters, loss contingencies, accounting estimates, concurring partner review, and subsequent events (among others). *Chapter 16* discusses audit and assurance reports and provides a broad overview of fundamental precepts that underscore all reporting. We provide examples of various types of audit reports, including reports on financial statements and reports on the effectiveness of internal control over financial reporting.

Chapter 17: Managing Audit Firm Risk and Minimizing Liabilities. Legal liability remains important. However, *Chapter 17* also considers the added importance of the regulatory environment and the need for auditors to operate in an environment in which the principles may not uniformly apply for each jurisdiction in which the auditor performs services. Further, we discuss various approaches to minimizing liability exposure.

Chapter 18: Complex Auditing Judgments. This chapter features coverage of various topics of both perennial importance and emerging contemporary interest, including discussions of (1) materiality judgments, (2) error correction, (3) the evaluation of significant deficiencies versus material weaknesses in internal control, (4) evaluating the quality of internal audit activities, including an evaluation of factors that should be considered by the external auditor when relying on or otherwise using the work performed by internal auditors, (5) auditing accounting estimates as well as evaluating the proper application of fair value within the financial statements, and (6) *new* sustainability reporting.

Ford and Toyota Case. Starting in Chapter 2, we introduce a case that extends throughout the textbook on Ford Motor Company and Toyota Motor Corporation. In Chapter 2 we discuss how we have conducted this case in our own classes. The textbook website contains relevant background resources such as company financial reports and regulatory filings. Using this case enables students to see the practical application of theoretical concepts using companies that are familiar, are high-profile (in the news), and vary in terms of their financial condition and U.S. versus international domicile.

New: **Academic Research Cases.** Many instructors use our textbook for both their undergraduate and graduate auditing classes. The **new** academic research cases are ideal for instructors who wish to extend students' theoretical understanding of the chapter concepts, particularly for graduate-level classes.

Biltrite Bicycle Case. Modules of this practice case are embedded in the end-of-chapter material of related chapters. Spreadsheet worksheets needed to complete the case appear on the Student Resources page of **CengageBrain** (**www.cengagebrain.com**).

ACL Cases Appendix. The ACL Appendix contains an overview of the basic functions of ACL followed by a brief, illustrated tutorial to help students learn how to use the basic features of *Version 9* of the *ACL Desktop Education Edition.* These are followed by four ACL cases:

1. **Pell Grants,** a fraud investigation case related to this student grant program
2. **Benford's Law case,** a fraud case dealing with employee expense reimbursements and the application of Benford's Law of numbers
3. **NSG Accounts Receivable,** which includes an audit program of procedures for which the students can use ACL and analyze the results
4. **NSG Inventory,** which requires students to develop an audit program and then perform those procedures and analyze the results

Download the ACL Case Appendix—and the data files for these cases—from the Student Resources page of **CengageBrain (www.cengagebrain.com)**.

Suitability for Alternate Presentation Formats

The eighth edition is designed to fit virtually all one-semester undergraduate courses in auditing or assurance services. The end-of-chapter Ford and Toyota cases, the material in Chapter 18 on complex audit judgments, and the **new** end-of-chapter academic research cases would be useful as additional materials to supplement a graduate-level auditing course, or a capstone course in which special audit topics are integrated with other discussions—such as fair value auditing integrated with fair value accounting presentations.

Supplements

The eighth edition contains a range of supplements that instructors and students need to get the most from the auditing course.

Instructor's Resource CD (IRCD). This all-in-one tool places all of the resources instructors need to plan and teach in one convenient location: Solutions Manual, PowerPoint® slides, Instructor's Manual, Test Bank in Microsoft® Word, and Exam-View® testing software. (**ISBN-10: 1111531846 | ISBN-13: 9781111531843**)

- **Solutions Manual.** This manual, written by the text authors, offers the highest accuracy as it provides solutions for all end-of-chapter material, plus solutions to ACL cases and the Biltrite Practice Case. The Solutions Manual is available on the IRCD.
- **Instructor PowerPoint® Presentation Slides.** Lectures come alive with these engaging PowerPoint® slides that are interesting, visually stimulating, and paced for student comprehension. These slides, are ideal as lecture tools and provide a clear guide for student study and note-taking. Instructor PowerPoint® slides, as well as a student version of the slides, are available on the IRCD and are downloadable by chapter on the Instructor's Resources page of **CengageBrain** (**www.cengagebrain.com**).
- **Instructor's Manual.** This manual contains all the resources instructors need to minimize class preparation time while maximizing teaching effectiveness. Chapter overviews, learning objectives, lecture notes with teaching suggestions, and guides equip you with the tools for positive outcomes throughout your course. The Instructor's Manual is available on the IRCD and is downloadable from **CengageBrain (www.cengagebrain.com)**.
- **Test Bank in Word.** The Test Bank has been substantially revised to reflect all the changes to the textbook for the eighth edition. The test bank is easy to access, use,

and modify for each instructor's unique purposes. Found on the Instructor's Resource CD, the Test Bank in Word features the questions instructors need to efficiently assess students' comprehension. The Test Bank in Word is available on the IRCD.

- **ExamView™ Computerized Testing Software.** This easy-to-use test-creation program contains all the questions from the Test Bank, making it simple to customize tests to your specific class needs as instructors edit or create questions and store customized exams. This is an ideal tool for online testing. This software is available on the IRCD.

ACL Desktop Education Edition, Version 9. Each NEW copy of the eighth edition comes with a CD containing **ACL's** *Desktop Education Edition, Version 9* at no additional cost for use with selected homework and cases. ACL is the most popular professional Audit Analytics software used in public accounting today. The software enhances the analysis of cases that are couched in significant account balances such as inventory and accounts receivable.

CengageBrain. Instructors and students can find additional support material online at **CengageBrain (www.cengagebrain.com)**.

- Students will find Student PowerPoint Slides, ACL case data files, chapter summaries, online quizzes, and other accounting resources for review.
- Instructors can easily download password-protected teaching resources, ACL case data files, and other materials.

Acknowledgments

We are grateful to members of the staff at Cengage Learning for their help in developing the seventh edition: Matt Filimonov, acquisitions editor; Kristen Hurd and Natalie Livingston, marketing managers; Jennifer Ziegler, content project manager; Stacy Shirley, art director; and Ann Mazzaro, editorial assistant. We would especially like to single out the contributions of Craig Avery, developmental editor, who has been with us since the first edition with Cengage and has always been constructive and supportive of our development; and Jared Sterzer, senior project manager, who is new to this edition but has been extremely helpful in making sure that the time spent in developing our content is not lost in the layout of the text. We believe, as we hope you do, that with the help of our publishing team the text is designed to support student understanding, learning, and application.

We appreciate the assistance of Jonathan Ellis and Susan Dempsey in integrating new features into this edition. We are appreciative of Douglas M. Boyle (University of Scranton) for his work on the new test bank and to LuAnn Bean (Florida Institute of Technology) for her work on the powerpoint slides.

We are again grateful to our students and to the instructors who have used the previous editions and have given their thoughtful feedback. We also thank Bradley Schwieger for his perceptive comments and efforts in building the foundation for this text.

We thank the many instructors listed below who responded to a survey on auditing conducted at the start of the revision. The findings from that survey helped us greatly.

Wafeek Abdelsayed, Southern Connecticut State University

Barbara Adams, South Carolina State University

Jack Armitage, University of Nebraska, Omaha

Dave Baglia, Grove City College

Anthony Barbera, State University of New York, Old Westbury

William Bernacchi, Mission College

James Bierstaker, Villanova University

Mike Bitter, Stetson University

Cynthia E. Bolt-Lee, The Citadel School of Business

Duane Brandon, Auburn University

Robert Braun, Southeastern Louisiana University

Rich Brody, University of New Mexico

Jeff W. Bruns, Bacone College

Alexander K. Buchholz, Brooklyn College of the City University of New York

Chuck Bunn, Wake Technical Community College

John Byrd, St. Leo University

David Camp, Blackburn College

Linda Campbell, Siena Heights University

Kay Carnes, Gonzaga University

James J. Carroll, Georgian Court University

Linda G. Chambers, Miles College

Barry Chapman, Davenport University

Gin Chong, Prairie View A&M University

Wayne Clark, Southwest Baptist University

Bob Cluskey, Troy University, Global Campus

Peggy Coady, Memorial University

Joe Coate, St. Bonaventure University

Jeffrey Cohen, Boston College

William D. Cooper, North Carolina A&T State University

John Coulter, Western New England College

Susann Cuperus, University of Mary

Charles D'Alessandro, St. Joseph's College

Donald Deis, Texas A&M University, Corpus Christi

William Dilla, Iowa State University

Richard Dumont, Post University

Ahmed Ebrahim, Fairfield University

Craig R. Ehlen, University of Southern Indiana

Rafik Elias, California State University, Los Angeles

Reza Espahbodi, Indiana University, South Bend

Jack R. Ethridge, Stephen F. Austin State University

Jack Fatica, Terra Community College

Patricia Feller, Nashville State Community College

Greg Della Franco, Lee University

Diana Franz, University of Toledo

Craig Froome, University of Queensland

Mary Geddie, University of Tennessee, Martin

George Andrew Gekas, Ryerson University

Marvin Gordon, Northwestern University

Brian Green, University of Michigan

Peggy Griffin, New Jersey City University

Kay Guess, St. Edward's University

Wendy Hahn, College of St. Elizabeth

James Hansen, Minnesota State University, Moorhead

Terri Herron, University of Montana

Dan Hinchliffe, University of North Carolina, Asheville

Mark Hogan, Elmhurst College

Sharon K. Howell, University of Texas at El Paso

Dan Hubbard, University of Mary Washington

Steve Jackson, The University of Southern Mississippi

Troy Janes, Rutgers University

Kate Jelinek, University of Rhode Island

Peggy Jenkins, State University of New York, Canton

Kevan Jensen, University of Oklahoma

Gail Kaciuba, St. Mary's University

Drummond Kahn, University of Oregon

Linda Kidwell, University of Wyoming

Tim Kizirian, Chico State University

Lauri Kremer, Lycoming College

Ellen Landgraf, Loyola University Chicago

Richard J. Lane, James Cook University

Joe Larkin, Saint Joseph's University

Randall LaSalle, John Jay College

Steven Laurion, Marian University

Yvette Lazdowski, Plymouth State University

Camillo Lento, Lakehead University

Fred Lerner, New York University

Gabriele Lingenfelter, Christopher Newport University

Steve Ludwig, Northwest Missouri State University

Joe Maffia, Hunter College

Julie Margret, La Trobe University

Jim W. Martin, University of Montevallo

Lizbeth Matz, University of Pittsburgh at Bradford

David J. McConomy, Queen's University (Canada)

D. David McIntyre, Mercer University

Michael McLain, Hampton University

David J. Medved, Thomas Edison State College

Sara Melendy, Gonzaga University

Dawn Miller, Trine University

Natalia Mintchik, University of Missouri, St. Louis

Jonathan G. Mitchell, Stark State College of Technology

Kathy Moffeit, University of West Georgia

Mark Morgan, Mississippi College

Barb Muller, Arizona State University

Joseph Nicassio, Westmoreland County Community College

Christine Z. J. Noel, Metropolitan State College of Denver

Kathy O'Donnell, University at Buffalo

Joseph Onyeocha, South Carolina State University

Soren Orley, University of Alaska, Anchorage

Karen Oxner, Hendrix College

Marshall Pitman, University of Texas at San Antonio

John Prendergast, Holy Family University

Ronald Reed, University of Northern Colorado

Michael Ridenour, Pennsylvania State University, Fayette Campus

Kim Rocha, Barton College

Phyllis Ross, Brown Mackie College, Salina

John D. Rossi III, Moravian College

Bradley Schwieger, St. Cloud State University

Mike Shapeero, Bloomsburg University of Pennsylvania

R. D. Sharma, Livingstone College

Gerald Smith, University of Northern Iowa

Eric Spires, The Ohio State University

Janice Stoudemire, Midlands Technical College

Kan Sugandh, La Sierra University

John Suroviak, Pacific University

Michael Sweeney, Hillsdale College

Paulette Tandy, University of Nevada, Las Vegas

Don Tecklenburg, Ohio Wesleyan University

Teresa Thamer, Brenau University

Michael Trebesh, Lansing Community College

Danny R. Vance, University of Central Arkansas

Scott Wallace, Blue Mountain Community College

Joan Wallwork, Kwantlen Polytechnic University

Tim Weiss, University of Northwestern Ohio

Donna Whitten, Purdue North Central

Terrence Willyard, Baker College

Rahnl Wood, Northwest Missouri State University

Darryl J. Woolley, University of Idaho

Emily Wright, MacMurray College

Jay Wright, Mountain State University

George Young, Florida Atlantic University

We also are indebted to the following reviewers, whose thoughts and ideas also helped us in the revision of the text:

Cynthia E. Bolt-Lee, The Citadel School of Business

Jeffrey Cohen, Boston College

Jan Colbert, Eastern Kentucky University

Rafik Elias, California State University, Los Angeles

Frederick L. Jones, University of Massachusetts, Dartmouth

Rose Layton, University of Southern California

Maureen Francis Mascha, Marquette University

Norma Montague, Wake Forest University

John H. Nugent, Texas Woman's University School of Management

Denise M. Patterson, California State University, Fresno

Ronald O. Reed, University of Northern Colorado

Daniel Selby, University of Richmond

Aamer Sheikh, Quinnipiac University

Eric Spires, The Ohio State University

We are very grateful to ACL Services, Ltd., for permission to distribute its software and tutorials, and for permission to reprint related images.

Larry E. Rittenberg

Karla M. Johnstone

Audrey A. Gramling

About the Authors

Larry E. Rittenberg

Larry E. Rittenberg, PhD, CPA, CIA, is the Ernst & Young Professor of Accounting & Information Systems at the University of Wisconsin–Madison, where he teaches courses in auditing and computer and operational auditing. He has served as the Chairman of

COSO (The Committee of Sponsoring Organizations of the Treadway Commission) and was instrumental in developing new guidance on internal control, and most recently, on monitoring the effectiveness of internal control over financial reporting. He has worked with both the PCAOB and the SEC in developing guidance that assists companies and auditors in evaluating and implementing cost-effective internal controls. He has served as vice-chair of Professional Practices for the Institute of Internal Auditors (IIA) and as president of the IIA Research Foundation. He has served as a member of the Auditing Standards Committee of the AAA Auditing Section, the AICPA's Computer Audit Subcommittee, the Information Technology Committee, and the Blue Ribbon Commission on Audit Committees. Professor Rittenberg, a Certified Internal Auditor®, has served as staff auditor for Ernst & Young and has coauthored five books and monographs and numerous articles. In January 2007, he received the "Outstanding Educator" award from the auditing section of the American Accounting Association. He is currently one of six members of the International Professional Practices Oversight Committee of the IIA that is reviewing the process by which internal auditors provide guidance and set standards for the professional practice of internal auditing.

Karla M. Johnstone

Karla M. Johnstone, PhD, CPA, is an Associate Professor of Accounting & Information Systems at the University of Wisconsin School of Business. She teaches both undergraduate and graduate-level auditing, and was awarded the 2008 School of Business Chipman Outstanding Faculty Teaching Award. Her research includes studies on corporate governance, internal controls, client acceptance, fraud, negotiation, internal auditing, audit committee decision-making, executive compensation, and budget-setting. She serves on the editorial boards at *The Accounting Review, Auditing: A Journal of Practice & Theory, The International Journal of Auditing*, and *Current Issues in Auditing*. She is an associate editor at *Accounting Horizons*. She has served the American Accounting Association (AAA) by co-chairing the 2010 and 2011 annual meetings, and as a member of the Notable Contributions to the Accounting Literature Award Committee. She has served the Auditing Section of the AAA as the co-chair of the 2007 Auditing Section Midyear Conference, as the chair of the Innovation in Auditing Education Award Committee, and as a member of the Outstanding Dissertation Award Committee, the Audit Standards Committee, and the Research Committee. She serves as a board member and audit committee member at the Center for Advanced Studies in Business at the University of Wisconsin–Madison. She has worked in practice as a corporate accountant and as a staff auditor for a CPA firm, and she was a doctoral fellow in residence at Coopers & Lybrand.

Audrey A. Gramling

Audrey A. Gramling, PhD, CIA, CPA, is Professor in the School of Accountancy at Kennesaw State University, where she teaches courses on auditing and SEC disclosure issues, and in 2010 was awarded the Coles College Distinguished Professor Award. She has served as an Academic Accounting Fellow in the Office of the Chief Accountant at the U.S. Securities and Exchange Commission. Audrey is currently, or has been, involved in a number of professional activities including serving as a member of Grant Thornton's Academic Advisory Council, as an Academic Fellow at Kennesaw State University's Corporate Governance Center, and as a member of COSO's Task Force on Monitoring Controls. She currently serves as a member of the Advisory Council of the COSO *Internal Control—Integrated Framework Update* project. Audrey serves on the editorial boards of *Accounting Horizons, Issues in Accounting Education, Journal of Accounting Education,* and *Current Issues in Auditing*. She has been an active member of the American Accounting Association, including serving as Secretary, Vice-President–Academic, and President of the AAA Auditing Section. Audrey worked as an external auditor at a predecessor firm of Deloitte and as an internal auditor at Georgia Institute of Technology. She has coauthored numerous books, monographs, and articles on various audit-related topics.

Brief Contents

Contents

All chapters contain the following end-of-chapter elements:

Summary
Significant Terms
Selected References to Relevant Professional Guidance
Review Questions
Multiple-Choice Questions
Discussion and Research Questions
Cases

CHAPTER 11

Audit of Acquisition and Payment Cycle and Inventory, 598

CHAPTER 12

Audit of Cash and Other Liquid Assets, 660

CHAPTER 13

Audit of Long-Lived Assets and Related Expense Accounts, 716

CHAPTER 14

Audit of Longer-Term Liabilities, Equity, Acquisitions, and Related-Entity Transactions, 758

Auditing

A Business Risk Approach

8e

1

Auditing: Integral to the Economy

LEARNING OBJECTIVES

The overriding objective of this textbook is to build a foundation with which to analyze current professional issues and adapt audit approaches to business and economic complexities. Through studying this chapter, you will be able to:

1 Define the objective of auditing and describe the role of auditing in meeting society's demands for unbiased financial and internal control information.

2 List the types of audit service providers and the knowledge needed by professionals entering the public accounting profession.

3 Identify organizations that affect the public accounting profession and the nature of their effects.

4 Identify the various auditing standards that affect the public accounting profession and compare these auditing standards on relevant dimensions.

5 Describe the audit opinion formulation process and list key steps in that process.

6 Identify and describe non-audit assurance and attestation services provided by external auditors and discuss the relevant professional standards.

7 Describe the unique roles of internal auditors and governmental auditors.

CHAPTER OVERVIEW

The capital markets depend on accurate, reliable, and objective (neutral) data that portray the economic nature of an entity's business and in turn provide a base to judge current progress toward long-term objectives. If the market does not receive reliable data, investors lose confidence in the system, make poor decisions, and may lose a great deal of money; ultimately, the system may fail. It is a complex process. However, the complexity goes further. Accounting transactions are becoming increasingly complicated as companies engage in more elaborate structures as well as in transactions that are difficult to measure. Further, complexity can only increase, as most companies and regulators recognize, because we are becoming a global economy and accounting is moving towards global harmonization.

As a profession, we are in a period of change in which auditors and accountants are called upon to make professional judgments that best reflect the economics of transactions or current states of economic holdings. Further, audit firms need professionals who make consistent judgments across a wide variety of companies, countries, and types of transactions. Thus, professional judgment and processes with which to make such judgments are critical to the success of each auditing firm. The focus of this text is on the audit of financial statements, although we recognize the importance of internal auditing and governmental auditing. This textbook addresses the unique challenges that independent external auditors face every day. This textbook is designed to help you develop the skills, including the development of professional judgment, needed to excel in performing this very important societal function.

Exhibit 1.1   Audit Opinion Formulation Process

I. Assessing Client Acceptance and Retention Decisions	II. Understanding the Client	III. Obtaining Evidence about Controls and Determining the Impact on the Financial Statement Audit	IV. Obtaining Substantive Evidence about Account Assertions	V. Wrapping Up the Audit and Making Reporting Decisions
CHAPTER 4	CHAPTERS 2, 4–6, and 9	CHAPTERS 5–14 and 18	CHAPTERS 7–14 and 18	CHAPTERS 15 and 16

The Auditing Profession, Regulation, and Corporate Governance	Decision-Making, Professional Conduct, and Ethics	Professional Liability
CHAPTERS 1 and 2	CHAPTER 3	CHAPTER 17

The overall purpose of this introductory chapter is to acquaint you with the auditing profession. We have divided the chapter into three parts, with each part representing an important aspect of the auditing profession. Part A provides an overall view of the nature of audit services, including the demand for such services, and identifies various parties that influence the profession. Part B introduces auditing standards used in the public accounting profession, and describes an audit opinion formulation process necessary to make professional judgments in a financial statement audit. We provide an overview of that process in Exhibit 1.1, and we will return to it throughout the text. Part C extends beyond the financial statement audit by providing an overview of assurance services other than the financial statement audit, and describing the internal auditing and governmental auditing professions.

PROFESSIONAL JUDGMENT IN CONTEXT

The Importance of Economic Factors When Conducting an Audit

In September 2010, the Public Company Accounting Oversight Board (PCAOB), an organization that provides oversight of public company auditors, issued a report based on its inspections of public company audits. The report summarizes issues discovered by the PCAOB during its 2007, 2008, and 2009 inspections. These issues relate to audit risks and challenges as a result of the disruptions in the credit and financial markets and the broader economic downturn. These economic factors presented increased risks to auditors, and many firms responded to these risks by issuing technical guidance, providing additional training, developing new audit tools, requiring additional audit procedures be performed, and increasing supervision of audit engagement personnel. While the PCAOB notes that audit firms made these efforts to respond to the increased risks, the report identifies instances where auditors appeared not to have complied with auditing standards in audit areas significantly affected by the economic crisis. These areas include fair value measurements, goodwill impairment, indefinite-lived intangible assets and other long-lived assets, allowance for loan losses, off-balance sheet structures, revenue recognition, inventory, and income taxes.

As an example of the connection between economic conditions and audit procedures, the PCAOB report notes that the uncertainty of fair value measurements, which are important to

users in valuing many assets and liabilities, is greatly increased during an economic crisis. The uncertainty created by the economic crisis in turn increases audit risk. In response to this risk, auditors need to properly test their clients' fair value measurements or they may fail to detect material misstatements related to these measurements, thereby providing users with unreliable information.

The PCAOB report illustrates the importance of the auditing profession to a successful economy. At the same time, it illustrates the difficult task that auditors face. As you read through this chapter and the text, consider the following questions:

- What is the objective of auditing and what process do auditors follow to accomplish this objective?
- How do external factors, such as economic trends, affect the audit process?
- What is the value of auditing in our capital markets?
- Who are the users of audited financial statements?
- What skills and knowledge are needed to be a competent audit professional?
- What organizations affect the public accounting profession?

Part A
OVERVIEW OF PUBLIC ACCOUNTING
Introduction to the Public Accounting Profession

LO 1

Define the objective of auditing and describe the role of auditing in meeting society's demands for unbiased financial and internal control information.

The external audit profession performs a unique task. It does not create the financial statements and it is precluded from designing the internal control systems for a public audit client. However, auditors provide opinions on financial statements and, as part of an **integrated audit**, auditors provide opinions on internal control effectiveness. It is a profession rife with risks and potential conflicts. Its value is affirmed when the public has confidence in its objectivity and the accuracy of its reports. When it fails, confidence in the financial system decreases.

A free-market economy can exist only if there is sharing of accurate, reliable information among parties that have a vested interest in the financial performance of an organization. The market is further strengthened if the data are transparent and neutral—that is, the data do not favor one party over another. The reported data must reflect the economics of transactions and the current economic condition of assets controlled and obligations owed. The audit process is intended to enhance the confidence that users can place on management-prepared financial statements. When the auditor has no reservations about management's financial statements or internal controls, the report is referred to as an **unqualified audit report**. Such a report is shown in Exhibit 1.2. If the auditor had reservations about the fair presentation of the financial statements, the audit report would be expanded to explain the nature of the auditor's reservations (covered in Chapter 16).

PRACTICAL POINT

The audit opinion formulation process needs to be completed by auditors who perform their professional responsibilities in an objective, unbiased, and professionally skeptical manner.

Exhibit 1.2   Integrated Audit Report

REPORT OF INDEPENDENT REGISTERED PUBLIC ACCOUNTING FIRM

To the Board of Directors and Shareholders of NSG Company:

We have audited the accompanying balance sheets of NSG Company (the Company) as of December 31, 2012 and 2011, and the related consolidated statements of income, stockholders' equity, and cash flows for each of the three years in the period ended December 31, 2012. These financial statements are the responsibility of the Company's management. Our responsibility is to express an opinion on these financial statements based on our audits.

We conducted our audits in accordance with the standards of the Public Company Accounting Oversight Board (United States). Those standards require that we plan and perform the audit to obtain reasonable assurance about whether the financial statements are free of material misstatement. An audit includes examining, on a test basis, evidence supporting the amounts and disclosures in the financial statements. An audit also includes assessing the accounting principles used and significant estimates made by management, as well as evaluating the overall financial statement presentation. We believe that our audits provide a reasonable basis for our opinion.

In our opinion, such consolidated financial statements present fairly, in all material respects, the financial position of the Company as of December 31, 2012 and 2011, and the results of their operations and their cash flows for each of the three years in the period ended December 31, 2012, in conformity with accounting principles generally accepted in the United States of America.

We have also audited, in accordance with the standards of the Public Company Accounting Oversight Board (United States), NSG's internal control over financial reporting as of December 31, 2012, based on the criteria established in *Internal Control—Integrated Framework* issued by the Committee of Sponsoring Organizations of the Treadway Commission and our report dated March 14, 2013 expressed an unqualified opinion on the effectiveness of the Company's internal control over financial reporting.

Rittenberg, Johnstone, & Gramling CPAs
Madison, Wisconsin
March 14, 2013

Auditing Defined

A **financial statement audit** has been defined as a:

> systematic process of *objectively obtaining and evaluating evidence* regarding *assertions* about economic actions and events to ascertain the degree of correspondence between those assertions and *established criteria* and *communicating the results* to interested users.[1]

There are a variety of parties involved in the production and use of audited financial statements. The board of directors, typically through the audit committee, has oversight responsibility over management and engages the auditor to audit the financial statements and prepare an independent opinion on the financial statements. Management has responsibilities for (a) preparing and presenting financial statements in accordance with the applicable financial reporting framework, (b) designing, implementing, and maintaining internal control over financial reporting, and (c) providing the auditors with information relevant to the financial statements. The auditor's job is to obtain reasonable assurance about whether management's statements are materially accurate and to provide a publicly available report based on the auditor's findings. The audited financial statements are provided to third-party users who have a vested interest in the organization.

Auditing: A Special Function

Auditing is a "special function" as described by Chief Justice Warren Burger in a 1984 Supreme Court decision:

> By certifying the public reports that collectively depict a corporation's financial status, the independent auditor assumes a public responsibility transcending any employment relationship with the client. The independent public accountant performing this special function owes ultimate allegiance to the corporation's creditors and stockholders, as well as to the investing public. This "public watchdog" function demands ... complete fidelity to the public trust.[2]

Chief Justice Burger's statement captures the essence of public accounting. Certified public accountants serve a number of diverse parties, but the most important is the public, as represented by investors, lenders, workers, and others who make decisions based on financial information about an organization. Auditing requires the highest level of technical competence, freedom from bias in assessing the fairness of financial presentations, and concern for the integrity of the financial reporting process. In essence, certified public accountants should view themselves as guardians of the capital markets. Unfortunately, that guardianship role has not always been embraced by the profession in the manner that the public expects. What might cause the auditing profession to forget its guardianship role? There is no single answer, but some problems during the late 1990s and early 2000s included the following:

1. Some members of the profession lost track of their responsibilities to the public.
2. Financial accounting rules came to be viewed as a set of rules that could be interpreted (with very minor boundaries) to suit the reporting objectives of management. Also, many auditors felt it was perfectly acceptable to apply accounting principles in a manner designed to achieve management objectives. In other words, the mindset was wrong: "If the FASB does not

> **PRACTICAL POINT**
>
> Auditing is a unique function that is licensed by the government to promote the effective functioning of the capital markets. But that unique license comes with a price—accountability and responsibility to the public.

---

[1] Auditing Concepts Committee, "Report of the Committee on Basic Auditing Concepts," *The Accounting Review*, 47, Supp. (1972), 18.

[2] *United States v. Arthur Young & Co. et al.,* U.S. Supreme Court, No. 82-687 [52 U.S.L.W.4355 (U.S., Mar. 21, 1984)].

prohibit the accounting, it must be acceptable." In short, some members of the profession were not independent of management.

3. Finding a way to accomplish a management reporting objective—e.g., moving losses off the balance sheet as in the Enron case—often resulted in lucrative consulting contracts for the audit firms, causing issues with independence.

4. Auditors were, in essence, hired and fired by management even though companies were required to have board members who were independent of management. Thus, auditors had strong motivation to please management. And management was often motivated to increase stock price—even if operations did not justify an increase in stock price.

5. The profession was not ready for the judgment required to implement principles-based accounting. This is an issue that will affect auditors in the future, as the demand for principles-based judgment will likely continue to accelerate.

6. The profession needed to be sufficiently profitable to retain partners and managers. To be more profitable, many audit firms reduced the amount of audit testing by inappropriately applying a risk-based approach to auditing.

The public accounting profession has been one of the most highly regarded professions in the country. However, like a baseball player, the auditor is only as good as the next at-bat—and that next at-bat must be played well and within the rules of the profession. Today's audit professional must be more than a "rules person." He or she must be able to apply professional judgment and adhere to standards of professional excellence and ethics.

The Need for Unbiased Reporting and Independent Assurance

The capital markets are built on transparent financial reporting. An organization's financial statements reflect, within the limits of the accounting model, a true and fair view of the organization's financial results. The statements do not favor one user over another. All users are considered important. However, the interests of the various users can conflict. Current shareholders might want management to use accounting principles that result in higher levels of reported income, but lending institutions generally prefer a conservative approach to valuation and income recognition. Exhibit 1.3 presents an overview of potential financial statement users and their primary use of financial reports.

Exhibit 1.3	Users of Audited Financial Statements
User	**Primary Use of Report**
Management	Review performance, make decisions, report results to capital markets
Stockholders	Assess performance, vote on organizational matters including the board of directors, make decision to buy or sell stock, or purchase more stock as part of a stock offering
Financial Institutions	Loan decisions—interest rates, terms, and risk
Taxing Authorities	Determine taxable income and tax due
Investors	Buy or sell stocks, bonds or other securities
Regulatory Agencies	Compliance with regulations, need for regulatory action
Labor and Labor Unions	Collective bargaining decisions
Bondholders	Buy or sell bonds
Court System	Assess the financial position of a company in litigation involving valuation
Vendors	Assess credit risk
Retired Employees	Protect employees from surprises concerning pensions and other post-retirement benefits due to accounting restatements

Need for Independent Assurance

Why do financial statement users need independent assurance about information provided by management? Shouldn't the information provided by management be reliable? The need for independent assurance arises from several factors that suggest there is a risk that information provided by management may not be accurate:

- *Potential bias* in providing information, that is, management may want to convey a better impression of the financial data than real circumstances merit
- *Remoteness* between a user and the organization or trading partner
- *Complexity* of the transactions, information, or processing systems such that it is difficult to determine their proper presentation without a review by an independent expert
- Investors need to manage their risk and thereby minimize financial surprises.
    - *Consequences* to investors, and others, of relying on inaccurate information can be quite significant.

Potential Bias in Providing Information Management has a vested interest in providing information that will make them look good. Management has inside information that it may or may not want to share with users. For example, management's compensation may be tied to company profitability or stock price and managers may be tempted to "bend" GAAP to make the organization's performance look better. There must be an unbiased arbiter to ensure fairness to users.

Remoteness of Users The Internet, coupled with global communication and transportation, has enabled us to become a global society. The advantages are tremendous, but a significant disadvantage is that we no longer either know or interact directly with many parties. Most users cannot interview management, tour a company's plant, or review its financial records firsthand; instead, they must rely on the financial statements to communicate the results of management's performance.

Complexity Many business transactions are more complex than ever. Third-party users depend on managers and auditors to deal with such complexities as financial instruments, derivatives, long-term contracts, and other complex transactions to ensure that they are fairly presented and fully disclosed in financial statements.

Consequences of Inaccurate Information During the past decade, many financial statement users—pension funds, private investors, venture capitalists, and banks—lost billions of dollars because financial information and, in some instances, the audit function, had become unreliable. When audits are not reliable, investors and other users lose a significant source of information that they need to manage risk.

Providers of Public Accounting Services

The public accounting profession includes sole-practitioner firms, local and regional firms, and large multinational professional services firms such as the Big 4. The organizational structure of accounting firms varies dramatically. For example, most of the Big 4 firms operate under one firm name across all countries. However, each of the Big 4 firms is actually a network of member firms. Each of the member firms enters into agreements to share a common name, brand, and quality standards. In most cases, member firms are organized as a partnership or limited liability corporation within each country. Some smaller firms also

---

PRACTICAL POINT

Increased reliability in financial reporting should lead to decreased variability in the capital markets because there will be fewer unwelcome "surprises" or fraud. The capital markets will be more efficient. Thus, to the extent that audits increase financial reporting reliability, they improve market efficiency.

PRACTICAL POINT

The factors leading up to, and the consequences of, inaccurate information can be seen in the subprime mortgage crisis in the United States. Many borrowers did not provide correct information on their loan applications; there was remoteness between the lenders and the subsequent buyers of the mortgages; and the derivative securities were very complex. Consequently, various financial statement users and others suffered significant losses.

LO 2

List the types of audit service providers and the knowledge needed by professionals entering the public accounting profession.

practice internationally through an affiliation with a network of firms. For example, a number of regional or local firms belong to an affiliation of such firms under the name of Moore Stephens, and another group operates under the name of Baker Tilly.

The organizational hierarchy of CPA firms has most often taken a pyramidal structure. Partners (or owners) form the top of the pyramid and are responsible for the overall conduct of each audit. Next in the hierarchy are the managers, who review the audit work performed by staff personnel (the base of the pyramid). Seniors are responsible for overseeing the day-to-day activities on a specific audit. Staff personnel typically spend two to four years at a staff level, after which they assume increasing supervisory responsibilities as seniors, managers, and ultimately partners. Partners and managers are responsible for many audit engagements that are being conducted simultaneously, whereas seniors and staff are usually assigned to fewer audits at a time.

Many public accounting firms have also organized their practices along industry lines to better serve clients in those industries. These often include categories such as financial services, retailing, not-for-profit, manufacturing, and government. The rationale is that an auditor needs to understand the industry as well as management does in order to identify (1) risks that the organization faces and the controls used to mitigate those risks, (2) risks of financial statement misstatements, and (3) opportunities to improve business operations.

Knowledge and Expertise Needed to Enter the Public Accounting Profession

The requirements of those entering the public accounting profession are demanding. Audits are performed in teams where each auditor is expected to:

- Contribute to analyzing and understanding the client's business.
- Be engaged in analyzing potential fraud risks at their clients.
- Understand computer processing and be able to access and audit electronic data.

Meeting these expectations requires considerable technical knowledge and expertise.

AUDITING *in Practice*

WHAT IS NEEDED FOR SUCCESS IN PUBLIC ACCOUNTING?

A review of public accounting firms' websites and relevant articles indicates that the knowledge and skills needed for success as an auditor generally fall into two categories: technical skills and leadership and professional skills (sometimes called "soft skills").

Technical Knowledge and Expertise	Leadership and Professional Abilities
• Accounting and auditing authoritative literature	• Make presentations to management and audit committee members
• Industry and client-specific knowledge and risks	• Exercise Logical reasoning that is documented and communicated to others
• Computer skills and accounting systems	• Manage and supervise others
• Internal controls	• Act with integrity and ethics
• Fraud and fraud detection techniques	• Provide meaningful feedback
	• Build a successful team
	• Collaborate with others
	• Maintain a professional personal presence

Accounting and Auditing The complexity of today's environment demands that the auditor be fully versed in the technical accounting and auditing authoritative literature. In addition, the auditor must have a sound conceptual understanding of the basic elements underlying financial reporting. This conceptual understanding is necessary to address the ever-increasing infusion of new types of transactions and contracts for which accounting pronouncements may not exist, or where the international standards may differ from U.S. accounting standards. As an example, the auditing profession was criticized because many financial instruments recorded in connection with subprime housing markets were not properly shown at market value. The auditor must also fully understand the fundamental concepts of auditing. Developing an understanding of audit concepts enables the auditor to adapt to changing economic situations or plan different audit approaches for clients in differing industries or those facing differing risks.

Knowledge of the Client's Industry, Business, and Risks Most audit firms use a "risk-based" approach to performing audits. The fundamental premise behind the risk-based approach is that the auditor must understand the basic structure of the client's business and industry in order to identify significant risks affecting that client. For example, an auditor of a bank should have substantial knowledge about the business economy in the area served by the bank, the bank's capital structure, the types of loans the bank has made, and other risks that will affect the likelihood that the loans will be repaid and the bank will survive. In a similar fashion, an understanding of the strategies used by management will assist the auditor in evaluating preliminary financial results and pinpointing areas needing more audit attention.

Computer Skills and Accounting Systems Today's companies are actively involved in e-commerce and electronic data interchange (EDI). As an example, most paychecks are deposited directly in bank accounts and debit or credit cards are used for many transactions. Most financial assets exist as digital images in computer systems. Traditional paper documents are disappearing. Systems are increasingly integrated across companies. Auditors must be prepared to address the audit challenges posed by electronic systems in which traditional source documents do not exist.

Internal Control Expertise An auditor of a larger public company must perform an "integrated audit," i.e., an audit of both the company's internal control and its financial statements. The auditor must be able to assess and test an organization's internal controls to determine if there are weaknesses that should be reported to the general public, to the audit committee, and to management.

Fraud A major concern that auditors face is that fraud may exist in the organization that they are auditing. Fraud can relate to inaccuracies in the financial statements and to outright theft of the organization's resources. Auditors need to be aware of the incentives for employees (including upper-level management) to commit fraud, the opportunities that weak internal controls may create that will allow a fraud to be perpetrated or concealed, and the rationalizations that employees may use to justify their actions and to continue or escalate the fraud over time.

Organizations Affecting the Public Accounting Profession

LO 3

Identify organizations that affect the public accounting profession and the nature of their effects.

Public accounting is a unique profession with a number of organizations shaping and regulating the nature of services provided by those in the profession.

Congress

The accounting profession has undergone a decade of unprecedented change.[3] Some of the factors leading up to the change include (a) the failure of one of the largest public accounting firms in the world (Arthur Andersen & Co.); (b) four of the largest bankruptcies in history—and each of the bankruptcies occurred in companies where financial statement misrepresentation had taken place; (c) billions of dollars in investment and retirement fund losses; (d) a sense that auditors were not independent of management; and (e) a question as to whether the public accounting profession could sufficiently govern itself to ensure that it would always act in the public interest. In response to these failures, Congress passed the **Sarbanes-Oxley Act of 2002**.[4] This legislation has had a significant impact on public company audit firms in the areas of:

- Auditor independence and the role of the audit committee
- Required reporting on internal control over financial reporting
- Oversight of the accounting profession

Auditor Independence and the Role of the Audit Committee   The Sarbanes-Oxley Act includes requirements to help ensure the **independence** of public company auditors. Independence refers to having the auditor be objective and unbiased while performing audit services. The Act requires companies to establish an independent audit committee as a subcommittee of the board of directors to provide oversight of the external auditors. The audit committee becomes "the audit client" and should have the sole power to hire or fire an audit firm. The audit committee also has oversight of potential independence conflicts, including those that may affect performance by the independent auditing firm. Other independence-related requirements of the Sarbanes-Oxley Act include mandatory rotation every five years of the partner in charge of the audit engagement and a prohibition on consulting work that auditors can perform for their audit clients.

Required Reporting on Internal Control over Financial Reporting
Congress and financial statement users were shocked with billion-dollar frauds at companies such as WorldCom, Adelphia, and Enron, as well as the poor risk-management processes and controls at financial institutions such as Bear Stearns and Lehman Brothers. In many of these organizations, senior management had overridden the accounting system, and in virtually all cases, the companies had poor internal control over financial reporting. Section 404 of the Sarbanes-Oxley Act requires management to independently assess and publicly report on the effectiveness of its internal control over financial reporting. Further, the external auditors a required to independently test the internal controls and give an opinion on them.

The internal control reporting and auditing requirements in Sarbanes-Oxley did not allow for exemptions based on company size. However, in 2010, with the passage of the Dodd-Frank Wall Street Reform and Consumer Protection Act, Congress exempted smaller public companies from having an independent auditor report on the effectiveness of their internal controls over financial reporting.

Oversight of the Accounting Profession   One of the most significant changes for the profession resulting from Sarbanes-Oxley was a change in

---

> **PRACTICAL POINT**
>
> Internal control reporting allows the financial statement users to assess the impact of any identified control deficiencies on the performance of management and the potential impact on the future of the organization. For example, a company with poor controls often does not have reliable information with which to make good management decisions.

> **PRACTICAL POINT**
>
> See http://www.pcaobus.org for information about the PCAOB, its standards, rules, and recent activities.

---

[3] The other change of the magnitude described here occurred in 1933 when the Securities and Exchange Commission was established in response to abuses in financial reporting that took place in the 1920s and fired speculation on Wall Street.

[4] Sarbanes-Oxley Act of 2002, H.R. Bill 3762.

AUDITING *in Practice*

PUBLIC REPORTING ON INTERNAL CONTROLS

There is a growing body of evidence to support the concept that good internal control is good business. The need for public reporting on internal control was advanced by the Treadway Commission's report on Fraudulent Financial Reporting in 1987, when that group identified a high correlation between fraudulent reporting and poor internal controls. Don Nicolaisen, former Chief Accountant of the SEC, reinforced this concept in a speech in 2004:

I believe that, of all of the recent reforms, the internal control requirements have the greatest potential to improve the reliability of financial reporting. Our capital markets run on faith and trust that the vast majority of companies present reliable and complete financial data for investment and policy decision-making.... It is absolutely critical that we get the internal control requirements right.[5]

oversight of the profession. Prior to 2002, the public accounting profession was self-regulated. However, with the passage of Sarbanes-Oxley, Congress created the Public Company Accounting Oversight Board (PCAOB) to oversee the auditors of public companies.

Public Company Accounting Oversight Board

The PCAOB is a private sector, nonprofit organization that oversees auditors of public companies. The overall goal of the PCAOB is to "protect the interests of investors and further the public interest in the preparation of informative, fair and independent audit reports." The PCAOB has four primary responsibilities: (1) *registration* of accounting firms that audit U.S. public companies, (2) periodic *inspections* of registered public accounting firms, (3) establishment of auditing and related *standards* for registered public accounting firms, and (4) *investigation and discipline* of registered public accounting firms for violations of relevant laws or professional standards.

The Securities and Exchange Commission

The **Securities and Exchange Commission** (SEC) was established by Congress in 1934 to regulate the capital market system. The SEC has oversight responsibilities for the PCAOB and for all public companies that are required to register with it to gain access to the U.S. capital markets. The SEC has the authority to establish GAAP for companies whose stock is publicly traded, although it has generally delegated this authority to the FASB.

Actions by the SEC have important implications for public company auditors. In response to the independence requirements of Sarbanes-Oxley, the SEC modified its auditor independence rules. Further, the SEC has issued staff accounting bulletins (SABs) clarifying concepts of revenue recognition and materiality. The SEC also has a responsibility to prosecute public companies and their auditors for violating SEC laws, including fraudulent accounting. For example, in recent years, the SEC has brought actions against companies and auditors including (a) Dell for failing to disclose material information and for improper accounting related to the use of "cookie jar" reserves, (b) Lucent for inappropriate revenue recognition, (c) a former Deloitte & Touche partner for a lack of independence, and (d) Ernst & Young for allowing premature revenue recognition and improper deferral of costs in its audits of Bally Total Fitness Holding Corporation, among many others.

PRACTICAL POINT

The initial focus of the PCAOB was on audits of public companies. However, the legislation did not require that certain hedge funds taking the public's money be audited by firms registered with the PCAOB. The hedge funds run by Bernie Madoff in his famous Ponzi scheme were purportedly audited by a three-person audit firm that told the New York Society of CPAs that they did not perform audits. The PCAOB has moved to require that companies like those of Madoff's hedge fund be audited by firms that are registered with it and that undergo periodic quality inspections by the PCAOB.

PRACTICAL POINT

See http://www.sec.gov for information about the SEC, including current staff accounting bulletins and legal actions brought against companies and auditors for accounting fraud or securities violations.

---

[5] Don Nicolaisen, Securities and Exchange Commission, October 7, 2004. Keynote Speech to the 11th Annual Midwestern Financial Reporting Symposium, http://www.sec.gov.

PRACTICAL POINT

See http://www.aicpa.org for information about the AICPA, the public accounting profession, professional standards, and the CPA exam.

American Institute of Certified Public Accountants

The **American Institute of Certified Public Accountants** (AICPA) has long served as the primary governing organization of the public accounting profession. That role has changed with the establishment of the PCAOB as the body for setting auditing standards for the audits of public companies. However, the AICPA continues to develop standards for audits of nonpublic companies. The AICPA provides continuing education programs and, through its Board of Examiners, prepares and administers the Uniform CPA Examination.

PRACTICAL POINT

See http://www.ifac.org/iaasb/ for information about the IAASB.

International Auditing and Assurance Standards Board

The **International Auditing and Assurance Standards Board** (IAASB) is a part of the International Federation of Accountants (IFAC), a global organization for the accounting profession that, as of the end of 2009, has 159 members in 124 countries. The IAASB sets **International Standards on Auditing** (ISAs) and facilitates the convergence of national and international auditing standards.

PRACTICAL POINT

See http://www.coso.org for information about COSO guidelines, fraud studies, and recommendations for improving internal control in organizations.

Committee of Sponsoring Organizations

The **Committee of Sponsoring Organizations of the Treadway Commission** (COSO) is a recognized provider of guidance on aspects of organizational governance, business ethics, internal control, enterprise risk management, and fraudulent financial reporting. COSO is sponsored by five organizations, including the Financial Executives International, the American Institute of Certified Public Accountants, the American Accounting Association, the Institute of Internal Auditors, and the Institute of Management Accountants. Important guidance issued by COSO includes:

- *Internal Control, Integrated Framework* (1992)—primary criterion for evaluating the effectiveness of internal control;
- *Internal Control over Financial Reporting—Guidance for Smaller Public Companies* (2006)—although designated for smaller companies, this guidance is applicable to companies of all sizes;
- *Guidance on Monitoring Internal Control Systems* (2009)—provides insight to management on recognizing high quality monitoring controls in their organizations;
- *Fraudulent Financial Reporting: 1987–1997—An Analysis of U.S. Public Companies* (1999)—seminal study in fraudulent financial reporting;
- *Fraudulent Financial Reporting: 1998–2007—An Analysis of U.S. Public Companies*—an update of the 1999 study.

PRACTICAL POINT

In late 2010 a Blue Ribbon Panel recommended that a separate set of accounting rules be developed for private companies doing business in the United States. This approach is somewhat similar to companies that use a scaled-down version of IFRS for small and medium-sized entities.

Accounting Standard Setters

Generally accepted accounting principles (GAAP) in the United States have traditionally been set by the Financial Accounting Standards Board (FASB), with approval by the Securities and Exchange Commission (SEC). However, over the past several years there has been a trend toward global harmonization of U.S. and international accounting standards. Within the foreseeable future, accounting standards for public companies worldwide (IFRS—International Financial Reporting Standards) could be set by the **International Accounting Standards Board** (IASB).[6]

---

[6] When referring to financial reporting requirements we will use GAAP to refer to generally accepted accounting principles for financial reporting, recognizing that the criteria may be developed by either FASB or the IASB. In some instances we will use the term applicable financial reporting framework. The auditor will determine which of the financial reporting frameworks is applicable to the audit and then apply that framework to determine whether the principles underlying that framework are properly applied.

State Boards of Accountancy

CPAs are licensed by state boards of accountancy, which are charged with regulating the profession at the state level. All state boards require passage of the Uniform CPA Examination as one criterion for licensure. However, education and experience requirements vary by state. Some states require candidates to have public accounting audit experience before issuing them a license to practice; other states give credit for audit experience related to private or governmental accounting. The work experience requirement can also vary with the level of education. Most states have reciprocal agreements for recognizing public accountants from other states; in some instances, however, a state may require either additional experience or coursework before issuing a license.

The Court System

The court system acts as a quality-control mechanism for the practice of auditing. Third parties may sue CPAs under federal securities laws, various state statutes, and common law for substandard audit work. Although the profession often becomes alarmed when large damages are awarded to plaintiffs in suits against CPA firms, the courts help ensure that the profession meets its responsibilities to third parties. During the past several decades, court cases have led to the codification of additional auditing standards for such areas as related-party transactions, "subsequent events" affecting the financial statements, and clarification of the auditor's report.

PRACTICAL POINT

Most states now require 150 college semester hours for CPA licensure, although a candidate may be able to sit for the CPA exam with only 120 semester hours in some states.

Part B
A STANDARDS BASED PROCESS FOR CONDUCTING AN AUDIT

Audit Standard Setting in the Public Accounting Profession

Auditors in the United States follow auditing guidance issued by the AICPA, PCAOB, and IAASB. Auditing standards set by these various authorities have a common objective—to provide assurance to the public that audits are

LO 4

Identify the various auditing standards that affect the public accounting profession and compare these auditing standards on relevant dimensions.

AUDITING *in Practice*

THE AICPA'S CLARITY AND CONVERGENCE PROJECT

In 2004 the AICPA's Auditing Standards Board (ASB) developed a plan to converge U.S. generally accepted auditing standards (GAAS) with the International Standards on Auditing (ISAs). The ASB's plan also included avoiding unnecessary conflict with PCAOB Auditing Standards (ASs). As part of its project, the ASB began redrafting all of the auditing sections in *Codification of Statements on Auditing Standards* (i.e., GAAS) and converging its standards with the ISAs. The ASB expects that nearly all ISA requirements will also be requirements of U.S. GAAS.

However, the ASB has noted that some differences between its new standards and those of both the IAASB and the PCAOB are necessary because of legal, regulatory, and other considerations. The ASB proposes that all redrafted standards be effective on the same date, and, as of late 2010, that proposed date is December 15, 2012. As the clarity project is moving toward finalization, auditors should monitor the new standards and be prepared for any changes in audit practices required by the new standards.

conducted in a professional manner. Auditing standards apply to the auditor's task of developing and communicating an opinion on financial statements and, as part of an integrated audit, on a client's internal control over financial reporting. The auditing standards used will vary according to the nature of the organization audited, such as whether an entity is public or nonpublic. For example, U.S. public companies are subject to SEC regulation and must be audited in accordance with the auditing standards established by the PCAOB, while U.S. nonpublic companies will have an audit performed in accordance with generally accepted auditing standards that have been promulgated by the AICPA. Further, the domicile of the organization that is being audited and, more importantly, where its stock is publicly traded (if applicable), determine whether the auditor must comply with PCAOB or AICPA standards or those developed by IAASB.

Fortunately, there is a great deal of commonality among the auditing standards. All of the standards start from fundamental principles on how an audit engagement should be planned and conducted and how the results should be communicated. An overview of these auditing standards is shown in *Comparison*

Comparison of Worldwide Professional Auditing Guidance

U. S. AND INTERNATIONAL AUDITING STANDARDS: COMMONALITIES AND DIFFERENCES

Standard Setters	IAASB	PCAOB	AICPA
Authority	International Federation of Accountants, and as agreed upon by countries who agree to abide by these standards	U.S Congress, as expressed in the Sarbanes-Oxley Act of 2002	Historical, as self-regulatory organization that had earned the public's trust
Terminology	International Standards on Auditing (ISAs)	Auditing Standards (ASs)	Statements on Auditing Standards (SASs)
Scope of Applicability of Standards	Audits in countries for which international standards are required, including most of Europe and many emerging markets.	Audits of all public U.S. companies—referred to as registered accounting firms.	Audits of nonpublic U.S. entities, except governmental units, for which standards are set by the Government Accountability Office (GAO).
Convergence	Committed to international convergence on auditing standards.	As a new regulatory body, the PCAOB does not currently have a mandate for international convergence.	The AICPA is committed to international convergence and works with the IAASB in developing many standards.

Commonalities Among the Standards	All are principles-based supplemented by more detailed guidance. Standards are similar in key areas such as: • Planning the Audit to Minimize Risk • Auditor Documentation • Audit Evidence • Due Professional Care or Reasonable Care • Nature of the Audit Report • Independence (U.S.) is similar to, but less comprehensive than Professional Skepticism (IAASB) As the AICPA and IAASB work towards convergence, there will be even greater similarities between their two sets of standards.
Key Differences Between the Standards	Areas where there are important differences across the standards include: • Opinions on accounting treatment and financial reporting framework • Reporting on internal control over financial reporting • Focus on independence vs. professional skepticism

of Worldwide Professional Auditing Guidance features throughout the text, in which we provide more detailed comparisons of these standards on topics specific to the chapter.

Overall Objectives in Conducting an Audit— Guidance Issued by the AICPA and the IAASB

Both the AICPA and the IAASB have provided guidance on the overall objectives in conducting an audit. The guidance, which is almost identical, recognizes that the objective of an audit is to obtain reasonable assurance about whether the financial statements are free from material misstatement and to report on the financial statements based on the auditor's findings. In completing these objectives, the auditor:

- Complies with relevant ethical requirements
- Plans and performs an audit with **professional skepticism** (i.e., an attitude that includes a questioning mind and critical assessment of audit evidence)
- Exercises professional judgment
- Obtains sufficient appropriate evidence on which to base the auditor's opinion
- Conducts the audit in accordance with professional auditing standards

This overall guidance is supplemented with specific auditing standards—SASs issued by the AICPA and ISAs issued by the IAASB.

Auditing Standards Issued by the AICPA (Statements on Auditing Standards)

Auditing standards in the United States have historically been based on ten generally accepted auditing standards ("the ten standards") that have served as the foundation for the audit of financial statements and the development of additional Statements on Auditing Standards (SASs). The ten standards were developed by the ASB of the AICPA and have been adopted by the PCAOB. However, as described in the *Auditing in Practice* feature, the AICPA is working on converging its standards with those of the IAASB. As part of that convergence, the ten standards will be replaced by principles. Because of their historical significance, we will briefly discuss the ten standards and then provide an overview of the principles proposed by the ASB.

The Ten Standards Issued by the AICPA

The ten standards fall within three categories:

- General standards—applicable to the auditor and audit firm
- Fieldwork standards—applicable to the conduct of the audit
- Reporting standards—applicable to communicating the auditor's opinion

General Standards   The **general standards** guide the profession in selecting and training its professionals to meet the public trust. The general standards require that:

1. The audit be performed by individuals having adequate technical training and proficiency as an auditor
2. Auditors be independent in their mental attitude in conducting the audit (independence *in fact*) and be perceived by users as independent of the client (independence *in appearance*)

PRACTICAL POINT

Maintaining professional skepticism helps the auditor reduce the risk of overlooking unusual transactions and is necessary for the critical assessment of audit evidence.

PRACTICAL POINT

The auditor is to conduct the audit with due care. Due care requires the auditor to discharge professional responsibilities with competence and to have the appropriate capabilities to perform the audit.

3. The audit be conducted *with* **due professional care** which is a standard of care that would be expected of a reasonably prudent auditor

Fieldwork Standards   The **fieldwork standards** require that:

1. An audit be properly planned and supervised
2. Auditors develop an understanding of the client's controls as an important prerequisite to developing specific audit tests
3. Auditors obtain sufficient appropriate audit evidence by performing audit procedures to provide a reasonable basis for the audit opinion being provided

Reporting Standards   The **reporting standards** require:

1. The auditor to state explicitly whether the financial statements are fairly presented in accordance with the applicable financial reporting framework, which may be GAAP or IFRS
2. The auditor, to identify, in the auditor's report, those circumstances in which accounting principles have not been consistently observed in the current period in comparison to the preceding period
3. The auditor to review disclosures for adequacy, and if the auditor concludes that informative disclosures are not reasonably adequate, the auditor must so state in the auditor's report
4. The auditor to express an opinion on the financial statements as a whole or state that an opinion can not be expressed

Principles Governing an Audit Conducted in Accordance with Generally Accepted Auditing Standards—Issued by the AICPA

In place of the ten standards, the AICPA has now developed fundamental principles that govern an audit conducted in accordance with generally accepted auditing standards. The four categories, with their specific principles, are:

Purpose of an Audit and Premise Upon Which an Audit Is Conducted

1. The purpose of an audit is to enhance the degree of confidence that users can place in the financial statement. This purpose is achieved when an auditor expresses an opinion on the financial statements.
2. An audit is based on the premise that management has responsibility to prepare the financial statements, maintain internal control over financial reporting, and provide the auditor with relevant information and access to personnel.

Responsibilities

1. Auditors are responsible for having the appropriate competence and capabilities to perform the audit, should comply with ethical requirements, and maintain professional skepticism throughout the audit.

Performance

1. The auditor needs to obtain reasonable assurance as to whether the financial statements are free from material misstatement.
2. Obtaining reasonable assurance requires the auditor to plan and supervise the work, determine materiality levels, identify risks of material misstatement, and design and implement appropriate audit responses to the assessed risks.
3. An audit has inherent limitations such that the auditor is not able to obtain absolute assurance about whether the financial statements are free from misstatement.

PRACTICAL POINT

Independence requires objectivity and freedom from bias and is often referred to as the *cornerstone* of auditing. Without independence, the value of the audit function would be lacking.

PRACTICAL POINT

The development of an **audit program** is the most visible product of the planning process. An audit program lists the audit objectives and the procedures to be followed in gathering audit evidence and helps those in charge of the audit to monitor the progress and supervise the work.

PRACTICAL POINT

Auditing involves assessing assertions against criteria. If it is a GAAP-based statement, then GAAP forms the criteria. If it is an IFRS-based statement, then the criteria for fairness is accounting principles promulgated under IFRS.

Reporting

1. The auditor expresses an opinion as to whether the financial statements are free of material misstatement or states that an opinion can not be expressed.

Auditing Standards Issued by the IAASB (International Standards on Auditing)

As of 2010, the IAASB auditing standards comprise thirty-six International Standards on Auditing (ISAs). Over 100 countries have national auditing standards that are based on the ISA. As indicated in the convergence project discussed in the *Auditing in Practice* feature, it is expected that the standards of the AICPA and IAASB will converge.

Auditing Standards Issued by the PCAOB (Auditing Standards)

The PCAOB, which came into existence in 2002, issues auditing standards that apply to auditors of U.S. public companies. As of 2010, the PCAOB has issued fifteen Auditing Standards (ASs). Further, the PCAOB adopted the AICPA standards that were in place on April 16, 2003 (referred to as interim standards). Thus, public company auditors must follow these standards of the AICPA unless they have been superseded by a PCAOB standard. Standards issued by the AICPA after April 16, 2003 are not part of the standards that public company auditors are required to follow.

An Overview of the Audit Opinion Formulation Process

Earlier in the chapter, we introduced you to Exhibit 1.1, which outlines the process that auditors follow in conducting an audit. The objective is to reach Phase V, where a decision is unequivocally made about the fairness of an organization's financial statements and, for integrated audits, the effectiveness of their internal controls. However, making this decision is not enough for an auditing firm to succeed. The auditor must make a decision that carries a very low risk of being in error. For example, an audit opinion where the auditor says the financial statements are fairly presented when, in fact, they are not fairly presented, will often lead to lawsuits or regulatory action. To minimize risk, the auditor pays a great deal of attention to client selection and retention (Phase I). Auditors are not required to perform audits for any company that asks; i.e., it is the audit firm's choice whether to provide that service. Thus, most audit firms have procedures to help them ensure that they are not associated with clients where management integrity is in question or where a company might otherwise present the audit firm with unnecessarily high risk (e.g., client financial failure, regulatory action against the client). Once a client is accepted (or the audit firm decides to retain a continuing client), the auditor needs to thoroughly understand the client's business (or update prior knowledge in the case of a continuing client), its industry, its competition, and its management and governance processes to determine the likelihood that financial accounts might be in error (Phase II). The auditor will also gain an understanding of the client's internal control over financial reporting, and in some audits, will decide to test those controls (Phase III). Much of what most people think of as auditing, the testing of account balances, occurs in Phase IV. The information gathered in Phases I through III will greatly influence the amount of testing to be performed in Phase IV. Finally, in Phase V the auditor will make a decision about (a) whether enough evidence has been gathered to support an audit opinion and (b) what type of opinion should be issued.

LO 5

Describe the audit opinion formulation process and list key steps in that process.

PRACTICAL POINT

Accounting students know that interpreting authoritative financial accounting pronouncements is difficult. The auditor's task is to consider whether the application of a generally accepted accounting principle best portrays the economic activity of the company.

AUDITING *in Practice*

DEVELOPING AN UNDERSTANDING OF MATERIALITY

The audit must be planned to provide reasonable assurance that material misstatements will be detected. The concept of materiality is pervasive and guides the nature and extent of auditing both financial statements and a company's internal control over financial reporting. Within an auditing context, materiality is a concept that relates to the importance or significance of an item, such as a financial statement amount, transaction, or discrepancy. But materiality is not simply a function of specific dollar amounts in the organization's financial statements. The auditor should consider qualitative, as well as quantitative, dimensions of materiality as a basis for designing the audit process to address material misstatements.

Phases I and II: Making Client Decisions and Gaining an Understanding of the Client

After deciding whether to accept a new client or retain an existing client, the auditor continues to develop an understanding of the client. Much of the information gained during the acceptance/retention decision is used in developing this understanding. Additionally, auditors will obtain an understanding of:

PRACTICAL POINT

Although the overall audit approach is shared with management and the audit committee, the specific details of the plan and audit program are not. Sharing such detailed information would enable management to circumvent the audit, e.g., if management were perpetrating a fraud and was trying to deceive the auditors.

- The client's business and the industry within which it operates
- Business risks the company faces and determining how those risks might affect the presentation of a company's financial results
- Potential fraud risks
- Management compensation plans and how those plans may motivate management actions that could affect the financial statements
- Appropriate level(s) of **materiality**
- The quality of the design of the client's internal controls over financial reporting
- Management's approach to assessing internal control over financial reporting and whether management has sufficient documentation of the design and operation of internal controls over financial reporting
- The client's accounting policies and procedures
- The financial statement items more likely to require adjustment, as well as those that are subjective in nature
- Factors that may require the extension or modification of audit tests, such as potential related-party transactions or the possibility of material misstatements
- Potential coordination of work with the client's internal audit function
- The type of reports to be issued, such as consolidated statements or single-company statements, special reports, internal control reports, or other reports to be filed with the SEC or other regulatory agencies.

PRACTICAL POINT

Materiality guidelines usually involve applying percentages to some base, such as total assets, total revenue, or pretax income. For example, an auditor might use a guideline that sets overall materiality at 1% of total assets or revenue, whichever is higher. However, any guideline is just a starting point that is adjusted for other relevant information, some of which may be qualitative. For example, if the client has a loan with a restrictive covenant that requires a current ratio of 2:1, any potential misstatement or adjustment amount that would bring that ratio under 2:1 would be judged to be qualitatively material.

This information is shared among audit team members in an audit planning meeting and is used to determine the overall audit approach. The overall audit approach is documented by the auditor in an audit program.

Phases III and IV: Obtaining Evidence

The third and fourth phases of the audit opinion formulation process involve obtaining evidence about controls, determining their impact on the financial statement audit, and obtaining substantive evidence about specific account assertions. An **assertion** is a statement about an action, event, condition, or performance over a specified period of time.

Management Assertions

The audit process is designed around assertions inherent in the accounting communication. For example, if a company represents that it has property, plant, and equipment net of depreciation of $42 million, some of the assertions being made by the company are that:

- The equipment is physically present and under control of the company (*existence*).
- All purchases of assets are fully recorded (*completeness*).
- It owns the equipment and has title to the equipment (*rights and obligations*).
- The equipment is properly valued at cost and the cost amounts add up to the balance shown in the financial statements (*valuation*).
- The equipment is appropriately classified and described (*presentation and disclosure*)
- The equipment shown on the financial statements is properly valued at cost (not to exceed its assessed value) with applicable allowances for depreciation (*valuation*).

> **PRACTICAL POINT**
>
> Auditors gather a considerable amount of information about the client before beginning any audit testing. That information allows the auditor to better control the risk of issuing an incorrect audit opinion.

Audit Procedures to Test Assertions

The auditor performs various audit procedures to test the assertions in each account balance. Consider an audit of property, plant, and equipment (PPE) and the valuation assertion implied in a company's financial statement:

The equipment shown on the financial statements is properly valued at cost (not to exceed its assessed value) with applicable allowances for depreciation.

This assertion can be broken down into four major components:

- The valuation of new assets added this year
- The valuation of assets that were acquired in previous years
- The proper recording of depreciation
- Potential impairment of the existing assets due to changed economic conditions or management plans regarding the manufacture of some of its products.

For illustration purposes, we focus on whether the current year's additions to equipment are properly valued. Audit procedures that would address this assertion include:

- *Auditing Additions to PPE*—Take a *sample* of all additions to property, plant, and equipment, and verify the cost through reference to vendor invoices to determine that cost is accurately recorded. If there is a high risk that the valuation may be misstated, the auditor may choose to take a larger sample.
- *Assessing the Potential Impairment of the Asset Additions*—Review continued operation of the assets through inquiry of management, and observation of operations to determine if the assets should be written down to an impaired value. Gather current economic information and independent evidence as to the current market price of the assets to corroborate management's statements.

Important elements in these audit procedures highlight the following:

- *Select a sample* of items to test. The auditor needs to take a representative sample because it is often too costly to examine all additions to PPE. The sample size could be increased in order to respond to a heightened risk of misstatement increases.
- *Review documentary evidence* of cost. The auditor examines external, objective evidence of the amount paid and the nature of the equipment purchased, e.g., an invoice.
- *Inquire and corroborate.* While the auditor will likely inquire of management to obtain some audit evidence, it is important that the auditor corroborate what management has said by using complementary evidence.

In determining the appropriate audit procedures to perform, the auditor needs to understand the following fundamentals:

- Audit procedures reflect a thorough understanding of the underlying assertions.
- Audit procedures are adjusted for the risk of potential misstatement in the account balance.
- There are many factors that influence the risk of misstatement. The auditor must understand these risks.

Phase V: Wrapping Up the Audit and Making Reporting Decisions

The fifth and final phase in the audit opinion formulation process involves summarizing the audit evidence related to the assertions tested and reaching a conclusion about the fairness of the client's financial presentation. If the evidence supports that an account balance is fairly represented, the auditor will continue with the audit of other account balances. If the evidence does not support a fair presentation, the auditor will gather additional evidence through detailed testing. The additional information gathered will lead the auditor to one of three conclusions:

- The account balance is misstated and the client agrees to adjust the financial statements to eliminate the misstatement. The audit report indicates that the financial statements are fairly presented and the auditor issues an unqualified audit report.
- The account balance is misstated, but the client disagrees. The auditor will issue an audit report indicating that the financial statements, in his or her opinion, are not fairly presented.
- Sufficient evidence has not been gathered to reach a conclusion on whether there is a misstatement in the accounts. For example, the client's controls may be so poor that documentary evidence does not exist. The auditor would issue a report that he or she cannot render an opinion on the fairness of the financial statements.

Note that in this list, the first outcome is by far the most common conclusion that the auditor reaches. Managers will face negative consequences if the auditor does not issue an unqualified audit report. Thus, while the latter two conclusions are possible, they are less common. Most of the time, when faced with an auditor issuing other than an unqualified audit report, management will acquiesce to the auditor's evidential findings.

Part C
OTHER ASSURANCE SERVICES AND AUDITING PROFESSIONS

Other Assurance and Attestation Services Provided by Public Accounting Firms

LO 6

Identify and describe non-audit assurance and attestation services provided by external auditors and discuss the relevant professional standards.

Financial statement audits represent only a part of the demand by various parties for assurance to be provided by independent auditors. In a financial statement audit, the auditor attests to the financial assertions made by management.

An auditor can also provide services attesting to other assertions such as the quality of internal control, compliance with regulatory requirements, or a wide variety of other items where there is a market for such services.

Assurance vs. Attestation vs. Audit

Sometimes the terms *assurance, attestation,* and *audit* are used interchangeably. However, these services differ on two fundamental dimensions:

- Existence of an outside third party that relies on the auditor's opinion
- Nature of services provided

The broadest of these services is **assurances services**. The AICPA's Special Committee on Assurance Services defines assurance services as "independent professional services that improve the quality of information, or its context, for decision makers." Assurance is a broad concept. The items on which assurance is provided can range from financial statements to computer system integrity to quality of products and services being sold to compliance with regulatory requirements. The assurance can be on information or processes. The adequacy of a process is just as important to most users as the information that goes into the process. Examples of assurance services that have been performed by auditing firms include:

- The adequacy of the process for capturing and reporting medical data
- The adequacy and reasonableness of the economic plans to build a new convention center in a major U.S. city

Attestation services are a subset of assurance services and *always* involve a report that goes to external users. For example, the auditor might provide a report to third parties about the quality of a company's internal controls over compliance with regulation. The narrowest attestation service is the audit of a company's financial statements. An audit is a subset of the other services that an auditor can provide. An overview of the three different levels of services is shown in Exhibit 1.4. Exhibit 1.5 describes the attributes needed to perform assurance services.

All types of assurance services involve three critical components:

- *Information* or a *process* on which the assurance service is provided
- A *user* or a *group of users* who derive value from the assurance services provided
- An *assurance service provider*

PRACTICAL POINT

Assurance services are designed to improve the quality of decision-making by improving confidence in the information on which decisions are based, the process by which that information is developed, and the context in which the information is presented to users. These services can be provided to management only or to external users.

PRACTICAL POINT

The IAASB's definition of assurance services, which follows, more closely mirrors the definition of attestation services used by U.S. practitioners:

An engagement in which a practitioner expresses a conclusion designed to enhance the degree of confidence of the intended users other than the responsible party about the outcome of the evaluation or measurement of a subject matter against criteria.

Thus, there are differences in definitions of and parameters used to articulate the similarities and differences of assurance vs. attestation vs. audit depending on locale.

AUDITING *in Practice*

ASSURANCE SERVICES

Two growth areas in assurance services include risk assessment and business performance measurement. For risk assessment services, the nature of the assurance provided relates to the quality of the processes implemented by an organization to identify, assess, and manage risks. For business performance measurement services, the nature of assurance provided relates to the processes used to identify, measure, and communicate measures of performance, and it could include assurance on the performance measures used by an organization.

Exhibit 1.4	Interrelationship of Assurance, Attestation, and Audit Services	
Type of Service	**Report to Third Party**	**Scope of Items Reported On**
Assurance Service	Optional, but not required Can include report only to party requesting the assurance	Broad, can include: • business processes • control processes • risk analysis • non-financial performance data • financial information
Attestation Service	Independent Auditor's Report is used by third party as part of the decision-making process	Same as assurance services Can be broad as long as objective criteria exist on which to evalu- ate fairness of management's report or information reported on
Audit Service	Third parties are primary users of the audit report	Audit of financial statements and related financial information

Exhibit 1.5	Attributes Needed to Perform Assurance Services

The attributes of individuals providing assurance services include:
• Subject-matter knowledge, such as information system knowledge
• Independence
• Agreed-upon criteria to evaluate quality of presentation, such as standards for internal control, or agreed-upon standards between
  the auditor and the user of the service
• Expertise in the process of gathering and evaluating evidence related to the subject matter

Providers of Assurance Services

The approach used in performing audits of financial statements applies equally well to other types of assurance services. The difference is in the subject-area knowledge required and the specific evidence that will need to be gathered to provide the assurance. Thus, the concepts covered in this text can be easily generalized to other types of assurance services beyond financial statement audits.

Many regional and local CPA firms provide a variety of assurance services to both audit and nonaudit clients. The large public accounting firms may provide many of the same consulting-type services—but they are not allowed to provide such services for their publicly traded audit clients. For example, all of the Big 4 firms provide significant internal audit services to companies that are not audit clients. As an example, at one of the companies for which a coauthor serves on the board, the company's external auditor is Deloitte and much of its internal audit work is outsourced to KPMG. The dollar value of the internal audit work can often rival of, or even exceed, the dollar amount for external audit work for a company.

Smaller accounting firms that do not have public clients follow standards developed by the AICPA regarding services that they may perform for an audit client. Many smaller public accounting firms provide information systems consulting, financial planning, tax planning, and internal audit services to both audit clients and nonaudit clients.

Levels of Assurance Provided

The IAASB has taken a two-pronged approach to the level of assurance provided that ultimately parallels the approach developed in the United States. The IAASB identifies two levels of assurance that can be provided:

1. Reasonable assurance
2. Limited assurance

Reasonable assurance engagements are "engagements in which a practitioner expresses a conclusion designed to enhance the degree of confidence of the intended users other than the responsible party about the outcome of the evaluation or measurement of a subject matter against criteria." There are some key elements in this definition that are important:

- There is always a third party involved, and the assurance is provided to the third party.
- There is measurement or evaluation against specific criteria. Those criteria may be part of a framework or might be related to criteria that have been agreed upon prior to the assurance engagement.
- The auditor is expected to communicate a definitive report, with reasonable assurance, on the information being presented.

A "limited assurance" engagement is one in which the objective is to provide less assurance by doing less work (thereby leading to a higher level of risk of being incorrect) that may be appropriately understood by all involved parties. Limited assurance engagements normally result in "negative assurance"; i.e., auditors perform limited procedures (usually analysis of an issue but without significant testing) and check to see if anything comes to their attention indicating a problem. In the United States, a limited assurance engagement related to financial statements is referred to as a **review**.

Professional Standards for Non-Audit Assurance Engagements

Auditors providing non-audit assurance services have standards to guide them and to help ensure quality for services beyond financial statement audits.

- *Attestation standards* is a term used by the AICPA to describe assurance services that involve gathering evidence regarding specific assertions and communicating an opinion on the fairness of the presentation to a third party. In the United States, whenever the auditor is performing a "reasonable assurance" engagement, the AICPA standards refer to the assurance as an "attestation service." Statements on Standards for Attestation Engagements (SSAEs) are issued by the AICPA. The AICPA has established specific standards for attesting to financial forecasts and projections, pro forma financial information, management discussion and analysis (MD&A), compliance with contracts or regulatory requirements, agreed-upon procedures, and controls at a service organization. Because it is difficult to anticipate all the areas into which the demand for attestation services might evolve, the attestation standards framework includes a set of general attestation standards to cover newly evolving services.
- *Compilation and review standards* refer to AICPA financial reporting standards that apply only to nonpublic companies where the board or a user has requested a lower level of assurance than that provided by an audit. In performing these services, the auditor does not gather enough evidence to support a statement as to whether the financial statements are fairly presented. Statements on Standards for Accounting and Review Services (SSARSs) are issued by the AICPA's Accounting and Review Services Committee (ARSC).

The IAASB has also issued standards that can be used by auditors who are performing assertion based assurance services (what the AICPA would refer to as attestation standards). These standards, International Standards on Assurance Engagements (ISAEs), are to be applied in assurance engagements other than audits or reviews of historical financial information.

Other Auditing Professions
The Internal Audit Profession

Internal auditing is defined as:

an independent, objective assurance and consulting activity designed to add value and improve an organization's operations. It helps an organization accomplish its

PRACTICAL POINT

Auditors can perform assurance engagements on a wide variety of information or processes, as might be demanded by third parties that desire greater confidence in the area subject to assurance.

PRACTICAL POINT

The auditor can be associated with information in a number of ways and the assurance that can be given by the auditor ranges from no assurance to limited assurance to reasonable assurance. The level of assurance is inversely related to the risk that the auditor's assurance could be incorrect.

PRACTICAL POINT

The limitation of compilation and review standards to nonpublic companies limits the auditor's legal exposure to some extent because the users often have specific relationships with the client, and in many cases, other access to client data.

LO 7

Describe the unique roles of internal auditors and governmental auditors.

objectives by bringing a systematic, disciplined approach to evaluate and improve the effectiveness of risk management, control, and governance processes.[7]

Internal auditing has emerged as an exciting discipline and an excellent training ground for future management positions. The emphasis on adding value and improving operations squarely aligns internal auditing with stockholders, the board of directors, and management.

Internal auditing, whether it is performed by auditors housed within a company or by auditors that participate in outsourcing functions of a public accounting or consulting firm, is increasingly becoming a strong alternative entry point into the auditing profession. The role of internal auditing is enhanced by the requirements of stock exchanges that listed companies should retain an internal audit function. The existence of an effective internal audit function is considered an important part of an organization's internal controls.

Services Provided by Internal Auditors

Internal auditors may provide both assurance and consulting services. Assurance comes in the form of assuring management and the board of directors about the company's compliance with policies or regulatory requirements or the effectiveness of processes and operations. Specific assurance services that internal auditors perform for an organization include:

- Effectiveness of a company's process for identifying and managing risk
- Quality of an organization's governance processes
- Effectiveness and efficiency of an organization's control processes
- Effectiveness and efficiency of operations, with suggestions for operational improvements
- Compliance of company operations with company policies and/or regulatory policies

Internal audit consulting activities often identify areas where the company can make significant operating improvements, or areas in which a company is not effectively managing its risk. Internal audit departments must maintain independence and recognize that they have unique data analysis skills and an independence from operations that can add value to assist management in addressing important problem areas. The internal audit function can analyze and identify potential solutions. However, management is responsible for choosing which solution to implement and must take responsibility for implementing the solution.

Internal auditing has been a leader in assisting organizations in documenting and evaluating the quality of internal control as part of the organization's Section 404 compliance with the Sarbanes-Oxley Act. Internal audit may have performed these services as a consulting service or an assurance service.

One type of internal audit activity involves the analysis of company operations, often referred to as an **operational audit**. Operational audits are designed to evaluate the effectiveness, economy, and efficiency with which resources are employed and can be applied to virtually every facet of an organization's operations. Operational audits are both challenging and interesting because the auditor must develop objective criteria to evaluate the effectiveness of an operation. The auditor must become familiar with best practices across companies as well as within the organization to develop such criteria. The auditor then must develop methodology, including the analysis of market data as well as internal information, to evaluate the effectiveness of operations. The auditor will have to thoroughly understand business processes and how various processes fit together across the organization.

---

[7] The Institute of Internal Auditors, http://www.theiia.org/guidance/standards-and-guidance/ippf/definition-of-internal-auditing/

The Institute of Internal Auditors

The Institute of Internal Auditors (IIA) is a voluntary organization dedicated to enhancing the professionalism and status of the internal auditing profession. With more than 170,000 members located in over 100 countries, the IIA is responsible for issuing standards for the profession. The IIA's International Internal Auditing Standards Board is recognized as the premier standard setter for the professional practice of internal auditing worldwide. The IIA administers the Certified Internal Auditor (CIA) program and has established a peer review process to help ensure that the practice of internal auditing around the globe is consistent with the professional standards.

The Governmental Auditing Profession

Governmental auditors are employed by various federal, state, and local agencies. The work performed by these auditors ranges from audits of a specific agency to audits of other governmental units to audits of reports furnished to the government by outside organizations. The requirement of accountability has created a demand for more information about government programs and services. Public officials, legislators, and private citizens want and need to know not only whether government funds are being handled properly and in compliance with laws and regulations, but also whether government organizations, programs, and services are achieving the purposes for which they were authorized and funded and whether they are doing so economically and efficiently.

Services Provided by Governmental Auditors

Governmental auditors perform all the types of audits that internal auditors perform; the major difference is the governmental orientation. The U.S. Government Accountability Office (GAO), headed by the Comptroller General, places a great deal of emphasis on performance audits. These audits determine (1) whether the entity is acquiring, protecting, and using its resources economically and efficiently; (2) the causes of inefficiencies or uneconomical practices; (3) whether the entity has complied with laws and regulations; (4) the extent to which the desired results or benefits established by the legislature or other authorizing body are being achieved; and (5) the effectiveness of organizations, programs, activities, or functions.

The U.S. Government Accountability Office

The U.S. GAO is the nonpartisan audit agency for Congress, which has delegated to the GAO the responsibility for developing auditing standards for governmental audits. The GAO periodically updates Governmental Auditing Standards, which includes standards for the conduct of audits of governmental organizations, programs, activities, and functions, and of government funds received by contractors, nonprofit organizations, and other nongovernmental entities. The standards cover the auditor's professional qualifications, the quality of the audit effort, and the audit reports appropriate. The standards are similar to those established by the AICPA and the IIA but relate to the nature of the work performed by governmental auditors.

> **PRACTICAL POINT**
>
> The GAO is a major player in setting auditing standards for all audits of governmental entities— even those entities audited by CPA firms. See http://www.gao.gov.

Summary

Efficient operation of the capital markets requires reliable financial information. The crucial importance of the fundamental product of the auditing profession— the financial statement audit—has been reinforced by events of the past century. Financial statement users need independent assurance on financial statement data. Auditors providing this assurance go through a structured process to gather and evaluate evidence and to communicate their findings to the public.

Recent failures in the auditing profession led Congress to enact the Sarbanes-Oxley Act of 2002, which has changed the regulatory oversight of the auditing profession. Oversight of the public accounting profession has shifted from the AICPA to the PCAOB for audits of public companies. The AICPA has now positioned itself as a standard setter for audit firms that do not audit public companies, as well as a promoter of a broader array of assurance services beyond financial statement audits. Audit standard setting continues to evolve with convergence projects between the AICPA and the IAASB. Auditors will need to understand the context of a particular audit engagement in order to reference the appropriate standards for the conduct of the audit. Fortunately, there is a great deal of consistency among all the standards.

Internal and governmental auditors also provide valuable services for organizations. These professions are broader than public accounting, and expose auditors to more aspects of a business, including risk management and operational efficiencies.

Significant Terms

American Institute of Certified Public Accountants (AICPA)   The primary professional organization for CPAs, it has a number of committees to develop professional standards for the conduct of nonpublic company audits and other services performed by its members and to self-regulate the profession.

Assertion   A positive statement about an action, event, condition, or the performance of an entity or product over a specified period of time; the subject of attestation services.

Assurance services   Independent professional services that improve the context or quality of information for decision-making purposes.

Attestation services   Services where an expression of opinion by an auditor is made to third parties concerning the correctness of assertions contained in financial statements or other reports against which objective criteria can be identified and measured.

Audit program   An auditor-prepared document that lists the specific procedures and audit tests to be performed in gathering evidence to test assertions.

Auditing   A systematic process of objectively obtaining evidence regarding assertions about economic actions and events to ascertain the degree of correspondence between those assertions and established criteria and communicating the results to interested users.

Due professional care   A standard of care expected to be demonstrated by a competent professional in his or her field of expertise, set by the generally accepted auditing standards but supplemented in specific implementation instances by the standard of care expected by a reasonably prudent auditor.

Financial statement audit   A systematic process to determine whether an entity's financial statements are fairly presented in accordance with GAAP, or other appropriate financial reporting framework.

Fieldwork standards   The three generally accepted auditing standards that deal with the actual conduct of an audit.

General standards   The three generally accepted auditing standards that deal with the qualification of individuals conducting an audit and the standard of care expected of those conducting an audit.

Generally accepted accounting principles (GAAP)   GAAP refers to generally accepted accounting principles for financial reporting. Throughout the text we recognize that the criteria may be developed by either FASB or the IASB. GAAP has general acceptance and provides criteria by which to assess the fairness of a financial statement presentation.

Government Accountability Office (GAO)   Governmental organization directly accountable to the Congress of the United States that performs special investigations for the Congress and establishes broad standards for the conduct of governmental audits.

Independence   Being objective and unbiased while performing professional services; being independent in fact and in appearance.

Integrated audit   Type of audit provided when an external auditor is engaged to perform an audit of the effectiveness of internal control over financial reporting ("the audit of internal control over financial reporting") that is integrated with an audit of the financial statements.

Internal auditing   An independent, objective assurance and consulting activity designed to add value and improve an organization's operations. It helps an organization accomplish its objectives by bringing a systematic, disciplined approach to evaluate and improve the effectiveness of risk management, control, and governance processes.

International Internal Auditing Standards Board   A part of the Institute of Internal Auditors that sets international standards for the professional practice of internal auditing.

International Accounting Standards Board (IASB)   It issues IFRS (International Financial Reporting Standards) and is working to be the one provider of accounting standards around the world.

International Auditing and Assurance Standards Board (IAASB)   A part of the International Federation of Accountants that is responsible for issuing auditing and assurance standards. Its goal is to harmonize auditing standards on a global basis.

International Standards for Auditing (ISAs)   Standards issued by the IAASB *for all* auditors who are following international auditing standards.

Materiality   Magnitude of an omission or misstatement of accounting information that, in light of surrounding circumstances, makes it probable that the judgment of a reasonable person relying on the information would have been changed or influenced by the omission or misstatement.

Operational audit   A systematic appraisal of an entity's operations to determine whether they are being carried out in an efficient manner and whether constructive recommendations for operational improvements can be made.

Professional skepticism   An attitude that includes a questioning mind and critical assessment of audit evidence.

Public Company Accounting Oversight Board (PCAOB)   A quasi-public board, appointed by the SEC, to provide oversight of the firms that audit public companies registered with the SEC. It has the authority to set auditing standards for the audits of public companies.

Reporting standards   The four generally accepted auditing standards that deal with the nature of the auditor's report and required communication.

Review   A type of assurance service that provides a lower level of assurance than does "reasonable assurance" because the audit-type procedures are limited. It results in a "negative assurance" opinion in which the auditor does not state that the amounts are fairly presented, rather the auditor states that nothing appeared that would cause him or her to believe there were misstatements.

Sarbanes–Oxley Act of 2002   Broad legislation mandating new standard setting for audits of public companies and new standards for corporate governance.

Securities and Exchange Commission (SEC)   The governmental body with the oversight responsibility to ensure the proper and efficient operation of capital markets in the United States.

Unqualified audit report   The standard three-paragraph audit report that describes the auditor's work and communicates the auditor's opinion that the financial statements are fairly presented in accordance with GAAP.

SELECTED REFERENCES TO RELEVANT PROFESSIONAL GUIDANCE	
TOPIC	**SELECTED GUIDANCE**
Conducting an Audit in Accordance with Professional Standards	SAS 1 *Codification of Auditing Standards and Procedures*
	SAS 95 *Generally Accepted Auditing Standards*
	SAS 102 *Defining Professional Responsibilities in Statements on Auditing Standards*
	SAS *Overall Objectives of the Independent Auditor and Conduct of an Audit in Accordance with Generally Accepted Auditing Standards* (issued but not effective; proposed effective date is December 2012)
	SAS *Preface to Codification of Statements on Auditing Standards, Principles Underlying an Audit Conducted in Accordance With Generally Accepted Auditing Standards* (issued but not effective; proposed effective date is December 2012)
	ISA 200 *Overall Objectives of the Independent Auditor and the Conduct of an Audit in Accordance with International Standards on Auditing*

Note: *Acronyms for Relevant Professional Guidance*
STANDARDS: **AS**—Auditing Standard issued by the PCAOB; **ISA**—International Standard on Auditing issued by the IAASB; **SAS**—Statement on Auditing Standards issued by the Auditing Standards Board of the AICPA; **SSAE**—Statement on Standards for Attestation Engagements issued by the AICPA.
ORGANIZATIONS: **AICPA**—American Institute of Certified Public Accountants; **COSO**—Committee of Sponsoring Organizations; **IAASB**—International Auditing and Assurance Standards Board; **PCAOB**—Public Company Accounting Oversight Board; **SEC**—Securities and Exchange Commission.

Review Questions

1-1   **(LO 1)** What is the "special function" that auditors perform? Whom does the public accounting profession serve in performing this special function?

1-2   **(LO 5)** Describe the audit opinion formulation process. What are the key steps within each of the five phases in the process?

1-3   **(LO 3)** What failures was Congress trying to address in passing the Sarbanes-Oxley Act of 2002? Identify some ways in which that Act affected the public accounting profession.

1-4   **(LO 6)** How does a financial statement audit differ from broader assurance services with respect to providing reports to third parties? Explain in terms of the scope of the activity and the potential users.

1-5   **(LO 1)** The term *professional judgment* is used throughout the chapter. In what ways might an auditor be called upon to exercise professional judgment in the course of performing an audit? To what extent does professional judgment rely on principles rather than rules? Explain.

1-6   **(LO 1)** What factors create a need for independent assurance? Explain how these factors are important to the public accounting profession.

1-7   **(LO 1)** A financial statement audit involves attesting to management assertions by reference to pre-established criteria. What serves as the criteria to judge the fairness of financial statements? Explain why "reference to criteria" is important to the audit function and the results communicated by the audit function.

1-8   **(LO 1)** How does complexity affect (1) the demand for auditing services and (2) the performance of auditing services?

1-9   **(LO 4)** Compare the AICPA's "ten generally accepted auditing standards"(historically used) with the newly issued "Principles Governing an Audit in Accordance with Generally Accepted Auditing Standards"

1-10   **(LO 1)** Who is the most important user of an auditor's report on a company's financial statements: company management, the company's shareholders, or the company's creditors? Briefly explain your rationale and indicate how auditors should resolve potential conflicts in the needs of the three parties.

1-11   **(LO 1)** How does an audit enhance the quality of financial statements and management's reports on internal control? Does an audit ensure a fair presentation of a company's financial statements or that internal control systems are free of material weaknesses? Explain.

1-12   **(LO 1)** Explain the concept of "due professional care." How does an independent third party evaluate whether or not an auditor met the standard of due professional care?

1-13   **(LO 3)** How might economic trends affecting a business impact the planning and execution of an audit? Give one example.

International

1-14   **(LO 4)** In what ways are the standards issued by the IAASB different from the standards issued by the AICPA and the PCAOB? In what ways are the standards issued by the IAASB consistent with the standards issued by the AICPA and the PCAOB?

1-15   **(LO 4)**   What is the difference between a reasonable assurance engagement and a limited assurance engagement?

1-16   **(LO 1)**   Why is it important that users perceive auditors to be independent?

1-17   **(LO 7)**   In what ways does the practice of internal auditing differ from the practice of public accounting? To whom is the internal auditing function responsible?

1-18   **(LO 2)**   In what ways might a public accounting practice of an audit firm with no public audit clients differ from that of one emphasizing public clients?

1-19   **(LO 7)**   What is the GAO? What types of audits does it perform? What is its role in setting standards for governmental audits?

1-20   **(LO 3)**   What is the role of the SEC in setting accounting and auditing standards?

1-21   **(LO 3, 4)**   Distinguish between the roles of the PCAOB and the AICPA in (a) setting audit standards, (b) performing quality-control reviews of member firms, and (c) setting accounting standards.

1-22   **(LO 3)**   What is COSO? Why is COSO, as a nonregulatory body, important to the auditing profession?

1-23   **(LO 2)**   Are small, local CPA firms that serve only small businesses and other local clients subject to the same auditing and accounting standards as the large international CPA firms?

1-24   **(LO 5)**   Describe how audit standards affect the design of audit programs.

1-25   **(LO 3)**   In what ways does the court system serve as a major regulatory body for the public accounting profession? Does the court system have a role in setting either accounting or auditing standards? Explain.

1-26   **(LO 5)**   What is an audit program? What information should an auditor gather before developing an audit program for a client?

1-27   **(LO 5)**   Define the term *materiality* and describe how an auditor would go about determining materiality to be used in planning an audit an organization's financial statements.

1-28   **(LO 5)**   What procedures should an auditor use to determine that all purchases debited to a fixed asset account in the current year are properly valued?

Multiple-Choice Questions

1-29   **(LO 1)**   In determining the primary responsibility of the external auditor for the audit of a company's financial statements, the auditor owes primary allegiance to which of the following parties?

    a. The management of the company being audited because the auditor is hired and paid by management.

b. The audit committee of the company being audited because that committee is responsible for coordinating and reviewing all audit activities within the company.

c. Stockholders, creditors, and the investing public.

d. The SEC because it determines accounting principles and auditor responsibility.

1-30 **(LO 1)** Which of the following would *not* represent one of the primary problems that create the demand for independent audits of a company's financial statements?

a. Potential management bias in preparing financial statements.

b. The downsizing of business and financial markets.

c. The complexity of transactions affecting financial statements.

d. The remoteness of the user from the organization and thus the inability of the user to directly obtain financial information from the company.

1-31 **(LO 6)** Which of the following statements is true regarding the provision of assurance services?

I. The third party who receives the assurance generally pays for the assurance received.

II. Assurance services always involve a report by one party to a third party on which an independent organization provides assurance.

III. Assurance services can be provided either on information or on processes.

  a. I and III

  b. II only

  c. III only

  d. I, II, and III

1-32 **(LO 3, 4)** Which of the following statements are correct regarding the setting of auditing standards in the United States?

a. The AICPA is responsible for the setting of audit standards for audits of nonpublic entities.

b. The GAO is responsible for setting audit standards for audits of governmental entities.

c. The PCAOB is responsible for setting audit standards for audits of public companies.

d. All of the above.

1-33 **(LO 3)** Which of the following statements are correct? As a result of the Sarbanes-Oxley Act of 2002

a. Public companies must report on the quality of their internal controls over financial reporting.

b. CPA firms cannot provide consulting services to any public company.

c. CPA firms can provide tax services only to nonpublic companies.

d. Accounting standards are set by the PCAOB.

e. All of the above.

1-34 **(LO 7)** The GAO is responsible for all of the following *except:*

a. Developing standards for audits of federal agencies.

b. Developing standards for audits of state agencies.

c. Performing special investigations at the request of Congress.

d. Developing standards for external audits of public companies.

1-35   **(LO 3)** The AICPA is a private governing organization of the public accounting profession that does all of the following except:

a. Perform quality peer reviews of companies performing audits.

b. Issue auditing standards dictating acceptable auditing practice for financial audits of public companies in the United States.

c. Establish standards for attestation services other than audits.

d. Prepare and grade the Uniform CPA Examination.

1-36   **(LO 1)** The application of due professional care means that the auditor's work conforms with all of the following except:

a. Current auditing standards.

b. The work that a reasonably prudent auditor would have performed in the same situation.

c. The work was at least equal to that which had been performed on the audit engagement during the preceding year.

d. All of the above are accurate regarding the application of due professional care.

1-37   **(LO 4)** The fieldwork standards require all of the following except:

a. An audit be properly planned and supervised.

b. Auditors develop an understanding of the client's controls as an important prerequisite to developing specific audit tests.

c. Auditors obtain sufficient appropriate audit evidence by performing audit procedures to provide a reasonable basis for the audit opinion being provided.

d. All of the above are required by the fieldwork standards.

1-38   **(LO 4)** The following describes a situation in which an auditor has to determine the most appropriate standards to follow. The audited company is headquartered in Paris but has substantial operations within the United States (60% of all operations) and has securities registered with the SEC and traded on the NYSE. The company uses IFRS for its accounting framework. What would be the most appropriate set of audit standards to follow?

International

a. Either PCAOB or IAASB

b. Either PCAOB or AICPA

c. Either IAASB or IASB

d. Either GAO or PCAOB

1-39   **(LO 5)** The auditor uses the following audit procedure as part of the audit of fixed assets that included material additions during the year: "take a *sample* of all additions to property, plant, and equipment, and trace to invoices received from the vendor." Which of the following outcomes would most likely alert the auditor to the possibility of a misstatement of the account balance?

a. Most of the items chosen are small in dollar amount even though the invoices are typical of items that last three to five years.

b. About one-third of the items chosen are large-dollar items that are traced to journal entries, but there are no underlying purchase documents.

   c. About one-fourth of the items are from the same vendor and relate to the equipment purchased for a new factory.

   d. Vendor invoices cannot be located for a number of purchases. However, all the items for which the invoices cannot be found relate to purchases from a related company.

   e. All of the above.

   f. (b) and (d) only

Discussion and Research Questions

1-40   **(Users of Financial Statements, LO 1)** It has been stated that auditing must be neutral because audited financial statements must serve the needs of a wide variety of users. If the auditor were to favor one group, such as existing shareholders, there might be a bias against another group, such as prospective investors.

Required

   a. What steps has the public accounting profession taken to minimize potential bias toward important users and thereby encourage neutrality in financial reporting and auditing?

   b. Who are the primary users of audited financial statements? Identify four user groups you believe are the most important. For each one identified, (1) briefly indicate their primary use of the financial statements and (2) indicate how an accounting treatment might benefit one party and potentially act to the detriment of another user.

1-41   **(Purposes of an External Audit, LO 1, 3)** The Rasmus Company manufactures small gas engines for use on lawnmowers and other power equipment. Most of its manufacturing has historically been in the Midwest, but it has recently opened plants in Asia that account for about 30% of its production. The company's stock is listed on the New York Stock Exchange.

Required

   a. Explain the rationale and value of an audit of a publicly held company to investors, creditors, and to the broader community as a whole.

   b. Explain why an audit of internal control provides value to the investing public.

   c. Explain the importance of an audit committee to the reliability of the financial statements and the audit function.

1-42   **(Smaller Company and Purpose of an External Audit, LO 1, 3)** Quello Golf Distributors is a relatively small, privately held golf distributing company handling several product lines, including Ping, Callaway, and Taylor-Made, in the Midwest. It sells directly to golf shops, pro shops, etc. but does not sell to the big retailers. It has approximately $8 million in sales and wants to grow at about 20% per year for the next five years. It is also thinking of a takeover or a merger with another golf distributorship that operates in many of the same areas.

Required

a. Explain why management might want an independent audit of its financial statements. Identify the specific benefits to Quello Golf Distributors.

b. What are the factors that Quello might consider in deciding whether to seek an audit from a large national public accounting firm, a regional public accounting firm, or a local firm?

c. Is Quello required to have an audit committee? Explain.

d. Is Quello required to issue a report on the quality of its internal control over financial reporting when it issues audited financial statements? Explain.

1-43   **(Nature of Auditing and the Public Accounting Profession, LO 1, 3, 4)** Do you agree or disagree with the following statements? Explain your rationale.

Fraud

a. A primary purpose of an audit is to ensure that all fraud that might be significant to a user is detected and reported.

b. There is a not an independence problem in a privately held company when the auditor is to be engaged by the manager because the manager is also the owner.

c. Congress, through Sarbanes-Oxley, requires mandatory reporting on internal control for public companies. That requirement should be extended to major charities like the Red Cross.

d. Users' expectations of the auditors of public companies are too high; the expectations simply cannot be met; the public should be better educated on what the auditor does and is capable of doing.

e. Consulting by public accounting firms for privately held companies is a value-added proposition and does not impair the independence of the audit; rather, it enhances the effectiveness of the audit because of greater knowledge of the company.

f. The PCAOB greatly enhances the reputation of the public accounting profession because it not only sets standards, but also determines whether firms audit according to those standards.

g. Fairly presented in accordance to GAAP is not as precise a criterion as one thinks because GAAP allows a wide variety of choices, e.g., FIFO vs. LIFO, accelerated vs. straight-line depreciation.

h. The auditor should be forced to state both (a) whether the financial statements are prepared in accordance with GAAP and (b) whether he or she feels that the choices made by the client best portray the economic substance of transactions within the GAAP framework.

i. Tax consulting, including preparing the tax return for top management, does not create a conflict of interest with the conduct of the audit.

1-44   **(Auditor Judgment, LO 1, 2, 3, 5)** Auditors often refer to the need for "professional judgment."

International

Required

a. In examining the audit opinion formulation process, identify the areas in which auditor judgment must be made. To what extent does that judgment extend beyond accounting issues?

b. It is claimed by some (although not always correctly) that they favor international accounting standards because they are more principles-based. Should principles-based accounting lead to more or less consistent audit judgments? Explain.

c. Should a public accounting firm expect that "professional judgments" made by its staff be, for the most part, consistent with each other? If not, why not? If yes, how are public accounting firms structured to help ensure consistent audit judgments?

1-45   (Understanding the Economic Environment and Client Business, LO 5) It is stated in the chapter that understanding a client's business is important to the conduct of an audit.

Required

a. Explain how an understanding of a business and the business environment would be important to the auditor in evaluating accounts such as:

1. Inventory
2. Allowance for uncollectible accounts
3. Warranty liability and warranty expenses

b. Explain how the understanding of the business may provide value-added services that the auditor might be able to use in order to assist a privately held client.

1-46   (Implementing an Assurance Service, LO 6) Assume an e-commerce company that sells various products over the Internet to consumers (e.g., Amazon.com, E-Toys, or eBay) wants certification from an auditor that states the company has (a) effective policies to ensure the following objectives and (b) those policies are implemented in a manner to achieve those objectives:

a. All goods are shipped in a timely fashion.
b. The goods are exactly as advertised.
c. The company stands behind any goods that are damaged in transit.
d. The company fulfills promises made in its credit policies.
e. Credit card and billing information is kept safe and is not sold to other e-tailers or retailers.

Required

a. For each of the assurances (a–e), indicate the evidence the auditor would gather in order to provide the assurance desired.

b. How often would the assurances have to be provided in order to meet the objectives sought by both the merchant and consumers?

c. What would be the best way to present the assurance, i.e., how would a potential user become aware of the assurances provided?

d. Why would a CPA be a good provider of such assurances?

e. What are the major attributes of companies that might not need such assurances?

f. Who are alternative providers of the above assurances?

Internet

1-47   (Internal Audit Profession, LO 7) The internal audit profession has grown rapidly in the past decade and has developed its own professional certification programs. Some companies are developing policies to recruit new personnel into internal audit departments directly from college campuses.

Required

a. Briefly describe the nature of internal auditing. What does it mean when it is described as an assurance and consulting activity? How does consulting differ from assurance?

b. Briefly explain what the internal auditor's role is regarding risk management and controls.

c. What are some of the reasons for pursuing a career in internal auditing?

d. Can some (all) of internal auditing be outsourced to a public accounting firm? Explain.

e. Access the website of the Institute of Internal Auditors (www. theiia.org) to determine the certification programs offered by the IIA. Prepare a brief memo summarizing these certifications.

1-48 **(Professional Organizations, LO 3, 4, 7)** Briefly describe the roles and responsibilities of the following professional organizations in developing and maintaining auditing standards and monitoring the quality of the various auditing professions:

Internet

a. AICPA

b. IIA

c. GAO

International

d. SEC

e. PCAOB

f. IAASB

1-49 **(Internal Auditing, LO 7)** You are aware that most of the first courses in auditing focus on public accounting rather than internal auditing. Yet your professor states that most of the concepts related to an audit approach and evidence gathering are applicable to both internal and external auditing.

Internet

Required
Conduct research using internet resources to answer the following questions.

a. If you decide to start your career in internal auditing, how will your first two years of work differ from your first two years in public accounting?

b. Assume that you are interested in eventually developing your skills as a manager in a large organization. Explain why beginning a career in internal auditing would be compatible with that objective.

1-50 **(Nature of Auditing and the Public Accounting Profession, LO 1, 3, 4)** You and a colleague are carrying on a heated discussion. The colleague makes a number of statements about the public accounting profession that you believe are in error. Welcoming an opportunity for rebuttal, you are ready to reply.

Fraud

Required

a. For each of the following colleague statements, develop a brief response indicating erroneous assumptions made by the colleague or your agreement with the statements.

International

b. Perform appropriate research using relevant Internet resources and cite relevant evidence in support of your response.

Colleague's Statements

1. "Auditing neither creates goods nor adds utility to existing goods and therefore does not add value to business. Auditing exists only because it has been legally mandated."

2. "The failure of the public accounting profession to warn us of the problems that existed in the economy is an example of a profession not adding utility to society."

3. "The only reason I would hire an auditor is with the expectation that the auditor search for and find any fraud that might exist within my company. Searching for fraud should be the primary focus of an audit."

4. "Auditors cannot legitimately serve the public when they are hired and fired by the management of the company being audited."

5. "The switch to the PCAOB in setting audit standards will enhance the reputation of the profession because the auditors must act in the public's interest."

6. "Auditors cannot add significant value to financial statements as long as GAAP allow such diversity in accounting principles. How, for example, can the same auditor issue unqualified opinions on identical companies—one that uses FIFO and the other LIFO to account for the same set of transactions—recognizing that the reported income and balance sheets will be materially different? How can both be fairly presented?"

7. "Auditing is narrow—just nitpicking and challenging the organization in an attempt to find mistakes. I would rather pursue a career where I really understand a company's business and would be in a position to make recommendations that would improve it."

8. "Auditing would add greater value if it analyzed company performance and presented a report on company performance along with the audited financial statements."

9. "If auditors make recommendations to clients based on weaknesses in the company operations, the auditors ought to make those recommendations public. This would help increase the public trust by providing more accountability by both management and auditors."

10. "Adding reports on the quality of internal control will enhance the value of the audit function to society."

1-51 **(Public Accounting Profession, LO 1)** In their review of the public accounting profession, Lou Harris and Associates warn that an audit report too often is viewed as a "certificate of health" for a company. The report states:

> The most serious consequences stemming from such a misunderstanding are that the independent auditor can quickly be portrayed as the force that represents all good in financial accounting and the guarantor of anything positive anyone wants to feel about a given company.

Required

a. Why is public accounting often viewed as a guarantor of results or even as a provider of assurance that one's investment is of high quality?

b. To what extent is it reasonable to view the auditor as a guarantor of an organization's financial quality? Explain.

c. To what extent do you believe that user expectations of the public accounting profession appear to you to be unwarranted? Explain.

1-52 **(PCAOB, LO 3)** Access the PCAOB home page at http://www .pcaobus.org.

a. Identify the members of the Board and their background. What is their background in accounting or using financial statements?

b. Identify the most recent auditing standard issued or in exposure draft form. Identify the nature of the standard and discuss the reason that the Board is issuing the standard.

1-53 **(SEC, LO 3)** Access the SEC home page at http://www.sec.gov.

a. Identify the most recent litigation brought by the SEC against a public company or against an accounting firm. Read the abstract of the complaint and download the document filed with the court. Comment on the nature of the litigation.

b. Identify the most recent Staff Accounting Bulletin that provides guidance to the profession. Identify the guidance given.

1-54 **(Public Accounting Firms, LO 2, 6)** The large public accounting firms no longer provide consulting services for their public audit clients. However, many public accounting firms that do not audit public companies continue to provide such services to their clients.

Required

a. Log on to the website of one of the Big 4 firms and identify the breadth of services that the firm provides to nonaudit clients.

b. Log on to the website of two firms in your area that provide services primarily to nonpublic companies. Identify their "business motto" and identify the nature of nonaudit services provided to clients.

c. Contrast the breadth and nature of services provided by the Big 4 firms vs. the local firms that you have examined.

1-55 **(Audit Standard Setters, LO 3, 4)** As companies become more global, auditors are becoming aware that there are a number of different standard setters for audit and assurance services, including the PCAOB, the AICPA, and the IAASB. Further, the GAO does not have an audit standards board, but it sets the standards for governmental audits within the United States.

Required

Access the websites of these various organizations to assist you in answering the following questions: Who appoints members to each of these boards? What are the differences in legal authority for each of these standard setting boards? Which of the boards have the most (a) CPAs or Chartered Accountants and (b) public members?

1-56 **(Audit Standards for NonPublic Companies, LO 3, 4)** The PCAOB has the authority to set audit standards for all audits of public companies registered in the U.S. The AICPA continues to set audit standards for nonpublic companies through its auditing standards board.

Required

a. What are the pros and cons of having the same audit standards for both public and nonpublic entities?

b. In what ways might you expect auditing standards for audits of nonpublic companies to differ from the standards for public companies? Identify three (there are not necessarily three right or wrong answers—this is an opinion and discussion question only). Identify the rationale for your answers.

c. A CPA is performing an audit of a local municipality. Where should the auditor look to determine audit standards that must be followed?

d. What role should an audit committee play in determining which standards an audit firm will use in auditing their company? Explain.

1-57   **(GAAS, LO 4)** Ray, the owner of a small company, asked Holmes, CPA, to conduct an audit of the company's records. Ray told Holmes that the audit must be completed in time to submit audited financial statements to a bank as part of a loan application. Holmes immediately accepted the engagement and agreed to provide an auditor's report within three weeks. Ray agreed to pay Holmes a fixed fee plus a bonus if the loan was granted.

Holmes hired two accounting students to conduct the audit and spent several hours telling them exactly what to do. Holmes told the students not to spend time reviewing the controls, but instead to concentrate on proving the mathematical accuracy of the ledger accounts and to summarize the data in the accounting records that support Ray's financial statements. The students followed Holmes's instructions and after two weeks gave Holmes the financial statements, which did not include footnotes because the company did not have any unusual transactions. Holmes reviewed the statements and prepared an unqualified auditor's report. The report, however, did not refer to GAAP or to the year-to-year application of such principles.

Required

Briefly describe each of GAAS's ten standards and indicate how the action(s) of Holmes resulted in a failure to comply with each standard.

Professional Skepticism

1-58   **(Auditing Standards, LO 4)** The ten generally accepted auditing standards (GAAS) have historically provided the foundation for the conduct of audits. More recently, the AICPA has a proposed standard, *Overall Objectives of the Independent Auditor and Conduct of an Audit in Accordance with Generally Accepted Auditing Standards* (which has been issued but is not effective as the proposed effective date is December 2012). Both sources of guidance address important concepts related to the conduct of the audit.

Required

a. Define the standard of "due professional care" and indicate how a court might decide whether an audit firm met the standard.

b. Explain why independence is often considered the cornerstone of the auditing profession. Explain why independence issues were a primary concern of Congress when it developed the Sarbanes-Oxley Act.

    c. Assume you work on an audit engagement for a client for some period of time. Further, assume there have never been any audit issues with the client, management is very honest and forthcoming, and the company is well run. Explain how you would retain your professional skepticism.

    d. If an auditor is engaged to conduct an audit and finds numerous mistakes, is it possible for the auditor to resign and not issue an audit opinion? Explain.

1-59   **(Materiality, LO 5)** Materiality is an important audit concept because audits must be designed to detect "material" misstatements.

Required

    a. Based on research using the Internet and other resources, define materiality and describe how it is used in both accounting and auditing.

    b. Should the determination of the materiality be discussed with (1) the audit committee and (2) management before the beginning of the audit engagement? Explain your rationale.

    c. What factors might an auditor look at in determining materiality for an audit client prior to the start of the audit?

1-60   **(Audit Procedures, LO 5)** Audits of financial statements are designed to test the correctness of account balances.

Required

    a. A construction company shows the following assets on its balance sheet:

- Construction equipment $1,278,000
- Accumulated depreciation $386,000
- Leased equipment—construction $550,000

    Explain how the three accounts differ from each other and the underlying accounting required for each.

    b. Is the equipment held by the company fairly old or new? Explain.

    c. Develop an audit procedure to determine that all leased equipment that should have been capitalized during the year was actually capitalized (as opposed to being treated as a lease expense).

    d. The construction equipment account shows that the company purchased approximately $400,000 of new equipment this year. Identify an audit procedure that will determine whether the equipment account was properly accounted for during the year.

    e. Assuming the auditor determines the debits to construction equipment were proper during the year, what other information does the auditor need to know in order to ensure that the construction equipment—net of depreciation—is properly reflected on the balance sheet?

    f. How can an auditor determine that the client has assigned an appropriate useful life to the equipment and has depreciated it accurately?

Cases

1-61   (GAO and the Public Accounting Profession, LO 1, 7) In a report to Congress entitled "Superfund: A More Vigorous and Better Managed Enforcement Program Is Needed," the GAO made the following observations:

> Because cost recovery has been considered a low priority within EPA [the Environmental Protection Agency] and received limited staff resources, it has faltered. To provide a systematic approach for implementing its Superfund enforcement initiatives, EPA should establish long-term, measurable goals for implementing the Administrator's Superfund strategy and identify the resource requirements that will be needed to meet these long-term goals. GAO also makes other recommendations to improve EPA's enforcement activities.

Discussion Issues

a. How would the GAO go about developing evidence to reach the conclusion that cost recovery has been a low priority within the EPA?

b. Why is it important to the EPA, Congress, and the GAO that the EPA establish long-term, measurable goals? How would the establishment of such goals facilitate future audits of the EPA?

c. Based on the conclusions identified earlier, would you consider the work performed on the EPA by the GAO to be an audit? Explain why or why not.

d. In what substantive ways does it appear that the audit work of the GAO differs from that of the public accounting profession?

Professional Skepticism

1-62   (PCAOB and Auditor Responsibilities, LO 1, 3, 4, 5) In April 2010 the PCAOB issued a disciplinary order instituting disciplinary proceedings, making findings, and imposing sanctions in the case of Robert T. Taylor, CPA (both the firm and the individual auditor). The order can be found in PCAOB Release No. 105-2010-006 at www.pcaobus.org. Review the PCAOB website, access this release, and answer the following questions.

a. What is the PCAOB and what authority does it have to issue disciplinary orders and impose sanctions?

b. What is the PCAOB's source of potential violations of law or PCAOB rules?

c. How many disciplinary orders has the PCAOB issued?

d. The order in the case of Robert T. Taylor recognizes that PCAOB standards require that an auditor exercise due professional care, exercise professional skepticism, and obtain sufficient evidence on which to base an opinion on the financial statements. Describe instances in which the respondents in the order did not adhere to these requirements.

e. What sanctions were imposed in this case? Do the sanctions seem appropriate?

Academic Research Case (LO 1)

Knechel, W.R. and Willekens, M. (2006). The Role of Risk Management and Governance in Determining Audit Demand. *Journal of Business Finance & Accounting: 33(9) & (10), 1344–1367.*

   i. What is the issue being addressed in the paper?
  ii. Why is this issue important to practicing auditors?
 iii. What are the findings of the paper?
  iv. What are the implications of these findings for audit quality (or audit practice) on the audit profession?
   v. Describe the research methodology used as a basis for the conclusions.
  vi. Describe any limitations of the research that the student (and practice) should be aware of.

SEARCH HINT

It is easy to locate these academic research articles! Simply use a search engine (e.g., Google Scholar) or an electronic research platform (e.g., ABI Inform) and search using the author names and part of the article title.

2

Corporate Governance and Audits

LEARNING OBJECTIVES

The overriding objective of this textbook is to build a foundation for analyzing current professional issues and adapting audit approaches to business and economic complexities. Through studying this chapter, you will be able to:

1 Define corporate governance and identify the parties involved in corporate governance and their respective roles.

2 List and analyze principles of effective corporate governance.

3 Describe events of the last decade that have had significant impact on corporate governance, including the corporate governance failures of various parties.

4 Identify recent governance and disclosure-related regulations that were the response to calls for increased governance and describe how various parties are affected by those regulations.

5 Articulate the responsibilities of audit committees.

6 List and analyze principles of effective audit committees.

7 Describe required communications between the audit firm and the audit committee.

8 Analyze the relationship between corporate governance and the audit.

CHAPTER OVERVIEW

Poorly governed companies, such as Enron, WorldCom, Bear Stearns, and Lehman Brothers, turned out to be risky investments for investors. The public accounting profession has been widely criticized for not doing enough to protect investors' interests as they relate to these types of companies. Therefore, audit firms view companies with poor governance as riskier audit clients. Corporate failures during the past decade have resulted in important changes in corporate governance. Congress reacted to these failures by enacting the Sarbanes-Oxley Act of 2002. The failures leading up the Act involved individuals in the audit profession and within organizations, including management and individuals charged with corporate governance. For example, questions have been raised about management greed associated with backdating of stock options and about whether a board of directors has enough power, time, and resources to provide proper oversight of management. The Sarbanes-Oxley Act contains provisions that affect the conduct of the audit and the responsibilities of management and the audit committee.

This chapter describes what is meant by corporate governance and the relationship between a client's corporate governance and the audit. In terms of the audit opinion formulation process, this chapter focuses on the basic notions of the auditing profession, regulation, and corporate governance in general and Phase II of the process, i.e., understanding the client in terms of the quality of its corporate governance.

The Audit Opinion Formulation Process

| I. Assessing Client Acceptance and Retention Decisions

CHAPTER 4 | II. Understanding the Client

CHAPTERS 2, 4–6, and 9 | III. Obtaining Evidence about Controls and Determining the Impact on the Financial Statement Audit

CHAPTERS 5–14 and 18 | IV. Obtaining Substantive Evidence about Account Assertions

CHAPTERS 7–14 and 18 | V. Wrapping Up the Audit and Making Reporting Decisions

CHAPTERS 15 and 16 |

| The Auditing Profession, Regulation, and Corporate Governance

CHAPTERS 1 and 2 | | Decision-Making, Professional Conduct, and Ethics

CHAPTER 3 | | Professional Liability

CHAPTER 17 |

PROFESSIONAL JUDGMENT IN CONTEXT

Responsibilities of Board Members

Periodically, the SEC emphasizes the important role that a company's board of directors has in protecting investors' interests. Although it is rare, the SEC can pursue actions against outside directors if the directors fail to fulfill their role. In March 2010, the SEC filed an action against a former director of InfoGroup who served as the chair of the board's audit committee. The SEC alleges that the company's CEO had used almost $9.5 million in corporate funds for personal expenses, including expenses related to the CEO's yacht, personal jet travel, personal insurance policies, and upkeep of three homes and twenty automobiles, and that the company entered into $9.3 million of transactions with companies in which the CEO had a personal role. The SEC's action against Vasant Raval, the former audit committee chair, alleges that Raval became aware of the CEO's expenses and related party transactions and was asked by the board to investigate. Raval conducted the investigation on his own and found that documentation for many of the expenses and related party transactions was not sufficient. Further, two internal auditors alerted Raval to the questionable purpose of many of the expenses. The SEC stated that Raval failed to take meaningful action to further investigate the matter and omitted critical facts in a report to the board. The SEC charged Raval with committing and causing a public company's securities law violations relating to the company's regulatory disclosures. Specifically, Raval did not take steps to ensure the accuracy of SEC filings. The SEC complaint alleges that Raval had a broad duty "to ensure the accuracy and completeness of the statements contained in the company's Commission filings" and that he "failed to take appropriate action with respect to significant red flags

concerning [the CEO's] expenses and Info's related party transactions with [the CEO's] entities." Raval settled the matter without admitting or denying the SEC's allegations and agreed to a bar from serving as an officer or director of a public company for five years, and agreed to pay a $50,000 civil penalty.

As you read through this chapter, consider the following questions:

- Why is the corporate governance of an organization important to both investors and auditors?
- What roles do the board of directors and the audit committee play with respect to corporate governance?
- What relationships do the board of directors and the audit committee have with the audit function?
- Why is it important that organizations have directors and audit committee members who are competent and independent of management?
- Why would the quality of corporate governance affect the quality of an organization's financial performance and the conduct of the external audit?
- What are the risks to the auditor if the organization does not have good corporate governance?
- Should an auditor accept an audit engagement with an organization that does not have good governance?
- What principles are associated with high-quality governance?
- What principles are associated with effective audit committees?

Sources: See SEC press release at http://www.sec.gov/news/press/2010/2010-39.htm; see SEC complaint at http://www.sec.gov/litigation/complaints/2010/comp21451-raval.pdf; and see SEC Litigation Release No. 21451/March 15, 2010.

What Is Corporate Governance?

LO 1

Define corporate governance and identify the parties involved in corporate governance and their respective roles.

Corporate governance is a process by which the owners and creditors of an organization exert control and require accountability for the resources entrusted to the organization. The owners (stockholders) elect a board of directors to provide oversight of the organization's activities and accountability to stakeholders. Many parties have a vested interest in the quality of an organization's corporate governance, including the following:

- Stockholders
- Boards of directors
- Audit committees (as a subcommittee of the board)
- Management (financial and operational)
- Internal auditors
- Self-regulatory organizations, such as the AICPA and the New York Stock Exchange
- Regulatory agencies, such as the SEC and the Environmental Protection Agency
- External auditors

Exhibit 2.1 provides a broad schematic of the overall governance process, while Exhibit 2.2 provides details on responsibilities of various parties involved in corporate governance. Governance starts with the stockholders/owners delegating responsibilities through an elected board of directors to management and, in turn, to operating units with oversight and assistance from internal auditors. The board of directors and its audit committee oversee management and, in that role, are expected to protect the stockholders' rights. However, it is important to recognize that management is part of the governance framework; management can influence who sits on the board and the audit committee as well as other governance controls that might be put into place.

In return for the responsibilities (and power) given to management and the board, governance demands accountability back through the system to the shareholders. However, the accountabilities do not extend to only the shareholders. Companies also have responsibilities to other **stakeholders**.

PRACTICAL POINT

Corporate governance and financial reporting reliability are receiving considerable attention from a number of parties including regulators, standard setting bodies, the accounting profession, lawmakers, and financial statement users.

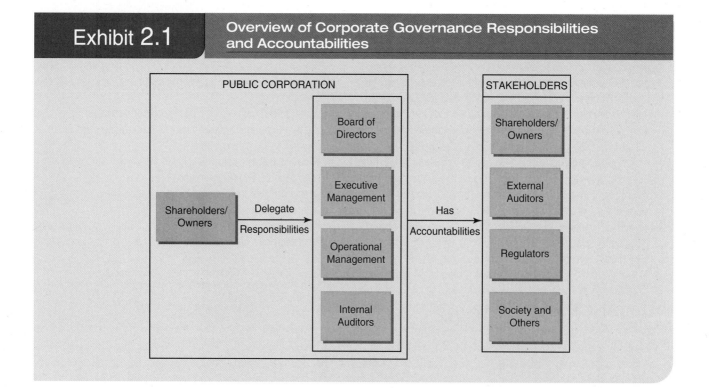

| Exhibit 2.1 | Overview of Corporate Governance Responsibilities and Accountabilities |

Stakeholders can be anyone who is influenced, either directly or indirectly, by the actions of a company. Management and the board have responsibilities to act within the laws of society and to meet various requirements of creditors and employees and other stakeholders.

A broad group of stakeholders has an interest in the quality of corporate governance because it has a relationship to economic performance and the quality of financial reporting. For example, it is likely that many employees in your state have significant funds invested in pension plans. Those pension plans are designed to protect the financial interests of those employees in their retirement. We use the word *society* in Exhibit 2.1 to indicate those broad interests. In a similar fashion, employees and creditors have a vested interest in the organization and how it is governed. Regulators are a response to society's wishes to ensure that organizations, in their pursuit of returns for their owners, act responsibly and operate in compliance with relevant laws.

While stockholders/owners delegate responsibilities to various parties within the corporation, they also require accountability as to how well the resources that have been entrusted to management and the board have been used. For example, the owners want accountability on such things as:

- Financial performance
- Financial transparency—financial statements that are clear with full disclosure and that reflect the underlying economics of the company
- Stewardship, including how well the company protects and manages the resources entrusted to it
- Quality of internal controls
- Composition of the board of directors and the nature of its activities, including information on how well management incentive systems are aligned with the stockholders' best interests

The owners want disclosures from management that are accurate and objectively verifiable. For example, management has a responsibility to provide financial reports, and in some cases, reports on internal control effectiveness. Management has always had the primary responsibility for the accuracy and completeness of an organization's financial statements. From a financial reporting perspective, it is management's responsibility to:

- Choose which accounting principles best portray the economic substance of company transactions.
- Implement a system of internal control that assures completeness and accuracy in financial reporting.
- Ensure that the financial statements contain accurate and complete disclosure.

Principles of Good Corporate Governance

What characteristics and actions on the part of organizations are key to ensuring high-quality corporate governance? Over the years governance consultants and proxy advisors have developed checklists of best practices of good governance. For example, in 2010, a commission sponsored by the New York Stock Exchange issued a report identifying ten core governance principles directed at various parties including boards, management, proxy advisory firms, shareholders, and the SEC. This report was in response to the financial crisis of 2008 and 2009. The principles related to boards and management include:

- The board's fundamental objective should be to build long-term sustainable growth in shareholder value for the corporation.
- Successful corporate governance depends upon successful management of the company, as management has the primary responsibility for creating a culture of performance with integrity and ethical behavior.

PRACTICAL POINT

In some parts of the world, such as Europe, organizations issue "triple-bottom-line reporting" that delineates the organization's contributions to the broader goals of society. Further, many corporations issue reports on sustainability and corporate responsibility. Most of these reports are not audited, but they contain a wealth of information about the company's philosophy and corporate governance that will be of interest to the auditor and other stakeholders.

PRACTICAL POINT

Section 304 of the Sarbanes-Oxley Act requires executives to forfeit any bonus or incentive-based pay or profits (including stock options) from the sale of stock received in the twelve months prior to an earnings restatement. This is often referred to as a "claw back" provision; many management contracts now also have such provisions. Such provisions are intended to ensure that management's economic incentives are aligned with their responsibilities.

PRACTICAL POINT

Good governance requires that organizations achieve objectives related to financial performance, financial reporting, and compliance with their own policies, as well as with applicable laws and regulations.

LO 2

List and analyze principles of effective corporate governance.

PRACTICAL POINT

A commission sponsored by the New York Stock Exchange issued a report in 2010 indicating that successful governance depends heavily upon honest, competent, and industrious managers.

- Good corporate governance should be integrated with the company's business strategy and not viewed as simply a compliance obligation.
- Transparency is a critical element of good corporate governance, and companies should make regular efforts to ensure that they have sound disclosure policies and practices.
- Independence and objectivity are necessary attributes of board members; however, companies must also strike the right balance in the appointment of independent and non-independent directors to ensure an appropriate range and mix of expertise, diversity, and knowledge on the board.

PRACTICAL POINT

An important aspect of governance is the *independent* judgment of boards about what is in the best interests of the company and its shareholders. Therefore, just as auditors need to be independent, other individuals charged with corporate governance also need to be independent.

The report notes that there are various implications of these principles. Given that the board's fundamental objective is to build long-term sustainable growth, corporate policies that encourage excessive risk-taking for the sake of short-term increases in stock price would typically be inconsistent with sound corporate governance. Similarly, compensation policies that do not encourage long-term value creation would not be viewed as good corporate governance. Corporate management has a responsibility for creating an environment in which a culture of performance with integrity can flourish. Additional management responsibilities would include establishing risk management processes and proper internal controls, requiring high ethical standards, ensuring open internal communications about potential problems, and providing accurate information to relevant parties including the board of directors and other stakeholders. Integrating corporate governance into the business strategy recognizes that governance must be part of the culture of the organization and must not just be an added checklist of things to do. While disclosure is the primary method of communication with stakeholders, organizations should determine if it is also appropriate for management or directors to engage in direct dialogue with investors and other stakeholders on governance, performance, or strategy concerns. A board should include directors who possess in-depth knowledge of the company and its industry.

PRACTICAL POINT

In December 2009 the SEC released rules requiring public companies to disclose their governance measures, including their board structure.

PRACTICAL POINT

Boards should take care to not adopt a "check the box" mentality when implementing and complying with governance mandates and best practices.

LO 3

Describe events of the last decade that have had significant impact on corporate governance, including the corporate governance failures of various parties.

Corporate Governance Challenges and Changes During the Last Decade

The first decade of the twenty-first century has seen more changes in corporate governance than at any time since the Great Depression. Various factors were in play that resulted in calls for increased governance. For example, there was incredible volatility in the financial markets beginning in 2000, leading to the financial crisis and recession hitting the markets in 2008 and 2009, and continuing into the next decade. There were also a number of financial failures—e.g., Enron and WorldCom—which represented fundamental breakdowns in the structure of corporate governance and involved many parties.

As summarized in Exhibit 2.2, the corporate governance failures were broad and a number of different parties contributed to those failures. Importantly, there was much finger pointing at the auditing profession for its failures. In the late 1990s, the SEC, led by Arthur Levitt, pushed for reform of the auditing profession. Levitt summed up the problem as follows:

PRACTICAL POINT

Governance failures over the past decade were not limited to the United States. Similar failures occurred in major companies located in Italy, France, India, Japan, the UK, as well as other parts of the world.

> Auditors are the public's watchdogs in the financial reporting process. We rely on auditors to put something like the good housekeeping seal of approval on the information investors receive. The integrity of that information must take priority.[1]

Levitt pushed the SEC to further develop concepts of audit independence because the consulting fees (mostly from audit clients) of public accounting firms

---

[1] Arthur Levitt, "The Numbers Game." Remarks at the NYU Center for Law and Business Reporting, September 28, 1998.

Exhibit 2.2	Corporate Governance Responsibilities and Failures	

Party	Overview of Responsibilities	Overview of Corporate Governance Failures
Stockholders	**Broad Role:** Provide effective oversight through election of board members, approval of major initiatives such as buying or selling stock, annual reports on management compensation from the board	• Focused on short-term prices • failed to perform long-term growth analysis • abdicated most responsibilities to management and analysts as long as stock price increased
Board of Directors	**Broad Role:** The major representative of stockholders to ensure that the organization is run according to the organization's charter and that there is proper accountability **Specific activities include:** • Selecting management • Reviewing management performance and determining compensation • Declaring dividends • Approving major changes, e.g., mergers • Approving corporate strategy • Overseeing accountability activities	• Inadequate oversight of management • Approval of management compensation plans, particularly stock options that provided perverse incentives, including incentives to manage earnings • Directors often dominated by management • Did not spend sufficient time or have sufficient expertise to perform duties • Continually re-priced stock options when market price declined
Management	**Broad Role:** Operations and accountability. Manage the organization effectively; provide accurate and timely accountability to shareholders and other stakeholders **Specific activities include:** • Formulating strategy and risk management • Implementing effective internal controls • Developing financial and other reports to meet public, stakeholder, and regulatory requirements • Managing and reviewing operations • Implementing an effective ethical environment	• Earnings management to meet analyst expectations • Fraudulent financial reporting • Using accounting concepts to achieve reporting objectives • Created an environment of greed, rather than one of high ethical conduct
Audit Committees of the Board of Directors	**Broad Role:** Provide oversight of the internal and external audit function and the process of preparing the annual financial statements and public reports on internal control **Specific activities include:** • Selecting the external audit firm • Approving any nonaudit work performed by the audit firm • Selecting and/or approving the appointment of the Chief Audit Executive (Internal Auditor) • Reviewing and approving the scope and budget of the internal audit function • Discussing audit findings with internal auditor and external auditor and advising the board (and management) on specific actions that should be taken	• Similar to board members—did not have expertise or time to provide effective oversight of audit functions • Were not viewed by auditors as the "audit client"; Rather, the power to hire and fire the auditors often rested with management
Self-Regulatory Organizations: AICPA, FASB	**Broad Role:** Set accounting and auditing standards dictating underlying financial reporting and auditing concepts; set the expectations of audit quality and accounting quality **Specific activities include:** • Establishing accounting principles • Establishing auditing standards • Interpreting previously issued standards	• **AICPA:** Peer reviews did not take a public perspective; rather, the reviews looked at standards that were developed and reinforced internally • Inadequate enforcement of existing audit standards • **AICPA:** Did not actively involve third parties in standard setting

Exhibit 2.2	Corporate Governance Responsibilities and Failures (*continued*)	
Party	**Overview of Responsibilities**	**Overview of Corporate Governance Failures**
	• Implementing quality control processes to ensure audit quality • Educating members on audit and accounting requirements	• **FASB:** Became more rule-oriented in response to (a) complex economic transactions, and (b) an auditing profession that was more oriented to pushing the rules rather than enforcing concepts • **FASB:** Pressure from Congress to develop rules that enhanced economic growth, e.g., allowing organizations to not expense stock options
Other Self-Regulatory Organizations: NYSE, NASDAQ	**Broad Role:** Ensure the efficiency of the financial markets including oversight of trading and oversight of companies that are allowed to trade on the exchange **Specific activities include:** • Establishing listing requirements—including accounting requirements and governance requirements • Overseeing trading activities	Pushed for improvements for better corporate governance procedures by its members, but failed to implement those same procedures for its governing board, management, and trading specialists
Regulatory Agencies: the SEC	**Broad Role:** Ensure the accuracy, timeliness, and fairness of public reporting of financial and other in formation for public companies **Specific activities include:** • Reviewing filings with the SEC • Interacting with the FASB in setting accounting standards • Specifying independence standards required of auditors that report on public financial statements • Identify corporate frauds, investigate causes, and suggest remedial actions	Identified problems but was not granted sufficient resources by Congress or the Administration to deal with the issues
External Auditors	**Broad Role:** Perform audits of company financial statements to ensure that the statements are free of material misstatements including misstatements that may be due to fraud **Specific activities include:** • Audits of public company financial statements • Audits of nonpublic company financial statements • Other services such as tax or consulting	• Helped companies use accounting concepts to achieve earnings objectives • Promoted personnel based on ability to sell "nonaudit products" • Replaced direct tests of accounting balances with inquiries, risk analysis, and analytics • Failed to uncover basic frauds in cases such as WorldCom and HealthSouth because fundamental audit procedures were not performed
Internal Auditors	**Broad Role:** Perform audits of companies for compliance with company policies and laws, audits to evaluate the efficiency of operations, and periodic evaluation and tests of controls **Specific activities include:** • Reporting results and analyses to management (including operational management) and audit committees • Evaluating internal controls	• Focused efforts on "operational audits" and assumed that financial auditing was addressed by the external audit function • Reported primarily to management with little reporting to the audit committee • In some instances (HealthSouth, WorldCom) did not have access to the corporate financial accounting records

had become higher than audit fees. The problem had been recognized for over a decade but audit firms argued that the consulting work helped, not hindered, an audit. As early as 1988, Arthur Wyatt, a long-time accounting standard setter, said:

> Practicing professionals should place the public interest above the interests of clients, particularly when participating in a process designed to develop standards expected to achieve fair presentation.... Unfortunately, the auditor today is often a participant in aggressively seeking loopholes.[2]

The SEC was increasingly concerned with what it viewed as a decline in professionalism and cited numerous instances in which the accounting that had been certified by public accounting firms did not reflect economic reality, although they might be in accordance with GAAP. Chairman Levitt cited numerous problems, including the use of the following:

- "Cookie jar reserves" to manage earnings
- Improper revenue recognition
- Creative accounting for mergers and acquisitions that did not reflect economic reality
- Increased use of stock-based compensation that put increased pressure on meeting earnings targets

Chairman Levitt was concerned that public accounting firms did not have the aptitude, desire, or independence necessary to say "no" to client accounting that pushed the bounds of financial reporting reasonableness. He proposed a change that would require auditors to make judgments on the economic substance of transactions and certify reports of company activities that were fully transparent.

In a separate study of the auditing profession, the Public Oversight Board (POB)—an independent board that preceded the PCAOB to look at professional issues—issued a report citing concerns with the audit process and methods of audit partner compensation. Specifically, the POB concerns were:

- Analytical procedures were being used inappropriately to replace direct tests of account balances.
- Audit firms were not thoroughly evaluating internal control and applying substantive procedures to address weaknesses in control.
- Audit documentation, especially related to the planning of the audit, was not in compliance with professional standards.
- Auditors were ignoring warning signals of fraud and other problems.
- Auditors were not providing sufficient warning to investors about companies that might not continue as "going concerns."

Compounding the audit profession's problems, self-regulatory organizations (professional accounting organizations such as the AICPA) failed in holding their members to the highest level of corporate accountability. Further, the AICPA pursued an aggressive and vocal strategy of promoting consulting activities by auditors for their audit clients. When financial failures later occurred in which audit firms appeared to lack independence because of high levels of consulting activities, regulators blamed the AICPA for its role in promoting consulting activities.

Individuals within companies also contributed to governance failures. For example, stock options were a major part of management compensation. Management had the ability to make accounting judgments to manipulate reported earnings through estimates or other accounting choices in order to maximize their option-based compensation. Boards did not provide adequate oversight of management and audit committees did not provide adequate oversight of

PRACTICAL POINT

Portraying the economic substance of transactions is a laudable goal. However, this goal requires the auditor to fully understand all facets of a transaction and to be independent enough of management to be willing to challenge them when they are not achieving this goal.

---

[2] Arthur Wyatt, "Professionalism in Standard Setting," *CPA Journal* (July 1988), 20–26.

the audit functions. Internal auditors also bear some responsibility in that often they did not focus sufficient efforts on ensuring accurate financial accounting.

In response to the failures presented in Exhibit 2.2, there were a number of new regulations, such as the **Sarbanes-Oxley Act of 2002**, requiring increased governance and disclosure.

The Sarbanes-Oxley Act of 2002

LO 4

Identify recent governance- and disclosure-related regulations that were the response to calls for increased governance and describe how various parties are affected by those regulations.

Given the governance failures and frauds at companies like Enron and World-Com, Congress felt it necessary to act to protect the investing public. In these companies and many others, significant operational failures were covered up with clever accounting frauds that were not detected by the public accounting firms. The press, Congress, and the general public continued to ask why such failures could have occurred given the governance responsibilities of so many parties including management, audit committees, and external auditors.

Some of the more significant provisions of the Act that affect management, audit committees, and external auditors include:

- Establishing the Public Company Accounting Oversight Board (PCAOB) with broad powers, including the power to set auditing standards for audits of public companies
- Requiring that the CEO and CFO *certify* quarterly and annual reports
- Requiring management of public companies to provide a comprehensive report on internal controls over financial reporting
- Requiring management forfeiture of certain compensation in instances where there is a restatement as a result of misconduct
- Empowering audit committees to be the formal "audit client," with responsibilities to hire and fire its external auditors and preapprove any nonaudit services provided by its external auditors; audit committees must also publicly report their charter and issue an annual report on their activities
- Requiring that audit committees have at least one person who is a financial expert and to disclose the name and characteristics of that individual; other members must be knowledgeable in financial accounting as well as internal control
- Requiring partners in charge of audit engagements, as well as all other partners with a significant role in the audit, to be rotated off public company engagements every five years
- Increasing the disclosure of all "off-balance-sheet" transactions or agreements that may have a material current or future effect on the financial condition of the company
- Requiring the establishment of an effective "whistle-blowing program" whereby important violations of the company's ethical code (including those related to accounting transparency) are reported to the appropriate levels of the organization and the audit committee
- Requiring a "cooling-off" period before audit team members can take a high-level position with an audit client; without the cooling-off period, it is presumed that the independence of the public accounting firm is jeopardized
- Limiting the nonaudit services that audit firms can provide to their audit clients
- Mandating analyses of audit firm competition and the potential need for audit firm rotation

PRACTICAL POINT

The Sarbanes-Oxley Act of 2002 is comprehensive and will be subject to regulatory adjustment for many years to come. For example, in 2010, the Dodd-Frank Wall Street Reform and Consumer Protection Act altered provisions of the Sarbanes-Oxley Act.

PRACTICAL POINT

The Sarbanes-Oxley Act applies only to public companies; privately held entities are not governed by the Act. However, private entities often look to the Act as an indication of "best practices." Further, entities that are planning to issue an initial public offering of stock in the near future will generally begin complying with requirements in the Act in preparation for subsequent compliance.

The PCAOB

With the establishment of the PCAOB, Congress removed auditors' self-regulatory privileges, in essence saying that the profession was not capable of setting its own standards for the audits of public companies. The PCAOB—which has five members, only two of whom can be CPAs—has been given the authority to set standards for audits of public companies. The board has broad powers affecting the audit profession, including:

- Requiring all public accounting firms that audit public companies to register with the PCAOB and become licensed to perform such audits
- Setting auditing standards for auditors of public companies
- Performing inspections of public accounting firms to determine their performance and requiring, where necessary, improvements in order to retain their status as a registered accounting firm
- Investigating and disciplining registered public accounting firms for violations of relevant laws or professional standards.

The PCAOB has issued standards on internal control, documentation, and engagement quality review and has most recently issued standards on audit risk, planning, supervision, materiality, and audit evidence, among others. It has also established an inspection process to look not only at the effectiveness of the audits of public companies, but also at whether the audits have been carried out efficiently.

Besides setting standards, the PCAOB influences the public accounting profession through its annual inspection of registered audit firms. The PCAOB's inspection reports usually come in two parts. The first part is public and describes major deficiencies the PCAOB encountered in its examination of audits of the registered firm. The second part is nonpublic and describes quality control areas that they recommend the registered audit firm address. If the firm addresses the PCAOB's concerns in a timely fashion, the nonpublic part remains confidential. However, if the registered firm does not take actions to improve its audit and quality process, the PCAOB will take stronger action against the firm ranging from making the recommendations to public, to an extreme situation in which the audit firm would be sanctioned from performing audits.

> **PRACTICAL POINT**
>
> All public accounting firms that audit U.S. registrants must register with the PCAOB and are subject to its inspection reporting process.

Stock Exchange Listing Requirements

Prior to the Sarbanes-Oxley Act, the New York Stock Exchange (NYSE) recommended several corporate governance improvements for its listed companies and has since adopted listing requirements including:

- Boards need to consist of a majority of independent directors
- Boards need to hold regular executive sessions of independent directors without management directors present
- Certain committees of the board (nominating/governance, compensation, audit) need to publish charters
- CEOs need to provide an annual certification of compliance with corporate governance standards
- Website disclosure of specific corporate governance issues.

Dodd-Frank Wall Street Reform and Consumer Protection Act of 2010

In response to the financial crisis of 2008 and 2009 and the difficulties faced by companies like Lehman Brothers, President Obama signed the Dodd-Frank Wall Street Reform and Consumer Protection Act of 2010 on July 21, 2010 (Dodd-Frank Act). The Dodd-Frank Act is a financial reform bill making significant changes to the financial sector. Although the corporate governance requirements of the Act are not the primary purposes of the legislation, they are nonetheless important. The Dodd-Frank Act:

- Mandates enhanced stock exchange listing standards on compensation committee independence
- Requires additional disclosure of the relationship between executive compensation and financial performance, as well as internal pay equity
- Mandates corporate policies on the forfeiture of executive compensation in certain circumstances

Role of Audit Committees

PRACTICAL POINT

At many companies the overall board is responsible for oversight of the risk management processes implemented by the organization. The audit committee then focuses on the financial reporting and related risks of the company.

PRACTICAL POINT

The audit committee acts as an independent check on management. The audit committee relies on the internal and external auditors to develop and communicate objective information needed by the audit committee to effectively perform its oversight functions.

As indicated in the Sarbanes-Oxley Act, a committee of the board of directors that has important significance to the auditor is the **audit committee**. The audit committee is a standing committee of the board of directors whose purpose is to oversee the accounting and financial reporting processes of the company and the financial statement audits. That committee is designated as the "audit client" to whom the external auditor should report.

For public companies, the audit committee must be composed of **outside directors**, i.e., directors who are not members of management and do not have other relationships with the firm (e.g., as vendor, consultant, or general counsel). Further, the audit committee should include at least one financial expert who has an understanding of GAAP and has relevant accounting and audit experience. As summarized in Exhibit 2.3, the audit committee has three primary responsibilities related to the financial reporting process:

- Provide oversight of the accounting and financial reporting processes and of the financial statement audits
- Appoint, compensate, and oversee the external auditor, including approving any nonaudit services to be provided by the external auditor
- Ensure that the board establishes a whistleblower program.

In addition to these responsibilities, in many companies the audit committee will also have the authority to hire and fire the head of the internal audit function, set the budget for the internal audit activity, and review the internal audit plan and discuss all significant internal audit results. Other responsibilities might include performing or supervising special investigations, reviewing policies on sensitive payments, maintaining communication between the board, management, the external auditors, and the internal auditors, and coordinating periodic reviews of compliance with company policies such as corporate governance policies.

The audit committee is not intended to replace the important processes performed by the auditors; however, the audit committee must make informed

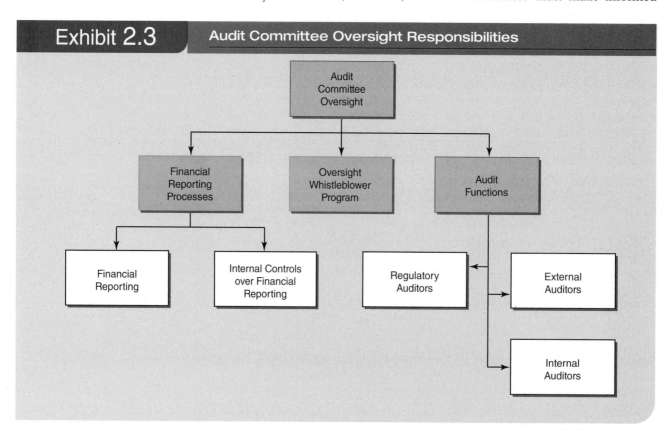

Exhibit 2.3   Audit Committee Oversight Responsibilities

choices about the quality of work it receives from the auditors. For example, the audit committee must monitor and assess the independence and competence of all audit functions. It should review quality-control reports on both the external audit firm and the internal audit function, and it should evaluate the quality of reports it receives from the auditors and the quality of financial reporting and control discussions. The audit committee will receive feedback from both the internal and external auditors on a number of issues including the quality of internal controls over financial reporting. Further, as part of its oversight responsibility, the audit committee expects the external auditor to report to the audit committee (1) all critical accounting policies and practices used by management, (2) all material alternative GAAP treatments that have been discussed with management, and (3) other material written communications between the auditor and management. Finally, the audit committee should review all regulatory audit findings, where applicable, to determine if they provide important feedback on the quality of controls, operational problems, or financial issues.

Prior to the introduction of the Sarbanes-Oxley Act, audit committees typically met three to four times a year—usually an hour before the annual board meeting. A survey of audit committee members conducted by KPMG in 2010 indicated that, on average, companies now hold five audit committee meetings annually, which each lasting about three hours. Further, the majority of the audit committees indicated that they spent more than eight hours each month on board and committee matters. The audit committee is now a key component of effective corporate governance; its members must have both sufficient time and expertise to fulfill its function. Further, the chair of the audit committee must be a strong individual who is willing to have frequent contacts with auditors and management. Given the significant financial reporting role of the audit committee, the financial statement auditor is very interested in the quality and effectiveness of the audit committee.

Principles of Effective Audit Committees

When the external auditor is evaluating the audit committee, you may wonder if there are fundamental principles of an audit committee that the external auditor should expect to find. Similar to the principles of corporate governance, there is not one set of legislated or required principles. However, a number of organizations have put forth various sets of principles of effective audit committees. Exhibit 2.4 provides one such listing.

There are numerous implications of the principles listed in Exhibit 2.4. These principles address the important topics of audit committee member independence and financial expertise, audit committee responsibilities, philosophy and culture issues, and risk assessment. Auditors assessing a client's audit committee will want to make sure that the audit committee is focused on getting the right people on the audit committee, instituting the right committee processes, and staying current on relevant emerging issues. In terms of getting the right people on the committee, financial expertise is an important requirement of audit committee members. However, as indicated in a subsequent *Auditing in Practice* feature, audit committee members must also have the willingness and ability to ask tough questions. In terms of the audit committee's process, the audit committee should have a charter, which identifies the scope of the committee's responsibilities and establishes the framework for the audit committee's activities. As part of its process, the audit committee should meet as needed, with sufficient time for discussion of key risk issues. Finally, for audit committees to be effective, their members must stay current on developments in business, accounting, and auditing.

Required Audit Firm Communication to the Audit Committee

As indicated in Exhibit 2.4, the audit committee should be responsible for hiring the external auditor. Then, throughout the remainder of audit opinion

PRACTICAL POINT

Some audit committees are expanding their functions to include oversight over organizational risk management processes. In most organizations, the audit committee also reviews the annual report filed with the SEC, including an analysis of the Management Discussion and Analysis section of the report to determine that management's discussion is consistent with the committee's understanding of operational performance.

LO 6

List and analyze principles of effective audit committees.

PRACTICAL POINT

Recent research indicates that audit committee effectiveness has improved following the implementation of the Sarbanes-Oxley Act. There have been improvements in terms of financial expertise and power. However, some smaller public companies are still struggling to develop effective audit committees.

LO 7

Describe required communications between the audit firm and the audit committee.

Exhibit 2.4	Twenty-first Century *Audit Committee* Principles for U.S. Public Companies

1. **Committee Purpose**—The purpose of the audit committee is to oversee all aspects of the financial reporting process, including preparation and filing of financial statements, internal control over financial reporting, and related risks.

2. **Committee Responsibilities**—The audit committee's major areas of responsibility include (1) oversight of the internal control system, (2) oversight of the internal audit function and external auditor, (3) review of financial filings, and (4) establishment and oversight of a "whistleblower" process.

3. **Interaction**—Audit committee effectiveness requires ongoing, timely, and substantive interaction among the board, management, the external auditor, the internal auditor, and legal counsel.

4. **Independence**—The audit committee should be composed of independent directors only, and these directors should be chosen by an independent nominating committee. The CEO's role in selecting new directors, especially those who are targeted for audit committee service, should be limited.

5. **Expertise and Integrity**—The audit committee should have at least one financial expert, and all other members should have a high level of financial literacy. The financial expert should have a background in accounting, and there should be increased proxy disclosure as to the nature and timing of this accounting background. The committee members should reflect a mix of backgrounds and perspectives, and each member should be familiar with the company's risks and controls and capable of inquisitive and independent judgment. All members should receive detailed orientation and continuing education on financial accounting and reporting issues to assure they achieve and maintain the necessary level of expertise.

6. **Philosophy and Culture**—The audit committee should clearly set expectations that financial statements and supporting disclosures reflect economic substance and that they be prepared in a manner that is informative and transparent. A legalistic view of accounting and auditing (e.g., "can we get away with recording it this way?") is not appropriate. Management integrity and a strong control environment are critical to reliable financial reporting.

7. **Internal Control**—The audit committee is responsible for ensuring that management designs and implements sound internal control, which is essential for reliable financial reporting for any organization. Section 404 of the Sarbanes-Oxley Act should apply to all public companies, and the primary focus of reporting on internal control should be effectiveness.

8. **Risk Assessment**—The audit committee should lead the board's assessment of enterprise risk, including the risk of management override of internal control. The board also should discuss the audit committee's fraud risk assessments and the fraud risk assessments developed by internal and external auditors.

9. **Meetings and Information**—The audit committee members should meet frequently for extended periods of time and should have unrestricted access to the information and personnel they need to perform their duties. Face-to-face meetings should occur at least quarterly, and executive sessions should be held at each of these meetings. Additionally, the committee should meet in separate executive sessions with management, the external auditor, the internal auditor, legal counsel, and other advisors.

10. **External Auditor**—The audit committee should hire, evaluate, fire (if appropriate), and determine the fee of the external auditor with only minimal input from senior management. The committee should review the proposed audit scope and approach, as well as the external auditor's independence. Additionally, the committee should seek audit firms whose personnel are selected, evaluated, compensated, and promoted primarily on the basis of technical competence, not on their ability to generate new business.

11. **Internal Audit**—The chief (internal) audit executive should have direct reporting access to the audit committee, and the committee should oversee the activities and budget of the internal audit function.

12. **Oversight of "Whistleblower" Procedures**—Whistleblower allegations should be initially screened by internal audit or an external whistleblower system provider and reported directly to the audit committee. Access to the whistleblower process should be extended to outside parties (customers, suppliers, etc.).

13. **Compensation and Stock Ownership**—The board should consider any risks of audit committee member stock/stock option holdings and should set compensation at a level that is appropriate for the expanded duties and risks these members face.

14. **Service and Term Limits**—The board should limit the number of other audit committees on which its audit committee members can sit to no more than one other public company if the member holds a full-time position (three others for members who are retired). The board should consider limiting the number of years an individual can serve on the audit committee to ensure adequate rotation of its members.

15. **Disclosure**—In addition to disclosure of the audit committee responsibilities in the charter, the annual proxy statement should contain an audit committee report on actual activities performed. The audit committee should disclose the processes it uses in discharging its responsibilities, including (1) the length of its meetings; (2) meeting participants; (3) use of executive sessions; (4) how the committee selects, compensates, and oversees the external auditor; (5) how the committee oversees the internal audit function; (6) the committee's role in overseeing internal control; (7) committee activities performed to assess the risk of fraudulent financial reporting, especially via management override of internal control; and (8) activities performed by the committee to review financial filings before their release to the public.

Source: Lapides, P. D., M. S. Beasley, J. V. Carcello, F. T. DeZoort, D. R. Hermanson, T. L. Neal, and J. G. Tompkins. May 8, 2007. 21st Century Governance and Audit Committee Principles by Corporate Governance Center, Kennesaw State University • Corporate Governance Center, University of Tennessee • Enterprise Risk Management Initiative, North Carolina State University, Culverhouse School of Accountancy, The University of Alabama

AUDITING *in Practice*

AUDITORS SHOULD EXPECT QUESTIONS FROM THE AUDIT COMMITTEE

External auditors should expect the audit committees at their clients to ask them relevant and probing questions. Some of the relevant questions include:

- What are the most significant risks to financial reporting at this company?

- What level of assurance do your procedures provide with respect to the annual financial statements?

- How do you assess the competence of company personnel engaged in financial reporting and related processes?

- How do you ensure that your staff members and their managers understand the business and perform quality audit procedures?

- What is your process if you determine that although the financial statements comply with GAAP they are not a fair presentation of the company's results and financial condition?

- How do you ensure that managers and partners reviewing the audit apply the appropriate judgment in most complex situations?

- How have you tested management's assumptions that influence account balances? Are you satisfied that management's assumptions are accurate?

- Does your audit team have experience in our industry, including an understanding of the risks associated with the industry?

- Does the audit firm pay sufficient attention to the compliance risks, especially regarding governmental contracting, that affects our company?

- What is your assessment of the competence of the financial function within this organization, as well as the depth of the expertise?

Source: McKenna, F. 2010. Asking Difficult Questions. *Internal Auditor* (July): 29–31.

formulation process, there should be ongoing communication between the auditor and the audit committee, to continue until the audit opinion is actually issued. For example, auditors will often meet with the audit committee before their committee meetings to have a dialogue about important issues.

It is important that audit committee members have clear expectations of the audit profession and process. Professional auditing standards promote better communication between auditors and audit committees by specifying certain things that must be communicated on every engagement. Examples of required communications, which vary across standard setters, are shown in Exhibit 2.5. A comparison of requirements across the various auditing standards is provided in the *Comparison of Worldwide Professional Auditing Guidance* feature. These communications form the foundation upon which all communication takes place with the audit committee. For example, the auditor must discuss all significant accounting and audit issues, including any restrictions by management on the conduct of the audit or any disagreements with management on how to account for something. As another example, auditors have a responsibility to exercise informed judgment beyond simply determining whether the statements reflect generally accepted accounting principles (GAAP). The auditor must have a discussion with the audit committee not only about the acceptance of a chosen accounting principle, but about whether or not the auditor believes the accounting choices made by the organization best portray the economic substance of the transactions and accurately represent its current financial state.

The audit committee must be assured that the auditor is free of any restrictions and has not been influenced by management during the course of the audit. Thus, the auditor must also communicate whether major issues were discussed with management before the auditor was engaged or whether management has consulted with other audit firms on accounting issues. It is important to note that this required communication is not limited to public companies only, but it is required for all companies that have an audit committee. If a

PRACTICAL POINT

Many public accounting firms discuss their annual inspection report from the PCAOB with audit committees. Most firms also discuss litigation that may adversely affect the auditing firm.

Comparison of Worldwide Professional Auditing Guidance

U.S. AND INTERNATIONAL GUIDANCE ON COMMUNICATION WITH AUDIT COMMITTEES

AICPA Auditing Standards Board (ASB)	SAS 114 describes the communication requirements for nonpublic companies. Required communications include:
	• The auditor's responsibilities under generally accepted auditing standards
	• An overview of the planned scope and timing of the audit
	• Significant findings from the audit including:
	   • Qualitative aspects of the entity's significant accounting practices
	   • Significant difficulties encountered during the audit
	   • Uncorrected misstatements
	   • Disagreements with management
	   • Management's consultations with other accountants
	   • Significant issues discussed, or subject to correspondence, with management
	In terms of timing of the communications, SAS 114 notes that the auditor should communicate with those charged with governance on a sufficiently timely basis to enable those charged with governance to take appropriate action. The appropriate timing for communications will vary with the circumstances of the engagement, but the standard encourages communications on an ongoing basis.
	
	SAS 114 is an important example of the AICPA's convergence with the ISAs of the IAASB.

Public Company Accounting Oversight Board (PCAOB)	The PCAOB has adopted as its interim standard SAS 61 which requires that the following topics be communicated to the audit committee: • The auditor's responsibility under Generally Accepted Auditing Standards • Significant accounting policies • Management judgments and accounting estimates • Significant audit adjustments • Other information in documents containing audited financial statements • Disagreements with management • Consultation with other accountants • Major issues discussed with management prior to retention • Difficulties encountered in performing the audit SAS 61 notes that the communications specified in the standard are incidental to the audit and therefore are not required to occur before the issuance of the auditor's report on the entity's financial statements so long as the communications occur on a timely basis. Since 2008 the PCAOB has been working on drafting a new standard in this area which, when finalized and approved, would strengthen the required communications.
International Auditing and Assurance Standards Board (IAASB)	The requirements in ISA 260 are virtually identical to the requirements of SAS 114.
SUMMARY	Audit committees that are well-informed about matters relating to the audit may be better able to carry out their role of overseeing the financial reporting process. While the specific requirements differ somewhat across these standards, all three standard-setting bodies recognize the importance of quality communication between the auditor and the audit committee. However, SAS 61 does not emphasize the critical importance of the communication and only considers the communication to be incidental to the audit.

company does not have an audit committee, the issues must be communicated to the board as a whole.

The required communication between auditors and the audit committee gives the audit committee a pivotal role in corporate governance, a role enhanced by the Sarbanes-Oxley Act requirement that CPA firms cannot provide nonaudit services without the explicit approval of the audit committee. Further, audit committees are motivated to make sure the auditors do their job, because poor performance on the part of the auditors will directly reflect on the performance of the audit committee members.

Exhibit 2.5	Communication to Audit Committees

EXAMPLES OF REQUIRED COMMUNICATIONS TO AUDIT COMMITTEES

Auditor's Responsibility under Generally Accepted Auditing Standards

The auditor must clearly communicate the audit firm's responsibility to perform the audit according to relevant auditing standards and independently assess the fairness of the financial statements, to assess the quality of the entity's internal controls over financial reporting, and to design the audit to detect material misstatements.

Significant Accounting Policies

The auditor should ensure that the audit committee is informed about the initial selection of, and changes in, significant accounting policies or their application, and discuss the quality of accounting principles used.

Management Judgments and Accounting Estimates

Many corporate failures have involved manipulation of accounting estimates such as loan loss reserves. The auditor should ensure that the audit committee is aware of the processes used by management in making sensitive accounting estimates, and the auditor's assessment of those processes and accompanying estimates.

Significant Audit Adjustments

Significant audit adjustments may reflect on the stewardship and accountability of management. The audit committee should be made aware of such adjustments, even if management readily agrees to make them. Significant adjustments, by definition, suggest that there have been internal control failures that must be communicated to management and the audit committee.

Judgments about the Quality of the Company's Accounting Principles

The auditor needs to discuss with the audit committee the quality of the company's financial statements and ensure that they are acceptable under GAAP. Auditors should be prepared to have a frank discussion about differences in assessments of the quality of the financial statements.

Other Information in Annual Reports

The auditor should briefly describe his or her responsibility to review other information contained in an annual report and whether such information is consistent with the audited financial statements.

Disagreements with Management

All major accounting disagreements with management, even if eventually resolved, should be discussed with the audit committee. This requirement is intended to insulate the auditors from management pressure to change or bend accounting treatments to suit management and should remove any subtle hints that the auditing firm may be replaced because it disagrees with management's proposed accounting treatments.

Consultation with Other Accountants

In some instances the auditor may become aware that management has consulted with other accounting firms about an accounting policy or its application. In those instances, the auditor should inform the audit committee of this consultation and possibly provide an assessment of the consultation.

Major Issues Discussed with Management Before Retention

During the proposal and hiring stages of the engagement, management and the auditor likely discussed issues related to accounting principles and audit standards. These issues should be discussed with the audit committee.

Overview and Planned Scope of the Audit

The auditor needs to communicate the planned scope of the audit engagement to the audit committee and have a discussion with it on the adequacy of the planned scope, as well as the materiality chosen for the audit.

Difficulties in Performing the Audit

Auditors may experience various difficulties in performing the audit (e.g., scheduling, cooperation). The auditor should discuss these issues with the audit committee.

Representations Requested from Management

The auditor normally requests representations from management on a number of important issues, such as management's responsibility for the financial statements, the appropriate allowances for accounts that need to be adjusted to market value, and the quality of controls. The nature of these requests, as well as management's responses, should be shared with the audit committee.

Corporate Governance and the Audit

LO 8

Analyze the relationship between corporate governance and the audit.

Good governance is important to the conduct of an audit for one very simple reason: companies with good corporate governance are less risky to audit. These companies generally have the following characteristics:

- Are less likely to engage in "financial engineering"
- Have a code of conduct that is reinforced by actions of top management
- Have independent board members who take their jobs seriously and have sufficient time and resources to perform their work
- Take the requirements of good internal control over financial reporting seriously
- Make a commitment to financial competencies needed

PRACTICAL POINT

Recent academic research shows that companies with good corporate governance have higher returns on equity than other companies. They also have lower costs of capital and superior stock returns compared to companies with weaker corporate governance.

Many audit firms are not willing to accept potential audit clients unless the clients demonstrate a strong commitment to good corporate governance. Stated simply, a public company that does not commit to good corporate governance is too much of a risk for an audit firm. Most audit firms look at the governance issues when making a decision to become associated with, or to remain associated with, an audit client.

Recall that stockholders and other stakeholders want disclosures from management that are accurate and objectively verifiable. The role of the audit is to provide independent verification. The auditor is in a much better position to provide accurate verification when governance mechanisms, such as the board and the audit committee, adhere to and embrace fundamental principles of good governance. At those types of organizations, the auditor can serve as an independent party working with other governance parties such as management, the board, the audit committee, to help ensure accurate financial reporting. However, in organizations where governance is not well developed or is heavily influenced by management, the auditor may decide that the audit firm is going to have to bear too much responsibility for assuring accurate financial reporting and so the client is, in essence, not auditable from a risk-mitigation standpoint.

Summary

The business and financial failures of the past decade have been closely associated with corporate governance failures. The governance failures involved a number of parties: management, boards of directors, auditors, audit committees, and other external parties. The Sarbanes-Oxley Act of 2002 and other regulatory actions address many of the causes of corporate governance failures, with specific governance requirements directed at audit committees, auditors, and management. The quality of a company's governance is critically important to the external auditor because well-governed companies pose less of a risk to the audit firm. In assessing a company's corporate governance, the auditor will consider factors associated with the board of directors and with the audit committee and whether these bodies have embraced fundamental principles associated with good governance. The quality of governance at a company will affect the auditor's willingness to accept the company as a client and, for accepted clients, will affect the approach to the audit.

Significant Terms

Audit committee   A subcommittee of the board of directors responsible for monitoring audit activities and serving as a surrogate for the interests of shareholders; it should be composed of outside members of the board, that is, members who do not hold company management positions.

Corporate governance   A process by which the owners and creditors of an organization exert control and require accountability for the resources entrusted to the organization. The owners (stockholders) elect a board of directors to provide oversight of the organization's activities and accountability to stakeholders.

Dodd–Frank Wall Street Reform and Consumer Protection Act of 2010   Signed on July 21, 2010, this financial reform bill makes significant changes to the financial sector and updates some of the requirements of the Sarbanes-Oxley Act of 2002.

Outside directors   Independent directors who are not members of management and do not have other relationships with the firm (e.g., as vendor, consultant, or general counsel).

Sarbanes–Oxley Act of 2002   Broad legislation mandating new standard setting for audits of public companies and new standards for corporate governance.

Stakeholders   Anyone who is influenced, either directly or indirectly, by the actions of a company; extends beyond the shareholders of a company.

SELECTED REFERENCES TO RELEVANT PROFESSIONAL GUIDANCE	
Topic	**Selected Guidance**
Auditors' Communications with the Audit Committee	SAS 61 *Communication with Audit Committees* (superseded by SAS 114 for nonpublic companies)
	SAS 90 *Audit Committee Communications*
	SAS 114 *The Auditor's Communication with Those Charged with Governance*
	SAS *The Auditor's Communication with Those Charged with Governance* (Redrafted) (issued but not effective; proposed effective date is December 2012)
	Proposed AS *Communications with Audit Committees*
	ISA 260 *Communication with Those Charged with Governance*

Note: *Acronyms for Relevant Professional Guidance*
STANDARDS: **AS**—Auditing Standard issued by the PCAOB; **ISA**—International Standard on Auditing issued by the IAASB; **SAS**—Statement on Auditing Standards issued by the Auditing Standards Board of the AICPA; **SSAE**—Statement on Standards for Attestation Engagements issued by the AICPA.
ORGANIZATIONS: **AICPA**—American Institute of Certified Public Accountants; **COSO**—Committee of Sponsoring Organizations; **IAASB**—International Auditing and Assurance Standards Board; **PCAOB**—Public Company Accounting Oversight Board; **SEC**—Securities and Exchange Commission.

Review Questions

2-1   **(LO 1)** Define *corporate governance* and identify the key parties involved in corporate governance.

2-2   **(LO 3)** Identify the parties that, at least to some degree, failed to meet their corporate governance objectives in the past decade.

2-3   **(LO 3)** In what ways were boards of directors responsible for corporate governance failures in the past decade?

2-4   **(LO 3)** In what ways was the auditing profession partially responsible for corporate governance failures in the past decade?

2-5   **(LO 3)** Arthur Levitt criticizes companies for using "cookie jar reserves" to help manage earnings. What are "cookie jar reserves" and how might they be used to manage corporate earnings?

2-6   **(LO 1, 3)** What should users reasonably expect from the audit profession?

2-7   **(LO 3, 4)** What was the Sarbanes-Oxley Act designed to accomplish? What were the major factors that led Congress to develop the Sarbanes-Oxley Act?

2-8   **(LO 4)** What is the PCAOB and what is its authority?

2-9   **(LO 4)** The Sarbanes-Oxley Act contains requirements of management. What are some of these requirements?

2-10   **(LO 4, 5, 6)** The Sarbanes-Oxley Act included a "whistleblowing" provision. What is "whistleblowing" and why is it an important element of corporate governance? Who should provide oversight of this program?

2-11   **(LO 4)** What requirements of the Sarbanes-Oxley Act are intended to strengthen the independence of the external auditor?

2-12   **(LO 1)** To whom do a company's financial statements belong: management, the audit committee, or the auditor? Explain and discuss why the ownership issue is important.

2-13   **(LO 5, 6)** What is an audit committee? What critical role does the audit committee play in corporate governance?

2-14   **(LO 5)** An audit committee should be composed of outside directors. Define "outside directors" within the context of an audit committee. How does the existence of an audit committee affect the auditor's independence? Explain.

2-15   **(LO 5, 6)** What oversight responsibilities does an audit committee have? Explain the difference between an "oversight responsibility" and a "primary responsibility."

2-16   **(LO 5)** Explain the difference between the audit committee's responsibilities regarding the external auditor and the audit committee's relationship to the internal audit and regulatory audit functions.

2-17   **(LO 5)**   Are nonpublic companies, such as a small private business, required to have audit committees that represent outside stakeholders such as banks or other lending institutions?

2-18   **(LO 7)**   Identify the specific items that must be communicated by the external auditor to the audit committee on every engagement.

2-19   **(LO 5, 6)**   What responsibility does the audit committee have regarding the provision of nonaudit services to a company and its management? Explain.

2-20   **(LO 8)**   Why is the governance structure of an organization important to the external auditor? What are the implications for the auditor if a company has not made a commitment to good governance practices?

2-21   **(LO 2, 6)**   How would an auditor assess the quality of an organization's corporate governance? In formulating your answer, consider the possibility that a company may have a good governance structure on paper but its actual implementation may be significantly less than that.

2-22   **(LO 1, 8)**   What is the relationship between good corporate governance and (a) entity performance and (b) audit risk? In what ways does poor corporate governance affect audit risk?

2-23   **(LO 6)**   What characteristics should audit committee members possess?

2-24   **(LO 5, 6)**   Explain how an independent and competent audit committee improves corporate governance.

Multiple-Choice Questions

2-25   **(LO 1)**   Which of the following is not a component of corporate governance?
    a. Oversight of management by the board of directors.
    b. Established processes to provide accountability to stockholders.
    c. Whistleblowing processes.
    d. Independent review of financial statements by the SEC.

2-26   **(LO 3)**   Which of the following would *not* be correct regarding corporate governance failures that took place in the past two decades?
    a. Boards of directors approved stock option plans that did not align management and shareholder objectives.
    b. Audit committees met infrequently, often for only an hour at a time.
    c. Boards of directors were often dominated by management.
    d. Accounting rules became more specific to address the complexities that existed in new transactions.

2-27   **(LO 4, 5, 6)**   Which of the following is not a Sarbanes-Oxley requirement of audit committees of public companies?
    a. The audit committee must be chaired by the chair of the board of directors.

b. Audit committee members must be financially literate.

c. Audit committee members must be independent directors.

d. The audit committee should view itself as the "client" of the external auditor.

2-28   **(LO 3)** In which way(s) did the public accounting profession bring about the problems that resulted in Congress's passing the Sarbanes-Oxley Act of 2002?

a. Failed to detect egregious frauds

b. Emphasized generating revenues over audit quality

c. Viewed helping clients find an accounting solution to show increased earnings as value-added auditing

d. All of the above

2-29   **(LO 1)** Which of the following is an *inappropriate* description of management's role in preparing financial statements and reports on internal control over financial reporting? Management has the primary responsibility for:

a. Determining the scope of internal and external audit activities.

b. Preparing financial statements that are fairly presented in accordance with GAAP.

c. Selecting accounting principles that best portray the economic reality of the organization's transactions and current state.

d. Developing, implementing, and assessing the internal control processes over financial reporting.

2-30   **(LO 7)** Which of the following would *not* be required to be communicated to the audit committee by the outside auditor?

a. Significant audit adjustments made during the course of the audit

b. Significant disagreements with management regarding accounting principles

c. The auditor's knowledge of management's consultation with other public accounting firms regarding the proposed treatment of a controversial accounting item

d. The extent to which the internal auditors assisted in the conduct of the audit

2-31   **(LO 4, 5)** Which of the following are critical improvements related to auditing and financial statements that the Sarbanes-Oxley Act was intended to provide?

a. Improved corporate governance

b. Required reporting on internal controls

c. Acknowledgment of greater audit committee responsibility

d. All of the above

2-32   **(LO 8)** In which of the following ways can an audit firm respond to poor corporate governance?

a. Not accept a client with poor corporate governance

b. Perform a more rigorous audit

c. Work more closely with management in performing the audit

d. Either (a) and (b) would be appropriate responses

e. (a), (b), and (c) would all be appropriate responses

2-33   **(LO 5, 6)** Effective audit committees should have ongoing, timely, and substantive interaction with which of the following parties?

   a. Board

   b. Management

   c. External auditor

   d. Internal auditor

   e. Legal counsel

   f. All of the above

2-34   **(LO 2)** Which of the following statements about effective corporate governance is least accurate?

   a. The board's fundamental objective should be to build long-term sustainable growth in shareholder value for the corporation.

   b. Management has the primary responsibility for creating a culture of performance with integrity and ethical behavior.

   c. Good corporate governance should be viewed as primarily a compliance obligation.

   d. Companies should make regular efforts to ensure that they have sound disclosure policies and practices.

   e. Independence and objectivity are necessary attributes of board members.

2-35   **(LO 1, 5)** In a well-governed organization, which of the following is not management's responsibility in the area of financial reporting and disclosure?

   a. Choose which accounting principles best portray the economic substance of company transactions.

   b. Implement a system of internal control that assures completeness and accuracy in financial reporting.

   c. Ensure that the financial statements contain accurate and complete disclosure.

   d. Hire the external audit firm.

Discussion and Research Questions

2-36   **(Components of Corporate Governance, LO 1, 2, 5, 6)** Auditors are required to assess various components of corporate governance. Respond to the following questions related to this important assessment.

Ethics

Required

   a. An important aspect of corporate governance is a company code of ethics. For example, Enron had one of the most complete codes of ethics in corporate America. What evidence would an auditor gather to determine whether a corporate code of ethics is actually being adhered to?

   b. Can an auditor make meaningful decisions about areas such as corporate governance where considerable judgment must be applied in making the decision? Are auditors equipped to make subjective judgments of this type?

　　c. How would an auditor assess the financial competence of an audit committee? What are the implications for accepting an audit engagement if the auditor does not believe the audit committee has sufficient expertise?

　　d. In what ways is an effective internal audit department a part of good corporate governance? Explain.

2-37　**(Corporate Governance, LO 1, 3, 8)** One of the criticisms of corporate America in the last decade was that there was a failure in corporate governance.

Required

　　a. Define the term *corporate governance* and identify the major parties involved in corporate governance, as well as their roles.

　　b. Identify the failures in corporate governance that took place in the past decade. Include the failures of each major party in the process.

　　c. Briefly explain why there is a relationship between corporate governance and risk to the auditor.

2-38　**(Corporate Governance Characteristics, LO 1, 2, 6, 8)** The following describes a potential audit client:

- The company is in the financial services sector and has a large number of consumer loans, including mortgages, outstanding.

- The CEO and CFO's compensation is based on three components: (a) base salary, (b) bonus based on growth in assets and profits, and (c) significant stock options.

- The audit committee meets semiannually. It is chaired by a retired CFO who knows the company well because she had served as the CFO of a division of the firm. The other two members are local community members—one is the president of the Chamber of Commerce and the other is a retired executive from a successful local manufacturing firm.

- The company has an internal auditor who reports directly to the CFO and makes an annual report to the audit committee.

- The CEO is a dominating personality—not unusual in this environment. He has been on the job for six months and has decreed that he is streamlining the organization to reduce costs and centralize authority (most of it in him).

- The company has a loan committee. It meets quarterly to approve, on an ex-post basis, all loans over $300 million (top 5% for this institution).

- The previous auditor has resigned because of a dispute regarding the accounting treatment and fair value assessment of some of the loans.

Required

For each of the factors listed above, indicate whether it is indicative of poor corporate governance. Explain your reasoning for your assessment. Identify the risks associated with each element and indicate how that risk might affect the financial statements and the audit.

2-39　**(Public Accounting and Corporate Governance, LO 1, 3, 8)** Public accounting serves an important role in corporate governance.

Required

a. Describe the role that external auditing fills in promoting good corporate governance.

b. In what ways might the public accounting profession have failed in its important role prior to the issuance of the Sarbanes-Oxley Act of 2002?

c. A former chairman of the SEC described auditors as "public watchdogs." What does the term convey regarding the responsibility of the external auditor to the public?

2-40 **(Expectations of External Auditors, LO 3, 4)** In a major speech, Arthur Levitt, former chairman of the SEC, chided auditors for failures in four areas:

- Allowing companies to use "cookie jar reserves" to manage earnings

- Allowing improper revenue recognition

- Assisting companies in using creative accounting for mergers and acquisitions that did not reflect economic reality

- Assisting management in meeting earnings targets that helped managers achieve stock option price targets

Required

a. Describe each of the four activities identified by Levitt and give an example of each. For example, give an example of how a firm would use "cookie jar reserves" to manage earnings.

b. If we assume that there were some instances in which auditors acted the way Levitt described, identify the potential motivation for auditors to provide such assistance to management.

c. For each item identified in part (b), describe how the Sarbanes-Oxley Act addressed the issue.

2-41 **(Sarbanes-Oxley Act of 2002, LO 4)** The Sarbanes-Oxley Act of 2002 has been described as the most far-reaching legislation affecting business since the passage of the 1933 Securities Act.

Required

a. Identify the portions of the legislation that specifically affect the external audit profession and discuss how they affect the profession.

b. How does the legislation affect the internal audit profession?

c. Do you believe the legislation enhances the power and prestige of the audit profession or, alternatively, that it decreases both the power and prestige of the profession?

2-42 **(Sarbanes-Oxley: Management Implications, LO 1, 4, 5)** The Sarbanes-Oxley Act of 2002 dramatically changes the responsibilities of top management.

Required

a. Briefly indicate how Sarbanes-Oxley changes the responsibilities of top management.

b. How has the relationship between management and the external auditor changed with Sarbanes-Oxley?

c. Who is primarily responsible for the fairness and completeness of financial statement presentations? Discuss the relative roles of the chief executive officer (CEO), the chief financial officer (CFO), the director of internal audit (CAE), the chair of the audit committee, and the external auditor (CPA).

2-43 **(Audit Committees, LO 1, 4, 5, 6, 7)** Audit committees are taking on added responsibilities after Sarbanes-Oxley.

Required

a. Describe the changes in audit committee membership and duties that were mandated by the Sarbanes-Oxley Act of 2002.

b. The audit committee now has the "ownership of the relationship with the public accounting firm." What are the implications (a) for the audit committee and (b) for the public accounting firm of the new auditor-client relationship with the audit committee?

c. Assume that management and the auditor disagree on the appropriate accounting for a complex transaction. The auditor has conveyed the disagreement to the audit committee along with an assessment that the disagreement is on the economics of the transaction and has nothing to do with earnings management. What is the responsibility of the audit committee? What skills must exist on the audit committee to meet its responsibility?

d. Assume the auditor and the management disagree on an accounting treatment. However, the auditor concludes that the choice management made is an acceptable application of GAAP. What is the auditor's responsibility regarding communicating its preferred accounting treatment to (a) management, (b) the audit committee, (c) users of the audited financial statements?

2-44 **(Audit Committees and External Auditors, LO 5, 6, 7)** Audit committees are mandatory for all public companies. The AICPA and IIA have endorsed the formation of audit committees (or their equivalent) for most organizations, including governmental entities and larger privately held companies.

Required

a. Define the term *audit committee*. Indicate its ideal composition.

b. Identify information that the external auditor must communicate to the audit committee.

c. Explain why nonpublic entities might want to have audit committees. Consider the following entities in formulating your answer:

- Governmental unit, e.g., a school that must be audited
- A charity, e.g., United Way
- A larger privately held company

2-45 **(Audit Committees and Auditor Independence, LO 4, 5, 6)** The audit committee is required to evaluate the independence of both the internal and external audit functions.

Required

a. What factors would you suggest an audit committee look at in evaluating the external auditor's independence?

b. How can the audit committee influence the independence of the internal audit function?

c. The audit committee must pre-approve all nonaudit services provided by the external auditor. Assume the audit committee must make a decision to allow or not allow the external audit firm to perform the following activities. Indicate whether you would approve or not approve each activity and state the rationale for your decision.

Proposed Service Reason for Approval or Disapproval

(1) Prepare the company's income tax return after the completion of the audit.

(2) Prepare the tax returns for all directors and managers as part of the fees paid for the overall audit.

(3) Prepare tax returns for managers and directors as requested and paid for by the individuals.

(4) Assist the internal audit department in their control reviews of an overseas operation (audit firm has personnel based in the country who speak the language but the internal audit department does not).

(5) Perform an independent security audit of information systems and report the results to management and the audit committee.

(6) Train operating personnel on internal control concepts and a framework to implement to improve the quality of internal controls.

(7) Take over the internal audit function to provide a full "integrated" audit of the company's operations and controls to achieve audit efficiency.

(8) Provide, at no cost, seminars on updates to accounting and auditing standards to clients' audit committee members.

(9) Same as item 8 except the seminars are provided to both audit clients and nonaudit clients, but by invitation only.

2-46   **(PCAOB, LO 4)** The development of the Public Company Accounting Oversight Board (PCAOB) was one of the most significant portions of the Sarbanes-Oxley Act of 2002.

Required

a. What is the main rationale that led Congress to develop the PCAOB as the public company audit standard setter? For example, why do you think Congress didn't suggest instead overhauling the Auditing Standards Board of the AICPA?

b. Identify the responsibilities of the PCAOB. How does the inspection process performed by the PCAOB affect the practice of public accounting?

c. The PCAOB can have no more than two CPAs among its five members. What might be the rationale for such a requirement? What are the advantages and disadvantages of the limitation concerning CPA members on the board?

d. Who are the current members of the PCAOB and what is their background and experience related to accounting?

e. Do the audit standards set by the PCAOB apply to audits of nonpublic companies? Explain.

2-47   **(Governance, Performance, and Audit Risk, LO 1, 2, 5, 6, 8)** The opening scenario of this chapter lists several questions for your group to consider.

Group Activity

Required

Address the following questions raised at the beginning of the chapter.

a. Why is the corporate governance of an organization important to both investors and auditors?

b. What roles do the board of directors and the audit committee play with respect to corporate governance?

c. What relationships do the board of directors and the audit committee have with the audit function?

d. Why is it important that organizations have directors and audit committee members that are competent and independent of management?

e. Why would the quality of corporate governance affect the quality of an organization's financial performance and the conduct of the external audit?

f. What are the risks to the auditor if the organization does not have good corporate governance?

g. Should an auditor accept an audit engagement with an organization that does not have good governance?

h. What principles are associated with high-quality governance as it relates to boards and management?

i. What principles are associated with effective audit committees?

2-48   **(Research Question, LO 4)** The Sarbanes-Oxley Act required the GAO to make numerous studies of the accounting profession and report to the SEC within one year of its enactment.

Required

In consultation with your instructor, select one of the following GAO studies of the accounting profession:

- *Consolidation of Public Accounting Firms and the Effect on Competition*

- *Principles-Based Accounting*

- *Mandatory Rotation of Audit Firms*

Present a report of the study in class.

Internet

2-49   **(Practical Research: Corporate Governance, LO 1, 2, 5, 6)** Select either a public company or a company that is near your university and perform a preliminary review of its corporate governance. Identify all the sources, including Internet sources, of evidence for your conclusion regarding corporate governance. Identify the strengths and weaknesses of the governance and describe the implications of the governance structure for the auditor.

Group Activity

2-50   **(Practical Research: Audit Committees, LO 5, 6)** Audit committees have taken on much more responsibility in the past few years. However, it must also be remembered that audit committee service is not a full-time appointment.

Required

a. Search annual reports via Edgar or by looking up the home page of selected companies. Select five companies (preferably in different industries) and prepare a report that describes the following:

- An analysis of the audit committee charters that identifies the commonalities in all the charters as well as any differences

- The characteristics of audit committee members (whether a CPA, other experience, etc.)

- The individual(s) identified as a "financial expert"
- The number of times the audit committee met during the year

b. Discuss in your group and report to the entire class your answers to the following:

- How do the companies differ in terms of audit committee characteristics? What do you think are the underlying causes of the differences?
- What are the professional backgrounds of individuals designated as financial experts? How do those differ across the various organizations?
- What are the implications of variations in the amount of time that the audit committee met during the year?

2-51   **(Research on Corporate Governance, LO 1, 2)** The chapter presents a list of corporate governance principles directed at management and the board based on a 2010 report of a commission sponsored by the New York Stock Exchange. Other organizations have also developed "best practices" related to corporate governance. For example, Business Roundtable issued a report entitled *2010 Principles of Corporate Governance* in April 2010 (available at http://businessroundtable.org/). As another example, in February 2010, the California Public Employees' Retirement System updated a report entitled *Global Principles of Accountable Corporate Governance* (available at http://www.calpers-governance.org/). Required Obtain one or more "best practices" lists of corporate governance principles, then compare and contrast those lists with the principles related to management and the board presented in this chapter. Prepare a report that (1) summarizes the similarities and differences across the different reports and that (2) provides your "Top Ten" list of governance principles for management and the board.

Internet

2-52   **(Defining Corporate Governance, LO 1)** This chapter defines corporate governance as a process by which the owners and creditors of an organization exert control and require accountability for the resources entrusted to the organization. However, many individuals (e.g., Arthur Levitt; Monks and Minow) and organizations (e.g., OECD) have provided alternative definitions of corporate governance. Required Perform research to obtain alternative definitions of corporate governance. Compare and contrast these definitions on relevant factors including how broad the definition is, the concepts included in the definition, etc. Based on your research and your understanding of corporate governance, draft your own definition of corporate governance.

Internet

2-53   **(International Perspectives on Corporate Governance, LO 1, 2)** Corporate governance is not just an issue for U.S. companies; companies throughout the world need to focus on corporate governance issues. However, the principles and challenges of corporate governance vary across countries. Required With input from your instructor, select a country and research the corporate governance issues in that country. A good starting point is the website of the OECD (www.oecd.org) or the World Bank (www.worldbank.org), which provides corporate governance information by country. Using information from these websites, along with other resources, prepare a report that addresses the following issues, as well as others, for your selected country: (1) compare and contrast the corporate governance principles of your selected country with the United States, (2) identify the relevant corporate governance parties and their roles, (3) describe the corporate governance challenges for your selected country, and (4) list and describe recent corporate governance activities in your selected country.

International

Internet

International

Internet

2-54 **(Research Alternative Board Structures, LO 1, 2)** The board structure that is in U.S. companies differs from board structures found in companies in some European and Asian countries. The corporate governance system in these countries separates the board of directors into a supervisory board and a management board. The management board is composed of insiders who are responsible for the company's daily business activities, while the supervisory board provides general oversight. This two-tiered system has been both criticized and applauded. Required research the two-tiered system and prepare a report that (1) compares the two-tiered system with the one-tier system used in the United States, (2) identifies countries and companies that use a two-tiered board system, (3) assesses the positive and negative aspects of the two-tiered board system, and (4) analyzes which system might be more effective in protecting stakeholders.

Cases

Internet

2-55 **(Audit Committees, LO 5, 6)** A $6 billion privately held consumer products company has approached you to help them implement an audit committee charter and to identify the elements needed to develop an effective audit committee.

Required

a. Identify the major stakeholders, in addition to the stockholders (usually a family), who would be likely candidates to serve on the company's audit committee.

b. Identify the key attributes that should be used in choosing audit committee members.

c. Obtain and review the annual report of a public company and locate its audit committee charter. What are the key features of the charter? What are its strengths? What are its weaknesses?

Group Activity

Ethics

Professional Skepticism

2-56 **(Corporate Governance at Dell, LO 1, 2, 8)** In August 2010, Michael Dell, Dell Inc.'s CEO and chairman of the board, was reelected to Dell's board of directors by Dell's shareholders. However, not all of the shareholders were happy with Mr. Dell's reappointment. Specifically, two labor groups that own shares of Dell stock wanted Mr. Dell removed from the board because of a Securities and Exchange Commission (SEC) action and settlement involving the company and Mr. Dell. The SEC complaint alleged various accounting manipulations that called into question Dell's reported financial success from 2002 to 2006. In July 2010, Dell, Inc. agreed to pay $100 million to settle SEC charges, without admitting or denying guilt. Mr. Dell agreed to pay a $4 million fine, also without admitting or denying guilt. In your groups consider the principles of effective corporate governance presented in this chapter and discuss the following:

a. What principles of corporate governance appear to be missing at Dell?

b. Given the apparent actions of Mr. Dell, and his management and board roles, should Dell's external auditor expect the corporate governance at Dell to be effective?

c. How might Dell's external auditor respond to concerns about the quality of governance at Dell?

d. Given the SEC settlement, should Dell's board have an independent chair?

e. Given the SEC settlement, should Mr. Dell be removed from his CEO position?

Academic Research Case (LO 1)

Archambeault, D., DeZoort, F. T., & Holt, T. (2008). The Need for an Internal Auditor Report to External Stakeholders to Improve Governance Transparency. *Accounting Horizons 22(4): 375–388.*

i. What is the issue being addressed in the paper?

ii. Why is this issue important to practicing auditors?

iii. What are the findings of the paper?

iv. What are the implications of these findings for audit quality (or audit practice) on the audit profession?

v. Describe the research methodology used as a basis for the conclusions.

vi. Describe any limitations of the research that the student (and practice) should be aware of.

SEARCH HINT

It is easy to locate these academic research articles! Simply use a search engine (e.g., Google Scholar) or an electronic research platform (e.g., ABI Inform) and search using the author names and part of the article title.

Go to www.cengage.com/accounting/rittenberg for the Ford and Toyota materials.

Within each subsequent chapter of this textbook, we highlight chapter-relevant material using Ford Motor Company (Ford) and Toyota Motor Corporation (Toyota) as practical examples. We pose questions that will require you to apply the concepts introduced in that chapter to the facts of Ford and Toyota. We have selected these companies because they (1) are large, well-known manufacturers of products that are familiar to you, (2) operate in dynamic industries that present serious risks and challenges, (3) are both publicly traded on the New York Stock Exchange, and (4) differ in terms of their issuer status with the Securities and Exchange Commission (Ford is a U.S.-based company and therefore files an annual Form 10-K and Form Def 14A, whereas Toyota is not a U.S.-based company and therefore files an annual Form 20-F).

On the textbook website (www.cengage.com/accounting/rittenberg), we include a large set of materials for both Ford and Toyota. These materials include Ford's annual report, 10-K and Def 14A (i.e., proxy statement), and an 8-K. Materials for Toyota include its annual report and 20-F. Chapter-end materials concerning Ford and Toyota contain questions referenced to specific pages within these sources. These materials will introduce you to the companies, provide you with insight into the automotive industry, detail financial results, and describe relevant corporate governance issues. In subsequent chapters, we present additional materials from these sources tailored to the topics of those chapters.

For Chapter 2, you should answer the following questions.

Source and Reference	Question
General Background Questions	
Ford Annual Report or 10-K *Toyota Annual Report or 20-F*	**1a.** Describe the history of Ford, its current business, operating sectors, and reportable segments. **1b.** Describe the factors affecting Ford's profitability, and factors affecting the automotive industry in general. **1c.** Compare the nature of Ford's history, business sectors, and reportable segments to those of Toyota.
Corporate Governance Questions	
Ford Def 14A	**2a.** What is the purpose of the Form Def 14A? **2b.** What does "Def" stand for? **2c.** What types of information does a proxy contain?
	3a. Who are the board members that are standing for election at Ford in 2010? **3b.** Which of them has been deemed "independent" of Ford? **3c.** How does Ford determine director independence? **3d.** Why does independence matter to shareholders?

3e. What characteristics is Ford seeking when considering individuals to serve on its board?

3f. How are non-employee board members compensated? Could the nature of the compensation potentially affect the director's independence? Explain.

4a. Describe Ford's audit committee and its duties.

4b. Who is the designated financial expert on the audit committee? Does the designation of only one individual as a financial expert seem adequate for the complexity of Ford and the requirements of the Sarbanes-Oxley Act?

4c. Review the audit committee's report and describe its primary contents.

Toyota Annual Report or 20-F

5a. Who is the auditor for Ford? Who is the auditor for Toyota?

5b. What were the Ford 2009 audit fees as a percentage of (a) total revenue, and (b) total assets?

5c. What were the Toyota 2009 audit fees as a percentage of (a) total revenue, and (b) total assets? Compare these amounts to those for Ford and discuss possible reasons for and implications of the differences.

5d. Audit fees were not always publicly disclosed. In fact, such disclosure only became mandatory since the year 2000 in the United States. Why is public disclosure of audit and other fees paid to the audit firm important?

Ford 10-K, Exhibits 31 and 32

6a. The Sarbanes-Oxley Act of 2002, Section 302, modified the requirements in the Exchange Act rules such that, effective starting in 2002, principal executive officers of publicly traded companies must certify their companies' financial statements and internal control processes. Read the officer certifications in Ford's Exhibits 31.1, 31.2, 32.1, and 32.2. What are your impressions of these disclosures?

6b. Obtain a copy of the Sarbanes-Oxley Act of 2002 (http://frwebgate.access. gpo.gov/cgi-bin/getdoc.cgi?dbname=107_cong_bills&docid=f:h3763enr. txt.pdf). What are the specific certifications required in SOX Section 302?

6c. Why do you think Congress felt that it was necessary to require executive officers to make affirmative claims such as those found in Ford's 10-K Exhibits 31 and 32?

6d. How do you think that signing these certifications affects the judgment processes of these executive officers, if at all?

6e. Would you feel comfortable making these certifications if you were in executive management at Ford? What steps would you have to take in order to reach that level of comfort? Remember, management cannot rely on the work of the external auditor in developing a basis for its certification.

6f. Explain how management would (a) utilize the internal audit function and (b) develop requirements of mid-level managers in the process of developing support for its certifications?

Toyota 20-F

7. Read Toyota's corporate governance disclosures. What are the significant differences in corporate governance between Toyota and Ford?

Ethics-Related Questions

Ford website, www.ford.com; hint – go to the "corporate" part of the website and then the "investor" part of the website and then search on "code of ethics"

8a. Review the code of ethics for senior management and the board of directors. What are the main components of these codes? Provide a critique of the components and overall message contained in the codes.

8b. What guidelines are provided as to how deviations from the company's code of ethics will be handled?

3

Judgmental and Ethical Decision-Making Frameworks and Associated Professional Standards

LEARNING OBJECTIVES

The overriding objective of this textbook is to build a foundation with which to analyze current professional issues and adapt audit approaches to business and economic complexities. Through studying this chapter, you will be able to:

1 Articulate a general framework for making high-quality professional decisions and apply this framework in selected audit settings.

2 Describe why ethical behavior by auditors is required to justify the public's trust.

3 Describe ethical theories that can be used in addressing ethical problems.

4 Articulate a framework for making high-quality ethical decisions and apply this framework in selected settings.

5 Explain how various requirements in the Sarbanes-Oxley Act of 2002 reflect previous ethical lapses in professional judgment on the part of financial market participants and set the tone for improved ethical decision-making.

6 Describe and apply the AICPA's Code of Professional Conduct.

7 Explain the principles used by the SEC in judging independence and discuss specific independence rules of the SEC and the PCAOB.

8 Discuss the importance of independence to the public accounting profession.

9 Discuss the major threats to independence and approaches to mitigate those threats.

10 Discuss the audit committee's responsibilities related to the independence of the external auditor.

11 Explain the role of professional skepticism in auditors' judgments, including the relationship between auditor independence and professional skepticism.

CHAPTER OVERVIEW

A profession that exists to serve the public must assure that its services are performed at the highest level of quality, integrity, and independence. This chapter introduces a general framework depicting how to make high-quality professional decisions. In addition, the chapter introduces a more specific ethical decision-making framework, illustrating considerations that professionals should weigh as they attempt to make challenging ethical judgments. We introduce the Sarbanes-Oxley Act of 2002 by illustrating how many of its requirements seek to curb the ethical lapses in professional judgment on the part of auditors, management, and other parties involved in corporate governance. We also describe the AICPA's Principles and Code of Professional Conduct.

The Audit Opinion Formulation Process

I. Assessing Client Acceptance and Retention Decisions	II. Understanding the Client	III. Obtaining Evidence about Controls and Determining the Impact on the Financial Statement Audit	IV. Obtaining Substantive Evidence about Account Assertions	V. Wrapping Up the Audit and Making Reporting Decisions
CHAPTER 4	CHAPTERS 2, 4–6, and 9	CHAPTERS 5–14 and 18	CHAPTERS 7–14 and 18	CHAPTERS 15 and 16

The Auditing Profession, Regulation, and Corporate Governance	Decision-Making, Professional Conduct, and Ethics	Professional Liability
CHAPTERS 1 and 2	CHAPTER 3	CHAPTER 17

Finally, we articulate the fundamental importance of auditor independence and detail the SEC's and PCAOB's rules concerning this issue for auditors of public companies. In terms of the audit opinion formulation process, this chapter focuses on the fundamental building blocks regarding decision-making, professional conduct, and ethics.

PROFESSIONAL JUDGMENT IN CONTEXT

A Case of Ethical Decisions Concerning Auditor Independence

Thomas Flanagan was an audit partner and key member of management (Vice Chairman) at Deloitte LLP, based out of the firm's Chicago office. During the latter part of his career, he managed a large number of public company audit engagements. Based on knowledge obtained from key members of management of one of his audit clients, Flanagan learned that the client would soon be purchasing another company. Knowing that the value of the acquired company would rise upon the news of the purchase, Flanagan purchased stock in the acquired company. As such, he engaged in insider trading. As the subsequent investigation would reveal, Flanagan traded in securities of at least 12 of his audit clients during 2005–2008. In fact, he made more than 300 trades in shares of the firm's clients over this period. He concealed his actions by lying on his independence disclosure filings with Deloitte, not revealing the existence of several of his brokerage accounts that would have identified his actions. Ultimately, the SEC uncovered his actions and notified Deloitte. Flanagan resigned from the firm, and Deloitte subsequently sued him for breach of fiduciary duty, fraud, and breach of contract based upon his misconduct. The firm ultimately won a judgment against him. A spokesperson for the firm stated "Deloitte unequivocally condemns the actions of this individual, which are unprecedented in our experience. His personal trading activities were in blatant violation of Deloitte's strict and clearly stated policies for investments by partners and other professional personnel."

In August 2010 the Securities and Exchange Commission charged Thomas Flanagan and his son with insider trading in the securities of several of the firm's audit clients. The SEC alleges that Flanagan's illegal trading resulted in profits of more than $430,000. On four occasions, Flanagan shared the nonpublic information with his son, who then traded based on that information for illegal profits of more than $57,000. The SEC also instituted administrative proceedings against Thomas Flanagan, finding that he violated the SEC's auditor independence rules on 71 occasions between 2003 and 2008 by trading in the securities of nine Deloitte audit clients. The Flanagans agreed to pay more than $1.1 million to settle the SEC's charges.

As you read the following chapter, consider this case and the following questions:

- Why is owning stock in one's client considered inappropriate?
- Why is it important that auditors be independent of their clients?
- Why did Deloitte take Flanagan's actions so seriously?
- What do you think might have led Flanagan to conclude that such insider trading was acceptable?
- Assume that you were working on one of Flanagan's engagements and you discovered that insider trading was occurring. What procedures should the audit firm have in place to encourage you to report the inappropriate behavior and yet protect your career?

Note: This case is based on facts disclosed in the case Deloitte LLP v. Thomas P. Flanagan, Court of Chancery of the State of Delaware, No. 4125-VCN and SEC Accounting and Auditing Enforcement Release No. 3164

Introduction
Decision-Making, Ethics, and Organizational Performance

Research shows that companies with strong corporate governance, high-quality decision-making, and high ethical standards generally perform better and have higher-quality financial information than those that are weak on these dimensions. Investigations into the world's largest bankruptcies to date (WorldCom, Lehman Brothers, and Enron) show that poor decision-making, inappropriate corporate cultures and ethical standards, and weak governance were important factors in their collapse. Top management was overly concerned about meeting Wall Street's earnings expectations and generating personal fortunes and took extreme measures to create the illusion of companies that looked good on paper but were actually free-falling toward collapse. The corporate culture was one where employees knew about, or were concerned about, fraud but were afraid to report it; the boards of directors were passive and ineffective; the outside auditors were preoccupied with keeping the clients' business; and bankers were so permissive they failed to uncover routine warning signs. Management's philosophy was "Do whatever it takes to increase the market value of our stock."

Some of the partners of Arthur Andersen, at one time the largest CPA firm in the world, got drawn into the delusion of sharing these fortunes and turned a blind eye to the financial reporting frauds management was perpetrating. Barbara Ley Toffler was partner-in-charge of Andersen's Ethics & Responsible Business Practices consulting services. In her book *Final Accounting—Ambition, Greed, and the Fall of Arthur Andersen,* she chronicles how a culture of arrogance and greed infected her company and led to enormous lapses in judgment among her peers.[1] The firm, once regarded by many as the best CPA firm in the world, changed its philosophy from "we do it right" to "keep the client happy." Andersen was forced into bankruptcy after being in business for 88 years.

In this chapter, we first introduce a general framework for making professional decisions, and then follow up with a more specific framework for making ethically difficult decisions. Throughout the textbook, we will ask you to return to these frameworks, applying them in the various auditing contexts that are the subject of subsequent chapters. We provide an overview of the Sarbanes-Oxley Act of 2002. Next, we discuss the AICPA's principles and rules of professional conduct, which serve as guides in making professional decisions, both general and ethically charged. We discuss the notion of auditor independence in detail, including an examination of why independence is fundamental to the auditing profession. Finally, we discuss the role of professional skepticism in auditors' professional judgment. We summarize relevant professional pronouncements at the end of the chapter.

LO 1

Articulate a general framework for making high-quality professional decisions and apply this framework in selected audit settings.

A General Decision-Making Framework
A Framework for Professional Decision-Making

Auditors add value to the financial markets by making high-quality decisions associated with their evaluation of client financial statements. High-quality

---

[1] Barbara Ley Toffler, Final *Accounting-Ambition, Greed, and the Fall of Arthur Andersen.* (New York: Broadway Books, 2003).

decisions are unbiased, meet the expectations of users, are in compliance with professional standards, and are based on sufficient factual information to justify the decision that is rendered. For example, auditors have to make decisions about the types of evidence to gather, how to evaluate that evidence, when to gather additional evidence, and what conclusions are appropriate given the knowledge that they have gained via the evidence. Ultimately, auditors have to decide whether the client's financial statements contain any departures from generally accepted accounting principles that would materially affect the judgment of users of the financial statements.

This type of decision-making situation is common among professionals. For example, consider a doctor trying to diagnose the illness of a patient. The doctor must decide what tests to order, how to interpret the test results, and when to order additional tests (how many and what type), and must ultimately diagnose any potential illness in the patient. In order to make complex, difficult, and important decisions such as these, professionals can benefit from a structured approach to their decision-making, as depicted in Exhibit 3.1.

In **Step 1**, the auditor structures the problem, considering the relevant parties to involve in the decision process, identifying various feasible alternatives, considering how to evaluate the alternatives, identifying uncertainties or risks, and determining how to structure the problem. To illustrate these tasks, consider a common decision that auditors face—determining whether a client's inventory values are fairly stated in accordance with generally accepted accounting principles. Auditors work within an organizational hierarchy with clearly defined roles about appropriate types of auditors that should participate in inventory testing (e.g., less experienced auditors may conduct inventory test counts, but industry experts may consider the valuation of complex inventory items). In addition,

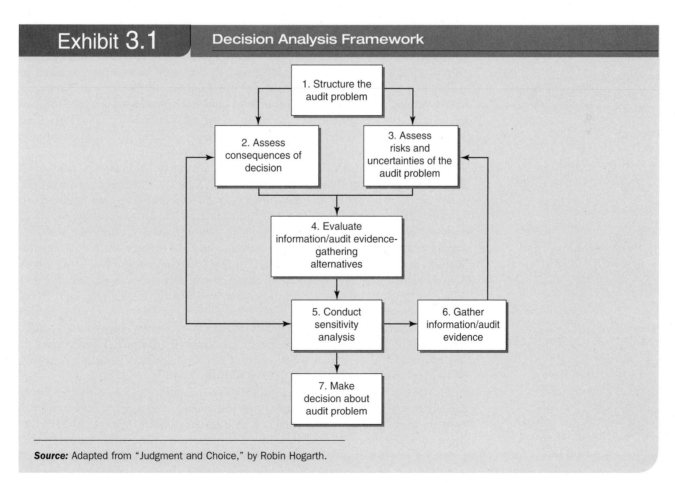

Exhibit 3.1 | **Decision Analysis Framework**

Source: Adapted from "Judgment and Choice," by Robin Hogarth.

auditors consider which individuals at the client are most qualified to assess inventory values. Auditors also identify feasible alternatives about the inventory balance. For example, is it fairly stated, overstated, understated? Consideration will also be given to the evidence necessary to determine accurate inventory valuation (e.g., observing the inventory, consulting outside prices of the inventory, and evaluating potential obsolescence). Auditors also have to evaluate the risk that the evidence they collect may not necessarily be diagnostic of the true, underlying value of the inventory. In other words, there is a risk that despite the work that they perform, their conclusions may be incorrect. The final stage of Step 1 includes structuring the problem, and professional guidance exists to assist in this process.

In **Step 2**, the auditor assesses the consequences of the potential alternatives. Considerations at this stage include determining the dimensions on which to evaluate the alternatives and how to weight those dimensions. Continuing the preceding example, the auditor will have to consider the consequences of various inventory valuation alternatives and whether a particular valuation alternative is more or less appropriate than the other available alternatives. If the auditor decides that the inventory is fairly stated and that the valuation methodology is appropriate, and that is in fact the case, then there are no negative consequences to the decision. However, if the auditor reaches an incorrect conclusion, then stakeholders may be misled, exposing auditors to litigation and reputation damage.

In **Step 3**, the auditor assesses the risks and uncertainties in the situation. Those risks and uncertainties are related to (a) the risks the audit client faces, (b) the quality of evidence the auditor gathers, and (c) the sufficiency of audit evidence gathered. In other words, there are risks related to a particular client, and there are risks in gathering sufficient audit evidence. All of these risks need to be assessed in determining the appropriate audit evidence to gather.

In **Step 4**, the auditor evaluates the various information/audit evidence-gathering alternatives against an appropriate decision rule. For auditors, decision rules are often articulated in terms of generally accepted accounting principles or generally accepted auditing standards. In our example, inventory valuation rules under generally accepted accounting principles may provide necessary guidance to assist in the decision-making process. Further, generally accepted auditing standards articulate rules regarding appropriate evidence-gathering strategies that must be followed when auditing inventory values.

In **Step 5**, the auditor considers the sensitivity of the conclusions reached in Steps 2, 3, and 4 to incorrect assumptions. It may be, given the results of the earlier steps, the auditor can determine enough evidence has been gathered to support (or not support), at a convincing level of certainty, and that the audit problem being evaluated can be answered appropriately. Continuing the preceding example, it may be that the auditor's initial evidence gathering and risk analysis enable a definitive conclusion. In that case, the auditor can move on to Step 7. However, there may still be significant uncertainties to resolve. For example, in the case of inventory, there may be variation in available market values against which to compare the historical costs of inventory on the client's financial statements. As such, the true inventory value may fall within a range, so the client and auditor will have to use their **professional judgment** to determine a value that is most reflective of economic reality. In such a situation, the auditor will have to complete Step 6 of the process.

In **Step 6**, the auditor gathers information and audit evidence in an iterative process that affects considerations about the consequences of potential alternatives and the uncertainties associated with those judgments. Importantly, the auditor considers the costs and benefits of information acquisition, knowing that gathering additional evidence requires time, effort, and money. Given that an audit is a for-profit enterprise, cost-benefit considerations in evidence gathering are particularly important. A good auditor knows "when to say when" and

AUDITING *in Practice*

WHAT IS PROFESSIONAL JUDGMENT?

Professional judgment involves applying relevant professional knowledge and experience to unique and potentially uncertain facts and circumstances in order to reach a conclusion or make a decision. Thus, a first part of professional judgment is determining when the auditor has sufficient, appropriate evidence to make a decision. Then, when an auditor makes high-quality professional judgments, he or she competently applies auditing and/or accounting principles, and makes decisions that are appropriate given the evidence that should be known to the auditor at the time of the judgment. Importantly,

professional judgment cannot be used to justify conclusions or decisions that would otherwise not be supported by the existing evidence. Documenting a professional judgment is critical. Professional standards in the United States and internationally require that documentation is sufficient to enable an experienced auditor, having no previous connection with the audit, to understand the significant judgments made in reaching conclusions on significant matters arising during the audit. Professional judgment is the key to conducting a quality audit.

decides to stop collecting evidence at the right time. In contrast, some auditors stop evidence collection too soon, thereby yielding inadequate evidence on which to make a decision. Still others continue evidence collection even though the current evidence is adequate, thereby contributing to inefficiency and reduced profitability in the audit.

The auditor iterates through Steps 1 through 6 repeatedly until satisfied that a decision can prudently be made. In **Step 7**, the auditor needs to make the difficult determination of whether the problem has been sufficiently analyzed and whether the risk of making an incorrect decision has been minimized to an acceptable level by collecting adequate, convincing evidence. Ultimately, the auditor must make and document the decision reached. Throughout the text and chapter problems, we will illustrate other applications of this decision analysis framework. Next, we turn to a more specific decision setting, one involving the resolution of ethically charged issues.

An Ethical Decision-Making Framework

Accepting a Public Trust

The public accounting profession has worked hard to gain the public trust, and it benefits monetarily from that trust as the sole legally acceptable provider of audit services for companies and other organizations. For that trust and economic advantage to be maintained, it is essential that professional integrity be based on personal moral standards and reinforced by codes of conduct. Whenever a "scandal" surfaces, the profession is diminished and auditors are personally ruined. It is not difficult to find oneself in ethically compromising situations without realizing it. During the course of an audit, for example, an auditor may become aware of a client's plans that will likely double the market value of its stock. Suppose the auditor has a roommate from college who would like to know about the investment opportunity. The roommate does not have a large investment portfolio, so sharing this knowledge would not affect the market. Should the auditor be allowed to share the information with the roommate? Or consider the Susan Birkert case from the "Auditing in Practice" feature. The anonymous tipster in that case was rumored to be a friend and colleague of Birkert's on the Comtech engagement. Imagine the ethical choice that the friend faced upon learning of Birkert's deception—to whistleblow and

PRACTICAL POINT

As accounting and auditing standards become less "rules-based" and become more "principles-based," the role of professional judgment in decision-making will become increasingly important to auditors' effectiveness. What is currently unknown, however, is the extent to which auditors' professional judgments will be second-guessed by third-party users in this environment of less-precise standards. This potential unknown questioning makes it even more important that auditors exercise professional judgment throughout an audit engagement.

LO 2

Describe why ethical behavior by auditors is required to justify the public's trust.

AUDITING *in Practice*

A YOUNG AUDITOR MAKES AN ETHICAL MISTAKE IN PROFESSIONAL JUDGMENT

Susan Birkert, age 27, was a lead senior on the KPMG audits of Comtech during fiscal years 2004–2006. During 2005, an acquaintance of Birkert agreed to purchase $5,000 of Comtech stock for her, in violation of professional rules regarding auditor independence. In May 2006, Birkert falsely asserted to KPMG that she was in compliance with audit firm and professional rules regarding independence. Following an anonymous tip and an ensuing KPMG internal investigation, Birkert admitted to the deception, and KPMG fired her. Subsequently, the PCAOB barred her from serving before it for a period of at least one year. For further details on this case, see the facts disclosed in PCAOB Release No. 105-2007-003, November 14, 2007.

inevitably damage Birkert's career or to ignore the matter and possibly rationalize Birkert's actions as inconsequential given the relatively small size of the impact on the market.

Accounting professionals are often faced with these types of difficult ethical choices. In such situations, a defined methodology is helpful in resolving the situation in a thoughtful, high-quality manner. An **ethical problem** occurs when an individual is morally or ethically required to take an action that may conflict with his or her immediate self-interest. An **ethical dilemma** occurs when there are conflicting moral duties or obligations, such as paying a debt to one person when there is equal indebtedness to another person and sufficient funds do not exist to repay both. Complex ethical dilemmas do not lend themselves to simple "right" or "wrong" decisions.

Ethical Theories

LO 3

Describe ethical theories that can be used in addressing ethical problems.

Ethical theories are helpful in assisting individuals in dealing with both ethical problems and ethical dilemmas. Two such theories—the utilitarian theory and the rights theory—provide references that have influenced the development of codes of conduct and can be used by professionals in dealing with ethically challenging situations.

Utilitarian Theory

Utilitarian theory holds that what is ethical is the action that achieves the greatest good for the greatest number of people. Actions that result in outcomes that fall short of the greatest good for the greatest number and those that represent inefficient means to accomplish such ends are less desirable. Utilitarianism requires the following:

- An identification of the potential problem and courses of action
- An identification of the potential direct or indirect impact of actions on each affected party (often referred to as **stakeholders**) who may have a vested interest in the outcome of actions taken
- An assessment of the desirability (goodness) of each action
- An overall assessment of the greatest good for the greatest number

Utilitarianism requires that individuals not advocate or choose alternatives that favor narrow interests or that serve the greatest good in an inefficient manner. There can be honest disagreements about the likely impact of actions or the relative efficiency of different actions in attaining desired ends. There are also potential problems in measuring what constitutes "the greatest good" in a particular circumstance. One problem with the utilitarian theory is the implicit assumption that the "ends achieved" justify the means. Unfortunately, such an approach can lead to disastrous courses of actions when those making the decisions fail to adequately measure or assess the potential costs and benefits. Thus, ethicists generally argue that utilitarian arguments should be mitigated by some "value-based" approach. The rights theory approach presents such a framework.

Rights Theory

Rights theory focuses on evaluating actions based on the fundamental rights of the parties involved. However, not all rights are equal. In the hierarchy of rights, higher-order rights take precedence over lower-order rights. The highest-order rights include the right to life, to autonomy, and to human dignity. Second-order rights include rights granted by the government, such as civil rights, legal rights, rights to own property, and license privileges. Third-order rights are social rights, such as the right to higher education, to good health care, and to earning a living. The lowest-level, fourth-order rights, are related to one's nonessential interests or one's tastes, such as the right to get rich, to play golf, or to be attractively dressed.

Rights theory requires that the "rights" of affected parties should be examined as a constraint on ethical decision-making. The rights approach is most effective in identifying outcomes that ought to be automatically eliminated, such as the "Robin Hood approach" of robbing from the rich to give to the poor, or in identifying situations in which the utilitarian answer would be at odds with most societal values.

An Ethical Framework

The following framework is derived from the utilitarianism and rights theories and defines an approach to addressing complex issues not addressed by the profession's code or when elements of the code seem to be in conflict:

LO 4

Articulate a framework for making high-quality ethical decisions and apply this framework in selected settings.

- Identify the ethical issue(s).
- Determine who are the affected parties and identify their rights.
- Determine the most important rights.
- Develop alternative courses of action.
- Determine the likely consequences of each proposed course of action.
- Assess the possible consequences, including an estimation of the greatest good for the greatest number. Determine whether the rights framework would cause any course of action to be eliminated.
- Decide on the appropriate course of action.

The following case, similar to an actual situation, is presented to show how to apply this framework to auditing situations.

Applying the Ethical Framework

Identify the Ethical Issue(s) The CPAs providing audit services for a client, Payroll Processors, Inc., believe Payroll Processors might go bankrupt. Several clients of the CPA firm use the payroll processing services of Payroll Processors. Should the other clients be provided with this confidential information prior to the information being publicly available through the audit report—which might be delayed as auditors further assess the potential for bankruptcy?

Determine Who Are the Affected Parties and Identify Their Rights The relevant parties to the issue include the following:

- Payroll Processors and its management
- Payroll Processors' current and prospective customers, creditors, and investors
- The CPA firm and its other clients
- The public accounting profession

Listing those potentially affected by the decision is easier than identifying their rights. The following, however, are some of the rights involved:

- Company management has the right to assume that confidential information obtained by its auditors will remain confidential unless disclosure is permitted by the company or is required by accounting or auditing standards.
- Payroll Processors' current and prospective customers, creditors, and investors have a right to receive reliable information and not be denied information that others receive.
- The CPA firm has the right to expect its professionals to follow the professional standards. However, some may feel pressure to protect their existing clients' welfare.
- The public accounting profession has the right to expect all its members to uphold the Code of Professional Conduct and to take actions that enhance the general reputation and perception of the integrity of the profession. The ethics ruling on confidentiality was designed to assure a free flow of information between the client and the auditor. Such information flow is considered necessary to the efficient and effective conduct of an audit engagement.

Determine the Most Important Rights   Many auditors would assess that the most important rights are those of (1) Payroll Processors to not have confidential information improperly disclosed; (2) users to receive reliable information; (3) the client, who expects that confidentiality of private information will be maintained; and (4) the profession to retain its reputation for trust and assurance that effective audits will occur without leaking information prematurely to selected parties.

Develop Alternative Courses of Action   The possible courses of action are (1) share the confidential information with the other clients of the public accounting firm prior to issuing an audit opinion on the client's financial statements or (2) do not share that information prior to issuing an audit opinion on the client's financial statements. The CPA firm was performing audit work, and the professional standards require that the auditors disclose their reservations about Payroll Processors remaining a going concern in their audit report, not in private information given to selected entities. Thus, that going-concern reservation would serve as a flag to anyone who reads the annual report.

Determine the Likely Consequences

1. *Share the Information Prior to Issuing the Audit Opinion*—Sharing this information with the other clients prior to issuing an audit report with a going-concern reservation may cause these other clients to take their business away from Payroll Processors, thus increasing the likelihood of bankruptcy for Payroll Processors. It might also increase the possibility of the CPA firm being found in violation of the rules of conduct and being sued by Payroll Processors or others for inappropriately providing confidential information to selected parties outside of the public role that CPAs fulfill. The CPA may also have his or her license suspended or revoked. Other Payroll Processors' clients who do not receive the information because they are not the CPA firm's clients will be put at a competitive disadvantage, and they may sue the auditor because of discriminatory disclosure.
2. *Do Not Share the Information Until the Audit Report Has Been Issued*—If the information is not shared with the other clients, those clients might take their audit business elsewhere if they find out the auditors knew of this problem and did not share it with them. Other clients of Payroll Processors may suffer losses because of the financial problems of Payroll Processors.

AUDITING *in Practice*

ABUSES OF POWER

One of the many problems encountered in the Enron engagement was that the lead audit partner was responsible for being a "relationship manager," that is, responsible for keeping the client happy. Enron used its resulting power over the audit partner and magnified it by paying Arthur Andersen consulting fees that were much greater than the audit fees. As a result, the Enron audit engagement at the Andersen overall partnership level was more important than it would have otherwise been to the audit firm. The loss of the Enron audit engagement, or the dissatisfaction of Enron as a client, could potentially result in the loss of very significant consulting revenues, which would be a big blow to the partnership's income.

Assess the Possible Consequences and Estimate the Greatest Good for the Greatest Number   Sharing the information may help other clients move their payroll processing business to other service providers in a more orderly manner and more quickly than would happen if they had to wait until the audit opinion was issued. However, other Payroll Processors' customers may be placed at a disadvantage if Payroll Processors does go bankrupt and their payroll processing is disrupted. Payroll Processors' employees will lose their jobs more quickly, and its investors are likely to lose more money more quickly. Its right to have confidential information remain confidential will be violated. There may be less confidence in the profession because of discriminatory or unauthorized disclosure of information. Management of other firms may be reluctant to share other nonfinancial information with auditing firms. After assessing the relative benefits of disclosing vs. not disclosing the information prior to issuing the audit opinion, it appears that the greatest good is served by not sharing the information selectively with current audit clients, but to complete the audit and issue the audit opinion in a timely manner.

Decide on the Appropriate Course of Action   The CPA should not share the information prior to issuing the audit opinion. The CPA may encourage Payroll Processors to share its state of affairs with its clients but cannot dictate that it do so. The need for equity and confidentiality of information dictates that the CPA's major course of communication is through formal audit reports associated with the financial statements.

The Sarbanes-Oxley Act of 2002 as a Reaction to Ethical Lapses

The financial scandals and associated market fallout in the late 1990s and early 2000s were a dramatic illustration of the costs of inappropriate ethical decisions by various parties, weak corporate governance, poor auditor decision-making, and insufficient auditor independence. The bankruptcies of Enron and World-Com and the subsequent collapse of Arthur Andersen LLP were such dramatic and large-scale events that Congress was compelled to respond, and it did so in the form of the Sarbanes-Oxley Act of 2002. Exhibit 3.2 summarizes the major provisions of the Sarbanes-Oxley Act.

As is clear from reading Exhibit 3.2, various sections of the Sarbanes-Oxley Act were written to respond to various abuses of the financial reporting process in the late 1990s and early 2000s, and many provisions affect auditors and the auditing profession directly. For example, Title I and its relevant sections effectively remove self-regulation of the auditing profession and replace it with

PRACTICAL POINT

The financial crisis of 2008–2010 followed a similar pattern to that of the market fallout in the late 1990s and early 2000s. There were serious ethical and governance failures in large investment banks. This led Congress to pass comprehensive legislation to significantly change the regulation of financial institutions.

LO 5

Explain how various requirements in the Sarbanes-Oxley Act of 2002 reflect previous ethical lapses in professional judgment on the part of financial market participants and set the tone for improved ethical decision-making.

Exhibit 3.2	Significant Provisions of the Sarbanes-Oxley Act of 2002

Section	Requirements

TITLE I: Public Company Accounting Oversight Board

101	Establishment and administrative provisions. The Board:
	• Is a nonprofit corporation, not an agency of the U.S. government.
	• Will have five financially literate members who are prominent individuals of integrity and reputation with a commitment to the interests of investors and the public.
	• Has authority to set standards related to audit reports and to conduct inspections of registered public accounting firms.
102	Registration with the Board:
	• Accounting firms auditing public companies must register with the PCAOB.
103	Auditing, quality control, and independence standards and rules. The Board:
	• Will establish or adopt rules regarding the conduct of audits and regarding audit firm quality control standards.
	• Will require audit firms to describe the scope of testing of issuers' internal control structure.
104	Inspections of registered public accounting firms. The Board will:
	• Inspect annually registered accounting firms that audit more than 100 issuers.
	• Inspect at least every three years registered accounting firms that audit fewer than 100 issuers.
	• Publicly report results of its inspections.
105	Investigations and disciplinary proceedings. The Board will:
	• Adopt procedures for disciplining registered accounting firms.
	• Require registered accounting firms to provide documentation and testimony that the Board deems necessary to conduct investigations.
	• Be able to sanction registered accounting firms for noncooperation with investigations.
106	Foreign public accounting firms. Foreign accounting firms must comply with the same rules related to the PCAOB as domestic accounting firms.
107	Commission oversight of the Board. The SEC has oversight and enforcement authority over the Board, including in processes involving standards setting, enforcement, and disciplinary procedures.
108	Accounting standards. The SEC will recognize as "generally accepted" accounting principles that are established by a standard setter that meets the Act's criteria.
109	Funding. Registered accounting firms and issuers will pay for the operations of the Board.

TITLE II: Auditor Independence

201	Services outside the scope of practice of auditors. There exist a variety of services that registered accounting firms may not perform for issuers, e.g., bookkeeping, systems design, appraisal services, and internal auditing, among others. Tax services may be performed, but only with preapproval by the audit committee.
202	Preapproval requirements. All audit and nonaudit services (with certain exceptions based on size and practicality) must be approved by the audit committee of the issuer.
203	Audit partner rotation. The lead partner and reviewing partner must rotate off the issuer engagement at least every five years.
204	Auditor reports to audit committees. Registered accounting firms must report to the audit committee issues concerning:
	• Critical accounting policies and practices.
	• Alternative treatments of financial information within generally accepted accounting principles that have been considered by management, and the preferred treatment of the accounting firm.
	• Significant written communications between the accounting firm and management.
205	Conforming amendments. This section details minor wording changes between the Sarbanes-Oxley Act and the Securities Act of 1934.
206	Conflicts of interest. Registered accounting firms may not perform audits for an issuer whose CEO, CFO, controller, chief accounting officer, or other equivalent position was employed by the accounting firm during the one-year period preceding the audit, i.e., a "cooling off period."
207	Study of mandatory rotation of registered public accounting firms. The Comptroller General of the United States shall conduct a study addressing this issue.

Exhibit 3.2	Significant Provisions of the Sarbanes-Oxley Act of 2002 *(continued)*

Section	Requirements

TITLE III: Corporate Responsibility

301   Public company audit committees.
- Audit committees are to be directly responsible for the appointment, compensation, and oversight of the work of registered accounting firms.
- Each audit committee member shall be independent.
- Audit committees must establish "whistleblowing" mechanisms within issuers.
- Audit committees have the authority to engage their own independent counsel.
- Issuers must provide adequate funding for audit committees.

302   Corporate responsibility for financial reports. The signing officers (i.e., CEO and CFO):
- Will certify in quarterly and annual reports filed with the SEC that the report does not contain untrue statements of material facts, and that the financial statements and disclosures present fairly (in all material respects) the financial condition and results of operations of the issuer.
- Must establish and maintain effective internal controls to ensure reliable financial statements and disclosures.
- Are responsible for designing internal controls, assessing their effectiveness, and disclosing material deficiencies in controls to the audit committee and registered accounting firm.

303   Improper influence on conduct of audits. Officers of issuers may not take action to fraudulently influence, coerce, manipulate, or mislead the registered accounting firm or its employees.

TITLE IV: Enhanced Financial Disclosures

401   Disclosures in periodic reports.
- Financial reports must be in accordance with generally accepted accounting principles, and must reflect material correcting adjustments proposed by the registered accounting firm.
- Material off-balance-sheet transactions and other relationships with unconsolidated entities or persons must be disclosed.
- The SEC must issue new rules on pro forma figures, and must study the issues of off-balance-sheet transactions and the use of special-purpose entities.

402   Enhanced conflict of interest provisions. Issuers may not extend credit to directors or executive offers.

404   Management assessment of internal controls.
- Annual reports must state the responsibility of management for establishing and maintaining an adequate internal control structure and procedures for financial reporting.
- Annual reports must contain an assessment of the effectiveness of the internal control structure and procedures of the issuer for financial reporting.
- Each registered accounting firm must attest to and report on the assessment made by the management of the issuer, and such attestation must not be the subject of a separate engagement (i.e., requires an integrated audit).

406   Code of ethics for senior financial officers. The SEC must issue rules requiring issuers to disclose whether or not the issuer has adopted a code of ethics for senior financial officers (and if not, the issuer must explain the rationale).

407   Disclosure of audit committee financial expert. The SEC must issue rules to require issuers to disclose whether or not the audit committee of the issuer is comprised of at least one member who is a financial expert (and if not, the issuer must explain the rationale).

SECTION V: Analyst Conflicts of Interest

501   Treatment of securities analysts. Registered securities associations and national securities exchanges must adopt rules to address concerns about conflicts of interest for analysts that recommend equity securities.

SECTION VI: Commission Resources and Authority

601   Enhanced funding for the SEC. The SEC's budget is increased to enable stronger enforcement and regulation of parties involved in the securities markets.

602   The SEC may censure any person, or deny, temporarily or permanently, the privilege of appearing or practicing before the SEC if that person is found:
- Not to possess the requisite qualifications to represent others.
- To be lacking in character or integrity, or to have engaged in unethical or improper professional conduct.
- To have willfully violated, or willfully aided and abetted the violation of any provision of the securities laws.

Exhibit 3.2	Significant Provisions of the Sarbanes-Oxley Act of 2002 *(continued)*

Section	Requirements

SECTION VII: Studies and Reports

701	GAO study and report regarding consolidation of public accounting firms. The Comptroller General of the United States shall conduct a study addressing factors leading to consolidation of public accounting firms since 1989 and the reduction in the number of firms capable of providing audit services to large national and multinational businesses subject to the securities laws.
702	Commission study and report regarding credit rating agencies. The SEC shall conduct a study on the role and function of credit rating agencies in the operation of the securities market.
703	Study and report on violators and violations. The SEC shall conduct a study to determine the number of securities professionals (e.g., public accountants, public accounting firms, investment bankers, brokers, dealers, attorneys) who have aided and abetted a violation of the federal securities laws, but have not been sanctioned, disciplined, or otherwise penalized.
704	Study of enforcement actions. The Comptroller General of the United States shall review and analyze all enforcement actions by the SEC involving violations of reporting requirements imposed under the securities laws and restatements over the five-year period preceding the Sarbanes-Oxley Act.
705	Study of investment banks. The Comptroller General of the United States shall conduct a study on whether investment banks and financial advisers assisted public companies in manipulating their earnings and obfuscating their true financial condition.

SECTION VIII: Corporate and Criminal Fraud Accountability

802	Criminal penalties for altering documents. Stronger penalties are now imposed for crimes involving the destruction, alteration, falsification, or destruction of financial records or corporate audit records.
805	Review of federal sentencing guidelines for obstruction of justice and extensive criminal fraud. Sentencing guidelines are enhanced for fraud and obstruction of justice sentences.
806	Protection for employees of publicly traded companies who provide evidence of fraud. This section provides whistleblower protection to protect against retaliation in fraud cases.
807	Criminal penalties for defrauding shareholders of publicly traded companies. Stronger penalties are now imposed for crimes involving securities fraud.

TITLE IX: White-Collar Crime Penalty Enhancements

903	Criminal penalties for mail and wire fraud. This section increases penalties for these violations.
904	Criminal penalties for violations of the Employee Retirement Income Security Act of 1974. This section increases penalties for violations of this Act.
905	Amendment to sentencing guidelines relating to certain white-collar offenses. The United States Sentencing Commission shall review and amend Federal Sentencing Guidelines related to provisions of the Sarbanes-Oxley Act.
906	Corporate responsibility for financial reports. This section provides penalties for corporate directors who knowingly provide incorrect certifications of financial statements and reports.

TITLE X: Corporate Tax Returns

1001	The CEO must sign the corporate tax return.

TITLE XI: Corporate Fraud and Accountability

1102	Tampering with a record or otherwise impeding an official proceeding. This section provides penalties for whoever corruptly alters, destroys, mutilates, or conceals a record, document, or other object, or attempts to do so, with the intent to impair the object's integrity and availability for use in an official proceeding, or otherwise obstructs, influences, or impedes any official proceeding, or attempts to do so.
1105	Authority of the Commission to prohibit persons from serving as officers or directors. The SEC may prohibit from serving before it as an officer or director any individual who has violated Section 10(b) of the Securities Act of 1934 or Section 8A of the Securities Act of 1933.
1106	Increased criminal penalties under Securities Act of 1934. This section provides increased penalties for violations of the Securities Act of 1934.

independent oversight by the Public Company Accounting Oversight Board (PCAOB). Section 201 eliminates the ability of accounting firms to provide many consulting services to audit clients, which was an issue cited as a significant driver of the failed audits of Enron. Sections 204, 301, and 407 significantly expand the power, responsibilities, and disclosures of corporate audit committees, thereby addressing concerns over weak corporate governance. Audit committees are directly responsible for the oversight of the company's external auditors and have the power to hire and fire the auditors. Section 404 requires management assurance and accounting firm attestation regarding the effectiveness of internal controls over financial reporting, a key structural problem in many organizations experiencing fraud. Finally, many sections of the Sarbanes-Oxley Act significantly enhance the penalties for criminal wrongdoing that affects the securities markets, individual shareholders, and the general public.

Approaches to Professional Codes of Ethics

Auditors need to exhibit the highest standard of ethical principles in order to function. For example, if the public does not have confidence in the independence and integrity of auditors, it will not subscribe any value to the auditors' work. However, not all CPAs serve the same audience. Some auditors perform audits of public companies and are guided by standards issued by the PCAOB. Most auditors belong to the AICPA and are subject to the ethical standards of the AICPA. Finally, there is a need for ethical behavior across global entities. Thus auditors should also be aware of the ethical standards issued by the International Federation of Accountants via the International Ethics Standards Board for Accountants. Fortunately, there is a great deal of consistency among these codes of ethics.

International Ethics Standards Board for Accountants

The International Ethics Standards Board for Accountants (IESBA) has taken a broad approach to ethical conduct. We present this first because it sets out principles that permeate all of the other standards. The Code of Ethics requires accountants to adhere to five fundamental principles:

- *Integrity*—A professional accountant should be straightforward and honest in performing professional services.
- *Objectivity*—A professional accountant should not allow bias, conflict of interest, or undue influence of others to override professional or business judgments.
- *Professional Competence and Due Care*—A professional accountant has a continuing duty to maintain professional knowledge and skill at the level required to assure that a client or employer receives competent professional service based on current developments. A professional accountant should act diligently and in accordance with applicable technical and professional standards when providing professional services.
- *Confidentiality*—A professional accountant should respect the confidentiality of information acquired as a result of professional and business relationships and should not disclose any such information to third parties without proper and specific authority unless there is a legal or professional right or duty to disclose. Confidential information acquired as a result of professional and business relationships should not be used for the personal advantage of the professional accountant or third parties.

- *Professional Behavior*—A professional accountant should comply with relevant laws and regulations and should avoid any action that discredits the profession.

Source: © 2008 by The International Federation of Accountants (IFAC). All rights reserved. Used with permission of IFAC. This text is an extract from the Handbook of International Standards on Auditing, Assurance, and Ethics Pronouncements of the International Auditing and Assurance Standards Board (IAASB), published by the International Federation of Accountants (IFAC) in April 2009 and is used with permission of IFAC.

The IESBA focuses on fundamental principles that should guide auditor decision-making in every situation. For example, there is a strong focus on objectivity and integrity. We find a similar approach in the AICPA Code of Ethics, but the terminology focuses more on audit independence, rather than objectivity.

AICPA Code of Professional Conduct

LO 6

Describe and apply the AICPA's Code of Professional Conduct.

Although the Sarbanes-Oxley Act, and the general decision-making framework or the specific ethical decision-making framework above will clearly be helpful in limiting management and auditor misbehavior and resolving difficult professional situations, the accounting profession also uses formal self-regulatory mechanisms to achieve consistency in judgment and defensibility to the public and regulators. For example, the AICPA, the Institute of Internal Auditors, and the Institute of Management Accountants have each developed codes of professional conduct as a means of self-regulation of their membership. When ethical problems are not specifically covered by these codes, the auditor must use common sense, moral values, and the frameworks outlined previously to resolve the difficult situations.

The Code of Professional Conduct was adopted by the AICPA membership to provide guidance and rules to all members—those in public practice, in industry, in government, and in education—in the performance of their professional responsibilities. The AICPA's Code of Professional Conduct is made up of a set of principles that provide the basis for the rules of conduct. In addition, there are interpretations of the rules, as well as ethics rulings. The Principles, shown in Exhibit 3.3, provide a broad standard for professional conduct and represent the highest guide for professional action. Auditors should always look to these principles for professional guidance. Many significant ethical dilemmas that auditors encounter can be solved by focusing on the application of these underlying principles. Too often, auditors have become so involved in looking at and interpreting specific rules that they have overlooked the underlying guiding principles. Thus, while specific rules are important, auditors must be sure that when they interpret and apply specific rules, they do so in a manner consistent with the guiding principles underlying those rules.

The **Rules of Conduct** are specific guidelines that reflect the broad principles of the profession. They provide more detailed guidance to help CPAs in carrying out their public responsibilities. The rules are specifically enforceable under the bylaws of the AICPA. Most rules apply to all CPAs, even if those individuals are not in public practice. The Rules of Conduct are intended to be specific enough to guide auditors in most situations they are likely to encounter and cover the broad areas of **independence**, **integrity**, adherence to professional pronouncements, and responsibilities to the public and colleagues.

The profession augments the rules with specific interpretations to provide additional guidance. The Rules of Conduct are presented in Exhibit 3.4. We highlight several of the most important rules in the following discussion.

The AICPA's rules, in part, reflect the nature of the profession's current role as a self-regulator of audits of companies in the private sector or organizations that include not-for-profit and governmental organizations. The tendency of the AICPA has been to react to specific issues with detailed rules in order to provide clear guidance when auditors or audit firms face issues that may be viewed by some as in the "gray area" of being acceptable or not acceptable.

Exhibit 3.3	AICPA Principles of Professional Conduct

Responsibilities In carrying out their responsibilities as professionals, members should exercise sensitive professional and moral judgments in all their activities.

Public interest Members should accept the obligation to act in a way that will serve the public interest, honor the public trust, and demonstrate commitment to professionalism.

Integrity To maintain and broaden public confidence, members should perform all professional responsibilities with the highest sense of integrity.

Objectivity and independence A member should maintain objectivity and be free of conflicts in discharging professional responsibilities. A member in public practice should be independent in fact and appearance when providing auditing and other attestation services.

Due care A member should observe the profession's technical and ethical standards, strive continually to improve competence and the quality of services, and discharge professional responsibility to the best of the member's ability.

Scope and nature of services A member in public practice should observe the principles of the Code of Professional Conduct in determining the scope and nature of services to be provided.

Source: Copyright American Institute of Certified Public Accountants, Inc. All rights reserved. Used with permission.

Exhibit 3.4	AICPA Rules of Conduct

Rule 101
Independence

A member in public practice shall be independent in the performance of professional services as required by standards promulgated by bodies designated by Council.

Rule 102
Integrity and Objectivity

In the performance of any professional service, a member shall maintain objectivity and integrity, shall be free of conflicts of interest, and shall not knowingly misrepresent facts or subordinate his or her judgment to others.

Rule 201
General Standards

A member shall comply with the following standards and with any interpretations thereof by bodies designated by Council.

A. *Professional Competence.* Undertake only those professional services that the member or the member's firm can reasonably expect to be completed with professional competence.

B. *Due Professional Care.* Exercise due professional care in the performance of professional services.

C. *Planning and Supervision.* Adequately plan and supervise the performance of professional services.

D. *Sufficient Relevant Data.* Obtain sufficient relevant data to afford a reasonable basis for conclusions or recommendations in relation to any professional services performed.

Rule 202
Compliance with Standards

A member who performs auditing, review, compilation, consulting, tax, or other professional services shall comply with standards promulgated by bodies designated by Council.

Rule 203
Accounting Principles

A member shall not (1) express an opinion that the financial statements or other financial data of any entity are presented in conformity with generally accepted accounting principles or (2) state that he or she is not aware of any material modifications that should be made to such statements or data in order for them to be in conformity with generally accepted accounting principles, if such statements or data contain any departure from an accounting principle promulgated by bodies designated by council to establish such principles that has a material effect on the statements or data taken as a whole. If, however, the statements or data contain such a departure and the member can demonstrate that due to unusual circumstances the financial statements or data would otherwise have been misleading, the member can comply with the rule by describing the departure, its approximate effects, if practicable, and the reasons why compliance with the principle would result in a misleading statement.

Exhibit 3.4	AICPA Rules of Conduct *(continued)*
Rule 301 Confidential Client Information	A member in public practice shall not disclose any confidential client information without the specific consent of the client.

Rule 302
Contingent Fees
	A member in public practice shall not:
	(1) perform for a contingent fee any professional services for, or receive such a fee from a client for whom the member or the member's firm also performs:
	    (a) an audit or review of a financial statement, or
	    (b) a compilation of a financial statement when the member expects, or reasonably might expect, that a third party will use the financial statement and the member's compilation report does not describe a lack of independence, or
	    (c) an examination of prospective financial information, or
	(2) prepare an original or amended tax return or claim for a tax refund for a contingent fee for any client. This prohibition applies during the period in which the member or the member's firm is engaged to perform any of the services listed above and the period covered by any historical financial statements involved in any such listed services.

Rule 501 Acts Discreditable	A member shall not commit an act discreditable to the profession.
Rule 502 Advertising and Other Forms of Solicitation	A member in public practice shall not seek to obtain clients by advertising or other forms of solicitation in a manner that is false, misleading, or deceptive. Solicitation by the use of coercion, overreaching, or harassing conduct is prohibited.
Rule 503 Commissions and Referral Fees	A. *Prohibited Commissions*. A member in public practice shall not for a commission recommend or refer to a client any product or service, or for a commission recommend or refer any product or service to be supplied by a client, or receive a commission, when the member or the member's firm also performs (attestation services referred to in Rule 302) for the client. This prohibition applies to the period covered by the attestation service and the related historical financial statements. B. *Disclosure of Permitted Commissions*. A member in public practice who is not prohibited by this rule from performing services for or receiving a commission and who is paid or expects to be paid a commission shall disclose that fact to any person or entity to whom the member recommends or refers a product or service to which the commission relates. C. *Referral Fees*. Any member who accepts a referral fee for recommending or referring any service of a CPA to any person or entity or who pays a referral fee to obtain a client shall disclose such acceptance or payment to the client.

Rule 505
Form of Organization and Name
	A member may practice public accounting only in a form of organization permitted by state law or regulation whose characteristics conform to resolutions of Council.
	    A member shall not practice public accounting under a firm name that is misleading. Names of one or more past owners may be included in the firm name or a successor organization.
	    A firm may not designate itself as "Members of the American Institute of Certified Public Accountants" unless all of its CPA owners are members of the Institute.

Source: Copyright American Institute of Certified Public Accountants, Inc. All rights reserved. Used with permission.

Independence—Rule 101

The auditor is required to be independent when providing attestation services, including audit services, to private or public entities. Independence is considered the cornerstone of the auditing profession. However, the AICPA also provides rules for other services that audit firms may supply to the public, such as consulting, tax, or bookkeeping services, which do *not* require the same degree of independence as an audit. There are several interpretations of Rule 101 and many specific rulings that provide detailed guidance concerning such matters as financial interests in the client, family relationships, loans with a client, and performance of nonaudit services.

Financial Interests An important point concerning Rule 101 is that it applies only to **covered members**. A covered member is, among other things, defined as:

- An individual on the attest engagement team
- An individual in a position to influence the attest engagement
- A partner in the office in which the lead attest engagement partner primarily practices in connection with the attest engagement

A covered member's *immediate family* is also subject to Rule 101 and its interpretations, with some exceptions. If you are a new staff person, manager, or partner working on an audit, you and your immediate family should not have any direct or material indirect financial interest in that client. A **direct financial interest** is a financial interest owned directly by, or under the control of, an individual or entity or beneficially owned through an investment vehicle, estate, or trust when the beneficiary controls the intermediary or has the authority to supervise or participate in the intermediary's investment decisions. An **indirect financial interest** occurs when the beneficiary neither controls the intermediary nor has the authority to supervise or participate in the intermediary's investment decisions.

For example, an auditor has an investment in a mutual fund that has an investment in an audit client. The auditor does not make the decisions to buy or sell the security held by the mutual fund. The ownership of mutual fund shares is a direct financial interest. The underlying investments of a mutual fund are considered to be indirect financial interests. If the mutual fund is diversified, a covered member's ownership of 5% or less of the outstanding shares of the mutual fund would not be considered to constitute a material indirect financial interest in the underlying investments. For purposes of determining materiality, the financial interests of the covered member and immediate family should be aggregated. No partner or professional employee of the CPA firm, whether a covered member or not, may be employed by an attest client or own more than 5% of an attest client's outstanding equity securities or other ownership interests.

Family Relationships A covered member's independence would be considered impaired if an immediate family member was employed by an audit client in a *key position* in which he or she can exercise influence over the contents of the financial statements, such as the CEO, CFO, chief accountant, member of the board of directors, chief internal audit executive, or treasurer. Independence is impaired if a covered member has a *close relative* who has a key position with the client or has a material financial interest in the client of which the CPA has knowledge.

Loans There are limits on the types and amounts of loans covered members may obtain from a financial institution that is also an audit client. Essentially, auditors cannot obtain large loans, or loans for investment purposes, from a client. However, auditors are permitted to obtain normal loans—if they are at standard terms, such as automobile loans or leases.

Performing Nonaudit Services The AICPA's code does not prohibit auditors from *performing other services such as bookkeeping* for their private clients, but auditors must take care to assure that working too closely with the client does not compromise the appearance of independence. If, for example, the auditor does bookkeeping, prepares tax returns, and performs several management

PRACTICAL POINT

Many vendors, such as software services on information system networks, pay commissions to all consultants who recommend their product. Some CPA firms accept these commissions for nonattest clients. However, they should (a) accept the commission only if they have formed an objective opinion that these are the best products for the client and (b) disclose the fact they are accepting the commission to the client.

PRACTICAL POINT

The AICPA has been criticized for "bright lines" tests for audit independence. The alternative approach would be that an auditor could never have any investment—direct or indirect—with an existing or potential client.

consulting services, the appearance, if not the fact, of independence has disappeared. A fundamental premise in these standards is that management must not cede decision-making authority to the CPA. For example, it is acceptable for the auditor of a *nonpublic company* to design, install, or integrate a client's information system, provided the client makes all management decisions. It is not acceptable to supervise client personnel in the daily operation of a client's information system.

Integrity and Objectivity—Rule 102

Rule 102 requires the AICPA member to act with integrity and **objectivity** in all services that may be provided to a client. Note that this applies also to CPAs who are not in public practice. For example, if the CFO of a company knowingly makes or permits others to make materially false and misleading entries in the financial statements or records, fails to correct an entity's financial statements or records, or signs—or directs another to sign—a document containing materially false and misleading information, that person has violated the AICPA Code of Ethics. A CPA is a special certificate that holds its owner to a high standard of ethical conduct, no matter where the individual is in his or her career.

A *conflict of interest* may occur, for example, if a member serves a client both as the auditor and legal counsel. Auditors must be objective. Legal counsel is an advocate for the client. One person cannot be both by turning objectivity on and off as needed.

Confidentiality—Rule 301

During the course of an audit, the auditor develops a complete understanding of the client and obtains **confidential information**, such as its operating strengths, weaknesses, and plans for financing or expanding into new markets. To assure a free flow and sharing of information between the client and the auditor, the client must be assured that the auditor will not communicate confidential information to outside parties. The only exceptions to this general rule are that auditors are not precluded from communicating information for any of the following purposes:

- To assure the adequacy of accounting disclosures required by GAAP
- To comply with a validly issued and enforceable subpoena or summons or to comply with applicable laws and government regulations
- To provide relevant information for an outside quality review of the firm's practice under PCAOB, AICPA, or state board of accountancy authorization
- To initiate a complaint with, or respond to an inquiry made by, the AICPA's professional ethics division or trial board or investigative or disciplinary body of a state CPA society or board of accountancy

Privileged communication means that confidential information obtained about a client cannot be subpoenaed by a court of law to be used against that

AUDITING *in Practice*

CYNTHIA COOPER AND THE WORLDCOM FRAUD

As the internal auditor of WorldCom, Cynthia Cooper was both a CPA and a CIA (certified internal auditor). As such, her professional ethics told her that she could not approve of journal entries that did not have sufficient support and that were designed to mislead the public.

client. Most states allow privileged communication for lawyers, but not for auditors.

A potentially troublesome area for accountants is confidential information obtained in one engagement that may be applicable to another. This is similar to the case used in developing the ethical framework earlier in the chapter. In the case of *Fund of Funds, Ltd. v. Arthur Andersen & Co.* (AA&Co.), a federal court jury ruled against the auditors because the jury expected the auditor to use information from one audit client to protect the interests of another audit client. The *Wall Street Journal* reported:

> According to court papers in the suit, John M. King, a Denver oil and gas fund promoter, convinced Fund of Funds to purchase natural resource assets from two concerns he controlled. Fund of Funds eventually paid about $120 million for over 400 natural resource assets.
>
> Fund of Funds alleged that many of the assets were sold at "unrealistically high and fraudulent prices" and that AA&Co. had "knowledge of or recklessly disregarded" the fraudulent activities because AA&Co. was also the auditor for the King concern.[2]

AA&Co. audited both Fund of Funds and King Resources, the entity that sold the assets to Fund of Funds. According to the court proceedings, the plaintiffs alleged that the same key audit personnel were involved in both audits and knew, or should have known, that the assets in question were sold at a price that generated profits much higher than comparable sales to other customers of King Resources. AA&Co. admitted knowledge of these overcharges but stated that it had a responsibility under the Code of Professional Conduct to keep the information confidential. The jury was convinced that information obtained while auditing King Resources should have been used during the audit of Fund of Funds.[3]

However, courts do not always give clear signals. In another case, *Consolidata Services v. Alexander Grant,* the court found the CPA firm guilty of providing confidential information to other clients. Alexander Grant (now Grant Thornton) did tax work for Consolidata Services, a company that provided computerized payroll services to other companies. On learning that Consolidata was in financial trouble, Grant warned some of its other clients, who were also Consolidata customers. Consolidata sued Grant charging that the accounting firm's disclosures effectively put it out of business. The jury ruled in favor of Consolidata. Grant was also found guilty of providing the information only to selected parties; that is, it provided the information only to its clients—not all customers of Consolidata.

These types of situations create true ethical dilemmas for auditors. Should they use knowledge obtained during the performance of work for one client when reporting on the statements of another client, as the Fund of Funds decision seems to indicate, or should they follow a narrower interpretation of the rules to keep the information confidential? Unfortunately, the rules do not directly answer this question. Two principles, however, seem to evolve from the cases. First, the audit firm was common for the two audit engagements with Fund of Funds and therefore the auditor could obtain and apply the information. Second, in the Consolidata case, the jury believed that the auditor had selectively used confidential information, thus violating the public trust. Moreover, although the courts generally uphold the confidentiality standard, they have not been reluctant to appeal to a higher standard of public trust when they perceive a conflict between confidentiality and the public trust. We expect

---

[2] *The Wall Street Journal,* November 6, 1981, p. 24.

[3] *Fund of Funds, Ltd. v. Arthur Andersen & Co.,* 545 F Supp. 1314 (S.D.N.Y. 1982).

that this area will continue to evolve. Auditors facing a potential conflict regarding confidentiality are advised to consult legal counsel.

Contingent Fees—Rule 302

A **contingent fee** is defined as a fee established for the performance of any service in which a fee will not be collected unless a specified finding or result is attained, or in which the amount of the fee depends on the finding or results of such services. An example of a contingent fee is a consulting firm agreeing to perform an information systems project for a fee of 50% of the defined cost savings attributable to the system for a period of three years. Contingent fees are attractive to clients because they do not pay unless the consultant delivers real value. Consulting firms often use contingent fees to compete with each other.

Contingent fees are prohibited from any client for whom the auditor performs attestation services. However, an auditor's fees may vary, depending on the complexity of services rendered or the time taken to perform the services. Contingent fees have not been prohibited for services provided to nonaudit clients. However, the auditor must still assure that the use of such fees does not impair the auditor's objectivity or need to uphold the public trust. For example, some auditors crossed the line in developing aggressive tax shelters for clients and were subject to civil suits by the government (and in some cases, criminal penalties).

Enforcement of the Code

Compliance with the Code depends primarily on the voluntary cooperation of AICPA members and secondarily on public opinion, reinforcement by peers, and, ultimately, on disciplinary proceedings by the Joint Ethics Enforcement Program, sponsored by the AICPA and state CPA societies. Disciplinary proceedings are initiated by complaints received by the AICPA's Professional Ethics Division.

Audit and other attestation reports on financial statements can be signed only by those who are licensed as CPAs by their state board of accountancy. Anyone can provide consulting, bookkeeping, and tax services. To become a licensed CPA, a person must pass the CPA exam, meet specific education and experience requirements, and agree to uphold the profession and its code of professional conduct. The member's CPA certificate may be suspended or revoked by the state board of accountancy. Without that certificate or license, a person is legally prohibited from issuing an audit opinion or a review report on financial statements. The state board may also require additional continuing education to retain or reinstate the CPA certificate.

Independence Rules of the SEC and the PCAOB

LO 7

Explain the principles used by the SEC in judging independence and discuss specific independence rules of the SEC and the PCAOB.

Now that you are familiar with the ethics principles and codes of the International Federation of Accountants and the AICPA, we move on to discussing the ethics rules that are specifically designed for auditors of public companies and are articulated via the rules of the SEC and the PCAOB.

In addition to the AICPA Rule 101 discussed previously, the SEC and PCAOB have established independence guidance and rules that apply to auditors of publicly held companies. The SEC's commitment to independence is summarized in the following two paragraphs:

> The independence requirement serves two related, but distinct, public policy goals. One goal is to foster high quality audits by minimizing the possibility that any external factors will influence an auditor's judgments. The auditor must approach each audit with professional skepticism and must have the capacity and the willingness to decide issues in an unbiased and objective manner, even when the auditor's decisions may be against the interests of management of the audit client or against the interests of the auditor's own accounting firm.

The other related goal is to promote investor confidence in the financial statements of public companies. Investor confidence in the integrity of publicly available financial information is the cornerstone of our securities market.... Investors are more likely to invest, and pricing is more likely to be efficient, where there is greater assurance that the financial information disclosed by issuers is reliable ... [that] assurance will flow from knowledge that the financial information has been subjected to rigorous examination by competent and objective auditors.[4]

The SEC has taken a principles-based approach in dealing with independence issues. All of the SEC statements on independence follow from four basic principles that define when an auditor is in a position that impairs independence. Those principles dictate that auditor independence is impaired when the auditor has a relationship that:

- Creates a mutual or conflicting interest between the accountant and the audit client
- Places the accountant in the position of auditing his or her own work
- Results in the accountant acting as management or an employee of the audit client
- Places the accountant in a position of being an advocate for the audit client[5]

In addition to these overarching independence principles, the SEC's independence rules, similar to the AICPA rules, prohibit specific relationships, including certain financial relationships, employment relationships, business relationships, and contingent fee contracts. The SEC's independence rules are applicable to public company auditors and their close family members, public company auditing firms and their associated entities, and publicly held companies and their affiliates. Rule 2-01 is designed to ensure that auditors are independent of their public audit clients, both *in fact* and *in appearance*. The Sarbanes-Oxley Act of 2002 required the SEC to strengthen auditor independence regulations, which resulted in the SEC establishing rules to prohibit auditors from providing various nonaudit services to their public audit clients. These prohibited nonaudit services include:

- Bookkeeping or other services related to the accounting records or financial statements of the audit client
- Financial information systems design and implementation
- Appraisal and valuation services, fairness opinions, or contribution-in-kind reports
- Actuarial services
- Internal audit outsourcing services
- Management functions
- Human resources
- Broker-dealer, investment adviser, or investment banking services
- Legal services
- Expert services unrelated to the audit

Section 103 of the Sarbanes-Oxley Act provides the PCAOB with rule-making authority in the area of auditor independence. Public company auditors must therefore comply with the independence rules of both the SEC and the PCAOB. The PCAOB adopted rules in 2005 and 2008 related to tax services. These rules prohibit registered public accounting firms from performing the following tax-related services for audit clients:

- Providing tax services to certain members of management serving in financial reporting oversight roles or to their immediate family members, and

PRACTICAL POINT

The independence rules of the SEC and the PCAOB apply only to public company auditors. However, many CPA firms that do not have public clients provide some nonaudit services—for example, bookkeeping, information systems design, appraisals, and in some cases internal audit work—to their audit clients. The client, as well as important third-party stakeholders, should make an assessment of the potential impairment of the auditor's independence when this additional work is performed on clients where attestation work is also provided.

---

[4]U.S. Securities and Exchange Commission, Final Rule: Revision of the Commission's Auditor Independence Requirements, February 5, 2001.

[5]Op. cit.

AUDITING *in Practice*

NONAUDIT SERVICES

An SEC disclosure made by DreamWorks Animation SKG, Inc. indicated that international affiliates of DreamWorks' auditor, E&Y, had performed nonaudit services for DreamWorks Studios that were not in accordance with the auditor independence rules. The nonaudit services included providing payroll-related services and making tax-related disbursements on behalf of DreamWorks. E&Y's fees for providing payroll services at one international location were $495 per month, while the total fees received for providing similar services at other international locations totaled $2,600.

DreamWorks' disclosure indicated that both its audit committee and the auditors had concluded that the auditors' independence was not impaired by the provision of these services, and in arriving at their conclusions, they had considered, among other things, the *de minimis* amount of fees involved and the ministerial nature of the services that were provided.

Source: SEC filing available at http://sec.freeedgar.com/displayHTML.asp?ID=3241135.

- Providing services related to marketing, planning, or opining in favor of the tax treatment of certain confidential transactions or based on an aggressive interpretation of applicable tax laws and regulations

The PCAOB has also adopted an independence rule related to contingent fees that is generally consistent with the SEC's contingent fee rule.

Further Considerations Regarding Auditor Independence

LO 8

Discuss the importance of independence to the public accounting profession.

Although we discussed various principles and rules regarding auditor independence in the previous section, we return in detail to this topic because independence is the cornerstone of the auditing profession. Without it, the profession would not have the necessary credibility to add value to corporate governance. Auditors must be independent *in fact* and *in appearance*. To be independent *in fact,* auditors must be objective and unbiased in their actions and evaluations and not be influenced by management. Auditors must be professionally skeptical as they gather evidence. They should not accept management's explanations without corroborating evidence.

To meet the objective of independence *in appearance,* the auditors must be perceived by knowledgeable users of financial statements as independent. An auditor could be independent in fact, but not appear to be independent. For example, an auditor may have an immaterial investment in an audit client and remain independent in fact. However, a financial statement user who knows of that investment may perceive that the auditor's judgment is impaired by a desire to increase the market value of that stock.

The major standard setters agree on the importance of independence. A comparison of the standards is shown in the *Comparison of Worldwide Professional Auditing Guidance* feature.

Major Threats to Independence

LO 9

Discuss the major threats to independence and approaches to mitigate those threats.

Independence is a state of mind that can be impaired by several potential threats. It starts with basic objectivity. The auditor and the audit firm must manage these threats to objectivity. We describe those threats and then approaches to mitigate those threats.

Compensation Schemes

Partners' compensation in many CPA firms has historically been based in large part on attracting and retaining profitable clients. This incentive creates a temptation

Comparison of Worldwide Professional Auditing Guidance

U. S. and International Guidance on Independence

AICPA Auditing Standards Board (ASB)	Statement on Auditing Standards (SAS) 1, section 220 addresses the topic of auditor independence. The auditor should be independent of the client in order to: • maintain the strong reputation of accountants in general • fairly and accurately report an audit so that stakeholders can make sound decisions • maintain the confidence of the public at large SAS 1 broaches the subject "independence in fact" and "independence in appearance" (although SAS 1 does not use those terms specifically). An auditor must both "be" independent and also "appear" independent.
Public Company Accounting Oversight Board (PCAOB)	Rule 3520 of the PCAOB Rules addresses independence of auditors. It states: "A registered public accounting firm and its associated persons must be independent of the firm's audit client throughout the audit and professional engagement period." Notes also refer to the independence principles as promulgated by the Securities and Exchange Commission.
International Auditing and Assurance Standards Board (IAASB)	The IAASB defines "independence" as "comprising both independence of mind and independence in appearance." The "auditor's ability to act with integrity, to be objective and to maintain an attitude of professional skepticism" is stressed in ISA 200.
SUMMARY	All three standards boards emphasize the necessity of auditors being independent from their clients. The IAASB builds an objective of professional skepticism into the concept of independence.

to accede to client wishes in order to keep the client happy. The wish to retain profitable clients can impair independence. The profession has responded in two ways: (a) providing the audit committee with more powers and responsibilities related to the audit, including hiring and firing the audit firm; and (b) structuring partner compensation schemes to focus more on quality of services rendered and training of staff personnel. Keeping a bad client is not good business; and a client who wants the auditor to potentially sacrifice independence is not a good client.

Who Is the Client?   The auditor of a public company should view the shareholders as the ultimate client. The shareholders are represented by the audit committee, who has the authority to hire and fire the auditor. Although the audit client is the shareholders, the auditor is getting paid by the company and interacts with management on a daily basis, so there is a potential threat to auditor independence based on monetary incentives and personal familiarity. Although the fee is paid by the company, all the important decisions related to the audit are supposed to be made by the audit committee and should represent the best interests of the shareholders.

For nonpublic companies, the client is whoever has the authority to hire and fire the auditor. That may be the owners, management, the board of directors, or, if it has one, the audit committee. The key point is that no matter who the client is, the auditor must make an objective, unbiased judgment about the fairness of the financial statements and should not favor the interests of one party over another. Every audit firm needs policies that influence its audit partners, managers, and staff to take actions every day that show that maintaining the public trust is more important than retaining a client.

Familiarity with the Client

Auditors serving a client for several years may develop relationships and friendships that cause them to become less skeptical than they would have been otherwise. The Sarbanes-Oxley Act requires that various engagement partners on public company audits, including the partner-in-charge of the audit and the

> **PRACTICAL POINT**
>
> Most of the international public accounting firms have changed partner compensation schemes to emphasize factors other than revenue generated, such as mentoring staff auditors, expanding the firm's expertise, surveys of client satisfaction, and so forth. However, the major factor remains "how much revenue is generated given the risk taken on by the firm"?

> **PRACTICAL POINT**
>
> While many nonpublic companies do not have audit committees, the auditor should always view the real client as a third-party user. It is only with such an attitude that the auditor can maintain complete independence and serve the public interest.

concurring partner (sometimes referred to an engagement quality review partner), rotate off the audit at least every five years. The *Auditing in Practice: Partner Rotation Rules* feature notes the difficulty that smaller audit firms may have in complying with the partner rotation rules. No such requirements exist for auditor rotation on nonpublic companies.

Some argue that public companies should periodically change CPA firms to help assure an objective and fresh approach to the audit. The GAO has issued a study on the costs of mandatory audit firm rotation and concluded that they were high and that other safeguards could be built into the process to protect the public without mandatory rotation of the audit firm.

Time Pressures

CPA firms often compete for clients through bids. The low bidder is often likely to get the job. However, in order to make a sufficient return on the audit, there will be time pressures to get the audit done as quickly as possible. Those in charge of audits are evaluated not only on the quality of their work but also on the efficiency with which the audit is conducted. This may create an environment in which the auditors do not look as deeply into potential problem areas as they should.

Additionally, auditors facing time pressure may choose to "eat" time and not record all of the time that they spent working on the audit engagement. Eating time allows for the auditor to make it appear as if the tasks were completed within the budgeted time period. However, such an approach makes it difficult for the audit team to properly prepare a time budget for future years, thereby continuing the possible negative consequences of time pressure. Behavior such as eating time is typically formally prohibited by audit firms, but anecdotal reports by practicing auditors indicate that the practice still sometimes occurs.

Rationalizing Behavior

When potential misstatements are detected, it takes time to investigate and determine if they could be material. To save time, the auditor may rationalize that the misstatement is not likely to be material, when in fact it could be. Research has shown that auditors often rationalize potential misstatements away by assuming that a misstatement that occurred in a small sample of transactions was a "unique" occurrence and therefore does not require further investigation. Auditors need to be aware of the human tendency to rationalize away

AUDITING *in Practice*

PARTNER ROTATION RULES

An example of the difficulty of adhering to the partner rotation rules, especially for smaller firms, can be found in an SEC filing by Signature Leisure, Inc. The filing notes that the audit firm of Cordovano and Honeck, LLP cited difficulties in adhering to the partner rotation rules as the reason for severing its relationship with its audit client. For small audit firms, there may simply not be enough partners to rotate on and off public client engagements. However,

since independence is fundamental and the public, through its legislators, views rotation as important, audit firms that cannot properly rotate partners should not perform public audits.

Source: 8K filed by Signature Leisure, Inc., which is available at http://www.sec.gov/Archives/edgar/data/1135194/000110313207000030/sl8kaud.htm

unpleasant or unwanted issues and be on guard against having that tendency affect their professional judgment.

Providing Nonaudit Services

CPAs may help organizations improve their information systems, suggest and help the client implement "best practices," do the client's bookkeeping, identify potential candidates for management positions, and perform other nonaudit tasks. However, when CPAs provide these types of nonaudit services to audit clients, they may find themselves in the position of auditing their own work or some of their own decisions. Independence is likely to be compromised if auditors are put into the position of auditing their own work or if auditors identify too closely with the company.

Providing nonaudit services to audit clients can also result in the CPA having an increased economic dependence on the client. As noted in the *Auditing in Practice: Audit and Nonaudit Fees* box, the fees received from nonaudit services can be much larger than the fees received from the audit services. In those situations, independence in the audit may be compromised, as the auditors may choose to "go easy" on the client in the audit so that the firm can retain the client and fees from both audit and nonaudit services. This example also shows that concerns of this type resulted in the SEC establishing rules that prohibit a public company auditor from providing many of these nonaudit services to its audit clients.

Managing Threats to Independence

Recognizing that there are threats to auditor independence is the first step in managing independence. Fortunately, audit firms have developed effective approaches to managing the threats to independence, including the following:

- Establishing and monitoring corporate codes of conduct
- Developing appropriate compensation schemes
- Implementing high-level reviews of decisions to accept or retain clients
- Separating consulting activities from audit activities
- Performing within-firm reviews of audit work and audit documentation
- Performing reviews and inspections within the profession

AUDITING *in Practice*

AUDIT AND NONAUDIT FEES

On April 11, 2000, the *European Wall Street Journal* reported that in a study of 307 U.S.-listed companies, on average, the fees for those other services were nearly three times as large as the audit fees.

Some of the audit-to-nonaudit fee relationships were:

- Sprint Corp. paid Ernst & Young, LLP $2.5 million for audit services and $63.8 million for other services.
- General Electric Co. paid KPMG $23.9 million for auditing work and $79.7 million for other services.
- J. P. Morgan Chase & Co. paid PricewaterhouseCoopers $21.3 million in audit fees and $84.2 million for additional work.

- Motorola Inc. paid KPMG $3.9 million for audit services and $62.3 million for other services.
- Delphi Automotive Systems Corp. paid Deloitte & Touche $6.6 million in audit fees and an additional $50.8 million for other services.

The SEC was concerned that the fees from nonaudit services were much higher than had been expected. In response to these concerns, and as a result of the Sarbanes-Oxley Act, the SEC modified its independence rules to prohibit a public company auditor from providing many types of nonaudit services to its audit clients.

CPA Firm Codes of Conduct

Establishing a strong code of conduct is a first step. However, the code must be accompanied by an understanding that the audit firm "lives" the code and that any deviation from the code will not be tolerated. The tone is established at the top and is reflected in compensation schemes that reiterate the importance of the code. It is reinforced through training and constant evaluation.

Appropriate Compensation Schemes

Most firms have modified their compensation schemes to recognize that walking away from a "bad" client is in the firm's best interest, that taking hard stances on the acceptability of accounting is good business, and that the quality of audit documentation is key to demonstrating high-quality audit decisions.

Reviews of Client Acceptance or Retention Decisions

Many audit firms have a high-level committee that evaluates decisions on accepting and retaining audit clients. Most of these decisions are based on risk models; that is, does the nature of the operations or the quality of management present a risk to the audit firm? The review of these decisions recognizes that simply increasing fees is not the sole objective of the firm. The firm must minimize the risk caused by being associated with an unscrupulous client.

Separation of Consulting Activities

Public accounting firms have taken two kinds of approaches to consulting in the past. They are:

1. Audit functions are separated from consulting functions, or
2. Consulting-type functions are performed only for nonaudit clients.

> **PRACTICAL POINT**
>
> CPA firms that perform audits of public companies still provide substantial consulting services that are not marketed to audit clients. Firms continue to provide full-service audit and consulting services to nonpublic audit clients, subject to restrictions in the AICPA's Code of Conduct.

Most public accounting firms continue to perform audits. Audit firms with a nonpublic client focus have generally opted to retain consulting services that they provide for both audit clients and nonaudit clients. Often, but not always, the consulting function is performed by groups that are distinct from the audit function. For example, information system consultants are generally not part of the audit staff.

Most of the Big 4 firms have developed various consulting services that are provided only to nonaudit clients. The fees from these services continue to grow and will likely approach the size of audit fees again in the future. These services include business risk consulting, computer security evaluations, internal audit outsourcing, tax planning, and related services.

Within-Firm Reviews of Audit Work

> **PRACTICAL POINT**
>
> Small accounting firms may experience difficulty finding an adequate number of engagement quality reviewers. To accommodate this practical difficulty, both the U.S. and international standards allow firms to hire engagement quality reviewers from an outside accounting firm.

Knowing that your work will be reviewed during, prior to completion, and after completion of the engagement reinforces the need for high-quality decision-making. CPA firms have audit partners and managers who review the work of staff auditors. Further, all public company audits, and many other engagements, are reviewed by an independent audit partner to provide a second, objective review of the engagement prior to the issuance of an audit opinion (such an individual is referred to as a *concurring partner* or *engagement quality review partner*). In addition, most large firms have internal quality review programs whereby independent groups of partners and managers perform a review of the audit work and documentation of selected audits that have been completed to determine that (a) the work meets professional standards and (b) the work was carried out objectively.

Comparison of Worldwide Professional Auditing Guidance

Comparison of the standards for engagement quality/concurring partner review is shown in the *Comparison of Worldwide Professional Auditing Guidance*. In short, such reviews are not required for non-public entities (i.e., privately held entities) in the United States, but they are required for publicly traded entities in the United States and in audit engagements internationally.

U.S. and International Standards on Engagement Quality Review/Concurring Partner Review

AICPA Auditing Standards Board (ASB)	The AICPA has no formal requirement for engagement quality/concurring partner review on individual audit engagements. However, the AICPA does require that firms establish specific criteria by which they will decide on a systematic basis the clients that should have such a review. The AICPA still requires the firms to undergo a quality review process at the overall audit firm level on a periodic basis and (a) the absence of specific criteria for engagement quality reviews, or (b) absence of adherence to those criteria would be considered a deficiency when overall audit firm reviews are performed. Recall that the AICPA standards concern non-publicly traded entities, and many of the firm's clients may be very small and only have one or two people assigned to the total audit. Thus, in the view of the AICPA (and many smaller firms), it would not make economic sense to have an engagement quality review for clients that are both uncomplicated and small. Some of the criteria that the firms use to decide that an engagement quality review is needed include: riskiness of client, size of client, and the extent of outside distribution of audit report (and thus, potentially the legal liability for the auditor).
PCAOB	Section 103 of the Sarbanes-Oxley Act of 2002 requires the PCAOB to ensure that public company audit firms provide an engagement quality review (sometimes known as a concurring partner review or a second partner review) for each audit. The PCAOB's Auditing Standard No. 7, "Engagement Quality Review" requires the engagement quality reviewer to evaluate all significant judgments made by the engagement team and to consider their evaluation of the client's risks. The standard specifically states that the engagement quality reviewer must have competence, independence, integrity, and objectivity, and the standard requires that all phases of the review be carefully documented.
IAASB	The IAASB standard on engagement quality review ("International Standard on Quality Control 1") is similar to AS No. 7, requiring that the engagement quality reviewer evaluate significant risks and the engagement team's responses to those risks, judgments made (particularly relating to addressing risks and materiality), the disposition of misstatements identified during the engagement (whether corrected or not), and matters communicated to management and others charged with governance over the organization.
SUMMARY	The standards setters diverge concerning engagement quality review, with the AICPA not requiring this audit procedure for the non-public entities over which it provides assurance guidance.

Reviews and Inspections Within the Profession

Section 104 of the Sarbanes-Oxley Act requires the PCAOB to conduct regular reviews (inspections) of accounting firms that are registered with it. Large accounting firms (i.e., firms with more than 100 issuers as clients) are inspected every year, and small accounting firms (i.e., firms with 100 or fewer issuers as clients) are inspected once every three years.

Firms currently required to be registered with and inspected by the PCAOB must also be enrolled in the AICPA's Peer Review Program (PRP), which requires the firm to have a peer review performed every three years. This peer review is designed to review and evaluate those portions of a firm's accounting and auditing practice that are not inspected by the PCAOB; therefore, the focus of the peer reviews is on the non-SEC issuer practice of the audit firm.

PRACTICAL POINT

External reviews help to serve the public interest by promoting quality in accounting and auditing services. A summary of the PCAOB's review of every firm can be found on their website at www.pcaobus.org.

Important Role of Audit Committees

The Sarbanes-Oxley Act mandates that the audit committee be responsible for the oversight of the engagement of the company's external auditor, including the hiring and firing of the auditor, and oversight of the external auditor's independence. Further, the independence rules of the PCAOB and the SEC require that the audit committee preapprove permitted services provided by the auditor.

LO 10

Discuss the audit committee's responsibilities related to the independence of the external auditor.

LO 11

Explain the role of professional skepticism in auditors' judgments, including the relationship between auditor independence and professional skepticism.

In addition, the PCAOB requires public accounting firms to communicate information related to the firm's independence to the client's audit committee. This information includes relationships the accounting firm has with the client that may reasonably be thought to bear on its independence.

These rules highlight the important role that the audit committee plays in helping assure auditor independence. Audit committees should consider all factors that might affect the independence of the auditor and should not approve nonaudit services that they believe might impair independence.

The Role of Professional Skepticism in Auditors' Judgments

International Standard on Auditing 200 states that "independence enhances the auditor's ability to act with integrity, to be objective and to maintain an attitude of professional skepticism" (paragraph A16). U.S. auditing standards define skepticism as involving "an attitude that includes a questioning mind and a critical assessment of audit evidence" (AU Section 230.07). According to international standards, professional skepticism includes being alert to, for example:

- Audit evidence that contradicts other audit evidence obtained.
- Information that brings into question the reliability of documents and responses to inquiries to be used as audit evidence.
- Conditions that may indicate possible fraud.
- Circumstances that suggest the need for audit procedures in addition to those required by the ISAs. (ISA 200, paragraph A18).

Professional skepticism is important because without it auditors are susceptible to accepting weak or inaccurate audit evidence. By exercising adequate professional skepticism, auditors are less likely to overlook unusual circumstances, to over-generalize from limited audit evidence, or to use inappropriate assumptions in determining the nature, timing, and extent of audit procedures. An auditor who is professionally skeptical will do the following:

- Critically question contradictory audit evidence
- Carefully evaluate the reliability of audit evidence, especially in situations in which fraud risk is high and/or only a single piece of evidence exists to support a material financial accounting transaction or amount
- Reasonably question the authenticity of documentation, while accepting that documents are to be considered genuine unless there is reason to believe the contrary, and will
- Reasonably question the honesty and integrity of management, individuals charged with governance, and third-party providers of audit evidence.

Given that auditors operate in an environment of significant litigation risk and one in which there is ample evidence of past frauds involving deception against auditors, it may seem that auditors will intuitively act with professional skepticism. However, the difficulty that auditors face is one inherent in the human condition—we are taught to trust others and to accept information and assertions as the truth. Further, if an auditor did not trust management, for example, that auditor would presumably cease to perform audit services for the client. These difficulties sometimes cause auditors to be less professionally skeptical than is optimal. The PCAOB's Report on its 2004–2007 inspections of domestic annually inspected audit firms reveals that the Board finds a lack of professional skepticism to be an important weakness in the current practice of auditing. For example, the Report notes "certain of the deficiencies also raised concerns about the sufficiency of firms' application of professional skepticism.... In some instances, firms did not sufficiently test or challenge management's forecasts, views, or representations that constituted critical support for the amounts recorded in the financial statements. In many of these instances, they limited their audit procedures to obtaining management's oral representations."

This view regarding professional skepticism is not limited to U.S. regulators. In a July 2010 periodical release, the UK Financial Services Authority (their chief regulator) stated, "In some cases that the FSA has seen, the auditor's approach seems to focus too much on gathering and accepting evidence to support management's assertions" (*Accountancy Age*, June 29, 2010). This is a human bias: if we think someone has integrity, then there is a tendency to overweight information that favors that person's view and underweight other evidence. Therefore, developing a "balanced" approach to gathering and evaluating evidence regarding management assertions is the fundamental value associated with an audit.

So how can audit firms and individual auditors be sure that they maintain and exercise their professional skepticism? At the audit firm level, leaders must ensure that auditors receive training on how to be skeptical, and firm policies and procedures should encourage skepticism as well. At the individual auditor level, the following tips can encourage a skeptical mindset:

- Be sure to collect sufficient evidence so that judgments are not made in haste or without adequate support.
- When evidence is contradictory, be particularly diligent in evaluating the reliability of the individuals or processes that provided that evidence.
- Generate independent ideas about reasons for unexpected trends or financial ratios rather than simply relying on management's explanations.
- Question trends or outcomes that appear "too good to be true."
- Wait to make professional judgments until all the relevant facts are known.
- Have confidence in your own knowledge and do not assume that the explanation for unexpected trends or financial ratios simply reflects your lack of understanding.

We encourage you to keep these ideas in mind as you proceed throughout this textbook. Because of the importance of professional skepticism to making high-quality auditing judgments, we will return to this concept throughout the textbook, including examples and problems to help you learn about and apply this concept.

Summary

Certified public accountants can serve the public only if they safeguard their reputation for high-quality decision-making, ethics, and independence. For most of the past century, the AICPA had the primary responsibility to provide guidance to the profession on pervasive ethics and independence concepts. All CPAs are expected to follow the basic principles of the AICPA's Code of Professional Conduct. However, as with accounting, the profession became more rule-focused. In turn, the AICPA issued over 100 interpretations and rulings dealing with independence.

As the accounting profession followed a hyper-growth pattern of expanding the nature of services during the 1980s and 1990s, the SEC and others, including Congress, became critical that the profession was losing independence as one of its core values. The SEC has called for the profession to return to fundamental concepts, and prohibits firms from performing specific nonaudit activities for public company audit clients. Auditors of public companies in the U.S. must adhere to the independence rules of the SEC and the PCAOB.

The decision-making framework that we introduced in this chapter can be used by auditors to analyze many professional audit judgments. When those judgments involve ethically charged issues, an ethical framework, such as the one outlined in this chapter, can help resolve an ethical dilemma in a thoughtful manner. Such a framework is useful in situations for which specific ethics and independence rules have not been developed. Finally, auditors who are independent are better able to act ethically, to be objective, and to exercise an appropriate level of professional skepticism.

Significant Terms

Concurring partner   An audit partner who is not otherwise connected with the audit client or involved in the conduct of the audit engagement who provides an independent review of the engagement prior to the issuance of an audit opinion. Also referred to as engagement quality review partner.

Confidential information   Information obtained during the conduct of an audit related to the client's business or business plans; the auditor is prohibited from communicating confidential information except in very specific instances defined by the Code or with the client's specific authorization.

Contingent fee   A fee established for the performance of any service pursuant to an arrangement in which no fee will be charged unless a specified finding or result is attained or in which the amount of the fee otherwise depends on the finding or results of such services.

Covered member   An individual on the attestation engagement team, an individual in a position to influence the attestation engagement, or a partner in the office in which the lead attestation engagement partner primarily practices in connection with the attestation engagement.

Direct financial interest   A financial interest owned directly by, or under the control of, an individual or entity or beneficially owned through an investment vehicle, estate, or trust when the beneficiary controls the intermediary or has the authority to supervise or participate in the intermediary's investment decisions.

Ethical dilemma   A situation in which moral duties or obligations conflict; one action is not necessarily the correct action.

Ethical problem   A situation in which an individual is morally or ethically required to do something that conflicts with his or her immediate self-interest.

Independence   Being objective and unbiased while performing professional services. It requires being independent in fact and in appearance.

Indirect financial interest   A financial interest in which the beneficiary neither controls the intermediary nor has the authority to supervise or participate in the intermediary's investment decisions.

Integrity   Adherence to a moral or ethical code that results in the state of being unimpaired.

Objectivity   A mental attitude that auditors should maintain while performing engagements. The auditor should have an impartial, unbiased attitude and avoid conflict-of-interest situations that could hinder the auditor's ability to perform audit duties objectively.

Privileged communication   Information about a client that cannot be subpoenaed by a court of law to be used against a client; it allows no exceptions to confidentiality.

Professional judgment   The application of relevant professional knowledge and experience to the facts and circumstances in order to reach a conclusion or make a decision.

Professional skepticism   An attitude that includes a questioning mind and a critical assessment of audit evidence.

Rights theory   An approach (framework) for addressing ethical problems by identifying a hierarchy of rights that should be considered in solving ethical problems or dilemmas.

Rules of conduct   Detailed guidance to assist the CPA in applying the broad principles contained in the AICPA's Code of Professional Conduct; the rules have evolved over time as members of the profession have encountered specific ethical dilemmas in complying with the principles of the Code.

Stakeholders   Those parties who have a vested interest in, or are affected by, the decision resulting from an ethical problem or dilemma.

Utilitarian theory   An ethical theory (framework) that systematically considers all the potential stakeholders who may be affected by an ethical decision and seeks to measure the effects of the decision on each party; it seeks to assist individuals in making decisions resulting in the greatest amount of good for the greatest number of people.

	SELECTED REFERENCES TO RELEVANT PROFESSIONAL GUIDANCE	
Topic	**Selected Guidance**
Communications with Audit Committees Regarding Independence	ISA 200 *Objective and General Principles Governing an Audit of Financial Statements*
	SAS *Overall Objectives of the Independent Auditor and Conduct of an Audit in Accordance with Generally Accepted Auditing Standards* (issued but not effective, proposed effective date is December 2012)
	PCAOB Rule 3526 *Communication with Audit Committees Concerning Independence*
	PCAOB Rule 3525 *Audit Committee Pre-Approval of Nonaudit Services Related to Internal Control over Financial Reporting*
	PCAOB Rule 3524 *Audit Committee Pre-Approval of Certain Tax Services*
Code of Professional Conduct	International Federation of Accountants (IFAC) *Code of Ethics for Professional Accountants*
	AICPA *Code of Professional Conduct*
Independence	ISA 200 *Overall Objectives of the Independent Auditor and the Conduct of an Audit in Accordance with International Standards on Auditing*
	SAS *Overall Objectives of the Independent Auditor and Conduct of an Audit in Accordance with Generally Accepted Auditing Standards* (issued but not effective, proposed effective date is December 2012)
	SAS 1 *Codification of Auditing Standards and Procedures*
	PCAOB Rule 3520 *Auditor Independence*
	PCAOB Rule 3523 *Tax Services for Persons in Financial Reporting Oversight Roles*
	SEC Regulation S-X Rule 201 *Qualifications of Accountants*
Qualifications of Accountants	IFAC *Code of Ethics for Professional Accountants,* Section 130
	SAS 1 *Codification of Auditing Standards and Procedures,* Sections 110 and 210
Engagement Quality Review	AS No. 7 *Engagement Quality Review*
	IAASB International Standard on Quality Control 1 *Quality Control For Firms That Perform Audits and Reviews of Financial Statements, And Other Assurance and Related Services Engagements*

Note: *Acronyms for Relevant Professional Guidance*

 STANDARDS: **AS**—Auditing Standard issued by the PCAOB; **ISA**—International Standard on Auditing issued by the IAASB; **SAS**—Statement on Auditing Standards issued by the Auditing Standards Board of the AICPA; **SSAE**—Statement on Standards for Attestation Engagements issued by the AICPA.

 ORGANIZATIONS: **AICPA**—American Institute of Certified Public Accountants; **COSO**—Committee of Sponsoring Organizations; **IAASB**—International Auditing and Assurance Standards Board; **PCAOB**—Public Company Accounting Oversight Board; **SEC**—Securities and Exchange Commission.

Review Questions

3-1   **(LO 2)** How is ethical behavior related to organizational success?

                           Ethics

3-2   **(LO 2)** Why is ethical behavior by auditors required to justify the public's trust in the profession?

3-3   **(LO 8)** Why is independence considered the most important characteristic of an auditor?

3-4   **(LO 9)** What are the major threats to auditor independence? Explain why each item represents a threat to auditor independence.

3-5   **(LO 9)** What can a CPA firm do to manage the threats to auditor independence? Explain why each management approach should be effective and how it would be implemented.

3-6   **(LO 7)** What are the major principles that have guided the SEC's actions on auditor independence?

3-7   **(LO 7)** What are the services that a CPA or CPA firm *cannot* provide for a public company audit client?

3-8   **(LO 6)** Describe the principles that form the basis of the AICPA's Rules of Conduct.

3-9   **(LO 6, 7)** Are there nonaudit services that can be performed for nonpublic companies that cannot be performed for public companies? Explain and identify such services.

3-10   **(LO 6, 7)** Why might the profession allow some services to be performed for nonpublic company clients that cannot be performed for public company clients?

3-11   **(LO 6, 7)** How do the AICPA's and the SEC's independence rules differ on providing data processing and consulting services for an audit client?

3-12   **(LO 8)** What is meant by independence (a) in fact and (b) in appearance? Give an example of an auditor being independent in fact but not in appearance.

3-13   **(LO 6, 7)** Describe the difference between a direct financial interest and an indirect financial interest in an audit client.

Ethics

3-14   **(LO 2, 5)** The Sarbanes-Oxley Act contains various requirements that reflect responses to ethical lapses in professional judgment on the part of various financial market participants. Refer to Exhibit 3.2 for an overview of Section 201 of the Act, and identify what ethical lapses may have occurred to result in these new requirements. Discuss how these new requirements help to justify the public's trust in the auditor.

3-15   **(LO 6)** Would independence be impaired, according to the AICPA, if a CPA:

a. Obtained a home mortgage with a bank that later became an audit client while the mortgage was still in effect?

b. Had been the audit client's controller during the first six months of the period covered by the audited financial statements?

c. Obtained a home mortgage while the lending institution was an audit client?

3-16   **(LO 7, 10)** What role does the audit committee have in making judgments about auditor independence?

3-17   **(LO 6)** Under what circumstances is it appropriate for a CPA to disclose confidential information about a client?

3-18   **(LO 6)** Would a CPA violate the AICPA's Code if he or she served a client both as its auditor and legal counsel? Explain your answer.

3-19   **(LO 6)** In considering the AICPA's Code, under what circumstances is it appropriate for a CPA to:

a. Provide services on a contingent fee basis?

b. Accept a commission for referring a product or service to the client?

c. Pay a referral fee to another CPA?

3-20   **(LO 6)** Describe the various ways in which the AICPA's Code is enforced.

3-21   **(LO 3)** Briefly describe the concepts and approaches underlying the utilitarian theory and the rights theory.

3-22   **(LO 1)** Explain the decision process used to encourage high-quality decision-making. Discuss how the concepts of audit evidence, uncertainty, risk, and professional skepticism affect the approach to developing sufficient information to support high-quality decisions.

Professional Skepticism

3-23   **(LO 6, 7)** What are the major differences in the guidance on auditor independence as put forth by the IESBA, the AICPA, and the SEC? How might the AICPA justify differences that might appear to create a conflict of interest when viewed by the SEC?

3-24   **(LO 11)** Compare the meaning of the terms *professional judgment* and *professional skepticism*.

3-25   **(LO 11)** How does auditor independence facilitate professional skepticism?

Professional Skepticism

Multiple-Choice Questions

Ethics

*3-26   **(LO 2, 6)** Which of the following statements best explains why the CPA profession has found it essential to promulgate ethical standards and to establish means for ensuring their observance?

   a. Vigorous enforcement of an established code of ethics is the best way to prevent unscrupulous acts.

   b. Ethical standards that emphasize excellence in performance over material rewards establish a reputation for competence and character.

   c. A distinguishing mark of a profession is its acceptance of responsibility to the public.

   d. A requirement for a profession is to establish ethical standards that stress primarily a responsibility to clients and colleagues.

3-27   **(LO 9)** Which of the following is not a major threat to an auditor's independence?

   a. Audit partner's compensation based on obtaining and retaining clients.

   b. Becoming too friendly with the client's management.

   c. Significant time pressures to get the audit done quickly.

   d. Auditing records maintained by the public accounting firm.

   e. All of the above are threats.

3-28   **(LO 6)** According to the AICPA's ethical standards, an auditor would be considered independent in which of the following instances?

   a. The auditor has an automobile loan from a client bank.

   b. The auditor is also an attorney who advises the client as its general counsel.

Ethics

---

*All problems marked with an asterisk are adapted from the Uniform CPA Examination.

    c. An employee of the auditor donates service as treasurer to a charitable organization that is a client.

    d. The client owes the auditor fees for two consecutive annual audits.

*3-29 **(LO 6)** A violation of the profession's ethical standards would most likely have occurred when a CPA:

    a. Purchased a bookkeeping firm's practice of monthly write-ups for a percentage of fees received over a three-year period.

    b. Made arrangements with a bank to collect notes issued by a client in payment of fees due.

    c. Whose name is Smith formed a partnership with two other CPAs and uses Smith & Co. as the firm name.

    d. Issued an unqualified opinion on the 2012 financial statements when fees for the 2011 audit were unpaid.

*3-30 **(LO 6)** A CPA is permitted to disclose confidential client information without the consent of the client to:

    I. Another CPA who has purchased the CPA's tax practice.

    II. Another CPA firm if the information concerns suspected tax return irregularities.

    III. A state CPA society's voluntary quality-control review board.

        a. I and III

        b. II and III

        c. II

        d. III

*3-31 **(LO 6)** Manny Tallents is a CPA and a lawyer. In which of the following situations is Tallents violating the AICPA's Rules of Conduct?

    a. He uses his legal training to help determine the legality of an audit client's actions.

    b. He researches a tax question to help the client make a management decision.

    c. He defends his audit client in a patent infringement suit.

    d. He uses his legal training to help determine the accounting implications of a complicated contract of an audit client.

3-32 **(LO 3)** Applying utilitarianism as a concept in addressing ethical situations requires the auditor to perform all of the following except:

    a. Identify the potential stakeholders that will be affected by the alternative outcomes.

    b. Determine the effect of the potential alternative courses of action on the affected parties.

    c. Choose the alternative that provides either the greatest good for the greatest number or the lowest cost (from a societal view) for the greatest number.

    d. Examine the potential outcomes to see whether the results are inconsistent with the rights or justice theories.

3-33   **(LO 7)** Which of the following nonaudit services does the SEC prohibit audit firms from providing to its publicly traded clients?

   a. Bookkeeping or other services related to the accounting records or financial statements of the audit client.

   b. Financial information systems design and implementation.

   c. Appraisal and valuation services, fairness opinions, or contribution-in-kind reports.

   d. Actuarial services.

   e. All of the above.

3-34   **(LO 11)** Professional skepticism includes being alert to the following:

   a. Audit evidence that contradicts other audit evidence obtained.

   b. Information that brings into question the reliability of documents and responses to inquiries to be used as audit evidence.

   c. Conditions that may indicate possible fraud.

   d. Circumstances that suggest the need for audit procedures in addition to those required by professional standards.

   e. All of the above.

**Professional
Skepticism**

Discussion and Research Questions

3-35   **(Applying Audit Independence Principles and Rules, LO 7)** In small groups, consider the following situations. Based on your discussion, determine which of the following would not be considered a violation of the four underlying independence principles issued by the SEC. Assume the situation involves a public client.

Group Activity

   a. Virchow John (VJ), CPAs, has a separate division that performs personal financial planning (wealth management) for high-income individuals. It is a separate profit center and is evaluated on its results. It performs this service for a select number of senior management, at customary fees and at the client's request, for some audit clients.

   b. Virchow John, CPAs, is retained and can be fired only by the audit committee of the client, but its fees are paid by the client.

   c. Virchow John, CPAs, has a separate unit that performs temporary accounting services. One of the clients lost a divisional controller of a unit that represents 7% of its revenue. VJ used its temporary accounting services to provide the controllership activity for 45 days while the client searched for a new controller.

   d. Virchow John, CPAs, recommends that the company improve its controls and accepts a 90-day engagement to train the company on how it should go about implementing better controls.

3-36   **(Professional Codes of Conduct, LO 6)** Many professions have developed codes of conduct. The public accounting profession, through its various professional organizations around the world, has developed detailed guidance in its various codes of conduct.

   Required

   a. What is the major purpose of professional codes of conduct?

   b. What are the potential sanctions if a CPA is found to have violated the various professional codes of conduct?

Ethics

3-37   **(Threats to Independence, LO 9)**

Scene 1—You are the senior in charge of the audit of NOB Company. The CFO is pressuring you to complete the audit in two weeks. Some of the audit team members are new staff and have required a significant amount of training to bring them up to speed for the audit. As a result, your audit is behind schedule. However, you know that even with extended overtime, your audit team cannot complete all of the planned audit work in two weeks.

Required

a. What should you do in this situation?

b. What could have been done to prevent this situation?

Scene 2—Partners in the public accounting firm of Noble, Wishman, & Kant, LLP, earn compensation points for (1) obtaining new clients, (2) retaining clients, and (3) selling additional services to existing clients. Depending on the number of points, each partner's compensation can be increased by up to 150% of their base salary.

Required

a. Explain why this arrangement can be a threat to independence.

b. What could be done to eliminate this threat but yet encourage the audit firm to seek out sufficient profitability to attract and retain qualified auditors?

Internet

3-38   **(Audit Committee Responsibilities, LO 5, 10)** The Sarbanes-Oxley Act mandates that the audit committee of the board of directors of public companies be directly responsible for the appointment, compensation, and oversight of the external auditors. In addition, the audit committee must preapprove all nonaudit services that might be performed by the auditing firm.

Required

a. Discuss the rationale for this mandate as opposed to letting the shareholders, CFO, or CEO have these responsibilities.

b. What factors should the audit committee consider in evaluating the independence of the external auditor?

c. Locate the proxy statement for a publicly traded company of your choice. To do so, go to the SEC's website. Search for your company's filings using the Edgar data system on the website. Once you have located your company's filings, you may narrow your search by typing in the phrase "Def 14A," which is the proxy filing. Once you have found the proxy, read and summarize the disclosures provided concerning the audit committee members, their compensation, their responsibilities, and their activities.

3-39   **(SEC Independence Principles, LO 7)**

Required

a. What are the four guiding principles that have been developed by the SEC for auditor independence?

b. Are the principles applicable only to auditors of SEC companies, or do they apply to auditors of smaller, privately held companies as well?

c. The following are five situations in which auditors may find themselves. For each of the situations, indicate whether it appears to violate the SEC's independence principles. Explain your answer.

(1) Spencer is the partner in charge of the audit of Flip Company. He has half interest in a joint venture with Flip's CFO, but the joint venture is audited by a separate independent CPA firm.

(2) Victoria is the senior-in-charge of the audit of Holder Company. During the past year, she filled in for the chief accountant, who had emergency surgery and was out for six weeks.

(3) Brandon has been asked by an audit client to represent the client in negotiations with the management of another company that the client wants to acquire.

(4) Sanders is the partner-in-charge of the audit of the Marshall Co. The CEO and CFO have asked Sanders to prepare their personal federal and state income tax returns as well as the tax returns for the company.

(5) Marianne Keuhn is an audit partner and a member of Blackhawk Country Club. She is a low-handicap golfer and plays in a regular foursome every Saturday morning that includes Shelly Paris, the CFO of one audit client, and Nancy Sprague, the CEO of another audit client.

3-40   **(SEC Independence Principles, LO 7)** In small groups, consider the following situations. In your discussions, consider the SEC's four basic principles regarding independence. Using only those principles, discuss and reach a conclusion as to whether any of the following four situations, representing services performed by a CPA for an audit client, violate audit independence principles. If you believe that the services can be performed if safeguards are in place, state the safeguards:

Group Activity

a. A CPA firm prepares the client's tax return.

b. For an audit client, a CPA performs business risk analysis with a focus on economic and business risk rather than accounting risks. The intent is to help the company better identify and manage its risks. Management makes all decisions about risk priorities and approaches to mitigating the risk.

c. A CPA performs marketing research, but only for nonaudit clients. However, it does have a significant number of audit clients who are in the same industry for which it performs marketing research.

d. A client board member performs consulting work for the consulting division of the CPA firm. However, the board member has no relationship with the auditors except that of being a board member.

3-41   **(Mitigating Threats to Independence, LO 9)** Public accounting firms have taken many positive steps to assure the independence of their firms in conducting audits.

Internet

Required

a. Identify five ways in which a public accounting firm can take positive actions to improve the firm's independence in conducting an audit.

b. Identify a small public accounting firm near your school. Visit the firm's website and determine the scope of the firm's services. Are independence issues different for small firms that audit only privately held companies than for firms that audit mostly public companies? Explain and be prepared to describe the breadth of services performed by the firm and the independence issues you believe it must manage.

c. Identify three unique challenges that smaller public accounting firms face in maintaining audit independence.

d. What are the requirements for independence and objectivity if an audit firm performs consulting services for a nonaudit client? Explain the rationale for the requirements.

Professional Skepticism

3-42   **(Auditor Independence and Professional Skepticism, LO 8, 11)** Independence is often hailed as the "cornerstone of auditing" and recognized as the most important characteristic of an auditor. In addition, professional skepticism is a key aspect of professional judgment.

Required

a. What is meant by independence as applied to the CPA?

b. Compare the independence of an auditor with that of a

(1) Judge

(2) Lawyer

c. Describe the difference between *auditor independence* and *professional skepticism*.

Ethics

3-43   **(AICPA Code of Conduct, LO 6)** The following are a number of scenarios that might constitute a violation of the AICPA Code of Professional Conduct.

Required

For each of the six situations, identify whether it involves a violation of the ethical standards of the profession and indicate which principle or rule would be violated.

a. Tom Hart, CPA, does the bookkeeping, prepares the tax returns, and performs various management services for Sanders, Inc., but does not do the audit. One management service involved the assessment of the computer needs and the identification of equipment to meet those needs. Hart recommended a product sold by Computer Co., which has agreed to pay Hart a 10% commission if Sanders buys its product.

b. Irma Stone, CPA, was scheduled to be extremely busy for the next few months. When a prospective client asked if Stone would do its next year's audit, she declined but referred them to Joe Rock, CPA. Rock paid Stone $2,000 for the referral.

c. Nancy Heck, CPA, has agreed to perform an inventory control study and recommend a new inventory control system for Ettes, Inc., a new client. Currently, Ettes engages another CPA firm to audit its financial statements. The financial arrangement is that Ettes, Inc. will pay Heck 50% of the savings in inventory costs over the two-year period following the implementation of the new system.

d. Brad Gage, CPA, has served Hi-Dee Co. as auditor for several years. In addition, Gage has performed other services for the company. This year, the financial vice president has asked Gage to perform a major computer system evaluation.

e. Due to the death of its controller, an audit client had its external auditor, Gail Klate, CPA, perform the controller's job for a month until a replacement was found.

f. Chris Holt, CPA, conducted an audit and issued a report on the 20X1 financial statements of Tree, Inc. Tree has not yet paid the audit fees for that audit prior to issuing the audit report on 19X2 statements.

3-44   **(AICPA Code of Conduct and Ethical Dilemmas, LO 4, 6)** Rule 301 on confidentiality recognizes a fundamental public trust between the client and the auditor and reflects the manner in which all professionals conduct themselves. However, in certain instances the auditor may be required to communicate confidential information.

Ethics

Required

a. Briefly explain the purpose of the confidentiality rule. Why is it important to assure the client of the confidentiality of information?

b. Under what circumstances is the CPA allowed to communicate confidential information, and who are the parties to which the information can be communicated?

c. Assume that an auditor is the partner-in-charge of two separate engagements, but during the conduct of the audit of Client A, the auditor learns of information that will materially affect the audit of Client B. Client B is not aware of the information (the inability of Client A to pay its debts). What alternative courses of action are available to the auditor? Would communication of the information to Client B be considered a violation of confidentiality? What guidance might the auditor seek other than Rule 301 in developing an answer to this ethical dilemma?

d. Is the auditor's report considered a confidential communication? Explain.

3-45   **(Application of Ethical Framework and AICPA Code of Conduct, LO 4, 6)** Robert, CPA, has a large one-office firm in a growing city, but his practice is shrinking. Several other firms recently opened offices in the city, and Robert lost several key clients to his new competitors. Because of the changed competitive climate, Robert decided his firm needed to offer a wider array of services and seek clients in industries in which the firm had not previously ventured. For example, Robert bid on a nearby community college's annual audit, even though his firm had never before audited a college. The college receives a significant amount of federal financial assistance. The bid was successful, and Robert's firm conducted and completed what he thought was an appropriate audit. Shortly after its conclusion, however, Robert was informed by the ethics committee that an investigation was being considered to determine if he had violated any of the AICPA's Rules of Conduct or related interpretations.

Ethics

Required

a. What rules of conduct and interpretations would the ethics committee most likely refer to for this investigation?

b. Using the ethical framework outlined in this chapter, describe how Robert might have avoided violation of those rules and interpretations.

3-46   **(Application of Ethical Framework, LO 4)** As the auditor for XYZ Company, you discover that a material sale ($500,000 sale, cost of goods of $300,000) was made to a customer this year. Because of poor internal accounting controls, the sale was never recorded. Your client makes a management decision not to bill the customer because such a long time has passed since the shipment was made. You determine, to the best of your ability, that the sale was not fraudulent.

Ethics

Required

a. Does GAAP require disclosure of this situation? Cite specific applicable standards.

b. Regardless of your answer to part (a), use the ethical framework developed in the chapter to determine whether the auditor should require either a recording or disclosure of the transaction. If you conclude that the transaction should be disclosed or recorded, indicate the nature of disclosure and your rationale for it.

Ethics

3-47   **(Application of Ethical Framework and AICPA Code of Conduct, LO 4, 6)** Your audit client, Germane Industries, has developed a new financial instrument, the major purpose of which is to boost earnings and to keep a significant amount of debt off the balance sheet. Its investment banker tells the firm that the instrument is structured explicitly to keep it off the balance sheet and that she has discussed the treatment with three other Big 4 firms that have indicated some support for the client's position. The transaction is not covered by any current authoritative pronouncement.

Your initial reaction is that the item, when viewed in its substance as opposed to its form, is debt. The client reacts that GAAP does not prohibit the treatment of the item it advocates and that the financial statements are those of management. The client notes further, and you corroborate, that some other firms would account for the item in the manner suggested by management, although it is not clear that a majority of other firms would accept such accounting.

Required

a. What is the ethical dilemma?

b. Does competition lead to a lower ethical standard in the profession?

c. What safeguards are built into the profession's standards and Code of Professional Conduct that would mitigate the potential effect of competition on the quality of the profession's work?

Ethics

3-48   **(Ethics in Practice, LO 2, 3, 4)** In her book *Extraordinary Circumstances,*[6] Cynthia Cooper describes her life as going from an internal auditor to a whistleblower. In the book, she states that she never believed she was a whistleblower; rather she believed she was "just doing her job."

Required

a. What is the difference between an "ethical dilemma" and "just doing one's job"? Respond in relationship to both internal and external auditing.

b. External auditors are not thought of as "whistleblowers." However, the external auditor may find situations in which he or she concludes that the company has fraudulently violated GAAP. Management disagrees and refuses to change the financial statements. To whom does the auditor report the findings?

---

[6] Cynthia Cooper, *Extraordinary Circumstances.* (New York: John Wiley & Co, 2008).

c. Assume an external auditor finds that an internal employee has perpetrated a fraud against the company. The amounts are material to the individual, but not to the company. Does this constitute an ethical dilemma or an ethical problem? How should the auditor decide the appropriate course of action to take? Suggest and defend your suggested action.

3-49 **(Professional Decision-Making Framework, LO 1)** This chapter lays out a framework for high-quality decision-making that has been applied across a number of different professions, including the medical profession. The framework has been adapted in this textbook to fit audit terminology.

Required

a. What is meant by the term *high quality decision-making*? How is that term operationalized in an audit situation?

b. How are both (i) the risk of making an incorrect decision and (ii) the risk that errors exist in the accounting records implemented in the decision-making model?

c. What does the decision-making model infer about the sufficiency and persuasiveness of information needed to make high-quality decisions? What is meant by the term *sensitivity analysis*?

d. What is the major decision auditors have to make regarding audits of a company's financial statements? For example, assume that the statements are only "a little bit wrong." What are the consequences for the auditor? What if the statements are significantly in error? What are the consequences for the auditor?

3-50 **(Professional Skepticism, LO 11)**

a. Why is it sometimes difficult for auditors to exercise appropriate levels of professional skepticism in practice?

b. What practices can individual auditors apply to help them to remember to be professionally skeptical?

c. Imagine that you are working on an audit engagement. What are the personal characteristics of management or other company employees that might make you skeptical about whether or not they are providing you accurate audit evidence? Aside from personal observations, what publicly available information about management or other company employees could you obtain to determine whether you should exercise heightened professional skepticism in your dealings with these individuals?

Professional Skepticism

Cases

3-51 **(Professional Skepticism, LO 11)** During the Fall of 2009, Koss Corporation, a Wisconsin-based manufacturer of stereo headphone equipment, revealed that its Vice President of Finance (Sujata "Sue" Sachdeva) had defrauded the company of approximately $31 million over a period of at least five years. Grant Thornton LLP was the company's auditor, and the firm issued unqualified audit opinions for the entire period in which they worked for Koss. According to reports, Sachdeva's theft accelerated over a period of years as follows:

Professional Skepticism

Fraud

FY 2005:	$2,195,477
FY 2006:	$2,227,669
FY 2007:	$3,160,310
FY 2008:	$5,040,968
FY 2009:	$8,485,937
Q1 FY 2010:	$5,326,305
Q2 FY 2010:	$4,917,005

To give you a sense of the magnitude of the fraud, annual revenues for Koss Corporation are in the range of $40–$45 million annually, and previously reported pre-tax income for fiscal years 2007 and through Q1 2010 was as follows:

FY 2007:	$8,344,715
FY 2008:	$7,410,569
FY 2009:	$2,887,730
FY 20010:	$ 928,491

How could Sachdeva have stolen so much money and fooled so many people over a long period? It is thought that Sachdeva hid the theft in the company's cost of goods sold accounts, and that weak internal controls and poor corporate governance and oversight enabled her to conceal the theft from corporate officials. Certainly, there must have been questions raised about the Company's deteriorating financial condition. But any number of excuses could have been used by Sachdeva to explain the missing money. For example, she might have blamed higher cost of goods sold on a change in suppliers or rising raw materials prices. Further, the Company had no internal audit function, nor was it required to have its auditor evaluate its internal control system (Koss is a non-accelerated public filers not yet subject to the requirements concerning internal control audits in SOX). Another contributing factor in Sachdeva's ability to conceal her thefts was that top-management of Koss had a high degree of trust in her, and did not monitor the accounts that she controlled at the company.

Sachdeva's total compensation for fiscal year 2009 was $173,734. But according to published reports, Sachdeva was known for her unusually lavish lifestyle and shopping sprees. It is reported that she spent $225,000 at a single Houston, Texas, jewelry store. Another report describes a $1.4 million shopping spree at Valentina Boutique in Mequon, Wisconsin. People familiar with her spending habits assumed that she used family money and that her husband's job as a prominent pediatrician funded her extravagant lifestyle. The fraud was ultimately uncovered because American Express became concerned when it realized that Sachdeva was paying for large balances on her personal account with wire transfers from a Koss Corporation account. American Express then notified the FBI and relayed its concerns.

Upon learning of the fraud, Koss Corporation executives fired Sachdeva, along with the company's audit firm, Grant Thornton LLP. Koss Corporation is attempting to recover its monetary losses through the recovery and sale of merchandise that was purchased by Sachdeva as part of the unauthorized transactions, and through insurance proceeds and possible claims against third parties (including Grant Thornton LLP). Law enforcement authorities notified Koss Corporation that at least 22,000 items—including high-end women's clothing, shoes, handbags, and jewelry—have been recovered to date. Sachdeva stored the bulk of the items she purchased in rented storage units in order to conceal the items from her husband.

After considering this situation, answer the following questions:

1. Why might Koss management have placed so much trust in Sachdeva, along with minimal supervision and monitoring?
2. What was Grant Thornton's obligation to uncover the fraud?

3. Why should Sachdeva's lavish lifestyle have raised suspicions? Why might it have been ignored or explained away by her professional colleagues?

4. How could management, the audit committee, and the auditors have been more professionally skeptical in this situation?

5. What was the audit committee's responsibility to notice that something looked amiss in the financial statements?

6. Sachdeva paid for her purchases using corporate credit cards. What internal controls could the company have used to prevent inappropriate use of the credit cards?

7. Some reports have described Sachdeva as having a very dominating personality, and revelations were made about the fact that she would often be verbally abusive of her subordinates in front of top-level managers at Koss. How should top-level managers have responded to this behavior? What actions could the subordinates have taken to respond to this behavior?

3-52 **(Audit Committee Oversight, Expertise, and Professional Skepticism, LO 4, 11)** Read the facts of the case in Problem 3-51 to become familiar with the fraud involving Koss Corporation. From the Company's October 7, 2009 proxy statement (Def 14A filing with the SEC), we know the following facts about the Company's audit committee.

Professional Skepticism

• Members, ages, and descriptions of the audit committee members are as follows:

Thomas L. Doerr, 65, has been a director of the Company since 1987. In 1972, Mr. Doerr co-founded Leeson Electric Corporation and served as its President and Chief Executive Officer until 1982. The company manufactures industrial electric motors. In 1983, Mr. Doerr incorporated Doerr Corporation as a holding company for the purpose of acquiring established companies involved in distributing products to industrial and commercial markets. Currently, Mr. Doerr serves as President of Doerr Corporation. Mr. Doerr owns no stock in Koss Corporation, and received $24,000 in cash compensation during 2009 to serve on the audit committee.

Lawrence S. Mattson, 77, has been a director of the Company since 1978. Mr. Mattson is the retired President of Oster Company, a division of Sunbeam Corporation, which manufactures and sells portable household appliances. Mr. Mattson is the designated audit committee financial expert. Mr. Mattson owns no stock in Koss Corporation, and received $23,000 in cash compensation during 2009 to serve on the audit committee.

Theodore H. Nixon, 57, has been a director of the Company since 2006. Since 1992, Mr. Nixon has been the Chief Executive Officer of D.D. Williamson, which is a manufacturer of caramel coloring used in the food and beverage industries. Mr. Nixon joined D.D. Williamson in 1974 and was promoted to President and Chief Operating Officer in 1982. Mr. Nixon is also a director of the non-profit Center for Quality of Management. Mr. Nixon owns 2,480 shares of common stock of the Company (less than 1% of outstanding shares), and received $21,000 in cash compensation during 2009 to serve on the audit committee.

John J. Stollenwerk, 69, has been a director of the Company since 1986. Mr. Stollenwerk is the Chairman of the Allen-Edmonds Shoe Corporation, an international manufacturer and retailer of high-quality footwear. He is also a director of Allen-Edmonds Shoe Corporation, Badger Meter, Inc., U.S. Bancorp, and Northwestern Mutual Life Insurance Company. Mr. Stollenwerk owns 13,551 shares of common stock of the Company (less than 1% of outstanding shares), and received $23,000 in cash compensation during 2009 to serve on the audit committee.

- The Audit Committee met three times during the fiscal year ended June 30, 2009. The independent accountants (Grant Thornton LLP) were present at two of these meetings to discuss their audit scope and the results of their audit.
- Koss claims that each member of the Audit Committee is "independent" as defined in Nasdaq Marketplace Rule 4200.
- The proxy statement describes the responsibilities of the audit committee as follows: "the Audit Committee, among other things, monitors the integrity of the financial reporting process, systems of internal controls, and financial statements and reports of the Company; appoints, compensates, retains, and oversees the Company's independent auditors, including reviewing the qualifications, performance and independence of the independent auditors; reviews and pre-approves all audit, attest and review services and permitted non-audit services; oversees the audit work performed by the Company's internal accounting staff; and oversees the Company's compliance with legal and regulatory requirements. The Audit Committee meets twice a year with the Company's independent accountants to discuss the results of their examinations, their evaluations of the Company's internal controls, and the overall quality of the Company's financial reporting."

Part 1. Does the description of the audit committee members bear a conclusion that its members appear to be professionally qualified for their positions? Do they meet enough times during the year to accomplish their responsibilities? What additional information might you need to answer this question, and how would the auditor obtain that information?

Part 2. Who was the audit committee financial expert? Do you think that the experiences of this individual as described should ensure that he is truly a financial expert capable of fulfilling his roles in this regard? Why is financial expertise important for audit committee members in general?

Part 3. Was the compensation that the audit committee members received for their services adequate in your opinion?

Part 4. Based on the information that you have learned in Parts 1–3 of this problem, what weaknesses in the audit committee governance structure existed at Koss Corporation immediately preceding the discovery of fraud? Should those weaknesses be reported to shareholders if a report on internal control was required? If yes, how might such information affect shareholders? If no, what is the basis for your conclusion?

Part 5. Consider a potential ethical dilemma. The audit firm is hired and/ or fired by the audit committee. Assume that Koss was a public company in which the auditor had to report on internal control, and the auditor concluded that the audit committee had such weaknesses that it constituted a material weakness in internal control. Should the audit firm report such a weakness when it would likely mean the audit firm would be fired? How might the audit firm and shareholders protect themselves from such pressure?

3-53 **(Public Trust, LO 2)** In a 1988 article, Arthur Wyatt, a former member of the FASB, stated, "Practicing professionals should place the public interest above the interests of clients, particularly when participating in a process designed to develop standards expected to achieve fair presentation…. Granted that the increasingly detailed nature of FASB standards encourages efforts to find loopholes, a professional ought to strive to apply standards in a manner that will best achieve the objectives sought by the standards. *Unfortunately, the auditor today is often a participant in aggressively seeking loopholes.* The public, on the other hand, views auditors as their protection against aggressive standard application." [Emphasis added].

Ethics

Required

a. What does it mean to find "loopholes" in FASB pronouncements? How would finding loopholes be potentially valued by the management of a client? How would finding loopholes affect the public's trust in the auditors' work?

b. Explain how auditors could be participants in "aggressively seeking loopholes" when the independence standard requires the pursuit of fairness in financial presentation.

c. How is professionalism related to the concept of fairness in financial reporting? Explain.

d. Is there evidence that the behavior Arthur Wyatt is referring to changed after the implementation of the Sarbanes-Oxley Act of 2002? What features of the Act may have led to improved auditor performance on these issues?

3-54 **(Application of Ethical Framework and AICPA Code of Conduct, LO 4, 6)** In *Fund of Funds, Ltd. v. Arthur Andersen & Co.*, Arthur Andersen auditors completed the audit of Fund of Funds with no problems encountered and issued an unqualified opinion. Shortly thereafter, essentially the same audit team began the audit of King Resources. While conducting that audit, the auditors realized that there was a significant contract between King Resources and Fund of Funds. The auditors continued with the audit and were surprised to find that King Resources had not dealt fairly with Fund of Funds by selling them property that was significantly overpriced. Now the auditors were caught in a dilemma: They could tell Fund of Funds; alternatively, they could refrain from telling Fund of Funds and hope that Fund of Funds would never find out.

Ethics

Required

a. Discuss what course of action you would recommend the auditors take and potential results of that action.

b. How could this situation have been avoided?

c. Discuss how this case differs from the *Consolidata* case described in the chapter in terms of disclosing confidential information.

3-55 **(Application of Ethical Framework, LO 4)** You have been engaged to examine the balance sheet of Hi-Sail Company, which provides services to financial institutions. Its revenue source comes from fees for performing these services. Its primary expenses are related to selling and general and administrative costs. The company has assets and liabilities of approximately $1 million. Operating losses in recent years have resulted in a retained earnings deficit and stockholder's equity close to zero. The assets consist primarily of restricted cash and accounts receivable. Its liabilities consist of accounts payable, accrued expenses, and reserves for potential losses on services previously provided.

Ethics

Your preliminary audit work indicated that the company generates a high volume of transactions. The internal control system surrounding these transactions is weak. It is also apparent that management is involved only moderately in day-to-day activities and spends most of its time dealing with nonroutine transactions and events.

You expended a significant amount of time and money to complete your examination of the balance sheet. The client understood the extended efforts and stated a willingness to pay whatever it cost to complete this engagement. However, monthly progress billings have not been paid.

On completion of the audit fieldwork, you reviewed a draft of the balance sheet and related notes with the company's president and chief financial officer/controller.

With minor wording modification, they agreed with the draft. They requested that you issue this report as soon as possible. You committed to the issuance of your opinion, subject to a review of the draft with the company's chairperson of the board.

After the chairperson reviewed the draft, she requested a special meeting outside the company's office. At the subsequent meeting, she stated that the drafted balance sheet and notes were severely in error. Included in her comments are the following:

1. The previous year's tax returns have not been filed, and the company has extensive potential tax liabilities.
2. The company has guaranteed significant amounts of debt related to joint ventures. These ventures have failed, and the company's partners are insolvent.
3. Significant notes payable to the chairperson have not been recorded.
4. Amounts payable to the chairperson and other officers related to reimbursement of monies expended by these individuals personally for travel, entertainment, and related expenses on the company's behalf have also not been recorded.

The chairperson surmised that the president and the chief financial officer/controller did not disclose these items because of their detrimental impact on the company. She believed that those officers were trying to stage a shareholder dispute to unseat her.

You continued to have separate meetings with these individuals. It became clear that the parties were in dispute, and you found it increasingly difficult to understand what was factual and what was not. The two officers, in particular, requested an urgent conclusion of the audit and delivery of your opinion. They claimed the chairperson's position was self-serving and not representative of the company's financial position.

You discovered the reason the two officers were anxious for the opinion and balance sheet was that they were attempting to sell the company. You also learned from the company and from another of your clients that the second client was interested in purchasing the company. This second client has asked you why you have not yet issued your report on Hi-Sail.

Discussion Issues

a. Write a report using the ethical framework in the chapter to describe what course of action you would take concerning the audit and how you decided on that course of action. The report should include all components of the framework presented in this chapter.

b. Indicate what you would do in response to the second client's inquiry and why.

3-56   **(Application of Ethical Framework, LO 4)** The following case requires you to read published academic papers that discuss ethics in auditing and accounting, and that will provide you with insight on opinions regarding how ethics training can be accomplished.

Read the following two published research papers:

1. "Hollow men and women at the helm … Hollow accounting ethics?" by Sandra Waddock, *Issues in Accounting Education* 2005 (Vol. 20, No. 2) pp. 145–150.
2. "Danish evidence of auditors' level of moral reasoning and predisposition to provide fair judgments," by Bent Warming-Rasmussen and Carolyn A. Windsor, *Journal of Business Ethics* 2003 (Vol. 47), pp. 77–87.

    Based on your reading of the two articles, answer the following four questions.

   a. What are the major arguments made in the first paper? Do you agree with them? What are the strengths of Professor Waddock's analysis? What are the weaknesses? What does the fact that there were frauds and unethical behavior long before the advent of formal business school education imply regarding Professor Waddock's views?

   b. What was the average level of moral reasoning for the auditors surveyed in the second paper? What does this imply for potential audit judgments made by those auditors and the extent to which they may be influenced by client preferences?

   c. Discuss whether you believe that ethics interventions during your college education will be helpful in assuring that your ethical framework will be appropriate for the duties you will be expected to perform as a professional accountant.

   d. Nearly all of the students in your class will be entering the professional workplace during the next year or so. It is important that you consciously consider how you might react if you encounter an ethical dilemma. Most importantly, you need to recognize that you are encountering an ethical dilemma and to think very carefully about the nature of that dilemma, how you might handle the situation itself, and how you might anticipate the outcomes of that situation. Toward that end, you are to "imagine" an ethical dilemma that you may encounter in your new professional life.

      • Describe the nature of the dilemma.

      • Describe how you plan to handle the situation.

      • Describe potential outcomes of your reaction to the situation.

Academic Research Case (LO 8, 9, 10)

Academic research addresses the conceptual issues outlined in this chapter. To help you consider the linkage between academic research and the practice of auditing, read the following research article and answer the questions below.

Johnstone, K., Sutton, M., & Warfield, T. (2008). Antecedents and Consequences of Independence Risk: Framework for Analysis. *Accounting Horizons. Sarasota: 15(1): 1–18.*

   i. What is the issue being addressed in the paper?

   ii. Why is this issue important to practicing auditors?

   iii. What factors are identified as contributing to the issue? What factors are identified as mitigating the issues?

   iv. What are some actions that can be taken to address this issue?

   v. What are the implications of these findings for audit quality (or audit practice) on the audit profession?

   vi. Describe any limitations of the research that the student (and practice) should be aware of.

SEARCH HINT

It is easy to locate these academic research articles! Simply use a search engine (e.g., Google Scholar) or an electronic research platform (e.g., ABI Inform) and search using the author names and part of the article title.

Go to www.cengage.com/accounting/rittenberg for the Ford and Toyota materials. Read the following excerpt from the 2010 Ford Motor Company Proxy Statement and then complete the discussion question.

The Audit Committee is composed of four directors, all of whom meet the independence standards contained in the NYSE Listed Company rules, SEC rules and Ford's Corporate Governance Principles, and operates under a written charter adopted by the Board of Directors. A copy of the Audit Committee Charter may be found on the Company's website, www.ford.com. The Audit Committee selects, subject to shareholder ratification, the Company's independent registered public accounting firm.

Ford management is responsible for the Company's internal controls and the financial reporting process. The independent registered public accounting firm, PricewaterhouseCoopers LLP ("PricewaterhouseCoopers"), is responsible for performing independent audits of the Company's consolidated financial statements and internal control over financial reporting and issuing an opinion on the conformity of those audited financial statements with United States generally accepted accounting principles and on the effectiveness of the Company's internal control over financial reporting. The Audit Committee monitors the Company's financial reporting process and reports to the Board of Directors on its findings.

Audit Fees

PricewaterhouseCoopers served as the Company's independent registered public accounting firm in 2009 and 2008. The Company paid PricewaterhouseCoopers $42.7 million and $43.7 million for audit services for the years ended December 31, 2009 and 2008, respectively. Audit services consisted of the audit of the financial statements included in the Company's Annual Report on Form 10-K, reviews of the financial statements included in the Company's Quarterly Reports on Form 10-Q, attestation of the effectiveness of the Company's internal controls over financial reporting, preparation of statutory audit reports, and providing comfort letters in connection with Ford and Ford Motor Credit Company funding transactions.

Audit-Related Fees

The Company paid PricewaterhouseCoopers $4.4 million and $7.7 million for audit-related services for the years ended December 31, 2009 and 2008, respectively. Audit-related services included support of funding transactions, due diligence for mergers, acquisitions and divestitures, employee benefit plan audits, attestation services, internal control reviews, and assistance with interpretation of accounting standards.

Tax Fees

The Company paid PricewaterhouseCoopers $4.1 million and $5.7 million for tax services for the years ended December 31, 2009 and 2008, respectively. The types of tax services provided included assistance with tax compliance and the preparation of tax returns, tax consultation, planning and implementation services, assistance in connection with tax audits, tax advice related to mergers, acquisitions and divestitures, and tax return preparation services provided to international service employees ("ISEs") to minimize the cost to the Company of these assignments. In 2005, the Company began the transition to a new service provider for tax return preparation services to ISEs. Of the fees paid for tax services, the Company paid 59% and 57% for tax compliance and the preparation of Company tax returns in 2009 and 2008, respectively.

All Other Fees

The Company did not engage PricewaterhouseCoopers for any other services for the years ended December 31, 2009 and 2008.

Total Fees

The Company paid PricewaterhouseCoopers a total of $51.2 and $57.1 million in fees for the years ended December 31, 2009 and 2008, respectively.

Auditor Independence

During the last year, the Audit Committee met and held discussions with management and PricewaterhouseCoopers. The Audit Committee reviewed and discussed with Ford management and PricewaterhouseCoopers the audited financial statements and the assessment of the effectiveness of internal controls over financial reporting, contained in the Company's Annual Report on Form 10-K for the year ended December 31, 2009. The Audit Committee also discussed with PricewaterhouseCoopers the matters required to be discussed by applicable requirements of the Public Company Accounting Oversight Board regarding the independent registered public accounting firm's communications with the Audit Committee concerning independence, as well as by SEC regulations. PricewaterhouseCoopers submitted to the Audit Committee the written disclosures and the letter required by applicable requirements of the Public Company Accounting Oversight Board regarding the independent registered public accounting firm's communications with the audit committee concerning independence. The Audit Committee discussed with PricewaterhouseCoopers such firm's independence. Based on the reviews and discussions referred to above, the Audit Committee recommended to the Board of Directors that the audited financial statements be included in the Company's Annual Report on Form 10-K for the year ended December 31, 2009, filed with the SEC.

The Audit Committee also considered whether the provision of other non-audit services by PricewaterhouseCoopers to the Company is compatible with maintaining the independence of PricewaterhouseCoopers and concluded that the independence of PricewaterhouseCoopers is not compromised by the provision of such services. Annually, the Audit Committee pre-approves categories of services to be performed (rather than individual engagements) by PricewaterhouseCoopers. As part of this approval, an amount is established for each category of services (Audit, Audit-Related, and Tax Services). In the event the pre-approved amounts prove to be insufficient, a request for incremental funding will be submitted to the Audit Committee for approval during the next regularly scheduled meeting. In addition, all new engagements greater than $250,000 will be presented in advance to the Audit Committee for approval. A regular report is prepared for each regular Audit Committee meeting outlining actual fees and expenses paid or committed against approved fees.

Audit Committee
Stephen G. Butler (Chair)
Kimberly A. Casiano
Irvine O. Hockaday, Jr.
Gerald L. Shaheen

Required

The audit committee "considered whether the provision of other nonaudit services by PricewaterhouseCoopers to the Company is compatible with maintaining the independence of PricewaterhouseCoopers and concluded that the independence of PricewaterhouseCoopers is not compromised by the provision of such services." Use the information revealed above regarding audit fees, audit-related fees, and tax fees, along with the decision analysis framework in Exhibit 3.1, to make your own decision about whether the provision of other nonaudit services might compromise the independence, or perception of independence, of PricewaterhouseCoopers from Ford management.

Audit Risk, Business Risk, and Audit Planning

LEARNING OBJECTIVES

The overriding objective of this textbook is to build a foundation with which to analyze current professional issues and adapt audit approaches to business and economic complexities. Through studying this chapter, you will be able to:

1 Identify the various types of risk relevant to conducting an audit.

2 Describe how audit firms manage engagement risk by making high-quality client acceptance and retention decisions.

3 Discuss the relevance of materiality in an audit context, and articulate the relationship between materiality and audit risk.

4 Describe the audit risk model and its components.

5 Articulate some limitations of the audit risk model.

6 Use the audit risk model to plan the nature of procedures to be performed on an audit engagement.

7 Use preliminary analytical techniques to identify areas of heightened risk of misstatement.

8 Apply the decision analysis and ethical decision-making frameworks to situations involving audit risk, business risk, and audit planning.

CHAPTER OVERVIEW

PRACTICAL POINT

An example of a recent risk management failure can be seen with the BP oil spill. Some have suggested that BP's lack of effective risk management may explain why BP did not take extra precautions such as relief wells or back-up systems. Had BP's management realized the magnitude of financial exposure they might have insisted on appropriate precautions, even if the precautions were very costly.

Risk is a natural part of business activity. However, as we have been reminded by the financial crisis and economic recession, risks that are not controlled and addressed can jeopardize the operation of companies—both large and small. Risk occurs on a daily basis; there is always a risk that a new product will fail, unanticipated economic events will occur, or an unlikely outcome may occur. The manner in which an organization manages those risks affects both the financial viability of the organization and the auditor's approach to auditing it.

Some organizations have management control mechanisms to identify, manage, mitigate, or control risks. The auditor needs to understand (a) the risks that affect the operations of the client and (b) how well management identifies and deals with those risks. In this chapter, we describe the nature of risks, the procedures the auditor uses to identify risks, and the methodologies organizations use to manage, mitigate, or control the risks.

In terms of the audit opinion formulation process, this chapter involves Phase I, i.e., client acceptance and retention decisions, and Phase II, i.e., understanding the client's risks. The analysis of risks directly affects the nature and amount of audit work performed. We introduce the concept of audit risk and the audit risk model to describe the auditor's risk that an audit may fail to detect material misstatements.

The Audit Opinion Formulation Process

I. Assessing Client Acceptance and Retention Decisions	II. Understanding the Client	III. Obtaining Evidence about Controls and Determining the Impact on the Financial Statement Audit	IV. Obtaining Substantive Evidence about Account Assertions	V. Wrapping Up the Audit and Making Reporting Decisions
CHAPTER 4	CHAPTERS 2, 4–6, and 9	CHAPTERS 5–14 and 18	CHAPTERS 7–14 and 18	CHAPTERS 15 and 16

The Auditing Profession, Regulation, and Corporate Governance	Decision-Making, Professional Conduct, and Ethics	Professional Liability
CHAPTERS 1 and 2	CHAPTER 3	CHAPTER 17

PROFESSIONAL JUDGMENT IN CONTEXT

Reacting to the Financial Crisis and the Government Rescue Package

In October 2008, the U.S. economy suffered the largest stock market loss in its history. Many large banks failed because they did not adequately manage risks. For the most part, the banks borrowed large amounts of funds (i.e., they were highly leveraged) to invest in mortgage-backed securities—often without a sufficient analysis of the risks associated with those securities. The subprime mortgage market failed, and banks did not know the real value of the assets that they held, which ultimately cost the American taxpayer enormous sums of money. Many questioned why companies and auditors did not identify the problem earlier. For example, why didn't we know the risk associated with these companies? Why didn't the Sarbanes-Oxley Act of 2002 protect investors and consumers against this kind of calamity? Moreover, the risks in the financial system should have been foreseen with proper risk management and regulation.

Given this economic turmoil, put yourself in the position of an audit partner who realizes that the current economic environment will make each of his or her audits more risky this year. As the partner plans each audit, he or she will need to articulate unique client risks, link those risks to specific account balances and relevant assertions in the financial statements, and identify the types of audit procedures that should be performed to adequately address the risks. Further, consider the following facts relevant to today's environment:

- For many manufacturing companies, goodwill is now one of the largest assets on their books.

- Many companies are downsizing, and not only will they be laying people off, they will be reducing inventories and closing plants.
- Sales have declined in the recent past, and economic recovery from the recession is slow and unpredictable.
- Many customers have declared bankruptcy, and many others are paying more slowly than they had in the past.

In planning each audit, the partner will have to think about accounting standards relating to impairment of assets, uncollectibility of accounts, net realizable value of inventory, and pension adjustments, among other issues. In addition, the team must consider the subjective nature of some of the evidence that might be gathered and evaluated. In this setting, professional judgment and skepticism are paramount. More fundamentally, without a good understanding of risk and markets, the audit firm's personnel cannot carry out their responsibilities.

As you read this chapter, think about the risks that are a natural part of running a business. Then, think about whether there is risk to audit firms who are associated with clients who have a high risk of failure, or a high risk of material misstatements in the financial statements. Finally, think about the risks that the auditor may face in determining whether there is a material misstatement in a client's financial statements because of the difficult economic environment that organizations are currently facing.

Nature of Risk

Risk is a pervasive concept. We are at risk every time we cross the road. Organizations are at risk every day they operate. There are many definitions of risk and approaches taken to manage risk. In this chapter, we identify four critical components of risk that are relevant to conducting an audit:

- *Business Risk*—risk that affects the operations and potential outcomes of organizational activities

LO 1

Identify the various types of risk relevant to conducting an audit.

- *Financial Reporting Risk*—risk that relates to the recording of transactions and the presentation of financial data in an organization's financial statements
- *Engagement Risk*—risk that auditors encounter by being associated with a particular client, including loss of reputation, inability of the client to pay the auditor, or financial loss because management is not honest and inhibits the audit process
- *Audit Risk*—the risk that the auditor expresses an audit opinion that the financial statements are fairly presented when they are materially misstated.

Exhibit 4.1 illustrates the relationships among these risks. At the broadest level, **business risk** and **financial reporting risk** originate with the audit client and its environment, and these risks then affect the auditor's **engagement risk** and **audit risk**. The effectiveness of risk management processes will determine whether a company or audit firm continues to exist. This chapter describes a framework for identifying and managing risks to minimize the auditor's risk associated with issuing an audit opinion on a company's financial statements or on the effectiveness of its internal accounting controls.

A number of factors affect a client's business risk. The overall economic climate—favorable or unfavorable—can have a tremendous effect on the organization's ability to operate effectively and profitably. Economic downturns are often associated with the failure of otherwise successful organizations. Technological change also presents risk for many companies. For example, Google and Apple's new communication products affected the phone business of Motorola and Nokia. Competitor actions, such as discounting prices or adding new product lines, also affect business risk. As we learned in the financial crisis, the complexity of financial instruments and transactions may increase business risk,

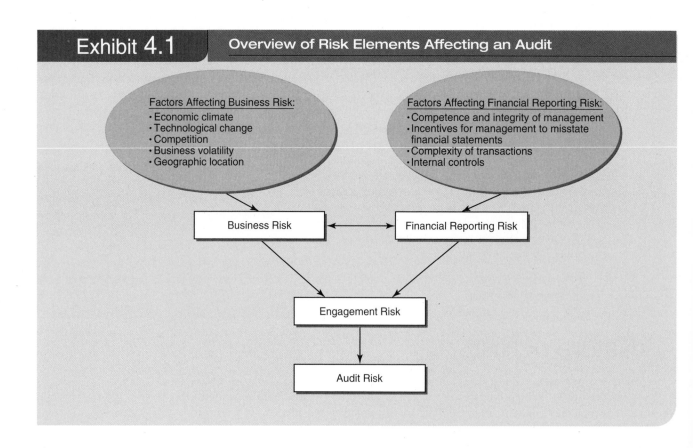

Exhibit 4.1   **Overview of Risk Elements Affecting an Audit**

Factors Affecting Business Risk:
- Economic climate
- Technological change
- Competition
- Business volatility
- Geographic location

Factors Affecting Financial Reporting Risk:
- Competence and integrity of management
- Incentives for management to misstate financial statements
- Complexity of transactions
- Internal controls

Business Risk ⟷ Financial Reporting Risk

Engagement Risk

Audit Risk

and, in turn, financial reporting risk. Finally, geographic locations of suppliers can also affect business risk. For example, sourcing products in China might be a competitive advantage but might also expose the company to risk if it finds that its products contain lead and cannot be sold in the United States or Europe. It is up to management to properly manage its business risk. All organizations are subject to business risk; management reactions may exacerbate it (make it more likely) or, conversely, good management can mitigate it.

When thinking about **financial reporting risk**, consider all of the items on a company's balance sheet that are subjective and based on judgment. There are judgments associated with issues such as asset impairments, mark-to-market accounting, warranties, returns, pensions, and estimates regarding the useful lives of assets, among others. Because of these estimates, financial reporting risk is affected by the competence and integrity of management and potential incentives to misstate the financial statements (e.g., due to stock options or bonus agreements). In addition, the sheer complexity of certain transactions can affect financial reporting risk. Finally, the entity's internal controls can affect financial reporting risk by either preventing or detecting errors or intentional misstatements. In order to understand business risk and financial reporting risk, the auditor will gather information through reviews of previous audits, reviews of the client's internal control and risk management processes, discussions with management, and analysis of the current economic environment.

Business risk and financial reporting risk may affect each other; e.g., management facing strong competition and weak financial results may be motivated to circumvent a weak internal control system or to take advantage of complex financial instruments to achieve desired financial reporting results even if the financial statements to not accurately portray economic reality. In addition, both business risk and financial reporting risk affect the auditor's engagement risk. For example, if the client declares bankruptcy or suffers extremely large losses, it is more likely that an audit firm will be sued. Audit firms have discovered that being associated with companies with poor integrity—e.g., Lehman Brothers, WorldCom, Parmalat, AIG, Enron—creates risks that can destroy the audit firm, lead to litigation costs and reputation declines, or increase the cost of conducting the audit.

> **PRACTICAL POINT**
>
> Risk is cumulative. If business risk is very high, the auditor may decide to not be associated with a client because engagement risk will be too high.

Audit risk is defined as the risk that the auditor expresses an inappropriate audit opinion when the financial statements are materially misstated, i.e., the financial statements are not presented fairly in conformity with the applicable financial reporting framework. The auditor can control audit risk in two different ways:

1. Avoid audit risk by not accepting certain companies as clients thereby reducing engagement risk to zero.
2. Set audit risk at a level that the auditor believes will mitigate the likelihood that the auditor will fail to identify material misstatements.

In controlling audit risk, the auditor must recognize that once a client is accepted, audit risk cannot be eliminated. However, it can be reduced by doing more work targeted to specific areas where financial reporting risk is high. However, doing more work raises audit fees, which may create tension with the client and its management. For example, if another audit firm would do the audit for less money, the current audit firm has a choice as to whether (a) to convince the audit client that it is mutually beneficial to the client and auditor to reduce audit risk, (b) to accept greater audit risk through reducing audit work and pass along the fee savings to the client, (c) to reduce the amount of revenue received for the same amount of work performed, or (d) to potentially lose the audit client.

AUDITING *in Practice*

MANAGING ENGAGEMENT RISK

AIG was a large insurance company that posted a $3.9 billion restatement of earnings in May 2005. AIG purposely hid many of the transactions related to the restatement from its audit firm, PwC. Following the restatement, PwC was sued for damages, and ultimately paid a settlement of $97.5 million. In short, management's lack of integrity ultimately cost the CPA firm many millions of dollars.

Does every company have a "right" to a financial statement audit? In the last decade, failures of public accounting firms because of the actions of their clients have led auditors to answer "no" to that question. Audit firms have implemented specific procedures to avoid being associated with audit clients they think are too risky. An important takeaway from Exhibit 4.1 is that each client brings certain unique business and financial reporting risks to bear on individual audit engagement. These risks, in turn, affect the engagement risk and audit risk that the audit firm must manage. In the next two sections, we focus on articulating how auditors manage engagement and audit risks.

Managing Engagement Risk Through Client Acceptance and Retention Decisions

LO 2

Describe how audit firms manage engagement risk by making high-quality client acceptance and retention decisions.

Perhaps the most important audit decision made on every audit engagement is determining whether a client will be accepted or retained. Most audit firms have developed detailed checklists and review procedures to help them decide whether to add a potential client to their existing portfolio of clients (i.e., the client acceptance decision) and whether to continue their relationship with existing clients (the client retention decision). There are a number of factors that affect the auditor's decision to accept or retain an audit client:

- Management integrity
- Independence and competence of management and the board of directors
- The quality of the organization's risk management process and controls
- Reporting requirements, including regulatory requirements
- Participation of key stakeholders
- Existence of related-party transactions
- The financial health of the organization

Management Integrity

Probably the most important factor for the auditor to assess and understand in every audit engagement is **management integrity**. The auditor must understand and assess (a) management integrity and (b) economic incentives that affect

AUDITING *in Practice*

STOCK OPTION BACKDATING FRAUD

During the last decade, a number of companies disclosed that management had cheated on its compensation by backdating stock options. It is not surprising that if management would cheat on one thing, it would also cheat by misstating financial statements. As an example, on April 23, 2010, a jury found Carl Jasper (the former CFO of Maxim Integrated Products) liable for securities fraud for engaging in a scheme to backdate stock option grants that allowed the company to conceal hundreds of millions of dollars of compensation costs and to thereby report significantly inflated income to investors.

The jury found that Jasper engaged in fraud, lied to auditors, and aided Maxim's failure to maintain accurate accounting records. Evidence from the trial showed that, with his knowledge, Jasper's staff granted stock options by using hindsight to identify dates with historically low stock prices. The staff then drafted false documentation to make it seem that the options had been granted at earlier dates, which enabled the company to conceal its true compensation expenses. For more information about this case, see SEC Litigation Release No. 20381.

management. The latter was clearly an influence in fraudulent financial reporting that occurred in the past decade.

There are a number of potential sources that the auditor should consult in gathering information about management integrity; these include previous auditors, prior-year audit experience, and independent sources of information.

Previous Auditors

A client acceptance or retention decision should include interviews with previous partners and audit staff to learn of their experiences with the client. If there is a change in auditors, the auditor should meet with the previous auditor to find out his or her view of reasons for the change, including information regarding any disputes with management and the quality of the client's controls. Client permission is required before the auditor can meet with the previous auditor because of the confidentiality of the information. Refusal to provide such access should represent a clear warning signal to the auditor.

All SEC-registered companies are required to report, on Form 8-K, a change in the auditing firm, and the reasons for that change, within four business days of the change. The registrant must specifically comment on whether the company had any significant disagreements with its auditors over accounting principles, auditing procedures, or other financial reporting matters and must indicate the name of the new audit firm. The dismissed audit firm must communicate with the SEC, stating whether it agrees with the information reported by the client.

In addition, the new auditor of a public company is required to communicate with the previous auditor and management to determine the reason for the change. The new auditor is particularly interested in determining whether there were any disagreements with the client on auditing or accounting procedures that would have led to the predecessor auditor's dismissal or resignation. Audit standards suggest inquiries that focus on the following:

- Integrity of management
- Disagreements with management as to accounting principles, auditing procedures, or other similarly significant matters
- The predecessor auditor's understanding of the reasons for the change of auditors

> **PRACTICAL POINT**
>
> All of the national CPA firms have formal client acceptance procedures whereby the firm considers factors in both (a) accepting new clients and (b) retaining existing clients where either audit risk is increasing or fee realization is decreasing. Usually these decisions are reviewed at the regional or national management level, especially if they involve high-risk clients.

> **PRACTICAL POINT**
>
> There is no formal filing of a report describing changes in auditors of a nonpublic company.

- Any communications by the predecessor to the client's management or audit committee concerning fraud, illegal acts by the client, and matters related to internal control

Prior-Year Audit Experience

The auditor has a wealth of information that should be in current or prior year's audit workpapers. The auditor should evaluate management's:

- Cooperation in dealing with financial reporting problems
- Attitude in identifying and reporting on complex accounting issues
- Commitment to implementing effective risk management and internal control processes
- Knowledge of the industry and business forces
- Approach to dealing with problems strategically vs. an alternative approach that focuses on managing earnings
- Handling of disputes regarding accounting treatments
- Attitude toward private meetings with the audit committee
- Cooperation in preparing schedules for audit analysis

Independent Sources of Information

The auditor should consider, where appropriate, obtaining evidence from the following sources:

- Independent, private investigations, e.g., those done by a private investigation firm—used when considering accepting an unknown client with unknown managers or board members
- References from key business leaders such as bankers and lawyers
- Background search records—such inquiries are routine and are usually conducted annually for all top management and members of the board of directors
- Past filings with regulatory agencies such as the SEC

A summary of sources of information about management integrity is shown in Exhibit 4.2.

> **PRACTICAL POINT**
>
> Many small businesses will not have audit committees but may have a board that acts as an audit committee. The board may include outside stakeholders.

Independence and Competence of the Audit Committee and Board

In public companies, the audit committee represents the shareholders and, in that role, is the audit firm's primary client. The auditor should gather enough information to assess whether the audit committee is both competent and acts in an independent fashion. The auditor should also understand the audit committee's commitment to transparent financial reporting and its approach in supporting internal auditing as an independent review function. The auditor should also evaluate whether the board, as a whole, is sufficiently knowledgeable and engaged to perform its required oversight role.

> **PRACTICAL POINT**
>
> Inadequate controls and risk management processes constitute a sufficient reason to not accept a potential audit client.

> **PRACTICAL POINT**
>
> Prior to the financial crisis, Bear Stearns engaged in high-risk transactions that resulted in a dangerous level of mortgage-backed securities. This risky management practice was likely the result of Bear Stearns's lack of attention to its risk management policies.

Quality of Management's Risk Management Process and Controls

The auditor should assess management's commitment to implementing an effective risk management system. The commitment to risk management and internal control signals much about the direction of management and its focus on long-term operations. A company without such a commitment

Exhibit 4.2 | Sources of Information Regarding Management Integrity

1. *Predecessor auditor.* Information obtained directly through inquiries is required by professional standards. The predecessor is required to respond to the auditor unless such data are under a court order, or if the client will not approve communicating confidential information.

2. *Other professionals in the business community.* Examples include lawyers and bankers with whom the auditor will normally have good working relationships and of whom the auditor will make inquiries as part of the process of getting to know the client.

3. *Other auditors within the audit firm.* Other auditors within the firm may have dealt with current management in connection with other engagements or with other clients.

4. *News media and Web searches.* Information about the company and its management may be available in financial journals, magazines, industry trade magazines, or more importantly on the Web.

5. *Public databases.* Computerized databases can be searched for public documents dealing with management or any articles on the company. Similarly, public databases such as LEXIS can be searched for the existence of legal proceedings against the company or key members of management.

6. *Preliminary interviews with management.* Such interviews can be helpful in understanding the amount, extent, and reasons for turnover in key positions. Personal interviews can also be helpful in analyzing the "frankness" or "evasiveness" of management in dealing with important company issues affecting the audit.

7. *Audit committee members.* Members of the audit committee may have been involved in disputes between the previous auditors and management and may be able to provide additional insight.

8. *Inquiries of federal regulatory agencies.* Although this is not a primary source of information, the auditor may have reason to make inquiries of specific regulatory agencies regarding pending actions against the company or the history of regulatory actions taken with respect to the company and its management.

9. *Private investigation firms.* Use of such firms is rare, but is increasingly being done when the auditor becomes aware of issues that merit further inquiry about management integrity or management's involvement in potential illegal activities.

should be viewed as one that heightens engagement risk. Sometimes the risk can be compensated for by performing additional audit procedures. However, research has shown that auditors cannot always perform enough audit procedures to adequately compensate for deficiencies in internal controls.

PRACTICAL POINT

The auditor should always review regulatory and internal audit reports to determine how management has reacted to problems that were identified previously.

Regulatory and Reporting Requirements

The auditor should review previous reports to regulatory agencies such as those filed with the SEC. In addition, some industries—banking, insurance, proprietary drugs, and transportation—are subject to regulatory oversight. Those agencies often conduct regulatory audits that auditors should review to determine if the regulatory auditors have identified problems with the company or its management.

Participation of Key Stakeholders

Outside stakeholders, including major stockholders, have an important stake in the audit. Generally, their views are represented on the board of directors. However, in some circumstances, it may make sense for the auditor to make inquiries of such stakeholders to (a) understand their concerns and (b) understand key compliance issues, e.g., lending agreements that will affect the conduct of the audit.

PRACTICAL POINT

Although auditors are generally anxious to get new audit clients, the auditor needs to thoroughly explore all the reasons that the company decided to change auditors to assess the risk of being associated with a new audit client.

Existence of Related-Party Transactions

The auditor should gather information, on a preliminary basis, to determine if a potential client is engaged in related-party transactions. Small companies in particular use related-party transactions to facilitate financing or to achieve tax benefits. However, such transactions often are used to manage earnings or to render the real financial condition of the company less transparent. For example, Tyco made numerous loans to top executives, which were then forgiven by company management and were used to entice the executives into more fraudulent cover-ups of transactions. WorldCom made loans to its top officers with no apparent schedule for repayment and engaged in financial transactions with companies owned by senior management. All of these transactions represent (a) conflicts of interest and (b) opportunities to influence the reported financial statements of the entity.

The Financial Health of the Organization

No business operates independently of the basic economy of the country in which it is located and, increasingly, of the overall global economy. The financial crisis of 2008 and the ensuing worldwide economic recession reiterate the interdependency of all organizations on global financial management. Every auditor must consider the condition of the current economy and its potential effect on the audit client. The financial crisis impaired the ability of companies to grow or forced companies to scale back operations and in some cases forced some businesses to fail in bankruptcy and to go out of business. A downward trend in the economy implies that:

- More companies will fail
- Companies will scale back their operations
- Companies will experience greater problems in collecting receivables or realizing the value of their inventory
- Many financial instruments will not be realized at their cost

The accounting model requires more market information be included in financial statements. In an economy with a downward trend, more companies will be assessing:

- Fixed assets for impairment, particularly when plants are being closed and operations scaled back
- Goodwill for impairment
- Accounts receivable for collectibility
- Inventory for net realizable value
- Significant financial instruments for current market value
- Pension plans and related pension assets for significant changes in value, and
- Liabilities, such as warranties or other accruals, for potential understatement

Auditors will have to test management's assertions related to these accounts, and we will fully develop the approach to testing these accounts throughout this text. The auditor must approach these accounts with an understanding that while there may be some subjectivity in valuing the assets and liabilities, the company needs to have a systematic approach determine the proper valuation.

In addition to performing traditional financial analysis, the auditor should seek to understand important financial-based contracts such as bank loan covenants, employee compensation, as well as regulatory requirements, existing litigation against the firm, and stock exchange listing requirements. Those contracts may provide motivation for management to misstate financial results.

Summary: High-Risk Audit Clients

The auditor evaluates the economic prospects of the company to help ensure that (a) important areas will be investigated and (b) the company will likely stay in business. High-risk companies are generally characterized by the following:

- Inadequate capital
- Lack of long-run strategic and operational plans
- Low cost of entry into the market
- Dependence on a limited product range
- Dependence on technology that may quickly become obsolete
- Instability of future cash flows
- History of questionable accounting practices
- Previous inquiries by the SEC or other regulatory agencies

A summary of international auditing standards that identify risks associated with financial statement misstatements is shown in the Auditing in Practice section below.

AUDITING *in Practice*

RISKS ASSOCIATED WITH FINANCIAL STATEMENT MISSTATEMENTS

International Standard on Auditing No. 315 provides an excellent summary of the varied risks that may be present in a company, and that may be associated with material misstatements in the company's financial statements. The existence of one or more of these risk factors does not necessarily mean that there is a material misstatement present, but it does indicate that the auditor will need to carefully consider and investigate that possibility, obviously leading to more audit work. As you read the list, notice that (1) the risks are associated with a wide range of both operations and financial reporting decisions, (2) the risks are sometimes hard to quantify and are judgmental in nature, and (3) many companies will have these risks but *not* have material misstatements, thus making it difficult for auditors to know when a risk factor truly is leading to a misstatement for their particular client. The list is as follows:

- Operations in regions that are economically unstable, e.g., countries with significant currency devaluation or highly inflationary economies
- Operations exposed to volatile markets, e.g., futures trading
- Operations that are subject to a high degree of complex regulation
- Going concern and liquidity issues including loss of significant customers, or constraints on the availability of capital or credit
- Offering new products, or moving into new lines of business
- Changes in the entity such as acquisitions or reorganizations

- Entities or business segments likely to be sold
- The existence of complex alliances and joint ventures
- Use of off balance sheet finance, special-purpose entities, and other complex financing arrangements
- Significant transactions with related parties
- Lack of personnel with appropriate accounting and financial reporting skills
- Changes in key personnel, including departure of key executives
- Deficiencies in internal control, especially those not addressed by management
- Changes in the IT system or environment, and inconsistencies between the entity's IT strategy and its business strategies
- Inquiries into the entity's operations or financial results by regulatory bodies
- Past misstatements, history of errors or significant adjustments at period end
- Significant amount of non-routine or non-systematic transactions, including intercompany transactions and large revenue transactions at period end
- Transactions that are recorded based on management's intent, e.g., debt refinancing, assets to be sold and classification of marketable securities
- Accounting measurements that involve complex processes
- Pending litigation and contingent liabilities, e.g., sales warranties, financial guarantees and environmental remediation

The Purpose of an Engagement Letter

The auditor and client (the audit committee) should have a mutual understanding of the nature of the audit services to be performed, the timing of these services, the expected fees and the basis on which they will be billed, the responsibilities of the auditor in searching for fraud, the client's responsibilities for preparing information for the audit, and the need for other services to be performed by the audit firm. The audit firm should prepare an engagement letter summarizing and documenting this understanding between the auditor and the client. The **engagement letter** clarifies the responsibilities and expectations of each party and thus is an important element of managing engagement risk—especially the risk related to litigation. The client also acknowledges those expectations (see Exhibit 4.3).

Exhibit 4.3	Audit Engagement Letter

Rittenberg, Johnstone, and Gramling
5823 Monticello Court
Madison, WI 53711

June 1, 2011

Mr. Dan Finneran, President
Mr. Paul Donovan, Chair, Audit Committee
President Rhinelander Equipment Co., Inc.
700 East Main Street
Rhinelander, WI 56002
Dear Mr. Finneran and Mr. Donovan:

Thank you for meeting with us to discuss the requirements of our forthcoming engagement. We will audit the consolidated balance sheet of Rhinelander Equipment Co., and its subsidiaries, Black Warehouse Co., Inc., and Green Machinery Corporation, as of December 31, 2011, and the related consolidated statements of income, retained earnings, and cash flows for the year then ended. We will also perform an audit of your internal accounting controls. Our audit work will be performed in accordance with auditing standards in the United States established by the Public Company Accounting Oversight Board, and will include examining, on a test basis, evidence supporting the amounts and disclosures in the financial statements, testing the operation of significant controls, assessing the accounting principles used and significant estimates made by management, as well as evaluating the overall financial statement presentation.

The objective of our engagement is the completion of the foregoing audit and, upon its completion and subject to its findings, the rendering of our report. As you know, the financial statements are the responsibility of the management and board of directors of your company, who are primarily responsible for the data and information set forth therein as well as for the maintenance of an appropriate internal control structure (which includes adequate accounting records and procedures to safeguard the company's assets). Accordingly, as required by the standards of the Public Company Accounting Oversight Board, our procedures will include obtaining written confirmation from management concerning important representations on which we will rely.

Also as required by auditing standards, we will plan and perform our audit to obtain reasonable, but not absolute, assurance about whether the financial statements are free of material misstatement. Accordingly, any such audit is not a guarantee of the accuracy of the financial statements and is subject to the inherent risk that errors and fraud (or illegal acts), if they exist, might not be detected. If we become aware of any unusual matters during the course of our audit, we will bring them to your attention. Should you then wish us to expand our normal auditing procedures, we would be pleased to work with you to develop a separate engagement for that purpose.

Our engagement will also include preparation of federal income tax returns for the three corporations for the year ended December 31, 2011, and a review of federal and state income tax returns for the same period prepared by your accounting staff. However, in order to maintain a detachment from management, our firm will not be preparing the tax returns of management.

Our billings for the services set forth in this letter will be based upon our per diem rates for this type of work plus out-of-pocket expenses; billings will be rendered at the beginning of each month on an estimated basis and are payable upon receipt. This engagement includes only those services specifically described in this letter; appearances before judicial proceedings or government organizations, such as the Internal Revenue Service, the Securities and Exchange Commission, or other regulatory bodies, arising out of this engagement will be billed to you separately.

We are enclosing an explanation of certain of our Firm's Client Service Concepts. We have found that such explanation helps communicate our commitment to the highest level of customer service.

We look forward to providing the services described in this letter, as well as other services agreeable to us both. In the unlikely event that any differences concerning our services or fees should arise that are not resolved by mutual agreement, we both recognize that the matter will probably involve complex business or accounting issues that would be decided most equitably to both parties by a judge hearing the evidence without a jury. Accordingly, you and we agree to waive any right to a trial by jury in any action, proceeding, or counterclaim arising out of or relating to our services and fees. If you are in agreement with the terms of this letter, please sign one copy and return it for our files. We appreciate the opportunity to work with you.

Very truly yours,

Larry E. Rittenberg

RITTENBERG, JOHNSTONE, and GRAMLING

Larry E. Rittenberg
Engagement Partner

LER:lk
Enc.

The foregoing letter fully describes our understanding and is accepted by us.
RHINELANDER EQUIPMENT CO., INC.

June 5, 2011

Mr. Dan Finneran, President
Mr. Paul Donovan, Chair, Audit Committee

Managing Audit Risk
Materiality

The auditor is expected to design and conduct an audit that provides reasonable assurance that material misstatements will be detected. Audit risk and materiality are interrelated in that audit risk is defined in terms of materiality; i.e., audit risk is the risk that unknown, but material, misstatement(s) exist in the financial statements after the audit has been performed.

Materiality is a concept that conveys a sense of significance or importance of an item. But, we must ask, Significant to whom? And how important? The auditor and management can often disagree on whether a transaction or misstatement is material. Further, a dollar amount that may be significant to one person may not be significant to another. Despite these measurement difficulties, the concept of materiality is pervasive and guides the nature and extent of auditing, so it is essential to understand it in the context of designing and conducting a high quality audit. There are various definitions of materiality, and we highlight two below that capture the essential elements of this idea.

The FASB defines **materiality** as the

magnitude of an omission or misstatement of accounting information that, in light of surrounding circumstances, makes it *probable* that the judgment of a reasonable person relying on the information would have been changed or influenced by the omission or misstatement.

LO 3

Discuss the relevance of materiality in an audit context, and articulate the relationship between materiality and audit risk.

The Supreme Court of the United States offers a somewhat different definition and states that

a fact is material if there is a substantial likelihood that the ... fact would have been viewed by the reasonable investor as having significantly altered the "total mix" of information made available (see AS No. 11).

Regardless of how it is specifically defined, materiality includes both the nature of the misstatement as well as the dollar amount of misstatement and must be judged in relation to importance placed on the amount by financial statement users. Thus, auditors need to understand the needs of financial statements users in order to make appropriate materiality judgments.

Materiality Guidance

Most public accounting firms provide specific written guidance and decision aids to assist auditors in making consistent materiality judgments. The guidelines usually involve applying percentages to some base, such as total assets, total revenue, or pretax income (e.g., 5% of net income). In choosing a base, the auditor considers the stability of the base from year to year so that materiality does not fluctuate significantly between annual audits. Income is often more volatile than total assets or revenue.

A simple guideline for small business audits could be, for example, to set overall materiality at 1% of total assets or revenue, whichever is higher. A traditional starting point for many companies is 5% of net income. The percentage may be smaller for large clients. Some CPA firms have more complicated guidance that may be based on the nature of the industry or a composite of materiality decisions made by experts in the firm. Still, any guidance is just that. The auditor may use the guidance as a starting point that should be adjusted for the qualitative conditions of the particular audit. For example, a company may have restrictive covenants on its bond indenture to maintain a current ratio of at least 2:1. If that ratio per the books is near the requirement, a smaller overall materiality may be required for auditing current assets and liabilities.

Statement on Auditing Standards No. 107 provides the AICPA's basic guidance on materiality judgments, and it is consistent with the PCAOB's AS No. 11, and the IAASB's ISA 320, which also address this topic. Overall, existing professional guidance notes that auditors must make materiality assessments for (1) audit planning and (2) evidence evaluation after audit tests are completed. The auditor considers materiality at both the overall financial statement level and in relation to classes of transactions, account balances, and disclosures. To determine the nature, timing, and extent of audit procedures, the materiality level for the financial statements as a whole should be stated as a specific monetary amount. For purposes of planning the audit, auditors should consider overall materiality in terms of the smallest aggregate level of misstatements that could be material to any one of the financial statements. For example, if the auditor believes that misstatements aggregating approximately $100,000 would be material to the income statement, but misstatements aggregating approximately $200,000 would be material to the balance sheet, the auditor typically assesses overall materiality at $100,000 or less (not $200,000 or less).

After establishing overall materiality at the financial statement level, auditors may decide to set a planning level of materiality that is relevant at the transaction or account balance level. **Planning materiality** is typically less than overall materiality and helps the auditor determine the extent of audit evidence needed. Planning materiality allows for the possibility that some misstatements that are less than overall materiality could, when aggregated with other misstatements, result in a material misstatement of the financial

AUDITING *in Practice*

AICPA CLARITY PROJECT AND MATERIALITY OF IDENTIFIED MISSTATEMENTS

A new SAS, *Evaluation of Misstatements Identified During the Audit,* is effective for audits of financial statements for periods ending on or after December 15, 2012.

The requirements in the SAS state that auditors must document the following items regarding their materiality judgments:

- "The amount below which misstatements are considered to be clearly trivial;

- All misstatements accumulated during the audit (other than those considered to be clearly trivial) and whether they have been corrected; and
- A conclusion as to whether uncorrected misstatements are material, either individually or in the aggregate, and the basis for that conclusion."

---

statements overall. Planning materiality relates to the concept of **tolerable misstatement**, which is the amount of misstatement in an account balance that the auditor could tolerate and still not judge the underlying account balance to be materially misstated. Planning materiality and tolerable misstatement move together; when planning materiality is set at a low level, tolerable misstatement is also set at a low level.

Auditors need to aggregate all potential misstatements in a place where the audit team can assess the materiality of misstatements. The accumulation of such information is often based on **posting materiality**—a materiality level where the auditor believes errors below that level would not, even when aggregated with all other misstatements, be material to the financial statements. For example, if posting materiality is set at $5,000, misstatements that the auditor detects that are below that amount would essentially be ignored for purposes of suggesting corrections to the client regarding misstatements that were detected during the course of the audit.

Changes in Materiality Judgments as the Audit Progresses

The auditor makes judgments about materiality at the overall financial statement level, planning materiality, tolerable misstatements, and posting materiality during the planning phase of the audit. Sometimes these judgments need to be revised after more facts about the client and its circumstances become known during the audit. Situations that would necessitate a change in materiality judgments include the following:

- Initial materiality judgments were based on estimated or preliminary financial statement amounts that turn out to be different from the audited amounts at the end of the audit.
- The financial statement amounts used in initially making the materiality judgments have changed significantly. For example, if during the course of the audit, the financial statements were adjusted significantly, then the initial materiality judgments may need to be adjusted accordingly.

If materiality judgments change during the course of the audit, then auditors will have to re-assess their decisions that relied on these judgments. For example, if planning materiality turns out to have been set too high, then detected misstatements that were deemed "immaterial" may later turn out to be deemed "material." Further, if planning materiality had been set too high, then the auditor may need to go back and modify the nature, timing, and extent of audit procedures.

SEC Guidance on Materiality

The SEC has been critical of the accounting profession for not sufficiently examining qualitative factors in making materiality decisions. In particular, the SEC has criticized the profession for:

- *Netting (offsetting) material misstatements* and not making adjustments because the net effect may not be material to net income. However, each account item may have been affected by a material amount.
- *Not applying the materiality concept to "swings" in accounting estimates.* For example, an accounting estimate could be misstated by just under a material amount in one direction one year and just under a material amount in the opposite direction the next year. The SEC says the materiality amount should be figured by looking at the total "swing" in estimates over the two-year period rather than by using the "best estimate" each year.
- *Consistently "passing" on individual adjustments that may not be considered material.* The SEC believes that the auditor should look at the qualitative nature of each misstatement and the potential aggregate effect of the misstatement. The SEC does not understand why a client would not be willing to adjust for a known error—even if it believes it is immaterial. The SEC often asks, if it is not material, why would management object to a change in the account balance?

We expand on concepts concerning materiality in Chapter 18.

Understanding the Audit Risk Model

Audit Risk Defined

LO 4

Describe the audit risk model and its components.

The risk that the auditor may give an unqualified opinion on materially misstated financial statements is called **audit risk**. Audit risk is determined and managed by the auditor. It is intertwined with materiality and is influenced by

AUDITING *in Practice*

WHAT MAKES A QUANTITATIVELY SMALL MISSTATEMENT MATERIAL?

The SEC provides guidance on situations in which a *quantitatively* small misstatement may still be considered material because of *qualitative* reasons. These include the following:

- the misstatement hides a failure to meet analysts' consensus expectations for the company
- the misstatement changes a loss into income or vice versa
- the misstatement concerns a segment or other portion of the company's business that plays a significant role in the company's operations or profitability
- the misstatement affects the company's compliance with regulatory requirements
- the misstatement affects the company's compliance with loan covenants or other contractual requirements
- the misstatement has the effect of increasing management's compensation—e.g., by satisfying requirements for the

award of bonuses or other forms of incentive compensation
- the misstatement involves concealment of an unlawful transaction

The above examples highlight situations in which management may argue that an amount is quantitatively immaterial and therefore should be allowed to remain uncorrected in the audited financial statements. This guidance from the SEC helps auditors to provide a rationale to managers about why such misstatements need to be corrected. Further, the auditors should consider these factors when setting planning materiality so that the audit will be designed to identify misstatements that might seem small but could make a difference to the user of the financial statements.

Exhibit 4.4	Relationship Between Engagement Risk and Audit Risk		
	ENGAGEMENT RISK		
	High	**Moderate**	**Low**
AUDIT RISK	Do not accept client	Set very low	Set within professional standards, but can be higher than companies with higher engagement risk
NUMERICAL EXAMPLE OF AUDIT RISK	None—Do not accept client (0.0)	0.01	0.05

engagement risk. The interrelationship of audit risk and engagement risk is shown in Exhibit 4.4, which shows that the auditor *assesses* engagement risk and then *sets* audit risk.

Inseparability of Audit Risk and Materiality

Audit risk and engagement risk relate to factors that would likely encourage someone to challenge the auditor's work. If a company is on the brink of bankruptcy, transactions that might not be material to a "healthy" company of similar size may be material to the users of the potentially bankrupt company's financial statements.

The following factors are important in integrating concepts of risk and materiality in the conduct of an audit:

1. *All audits involve testing* and thus cannot provide 100% assurance that the company's financial statements are correct without inordinately driving up the cost of audits. Thus, there is always some risk that some material misstatement might not be uncovered.
2. *Some clients are not worth accepting.* Because audits rely on testing, and to some extent on the integrity of management, there are some clients that an audit firm should not accept (engagement risk is too high).
3. Auditing firms must *compete in an active marketplace* for clients who choose auditors based on such factors as fees, service, personal rapport, industry knowledge, and the ability to assist the client.
4. Auditors need to *understand society's expectations* of financial reporting to minimize audit risk and formulate reasonable materiality judgments. Society's expectations are often articulated in lawsuits that the auditor wants to avoid.
5. Auditors must *identify the risky areas of a business* to determine which account balances are more susceptible to material misstatement, how the misstatements might occur, and how a client might be able to cover them up.
6. Auditors need to develop methodologies to *allocate overall assessments of materiality* to individual account balances because some account balances may be more important to *users*.

PRACTICAL POINT

Engagement risk deals with whether the auditor wants to be associated with a client. Audit risk comes into play when the auditor accepts an association with a client and is related to the planning of that audit.

PRACTICAL POINT

Auditors must always balance audit risk and audit fees. When audit risk is set low (i.e., the auditor is only willing to accept a low risk of issuing an unqualified opinion on materially misstated financial statements), more audit work is required, thus potentially driving up audit fees. But when fees are high, the audit client may decide to put the audit out for bid, thus inviting competition from other audit firms for the audit engagement.

The Audit Risk Model

The auditor sets the desired audit risk based on the assessment of engagement risk. Audit risk is often illustrated using numeric examples. Many audit firms utilize the measures associated with statistical sampling to set audit risk, e.g., setting audit risk at a 1% level for clients with high engagement risk and at 5% for lower engagement risk clients. Other auditing firms work with the broader descriptions of audit risk as high, moderate, or low and adjust the nature of their audit procedures accordingly. Setting audit risk at 1% is equivalent to performing a statistical test using a 99% confidence level. Audit risk set at 1% implies that the auditor is willing to take a 1% chance of issuing an unqualified audit opinion on materially misstated financial statements. Audit risk set at 5% implies that the auditor is willing to take a 5% chance of issuing an unqualified audit opinion on materially misstated financial statements. It is acceptable for auditors to take on higher levels of audit risk for clients with lower levels of engagement risk.

The following general observations influence the implementation of the audit risk model:

- Complex or unusual transactions are more likely to be recorded in error than are recurring or routine transactions.
- The better the organization's internal controls, the lower the likelihood of material misstatements.
- The amount and persuasiveness of audit evidence gathered should vary inversely with audit risk; i.e., lower audit risk requires gathering more persuasive evidence.

These general premises have been incorporated into an audit risk (*AR*) model with three components: inherent risk (*IR*), control risk (*CR*), and detection risk (*DR*) as follows:

$$AR = f(IR, CR, DR)$$

PRACTICAL POINT

The auditor's assessment of risk of material misstatement, including fraud risks, should continue throughout the audit. As the auditor obtains new audit evidence, the auditor may need to revise the initial risk assessments and modify planned audit procedures.

where

Inherent risk (*IR*) is the susceptibility of an assertion to a misstatement, because of error or fraud, that could be material, individually or in combination with other misstatements, before consideration of any related controls. Stated simply, inherent risk is the initial susceptibility of a transaction or accounting adjustment to be recorded in error, or for the transaction not to be recorded in the absence of internal controls.

Control risk (*CR*) is the risk that a misstatement because of error or fraud that could occur in an assertion and that could be material, individually or in combination with other misstatements, will not be prevented or detected on a timely basis by the company's internal control. Stated simply, control risk is the risk that the client's internal control system will fail to prevent or detect a misstatement.

Detection risk (*DR*) is the risk that the procedures performed by the auditor will not detect a misstatement that exists and that could be material, individually or in combination with other misstatements. Stated simply, detection risk is the risk that the audit procedures will fail to detect a material misstatement.

The audit risk model is sometimes written as a multiplicative model in the following form to illustrate the logical relationships within the model:

$$AR = IR \times CR \times DR$$

PRACTICAL POINT

Although the audit risk model does not include a term for fraud risk, a well-developed risk assessment process considers the risk of fraud throughout the entire audit process rather than approaching the assessment of fraud risk as a separate component of the audit.

Stated simply, audit risk is the risk that the auditor may give an unqualified opinion on materially misstated financial statements. It is influenced by (*IR*) the likelihood that a transaction, estimate, or adjustment might be recorded incorrectly; (*CR*) the likelihood that the client's internal control processes would fail to prevent or detect the misstatement; and (*DR*) the likelihood that, if a misstatement occurred, the auditor's procedures would fail to detect the misstatement.

Audit risk is a planning judgment that is *set* by the auditor. The auditor *assesses* the inherent and control risks (the **risk of material misstatement** existing in the accounting records) for each significant component of the financial statements of the organization. From these two assessments, the auditor *determines* the level of detection risk that the audit firm needs to control for the potential misstatement in each significant component of the financial statements.

Inherent risk recognizes that an error is more likely to occur in some areas than in others. For example, an error is more likely to occur in calculating foreign currency translation amounts or in making deferred income tax projections than in recording a normal sale. As the auditor identifies accounts that are more susceptible to material misstatement, the audit plan should be adjusted to reflect the increased inherent risk. **Control risk** reflects the possibility that the client's system of controls will allow erroneous items to be recorded and not detected in the ordinary course of processing.

Internal control may vary with classes of transactions: Controls over the recording of receivables, for example, may be strong, but those for recording foreign currency transactions may be much weaker. Because of the inherent limitations associated with all internal controls, the professional standards recognize that some control risk is present in every audit engagement.

There is a relationship of internal control to **financial reporting risk** that should be understood: *The only purpose of controls is to mitigate risk.* In other words, internal controls do not exist in a vacuum; rather they are developed to address specific risk concerns. For example, when dealing with financial reporting risk, the auditor understands that there are specific risks associated with processing a transaction; e.g., the transaction may be lost, duplicated, inaccurately recorded, or recorded in the wrong period. Controls—and control risk—must be assessed in relationship to their ability to mitigate the risks that affect the account balance.

Detection risk is controlled by the auditor and is an integral part of audit planning. Detection risk is affected by both the effectiveness of the auditing procedures that the auditor performs and the extent to which those procedures were performed with due professional care. The auditor's determination of detection risk influences the nature, amount, and timing of audit procedures to ensure that the audit achieves no more than the desired audit risk.

In summary, inherent risk and control risk are existing features of the audit client that the auditor cannot control. A high level of inherent or control risk means that the company is more likely to have misstatements associated with these risks. On the other hand, audit risk and detection risk are risks that the auditor faces, and that the auditor can (and has the obligation to) therefore manage. A high level of audit or detection risk means that the audit firm is willing to take a higher risk of issuing an unqualified opinion on materially misstated financial statements; an audit firm would only accept such a heightened risk if the client's inherent and control risks are *low*.

Illustration of the Audit Risk Model   Consider the typical accounting system as an input-process-output model (Exhibit 4.5). The output is the financial statement account balance. The input and process represent the client's internal controls and the difficulty in recording the transaction or accounting entry. If the input and process are reliable, then there is little likelihood that the account balance is misstated. The auditor would need to perform only a minimal amount of work to ensure that the account balance is correct. However, as

PRACTICAL POINT

Setting audit risk is an auditor judgment that is affected by the riskiness of the client. It is a starting point for planning what audit work should be performed and how much work should be performed.

PRACTICAL POINT

Auditors can only assess the inherent risk and control risk; managers of the company are charged with managing these risks. When assessing control risk the auditor will make a preliminary assessment based on an understanding of the client's internal controls. In some cases, that assessment will be updated according to the evidence the auditor obtains as to whether the controls are effectively working.

PRACTICAL POINT

Risks and controls are always interrelated. Controls exist only to address risks, and the quality of internal controls must be assessed by whether or not they effectively mitigate a risk.

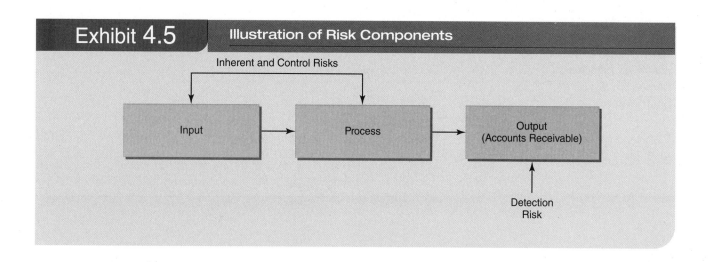

| Exhibit 4.5 | Illustration of Risk Components |

PRACTICAL POINT

Direct tests of account balances represent one type of testing, referred to as "substantive testing." The auditor's decision on direct tests includes both the type of procedures to perform and how much audit evidence should be gathered.

part of ensuring that the input and process are reliable, the auditor would need to test whether the input and process controls were operating effectively.

However, if the client's internal controls are inadequate, or management is motivated to misstate the account balance, or if the nature of the transactions are inherently difficult, then the risk of material misstatements occurring and not being detected and corrected is quite high. Consequently, the auditor will do more work in testing the account balance. Audit risk is held constant, but the high levels of inherent and control risk demand that the auditor's detection risk be small in order to control audit risk at the predetermined level.

The audit risk model may also be illustrated using a quantitative approach with probability assessments applied to each of the model's components. Although useful, a strictly quantitative approach tends to give the appearance that all components can be precisely measured—when they cannot be. Therefore, many public accounting firms apply subjective, qualitative assessments to each model component; control risk, for example, is identified as high, moderate, or low.

Quantitative Example of Audit Risk: High Risk of Material Misstatement
Assume an audit of an organization with many complex transactions and weak internal controls. The auditor assesses both inherent risk and control risk at their maximum, implying that the client does not have effective internal control and there is a high risk that a transaction would be recorded incorrectly. Assume that engagement risk is high and the auditor has set audit risk at the 0.01 level; i.e., the auditor does not want to take much of a risk that a misstatement goes unfound in the financial statements.

The effect on detection risk, and, thus, the extent of audit procedures, is as follows:

$$AR = IR \times CR \times DR$$
$$\text{therefore,} \quad DR = AR \div (IR \times CR)$$
$$DR = 0.01 \div (1.0 \times 1.0) = 0.01, \text{ or } 1\%$$

In this case, detection risk and audit risk are the same because the auditor cannot rely on internal controls to prevent or detect misstatements. The illustration yields the intuitive result: Poor controls and a high likelihood of misstatement lead to extended audit work to maintain audit risk at an acceptable level.

PRACTICAL POINT

Because of the Sarbanes-Oxley Act, many companies have invested in internal controls over transactions and have reduced control risk. However, there may be high control risk in some areas, e.g., estimates or complex financial instruments. Thus, control risk assessments are account-specific, and are often assertion-specific as well.

Quantitative Example: Low Risk of Material Misstatement   Assume that the client has simple transactions, well-trained accounting personnel, no incentive to misstate the financial statements, and effective internal control. The auditor's previous experience with the client, an understanding of the client's internal controls, and the results of preliminary testing this year indicate a low risk of material misstatement existing in the accounting records. The auditor assesses inherent and control risk as low as 50% and 20%, respectively. Audit risk is set at 0.05 consistent with a low engagement risk.

The auditor's determination of detection risk for this engagement would be

$$DR = AR \div (IR \times CR)$$
$$DR = 0.05 \div (0.50 \times 0.20) = 0.50, \text{ or } 50\%$$

In other words, the auditor could design tests of the accounting records with a lower detection risk, in this case 50%, because only minimal substantive tests of account balances are needed to provide corroborating evidence on the expectations that the accounts are not materially misstated. However, the auditor would have had to test whether the controls were operating effectively in order to support a control risk assessment below 100%.

Limitations of the Audit Risk Model

The audit risk model has some limitations that make its actual implementation difficult. In addition to the danger that auditors will look at the model too mechanically, CPA firms in determining their approach to implementing the model have considered the following limitations:

1. *Inherent risk is difficult to formally assess.* Some transactions are more susceptible to error, but it is difficult to assess that level of risk independent of the client's accounting system.
2. *Audit risk is judgmentally determined.* Many auditors set audit risk at a nominal level, such as 5%. However, no firm could survive if 5% of its audits were in error. Audit risk on most engagements is much lower than 5% because of conservative assumptions that take place when inherent risk is assessed at the maximum. Setting inherent risk at 100% implies that every transaction is initially recorded in error. It is very rare that every transaction would be in error. Because such a conservative assessment leads to more audit work, the real level of audit risk will be significantly less than 5%.
3. The model *treats each risk component as separate and independent* when in fact the components are not independent. It is difficult to separate an organization's internal controls and inherent risk.
4. *Audit technology is not so precisely developed that each component of the model can be accurately assessed.* Auditing is based on testing; precise estimates of the model's components are not possible. Auditors can, however, make subjective assessments and use the audit risk model as a guide.
5. The model is *not particularly useful for helping auditors determine the necessary control testing for issuing an opinion on the effectiveness of internal controls* as is be required in an integrated audit.

Planning the Audit Using the Audit Risk Model

Lessons Learned: The Lincoln Savings and Loan Case

Professors Erickson, Mayhew, and Felix make the case for a greater understanding of business risk in an article entitled "Why Do Audits Fail? Evidence from Lincoln Savings and Loan."[1] In examining one of the major savings and loan failures of the 1980s, the authors noted that the auditors had apparently followed standard audit procedures and yet failed to discover major misstatements in the financial statements. They concluded that the auditors would have done a much better job of finding the misstatements had they understood more about the business, economic trends affecting the client, and the risks inherent in the client's transactions. The authors cited two major reasons for their conclusions:

> First, in cases of management fraud, auditors are unlikely to receive reliable evidence from a client.... Second, a business understanding approach can provide reliable audit evidence even in the presence of management fraud. Specifically, economic data and information in the financial press provided a reliable basis from which Lincoln Savings and Loan's (LSL) auditors could have developed expectations about LSL's operations.[2]

Let's examine their conclusions a little further. If there are major problems within a company, it is likely that the reliability of evidence gathered from

LO 5

Articulate some limitations of the audit risk model.

PRACTICAL POINT

Audit risk is a concept that drives the auditor's planning and executing an audit. The illustrations are designed to provide guidance, but should not be rotely applied to any audit client. The key to auditing in applying professional judgment based on the specifics of a given client situation.

LO 6

Use the audit risk model to plan the nature of procedures to be performed on an audit engagement.

---

[1]Erickson, M., Mayhew, B., & Felix, W. L. "Why Do Audits Fail? Evidence from Lincoln Savings and Loan," *Journal of Accounting Research,* Spring 2000.

[2]*Ibid.*

within the company will be reduced. Because of the reduced reliability of internally generated evidence, the auditor should (a) understand the company, its strategies, and operations in depth; (b) develop an understanding of the market in which the company operates, including economic trends, product trends, and competitor actions; (c) develop an understanding of the economics of the client's transactions; and (d) develop a set of expectations about financial results or transaction outcomes.

Lincoln Savings and Loan (LSL), although a savings and loan company, had made a number of real estate deals in the Phoenix area. If the auditors had followed a risk-based approach to determine where and how much audit evidence was needed, they would have learned the following:

- The company had increasingly moved to high-risk real estate transactions; that is, it moved beyond lending to real estate development and speculation.
- The real estate market in Phoenix, as well as in the rest of the Southwest, was in a significant downturn with fewer new housing starts.
- Most of the funds used to finance the sales that accounted for most of LSL's net income came from one single LSL subsidiary; that is, all the risks of the sale remained with LSL.
- Many of the real estate sales transactions that eventually defaulted would affect the parent company and not be isolated to a subsidiary that was partially kept off the books.

Erickson et al.'s description of the audit failure at LSL leads us to a better understanding of how to conduct a risk-based audit. The fundamental concept is simple. By understanding the nature of the business, management motivation, the client's control system, and the complexity of transactions, the auditor can better determine the risks that a particular account balance may be misstated. The auditor should focus greater skepticism and greater audit testing on the account balances and disclosures that contain the highest risk of material misstatement.

The PCAOB's AS 12, *Identifying and Assessing Risks of Material Misstatement*, provides excellent examples of situations in which business risks may ultimately result in material misstatements in the financial statements:

- Industry developments (a potential related business risk might be, e.g., that the company does not have the personnel or expertise to deal with the changes in the industry.)
- New products and services (a potential related business risk might be, e.g., that the new product or service will not be successful.)
- Use of information technology ("IT") (a potential related business risk might be, e.g., that systems and processes are incompatible.)
- New accounting requirements (a potential related business risk might be, e.g., incomplete or improper implementation of a new accounting requirement.)
- Expansion of the business (a potential related business risk might be, e.g., that the demand for the company's products or services has not been accurately estimated.)
- The effects of implementing a strategy, particularly any effects that will lead to new accounting requirements (a potential related business risk might be, e.g., incomplete or improper implementation of the strategy.)
- Current and prospective financing requirements (a potential related business risk might be, e.g., the loss of financing due to the company's inability to meet financing requirements.)
- Regulatory requirements (a potential related business risk might be, e.g., that there is increased legal exposure.)

Importantly, both U.S. and international auditing standards emphasize the essential leadership role that the engagement partner should play in planning the audit. As the LSL example illustrates, audit planning often involves a high-level and sophisticated understanding of the client and its business model;

usually such an understanding is only attained through many years of auditing experience. Thus, auditing standards point out that early planning led by the engagement partner and informed by a careful consideration of each organization's unique business risks is critical to audit quality.

Every audit engagement should start with a thorough analysis of the company's business, its strategy, the nature of its transactions, its processes to identify and manage risk, and the economics of its transactions. The approach is summed up as follows:

- Develop an independent understanding of the business as well as the risks the organization faces.
- Use the risks identified to develop expectations about account balances and financial results.
- Assess the quality of the control system to manage risks.
- Determine residual risks and update expectations about financial account balances.
- Manage the remaining risk of account balance misstatement by responding to the risks of material misstatement.

An overview of this process and the activities involved in each step are shown in Exhibit 4.6. The exhibit also identifies the typical procedures performed in

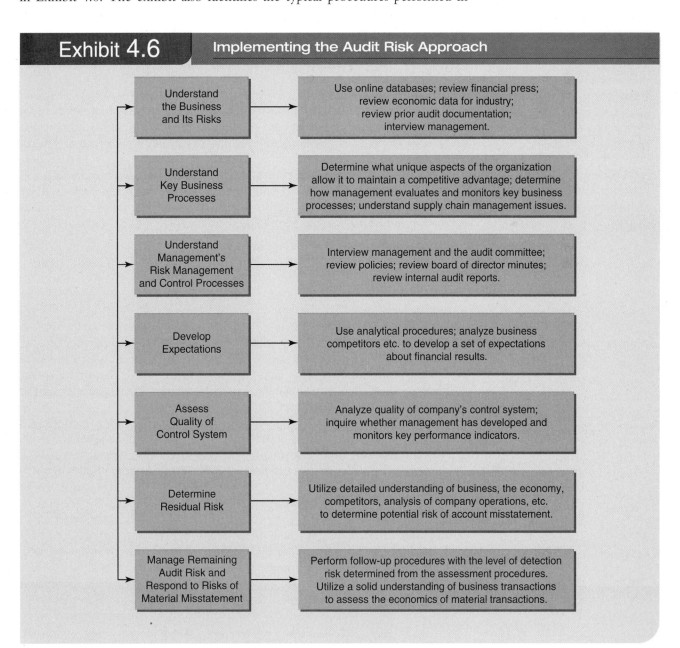

Exhibit 4.6 — Implementing the Audit Risk Approach

Understand the Business and Its Risks	Use online databases; review financial press; review economic data for industry; review prior audit documentation; interview management.
Understand Key Business Processes	Determine what unique aspects of the organization allow it to maintain a competitive advantage; determine how management evaluates and monitors key business processes; understand supply chain management issues.
Understand Management's Risk Management and Control Processes	Interview management and the audit committee; review policies; review board of director minutes; review internal audit reports.
Develop Expectations	Use analytical procedures; analyze business competitors etc. to develop a set of expectations about financial results.
Assess Quality of Control System	Analyze quality of company's control system; inquire whether management has developed and monitors key performance indicators.
Determine Residual Risk	Utilize detailed understanding of business, the economy, competitors, analysis of company operations, etc. to determine potential risk of account misstatement.
Manage Remaining Audit Risk and Respond to Risks of Material Misstatement	Perform follow-up procedures with the level of detection risk determined from the assessment procedures. Utilize a solid understanding of business transactions to assess the economics of material transactions.

each step of the audit process and how the auditor analyzes the risk of financial statement misstatement from the top down. Much of the risk of misstatement can be analyzed without directly testing the account balance.

Applying the process to the LSL example, the auditor would have seen that there were significant risks in the real estate loans and that the audit would need to go beyond traditional confirmations of account balances to gain a better understanding of significant transactions, the underlying collateral for the loans, and the relationship of the loans to other entities that make up the consolidated financial statements. The financial results that were at odds with the industry should have alerted the auditor to focus on the accounts that were most out of line and susceptible to financial manipulation. This point is important enough to repeat: The **risk-based approach** to auditing is dependent on the auditor's ability to understand the business sufficiently to identify account balances that are more likely to be materially misstated and then adjust audit procedures to increase the likelihood of detecting material misstatements—if they had occurred.

Implementing the Audit Risk Approach

Understand the Business and Its Risks

The auditor will make use of a variety of tools to understand the client's business and its business risk. Much of the work will be done by monitoring the financial press and SEC filings and broker analyses, developing a firm and industry-based knowledge management system, and utilizing other online information sources about a company. Some traditional approaches will continue to be used, including inquiries of management, reviews of internal risk management documentation, inquiries of business people, and review of legal or regulatory proceedings against the company. The following are some of the major online resources an auditor can use to learn more about a company:

- *Knowledge management systems*—Public accounting firms have developed these systems around industries, clients, and best practices. These systems also capture information about relevant accounting or regulatory requirements for the companies and can be utilized to develop "risk alerts" for the companies.
- *Online searches*—Internet search companies such as Hoovers On-Line are an excellent source of information about companies. Other online searches can be conducted through other portals such as Google. Yahoo has two excellent sources of information: (1) a financial section that provides data about most companies and (2) a "chat" line that contains current conversations about the company (much of which may be unreliable).
- *Review of SEC filings*—The SEC filings can be searched online through the EDGAR and IDEA systems. The filings include company annual and quarterly reports, proxy information, and registration statements for new security issues. These filings contain substantial information about the company and its affiliates, its officers, and directors. This information can be used to obtain an understanding of management's compensation arrangements, including incentive compensation that may provide important information about management incentives and bonus arrangements. Further, the auditor should monitor trading activity of the organization's securities, along with the relevant holdings of top-level management and/or board members.
- *Company websites*—A company's website may contain information that is useful in understanding its products and strategies. As companies move to

provide more financial information online, auditors will want to review these websites to keep abreast of developments.

- *Economic statistics*—Most industry data, including regional data, can now be found online. The auditor can compare the results of a client with regional economic data. For example, the auditor could easily question why a company is growing at a rate of 50% while the overall industry is declining by 20% or more. However, that question can be asked only if the auditor has industry information.
- *Professional practice bulletins*—The AICPA publishes "Audit Risk Alerts" online, and the SEC often issues practice bulletins to draw the profession's attention to important issues. The PCAOB has also published several "Staff Audit Practice Alerts" dealing with topics such as significant unusual transactions, fair value measurements, and the economic environment.
- *Stock analysts' reports*—Brokerage firms invest millions of dollars in conducting research about companies, their strategies, competitors, quality of management, and likelihood of success. Many of the major investment analysts are granted access to top management and are the beneficiaries of frequent analysts' meetings. These reports may contain a wealth of useful information about a client.
- *Company earnings calls*—The auditor can observe or read the transcripts of management's earnings calls in order to understand the most up-to-date issues that the organization is facing, along with management's publicly disclosed plans.

Application of Accounting Principles and Related Disclosures

One issue critical to understanding the client's business and its risks involves an analysis of management's selection and application of accounting principles, including related disclosures. The auditor needs to determine whether or not management's choices in this regard are appropriate for its business and are consistent with the applicable financial reporting framework for its industry. The auditor should develop expectations about the appropriate disclosures that are necessary and should compare those expectations to the reality of the disclosures made by management.

For example, the PCAOB's AS 12, *Identifying and Assessing Risks of Material Misstatement*, requires that the auditor obtain an understanding of the following types of matters relevant to understanding management's application of accounting principles and related disclosures:

- "Significant changes in the company's accounting principles, financial reporting policies, or disclosures and the reasons for such changes;
- The financial reporting competencies of personnel involved in selecting and applying significant new or complex accounting principles;
- The accounts or disclosures for which judgment is used in the application of significant accounting principles, especially in determining management's estimates and assumptions;
- The effect of significant accounting principles in controversial or emerging areas for which there is a lack of authoritative guidance or consensus;
- The methods the company uses to account for significant and unusual transactions; and
- Financial reporting standards and laws and regulations that are new to the company, including when and how the company will adopt such requirements."

Multi-Location Audit Engagements

Many companies are of sufficient complexity that they operate in many locations and are organized in terms of multiple business units (subsidiaries, divisions, branches, etc.). When planning the audit, it is essential that the auditor carefully considers the extent to which audit procedures will need to be performed at these different locations or business units, along with the timing of those procedures. In conducting this planning, there should be a correlation between the risk of material misstatement at the location or business unit and the extent to which the auditor will focus audit effort on that location or business unit. In other words, risky locations or business units should receive relatively more audit attention than other parts of the organization. Risk factors relevant to assessing the risk of material misstatement at a particular location or business unit include:

- The nature and amount of assets, liabilities, and transactions executed at the location or business unit. For example, are significant transactions executed at the location that are unusual or inappropriate for the normal business operations of the organization?
- The materiality of the location or business unit in terms of relative size or importance to the overall organization.
- Specific or unique risks of the location or business unit that heighten the risk of material misstatement.
- The extent to which the organization has centralized its record-keeping and information-processing systems.
- The effectiveness of the organization's control environment. For example, does management appear to have effectively delegated control over the organization to others? Does management appear to effectively supervise activities at various locations or business units?
- The extent to which management monitors activities of the organization at various locations or business units.

Understand Key Business Processes

Each organization has a key processes that give it a competitive advantage (or disadvantage). The auditor should gather sufficient information to understand these processes, the industry factors affecting key processes, how management monitors the processes and performance, and the potential operational and financial effects associated with key processes. For example, a major computer manufacturer may have important processes focusing on distribution and supply chain management. The auditor wants to gain assurance that management identifies the risks associated with the supply chain and how those risks might affect:

- Inventory levels
- Potential obsolescence of inventory
- Likelihood of goods being returned because of defective parts
- Ability to charge back returns to a supplier

If the supply chain is well controlled, inventory levels should be low and there will be only a small likelihood of obsolete inventory at year end. However, if the process is not well controlled, the likelihood of obsolete inventory at year end increases and the auditor will respond with more direct tests of ending inventory to determine the extent of inventory obsolescence.

Sources of Information about Key Processes

The following are other sources of information about the company:

- *Management inquiries*—The auditor should interview management to identify its strategic plans, its analysis of industry trends, the potential impact of actions it has taken or might take, and its management style.
- *Review of client's budget*—The budget represents management's fiscal plan for the forthcoming year. It provides insight into management's approach to operations and to risks the organization may face. The auditor looks for significant changes in plans and deviations from budgets, such as planned disposition of a line of business, significant research or promotion costs

associated with a new product introduction, new financing or capital requirements, changes in compensation or product costs due to union agreements, and significant additions to property, plant, and equipment.

- *Tour of client's plant and operations*—A tour of the client's production and distribution facilities offers much insight into potential audit issues. The auditor can visualize cost centers as well as shipping and receiving procedures, inventory controls, potentially obsolete inventory, and possible inefficiencies. The tour increases the auditor's awareness of company procedures and operations, giving him or her direct experience into sites and situations that are otherwise encountered only in company documents or observations of client personnel.
- *Review of data processing center*—The auditor should tour the data processing center and meet with the center's director to understand the computing structure and controls.
- *Review important debt covenants and board of director minutes*—Most bond issues and other debt agreements contain covenants, often referred to as **debt covenants**, which the organization must adhere to or risk default on the debt. Common forms of debt covenants include restrictions on the payment of dividends, requirements for maintaining minimum current ratios, or requiring annual audits.
- *Review relevant government regulations and client's legal obligations*—Few industries are unaffected by governmental regulation, and much of that regulation affects the audit. An example is the need to determine potential liabilities associated with cleanup costs defined by the Environmental Protection Agency. The auditor normally seeks information on litigation risks through an inquiry of management but follows up that inquiry with an analysis of litigation prepared by the client's legal counsel.

Understand Management's Risk Management and Control Processes

To understand the risk management and control processes in place, the auditor will normally use some or all of the following techniques:

- Develop an understanding of the processes used by the board of directors and management to evaluate and manage risks.
- Review the risk-based approach used by internal auditing with the director of internal auditing and the audit committee.
- Interview management about its risk approach, risk preferences, risk appetite, and the relationship of risk analysis to strategic planning.
- Review outside regulatory reports, where applicable, that address the company's policies and procedures toward risk.
- Review company policies and procedures for addressing risk.
- Gain a knowledge of company compensation schemes to determine if they are consistent with the risk policies adopted by the company.
- Review prior years' work to determine if current actions are consistent with risk approaches discussed with management.
- Review risk management documents.
- Determine how management and the board monitor risk, identify changes in risk, and react to mitigate, manage, or control the risk.

Exhibit 4.7 highlights the types of questions the auditor may want to ask when making inquiries of management and in analyzing the information from other sources.

Exhibit 4.7   Gathering Information: Sample Questions for Management

SAMPLE QUESTIONS AND AREAS OF INTEREST

Risks—Industry

- How is the industry changing?
- Who are your major competitors? What are their competitive advantages? What are your competitive advantages?
- How fast do you expect the industry to grow over the next five years?
- How fast do you expect to grow? What accounts for the difference between your growth expectations and that of the industry?

Risks—Financial and Other

- What process do you have in place to identify important business risks to the company?
- What are the company's principal business risks and what procedures are employed to monitor these risks?
- What are the company's principal financial statement and internal control risks, and what procedures are employed to monitor and manage those risks?
- What is the overall level of sophistication of the existing financial systems? Does the level of complexity create unusual business or financial risks? How does management address these risks?
- What subsidiaries, operating divisions, or corporate activities, not subject to audit, offer unusual business or financial risk but are viewed as "not material" in establishing the external audit scope? How does management view this "exposure"?

Controls

- What is your assessment of the overall control environment, including key business information systems? What are the principal criteria for your assessment of controls?
- Are there any significant deficiencies in the accounting systems or accounting personnel that should be addressed? Where improvements should be made? What process has management implemented to encourage these improvements?
- What process is used to assess and assure the integrity of new or revised operating or financial systems?
- Have the internal auditors identified control deficiencies? If so, what is management's view about the seriousness of the control deficiencies? What is the plan and timetable for corrective action?

Legal and Regulatory Issues

- Is there a specific management-level person designated as responsible for knowing and understanding relevant legal and regulatory requirements? What are the key risks and how are the risks of noncompliance identified and managed?

Code of Ethical Conduct

- Were there any reported conflicts of interest or irregularities or other violations of the code of ethical conduct identified during the year? What are the procedures for resolution? How were conflicts, irregularities, or other violations resolved?
- Were any significant, or potentially significant, regulatory noncompliance issues identified? If so, what is the status and what is the potential risk?
- Does the company have a comprehensive "whistleblower policy" and processes in place to implement the whistleblower function? Are complaints regularly reviewed by the audit committee and senior management?

PRACTICAL POINT

Auditing standards require that key engagement team members discuss the susceptibility of the organization's financial statements to material misstatement caused by error or fraud. In considering the possibility of fraud, engagement team members should have an attitude that includes a questioning mind, and they should be careful to set aside prior personal beliefs that management is honest and has integrity. In short, auditors need to exercise professional skepticism when they engage in this discussion.

Develop Expectations

The auditor should, and can, develop informed expectations about company results without having set foot in the company. The expectations should be documented, along with a rationale for the expectations. The analysis of the company should be communicated to all audit team members, emphasizing an understanding of the areas they are assigned to audit. Audit planning is not complete when the expectations are set. However, research has shown that audits are more effective when auditors develop expectations in advance. These expectations are the starting point for performing preliminary analytical techniques, which are discussed later in this chapter.

Assess Quality of Control System

Internal controls exist to manage risks. Controls range from broad policies to effective oversight, starting with the board of directors and permeating through management to every level in the organization. The auditor may gain a great deal of confidence about the correctness of financial account balances based on an understanding of the client's system and the consistency of its operations with objectively developed expectations. During the planning of the audit, the auditor will assess the design and implementation of the client's controls. If the auditor believes that the controls are well designed and have been implemented, the auditor may test those controls to determine if they are, indeed, operating effectively.

Management should also have controls in place to monitor operations, and the auditor is interested in those controls because operational efficiency will affect the valuation of many account balances. The auditor will usually inquire whether a company has developed key performance indicators on such areas as:

- Backlog of work in progress
- Dollar amount of return items (overall and by product line)
- Increased disputes regarding accounts receivable or accounts payable
- Surveys of customer satisfaction
- Assessment of risks associated with financial instruments
- Current level of collections (loans or receivables) in comparison with past years
- Employee absenteeism
- Decreased productivity by product line, process, or department
- Information processing errors
- Increased delays in important processes

The key performance indicators may indicate that some areas are managed very well, while others are not managed as well and constitute a high-risk concern. The absence of implementation of key performance indicators may indicate an overall high risk.

Determine Residual Risk

Based on the foregoing, the auditor develops expectations and makes an assessment of the risk that a particular account balance or assertion may be misstated. If the auditor has reason to believe the risk of misstatement is low, the auditor may be able to gain satisfaction regarding the account balance without directly testing it. Other techniques, such as using substantive analytical procedures or analyzing the quality of the control system, may yield persuasive evidence about the correctness of an account balance. This is not meant to imply that an auditor can perform a complete audit without ever directly testing some account balances; it means that the amount of testing can be minimized if risks are adequately addressed. However, if there is a high risk that an account balance may be misstated, the auditor should direct more attention to the audit of that account.

Manage Remaining Audit Risk by Responding to Risks of Material Misstatement

The auditor must design effective responses to address assessed risks. Such responses can be categorized as overall responses, i.e., those that affect how the audit is conducted at a global level, and responses involving altering the nature, timing, and extent of audit procedures that the auditor will perform.

Overall Responses

Overall responses to assessed risk may include the following:

- Making appropriate assignment of engagement personnel, matching individual knowledge, skill, and ability to the assessed risks of material misstatement
- Providing adequate supervision, and being careful to heighten supervision in response to assessed risks of material misstatement

PRACTICAL POINT

Auditors should use tools similar to those of financial analysts to develop expectations about the industry and the audit client. Those expectations allow the auditor to better implement a risk-based approach to the conduct of an audit.

PRACTICAL POINT

Obtaining an understanding of internal control includes evaluating the design of controls that are relevant to the audit and determining whether those controls have been implemented.

PRACTICAL POINT

For public clients the auditor will test the operating effectiveness of controls as part of an integrated audit. For nonpublic clients the auditor will test the operating effectiveness of controls only when the auditor wants to support an assessment of control risk below a high level.

PRACTICAL POINT

In the absence of a risk-based audit approach, the auditor will apply a standard audit program for the audit of material account balances. A standard audit program would include all the basic procedures of an audit, but *not* tailored to the specific facts or risks of the particular client engagement. Such an approach can be both ineffective and inefficient.

- Evaluating the organization's selection and application of significant accounting principles and associated disclosures.
- Selecting audit procedures in a way that incorporates an element of unpredictability so that client management is unable to anticipate and prepare for upcoming audit tests. Examples of ways to incorporate unpredictability include the following:
  - Perform some audit procedures on accounts, disclosures, and assertions that would otherwise not receive scrutiny because they are considered "low risk"
  - Change the timing of audit procedures from year to year
  - Select items for testing that are outside the normal boundaries for testing, i.e., are lower than prior-year materiality
  - Perform audit procedures on a surprise/unannounced basis
  - Vary the location or procedures year to year for multi-location audits

Responses Involving Altering the Nature, Timing, and Extent of Procedures

Other responses to assessed risks involve altering the nature, timing, and extent of procedures. Please refer to Chapter 7 for discussion of a framework for collecting such audit evidence. Importantly, the auditor should plan and perform audit procedures that address assessed risks of material misstatement. The auditor should conduct a more intensive audit when the risks of material misstatement are elevated. For example, a company with high engagement risk, and thus low audit risk, requires a more experienced audit staff and direct tests of account balances performed at year end. In contrast, a company with low engagement risk, and thus higher acceptable levels of audit risk, requires less direct tests of account balances at year end and could rely more on substantive analytical procedures.

The auditor should consider the types of misstatements that could occur, given the specific assessed risks, and should consider the likelihood of misstatement. If the auditor determines, through inquiry and other testing, that the company has strong risk management and control processes in place, the auditor may be able to focus the audit program on testing internal controls and developing corroborative evidence based on more limited direct tests of account balances. On the other hand, if the company does not have an effective risk management process in place, the auditor will identify areas where account balances are more likely to be misstated and concentrate direct tests of account balances in those areas.

A practical way of managing remaining audit risk is to think of material misstatements as analogous to water from a rain shower getting us wet. Risks may result in material misstatements (rain); management is responsible for keeping the financial statements free of material misstatements (dry). The auditor's objective is to gather enough information to objectively assess how well management is doing in keeping the financial statements free from material misstatement (dry). Exhibit 4.8 shows that Client A has an effective risk management and control system (the umbrella without holes) that prevents material misstatements (rain) from getting into the accounting records. However, we know that umbrellas are not always perfect—they may spring leaks when least expected, or one of the supporting arms may fail and all of the rain may come through on one side. The auditor has to test the umbrella (controls) to see that it is working but must do enough substantive testing of the account balance to determine that leaks (misstatements) had not occurred in an amount that would be noticeable (material misstatement). Client B's umbrella has holes in it (weak risk control system), resulting in wet accounting records (they are likely to contain material misstatements). Because of the weak controls, it is unlikely that the auditor will perform any testing of controls. Thus, the auditor must perform extensive direct tests of the account balances to identify the misstatements and get them corrected.

| Exhibit 4.8 | Effect of Risk Analysis on Audit Plan |

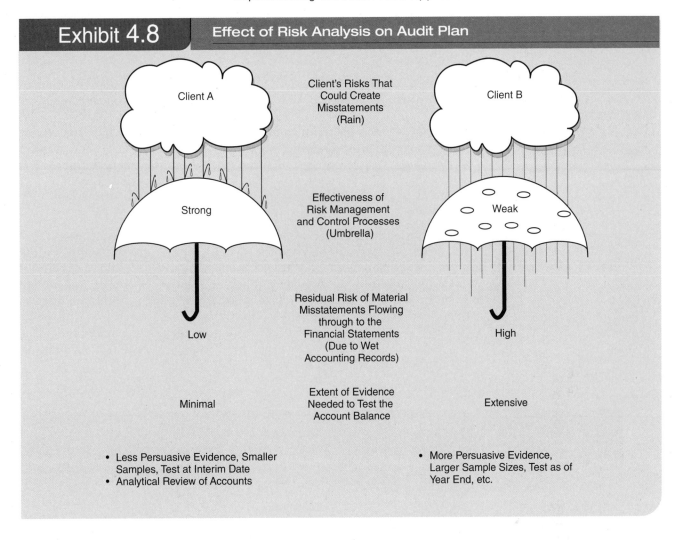

Risk Analysis and the Conduct of the Audit

Auditors must be business savvy and business alert. The auditor must understand the company and its risks as a basis for determining which account balances should be directly tested as well as which ones can be corroborated by substantive analytical procedures.

Linkage to Tests of Account Balances

The auditor assesses the likelihood that an account balance contains a material misstatement. For example, assume that the auditor concludes there is a high risk that management is using "reserves" or account balance estimates to manage earnings. In such a case, the auditor must set materiality at an appropriate level and undertake procedures to determine if there is an apparent manipulation of the reserves to influence reported net income.

Quality of Accounting Principles Used

There is a significant risk that a client may record a transaction but not make correct accounting judgments. Further, the auditor is required to discuss with the audit committee not only whether the financial statements are fairly presented in accordance with the applicable financial reporting framework but also whether the accounting principles chosen by management are the most appropriate. Although the phrase *most appropriate* may be somewhat ill defined,

PRACTICAL POINT

The auditor should modify the overall audit strategy and audit plan as necessary if circumstances change significantly during the course of the audit. These changes might be due to a revised assessment of the risks of material misstatement or the discovery of a previously unidentified risk of material misstatement.

PRACTICAL POINT

As global companies increasingly move to IFRS, the auditor will increasingly be challenged to document the reasoning for the accounting choices made under a "principles-based" approach to accounting.

the FASB has developed guidelines that auditors can implement to help evaluate the most appropriate accounting treatment. These guidelines include the following.

- *Representational faithfulness*—That is, are the transactions recorded according to their economic substance, fairly reflecting the relative risks of all parties involved?
- *Consistency*—Are the transactions reported consistently over time and across divisions within the company?
- *Accounting estimates*—Are the estimates based on proven models? Does the client reconcile actual costs with estimates over a period of time? Are there valid economic reasons for significant changes in accounting estimates?

The National Association of Corporate Directors (NACD) has suggested specific items for discussion between the auditor and the audit committee on the quality of accounting. The nature of the questions posed provides an additional guide to the quality of accounting issues. Selected excerpts from the NACD guide are shown in Exhibit 4.9. The questions probe the rationale and motivation for accounting choices.

There exist certain differences internationally regarding auditors' assessment and responses to risk. We articulate the relevant standards in the following Comparison of *Worldwide Professional Auditing Guidance*.

Exhibit 4.9 **Guides in Determining the Quality of Accounting: Selected Excerpts from the NACD Blue Ribbon Commission on Audit Committees**

Financial Statements—Accounting Choices

- What are the significant judgment areas (reserves, contingencies, asset values, note disclosures) that affect the current-year financial statements? What considerations were involved in resolving these judgment matters? What is the range of potential impact on future reported financial results?
- What issues or concerns exist that could adversely affect the future operations and/or financial condition of the company? What is the plan to deal with these future risks?
- What is the overall "quality" of the company's financial reporting, including the appropriateness of important accounting principles followed by the company?
- What is the range of acceptable accounting choices the company has available to it?
- Were there any significant changes in accounting policies, or in the application of accounting principles during the year? If yes, why were the changes made and what impact did the changes have on earnings per share (EPS) or other key financial measures?
- Were there any significant changes in accounting estimates, or models used in making accounting estimates during the year? If yes, why were the changes made and what impact did the changes have on earnings per share (EPS) or other key financial measures?
- What are our revenue recognition policies? Are there any instances where the company may be thought of as "pushing the limits" of revenue recognition? If so, what is the rationale for the treatment chosen?
- Have similar transactions and events been treated in a consistent manner across divisions of our company and across countries in which we operate? If not, what are the exceptions and the reasons for them?
- Do the accounting choices made reflect the economic substance of transactions and the strategic management of the business? If not, where are the exceptions and why do they exist?
- To what extent are the financial reporting choices consistent with the manner in which the company measures its progress toward achieving its mission internally? If not, what are the differences? Do the financial statements reflect the company's progress, or lack thereof, in accomplishing its overall strategies?
- How do the significant accounting principles used by our company compare with leading companies in our industry, or with other companies that are considered leaders in financial disclosure? What is the rationale for any differences?
- Has there been any instance where short-run reporting objectives (e.g., achieving a profit objective or meeting bonus or stock option requirements) were allowed to influence accounting choices? If yes, what choices were made and why?

Comparison of Worldwide Professional Guidance

ASSESSING AND RESPONDING TO RISK

AICPA Auditing Standards Board (ASB)

SAS 107 addresses audit risk and materiality. It notes that audit risk and materiality should be assessed at different levels of the audit, e.g., the financial statement level and at the individual account level. SAS 107 also discusses the need to communicate with a client's management about risk and materiality.

SAS 109 emphasizes the need for an auditor to understand a client's business. The reason that an auditor needs to understand the client's business is stated as follows:

> The auditor must obtain a sufficient understanding of the entity and its environment, including its internal control, to assess the risk of material misstatement of the financial statements whether due to error or fraud, and to design the nature, timing, and extent of further audit procedures.

SAS 109 provides extensive guidance on how to design risk assessment procedures and how to examine the client's internal control, among other procedures to be followed in order to gain an understanding of the client's business.

Public Company Accounting Oversight Board (PCAOB)

The PCAOB recently issued a series of standards that address various topics relating to how auditors should assess and respond to risk. These standards, which greatly emphasize the importance of professional judgment, address the following topics:

- Audit Risk
- Audit Planning
- Supervision of the Audit Engagement
- Consideration of Materiality in Planning and Performing an Audit
- Identifying and Assessing Risks of Material Misstatement
- The Auditor's Responses to the Risks of Material Misstatement
- Evaluating Audit Results
- Audit Evidence

International Auditing and Assurance Standards Board (IAASB)

There are three ISAs that address audit risk and materiality: ISAs 315, 320, and 330. These three ISAs discuss the materiality of errors in financial records and the possibility of this leading to material misstatement of financial information. These ISAs also give guidance as to how auditors should make consideration for the risk of material misstatement. ISA 315, entitled "Identifying and Assessing the Risks of Material Misstatement Through Understanding the Entity and Its Environment," addresses the need for an auditor to understand his/her client's business. Like SAS 109 (discussed above), ISA 315 offers extensive guidance on how an auditor should gain an understanding of a client's business. ISA 330 requires the auditor to determine the overall responses to identified risks at both the financial statement level and the assertion level.

SUMMARY

The three sets of standards are similar in the requirements to assess and respond to risk, and recognize the importance of applying professional judgment.

Preliminary Financial Statement Review: Using Analytical Techniques to Identify Areas of Heightened Risk

The auditor should apply preliminary financial analysis techniques to the client's unaudited financial statements and industry data to better identify the risk of misstatement in particular account balances. This analysis improves the auditor's understanding of the client's business and directs the auditor's attention to high-risk areas. Therefore, the auditor will be better informed when planning the nature, timing, and extent of procedures to test the client's account balances.

LO 7

Use preliminary analytical techniques to identify areas of heightened risk of misstatement.

Assumptions Underlying Analytical Techniques

A basic premise underlying the application of analytical procedures is that plausible relationships among data may reasonably be expected to exist and continue in the absence of known conditions to the contrary. Typical examples of relationships and sources of data commonly used in an audit process include the following:

- Financial information for equivalent prior periods, such as comparing the trend of fourth-quarter sales for the past three years and analyzing dollar and percent changes from the prior year
- Expected or planned results developed from budgets or other forecasts, such as comparing actual division performance with budgeted performance
- Comparison of linked account relationships, such as interest expense and interest-bearing debt
- Ratios of financial information, such as examining the relationship between sales and cost of goods sold or developing and analyzing common-sized financial statements
- Company and industry trends, such as comparing gross margin percentages of product lines or inventory turnover with industry averages
- Survey of relevant nonfinancial information, such as analyzing the relationship between the numbers of items shipped and royalty expense or the number of employees and payroll expense

A Process for Performing Analytical Procedures

The process used by the auditor in performing analytical procedures involves a number of steps. The first step is to develop an expectation. This expectation is basically an informed prediction about an account balance or a ratio. The prediction can be very precise, such as a specific number or ratio, or it can be less precise, such as a direction of change (increase or decrease) without an indication of the extent of the change. The auditor's expectation will be based on plausible relationships informed by the auditor's knowledge of the business, industry, trends, and other accounts and relationships present in the financial statements.

Developing informed expectations, and critically appraising client performance in relationship to those expectations, is fundamental to a risk analysis approach to auditing. The auditor needs to understand developments in the client's industry, general economic factors, and the client's strategic development plans in order to generate informed expectations about client results. Critical analysis based on these expectations could lead the auditor to detect many material misstatements. The analytical results are important in implementing the risk-based approach to auditing. It is only when these expectations are properly developed that the auditor can determine the amount of residual risk in key account balances.

After developing an expectation, the auditor will determine how big a difference can occur between the auditor's expectation and what the client has recorded before doing additional audit work. It would be rare for the auditor's expectation to exactly match the client's records. The maximum acceptable difference is sometimes referred to as a threshold. The threshold could be either a numerical value or a percentage. Differences in excess of the threshold will have to be investigated by the auditor.

Once the auditor has determined the threshold, the auditor will then compare the expectation with what the client has recorded. This comparison will allow the auditor to determine which differences need to be investigated in greater detail. These differences are areas where there is a heightened risk of misstatement. Fundamental questions arising from comparing expectations to the client's records might be as simple as these:

- Why is this company experiencing such a rapid growth in insurance sales when its product depends on an ever-rising stock market and the stock market has been declining for the past three years?

- Why is this company experiencing rapid sales growth when the rest of the industry is showing a downturn?
- Why are a bank client's loan repayments on a more current basis than those of similar banks operating in the same region with the same type of customers?

The analytical procedures process culminates in the auditor investigating significant differences and making conclusions. For preliminary analytical procedures, where there is a difference in excess of the threshold, the auditor will conclude that there is a heightened risk of misstatement and will plan the nature, timing, and extent of audit procedures in a way that will most effectively address that risk.

Types of Analytical Procedures

Two of the most frequently used analytical procedures when planning the audit are trend analysis and ratio analysis. Most commonly, the auditor will import the client's unaudited data into a spreadsheet or a software program to calculate trends and ratios and help pinpoint areas for further investigation. These trends and ratios will be compared with auditor expectations that were developed from knowledge obtained in previous years, industry trends, and current economic development in the geographic area served by the client.

Trend Analysis

Trend analysis includes simple year-to-year comparisons of account balances, graphic presentations, and analysis of financial data, histograms of ratios, and projections of account balances based on the history of changes in the account. It is imperative for the auditor to develop expectations and to establish decision rules, or thresholds, in advance in order to identify unexpected results for additional investigation. One potential decision rule, for example, is that dollar variances exceeding one-third or one-fourth of planning materiality should be investigated. Such a rule is based on the statistical theory of regression models, even though regression is not used. Another decision rule, or threshold, is to investigate any change exceeding some percentage. This percent threshold is often set higher for balance sheet accounts than for income statement accounts because balance sheet accounts tend to have greater year-to-year fluctuations.

Auditors often use a trend analysis over several years for key accounts, as shown in the following example in planning for the 2011 audit (2011 data are unaudited).

	2011	2010	2009	2008	2007
Gross sales ($000)	$29,500	$24,900	$24,369	$21,700	$17,600
Sales returns ($000)	600	400	300	250	200
Gross margin ($000)	8,093	6,700	6,869	6,450	5,000
Percent of prior year: Sales	118.5%	102.2%	112.3%	123.3%	105.2%
Sales returns	150.0%	133.3%	120.0%	125.0%	104.6%
Gross margin	132.8%	97.5%	106.5%	129.0%	100.0%
Sales as a percentage of 2007 sales	167.6%	141.5%	138.5%	123.3%	100.0%

In this example, the auditor's expectation might be that gross margin percentage and sales percentage would increase at about the same rate. Further, the auditor might have an expectation that sales returns would be relatively stable in comparison with the prior year. After setting a threshold and comparing the expectation to the client's data, the auditor in this example might

PRACTICAL POINT

The auditor's steps in the process of performing preliminary analytical procedures, including the development of the auditor's expectations, the identification of the threshold, and appropriate follow-up, should be appropriately documented. This ensures that reviewers of the file understand the judgments made during the audit process.

PRACTICAL POINT

If the threshold in analytical procedures is set too low, the auditor will be following up on immaterial differences and will be inefficient in performing the audit. If the threshold is set too high, the auditor may end up not investigating important differences, thereby reducing audit effectiveness.

conclude that the changes in gross margin and sales returns are worthy of further investigation. The auditor would want to gain an understanding about why gross margin is increasing more rapidly than sales and why sales returns are increasing. More importantly, the auditor should develop some potential hypotheses as to why there was an increase in gross margin along with the reason for the substantial increase in sales. Then, once the hypotheses are developed, the auditor should determine which set of hypotheses is most likely and then use those for prioritizing audit work. Potential hypotheses for the increase in gross margin might be:

1. The company has introduced a new product that is a huge market success, e.g., the initial introduction of the iPad by Apple.
2. The company has changed its product mix.
3. The company has improved its operational efficiencies.
4. The company has fictitious sales (and consequently no cost of goods associated with those sales).

Upon analysis, two of the hypotheses above would best explain the unaudited changes in sales and gross margin for 2011: (a) a significant new product introduction that allows higher margins or (b) fictitious sales. With this analysis, the auditor can prioritize which hypothesis to investigate first and thus achieve audit efficiency. For example, if the company has not introduced a new product and the company's sales growth and gross margin are significantly higher than the competition, then it is likely that Hypothesis 4 (fictitious sales) is the most likely. Going through this process of preliminary analytical procedures helps the auditor identify areas where the risk of material misstatement is high and then allows for the auditor to plan appropriate procedures to address those risks.

Ratio Analysis

Ratio analysis is more effective than simple trend analysis because it takes advantage of economic relationships between two or more accounts. It is widely used because of its power to identify unusual or unexpected changes in relationships. Ratio analysis is useful in identifying significant differences between the client results and a norm (such as industry ratios) or between auditor expectations and actual results. It is also useful in identifying potential audit problems that may be found in ratio changes between years (such as inventory turnover).

Comparing ratio data over time for the client and its industry can yield useful insights. The auditor could rely on industry data to develop expectations for preliminary analytics. For example, if a particular industry ratio increased over time, the auditor's expectation might be that the client's ratio would also increase over time. In the following example, the percentage of sales returns and allowances to net sales for the client does not vary significantly from the industry average for the current period, but comparing the trend over time yields an unexpected result.

| | SALES RETURNS AS A % OF NET SALES | | | | |
	2011	2010	2009	2008	2007
Client	2.1%	2.6%	2.5%	2.7%	2.5%
Industry	2.3%	2.1%	2.2%	2.1%	2.0%

This comparison shows that even though the percentage of sales returns for 2011 is close to the industry average, the client's percentage declined significantly from 2010 while the industry's percentage increased. In addition, except for the current year, the client's percentages exceeded the industry average. The result is different from the auditor's expectation that the percentage would increase from the prior period, likely exceeds the auditor's threshold, and thus, the auditor should investigate the potential cause. Here are some possible explanations for the differences:

- The client has improved its quality control.
- Fictitious sales have been recorded in 2011.
- The client is not properly recording sales returns in 2011.

The auditor must design audit procedures to identify the cause of this difference to determine whether a material misstatement exists.

Commonly Used Financial Ratios

Exhibit 4.10 shows several commonly used financial ratios. The first three ratios provide information on potential liquidity problems. The turnover and gross margin ratios are often helpful in identifying fraudulent activity or items recorded more than once, such as fictitious sales or inventory. The leverage and capital turnover ratios are useful in evaluating going-concern problems or adherence to debt covenants. Although the auditor chooses the ratios deemed most useful for a client, many auditors routinely calculate and analyze the ratios listed in Exhibit 4.10 on a trend basis over time. Other ratios are specifically designed for an industry. In the banking industry, for example, auditors calculate ratios on percentages of nonperforming loans, operating margin, and average interest rates by loan categories.

Ratio and trend analysis are generally carried out at three levels:

- Comparison of client data with industry data
- Comparison of client data with similar prior-period data
- Comparison of preliminary client data with expectations developed from industry trends, client budgets, other account balances, or other bases of expectations

PRACTICAL POINT

Analytical techniques contain a combination of both quantitative and qualitative judgments. Analytics are required as part of planning the audit and during the wrap-up of the audit. Substantive analytics, which are optional, may be performed as a substantive procedure providing evidence about account balances.

Exhibit 4.10 — Commonly Used Ratios

Ratio	Formula
Short-term liquidity ratios:	
Current ratio	Current Assets/Current Liabilities
Quick ratio	(Cash + Cash Equivalents + Net Receivables)/Current Liabilities
Current debt-to-assets ratio	Current Liabilities/Total Assets
Receivable ratios:	
Accounts receivable turnover	Credit Sales/Accounts Receivable
Days' sales in accounts receivable	365/Turnover
Inventory ratios:	
Inventory turnover	Cost of Sales/Ending Inventory
Days' sales in inventory	365/Turnover
Profitability measures:	
Net profit margin	Net Income/Net Sales
Return on equity	Net Income/Common Stockholders' Equity
Financial leverage ratios:	
Debt-to-equity ratio	Total Liabilities/Stockholders' Equity
Liabilities to assets	Total Liabilities/Total Assets
Capital turnover ratios:	
Asset liquidity	Current Assets/Total Assets
Sales to assets	Net Sales/Total Assets
Net worth to sales	Owners' Equity/Net Sales

Comparison with Industry Data   A comparison of client data with industry data may identify potential problems. For example, if the average collection period for accounts receivable in an industry is 43 days, but the client's average collection period is 65 days, this might indicate problems with product quality or credit risk. Or, as another example a bank's concentration of loans in a particular industry may indicate greater problems if that industry is encountering economic problems.

One potential limitation to using industry data is that such data might not be directly comparable to the client's. Companies may be quite different but still classified within one broad industry. Also, other companies in the industry may use accounting principles different from the client's (e.g., LIFO vs. FIFO).

Comparison with Previous Year Data   Simple ratio analysis comparing current and past data that is prepared as a routine part of planning an audit can highlight risks of misstatement. The auditor often develops ratios on asset turnover, liquidity, and product-line profitability to search for potential signals of risk. For example, an inventory turnover ratio might indicate that a particular product line had a turnover of four times for the past three years, but only three times this year. The change may indicate potential obsolescence, realizability problems, or errors in the accounting records. Even when performing simple ratio analysis, it is important that the auditor go through each of the steps in the process, beginning with the development of expectations.

Summary

Audit clients have their own business and financial reporting risk, and those risks in turn affect the auditor's engagement risk and audit risk. In order to effectively manage those risks, the auditor must make informed client acceptance and retention decisions and must use the audit risk model to plan and conduct the audit. To accomplish effective risk management, the auditor needs to be thoroughly knowledgeable about the client, its industry, products, controls, financing, and risk management plans. In fact, auditors are increasingly urged by the SEC and auditing standard setters to use a risk-based approach to auditing. Auditors perform financial statement review and preliminary analytical procedures to identify areas having a heightened risk of misstatement. This identification helps the auditors determine how to plan and perform the audit to provide reasonable assurance that no material errors exist in the client's financial statements.

Significant Terms

Audit risk   The risk that the auditor expresses an inappropriate audit opinion when the financial statements are materially misstated, i.e., the financial statements are not presented fairly in conformity with the applicable financial reporting framework.

Business risk   Those risks that affect the operations and potential outcomes of organizational activities.

Control risk   The risk that a misstatement because of error or fraud that could occur in an assertion and that could be material, individually or in combination with other misstatements, will not be prevented or detected on a timely basis by the company's internal control. Thus, control risk is the risk that the client's internal control system will fail to prevent or detect a misstatement.

Debt covenant   An agreement between an entity and its lender that places limitations on the organization; usually associated with debentures or large credit lines.

Detection risk   The risk that the procedures performed by the auditor will not detect a misstatement that exists and that could be material, individually or in combination with other misstatements. Detection risk is the risk that the audit procedures will fail to detect a material misstatement. The auditor controls detection risk after specifying audit risk and assessing inherent and control risk.

Engagement letter   Specifies the understanding between the client and the auditor as to the nature of audit services to be conducted and, in the absence of any other formal contract, is viewed by the courts as a contract between the auditor and the client; generally covers items such as client responsibilities, auditor responsibilities, billing procedures, and the timing and target completion date of the audit.

Engagement risk   The economic risk that a CPA firm is exposed to simply because it is associated with a client. Engagement risk is controlled by careful selection and retention of clients.

Financial reporting risk   Those risks that relate directly to the recording of transactions and the presentation of financial data in an organization's financial statements.

Inherent risk   The susceptibility of an assertion to a misstatement, because of error or fraud, that could be material, individually or in combination with other misstatements, before consideration of any related controls. Stated simply, inherent risk is the initial susceptibility of a transaction or accounting adjustment to be recorded in error, or for the transaction not to be recorded in the absence of internal controls.

Management integrity   The honesty and trustworthiness of management as exemplified by past and current actions; auditors' assessment of management integrity reflects the extent to which the auditors believe they can trust management and its representations to be honest and forthright.

Materiality   The magnitude of an omission or misstatement of accounting information that, in view of surrounding circumstances, makes it probable that the judgment of a reasonable person relying on the information would have been changed or influenced by the omission or misstatement.

Planning materiality   The materiality level that is relevant at the transaction or account balance level, which is typically less than overall materiality.

Posting materiality   The amount below which errors are treated as inconsequential.

Risk of material misstatement   An auditor's combined assessment of inherent and control risk.

Risk   A concept used to express uncertainty about events and/or their outcomes that could have a material effect on the organization.

Risk-based approach   An audit approach that begins with an assessment of the types and likelihood of misstatements in account balances and then adjusts the amount and type of audit work to the likelihood of material misstatements occurring in account balances.

Tolerable misstatement   The amount of misstatement in an account balance that the auditor could tolerate and still not judge the underlying account balance to be materially misstated.

SELECTED REFERENCES TO RELEVANT PROFESSIONAL GUIDANCE	
TOPIC	**SELECTED GUIDANCE**
Risk Management	COSO *Enterprise Risk Management: Integrated Framework, 2004*
Audit Risk and Materiality	AS No. 8 *Audit Risk*
	AS No. 11 *Consideration of Materiality in Planning and Performing an Audit*
	SAS 47 *Audit Risk and Materiality in Conducting an Audit*
	SAS 107 *Audit Risk and Materiality in Conducting an Audit*
	SAS *Materiality in Planning and Performing an Audit* (issued but not effective, proposed effective date is December 2012)
	SAS *Overall Objectives of the Independent Auditor and Conduct of an Audit in Accordance with Generally Accepted Auditing Standards* (issued but not effective, proposed effective date is December 2012)
	ISA 200 *Overall Objectives of the Independent Auditor and Conduct of an Audit in Accordance with International Standards on Auditing*
	ISA 320 *Materiality in Planning and Performing an Audit*
Planning and Supervision	AS No. 9 *Audit Planning*
	AS No. 10 *Supervision of the Audit Engagement*

	SAS 108 *Planning and Supervision*
	SAS *Planning an Audit* (issued but not effective, proposed effective date is December 2012)
	ISA 300 *Planning an Audit of Financial Statements*
Assessing and Responding to Risk	AS No. 12 *Identifying and Assessing Risks of Material Misstatement*
	AS No. 13 *The Auditor's Responses to the Risks of Material Misstatement*
	SAS 109 *Understanding the Entity and Its Environment and Assessing the Risks of Material Misstatement*
	SAS *Understanding the Entity and Its Environment and Assessing the Risks of Material Misstatement* (Redrafted) (issued but not effective, proposed effective date is December 2012)
	SAS 110 *Performing Audit Procedures in Response to Assessed Risks and Evaluating the Audit Evidence Obtained*
	SAS *Performing Audit Procedures in Response to Assessed Risks and Evaluating the Audit Evidence Obtained* (Redrafted) (issued but not effective, proposed effective date is December 2012)
	AICPA Audit Risk Alert *Understanding the New Auditing Standards Related to Risk Assessment—2005/2006*
	AICPA Audit Risk Alert *Current Economic Instability: Accounting and Auditing Considerations—2009*
	ISA 315 *Identifying and Assessing the Risks of Material Misstatement Through Understanding the Entity and Its Environment*
	Proposed ISA 315 (Revised) *Identifying and Assessing the Risks of Material Misstatement through Understanding the Entity and Its Environment*
	ISA 330 *The Auditor's Responses to Assessed Risks*
Analytical Procedures	SAS 56 *Analytical Procedures*
	Proposed SAS *Analytical Procedures* (Redrafted)
	ISA 520 *Analytical Procedures*
Client Acceptance	SAS 84 *Communications Between Predecessor and Successor Auditors*
	Proposed SAS *Terms of Engagement*
	ISA 210 *Agreeing the Terms of Audit Engagements*
Quality Control for Audits	Proposed SAS *Quality Control for an Audit of Financial Statements*
	ISA 220 *Quality Control for an Audit of Financial Statements*

Note: *Acronyms for Relevant Professional Guidance*

STANDARDS: **AS**—Auditing Standard issued by the PCAOB; **ISA**—International Standard on Auditing issued by the IAASB; **SAS**—Statement on Auditing Standards issued by the Auditing Standards Board of the AICPA; **SSAE**—Statement on Standards for Attestation Engagements issued by the AICPA.

ORGANIZATIONS: **AICPA**—American Institute of Certified Public Accountants; **COSO**—Committee of Sponsoring Organizations; **IAASB**—International Auditing and Assurance Standards Board; **PCAOB**—Public Company Accounting Oversight Board; **SEC**—Securities and Exchange Commission.

Review Questions

4-1   **(LO 1)** Define the following terms:
- Business risk
- Engagement risk
- Financial reporting risk
- Audit risk

4-2   **(LO 1)** What is risk management and why is it important that an organization implement effective risk management? Who has the primary responsibility for the effective implementation of a risk management program (sometimes referred to an Enterprise Risk Management or ERM) to identify and then manage or mitigate risks?

4-3   **(LO 1)**   Explain why so many corporate losses are tied to poor risk management. How does the quality of risk management relate to the long-term viability of an organization?

4-4   **(LO 1)**   How are risks and controls related? Why is it important to assess risks prior to evaluating the quality of an organization's controls?

4-5   **(LO 1)**   What kinds of risks does a company encounter if it decides to develop a new product?

4-6   **(LO 2)**   What are the major procedures an auditor will use to identify the risks associated with an existing or a potential new client?

4-7   **(LO 2)**   How would an auditor go about assessing management integrity? Why is management integrity considered the most important factor affecting the client acceptance or continuation decision?

4-8   **(LO 2)**   What are the primary factors an auditor will want to investigate before accepting a new audit client?

4-9   **(LO 1)**   How does financial reporting risk relate to audit risk and the planning of the audit engagement? What are the most important factors that affect financial reporting risk?

4-10   **(LO 1)**   What is a "high-risk" audit client? What are the characteristics of clients that are considered high risk?

4-11   **(LO 1, 2)**   Why do related-party transactions represent special risks to the auditor and the conduct of an audit?

4-12   **(LO 2)**   What sources of information should an auditor look at in determining whether to accept a new client? Why is it important that the auditor make the acceptance decision systematically?

4-13   **(LO 2)**   What information should the auditor seek from the predecessor auditor when considering the acceptance of a new audit client?

4-14   **(LO 2)**   What is an engagement letter? What is its purpose?

4-15   **(LO 2)**   How will an auditor find out whether there has been a dispute between the client and the preceding auditor regarding accounting principles?

4-16   **(LO 3, 4)**   What is audit risk? Does the auditor determine audit risk or does the auditor assess it? What factors most influence audit risk?

4-17   **(LO 3, 4)**   Explain how the concepts of audit risk and materiality are related. Must an auditor make a decision on materiality in order to implement the audit risk model?

4-18   **(LO 3)**   Some audit firms develop very specific quantitative guidelines, either through quantitative measures or in tables, relating planning materiality to the size of sales or assets for a client. Other audit firms leave the materiality judgments up to the individual partner or manager in charge of the audit. What are the major advantages and disadvantages of each approach? Which approach would you favor? Explain.

4-19   **(LO 3)** The SEC has criticized the auditing profession for not looking at significant changes in accounting estimates. For example, a reserve (liability estimate) may be estimated very high one year, and then very low the next year. Explain how an accounting estimate might not be materially misstated for two consecutive years but because of the "swing" in the accounting estimate, net income could be misstated by a material amount.

4-20   **(LO 3)** The SEC is very concerned that auditors recognize the qualitative aspect of materiality judgments. Explain what the "qualitative" aspect of materiality means. List some factors that would make a quantitatively small misstatement be judged as qualitatively material.

4-21   **(LO 4)** A recent graduate of an accounting program went to work for a large international accounting firm and noted that the firm sets audit risk at 5% for all major engagements. What does a literal interpretation of setting audit risk at 5% mean? How could an audit firm set audit risk at 5% (i.e., what assumptions must the auditor make in the audit risk model to set audit risk at 5%)?

4-22   **(LO 4)** What is inherent risk? How can the auditor measure it? What are the implications for the audit risk model if the auditor assesses inherent risk at less than 100%?

4-23   **(LO 5)** What are the major limitations of the audit risk model? How should those limitations affect the auditor's implementation of the audit risk model?

4-24   **(LO 6)** What are the major lessons learned in the analysis of the audits of Lincoln Savings and Loan? Where would the auditor obtain information regarding the real estate market in the Phoenix area or in the southwestern United States? Why is it important that the auditor have such information during an audit of a savings and loan organization?

4-25   **(LO 6)** Consider a manufacturing company in an environment in which the overall business conditions are declining. What are the major risks associated with the inventory account balance? Explain how those risks would affect the auditor's approach to auditing inventory.

4-26   **(LO 2, 4)** List at least five risks that may be present in a company, and that may be associated with material misstatements in the company's financial statements. Does the existence of one or more of these risk factors necessarily mean that there is a material misstatement present? What does the presence of one or more of these risks imply in terms of planned audit work?

4-27   **(LO 6, 7)** Why is it important for the auditor to use risk analysis to develop expectations about client performance?

4-28   **(LO 6)** What background information might be useful to the auditor in planning the audit to assist in determining whether the client has potential inventory obsolescence or receivables problems? Identify the various sources the auditor would use to develop this background information.

4-29   **(LO 2, 6)**   In deciding whether to accept a new manufacturing client, the auditor usually arranges to take a tour of the manufacturing plant. Assuming that the client has one major manufacturing plant, identify the information the auditor might obtain during the tour that will help in planning and conducting the audit, if the client is accepted.

4-30   **(LO 7)**   Explain how ratio analysis and industry comparisons can be useful to the auditor in identifying potential risk on an audit engagement. How can such analysis also help the auditor plan the audit?

4-31   **(LO 7)**   What ratios would best indicate problems with potential inventory obsolescence or collectibility of receivables? How are those ratios calculated?

4-32   **(LO 6)**   How does risk analysis affect the nature of procedures performed on specific account balances? How would an auditor's professional skepticism affect the nature of procedures performed? Use as an example the following accounts for illustration:

**Professional
Skepticism**

- Allowance for loan losses
- Inventory
- Sales commissions
- Accounts receivable

Multiple-Choice Questions

4-33   **(LO 1)**   Business risk is the risk that:
a. The auditor will fail to detect material misstatements in the financial statements.
b. The control system will fail to detect material misstatements.
c. The client will experience difficulties associated with managing and growing the business.
d. The client will change auditors often.

4-34   **(LO 1)**   An external auditor is interested in whether or not a company has implemented an effective risk management process because:
a. It reduces the likelihood that an organization will fail.
b. It provides a framework for the company to develop controls to manage or mitigate those risks.
c. It provides a framework to reduce financial statement misstatements.
d. All of the above.

4-35   **(LO 2)**   Which of the following would not be a source of information about the risk of a potential new audit client?
a. The previous auditor
b. Management
c. SEC filings and statements
d. The PCAOB quality-control reports

4-36   **(LO 2)**   An engagement letter should be written before the start of an audit because:
a. It may limit the auditor's legal liability by specifying the auditor's responsibilities.
b. It specifies the client's responsibility for preparing schedules and making the records available to the auditor.

c. It specifies the expected cost of the audit for the upcoming year.

d. All of the above.

Professional Skepticism

4-37 **(LO 2, 6)** If the auditor has concerns about the integrity of management, which of the following *would not* be an appropriate action?

a. Refuse to accept the engagement because a client does not have an inalienable right to an audit

b. Expand audit procedures in areas where management representations are normally important by requesting outside verifiable evidence

c. Raise the audit fees to compensate for the risk inherent in the audit but do not plan any extended audit procedures

d. Plan the audit with a higher degree of skepticism, including specific procedures that should be effective in uncovering management fraud

4-38 **(LO 3, 4, 6)** Which of the following combinations of engagement risk, audit risk, and materiality would lead to the most audit work?

Engagement Risk	Audit Risk	Materiality
a. Low	High	High
B. Moderate	Lowest	Lowest
c. Low	Moderate	Lowest
d. High	High	High

4-39 **(LO 5)** All of the following would be considered a limitation of the audit risk model *except:*

a. The model treats each risk component as a separate and independent factor when the factors are interrelated.

b. Inherent risk is difficult, if not impossible, to formally assess.

c. It is not possible to assess control risk.

d. The model does not support qualitative judgments.

4-40 **(LO 3)** All of the following are true except:

a. Materiality at the financial statement level is set at a higher level than planning materiality.

b. Planning materiality moves in the same direction as tolerable misstatement.

c. A materiality level where the audit believes errors below that level would not, even when aggregated with all other misstatements, be material to the financial statements is referred to as posting materiality.

d. The FASB, PCAOB, and the U.S. Supreme Court have all agreed to a uniform definition of materiality.

4-41 **(LO 7)** Which of the following would indicate that inventory will be a high-risk account for the upcoming audit?

a. Inventory has decreased even though sales have increased.

b. Sales growth is lower than inventory growth.

c. Average inventory age is higher than the industry and the auditor had expected the client's activities to be in line with the industry.

d. All of the above.

e. (b) and (c) above.

4-42   **(LO 7)** Comparing client data with industry data and with its own results for the previous year, the auditor finds that the number of days' sales in accounts receivable for this year is 66 for the client, 42 for the industry average, and 38 for the previous year. Inventory levels have remained the same. The auditor expects that the client's activities will be similar to last year and to the industry. The least likely valid explanation of this increase would be:

Fraud

    a. Fictitious sales during the current year.

    b. A policy to promote sales through less strenuous credit policies.

    c. Potential problems with product quality and the inability of the client to meet warranty claims.

    d. Increased production of products for expected increases in demand.

4-43   **(LO 7)** An auditor suspects that fictitious sales may have been recorded during the year. Which of the following analytical review results would *most likely* indicate that fictitious sales were recorded?

Fraud

    a. Uncollectible account write-offs increased by 10%, sales increased by 10%, and accounts receivable increased by 10%.

    b. Gross margin decreased from 40 to 35%.

    c. The number of days' sales in accounts receivable decreased from 64 to 38.

    d. Accounts receivable turnover decreased from 7.1:1 to 4.3:1.

Discussion and Research Questions

4-44   **(Types of Audit Risks, LO 1)** The auditor can control some types of risks but must assess other types of risks. A number of different types of risk were introduced in this chapter.

Required

Using the format below:

    a. Define each of the following risk concepts that were introduced in this chapter.

    b. Indicate the importance of the risk to the conduct of the audit.

    c. Indicate whether the auditor either assesses the risk or whether the auditor controls the risk.

Risk	Definition	Importance to Audit	Assessed or Controlled
Business risk			
Engagement risk			
Financial reporting risk			
Audit risk			
Inherent risk			
Control risk			
Detection risk			

4-45   **(Relationship of Risk and Controls, LO 1)** Auditors need to understand the relationship of business risk to the planning of an audit.

Required

    a. Explain how the existence, or nonexistence, of a good risk management process by an organization affects the planning of an audit engagement.

b. What risks does a company have in developing and introducing a new product? Take the example of the process of introducing a new product in any industry that you are interested in and (a) identify the risks, (b) identify the controls that you would recommend to address those risks, and (c) identify the possible effect on the organization and the audit if the controls are not in place.

c. What is the relationship between risk and controls? In other words, is there a need for control if there are no risks?

4-46   (Relationship of Risks and Controls, LO 1) Consider the payment of individuals working in a factory who are paid by the hour. According to union contract, they have extensive benefits.

Required

a. What are the risks that affect the processing and payment of the employees?

b. What controls do you suggest to address those risks? Be specific in relating the controls to the risks that are being addressed.

Group Activity

4-47   (Risk Analysis and Financial Statement Audits, LO 1, 4, 6, 7) In a small group, discuss the views expressed by the following three auditors.

Auditor 1: "Risk analysis is good. But, when all is said and done, it does not add much to the audit. You still need to directly test the account balances with procedures such as confirmations or observation. You can't ever get away from good old-fashioned auditing."

Auditor 2: "The problem with 'good old-fashioned auditing' is that there is a tendency to overaudit. We spend a lot of time on areas in which the likelihood of material misstatement is almost nil. At the same time, we don't spend enough time understanding the company's strategy and the structure of its transactions to determine where the real risk of misstatement may be occurring."

Auditor 3: "I have been trained as an accountant and an auditor. I am prepared to deal with financial statements. I have not been trained to analyze or perform business risk analysis. I have taken financial statement analysis and can perform analytical review to identify trends and potential misstatements, but it is unrealistic to expect me, or my audit firm, to do business risk analysis. It is not part of auditing."

Required

a. Analyze the arguments made by the three auditors. Which has the more persuasive argument? Why is the argument more persuasive?

b. Do auditors need to be trained in risk management—at least to the extent of evaluating whether or not an organization has effective risk management? Explain.

c. The SEC and audit standard setters have implored auditors to implement more of a risk-based approach to auditing. At the same time, it has criticized audit firms that overreacted to companies with good risk management and tried to perform an audit primarily using substantive analytical procedures. Are these two views reconcilable? Explain what is meant by a "risk-based" approach to auditing.

d. Explain how the auditor would adjust audit procedures in relationship to the trend analysis shown in the text where sales has gone up by 118% over the previous year while gross margin has gone up by 132%. You may further assume that the industry as a whole had an increase of 5% on both revenue and gross margin.

4-48 **(Management Integrity and Audit Risk, LO 2, 4, 6)** The auditor needs to assess management integrity as a potential indicator of risk. Although the assessment of management integrity takes place on every audit engagement, it is difficult to do and is not often well documented.

Ethics

Group Activity

Required

a. Define management integrity and discuss its importance to the auditor in determining the type of evidence to be gathered on an audit and in evaluating the evidence.

b. Identify the types of evidence the auditor would gather in assessing the integrity of management. What are sources of each type of evidence?

c. For each of the following management scenarios, (1) indicate whether you believe the scenario reflects negatively on management integrity, and explain why; and (2) indicate how the assessment would affect the auditor's planning of the audit.

Management Scenarios

i. The owner/manager of a privately held company also owns three other companies. The entities could all be run as one entity, but they engage extensively in related-party transactions to minimize the overall tax burden for the owner/manager.

ii. The president of a publicly held company has a reputation for being a "hard nose" with a violent temper. He has been known to fire a divisional manager on the spot if the manager did not achieve profit goals.

iii. The financial vice president of a publicly held company has worked her way to the top by gaining a reputation as a great accounting manipulator. She has earned the reputation by being very creative in finding ways to circumvent FASB pronouncements to keep debt off the balance sheet and in manipulating accounting to achieve short-term earnings. After each short-term success, she has moved on to another company to utilize her skills.

iv. The president of a small publicly held firm was indicted on tax evasion charges seven years ago. He settled with the IRS and served time doing community service. Since then, he has been considered a pillar of the community, making significant contributions to local charities. Inquiries of local bankers yield information that he is the partial or controlling owner of several corporations that may serve as "shell" organizations whose sole purpose is to assist the manager in moving income around to avoid taxes.

v. James J. James is the president of a privately held company that has been accused of illegally dumping waste and failing to meet government standards for worker safety. James responds that his attitude is to meet the minimum requirements of the law and if the government deems that he has not, he will clean up. "Besides," he asserts, "it is good business; it is less costly to clean up only when I have to, even if small fines are involved, than it is to take leadership positions and exceed government standards."

vi. Carla C. Charles is the young, dynamic chairperson of Golden-Glow Enterprises, a rapidly growing company that makes ceramic specialty items, such as Christmas villages for indoor decorations. Golden-Glow recently went public after five years of 20% annual growth. Carla has a reputation for being a fast-living party animal, and the society pages have carried reports of "extravagant" parties at her home. However, she is well respected as an astute businessperson.

d. **(Group Discussion)** There are a number of success stories where managers exhibited both (a) great strategic thinking and (b) lack of integrity. Sometimes the two intermixed, but often they did not. Examples include the CEOs of AIG, United Health, HealthSouth, Tyco, as well as the legendary CEOs at Enron and WorldCom. Describe the major individual characteristics that might contribute to a lack of management integrity and how the auditor would know about these characteristics. Sometimes the characteristics are directly observable; at other times, they are observable only by the individual's actions.

*4-49 **(Sources of Information for Audit Planning, LO 6)** In early summer, an auditor is advised of a new assignment as the senior auditor for Lancer Company, a major client for the past five years. She is given the engagement letter for the audit covering the current calendar year and a list of personnel assigned to the engagement. It is her responsibility to plan and supervise the fieldwork for the engagement.

Required

Discuss the necessary preparation and planning for the Lancer Company annual audit before beginning fieldwork at the client's office. In your discussion, include the sources that should be consulted, the type of information that should be sought, the preliminary plans and preparation that should be made for the fieldwork, and any actions that should be taken relative to the staff assigned to the engagement.

Professional Skepticism

4-50 **(Materiality and Professional Skepticism, LO 3)** Auditors make materiality judgments during the planning phase of the audit in order to be sure they ultimately gather sufficient evidence during the audit to assure that the financial statements are free of material misstatements. The lower the materiality threshold that an auditor has for an account balance, the more the evidence that the auditor must collect to be sure the account balance is correctly stated. Auditors often use quantitative benchmarks such as 1% of total assets or 5% of net income to determine whether misstatements materially affect the financial statements, but ultimately it is an auditor's individual professional judgment as to whether a given misstatement is or is not considered material.

Required

a. What is the relationship between the level of riskiness of the client and the level of misstatement in an account balance that an auditor would consider material? For example, assume that Client A has weaker controls over accounts receivable compared to Client B (i.e., Client A is riskier than Client B). Assume that Client B is similar in size to Client A, and that the auditor has concluded that a misstatement exceeding $5,000 would be material for Client B's accounts receivable account. Should the materiality threshold for Client A be the same as, more than, or less than that for Client B? Further, which client will require more audit evidence to be collected, Client A or Client B?

b. How might an auditor's individual characteristics affect his or her professional judgments about materiality?

c. Assume that one auditor is more professionally skeptical than another auditor, and that they are making the materiality judgment in part (a) of this problem. Compare the possible alternative monetary thresholds that a more versus less-skeptical auditor might make for Client A.

4-51　**(Accepting a New Client, LO 2)** Bob Jones, a relatively new partner for Kinde & McNally, CPAs, has recently received a request to provide a bid to perform audit and other services for Wolf River Outfitting, a large regional retailing organization with more than fifty stores in the surrounding five-state area. Wolf River is a fast-growing company specializing in premium outerwear and outdoor sports equipment. It is not publicly traded. Bob realizes that bringing in new clients is important to his success in the firm. Wolf River looks like a good audit that might provide opportunity to sell other services. Consequently, Bob is thinking about "lowballing" the audit (i.e., bidding very low on audit fees) in an effort to gain a foothold for providing other services to the client.

Required

a. What other information should Bob gather about Wolf River before proposing to perform the audit? For each item of information, indicate the most efficient way for Bob to gather the information.

b. Auditing firms are often encouraged to bid low for the audit work in order to get the more lucrative consulting work. Explain both the positive and negative effects of such behavior on the public accounting profession. In particular, discuss the potential effect on the audit function within a public accounting firm.

c. Explain how the auditor could use the SEC filings and industry as well as personal data that may be available on the Internet or other data services to gather information about the potential client.

d. Explain why Bob would want an engagement letter before beginning the audit.

4-52　**(Audit Risk Model, LO 3, 4, 5)** A staff auditor was listening to a conversation between two senior auditors regarding the audit risk model. The following are some statements made in that conversation regarding the audit risk model.

Group Activity

Required

In small groups, discuss whether you agree or disagree with each of the statements. Select a representative of your group who will be responsible for describing your group's rationale to the entire class following this exercise.

1. Materiality is a concept that can be applied quantitatively or qualitatively. In essence, it is a concept used to ensure that the auditor gathers sufficient evidence to render an opinion on the financial statements without adversely affecting the decision of a reasonable person relying on the financial statements.

2. Setting audit risk at 5% is a valid setting for controlling audit risk at a low level only if the auditor assumes that inherent risk is 100%, or significantly greater than the real level of inherent risk.

3. Inherent risk may be very small for some accounts (e.g., the recording of sales transactions at a Wal-Mart). In fact, some inherent risks may be close to 0.01%. In such cases, the auditor does not need to perform direct tests of account balances if he or she can be assured that inherent risk is indeed that low and that internal controls, as designed, are working appropriately.

4. Control risk refers to both (a) the design of controls and (b) the operation of controls. To assess control risk as low, the auditor must gather evidence on both the design and operation of controls.

5. Detection risk at 50% implies that the direct test of the account balance has a 50% chance of not detecting a material misstatement and that the auditor is relying on the assessment of inherent and control risk to address the additional uncertainty regarding the possibility of a material misstatement.

6. Audit risk should vary inversely with engagement risk: The higher the risk with being associated with the client, the lower should be the audit risk taken.

7. In analyzing the audit risk model, it is important to understand that much of it is judgmental. For example, setting audit risk is judgmental, assessing inherent and control risk is judgmental, and setting detection risk is simply a matter of the individual risk preferences of the auditor.

4-53 **(Audit Assessment of Materiality, LO 3)** The audit report provides reasonable assurance that the financial statements are free from material misstatements. The auditor is put in a difficult situation because materiality is defined from a user's viewpoint, but the auditor must assess materiality in planning the audit to ensure that sufficient audit work is performed to detect material misstatements.

Required

a. Define materiality as used in accounting and auditing, particularly emphasizing the differences in materiality definitions that exist from the FASB, the PCAOB, and the U.S. Supreme Court.

b. Three major dimensions of materiality are (1) the dollar magnitude of the item, (2) the nature of the item under consideration, (3) the perspective of a particular user. Give an example of each. Is one dimension more important than the other? Explain.

c. Once the auditor develops an assessment of materiality, can it change during the course of the audit? Explain. If it does change, what is the implication of a change for audit work that has already been completed? Explain.

4-54 **(Materiality and Audit Adjustments, LO 3)** Assume that the auditor has set planning materiality at $100,000 for misstatements affecting income and $125,000 for asset or liability misstatements that do not affect income. The auditor tests some accounts and has a great deal of confidence in the correct determination of the account balance. For other accounts, such as estimates, the auditor has a best estimate and a range in which he or she believes the correct amount exists. The following information is available upon completion of the audit:

	This Year Balance	Auditor Estimated Balance	Last Year Unadjusted Misstatement
Accounts Receivable	$1.2 million	$1.15 Range: 1.0–1.25	$80,000 over
Prepaid Insurance	120,000	100,000	5,000 under
Prepaid Revenue	1.8 million	1.95 million Range: 1.92–1.98	90,000 over

Auditors often deal with uncertainty—including uncertainty about the correct amount of an account balance. The uncertainty occurs because (a) the auditor uses sampling and (b) some estimates are imprecise.

Required

a. How should the auditor deal with uncertainty when making materiality judgments regarding account balances and the company's financial statements? For example, should the auditor use the best estimate or the upper or lower limit of the estimated range in determining whether an account balance is materially misstated? Explain.

b. How much is net income misstated for this year? Is the amount of misstatement considered material? Explain.

c. What is the minimum amount of adjustment that needs to be made this year in order for the financial statements to not be materially misstated? Explain.

d. What adjustments do you recommend making to the current year's financial statements? Prepare a list of adjustments.

e. What is the rationale for not booking immaterial adjustments? Do you agree with the rationale?

f. An estimate is an estimate; it is not a precise answer. Assume that management is absolutely convinced that its estimates are correct and the auditor's estimates are incorrect. What options are open to the auditor regarding the account balance? Could the auditor give an unqualified opinion on the financial statements because the financial statements are management's statements and management is convinced that it is correct?

4-55 **(Risks Associated with a Client, LO 2)** James Johnson has just completed a detailed analysis of a potential new audit client, Rural Railroad and Pipeline, Inc. (RRP). James reports that the name is deceiving. The company is no longer in the railroad business but owns a significant amount of land rights along former railway lines. The land rights have been leased to pipeline companies for transporting

Professional Skepticism

natural gas. It has also leased some land rights to communications companies for laying fiber-optic cable. The company is traded over the counter. James interviewed the current auditors and members of management in preparing the following outline report:

> The company is dominated by Keelyn Kravits. Ms. Kravits has recently acquired the company through a leveraged buyout (LBO). The LBO was achieved through a substantial borrowing that is now recorded on the books of RRP. The debt is at 3% over prime and requires the maintenance of minimum profitability and current ratios. If those ratios are not attained, the debt will either be immediately due—or, at the option of the lender, the interest rate can be raised anywhere from 2% to 4%.

Ms. Kravits has a reputation for coming into a company, slashing expenses, and making the company profitable. At the end of three to five years, she often takes the company back to being publicly traded. Although most of this is commendable, it should also be noted that Ms. Kravits has been very aggressive in using the flexibility in accounting principles to achieve profitability objectives.

The LBO has generated a large amount of recorded goodwill. In fact, the recorded goodwill represents 43% of total assets. The company recently acquired a small communications company that is providing local phone service in one part of the region covered by RRP. The company has older technology and appears to have lagged behind the industry in developing computerized billing procedures. Its billing is all computerized, but it appears to be more error prone than that of some of its competitors, judging by the number of phone calls to the customer service department.

The company has been subject to governmental investigations and has constantly pushed the limit in acquiring and marketing additional rights of way. The governmental complaints have often focused on environmental issues and noncompliance with land-use approvals for new developments.

The previous auditor had no significant problems with the company under its old management. Ms. Kravits believes the previous audit firm was not large enough to render the services needed; she wants an auditor who acts like a "business partner" and will not be reluctant to offer constructive suggestions.

Ms. Kravits states that she will look to the new audit firm to do a substantial amount of consulting work.

One recent acquisition is a small casino that will operate on the company's property in Las Vegas. Although the company is not experienced in this area, it plans to retain existing management to run this operation. Ms. Kravits believes this acquisition is an ideal fit, because she would like to use communications technology to bring the excitement of Las Vegas to the Internet.

Required

a. The audit partner wants a report summarizing the potential benefits and disadvantages of becoming the auditor for RRP. In your memo, identify all the pertinent risks the audit partner should consider in determining whether to make a proposal to become the auditor for RRP.

b. What factors should the audit partner consider in determining how much to bid to become the auditor for RRP? For each factor identified, indicate its effect on the cost and conduct of the potential audit.

c. What other information would you want to gather before developing a proposal for the audit of RRP?

d. How might auditors with more versus less professional skepticism view the facts in this case differently?

4-56   **(Understanding a Business: Risk Assessment, LO 1, 4, 6)** The auditor needs to understand the business in order to assess the risk of potential account misstatements. In preparing for a new audit, the auditor arranges to take a tour of the manufacturing plant and the distribution center. The client is a manufacturer of heavy machinery. Its major distribution center is located in a building next to the manufacturing facility.

Required

The auditor made the following list of observations during the tour of the plant and distribution center. For each observation, indicate:

a. The potential audit risk associated with the observation.

b. How the audit should be adjusted for the knowledge of the risk.

Tour of Plant Observations

1. The auditor notes three separate lines of production for three distinct product lines. Two seem to be highly automated, but one seems antique.

2. The auditor notes that a large number of production machines are sitting idle outside and that a second line of one of the company's main products is not in operation.

3. The client uses a large amount of chemicals. The waste chemicals are stored in vats and barrels in the yard before being shipped for disposal to an independent disposal firm.

4. The distribution center seems busy and messy. Although there appear to be defined procedures, the supervisor indicates that during peak times when orders must be shipped, the priority is to get them shipped. Employees "catch up" on paperwork during slack time.

5. One area of the distribution center contains some products that seem to have been there for a long time. They are dusty and the packaging looks old.

6. Some products are sitting in a transition room outside the receiving area. The supervisor indicates that the products either have not been inspected yet, or they have failed inspection and he is awaiting orders on what to do with them.

7. The receiving area is fairly automated. Many products come packaged in cartons or boxes. The receiving department uses computer scanners to read the contents on a bar code, and when bar codes are used, the boxes or containers are moved immediately to the production area where they are to be used.

8. One production line uses just-in-time inventory for its major component products. These goods are received in rail cars that sit just outside the production area. When production begins, the rail cars are moved directly into production. There is no receiving function for these goods.

9. The company uses minimum security procedures at the warehouse. There is a fence around the facilities, but employees and others seem to be able to come and go with ease.

Professional Skepticism

4-57   (Analytical Review in Planning an Audit, LO 7) Analytical review can be an extremely powerful tool in identifying potential problem areas in an audit. Analytical review can consist of trend and ratio analysis and can be performed by comparisons within the same company or comparisons across the industry. The following information shows the past two periods of results for a company and a comparison with industry data for the same period:

ANALYTICAL DATA FOR JONES MANUFACTURING

	Prior Period (000 omitted)	Percent of Sales	Current Period (000 omitted)	Percent of Sales	Percent Change	Industry Average as a Percent of Sales
Sales	$10,000	100	$11,000	100	10	100
Inventory	$2,000	20	$3,250	29.5	57.5	22.5
Cost of goods sold	$6,000	60	$6,050	55	0.83	59.5
Accounts payable	$1,200	12	$1,980	18	65	14.5
Sales commissions	$500	5	$550	5	10	Not available
Inventory turnover	6.3	—	4.2	—	(33)	5.85
Average number of days to collect	39	—	48	—	23	36
Employee turnover	5%	—	8%	—	60	4
Return on investment	14%	—	14.3%	—	—	13.8
Debt/Equity	35%	—	60%	—	71	30

Required

a. What are the advantages and limitations of comparing company data with industry data during the planning portion of an audit?

b. From the preceding data, identify potential risk areas and explain why they represent potential risk. Briefly indicate how the risk analysis should affect the planning of the audit engagement.

c. Identify any of the above data that should cause the auditor to increase the level of professional skepticism.

4-58   (Analytical Review and Planning the Audit, LO 7) The following table contains calculations of several key ratios for Indianola Pharmaceutical Company, a maker of proprietary and prescription drugs. The company is publicly held and is considered a small- to medium-size pharmaceutical company. Approximately 80% of its sales have been in prescription drugs; the remaining 20% are in medical supplies normally found in a drugstore. The primary purpose of the auditor's calculations is to identify potential risk areas for the upcoming audit. The auditor recognizes that some of the data may signal the need to gather other industry- or company-specific data.

A number of the company's drugs are patented. Its best-selling drug, Anecillin, which will come off of patent in two years, has accounted for approximately 20% of the company's sales during the past five years.

INDIANOLA PHARMACEUTICAL RATIO ANALYSIS

Ratio	Current Year	One Year Previous	Two Years Previous	Three Years Previous	Current Industry
Current ratio	1.85	1.89	2.28	2.51	2.13
Quick ratio	0.85	0.93	1.32	1.76	1.40
Interest coverage:					
Times interest earned	1.30	1.45	5.89	6.3	4.50
Days' sales in receivables	109	96	100	72	69
Inventory turnover	2.40	2.21	3.96	5.31	4.33
Days' sales in inventory	152	165	92	69	84
Research & development as % of sales	1.3	1.4	1.94	2.03	4.26
Cost of goods sold as % of sales	38.5	40.2	41.2	43.8	44.5
Debt/equity ratio	4.85	4.88	1.25	1.13	1.25
Earnings per share	$1.12	$2.50	$4.32	$4.26	n/a
Sales/tangible assets	0.68	0.64	0.89	0.87	0.99
Sales/total assets	0.33	0.35	0.89	0.87	0.78
Sales growth over past year	3%	15%	2%	4%	6%

Required

a. What major conclusions regarding financial reporting risk can be drawn from the information shown in the table? Be specific in identifying specific account balances that have a high risk of misstatement. State how that risk analysis will be used in planning the audit. Be very specific in your answer. You should identify a minimum of four financial reporting risks that should be addressed during the audit and how they should be addressed.

b. What other critical background information might you want to obtain as part of the planning of the audit or would you gather during the conduct of the audit? Briefly indicate the probable sources of the information.

c. Based on the information, what major actions did the company take during the immediately preceding year? Explain.

4-59   **(Ethical Considerations in Obtaining a New Audit Client, LO 2, 6, 8)**
Keune and Keune, CPAs, a regional audit firm with most of its activities located in one state, just accepted a new privately held company as an audit client. The company is considered a plum because it is one of the largest companies in that region of the state. It is well known in the home building business and its owner, Paul Maynard, sponsors race cars in both the Indy League and NASCAR with the company's logo and name on the cars. Because the company is well known, the audit partners concentrated on scoping and pricing the engagement. The auditors are well aware of the previous auditors, but given the reputation of the company, they did not feel a need to contact the predecessor auditors because it was a routine "bid for audit" and the current auditors were also bidding. Because it was routine, the auditors did not feel it necessary to write an engagement letter.

After beginning the audit, the auditors find out the following:

- The audit committee was not involved in the decision to change auditors, and only two of the three audit committee members are outside directors.

Ethics

Professional Skepticism

- The company engages in significant related-party transactions to minimize its tax liability. Although not illegal, the transactions do not meet the substance criteria required by the IRS. Company management is adamant that it will not change unless the IRS requires it to change.

- There are a significant number of related-party transactions with the owner, and no valid business reason or economic benefit to the company is associated with these transactions.

- The decision to invest $15 million in sponsoring race cars was not approved by the board, but came at the dictate of the company CEO, Paul Maynard, who has a passion for racing.

- The board consists of mostly family members, with only two members who might be considered outside directors.

- The company wants to file to obtain public debt but has not done so yet. However, it does not feel that Sarbanes-Oxley 404 is effective and has told the auditors that they need to rely on their existing tests of account balances and controls in order to issue the required report on internal control over financial reporting.

- There is a very casual attitude toward accounting. The CFO states: "Most accounts are estimates, and my estimate is as good as anybody else's." Thus, there is no need to spend a great deal of time on those accounts.

Required

a. What are the important deficiencies in the auditor's process of accepting the audit client? What should have been done prior to accepting the client?

b. Many of the issues identified above reflect negatively on the integrity of management.

1. What choices does the auditor have regarding continuing the audit or resigning from the audit? What choice do you recommend and why? If the auditor resigns from the audit, to whom must the reasons for the resignation be communicated?

2. How would an engagement letter have been useful to the audit firm in this engagement? Will an engagement letter normally cover the types of issues that were subsequently identified by the auditor? How would an engagement letter assist the auditor should the auditor decide to resign?

3. How would the audit be expanded given the findings stated above? How will professional skepticism impact the planning of the audit? Be specific in your answer.

4. If the auditor has to significantly expand the audit because of the problems identified above, and the auditor had bid the audit for a fixed fee for the first three years, is it permissible to (a) raise the audit rates or (b) resign? Explain your answer.

c. Is it ethically appropriate for the audit firm to resign from this client at this point? Is it obligated to continue providing services to this client? In structuring your answer, consider the ethical decision-making framework that was introduced in Chapter 3 and recall that it consists of the following steps: (1) identify the ethical issue(s); (2) determine who are the affected parties and identify their rights; (3) determine the most important rights; (4) develop alternative courses of action; (5) determine the likely consequences of each proposed course of action; (6) assess the possible consequences, including an estimation of the greatest good for the greatest number; (7) determine whether the rights framework would cause any course of action to be eliminated; and (8) decide on the appropriate course of action.

4-60   **(Assessing Changing Risk Conditions and Audit Planning, LO 1, 4, 6)**
The introductory material to the chapter painted a scenario that was based on the financial crisis that first came to light in the fall of 2008. In that scenario, it was stated that:

- For many manufacturing companies, goodwill is now one of the largest assets on their books.

- Many companies are downsizing, and not only will they be laying people off, they will be reducing inventories and closing plants.

- Sales are expected to be down.

- Customers will be paying more slowly, and some may not be able to pay at all.

- Return on the company's pension assets may be significantly lower.

Required

Assume you are auditing a manufacturing firm headquartered in the United States, 80% of its sales are made in the United States, and 60% of its manufacturing is also located in the United States. The two largest assets are property, plant, and equipment (31% of assets) and goodwill (24% of assets). It is likely that the firm will be scaling back operations. The other large assets are receivables and inventory.

a. Identify the accounting decisions that must be made by the company regarding the five significant trends identified above.

b. For four asset accounts identified above (PPE, goodwill, receivables, and inventory), indicate how the audit will change this year because of the economic downturn. Be specific as to how the auditor should gather the information regarding each of these accounts to assess their proper valuation.

c. How important are both economic trends and industry trends regarding the valuation of the above assets? Management asserts that the trends are only temporary and that there is no need to write down any of the assets. However, assume that current economic data does not justify that optimism; i.e., the industry is down, the clients are slow in paying, and inventory is building up. How does the auditor deal with the optimism of management—who might be right—and the accounting requirements?

4-61   **(New PCAOB Auditing Standard on Identifying and Assessing Risks, LO 6)** In August 2010 the PCAOB approved AS No. 12. Access this standard at the PCAOB website (www.pcaob.org). Paragraph 5 of the standard lists five risk assessment procedures that the auditor is to perform. Assume that you are a senior on an audit engagement and need to explain to your intern what each of these procedures involves and why the auditor performs these procedures. In your own words, and using terminology that is understandable to an intern who has not yet taken an auditing course, describe these procedures and the reason that the auditor performs these procedures. Be brief; you should only use one or two paragraphs for each procedure.

Internet

Cases

**Professional
Skepticism**

4-62   **(Risk Analysis, LO 1, 4, 6, 7)** The auditor for ABC Wholesaling Company has just begun to perform preliminary analytical procedures as part of planning the audit for the coming year. ABC Wholesaling is in a competitive industry, selling products such as STP Brand products and Ortho Grow products to companies such as Wal-Mart, Kmart, and regional retail discount chains. The company is privately owned and has experienced financial difficulty this past year. The difficulty could lead to its major line of credit being pulled if the company does not make a profit in the current year. In performing the analytical procedures, the auditor notes the following changes in accounts related to accounts receivable:

	Current Year (000) omitted	Previous Year (000) omitted
Sales	$60,000	$59,000
Accounts receivable	$11,000	$7,200
Percent of accounts receivable current	72%	65%
No. of days' sales in accounts receivable	64	42
Gross margin	18.7%	15.9%
Industry gross margin	16.3%	16.3%
Increase in Nov.–Dec. sales over previous year	12%	3.1%

The auditor had expected the receivables balance to remain stable, but notes the large increase in receivables. After considering possible reasons for this increase, the auditor decides to make inquiries of management. Management explains that the change is due to two things: (1) a new computer system that has increased productivity, and (2) a new policy of rebilling items previously sold to customers, thereby extending the due dates from October to April. The rebilling is explained as follows: Many of the clients' products are seasonal; for example, lawn care products. To provide better service to ABC's customers, management instituted a new policy whereby management negotiated with a customer to determine the approximate amount of seasonal goods on hand at the end of the selling season (October). If the customer would continue to purchase from the client, management would rebill the existing inventory, thereby extending the due date from October until the following April, essentially giving an interest-free loan to the customer. The customer, in turn, agreed to keep the existing goods and store them on its site for next year's retail sales.

The key to analytical procedures is to determine whether potential explanations satisfy all the changes that are observed in account balances. Further, it is important to be professionally skeptical of management-provided explanations. For example, does the explanation of a new computer system and the rebilling adequately explain all the changes, or are there other explanations that are more viable? The auditor must be able to answer these questions to properly apply the risk-based approach to auditing. There are several factors that would indicate to a skeptical auditor that these explanations might not hold:

1. The company has a large increase in gross margin. This seems unlikely, because it is selling to large chains with considerable purchasing power. Further, other competitors are also likely to have effective computer systems.

2. If the rebilling items are properly accounted for, there should not be a large increase in sales for the last two months of this year when the total sales for the previous year is practically the same as that of the preceding year.

3. If the rebillings are for holding the inventory at customers' locations, the auditor should investigate to determine (a) if the items were properly recorded as a sale in the first place or if they should still be recorded as inventory, (b) what the client's motivation is for extending credit to the customers indicated, and (c) whether it is a coincidence that all of the rebilled items were to large retailers who do not respond to accounts receivable confirmations received from auditors.

Required

a. What potential hypotheses would likely explain the changes in the financial data given? Identify all that might explain the change in ratios, including those identified by management.

b. Of those identified, which hypothesis would best explain all the changes in the ratios and financial account balances? Explain the rationale for your answer.

c. Given the most important hypothesis identified, what specific audit procedures do you recommend as highest priority? Why?

4-63   **(Using Electronic Information in Performing Risk Analysis, LO 1, 4, 6)** The auditor increasingly relies on electronic sources of information to keep up-to-date on industry developments, new trends in the economy, regulatory requirements, and other coverage of the client in the financial press.

Internet

Required

Select a publicly owned company that is of interest to you. Access the Internet to gather information about the company, the industry, and the risks associated with the company. In your online search, include the following:

- The company's annual report, either on its home page or as filed with the SEC, using EDGAR or IDEA or SEC.gov (look at the management discussion and analysis section as well as other information)

- A company chat line, such as Yahoo Finance

- Another source of industry data such as Yahoo Finance or Hoover's Online

- A stockbroker analysis or investment analyst

  a. Develop an industry analysis and a business risk analysis for the company (ask your instructor about length of paper).

  b. Consider the online search sources and answer the following issues for each source:

1. Usefulness of the site in providing relevant background information about the company, including its strategies and competitors.

2. Ease of use in obtaining the information.

3. Reliability of information. Contrast the information received from (a) the chat line, (b) the stockbroker/investment analyst, (c) management's discussion and analysis section of the annual report, and (d) the other financial sources of industry data.

4. Comprehensiveness of information obtained.

5. Usefulness of the data in identifying risks.

Internet

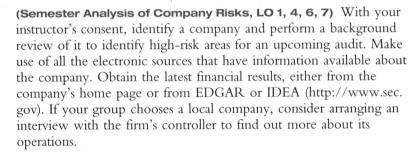

Group Activity

4-64   **(Semester Analysis of Company Risks, LO 1, 4, 6, 7)** With your instructor's consent, identify a company and perform a background review of it to identify high-risk areas for an upcoming audit. Make use of all the electronic sources that have information available about the company. Obtain the latest financial results, either from the company's home page or from EDGAR or IDEA (http://www.sec.gov). If your group chooses a local company, consider arranging an interview with the firm's controller to find out more about its operations.

Required

Prepare a detailed analysis of risk for the company and discuss the implications of the risk areas for the audit of that company. In preparing the analysis, be sure to include the following:

- Business strategies
- Key competitors
- Industry trends
- Key business processes
- Financial resources and availability
- Major risks
- Implications of those risks for the conduct of the audit

Fraud

4-65   **(Lincoln Federal Savings and Loan, LO 1, 4, 6)** The following is a description of various factors that affected the operations of Lincoln Federal Savings and Loan, a California savings and loan (S&L) that was a subsidiary of American Continental Company, a real estate development company run by Charles Keating.

Required

a. After reading the discussion of Lincoln Federal Savings and Loan, identify the risk areas that should be identified in planning for the audit.

b. Briefly discuss the risks identified and the implication of those risks for the conduct of the audit.

c. The auditor did review a few independent appraisals indicating the market value of the real estate in folders for loans. How convincing are such appraisals? In other words, what attributes are necessary in order for the appraisals to constitute persuasive evidence?

Lincoln Federal Savings & Loan

Savings and Loan industry background—The S&L industry was developed in the early part of the twentieth century in response to a perceived need to provide low-cost financing to encourage home ownership. As such, legislation by Congress made the S&L industry the primary financial group allowed to make low-cost home ownership loans (mortgages).

For many years, the industry operated by accepting relatively long-term deposits from customers and making 25- to 30-year loans at fixed rates on home mortgages. The industry was generally considered to be safe. Most of the S&Ls (also known as thrifts) were small, federally chartered institutions with deposits insured by the FSLIC. "Get your deposits in, make loans, sit back, and earn your returns. Get to work by 9 a.m. and out to the golf course by noon" seemed to be the motto of many S&L managers.

Changing economic environment—During the 1970s, two major economic events hit the S&L industry. First, the rate of inflation had reached an all-time high. Prime interest rates had gone as high as 19.5%. Second, deposits were being drawn away from the S&Ls by new competitors that offered short-term variable rates substantially higher than current passbook savings rates. The S&Ls responded by increasing the rates on certificates of deposit to extraordinary levels (15–16%) while servicing mortgages with 20- to 30-year maturities made at old rates of 7–8%. The S&Ls attempted to mitigate the problem by offering variable-rate mortgages or by selling off some of their mortgages (at substantial losses) to other firms.

However, following regulatory accounting principles, the S&Ls were not required to recognize market values of loans that were not sold. Thus, even if loan values were substantially less than the book value, they would continue to be carried at book value as long as the mortgage holder was not in default.

Changing regulatory environment—Congress moved to deregulate the S&L industry. During the first half of 1982, the S&L industry lost a record $3.3 billion (even without marking loans down to real value). In August 1982, President Reagan signed the Garn-St. Germain Depository Institutions Act of 1982, hailing it as "the most important legislation for financial institutions in 50 years." The bill had several key elements:

- S&Ls would be allowed to offer money market funds free from withdrawal penalties or interest rate regulation.

- S&Ls could invest up to 40% of their assets in nonresidential real estate lending. Commercial lending was much riskier than home lending, but the potential returns were greater. In addition, the regulators helped the deregulatory fever by removing a regulation that had required a savings and loan institution to have 400 stockholders with no one owning more than 25%—allowing a single shareholder to own a savings and loan institution.

- The bill made it easier for an entrepreneur to purchase a savings and loan. Regulators allowed buyers to start (capitalize) their thrift with land or other "noncash" assets rather than money.

- The bill allowed thrifts to stop requiring traditional down payments and to provide 100% financing, with the borrower not required to invest a dime of personal money in the deal.

- The bill permitted thrifts to make real estate loans anywhere. They had previously been required to make loans on property located only in their own geographic area.

Accounting—In addition to these revolutionary changes, owners of troubled thrifts began stretching already liberal accounting rules—with regulators' blessings—to squeeze their balance sheets into (regulatory) compliance. For example, goodwill, defined as customer loyalty, market share, and other intangible "warm fuzzies," accounted for over 40% of the thrift industry's net worth by 1986.

Lincoln Federal S&L—American Continental Corporation, a land development company run by Charles Keating and headquartered in Phoenix, purchased Lincoln Federal S&L. Immediately, Keating expanded the lending activity of Lincoln to assist in the development of American Continental projects, including the Phoenician Resort in Scottsdale.[3] Additionally, Keating sought higher returns by purchasing junk bonds marketed by Drexel Burnham and Michael Millken. Nine of Keating's relatives were on the Lincoln payroll at salaries ranging from over $500,000 to over $1 million.

Keating came up with novel ideas to raise capital. Rather than raising funds through deposits, he had commissioned agents working in the Lincoln offices who sold special bonds of American Continental Corp. The investors were assured that their investments would be safe. Unfortunately, many elderly individuals put their life savings into these bonds, thinking they were backed by the FSLIC because they were sold at an S&L, but they were not.

Keating continued investments in real estate deals, such as a planned megacommunity in the desert outside of Phoenix. He relied on appraisals, some obviously of dubious value, to serve as a basis for the loan valuation.

Academic Research Case (LO 2)

SEARCH HINT

It is easy to locate these academic research articles! Simply use a search engine (e.g., Google Scholar) or an electronic research platform (e.g., ABI Inform) and search using the author names and part of the article title.

Academic research addresses the conceptual issues outlined in this chapter. To help you consider the linkage between academic research and the practice of auditing, read the following research article and answer the questions below.

Johnstone, K. (2000). Client-Acceptance Decisions: Simultaneous Effects of Client Business Risk, Audit Risk, Auditor Business Risk, and Risk Adaptation. *Auditing, A Journal of Practice & Theory. Sarasota: 19(1): 1–25.*

i. What is the issue being addressed in the paper?

ii. Why is this issue important to practicing auditors?

iii. What are the findings of the paper?

iv. What are the implications of these findings for audit quality (or audit practice) on the audit profession?

v. Describe the research methodology used as a basis for the conclusions.

vi. Describe any limitations of the research that the student (and practice) should be aware of.

---

[3]The Phoenician was so lavishly constructed that a regulator estimated that just to break even, the resort would have to charge $500 per room per night at a 70% occupancy rate. Similar resort rooms in the area were available at $125 a night.

Go to www.cengage.com/accounting/rittenberg for the Ford and Toyota materials.

Source and Reference	Question
Ford 10-K	**1a.** Describe the primary risks facing Ford.
Toyota 20-F	**1b.** Describe the primary risks facing Toyota.
	1c. Compare the risks of Ford and Toyota.
	1d. Why would auditors want to know about their clients' business-related risks?
Ford Def 14A, Toyota 20-F	**2a.** What are related-party transactions?
	2b. Why do related-party transactions pose a risk to audit firms?
	2c. Read about the related parties at Ford and Toyota. Does one firm have more related-party transactions than the other? If so, what might be the rationale? Are there any situations that cause you particular concern? Explain your concern.

A Computerized Audit Practice Case

Description of the Practice Case

This case has two learning objectives. First, it provides the student an opportunity to apply auditing concepts to a "real-life" audit client. The client, Biltrite Bicycles, Inc., operates within a unique business climate and internal control environment, and the student must assess inherent risk and control risk accordingly. The case contains modules involving sampling applications, risk assessment, audit documentation, analysis of design of controls, tests of details, audit adjustments, and an audit report upon completion of the 2009 engagement. Second, the case enables the student to use the computer as an audit-assist device. The student may use the computer in the Biltrite case to both automate the fieldwork and assist in decision-making.

The case consists of modules. At the end of each module is a set of requirements. The student will need an PC and an Excel or Excel-compatible spreadsheet program, and the student should download the data files from the website www.rittenberg.swlearning.com under the tab "Student Resources."

The modules parallel the phases of a financial statement audit. Many of the modules require both qualitative and quantitative analyses. Based on narrative material and on partially completed audit documentation, the student will be asked to complete the documentation, arrive at audit conclusions, and/or answer questions relating to specific auditing standards and interpretations. The following modules make up the Biltrite case:

Module I: Assessment of inherent risk
Module II: Assessment of control risk
Module III: Control testing the sales processing subset of the revenue cycle
Module IV: PPS sampling—factory equipment additions
Module V: Accounts receivable aging analysis and adequacy of allowance
                 for doubtful accounts
Module VI: Sales and purchases cutoff tests
Module VII: Search for unrecorded liabilities
Module VIII: Dallas Dollar Bank—bank reconciliation
Module IX: Analysis of inter-bank transfers
Module X: Analysis of marketable securities
Module XI: Plant asset additions and disposals
Module XII: Estimated liability for product warranty
Module XIII: Mortgage note payable and note payable to Bank Two
Module XIV: Working trial balance
Module XV: Audit report

We recommend that the modules be completed in the following order:

Module I: Following Chapter 4
Module II: Following Chapter 6
Module III, IV, and V: Following Chapter 10★
Modules VI and VII: Following Chapter 11
Modules VIII, IX, and X: Following Chapter 12
Module XI: Following Chapter 13

★Module IV may be completed after either Chapter 10 or Chapter 14. Check with your instructor.

Modules IV, XII and XIII: Following Chapter 14★
Module XIV: Following Chapter 15
Module XV: Following Chapter 16

For purposes of this case, the income tax effects of audit adjustments have been ignored.

Description of the Company

Operations   Biltrite was incorporated in 1970 to manufacture ten-speed touring bikes. An exercise bike was added to the product line in 1980, and mountain bikes were added in 1987.

Currently, the company makes the following products:

Grand Prix: Ten-speed touring bike
Phoenix: Deluxe eighteen-speed racing bike
Pike's Peak: Twelve-speed mountain bike
Himalaya: Eighteen-speed deluxe mountain bike
Waistliner: Stationary exercise bike

All of these products are manufactured in one plant, which is located in eastern Texas. Derailleurs (front and rear) comprise a major portion of the parts inventory. Other purchased parts consist of tires, handle grips, pedals, wheels, and spokes. Materials and supplies consist primarily of paint and steel. Biltrite manufactures the frames and handlebars, and assembles and paints the bikes.

The factory, which employs 2,000 workers, was built in 1970, was refurbished and updated five years ago, and it is now quite automated. Increased automation enabled Biltrite to decrease its factory workers from 3,000 workers ten years ago to 2,000 workers just two years ago. The vice president of production observed that automation enabled Biltrite to significantly increase production-worker productivity. The marketing vice president agrees and predicts revenue and profit growth for at least the next two to three years. In addition to the 2,000 production workers, the company employs 200 salaried administrative employees, including the corporate management staff, warehouse superintendents, and regional sales managers. In addition, the regional units employ 100 warehouse personnel and 120 salespersons. Hourly employees, consisting of the production workers and warehouse personnel, are paid weekly; salaried employees are paid biweekly. Salespersons receive a salary plus 5 percent commission, based on gross sales.

Biltrite's administrative offices are located in another building in the same complex. The company has ten regional distribution locations in various parts of the United States; each location consists of a warehouse headed by a warehouse superintendent and a sales office directed by a regional sales manager. Products are shipped to the warehouses upon completion, and from the warehouses they are shipped to licensed dealers in the respective regions. The dealer network consists of approximately 1,500 outlets located throughout the United States and Canada.

All products carry a full one-year warranty covering parts and labor. The company is known for the quality of its products and for its strong service support. As of the end of 2009, the company had a total of 60 customer accounts ranging in amounts from $2,200 to approximately $1,350,000. The cumulative accounts receivable at year-end December 31, 2009, was $12 million.

Biltrite experienced steady growth in sales and profitability of all product lines from the date of incorporation until about four years ago. From about four years ago until the current year, competition from international manufacturers has had a significant impact on Biltrite's revenue and net profit

---

★Module IV may be completed after either Chapter 10 or Chapter 14. Check with your instructor.

(see Exhibit BR.1). However, Biltrite has experienced significant growth in sales and profitability for the current year.

In an attempt to combat the strong competition from foreign bicycle producers, managers at Biltrite, particularly those responsible for marketing and controlling production costs, have been given demanding performance targets in recent years. While the financial rewards for meeting or exceeding these targets are great, the targets are deemed very challenging. In response, many marketing and production-control managers have left the firm for opportunities elsewhere, leaving Biltrite relatively understaffed in some areas. In addition, many recent hires to the management team have not been provided with sufficient descriptions of or training for the tasks, knowledge, and skills needed to succeed.

Audit Engagement Your firm, Denise Vaughan & Co., Certified Public Accountants, has audited Biltrite since its incorporation in 1970. Denise Vaughan is presently the partner in charge of the engagement and Carolyn Volmar is the audit manager. The audit team consists of Richard Derick, senior auditor in charge of the Biltrite audit; Cheryl Lucas, assistant auditor, in her third year with the firm and her third year on the Biltrite audit; Shelly Ross, assistant auditor in her second year with the firm and her second year on the Biltrite audit; and a student (you), assistant auditor, newly hired. Biltrite will be your first audit.

Derick has been in charge of the Biltrite audit fieldwork for the past two years. Prior to that time he had been a part of the Biltrite audit team as an assistant. He is very familiar with the client's operations and internal controls and works well with Biltrite personnel. Richard Derick and his audit team were present at Biltrite's year-end physical inventory.

Biltrite Personnel In 2000, Trevor Lawton assumed control of Biltrite after the retirement of his father, the founder of the company. The Lawton family presently owns 25 percent of the outstanding Biltrite common stock; the remaining 75 percent is held by nonfamily members. Biltrite is not subject to SEC regulation. Lawton managed conservatively when first becoming CEO and president of Biltrite. In recent years he has become increasingly aggressive, believing that strategic changes must be bold, frequent, and swift in order to prevail in the highly competitive bicycle industry. He has worked to make his management perspective the basis of Biltrite's corporate culture. Lawton believes that success can be attained via aggressive marketing and containment of production costs. As a result of devoting most of his attention to sales and production, he is relatively detached from financial reporting matters. Lawton generally views the accounting function as a necessary evil conducted by "bean counters" that don't seem to understand the need for Biltrite's financial statements to "look good." Consistent with these views, the accounting group has received modest allocations of resources in recent years, and operates with a relatively small, but seemingly competent and trustworthy staff.

Reflecting Lawton's preference for centralized management, Lawton and the vice presidents of production and marketing determine Biltmore's objectives and strategic plan with little input from other managers. Once determined, the objectives and strategic plan are not widely disseminated to employees, but are presented for feedback and approval at board of directors' meetings. Privately, some managers and board members believe the financial objectives to be overly optimistic and unlikely to be attained. In addition, many middle- and lower-level managers feel the supporting budgets lack the necessary resources to meet financial objectives.

For the past couple of years, Lawton has been unable to devote the time he would like to identifying and managing an increasing array of risks. To address this problem, Lawton has begun forming a small enterprise risk management

Bittrite Bicycles, Inc., Comparative Income Statements, 2000–2009 (in thousands of dollars)

	2009*	2008	2007	2006	2005	2004	2003	2002	2001	2000
Sales	$335,000	$280,000	$272,000	$274,500	$266,800	$269,300	$268,700	$265,570	$263,440	$262,890
Cost of Goods Sold	227,800	215,600	209,440	211,365	205,436	188,510	188,090	185,899	184,408	184,023
Gross Profit	107,200	64,400	62,560	63,135	61,364	80,790	80,610	79,671	79,032	78,867
Operating Expenses	45,770	42,330	41,400	42,000	40,680	39,997	40,100	38,965	38,670	37,700
Operating Income	61,430	22,070	21,160	21,135	20,684	40,793	40,510	40,706	40,362	41,167
Other Expenses (net)	15,668	8,960	8,700	8,240	8,150	7,890	7,940	7,760	7,240	7,123
Net Income before Taxes and Extraordinary Item	45,762	13,110	12,460	12,895	12,534	32,903	32,570	32,946	33,122	34,044
Income Taxes	13,729	4,542	4,150	3,869	3,760	9,871	9,771	9,884	9,937	10,213
Net Income before Extraordinary Item	32,033	8,568	8,310	9,026	8,774	23,032	22,799	23,062	23,185	23,831
Extraordinary Gain (Loss)—Net of Tax	0	1,235	0	(2,650)	0	0	(1,540)	0	3,400	0
Net Income	$ 32,033	$ 9,803	$ 8,310	$ 6,376	$ 8,774	$ 23,032	$ 21,259	$ 23,062	$ 26,585	$ 23,831

*Unaudited.

team comprised of managers with finance, marketing, and production expertise. The team would manage risks from both internal and external sources, and report directly to Lawton. Because of heavy demands on his time, Lawton has not been able to finalize formation of the risk management team. Currently, the mechanisms in place for identifying, analyzing, and acting on risk matters are rather unstructured and vary in quality from department to department. For example, risk management in production and procurement is known to be rather weak, while the corporate controller is thought to be doing quality risk management regarding financial reporting and information systems matters.

Gerald Groth, the corporate controller of Biltrite, has been with the company since receiving his MBA ten years ago. Groth is also a CPA and was a staff accountant with Denise Vaughan & Co. for five years just prior to joining Biltrite. Other Biltrite personnel include:

Elmer Fennig, vice president, production;

Charles Gibson, vice president, marketing;

Marlene McAfee, treasurer;

Laura Schroeder, director of human resources;

John Mesarvey, chief accountant;

Glenn Florence, director of internal auditing; and

Malissa Rust, director of Computer Based Information Systems (CBIS).

Mesarvey, Florence, and Rust report to Groth. Emil Ransbottom, the director of purchasing, as well as the plant manager and the factory supervisors, report to Fennig. Three personnel officers report to the director of human resources. Biltrite has three product managers—one for touring bikes, one for mountain bikes, and one for stationary bikes. The sales staff report to the product managers and the product managers report to Gibson. Under Mesarvey, the chief accountant, are Harriet Smith, transaction processing; Oliver Perna, cost accounting; and Janice Hollins, financial statements.

The reporting relationships at Biltrite have changed little since the mid-1970s even though Biltrite has experienced considerable growth in production volume and the warehouse distribution network, as well as a major transformation of its information system. However, over time responsibilities and authority for decision-making have become more centralized.

Board of Directors and Audit Committee   Lawton is the chairman of the board of directors. Also on the board are two of Lawton's siblings, neither of whom is engaged in day-to-day management of Biltrite. The rest of the board is comprised of Biltrite's treasurer and vice presidents of production and marketing, as well as a number of external members that were longtime business associates of Lawton's father. The external members of the board have considerable financial expertise in their respective industries (insurance, road construction, banking, health care, and software). The board meets quarterly (March, June, September, and December). At the December meeting, Biltrite's top managers present the board with the budget for the upcoming year and analyses of budget variances for the current year through November. Board members receive the budget and variance analyses approximately two weeks prior to the meeting. Given their limited financial expertise in the bicycle industry, Board members question or challenge the upcoming budget on few matters and seldom have probing questions regarding budget variances.

The audit committee (one of three committees along with the compensation and nomination committees) is made up exclusively of external members. At the June and December board meetings, the audit committee holds a joint meeting with the external audit partner, director of internal audit, and controller to be briefed on audit findings and approve the scope of planned audit activities. In addition, significant changes in internal control over financial reporting are presented and explained. The audit committee, in joint consultation with the compensation committee, approves the recommendations of the controller regarding the annual appointment of the external auditor, and the compensation and retention of the director of internal audit.

Accounting and Information Systems   Transaction processing is divided into the following sections: General ledger, accounts receivable, accounts payable, and payroll. The managers of these sections report to Smith. Three staff auditors report to the director of internal auditing. Harold Cannon, information technology manager, and Nancy Karling, management information systems manager, report to the CBIS director. Cannon's department is divided into four sections: data entry, data processing, control, and systems analysis and programming. Karling's department is divided into three sections: statistical analysis, budget coordination, and report generation. Reporting to the treasurer are Lawrence White, credit manager; Paula Penelee, portfolio manager; and Mark Wilkins, cashier.

Biltrite closes its general ledger on a calendar-year basis. Unaudited financial statements are prepared quarterly and are reviewed by Denise Vaughan & Co. The accounting information system, including the general ledger, inventories, receivables, payables, and plant assets, was initially computerized in 1982, and it was upgraded to a real-time system about three years ago. After extensive "debugging," the real-time system seems to be functioning smoothly.

The company has provided the auditors with a year-end adjusted trial balance and a complete set of financial statements, together with supporting schedules (see Exhibits BR.2–BR.6).

Biltrite's internal audit staff of three members plus the director is viewed by our external audit firm as competent. The internal audit group conducts evaluations of important processes (e.g., sales, purchases, payroll) on a recurring basis, usually once every ten to fourteen months. In addition, the group works on special projects as warranted. Any weaknesses in accounting and information systems are reported immediately to Groth and the responsible function manager. The director of internal audit reports directly to Groth and also makes periodic presentations of recommendations and findings to Lawton and the audit committee.

Exhibit BR.2	Biltrite Bicycles, Inc., Adjusted Trial Balance as of December 31, 2009

	Account Number	Debit	Credit
		(in thousands of dollars)	
Bank Two Demand Deposit	1001	$ 10,200	
Dallas Dollar Bank Demand Deposit	1002	2,100	
Dallas Dollar Bank Payroll Account	1008	57	
Petty Cash	1012	5	
Investments in Marketable Securities	1101	7,000	
All for Decline in Market Value of Securities	1102		$ 2,800
Accounts Receivable—Trade	1201	11,920	
Notes Receivable—Trade	1202	80	
Notes Receivable—Officers	1203	0	
Allowance for Doubtful Accounts	1250		220
Raw Materials Inventory	1310	6,200	

(Continues)

Exhibit BR.2	Biltrite Bicycles, Inc., Adjusted Trial Balance as of December 31, 2009 (*continued*)

	Account Number	Debit	Credit
		(in thousands of dollars)	
Derailleurs Inventory	1320	5,500	
Purchased Parts Inventory	1330	15,100	
Goods in Process—Grand Prix Touring Bike	1350	800	
Goods in Process—Phoenix Touring Bike	1351	700	
Goods in Process—Pike's Peak Mountain Bike	1352	1,500	
Goods in Process—Himalaya Mountain Bike	1361	1,200	
Goods in Process—Waistliner Stationary Bike	1365	300	
Finished Goods—Grand Prix Touring Bike	1371	1,616	
Finished Goods—Phoenix Touring Bike	1372	2,300	
Finished Goods—Pike's Peak Mountain Bike	1373	5,800	
Finished Goods—Himalaya Mountain Bike	1376	4,600	
Finished Goods—Waistliner Stationary Bike	1379	1,200	
Indirect Materials	1385	800	
Repair Parts Inventory	1390	2,600	
Prepaid Insurance	1410	600	
Deferred Taxes—Warranty	1440	400	
Land	1510	4,000	
Factory Building	1520	50,000	
Accumulated Depreciation—Building	1525		14,140
Warehouses and Sales Offices	1527	200,000	
Accumulated Depreciation—Warehouses and Sales Offices	1529		105,000
Factory Equipment	1530	360,000	
Accumulated Depreciation—Factory Equipment	1535		144,660
Office Building	1540	20,000	
Accumulated Depreciation—Office Building	1545		8,000
Office Fixtures and Equipment	1550	10,000	
Accumulated Depreciation—Office Fixtures and Equipment	1555		6,150
Autos and Trucks	1560	1,000	
Accumulated Depreciation—Autos and Trucks	1565		620
Patents	1610	4,000	
Copyrights	1620	2,000	
Deposits	1710	340	
Cost of Goods Sold—Grand Prix Touring Bike	5100	34,448	
Cost of Goods Sold—Phoenix Touring Bike	5200	32,903	
Cost of Goods Sold—Pike's Peak Mountain Bike	5300	89,584	
Cost of Goods Sold—Himalaya Mountain Bike	5400	22,075	
Cost of Goods Sold—Waistliner Stationary Bike	5500	48,790	
Direct Labor	6100	35,600	
Direct Labor Applied	6200		35,600
Indirect Labor	7201	5,500	
Depreciation—Factory Building	7205	2,000	
Depreciation—Factory Equipment	7206	42,060	
Real Estate Taxes	7210	4,400	
Personal Property Taxes	7211	1,600	
Manufacturing Supplies	7220	15,042	
FICA Tax Expense	7230	3,980	
State Unemployment Tax Expense	7231	1,120	
Federal Unemployment Tax Expense	7232	880	
Workers' Compensation Premiums	7233	550	
Health Insurance Premiums—Factory	7234	2,860	

Exhibit BR.2	Biltrite Bicycles, Inc., Adjusted Trial Balance as of December 31, 2009 (*continued*)

	Account Number	Debit	Credit
		(in thousands of dollars)	
Employee Pension Expense	7235	3,810	
Repairs and Maintenance Expense	7236	1,222	
Utilities Expense	7241	16,100	
Miscellaneous Factory Expense	7242	2,200	
Manufacturing Overhead Applied	7250		103,324
Sales Commissions	8310	16,500	
Sales Salaries	8320	1,200	
Bad Debts Expense	8325	500	
Product Warranty	8330	1,139	
Advertising	8340	3,311	
Miscellaneous Selling Expense	8350	420	
Administrative Salaries	9410	7,550	
Research and Development Costs	9420	1,050	
Patent Amortization	9425	700	
FICA Tax Expense	9431	856	
State Unemployment Tax Expense	9432	224	
Federal Unemployment Tax Expense	9433	120	
Workers' Compensation Premiums	9434	100	
Health Insurance Premiums—Administrative	9435	500	
Employee Pension Expense	9436	100	
Employee Profit Sharing Expense	9437	345	
Depreciation—Office Building	9440	800	
Depreciation—Office Fixtures and Equipment	9445	1,875	
Depreciation—Autos and Trucks	9447	320	
Depreciation—Warehouses and Sales Offices	9449	10,000	
Accounting Fees	9450	320	
Legal Fees	9451	430	
Other Professional Services	9452	20	
Supplies Expense	9460	200	
Insurance Expense	9470	450	
Printing and Copying Expense	9480	235	
Postage Expense	9481	285	
Gain/Loss on Disposal of Plant Assets	9485		4,000
Miscellaneous Administrative Expense	9490	220	
Interest Expense	9701	12,890	
Loss on Decline in Market Value of Securities	9702	2,800	
Federal Income Tax Expense	9990	10,329	
State Income Tax Expense	9991	1,923	
City Income Tax Expense	9992	1,477	
Notes Payable—Trade	2010		3,660
Accounts Payable—Trade	2020		10,200
Interest Payable	2030		3,400
Sales Salaries Payable	2041		30
Administrative Salaries Payable	2042		870
Factory Wages Payable	2043		1,290
FICA Payable	2051		310
State Income Taxes Withheld	2052		150
City Income Taxes Withheld	2053		50
Unemployment and Workers' Compensation Premiums Payable	2054		25

(Continues)

Exhibit BR.2	Biltrite Bicycles, Inc., Adjusted Trial Balance as of December 31, 2009 (*continued*)

	Account Number	Debit	Credit
		(in thousands of dollars)	
Accrued Profit Sharing Payable	2055		345
Federal Income Taxes Payable	2061		4,000
State Income Taxes Payable	2062		1,200
City Income Taxes Payable	2063		800
Estimated Product Warranty Liability	2070		544
Accrued Commissions Payable	2080		1,400
Mortgage Note Payable (10%)	2110		60,000
Deferred Tax Liability—Depreciation	2120		10,600
12% Note Payable to Bank Two	2130		45,000
10% Preferred Stock	3110		120,000
Common Stock	3120		100,000
Additional Paid-in Capital	3130		50,000
Treasury Stock	3140	8,153	
Retained Earnings	3150		29,574
Dividends	3160	15,000	
Sales—Grand Prix Touring Bike	4100		50,659
Sales—Phoenix Touring Bike	4200		47,360
Sales—Pike's Peak Touring Bike	4300		132,892
Sales—Himalaya Mountain Bike	4400		34,299
Sales—Waistliner Stationary Bike	4500		69,790
Interest Earned	4901		115
Dividends Earned	4902		105
Loss on Disposal of Investments	4903	198	
		$1,203,182	$1,203,182

Exhibit BR.3	Biltrite Bicycles, Inc., Income Statements for the Years Ended December 31, 2009 and 2008 (in thousands of dollars)

	Year Ended 12/31/2008		Year Ended 12/31/2008	
Sales Revenue		$ 335,000		$ 280,000
Cost of Goods Sold:				
Beginning inventories	$ 10,142		$ 6,690	
Cost of goods manufactured (Schedule 1)	233,174		219,052	
Cost of goods available for sale	243,316		225,742	
Ending inventories	15,516		10,142	
Cost of Goods Sold		227,800		215,600
Gross Profit on Sales		107,200		64,400
Operating Expenses (Schedule 2)		45,770		42,330
Operating Income		61,430		22,070
Financial Income and Expense:				
Interest expense	12,890		9,682	
Interest and dividends earned	(220)		(220)	

Exhibit BR.3

Biltrite Bicycles, Inc., Income Statements for the Years Ended December 31, 2009 and 2008 (in thousands of dollars) (*continued*)

	Year Ended 12/31/2008		Year Ended 12/31/2008	
Loss (gain) on disposal of investments	198		-100	
Loss on decline in market value of securities	2,800		400	
Net Financial Expense		15,668		8,960
Net Income before Taxes and Extraordinary Items		45,762		13,110
Income Taxes		13,729		4,542
Net Income before Extraordinary Items		32,033		8,568
Extraordinary Gain from Eminent Domain Sale (net of tax)				1,235
		$32,033		$ 9,803

SCHEDULE 1
COST OF GOODS MANUFACTURED
(IN THOUSANDS OF DOLLARS)

	Year Ended 12/31/2009*		Year Ended 12/31/2008	
Beginning Work-in-Process Inventories		$ 4,000		$ 4,663
Manufacturing Costs:				
Direct Materials:				
Beginning inventories of materials and purchased parts	$ 16,150		$ 15,320	
Purchases	105,400		86,200	
Available for production	121,550		101,520	
Ending inventories of materials and purchased parts	26,800		16,150	
Cost of Materials Used in Production	94,750		85,370	
Direct Labor	35,600		31,300	
Manufacturing Overhead (Schedule 1A)	103,324		101,719	
Total manufacturing costs		233,674		218,389
Total Work in Process		237,674		223,052
Ending Work-in-Process Inventories		4,500		4,000
Cost of Goods Manufactured		$ 233,174		$ 219,052

SCHEDULE 1A
MANUFACTURING OVERHEAD

	Year Ended 12/31/09*	Year Ended 12/31/08
Indirect Labor	$ 5,500	$5,300
Depreciation of Factory Building	2,000	2,000
Depreciation of Factory Equipment	42,060	42,860
Property Taxes	6,000	5,800
Manufacturing Supplies	15,042	14,600
Payroll Taxes and Fringe Benefits	13,200	12,400
Utilities	16,100	15,600
Repairs and Maintenance	1,222	1,159
Miscellaneous	2,200	2,000
	$ 103,324	$ 101,719

(Continues)

Exhibit BR.3	Biltrite Bicycles, Inc., Income Statements for the Years Ended December 31, 2009 and 2008 (in thousands of dollars) (continued)

	Year Ended 12/31/2008	Year Ended 12/31/2008

SCHEDULE 2
OPERATING EXPENSES
(IN THOUSANDS OF DOLLARS)

	Year Ended 12/31/09*		Year Ended 12/31/2008	
Selling Expenses:				
Sales Commissions	$ 16,500		$ 13,800	
Sales Salaries	1,200		1,180	
Bad Debts Expense	500		900	
Product Warranty	1,139		1,078	
Advertising	3,311		2,522	
Miscellaneous Selling	420		146	
		$ 23,070		$ 19,626
General Expenses:				
Administrative Salaries	7,550		6,677	
Research and Development	1,050		2,200	
Patent Amortization	700		700	
Payroll Taxes and Fringe Benefits	2,245		2,200	
Depreciation—Office Building	800		800	
Depreciation—Office Fixtures and Equipment	1,875		2,260	
Depreciation—Autos and Trucks	320		300	
Depreciation—Warehouses	10,000		10,000	
Accounting and Legal Fees	750		720	
Other Professional Services	20		18	
Supplies	200		280	
Insurance	450		240	
Printing and Postage	520		115	
Gain/Loss on Disposal of Plant Assets	(4,000)		(3,850)	
Miscellaneous Administrative	200		44	
		22,700		22,704
		$ 45,770		$ 42,330

*Unaudited.

Exhibit BR.4	Biltrite Bicycles, Inc., Balance Sheets as of December 31, 2009 and 2008 (in thousands of dollars)

	12/31/09*		12/31/08	
ASSETS				
Current Assets				
Cash on hand and in banks		$ 12,362		$ 15,800
Investments in marketable securities		4,200		5,300
Accounts and notes receivable—trade	$ 12,000		$ 13,200	
Less allowance for doubtful accounts	(220)		(800)	
		11,780		12,400

Exhibit BR.4	Biltrite Bicycles, Inc., Balance Sheets as of December 31, 2009 and 2008 (in thousands of dollars) (*continued*)			

	12/31/09*		12/31/08	
Inventories				
Materials and purchased parts	26,800		16,150	
Goods in process	4,500		4,000	
Finished goods	15,516		10,142	
Indirect materials and repair parts	3,400		3,200	
		50,216		33,492
Prepaid Expenses		600		560
Deferred Tax Asset—warranty		400		460
Total current assets		79,558		68,012
Property, Plant, and Equipment				
Land		4,000		4,000
Factory building	50,000		50,000	
Less accumulated depreciation	(14,140)		(12,140)	
		35,860		37,860
Warehouses and sales offices	200,000		200,000	
Less accumulated depreciation	(105,000)		(95,000)	
		95,000		105,000
Factory equipment	360,000		320,000	
Less accumulated depreciation	(144,660)		(147,460)	
		215,340		172,540
Office building	20,000		20,000	
Less accumulated depreciation	(8,000)		(7,200)	
		12,000		12,800
Office fixtures and equipment	10,000		9,000	
Less accumulated depreciation	(6,150)		(5,075)	
		3,850		3,925
Autos and trucks	1,000		900	
Less accumulated depreciation	(620)		(300)	
		380		600
Total Property, Plant, and Equipment		366,430		336,725
Investments and Other Assets: Patents and Copyrights	6,000		6,700	
(net of accumulated amortization)				
Deposits	340		340	
Total investments and other assets		6,340		7,040
TOTAL ASSETS		$ 452,328*		$ 411,777
LIABILITIES				
Current Liabilities				
Notes payable	$ 3,660		$ 14,890	
Accounts payable	10,200		18,600	
Interest payable	3,400		2,200	
Salaries and wages payable	2,190		2,018	
Payroll withholdings	510		490	
Taxes and fringe benefits payable	370		345	
Income taxes payable	6,000		1,800	
Estimated product warranty liability	544		860	
Accrued commissions payable	1,400		1,200	
Total current liabilities		28,274		42,403
Long-Term Liabilities				
Mortgage note payable (10%)	60,000		60,000	
Deferred tax liability—depreciation	10,600		9,800	

(Continues)

Exhibit BR.4 — Biltrite Bicycles, Inc., Balance Sheets as of December 31, 2009 and 2008 (in thousands of dollars) (continued)

	12/31/09*		12/31/08
12% note payable to Bank Two	45,000		
Total long-term liabilities	115,600		69,800
TOTAL LIABILITIES	143,874		112,203
STOCKHOLDER'S EQUITY			
Invested Capital			
Preferred stock—$100 par value, 10% cumulative, 10,000,000 shares authorized,	120,000		120,000
Common stock, $10 par value, 90,000,000 shares authorized, 10,000,000 shares issued, of which 220,000 shares are in the treasury	100,000		100,000
Paid-in capital in excess of par value of capital stock	50,000		50,000
Total invested capital	270,000		270,000
Retained earnings	46,607		29,574
Total	316,607		299,574
Less cost of 220,000 shares of treasury stock	(8,153)		0
TOTAL STOCKHOLDERS' EQUITY	308,454		299,574
TOTAL LIABILITIES AND STOCKHOLDERS' EQUITY	$ 452,328		$ 411,777

*Unaudited.

Exhibit BR.5 — Biltrite Bicycles, Inc., Statement of Retained Earnings for the Years Ended December 31, 2009 and 2008

	(in thousands of dollars)	
	Year Ended 12/31/09*	Year Ended 12/31/08
Retained Earnings—beginning of year	$ 29,574	$ 29,771
Net Income	32,033	9,803
Dividends	(15,000)	(10,000)
Retained Earnings—end of year	$ 46,607	$ 29,574

*Unaudited.

Exhibit BR.6 — Biltrite Bicycles, Inc., Statement of Cash Flows for the Year Ended December 31, 2009 unaudited

CASH PROVIDED BY OPERATING ACTIVITIES	
Net Income	$ 32,033
Add (deduct)	
Increase in inventories	(16,724)
Decrease in accounts and notes receivable	620
Increase in prepaid expenses	(40)
Increase in deferred tax liability	800

Exhibit BR.6	Biltrite Bicycles, Inc., Statement of Cash Flows for the Year Ended December 31, 2009 unaudited (*continued*)

Decrease in deferred tax asset	60	
Decrease in accounts payable	(8,400)	
Increase in interest payable	1,200	
Increase in salaries and wages payable	172	
Increase in payroll withholdings	20	
Increase in taxes and fringe benefits payable	25	
Increase in income taxes payable	4,200	
Decrease in product warranty liability	(316)	
Increase in accrued commissions payable	200	
Depreciation and amortization	57,755	
Loss on sale of investments	198	
Gain on disposal of plant assets	(4,000)	
Loss on decline in market value of securities	2,800	
Total Cash Provided by Operating Activities		$ 70,603
CASH USED IN INVESTING ACTIVITIES		
Disposal of Property and Equipment		
Factory equipment	9,000	
Office equipment	200	
Purchase of Plant Assets		
Factory equipment	(89,860)	
Office fixtures and equipment	(2,000)	
Autos and trucks	(100)	
Sale of Marketable Securities	1,102	
Purchase of Marketable Securities	(3,000)	
Purchase of Treasury Stock	(8,153)	
Total Cash Used in Investing Activities		(92,811)
CASH PROVIDED BY FINANCING ACTIVITIES		
Issuance of 12% Note Payable to Bank Two	45,000	
Payment of Dividends	(15,000)	
Payment of Mortgage Note Installment	(10,000)	
Payment of Notes Payable	(1,230)	
Total Cash Provided by Investing Activities		18,770
INCREASE (DECREASE) IN CASH		$ (3,438)

Module I: Assessment of Inherent Risk

In this module, you will assess inherent risk after you have done the following:

1. Analyzed Biltrite's organizational structure and prepared an organization chart;

2. Applied preliminary analytical procedures to Biltrite's financial data; and

3. Studied Biltrite's business operations and the bicycle manufacturing industry generally.

In completing this assignment, you may assume that Derick has decided on the following initial risk assessments:

Inherent risk: 100%

Control risk: maximum

Audit risk: 5%

Overview of Biltrite's Business and Industry

As part of his continuing study of Biltrite's operations, Derick has extracted the following additional data from the computerized permanent file entitled "Business and Industry."

1. In 2009, in the face of increasing liquidity problems, payment of trade accounts payable within the specified credit terms became increasingly difficult. After much discussion with Harvey Bombenmyr, the president of Bank Two, and Bank Two's lending officers, Lawton was able to negotiate a ten-year 12% note payable for $45 million. The note is unsecured and is payable in equal annual installments, together with interest, beginning March 1, 2009, and contains restrictive covenants. Those relevant to the Biltrite audit are the following:

   a. A minimum balance of $10 million must be maintained in Biltrite's demand deposit account with Bank Two;

   b. Further borrowing is prohibited until the Bank Two note has been amortized below $10 million; and

   c. Dividends may be declared only from retained earnings in excess of $45 million.

   d. In April 2008, Lawton borrowed $3 million from the company in exchange for an unsecured note. The transaction resulted in a debit to Account 1203—Notes Receivable, Officers. According to Groth, Lawton plans to repay this note prior to December 31, 2009.

2. Legal action against the company was initiated by Rollfast, a competitor, in late 2008. The suit alleges that Biltrite infringed on a process already patented by Rollfast. The process, according to Rollfast's attorneys, enables a bicycle manufacturer to produce a frame in one piece, thereby adding strength to the bicycle by eliminating welding. Biltrite has responded to the action by demonstrating the unique characteristics of its patented bicycle frame. By July 2009, the suit had neither been heard by the court nor settled outside the courts by the litigants. Rollfast is suing Biltrite for $50 million.

3. Although Lawton and Groth have intensified efforts in recent years to establish and implement a sound internal control system, the independent auditors have not seen fit to reduce the assessed level of control risk below the maximum level. If the auditors' 2008 recommendations have been implemented, however, Derick anticipates a reduction in the assessed level of control risk in one or more of the transaction cycles.

4. In the past, our audit team has used the internal audit staff only when necessary to assist in various phases of the Biltrite audit.

Requirements

1. Prepare an organizational chart for Biltrite and identify the major strengths and weaknesses in Biltrite's organizational structure.

2. Using the downloaded data and the spreadsheet program, retrieve the file titled "Analy1." Scroll through the file and locate the following documentation:

   - WP A.1—Comparative income statements
   - WP A.2—Sales and cost of goods sold—by product line
   - WP A.3—Comparative schedule of manufacturing overhead and operating expenses
   - WP A.4—Inventories

3. In completing the preliminary analytical procedures, the audit team's expectations are that there will be some growth over the prior year, the relationships among financial statement items will remain relatively stable, and Biltrite's ratios will be comparable to reported industry ratios. After scrutinizing the documentation, perform the following:

   a. Using the "Comparative Income Statements" data in WP A.1, calculate each income statement component as a percentage of sales for 2009. (*Hint:* For help with the cell equations, examine the comparable cells for 2008.)

   b. Using the "Sales and Cost of Goods Sold—By Product Line" data in WP A.2, calculate the cost per unit as a percentage of sales price for 2009 by product line. (You may examine the comparable 2008 cell equations as you did in requirement (a).)

   c. Using the "Comparative Schedule of Manufacturing Overhead and Operating Expenses" data in WP A.3, calculate each component as a percentage of sales for 2009. (You may examine the comparable 2008 cell equations as you did in requirements (a) and (b).)

   d. Using the product line data from requirement (b) and the "Inventories" data from WP A.4, calculate finished goods inventory turnover for 2009 by product line. Calculate materials and purchased parts turnover for 2009 by component. (Again, you may refer to comparable cell equations for 2008.)

   e. Print the results of this analysis.

4. Using the downloaded data and spreadsheet program, load the file titled "Budget." Examine the worksheet carefully and locate the following schedules:

- WP A.6—Budgeted vs. actual income statements for 2009
- Schedule 1—Cost of goods manufactured
- Schedule 2—Operating expenses

Compare with the results of requirement (3). Do any of the variances, when considered in relation to the results of requirement (3), raise warning signals? Print the budget.

5. Using the downloaded data and spreadsheet program, load the file titled "Analy2" and locate the following in WP A.5:

- Comparative percentage balance sheets for 2009 and 2008
- Comparative ratios:

  2009 vs. 2008

  Industry ratios for 2008

After reviewing the documentation, perform the following:

a. Using the "Balance Sheets" data, calculate the percent of each asset component as a percentage of total assets for 2009, and calculate each liability and stockholders' equity component as a percentage of total liabilities and stockholders' equity for 2009. (*Note:* This has been done for 2008; as in requirement (3), you may refer to the comparable cell equations for 2008 to expedite calculating the 2009 percentages.)

b. Using the "Balance Sheets" and "Comparative Income Statements" data, calculate the following ratios for 2009:

- Current ratio
- Quick ratio
- Times interest earned
- Return on stockholders' equity

(*Note*: The 2008 calculations have already been done for you.)

c. Compare pertinent ratios with industry averages (these are located next to the 2008 Biltrite ratios). Are there any significant disparities between Biltrite's ratios and the industry averages?

d. Print the results of your analytical procedures.

e. Wheels-4-U Company is a competitor in the bicycle industry. Using the downloaded data, retrieve the file "Wheels-4-U." Using the data contained in that report, perform the following:

1. Compare Wheels-4-U's percentage income statements with Biltrite's percentage income statements for the same years.

2. Go to Wheels-4-U's comparative balance sheets and income statements and calculate the same ratios that you calculated for Biltrite in (b) above

3. On the basis of (1) and (2) above, what strengths and weaknesses of Biltrite relative to Wheels-4-U can you identify?

6. What is the purpose of performing analytical procedures during the planning phase of the audit? What is the purpose of including budgets and performance reports in the application of analytical procedures? Based on your analytical procedures performed in requirements (2), (3), (4), and (5), what, if any, concerns do you have? Relate your concerns to management's assertions contained in the financial statements (existence, completeness, valuation, etc). Can you suggest some specific audit procedures to allay your concerns?

7. Based on analytical procedures and study of the business and industry, in what specific transaction areas are you willing to reduce inherent risk below 100 percent? In deciding whether or not to reduce inherent risk, consider audit complexity and the probability of fraud.

5

Internal Control over Financial Reporting

LEARNING OBJECTIVES

The overriding objective of this textbook is to build a foundation with which to analyze current professional issues and adapt audit approaches to business and economic complexities. Through studying this chapter, you will be able to:

1 Discuss internal control as an integral part of an organization's corporate governance and risk management processes and its effect on the financial statement audit.

2 Identify and describe the components of internal control as presented in the COSO *Internal Control, Integrated Framework.*

3 Articulate the underlying principles of an effective control environment.

4 Identify common internal control activities found in many organizations.

5 Integrate an understanding of computer-based controls, including general computer and application controls, with the evaluation of internal control over financial reporting.

6 Describe components contained in management reports on internal control over financial reporting.

7 Describe the process that external auditors use to assess internal controls.

8 Describe the nature of documentation the auditor develops to support the understanding and assessment of internal control.

9 Apply the decision analysis and ethical decision-making frameworks to situations involving the understanding and assessment of internal control.

CHAPTER OVERVIEW

This chapter focuses on Phases II and III of the audit process with an emphasis on Phase III—obtaining evidence about internal controls. All organizations need effective internal control to operate over the long run. The fundamental concept of good internal control relates to assisting organizations in achieving their objectives. Organizations need strong internal controls to assure that all sales are recorded, all cash receipts are collected and properly deposited in the organization's bank accounts, and management has accurate data on which to make decisions. The Sarbanes-Oxley Act of 2002 (SOX) now requires management of public companies to independently assess the effectiveness of internal control over financial reporting. Nonpublic companies do not have this reporting requirement; however, the auditor still needs to understand the quality of internal controls to plan the audit engagement. Further, for larger public companies, the external auditor provides a separate opinion on the effectiveness of internal control.

This chapter also introduces the COSO *Internal Control, Integrated Framework,* which is used by companies and auditors as the criteria against which to assess the quality of internal controls. We identify the major components of an effective internal control system. We also describe the process management uses to independently document and assess the quality of its internal controls.

The Audit Opinion Formulation Process

I. Assessing Client Acceptance and Retention Decisions *CHAPTER 4*	II. Understanding the Client *CHAPTERS 2, 4–6, and 9*	III. Obtaining Evidence about Controls and Determining the Impact on the Financial Statement Audit *CHAPTERS 5–14 and 18*	IV. Obtaining Substantive Evidence about Account Assertions *CHAPTERS 7–14 and 18*	V. Wrapping Up the Audit and Making Reporting Decisions *CHAPTERS 15 and 16*

The Auditing Profession, Regulation, and Corporate Governance *CHAPTERS 1 and 2*	Decision-Making, Professional Conduct, and Ethics *CHAPTER 3*	Professional Liability *CHAPTER 17*

PROFESSIONAL JUDGMENT IN CONTEXT

Consolidated U.S. Financial Statements and Material Weaknesses

Good internal controls are needed in all types of organizations—including the U.S. government. Without quality controls and complete and accurate information, government officials will find it difficult to move forward in making important decisions, including decisions about the debt levels in the United States. The Government Accountability Office (GAO) is responsible for auditing the government's consolidated financial statements (which are referred to below as "CFS"). Following are excerpts from the GAO's report entitled FINANCIAL AUDIT: *Material Weaknesses in Internal Control Continue to Impact Preparation of the Consolidated Financial Statements of the U.S. Government,* issued in April 2010:

During its audit of the fiscal year 2009 CFS, GAO identified continuing and new control deficiencies in the federal government's processes used to prepare the CFS. The control deficiencies GAO identified involved enhancing policies and procedures for identifying and analyzing federal entities' reported restatements and changes in accounting principles; establishing and documenting policies and procedures for disclosing significant accounting policies and related party transactions; establishing and documenting procedures to assure the accuracy of Treasury staff's work in three areas: (1) social insurance, (2) legal contingencies, and (3) analytical procedures; and various other control deficiencies identified in previous years' audits.

These control deficiencies contribute to material weaknesses in internal control over the federal government's ability to (1) adequately account for and reconcile intergovernmental activity and balances between federal entities; (2) ensure that the accrual-based consolidated financial statements were consistent with the underlying audited entities' financial statements, properly balanced, and in conformity with U.S. generally accepted accounting principles; and (3) identify and either

resolve or explain material differences between components of the budget deficit reported in Treasury's records.... [and other agency records].

In our report dated December 9, 2008, we disclaimed an opinion on the consolidated financial statements of the U.S. government (CFS) for the fiscal years ended September 30, 2008 and 2007.... Since GAO's first audit of the fiscal year 1997 CFS, material weaknesses in financial reporting and other limitations on the scope of our work have prevented us from expressing an opinion on the federal government's accrual basis consolidated financial statements. We have reported that the federal government did not have adequate systems, controls, or procedures for preparing the CFS to ensure that the consolidated financial statements are consistent with the underlying audited agency financial statements, properly balanced, and in conformity with U.S. generally accepted accounting principles (GAAP).

As you read through this chapter, consider the inability of the GAO to perform an audit of the U.S. financial statements and address the following questions:

- What does it mean when an auditor says that an organization does not have adequate internal controls?

- What criteria does an external auditor, or a GAO auditor, use to reach a definite conclusion that internal controls are inadequate?

- When does an auditor draw a line in dealing with internal controls between simply (a) doing more audit work, or (b) determining that the controls are so bad that no amount of audit work can be performed to reach an audit opinion?

- In contrast to the GAO situation described above, how would an audit be affected if the internal controls were good?

Importance of Internal Control to Financial Statement Audits

The quality of internal control over financial reporting is an important part of an organization's commitment to good governance. Internal control is designed to provide accountability of those entrusted to run the enterprise by the stakeholders, who have provided resources to the organization. Internal controls are a response to the risks that stand between an organization and the accomplishment of its objectives. In other words, controls exist as a way to mitigate and manage risk and are necessary for good long-term decision-making. As seen on the previous page in the *Professional Judgment in Context,* an organization such as the U.S. government that does not have effective internal controls does not have sufficient information to support the kind of decisions that the organization (and, in this case, society) needs to make.

Internal controls are needed because every organization faces significant risks, ranging from (a) corporate failure, to (b) misuse of corporate assets, to (c) incorrect or incomplete preparation of financial statements and other external reports. Internal controls are designed to mitigate those risks. Applicable auditing standards reiterate the importance of the understanding of internal control. For example, ISA 200.7 notes that the ISAs require that the auditor

- exercise professional judgment and maintain professional skepticism throughout the planning and performance of the audit
- identify and assess risks of material misstatement, whether due to fraud or error, based on an understanding of the entity and its environment, including the entity's internal control.

The PCAOB, in AS 11, makes a similar observation:

> The auditor should obtain a sufficient understanding of each component of internal control over financial reporting to (a) identify the types of potential misstatements, (b) assess the factors that affect the risks of material misstatement, and (c) design further audit procedures. (AS 11, para. 18)

The PCAOB makes a very important point: The auditor needs to understand a company's internal controls in order to anticipate the types of misstatements that may occur and then develop appropriate audit procedures to determine if those misstatements exist in the financial statements. For example, if an auditor notes that a client does not have effective controls to assure that all sales are recorded in the correct time period, then the auditor needs to develop sufficient and appropriate substantive audit procedures to test whether sales and receivables are misstated because of the absence of effective controls.

COSO: A Framework for Internal Control

Just as a U.S. company might refer to GAAP as a basis for determining whether its financial statements are fairly presented, companies need to refer to a comprehensive framework of internal control when assessing the quality of internal control over financial reporting. The most widely used framework in the United States is referred to as **COSO** (Committee of Sponsoring Organizations of the Treadway Commission). The sponsoring organizations include the American Accounting Association, the American Institute of CPAs, Financial Executives International, the Institute of Internal Auditors, and the Institute of Management Accountants. The sponsoring organizations came together in the mid-1980s to address the increase of occurrences of financial fraud. One recommendation of COSO's earliest study was to develop a comprehensive framework of internal control.[1] COSO defines **internal control** as:

> a process, effected by an entity's board of directors, management, and other personnel, designed to provide reasonable assurance regarding the achievement of objectives in the following categories: (1) reliability of financial reporting, (2) compliance with applicable laws and regulations, and (3) effectiveness and efficiency of operations.

These objectives are designed to assist the organization in achieving one of its most important objectives, which is successfully implementing corporate strategies to achieve returns for shareholders. Internal control objectives are designed to assist the organization in assuring that it has effective and efficient operations related to its overall strategy, its activities are in compliance with applicable laws and regulations, it safeguards its assets from theft and fraud, and it prepares accurate financial information for internal decision-making and external reporting to the relevant stakeholders.

There are other elements of the definition that are important. Internal control:

- Is a *process* designed to accomplish the organization's objectives
- *Starts at the top* of the organization with the board of directors and management creating and reinforcing a structure and a tone for controls in the organization
- Directly or indirectly *includes all people* in the organization, ranging from shipping clerks to the internal auditor to the chief financial officer and chief executive officer
- Is *broader* than internal control over financial reporting
- Is applied across *all activities* of the organization, ranging from functional areas such as marketing, to operational units such as a division of a company, to interrelationships with other organizations

AUDITING *in Practice*

DECISIONS AND COMPANY FAILURE

Reliable Insurance Co. of Madison, Wisconsin, introduced a new insurance policy to provide supplemental coverage to Medicare benefits for the elderly. The insurance was well received by elderly policyholders, many of whom were in nursing homes. The insurance policy was competitively priced and sold very well. To estimate reserves (liabilities) for future claims against the policies, the client used initial claims data to estimate costs and to build a model to estimate the reserves. For example, claims data for the first year could be compared with premiums for the same time period to estimate the needed reserve for claims. Unfortunately, the client's accounting system had control deficiencies that delayed the processing of claims. As a result, the internal estimation model was comparing claims data for one month with premiums for three months,

which resulted in the model significantly underestimating the needed reserves for future claims.

Because the internal control system failed to record claims on a timely basis, the company (a) underpriced the policies and (b) misrepresented their financial health to shareholders and lenders. The low price attached to the policies allowed the company to greatly expand their sales. Unfortunately, the company was forced into bankruptcy when it could not meet policyholder claims. Had the internal control processes been properly designed, tested, and monitored, management would have made better decisions. The internal control deficiency led not only to misleading financial statements, but, more importantly, to the ultimate failure of the business.

---

[1] Report of the National Commission on Fraudulent Financial Reporting (Washington, DC, COSO: 1987), p. 28.

Components of Internal Control

> **PRACTICAL POINT**
> Internal control is a process related to the achievement of the organization's objectives. Organizations identify the risks to achieving those objectives and implement various controls to mitigate those risks.

Internal control consists of five interrelated components designed to work together as a process to accomplish the organization's objectives. These components are derived from the way management runs a business and are integrated with the management process.

The five components of the COSO *Internal Control, Integrated Framework* are shown in Exhibit 5.1.

The internal control process starts with the articulation of the organization's *financial reporting objectives*, i.e., to produce financial statements that are free from material misstatement. The framework has five important components:

1. *Risk Assessment.* Management must identify and *assess the risks* that may affect the accomplishment of those objectives, e.g., the risk of making judgmental mistakes about the appropriate accounting choices.
2. *Control Environment.* The *control environment* refers to the overall governance of the organization starting by the tone developed at the top level of the organization. It includes the organization's corporate culture, its ethics, the quality of its people, and how the organization is controlled.
3. *Control Activities.* Because errors can occur in processing, the organization needs to implement *control activities* that are designed to prevent or detect errors.
4. *Information and Communication.* Management must communicate its policies effectively, as well as receive upward information through the organization's *information and communication* process.
5. *Monitoring.* As internal control is implemented, management should *monitor* the operation of controls to provide assurance that all five components (including the monitoring function itself) continue to operate effectively.

> **PRACTICAL POINT**
> If internal controls are not enforced they are useless and can lead to waste and fraud. Monitoring provides evidence on whether internal controls are enforced.

> **PRACTICAL POINT**
> An organization's response to fraud helps set the control environment. If an organization is too lenient in its treatment of employees who committed fraud, the control environment will be seen as weaker than if the treatment were harsher.

Relationship of Internal Control Components to Each Other

The internal control process is continuous: management identifies and assesses risks to the accomplishment of its objectives, implements a control environment and control activities that reduce the risks to an acceptable level, develops effective information and communication processes, and monitors the effectiveness of the overall internal control system. We now describe the five components in more detail and discuss how management might assess the effectiveness of its internal control over financial reporting.

Exhibit 5.1 COSO Framework for Internal Control

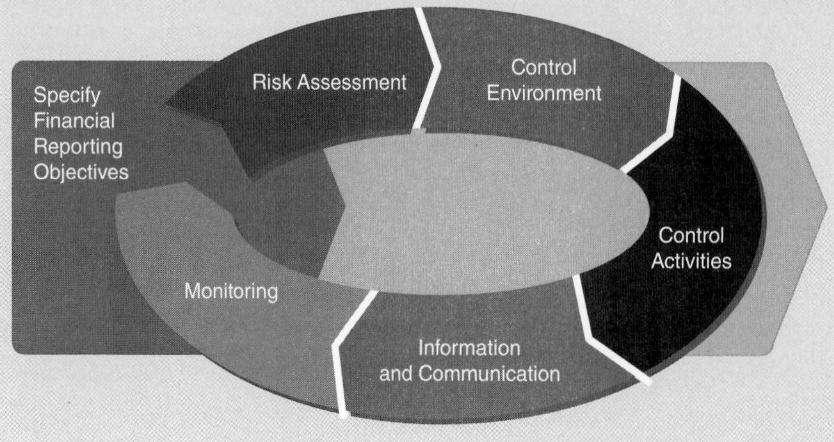

AUDITING *in Practice*

VENDOR RELATIONSHIPS AND INTERNAL CONTROL

As businesses become more integrated through mutual supply chain processes, the quality of a business partner's control system becomes increasingly important. Consider, for example, a manufacturer that enters into contracts with major suppliers to provide high-quality just-in-time manufacturing. The manufacturer needs to know that the supplier has controls in place that will ensure the following:

- Manufacture of high-quality components
- Shipment of goods such that they can be placed into the manufacturing process with no interruption of the process

- Acceptance of orders online with sufficient levels of privacy and security to avoid sharing secrets with competitors
- Proper accounting for receipts, transfers, and monetary payments

Many organizations are using internal or external auditors to review the controls of business partners before entering into such agreements.

Terminology: Entity-Level Controls

Some of the components of internal control operate at a high level across an entity and often are referred to as entity-level controls. Entity-level controls exist on a higher level than transaction-level controls and affect multiple processes, transactions, accounts, and assertions. At some level, each of the five components of COSO has some elements that can be considered to be entity-level controls. Auditing Standard No. 5 notes that the following should be considered entity-level controls:

- Controls related to the control environment;
- Controls over management override;
- The company's risk assessment process;
- Centralized processing and controls, including shared service environments;
- Controls to monitor results of operations;
- Controls to monitor other controls, including activities of the internal audit function, the audit committee, and self-assessment programs;
- Controls over the period-end financial reporting process; and
- Policies that address significant business control and risk management practices.

AS 5 encourages a top-down approach that first focuses important risks, the controls that are designed to mitigate those risks, and then an analysis of entity-level controls followed by analysis of specific control activities related to significant accounts and disclosures and their relevant assertions.

> **PRACTICAL POINT**
>
> Entity-level controls typically have an important, but indirect, effect on the likelihood that a misstatement will be detected or prevented on a timely basis.

Risk Assessment

Risk assessment involves the identification and analysis of the risks of material misstatement in financial reports. Congress, the courts, and the marketplace have clearly communicated that the risk of incorrect financial statements must be very low. To ignore the risks will subject both the company and its auditors to litigation and potential bankruptcy. The manner in which a misstatement might occur varies with both the organization's control environment and the nature of processing. For example, a company might fail to capture all transactions because someone does not scan shipments into a computer file, or alternatively, a clerk may fail to fill out a shipping order. Failure to sufficiently identify the risks likely results in deficiencies in the organization's controls. Management often uses a risk assessment questionnaire (see Exhibit 5.2) as a basis for identifying the significant risks related to financial reporting and documenting that it has an effective risk assessment approach.

> **PRACTICAL POINT**
>
> The economic financial crisis has highlighted the importance of an organization's risk assessment process as some have suggested that the crisis resulted, in part, from poor risk management. Auditors should be alert to changes in their client's risk assessment process.

Exhibit 5.2	Example of a Risk Assessment Questionnaire Concerning Financial Reporting

Financial Reporting Risk Issue   **Response (Yes/No)**

1. What is the history of past differences between the client and auditor on financial reporting? Is there a pattern of financial reporting problems indicated by trends in this regard?

2. What is the history regarding the accuracy and variability of accounting estimates? Have any of the transaction cycles historically been plagued with inaccurate estimates?

3. Are there inappropriate accounting policies identified by our external auditor that have not been reconsidered since last year?

4. What is the nature of related-party transactions?

5. Are there high-risk transactions involving:
   - Significant valuation judgments?
   - Up-front revenue or expense recognition?
   - Derivatives?
   - Aggressive accounting estimates?
   - Bill-and-hold transactions?
   - Unusually complex transactions?
   - Unusually large year-end transactions?
   - Issues currently the focus of SEC or PCAOB scrutiny?

PRACTICAL POINT

Internal control is a continuous process that addresses objectives relating to operating effectiveness and efficiency, compliance with policies and procedures, and reliability of financial reporting.

PRACTICAL POINT

Virtually all recent financial frauds were associated with organizations that had weaknesses in the control environment. These include companies such as WorldCom, Enron, Adelphia, and companies caught in the financial crisis, such as Lehman Brothers, Merrill Lynch, and Citi.

The auditor analyzes more than the financial statements in assessing the potential risk for misstatement. For example, there are important risks that exist related to the procurement of goods and services used. If those risks are not mitigated, then there will likely be misstatements in the company's financial accounts.

Control Environment

The **control environment** starts with the board of directors, audit committee, and management. Together this group constitutes the leadership of the organization and sets the tone for acceptable conduct through policies, codes of ethics, commitment to hiring competent employees, developing reward structures that promote good internal controls and reliable financial reporting, and effective governance. Weaknesses in the "tone at the top" have been associated with most financial frauds during the past decade. Thus, the control environment must establish and reinforce the organization's commitment to strong internal control, and management must demonstrate that commitment through its communications and actions.

The failures of major financial institutions such as Lehman Brothers and Bear Stearns were also linked to problems in the control environment, including weak board oversight and virtually no control over the risks related to subprime lending and collateralized debt obligations. Each organization had ineffective boards of directors that were dominated by top management. Management teams were driven to increase the stock price, either as a basis for expanding the company or for personally enriching themselves through stock compensation. All of the organizations developed complex reporting structures that obfuscated transactions. As an example, refer to the *Auditing in Practice* feature, which describes a control environment problem at HealthSouth.

A ringing indictment of the problem with the control environment at World-Com was given by Richard Breeden in a special report on WorldCom's collapse:

> Among other things, the board of directors of the Company consistently ceded power to Ebbers [Bernard Ebbers, CEO of WorldCom]. As CEO, Ebbers was

AUDITING *in Practice*

ETHICS AND THE CONTROL ENVIRONMENT

In testimony before the House Subcommittee in October 2003, the Director of Internal Audit of HealthSouth testified that she had inquired about expanding her department's work and that she needed access to corporate records. She reported directly to the HealthSouth CEO, Richard Scrushy. She told a congressional committee that Mr. Scrushy reminded her that she did not have a job before she came to HealthSouth and she should do the job she was hired to do. When asked by a congressman whether she had thought about reporting rumors of fraud to Ernst & Young, she indicated that she had run her concerns through the chain of command within the company and had done all she could do. Unfortunately, the chain of command was run by the CEO.

The internal auditor did not follow up with Ernst & Young. Others testified to the same effect—if they wanted to keep their jobs, they continued to do the work they were hired to do and let management take care of other items. The "tone at the top" sent a clear message: "Don't question management!"

In the case of HealthSouth, it did not matter that the organization had a code of ethics for its employees. The company and its board was dominated by management. The unwritten message was stronger than any written message: "Do what we want you to do or lose your job."

allowed nearly imperial reign over the affairs of the company, without the board of directors exercising any restraint on his actions, even though he did not possess the experience or training to be remotely qualified for his position. One cannot say that the checks and balances against excessive power within the old WorldCom did not work adequately. *Rather the sad fact is there were no checks and balances.* [emphasis added].[2]

COSO has identified seven underlying principles of an effective control environment. Those seven principles are:

1. *Integrity and Ethical Values*—Sound integrity and ethical values, particularly of top management, are developed and set the standard of conduct for financial reporting.
2. *Importance of the Board of Directors*—The board of directors understands and exercises oversight responsibility related to financial reporting and related internal control.
3. *Management's Philosophy and Operating Style*—Management's philosophy and operating style support achieving effective internal control over financial reporting.
4. *Organizational Structure*—The organizational structure supports effective internal control over financial reporting.
5. *Commitment to Financial Reporting Competencies*—The company retains individuals competent in financial reporting and related oversight roles.
6. *Authority and Responsibility*—Management and employees are assigned appropriate levels of authority and responsibility to facilitate effective internal control over financial reporting.
7. *Human Resources*—Human resource policies and practices, including compensation programs, are designed and implemented to facilitate effective internal control over financial reporting.

Together, these principles provide the overall guidance to the organization for implementing specific controls, and we expand on them next.

PRACTICAL POINT

Compensation plans are developed to influence the actions of top management. However, as noted in the HealthSouth example, the compensation program, or the threat of withholding compensation, can significantly influence those who are entrusted to carry out company policies in the best interests of the company's shareholders.

PRACTICAL POINT

COSO has developed additional guidance for smaller companies in implementing internal controls to meet Sarbanes-Oxley Section 404 reporting requirements.[3]

LO 3

Articulate the underlying principles of an effective control environment.

[2] Richard Breeden, *Restoring Trust: Corporate Governance for the Future of Enron*, August 2003, pp. 1–2.

[3] COSO, *Internal Control, Integrated Framework: Guidance for Smaller Public Companies*, 2006, available at http://www.coso.org.

AUDITING *in Practice*

INTEGRITY AND ETHICS ISSUES AT NAVISTAR LED TO CONTROL DEFICIENCIES

Navistar's restated 2005 financials issued December 2007:

Report from Deloitte:

Material Weakness Description

1. Control Environment: As of October 31, 2005, *management was unsuccessful in establishing an adequately strong consciousness regarding the consistent application of ethics across all areas of the company and the importance of internal controls over financial reporting, including adherence to GAAP.* This weakness in the overall control environment likely contributed to many of the other material weaknesses disclosed

herein. As identified by the Board of Directors' independent investigation, certain members of management and other employees, in place at that time, were involved in instances of intentional misconduct that resulted in some of the company's smaller, but material, restatement adjustments. With respect to these instances, most of these individuals are no longer employed by the company. In other instances, the Investigatory Oversight Special Committee of our Board of Directors has implemented appropriate remediation plans. [emphasis added]

PRACTICAL POINT

Auditors can, and are expected to, evaluate an organization's ethical climate and the potential effect of that climate on the preparation of the financial statements.

Integrity and Ethical Values

The effectiveness of internal control policies and procedures is tied to the integrity and ethical values of the people who create, administer, and monitor them. Integrity and ethical behavior are products of the entity's ethical and behavioral standards, including how they are communicated and how they are reinforced in practice. They include management's actions to remove or reduce incentives and temptations that might prompt personnel to engage in unethical acts. They also include the communication of ethical values and behavioral standards to personnel through policy statements, codes of conduct, and by example.

The importance of the control environment and ethical values cannot be overstated. As indicated in the *Auditing in Practice* feature regarding Navistar, a corrupt corporate culture will influence every other aspect of internal control.

Board of Directors and the Audit Committee

Members of the board of directors are the elected representatives of shareholders and have responsibility for management oversight, including evaluating and approving the organization's strategic plans. An effective board will be actively involved and will function as a check against a potentially dishonest or self-centered CEO. Good corporate governance requires that the majority of directors be "outside directors," i.e., directors who are not members of management and do not have business or personal relationships with management. It has been suggested that the chair of the board be independent of the CEO, or when the CEO is the chair, the independent board members appoint a "lead director" with authority to take action on behalf of the independent directors.

PRACTICAL POINT

Enron had one of the best "written" codes of ethics. However, the board routinely waived "conflict of interest" requirements, which allowed the company's treasurer to set up special-purpose entities whose sole aim was to either inflate Enron's earnings or hide Enron's losses.

Most boards will have three subcommittees: (1) the audit committee, (2) the compensation committee, and (3) a nominating and governance committee. The audit committee has responsibility for oversight of external financial reporting and all audit functions. The compensation committee is responsible for recommending the appointment of top officers and compensation packages for senior management. The nominating and governance committee must identify independent, competent directors who will serve stockholder interests and develop charters that spell out the responsibilities of the board and its subcommittees. Starting in 2010, the SEC is requiring a report on the board's oversight of risk management. Boards have responded by either forming a risk management committee at the board level, or alternatively, formally putting risk management on the agenda of every board meeting.

Management's Philosophy and Operating Style

Management performs three critical processes that are important in evaluating internal control:

1. *Sets the Tone*—Management's philosophy and operating style emphasize high-quality and transparent financial reporting.
2. *Articulates Objectives*—Management establishes and clearly articulates financial reporting objectives, including those related to internal control over financial reporting.
3. *Selects Accounting Principles and Oversees Estimates*—Management follows a disciplined, objective process in selecting accounting principles and developing accounting estimates.

Management must demonstrate that it sets the right tone for individual and company activities, clearly articulates objectives regarding financial reporting and assures that those objectives are understood and achieved, and sees that the company follows a disciplined approach in selecting accounting principles that best portray the economics of transactions.

Organizational Structure

Well-controlled organizations have clearly defined lines of responsibility, authority, and accountability. Internal audit is often considered an integral part of a good organizational structure because it provides management with independent assessments of other controls as well as the effectiveness of the organization's risk management, governance, and compliance processes.

Commitment to Financial Reporting Competencies

Competence is the knowledge and skills necessary to accomplish tasks that define the individual's job. Commitment to competence includes management's consideration of the competence levels for particular jobs and how those levels translate into requisite skills and knowledge.

Authority and Responsibility

Authority and responsibility are intertwined with the organization's structure. Everyone in the organization has some responsibility for the effective operation of internal control. COSO has identified the following considerations:

- *Board oversees financial reporting responsibility*—The board of directors oversees management's process for defining responsibilities for key financial reporting roles.
- *Defined responsibilities*—Assignment of responsibility and delegation of authority are clearly defined for all employees involved in the financial reporting process.
- *Limit of authority*—Assignment of authority and responsibility includes appropriate limitations.

An example of limited authority occurs when a unit manager is limited in the dollar amount of individual purchases that can be processed without further approval.

Human Resources

Organizations need to establish policies and procedures for hiring, training, supervising, evaluating, counseling, promoting, compensating, and taking remedial action regarding its employees. These procedures are most often found in personnel policies designed to assure that (a) the organization hires the right people,

PRACTICAL POINT

Three companies with major financial reporting frauds—Enron, WorldCom, and HealthSouth—all had ineffective internal audit functions.

PRACTICAL POINT

Internal auditors should meet periodically in executive sessions with the audit committee. The internal audit department is often described as the "last line of defense" within an organization. For that reason, budgets for the internal audit function and the appointment of the chief audit executive should be approved by the audit committee.

PRACTICAL POINT

Auditors think very carefully about management competence and must adjust the audit for areas they see as problems. As an example, during the evaluation phase of internal control of a publicly traded organization, the external auditors met privately with the audit committee and expressed concerns about the competence of the CFO. After further analysis, the audit committee recommended to the full board and management that the organization hire a new CFO.

(b) hiring and retention decisions comply with applicable federal and state laws and regulations, (c) employees are properly trained and supervised, and (d) the organization respects employee rights and delineates employee responsibilities.

The nature of compensation programs has become more important, and all public companies must describe their overall compensation program with particular emphasis on executive compensation. The auditor must consider the risks associated with potentially dysfunctional compensation programs such as basing a bonus on level of reported earnings.

Assessing the Control Environment

The evaluation of the control environment should include the seven principles of an effective control environment identified above. Management and the auditor independently assess the strength of the board of directors and the understanding of the company's ethical principles and adherence thereto. An example of this assessment is seen in Exhibit 5.3, which demonstrates the

Exhibit 5.3	Assessing Elements of the Control Environment
Underlying Principle	**Evidence Reviewed**
Integrity and Ethical Values	
1. The company has a Code of Conduct that is actively distributed throughout the organization.	Reviewed Code of Conduct. Viewed a prominent reference to the Code on the company's web site. Randomly interviewed 30 employees across multiple disciplines and determined that all but one had knowledge of the Code.
2. The Code of Conduct is signed by all the officers and directors of the company.	The corporate secretary maintains a file of all signed documents by officers and managers acknowledging that they have read the Code and commit to abide by its principles.
3. There is continuing training on the commitment to ethics.	Reviewed schedule of offerings with the training department. Covers all employees on an every–three-year basis.
4. Independent tests indicate that employees are aware of the Code of Conduct and are committed to its achievement.	Randomly interviewed 30 employees across multiple functional areas and determined that all but one had knowledge of the Code.
5. Violations of the Code of Conduct are identified and dealt with in a manner that reinforces the company's integrity.	The corporate secretary keeps a file of all known ethical violations and the disposition of the issue that led to a reporting of the violation. Reviewed the files of actions taken and noted they were within the company policies.
6. Employees and stakeholders view the company as one with high ethical standards.	In addition to the random survey of company employees, a second survey was sent to important vendors and customers of the company regarding their view of the organization's commitment to ethical values.
Importance of Board of Directors	
1. The board meets a sufficient number of times and appropriate length to address company issues.	Read the minutes of the meetings of the board of directors and considered sufficiency of meetings in addressing important issues.
2. The board contains a majority of independent directors.	Considered board of director relationships, and calculated the percentage of independent directors.
3. The board has an independent lead director and the board holds "executive sessions" without members of management present.	Discussed with lead director to understand the authority of independent directors and their view of management's commitment to the importance of this control.
4. The board has a governance and nominating, compensation, and audit committee made up of independent directors only.	Reviewed composition of subcommittees.

(continues)

| Exhibit 5.3 | Elements of the Control Environment (*continued*) |

Underlying Principle	Evidence Reviewed
5. The audit committee is composed of independent directors who have financial expertise.	Reviewed audit committee relationships, and evaluated resumes of audit committee members to consider expertise issues.
6. The audit committee meets in executive session with the external auditor and with the Director of Internal Audit.	Noted meetings during year in which this occurred.
7. The audit committee has a robust charter and the resources to carry out its mission.	Considered the audit committee's charter and compared budget to organizations of a similar size.

Management Philosophy and Operating Style

1. Management emphasizes to all employees the importance of integrity in financial reporting.	Discussed this issue with personnel involved in the financial reporting process.
2. Management has processes in place to review information before it goes public and to receive input, where applicable, from the audit functions.	Reviewed plans, and queried staff in financial reporting about whether there were instances when this did not occur.
3. Similar additional procedures to be performed as suited to the company.	

Organizational Structure

1. The organization maintains a structure that facilitates communication regarding financial reporting objectives and internal control.	Queried financial reporting staff and internal audit staff about what they perceive financial reporting objectives to be.
2. Performance evaluations are consistent with promoting internal control over financial reporting.	Reviewed performance evaluations of three employees in internal audit and two employees in financial reporting to understand link between performance and internal control–associated job activities. Discussed this issue with those employees.
3. Additional procedures as fits the organization.	

Commitment to Financial Reporting Competencies

1. The organization has a commitment to hire individuals with requisite financial competence. That competence is evidenced performance of the: • Corporate Controller • Director of Internal Audit • Divisional Controllers • Tax Manager • Other Accounting Managers	Evaluated resumes of the CFO, corporate controller, and director of internal audit to establish the existence of professional certifications. Considered the responses of these individuals to complex financial reporting issues during the past year, with a focus on evaluating competence.
2. Similar objectives and procedures as fits the organization.	

Authority and Responsibility

1. Clear lines of authority and responsibility are established for all individuals who can either commit financial resources on behalf of the company, or whose actions affect financial reporting.	Established a formal organization chart that reflects the manner in which the organization operates.
2. Independent reviews are performed to provide assurance that individuals do not exceed their limits of authority.	Asked Director of Internal Audit to discuss instances in which individuals exceeded their limits of authority.
3. Similar objectives and procedures as fits the organization.	

Human Resources

1. HR policies are designed to promote effective internal control specifying needed competencies and ethical values.	Asked internal audit to assess the entity's ethical values and how those values are communicated and reinforced.
2. HR policies are designed to ensure compliance with all federal state regulations.	Asked tax and internal audit personnel to discuss instances in which there were violations of federal and state regulations.
3. Similar objectives and procedures as fits the organization.	

key control elements and pertinent evidence that would be reviewed. As you read Exhibit 5.3, remember that most frauds and accounting restatements take place when there are significant deficiencies or material weaknesses in the control environment.

A strong control environment is the first, and most important, line of defense against the risks related to the accuracy and completeness of financial statements. However, a strong control environment cannot reduce all the financial reporting risks to zero. Therefore, management must implement specific control activities to minimize misstatements in the financial records.

Control Activities

Control activities are the policies and procedures that are established to assist organizations in accomplishing objectives and mitigating risks. Controls can be embedded in processes, e.g., edit controls designed into computer applications or segregation of duties required in processing transactions. Although there are some generic controls that are seen in most internal control processes—e.g., segregation of duties, independent reconciliations, and management review—it is important to remember that there is no universal set of controls applicable to all situations. Organizations implement control activities to mitigate the risks that are specific to their organization.

At a high level, control activities include management review and analysis of operations, as well as approaches to manage areas where accounting estimates are used. At a transaction level, controls are built into computer systems that limit access to programs or data (including data entry) or controls compare transactions with acceptable parameters. The control activities are linked to the risks identified to mitigate those risks.

As with all components of internal control, control activities involve two elements: (1) the design and implementation of the controls including a description of how the control activities operate, and (2) the operation of the controls, i.e., procedures implemented consistent with the design of the controls. Management (and the auditor) first assess that the design of controls is adequate and that the controls have been implemented. That is not enough, however; there must be evidence that the controls are working effectively. Three important processes affect the quality of data entering into the general ledger, as shown in Exhibit 5.4. They include entries from:

- Transactions processing
- Accounting estimates
- Adjusting and closing journal entries

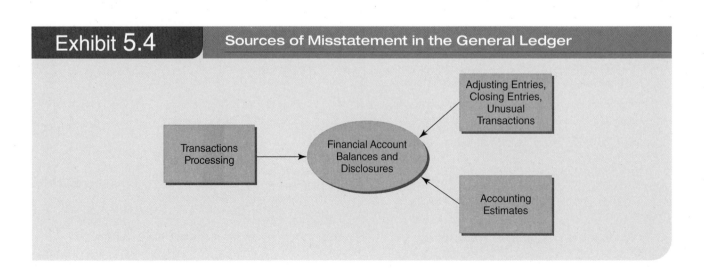

Exhibit 5.4   **Sources of Misstatement in the General Ledger**

There is a high risk, as well as a history, that fraud is accomplished through adjusting, closing, and other unusual journal entries. Controls over these areas should include the following:

- Documented support for all entries
- Reference to underlying supporting data with a well-developed audit trail
- Review by the CFO or controller
- Independent reviews, as needed, by internal audit to determine that all supporting items are present and entries are appropriate

Accounting estimates, such as those used in developing the allowance for doubtful accounts, pension liabilities, environmental obligations, and warranty reserves, should be based on underlying processes and data that have been proven to provide accurate estimates. Controls should be built around the processes to assure that the data are accurate, the estimates are faithful to the data, and the underlying data model reflects current economic conditions and has proven to provide reasonable estimates in the past.

> **PRACTICAL POINT**
>
> Year-end journal entries and estimates are almost always high risk. The risk varies inversely with the quality of the control environment.

Preventive and Detective Controls

Preventive controls are designed to prevent the occurrence of a misstatement and should be emphasized in the design of processes. As an example, access controls prevent the unauthorized entry of transactions into the general ledger. Edit controls may prevent some inappropriate transactions from being recorded. Preventive controls are usually the most cost-efficient when designing processes. However, they may not provide documentary evidence that controls are working effectively. For example, a control that prevents a fictitious transaction from being processed might not leave documentary evidence that it worked.

Many organizations supplement the preventive controls by building detective controls that provide evidence on whether processing has been effective in preventing errors. Reconciliations, for example, provide indirect evidence on the functioning of other controls. Other detective controls include continuous monitoring techniques that show whether transactions have been processed that should not have been processed.

Common Internal Control Activities

The evaluation of internal control is based on the presence and proper functioning of all five components of the internal control framework. However, the processing of transactions is fraught with risk. For example, transactions might be lost, altered, recorded incorrectly or, once recorded, they may be modified by someone using the computer system to alter existing records.

The objectives of transactions processing are related to financial statement assertions and can be expressed as follows:

- Recorded transactions are valid, exist, and have occurred
- All transactions are recorded
- Transactions are properly valued
- Transactions are properly presented and disclosed
- Transactions relate to rights or obligations of the entity

LO 4

Identify common internal control activities found in many organizations.

In evaluating the need for any particular control, the organization must assess the risk of not achieving a particular objective. For example, the organization has objectives to assure that all valid transactions are recorded, are recorded at the correct price, and in the appropriate time period. The organization implements controls to accomplish those objectives. Each control can be evaluated on whether it reduces the risk of not accomplishing the objectives to an acceptable level. Most of the controls identified next are ones that are familiar to accounting majors, and they are implemented in almost all accounting systems. These control activities include:

- Segregation of duties
- Authorization procedures
- Adequately documented transaction trail
- Physical controls to safeguard assets
- Reconciliation of control accounts with subsidiary ledgers, of transactions recorded with transactions submitted for processing, and of physical counts of assets with recorded assets

Segregation of Duties   The concept underlying segregation of duties is that individuals should not be put in situations in which they could both perpetrate and cover up fraudulent activity by manipulating the accounting records. Proper segregation of duties requires that at least two employees be involved such that one does not have (a) the authority and ability to process transactions and (b) custodial responsibilities. Separating these functions prevents someone from authorizing a fictitious or illegal transaction and then covering it up through the accounting process. Separating record keeping and physical custody of assets is designed to prevent someone with custodial responsibilities from taking assets and covering it up by making fictitious entries to the accounting records.

Authorization Procedures   Controls should be established to assure that only properly authorized transactions take place and that unauthorized personnel do not have access to—or the ability to change—already recorded transactions. For example, organizations do not want individuals to have access to computer records that are not needed for the performance of their jobs. The specific implementation of authorization policies varies with organizational size and degree of computerization. The following authorization guidelines are pertinent for all organizations:

- The *ability to commit* the organization to any long-range plans with substantial financial impact should be reserved for the highest functional level in the organization, including the board of directors.
- *Authorization policies* should be clearly spelled out, documented, and communicated to all affected parties within the organization.
- *Blanket authorizations*, for example, computer-generated purchase orders, should be periodically reviewed by supervisory personnel to determine compliance with the authorization procedure.
- *Authorization should be limited* to departments that are assigned responsibilities for a particular function. For example, the credit department, not the sales force, should have the authority to extend credit to customers.

Adequate Documentation   Documentation should exist to provide evidence of the **authorization** of transactions, the existence of transactions, the support for journal entries, and the financial commitments made by the organization. The following are guidelines for developing reliable documentation and assuring adequate control:

- *Prenumbered paper or computer-generated documents* facilitate the control of, and accountability for, transactions and are crucial to the completeness assertion.
- *Timely preparation* of documents, including electronic documents as part of an electronic audit trail, improves the creditability and accountability of the documents and decreases the rate of errors on all documents.
- *Authorization of* a transaction should be clearly evident in the client's records—whether paper-based or electronic.

- A *transaction trail* should exist to provide information in order to respond to customer inquiries and identify and correct errors.

These guidelines apply to both paper and electronic documents. For example, a computer application may be programmed to pay for merchandise when there is an electronic copy of receipt of merchandise. The computer program compares the receipts with a purchase order and may or may not require a vendor invoice before payment. Nor will it require any human review once the program and related procedures have been developed.

Physical Controls to Safeguard Assets   Physical controls are necessary to protect and safeguard assets from accidental or intentional destruction and theft. Examples of physical controls include the following:

- Security locks to limit access to computer facilities
- Inventory warehouses with fences, careful key distribution, and environmental (climate) control
- Vaults, safes, and similar items to limit access to cash and other liquid assets
- Physical segregation and custody to limit access to records and documents to those authorized
- Security controls regarding access to computer systems

Reconciliations   Reconciliation controls operate by checking for agreement between:

- Submitted transactions and processed transactions
- Detailed subsidiary accounts and the corresponding control account
- Physical counts of assets with the recorded assets

It is important that reconciliations be performed by someone other than the person originally recording the transaction, the individual with custody for the transaction, and the individual with the ability to authorize the transaction.

Information and Communication

Information and communication refers to the process of identifying, capturing, and exchanging information in a timely fashion to enable accomplishment of the organization's objectives. It includes the organization's accounting system and methods for recording and reporting on transactions. Information and communication usually involves a two-way flow: (a) from top management to the rest of the organization, communicating its key policies, its code of conduct, and strategies; and (b) from the bottom up, communicating economic information as well as deviations from the organization's policies.

Every organization should have an information system that facilitates timely identification of performance problems and control failures. The information system, by itself, is not sufficient. It must communicate to the right people to assure that action is taken when needed.

The Sarbanes-Oxley Act puts an additional emphasis on "upstream" communication, particularly when an employee is concerned that there is something inappropriate in the company's operations. This is referred to as a "whistleblower function" and often includes processes such that reporting can be anonymous and non-retributive. The whistleblower program should include a process to bring important financial issues to the audit committee.

Whistleblowers may choose to provide information to parties outside of the company. The 2010 Dodd–Frank Wall Street Reform and Consumer Protection Act creates whistleblower protection by prohibiting retaliation against individuals who provide information to the SEC relating to securities law and other violations.

PRACTICAL POINT

Reconciliations need to be performed on a timely basis. When properly implemented (including the investigation and rectification of differences), reconciliations are one of the most effective control activities within an organization.

PRACTICAL POINT

Reconciliations are an important control because they mitigate the risk related to incorrect processing as well as the risk of fictitious transactions.

PRACTICAL POINT

Lowe's, a large home-repair, building, and lumber retailer, has relationships with many vendors. Lowe's has a "hotline" where a vendor can communicate directly with the internal audit department if there has been any inappropriate action by a purchasing agent of the company, e.g., a suggestion of a "kickback" if a large order is placed.

AUDITING *in Practice*

MONITORING CONTROLS IN FAST-FOOD FRANCHISES

A company such as Wendy's or McDonald's that serves fast food across thousands of locations must be able to monitor the workings of its controls at each location. The company has written policies and procedures dealing with control issues ranging from the acceptance of product (must be from authorized vendor), disposal of waste, recording of sales (must offer a cash register receipt or the meal is free), and supervision of employees. The companies have standardized procedures for counting cash, reconciling cash with the cash register, depositing the cash daily, and transferring cash to corporate headquarters. From previous statistics and industry averages, the company knows that food costs should run approximately 36.7% of revenue.

The company develops a performance monitoring process that results in daily and weekly reports on:

- Store revenue compared with expected revenue and previous year's revenue for the same week
- Special promotions in effect
- Gross margin

The company then uses the monitoring reports to follow up with local stores and to determine which stores, if any, need further investigation. For example, the company identifies a group of stores—all managed by one person—for which store revenue is lower than expected; but more important, the gross margin is significantly less than expected (63% expected, but 60% attained). The monitoring report indicates that one of the following explanations may represent the problems at the stores: (a) not all revenue is being recorded; (b) product is unnecessarily wasted; (c) product is diverted to other places; or (d) some combination of these. Although the original focus is on operating data, the implication is that there is a breakdown of internal controls at those specific locations. The monitoring of performance has led to the monitoring of controls.

The report leads management to determine the cause of the problem and to take corrective action.

Monitoring

Monitoring is defined as a process that provides feedback on the effectiveness of the other four components of internal control. Monitoring can be done through *ongoing activities or separate evaluations*. Ongoing monitoring procedures are built into the normal recurring activities of an entity. Internal auditors, customers, and regulators can all contribute to the monitoring of internal controls. For an example, see the *Auditing in Practice* feature regarding monitoring controls in a fast-food franchise.

Monitoring is very important in a SOX 404 context because if management has developed effective monitoring of its other control components, then both management and the auditor should be able to reduce their tests of controls. Once a company establishes that controls are effective, attention can be turned to how well the company monitors the continuing functioning of those controls.

Internal auditing is often considered a highly effective monitoring control. Some monitoring activities are established and exercised by parties outside an entity that affect an entity's operations and practices. An example is that customers implicitly corroborate billing data by paying their invoices or complaining about their charges. Regulators may also communicate with the entity concerning matters that affect the functioning of internal controls.

IT Controls Integrated into Internal Control Evaluations

Virtually all financial reporting systems are computerized, and the auditor needs to assess the important computer controls in assessing internal controls. Some computer controls are pervasive and affect every computerized system. We refer to these controls as **general computer controls**. Other controls are built into specific processes, such as a control affecting the integrity of recording a sale and account receivable. These are referred to as **application controls** and include input, processing, and output controls.

General Computer Controls

General computer controls are pervasive control procedures that affect all computerized applications. These controls address the following:

- Planning and controlling the data processing function
- Controlling applications development and changes to programs and/or data files and records
- Controlling access to equipment, data, and programs
- Assuring business continuity such that control failures do not affect data or programs
- Controlling data transmission

Because general controls affect every computer process, the auditor usually starts with the general controls in evaluating the potential control weaknesses involving computerized processes.

Planning and Controlling the Data Processing Function The auditor should focus on seven fundamental control concepts in evaluating data processing:

1. The Authorization for All Transactions Should Originate Outside the Data Processing Department—This authorization includes the review and approval of program changes and reinforces a fundamental point that IT personnel should not be allowed to make unauthorized changes to programs or data.
2. The Users, Not Data Processing, Are Responsible for Authorization, Review, and Testing of All Application and Database Developments and Changes in Computer Programs.
3. Access to Data Is Provided Only to Authorized Users as determined by the owner of the data and consistent with organization policies and guidelines for information privacy.
4. The Data Processing Department Is Responsible for All Custodial Functions Associated with Data, Data Files, Software, and Related Documentation— This responsibility includes limiting access to authorized users, building integrity checks into programs and systems, and maintaining adequate backup and security of all applications, data files, and documentation.
5. Users, Jointly with Data Processing, Are Responsible for the Adequacy of Application Controls Built into Computer Applications or Database Systems—Organizations should develop control guidelines that specify minimum control objectives for every application, alternative controls that could be implemented, and responsibility for the controls.
6. Management Should Periodically Evaluate the Information System's Function for Operational Efficiency, Integrity, Security, and Consistency with Organizational Objectives for Information Technology—In many situations a separate unit of data processing performs this review. In other situations, the internal audit department performs this evaluation.
7. The Internal Audit Staff Should Be Adequately Trained in Computer Auditing and Should Periodically Audit Applications and Operations.

Controlling Applications Development and Program Changes Organizations run the risk that computer programs are not efficient, are not effective, or do not contain proper controls. Thus, every organization should have a process to determine that the right applications are developed or purchased, are built and installed within budget, and accomplish the objectives for which they were designed or purchased.

PRACTICAL POINT

Computer applications are computer programs and include all of the attendant procedures to accomplish a particular processing task such as payroll, purchasing, or sales.

PRACTICAL POINT

A client should have a risk management plan for information technology (IT). The auditor should begin an audit of computerized processing by reviewing the risk management plan for IT.

PRACTICAL POINT

Control over program changes is usually something that internal audit addresses on a frequent basis.

PRACTICAL POINT

Nearly all organizations depend on their IT functions to facilitate financial reporting. If those processes are not executed properly, there can be devastating consequences for the organization.

PRACTICAL POINT

In order to effectively implement access controls, the organization must identify *all users* who should have access to the organization's computer programs or data and then identify specific actions that each individual can take regarding a program or data. Care must be taken to update the table of authorizations on a frequent basis.

Controlling Access to Equipment, Data, and Programs   Restricting access to assets to authorized users for authorized purposes is a fundamental internal control concept. It can be argued that access controls in a computerized system are the most important and pervasive controls that need to be addressed by management. Information is highly concentrated in computer systems. Further, a perpetrator who gains unauthorized access to a computer system gains access to physical assets such as cash or inventory because those programs control access to actual physical assets. The auditor should determine the extent to which the client has instituted a data access program based on the following principles:

- Access to any data item is limited to those *with a need to know.*
- The ability to change, modify, or delete a data item is restricted to those *with the authorization to make such changes.*
- The access control system has the ability to identify and verify any potential users as authorized or unauthorized for the data item and function requested.
- *A security department should actively monitor* attempts to compromise the system and prepare periodic reports to those responsible for the integrity of data and access to the data.

These four principles require a comprehensive access control program that identifies all data items, users, user functions, and authorized functions that users may perform on each data item. An access control system must restrict access to data to authorized users for authorized purposes. Access is controlled by developing a detailed matrix in which users are assigned to groups. The three-dimensional matrix then matches user groups to data and authorized functions, such as an ability to read an item, change an item, or input a new item.

An example of an **authorization** table is shown in Exhibit 5.5. In order to implement access controls, the organization must first identify every data asset or program and then map users and allowable accesses. Once a security system is in place, the organization must implement an authentication procedure to assure that an individual is who he or she claims to be. A good access control system also monitors threats to the system and develops reports to address potential threats and vulnerabilities. Fortunately, some excellent software products provide the ability to restrict access according to the principles just specified.

Exhibit 5.5   Data Authorization Table

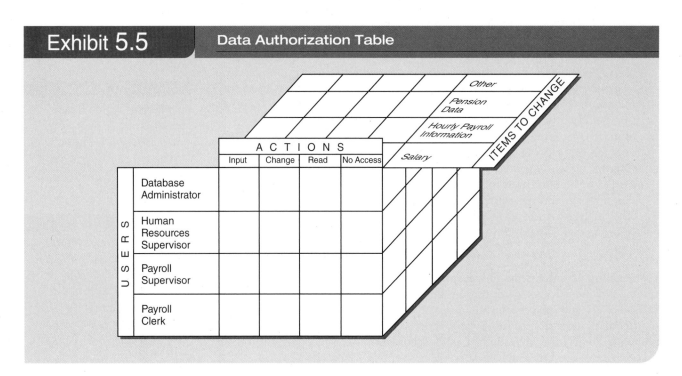

Once the system has been implemented and individuals are given the authority to access data or make changes, a system must be put in place to verify that users are indeed authorized to make changes or access data. That system is referred to as **authentication**, which is verifying to the system that the person is who she or he claims to be. Three primary methods are used to authenticate users:

- *Something they know,* such as a password or something that should be known only to them
- *Something they possess,* such as a card with a magnetic strip
- *Something about themselves,* such as a fingerprint, a voiceprint, or some other type of physical identification

The authentication method used should depend on the criticality of the program or data being protected. In many cases, a password to log on to a personal computer is sufficient. In other situations, a more sophisticated approach or a combination of approaches should be used. A password system is most widely used, but it is subject to problems associated with lost, stolen, or easily guessed passwords. To be effective, passwords must be changed frequently and should be difficult to guess. Something possessed is most often in the form of a plastic card with a magnetic strip to identify the user to the system. The card is often combined with passwords to provide a higher level of security than can be obtained if only one of the methods is used by itself. For example, individuals wishing to use an automated teller machine (ATM) must identify themselves to the computer terminal by something possessed (the bank card) and by a password. The user is allowed access to the ATM network only if the two agree with a list of authorized users.

Identification of users on the basis of physical characteristics continues to be the least widely used method because of cost and reliability concerns. However, the cost-effectiveness is improving and it is now widely used in restricting access to physical premises. The major risk associated with physical identification *where electronic transmission is required* is that the physical scan must be matched with the secured scan that is stored within the system. If someone were able to break into a system and obtain the physical scans of authorized users, those individuals could masquerade as the authorized personnel by submitting their profiles when logging on to the system. If a system administrator were aware of the compromise, the administrator would have to revoke the privilege of the authorized user. Then the individual who appropriately tries to log on to the system with his or her retina scan or fingerprint would be denied access.

Business Continuity   Each information system should have a security and backup plan to protect both physical assets (hardware and computer documentation) and programs and data files. If an audit client does not have adequate backup and recovery procedures, the auditor needs to discuss the risks with management and the audit committee to determine whether any disclosure of the risks is required.

Controlling Data Transmission   Communications controls are those specific controls to assure the completeness and correctness of data transmitted between a **computer** application and another device, such as a terminal or another computer system. The major control over Internet data transmission is encryption. Messages can be encrypted such that they are virtually impossible to decipher without having the proper code to decipher the message.

Application Controls

Application controls are specific control procedures (manual and computerized) designed into and around the computer program to ensure that processing objectives are attained. The application control procedures should match the complexity of the applications. The control procedures are often referred to as *input, processing,* and *output control procedures.*

Input Controls   The control procedures designed to assure that the organization fully captures all the transactions between itself and another entity, and to properly record those transactions, are referred to as **input controls**. Input controls to ensure the capture of transactions (once and only once) and identified for processing. Examples of important input controls include

- *A unique transaction identifier established by the computer,* along with all the audit trail information (for example, prenumbered documents)
- *Procedures to limit access* to transactions in accordance with management's specific policies
- *Formation of an audit trail*

An overview of an electronic **audit trail** is shown in Exhibit 5.6. An audit trail includes the documents and records that allow a user or auditor to trace a transaction from its origination through to its final disposition, or vice versa. If there are significant deficiencies in controls designed to assure that all transactions are captured, the auditor may be forced to conclude that an entity cannot be audited, that is, without an audit trail an entity is not auditable.

Input controls are designed to ensure that authorized transactions are correct, complete, and recorded in a timely fashion and that only authorized transactions exist. They include the following:

- Computerized input validation tests
- Self-checking digits
- Use of stored data reference items to eliminate input of frequently required data
- On-screen input verification techniques

Input validation tests are often referred to as *edit tests* because they are control tests built into the application to examine input data for obvious errors. Edit tests are designed to review transactions much like experienced personnel do

---

Exhibit 5.6   Electronic Audit Trail

Unique identification of transaction. Examples include the assignment of a unique number by the computer. The unique identifier could be assigned sequentially or could consist of a location identifier and unique number within a location. Sales invoices, for example, are sequentially numbered by the computer application.

Date and time of transaction. These could be assigned automatically by the computer application.

Individual responsible for the transaction. The log onto the computer terminal provides evidence of the party authorizing or initiating the transaction.

Location from which the transaction originated. The log onto the computer can identify the source of the transaction.

Details of the transaction. These should be noted in a computer log. Essentially, all the details normally found in a paper document, such as the quantities ordered, back-order provisions, and so forth, should also be captured and saved for the electronic audit trail.

Cross-reference to other transactions. When applicable, all cross-referencing to other transactions should be captured. For example, if a payment cross-references a specific invoice, the information needed to complete the cross-reference should be captured.

Authorization or approval of the transaction. If the transaction requires authorization by a party other than the one initiating the transaction, the proper electronic authorization should be captured.

Other information. As required, other information should also be recorded as part of the electronic audit trail.

The organization should make provisions to retain the electronic audit trail for a period of time as would be required for a paper audit trail.

in manual systems in which an employee would know, for example, that no one worked more than 55 hours in the past week. The following types of edit tests are found in most computer applications:

- Alphanumeric field
- Reasonableness of data (within prespecified ranges or in relationship to other data)
- Limits (data must be within specified limits)
- Validity (data must take on valid values)
- Missing data
- Sequence (items are in sequence and are not duplicated)
- Invalid combinations of items
- Other relations expected to exist in the data

Exhibit 5.7 contains a detailed description of each of these input validation tests. If an item entered online does not meet the required criteria, the user is notified and a correction is made or a decision is made about whether the transaction should be processed or reviewed further before processing.

Self-checking digit algorithms have been developed to test for transposition errors associated with identification numbers. Self-checking digits operate by computing an extra digit, or several digits, that are added (or inserted) into a numeric identifier. The algorithms are designed to detect the common types

PRACTICAL POINT

Some companies have developed continuous auditing approaches that consider what can go wrong in processing a transaction and then perform testing to see if any such error occurred. Examples of organizations that have implemented continuous monitoring can be found at www.oversightsystems.com.

Exhibit 5.7	Examples of Input Validation Tests
Alphanumeric	Each data field is compared with a prespecified type to determine whether the field contains appropriate alpha or numeric characters.
Reasonableness	Reasonable ranges for an item are prespecified based on past history and current expectations. For example, a company that trades commodities on the Chicago Mercantile Exchange can develop a reasonableness range for an exchange price because the exchange prohibits trades that differ by more than a specific percentage from the previous day's closing price.
Limits	Limit tests are specified for items that require supervisory review before processing. A limit test, for example, might be placed on the number of hours factory personnel work during a one-week period. If it is highly unlikely that anyone would work more than 55 hours in a week, a limit test of 55 hours could be incorporated into the edit test.
Validity	A specific set of values could be programmed into the application and the identified fields could be tested to determine whether they contain one of the valid values. For example, a company may have only five jobs in progress during a particular time period. The validity test could determine whether a job accounting entry contains one of the job classifications currently in progress.
Missing Data	Fields could be reviewed to see whether data were missing. If fields crucial to processing were incomplete, the edit tests would reject the transaction.
Sequence	If some transactions should be processed in a specific sequence, that sequence could be programmed as a validation test. Further, the system may be programmed to determine whether any items in a specified sequence are missing, such as prenumbered documents, or to search for potential duplicates. An example of the latter would be a retailer's accounts payable program that searches to determine whether a vendor had previously been paid for an invoice that has been submitted for processing.
Invalid Combinations of Items	If data items must logically be consistent, the computer application should test for that consistency. For example, if it is not possible for an employee to have a job code as janitor and machinist during the same time period, the program should test for the invalid combination.
Other	The designer of the computer application should build into the application any other test that would have been manually reviewed before the application was automated and that has the ability to be computerized.

PRACTICAL POINT

When computer processing is an integral part of internal controls, many companies can achieve greater efficiency through a continuous audit approach that provides assurance on the continued operation of controls rather than individual tests of controls once a year.

PRACTICAL POINT

Management's process of determining the continued effectiveness of internal control should be a normal part of the control process. It should not be an "add-on" that is performed once a year to meet regulatory reporting requirements.

of mistakes. Whenever the identifier is entered into the system, the application recalculates the self-checking digit to determine whether the identifier is correct.

Processing Controls   Processing controls are designed to assure that the correct program is used for processing, all transactions are processed, and the correct transactions update multiple files. The most important processing controls come before the program is put into operation. Users should use comprehensive test data to assure that the program does all computations correctly before the program is authorized for production.

Output Controls   Output controls are designed to assure that all data are completely processed and that output is distributed only to authorized recipients. Typical controls include reconciliation of control totals, output distribution schedules and procedures, and output reviews. For critical data, the user may perform a detailed review of the output contents with input to determine the completeness of a crucial process. The organization should also develop policies for protecting privacy and retaining records.

Management Evaluation of Internal Controls

Organizations develop good internal controls for one fundamental reason: *better internal controls lead to better data for decisions and increase the likelihood of organizational success and sustainability.* The assessment of internal control should be a by-product of good internal control processes. For example, monitoring is a key component of the COSO internal control framework. Management should

AUDITING *in Practice*

INTERNAL CONTROLS

The mandatory reporting required by the Sarbanes-Oxley Act has dramatically changed the way many organizations think about and evaluate controls. The process of identifying, documenting, and testing internal controls has created an awareness of deficiencies that were never addressed previously. There had been a tendency to not look at controls if operations were profitably managed. The reporting requirement has had the following effects on day-to-day management of organizations:

- Mid-level and lower-level managers now understand they are the owners of the control processes, not the auditors.
- Companies have identified risks and control deficiencies that are often ignored if subunits are profitable.
- Improved controls have led to improved efficiencies in operations.
- Companies have implemented more continuous monitoring processes in their computer systems and have identified control problems earlier.

- Management has become more risk-conscious and has developed better monitoring controls.

The bottom-line effect is that all managers realize they have responsibility for the effectiveness of internal controls, including processes that allow them to monitor controls and identify deviations from good practices. The new-found attention to internal controls has led to improvements in business practices. One of the intentions of the Sarbanes-Oxley Act is that boards of directors need to understand they have a responsibility to improve the governance of the organization, including the organization's responsibility to develop effective control systems that safeguard assets and improve the reliability of financial reporting. It appears that the Act is having the desired effect.

implement effective monitoring to gain assurance that controls are continuing to work properly.

Unfortunately, many companies have viewed management's assessment of internal controls as an "add-on" to meet regulatory reporting requirements and often complain about the cost of the compliance work.

Management Reports on Internal Control over Financial Reporting

The Sarbanes-Oxley Act of 2002 requires management to implement effective internal controls over financial reporting and to certify that the controls have been implemented properly and are operating effectively. The SEC is charged with setting guidelines to assist management in its assessment of the effectiveness of internal controls over financial reporting. The SEC guidelines require that suitable criteria, e.g., COSO, be used in assessing internal controls over financial reporting.

The reports must describe *material weaknesses* in internal controls over financial reporting. To guide both management and the auditor, the SEC and the PCAOB have provided the following definitions:

- *Material weakness in internal control*—A **material weakness** is a deficiency, or a combination of deficiencies, in internal control over financial reporting, such that there is a reasonable possibility that a material misstatement of the company's annual or interim financial statements will not be prevented or detected on a timely basis.
- *Significant deficiency in internal control*—A **significant deficiency** is a deficiency, or a combination of deficiencies, in internal control over financial reporting that is less severe than a material weakness, yet important enough to merit attention by those responsible for oversight of the company's financial reporting.

A material weakness is a deficiency where there is reasonable possibility that either the design of the control is poor, or the operation of the control is such that material misstatements could occur in the financial statements and not be detected or corrected on a timely basis. The absence of a misstatement does not mean that internal control does not have any material weaknesses; it just means that a misstatement did not occur. On the other hand, the discovery of a material misstatement of an account balance normally means that there was a breakdown in internal controls and that there was a material weakness. For example, if management did not employ individuals with sufficient competence to make judgments on the appropriateness of alternative accounting treatments for a transaction, it has a material weakness in internal controls. A significant deficiency is important enough that the auditor has to bring it to the attention of management and the audit committee, but the deficiency does not rise to the level of a material weakness. Thus, it is reported to management and the board but not to outsiders.

Examples of internal control weaknesses that have been identified in management reports in the past few years include those shown in Exhibit 5.8. Note that the control weaknesses are not limited to processing. Rather, the weaknesses often include shortcomings in an organization's control environment. Recall that a material weakness does not mean the control failure leads to material, or even significant, misstatements in the financial statements. Rather, there is a reasonable possibility that this type of control weakness *could* lead to a material misstatement.

An example of a management report is shown in Exhibit 5.9, from Ford Motor Company. Note that management, including the CEO and CFO, both supervised and participated in the evaluation of internal controls and they

PRACTICAL POINT

Although the internal control reporting requirement is only for large publicly held companies, the "best practice" of public reporting on internal control has carried over to large privately held companies as well. Those companies need to reassure their stakeholders, including lenders, suppliers, and other creditors, that they have control processes in place sufficient to achieve the broad internal control objectives.

LO 6

Describe components contained in management reports on internal control over financial reporting.

PRACTICAL POINT

Management considers a number of factors, including the likelihood that a control failure will result in a material misstatement in the accounts, the importance of the information to an external user, and the pervasiveness of a control failure in judging whether a control deficiency is a material weakness or a significant deficiency.

PRACTICAL POINT

Internal auditors can assist management in its assessment of internal controls over financial reporting.

AUDITING *in Practice*

INEFFECTIVE INTERNAL CONTROL OVER FINANCIAL REPORTING LEADS TO EMBEZZLEMENT

In August 2009 the management at Koss Corporation, a U.S.-based high-fidelity stereophonic leader, reported that its internal control over financial reporting was effective as of its fiscal year end (June 30, 2009). Because it was a smaller public company, it was not required to have its external auditor provide an opinion on its internal control. Just four months later the company reported that it did not have adequate internal controls and that unauthorized transactions since 2006 may have exceeded $20 million. These unauthorized transactions were the result of embezzlement by the company's vice president of finance and totaled more than the company's reported earnings during the same period. While an audit of internal control over financial reporting will not guarantee that internal controls are effective, it will provide reasonable assurance regarding internal control effectiveness.

Exhibit 5.8 — Examples of Control Weaknesses

Weaknesses in the Design of Controls over Processing

- Absence of appropriate segregation of duties over important processes.
- Absence of appropriate reviews and approvals of transactions, accounting entries, or systems output.
- Inadequate controls to safeguard assets.
- Absence of controls to ensure that all items in a population are recorded.
- Inadequate processes to develop significant estimates affecting the financial statements, e.g., estimates for pensions, warranties, and other reserves.
- Undue complexity in the design of the processing system that obfuscates an understanding of the system by key personnel.
- Inadequate controls over access to computer systems, data, and files.
- Inadequate controls over computer processing.
- Inadequate controls built into computer processing.

Weaknesses in the Control Environment

- A low level of control consciousness within the organization.
- Audit committee does not have outside members.
- There is no ethics policy or a reinforcement of ethical behavior within the company.
- Company does not have procedures to monitor the effectiveness of internal control.
- Audit committee is not viewed as the client of the external auditor.
- Failure to follow up and correct previously identified internal control deficiencies.
- Evidence of significant undisclosed related-party transactions.
- Ineffective internal audit, including restrictions on the scope of internal audit activities.
- Management overrides accounting transactions.
- Personnel do not have the competencies to carry out the assigned tasks.

Weaknesses in the Operation of Controls

- Independent tests of controls at a division level indicate that the control activities are not working properly, e.g., purchases have been made outside of the approved purchasing function.
- Controls fail to prevent or detect significant misstatements of accounting information.
- Misapplication of accounting principles.
- Credit authorization processes are overridden by the sales manager to achieve sales performance goals.
- Reconciliations (a) are not performed on a timely basis or (b) are performed by someone independent of the underlying process.

| Exhibit 5.8 | Examples of Control Weaknesses (*continued*) |

- Testing reveals evidence that accounting records have been manipulated or altered.
- Evidence is found of misrepresentation by accounting personnel.
- Computerized controls leading to items identified for non-processing are systematically overridden by employees to process the transactions.
- The completeness of a population, e.g., prenumbered documents or reconciling items logged onto the computer with those processed, are not accounted for on a regular basis.

| Exhibit 5.9 | Ford Motor Company Management Report on Internal Control over Financial Reporting (2009) |

Our management is responsible for establishing and maintaining adequate internal control over financial reporting, as such term is defined in Exchange Act Rule 13a-15(f). The Company's internal control over financial reporting is a process designed to provide reasonable assurance regarding the reliability of financial reporting and the preparation of financial statements for external purposes in accordance with generally accepted accounting principles.

Because of its inherent limitations, internal control over financial reporting may not prevent or detect misstatements. Also, projections of any evaluation of effectiveness to future periods are subject to the risk that controls may become inadequate because of changes in conditions or because the degree of compliance with policies or procedures may deteriorate.

Under the supervision and with the participation of our management, including our CEO and CFO, we conducted an assessment of the effectiveness of our internal control over financial reporting as of December 31, 2009. The assessment was based on criteria established in the framework *Internal Control—Integrated Framework,* issued by the Committee of Sponsoring Organizations of the Treadway Commission. Based on this assessment, management concluded that our internal control over financial reporting was effective as of December 31, 2009.

The effectiveness of the Company's internal control over financial reporting as of December 31, 2009 has been audited by PricewaterhouseCoopers LLP, an independent registered public accounting firm, as stated in its report included herein.

concluded that their internal control over financial reporting was effective as of December 31, 2009.

The auditor's evaluation of internal controls is discussed in the following section and an example of auditor reporting on internal control over financial reporting is provided in Chapter 6.

PRACTICAL POINT

Whether a control deficiency is classified as a material weakness does not depend on whether a misstatement in the financial statements actually occurred.

Auditor Evaluation of Internal Controls

Management's purpose in evaluating internal controls is to obtain high-quality data for making good business decisions; the auditor's purpose in evaluating internal controls is twofold: (a) determine control risk, which thereby affects the financial statement audit approach and (b) in an integrated audit of internal controls and the financial statements provide an opinion of the effectiveness of internal control. Only larger public companies are required to have an audit opinion on the effectiveness of internal control. In 2010, with the passage of the Dodd–Frank Wall Street Reform and Consumer Protection Act ("the Act"), smaller public companies were exempted from having an independent auditor test and report on the effectiveness of their internal controls over financial reporting. However, management in these smaller public companies need to continue doing their own assessment, testing, and reporting on the effectiveness of their internal controls over financial reporting, and auditors will continue to review management's assessment and testing as part of the year-end financial statement audit.

PRACTICAL POINT

When an external auditor points out material weaknesses, it is negligent of those charged with governance to not address the control deficiencies.

In determining control risk, the auditor will assess control risk on a scale from high (weak controls) to low (strong controls). Assessing control risk as high means the auditor does not have confidence that internal controls will prevent or detect material misstatements; assessing control risk as low has the opposite implication. If there are important deficiencies in the organization's internal controls over financial reporting, the auditor has to (1) assess control risk at a higher level, (b) determine the type of misstatements that are most likely to occur, and (c) design substantive audit tests that are most likely to discover the misstatements if they had occurred. If, on the other hand, the auditor's analysis of internal controls is that they are effective, the auditor (1) assesses control risk as low, (2) determines, by testing the controls, whether the controls are working as designed, and (3) determines the most effective and efficient way to integrate the audit of controls and the audit of financial statement account balances.

When performing an integrated audit, any identified material weaknesses would require specific reporting by the auditor and would cause the auditor to issue an adverse report on internal controls.

The process for evaluating controls, shown in Exhibit 5.10, involves important steps in the **integrated audit**. The steps in the integrated audit are presented below and are discussed in greater detail in Chapter 6. Steps 4 through 7 of the process of conducting an integrated audit relate to activities involved in auditor evaluation of internal controls.

LO 7

Describe the process that external auditors use to assess internal controls.

1. Update information about various risks.
2. Consider the possibility of account misstatements.
3. Complete preliminary analytical procedures.
4. Understand the client's internal controls.
5. Identify controls to test.
6. Make a plan to test the controls and execute that plan.
7. Consider the results of control testing.
8. Conduct substantive audit tests.

> **PRACTICAL POINT**
>
> If the auditor correctly determines that internal controls are effective, there is less risk that an individual account balance is misstated.

Step 4: Understand the Client's Internal Controls

The auditor needs to gain an understanding of the design of the five components of internal control. For continuing clients, much of the information is available from the previous year's audit and can be updated for changes. For new clients, this process is necessarily much more time-consuming. But, in either case, the auditor will concentrate on areas where the risk of material misstatement is greatest, focusing on understanding those controls related to the significant accounts and disclosures and their relevant assertions.

> **PRACTICAL POINT**
>
> Management's assessment of internal controls for the purpose of external reporting under SOX is similar to the process used by the external auditor and consists of both tests of controls and monitoring activities.

Management's Risk Assessment Process and the Control Environment

Understanding the risk assessment process is important because it reveals management's preferences, preparation, and risk tolerance. The control environment has a pervasive effect both on the culture of an organization and on the likelihood of errors or fraud. The control environment and risk assessment components must be based on the quality of the components rather than by simply looking at accounting transactions.

A partial sample of a risk assessment and control environment questionnaire is shown in Exhibit 5.11. Such a questionnaire serves as a basis for evaluating the control environment. In looking at the exhibit, it is important to understand that the auditor should not only gather information on the questions but should observe how well each element is implemented by management or the board.

Significant Accounts and Disclosures

The auditor will focus on those accounts and disclosures that are significant to the company's financial statements, e.g., sales and cost of sales. Each of the

Exhibit 5.10 Process for Evaluating Internal Controls—All Clients

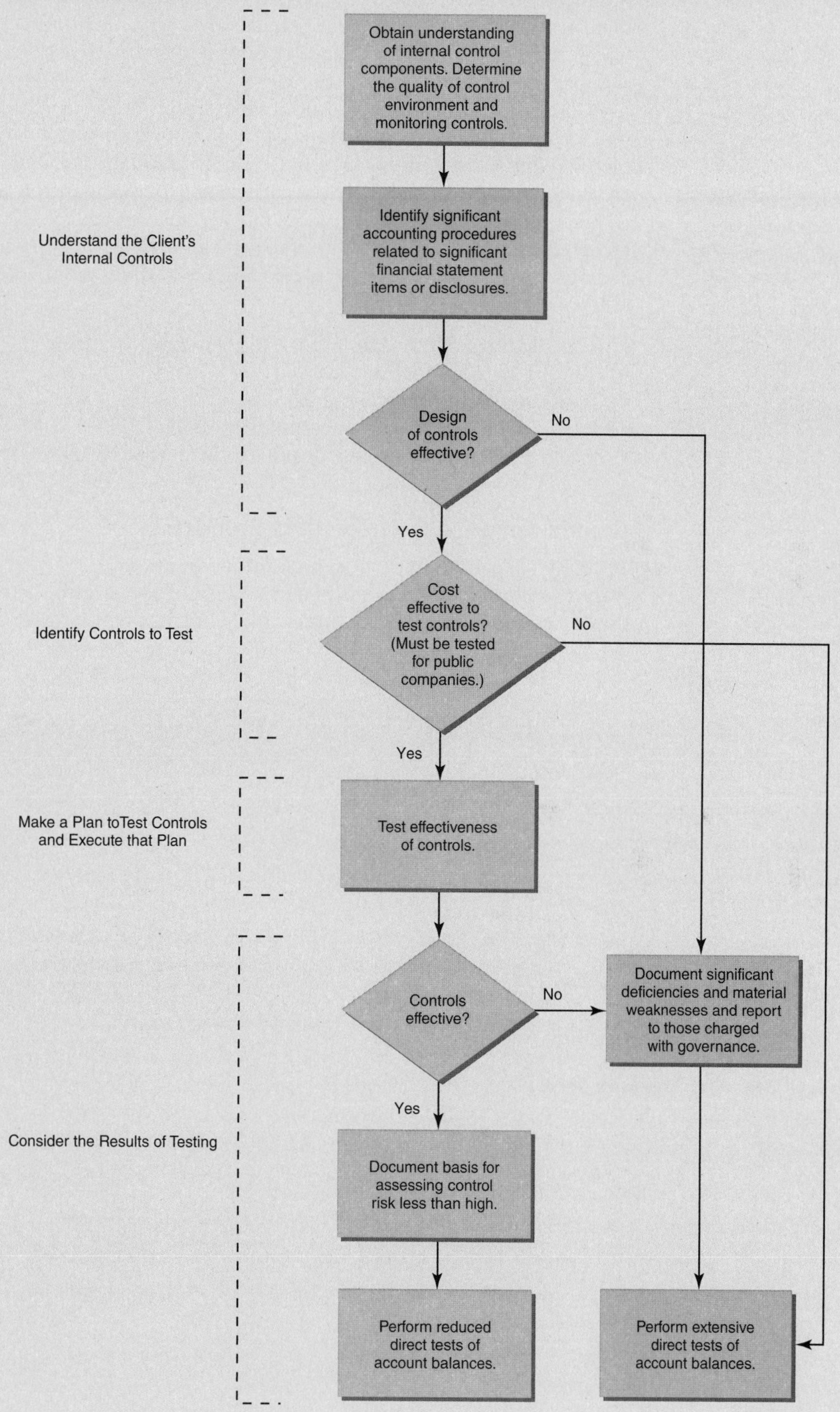

Understand the Client's Internal Controls

Obtain understanding of internal control components. Determine the quality of control environment and monitoring controls.

↓

Identify significant accounting procedures related to significant financial statement items or disclosures.

↓

Design of controls effective? — No →

↓ Yes

Identify Controls to Test

Cost effective to test controls? (Must be tested for public companies.) — No →

↓ Yes

Make a Plan to Test Controls and Execute that Plan

Test effectiveness of controls.

↓

Consider the Results of Testing

Controls effective? — No → Document significant deficiencies and material weaknesses and report to those charged with governance.

↓ Yes

Document basis for assessing control risk less than high.

↓

Perform reduced direct tests of account balances.

Perform extensive direct tests of account balances.

significant accounts is made up of a specific class or type of transaction and is part of a particular process. For example, consider a company that has both Internet and retail store sales. Revenue is a signification account for which there is two types of transactions (retail store sales and Internet sales), each of which may be subject to different controls that have to be evaluated by the auditor.

Auditors of both public and nonpublic clients are required to assess control risk for each **relevant assertion** for each important class of transactions and each significant account balance as a basis for planning the audit. The assertions provide a framework for both (a) analyzing whether controls are adequate to achieve a particular objective, e.g., making sure that all valid transactions are recorded and (b) determining how to test the controls and the accuracy of processing. The assertions which were presented earlier in the text include the following:

- Recorded transactions are valid, exist, and have occurred
- All valid transactions are recorded
- Transactions are properly valued
- Transactions are properly presented and disclosed
- Transactions relate to rights or obligations of the entity

Control Activities in Accounting Processes

With an understanding of significant accounts and relevant assertions, the auditor will then develop an understanding of the control activities related to those accounts and assertions. An example linking two of the financial statement

> **PRACTICAL POINT**
>
> The assertions provide both the framework for the assessment of the adequacy of internal controls and the direction the auditor should take in testing both the controls and the validity of processing.

Exhibit 5.11   **Partial Risk Assessment and Control Environment Questionnaire**

Nature of Company Operations and Strategy

1. Does the company have a sound strategy for future growth and meeting customer needs?

2. Is the company highly computerized? If yes, describe its computerization and the risks that should be considered during the course of the audit.

3. What main competitive factors are currently affecting the company? How is the company identifying and addressing the risks associated with these competitive factors? What are the potential implications of these factors for major account balances such as inventory or accounts receivable?

4. Are important legal or regulatory developments currently affecting the company? If yes, please describe.

Nature of Management's Risk Assessment Process

1. What risks does management view as most crucial to its success?

2. What new risks have been identified by management in the past year?

3. How long has it been since the company has updated its risk assessment process?

4. Does the entity have a planned reaction to respond to a lack of resources? What is the nature of that plan?

5. Are the risks regularly reviewed with the board and discussed in conjunction with the company's strategic plans?

6. Has management considered the risks associated with compensation plans for various levels of management and the potential impact of those compensation plans on behavior?

7. Are there identified "owners" of risk within the organization, and if so, how does management gain assurance that those risks are managed effectively?

8. Are the risks to financial reporting incorporated into a plan for developing controls over process transactions, adjusting entries, and accounting estimates?

assertions with control activities for payroll processing is shown in Exhibit 5.12. The affected accounts are payroll expense, accrued payroll, cash, fringe benefits, and payroll taxes.

Perhaps the easiest way to understand the design of control activities within a process is to perform a "**walkthrough**," which has been defined as tracing the processing of a transaction from its beginning to its recording in the general ledger and identifying the important controls over the process. The walkthrough provides the auditor with a visual image of processing and controls. Coupled with good interviewing skills, walkthroughs are the most commonly used approach to gaining an understanding of how the system actually operates.

A walkthrough designed to gain an understanding of controls is not the same as *testing those controls*. Walkthroughs are generally sufficient to evaluate design effectiveness and implementation. However, if the auditor wishes to reduce control risk to a low level, he or she must also gather evidence on the effective operation of those controls. Walkthroughs may include:

- Inquiries of accounting and operational personnel
- Plant and operational tours to observe control conscientiousness and financial risks associated to how items are processed
- Reviews of client-prepared documentation to determine how controls (a) are supposed to operate and (b) actually operate
- Reviews of prior-year's audit documentation to determine where control problems existed and the effect on related account balances

Management's Monitoring Activities

Monitoring is important because its implementation (or lack thereof) reflects management decisions about the importance of internal control and whether management is committed to identifying significant control failures as they occur. Monitoring activities can include both those that management completes itself and those that it delegates to the internal audit function. Monitoring is based on a few simple principles:

1. It is based on a foundation of effective control that has been established in the company,

> **PRACTICAL POINT**
>
> Understanding the assertions helps the auditor identify the underlying population from which to sample transactions. If the auditor is testing the assertion that all recorded transactions exist, the auditor always samples from the population of recorded items.

Exhibit 5.12	Financial Statement Assertions and Control Activities: Payroll
Financial Statement Assertion	**Control Activities**
Existence/Occurrence: Recorded transactions have occurred and pertain to the entity.	An employee is paid only if the employee already exists on the master payroll and is entered on that payroll by someone independent of payroll processing.
	A supervisor verifies that the employee worked, or the payroll department verifies by existence of time cards for that individual.
	Employees are required to electronically check-in and check-out for hours worked, thereby establishing an electronic trail of hours worked.
Completeness: All transactions have been recorded.	Employee expects a check within a specific time frame and acts as an independent check on performance.
	All instances of potential misstatements are sent to individuals other than those who have responsibility for preparing the payroll (independent check on performance).
	Payroll department reconciles total hours paid within the time period with total hours worked per supervisor or time cards.

2. It should be designed to address important risks to the achievement of reliable financial reporting, and

3. It should be sufficiently robust to identify control failures in a timely fashion such that corrective action can take place before the financial statements are materially misstated.

A partial questionnaire designed to assist auditors in understanding management's monitoring activities is shown in Exhibit 5.13.

Preliminary Assessment Based on Understanding of Controls

After gaining an understanding of the company's controls, the auditor makes a preliminary assessment of the effectiveness of internal controls as a basis for assessing control risk. This preliminary assessment, which is based on the auditor's understanding of the design and implementation of the controls, is important because it drives the planning for the rest of the audit. If the control risk is assessed as high, the auditor cannot plan on relying on the controls to reduce substantive tests of account balances. Therefore, the auditor will not perform tests of controls; instead, the auditor must plan for substantive testing of account balances so that no reliance is placed on the client's internal controls. The *Auditing in Practice* feature on the following page demonstrates the linkage of control weaknesses and audit tests.

If control risk is assessed as low, the auditor will plan to test the operating effectiveness of those controls in an effort to reduce substantive testing related to account balances.

Assessing Control Risk as Moderate   In some cases, the auditor may believe that control risk is not high, but that the cost of gathering evidence on the effectiveness of the controls will be higher than the savings obtained by reducing the substantive audit tests. This is applicable *only when the auditor is not reporting on internal control* (i.e., for nonpublic companies). If the auditor believes the design of controls is effective but does not test the controls, the best the auditor can do is to assess control risk at the moderate level. Auditors

---

Exhibit 5.13	Evaluating Management's Monitoring Activities: Sample Questions

Operational Monitoring Controls

1. How does management manage and evaluate the performance of key business processes?

2. How has management determined that its internal controls are operating properly? Do operational data identify control problems?

3. What types of business-activity monitoring occur in the organization? For example:

- What types of information technologies is management using to monitor business performance?

- What signals problems in operational units or systems?

- Is the monitoring system real-time or periodic?

Internal Audit

1. Is the internal audit function effective? Does the internal audit function view its budget as adequate?

2. Has the internal audit function adopted and followed professional standards?

3. Is there a clear internal audit mission statement from the audit committee? What is the relationship between the internal audit function and the audit committee?

4. Are there restrictions on internal audit access to records or on its scope of activities?

5. Is there any evidence that the internal audit department is inadequate?

AUDITING *in Practice*

WEAK CONTROLS AND LINKS TO AUDIT TESTS

Scenario. The auditor finds that the client does not use prenumbered receiving slips to record the return of sales merchandise nor does it have procedures to assure prompt recording of returned merchandise. Sales returns have been high, and the auditor is concerned that the overall control environment is weak and that management seems obsessed with increasing earnings.

Linkage to Audit Tests. The auditor is not able to rely on controls when testing the balance of sales returns. Therefore, the auditor expands the substantive tests for sales returns by (1) arranging to be on hand at the end of the year to observe the taking of physical inventory,

observing items received during the inventory counting process, and the client's procedures for documenting receipts; (2) tracing receipts for items returned by customers to credit memos to determine if they are issued in the correct time period; (3) reviewing all credit memos issued shortly after year end to determine whether they are recorded in the correct time period; and (4) increasing the number of accounts receivable confirmations sent to the client's customers. All four of these procedures represent an expansion of tests beyond what would be required if the company had good internal controls over receiving returned goods.

should assess risk at the moderate level without testing controls only if (1) the company is a continuing client, (2) past-year audit results did not yield any material misstatements in the financial statements, (3) preliminary analysis of the system indicates no significant changes since last year, (4) management has effective monitoring controls, and (5) the company is not issuing a report on internal control. Otherwise, basing an assessment of control risk only on a walk-through should lead to control risk being assessed as high.

Step 5: Identify Controls to Test

Once the auditor concludes that controls are well designed and implemented, the next step is to test the operating effectiveness of some of those controls in order to (a) provide an opinion on the entity's internal controls in an integrated audit and (b) reduce substantive testing for the financial statement audit. There is no need to test every control related to a relevant assertion, only those that are more important in reducing the risk.

The auditor will often test both the proper recording of transactions and the effectiveness of control activities at the same time. For example, a sales transaction and its proper recording might be tested by selecting sales orders and tracing through shipments to the recording in accounts. While tracing the transaction, the auditor will also test key controls, such as determining that there was proper credit authorization, prenumbered documents were used to uniquely identify each transaction, the sale was invoiced at an approved price, and reconciliations were properly used to determine that the transaction was recorded in the correct time period.

Step 6: Make a Plan to Test the Controls and Execute That Plan

The auditor's preliminary assessment of control risk is based on an understanding of the control system as it has operated in the past and how it is designed to operate. If the auditor is going to assess control risk as low for purposes of the financial statement audit, then the auditor must gain assurance that the controls are operating effectively throughout the fiscal period. If the auditor is planning on issuing an opinion on internal control effectiveness, then the auditor will need to gain assurance that the controls are operating effectively as of the client's

PRACTICAL POINT

A risk-based approach makes a great deal of sense—as long as the auditor is honest in evaluating the risk associated with transactions or account balances and has a justifiable basis for reducing risk. One of the reasons Arthur Andersen & Co. failed is because many of its audit partners viewed risk analysis as a way of reducing work and increasing the profitability of audits. Often, the risk analysis had no relationship to the actual risk that existed.

PRACTICAL POINT

Dual purpose testing, i.e., tests of proper recording of transactions and testing of internal controls at the same time, is an efficient way to implement an integrated audit.

PRACTICAL POINT

The auditor's risk assessment can, and should, be performed on each class of transactions. Thus, an auditor might assess control risk as high on sales and receivables, but might assess control risk as low on inventory and purchases.

year end. To accomplish this, the auditor examines the client's documentation of how controls work and develops an approach to test the controls.

The PCAOB, in Auditing Standard No. 5, indicates that auditors should use a "top-down approach" that begins at the financial-statement level. They should focus first on the entity-level controls and then work down to the significant accounts and disclosures and their relevant assertions. This risk-based approach eliminates from further consideration those accounts that have only a remote likelihood of containing a material misstatement.

The auditor uses a variety of procedures to test whether controls, at both the entity level and the transaction level, are operating effectively. These procedures include inquiry of client personnel, observation of control operations, examination of relevant documentation, and re-performance of the control. When examining documentation or reperforming a control, the audit tests involve taking a sample of transactions from either (a) initially identified transactions and tracing the processing of the transactions through to the final recording or (b) selecting items from those already recorded to determine that appropriate controls are tested. However, the auditor's knowledge of controls is not necessarily limited to just the immediate control testing. The PCAOB (AS No.11) also emphasizes that the auditor integrates knowledge from previous experience with the client, the preliminary assessment of controls, and information from the tests of financial account balances.

Example of Approaches to Testing Controls

As an example of alternative testing approaches, consider an important control in virtually every organization. That control is that the company *requires a financial review and specific approval for all customers that are granted credit, and the amount of credit for any one company is limited by customer policy which is based on financial health of the customer, past collection experience, and current credit rating of the customer.* There are three approaches that an auditor might consider in testing the control:

1. Take a sample of purchase orders and trace the purchase orders through the system to determine whether (a) there was proper review of credit and (b) credit authorization or denial was proper.
2. Take a sample of recorded items (accounts receivable) and trace back to the credit approval process to determine that it was performed appropriately.
3. Use a computer audit program to read all accounts receivable and develop a print-out of all account balances that exceed their credit authorization.

Clearly, there are different costs and advantages associated with each of these three methods. The third method is dependent on proper input of the credit limits into the computer system. If there are no exceptions, the auditor could infer that the control is working even though the auditor did not directly test the control. This approach is cost-effective, but it requires an inference about the control and covers only the operation of the controls related to the current account balances. The first method is the most effective because it not only requires that the auditor look at documentary evidence, but that the auditor determine that the control did work effectively, i.e., it led to the correct conclusion, either deny or provide credit. This method requires documentation of all credit applications and purchase orders, and will be based on audit sampling (not an examination of all transactions), whereas the third method was a 100% evaluation of each item currently recorded. The second method (sample from recorded items) can provide evidence on whether there was proper credit approval for all items that are presently recorded. However, it does not provide evidence as to whether other items should have been approved for credit, but had not been approved.

All three methods provide relevant evidence to the controls related to credit approval. Which one is the most appropriate? Auditors have to make decisions like this on every engagement. It seems trite to say "it depends," but as noted through the earlier chapters, the right choice does depend on the risk associated with the engagement, the auditor's experience with the credit level set by the company (i.e., the credit approval level seems appropriate), the auditor's assessment of the control environment, the auditor's assessment of the quality of controls surrounding the computer applications, and the overall cost of the audit procedure. If other controls are good and risk is low, the auditor will most likely use the third approach because (a) it is the least costly and (b) it tests 100% of the recorded population. The auditor might reason further that the major risk is overstatement of accounts receivable through bad credit. The auditor is not very concerned about customers who were turned down for credit; on the other hand, management, in its assessment, might prefer to test the control by sampling from all customer orders because they do not want valid customers to be turned down for credit.

An example of an audit program to test the effectiveness of internal controls over the shipment of items and recording of sales transactions is shown in Exhibit 5.14. Significant controls identified by the auditor include (1) use of prenumbered shipping documents, (2) review of sales order forms by supervisory personnel for completeness, (3) the requirement that all shipments have specific supervisory authorization, (4) the requirement that sales have credit approval before shipment, and (5) reconciliation of the total number of items billed with the number of items shipped. In reviewing Exhibit 5.14, note that the auditor has designed specific procedures that will be effective in determining whether each important control is operating effectively. However, the auditor may do more than that. For example, the auditor also traces selected transactions through the system and into the general ledger, thus providing information about the correctness of the recorded balance. This dual-purpose testing is an example of an approach that could be used in an integrated audit.

Guidance on Sample Size for Testing Controls

The auditor may choose to test a wide variety of controls. As a basis for developing guidance for testing, we classify control procedures into five types:

1. *Manual transaction-oriented* controls that are designed to operate on every transaction throughout the year
2. *Transaction controls built into computer applications* that are designed to operate independently of manual intervention throughout the year
3. *Monthly control procedures,* such as monthly bank reconciliations or reconciliation of subsidiary ledgers with control ledgers
4. *Year-end controls* that are more relevant to estimate account balances at the end of the year, e.g., allowance for uncollectible receivables
5. *Adjusting-entry controls* that affect the closing of the books at year end as well as adjustments that are made to significant estimates during the year

The amount of work the auditor will need to perform to test the controls depends on whether management or the internal auditors have tested the controls as a basis for their assertion on the effectiveness of internal control. The following guidelines assume that the company has a strong control environment and either management or the internal auditors have tested the controls. If neither of these assumptions is correct, the extent of testing should be increased.

Manual Transaction-Oriented Controls Transaction-oriented controls should be tested according to the guidelines developed for attribute testing using statistical sampling techniques (as discussed in Chapter 8). The criteria for these samples are developed later in this text, but for the most part, the sample sizes will vary between 30 and 100 transactions, though they could be higher in some instances.

Transaction Controls Built into Computer Applications The sample size must be sufficient to persuade the auditor that the control operates

PRACTICAL POINT

Inquiry alone is not sufficient to support a conclusion about the operating effectiveness of a control.

PRACTICAL POINT

If there are account balances that are not material (either individually or when aggregated into a line item on the balance sheet or income statement), and there is little risk of misstatement, the auditor does not need to test the controls related to the account balances.

Exhibit 5.14	Audit Program for Testing the Effectiveness of Control Procedures (Manual System)

Procedure	Performed by
1. Review shipping procedures and determine the shipping department's procedures for filing shipping documents. Statistically select a sample of shipping documents, and review to determine that all items are accounted for either by a sales invoice or voided. Investigate the disposition of any missing document numbers. [Completeness]	_____
2. Select a sample of sales orders and perform the following for each:	
a. Review sales order form for completeness and approval by an authorized agent of the company. [Authorization]	_____
b. Determine whether sales order requires additional credit approval. If so, determine whether such approval has been granted and documented. [Authorization]	_____
c. Trace sales order to the generation of a shipping document, and determine that appropriate items have been shipped. [Occurrence]	_____
d. Trace shipping document to sales invoice, noting that all items have been completely and correctly billed. [Completeness and Valuation]	_____
3. Review the daily error report generated by the computer run to process sales transactions, and note the type of transactions identified for correction. Take a sample of such transactions and trace them to resubmitted transactions, noting:	
a. Approval of the resubmitted transactions [Authorization]	_____
b. Correctness of the resubmitted transaction [Valuation]	_____
c. Proper update of the resubmitted transaction in the sales account [Completeness]	_____

effectively across a wide variety of transactions throughout the year. If the auditor has tested general computer controls, such as controls over program change, and has concluded those controls are effective, the tests of computerized application controls could be as small as one for each kind of control of interest to the auditor. However, in most cases, a control addresses a wide variety of circumstances and the auditor may choose to examine exception reports to identify how unusual transactions are handled.

Monthly Control Procedures   Assuming the design of these procedures is adequate, the auditor could choose one month and retest the client's tests of these accounts. For example, the auditor could reperform the bank reconciliation for one month.

Year-End Controls   The auditor is most concerned that year-end controls are working when it is likely that the amounts would be in year-end balance sheet accounts. The auditor would take a sample of transactions during the latter part of the year, e.g., the last quarter or after year-end for those controls related to the year-end close process.

Adjusting-Entry Controls   Adjusting entries represent a high risk of material misstatement. The auditor's testing of the controls over these processes will be inversely related to the control environment; i.e., the better the control environment, the smaller the sample size will be, and vice versa. The testing also varies directly with the materiality of the account balance and the auditor's assessment of risk that the account balance might be misstated. The auditor wants to review a number of transactions to determine that (a) other controls are not being overridden by management; (b) there is support for the adjusting entries, e.g., underlying data analyses; and (c) the entries receive proper approval by the appropriate level of management. If the number of transactions is high, the auditor might use statistical sampling. If the number of transactions is low, the auditor may choose to focus on the larger transactions.

Step 7: Consider the Results of Control Testing

The auditor's work related to the design and operation of a client's internal controls is not an end in itself. The results of control testing will influence the financial statement audit. If control risk is assessed as high, the extent of substantive testing of account balances must be higher. Recall, the major purpose of understanding the control processes is to help the auditor determine where the most risk exists of financial statement errors and to use that information to perform more efficient and effective tests of account balances—all to keep audit risk within desirable levels.

The results of control testing will also impact the nature of the auditor's report on internal control effectiveness. If the auditor has identified one or more material weaknesses—either in design effectiveness or operating effectiveness—the auditor will issue an adverse report on the client's internal controls.

Documenting the Auditor's Understanding and Assessment of an Organization's Internal Controls

Documentation should clearly identify each component of the internal control framework. Documentation of the auditor's assessment of control risk should clearly delineate implications for the substantive testing of accounts. More importantly, the documentation must clearly identify who did the audit work and provide the basis for supporting audit conclusions.

The documentation of the understanding of controls is most often captured using narratives and flowcharts that describe the control processes. Some firms also use questionnaires to assist in identifying important areas where controls are expected. There is no one right approach; each audit firm should choose an approach that fits the nature of its technology, its clients, and the nature of risks that each client must address. Once the overall internal control process has been documented, many audit firms will focus in subsequent years only on changes in the system and the effectiveness of monitoring controls to signal potential breakdowns in the overall control design. An example of a comprehensive questionnaire—one form of documentation—is shown in Exhibit 5.15.

PRACTICAL POINT

PricewaterhouseCoopers issued an adverse report on AIG Inc., in 2007 because of control weaknesses regarding financial instruments.

LO 8

Describe the nature of documentation the auditor develops to support the understanding and assessment of internal control.

PRACTICAL POINT

The PCAOB's requirement is that documentation must be able to be interpreted by an auditor not connected to the engagement and, therefore, that it "stand on its own" in support of the audit conclusions.

Exhibit 5.15	**Control Procedures Questionnaire—Accounts Payable (Manual System)**

	Yes	No	N/A
Purchases Authorized			
1. Purchase requests are signed by the department supervisor.	____	____	____
2. Approval of a purchase request is noted by the initials or signature of the purchasing manager.	____	____	____
3. An approved vendor listing is readily available to all department supervisors requesting goods or services.	____	____	____
Valid Recorded Purchases/Payables			
1. Receiving reports are independently signed and dated.	____	____	____
2. Receiving reports are prenumbered, controlled, and accounted for.	____	____	____
3. The purchase order, receiving report, and vendor invoice are agreed before recording the payable.	____	____	____
4. Vendor invoices and supporting documents are defaced (e.g., stamped when paid) to prevent duplicate recording.	____	____	____
Proper Account Distribution			
1. Account distribution is authorized by the department supervisor requesting the goods or services.	____	____	____

(continues)

Exhibit 5.15	Control Procedures Questionnaire—Accounts Payable (Manual System) (*continued*)

Purchases Authorized	Yes	No	N/A
2. Computer-generated account distribution reports are approved by an appropriate person signing or initialing the report. .	____	____	____

All Liabilities for Goods or Services Recorded			
1. Prenumbered purchase orders are accounted for.	____	____	____
2. Computer batch control tickets are reconciled to edit reports.	____	____	____
3. Edit reports identify invalid vendor numbers and part numbers.	____	____	____
4. Online entry includes the input of vendor invoice control totals.	____	____	____

All Payments Properly Supported			
1. Supporting documents are reviewed before the check is signed.	____	____	____
2. Vendor invoice approval for payment is noted by the initials of the department supervisor authorizing the account distribution.	____	____	____

Payments for Nonroutine Purchases			
1. Approved check request forms and/or billing statements accompany the check and are reviewed before the check is signed.	____	____	____

All Returns Accounted for Properly			
1. Debit memos are prenumbered, controlled, and accounted for.	____	____	____
2. Debit memos are approved by appropriate purchasing managers.	____	____	____

Exhibit 5.15 illustrates that these questionnaires are comprehensive and fairly simple to use, but they are sometimes not as helpful as flowcharts in documenting a walkthrough of transaction processing.

The documentation of internal controls is not finished until the auditor tests the controls that address major risks of financial misstatement. That documentation should show:

- How each significant control is tested,
- The sampling approach used and the size of the sample used in testing,
- The conclusions of the tests,
- The individual performing the test,
- The auditor's conclusion on the effectiveness of the control, and
- The implications for the audit of related financial account balances.

PRACTICAL POINT

Most larger public accounting firms use laptops connected to a network to facilitate the sharing and review of audit work, including the important elements of internal controls.

Summary

Management's responsibility is to design, operate, and maintain an effective internal control system. Management of public companies also has a responsibility to report publicly on the effectiveness of its internal control over financial reporting. The auditors' responsibility is to understand the design and operation of those controls as a basis for conducting the financial statement audit and, in the performance of an integrated audit, for independently reporting on the effectiveness of those controls. The COSO *Internal Control, Integrated Framework* provides criteria by which both management and auditors evaluate the effectiveness of internal control. This chapter provides the foundation for understanding the "integrated audit" of financial statements and internal controls, which is covered in Chapter 6.

Significant Terms

Application controls The controls built into computer applications (programs) to minimize the risk of processing misstatements. They are often referred to as input, processing, and output controls.

Audit trail A term used to describe the documents and records that allow a user or auditor to trace a transaction from its origination through to its final disposition, or vice versa.

Authentication The process by which people identify themselves to the computer system. Designed to prove that persons accessing computer applications are who they claim to be.

Authorization An important control that delegates authority, and the limits to that authority, to specific individuals or process owners in the organization.

Control activities The policies and procedures implemented by management to assure the accomplishment of organizational objectives and the mitigation of risks.

Control environment The overall control consciousness of an organization, effected by management through example, policies, procedures, ethical standards, and monitoring processes.

COSO *Internal Control, Integrated Framework* A comprehensive framework of internal control used to assess the quality of internal control over financial reporting as well as controls over operational and compliance objectives.

General computer controls The controls that address the operation and security of computer systems, covering such areas as new system developments, security, and access controls.

Information and communication One of the five components of internal control. Includes the process of identifying, capturing, and exchanging in a timely fashion to assist in the accomplishment of an organization's objectives.

Input controls The control procedures designed to assure that the organization fully captures all the transactions between itself and another entity and to properly record those transactions.

Integrated audit An audit in which the same auditor must attest to both the financial statements and management's assertions regarding the effectiveness of internal controls over financial reporting.

Internal control A process, effected by an entity's board of directors, management, and other personnel, designed to provide reasonable assurance regarding the achievement of objectives in the following categories: (1) reliability of financial reporting, (2) compliance with applicable laws and regulations, and (3) effectiveness and efficiency of operations.

Material weakness in internal control A deficiency, or a combination of deficiencies, in internal control over financial reporting such that there is a reasonable possibility that a material misstatement of the company's annual or interim financial statements will not be prevented or detected on a timely basis.

Monitoring One of the five components of internal control that assesses the quality of the other internal components and whether they continue to operate effectively. Monitoring includes the assessment of both the design and operation of controls on a timely basis.

Relevant assertion A financial statement assertion that, for a given account, is pertinent to determining the reasonable possibility of a misstatement that would cause the financial statements to be materially misstated. This determination is based on inherent risk, without regard to the effect of controls.

Risk assessment The process used to identify and evaluate the risks that may affect an organization's ability to achieve its objectives.

Self-checking digits An input edit control designed to detect common transposition errors in data submitted for processing. Most often used for critical data such as account numbers or product identifiers.

Significant accounts and disclosures Those accounts and disclosures that have a reasonable possibility of containing a misstatement that, individually or when aggregated with others, has a material effect on the financial statements. This determination is based on inherent risk, without regard to the effect of controls.

Significant deficiency in internal control A deficiency, or a combination of deficiencies, in internal control over financial reporting that is less severe than a material weakness, yet important enough to merit attention by those responsible for oversight of the company's financial reporting.

Walkthrough An audit approach whereby the auditor "walks through" the processing of a transaction to gain, and document, an understanding of how the controls work.

SELECTED REFERENCES TO RELEVANT PROFESSIONAL GUIDANCE	
Topic	**Selected Guidance**
Audit Documentation	SAS 103 *Audit Documentation* SAS *Audit Documentation (Redrafted) (issued but not effective; proposed effective date is December 2012)* AS No. 3 *Audit Documentation* ISA 230 *Audit Documentation*
Integrated Audits	AS No. 5 *An Audit of Internal Control over Financial Reporting That Is Integrated with an Audit of Financial Statements* SSAE 15 *An Examination of an Entity's Internal Control over Financial Reporting That Is Integrated with an Audit of Its Financial Statements*
Communication Regarding Internal Control-Related Matters	SAS 115 *Communicating Internal Control Related Matters Identified in an Audit* SAS Communicating Internal Control Related Matters Identified in an Audit (Redrafted) (issued but not effective; proposed effective date is December 2012) ISA 265 *Communicating Deficiencies in Internal Control to Those Charged with Governance and Management*
Internal Control	COSO *Internal Control, Integrated Framework, 1992* COSO *Internal Control over Financial Reporting: Guidance for Smaller Businesses, 2006* COSO *Guidance on Monitoring Internal Control Systems, 2009*

Note: *Acronyms for Relevant Professional Guidance*
STANDARDS: **AS**—Auditing Standard issued by the PCAOB; **ISA**—International Standard on Auditing issued by the IAASB; **SAS**—Statement on Auditing Standards issued by the Auditing Standards Board of the AICPA; **SSAE**—Statement on Standards for Attestation Engagements issued by the AICPA.
ORGANIZATIONS: **AICPA**—American Institute of Certified Public Accountants; **COSO**—Committee of Sponsoring Organizations; **IAASB**—International Auditing and Assurance Standards Board; **PCAOB**—Public Company Accounting Oversight Board; **SEC**—Securities and Exchange Commission.

Review Questions

5-1   **(LO 1)** What is the relationship between internal control and corporate governance? In what ways does internal control enhance corporate governance as well as economic performance?

5-2   **(LO 1)** How are the concepts of risk and internal control interrelated?

5-3   **(LO 2)** What are the components of the COSO *Internal Control, Integrated Framework*? How has the Sarbanes-Oxley Act affected the use of the COSO framework?

5-4   **(LO 1)** Define internal control over financial reporting. What is the difference between internal control and internal control over financial reporting? What are the implications of the difference to the auditor?

5-5   **(LO 3, 7)** What are the major elements of the control environment, including the tone at the top?? Why is the tone at the top so important? How would an auditor go about assessing the tone at the top and its potential effect on the quality of an organization's controls?

Ethics

5-6   **(LO 3, 7)** An important element of the control environment is the organization's commitment to ethics and integrity. How might an auditor assess the organization's commitment to ethics and integrity?

5-7   **(LO 3, 7)** One element of the control environment is the organization's commitment to financial reporting competencies.

In your view, is the auditor capable of evaluating the competency of the accounting staff? How would the auditor go about evaluating the competency of the accounting department and the competencies of those making judgments on financial reporting issues?

5-8 **(LO 3, 7)** What functions do an organization's board of directors and the audit committee of the board of directors perform in promoting a strong control environment? How might an auditor assess the effectiveness of an audit committee?

5-9 **(LO 2)** What is monitoring? Identify the two major types of monitoring and explain how they could be used by management. Does monitoring apply only to control activities, or does it also apply to other elements of the internal control framework, e.g., the control environment, risk assessment, and so forth?

5-10 **(LO 3, 4)** What types of controls might a large-scale organization use to assure that its divisional management is conducting business in a manner that will best achieve the objectives of the business? What financial misstatement risks might be associated with a compensation system that places a heavy emphasis on year-end bonuses based on divisional profit performance?

5-11 **(LO 6, 7)** Define the following:
- Significant deficiency in internal controls over financial reporting
- Material weakness in internal controls over financial reporting

5-12 **(LO 2, 3, 6, 7)** Assume an audit committee is not effective. For example, Lehman Brothers, Inc. had weak directors with little financial knowledge and those directors were not independent of management. How do the weaknesses at the board and audit committee affect the auditor's evaluation of internal control over financial reporting? Would an ineffective audit committee constitute a material weakness in internal control over financial reporting? State the rationale for your response.

5-13 **(LO 1, 6, 7)** What does it mean to have a "material weakness in internal control"? How does the auditor distinguish between a significant deficiency in internal control and a material weakness in internal control? How does the auditor use the knowledge that there is a weakness in internal control to design substantive tests of account balances?

5-14 **(LO 6)** What is the role of internal audit in assisting management in preparing its report on the effectiveness of internal control over financial reporting? Is internal audit considered to be independent of management or an extension of management? Explain.

5-15 **(LO 4)** Why do auditors and accountants place such a high emphasis on segregation of duties? What kinds of segregation of duties are important in accounting applications? Give an example of a segregation of duties you might recommend for the cash receipts process.

5-16 **(LO 2, 3, 7)** How do compensation programs generally affect individual performance? What is the auditor's responsibility to evaluate the effect of compensation schemes on the risk of financial statement misstatement? Discuss the importance of professional skepticism in this evaluation. What are the essential components of

Professional Skepticism

compensation practices that an auditor should look at when evaluating the control environment?

5-17   **(LO 5)** Briefly describe how each of the following edit controls works and the types of errors each is designed to detect. Give one example of each for a retail organization.

   a. Limit test
   b. Reasonableness test
   c. Validity test
   d. Missing data test
   e. Invalid combination of items

5-18   **(LO 5)** What major principles should guide the development of a comprehensive access control program for a data processing center? Assume that the organization uses automated access control software to implement the principles.

5-19   **(LO 5)** Identify the three primary methods for authenticating a user attempting to gain access to a restricted program or file. Briefly identify the major advantages and disadvantages of each method.

5-20   **(LO 5)** In a computer environment, what are general computer controls? What is the relationship between general computer controls and application controls?

5-21   **(LO 6)** How does management gain assurance about the effectiveness of internal control over financial reporting?

5-22   **(LO 4, 7)** Assume the auditor wishes to test controls over the shipment and recording of sales transactions. Identify the controls that the auditor would expect to find to achieve the objective that "all transactions are recorded correctly, and in the correct time period." For each control identified, briefly indicate how the auditor would go about testing whether the control operated effectively.

5-23   **(LO 4, 7)** The auditor wishes to test the controls around the assertion that all valid transactions are recorded at the correct time and at the correct price. Consider the revenue cycle and identify the types of controls the auditor might look to determine if they are in place.

5-24   **(LO 7)** Is the auditor required to test the operation of controls on every audit engagement? Explain.

5-25   **(LO 6, 7)** Is management required to assess the following issues in performing its evaluation of internal control? If yes, how might management and external auditors assess each one?

   • The independence and competence of the board of directors
   • The effectiveness of the audit committee
   • The competence of accounting personnel
   • Whether company employees are adhering to the company's code of conduct

5-26   **(LO 7)** What are the external auditor testing requirements of internal controls for:

   • A publicly held company
   • A nonpublicly held company

Identify situations in which an auditor might choose not to test internal controls.

5-27 **(LO 7)** What are the factors the auditor should consider in determining the sample size for tests of controls as part of the auditor's attestation on the effectiveness of internal control over financial reporting? Consider the following types of controls:

- Controls performed on every transaction
- Computerized controls as part of every transaction
- Monthly control procedures
- Controls over estimates
- Year-end adjusting entries

5-28 **(LO 7, 8)** Explain how a walkthrough would help the auditor understand and document the adequacy of controls in an accounting application. Explain how a tour of the client's plant or other facilities would also help the auditor in understanding internal controls.

Multiple-Choice Questions

5-29 **(LO 6, 7)** Which of the following would most likely be considered a significant deficiency in an organization's control environment?

a. The internal audit function is outsourced to a public accounting firm that is not performing the financial statement audit.

b. Management has approximately 60% of its compensation in stock options but the options cannot be exercised for five years.

c. Management relies on the external audit as its primary source of monitoring controls.

d. The audit committee meets with the external auditor and the internal auditor but does not allow the CFO to participate in these meetings.

5-30 **(LO 4)** Which of the following controls would be *most effective* in assisting the organization in achieving the completeness objective?

a. All employee time cards should be collected by the supervisor and transmitted directly to the payroll department for processing.

b. All shipments must be approved by the credit manager to assure that the total invoice amount does not exceed approved limits.

c. All receipts of merchandise must be independently counted or weighed by someone in the receiving department who also reviews the goods for quality-control deficiencies.

d. All shipments must be recorded on prenumbered shipping documents that are independently accounted for.

5-31 **(LO 1, 4, 7)** Assume the auditor has tested controls and determines that the company has weak controls related to pricing and dating of sales. Some of this weakness is based on inadequate segregation of duties. Based on this information, which of the following actions should the auditor take?

a. Resign from the audit because the entity is not auditable.

b. Discontinue testing controls over sales pricing and dating of sales transactions.

    c. Expand the direct tests of related account balances by selecting recorded sales and tracing back to shipping documents and authorized price lists.

    d. (b) and (c) above.

5-32 **(LO 5)** In order to implement an effective access control process for computerized processing, an organization must do all of the following *except:*

    a. Identify all users who can be granted access to any portion of computer records or computerized programs.

    b. Identify all activities that employees might legitimately perform on the data.

    c. Identify all data that someone might want to access.

    d. Identify a common physical ID of each employee and potential user, e.g., fingerprint.

The following information applies to Questions 5-33 and 5-34.

An auditor wishes to test controls over the sufficiency of the credit process. The various controls identified during the interview with the credit manager and IT director are:

- Credit limits are established for all companies by the credit manager and cannot exceed the amount without the explicit approval of the credit manager.

- Sales cannot be made to new customers on credit without the establishment of a credit limit by the credit manager.

- The credit manager regularly reviews the credit limits established by each customer and updates the credit rating and limit as new information is gathered.

- Access to the credit limit file is limited to the credit manager or her authorized assistant.

5-33 **(LO 5)** Which of the following statements are correct regarding the controls?

    i. The controls are only as good as the credit manager's process for establishing and reviewing credit limits.

    ii. Because the process of establishing credit limits is fairly time-consuming, the marketing manager should have the ability to approve sales on an ad hoc basis while waiting for the credit approval.

    iii. The credit manager should establish a credit limit for all related companies (parents, subsidiaries, etc.) even though each is a separate company.

      a. II and III only.

      b. I, II, and III

      c. I and III only

      d. II only

5-34 **(LO 6)** Assume the auditor concludes the controls are working properly based on inquiry and other appropriate tests. Which of the following is a correct inference regarding the auditor's conclusion?

    a. The auditor *will not* need to perform direct tests on the valuation of accounts receivable.

   b. The auditor *could not* have concluded that the internal controls over credit were effective unless the auditor determined that the credit limits are updated for changed conditions.

   c. The auditor does *not* need to confirm accounts receivable because the risk of a material misstatement of receivables is mitigated by the controls.

   d. The auditor does *not* need to perform any more direct tests of the account balances if the auditor has tested the IT general controls.

5-35   **(LO 4)** Proper implementation of reconciliation controls would be effective in detecting all of the following errors *except:*

   a. Transactions were appropriately posted to individual subsidiary accounts, but because of a computer malfunction, some of the transactions were not posted to the master account.

   b. The client has experienced inventory shrinkage that has caused the perpetual inventory records to be overstated.

   c. Three shipments were never invoiced because employees in the shipping room colluded with a shipper to deliver goods to their own private company for resale and never recorded the shipments on any documents.

   d. A bank teller properly recorded all transactions involving checks but pocketed all cash receipts, even though customers were given a receipt as evidence of the deposit to their accounts.

5-36   **(LO 4)** Segregation of duties is best accomplished when the auditor determines which of the following?

   a. Employees perform only one job, even though they might have access to other records.

   b. The internal audit department performs an independent test of transactions throughout the year and reports any errors to departmental managers.

   c. The person responsible for reconciling the bank account is responsible for cash disbursements but not for cash receipts.

   d. The payroll department cannot add employees to the payroll or change pay rates without the explicit authorization of the personnel department.

5-37   **(LO 4, 7)** The auditor wishes to test the assertion that controls are in place to ensure that all recorded sales transactions are valid. The auditor should:

   a. Take a sample of shipping documents and determine that all of the items shipped are invoiced.

   b. Use a computer audit program to list all recorded invoices and compare the invoices to individual credit limits that were properly authorized.

   c. Take a sample of recorded sales and trace back to locate a shipping document to determine that the recorded item was shipped.

   d. Take a sample of recorded invoices and match the invoice amounts with preauthorized prices that are in the computer system.

5-38   **(LO 2)** Which of the following would *not* be considered an effective implementation of the monitoring element of the COSO internal control framework?

a. Internal audit periodically performs an evaluation of internal controls that have been documented and tested in prior years.

b. Management reviews current economic performance against expectations and investigates to determine causes of significant deviations from the expectations.

c. The company implements software that captures all instances in which the underlying program is designed to capture processed transactions that exceed company-authorized limits.

d. The company builds in edit checks to determine whether all purchases are made from authorized vendors.

Discussion and Research Questions

Ethics

5-39   **(Integral Role of Internal Control to Corporate Governance, LO 1, 2, 6, 7)** Internal control has been identified as a crucial part of corporate governance.

Required

a. What is the relationship between internal control and good governance practices?

b. Consider the GAO Report on the quality of U.S. government processing and financial statements described in the *Professional Judgment in Context* feature at the beginning of the chapter. Is it unethical for government managers to allow the control system at the company to deteriorate to the level that it has?

c. Has mandatory reporting on internal control over financial reporting improved the quality of governance in organizations? Discuss the cost-benefit issues associated with mandatory reporting on internal control over financial reporting.

d. How might reports on internal control affect the valuation of a company's stock? Explain and justify your response.

5-40   **(Components of the COSO *Internal Control, Integrated Framework*, LO 1, 2, 6)** The COSO *Internal Control, Integrated Framework* (ICIF) describes an organization's internal controls as consisting of five components.

Required

a. Briefly describe each component of the ICIF and how the components help to accomplish organizational objectives.

b. For each component, explain how a deficiency in that component affects management's reporting requirements related to internal control over financial reporting.

c. For the purposes of conducting the financial statement audit, is an assessment of internal controls over financial reporting made at the overall organization level or for specific subsystems of the organization's transaction processing systems? Explain.

5-41   **(Tone at the Top, LO 1, 2, 3, 7, 8)** A review of corporate failures as described in the financial press, such as the *Wall Street Journal,* often describes the tone at the top (the overall control environment) as one of the major contributors to the failure. Often the tone at the top at the failed companies reflects a disdain for controls and an emphasis on accomplishing specific financial reporting objectives such as reporting increased profitability (whether it exists or not).

Required

a. Identify the key components an auditor will evaluate in assessing the control environment of an organization. How will the auditor's assessment of the control environment affect the design and conduct of an audit? Consider both a positive and negative evaluation.

b. For each component of the control environment identified in part (a), indicate the information (and the sources of the information) the auditor would gather in evaluating the factor.

c. What needs to be documented related to the auditor's evidence gathering, evaluation, and assessment of the client's control environment?

5-42   **(Monitoring Activities, LO 2, 7)**   Companies can gain efficiencies by implementing effective monitoring of their internal control processes.

Required

a. Define monitoring and how it relates to the other components of the internal control framework.

b. Identify the important monitoring procedures that a company might use in assessing its controls over revenue recognition and associated costs that might be used in each of the following situations:

- A convenience store such as a 7-Eleven

- A chain restaurant such as Olive Garden

- A manufacturing division of a larger company that makes rubberized containers for the consumer market

c. To what extent can the auditor focus the assessment of internal control on testing the effectiveness of the company's monitoring processes? Discuss and support your conclusion. Discuss, for example, the level of comfort the auditor can get about the effectiveness of other controls by testing the effectiveness of monitoring controls.

5-43   **(Control Environment Evidence, LO 2, 3, 7)**   Management and the auditor have to develop processes to assess the effectiveness of each element in the control environment.

Group Activity

Required

a. Exhibit 5.3 is an example of an approach to identifying the important elements of the company's control environment and an approach to gathering evidence to determine whether the underlying principle is being achieved. With your group members, select a company with which you are familiar and prepare an analysis of the control environment, using the format in Exhibit 5.3 as follows:

Underlying Principle	**Evidence Gathered and Analysis of Evidence**
Integrity and ethical values	
Board of directors	
Organizational structure	
Management philosophy and operating style	
Commitment to financial reporting competencies	
Authority and responsibility	
Human resources	

Group Activity

5-44   **(Reporting an Internal Control, LO 1, 2, 6)** Various parties are taking an increased interest in the quality of an entity's internal controls.

Required: In your groups address the following:

a. Briefly explain the difference between internal control and internal control over financial reporting. What are the major distinctions?

b. The Sarbanes-Oxley Act requires public reporting on the quality of internal controls over financial reporting. Who are the primary beneficiaries of public reporting on internal control and what are the primary benefits of such reporting?

c. Why might a company's trading partner (supplier or integrated customer) be interested in the quality of an organization's internal controls?

d. How would a negative report on internal controls over financial reporting likely affect stock prices? Does the nature of the material weakness make a difference in the likely effect on stock market prices? Explain by identifying, in your own view, the types of deficiencies that would most likely have a negative effect on stock market prices.

e. Does a report on internal control have to assess all of the COSO components or could it be based on the controls over the processing of transactions? Explain.

Professional Skepticism

Fraud

5-45   **(Evaluating the Effectiveness of Internal Controls, LO 1, 3, 4, 6, 7)** The following scenario describes the Pelleteri Plastics Company, a small plastics producer with $250 million in revenue and approximately 300 employees.

Pelleteri Plastics is a NASDAQ-listed public company that first became listed three years ago. It has been hit hard by the recent recession and its sales have dropped from $1.375 million to $1.250 million. It is barely profitable and is just meeting some of its most important debt covenants. During the past year, John Pelleteri, CEO and owner of 22% of the company's shares, has taken the following actions to reduce costs:

1. Laid off approximately 75 factory workers and streamlined receiving and shipping to be more efficient.

2. Cut hourly wages by $3 per hour.

3. Reduced the size of the board by eliminating three of the four independent directors and changed the compensation of remaining board members to 100% stock options to save cash outflow. The company granted options to the remaining six directors with a market value of $100,000 per director, but no cash outlay.

4. Eliminated the internal audit department at a savings of $450,000. The process owners (e.g., those responsible for accounts payable) are now required to objectively evaluate the quality of controls over their own areas and thus to serve as a basis for management's report on the effectiveness of internal control.

5. Changed from a Big 4 audit firm to a regional audit firm, resulting in an additional audit savings of $300,000. This is the first public company audit for the new firm.

6. Because internal audit no longer exists, the CEO relies on monitoring as the major form of control assessment. Most of the monitoring consists of comparing budget with actual results. Management argues this is very effective because the CEO is very much involved in operations and would know if there is a reporting problem.

7. Set tight performance goals for each manager and promised a bonus of 20% of their salary if they meet the performance objectives. The performance objectives relate to increased profitability and meeting existing volumes.

8. The purchasing department has been challenged to move away from single-supplier contracts to identify suppliers that can significantly reduce the cost of products purchased.

9. Put a freeze on all hiring, in spite of the fact that the accounting department has lost its assistant controller. This has required a great deal of extra overtime for most accounting personnel, who are quite stressed.

Required

a. For each of the items listed above, identify whether the item would be considered (a) an operational issue and not a weakness in internal control, (b) a material weakness in internal control, or (c) a significant deficiency in internal control. If additional information is needed in order to assess whether the item is a control deficiency, briefly indicate what information would be required.

b. How has the risk related to financial reporting increased during the year? Given the increase in risk, how might the auditor approach the audit differently this year? Be sure that your response addresses the relevance of professional skepticism and fraud risks.

5-46 **(Tests of Controls, LO 1, 3, 6)** Auditing standards indicate that if control risk is assessed as low, the auditor must gain assurance that the controls are operating effectively.

Required

a. What is meant by testing the operating effectiveness of control procedures? How does an auditor decide which controls to test?

b. The PCAOB urges auditors to take a "top-down, risk-based approach" to determining which controls to test. Explain how an auditor actually performs such an approach.

c. How is the auditor's assessment of control risk affected if a documented control procedure is not operating effectively? Explain the effect of such an assessment on the nature of audit tests of account balances.

d. Assume that an auditor needs to examine a document to determine that a control is working effectively and the client cannot locate the document. Should the auditor take another sample item to substitute for the one that could not be found? What should the auditor's conclusion be regarding the operation of the control if (1) the document cannot be found and (2) the auditor chooses another transaction and the documentation for that other transaction can be found?

5-47 **(Application Controls, LO 1, 4, 5, 7)** Cabelas is a catalog retailer emphasizing outdoor gear, with a focus on fishing and hunting equipment and clothing. It prints an annual catalog containing over 200 pages of products, as well as approximately six special sale catalogs during the year. Products range from fishing lures retailing for $1.29 to boat packages for over $25,000. It also has both a significant Web presence and a number of large retail locations. Purchases can be made through the mail, on the Internet, or at the retail store. There will sometimes be online specials that are not available elsewhere (e.g., close-outs). Merchandise can be paid for by personal check, credit card, or cash. Customers can (a) order online, (b) mail in their order (with check or credit card information included), or (c) place an order by calling the company's toll-free number.

Focusing on catalog operations, assume the company has implemented an order-entry system by which computer operators take the customer order, check the availability of items for shipment, and confirm the invoice amount with the customer. Once an order is taken, the system generates a shipping-and-packing document, places a hold on the inventory, and prepares an invoice (and recording of sales) when items are shipped.

Required

a. Identify the application control procedures (including edit controls) you would recommend for orders coming in over the Web or through calls to the online order taker.

b. Briefly indicate how control procedures might differ for the orders that are made directly over the Web.

c. For each control procedure identified in part (a), briefly indicate the potential types of errors or irregularities that could occur because the control is not present or is not operating effectively and (b) identify the audit steps the auditor might take to test the year-end account balance that is affected by the control.

5-48   **(Application Controls, LO 1, 5, 7)** The following represent errors that often occur in a computerized environment.

Required

For each error:

A. Identify a control procedure that would have been effective in either preventing or detecting the error,

B. Should the auditor expand the testing of controls? If yes, how should the tests be expanded?

C. What is the impact on auditing account balances?
Errors Found

a. The selling price for all products handled by a particular company salesperson was reduced from authorized prices by 25% to 40%. The salesperson was paid commission on gross sales made. Subsequently, the auditor found that other sales personnel also reduced prices in order to meet sales targets.

b. Duplicate paychecks were prepared for all employees in the company's warehouse for the week ended July 31. This occurred because the data processing department processed employee time cards twice.

c. An employee in the sales order department who was upset about an inadequate pay raise copied the client's product master file and sold it to a competitor. The master file contained information on the cost and sales price of each product as well as special discounts given to customers.

d. An individual in the sales department accessed the product master file and, in an attempt to change prices for a specific customer, ended up changing prices for the products for all customers.

e. A nonexistent part number was included in the description of goods on a shipping document. Fortunately, the individual packing the item for shipment was able to identify the product by its description and included it in the order. The item was not billed, however, because it was not correctly identified in the system.

f. A customer account number was transposed during the order-taking process. Consequently, the shipment was billed to another customer. By the time the error was identified, the original customer decided to take its business elsewhere.

g. An accounts receivable clerk with access to entering cash remittances misappropriated the cash remittances and recorded the credit to the customer's account as a discount.

h. An employee consistently misstated his time card by returning at night and punching out then, rather than when his shift was over at 3:30. Instead of being paid for 40 hours per week, he was paid, on average, for over 60 hours per week for almost one year. When accused of the error, he denied any wrongdoing and quit.

i. A customer order was filled and shipped to a former customer, who had already declared bankruptcy and already owed a large amount to the company that was most likely uncollectible. The company's standard billing terms are 2%, 10 days, or net 30.

5-49   **(Access Control Policies, LO 5)** A comprehensive program for controlling access to the computer equipment, computer programs, and data is an important control. In evaluating the comprehensiveness of an access policy, the auditor considers both physical and data access (i.e., access to data by gaining access to computer files through the computer).

Required

a. Identify the physical controls an auditor would expect to find regarding access to equipment and computer documentation.

b. Identify the three main ways an access control program can authenticate a user. What are the advantages and disadvantages of each approach?

c. What are the risks in using a physical identifier such as a retinal scan or a fingerprint as the major approach to authenticating users? What are the implications to the user if the authentication is compromised?

d. Assume that a client has software that does a good job in authenticating users. Explain how an access matrix works and the importance of developing an access matrix for security. Explain how users and access should be matched on a matrix.

Group Activity

5-50   **(Continuous Monitoring, LO 2, 5)** More firms are using the power of computing to develop continuous monitoring approaches to identify control problems early and to take corrective action on a timely basis.

Internet

Required

In your groups, address the following issues:

a. Explain how the concept of continuous monitoring might be applied in a computerized application that processes sales orders and records sales.

b. With the permission of your instructor, select one of the following websites:

- Oversightsystems.com
- Approva.com
- ACL.com

Explain the types of products that each firm provides to the market and how the products might help an organization implement effective monitoring over computer operations. To what extent are the software products (1) another control to be implemented versus (2) an approach to control monitoring? Explain.

5-51 **(Assessing Control Deficiencies, LO 4, 7)** Assume the auditor is testing management's assertion that internal control is effective. The company is a manufacturing company with high-dollar specialized machines used in the medical profession. The auditor is testing controls over the revenue recognition process, including the recording of accounts receivable, cost of goods sold, and inventory.

Required

a. The following table identifies important controls the auditor is testing regarding the revenue cycle. The first column describes the control and the second column describes the test results of the auditor. Based on the test results, determine whether the auditor's results support a conclusion that either a significant deficiency or material weakness exists. The assessment can apply to each control or the process as a whole. Briefly describe the rationale for your answer.

CONTROL TESTING OVER REVENUE

Control Tested	Test Results	Significant Deficiency?	Material Weakness?
(1) All sales over $10,000 require computer check of outstanding balances to see if approved balance is exceeded.	Tested throughout year with a sample size of 30. Only 3 failures, all in the last quarter, and all approved by sales manager.		
(2) The computer is programmed to record a sale only when an item is shipped.	Sampled 10 items during the last month. One indicated that it was recorded before shipped. Management was aware of the recording.		
(3) All prices are obtained from a standardized price list maintained within the computer and accessible only by the marketing manager.	Auditor selected 40 invoices and found 5 instances in which the price was less than the price list. All of the price changes were initiated by salespeople.		
(4) Sales are shipped only upon receiving an authorized purchase order from customer.	Auditor selects 15 transactions near the end of each quarter. On average, 3–4 are shipped each quarter based on salesperson's approval and without a customer purchase order.		

CONTROL TESTING OVER REVENUE

Control Tested	Test Results	Significant Deficiency?	Material Weakness?
(5) Every shipment is assigned a number by the computer when an order is taken. A report is prepared each month showing the status of all items where purchase orders have been received, items currently in progress, and items shipped.	Auditor examines three of the weekly reports and observes that the items shown as shipped do not reconcile with the number of items invoiced. Management says this is a regular timing issue and does not affect the correctness of the account balances.		

5-52   **(Segregation of Duties, LO 1, 4)** For each of the following situations, evaluate the segregation of duties implemented by the company and indicate the following:

a. Any deficiency in the segregation of duties described. (Indicate *None* if no deficiency is present.)

b. The potential errors or irregularities that might occur because of the inadequate segregation of duties.

c. Compensating, or other, controls that might be added to mitigate potential misstatements.

d. A specific audit test that ought to be performed to determine whether a misstatement in an account balance had occurred.

Situations

1. The company's payroll is computerized and is handled by one person in charge of payroll who enters all weekly time reports into the system. The payroll system is password protected so that only the payroll person can change pay rates or add/delete company personnel to the payroll file. Payroll checks are prepared weekly, and the payroll person batches the checks by supervisor or department head for subsequent distribution to employees.

2. XYZ is a relatively small organization but has segregated the duties of cash receipts and cash disbursements. However, the employee responsible for handling cash receipts also reconciles the monthly bank account.

3. Nick's is a small family-owned restaurant in a northern resort area whose employees are trusted. When the restaurant is very busy, any of the waitstaff has the ability to operate the cash register and collect the amounts due from the customer. All orders are tabulated on "tickets." Although there is a place to indicate the waiter or waitress on each ticket, most do not bother to do so, nor does management reconcile the ticket numbers and amounts with total cash receipts for the day.

4. A purchasing agent for JC Penney has the responsibility for ordering specific products, e.g., women's clothes, and setting the prices for those products. The purchasing agent is eligible for a bonus based on the profitability of his or her line of business. The receipt, demonstration, and sale of the goods are handled by individuals who are separate from the purchasing agent.

5. Bass Pro Shops takes customer orders via a toll-free phone number. The order taker sits at a terminal and has complete access to the customer's previous credit history and a list of inventory available for sale. The order clerk has the ability to input all the

customer's requests and generate a sales invoice and shipment with no additional supervisory review or approval.

6. The purchasing department of Big Dutch is organized around three purchasing agents. The first is responsible for ordering electrical gear and motors, the second orders fabrication material, and the third orders nuts and bolts and other smaller supplies that go into the assembly process. To improve the accountability to vendors, all receiving slips and vendor invoices are sent directly to the purchasing agent placing the order. This allows the purchasing agent to better monitor the performance of vendors. When approved by the purchasing agent for payment, the purchasing agent must forward (a) a copy of the purchase order, (b) a copy of the receiving slip, and (c) a copy of the vendor invoice to accounts payable for payment. Accounts payable will not pay an invoice unless all three items are present and match as to quantities, prices, and so forth. The receiving department reports to the purchasing department.

7. The employees of Americana TV and Appliance—a major electronics retailer—are paid based on their performance in generating profitable sales for the company. Each salesperson has the ability to modify a tagged sales price (within specified but very broad parameters). Once a sales price has been negotiated with the customer, an invoice is prepared. At the close of the day, the salesperson looks up the cost of the merchandise on a master price list. The salesperson then enters the cost of the merchandise on the copy of the invoice and submits it to accounting for data entry and processing. The salesperson's commission is determined by the gross margin realized on sales.

5-53   **(Testing Internal Controls, LO 1, 4, 5, 7)** If a company's control risk is assessed as low, the auditor needs to gather evidence on the operating effectiveness of the controls.

Required

a. For each of the following control activities, indicate the audit procedure the auditor would use to determine its operating effectiveness.

b. Briefly describe how substantive tests of account balances should be modified if the auditor finds that the control procedure is not working as planned. In doing so, indicate (a) what could happen because of the control deficiency, and (b) how the auditor's tests should be expanded to test for the potential misstatement.

Controls

1. Credit approval by the credit department is required before salespersons accept orders of more than $15,000 and for all customers who have a past-due balance higher than $22,000.

2. All merchandise receipts are recorded on prenumbered receiving slips. The controller's department periodically accounts for the numerical sequence of the receiving slips.

3. Payments for goods received are made only by the accounts payable department on receipt of a vendor invoice, which is then matched for prices and quantities with approved purchase orders and receiving slips.

4. The accounts receivable bookkeeper is not allowed to issue credit memos or to approve the write-off of accounts.

5. Cash receipts are opened by a mail clerk, who prepares remittances to send to accounts receivable for recording. The clerk prepares a daily deposit slip, which is sent to the controller. Deposits are made daily by the controller.

6. Employees are added to the payroll master file by the payroll department only after receiving a written authorization from the personnel department.

7. The only individuals who have access to the payroll master file are the payroll department head and the payroll clerk responsible for maintaining the payroll file. Access to the file is controlled by computer passwords.

8. Edit tests built into the computerized payroll program prohibit the processing of weekly payroll hours in excess of 53 and the payment to an employee for more than three different job classifications during a one-week period.

9. Credit memos are issued to customers only on the receipt of merchandise or the approval of the sales department for adjustments.

10. A salesperson cannot approve a sales return or price adjustment that exceeds 6% of the cumulative sales for the year for any one customer. The divisional sales manager must approve any subsequent approvals of adjustments for such a customer.

5-54   **(Authorizing Transactions, LO 4)** Authorization of transactions is considered a key control in most organizations. Authorizations should not be made by individuals who have incompatible functions.

Required

Indicate the individual or function (e.g., the head of a particular department) that should have the ability to authorize each of the following transactions. Briefly indicate the rationale for your answer.

Transactions

1. Writing off old accounts receivable
2. Committing the organization to acquire another company that is half the size of the existing company
3. Paying an employee for overtime
4. Shipping goods on account to a new customer
5. Purchasing goods from a new vendor
6. Temporarily investing funds in common stock investments instead of money market funds
7. Purchasing a new line of manufacturing equipment to remodel a production line at one of the company's major divisions (the purchase represents a major new investment for the organization)
8. Replacing an older machine at one of the company's major divisions
9. Rewriting the company's major computer program for processing purchase orders and accounts payable (the cost of rewriting the program will represent one quarter of the organization's computer development budget for the year)

5-55   **(Elements of Internal Control, LO 4)** Brown Company provides the following office support services for more than 100 small clients:

1. Supplying temporary personnel
2. Providing monthly bookkeeping services
3. Designing and printing small brochures
4. Copying and reproduction services
5. Preparing tax reports

Some clients pay for these services on a cash basis, some use 30-day charge accounts, and others operate on a contractual basis with quarterly payments. Brown's new office manager was concerned about the effectiveness of control procedures over sales and cash flow. At the manager's request, the process was reviewed and the following facts were disclosed:

a. Contracts were written by account executives and then passed to the accounts receivable department, where they were filed. Contracts had a limitation (ceiling) on the types of services and the amount of work covered. Contracts were payable quarterly in advance.

b. Client periodic payments on contracts were identified on the contract, and a payment receipt was placed in the contract file. Accounting records showed Credit Revenue; Debit Cash.

c. Periodically, a clerk reviewed the contract files to determine their status.

d. Work orders relating to contract services were placed in the contract file. Accounting records showed Debit Cost of Services; Credit Cash or Accounts Payable or Accrued Payroll.

e. Monthly bookkeeping services were usually paid for when the work was complete. If not paid in cash, a copy of the financial statement (marked "Unpaid $ _____") was put into a cash-pending file. It was removed when cash was received, and accounting records showed Debit Cash; Credit Revenue.

f. Design and printing work was handled like bookkeeping's work. However, a design and printing order form was used to accumulate costs and compute the charge to be made to the client. A copy of the order form served as a billing to the client and, when cash was received, as a remittance advice.

g. Reproduction (copy) work was generally a cash transaction that was rung up on a cash register and balanced at the end of the day. Some reproduction work was charged to open accounts. A billing form was given to the client with the work, and a copy was put in an open file. It was removed when paid. In both cases, when cash was received, the accounting entry was Debit Cash; Credit Revenue.

h. Tax work was handled like the bookkeeping services.

i. Cash from cash sales was deposited daily. Cash from receipts on account or quarterly payments on contracts was deposited after being matched with evidence of the receivable.

j. Bank reconciliations were performed using the deposit slips as original data for the deposits on the bank statements.

k. A cash log of all cash received in the mail was maintained and used for reference purposes when payment was disputed.

l. Monthly comparisons were made of the costs and revenues of printing, design, bookkeeping, and tax service. Unusual variations between revenues and costs were investigated. However, the handling of deferred payments made this analysis difficult.

Required

a. List at least eight elements of poor internal control that are evident.

b. List at least six elements of good internal control that are evident.

5-56 **(Control Failures, LO 1, 2, 3, 4)** It has been alleged that many recent corporate failures such as those at Enron, AIG, Citigroup, Merrill Lynch, and World Com were largely due to the lack of adequate controls in the organization. The financial press also contains many examples of frauds at the local level that have been perpetrated in organizations with weak controls.

Group Activity

Internet

Required

In your group, select a company that has recently failed or has been involved in a fraud. Research the company and its failure using appropriate Internet resources. Identify deficiencies in internal control that may have contributed to the decline and subsequent failure of the organization. Present your analysis to the class.

5-57 **(Assessing Control Risk, LO 4, 6, 7)** With your instructor's consent, select a place where you have worked part-time or an organization in which you have some acquaintance (relative or friend) and therefore have access. Choose one area of operations (cash receipts, sales, shipping, receiving, or payroll) for review. For the area selected for review:

a. Identify the major transactions processed.

b. Select a representative transaction and perform a walkthrough of the application to gain an understanding of processing and control procedures implemented to accomplish the control objectives described in the chapter.

c. Document the key control procedures using a control objectives framework.

d. Identify control procedures you would recommend to improve the organization's internal controls.

Cases

5-58 **(Control Deficiencies, LO 4)** You have been assigned to review the internal controls of the credit department of a recently acquired subsidiary. The subsidiary imports several lines of personal computers and sells them to retail stores throughout the country. The credit department consists of a new credit manager, a clerk, and a part-time secretary.

Sales are made by fifteen sales representatives: five are at company headquarters and handle large accounts with retail chains and ten are located throughout the country. Sales representatives visit current and prospective customers and, if a sale is made, either submit the order electronically or prepare a customer order form consisting of the original and three copies. One copy is retained by the customer, one by the sales representative, and one is sent to the warehouse; the original is sent to headquarters.

For new customers with orders of more than $100,000, a credit application is also completed and sent along with the order to headquarters. The credit application includes a bank reference and three credit references along with financial statements.

The sales order sent to headquarters goes first to the credit department for approval. The credit department looks up the customer's credit on a computerized file that is maintained for customers with "good credit." If the customer is in the file, the clerk examines a monthly report listing all accounts that have not been paid in 60 days. If the customer is not listed in the report, the clerk initials the order as approved and sends it to accounting for recording and billing. The credit manager holds orders from new customers or from customers listed on the 60-day report for review. For transactions submitted electronically, the computer is programmed to identify all accounts that are over 60 days old and all sales that are over $100,000 to be sent to the credit manager for review.

For orders of more than $100,000 from new customers, the credit manager reviews the credit application along with the financial statements and calls at least one of the credit references. If the order is approved, the manager initials it and gives it to the secretary, who enters the approved data into the database.

If the order is denied, the manager adds the customer's name to a list of past rejected credit applications and canceled accounts. For new customers placing orders for less than the $100,000 limit, there is no further review beyond the review of previously rejected credit applicants. If orders are not approved, the credit manager calls the warehouse to stop shipment. The order is marked "Credit Not Approved" and given to the secretary, who notifies the sales representative and the customer. The order and the credit application are then thrown away.

Once each quarter, the credit manager requests that the accounting department provide a list of all accounts more than 90 days old with supporting detail of account activity for the past 12 months. The credit manager reviews the information and determines whether action should be taken. Action consists of the following:

- The manager calls the sales representative and asks him or her to contact the client about payment.

- If payment is not made in three weeks, the credit manager calls the customer and requests payment. The customer is also put on the "no credit" list in the company's database.

- If payment is not made within four additional weeks, the account is turned over to a collection agency.

When an account has been with a collection agency for two months without receiving payment, it is written off. The credit manager prepares the necessary adjusting entries.

Required

a. Identify the deficiencies associated with the credit function as just described. Use the following format:

   Deficiency   *Associated Risk*   *Recommended Control*

b. Identify control improvements that could be made in the process.

5-59   **(Identification of Control Deficiencies, LO 2, 4, 7)** Waste Management is an $18 billion company that picks up solid waste and operates landfills, recycling centers, and electrical-generation facilities. It produces electricity from landfill by-products that serves about 1 million homes a year. It operates solely in North America and is organized as follows.

The company is headquartered in Houston, Texas, and is organized to serve five major regions across the United States and Canada (East, North, South, West, and Canada). The regions are further subdivided into market areas, such as New York, Philadelphia, and Eastern Ohio. Within each market area are the business units, e.g., a landfill, a waste transfer station, a waste hauling division, and a recycling center. Much of the accounting takes place at the business-unit level. The company operates about 300 landfill sites, 160 recycling centers, 400 solid-waste sites, and about 1,000 waste-hauling units. Thus, the company has approximately 2,000 separate business units.

Some of the company's applications operate at the corporate level (e.g., purchasing and accounts payable) and some at the market-area level (e.g., financial consolidation of units, development of monitoring reports, and payroll processing). The remainder of the activities, particularly revenue processes, takes place at the business-unit level. Principal revenue recording activities include the following:

- Billing governmental entities for contract prices for hauling solid waste. Billing is based on the target number of households but increases if the actual number of houses exceeds the set limit, and vice versa.

- Billing individuals for special-request pickups, e.g., disposing of appliances.

- Selling recycled products to the secondary market.

- Collecting cash for non–Waste Management haulers that show up at a landfill. This is done through weighing the full trucks and collecting cash from the hauler for the amount weighed.

At this point, Waste Management has only begun installing integrated weighing and billing scales at the landfills. For most of the landfills, a scale operator weighs the truck, calculates the amount of solid waste received, and charges the hauler (or consumer) an amount based on authorized landfill policies. The operator collects the cash, and later, when time permits, enters all the data into the revenue recognition and cash accounting system kept on the computer.

All decisions on hiring new workers take place at the business-unit level even though payroll processing takes place at the market-area level.

Required

a. Identify the control procedures that Waste Management should have in place for revenue processing and revenue recognition. Use the framework of internal control objectives for transaction processing to assist in the identification of needed controls. Also consider the risks associated with the processing, i.e., what things could go wrong with someone operating the weighing scales, collecting cash, and entering the data into the computer for revenue recognition purposes.

b. Identify two or three monitoring controls or exception reports that management might have in place to assure that all solid waste accepted at a transfer station (to later be trucked to a landfill) or at a landfill is recorded.

c. Identify the control procedures the company should have in place to assure that the internal control objectives for payroll processing are met.

d. Management has documented the controls and needs to develop tests to determine that the controls are operating effectively. For all the controls identified in part (a), indicate a test that would determine the effectiveness of the controls in operation.

e. Consider revenue recognition. Develop a comprehensive approach that would guide the external auditor in determining how many controls need to be tested, and at what level they need to be tested, for each of the three processes. Consider the amount of testing that must take place at the corporate level, the market-area level, and the business-unit level.

5-60   **(Supply Chain Controls, LO 4)** JC Penney is the largest retailer of men's shirts in North America. In order to reduce inventory and order time, and to better anticipate market trends, JC Penney has established a sole sourcing contract with TAL Industries of Hong Kong and has signed a long-term purchase contract with TAL regarding the quality of shirts, prices, shipping requirements, and inventory levels.

TAL downloads information on sales from all JC Penney stores each evening. It has a responsibility to predict market demand and to increase the sales of its shirts in each store. Having the advantage of analyzing diverse trends across the United States, TAL has been known to rush-order the manufacturing of new shirts in specific styles and air-freight them directly to some stores—not at JC Penney's request, but because of its own market analysis.

In a sense, JC Penney does not know the exact quantities of shirts that will be shipped to each store. Nor does JC Penney have a formal receiving function at each store that logs in the items received. However, it does have a receiving function if the shirts go to one of its twelve distribution centers. But if TAL labels and prices all the goods and ships directly to the stores, it saves time and effort for JC Penney.

TAL bills JC Penney electronically every week, and JC Penney transfers the authorized amount electronically to TAL's bank account on the 16th and 30th of each month.

Required

a. What information does JC Penney need to know about TAL Industries before entering into a contract such as the one described?

b. Identify the controls that JC Penney should have in place to assure that only goods that were received were billed and that the billing is at the authorized prices.

c. What kind of reconciling procedure would tell JC Penney whether or not it paid TAL for more shirts than actually received?

d. From TAL's viewpoint, what controls should JC Penney have on hand at the store level to assure that shirts are not taken off the receiving dock before they reach the shopping floor and that there is no shoplifting or other theft of the product? Why are these controls important to TAL?

5-61 **(Decision Analysis and Remediation of Material Weaknesses, LO 2, 3, 7, 9)**

The restated 2004 Annual Report of Milacron, Inc. contained the following description of a material weakness in the company's internal controls:

Review of Complex and Judgmental Accounting Issues—There are inadequate levels of review of complex and judgmental accounting issues. Various audit adjustments were needed to correct errors resulting from this internal control deficiency, which manifested itself in the determination of deferred tax valuation allowances as well as litigation reserves and recoverables from third-party insurers. These adjustments are reflected in the company's audited financial statements for the year ended December 31, 2004. In addition, during the fourth quarter of 2005, the company became aware of the need to restate its consolidated financial statements because of the failure to consider the effect of a beneficial conversion feature on the calculation of basic and diluted loss from continuing operations per common share and net loss per common share. This error also represents an effect of the material weakness in review of complex and judgmental accounting issues.

To address this material weakness, the company continues to implement remediation plans, including the following:

- The company implemented increased levels of review of complex and judgmental accounting issues.

- The company initiated a plan to add personnel with technical accounting expertise and began a search for qualified candidates.

- The company implemented a new policy and guidelines for increased, individualized professional development for finance and accounting personnel.

Milacron's 2005 Annual Report contained the following statement in the auditor's report on internal controls: "… in our opinion, Milacron Inc. and subsidiaries maintained, in all material respects, effective internal control over financial reporting as of December 31, 2005, based on the COSO criteria." Thus, the company successfully remediated the material weakness in internal controls concerning the complex and judgmental accounting issues that were the result of inadequate review and inadequate technical expertise and training of its accounting personnel.

Required

a. Use the decision analysis framework introduced in Chapter 3 to discuss how you would analyze whether the company's control remediation plans had been effective.

b. Assume that instead of remediating the material weakness, Milacron's controls over the complex and judgmental accounting issues continued to remain a problem because management did not have the cash resources necessary to hire more competent personnel or to improve training and professional development for its personnel. What are the ethical implications of such an outcome?

Academic Research Case (LO 1, 5)

Grant, G., Miller, K., & Alali, F. (2008). The Effect of IT Controls on Financial Reporting. *Managerial Auditing Journal 23(8): 247–271.*

  i.   What is the issue being addressed in the paper?
 ii.   Why is this issue important to practicing auditors?
iii.   What are the major findings of the paper?
 iv.   What are the implications of these findings for audit quality (or audit practice) on the audit profession?
  v.   Describe the research methodology used as a basis for the conclusions.
 vi.   Describe any limitations of the research that the readers should be aware of.

Go to www.cengage.com/accounting/rittenberg for the Ford and Toyota materials.

Source and Reference	Question
Ford 10-K and Toyota 20-F	**1a.** Both Ford and Toyota management comment on "disclosure controls." What are disclosure controls? Why are they important?
	1b. Both Ford and Toyota management comment on the fact that internal control over financial reporting has "inherent limitations." What are those inherent limitations?
	1c. Ford notes one change in internal control. What is it? What area of the audit would be affected by this change?
	1d. How does management obtain comfort that internal control does not contain any material weaknesses?
	1e. From a conceptual point of view, assume two companies are the same size, participate in the same industry, and have the same reported net income. However, one has a material weakness in internal control over financial reporting and the other does not have any material weaknesses. Should the stock price of the two be different? If yes, what is the rationale for the difference in the stock price?

6

Performing an Integrated Audit

LEARNING OBJECTIVES

The overriding objective of this textbook is to build a foundation with which to analyze current professional issues and adapt audit approaches to business and economic complexities. Through studying this chapter, you will be able to:

1 Discuss the requirements of the professional auditing standards related to the performance of integrated audits of internal control over financial reporting and audits of financial statements.

2 Describe external audit reports on internal control over financial reporting.

3 Describe the steps in performing an integrated audit.

4 Identify the potential outcomes concerning the results of control testing and their implications

for subsequent substantive tests of account balances.

5 Discuss factors that managers and auditors should consider in assessing control deficiencies, including distinguishing between a significant deficiency and a material weakness.

6 Apply the decision analysis and ethical decision-making frameworks to situations involving an integrated audit.

CHAPTER OVERVIEW

An **integrated audit** combines the audit of an organization's financial statements and an audit of its internal control over financial reporting. All audits are, to some extent, integrated, but only larger public companies are currently required to have integrated audits.

Auditors, on every engagement—large or small, public or private, not-for-profit or governmental—have a responsibility to develop an in-depth understanding of internal controls as a basis for determining the nature, timing, and extent of substantive tests of account balances. However, auditors are not always required to test controls. Testing is required when (a) information about internal controls is a significant part of audit evidence or (b) when an integrated audit of a public company is performed. In terms of the audit opinion formulation process, this chapter involves Phases II and III, that is, describing how auditors understand and test their public client's internal controls as they implement plans for conducting an integrated audit.

Audit Opinion Formulation Process

I. Assessing Client Acceptance and Retention Decisions	II. Understanding the Client	III. Obtaining Evidence about Controls and Determining the Impact on the Financial Statement Audit	IV. Obtaining Substantive Evidence about Account Assertions	V. Wrapping Up the Audit and Making Reporting Decisions
CHAPTER 4	CHAPTERS 2, 4–6, and 9	CHAPTERS 5–14 and 18	CHAPTERS 7–14 and 18	CHAPTERS 15 and 16

The Auditing Profession, Regulation, and Corporate Governance	Decision-Making, Professional Conduct, and Ethics	Professional Liability
CHAPTERS 1 and 2	CHAPTER 3	CHAPTER 17

PROFESSIONAL JUDGMENT IN CONTEXT

The Importance of Controls for Quality Financial Reporting and Auditing

During the initial period of the enactment of Sarbanes-Oxley, approximately 1 in 8 companies had financial statement restatements—some of relatively low amounts, others larger. Based on those restatements, Glass Lewis & Co [February 27, 2007, Yellow Card Trend Alert] stated:

Companies take note: If you restated, you must have had material weaknesses. We still have a hard time figuring out how so many companies that restated also could have reasonably concluded that their internal controls are effective and that they have no material weaknesses—or that no material weaknesses even existed at the time of the errors.

In a publication issued by the Institute of Management Accountants (IMA) entitled *The Missing Piece in the Restatement Puzzle* (2007), the authors quote Greg Jonas, Managing Director of Investor Services, as follows:

The requirement to report on internal control resulted from one particular type of internal control breakdown: senior management of some major public companies overrode their control systems and issued misleading financial statements. History has shown that senior management cooking the books has been most costly of control failures. It has caused billions in investor losses, undermined confidence in reporting affecting the liquidity and cost of capital for many companies, and triggered significant new regulations and requirements, including reporting on controls. Other forms of fraudulent financial reporting, such as misleading reporting by lower-level employees, have not had the same impact. (p. 19)

The same IMA publication also stated:

Based on our inquiries, we have not identified any external audit firms that maintain five-year historical records of all errors and irregularities they have identified during their audits. This data would allow pattern analysis, helping with *the identification of trends and patterns that would disclose systemic control weaknesses, including the frequency that management has not provided full and frank disclosure. As noted earlier, in order for full transparency and understanding of systemic root cause errors to be a reality, appropriate safe harbors for issuers and public audit firms need to be seriously considered. (p. 18)*

The IMA makes a strong statement that public accounting firms should develop "pattern analysis" that could be used in conjunction with automated tools to better identify situations in which misstatements may take place, or where controls are likely not working sufficiently. Integrated audits provide auditors with an opportunity to gather this data.

As you read through this chapter, consider the following questions:

- What judgments must be made during the course of developing and implementing an integrated audit?

- To what extent, and under what conditions, can an auditor focus primarily on testing controls and thereby reduce the amount of substantive testing of account balances?

- Does the discovery of material misstatements in any account balance (accruals, estimates, etc.) indicate that the company had a material weakness in internal controls?

- What are the difficulties in evaluating the control environment—particularly pressures by top management—and integrating those risks into the integrated audit?

- What efficiencies should be gained in performing an integrated audit? For example, by what extent should audit costs decrease for companies that have excellent internal controls?

- How should the substantive tests of account balances change when internal controls contain significant deficiencies or material weaknesses?

Auditing Standards for the Integrated Audit

LO 1

Discuss the requirements of the professional auditing standards related to the performance of integrated audits of internal control over financial reporting and audits of financial statements.

The audit requirements for public companies changed with the enactment of the Sarbanes-Oxley Act of 2002, which required that public companies and their auditors must report on internal control over financial reporting. In February 2007, the PCAOB issued Auditing Standard No. 5 entitled *An Audit of Internal Control over Financial Reporting That Is Integrated with an Audit of Financial Statements*; that standard has focused the auditing profession on risk analysis and more efficiency in performing evaluations of internal controls associated with a financial statement audit. This chapter describes approaches, and provides examples, of how auditors can efficiently perform integrated audits.

Auditing Standard No. 5, coupled with similar guidance for management from the SEC, has encouraged organizations and auditors to take a top-down, risk-based approach to implementing an integrated audit of internal controls and financial statements. AS 5 highlights the following significant and important points about an integrated audit:

1. Encourages management and auditors to implement a *top-down, risk-based approach* to identify significant accounts, relevant assertions, the risk of misstatement, and the controls that are important to mitigating those risks.
2. Indicates that a material weakness means that the control deficiency is such that there is a *reasonable possibility* that a *material misstatement* could occur, and not be detected, in the financial statements.
3. Recognizes, that to some extent, the external auditor can *rely* on some of the company's evaluation and/or testing of controls, particularly work performed by a competent and independent internal audit function.

PRACTICAL POINT

Recall from Chapter 5 that the Dodd-Frank Wall Street Reform and Consumer Protection Act (2010) exempts smaller public companies from having an auditor test and report on the effectiveness of internal controls. The definition of a "smaller public company" is a company that has less than $75 million of common equity.

Comparison of Worldwide Professional Guidance

PERFORMING INTEGRATED AUDITS

AICPA Auditing Standards Board (ASB)	While there are no specific SASs that discuss integrated audits, the AICPA has published Statement on Standards for Attestation Engagements (SSAE) No. 15, *An Examination of an Entity's Internal Control over Financial Reporting That Is Integrated with an Audit of Its Financial Statements*. SSAE 15 is a "bringing together" of the AICPA's AT section 501—*Reporting on an Entity's Internal Control over Financial Reporting*—and the PCAOB's AS 5 (described below). The general requirements of SSAE 15 are the same as those outlined in AS 5.
Public Company Accounting Oversight Board (PCAOB)	The PCAOB's AS 5 discusses integrated audits—that is an audit of both a client's internal control and of its financial statements. AS 5 supersedes AS 2 and outlines the general steps to perform in an integrated audit, as well as the required contents of the reports prepared as part of the integrated audit. AS 5 notes that the auditor (1) should use a top-down approach to the audit of internal control over financial reporting in selecting the controls to test, (2) should assess both design and operating effectiveness of controls, (3) must evaluate the severity of each identified control deficiency to determine whether the deficiencies, individually or in combination, are material weaknesses as of the date of management's assessment, and (4) must issue an adverse report on internal control over financial reporting if the client has one or more material weaknesses. AS 5 also provides guidance to the auditors on communicating control deficiencies to management and the audit committee.
International Auditing and Assurance Standards Board (IAASB)	The IAASB does not have any pronouncements regarding the performance of integrated audits.
SUMMARY	Two of the three boards—the ASB and the PCAOB—have pronouncements regarding integrated audits. These two boards' pronouncements are quite similar as to the requirements and process for performing an integrated audit.

4. Emphasizes the need to *document the auditor's reasoning process* linking risk and control deficiencies to specific tests of account balances.

5. Increases *audit effici*ency by getting auditors to think through areas where they can place greater reliance on effective internal controls in reducing the amount of substantive tests of account balances.

Further, AS 13, *The Auditor's Responses to the Risks of Material Misstatement*, reiterates that the auditor is required to perform the evaluation of internal controls and the audit of the financial statements at the same time (para. 09). Thus, the auditor is continuously integrating evidence about internal controls into the design of substantive tests of account balances, as well as integrating information from the tests of account balances back into the assessment of internal controls.

> **PRACTICAL POINT**
>
> To implement AS 5, auditors must be very good at identifying and assessing risk, analyzing the types of controls that may mitigate the risks, and analyzing the potential effect of control deficiencies on account balances—including explicitly how a misstatement might take place and how it would affect the account balance.

Audit Reports on Internal Control over Financial Reporting

The auditor's report on internal control provides a road map for planning the integrated audit by describing the responsibilities of the auditor and the evidence that must be gathered.

The requirements for the audit of internal control set out in Audit Standard No. 5 (AS 5), para. 3 are as follows:

> The auditor's objective in an audit of internal control over financial reporting is to express an opinion on the effectiveness of the company's internal control over financial reporting. Because a company's internal control cannot be considered effective if one or more material weaknesses exist, to form a basis for expressing an opinion, the auditor must plan and perform the audit to obtain competent evidence that is sufficient to obtain reasonable assurance about whether material weaknesses exist as of the date specified in management's assessment. A material weakness in internal control over financial reporting may exist even when financial statements are not materially misstated.

AS 5 further requires the auditor to plan and perform the audit of internal control and financial statements at the same time:

> the auditor should design his or her testing of controls to accomplish the objectives of both audits simultaneously.... Obtaining sufficient evidence to support control risk assessments of low for purposes of the financial statement audit ordinarily allows the auditor to reduce the amount of audit work that otherwise would have been necessary to opine on the financial statements. (AS 5, para. 7, 8)

The work is integrated to promote audit efficiency. It is further integrated because both the tests of controls and the substantive tests of account balances provide evidence related to each other. For example, the tests of controls provide indirect evidence on the likelihood that the financial statements are free from misstatement. If the controls are effective, it is more likely that the financial statements will be free from material misstatement. Further, if the auditor finds material misstatements in account balances or disclosures, those misstatements imply that there were material weaknesses in internal controls.

LO 2

Describe external audit reports on internal control over financial reporting.

> **PRACTICAL POINT**
>
> The client must report, on a quarterly basis, whether there are material changes in internal controls. Thus, the client should be monitoring the effectiveness of controls throughout the year even though its annual public report describes the effectiveness of internal controls at a specific point in time, usually the balance sheet date.

> **PRACTICAL POINT**
>
> Audit risks pertain to both reports on internal control and reports on the financial statements. However, most auditors believe there is the potential for much greater negative financial impact to the auditor of an incorrect report on financial statements. On the other hand, auditors are finding that adverse audit reports on internal controls, where merited, that preceded the financial crisis of 2008–2009 have had a positive effect on the reputation of the auditors.

Unqualified Opinion on Internal Control over Financial Reporting

The auditor's report on internal control is integrated with the report on the company's financial statements. An example of a "clean" opinion on internal control for Ford Motor Company is shown in Exhibit 6.1.

Exhibit 6.1   **Example of Unqualified Opinion on Internal Controls**

REPORT OF INDEPENDENT REGISTERED PUBLIC ACCOUNTING FIRM

To the Board of Directors and Stockholders
Ford Motor Company:

In our opinion, the accompanying consolidated balance sheets and the related consolidated statements of operations, of stockholder's equity and of cash flows present fairly, in all material respects, the financial position of Ford Motor Company and its subsidiaries at December 31, 2009 and December 31, 2008, and the results of their operations and their cash flows for each of the three years in the period ended December 31, 2009 in conformity with accounting principles generally accepted in the United States of America. Also in our opinion, the Company maintained, in all material respects, effective internal control over financial reporting as of December 31, 2009, based on criteria established in *Internal Control - Integrated Framework* issued by the Committee of Sponsoring Organizations of the Treadway Commission (COSO). The Company's management is responsible for these financial statements, for maintaining effective internal control over financial reporting and for its assessment of the effectiveness of internal control over financial reporting, included in Management's Report on Internal Control Over Financial Reporting in this Annual Report. Our responsibility is to express opinions on these financial statements and on the Company's internal control over financial reporting based on our integrated audits. We conducted our audits in accordance with the standards of the Public Company Accounting Oversight Board (United States). Those standards require that we plan and perform the audits to obtain reasonable assurance about whether the financial statements are free of material misstatement and whether effective internal control over financial reporting was maintained in all material respects. Our audits of the financial statements included examining, on a test basis, evidence supporting the amounts and disclosures in the financial statements, assessing the accounting principles used and significant estimates made by management, and evaluating the overall financial statement presentation. Our audit of internal control over financial reporting included obtaining an understanding of internal control over financial reporting, assessing the risk that a material weakness exists, and testing and evaluating the design and operating effectiveness or internal control based on the assessed risk. Our audits also included performing such other procedures as we considered necessary in the circumstances. We believe that our audits provide a reasonable basis for our opinions.

Our audits were conducted for the purpose of forming an opinion on the basic financial statements taken as a whole. The accompanying sector balance sheets and the related sector statements of income and of cash flows are presented for purposes of additional analysis and are not a required part of the basic financial statements. Such information has been subjected to the auditing procedures applied in the audit of the basic financial statements and, in our opinion, are fairly stated in all material respects in relation to the basic financial statements taken as a whole.

As discussed in Note 1 to the consolidated financial statements, the Company changed the manner in which it accounts for noncontrolling interests and convertible debt instruments that may be settled in cash upon conversion (including partial cash settlement) in 2009. As discussed in Note 23 to the consolidated financial statements, the Company changed the manner in which it accounts for uncertain tax positions in 2007.

A company's internal control over financial reporting is a process designed to provide reasonable assurance regarding the reliability of financial reporting and the preparation of financial statements for external purposes in accordance with generally accepted accounting principles. A company's internal control over financial reporting includes those policies and procedures that (i) pertain to the maintenance of records that, in reasonable detail, accurately and fairly reflect the transactions and dispositions of the assets of the company; (ii) provide reasonable assurance that transactions are recorded as necessary to permit preparation of financial statements in accordance with generally accepted accounting principles, and that receipts and expenditures of the company are being made only in accordance with authorizations of management and directors of the company; and (iii) provide reasonable assurance regarding prevention or timely detection of unauthorized acquisition, use, or disposition of the company's assets that could have a material effect on the financial statements.

Because of its inherent limitations, internal control over financial reporting may not prevent or detect misstatements. Also, projections of any evaluation of effectiveness to future periods are subject to the risk that controls may become inadequate because of changes in conditions, or that the degree of compliance with the policies or procedures may deteriorate.

PricewaterhouseCoopers LLP

PricewaterhouseCoopers LLP
Detroit, Michigan
February 25, 2010

Note that the auditor's unqualified report contains the following elements:

- The internal control report is contained in the same report that contains the opinion on the financial statements. An acceptable alternative is to issue two reports: one on the financial statements and the other on internal controls. However, if separate reports are issued, each report must refer to the other report.
- The auditor provides an opinion on the effectiveness of internal control in the context of agreed-upon criteria, that is, the *COSO Internal Control - Integrated Framework.*
- The auditor recognizes and conveys to users that there are limitations of internal control that can affect its effectiveness in the future.

Adverse Audit Opinion on Internal Control over Financial Reporting

During the first reporting year (2004), approximately 15% of the SEC registrants received adverse audit reports on the quality of their internal controls. As of the sixth year of reporting (2009), that percentage has dropped to under 3% for the largest public companies and a slightly larger percentage for relatively smaller public companies.

An **adverse report** is issued when the auditor finds one or more material weaknesses in the client's internal control over financial reporting. An example of an adverse report is shown in Exhibit 6.2. The auditor describes the weaknesses identified in management's report but does not discuss the actions being taken by the management team to remediate the problems. The report also does not discuss whether the control weakness was first identified by management or by the auditor. The auditor does not provide an opinion on management's plans to remediate the control deficiencies.

> **PRACTICAL POINT**
>
> The financial statement audit plan should address whether management has been effective in remediating control deficiencies identified in prior year audits.

Steps in an Integrated Audit

As indicated in Exhibit 6.2, the auditor's report on internal control covers both the design and the operation of internal controls. The auditor's evaluation includes all five components of the COSO internal control framework, and that evaluation includes testing of important controls to determine whether they are working effectively. Further, the testing by the auditor must be independent of the testing that management might have performed in developing its own assessment of internal control, although the auditor can consider using some of the work performed by management and others in the organization.[1]

> **LO 3**
>
> Describe the steps in performing an integrated audit.

Although an integrated audit is required only for larger public companies, the concepts underlying it are also applicable to any audit of financial statements. A financial statement audit focuses on significant accounts and disclosures where the likelihood of material misstatements is the greatest; an integrated audit helps identify those accounts and disclosures.

The components of internal control were presented in Chapter 5, along with approaches that the auditor and management might use to test the effectiveness of internal control. This chapter expands on the auditor's responsibility by analyzing how the auditor should integrate audit evidence from the internal control audit and the financial statement audit to perform the most efficient procedures necessary to issue the auditor's two separate opinions.

---

[1] For sake of brevity, we will use the term *internal control* in this chapter as a short-cut term for *internal control over financial reporting.* As described in the previous chapter, "internal control," is much broader than the financial reporting objectives.

Exhibit 6.2   Example of Adverse Opinion on Internal Control

**REPORT OF INDEPENDENT REGISTERED PUBLIC ACCOUNTING FIRM
ON INTERNAL CONTROL OVER FINANCIAL REPORTING**

Milacron Inc.

We have audited management's assessment, included in the accompanying "Management's Report on Internal Control over Financial Reporting" appearing in Item 9A of this Amended Annual Report on Form 10-K, that Milacron Inc. did not maintain effective internal control over financial reporting as of December 31, 2004, because of the effect of the three material weaknesses identified in management's assessment, based on criteria established in Internal Control—Integrated Framework issued by the Committee of Sponsoring Organizations of the Treadway Commission (the COSO criteria). Milacron Inc.'s management is responsible for maintaining effective internal control over financial reporting and for its assessment of the effectiveness of internal control over financial reporting. Our responsibility is to express an opinion on management's assessment and an opinion on the effectiveness of the company's internal control over financial reporting based on our audit.

[*scope paragraph eliminated for text only*]

[*description of internal control paragraph eliminated for text only*]

[*limitations of internal control paragraph eliminated*]

A material weakness is a control deficiency, or combination of control deficiencies, that results in more than a remote likelihood that a material misstatement of the annual or interim financial statements will not be prevented or detected. The following material weaknesses have been identified and included in management's assessment:

Review of Complex and Judgmental Accounting Issues—The Company does not have adequate levels of review of complex and judgmental accounting issues. Various audit adjustments to the financial statements as of and for the year ended December 31, 2004 were needed to correct errors resulting from this internal control deficiency, which manifested itself in the determination of deferred tax valuation allowances, litigation reserves, and receivable amounts due from third-party insurers.

In addition, during the fourth quarter of 2005, the Company became aware of the need to restate its consolidated financial statements for the year ended December 31, 2004 due to the failure to consider the effect of a beneficial conversion feature on the calculation of basic and diluted loss from continuing operations per common share and net loss per common share. This error also represents an effect of the material weakness in review of complex and judgmental accounting issues.

Segregation of Duties—There is inadequate segregation of incompatible duties within the Company's manual and computer-based business processes at the corporate and operating levels. The inadequate segregation of incompatible duties significantly reduced or eliminated the effectiveness of many of the Company's internal controls over the accounts which comprise the consolidated financial statements.

Accounting for Inventories—There are insufficient controls with respect to the accounting for inventories primarily at one major North American manufacturing location. Specifically, the Company did not have effective controls to ensure inventory was properly valued and to ensure inventory was properly relieved at the time of sale.

These material weaknesses were considered in determining the nature, timing, and extent of audit tests applied in our audit of the 2004 financial statements and this report does not affect our report dated March 25, 2005 except for the footnote titled Restatement of Financial Statements, as to which the date is October 10, 2005, on those financial statements.

In our opinion, management's assessment that Milacron Inc. did not maintain effective internal control over financial reporting as of December 31, 2004, is fairly stated, in all material respects, based on the COSO control criteria. Also, in our opinion, because of the effect of the material weaknesses described above on the achievement of the objectives of the control criteria, Milacron Inc. has not maintained effective internal control over financial reporting as of December 31, 2004 based on the COSO control criteria.

We do not express an opinion or any other form of assurance on management's statements referring to plans for corrective action and remediation of the material weaknesses identified in management's assessment.

Ernst & Young, LLP
Cincinnati, Ohio
June 28, 2005 (except for the second paragraph
under Review of Complex and Judgmental Accounting
Issues, as to which the date is October 10, 2005)

Exhibit 6.3   Overview of Client Process and Auditor Testing

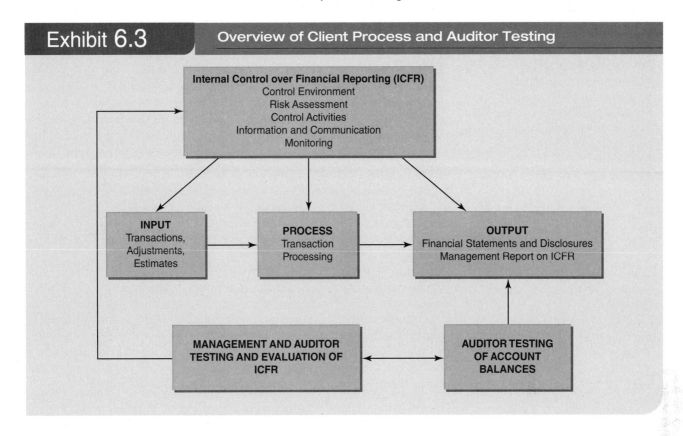

Framework for Audit Evidence in an Integrated Audit

Exhibit 6.3 shows the overall model leading to the client's preparation of its financial statements and management report on internal control, as well as the auditor's process for auditing the client's internal control and financial statements.

A number of important elements in Exhibit 6.3 have implications for the integrated audit:

- The quality of internal control affects the reliability of financial statement data.
- Internal control affects inputs into the client's reporting system, the process of recording transactions (including estimates and adjustments), and the outputs of the client's reporting system.
- If ICFR is strong and the controls over transaction processing, adjustments, and estimates are effective, then both management and the auditor would have a high degree of confidence that the financial accounts are fairly stated and financial disclosures are adequate.
- A potential for misstatements exists in the input, process, and output activities.
- There is always a need for the auditor to perform some substantive testing of material account balances, but the nature, timing, and extent of that testing will depend on the auditor's assessment of the quality of internal controls.
- Evidence obtained by the auditor during the testing of account balances can provide evidence about control effectiveness.
- The auditor's evidence is based on testing internal controls, understanding the relationship of control components to financial statement line items, performing substantive tests of account balances, including substantive analytical procedures and direct tests of account balances.

Implementing the Integrated Audit

The challenge in an integrated audit is to find the most cost-effective manner in which to develop sufficient evidence to render an opinion on the financial statements and the effectiveness of a company's internal control. A top-down, risk-based approach to an integrated audit, as described in AS No. 5, requires auditors to focus on accounts, disclosures, and assertions that have a reasonable possibility of material misstatement to the financial statements and related disclosures. The approach described in AS No. 5 highlights the importance of the following:

- Beginning the integrated audit at the financial statement level and developing an understanding of the overall risks
- Identifying entity-level controls that are important to the auditor's conclusion about whether the company has effective internal control over financial reporting
- Identifying significant accounts and related disclosures, as well as their relevant assertions
- Understanding likely sources of the misstatement in these significant accounts, disclosures, and assertions, including the client's controls that are designed to mitigate these risks of misstatement
- Selecting controls to test that are important to the auditor's conclusion about whether the company has effective internal control over financial reporting
- Testing the design and operating effectiveness of selected controls

The following steps, which are part of Phases I through IV of the audit opinion formulation process presented at the beginning of the chapter, outline the approach to implementing an integrated audit (with detail on each step provided below):

Phases I and II of the Audit Opinion Formulation Process

1. Update information about various risks.
2. Consider the possibility of account misstatements.
3. Complete preliminary analytical procedures.
4. Understand the client's internal controls.

Phases III and IV of the Audit Opinion Formulation Process

5. Identify controls to test.
6. Make a plan to test the controls and execute that plan.
7. Consider the results of control testing.
8. Conduct substantive audit tests.

AUDITING *in Practice*

CONTROLS TO ADDRESS FRAUD RISK

The PCAOB has identified the following as specific types of controls that the auditor should consider in evaluating whether or not a company has sufficiently addressed fraud risk:

- Controls over significant, unusual transactions, particularly those that result in late or unusual journal entries;

- Controls over journal entries and adjustments made in the period-end financial reporting process;
- Controls over related-party transactions;
- Controls related to significant management estimates; and
- Controls that mitigate incentives for, and pressures on, management to falsify or inappropriately manage financial results.

Phases I and II of the Audit Opinion Formulation Process

Step 1: Update Information about Various Risks. The auditor initially obtains risk-related information during the client acceptance or retention phase of the audit. The auditor should continually gather and update information on business risk, including the identification of any fraud risk factors noted during preliminary audit planning. In addition, the auditor should update audit planning for new risk information. The auditor needs to understand the overall risks, as well as risks at the account and assertion levels. Ultimately, the starting point of the integrated audit should be to understand (a) the risks that the business faces in meeting its objectives, with a focus on the objective of accurate financial reporting; (b) the incentives that may motivate management or other employees to misstate the financial statements; and (c) the risks inherent in important business processes.

Step 2: Consider the Possibility of Account Misstatements. The auditor should analyze potential management motivations to misstate account balances, as well as the existence of other fraud indicators, and determine the most likely method for misstating account balances.

Exhibit 6.4 contains an overview of the risk characteristics that the auditor should consider and illustrates how those risks relate to the possibility that particular account balances may contain misstatements.

The area of accounting judgments and estimates is almost always considered high risk. Oftentimes, misstatements occur because the company does not have the required accounting competencies. The auditor needs to determine if the organization has a commitment to build, or acquire, the competencies needed to address the complexity of the business and its processes. Auditors should determine that the organization (a) identifies the characteristics of individuals who can deal with those complexities, (b) hires and retains those individuals, and (c) periodically reevaluates the needed competencies.

Step 3: Complete Preliminary Analytical Procedures. The auditor is required to perform preliminary analytical procedures. These procedures help the auditor to determine whether unexpected relationships exist in the accounts and to

> **PRACTICAL POINT**
>
> A significant risk for many audit clients is the understatement of both liabilities and the related expenses. The audit plan should acknowledge those risks and design the audit to test controls related to those risks.

> **PRACTICAL POINT**
>
> The financial competencies needed by an organization are directly correlated with the complexity of transactions in which the company engages and the size of the company. Management and the auditor must make a subjective evaluation of the financial competencies of those involved in making accounting decisions.

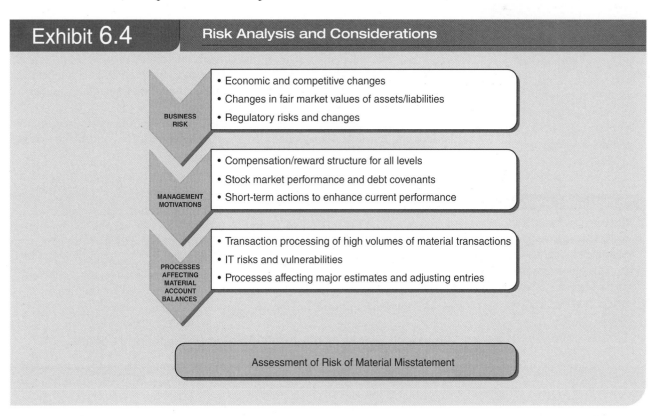

Exhibit 6.4   Risk Analysis and Considerations

BUSINESS RISK
- Economic and competitive changes
- Changes in fair market values of assets/liabilities
- Regulatory risks and changes

MANAGEMENT MOTIVATIONS
- Compensation/reward structure for all levels
- Stock market performance and debt covenants
- Short-term actions to enhance current performance

PROCESSES AFFECTING MATERIAL ACCOUNT BALANCES
- Transaction processing of high volumes of material transactions
- IT risks and vulnerabilities
- Processes affecting major estimates and adjusting entries

Assessment of Risk of Material Misstatement

PRACTICAL POINT

One of the criticisms of the audit profession in the late 1990s was that auditors focused on comparing account balances with past-years' balances (often referred to as fluctuation analysis). Auditors often ignored the processes that led to the recording of the balances as well as the economic factors driving potential changes in the account balance. Such a narrow view led to erroneous conclusions about the correctness of account balances.

PRACTICAL POINT

Once a company establishes that it has effective internal control over processes, monitoring can be effective by assuring that any changes made to the processes are fully documented and tested (including interfaces with other systems) and that controls have not deteriorated.

PRACTICAL POINT

The auditor's testing of the internal audit work can be limited, but should be sufficient to formulate an opinion on whether internal audit's conclusions are supported by independent evidence on the operation of controls.

PRACTICAL POINT

Walkthroughs are an effective way for auditors to better understand the likely sources of potential misstatements in the financial statements and to identify important controls to select for testing.

document how the audit testing should be modified because of any unusual relationships.

Step 4: Understand the Client's Internal Controls. The auditor will develop an understanding of the client's internal controls that are designed to address the risks identified in the three previous steps, including relevant entity-level controls and fraud-related controls. See the *Auditing in Practice* feature for examples of specific fraud-related controls the auditor should consider.

This step of the integrated audit process will include the following activities:

- Documenting significant accounts (including the relevant assertions of those accounts), the processes related to those accounts, and control activities within those processes. The processes drive the correct account balance. If a process is not performed correctly, it could result in significant misstatement of an account balance that would not be signaled by looking at the size of an account balance alone.
- Documenting the other COSO control components: the control environment, risk assessment, information and communication, and monitoring.
- Considering how management tests the effectiveness of important controls, including who does the testing, the objectivity of the testing process, and the nature of samples taken for the testing (both representativeness and sample size).
- Understanding how management addressed, and corrected, previously identified control deficiencies, where applicable.
- Understanding how management monitors previously identified effective controls.
- Evaluating how management assimilates data and the approach it uses to draw its conclusions on the effectiveness of internal control over financial reporting, including understanding how it has reached its conclusions regarding the report on internal control.

Completing these activities will include a review of the client's documentation of internal controls, and also includes gaining an understanding of the approach used by management to assess internal control.

Management's Process of Evaluating Internal Control   The amount of work performed by the independent auditor is dependent on the design, thoroughness, and independence of management's assessment process. Although AS 5 encourages the auditor to consider management's work, the auditor still needs to corroborate management's assessment with independent understanding and tests of all aspects of the organization's internal controls.

The external auditor will often consider the work performed by the internal auditor on behalf of management. In assessing whether the work of the internal auditor can be relied on, the auditor considers:

- The independence, objectivity, and competency of the internal audit function
- The design and comprehensiveness of the internal audit testing and evaluation approach, including an analysis and test of the organization's approach to remediating control problems
- The documentation of the internal audit testing
- The nature of the external auditor's corroborating evidence; e.g., selected tests of the same controls to validate the results achieved by internal audit
- The external auditor's independent test of important controls

Phases III and IV of the Audit Opinion Formulation Process

Step 5: Identify Controls to Test. The auditor determines the important controls that need to be tested for the purposes of (a) formulating an opinion on the entity's internal controls and (b) forming a basis for designing substantive tests of account balances. As management establishes the effectiveness of its controls, it may rely more on monitoring process as a basis for its assessment; the auditor must be prepared to take advantage of effective monitoring by management.

The auditor should select those controls that are important to the auditor's conclusion about whether the company's controls adequately address the assessed risk of misstatement for relevant assertions. The auditor will select both entity-level controls and control activities for testing. The selection of control activities to be tested will depend on the results of testing the selected entity-level controls. Effective entity-level controls may reduce the number of control activities selected for testing. Overall, risks associated with significant accounts, disclosures, and their relevant assertions should lead to the identification of important controls that need to be tested.

In selecting controls to test, the auditor recognizes that account balances are the culmination of the recording and adjustment processes and relate directly to assertions about account balances, such as existence, valuation, and so forth. The auditor needs to explicitly link controls and assertions when determining which controls to select for testing. The following table describes the assertions related to existence, completeness, and valuation and links the assertions to controls—all part of the process of selecting which controls to test.

Financial Statement Assertions	Examples of Controls That Might Be Selected for Testing
Existence—all recorded items are valid.	• Shipments recorded are reconciled with shipping documents daily. • Items cannot be recorded without underlying source documents and approvals.
Completeness—all valid items are recorded.	• Prenumbered shipping documents are used and reconciled with shipments recorded daily. • A list of cash receipts is developed when cash is collected and is reconciled with cash deposits and the debit to cash daily.
Valuation—all items are recorded at the correct valuation.	• Preauthorized sales prices are entered into the computer pricing table by authorized individuals. • Sales prices can be overridden only on the authorization of key management personnel. A record of any overrides is documented and independently reviewed by management, internal audit, or other parties performing control analysis.

Step 6: Make a Plan to Test the Controls and Execute That Plan. The auditor develops a plan for testing the design and operating effectiveness of internal controls and performs appropriate tests of key controls. For non-integrated audits, the auditor can choose to not test controls, but the auditor must determine where material misstatements could occur if controls are not present or may not be working. The PCAOB has mandated that the external auditor must gather appropriate and sufficient evidence, and that evidence should be based on the materiality of the account, i.e., the more material the account, the more independent tests should be conducted.

Auditors are required to assess control risk for each relevant assertion for important accounts and disclosures as a basis for planning the audit. In an integrated audit, the auditor has to understand *and test* controls that are important to preventing or detecting significant misstatements. Not all controls need to be tested. Further, controls for all assertions need not be tested if the auditor believes that a misstatement related to a particular assertion would not be material.

PRACTICAL POINT

By definition, material weaknesses in internal control mean that material misstatements could take place in financial statements and not be detected by the client's regular processes. The auditor uses knowledge of control deficiencies obtained through understanding and testing the client's controls to design substantive tests that would detect such misstatements should they have occurred.

PRACTICAL POINT

Large public companies are required to file their annual reports within sixty days after their fiscal year's end. The filing requirement supports gathering more evidence during the year as a basis for the auditor's opinions. Testing controls at an interim date may improve the effectiveness and efficiency of the integrated audit.

PRACTICAL POINT

To obtain evidence about whether a control is operating effectively, the auditor must directly test the control. The auditor cannot infer the effectiveness of a control from the absence of misstatements in the financial statements.

The auditor will test the design effectiveness of controls by determining whether the company's controls, as designed and implemented, can effectively prevent or detect material misstatements in the financial statements. Procedures to test design effectiveness include inquiry of appropriate personnel, observation of the company's operations, and inspection of relevant documentation. Walk-throughs may be the most efficient way to evaluate design effectiveness. The auditor will test the operating effectiveness by determining whether the control is operating as designed and by personnel who have the authority and competence to perform the control effectively. Procedures the auditor performs to test operating effectiveness include inquiry of appropriate personnel, observation of the company's operations, inspection of relevant documentation, and reperformance of the control.

The nature of the testing will vary with the nature of the process, the materiality of the account balance, and the control. For example, computerized edit controls built into a computer application could be tested by submitting test transactions to determine if the controls are working properly. For manual controls, such as authorizations, the auditor might select a number of transactions to determine if there is documented evidence that proper authorization has taken place. For the reconciliation of shipments with recorded sales, the auditor could select a number of day's sales and determine that the reconciliations were performed appropriately and differences were investigated. General concepts regarding control testing are summarized in the following diagram:

Concepts Affecting Control Testing

Computerized Controls	**Concept:** Determine whether there have been changes to important computer applications during the year.
	• Determine if there are changes in the computer program. If there are, test the integrity of the controls after the changes.
	• Consider submitting test transactions through the system to determine that it is working properly.
	• Take a random sample of transactions and determine that (a) key controls are operating and (b) processing is complete.
	• Review exception reports to determine (a) that proper exceptions are being noted and (b) that exceptions go to authorized personnel and there is adequate follow-up for proper processing.
Manual Controls: • Authorizations • Reconciliations • Segregation of duties • Review for unusual transactions	**Concept:** There should be documented evidence that a control is working. The auditor should take a sample of transactions to determine that there is evidence of the control's operation.
	• Take a sample of transactions and examine evidence supporting that the controls are working, e.g., review a document or a computer printout indicating proper approval.
	• Take a sample of reconciliations to determine that (a) they were performed by an authorized person and (b) they were performed properly.
	• Observe client personnel assigned to perform important controls and determine that they are performed properly.
	• Review selected transactions to determine whether they were properly authorized and recorded in the correct time period.
	• Take a sample of reports that management uses to identify unusual transactions. Review to determine (a) that they are used regularly and (b) that unusual items are identified and followed up.
Adjusting Entries	**Concept:** There should be documented evidence that there are controls over normal journal entries, such as depreciation, and that they are applied on a regular basis. All other adjusting entries should include documentation that spells out (a) the reason and support for the adjustment and (b) the authorization of the adjustment.

(continues)

- Take a sample of adjusting entries and review to determine (a) that there is supporting documentation for the entry, (b) the entry is appropriate, (c) the entry is made to the correct accounts, and (d) the entry was properly authorized.
- Give special attention to significant entries made near year end.

Accounting Estimates	**Concept:** There should be documented evidence regarding the estimate. Further, the auditor should determine that controls are sufficient to ensure (a) the estimate is made based on accurate data, (b) that the process of making the estimate is performed consistently, and (c) the model is updated for changing economic or business conditions. For example, estimates of a health care liability should be updated for changes in the trend of health care costs and required employee deductibles and co-pays.

- Review the process and supporting documentation noting that:
  - All entries are properly authorized.
  - There are controls to ensure that estimates are updated for current market or economic conditions.
  - There is evidence that data used to make the estimates come from reliable sources.

Testing the Control Environment, Risk Assessment, Information and Communication, and Monitoring Components   Auditors are often most comfortable focusing on control activities. However, research continues to show that fraud and serious misstatements in financial statements are often caused by control weaknesses in other control components—especially weaknesses in the control environment. We add the following observations that should be considered by the auditor in testing controls in the other four internal control components.

Control Environment—The auditor should select and test many of the so-called soft controls in the control environment, such as evaluating adherence to the company's ethical standards. As another example, the auditor regularly meets with the audit committee and thus has first-hand knowledge about the financial expertise and independence of the committee. The auditor will know how the audit committee reacts to areas where there are disagreements between management and the auditor or how the committee reacts when management "pushes the line" on accounting judgments. Further, the auditor will have first-hand knowledge of the client's attitude toward "pushing the accounting boundaries." These are all important aspects of the control environment that the auditor will want to test.

Risk Assessment—From a strict PCAOB perspective, the auditor is only required to assess whether the organization systematically evaluates the risks related to financial reporting as a basis to determine the nature of controls needed to mitigate those risks. Many auditors will also gather knowledge about the extent an organization uses enterprise risk management. For example, the auditor can determine if the company has a chief risk officer or if the company periodically engages employees in evaluating fraud risk. Much of the information is gathered through inquiry and review of documents. The auditor needs to understand whether the company uses a consistent framework in evaluating the risks associated with transaction processing, adjustments, estimates, and disclosures.

Information and Communication—The auditor should assess the company's information and communication systems through inquiry, observation, and review of documentation. For example, the auditor should ascertain (a) that there are processes in place to identify areas where corrective action needs to be taken and (b) that there are follow-up processes in place to determine if controls have failed. Further, the auditor needs to perform tests to know that there is communication about (a) the company's ethical values, (b) the availability of a

PRACTICAL POINT

The SEC has recognized that how individuals are compensated (see, e.g., the multiple references to the financial crisis, Lehman Brothers, etc. throughout the text) may cause deterioration of the control environment.

PRACTICAL POINT

The auditor will vary the nature, timing, and extent of testing of selected controls based upon the risk associated with a control.

PRACTICAL POINT

The auditor usually sits in on the full audit committee meeting and can observe whether there is evidence that whistleblowing complaints are identified and dealt with in a timely fashion.

LO 4

Identify the potential outcomes concerning the results of control testing and their implications for subsequent substantive tests of account balances.

whistleblower program, and (c) other areas where employees can go if they have concerns about the operations of the company.

As part of testing information and communication, the auditor should recognize that the Sarbanes-Oxley Act requires the establishment of an effective whistleblower program. The auditor should determine that the program is effective by evaluating whether employees are aware of the program, the number of complaints filed, who receives the complaints, who handles the complaints, and the ultimate disposition of the complaints. The auditor also wants to know what information the board or the audit committee receives regarding the nature of whistleblower complaints.

Monitoring—Monitoring can take many forms, ranging from testing by an internal audit department to independent review of control activities (e.g., reconciliations) by supervisory personnel to reviews of operating data by top management that are specifically designed to identify anomalies in the data that should be investigated. Monitoring applies to all five components of the COSO framework. For example, management should monitor for potential changes in the control environment or the effectiveness of its risk assessment activities. An audit approach to testing the effectiveness of monitoring is shown in Exhibit 6.5.

Step 7: Consider the Results of Control Testing. The auditor needs to analyze the results of the tests of controls. There are two potential outcomes, with associated alternative courses of action in the audit:

1. If deficiencies are identified, assess those deficiencies to determine whether they are significant deficiencies or material weaknesses. Determine whether the preliminary control risk assessment should be modified and document the implications for substantive testing. Determine the impact of these deficiencies, and any revision on the control risk assessment and on planned substantive audit procedures, by determining the types of misstatements that are most likely to occur.
2. If no control deficiencies are identified, assess whether the preliminary control risk assessment is still appropriate, determine the extent that controls can provide evidence on the correctness of account balances, and determine planned substantive audit procedures. The level of substantive testing in this situation will be less than what is required in circumstances where deficiencies in internal control were identified.

From the audit risk model, we know that companies with strong internal controls should require less substantive testing of account balances. We also know that greater computerization of processes increases the likelihood of consistent processing throughout the year. The fundamental questions that the auditor must address to determine the optimal amount of audit work are as follows:

1. How much assurance regarding the correctness of account balances can the auditor attribute to the effective operation of internal controls, and thereby decrease the amount of substantive testing of account balances?
2. What is the risk that the auditor's evaluation of internal controls might be incorrect? Many audit judgments, including some related to the effectiveness of internal controls, are subjective. Auditors within a firm may act inconsistently in making such judgments.
3. Which account balances contain more than an acceptable amount of risk that a material misstatement could occur and not be prevented or detected by internal controls?
4. How would a misstatement in a material account balance most likely occur?
5. What are the most effective substantive tests of account balances to determine whether there is a misstatement in the account balance?

The auditor must answer these five important questions to plan an effective integrated audit. There is no one right answer—all of the questions are interrelated.

| Exhibit 6.5 | Evaluating Effectiveness of Monitoring |

Audit Objectives	Evidence-Gathering Activities
1. Determine areas where the company performs separate evaluations of internal control through internal audit or other employees.	• Review the internal audit reports to determine the extent that tests of controls are covered. • Review management plans to test individual controls.
2. Determine the extent that management uses monitoring to continually evaluate components of the COSO Framework.	• Make inquiries of management as to monitoring methods. • Evaluate information gathered to assess whether the monitoring is performed at a level of precision that would identify a breakdown of controls. • Evaluate the comprehensiveness of the design of the monitoring process and whether, if performed correctly, monitoring will provide a basis for management's assessment of internal controls. • Determine how to independently test the effectiveness of management's monitoring.

3. Determine the effectiveness of the existing monitoring procedures.	*For understanding the effectiveness of internal audit:*
	• Review the internal audit programs and testing for the year.
	• Assess the independence and the competence of the internal audit function. If independent and competent, more reliance can be placed on its work.
	• Test, as deemed necessary, selected conclusions reached by the internal audit group.
	• Reach a conclusion regarding the effectiveness of the internal auditor's tests of controls.
	• Evaluate the internal auditor's tests and the independent testing of the controls.
	
	For understanding the effectiveness of other monitoring procedures:
	• Take a sample of documented monitoring by management. Review the documentation to determine:
	  a. that there is a documented management conclusion regarding the monitoring information.
	  b. that anomalies are investigated to determine whether there is a breakdown in either a control component or a control activity.
	  c. that problems are addressed, and corrective action is taken on a timely basis.

4. Consider the effect of the controls on the likely misstatement of financial account balances and on the substantive testing that needs to be performed.	• Analyze effectiveness of controls and consider effects on residual risks in account balances. • Reach a conclusion about the effectiveness of internal controls based, in part, on the quality of monitoring. • Determine if additional tests of controls are needed for areas in which monitoring is not effective. • Determine the risks that particular account balances might be misstated and how those accounts might be tested.

For example, the residual risk of a material misstatement is dependent on the joint answer to the first two questions. The remaining three questions address the identification of accounts that might be misstated, how a misstatement could occur, and how the auditor would most effectively determine if a misstatement did occur.

Account Balances Likely to Contain Misstatements   When the auditor finds that internal controls are effective, there is little risk that accounts are misstated. Still, there will always be some accounts that have more than an acceptable amount of **residual risk** (the probability that an account balance might be misstated after processing and the application of internal controls) that will require some substantive testing. In determining the amount of substantive testing needed, the auditor considers (a) the source of potential misstatement and (b) the extent and type of potential misstatement. This can be illustrated by looking at the typical entries into accounts receivable, including the related allowance, as follows:

Accounts Receivable

Previous Balance	Cash Receipts
Revenue (sales)	Write-Offs
Adjustments	Adjustments

Allowance for Uncollectible Accounts

| Write-Offs | Previous Balance |
| | Current Provision |

Note that multiple processes affect the account balances. Some of the processes contain subjectivity and are considered high risk, for example, determining how much of a receivable balance will ultimately be uncollectible. The following processes affect the accounts receivable balance:

- *Revenue*—The processing of normal transactions is usually computerized with consistent controls built into the process. However, the SEC has designated revenue recognition as "high risk," requiring the auditor to do some direct tests of account balances (including receivables) because there has been recurring evidence that companies who want to boost reported sales and/or earnings often do so by overriding controls related to the recording of revenue. These overrides often occur in the nature of "special contracts," or unusual shipments near the end of the year.
- *Cash Receipts*—The processing of cash receipts is usually automated with implementation of consistent controls. If a company has good segregation of duties, the likelihood of misstatement is relatively small.
- *Current Provision for Uncollectible Accounts*—Most companies rely heavily on previous experience in making these estimates. Recent SEC cases indicate that the allowance is often subject to misstatements based on (a) inaccurate or nonrelevant data fed into the model and (b) motivation of management to meet earnings goals and therefore allowing subjectivity and bias to enter into the estimate.
- *Write-Offs*—The determination of when to write off account balances is also subjective.
- *Adjustments*—Adjustments, other than those noted above, should be rare. If there are significant adjustments, the auditor will have to test the process or the adjustments to determine the correct balance.

Similar analyses will be made for other related accounts, and will include the concepts outlined below:

- The riskiness of the account dictates the nature, timing, and extent of substantive tests of the account that need to be performed.
- Account balances affected by highly subjective estimates usually require direct tests of the account balances.
- Nonstandard and large adjusting entries should be reviewed and tested using appropriate substantive procedures.
- The size of the account (materiality) influences, but does not totally dictate, whether substantive testing should be performed.
- The extent and results of control testing performed by management, as well as the control testing performed by the auditor, will influence the substantive testing of the account balance to be performed.

PRACTICAL POINT

The SEC initiated action against Gateway Computer because it changed its credit policy to sell products to a significant number of customers who had formerly been turned down for credit. Even though the customer base changed, the company did not change its process for estimating uncollectible receivables thereby resulting in a large overstatement of both receivables and reported earnings.

- The confidence the auditor has from all sources (knowledge of the business and industry, results of control testing, knowledge of system changes, previous misstatements) influences the substantive testing to be performed.
- The existence of other corroborating tests of the account balance, such as the knowledge gained from testing related accounts, also affects substantive testing to be performed.

The effects of other information on substantive testing are summarized as follows:

FACTORS AFFECTING EXTENT OF DIRECT TESTING TO BE PERFORMED

Audit Evidence Factors	Auditor Assessment	Effect on Direct Testing Performed
Audit risk	Low	More direct testing
Business risk	High	More direct testing
Subjectivity of accounting process	High	More direct testing
Materiality of account balance	High	More direct testing
Effectiveness of internal control as assessed by management and the auditor	Internal controls are effective	Less direct testing
Evidence from tests of other accounts	Directional tests indicate low risk of misstatement	Less direct testing

Likely Nature of Misstatements and Efficiency of Audit Tests   Ultimately, the auditor needs to consider which account balances might be misstated and how they might be misstated. We demonstrate the audit process using the accounts receivable example.

Assume the following scenario for illustration purposes. Consistent with the relevant professional guidance, the auditor has assessed revenue to be "high risk" even though management has concluded that internal controls over transactions processing are effective. A preliminary analytical review of the last quarter led to the identification of a large number of sales with nonstandard contractual terms. After reading a sample of the sales contracts and understanding and testing controls, the auditor concludes that there is an unacceptable level of residual risk in the revenue account. The auditor identified a number of ways in which the account could be misstated. For example, sales might:

- Be recorded in the wrong period.
- Contain unusual rights-of-return provisions that have not been accounted for correctly.
- Contain terms that are more consistent with a consignment rather than a sale.
- Be concentrated in a very few customers, many of whom are international customers and may have different credit risks than most other customers.

Given the identified risks, the auditor decides to expand substantive audit tests of the recorded transactions that have unusual sales terms and focus on the existence and valuation assertions. In order to bring the residual risk to an acceptable level, the auditor has to gather substantive evidence on the revenue (and receivables) associated with the unusual contracts and must identify for audit investigation the sales that have these special terms. In testing receivables, the auditor decides to concentrate accounts receivable tests on a combination of large accounts, plus all of those that have unusual sales terms. Confirmations will be sent to both of those groups, with extensive follow-up where confirmations are not returned, or where the auditor might suspect the validity of the contract, the customer, or the possibility of "side agreements" affecting the contracts.

The audit process to address the residual risk remaining in accounts receivable and revenue is captured in the following analysis of the auditor's thought process:

PRACTICAL POINT

Auditors must be prepared to think through audit implications to determine audit efficiency. Rotely applying routine audit procedures is both inefficient and ineffective.

Auditor's Thought Process

How are all of these "unusual" sales terms to be identified?	• Ask management for a listing of all such sales (not highly effective). • Use audit software to list all large sales in last quarter and all sales to foreign locations. • Use audit software to develop a list of all returns after the end of the year and develop an analysis of whether a pattern exists.
How much could revenue and accounts receivable be misstated if all of these transactions are incorrect?	• Once the transactions are identified, the auditor can summarize the dollar amount using audit software to determine if the amount would be material. If the amounts are not material, there is no need to perform additional audit work.

How does the auditor determine whether the sales are proper and the receivables are valid?	• Examine a sample of the contracts.
	
	• Have the contracts reviewed by legal counsel if there are any questions regarding the terms of sale and the rights of the customer.
	
	• Send confirmation to the customers inquiring of both the account balance and the terms of the contract.
	
	• Review subsequent payments to determine:
	  • Whether payments were subsequently made
	  • Terms of the payment, e.g., whether there is reference that payments were made in response to the customer selling the goods to a third party.

If revenue and receivables are determined to be valid, how likely is it that the client will collect the full amount of the receivable (realizability of the account)?	• Review subsequent payments and compare with contractual schedule of payments. • Review credit agency ratings and analysis of financial health of the customer. • Review past history of collections from the customer. • (Possibly) request current financial statements from the customer to evaluate financial health. • Review the customer's industry to determine if there are signs of financial distress in the industry.

PRACTICAL POINT

An important consideration for the auditor is the amount of time that exists after year end before the client is required to file its statements with the SEC. If that time is limited, then procedures that are dependent on gathering information after year end—e.g., subsequent collections—are also limited.

The key point to understand is that audit efficiency is gained only by auditing smarter. The auditor has to consider a number of important factors to reduce audit costs and, at the same time, manage audit risk at an acceptable level.

Step 8: Conduct Substantive Audit Tests. As discussed in Step 7, the auditor plans substantive procedures (substantive analytical procedures and direct tests of account balances) based on the potential for misstatement and the information gathered about the effectiveness of internal controls. When completing substantive procedures, the auditor will continue to assess whether the evidence obtained from all sources is sufficient and appropriate and the auditor may need to adjust the audit plan to ensure that sufficient and appropriate audit evidence is obtained. Finally, the auditor will integrate audit evidence from all sources and formulate an opinion on the fairness of the account balance, or perform additional audit work.

PRACTICAL POINT

Substantive procedures performed by the auditor will include procedures to address fraud risks.

Exhibit 6.6	Overview of Integrated Audit Decisions Leading up to Substantive Testing Decisions

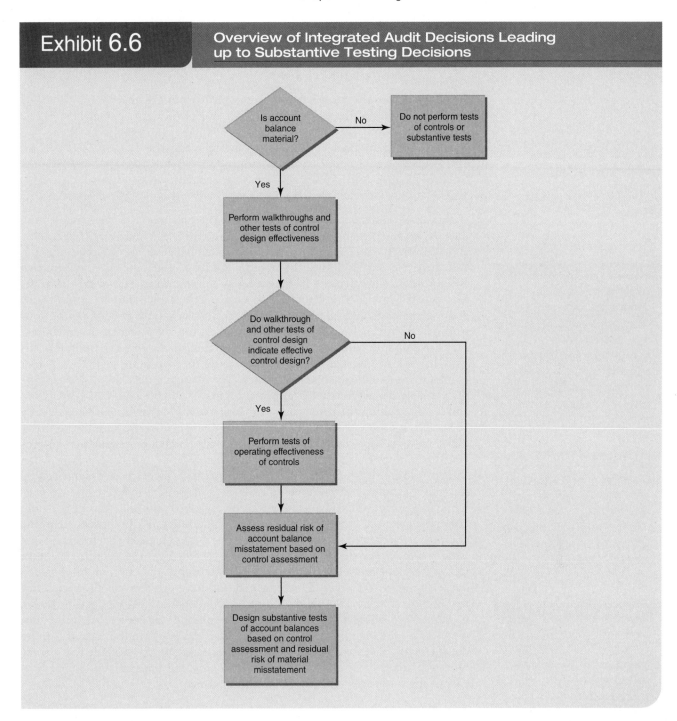

Summary of Integrated Audit Decisions

Exhibit 6.6 provides a summary overview of some of the integrated audit decisions leading up to the design of substantive tests. These decisions were discussed above as part of Steps 4, 5, 6, and 7 of the integrated audit and are summarized below.

The process outlined in Exhibit 6.6 should begin with the identification of material account balances and disclosures, and their relevant assertions. Materiality is a judgment that contains both a quantitative and qualitative dimension. The identification process includes consideration of factors such as reported earnings, size of the misstatement, trends in performance, and market expectations. Keep in mind that each account balance usually has a related income or a balance sheet account associated with it. For example, accounts receivable and

PRACTICAL POINT

Regardless of the level of assessed control risk, the auditor must conduct some substantive procedures for material account balances.

sales are related. The process of determining the important account balances should include the following:

- Input from the audit team's brainstorming analysis regarding potential for fraud
- Review of "market expectations" of company performance
- Trends in performance, including trends in key business segments
- The size of the account balance
- The subjectivity used in making accounting estimates
- Comparison of account balances with industry trends, averages, and so on
- How IT affects the company's flow of transactions
- The auditor's overall assessment of the company's control environment

For most companies, the material account balances will be obvious and include accounts such as revenue, cost of goods sold, inventory, receivables, and accounts payable. As part of identifying significant accounts and disclosures and their relevant assertions, the auditor should identify the types of risk that could cause a misstatement in the material account balances and the processes that would allow that misstatement to occur. The client's internal control process is designed to address these risks and the auditor should understand the controls that the client has implemented to address risks of potential misstatement.

As an example, assume the auditor determines that a mid-sized public company has risk of material misstatement because the controller is not competent in addressing complex accounting issues. The company decided to mitigate the risks, as a matter of policy, by (a) not engaging in complex business transactions and (b) minimizing the percentage of management compensation that is directly attributed to reported profit. The auditor further reviews the revenue accounting process and determines that there are control activities designed to (a) prevent unauthorized transactions, (b) assure that revenue is recorded only when earned, and (c) require that all unusual contracts be reviewed and approved by the CEO. Further, because there is a risk of management override, the controller develops a list of unusual contracts to be reviewed with the chair of the audit committee and the lead director. Thus, while there is a risk of misstatement, the controls are designed to mitigate the risks to the financial statements. If the auditor assesses the design of these controls as effective, the auditor will want to test their operating effectiveness. However, even if the controls are designed and operating effectively, the auditor may still have concerns about the residual risk of misstatements associated with revenue recognition because that process is most prone to misstatement because of the application of poor accounting judgments. The auditor may respond by planning and performing more, and more detailed, tests of revenue and receivables. For example, the auditor will review unusual transactions near year end and will examine unusual sales contracts as part of the substantive tests of the account balance.

Integrated Audit Example: Judging the Severity of Control Deficiencies and Implications for the Financial Statement Audit

To illustrate the concepts introduced in this chapter, we provide an abbreviated example of an integrated audit focusing on cost of goods sold, inventory, and accounts payable. For simplicity, we will assume that the company purchases and distributes products; i.e., the company is not a manufacturer, but it does hold a significant amount of inventory. The significant account balances are as follows:

PRACTICAL POINT

Recent research by COSO reinforces the concept that the control environment is one of the most important factors associated with fraud and should always be assessed along with the potential impact on residual risk in account balances.

PRACTICAL POINT

The integrated audit is built on professional judgment and a thorough understanding of risk, controls, and the manner in which account balances might be misstated.

PRACTICAL POINT

When the auditor has determined that internal control is effective, more of the substantive testing can be performed using analytical procedures that the auditor has determined will be effective in the circumstances in identifying potential misstatements.

LO 5

Discuss factors that managers and auditors should consider in assessing control deficiencies, including distinguishing between a significant deficiency and a material weakness.

- Inventory
- Revenue
- Accounts receivable
- Cost of goods sold
- Accounts payable

The auditor determines that there are five major processes that affect the significant account balances:

- Purchasing
- Revenue and cost of goods sold
- Inventory management and adjustments
- Cash disbursements
- Adjusting and closing processes

In planning for the most efficient audit, the auditor notes the following:

RELATIONSHIP OF PROCESSES AND ACCOUNTS

Process	Related Accounts
1. Purchasing	Accounts Payable
	Inventory
	Expenses
	Other Assets
2. Revenue and Cost of Goods Sold	Revenue
	Cost of Goods Sold
	Inventory
	Accounts Receivable
3. Cash Disbursements	Accounts Payable
	Cash
	Expenses
	Other Assets
4. Inventory Management and Adjustments (periodic counts, etc.)	Inventory
	Cost of Goods Sold
	Loss on inventory
5. Adjusting and Closing Processes	Inventory
	• Inventory shrinkage
	• Obsolescence
	• Lower of cost or market adjustments
	Cost of Goods Sold
	• Allowance for Uncollectible Accounts

Management and the auditor determine that all five of these processes are important to reliable financial reporting and that effective internal control over financial reporting is necessary in each of these processes. Therefore, controls in all five processes will be assessed for design and operating effectiveness.

Management Assessment of Controls

We will focus our example on the purchasing cycle. Management has identified the material accounts and relevant assertions in the process of procuring goods and recording the related accounts payable and inventory. After selecting and testing controls designed to mitigate risk of misstatement in these accounts, management identifies the following control deficiencies:

- *Segregation of duties:* At one location, the controls are not well designed, as there is not proper segregation of duties. However, the location is very small, accounting for less than 1% of purchases.

- *Lack of approval:* At a second location that handles 62% of the company purchases, management found that approximately 17% of the purchase orders did not contain proper approval. The reason for the lack of approval was the rush to procure material in a timely fashion to meet a contract requirement. This represents an operating deficiency.

Recall that the definitions for significant deficiency and material weakness are as follows:

- A *material weakness* is a deficiency, or a combination of deficiencies, in internal control over financial reporting, such that there is a reasonable possibility that a material misstatement of the company's annual or interim financial statements will not be prevented or detected on a timely basis.
- A *significant deficiency* is a deficiency, or a combination of deficiencies, in internal control over financial reporting that is less severe than a material weakness, yet important enough to merit attention by those responsible for oversight of the company's financial reporting.

In deciding how to categorize a deficiency, management and auditors should consider the following factors:

- The risk that is being mitigated and whether other controls operate effectively to mitigate the risk of material misstatement,
- The materiality of the related account balances,
- The nature of the deficiency,
- The volume of transactions affected,
- The subjectivity of the account balance that is subject to the control, and
- The rate at which the control fails to operate.

Management concluded that the first deficiency (related to segregation of duties) did not rise to the level of either a significant deficiency or a material weakness. However, management decides to use this deficiency as an opportunity to centralize purchases at headquarters.

The second deficiency (related to lack of approval) is more of a problem. Management determines this is a significant deficiency based on the following rationale:

- It is a major departure from an approved process.
- It could lead to the purchase of unauthorized goods.
- The unauthorized goods could lead to either (a) inferior products or (b) potential obsolescence.
- Those making the purchases could cause them to be shipped elsewhere (fraudulently) and could lead to a material misstatement in the financial statements.

PRACTICAL POINT

Management's evaluation of internal controls often presents opportunities to improve both the quality of controls and the efficiency of processing.

Management determines that other controls are in place that test for inferior products and obsolescence, and that cycle counting of inventory would discover goods that are shipped to a different location. Accordingly, management believes that because of these controls any potential misstatements in the financial statements would not be material. Management tests these controls and determines that they were operating effectively. If these other controls were not in place and operating effectively, then management would have assessed the control deficiency as a material weakness.

Auditor Assessment of Controls

After determining material accounts and relevant assertions, the auditor reviews management's documentation of its control evaluation and management's findings. The auditor had previously reviewed and tested the control environment and other entity-level controls and had evaluated them as strong. The auditor concluded the client had sufficient documentary evidence to test the operating effectiveness of the control activities.

The auditor then determined that the following were the key controls in the procurement process (for discussion purposes, we will again concentrate on the purchasing process and assume that the auditor did not find any material weaknesses in the other processes):

- Only authorized goods are purchased from authorized vendors.
- Purchase prices are negotiated by contract or from bids.
- All purchases are delivered to the company and received by a separate receiving department.
- All purchases are recorded in a timely fashion and are appropriately classified.
- Payments are made only for goods that are received.
- Payments are made consistent with the purchase orders or contracts.
- Payments are made in a timely fashion.

Because much of the process is computerized, the auditor performs computer security tests to assure that access controls are working properly and there is adequate control over program changes. The auditor determines that those controls are effective. An additional advantage of testing the computer access controls is that the controls may be applicable to many other processes.

The auditor takes a sample of fifty purchase orders to examine whether purchases are authorized and are processed properly. The auditor's sample size is influenced by previous information about the operation of the control. Although management had also taken a random sample of purchases and tested the operating effectiveness, the auditor needs to independently determine that the controls are working (or not working). The sample is randomly chosen and the auditor traces the transactions through the system to determine that the objectives identified above are addressed by controls.

The auditor's testing of controls identified the same two deficiencies identified by management. Management viewed the deficiency related to lack of approval as a *significant deficiency* because (a) the company has a good ethical climate and (b) management's tests confirmed that all goods were delivered to the company. The auditor's tentative conclusion is that this deficiency in internal controls is a *material weakness* because:

- The location was responsible for ordering 62% of all of the company's products.
- Management's tests showed a very high failure rate of over 17%.

The fact that all the goods were delivered to the company is important and a testament to the ethical culture of the company. However, not all individuals are ethical and someone else could be in the purchasing position with a lower commitment to ethical behavior. Stated another way, a weakness in internal control can exist even if there were no errors in processing or misstatement in the current period. The potential for misstatement is high because the auditor believes that existing controls do not mitigate the risk of material misstatement.

More specifically, the auditor notes the following related to the auditor's tests of controls:

- One of the fifty purchases was made from an unauthorized vendor. Investigation reveals that the vendor was subsequently authorized and it was a timing problem; that is, the vendor should have been authorized earlier.
- Seven of the fifty did not have proper authorization, corroborating the earlier finding by management.
- Three of the fifty purchases were paid even though there was no receiving report.
- All of the other controls were found to work properly.

The auditor is concerned that the system allowed a purchase to be made before the vendor was authorized. The auditor's analysis is focused primarily on the risks that may be caused by unauthorized purchases. The auditor believes that unauthorized purchases could lead to a material misstatement of inventory; that is, goods

---

PRACTICAL POINT

There can be reasonable differences of opinion as to whether a control deficiency is a significant deficiency or a material weakness. The auditor must be able to reason through the process, along with management, to determine the proper categorization of the deficiency. If a specific deficiency is mitigated by another control, then the risk is properly mitigated and there is no need to report a deficiency.

PRACTICAL POINT

The assessment of internal control is at the end of the client's reporting period. There is often an opportunity to correct a deficiency before the end of the year if it is identified early enough.

PRACTICAL POINT

The assessment of the seriousness of the deficiency is based on the risk that the control deficiencies *have a reasonable possibility* of leading to *material* misstatements in an account balance.

PRACTICAL POINT

Substantive tests of account balances are determined, in large part, by the specific nature of the identified control deficiencies.

were ordered and paid (even though there was no proof that they were actually received) but may have been delivered elsewhere. Based on this concern, the auditor decides that the deficiency related to lack of approval warrants a material weakness designation. Using this analysis, which represents an analysis of residual risk of misstatement, the auditor determines the following implications for substantive tests in the financial statement audit:

- The auditor will do limited testing of inventory quantities at year end, primarily through random tests of the perpetual inventory system.
- The auditor will examine the year-end inventory for potential obsolescence by looking at industry trends and recent prices within the firm and by using audit software to analyze the aging of inventory.
- The auditor will continue to examine all adjusting entries at the end of the year to determine whether there are unusual entries to inventory and related accounts.

Summary

An integrated audit follows the concepts developed earlier with the audit risk model. The SEC and PCAOB have encouraged the audit profession to implement an integrated audit to take advantage of the significant amount of control testing that is performed in conjunction with attesting to the effectiveness of internal control over financial reporting.

The audit can be more efficient when the auditor considers the risks in the financial statements and how those risks are effectively mitigated by controls. When the risks are effectively mitigated, the auditor can perform limited substantive testing of account balances. This chapter illustrates application of the integrated audit by applying concepts of internal control and audit evidence.

Significant Terms

Adverse report on internal controls A report in which the auditor communicates to shareholders that the company does not have effective internal control over financial reporting as of the balance sheet date.

Integrated audit An audit process that incorporates the knowledge obtained from internal control testing

to determine the optimal amount of evidence necessary to attest to the financial statements and to the effectiveness of internal controls.

Residual risk The probability that an account balance might be misstated after processing and the application of internal controls.

SELECTED REFERENCES TO RELEVANT PROFESSIONAL GUIDANCE	
Topic	**Selected Guidance**
Integrated Audits	AS 5 *An Audit of Internal Control over Financial Reporting That Is Integrated with an Audit of Financial Statements* SSAE 15 *An Examination of an Entity's Internal Control over Financial Reporting That Is Integrated with an Audit of Its Financial Statement*
Assessing and Responding to Risk	AS 12 *Identifying and Assessing Risks of Material Misstatement* AS 13 *The Auditor's Responses to the Risks of Material Misstatement* SAS 109 *Understanding the Entity and Its Environment and Assessing the Risks of Material Misstatement* SAS *Understanding the Entity and Its Environment and Assessing the Risks of Material Misstatement* (Redrafted) (issued but not effective; proposed effective date is December 2012) ISA 315 *Identifying and Assessing the Risks of Material Misstatement Through Understanding the Entity and Its Environment*

	Proposed ISA 315 (Revised) *Identifying and Assessing the Risks of Material Misstatement Through Understanding the Entity and Its Environment* ISA 330 *The Auditor's Responses to Assessed Risks*
Communication Regarding Internal Control-Related Matters	SAS 112 *Communicating Internal Control Related Matters Identified in an Audit* SAS 115 *Communicating Internal Control Related Matters Identified in an Audit* SAS *Communicating Internal Control Related Matters Identified in an Audit* (Redrafted) (issued but not effective; proposed effective date is December 2012) ISA 265 *Communicating Deficiencies in Internal Control to Those Charged with Governance and Management*
Internal Control	COSO *Internal Control - Integrated Framework, 1992* COSO *Internal Control over Financial Reporting: Guidance for Smaller Businesses, 2006* COSO *Guidance on Monitoring Internal Control Systems, 2009*

Note: *Acronyms for Relevant Professional Guidance.*

STANDARDS: **AS**—Auditing Standard issued by the PCAOB; **ISA**—International Standard on Auditing issued by the IAASB; **SAS**—Statement on Auditing Standards issued by the Auditing Standards Board of the AICPA; **SSAE**—Statement on Standards for Attestation Engagements issued by the AICPA.

ORGANIZATIONS: **AICPA**—American Institute of Certified Public Accountants; **COSO**—Committee of Sponsoring Organizations; **IAASB**—International Auditing and Assurance Standards Board; **ISB**—Independence Standards Board; **PCAOB**—Public Company Accounting Oversight Board; **SEC**—Securities and Exchange Commission.

Review Questions

6-1   **(LO 1)** Are integrated audits only required for publicly held companies, or is the requirement also applicable to privately held or not-for-profit organizations?

6-2   **(LO 1, 4)** What is an integrated audit? What are the major opportunities for efficiencies in an integrated audit?

6-3   **(LO 1, 4)** Assume that internal controls are effective as assessed by the auditor through testing the design and operating effectiveness. To what extent does the auditor still need to perform substantive testing for account balances? Explain.

6-4   **(LO 1, 3)** What is the implication of a material misstatement in the account balances at year end in terms of providing feedback on the effectiveness of internal control over financial reporting? Explain.

6-5   **(LO 4)** What are the primary factors that should be considered in determining whether the auditor needs to directly test year-end account balances?

6-6   **(LO 3)** Assume that the auditor's tests of internal controls did not reveal any material weaknesses in controls. However, during the audit, a material misstatement in an important account was found. Does the auditor have to analyze the cause of the misstatement and report a material weakness in internal control? Explain your answer.

6-7   **(LO 1, 3)** Describe the major elements of PCAOB Auditing Standard No. 5 and how it has affected practice.

6-8   **(LO 2)** Review the external auditor's report on the integrated audit of Ford Motor Co. contained in the chapter material. What are the important elements in that report related to internal control?

6-9   **(LO 3)** To what extent can the auditor use management's process in evaluating internal control, including evidence gathered, to plan and execute the auditor's integrated audit?

6-10   **(LO 3)** In applying a top-down, risk-based approach to an audit, should the auditor start with the ending account balances or does the auditor begin at the financial statement level? Is one approach preferred over the other? Explain.

6-11   **(LO 3)** Explain the relationship between risk analysis, internal control, and material account balances in designing an approach to an integrated audit. In doing so, explain the differences between business risk, control risk, and residual risk that an account balance may be misstated.

6-12   **(LO 3)** Define what constitutes an "acceptable level of residual risk" when evaluating the effectiveness of internal control over financial reporting.

6-13   **(LO 3)** What evidence might the auditor gather to evaluate whether or not a company has made a commitment to appropriate levels of financial competencies? How would the auditor assess whether the company's accountants and others in the process were competent?

6-14   **(LO 3)** Does the auditor test the same transactions that management and internal audit tested, or does the auditor test different transactions? Explain the rationale.

6-15   **(LO 3)** What are the important controls that the auditor should expect to find over management's process of making accounting estimates? Consider, e.g., the process of estimating the proper allowance for uncollectible accounts.

6-16   **(LO 3)** What risks must an auditor evaluate in preparing for a top-down, risk-based approach to performing an integrated audit?

6-17   **(LO 3, 4)** How does the subjectivity of an accounting process—e.g., making an accounting estimate—affect (a) the nature of the controls the auditor expects to find over the process and (b) the amount of substantive testing of the account balance that should be performed?

6-18   **(LO 3)** What factors most influence the auditor's assessment about the potential existence of material misstatements in an account balance? How are those factors addressed in an integrated audit?

6-19   **(LO 3)** What is monitoring? How should the auditor go about determining whether management's process for monitoring the effectiveness of internal controls is adequate?

6-20   **(LO 5)** What are the factors that should be considered by management and the auditor in determining whether a deficiency is a "significant deficiency" or a "material weakness"?

6-21   **(LO 3)** What are the important criteria that an auditor should use in selecting which controls to test when performing an integrated audit?

6-22   **(LO 3, 4)** In analyzing the results of the tests of controls, there are two potential outcomes: (1) deficiencies are identified and (2) deficiencies are not identified. What are alternative courses of action in the audit associated with these alternative outcomes?

6-23 **(LO 4)** The chapter emphasizes that when the auditor determines that controls are not working, the auditor needs to anticipate (a) what kind of misstatements could occur in the financial statements, (b) how those misstatements might occur, and (c) how the auditor should change the substantive testing of the affected account balance(s) to determine if a misstatement did occur. Assume that the authorization process for ordering goods was found to contain a material weakness. Use the framework above to identify the kind of misstatements that could occur, how they might occur, and how the auditor would adjust substantive audit procedures.

Multiple-Choice Questions

6-24 **(LO 3)** The auditor wants to develop a top-down, risk-based approach to perform an integrated audit of internal controls and financial statements for a public company. Which of the following statements is correct regarding the integrated audit?

a. The auditor should start with the errors detected in last year's audit.

b. The auditor should start by identifying material account balance, disclosures, and relevant assertions and assess the risks that those account balances may be misstated.

c. Because accounting estimates are subjective, the auditor should perform only substantive tests of accounts established by accounting estimates.

d. Accounting disclosures are separate and need not be included in the auditor's assessment of internal controls over financial reporting.

6-25 **(LO 4, 5)** The auditor discovers that there is a key control failure over sales contracts and that some contracts near the end of the year are not properly reviewed by management. Which of the following would be the best way for the auditor to respond to the control deficiency identified?

a. Expand the testing over the control with a larger sample from the last quarter of the year.

b. Wait to assess whether the deficiency is a material weakness or significant deficiency based on the actual number of errors or misstatements found in the related account balances.

c. Expand the sample size for substantive testing and review of contracts during the latter part of the year to determine if revenue is appropriately identified.

d. All of the above.

6-26 **(LO 1, 2)** Which of the following statements *is correct* regarding the auditor's report on a public company's internal control over financial reporting?

a. A company cannot have a material weakness in internal controls if the auditor does a GAAS audit and does not find a material misstatement.

b. The auditor must explicitly reference the criteria for evaluating internal control, e.g., the COSO framework.

c. The audit is performed in conjunction with the auditing standards promulgated by the AICPA Auditing Standards Board.

d. The audit must report on whether management used the appropriate tools in its assessment of internal control over financial reporting.

6-27   **(LO 5)** The auditor is auditing sales and accounts receivable and notes the following: (a) the company regularly does not follow its credit policies; rather it routinely overrides the credit policy when divisional management needs to meet its performance goals; and (b) the sales manager has the ability to override the credit policy for important customers. However, the controls over proper recording of sales transactions are working. Which of the following statements would be correct regarding an integrated audit of sales and receivables?

I. The most relevant assertion regarding receivables to test for this client is the existence assertion.

II. If the amount of credit overridden is such that the likely uncollectible amount is material, the auditor should conclude that the client has a material weakness in internal control.

III. The monitoring aspect of internal control is not working effectively.

a. I and II only

b. II only

c. II and III only

d. I, II, and III

6-28   **(LO 3, 4)** Using the descriptive information in Question 6-27, indicate the most appropriate action for the auditor to take regarding the expansion of the substantive tests of sales and receivables:

a. Expand the use of confirmations to determine the existence of the customers with bad credit.

b. Expand the search for new sales made to these same customers after year end.

c. Use generalized audit software to foot the file of receivables to determine that all items have been recorded.

d. Expand the use of collectibility tests, including aging of accounts receivable and reviewing credit scores for a large selection of sales made during the latter part of the year, and update the procedure for estimating the allowance for uncollectible accounts.

6-29   **(LO 3, 4, 5)** If management finds a material weakness in internal controls but remediates the control before year end and determines that no material misstatements have occurred because of the deficiency, the auditor should do which of the following?

a. Test the remediated control to determine that it is working effectively.

b. Issue an adverse opinion because the control was not working effectively throughout the year.

c. Expand tests of the affected account balances to develop an independent assessment as to whether there are material misstatements.

d. All of the above.

e. (a) and (c) above.

6-30 **(LO 1, 3)** The auditor's tests of internal control over financial reporting include all of the following *except* controls over:

a. Disclosures

b. Processes leading to accounting estimates

c. Adjusting journal entries

d. Determining the income tax liability

e. All of the above are included.

6-31 **(LO 5)** Which of the following would *not* be a primary consideration of the auditor in determining whether a deficiency was a significant deficiency or a material weakness?

a. The rate of failure of the control

b. The volume and dollar amount of transactions affected by the control

c. Whether the control is computerized or manual

d. Whether the control deficiency is mitigated by other control elements, e.g., the control environment

6-32 **(LO 3)** Which of the following are correct related to the auditor's tests of the client's monitoring controls?

  I. The auditor should test monitoring only if the management's evaluation of internal control indicates that management is relying on monitoring controls.

  II. Monitoring is a process to determine that other controls are working properly.

  III. Monitoring can substitute for a deficiency of other controls.

  a. I only

  b. I and II only

  c. I, II, and III

  d. II and III

6-33 **(LO 3)** All of the following would be included in the auditor's tests of controls over accounting estimates *except*:

a. Confirmation of the estimate with outside third parties

b. Review of documentation to determine that the estimate is properly reviewed and authorized

c. Review of processes used to determine if there are changes to the parameters used in the estimates, including management monitoring of the economic environment

d. Review of processes to approve changes to the estimation process

Discussion and Research Questions

6-34 **(Deficiencies in Internal Control, LO 2, 3, 4)** Following is a portion of management's report on internal control by Milacron Inc. in 2004.

Item 9A. *Controls and Procedures*

Disclosure Controls and Procedures (Interim Analysis)

Disclosure controls and procedures are controls and other procedures that are designed to ensure that information required to be disclosed by the company is recorded, processed, summarized, and reported within the time periods specified in the rules and forms of the Securities and Exchange Commission (SEC).... the company's chief executive officer and chief financial officer have concluded that the company's disclosure controls and procedures were not effective as of December 31, 2004, due to the material weakness in internal control over financial reporting described below.

Internal Control over Financial Reporting

While the company's assessment of the effectiveness of its internal control over financial reporting is not complete, a material weakness, as defined in standards established by the Public Company Accounting Oversight Board (United States), has been identified.... The identified material weakness consists of inadequate levels of review of complex and judgmental accounting issues. Various audit adjustments were needed to correct errors resulting from the internal control deficiency. This deficiency manifested itself in the determination of deferred tax valuation allowances as well as litigation reserves and recoverables from third-party insurers. These adjustments are reflected in the company's audited financial statements for the year ended December 31, 2004....

To address the identified material weakness, the company is in the process of implementing remediation plans, including the following:

- The company has increased its levels of review of complex and judgmental accounting issues.
- The company has initiated a plan to add personnel with technical accounting expertise.
- The company has made a commitment to increase professional development for finance and accounting personnel...

The indenture governing the company's 11 1/2% Senior Secured Notes due 2011 requires filing the Form 10-K in a timely manner. The failure to do so is a default under the indenture.

Updated Analysis Filed in Amended 10-K

The following is a description of the three material weaknesses in the company's internal control over financial reporting:

Review of Complex and Judgmental Accounting Issues—There are inadequate levels of review of complex and judgmental accounting issues. Various audit adjustments were needed to correct errors from this internal control deficiency... [remainder of paragraph describes these deficiencies in more detail].

Segregation of Duties—There is inadequate segregation of incompatible duties with respect to the company's manual and computer-based business processes at the corporate and operating levels. Such inadequacy in segregation of incompatible duties significantly reduced or eliminated the effectiveness of many of the company's internal controls over the accounts which comprise the consolidated financial statements. This material weakness has been caused primarily by two factors:

- Instances in which, as a result of the company's effort to stream-line business processes, individuals are in various conflicting roles; and
- The use of older computer systems which are not always capable of limiting user's access to certain transactions.

No audit adjustments to the company's audited financial statements for the year ended December 31, 2004 resulted from this material weakness.

To address this material weakness, the company will implement, based on specific circumstances, one or more measures, which will include:

- Reassignment of certain responsibilities in order to eliminate incompatible roles;
- Implementation of independent reviews of certain completed transactions; and
- Further restriction of access to certain sensitive, conflicting transactions.

Additionally, the company is in the process of implementing a company-wide [computer] system to upgrade its overall operating systems. In addition to the many operating benefits, the new system will also be capable of adequate segregation of duties.

Inventory Valuation—There are insufficient controls with respect to the accounting for inventories primarily at one major North American manufacturing location. Specifically, the Company did not have effective controls to ensure inventory was properly valued and to ensure inventory was properly relieved at the time of sale.

Because of the material weaknesses described above, management has concluded that, as of December 31, 2004, the company did not maintain effective internal control over financial reporting.

Ernst & Young LLP , the registered public accounting firm that audited the company's financial statements included in the Form 10-K, has issued an attestation report on management's assessment of the effectiveness of internal control over financial reporting as of December 31, 2004, which is included below.

Required

a. Identify the control deficiencies that management identified in its report on internal control.

b. For each control deficiency identified, answer the following:

(1) How would management identify the deficiency?

(2) How is management planning on remediating the deficiency?

(3) What evidence should the auditor gather to determine whether the control deficiency has been remediated?

c. Management indicates that the deficiencies may cause the company to violate its debt covenants.

(1) Explain why the deficiencies might violate debt covenants.

(2) What are the implications to the company if the debt covenants are violated?

(3) Why are lenders interested in the effectiveness of a company's internal control?

d. Management asserts that the control deficiencies did not lead to material misstatements in the financial statements:

(1) How would management know that there were no material misstatements?

(2) Is the auditor required to attest to this assertion by management? Explain why or why not.

6-35   **(Importance of the Control Environment, LO 3)** The auditor of a public company in the retailing industry is planning an integrated audit. The company has approximately 260 retail stores, primarily in the southeastern United States.

Ethics

Required

a. Explain why an analysis of the company's control environment is important to the planning of the integrated audit.

b. The company claims that it has a strong control environment, including a culture of high integrity and ethics; a commitment to financial reporting competencies; and an independent, active, and knowledgeable audit committee. For each of these items, develop an audit program to gather evidence that these elements are effective. Organize your answer around each of these three elements:

- Integrity and ethical climate

- Financial reporting competencies

- Effective audit committee

In developing your answer, be sure to include the following two components: (1) evidence that would convince the auditor that the component of the control environment was operating effectively and (2) procedures the auditor would use to gather the evidence.

6-36   **(Controls over Accounting Estimates, LO 3, 4)** Consider a company like General Motors that must make estimates on pension liabilities, health care liabilities, guarantees on the contracts with Delphi, warranty liabilities for its cars, uncollectible loans from its wholly owned subprime finance subsidiary (Americredit) acquired in July 2010, as well as the costs associated with restructuring.

Group Activity

Required

a. With the consent of your instructor, select one of the areas identified where General Motors makes accounting estimates and complete the following:

(1) Identify the economic and regulatory factors that may affect the computation of the liability.

(2) Identify the internal data that affect the computation of the liability.

(3) Identify the preciseness of the estimate that is expected.

(4) Identify the control activities that you would expect to be present in the process of making the estimate.

(5) Identify the approaches the auditor would use to determine whether the design of controls is appropriate and the controls are working properly.

(6) Discuss whether the approach you have taken to test the controls also tests the proper recording of the accounting estimate.

b. Assume that all of the controls your group has identified and tested are working as designed:

(1) To what extent do you believe the auditor still has to perform substantive tests of the account balances?

(2) If you conclude that substantive tests of the account balances still have to be performed, identify one or two procedures to gather additional audit evidence that the auditor should use.

(3) Report your analysis to the class.

6-37   **(Auditor's Report on Internal Control, LO 2, 4, 5)** The auditor prepares a report on internal control over financial reporting for one of its public companies.

Required

a. Is the auditor also required to audit the company's financial statements at the same time? Explain.

b. Does an unqualified report on internal controls over financial reporting imply that the company does not have any significant deficiencies in controls? Explain.

c. If no material misstatements can be found in the financial statements, can the auditor conclude that there are no material weaknesses in internal control? Explain.

Group Activity

Ethics

6-38   **(Ethical Decision-Making, LO 3, 5, 6)** The auditor is evaluating the internal control of a new client. Management has prepared its assessment of internal control and has concluded that it has some deficiencies but no significant deficiencies and no material weaknesses. However, in reviewing the work performed by management, including the internal auditor, the auditor observes the following:

• Sample sizes taken by the internal auditor were never more than ten transactions, and most of the tests of operating effectiveness were based on a sample of one performed as part of a walk-through of a transaction.

• Management has fired the former CFO and a new CFO has not been appointed, but management indicates it has depth in the accounting area and is searching for a new CFO.

- The company has no formal whistleblowing function because management has an "open-door" policy so that anyone with a problem can take it up the line.

- Management's approach to monitoring internal control is to compare budget with actual expenses and investigate differences.

In response to inquiries by the auditor, management responds that its procedures are sufficient to support its report on internal control. The auditor's subsequent work yields the following:

- Many control procedures do not operate in the way described by management, and the procedures are not effective (not designed effectively).

- There is no awareness of, or adherence to, the company's code of conduct.

- The accounting department does not have a depth of talent; moreover, although the department can handle most transactions, it is not capable of dealing with newer contracts that the firm has entered into. The response of management is, "That is why we pay you auditors the Big Bucks—Help us make these decisions."

The auditor reaches a conclusion that there are material weaknesses in internal control, thus differing from management's assessment. Management points out that every issue on which there is a disagreement is a subjective issue, and there is no one position that is better than the others. Management's position is that these are management's financial statements, and the auditor should accommodate management's view because there are no right answers.

Required

a. Identify the audit approach the auditor could use to gather evidence regarding the effectiveness of the organization's code of ethics.

b. The partner in charge of the job appears to be persuaded that the differences are only subjective and is proposing that an unqualified opinion on internal controls be issued. Recognize that this is a first-year client—and an important one to the office. Apply the ethical framework developed earlier to explore the actions that should be taken by the manager on the audit regarding (1) whether to disagree with the partner and (2) if there is a disagreement, to what level it should be taken in the firm.

c. Given the deficiencies noted, does the information support that there is a material weakness in internal control? If yes, what are the major factors that lead you to that conclusion?

d. Assume that the engagement team makes a decision that there is a material weakness in internal controls. Write two or three paragraphs that describe those weaknesses.

6-39 **(Phases of an Integrated Audit, LO 3)** Planning for an integrated audit consists of eight steps that lead to audit testing of controls and financial statement account balances.

Required

a. Describe the eight steps of an integrated audit.

b. Does the auditor need to evaluate each of the components of the COSO *Internal Control - Integrated Framework* to reach an opinion on the effectiveness of internal control?

c. Can one element of the framework be weak and yet be offset by another element? Explain.

6-40 **(LO 3)** **(Segregation of Duties)** Segregation of duties is an important concept in internal control. However, segregation of duties is often a challenge for smaller businesses because they do not have sufficient staff to segregate duties. Normally, the segregation of duties identified below results in either a significant deficiency or a material weakness in internal control.

Required

For each "segregation of duties" problem identified here:

a. Identify the risk to financial reporting that is associated with the inadequacy of the segregation of duties.

b. Identify other controls that might mitigate the segregation of duties risks.

c. If a control is identified that would mitigate the risks, briefly indicate what evidence the auditor would need to gather to determine that the control is operating effectively.

The inadequate segregation of duty situations to be considered are as follows:

- The same individual handles cash receipts, the bank reconciliation, and customer complaints.
- The same person prepares billings to customers and also collects cash receipts and applies them to customer accounts.
- The person who prepares billings to customers does not handle cash, but does the monthly bank reconciliation, which, in turn, is reviewed by the controller.
- The controller is responsible for making all accounting estimates and adjusting journal entries. The company does not have a CFO and has two clerks who report to the controller.
- A start-up company has very few transactions, less than $1 million in revenue per year, and has only one accounting person. The company's transactions are not complex.
- The company has one computer person who is responsible for running packaged software. The individual has access to the computer to update software and can also access records.

6-41 **(High-Risk Audit Area: Revenue Recognition, LO 3, 4)** Professional guidance has stated that revenue recognition should always be considered to be high risk in planning an audit of a company's financial statements.

Required

a. Identify the major accounting and operational processes that affect revenue.

b. Identify the other financial accounts normally associated with revenue recognition.

c. Assume management has identified effective controls over the recording of revenue transactions and the auditor concurs with that assessment:

(1) What risks still might exist in the account balance if the controls over the recording of shipments have been determined to be adequate?

(2) Identify the substantive tests of the revenue account that the auditor might still want to apply given that revenue recognition is high risk.

d. The auditor is concerned that the client may have been involved in special contracts for goods that were shipped at year end that may have "nonstandard" rights of return by the customer:

(1) What controls should be in place to mitigate this risk?

(2) How would the auditor find out about the special contracts; i.e., what audit procedures should the auditor perform to identify the possibility that the special contracts might exist?

6-42   **(Residual Risk, LO 3, 4)** The COSO internal control framework provides guidance to management to reduce residual risk to an acceptable level.

Required

a. Define the term *residual risk.*

b. Which of the following parties should determine residual risk?

- Management
- The external auditor
- The audit committee
- A regulatory body such as the PCAOB

c. What factors affect the auditor's assessment of residual risk remaining in an account balance before performing substantive tests of the account balance?

6-43   **(Factors Affecting Amount of Control Testing, LO 3, 4)** There are many factors that may affect the size of the sample the auditor takes to test controls.

Required

a. How is sample size affected by the nature of the processing?

b. Assume the auditor wishes to reduce the amount of substantive testing of an account based on the strength of internal controls. In thinking about sample size for internal control testing, the auditor will want to gather sufficient evidence to assess control risk as (high, low). Select one response and indicate how your choice would most likely affect the sample size for testing.

c. Assume that the auditor plans the audit to rely on internal controls based on a belief that they are very effective. Management also believes that controls are effective and has developed an effective system (in its view) to monitor the controls.

(1) What would constitute an effective monitoring process?

(2) If the monitoring process is effective, could the auditor rely mostly on a testing and evaluation of monitoring for an assessment of internal controls? Explain.

(3) Assume one form of monitoring is that management reviews year-end transactions for unusual sales or terms. Would this be an acceptable form of monitoring? How would the auditor determine that the monitoring is effective?

6-44   **(Factors Affecting Amount of Substantive Testing of Account Balances, LO 4)** There are many factors that affect the auditor's decision as to how much direct testing of an account balance will be required.

Required

a. Identify the factors (risks) that affect the auditor's decision as to whether to perform substantive tests of an account balance and, if so, how much testing is required.

b. For each factor identified, indicate how it affects the auditor's decision of how much substantive testing to perform.

6-45   **(Linking Deficiencies to Substantive Tests, LO 3, 4)** The auditor determines that there may be misstatements in the inventory and cost of goods sold accounts. During the conduct of the audit, the auditor found a material weakness in internal controls in that (a) some shipments were recorded before the actual shipment took place (this happened throughout the year at a rate of two out of thirty), (b) some shipping documents could not be found even though the shipment had been recorded (two out of thirty), and (c) some goods were received and sat on the shipping dock for up to seven days before the receipt was recorded. This happened at a rate of five out of thirty.

Required

a. For each of these deficiencies, indicate the potential misstatement affecting inventory and cost of goods sold.

b. Identify whether the potential misstatement of inventory identified above would be considered significant enough to require substantive testing of inventory, as opposed to relying on controls for the audit evidence of financial statement account balances. State the rationale for your answer.

c. For each deficiency or potential misstatement, indicate how you might test to see whether inventory was misstated.

d. Assume that no deficiencies were found in the auditor's tests of controls. How would the audit plan for substantive tests of inventory be changed? Describe both the nature of the tests performed and the sample sizes taken.

6-46   **(Deficiencies and Compensating Controls and Links to Substantive Testing, LO 3, 4)** For the company identified in Question 6-45, assume that the company has an internal audit department which makes periodic test counts of inventory and that management adjusts the inventory records to the test counts.

Required

a. What factors should the auditor consider in determining whether or not to rely on the work performed by the internal auditor?

b. If the internal auditor was doing a great job in testing controls over inventory record keeping, what would the auditor expect to see with respect to (1) the pattern of the control failures found in Question 6-45, and (2) recommendations made by the internal auditor to management?

c. Assume the following two scenarios:

   • The internal auditor's work on inventory consists primarily of making the test counts and seeing that the inventory is adjusted for differences.

   • The internal auditor's work meets all the criteria you have identified in part (b).

Explain how the two scenarios would affect the amount of direct testing of inventory the auditor should plan on performing.

6-47   **(Monitoring, LO 3, 4)** For the inventory scenario developed in Questions 6-45 and 6-46, consider the type of monitoring that might be performed by management.

Required

a. Explain the monitoring element of the COSO internal control framework. What is the purpose of monitoring?

b. Identify two or three types of monitoring that would be effective once the company has fixed all the control deficiencies that might have existed.

c. For the monitoring approaches you have identified, (1) describe how the approach would work and (2) what evidence the auditor might want to gather to determine the effectiveness of the monitoring control.

d. Explain why an improvement in the robustness of the monitoring element of internal controls should lead to a decrease in cost for a company to comply with Section 404 of Sarbanes-Oxley.

6-48   **(Using the Work of Others, LO 3)** The PCAOB allows the auditor to use the work of others, such as internal auditors or other company personnel, to alter the nature, timing, or extent of the auditor's own testing of internal controls.

Client A has an internal audit department that reports to the CFO and audit committee. The department is fully staffed with personnel who are experienced, highly qualified, and professional. It has an external peer review conducted every three years that shows it has fully complied with the Institute of Internal Auditor's professional standards. It has a charter that clearly allows full access to all areas of the company, company personnel, records, and other sources of information. It focuses a lot of attention on testing controls of the more significant control activities of the company as well as on corporate government issues and management's processes for risk identification and assessment.

Client B has an internal audit department that reports to the controller and audit committee. It is understaffed and most of its personnel are recent college graduates. The chief audit executive, however, has had a lot of experience with the company and is considered to be "one of the guys." Its audit scope is determined by the controller. The department focuses most of its attention on financial auditing but does some testing of controls in areas as directed by the controller. It does not have enough budget to undergo an external peer review of the quality of its performance.

Required

a. Discuss the factors the external auditor should consider in determining to what extent the work of the internal auditors can be relied on in forming an opinion on internal controls.

b. Is it likely that much reliance can be placed on the work performed by the internal auditors of Client A? Client B? Explain.

c. Why might the external auditor decide to test the effectiveness of the control environment itself rather than rely to any extent on the testing of corporate governance by the internal auditors of Client B?

6-49   **(Adjusting Entries, LO 3)** Adjusting entries have been utilized to improperly manage earnings.

Group Activity

Required

In your groups, perform the following:

a. Identify two types of "routine" adjusting entries and two types of nonroutine adjusting entries that might be made either monthly or quarterly.

b. Explain the types of controls that might be expected to be associated with routine adjusting entries. Illustrate with the types of entries you have identified in part (a).

c. For the adjusting entries, identify how the auditor would gather evidence on the one or two most important controls built into the process.

d. Assume the nonroutine adjusting entries can be material for the company. Identify two or three important controls that you would recommend be implemented for the nonroutine adjusting entries.

6-50 **(Testing Controls and Financial Statement Integration, LO 3, 4)** Assume the auditor is assigned to analyze and test the controls related to purchasing, including inventory items as well as items that are expensed. There are three purchasing agents for a medium-sized company ($750 million in sales) with each specializing in different areas. Department heads are authorized to purchase "expense-type" items up to $750 individually and up to $20,000 annually.

Required

a. Explain how the auditor would test to see that the following controls are working effectively:

- Authorization of purchases by department heads
- Authorization of inventory purchases by purchasing agents
- Independent receipt of inventory
- Reconciliation of inventory with perpetual records on a regular basis
- Limit of total purchases for a month to amount approved by budget or planned production
- Clear accounting policies regarding the accounts to be charged for purchases with periodic review by the controller's department

b. Assume management and auditors both conclude the controls are working properly. Of the total purchases made during the year, $520 million was for products (inventory and cost of goods sold) and another $120 million was for expenses, excluding legal and professional fees. These expenses ranged from office supplies, to production supplies, and so on, and one large item—advertising expense at $10 million.

(1) Identify the implications for the remaining substantive audit testing of expenses. Identify all the assumptions you have made about the nature of the auditor's tests of expense items. Explain your answer.

(2) Identify the implications for the remaining substantive testing of cost of goods sold.

Group Activity

6-51 **6-51 (LO 4, 5)** The introduction to this chapter contained the following quotes from an IMA paper:

The requirement to report on internal control resulted from one particular type of internal control breakdown: senior management of some major public companies overrode their control systems and issued misleading financial statements. History has shown that senior management cooking the books has been most costly of control failures. It has caused billions in investor losses, undermined confidence in reporting affecting the liquidity and cost of capital for many companies, and triggered significant new regulations and requirements, including reporting on controls. Other forms of fraudulent financial reporting, such as misleading reporting by lower-level employees, have not had the same impact. (p. 19)

The same IMA piece also stated:

Based on our inquiries, we have not identified any external audit firms that maintain five-year historical records of all errors and irregularities they have identified during their audits. This data would allow pattern analysis, helping with the identification of trends and patterns that would disclose systemic control weaknesses, including the frequency that management has not provided full and frank disclosure. As noted earlier, in order for full transparency and understanding of systemic root cause errors to be a reality, appropriate safe harbors for issuers and public audit firms need to be seriously considered.

Required

a. The Jonas comment included in the chapter introduction material implies that auditors can (should) identify control environment problems leading to "cooking the books." In your group, discuss the following: (1) Do you think, as future auditors, you can or should be responsible for identifying control environment problems that lead to "cooking the books"? and (2) What might some of those control environment problems be?

b. Do you think that firms should develop a "pattern analysis" database as suggested in the last part of the article? If yes, what are (a) the potential difficulties in developing such a database and (b) the potential problems in using such a database? What obstacles might a firm have to overcome to use such a database?

Cases

6-52   **(PCAOB Inspections and Controls, LO 1, 3)** One of the fundamental changes that occurred upon passage of the Sarbanes-Oxley Act of 2002 is that the audit profession is no longer allowed to be self-regulatory. The Public Company Accounting Oversight Board (PCAOB) has the authority to assess whether audit firms are conducting high-quality audits. To make that assessment, the PCAOB conducts formal inspections of audits completed by audit firms registered with the PCAOB, and the results of those inspections are made public on the PCAOB's website (www.pcaobus.org; follow the links to inspection reports). The inspection teams select certain higher-risk areas for review, inspect the engagement team's audit documentation, and interview engagement personnel regarding those areas. The areas subject to review include, e.g., revenues, reserves or estimated liabilities, derivatives, income taxes,

Internet

related-party transactions, supervision of work performed by foreign affiliates, assessment of risk by the audit team, and testing and documentation of internal controls by the audit team. The inspection team also analyzes potential adjustments to the issuer's financial statements that had been identified during the audit but not recorded in the financial statements. For some engagements, the inspection team reviews written communications between the audit firm and the issuer's audit committee.

The reports that have been released to the public contain a variety of examples of audit engagements in which auditors have had difficulty in properly assessing and responding to weaknesses in client internal controls. Excerpts from reports of these difficulties follow:

Audit Firm 1: "In this audit, the Firm's internal control testing and substantive procedures related to revenue were deficient. The Firm assessed control risk for revenue as 'below maximum' in an environment that the Firm concluded had 'pervasive weaknesses' in IT general controls. The nature and extent of the Firm's substantive procedures were not sufficient in a high control risk environment and inappropriately relied on system-generated information without testing the source data."

Audit Firm 2: "The issuer used a service organization for payroll services, and the Firm placed reliance on the controls at the service organization with respect to vacation expense and accrual testing. The Firm, however, had not obtained an understanding of the internal controls at the service organization through its own assessment, nor had it obtained an auditor's report on the service organization prepared in accordance with AU 324, *Service Organizations*. Thus, the Firm should not have relied on the controls at the service organization."

Audit Firm 3: "PCAOB standards require the auditor to test internal controls before relying on them for the purpose of designing and performing the substantive audit procedures. In 13 instances involving the audits of 10 issuers, the Firm failed to test, or failed to perform sufficient tests of, controls that the Firm relied on in designing and performing its substantive audit procedures. The instances included the following:

- The Firm relied on information technology ('IT') application controls that had not been tested for several years.

- The Firm did not sufficiently address the effects of deficiencies in IT program access controls, change-management controls, or application controls.

- The Firm relied on change-management controls that had been tested only for the first half of the year without performing appropriate updating procedures.

- The Firm relied on IT system–generated data without testing the IT general computer and/or application controls.

- The Firm tested controls using samples that were smaller than necessary to support reliance on the types of controls being tested."

Required

a. Comment on the PCAOB's inspection process, focusing on (1) why it is considered important to audit quality and (2) how it may improve audit quality.

b. Review the comments from the inspection reports provided above. What common problems did the PCAOB detect during the inspections?

c. Considering the problems detected by the PCAOB, why do you think it was concerned about those particular issues? How could the problems in the audit procedures have affected the nature of the audit opinion rendered on those engagements?

d. For two of the audit firms, the PCAOB detected problems involving information technology controls. Why are these controls so important to the proper functioning of an organization's financial reporting system? Why might auditors have particular difficulty in assessing these controls? What procedures could audit firms put into place to assure that auditor difficulty in this regard is minimized?

e. Visit the PCAOB's website and review two inspection reports of your choosing. Be prepared to discuss your findings during class.

6-53 **(General Motors, Accounting Controls, LO 3, 4, 5)** General Motors is in the process of restructuring its operations. In recent years, it has spun off its major parts supplier and its financing arm and is restructuring most of its operations. In March 2006, it announced that it needed to restate its prior year's financial statements. Excerpts from the *Wall Street Journal* describing the restatements include the following:

GM, which already faces an SEC probe into its accounting practices, also disclosed that its 10-K report, when filed, will outline a series of accounting mistakes that will force the car maker to restate its earnings from 2000 to the first quarter of 2005. GM also said it was widening by $2 billion the loss it reported for 2005.

Many of the other GM problems relate to rebates, or credits, from suppliers. Typically, suppliers offer an upfront payment in exchange for a promise by the customer to buy certain quantities of products over time. Under accounting rules, such rebates can't be recorded until after the promised purchases are made.

GM said it concluded it had mistakenly recorded some of these payments prematurely. The biggest impact was in 2001, when the company said it overstated pretax income by $405 million as a result of prematurely recording supplier credits.

Because the credits are being moved to later years, the impact in those years was less, and GM said it would have a deferred credit of $548 million that will help reduce costs in future periods. The issue of how to book rebates and other credits from suppliers is a thorny one that has tripped up other companies, ranging from supermarket chain Royal Ahold NV to Kmart Corp.

GM also said it had wrongly recorded a $27 million pretax gain from disposing of precious-metals inventory in 2000, which it was obliged to buy back the following year.

GM on Thursday told investors not to rely on its previously reported results for the first quarter of 2005, saying it had underreported its loss by $149 million. GM said it had "prematurely" boosted the value it ascribed to cars it was leasing to rental-car companies, assuming they would be worth more after the car-rental companies are done with them. GM previously had reported a loss of $1.1 billion, or $1.95 a share, for the first quarter. (March 18, 2006)

You may assume the amounts are material.

Required

a. Without assuming that the errors in accounting judgment were intentional or not intentional, discuss how the nature of the errors affects the auditor's judgment of the control environment and whether the auditor should conclude there are material weaknesses in internal control. What would your judgment be if the accounting treatment were deemed "acceptable, but aggressive" by the company's CFO and CEO? How would those judgments affect the auditor's assessment of the control environment?

b. Describe the nature of the accounting judgment made by the company regarding the residual value of the cars it leases. What information and communication system should exist regarding the residual value of the cars returned from leasing? What controls should be in place? What evidence would the auditor need to evaluate the reasonableness of the change made by the company?

c. Explain the rebates, or up-front rebates, from the company's suppliers. Why would the suppliers pay the up-front credits? What is the proper accounting for the up-front credits? What controls should be in place to account for the up-front credits? How would the auditor audit (1) the controls over the accounting for the up-front credits and (2) the expense-offset account, or the liability account?

Academic Research Case (LO 5)

Hermanson, D., & Ye, Z. (2009). Why Do Some Accelerated Filers with SOX Section 404 Material Weaknesses Provide Early Warning under Section 302? *Auditing: A Journal of Practice & Theory* 28(2): 247-271.

1. What is the issue being addressed in the paper?

2. Why is this issue important to practicing auditors?

3. What are the major findings of the paper?

4. What are the implications of these findings for audit quality (or audit practice) on the audit profession?

5. Describe the research methodology used as a basis for the conclusions.

6. Describe any limitations of the research that readers should be aware of.

Go to www.cengage.com/accounting/rittenberg for the Ford and Toyota materials.

Source and Reference	Question
Ford 10-K and Toyota 20-F	**1a.** Read the reports of the independent registered public accounting firm for Ford and Toyota. Notice that the reports clearly articulate differential responsibilities on the part of management versus the audit firm. Why is it important that the audit firm articulate these responsibilities in this way?
	1b. In Ford's report from the independent registered public accounting firm, how does PwC describe the way that it conducts the audit of internal controls?
	1c. Ford received an unqualified opinion on its internal controls, as did Toyota. How would you feel about the disclosures and reported financial results if this were not the case?
	1d. If you were a shareholder of Ford or Toyota and the company received an adverse report on internal controls, what would you do? In addition,
	• How does the adverse report affect the reliability of future reports, e.g., interim financial reports?
	• How does the report affect the current financial statements?
	• What does the report imply about management's stewardship function and its commitment to risk management?
	• Should the quality of a company's internal controls over financial reporting affect a company's stock price? Explain.

Module II: Preliminary Assessment of Control Risk Based on an Understanding of the Design of Controls

In this module, you will be asked to consider the information presented in the Description of the Practice case in order to develop a preliminary assessment of control risk. While Biltrite is not required to obtain an audit opinion on the effectiveness of its internal controls, the audit committee has asked your audit firm to provide feedback on its assessment of the design of its internal control over financial reporting, including the five components of internal control as described by COSO. Additional information you should consider is presented below.

The Accounting Information System and Internal Control over Financial Reporting

All computer-based information systems (CBIS) and accounting functions are centralized at the Texas home office. Some of the more significant features of the system are discussed in the following paragraphs.

Computerized Ledger　The general ledger software package, revised as part of the upgrade project, contains the following integrated modules: accounts receivable, accounts payable, inventories, plant assets, payroll, and general ledger.

Sales Processing　Customer sales orders received by salespersons are input directly into the system via terminals from each of the regional locations. The regional sales manager is responsible for entering the orders after checking for proper credit approval and determining the maximum credit limit. A transaction log is maintained at each remote terminal; the log shows date of order entry, identification number of the salesperson receiving the order, customer number, stock number, and quantity ordered. After determining stock availability, the computer prepares a consecutively numbered, three-part sales invoice. As part of the sales processing, the computer inserts the customer's name and address, product descriptions and prices, and extensions and footings. Terms of payment and discount availability also are determined by the computer and included on the invoice. For each order processed, the computer records the transaction, including costing the sale, and updates the accounts receivable and inventory modules. The original invoice is mailed to the customer, the first copy is faxed to the warehouse as shipping authorization, and the second copy is retained awaiting a signed bill of lading evidencing shipment. Upon its receipt from the regional unit, the bill of lading is attached to the second invoice copy and placed in a numeric file. Exhibit BR.7 describes the sales processing function in the form of a flowchart.

Cash Receipts　All mail is centrally received in the mailroom, opened, and distributed. Checks from customers are forwarded to CBIS, where the customer number, invoice numbers paid, discount taken, and net amount remitted are entered into the system based on the remittance advice information. The computer then updates the customer accounts, as well as the accounts receivable control and cash in bank accounts. At the end of the day, the computer produces a printout of detail and totals by customer, as well as a grand total.

Exhibit BR.7   Sales Processing Flowchart

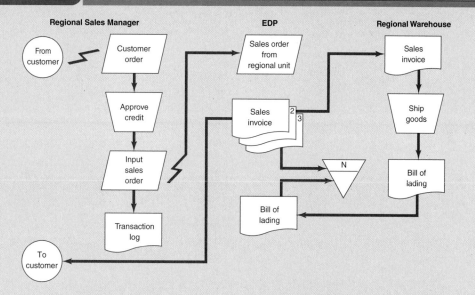

The checks and remittance advices are then separated and the checks are forwarded to Mark Wilkins, cashier. Wilkins prepares the deposit and deposits each day's remittances intact. Receipted deposit tickets are forwarded by the bank to the controller's office where a comparison is made with the daily printout of cash receipts.

Miscellaneous cash receipts are processed in a fashion similar to that accorded customer remittances, except that a recording form is prepared by the general ledger section and forwarded daily to CBIS for entry into the computer. Prepared from the remittance advice, the recording form contains the date, amount remitted, account number(s), and amount(s) to be credited. Exhibit BR.8 is a flowchart describing processing of customer cash receipts.

Purchases and Accounts Payable   Biltrite buys its derailleurs and other bicycle parts from three unrelated vendors; steel and paint are purchased from selected vendors, based on a bidding process. Supplies are purchased from various vendors. All parts, materials, and supplies are ordered as reorder points are reached on the basis of a three-part purchase order generated by the computer.

Emil Ransbottom, director of purchasing, reports to Elmer Fennig, production vice president. Prices, as agreed upon by Ransbottom and the respective vendors, also appear on the purchase order, which is mailed to the vendor after being reviewed and approved by Fennig. A copy of the purchase order is sent to accounts payable and another goes to the purchasing department for later comparison with the incoming goods.

When goods are received, they are counted and inspected by employees in the receiving department and a two-part receiving report is prepared. The original accompanies the goods to stores, where quantities and types of goods are compared with the receiving report, and the copy is filed numerically in the receiving department. The store's manager then signs the receiving report and forwards it to the director of purchasing for comparison with the purchase order for type, quantity, price, and discount terms. After signing for agreement, the director of purchasing forwards the receiving report to accounts payable, where it is filed by vendor, along with the purchase order copy, awaiting receipt of a vendor's invoice.

When the vendor's invoice is received, an accounts payable clerk compares it with the purchase order and receiving report, and then prepares a voucher for processing the invoice. The voucher contains the vendor number, vendor invoice number, stock number, quantities, price, and terms. Voucher copies are forwarded to CBIS for daily processing of vendors' invoices. A daily control tape of dollar totals appearing on the invoices is retained by accounts payable for later comparison with

Exhibit BR.8 — Processing Flowchart: Cash Receipts from Customers

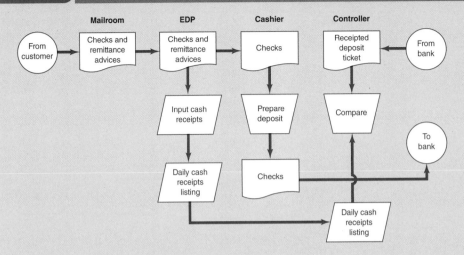

computer output. During the input of vouchers, the accounts payable software module of the general ledger package edits for the following characteristics: valid vendor number, valid stock number, price in agreement with vendor price, and agreement with discount and payment terms stored in the computer. During the processing run, the computer updates the accounts payable ledger, the manufacturing overhead detail, the operating expense detail, and the perpetual inventory records for purchased parts, materials, and supplies. The computer also performs a record count and compares output with input at the end of the processing run. Lastly, the due date of the invoice is stored in the computer for purposes of generating daily disbursement checks for invoices to be paid on that date.

Computer output consists of a purchases summary that is forwarded to accounts payable for review and comparison with the control tape. Accounts payable also files alphabetically the voucher, along with the attached purchase order, receiving report, and vendor's invoice in an unpaid vouchers file. All of these documents are prenumbered. Exhibit BR.9 is a flowchart depicting the documents and procedures just described.

Payments to Vendors   The daily computer check writing process produces a two-part check/remittance advice set. The remittance advice, indicating invoice number(s) being paid, gross amount, discount, and net amount of the check constitutes the lower part of the set. The check/remittance advice set is sent to accounts payable for comparison with the documents contained in the alphabetic vendors' invoice file. If the amounts appearing on the remittance advice agree with the vendor's invoice, an accounts payable clerk initials the voucher, attaches the purchase order, vendor's invoice, and receiving report, and forwards the documents to the treasurer. The treasurer examines the documentation received from accounts payable for agreement among the invoice, purchase order, and receiving report as to type, quantities, and prices. If everything is in agreement and the documents include initials evidencing proper approvals, the check is approved for signature. The checks are then signed by a check-signing machine and mailed directly to the vendor by the treasurer's office. The documents are effectively canceled to prevent reuse and are returned to accounts payable for filing in the paid vouchers file.

Responsibility for operating the check-signing machine is assigned to one individual. The machine is locked at all times when not being used to sign checks and the key is in the custody of the check signer. Exhibit BR.10 is a flowchart describing the payment process.

Payroll   Hourly production employees are paid weekly. Nonproduction employees are salaried and are paid biweekly. Salespersons also are paid biweekly, on a combination salary and commission compensation basis. The

Exhibit BR.9 — Purchases and Accounts Payable Processing Flowchart

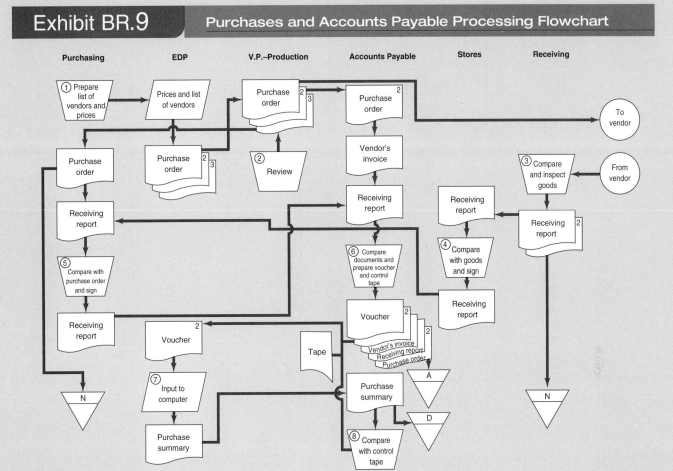

total time worked is accumulated for hourly employees by a time clock located at the factory entrance. The employee's name, Social Security number, and department number appear on the clock card. Factory supervisors approve the clock cards at the end of each week for employees working in their respective departments, before submitting them to payroll.

Each Monday morning the timekeepers summarize and assemble the clock cards by department number and forward the packets to payroll. The clock cards are examined in payroll for proper approval, a tape is run of total hours by department, and then the cards and tape are forwarded to CBIS for processing. A data entry clerk enters via a terminal the employee number, the department number, and the hours worked. Input editing consists of checking for valid employee number, valid department, and reasonableness of hours worked. The employee computer file contains the current pay rates, and the employee and department numbers.

Adjustments to the employee database for any rate changes, additions of new employees, and deletions of terminated employees are made only on the basis of authorization slips obtained from Laura Schroeder, director of human resources. Withholding information is also included in the database and is updated on the basis of authorization received from the human resources division.

The computer calculates gross pay, withholdings, and net pay. The employer's taxes (e.g., FICA, unemployment, and workers' compensation premium) also are calculated by the payroll module of the accounting software package. A record count is performed by the computer and compared with employee records updated at the end of the run. A register also accumulates hours by department for comparison with total hours at the end of the run.

Output consists of prenumbered payroll checks, a payroll summary, and a cost distribution summary. The control group is responsible for distributing the output. The checks, along with the summaries, are forwarded to the treasurer

Exhibit BR.10   Payment Processing Flowchart

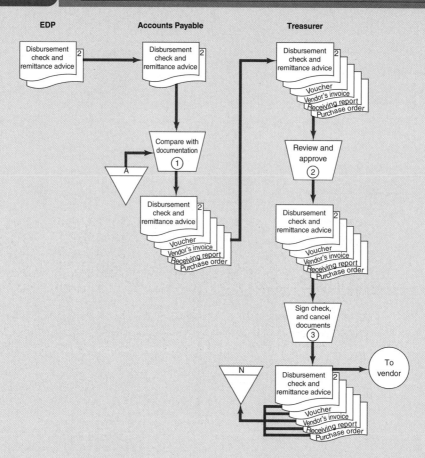

for signature and distribution. A check for the total amount of net pay is first drawn upon the general account for deposit in the payroll account; the treasurer signs this check and forwards it to the cashier for deposit.

After being compared with the payroll summary on a test basis, the individual payroll checks are signed with the aid of a check-signing machine and distributed by treasury personnel. Unclaimed checks are retained in safekeeping by the treasurer's office. The payroll summary and the control tape are forwarded to the payroll department as a basis for comparing total hours by department and for completing the various payroll tax returns and reports. The cost summary is sent to Oliver Perna, director of cost accounting, for review and filing. Exhibit BR.11 is a flowchart describing the production payroll process.

As part of the integrated software package, the payroll data serves as input for updating the goods-in-process inventory accounts. To complete the updating of goods-in-process and finished goods inventory, production reports and materials requisitions are entered into the system on a weekly basis. In addition to the perpetual inventory ledgers, the database includes a manufacturing overhead detail and an operating expense ledger. Current standard costs are also incorporated into the database. This enables the computer to calculate and print daily, weekly, and monthly variance reports for analysis by Perna and Malissa Rust, director of information systems and data processing.

The salaried payroll is prepared in a similar fashion. CBIS updates the employee database as written authorizations are received from human resources. As with production employees, the authorizations relate to changes in employee salaries, new employees, and terminated employees. Any overtime for salaried employees must be approved in writing by the respective department heads and routed to CBIS through payroll; the payroll department reviews the overtime for proper authorization and for reasonableness before transmitting the information to CBIS.

Exhibit BR.11 — Production Payroll Processing Flowchart

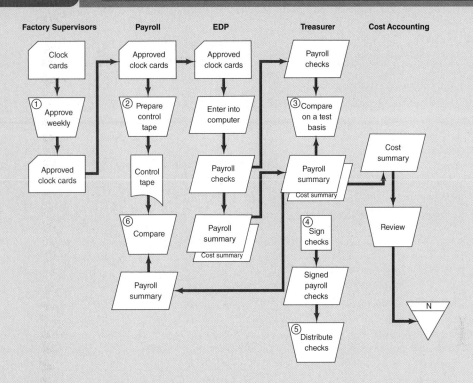

Other Accounting System Features Monthly financial statements consist of a balance sheet, an income statement, and a statement of cash flows and are generated automatically by the computer. Month-end adjustments for accruals (payroll, taxes, warranty, commissions, pension, profit sharing, interest, and fringe benefits) and apportionments (depreciation, insurance, bad debts, and amortization) are determined by John Mesarvey, Biltrite's chief accountant, and submitted to CBIS on standard recording forms. CBIS enters the data and invokes the command for printing the financial statements. In addition to the financial statements, the adjusting entries are printed and forwarded by the control group to Mesarvey for comparison with his copy of the adjustments as originally submitted to CBIS. Exhibit BR.12 contains the December 31, 2009, adjustments for inventories (perpetual records adjusted to year-end physical inventory) and unrecorded liabilities. Exhibits BR.13–BR.16 contains beginning and ending entries in the December 2009 transaction registers.

Sales invoices, purchase orders, disbursement checks, and payroll checks are prenumbered and generated by computer, as described previously. All manually prepared documents, such as vouchers and receiving reports, are also prenumbered. They are safeguarded and under the responsibility of designated individuals. Used documents are canceled to prevent reuse. Bills of lading are not prenumbered or otherwise accounted for. The internal auditing department regularly accounts for the numeric sequence of used documents. All voided documents are retained until the annual independent audit has been completed.

Within the CBIS department, duties are separated among the following functions:

1. Systems analysis and programming;
2. Data entry;
3. Data processing; and
4. Control.

Systems analysts and programmers provide extensive documentation of all programs and systems, as well as program changes. Complete instructions are provided for the computer operators who enter data as part of the various processing modules.

Exhibit BR.12   Biltrite Bicycles, Inc., Selected Client Adjusting Entries, December 31, 2009

UNRECORDED INVOICES

7210	Real Estate Taxes	$468,000	
7241	Utilities Expense	1,322,400	
7234	Health Insurance Premiums—Factory	240,980	
9435	Health Insurance Premiums—Administrative	47,560	
1320	Derailleurs Inventory	788,300	
1390	Repair Parts Inventory	177,650	
7220	Manufacturing Supplies	977,500	
9450	Accounting Fees	150,000	
9451	Legal Fees	212,000	
2020	Accounts Payable—Trade		$4,384,390

Client's entry to adjust for unrecorded invoices at 12/31/06

INVENTORY ADJUSTMENT

5100	Cost of Goods Sold—Grand Prix Touring Bike	$456,000	
5200	Cost of Goods Sold—Phoenix Touring Bike	244,300	
5300	Cost of Goods Sold—Pike's Peak Mountain Bike	455,690	
5400	Cost of Goods Sold—Himalaya Mountain Bike	88,700	
5500	Cost of Goods Sold—Waistliner Stationary Bike	22,300	
1310	Raw Materials Inventory	33,560	
1330	Purchased Parts Inventory	333,670	
1376	Finished Goods—Himalaya Mountain Bike	66,340	
1385	Indirect Materials	33,500	
1390	Repair Parts Inventory	61,140	
1320	Derailleurs Inventory		$222,600
1371	Finished Goods—Grand Prix Touring Bike		625,700
1372	Finished Goods—Phoenix Touring Bike		366,800
1373	Finished Goods—Pike's Peak Mountain Bike		557,800
1379	Finished Goods—Waistliner Stationary Bike		22,300

Client's entry to adjust perpetual inventory records to physical inventory taken as of 12/31/06. (Adjustments to materials and parts inventories were allocated proportionately to the five cost-of-goods-sold accounts.)

All program changes must be approved in writing by Rust, director of information systems and data processing, as well as by affected user departments. Current backup programs and data files are maintained in a location outside data processing. The internal auditors presumably have current copies of the programs, but they rarely test transaction processing on an unannounced basis.

All computer output is distributed by the control group to authorized recipients.

Any misstatements occurring during processing runs are logged into the console and are accessible only by the control group. The control group then monitors the reprocessing of the misstatements after satisfying themselves that the misstatements were unintentional. Data processing personnel have no access to the misstatement log and must contact the control group, inasmuch as processing cannot continue until any misstatement is corrected.

An accounts receivable aging analysis is produced monthly by the computer. This analysis is used by Lawrence White, credit manager, and John Mesarvey, chief accountant, for determining the monthly adjustment to the allowance for doubtful accounts; White also performs extensive follow-up of customers whose accounts are past due.

All bank accounts have been reconciled on a monthly basis, including the December 31, 2009, reconciliation.

Other controls following are other policies and procedures that relate to Biltrite's internal control over financial reporting:

1. Laura Schroeder, director of human resources, instituted a program for completely updating job descriptions after the data processing system was

Exhibit BR.13 Biltrite Bicycles, Inc., Voucher Register, December 31, 2009

Date	Voucher No.	Vendor	Accounts Payable Credit	Raw Materials Debit	Derailleurs Debit	Purchased Parts Debit	Indirect Materials Debit	Repair Parts Debit	Other Account Number	Other Debit
Dec. 1	12222	LaPrix Derailleurs, Ltd.	$ 415,000		$ 415,000					
Dec. 1	12223	Kryolock Steel Supply	212,480	$ 212,480						
Dec. 1	12224	Crown Manufacturing	122,169			$ 78,000	$ 44,169			
Dec. 30	12448	Crystal Manufacturing, Inc.	589,600		589,600					
Dec. 30	12449	Kryolock Steel Supply	266,800	266,800						
Dec. 31	12450	Crown Manufacturing	318,600			215,000	93,000	$ 10,600		
Dec. 31	12451	Palmer & Nile Advertising	112,800						8340	$ 112,800
Dec. 31	12452	MedCare HMO, Inc.	41,600						9435	41,600
Dec. 31	12453	Denise Vaughan & Co., CPAs	122,500						9450	122,500
Dec. 31	12454	Joelson & Wicks, Attorneys at Law	233,000						9451	233,000
Dec. 31	12455	Zebra Cleaning Supplies	7,865						9460	7,865
Dec. 31	12456	Crew Brothers Manufacturing	1,445,900			1,445,900				
Dec. 31	12457	LaPrix Derailleurs, Ltd.	962,200		962,200					
			$ 25,774,213	$ 3,822,900	$ 4,376,000	$ 12,430,975	$ 883,411	$ 776,500		$ 3,484,427

Exhibit BR.14   Biltrite Bicycles, Inc., Sales Summary, December 31, 2009

Date	Invoice No.	Customer	Accounts Receivable Debit	Sales—Credit				
				Grand Prix	Phoenix	Pike's Peak	Himalaya	Waistliner
Dec. 1	31662	Bikes and Parts	$ 67,000	$ 21,750	$ 12,600	$ 27,100	$ 5,550	$ 0
Dec. 1	31663	L Mart Department Stores	325,600	185,200	0	89,600	21,500	29,300
Dec. 30	33002	Texas Bike Emporium	266,800	55,300	42,800	92,300	44,600	31,800
Dec. 30	33003	Rear and Sawbuck	881,870	322,550	23,400	466,740	32,500	36,680
Dec. 30	33004	Southwest Spokes, Inc.	443,760	77,200	55,900	223,060	87,600	0
Dec. 31	33005	Great Lakes Fitness Centers	144,600	0	0	0	0	144,600
Dec. 31	33006	Big Mart Discount Centers	773,200	288,700	0	410,650	22,300	51,550
Dec. 31	33007	Leisure Time	338,700	44,860	62,375	122,400	88,500	20,565
Dec. 31	33008	Truly Bikes	122,900	15,600	31,600	35,500	40,200	0
Dec. 31	33009	L Mart Department Stores	1,322,800	497,310	88,760	714,580	22,150	0
			$ 21,656,900	$ 2,356,700	$ 9,234,500	$ 1,329,800	$ 7,988,600	$ 747,300

Exhibit BR.15 — Bittrite Bicycles, Inc., Cash Summary, December 31, 2009

Date	Received From	Cash Debit	Sales Discounts Debit	Accounts Receivable Credit	Account Number	Miscellaneous Debit	Miscellaneous Credit	Deposits
Dec. 1	Rear and Sawbuck	$ 662,461	$ 3,329	$ 665,790				
Dec. 1	Texas Bike Emporium	187,398	942	188,340				
Dec. 1	Florida Bike World	759,583	3,817	763,400				$ 1,609,442
Dec. 30	Major Acres Discount Centers	684,162	3,438	687,600				
Dec. 30	New England Bike Shops	88,177	443	88,620				
Dec. 30	Exercise World	43,979	221	44,200				
Dec. 30	Kaiser and Peabody Brokerage	24,223			4902		$ 24,223	
Dec. 30	West Coast Distributors	729,624	3,666	733,290				1,570,165
Dec. 31	L Mart Department Stores	287,207	1,443	288,650				
Dec. 31	Bikes and Parts	75,864	336	76,200				
Dec. 31	T. Lawton	3,000,000			1203		3,000,000	
Dec. 31	Dollar Discount Stores	335,017	1,683	336,700				
Dec. 31	Jimbob's Recreation & Leisure	86,230	0	86,230				
Dec. 31	Big Mart Discount Centers	887,640	4,460	892,100				4,641,958
		$ 20,006,675	$ 152,654	$ 15,988,652		$63,546	$ 4,234,223	$ 20,006,675

Exhibit BR.16　Biltrite Bicycles, Inc., Check Register, December 31, 2009

Date	Payee	Voucher Number	Bank Two Check Number	Dollar Bank Check Number	Accounts Payable Debit	Purchases Discounts Credit	Bank Two Credit	Dollar Bank Credit
Dec. 1	Kryolock Steel Supply	12188		44263	$ 388,700	$ 2,444		$ 386,256
Dec. 1	Crystal Manufacturing	12193		44264	654,980	3,228		651,752
Dec. 1	MedCare HMO, Inc.	12179	126880		46,400		$ 46,400	
Dec. 30	Crew Brothers Manufacturing	12378		44678	1,890,000	9,450		1,880,550
Dec. 30	Crown Manufacturing	12382		44679	422,300	2,112		420,188
Dec. 30	East Texas Power Company	12390	127329		455,380		455,380	
Dec. 31	Bell Southwest	12391	127330		75,688		75,688	
Dec. 31	LaPrix Derailleurs, Ltd.	12383		44680	1,340,000	6,700		1,333,300
Dec. 31	Zebra Cleaning Supplies	12344		44681	12,460	125		12,335
Dec. 31	Internal Revenue Service	12277		44682	3,600,000			3,600,000
Dec. 31	Jones Equipment	12198	127331		896,000	4,498	891,502	
Dec. 31	Jolly Roger Paints	12264		44683	326,000	1,630		324,370
Dec. 31	Rolla Deal Tires, Inc.	12234		44684	667,500	3,338		664,162
					$ 24,521,003	$ 87,665	$ 1,780,000	$ 22,653,338

converted to real time. This program is now finished, and training programs have been developed for data processing, as well as for new and existing employees in other functional areas.

2. Three years ago, human resources developed a code of conduct for Biltrite detailing expected standards of ethical behavior and distributed it to all existing employees. Since then, all new hires have been provided the code of conduct, along with other firm-related materials, at orientation. There are no formal employee training programs regarding the code but each monthly newsletter devotes one page to some aspect of the code. The six-page newsletter is mailed to the home address of each employee.

3. Inventories of materials, purchased parts, and finished goods are secured, and inventory managers have been assigned responsibility for their safekeeping. The internal audit staff, however, performs only infrequent test counts and comparisons with the perpetual records. Moreover, when they do plan for these counts, the auditors notify the inventory managers weeks in advance.

4. Directors and department heads are responsible for making hiring recommendations. The human resources division, however, screens and investigates all applicants for proper background and required education, training, and experience for the positions. In addition, final hiring and termination authority rests with the human resources director.

5. Groth has made efforts to minimize the chance of financial reporting improprieties at Biltrite. To date, no cases of improprieties have been documented. One approach has been to widely publicize among the accounting group the seriousness of and severe penalties (loss of job and prosecution to the full extent of the law) for any improprieties. Another approach taken by Groth to minimize improprieties was to create a process for anonymously communicating information upstream through someone other than a direct superior. The process promises that "whistleblowers" will be protected from possible reprisals. Finally, Groth has overseen the development of detailed job descriptions for each of the accounting and information systems managers. In addition to providing explicit responsibilities and authority for each manager, the job descriptions provide detailed guidance on the situations in which a manager may override established controls, and the process for documenting, explaining, and disclosing to superiors such overrides.

Requirements

1. Given the description of the company, the industry, the accounting information system, and the internal control over financial reporting, identify strengths and weaknesses in the internal control over financial reporting. Also, be sure to relate the strengths and weaknesses to management's assertions contained in the financial statements. Because of management's request for feedback on the design of its overall internal control over financial reporting, in addition to assessing control activities, your assessment of strengths and weaknesses should include controls that make up the Control Environment, Risk Assessment, Information and Communication, and Monitoring. If the case does not contain enough information for you to assess some aspect of internal control over financial reporting, develop a list of questions that you would want to ask management so that you could gain enough information to make those assessments. You may find it helpful to organize your identified strengths and weaknesses around the 20 principles outlined in COSO's 2006 guidance. The principles can be accessed at http://www.coso.org/documents/SB_Executive_Summary.pdf

2. Based on your review of the accounting information system and existing control procedures, in what specific transaction areas are you willing to assess control risk less than high?

7

A Framework for Audit Evidence

LEARNING OBJECTIVES

The overriding objective of this textbook is to build a foundation with which to analyze current professional issues and adapt audit approaches to business and economic complexities. Through studying this chapter, you will be able to:

1 Identify the overall framework by which audit evidence is identified, gathered, evaluated, and documented.

2 Describe financial statement assertions and how the assertions drive the choice of evidence to be gathered.

3 Describe factors that affect the appropriateness and sufficiency of audit evidence.

4 Explain how directional testing helps achieve both audit effectiveness and audit efficiency.

5 Identify basic audit procedures and how they relate to evaluating underlying financial statement assertions.

6 Explain the nature, design, and purposes of audit programs.

7 Describe the purposes and contents of good audit documentation.

8 Identify issues surrounding auditing management's estimates.

9 Apply the decision analysis and ethical decision-making frameworks to situations involving audit evidence.

CHAPTER OVERVIEW

Auditing is a process of objectively gathering and evaluating evidence pertaining to assertions. In terms of the audit opinion formulation process, this chapter focuses on Phases III and IV, with a focus on obtaining evidence about account assertions and determining the impact on the financial statement audit (audit evidence related to internal control was covered previously). As the auditor plans an audit, three basic evidence-related questions need to be answered: What audit evidence should be gathered? How much audit evidence is needed? And when should the evidence be gathered? See Exhibit 7.1. Audit programs are designed to show how these decisions result in specific audit activities to gather and evaluate audit evidence. The specific audit procedures used must address the risk of potential misstatement of financial statements or the likelihood that internal control over financial reporting contains material deficiencies. The auditor's process of gathering and assessing the evidence must be documented, clearly laying out the evidence gathered and the auditor's evaluation of that evidence, the auditor's judgments and reasoning process, and the conclusions reached. In this chapter, we focus on audit evidence related to financial statements and the underlying assertions contained in a company's financial statements, describing evidence-gathering tools typically used by auditors.

The Audit Opinion Formulation Process

| I. Assessing Client Acceptance and Retention Decisions CHAPTER 4 | II. Understanding the Client CHAPTERS 2, 4–6, and 9 | III. Obtaining Evidence about Controls and Determining the Impact on the Financial Statement Audit CHAPTERS 5–14 and 18 | IV. Obtaining Substantive Evidence about Account Assertions CHAPTERS 7–14 and 18 | V. Wrapping Up the Audit and Making Reporting Decisions CHAPTERS 15 and 16 |

| The Auditing Profession, Regulation, and Corporate Governance CHAPTERS 1 and 2 | Decision-Making, Professional Conduct, and Ethics CHAPTER 3 | Professional Liability CHAPTER 17 |

PROFESSIONAL JUDGMENT IN CONTEXT

PCAOB Inspection of Deloitte & Touche: Problems Uncovered Concerning Audit Evidence

On May 4, 2010, the PCAOB issued its public inspection report of Deloitte & Touche, LLP, describing its inspection of audits conducted during 2009. In the summary comments regarding the inspection, the PCAOB inspectors stated:

In some cases, the conclusion that the Firm failed to perform a procedure may be based on the absence of documentation and the absence of persuasive other evidence, even if the Firm claims to have performed the procedure. PCAOB Auditing Standard No. 3, Audit Documentation (AS No. 3) provides that, in various circumstances including PCAOB inspections, a firm that has not adequately documented that it performed a procedure, obtained evidence, or reached an appropriate conclusion must demonstrate with persuasive other evidence that it did so, and that oral assertions and explanations alone do not constitute persuasive other evidence (p. 3)

The inspection report went on to say:

In some cases, the deficiencies identified were of such significance that it appeared to the inspection team that the Firm, at the time it issued its audit report, had not obtained sufficient competent evidential matter to support its opinion on the issuer's financial statements or internal control over financial reporting ("ICFR").

Considering this, it is reasonable to ask the following questions: What is the nature of these deficiencies? Could this criticism happen to me? And why didn't Deloitte's reviewing partners detect the deficiencies? In order to understand how to answer these questions, the following excerpts describe the nature of deficiencies found on individual audits:

In this audit, the Firm failed in the following respects to obtain sufficient competent evidential matter to support its audit opinion—

- The Firm failed to perform adequate audit procedures to test the valuation of the issuer's inventory and investments in joint ventures (the primary assets of which were inventory). Specifically, the Firm:
  - Failed to re-evaluate, in light of a significant downturn in the issuer's industry and the general deterioration in economic conditions, whether the issuer's assumption, which it had also used in prior years, that certain inventory required no

review for impairment was still applicable in the year under audit;
  - Excluded from its impairment testing a significant portion of the inventory that may have been impaired, because the Firm selected inventory items for testing from those for which the issuer already had recorded impairment charges;
  - Failed to evaluate the reasonableness of certain of the significant assumptions that the issuer used in determining the fair value estimates of inventory and investments in joint ventures;
  - Failed to obtain support for certain of the significant assumptions that the Firm used when developing an independent estimate of the fair value of one category of inventory; and
  - Failed to test items in a significant category of inventory, which consisted of all items with book values per item below a Firm-specified amount that was over 70 percent of the Firm's planning materiality.

- The Firm failed to perform adequate audit procedures to evaluate the issuer's assertion that losses related to the issuer's guarantees of certain joint venture obligations were not probable, because the Firm's procedures were limited to inquiry of management.

As you read this chapter, consider the implications of the PCAOB's findings related to gathering evidence on the development of an audit program as you address the following questions:

- What is the auditor's responsibility to consider information outside of the client's records to develop sufficient and appropriate audit evidence?
- Why are the items identified above by the PCAOB considered "critical mistakes" in performing an audit?
- Why is "inquiry of management" not considered "sufficient information" by itself?
- Presumably Deloitte used a standardized audit program. How could a standardized audit program lead to some of the problems identified above, e.g., failing to test a category of inventory that had book value in excess of 70% of the firm's planning materiality, or limiting the testing of impairment to inventory that had already been assessed as impaired by management?

Exhibit 7.1 Basic Evidence Questions

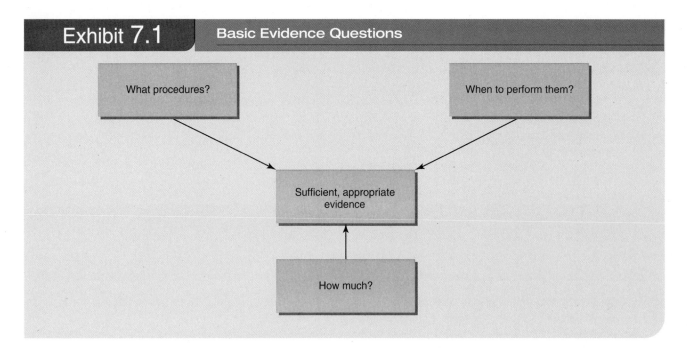

Overview of the Audit Evidence Framework

What Is Audit Evidence?

LO 1

Identify the overall framework by which audit evidence is identified, gathered, evaluated, and documented.

Audit evidence is all the information used by auditors in arriving at the conclusions on which the audit opinion is based. Auditors spend most of their time obtaining and evaluating evidence concerning the assertions contained in financial statements and reports on internal control. The evidence-gathering and evidence-evaluation process is the core of an audit. The standards are clear on the audit requirement. For example, the PCAOB's AS No. 15 (para. 3) states:

> The objective of the auditor is to plan and perform the audit to obtain appropriate audit evidence that is sufficient to support the opinion expressed in the auditor's report.

Management makes assertions about a number of different things: earnings and financial condition of the organization, the organization's internal controls and its operations, compliance with governmental regulations, and other measures of business performance, such as on-time arrival information for an airline. It appears that many organizations will soon be called upon to report on assertions related to the quality of their risk management processes, and then auditors may be called upon to assert to the quality of such reports. The scope of auditing is limited only by the demands for reliable information and an auditable information system.

The nature of audit evidence is broad—with a specific objective to reduce the auditor's level of risk that the financial statements may contain a material misstatement. It is instructive to examine the text of ISA 200 (A28) on the nature of audit evidence. It states:

> Audit evidence is necessary to support the auditor's opinion and report. It is cumulative in nature and is primarily obtained from audit procedures performed during the course of the audit. It may, however, also include information obtained from other sources such as previous audits … or a firm's quality control procedures for client acceptance and continuance. In addition to other sources inside and outside the entity, the entity's accounting records are an important

source of audit evidence. Also, information that may be used as audit evidence may have been prepared by an expert employed or engaged by the entity. Audit evidence comprises both information that supports and corroborates management's assertions, and any information that contradicts such assertions. In addition, in some cases, the absence of information (for example, management's refusal to provide a requested representation) is used by the auditor, and therefore, also constitutes audit evidence. Most of the auditor's work in forming the auditor's opinion consists of obtaining and evaluating audit evidence. (ISA 200, para. A28)

This brief statement makes a number of important points that should expand your thinking about the nature of audit evidence. Audit evidence:

- Includes both internally generated and external information,
- Includes information that both may support, or contradict, management's assertions,
- Is influenced by management actions, e.g., not producing requested documentation, or not producing such documentation in a timely manner,
- Can be developed using outside experts, and
- Can be obtained through other procedures the auditor normally performs (analysis of risk in deciding whether to accept or continue a client, previous year's audit data, and quality of a company's control system reflecting accuracy of internal processing).

Important Characteristics of Audit Evidence: Appropriateness and Sufficiency

ISA 300 describes the auditor's obligation regarding evidence: the auditor has to conclude whether sufficient, appropriate audit evidence has been obtained to justify the rendering of an audit opinion (ISA 330.26). However, determining what is "appropriate" and "sufficient" are not easy tasks! This chapter addresses these important concepts, and in the process provides the fundamental building blocks for understanding how to design and implement an audit program.

AUDITING *in Practice*

AICPA CLARITY PROJECT AND AUDIT EVIDENCE

There now exists a clarified SAS, *Audit Evidence,* resulting from the AICPA's Clarity Project. The redrafted SAS supersedes SAS 106 (AU Section 326), of the same name, and is effective for audits of financial statements for periods ending on or after December 15, 2012. The redrafted SAS 106 is condensed compared to the original, and has reorganized some of the content of the original into other related SASs. Also, other content of the original SAS 106 will be reorganized into other redrafted SASs as the AICPA Clarity Project progresses. The AICPA's Clarity Project is intended to help converge existing U.S. generally accepted auditing standards (GAAS) with International Standards on Auditing issued by the International Auditing and Assurance Standards Board.

Of interest, the redrafted SAS 106 formally introduces the term *accounting records* and distinguishes that term from *audit evidence*; accounting records are a subset of accounting evidence. The redrafted SAS 106 states that

"accounting records are the records of initial accounting entries and supporting records, for example:

- Checks;
- Records of electronic funds transfers;
- Invoices;
- Contracts;
- General ledgers;
- Subsidiary ledgers;
- Journal entries;
- Other adjustments to the financial statements not reflected in journal entries; and
- Records (e.g., worksheets or spreadsheets) supporting cost allocations, computations, reconciliations, and disclosures."

Exhibit 7.2	Interrelationship of Appropriateness and Sufficiency of Evidence

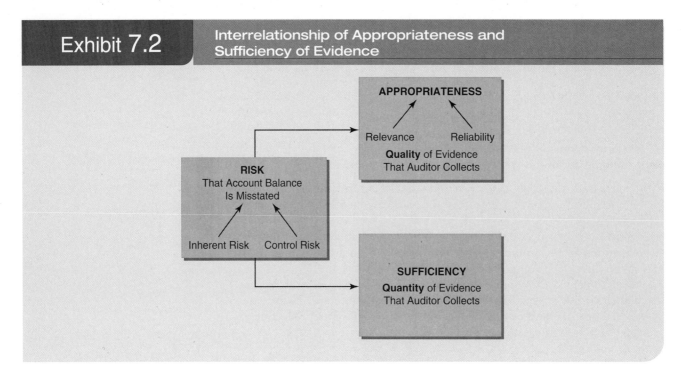

Appropriateness is defined as:

The measure of the quality of audit evidence; that is, its relevance and its reliability in providing support for the conclusions on which the auditor's opinion is based. (ISA 500.5)

Sufficiency is defined as:

The measure of the quantity of audit evidence. The quantity of the audit evidence needed is affected by the auditor's assessment of the risks of material misstatement and also by the quality of such audit evidence. (ISA 500.5)

The relationship between risk, appropriateness, and sufficiency of audit evidence is shown in Exhibit 7.2. When reviewing the exhibit, remember that the task of the auditor is to gather sufficient, appropriate evidence. Appropriateness is affected by the **relevance** of the evidence, i.e., it must provide insight on the validity of the assertion being tested, and by the **reliability** of the evidence, i.e., whether it is convincing. Sufficiency relates to the question of "how much" audit evidence must be collected. Both appropriateness and sufficiency are affected by the riskiness of the client (i.e., its inherent and control risk profile). In all cases, the auditor must collect appropriate evidence—it must always be of high quality. However, a high-risk client may make it more difficult to gather appropriate evidence because that client's financial accounting system may result in the production of evidence that lacks relevance and reliability. Therefore, the auditor will need to gather other, corroborating high-quality evidence from sources other than the client. In terms of sufficiency, higher-risk clients always require that the auditor collects a larger quantity of evidence.

Standards regarding audit evidence are similar across all three major standard-setting bodies. An overview of the various definitions is shown in the *Comparison of Worldwide Professional Guidance* on Audit Evidence.

Sources of Evidence

Exhibit 7.3 shows the various sources of potential audit evidence. Remember that the auditor needs to gather appropriate, sufficient evidence so that the risk

Comparison of Worldwide Professional Guidance

AUDIT EVIDENCE

AICPA Auditing Standards Board (ASB)

SAS 106 defines audit evidence as "all the information used by the auditor in arriving at the conclusions on which the audit opinion is based and includes the information contained in the accounting records underlying the financial statements and other information."

SAS 106 also discusses the importance of the concepts of sufficiency and appropriateness of evidence by noting that "The quantity of audit evidence needed is affected by the risk of misstatement (the greater the risk, the more audit evidence is likely to be required) and also by the quality of such audit evidence (the higher the quality, the less the audit evidence that may be required). Accordingly, the sufficiency and appropriateness of audit evidence are interrelated."

Public Company Accounting Oversight Board (PCAOB)

AS No. 15 defines audit evidence as "all the information, whether obtained from audit procedures or other sources, that is used by the auditor in arriving at the conclusions on which the auditor's opinion is based. Audit evidence consists of both information that supports and corroborates management's assertions regarding the financial statements or internal control over financial reporting and information that contradicts such assertions." Despite slight differences in the definition of audit evidence, the overall guidance is similar to SAS 106.

International Auditing and Assurance Standards Board (IAASB)

ISA 500 provides a general overview related to audit evidence and includes concepts similar to SAS 106. For example, ISA 500 notes that "The auditor shall design and perform audit procedures that are appropriate in the circumstances for the purpose of obtaining sufficient appropriate audit evidence."

SUMMARY

Obtaining quality evidence is critical to the success of an audit. The three boards have similar guidance regarding gathering and evaluating audit evidence.

---

of material misstatements is minimized. That assurance is gained through the gathering of evidence related to (a) knowledge of the client, its business, and its industry—gathered from previous audit work, client risk analysis, and client acceptance analysis; (b) outside information—gathered by the audit team itself using market data or through independent analyses by specialists; (c) accounting systems—gathered through direct tests of account balances and transactions, along with analytical analysis; and (d) the quality of internal control—gathered through an evaluation of the design of internal controls and the operation of those controls. While we will focus this chapter on developing audit tests for very specific assertions, it is important to recognize that the total evidence that the auditor must assess comes from a variety of sources and must be judgmentally analyzed by the auditor.

PRACTICAL POINT

The assessment of sufficient evidence is a judgment that incorporates evidence from a diverse set of sources. The auditor looks for consistency between the evidence sources, and when consistency is not present, the auditor must gather additional evidence until satisfied that there is little risk of a material misstatement.

Exhibit 7.3 Sources of Audit Evidence

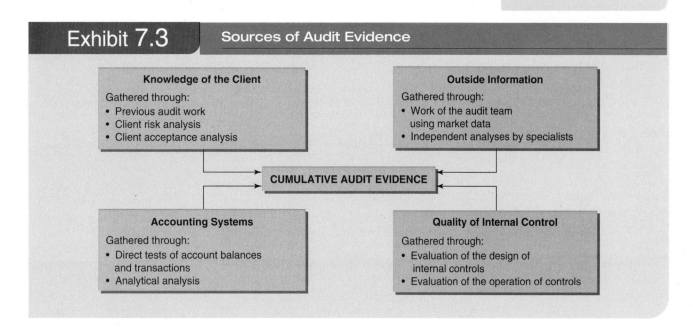

Assertion Model for Financial Statement Audits

LO 2

Describe financial statement assertions and how the assertions drive the source of evidence to be gathered.

In performing direct tests of account balances, the auditor is guided by the overall framework of assertions that are embodied in financial statements and individual accounts. The procedures to gather audit evidence to test the underlying assertions are referred to as an **audit program**.

The following primary assertions are embodied in the financial statements:

- Existence and occurrence
- Completeness
- Rights and obligations
- Valuation and allocation
- Presentation and disclosures

The specification of the assertions assists the auditor in planning audit tests. The following is a more explicit statement of the assertions. For account balances, management is asserting that:

- The assets, liabilities, and equity interests *exist* (***existence/occurrence***).
- All assets, liabilities, and equity interests that should have been recorded have been recorded (***completeness***).
- The entity holds or controls the *rights* to assets, and liabilities are the *obligations* of the entity (***rights*** and ***obligations***).
- Assets, liabilities, and equity interests are included in the financial statements at appropriate amounts and any resulting valuation or allocation adjustments are appropriately recorded (***valuation*** and ***allocation***).
- Assets, liabilities, and equity interests are appropriately classified on the financial statements, and are adequately described in the footnotes to the financial statements (***presentation*** and ***disclosure***).

The objective of gathering audit evidence is to determine the validity of these assertions as they apply to material financial statement accounts. To better understand how the auditor approaches the evidence-gathering process and tests these assertions, consider the inventory of Ford Motor Company, as described in Footnote 10 of its 2009 Annual Report.

Inventories at December 31, 2009 were as follows (in millions $):

Raw Materials, Work in Process, and Supplies	$2,783
Finished Products	3,465
Total Inventory Under First-in, First-out (FIFO)	6,248
Less: Last-in, First-out (LIFO) adjustment	(798)
Total Inventory	$5,450

Inventories are stated at lower of cost or market. About one-fourth of inventories were determined under the LIFO method. Further, Ford indicates that LIFO inventory quantities were liquidated, which decreased their cost of sales by $33 million.

The account balance represents the culmination of inventory transactions during the year. In addition to reflecting the various components of inventory, that is, from raw materials to finished products (i.e., cars and trucks), the inventory account also reflects risks related to holding the inventory until sale. Therefore, it is important to understand that the valuation of inventory is not based just on historical cost, but also must reflect market conditions.

There are other risks associated with the inventory account. For example, Ford management notes that it has several long-term supply arrangements that commit it to purchase minimum or fixed quantities of certain parts or materials or to pay a minimum amount to the seller ("take-or-pay" contracts). At the same time, Ford

PRACTICAL POINT

In 2006, Ford's inventory was about $12 billion, indicating an inventory reduction of about $6 billion over three years. During that period of time, the company focused considerable effort in restructuring, streamlining operations, and evaluating the potential impairment of inventory associated with changes in the nature of its operations and the cars it builds. Auditors need to understand management's strategies and execution of those strategies in performing an evaluation of inventory.

AUDITING *in Practice*

INDUSTRY RISKS AND AUDIT EVIDENCE

Excess capacity is a problem for the automotive industry. Excess capacity means that automotive producers such as Ford and Toyota have invested money in physical production capability (e.g., manufacturing plants and equipment) that exceeds customer demand. According to CSM Worldwide (an automotive research firm), the industry-wide global production capacity for automotive companies is about 86 million units, which exceeds actual global production by about 29 million units. In addition, it is expected that global excess capacity conditions will remain at about 21 million units per year from 2010 to 2014. This means that the currently unstable conditions in this industry can be expected to remain for a considerable time. The important point from an auditing perspective is that increased risk of the client represents increased risk for the audit firm, and that translates to an increased need to collect appropriate, sufficient audit evidence.

has committed to (a) producing fewer vehicles, and (b) producing smaller vehicles while still generating adequate profits. With these risks in mind, the auditor must develop an audit approach to gather appropriate, sufficient evidence to determine that inventory exists, is owned by the company, is properly valued, is recorded during the correct period, and is properly disclosed and presented in the financial statements and footnotes. When developing an audit approach, it is important to recognize that Ford is internationally diverse and carries inventory—often with different car platforms—at locations all around the world. Further, we know that some vehicles may have individual value problems, such as Ford's competitor, Toyota, experienced with their "sticking gas pedal" during 2009 and 2010. These are all risk factors that need to be addressed in an audit program.

The Economics of Gathering Appropriate, Sufficient Evidence

When considering the best approach to gathering audit evidence, the auditor considers factors affecting the relevance and reliability of the financial data. Important factors affecting relevance and reliability include management integrity, client economic risk, quality of the client's information system and internal controls, and current market conditions and competitor actions. Management's integrity and competence affect both the design and operation of the client's information system. Differences in these types of factors across clients affect whether various pieces of evidence are appropriate to gather in each client's unique circumstances. In addition, the client's business, by its nature, carries distinct risks that require judgments that may affect valuation. For example, competitors may be introducing new products that will affect the marketability of inventory on hand. The auditor cannot prepare an audit program to test financial statement assertions without simultaneously considering the risk factors that could cause the account balances to be incorrect.

Exhibit 7.4 presents four important steps in the audit evidence collection process that will help ensure that appropriate, sufficient evidence is collected:

1. Understand the client and its industry.
2. Assess the risk of material misstatement by assertion for each significant component of the client's financial statements.
3. Determine the most persuasive evidence to address assertions and the most economical approach to gather the evidence.
4. Assess adequacy of evidence and issue a report.

LO 3

Describe the factors that affect the appropriateness and sufficiency of audit evidence.

PRACTICAL POINT

The PCAOB's AS No. 15 states that if audit evidence obtained from one source is inconsistent with evidence obtained from another source the auditor should perform audit procedures to resolve the inconsistency and determine the effect on other aspects of the audit.

Exhibit 7.4	Overall Audit Evidence Collection Approach

Step	Concerns	Action
1. Understand client and industry.	• Industry characteristics • Management integrity and pressures that could influence reliability of the data • Nature and quality of information system • Economic influences	• Review database on client and industry. • Assess management integrity. • Identify red flags. • Perform preliminary analytical procedures.
2. Assess risk of material misstatement by assertion for each significant component of the client's financial statements.	• Inherent risk • Control risk • Computer systems	• Identify factors affecting reliability of client data. • Obtain an understanding of and, when appropriate, test internal controls.
3. Test details of account balances and transactions.	• How much evidence to collect? • Which procedures to perform? • When to perform those procedures?	• Perform analytical procedures, and/or direct tests of account balances and transactions to corroborate financial data or other information about organizational performance.
4. Assess adequacy of evidence documented and issue a report.	• Is there a need to make adjustments to the financial statements? • Are there any system deficiencies?	• Perform final analytical procedures and additional procedures when necessary. • Decide on the type of report the evidence supports.

Each of the first three steps is designed to develop and execute an appropriate and efficient gathering and assessment of audit evidence to conclude on the overall reliability of the company's financial statements. When considering the right set of audit evidence, there are two additional important points that need to be understood:

1. Client reports can be made at periodic intervals, such as quarterly or yearly for financial statements, or the reports can occur almost continuously as companies implement XBRL for public reporting.

AUDITING *in Practice*

ECONOMIC INCENTIVES VS. RISK MANAGEMENT FOR AUDIT FIRMS

When examining the development of the audit programs, keep in mind that auditing firms necessarily have two major objectives: (a) to make money, and (b) to manage audit risk effectively in order sustain long-term operations. To make money, audit firms have to:

• Perform audits efficiently, i.e., not complete unnecessary work, use an appropriate balance of more-experienced and less-inexperienced personnel, and use audit procedures that maximize effectiveness while minimizing cost where possible.

• Maintain existing client relationships and expand the number of new clients where possible. To do so, audit firms need to keep their fees reasonable (by being cost-effective) and provide high quality services that clients value.

• Expand work beyond audits. This includes some services that are allowable for audit clients, as well as expanding consulting and other services to non-audit clients.

• Perform integrated audits for public companies to take advantage of the work performed in assessing and opining on the quality of a company's internal control over financial reporting.

But, at the same time, auditing firms have to manage risk effectively. They do so by:

• Carefully assessing engagement risk and avoiding high-risk clients.

• Assuring that each audit team member is aware of the client's risks, including fraud risk.

• Providing adequate review, which in turn is dependent on adequate documentation of all audit work performed.

There is always tension between these two objectives. Most audit firms operate in a fashion that clearly ensures that the second objective (managing audit risk) is given priority. If this were not the case, audit firms would encounter litigation that would put them out of business in the long-term. However, it is important to remember that individual audit partners are evaluated, in part, on the number and types of clients that they retain and how profitable those clients are for the firm as a whole. So audit firms face a tricky balance of managing risk and also maintaining profitability and appropriate performance goals for employees.

2. The audit process is both simultaneous and sequential. Auditors are continually updating information relating to client risk, current market conditions, and current interactions with management. At the same time, the audit programs are sequential starting with risk, followed by an evaluation of controls to mitigate those risks, and the gathering of objective evidence regarding the correctness of account balances.

Both the U.S. and international auditing standards encourage auditors to focus on account balances that contain the greatest likelihood of material misstatement. With that in consideration, Exhibit 7.5 illustrates that there are cost implications associated with differences in evidence appropriateness and sufficiency in clients with varying risk profiles. For example, Panel A depicts a client in which there is little risk of misstatement, internal controls are effective, and the client has relatively non-complex transactions. Here, the available audit evidence is relevant and reliable, and the quality of that evidence is high. In such a case, the integrated audit would require only a minimal number of direct tests of transactions and account balances, and the audit would therefore be less costly to conduct. Conversely, Panel B depicts a client in which there is high risk of misstatement and internal controls are not effective. Here, the auditor is faced with a situation in which available audit evidence from the client is of lower quality. Therefore, the auditor will have to find other evidence that is high quality to corroborate evidence obtained from within the client's systems. Ultimately, all these factors result in the need for the auditor to perform more direct tests of transactions and account balances, and those tests are costly.

This example should illustrate the importance of client acceptance and retention procedures that yield good, low-risk clients. Such clients are less costly to audit, and they result in fewer problems for audit firms in the long run. Naturally, all audit firms find such clients to be desirable; therefore, competition for those clients is fierce and audit fees are thereby negotiated downward, squeezing profits for the audit firm. In the end, audit firms need to find a good "mix" of clients in a range of acceptable levels of risk, cost, and profitability.

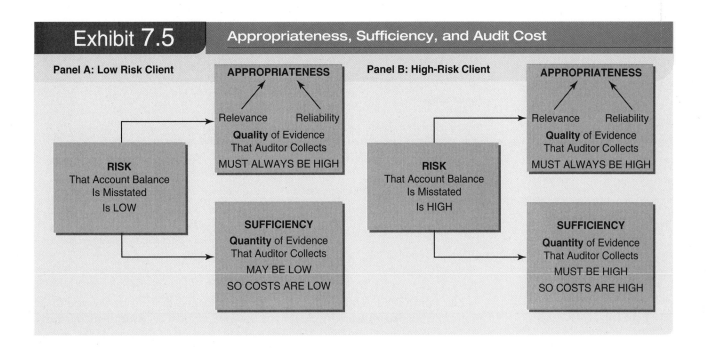

Exhibit 7.5   Appropriateness, Sufficiency, and Audit Cost

Panel A: Low Risk Client

APPROPRIATENESS
Relevance   Reliability
Quality of Evidence That Auditor Collects
MUST ALWAYS BE HIGH

RISK That Account Balance Is Misstated Is LOW

SUFFICIENCY
Quantity of Evidence That Auditor Collects
MAY BE LOW
SO COSTS ARE LOW

Panel B: High-Risk Client

APPROPRIATENESS
Relevance   Reliability
Quality of Evidence That Auditor Collects
MUST ALWAYS BE HIGH

RISK That Account Balance Is Misstated Is HIGH

SUFFICIENCY
Quantity of Evidence That Auditor Collects
MUST BE HIGH
SO COSTS ARE HIGH

Appropriateness: Relevance of Audit Evidence

Relevance deals with the logical connection with, or bearing on, the purpose of the audit procedure as related to the underlying assertion being tested. Some evidence is directly relevant to the assertion and is often referred to as **direct evidence**. As an example, communicating with a large sample of customers provides direct evidence on the existence of an accounts receivable balance. The only inference the auditor has to make is that (a) customers know their account balance, and (b) the sample is representative of the population as a whole. **Indirect evidence**, on the other hand, often requires more inferences and the logic for the conclusion relies on more complex inferences. For example, the auditor might perform analytical procedures on an account balance, e.g. analyzing expenses and comparing the expense account with previous years. Assuming the auditor does not find unexpected results, the auditor has to infer that (a) the analytical procedures capture important underlying relationships, (b) controls are such that management cannot manipulate the account balance to make the amounts look smooth, and (c) that the result is consistent with other information known about the client or the client's industry. In such a case, the indirect evidence is considered appropriate because it is both relevant and reliable.

It is important that the auditor guard against unwarranted inferences from the gathering of audit evidence. The following are examples of inferences that auditors may make because they use evidence that is not entirely relevant:

- The auditor believes that inventory is properly valued and only tests the existence of inventory. However, proving the existence of inventory does not provide relevant evidence that the inventory is properly valued.
- The auditor believes that accounts payable is properly valued. However, the evidence is based on a sample taken from the largest existing accounts payable balances. But, such evidence may be misleading because the larger, outstanding accounts payable balances do not provide the most appropriate evidence because the completeness assertion involves *under*statements, not *over*statements.

Appropriateness: Reliability of Audit Evidence

The reliability of audit evidence is judged by its ability to provide convincing evidence related to the audit objective being evaluated. The IAASB (ISA 500, para. A31) has established the following presumptions about the reliability of audit evidence:

More Reliable	Less Reliable
Directly obtained evidence (e.g., observation of a control)	Indirectly obtained evidence (e.g., an inquiry about the working of a control)
Evidence derived from a well-controlled information system	Evidence derived from a poorly controlled system or easily overridden information system
Evidence from independent outside sources	Evidence from within the client's organization
Evidence that exists in documentary form	Verbal evidence not supported by documentation
Original documents	Photocopies or facsimiles, or digitized data (would depend on quality of controls over their preparation and maintenance)

This guidance is common sense. Evidence obtained directly by the auditor is preferable to that obtained indirectly. Evidence from well-controlled information systems is preferable to that from poorly controlled systems. Independent third-party evidence obtained from knowledgeable individuals with adequate time and motivation to respond to audit inquiries is preferable to internally generated information (that could be fabricated) from the client. Evidence supported by original documents is preferable to photocopied documents. Finally, observable evidence is generally better than oral evidence (unless the auditor can determine the oral evidence is not in some way biased).

Some types of evidence better address specific assertions. As such, the auditor is influenced by both relevance and reliability to the assertion being tested. For example, if the auditor wishes to test warranty liabilities, it is likely that most of the information resides internally—some in the client's accounting system and some in operational data. Such data becomes persuasive only when the underlying internal control system is strong and the information contains relevant documentation that cannot be easily manipulated by management.

Internal Documentation

Internal documentation ranges from legal agreements (leases, sales contracts, and royalty arrangements) to business documents (purchase orders and receiving reports) to accounting documents (depreciation schedules and standard cost system records) to planning and control documents (original source documents such as time cards, inventory scrap reports, and market research surveys). Exhibit 7.6 provides examples of internal documents. The reliability of internal documentation varies according to the following:

- Effectiveness of internal controls
- Risk and management motivation to misstate individual accounts (fraud potential)
- Formality of the documentation, such as acknowledgment of its validity by parties outside the organization or independent of the accounting function
- Independence of those preparing the documentation from those recording the transactions

PRACTICAL POINT

As companies are generally computer-dependent and computer-integrated, paper-based documentary evidence decreases. Thus, auditors need to understand the attributes that underlie the evidence in paper form to determine if there are sufficient controls in the computer system to assure that the computerized information has the same attributes.

Exhibit 7.6	Examples of Internal Documents
Legal Documents	Labor and fringe benefit agreements
	Sales contracts
	Lease agreements
	Royalty agreements
	Maintenance contracts
Business Documents	Sales invoices
	Purchase orders
	Canceled checks
	Payment vouchers
	EDI agreements
Accounting Documents	Estimated warranty liability schedules
	Depreciation and amortization schedules
	Standard cost computations and schedules
	Management exception reports
Other Planning and Control Documents	Employee time cards
	Shipping and receiving reports
	Inventory movement documents such as scrap reports and transfer receipts
	Market research surveys
	Pending litigation reports
	Variance reports

Note: Many of the planning and control documents have analyses attached. Market research survey data usually appear as part of the marketing department's opinion of new product potential; variance reports are accompanied by explanations of the causes of the variances and recommendations with respect to them. These analyses are generally considered to be testimonial rather than documentary evidence.

Documentation may be paper-based or electronic. The quality of electronic evidence depends on the controls built into the information system; in particular, it depends on whether access to data and the documents are appropriately restricted. An example of internal documentation is a personnel record containing data about an employee's pay rates, benefit packages, and wages paid. The document is prepared by the payroll department and reviewed by supervisory employees. When developed under strong systems of internal control, such documentation assists the auditor in determining that payroll expense and payroll-related accruals are proper.

External Documentation

External documentation is generally considered to be highly reliable, but the reliability depends on whether (a) the documentation was prepared by a knowledgeable outside party and (b) is received directly by the auditor. Most external documentation, however, is directed to the client. For example, a customer order that specifies prices and quantities is received by the client, not the auditor. Therefore, in high-risk situations the auditor should confirm the contents of the document with the pertinent outside party.

External documentation can vary in content, ranging from business documents normally found in the client's possession (vendor invoices and monthly statements), to confirmations received directly from the client's legal counsel, banker, or customer, to trade and credit information. External documentation varies in reliability and is influenced by its formality, its source, and its independence. See Exhibit 7.7 for examples of external documentation.

One standard business document normally in the client's possession is a vendor invoice (see Exhibit 7.8). A vendor's invoice shows the purchase price (cost) of items in the client's inventory, dates of invoice and shipment, payment and ownership terms, shipping address (inventory location), purchase order reference, purchasing agent (evidence of authorization), and amount due (liability as well as asset valuation evidence). Because a vendor invoice is formal, it is generally not altered by clients, even though it is in the client's possession. It is therefore considered reliable except for situations in which the auditor questions management's integrity and has assessed the client and account balance being tested as high risk.

Paper vs. Electronic Documentation   Recognize, however, that as businesses change, the invoice may only exist in electronic fashion. Thus, the auditor must gain assurance that the data shown in Exhibit 7.8 is present in electronic fashion, and, more importantly, the information is safeguarded in the client's computer system and therefore cannot be easily manipulated.

Exhibit 7.7	Examples of External Documents
Business Documents	Vendor invoices and monthly statements
	Customer orders
	Sales or purchase contracts
	Loan agreements
	Other contracts
Third-Party Documents	Confirmation letters from legal counsel
	Confirmation statements from banks
	Confirmation replies from customers
	Vendor statements requested by auditors
General Business Information	Industry trade statistics
	Credit rating reports
	Data from computer service bureaus

Exhibit 7.8 Vendor Invoice

Nature Sporting Goods Manufacturing Company
200 Pine Way
Kirkville, WI 53800
Phone (607) 255-3311 Fax (607) 256-1109

Sold To:	**Ship To:**	**Invoice #** 44779
Bain's Sporting Goods	Bain's Sporting Goods	**Invoice Date** 8/30/11
123 Lock Avenue	123 Lock Avenue	**PO #** 32348
Cedar Rapids, Iowa 52404	Cedar Rapids, Iowa 52404	

Shipped Via
Roadway 8/30/11

Terms: Account # 127000
Net 30

Ordered	Quantity Shipped	Back Ordered	Item Number & Description	Unit Price	U/M	Extension
125	125	0	T-332B 2-person tents	34.99	Each	4,373.75
50	50	0	T-500Y Umbrella tents	55.75	Each	2,787.50

Freight Collect	**Comments:**	**Sale**	7,361.25
		Tax	
	Finance charge of 1½% per month on overdue invoices.	**Total**	7,361.25

As more organizations rely on electronic interaction, it is important that the audit procedures adapt to the use and analysis of electronic data.

Sufficiency

The amount of evidence must of sufficient quantity to convince the audit team of the correctness or incorrectness of an account balance. Similarly, the evidence must stand on its own such that another unbiased professional would reach the same conclusion. However, how much evidence is enough? This is partly a matter of experienced audit judgment and, as the example in Exhibit 7.5 reveals, it is also affected by client risk characteristics. Importantly, audit evidence is integrated from a number of sources. Documentation of that evidence from multiple sources, and the demonstrated testing of account balances, remain paramount and are the first things to be questioned when an audit fails.

In the James Fazio case from the *Auditing in Practice* feature below, we see the personal ramifications to the auditor of knowingly and recklessly not collecting sufficient evidence. In Fazio's case, he was aware of the existence of a variety of factors that called into question the adequacy of Ligand's reserves for returns (e.g., lack of actual return history, limited visibility into distribution channels, and significant increases in or excess levels of inventory), but he did not adequately analyze whether those factors impaired Ligand's ability to make reasonable estimates of returns. Consequently, the PCAOB concluded that Fazio did

PRACTICAL POINT

Most of us have made electronic purchases, whether from places such as Amazon.com, or via prepaid cards, such as from Starbucks. We often take the controls built into the systems for granted, but auditors must evaluate and test such controls.

AUDITING *in Practice*

WHEN AN AUDITOR FAILS TO COLLECT SUFFICIENT EVIDENCE

James L. Fazio, age 46, was a CPA and partner in the San Diego office of Deloitte LLP. He was the partner-in-charge of the audit of Ligand Pharmaceuticals. At the time of the 2003 Ligand audit, Deloitte's audit policies required that each client's engagement risk be assessed annually as normal, greater than normal, or much greater than normal. In Ligand's case, the engagement team assessed engagement risk as "greater than normal" because of concerns regarding product sales and sales returns. Specifically, the engagement team documented concern in the audit workpapers that Ligand's estimates of sales returns and reserves were not sufficient to cover actual returns. Given the heightened risk, the written audit plan called for the engagement team to perform procedures to address the issue and to increase their professional skepticism regarding the returns issues.

However, the PCAOB found that James Fazio failed to exercise due professional care, exercise professional skepticism, obtain sufficient competent evidential matter to afford a reasonable basis for an opinion regarding the financial statements, evaluate subsequent events, and supervise assistants. Specifically, he failed to (1) adequately assess whether Ligand had gathered sufficient evidence to properly estimate future returns, (2) adequately evaluate the reasonableness of Ligand's estimates of returns, and (3) identify and address issues concerning Ligand's exclusion of certain returns from its estimates of returns.

The PCAOB concluded that Fazio's conduct met conditions warranting sanctions because of "intentional or knowing conduct, including reckless conduct." As a result of this conclusion, the PCAOB ordered that Fazio not be allowed to associate with a registered public accounting firm, but he may file a petition for PCAOB consent to have such an association after two years.

Source: This case is based on facts disclosed in PCAOB Release No. 105-2007-006, December 10, 2007.

PRACTICAL POINT

While all of the sources of audit evidence are important, the auditor can never skimp on the direct testing of account balances. During the fall of 2009, Koss Corporation found that its vice president of finance had defrauded the company of approximately $31 million over a five-year period. Grant Thornton LLP was the company's auditor, and the firm issued unqualified audit opinions for the entire period. When the Koss fraud was found, the press' first question was "Why didn't their testing find the fraud?"

not have a sufficient basis to support the conclusion that Ligand's revenue recognition was appropriate.

Ultimately, Ligand restated its financial statements for 2003 and other periods because its revenue recognition did not follow the applicable financial reporting framework. In its restatement, Ligand recognized about $59 million less in revenues (a 52% decrease from what was originally reported), and revealed a net loss that was more than 2.5 times the net loss originally reported. Thus, investors were misled by Ligand's misstated financial statements and by Fazio's failure to conduct sufficient audit tests in a manner that would have led to more accurate financial statements. The punishment that Fazio received highlights an evidence-sufficiency dilemma for auditors: There are no "bright-line" requirements to tell auditors that they have collected enough evidence, yet if it is subsequently determined that they have not done so, then there can exist very severe ramifications for what is subsequently deemed improper professional judgment.

Nature of Audit Testing

Direct tests of account balances and transactions are designed by determining the most efficient manner to substantiate the assertions embodied in the account or transactions. There are many alternatives open to the auditor in planning audit tests. The following table summarizes some of those alternatives and provides an example of each type of test.

PRACTICAL POINT

Evidence is persuasive only when other trained professionals in the field would reach a similar conclusion based only on the evidence examined.

Types of Audit Tests	Example	Purpose
Tests of Effectiveness of Internal Control	a. Test a sample of cash disbursements for evidence that vendor invoices are matched with receiving reports and purchase orders before authorizing payment.	a. Determine whether the controls are effective over cash disbursements. Use the information performing an integrated audit of controls and account balances.

Types of Audit Tests	Example	Purpose
	b. Process test transactions through the client's computer system to test the operation of computer controls.	b. Determine whether controls in the application program work.
Dual-Purpose Tests of Controls and Account Balances	Same as tests of controls plus the auditor matches the information on the vendor's invoice with the receiving report and purchase order and verifies that the appropriate account was charged for the purchase (e.g., inventory, expense, or equipment).	Determine whether the controls are effective to help plan the nature, timing, and extent of other audit tests, and test the accuracy of recording the related transactions.
Substantive Analytical Tests	a. Calculate the number of day's sales in accounts receivable and compare with prior years and industry information.	a. Help determine whether some of the receivables are not collectible.
	b. Estimate depreciation expense using the average of the beginning and ending balances of a class of equipment.	b. Establish the reasonableness of depreciation expense. Further testing may not be needed.
Direct Tests of Account Balances	Confirm customer balances with a sample of customers.	To test the existence and dollar accuracy of account balances as stated at historical cost.
Direct Tests of Transactions	Select a sample of recorded sales and vouch them back to evidence that the sale actually took place (evidence of shipment and customer orders).	To test the existence of sales transactions.

When directly testing an account balance or related transactions, the auditor considers two basic types of **evidence**:

1. The *underlying accounting records*, including evidence of internal controls over financial reporting, as well as supporting records such as checks, invoices, contracts; the general and subsidiary ledgers; journal entries; and worksheets supporting cost allocations, computations, reconciliations, and disclosures.
2. *Corroborating information* that validates the underlying accounting records, such as minutes of meetings, confirmations from independent parties, industry data, inquiry, observation, physical examination, and inspection of documents.

Auditors have traditionally focused audit procedures on the direct tests of asset and liability account balances, as opposed to examining transactions during the year, because:

- There are usually *fewer items* in the ending balance than are contained in the transactions that have taken place during the year. Most companies, for example, have fewer items in ending inventory than the number of purchase and sales transactions recorded during the year.
- *Reliable evidence*, which can be gathered efficiently, usually exists for items making up an ending balance more so than for transactions. Ending inventory can be physically observed, but goods sold are gone and it is more difficult to verify both the quantity and cost of those items.
- It is easier to *focus on changes in assets or liabilities, rather than testing all the details that affected the accounts*. For many long-term assets and liabilities, such as fixed assets or bonds payable, audit attention is often directed toward the changes in the account balances during the year if the opening balances were audited the previous year. The auditor can then investigate the changes.

Audit Procedures
A Framework for Audit Procedures

Audit procedures vary according to the risks associated with the client and the methods used to record transactions. The following framework identifies audit procedures relevant to five different activities conducted during the audit:

1. **Understand Client and Industry: Preliminary Planning and Risk Analysis**

   a. Review prior-year audit work.

   b. Update client acceptance or client continuation process—which might include many of the procedures identified below.

   c. Review publicly available data about the organization.

   d. Perform analytical procedures to determine items that seem inconsistent with the overall direction of the industry and prior direction of the company.

   e. Inquire of management and employees regarding changes in strategy, operations, or competition.

   f. Perform internal control walkthroughs.

2. **Assess Risk of Material Misstatement: Understand and Test Internal Controls and System Processing**

   a. Inquire of management and supervisory personnel.

   b. Review system documentation and perform a walkthrough of processes.

   c. Observe system in operation. For computer applications, consider tracing transactions through the system.

   d. Document process flow and control points.

   e. Determine the effectiveness of procedures that the client has developed to monitor the continued effectiveness of internal controls over financial reporting.

   f. Select transactions and trace through processing to determine if controls are working properly.

3. **Gather Evidence Related to Account Balances and Transactions**

   a. Review authoritative documents and client records:

      (1) Vendor invoices and monthly statements

      (2) Receiving and shipping records

      (3) Legal documents and others

   b. Make inquiries to independently verify data, or to determine management intent and/or plans:

      (1) Inquire of management and other client personnel

      (2) Inquire of outside parties

   c. Prepare auditor-generated evidence of tests performed or evidence gathered:

      (1) Direct observation

      (2) Perform recomputations, including recalculations and mathematical tests

      (3) Reprocess transactions from origin to final records

      (4) Vouch transactions from final records back to origin

      (5) Physically examine assets for existence, working condition, marketability, etc.

      (6) Perform analytical procedures, where appropriate, to determine consistency of account balances with expectations.

      (7) Auditor analysis through reasoning and examining integrated portions of the evidence.

   d. Compare internal evidence with specific external, economic data that also pertains to the underlying assertions being tested.

4. Determine Need to Engage Outside Specialists

a. Consider valuation specialists for areas such as evaluating potential impairment of goodwill, or the costs to be allocated to various assets/liabilities related to an acquisition.

b. Consider use of outside specialists in other areas such as pension estimates, valuation of stock options, and valuation of complex financial instruments.

5. Assess the Consistency of Evidence Gathered and Document Conclusions

a. Consider internal consistency of evidence gathered.

b. Consider the consistency of internal evidence generated with external evidence gathered that reflects economic conditions and client operations.

c. Expand evidence-gathering procedures for areas where results are inconsistent, or where results raise questions on correctness of account balances.

d. Document conclusions based on the evidence gathered such that someone knowledgeable in auditing can follow the reasoning process.

Each of these procedures has strengths and weaknesses that should be considered in determining the optimal approach for a client. The auditor looks at the relative weight and internal consistency of evidence in formulating an audit opinion. AS No. 15 issued by the PCAOB in 2010 assists the auditor by stating:

> If audit evidence obtained from one source is inconsistent with that obtained from another, or if the auditor has doubts about the reliability of information to be used as audit evidence, the auditor should perform the audit procedures necessary to resolve the matter and should determine the effect, if any, on other aspects of the audit. (para. 29)

The key point made in AS No. 15 is that the auditor needs to consider all sources of information, as well as the internal consistency of the information, in formulating a judgment as to whether (a) sufficient evidence has been obtained, and (b) the evidence clearly leads to a conclusion about the fairness of the financial statement presentation.

Directional Testing

Directional testing involves testing balances primarily for either over- or understatement (but not both) and creates audit efficiency by taking advantage of the double-entry bookkeeping system. Directional testing leads to audit efficiency because:

- Misstatements of some accounts are more likely to occur in one direction than the other. For example, management may be more motivated to overstate sales and assets than to understate them. Alternatively, a company is more likely to understate liabilities.
- Directional testing of an account balance provides evidence on a complementary set of accounts. For example, testing accounts receivable for overstatement provides evidence on the possible overstatement of sales.
- Some assertions are directional by nature. Existence assertions address overstatement, whereas completeness assertions address understatement.

Assets are most often tested for overstatement. A test of an asset for overstatement also provides corollary evidence on the potential overstatement of revenue and liabilities or the potential understatement of other asset or expense accounts. For example, if accounts receivable are overstated, it is likely that revenue is overstated or cash is understated.

Similarly, testing liabilities for understatement provides indirect evidence on the potential understatement of expenses or assets, or the potential overstatement of revenue and other liabilities. For example, if there are unrecorded

PRACTICAL POINT

The PCAOB's AS Nos. 12, 13, and 15 address concepts concerning audit procedures. These standards state that audit procedures include risk assessments, tests of controls, and substantive procedures—including both tests of details and substantive analytical procedures.

LO 4

Explain how directional testing helps achieve both audit effectiveness and audit efficiency.

PRACTICAL POINT

Directional testing often provides evidence relating to more than one account balance at a time.

liabilities, such as a failure to accrue payroll expense, the related payroll expense is understated, and possibly inventory is understated if payroll costs are not properly allocated to inventory.

Commonly Used Audit Procedures for Direct Tests of Account Balances and Transactions

LO 5

Identify basic audit procedures and how they relate to evaluating the underlying financial statement assertions.

A wide variety of audit procedures are used to perform direct tests of account balances and transactions. The primary types of procedures used by auditors to directly gather evidence on account balances include the following:

- Observation of client personnel and procedures
- Inquiry of knowledgeable persons
- Obtaining external confirmations
- Inspection of documents
- Inspection of physical assets
- Recalculation of data—including independent tests of mathematical accuracy
- Data analysis
- Reperformance
- Reprocessing transactions by tracing documents from origination through accounting records to the general ledger
- Vouching of transactions by selecting recorded transactions and tracing backward through accounting records to original documentation
- Analytical procedures

PRACTICAL POINT

The PCAOB emphasizes the usefulness of "walkthroughs" as an important part of the auditor's process of evaluating internal control. Walkthroughs represent a combination of inquiries, observations, and physical examination. In a walkthrough, the auditor traces a transaction from origination through the company's information systems until it is reflected in a company's financial reports.

Observation   Observation is most often used to gain an understanding of a client's processing system, including a "walkthrough" of processes. It is also a common practice to observe the client's process of taking physical inventory to establish existence and valuation.

Although intuitively appealing, observation suffers from some major limitations. Observation of processing is rarely unobtrusive. Individuals who know they are being observed typically act differently than when not observed. There is also a problem in generalizing the results from a single set of observations. Observation of processing on one day does not necessarily indicate how the transactions were processed on a different day. Finally, observation is rarely sufficient to satisfy any assertion other than existence. For example, simply observing a fixed asset does not necessarily mean that the client actually owns it; observing an inventory item does not necessarily mean that the auditor will be able to accurately assess its value.

Inquiries of Knowledgeable Persons   Inquiry is used extensively to gain an understanding of the following:

- The accounting system
- Management's plans for such things as marketable investments, new products, disposal of lines of business, and new investments
- Pending or actual litigation against the organization
- Changes in accounting procedures or accounting principles
- Management's approach and assumptions used in the valuation of key accounts, (e.g., the collectibility of accounts receivable or the salability of inventory)
- Management's or the controller's assessment of complex financial matters

Inquiry is stronger when it can be corroborated with other forms of audit evidence. As noted earlier, the strength of inquiry as evidence is related to management integrity and the business risk associated with the client.

External Confirmations   Confirmations consist of sending an inquiry to an outside party to corroborate information. The outside parties are asked to respond directly to the auditor as to whether they agree or disagree with information, or to provide additional information that will assist the auditor in evaluating the correctness of an account balance. Confirmations often include requests to legal counsel for an assessment of current litigation and the client's potential liability, letters to customers asking whether they owe the amount on the client's accounts receivable records, and letters to banks confirming bank balances and loans. In some cases, the auditor will confirm the terms of sales agreements or other contracts.

Although confirmations can be a strong source of evidence, auditors must not rely on them unduly. When using confirmations with outside parties, the auditor must gain assurance that the outside party:

- Exists.
- Is able to respond objectively and independently.
- Is likely to respond conscientiously, appropriately, and in a timely fashion.
- Is unbiased in responding.

Professional standards presume, but do not require, that the auditor separately confirms accounts receivable. The auditor often complements confirmations with other sources of evidence, such as the customer's subsequent payment of the outstanding balance, as persuasive evidence of the amount owed at year end.

Confirmations primarily address the existence assertion and can only indirectly address the valuation assertion. Confirmation that the customer owes an amount to the client does not necessarily indicate that the client will collect the full amount due (valuation) or that the receivable has not been sold to a third party (rights). Finally, confirmations must be sent independently of the client. (See the *Auditing in Practice—The Parmalat Confirmation Fraud*.)

Inspection of Documents   Much of the audit process depends on examining documents—either in paper or electronic form. Documents exist in forms such as invoices, payroll time cards, and bank statements. Auditors examine invoices from suppliers, for example, to establish the cost and ownership of inventory or various expenses (i.e., valuation). They also read contracts to help establish the potential existence of liabilities. Auditors should be sure to use original source documents rather than copies, because copies are easy for an unscrupulous management to falsify.

AUDITING *in Practice*

THE PARMALAT CONFIRMATION FRAUD

The Parmalat fraud involved a large family-held Italian company that produced dairy products around the world. The company's management perpetrated a fraud that involved taking cash from the business for family purposes, but not recording the transactions in the books, thereby resulting in an overstatement of cash on the company's books. They also shifted monetary assets in and out of banks located in the Bahamas Islands. The audit firm decided they should independently confirm the existence of Parmalat's $3.2 billion account with the Bank of America in New York. Unfortunately, the audit senior was careless and after preparing the confirmation,

he put it in the client's mail room where it was intercepted by management. Management was able to scan the signature of a Bank of America employee from another document and put it on a copy of the confirmation form. A Parmalat employee then flew to New York from Italy just to mail that confirmation to the auditors with the appropriate postmark. The auditors received the fraudulent confirmation and concluded that the cash balance existed. There is an important point here: There are no trivial tasks in an audit—each procedure must be done professionally and with care!

Inspection of Physical Assets   Observation or inspection is useful in verifying the existence of tangible assets and in identifying potential obsolescence or signs of wear and tear. However, observation alone does not provide evidence on completeness, ownership, or valuation. For example, the inventory might be held on consignment from others and is therefore not owned by the entity under audit. In addition, observation does not provide evidence about the cost of inventory and may not uncover problems of obsolescence or quality control.

Recalculation of Data   Auditors often find it useful to recalculate a number of client computations. Recalculations include the following:

- *Footing*—Adding a column of figures to verify the correctness of the client's totals.
- *Cross-footing*—Checking the agreement of the cross-addition of a number of columns of figures that sum to a grand total. For example, the sum of net sales and sales discounts should equal total sales.
- *Tests of extensions*—Recomputing items involving multiplication (e.g., multiplying unit cost by quantity on hand to arrive at extended cost).
- *Recalculating estimated amounts* for account estimates or allowances (e.g., recomputing the allowance for doubtful accounts based on a formula related to the aging of accounts receivable ending balances).

There are many court cases involving auditors where the detail in the records did not agree with the balances in the financial statements. Moreover, clients often used spreadsheets to calculate accounting estimates. Auditors can test the accuracy of the estimates by recalculating them using an auditor-developed spreadsheet or evaluating the logic incorporated in the client's spreadsheet.

Data Analysis—A Hybrid of Recalculation and Analytical Procedures

A common term used in both internal and external auditing is *data analysis*. Auditors are now using sophisticated software to look for unusual patterns in the underlying data, or assessing the mathematical correctness of data. They are also using software (covered in Chapter 8) to help them perform independent recalculations to determine the underlying correctness of computations or completeness of the population being tested. Data analysis is particularly important in search for fraud.

Data analysis is a hybrid of both recalculation and analytical procedures because it uses mathematical techniques, e.g., regression analysis, or pattern analysis to identify potentially unusual patterns of data that merit additional audit inquiry. Other hybrid approaches, including forms of continuous monitoring of controls or transactions, are increasingly being used by auditors.

Reperformance of Client Procedures   Reperformance involves the auditor's independent execution of controls that were originally performed as part of the entity's internal control. In other words, the auditor must not only observe that personnel said they performed a control; the auditor should do what is necessary to determine that the control actually worked.

Reprocessing of Transactions   Reprocessing involves selecting a sample from a population of source documents and reprocessing them to be sure they have all been properly recorded. For example, reprocessing would include taking a sample from the client's shipping records and tracing that sample through internal processes and into the sales journal and general ledger (see Exhibit 7.9). Reprocessing provides evidence that valid transactions have been recorded (completeness). Auditors often use reprocessing to test the effectiveness of internal controls at the same time they are testing proper recording of the transactions. For example, when testing sales transactions, the auditor might also

---

PRACTICAL POINT

Some things never seem to change. For almost a century, frauds have been hidden by misfooting data, or inappropriately cross-footing columns. More recently, this same technique has been used to cover up frauds by making spreadsheets appear to tie out when they do not. Recalculating remains an important audit technique—even in an electronic environment.

PRACTICAL POINT

Data analysis techniques are increasingly important as audit firms and internal auditors implement continuous monitoring of computer software into their suite of audit procedures. Students who are comfortable in such environments and are adept at using software for analysis purposes will have a competitive advantage—provided that the data analysis is coupled with an ability to use judgment to understand the causes of unusual or unexpected patterns in the data.

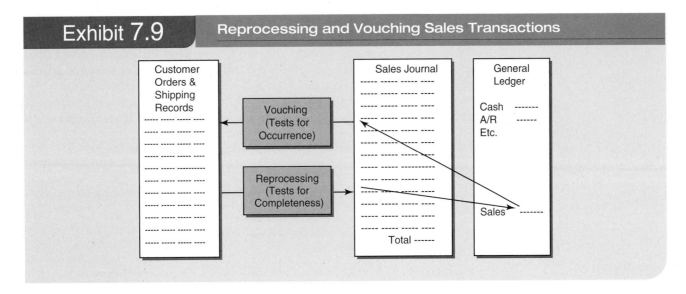

Exhibit 7.9 — **Reprocessing and Vouching Sales Transactions**

examine whether controls involving credit approval, sequencing of shipping documents, authorized billing prices are operating properly.

Vouching of Transactions **Vouching** is complementary to reprocessing. Vouching involves taking a sample of already recorded transactions and tracing them back to their original source. For example, a sample of items recorded in the sales journal is traced back to shipping documents and customer orders (see Exhibit 7.10). Vouching provides evidence on the assertion that recorded transactions are valid (existence). For a graphical comparison of the differences between vouching and reprocessing, see Exhibit 7.10.

Analytical Procedures **Analytical procedures** involve comparisons, either judgmentally or statistically, of data over time, across operating units, or between related components of the financial statements to develop insight concerning expected relationships. If there are no unexpected differences and the organization has strong internal controls over financial reporting, the auditor may conclude that little additional audit evidence needs to be examined. However, if there are unexpected differences, the auditor will need to perform extensive additional tests of the underlying account balance.

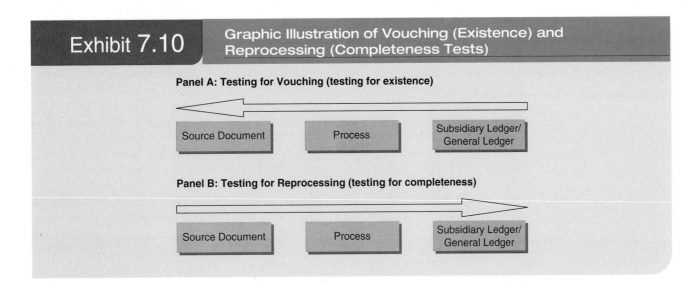

Exhibit 7.10 — **Graphic Illustration of Vouching (Existence) and Reprocessing (Completeness Tests)**

Application to Assertions

An audit procedure may provide evidence for one or more assertions affecting an account balance. The following table presents examples of procedures that address specific assertions regarding fixed assets and contingencies. The procedures are organized according to the assertion and some of the procedures cover more than one assertion. A good audit program consolidates the procedures to gain audit efficiency.

Assertions	Fixed Assets	Contingencies
Existence	• Physically examine the assets. • Vouch selected new additions to vendor's invoice to determine it is an asset and not an expense. • Inquiry to determine rationale for expected life.	• Inquiry of management. • Send confirmation request to legal counsel.
Completeness	• Vouch repairs/maintenance expense to determine if a fixed asset was inappropriately expensed. • Inquiry regarding process of determining whether an expenditure is an asset or an expense.	• Inquiry of management. • Vouch legal expense. • Review nature of legal services to determine if a liability might exist.
Rights/ Obligations	• Vouch to vendor's invoice recognizing ownership. • Review purchase contracts.	• Inquiry of management. • Confirmation from legal counsel. • Examine payments related to in-progress litigation.
Valuation/ Allocation	• Vouch to vendor's invoice to establish purchase price. • Determine that estimated life and salvage value are consistent with similar purchases, company policies, expected future use, and past experience. • Recalculate depreciation expense. • Estimate total depreciation using analytical procedures.	• Inquiry of management. • Confirmation from legal counsel. • Recalculation of potential damages sought by plaintiff. • Review court filings.
Presentation/ Disclosure	• Review presentation within the financial statements to ensure completeness and conformance with the applicable financial reporting financial reporting framework • Review disclosures to ensure that they are adequate and understandable.	• Review presentation on financial statements to ensure completeness and conformance with compliance with the applicable financial reporting financial reporting framework. • Review disclosures to ensure that they are adequate and understandable.

Fixed Assets Physical examination addresses the existence assertion for many assets, including fixed assets. Vouching to vendor invoices helps establish existence, ownership (rights), and the obligation to pay as well as establishing that the item is properly classified as an asset. Inquiry of management can help identify the intended use of the asset and whether they may be any unrecorded disposals of assets (existence). Examining the repairs and maintenance expense account may uncover costs that should have been capitalized (completeness). Review of intended use, industry trends, and past history can provide insight on whether the client has chosen an appropriate asset life and salvage value. Recalculating depreciation expense or estimating depreciation expense using analytical procedures helps determine the appropriateness of the book value of depreciable assets (valuation). Reading related notes to the financial statements helps assure that appropriate disclosures have been made by management.

Contingencies (Pending Litigation)   Management is the primary source of information concerning the existence of pending litigation, the probability of an unfavorable outcome, and the potential amount of damages. Vouching major legal expense transactions back to source documents will help establish the reasons the client is paying lawyers. Corroboration of management's information should be obtained from the client's legal counsel. The lawyers will be asked to comment on the completeness and reasonableness of the information provided by management. Related notes to the financial statements should be reviewed to assure that appropriate disclosures have been made by management.

PRACTICAL POINT

It is often difficult to establish the potential liability or claims associated with litigation. The auditor will need to solicit accurate assessments of the litigation and the likely outcome from both management and outside legal counsel.

Timing of Procedures

In addition to determining which procedures to perform, the auditor must determine when to perform them—at the balance sheet date, earlier than the balance sheet date, or after the balance sheet date. Performing procedures prior to the balance sheet date will allow earlier completion of the audit and require less overtime of the audit staff. It may also meet management's desire to distribute the financial statements shortly after year end. However, performing the procedures at an interim date increases the risk of material misstatements occurring between the interim date and the year-end balance. Performing procedures after year end may provide the most convincing evidence; for example, a collection of a receivable after year end is persuasive regarding both the existence and valuation of the receivable. The timing decision is usually based on the assessment of risk associated with the account, the effectiveness of internal controls, the nature of the account, and the availability of audit staff.

When an organization has effective internal controls over financial reporting, the risk of misstatements occurring between the interim audit date and year end is decreased. There are several accounts for which the auditor can effectively and efficiently test the transactions during the year rather than the final balance. For example, the auditor can test property, plant, and equipment additions and disposals during the year. Accounts receivable may be confirmed prior to year end and any major new additions can be confirmed at year end. A similar approach can often be used for other noncurrent assets, long-term debt, and owners' equity transactions.

Audit Programs and Documenting Audit Evidence
Audit Program Development

An audit program specifies the audit objectives, the procedures that should be followed in gathering, documenting, and evaluating audit evidence, and the auditor's reasoning process in reaching an audit conclusion. Audit programs address issues such as how many transactions need to be examined or what population should be sampled to determine the validity of a particular account balance. The auditor makes decisions on the best combination of procedures to use in gathering evidence to evaluate assertions for each client.

Consider the Ford Motor Company inventory example earlier in the chapter. Auditor inspection of raw materials provides evidence on the existence and condition of the inventory, but not its ownership or valuation. Examination of purchase documents provides evidence of ownership and valuation because the documents indicate the cost of the purchases as well as transfer of ownership to the company. An analysis of current market conditions provides evidence on marketability and indicates whether there may be a permanent decline in inventory value. Examination of year-end shipping and receiving documents

LO 6

Explain the nature, design, and purposes of audit programs.

provides evidence on the proper cutoff of transactions (assuming that the dealers do not have any unusual right of return for cars purchased). Finally, reading the footnotes to the financial statements will help the auditor determine whether proper disclosures have been made.

However, the procedures identified only partially address the question "What is the optimal amount and type of evidence to be gathered?" Ford may have its cars at various plants all around the world, and some of the cars may be in transit at year end, or some may be on consignment with dealers until they are sold. How many locations should the auditor visit to observe Ford's procedures for handling inventory? In answering these questions, and as part of audit planning, the auditor may use analytical procedures to determine inventory locations, age of inventory, and dollar amounts at each location to determine the risk that inventory might be overstated in specific locations. In addition, the auditor will consider tests of the quality of internal controls over financial reporting to further identify areas where risk of misstatement exists. In general, if controls are good, the risks are lower and the need for direct tests or observation will be smaller. The main thing to remember, though, is that all of these decisions about evidence collection must be detailed in the audit program.

Documenting Audit Evidence

LO 7

Describe the purposes and contents of good audit documentation.

Auditors like to assume that their work will never be questioned, but that is an unrealistic assumption! The documentation of audit work must stand on its own. It should be possible for an experienced auditor to evaluate the evidence independently of the individuals who performed the audit and reach the same conclusion.

Audit documentation is the written record that forms the basis for the auditor's conclusions. It provides support for the auditor's representations, whether those representations are contained in the auditor's report or otherwise. Audit Standard No. 3, *Audit Documentation*, makes it clear that the documentation must also clearly show the auditor's reasoning process and the basis for conclusions reached on the audit. AS No. 3 states that:

> Audit documentation should be prepared in sufficient detail to provide a clear understanding of its purpose, source, and the conclusions reached. Also, the documentation should be appropriately organized to provide a clear link to the significant findings or issues (addressed in the audit). (para. 4)

Audit documentation, also referred to as workpapers or working papers (even if they are all electronic), facilitates the planning, performance, and supervision of the audit and forms the basis of the review of the quality of the work performed. Audit documentation includes records of the planning and performance of the work, the procedures performed, evidence obtained, and conclusions reached by the auditor. Together, these items serve as the primary evidence in support of audit conclusions.

Audit documentation, paper and/or electronic, should typically include the following:

Audit Planning and Risk Analysis

- Evidence of planning, including the audit program.
- Audit approach and basic data utilized to identify risk, including fraud risk.
- Updates on how significant issues from previous year's audits are addressed during the current audit.
- An analysis of the auditor's assessment of internal control and a linkage of control deficiencies to expanded (or different) audit tests for accounts where there is high risk of material misstatements.
- Memoranda that describe the auditor's conclusions regarding risk associated with acceptance or continuance of the client.

Audit Work Performed

- The client's trial balance and any auditor adjustments to it.
- Copies of selected internal and external documents.
- Memos describing the auditor's approach to gathering evidence and the reasoning process in support of account balances.
- Results of analytical procedures and tests of client records, and the individuals responsible for performance, and subsequently the review, of the procedures.
- Correspondence with outside specialists who provided evidence significant to the evaluation or accounting for assets/liabilities and the related revenue expense effects (e.g., valuation specialists); must include an analysis of the independence and credentials of the specialists.
- Auditor-generated analysis of account balances (e.g., audit software analysis of accounts and relationships).

Identification of Significant Issues and Conclusions

- Identification of significant accounting issues that were identified during the course of audit and how they were resolved, including any correspondence with national office experts.
- A clear articulation of the auditor's judgment and the reasoning process that led to the judgment on the fairness of the financial statements.

Audit documentation must conform to a very high standard of quality. Importantly, the documentation must demonstrate definitively that the work was in fact performed. Further, it must contain sufficient information to enable an experienced auditor, having no previous connection with the engagement, to understand the nature, timing, extent, and results of the procedures performed, evidence obtained, and conclusions reached; and to determine who performed the work, the date such work was completed, and the person who reviewed the work and the date of such review. These documentation requirements enable PCAOB inspectors who examine the quality of audit work to understand the nature of audit evidence contained within the documentation. The AICPA and international standards require that the audit documentation contain similar attributes.

The PCAOB requires that all audit engagements document **significant issues or audit findings**, as well as the actions taken to address them (including additional evidence obtained, where applicable). Significant findings or issues are defined as substantive matters that are important to the analysis of the fair presentation of the financial statements; they include the following:

a. Significant matters involving the selection, application, and consistency of accounting principles, including related disclosures. Significant matters include, but are not limited to, accounting for complex or unusual transactions, accounting estimates, and uncertainties, as well as related management assumptions.

b. Results of auditing procedures that indicated a need for modification of planned auditing procedures, or the existence of material misstatements, omissions in the financial statements, significant deficiencies, or material weaknesses in internal control over financial reporting.

c. Audit adjustments. For purposes of this standard, an **audit adjustment** is a correction of a misstatement of the financial statements that was or should have been proposed by the auditor, whether or not recorded by management, that could, either individually or when aggregated with other misstatements, have a material effect on the company's financial statements.

d. Disagreements among members of the engagement team or with others consulted on the engagement about final conclusions reached on significant accounting or auditing matters.

e. Circumstances that cause significant difficulty in applying auditing procedures.

f. Significant changes in the assessed level of audit risk for particular audit areas and the auditor's response to those changes.

g. Any matters that could result in modification of the auditor's report. (PCAOB Auditing Standard No. 3).

As is evident from this list, the PCAOB wants clearly documented evidence regarding difficulties that auditors experience on audit engagements, and it wants auditors to document what they did to resolve those difficulties.

Revisions and Retention of Audit Documentation

Audit documentation should be completed and assembled within 60 days following the audit report release date. After that date, the auditor must not delete or discard audit documentation before the end of the required retention period (7 years). Occasionally, because of an internal or external quality review process, it may be determined that procedures considered necessary were omitted from the audit or the auditor subsequently becomes aware of information related to financial statements that have already been issued. The auditor should then perform any necessary procedures and make the necessary changes to the audit documentation.

Audit Planning Documentation

The planning process lays the foundation for the audit and should be carefully documented. Interviews with key executives should be summarized with implications clearly drawn for the conduct of the audit. Business risk analysis, fraud risk analysis, and analytical procedures should be documented with a clear identification of accounts requiring special audit attention. The auditor's assessment of materiality, overall audit approach, and personnel needed should also be summarized. The documentation serves an important planning function for the audit; it also serves as evidence that the auditors took their responsibilities seriously in evaluating potential problems or special circumstances involved in, or related to, the audit.

The Audit Program as an Integral Part of Documentation

An audit program specifies the *procedures* to be performed in gathering audit evidence and is used to record the *successful* completion of each audit step. The audit program *is the single most important piece of documentation in an audit engagement* and provides an effective means for:

- Organizing and distributing audit work
- Monitoring the audit process and progress
- Recording the audit work performed and those responsible for performing the work
- Reviewing the completeness and persuasiveness of procedures performed

Most audit firms have standardized audit programs that can be modified to fit a client's unique features. For example, the audit of accounts receivable might appear to be the same for most businesses. However, there may be significant differences in how each organization processes receivables, or their credit terms, or in the economic health of their industry that might cause an audit team to modify a standard audit program to fit the particular circumstances of the client. A partial audit program for accounts receivable is presented in Exhibit 7.11. Please note that although audit programs are organized to promote the efficient gathering and evaluation of audit evidence, the program is always based on testing assertions. A good habit for all auditors is to examine audit programs to determine that all relevant assertions are addressed.

PRACTICAL POINT

One of the most important things an auditor can do is to document his or her reasoning process, including all the facts that were relied on in reaching a decision. This protects the auditor from the "20-20 hindsight bias," where someone looking at a significant issue later might use facts that were not known to the auditor to reach a different conclusion.

PRACTICAL POINT

Audit programs are always built to test the underlying assertions introduced earlier in the chapter in an efficient and comprehensive fashion.

PRACTICAL POINT

Once the audit programs have been developed, they may need to be modified to address unexpected problems or issues that arise.

| Exhibit 7.11 | Partial Audit Program for Accounts Receivable |

AUDIT OBJECTIVES

1. Determine that accounts receivable are authentic obligations owed to the company (existence, rights).
2. Verify that accounts receivable include all amounts owed to the company (completeness).
3. Determine that the allowance for doubtful accounts is adequate but not excessive. Determine that all significant doubtful accounts have been written off (valuation).
4. Verify that pledged, discounted, or assigned accounts receivable are properly disclosed. Related-party receivables are properly disclosed (presentation and disclosure).
5. Determine that accounts receivable are appropriately classified in the balance sheet (presentation and disclosure).

Audit Procedures	Performed by	Ref
1. Test the accuracy and completeness of the underlying accounting records by footing the accounts receivable file and agreeing it to the general ledger (valuation).		
2. Take a sample of recorded accounts receivable balances and confirm the balances with the customers (existence, valuation, rights).		
3. Vouch aging details to supporting documents, discuss collectibility of receivables with responsible officials, and review correspondence with customers (valuation).		
4. Analyze allowance for doubtful accounts; compare to past history and industry trends to determine adequacy (valuation).		
5. Take a sample of recorded receivables and prepare a list of subsequent cash receipts to determine if they are fully paid before the end of the audit (existence, valuation, rights).		
6. Verify cutoff for sales, cash receipts, and returns by examining transactions near the end of the year (completeness, existence).		
7. Determine adequacy of disclosure of related-party, pledged, discounted, or assigned receivables (presentation).		

Copies of Documents

Some client documents are of such importance that a copy should be included in the audit documentation. Such documents usually have legal significance, such as lease agreements, bond covenant agreements, significant portions of the board of directors' minutes, government correspondence regarding client investigations, and loan agreements. Responses to the auditor's confirmation requests for accounts receivable, pending litigation, or bank loans are examples of documents from outside parties that are retained. Finally, management representations are formally documented in a management representation letter, which is signed by management to acknowledge the accuracy of its verbal or written assertions.

Auditor-Generated Memos

Auditors assimilate diverse evidence to reach an opinion as to whether a particular account balance is fairly stated. The auditor's reasoning process in assembling and analyzing evidence is important and should be documented via auditor-generated memos. At first you might think that documenting your own opinion is unnecessary. After all, you will have documented all the evidence underlying that opinion. However, the documentation must stand on its own; in other words, another auditor must be able to understand the reasoning process by which you evaluated that evidence and formulated your opinion. In order to gain that understanding, another auditor will not be able to rely on just talking to you. Over time you will likely forget important details about how you reached your opinions; therefore, documenting them for the audit file via an auditor-generated memo is essential.

Characteristics of Good Audit Documentation

Audit documentation serves as the primary evidence of an audit. Well-developed audit documentation contains the following:

- A heading that includes the name of the audit client, an explanatory title, and the balance sheet date
- The initials or electronic signature of the auditor performing the audit test and the date the test was completed
- The initials or electronic signature of the manager or partner who reviewed the documentation and the date the review was completed
- A description of the tests performed and the findings
- Tick marks and legend indicating the nature of the work performed by the auditor
- An assessment of whether the tests indicate the possibility of material misstatement in an account

Comparison of Worldwide Professional Guidance

AUDIT DOCUMENTATION

AICPA Auditing Standards Board (ASB)

SAS 103 requires that:

"The auditor must prepare audit documentation in connection with each engagement in sufficient detail to provide a clear understanding of the work performed (including the nature, timing, extent, and results of audit procedures performed), the audit evidence obtained and its source, and the conclusions reached."

Further, the auditor is required to "document significant findings or issues, actions taken to address them (including any additional evidence obtained), and the basis for the final conclusions reached."

With respect to specific items tested, SAS 103 notes that for tests of controls and substantive tests, that involve inspection of documents or confirmation should include the identifying characteristics of the specific items tested.

Public Company Accounting Oversight Board (PCAOB)

AS 3 notes that "audit documentation includes records of the planning and performance of the work, the procedures performed, evidence obtained, and conclusions reached by the auditor."

Further, AS 3 requires that "Audit documentation should be prepared in sufficient detail to provide a clear understanding of its purpose, source, and the conclusions reached. Also, the documentation should be appropriately organized to provide a clear link to the significant findings or issues."

With respect to documenting items that were tested AS 3 notes that "Documentation of auditing procedures that involve the inspection of documents or confirmation, including tests of details, tests of operating effectiveness of controls, and walkthroughs, should include identification of the items inspected. Documentation of auditing procedures related to the inspection of significant contracts or agreements should include abstracts or copies of the documents."

International Auditing and Assurance Standards Board (IAASB)

ISA 230 documentation requirements are very similar to AS 3 and SAS 103 in that the standard states that documentation is intended to provide "(a) A sufficient and appropriate record of the basis for the auditor's report; and (b) Evidence that the audit was planned and performed in accordance with ISAs and applicable legal and regulatory requirements."

With respect to testing of specific items, the auditor is required to document the identifying characteristics of the specific items or matters tested.

SUMMARY

Audit documentation is critical to providing evidence that an audit has been completed in accordance with relevant auditing standards. The three boards have similar requirements regarding the purpose and extent of audit documentation.

- An index to identify the location of relevant evidence
- A cross-reference to related documentation, when applicable
- A section that identifies all significant audit and/or accounting issues that arose during the audit and how they were resolved
- A comprehensive and clear memorandum that delineates the auditor's analysis of the consistency of audit evidence and the conclusions reached regarding the fairness of the financial presentation

An example of an audit document used as the basis to document the performance of a price test on a client's inventory is shown in Exhibit 7.12. The documentation indicates the tests performed, the source of evidence examined, and the conclusion of the audit tests. It also indicates the dollar amounts tested and those not tested. If exceptions had been noted, the auditor would have documented them and would have projected the potential misstatement to the total account balance to determine whether the work might indicate material misstatements in the account balance.

Example of Audit Program to Directly Test Account Balances

We illustrate the design of an audit program by examining the inventory account of Shirt Shak Stores, Inc. For illustration purposes, we focus only on

Exhibit 7.12	Working Paper for Inventory Price Test

C-1/3

CMI Manufacturing Company
Inventory Price Test
Year Ended December 31, 2011

Prepared by: *ACM*
Date: *1/21/12*
Reviewed by: *BJS*
Date: *1/24/12*

Item No.	Item Name	Quantity	Cost Per Unit	Extended Cost
4287	Advanced Micro stamping machine	22*	$5,128†	112,816.00‡
5203	1/4 HP electric motor	10*	$39†	390.00‡
2208	Assembly kit for motor housing	25*	$12†	300.00‡
1513	Micro stamping machine, Model 25	200*	$2,100†	420,000.00‡
0068	Rack & Pinion component	300*	$42†	12,600.00‡
8890	Repair kits for stamping machines	1,000*	$48†	48,000.00‡
	Total value of items tested			594,106.00
	Items not tested			1,802,000.00
	Balance per general ledger			2,396,106.00§

F T/B

Note: Sampled items were selected using a dollar unit sampling technique with materiality set at $50,000, and internal control judged to be good.

Tick Mark Legend:

*Quantities agree with client physical inventory tested earlier.

†Traced to client's standard cost system that was independently tested. Amount agrees with client's standard cost.

‡Tested extension, no exceptions.

§ Footed, no exceptions; agrees with trial balance.

Conclusion: In my opinion, the pricing and clerical accuracy of inventory is proper.

the direct tests of inventory (rather than also focusing on tests of controls). Shirt Shak is a retailer of swimwear, water sport equipment, and gifts, with several locations along the Florida coast. Its home office is in Cocoa Beach and serves as the central purchasing and distribution center. The inventory account represents assertions made by management as to the existence, completeness, ownership, and valuation of the inventory.

An example of an audit program for the direct testing of inventory is shown in Exhibit 7.13. The audit program is based on these assumptions: (1) the company has effective internal control, (2) the inventory is relatively homogenous and is valued according to the FIFO cost assumption, and (3) the client's records are computerized. The auditor has previously tested purchase and sales transactions and has determined that they have been appropriately recorded in the inventory accounts. The audit program does not indicate the sample size for items selected. Determining the appropriate sample size is covered in Chapter 8.

Exhibit 7.13   Audit Program for Inventory

Shirt Shak Stores, Inc.
Audit of Inventory, Year Ended December 31, 2011

Audit Procedures	Done by	Ref
1. General		
a. Review industry trends and determine potential implications for the realizability of Shirt Shak's inventory.	_____	_____
b. Inquire of management regarding any changes in lines of business or product mix that may affect inventory.	_____	_____
c. Review prior year documentation to identify problem areas and determine the potential effect on this year's audit.	_____	_____
2. Planning		
a. Perform an analytical review of inventory by product line and by location to determine whether there are any significant changes from the prior period.	_____	_____
b. Perform a cross-sectional analysis of inventory by store to identify any outliers. If there are outliers, include them in step 3a.	_____	_____
c. Inquire of management as to whether any product lines have been disposed of or added.	_____	_____
d. Inquire of management as to whether there have been any significant pricing or other changes that may affect the valuation of inventory.	_____	_____
e. Determine the location of computer records and the computer applications and file structures on which inventory data are located.	_____	_____
f. Determine the need for specialized personnel, either computer audit or inventory specialists.	_____	_____
3. Audit Procedures		
a. Select specific locations including the distribution center and any outliers identified in 2b. Take a statistical sample of items at those locations from the client's perpetual inventory records, and do the following:	_____	_____
(1) Identify the location of the items, observe their existence, and count them. Statistically analyze any exceptions and determine whether the exceptions could lead to a material error in the inventory account balance (existence).	_____	_____
(2) For items selected, observe their condition and determine whether they appear to be in saleable condition (valuation).	_____	_____
b. Using a computerized audit program (such as ACL), do the following:	_____	_____
(1) Foot the inventory file and verify that it agrees with the general ledger (valuation).	_____	_____
(2) Select a statistical sample for performing price tests by examining purchase documents (valuation).	_____	_____

Exhibit 7.13	Audit Program for Inventory *(continued)*

Audit Procedures	Done by	Ref
(3) Compute inventory turnover by product and prepare a printout of any product whose turnover is less than 6. Inquire of management as to the possibility that the goods cannot be sold (valuation).	___	___
(4) Based on previous tests that show net realizable value to be 93% of sales price, compute net realizable value by multiplying sales price by 0.93 and prepare a printout of all items for which net realizable value is less than cost. Determine the amount of write-down needed to reflect LOCOM (valuation).	___	___
(5) Verify extensions by multiplying quantity by cost for all items (valuation).	___	___
c. For the items selected in 3b (2), perform price tests by tracing the product FIFO cost per the printout to the latest purchases.	___	___
(1) Note and statistically analyze any exceptions and project the results to the population as a whole.	___	___
(2) Based on the exceptions, determine whether there is any pattern to the errors such that they might be isolated to a particular time period, product, or location.	___	___
(3) Based on the exceptions and any pattern to the errors found, determine whether there is an unacceptable risk of material error existing in the account balance. If such a risk exists, consult with the partner in charge regarding the expansion of audit tests.	___	___
(4) Determine the ownership of the items by inspecting relevant purchase documents, receiving documents, and other related documentation.	___	___
d. Observe the receiving and sales cutoff procedures of the client to determine that all goods are recorded in the proper period. Obtain the last number of receiving documents at the distribution center. Review the December and January purchases journal to determine that all purchases have been recorded in the proper time period (cutoff, completeness, existence).	___	___
e. Review the client's presentation of the balance sheet inventory items and related footnotes for completeness and accuracy of presentation (disclosure).	___	___
4. Completion		
a. Perform an analytical review of inventory by comparing current year inventory by product line with previous inventory levels in relation to sales. Determine whether there are any large or unusual increases in inventory that have not been adequately explained. Determine the extent to which investigation ought to be extended.	___	___
b. Formulate an opinion on the fairness of the financial statement presentation. Document that conclusion and the adequacy of the testing performed on inventory in a memo to be included in the inventory file.	___	___

Auditing Account Balances Affected by Management's Estimates

Many account balances are subject to estimates, appraisals, or other management assumptions. These accounts include estimated warranty liabilities, allowance for doubtful accounts or loan loss reserves, pension costs and liabilities, evaluations of fixed assets, and analysis of goodwill for possible impairment. Although management judgment is important, the auditor must determine that those judgments are substantiated by independent, objective, and verifiable data that support the estimates. Unfortunately, accounting estimates have too often been subject to earnings manipulation (see the *Auditing in Practice* feature.) Auditors must take special care to exercise appropriate professional skepticism in evaluating the reasonableness of these estimates.

LO 8

Identify issues surrounding auditing management's estimates.

AUDITING *in Practice*

"GENERAL MOTORS, FORD OFFSET LOSSES BY DIPPING INTO COOKIE-JAR FUNDS"

The *Wall Street Journal* reported the following:

> General Motors Acceptance Corp (GMAC), the credit arm of General Motors, and Ford Motor Credit, the credit arm of Ford Motor Company, must establish reserves to cover bad loans, such as foreclosures or repossessions. They have flexibility with these rainy-day funds and have allowed their loan-loss reserves to dwindle during 2005. The auto makers each lost more than $1.3 billion in the third quarter of 2005 in their world-wide automotive operations. GMAC reduced its reserves through the first three quarters of 2005 by $525 million that helped boost GMAC's pretax profit by nearly 20% for the year. Ford Motor Credit's reserves fell $1.85 billion between 2002 and 2004 and another $813 million during the first three quarters of 2005.

The *Wall Street Journal* also reported that the reserves (allowance for uncollectible accounts) had decreased even though (a) the amount of total loans was increasing and (b) economic signs pointed to a downturn for the portion of the economy that held those loans. The *Journal* was questioning whether the estimates were realistic assumptions or ploys to meeting earnings objectives. General Motors and Ford responded that their previous estimates were too high and that these changes just brought the estimates more in line. The auditor has to determine which "story" was correct before signing off on audit reports; that is, the estimates should be reasonable based on the data available at the time of the audit engagement.

Source: The Wall Street Journal Online, November 22, 2005.

Evidence Used in Auditing Management's Estimates

Objective and independent evidence must be gathered to evaluate management's accounting estimates. First, auditors must understand the processes used by management in developing estimates. That understanding should include an understanding of (a) controls over the process, (b) the reliability of underlying data in developing the estimate, (c) use of outside experts (how used, expertise, etc.) and (d) how management reviews the results of the estimates for reasonableness. Second, once the auditor understands the process, there are two approaches that the auditor can use. They are:

- Test the process used, including the reliability of the underlying data, or
- Develop independent estimates and compare those with that developed by management.

The choice between these two approaches will depend on the magnitude and complexity of the account balance. An example of the latter process is the comparison of warranty costs incurred or bad debt write-offs with the estimates in recent years to determine reasonableness of the estimates.

Estimates that are based on industry-wide or economy-wide trends need to be independently evaluated. For example, the earnings assumptions related to returns on pension funds should be based on how well stocks, as a whole, are doing within the economy and long-run predicted growth within the economy. Other pension data include actuarial reports on life expectancies and benefits that rely on experts. The auditor should review such evidence for consistency with economic reports, actuarial reports, and compare with the assumptions used by other clients and other companies in the same industry.

Asset impairment is based on either appraisals of current market value or estimates of future cash flows. If appraisals are done by professional appraisers, the auditor should determine the qualifications and reputation of the appraisers. Estimates of future cash flows provided by management need to be analyzed for the reasonableness of the assumptions and consistency with current and predicted future results.

Summary

Each audit is unique, but the approach to all audits is essentially the same. Management makes assertions in financial statements about the existence, completeness, rights or obligations, valuation, and presentation/disclosure of financial data. Evidence about these assertions is gathered, analyzed, and documented to enable to the auditor to reach a justified opinion on the fairness of the financial statements. The audit requires the auditor to gather sufficient, appropriate evidence. The auditor uses the risk assessments discussed in previous chapters to assist in determining the potential reliance on internally generated audit evidence. An effective audit combines relevant and persuasive audit evidence to provide reasonable assurance that the financial statements are free of material misstatement. It is also important to perform each audit as efficiently as possible without jeopardizing quality. Determining the sufficiency of evidence is a matter of professional judgment, but there are guidelines outlined in this chapter that can assist the auditor in making that judgment.

Significant Terms

Accounting records   The records of initial accounting entries and supporting records.

Analytical procedures   Comparisons, either judgmentally or statistically, of data over time, across operating units, or between components of the financial statements to develop insight concerning expected relationships.

Appropriateness of audit evidence   "The measure of the quality of audit evidence; that is, its relevance and its reliability in providing support for the conclusions on which the auditor's opinion is based." (ISA 500.5)

Audit adjustment   A correction of a misstatement of the financial statements that was or should have been proposed by the auditor, whether or not recorded by management, that could, either individually or when aggregated with other misstatements, have a material effect on the company's financial statements.

Audit documentation   The written record that forms the basis for the auditor's conclusions.

Audit evidence   All the information used by auditors in arriving at the conclusions on which the audit opinion is based.

Audit program   A list of the procedures to gather audit evidence, including specific procedures that are tailored to a specific client setting; it is the most important piece of documentation in an audit engagement.

Completeness   All assets, liabilities, and equity interests that should have been recorded have been recorded; i.e., nothing is left out of the financial statements.

Direct evidence   Audit evidence that requires only one inference to reach a conclusion about the assertion being tested. Usually that inference is that the sample taken is representative of the population as a whole.

Directional testing   An approach to testing account balances that considers the type of misstatement likely to occur in the account balance and the corresponding evidence provided by other accounts that have been tested. The auditor normally tests assets and expenses for overstatement, and liabilities and revenues for understatement, because (1) the major risks of misstatements on those accounts are in those directions or (2) tests of other accounts provide evidence of possible misstatements in the other direction.

Evidence   The underlying accounting data and all corroborating information used by the auditor to gain reasonable assurance as to the fairness of an entity's financial statements.

Existence/occurrence   The assets, liabilities, and equity interests are able to be accounted for, either physically or via verification in the accounting system.

Indirect evidence   Audit evidence that requires a linkage of inferences to provide assurance about the assertion being tested, i.e., one or more inferences are made. Examples include inferences made when using analytical procedures as audit evidence.

Presentation/disclosure   Assets, liabilities, and equity interests are appropriately classified on the financial statements and are adequately described in the footnotes to the financial statements.

Recalculation of data   Performing mathematical double-checks of client computations.

Relevance of audit evidence   Evidence that provides insight on the validity of the assertion being tested, i.e., the evidence bears directly on the assertion being tested.

Reliability of audit evidence   A measure of the quality of the underlying evidence. It is influenced by risk, potential management bias associated with the evidence, and the quality of the internal control system underlying the preparation of the evidence.

Reprocessing   Selecting a sample from a population of source documents and processing them through the client's system again to be sure they have all been properly recorded.

Rights/obligations   The entity holds or controls the legal ownership to assets, and liabilities are those legally owed by the entity.

Significant issues or audit findings   Substantive matters that are important to the procedures performed, evidence obtained, or conclusions reached on an audit.

Sufficiency of audit evidence   "The measure of the quantity of audit evidence. The quantity of the audit evidence needed is affected by the auditor's assessment of the risks of material misstatement and also by the quality of such audit evidence." (ISA 500.5)

Valuation/allocation   Assets, liabilities, and equity interests are included in the financial statements at appropriate amounts and any resulting valuation or allocation adjustments are appropriately recorded.

Vouching   Taking a sample of already recorded transactions and tracing them back to their original source.

SELECTED REFERENCES TO RELEVANT PROFESSIONAL GUIDANCE	
Topic	**Selected Guidance**
Audit Evidence	SAS 31 *Evidential Matter*
	SAS 80 *Amendment to Statement on Auditing Standards No. 31, Evidential Matter*
	SAS 106 *Audit Evidence*
	SAS *Audit Evidence* (Redrafted) (issued but not effective; proposed effective date is December 2012)
	SAS 110 *Performing Audit Procedures in Response to Assessed Risks and Evaluating the Audit Evidence Obtained*
	Statement on Auditing Standards (SAS) *Performing Audit Procedures in Response to Assessed Risks and Evaluating the Audit Evidence Obtained* (Redrafted) (issued but not effective; proposed effective date is December 2012)
	SAS *Audit Evidence—Specific Considerations for Selected Items* (issued but not effective; proposed effective date is December 2012)
	AS No. 13 *The Auditor's Responses to the Risks of Material Misstatement*
	AS No. 14 *Evaluating Audit Results*
	AS No. 15 *Audit Evidence*
	ISA 500 *Audit Evidence*
	ISA 501 *Audit Evidence—Specific Considerations for Selected Items*
Audit Documentation	SAS 103 *Audit Documentation*
	SAS *Audit Documentation* (Redrafted) (issued but not effective; proposed effective date is December 2012)
	AS No. 3 *Audit Documentation*
	ISA 230 *Audit Documentation*

Note: *Acronyms for Relevant Professional Guidance*

STANDARDS: **AS**—Auditing Standard issued by the PCAOB; **ISA**—International Standard on Auditing issued by the IAASB; **SAS**—Statement on Auditing Standards issued by the Auditing Standards Board of the AICPA; **SSAE**—Statement on Standards for Attestation Engagements issued by the AICPA.

ORGANIZATIONS: **AICPA**—American Institute of Certified Public Accountants; **COSO**—Committee of Sponsoring Organizations; **IAASB**—International Auditing and Assurance Standards Board; **PCAOB**—Public Company Accounting Oversight Board; **SEC**—Securities and Exchange Commission.

Review Questions

7-1   **(LO 1)**   What is "audit evidence"? Describe the primary sources of audit evidence.

7-2   **(LO 1, 3)**   What are the three basic decisions auditors must make concerning audit evidence during the planning process?

7-3   **(LO 2)** Explain the importance of audit assertions for financial statement audits. Define each of the following assertions:
- Existence/occurrence
- Completeness
- Rights/obligations
- Valuation/allocation
- Presentation/disclosure

7-4   **(LO 2)** The valuation assertion is often difficult to audit. Identify all the components of the valuation assertion for short-term investments in marketable securities.

7-5   **(LO 1, 3)** The International Standards on Auditing require the auditor to gather sufficient appropriate evidence to ensure that the auditor has a reasonable basis for an opinion regarding the financial statements. What are the characteristics of (a) sufficient audit evidence and (b) appropriate audit evidence? How are sufficiency and appropriateness related?

International

7-6   **(LO 1, 3)** To what extent are the concepts of sufficiency and relevance related to audit risk? Explain in terms of audits for which the auditor has determined that the level of audit risk will be low vs. an engagement in which the auditor has determined that the level of audit risk is higher.

7-7   **(LO 3)** ISA 200 identifies four major sources of audit evidence. What are these sources of evidence, and what are the components of each? Why is it important for the auditor to consider all four sources of evidence when auditing an organization?

International

7-8   **(LO 1, 2, 3)** Explain how information about the client, including previous audit work, client acceptance/continuance judgments, and the client's business risk are each relevant in developing comprehensive evidence used in assessing whether the financial statements are fairly presented.

7-9   **(LO 3)** Audit firms must be profitable and at the same time manage audit risk at a sufficient level to remain in business. Explain the tension between "making money" and managing the risk of the audit firm, and how the audit firm can minimize that tension. How might partner compensation affect audit risk?

7-10   **(LO 5)** In the overview of audit procedures, five different activities are identified in the evidence gathering and evaluation process. What are those activities and why is it important that each is considered and integrated into an overall assessment of audit evidence?

7-11   **(LO 4)** What is directional testing? How can the concept of directional testing assist the auditor in attaining audit efficiency?

7-12   **(LO 4)** Explain how testing an asset account for overstatement provides evidence on potential overstatements of revenue and understatement of expenses. Illustrate using accounts receivable and inventory as examples.

7-13   **(LO 1, 3)** Discuss the relative reliability and usefulness of internal and external documentation. Give two examples of each.

7-14 **(LO 7)** For audits under the jurisdiction of the PCAOB, auditors must document significant findings or issues and actions taken to address them. One of the significant findings that auditors are required to document and address are audit adjustments. What are audit adjustments? Why might the PCAOB care if management refuses to make an audit adjustment that the auditor recommends?

7-15 **(LO 3, 5)** Are inquiries of management considered reliable evidence? Under what conditions and for what assertions would inquiry of management be considered reliable evidence?

7-16 **(LO 1, 3)** Is paper-based evidence more reliable than the same evidence generated electronically and stored on a computer system? Explain. Under what conditions is electronically stored evidence as reliable as paper-based evidence?

7-17 **(LO 5)** What is the difference between reprocessing a transaction and vouching a transaction? What underlying assertion does each test address?

Professional Skepticism

7-18 **(LO 3, 5)** Confirmations can sometimes be unreliable even if they involve external documentation. What assumptions should the auditor address concerning confirmations before concluding that using confirmations will result in reliable audit evidence? Explain the role of professional skepticism in the context of evaluating evidence obtained from confirmations.

7-19 **(LO 3)** Why is it generally more efficient to test ending account balances rather than testing transactions throughout the year? Explain why the efficiency might change in a computerized environment with effective internal controls.

7-20 **(LO 6)** What are the purposes of an audit program? What are the major issues that should be addressed in an audit program?

7-21 **(LO 7)** What is audit documentation? What key components should each audit document contain?

7-22 **(LO 3)** Many organizations are consciously eliminating paper documents by integrating their computer system with those of their suppliers and customers. Paper documents, such as purchase orders, are being replaced by machine-generated purchase orders. How is this change in documentation likely to affect the audit approach for such clients? Explain and give an example.

7-23 **(LO 7)** What is meant by the statement "audit documentation ought to stand on its own"? What is the importance of this concept?

7-24 **(LO 3)** Assume an auditor wishes to estimate an account balance by reference to outside data or other information generated from outside the accounting system. Under what conditions would such a procedure generate reliable audit evidence?

Professional Skepticism

7-25 **(LO 8)** Consider the "Earnings Management" example for Ford and General Motors in the chapter section "Auditing Account Balances Affected by Management's Estimates" as background. Why might it be difficult for auditors to disallow companies' preferences to decrease existing reserves? Explain the role of professional skepticism in the context of evaluating management's explanations for their accounting for reserves in this context.

Multiple-Choice Questions

7-26 **(LO 3)** The auditor wishes to gather evidence to test the assertion that the client's capitalization of leased equipment assets is properly valued. Which of the following sources of evidence will the auditor find to be the most persuasive (most reliable and relevant)?

a. Direct observation of the leased equipment.

b. Examination of the lease contract and recalculation of capitalized amount and current amortization.

c. Confirmation of the current purchase price for similar equipment with vendors.

d. Confirmation of the original cost of the equipment with the lessor.

7-27 **(LO 3, 5)** The sufficiency of audit evidence is determined by:

a. The reliability of the audit evidence.

b. The quantity of evidence gathered.

c. The risk of material misstatement of the assertion being examined.

d. All of the above.

7-28 **(LO 3, 5)** An auditor determines that management integrity is high, the risk of account misstatements is low, and the client's internal controls are effective. Which of the following conclusions can be reached regarding the need to perform direct evidence regarding the correctness of account balances? Direct tests

a. Should be limited to material account balances, and the extent of testing should be sufficient to corroborate the auditor's assessment of low risk.

b. Of account balances are not needed.

c. Can be limited to analytical procedures.

d. Should be performed on all material account balances regardless of the auditor's assessment of internal control.

7-29 **(LO 4)** A test of inventory for overstatement provides corresponding evidence on:

	Cost of Goods Sold	Revenue	Accounts Payable
a.	Overstatement	Overstatement	Understatement
b.	Understatement	Overstatement	Overstatement
c.	Understatement	Understatement	Understatement
d.	Overstatement	Overstatement	Overstatement

7-30 **(LO 3, 5)** Observation is considered a reliable audit procedure but one that is limited in its usefulness. Which of the following is not correct regarding a limitation of the use of observation as an audit technique?

a. Individuals may act differently when being observed than they do otherwise.

b. It is rarely sufficient to satisfy any assertion other than existence.

c. It is rarely sufficient to satisfy any assertion other than valuation.

d. It is difficult to generalize from one observation as to the correctness of processing throughout the period under audit.

*7-31   **(LO 2, 5)** Confirmation is most likely to be a relevant form of evidence with regard to assertions about accounts receivable when the auditor has concern about the receivables'

a. Valuation

b. Classification

c. Existence

d. Completeness

7-32   **(LO 7)** Regarding the auditor's reasoning process about an account balance, the auditor should

a. Simply state a conclusion because anything else would lead to second-guessing by another auditor or a lawyer.

b. Identify and document all of the elements of the reasoning process, but only for accounts where audit adjustments were needed.

c. Assure that audit documentation, by itself, is sufficient to support the auditor's opinion without an explicit description of the reasoning process, that is, the evidence should be able to stand on its own.

d. Be limited to analysis made by the partner in charge of the engagement.

7-33   **(LO 5)** An auditor observes inventory held by the client and notes that some of the inventory appears to be very old but still in reasonable condition for sale. Which of the following conclusions is justified by the audit procedure?

   I. The older inventory is obsolete.

  II. The inventory is owned by the company.

III. Inventory may need to be reduced to current market value.

a. I only

b. II only

c. I and III only

d. III only

7-34   **(LO 2, 5)** The auditor wishes to test the completeness assertion regarding revenue. Which of the following procedures would be most effective in addressing that assertion?

a. Take a sample of recorded revenue and trace to the underlying shipping document.

b. Take a sample of shipping documents and trace to related invoice and into the general ledger.

c. Perform analytical review comparing recorded sales revenue with the two previous years.

d. Take a sample of invoices and trace to related source document.

---

*All problems marked with an asterisk are adapted from the uniform CPA examination.

Discussion and Research Questions

7-35 **(Financial Statement Assertions for a Liability Account, LO 2, 5)**
Accounts payable is generally one of the larger, and most volatile,
liability accounts to audit. Assume that you are auditing the accounts
payable account for Appleton Electronics, a wholesaler of hardware
equipment. You can assume that the company has good internal
controls and is not designated as a high-risk audit client. You are the
continuing auditor. During the previous audit, adjustments were made
regarding accounts payable, but none of them was considered material.

**Professional
Skepticism**

Required

a. Identify the financial statement assertions that apply to accounts
payable.

b. For each assertion identified, list two or three types of audit evidence that would address the assertion and the procedures used to
gather the audit evidence. Organize your answer as follows:

Financial Statement Assertion   *Audit Evidence and Procedures*

c. How would the evidence-gathering procedures be affected if you
had assessed the client as a high-risk client because (1) there are
questions of management integrity, (2) the company is in a peril-
ous financial situation, and (3) the company has inadequate internal
controls? Be specific in your answer, explaining what additional
evidence, or alternative types of evidence, you would gather.

d. Why should the auditor be more skeptical of management in the
scenario in part (c) versus a scenario in which the company is
low-risk on these dimensions?

7-36 **(Financial Statement Assertions, LO 2, 5)** Auditors routinely
encounter client entries or financial accounting choices that are
inconsistent with the financial statement assertions.

Required

a. For each of the following, indicate what *account balance* assertion(s)
is violated.

1. Sales shipped FOB destination are recorded when shipped.
Some of these are in transit at the balance sheet date.

2. An inventory purchase is received but not recorded until the
company pays for the goods.

3. Repair costs that should be expensed are capitalized.

4. No loss is recorded or disclosed for a pending lawsuit against
the client that is material, probable, and can be estimated.

5. Sales shipped FOB shipping point are recorded before the balance sheet date but not shipped until after the balance sheet date.

6. Wages earned but not paid by the balance sheet date are not recorded.

7. Some checks in payment of accounts payable are recorded
before the balance sheet date but not mailed until after the
balance sheet date.

8. Collections from customers received after the balance sheet
date are recorded as of the balance sheet date.

9. A capital lease is improperly accounted for as an operating
lease.

10. A $56,000 sale on account near year end was recorded at $65,000.

b. Which of the items in part (a) affect net income? Explain.

7-37   **(Procedures and Assertions—Inventory, LO 5)** You are planning the audit of the PageDoc Company's inventory. PageDoc manufactures a variety of office equipment.

Required

Describe how each of the following procedures could be used in the audit of inventory and the related assertion(s) it tests:

Procedure	How used	Assertion(s) tested
Observation		
Physical inspection		
Inquiry		
Confirmation		
Inspection of documents		
Recalculation		
Reprocessing		
Vouching		
Analytical procedures		

7-38   **(Relevance and Reliability of Audit Evidence, LO 1, 3, 5)** An auditor has to determine both the reliability and the relevance of potential audit evidence in order to determine that "appropriate" audit evidence is gathered.

Required

a. Explain the difference between relevance and reliability.

b. How does an auditor go about determining the reliability of potential audit evidence?

c. Sufficiency is a separate attribute of audit evidence, but it is related to both relevance and reliability. For each of the following items, identify whether or not the auditor has made a judgment error, and if there is a judgment error whether the error relates to sufficiency, reliability, or relevance of the audit evidence. Arrange your answer as follows:

Judgment Error	Nature of Error	Explanation
Yes or No	Relevance, etc.	Description of error

1. The auditor receives only 20% of the confirmations that were sent to customers to verify their account balance. The auditor responds by taking another sample of receivables to send out in place of the first sample. The auditor is convinced the first sample is not representative of the population as a whole.

2. The auditor sent a confirmation to an independent warehouse to confirm that the inventory was owned by the audit client. There was no response. The auditor decided to visit the warehouse to independently verify the inventory on hand.

3. The auditor decides to test the completeness of accounts payable by taking a sample of recorded accounts payable and tracing to the source document evidencing receipt of the goods or services. No exceptions were noted so the auditor does not expand the audit work.

4. An auditor wishes to test the valuation of a marketable security and inquires about management's intent for using the securities. Management indicates that they are intending to hold the securities as a long-term investment. The auditor decides that no further evidence is needed and that the securities are properly valued at cost.

5. The auditor notes that there are some problems with segregation of duties over accounts receivable. The client is aware that the auditor normally sends out accounts receivable confirmations. The auditor decides to expand the audit work by sending additional confirmations.

6. During the observation of inventory, the auditor notes a number of items that look old and apparently not used. The auditor discusses each item with the marketing manager to determine whether or not the item is considered saleable at normal prices.

7-39   **(Relevance and Reliability of Audit Evidence, LO 3, 5)** In this chapter, several different kinds of audit evidence were identified. The following questions concern the relevance and reliability of audit evidence.

Required

a. Explain why confirmations are normally considered more reliable than inquiries of the client. Under what situations might the opposite hold true?

b. Give three examples of reliable evidence and three examples of less reliable evidence. What characteristics distinguish them?

c. Explain why physical inspection is considered strong, but limited, evidence. What knowledge about inventory should the auditor possess in order to make observation of inventory both relevant and reliable?

d. What characteristics must internal evidence have to cause the auditor to assess the evidence as reliable?

e. Explain why tests of details may be more relevant than analytical procedures.

f. Explain how analytical procedures might be more relevant to assessing the correctness of an account balance than would be tests of details. In formulating your answer, think in terms of particular account balances.

g. There is always tension between the cost of obtaining evidence and the risk of making an incorrect assessment of the fairness of the financial statements. Explain the relationship between cost, relevance, and reliability of information and the criteria auditors use to balance those three factors.

h. Identify three instances when an auditor is likely to use recalculation and reperformance as audit procedures in gathering audit evidence. Is an auditor-prepared spreadsheet a recalculation or an independent estimate of an account balance? Explain.

7-40   **(Account Relationships and Audit Efficiency, LO 3, 4)** One way that the auditor might achieve audit efficiency is to recognize the interrelationship between accounts. In many situations, evidence gathered in auditing a balance sheet account (asset, liability, or equity) can be easily expanded to auditing a related income statement account.

Required

a. For each of the accounts identified below:

　1. Identify one or more related accounts that could be audited efficiently by expanding on the audit evidence gathered during the audit of the account.

　2. Identify how the evidence gathered from auditing the balance sheet account could be used in auditing the related income, equity, or expense account.

Account Balances Audited

1. Marketable Equity Securities
2. Bond Payable
3. Property, Plant, and Equipment
4. Equity Method Investments
5. Capitalized Leases
6. Capitalized Lease Obligations
7. Notes Payable
8. Estimated Warranty Liability (Reserve)
9. Preferred Stock

b. Explain why auditors generally consider it more efficient to directly test a year-end balance sheet account rather than test transactions during the year. Does this mean that auditors do not need to test the transactions that make up an account balance; that is, they need to test only the year-end balance? Explain your answer in terms of the reliability and persuasiveness of audit evidence.

7-41　**(Complementary Effect of Audit Tests, LO 2, 4)** With the double-entry accounting system, testing one account balance produces audit evidence concerning another account balance or class of transactions. For example, testing for overstatement of current marketable securities may uncover an understatement of long-term investments due to a misclassification (presentation and disclosure).

Required

For each of the following tests of account balances:

a. Indicate at least two other account balances or classes of transactions for which evidence is also provided, as well as the related assertions.

b. Identify at least one procedure that the auditor might use to test the identified account for the assertion identified below. Be explicit in the audit procedure. For example, if you are suggesting that the auditor take a sample of something, be clear as to what population the sample is taken from.

　1. Testing inventory for overstatement (existence and valuation)

　2. Testing revenue for understatement (completeness)

　3. Testing accounts receivable for overstatement (existence)

　4. Testing accrued salaries or wages for understatement (completeness)

　5. Testing repairs and maintenance expense for overstatement (existence)

　6. Testing the adequacy of the allowance for doubtful accounts (valuation)

7-42   **(Types of Audit Procedures, LO 2, 5)** Ten types of audit procedures are identified as part of the audit evidence-gathering process. These procedures are as follows:

Observation	Inspection of physical assets
Examination of documents	Inquiry of knowledgeable persons (internal and external)
Reprocessing	Recalculation
Reperformance	Vouching
External confirmations	Analytical procedures

Required

Following is a list of audit procedures performed. For each procedure, classify the evidence gathered according to one (or more, if applicable) of the audit procedure types and identify the assertion(s) being tested. Organize your answer as follows:

Procedure	Type of Procedure	Assertion Tested
a.		
b.		

Auditing Procedures Performed

a. Calculate the ratio of Cost of Goods Sold to Sales as a test of overall reasonableness of the balance for Cost of Goods Sold.

b. Trace a sales transaction from the origination of an incoming sales order to the shipment of merchandise to an invoice and to the proper recording in the sales journal.

c. Test the accuracy of the sales invoice by multiplying the number of items shipped by the authorized price list to determine extended cost. Foot the total and reconcile it with the total invoiced.

d. Select recorded sales invoices and trace the corresponding shipping documents to verify the existence of goods shipped.

e. Examine canceled checks returned with the client's January bank statement as support of outstanding checks listed on the client's December year-end bank reconciliation.

f. Perform inspection and independently count a sample of the client's marketable securities held in a safe deposit box.

g. Tour the plant to determine that a major equipment acquisition was received and is in working condition.

h. Review a lease contract to determine the items it covers and its major provisions.

i. Request a statement from a major customer as to its agreement or disagreement with a year-end receivable balance shown to be due to the audit client.

j. Develop a spreadsheet to calculate an independent estimate of the client's warranty liability (reserve) based on production data and current warranty repair expenditures.

k. Meet with the client's internal legal department to determine its assessment of the potential outcome of pending litigation regarding a patent infringement suit against the company.

l. Review all major past-due accounts receivable with the credit manager to determine whether the client's allowance for doubtful accounts is adequate.

m. Make test counts of inventory items inspected and record the items in the audit documentation for subsequent testing.

n. Obtain information about the client's processing system and associated controls by asking the client's personnel to fill out a questionnaire.

o. Examine board of directors' minutes for the approval of a major bond issued during the year.

p. Have the client's outside law firm send a letter directly to the auditor providing a description of any differences between the lawyer's assessment of litigation and that of the client.

Professional Skepticism

7-43 **(Inquiry of Knowledgeable Persons and Including Confirmations, LO 3, 5)** One major task for an auditor is to evaluate the reliability of evidence obtained through inquiry of knowledgeable persons—both internal to and external to the organization. The evidence may come in the form of oral or written representations from management or in written form from parties outside the organization.

Required

a. In the course of an audit, the auditor asks many questions of client officers and employees. Describe the factors the auditor should consider in evaluating oral evidence provided by client officers and employees. How should professional skepticism affect auditors' evaluations of oral evidence?

b. For each of the following examples of evidence obtained from inquiry, identify either (1) an alternative source of evidence or (2) corroborative evidence the auditor might seek to increase the overall reliability of the evidence.

Examples of Testimonial Evidence:

1. Confirmation is received from customers as to the balance of accounts receivable shown by the client.

2. Management is optimistic that all items in a product line will be sold at normal prices in spite of a temporary downturn in sales.

3. Management indicates a strategy to both grow revenue and profits, thereby offsetting the potential need to write down recorded goodwill for impairment.

4. Management tells the auditor that the Food and Drug Administration has approved its new drug for commercial sale. Although sales have not yet been made, the company anticipates a major increase in the value of the company's stock.

5. The auditor interviews the production manager, who candidly identifies quality-control problems and points out substantial pieces of inventory that should be reworked before shipment.

7-44 **(Alternative Sources of Evidence, LO 2, 3, 5)** The following situations present the auditor with alternative sources of evidence regarding a particular assertion.

Required

a. For each of the following situations, identify the assertion(s) the auditor is most likely testing with the procedure.

b. For each situation, identify which of the two sources presents the most appropriate evidence and briefly indicate the rationale for your answer.

Sources of Audit Evidence

1. Confirming accounts receivable with business organizations vs. confirming receivables with consumers.

2. Visually inspecting an inventory of electronic components vs. performing an inventory turnover and sales analysis by products and product lines.

3. Observing the counting of a client's year-end physical inventory vs. confirming the inventory held at an independent warehouse by requesting a confirmation from the owner of the warehouse.

4. Confirming a year-end bank balance with the client's banking institution vs. reviewing the client's year-end bank statement vs. having a cutoff bank statement as of January 20 for all activity from December 31 to January 20 sent to the auditor.

5. Observing the client's inventory composed primarily of sophisticated radar detectors and similar electronic equipment vs. observing the client's inventory composed primarily of sheet metal.

6. Confirming the client's year-end bank balance with the bank vs. confirming the potential loss because of a lawsuit with the client's outside legal counsel.

7. Testing the client's estimate of warranty liability by (a) recalculating amounts by inputting data into the client's spreadsheet used in calculating the liability, or (b) independently creating an independent spreadsheet that uses regression analysis to estimate the warranty liability using client sales and warranty return data.

8. Inspecting payments made to vendors after year end to determine if they were properly recorded as accounts payable at year end vs. requesting vendor statements at year end for all significant vendors from whom the client made purchases during the year.

9. For a financial institution, testing the organization's controls for recording customer savings deposits, including the effective operation of an independent department to explore any inquiries by customers vs. confirming year-end savings account balances with customers.

10. For a financial institution, testing the organization's controls for making and recording business loans vs. confirming year-end loan balances directly with customers.

7-45   **(Audit Program and Assertions, LO 2, 5)** You have been assigned to audit the notes receivable of a medium-size audit client, Eagle River Distributing. The notes receivable account is new this year and, per discussion with the controller, it came about because three major customers were experiencing payment difficulties. The three customers account for approximately 15% of the client's annual sales. The account was first used in July with a $300,000 balance and now has a year-end balance of $2.5 million (this compares to an accounts receivable year-end balance of $6.0 million).

Group Activity

On further investigation, you determine that the year-end balance is composed of the following notes:

J.P. McCarthur Printing, 10%, due July 1 of next year	$1.2 million
Stevens Point Newspaper, 11%, due Sept. 30 of next year	$0.8 million
Orbison Enterprises, 12%, due in 18 months	$0.5 million

You further discover the following:

1. Orbison Enterprises is a company wholly owned by the president of Eagle River Distributing and is backed by the personal guarantee of the president (including the pledging of personal assets).
2. The company continues to make sales to each of these companies. The notes represent a consolidation of previous outstanding receivables. All three companies are current in their payments of existing receivables.

Required

a. In a small group, work together to identify and discuss any special risk concerns that you might have regarding the audit of this new account.

b. Identify the major assertions to be tested by the auditor in auditing this account. For each assertion, identify one or two auditing procedures that could be used to gather evidence in determining the correct financial statement presentation of the account.

7-46 **(Audit Documentation, LO 7)** Audit documentation represents the auditor's accumulation of evidence and conclusions reached on an audit engagement. Prior-year audit documentation can provide insight into an audit engagement that will be useful in planning the current year audit.

Required

a. What are the purposes or primary functions of audit documentation?

b. Who owns the documentation, the auditor or the client?

c. What important planning information might an auditor learn when reviewing the prior-year audit documentation of a client?

d. The auditor often asks the client to prepare a schedule, such as a schedule listing all repair and maintenance expenses over $5,000 for the past year. Assume that the client requests a copy of the previous year's documentation to serve as a guide and the auditor is reluctant to furnish the documentation to the client.

   1. Is it permissible to provide the client copies of the auditor's previous documentation? If so, are there any particular conditions the auditor should examine before furnishing the documentation to the client?

   2. What procedures should the auditor use to assure that the client has properly prepared the requested documentation?

e. Assume the auditor found a weakness in internal control that suggested that the company had higher than normal risk that revenue might be recorded in the wrong period. Given this weakness, what information should be included in audit documentation?

7-47 **(Audit Documentation, LO 7)** The following equipment schedule was prepared by the client and audited by Sam Staff, an audit assistant, during the calendar year 2011 audit of Roberta Enterprises, a continuing audit client. As engagement supervisor, you are reviewing the documentation.

Required

Identify the deficiencies in the audit documentation.

ROBERTA ENTERPRISES
12/31/2011

		COST				ACCUMULATED DEPRECIATION			
Description	Date Purchased	Beginning Balance	Additions	Disposals	Ending Balance	Beginning Balance	Depreciation Expense	Disposals	Ending Balance
1020 Press	10/25/08	15,250		15,250*	0	10,500†	1,575‡	12,075§	0
40" Lathe	10/30/06	9,852		9,852	0	7,444†	1,250‡	8,694§	0
505 Router	10/15/08	4,635			4,635	3,395†	875		4,270
MP Welder	9/10/07	1,222			1,222	850†	215		1,065
1040 Press	3/25/11		18,956§		18,956	0	3,566		3,566
IBM 400AS Computer	7/16/07	12,547			12,547	7,662†	3,065†		10,727
60" Lathe	5/29/11		13,903§		13,903	0	950†		950
Fork Lift	6/2/05	7,881			7,881	3,578†	810†		4,388
Totals		51,387	32,859§	25,102	59,144	33,429†	12,306†	20,769§	24,966
			‖		‖	‖	‖	‖**	‖

† Traced to 12/31/2010 audit documentation
‡ Recalculated
§ Verified
‖ Footed/cross-footed
* Traced to sales document and cash receipt
** Traced to trial balance

Cases

7-48   **(Assimilating Audit Evidence, LO 1, 2, 7)** Exhibit 7.3 is a depiction of the sources of evidence. The auditor gathers:

- Knowledge about the client
- Information about internal controls
- Accounting process information—tests of account balances and accounting processes
- Outside information, including market information

Professional Skepticism

Required

a. Exhibit 7.3 shows each of these four items with an arrow going to cumulative audit evidence. However, each component may have an effect on other components. Explain how the components interact, e.g., how information about internal control affects client acceptance, tests of account balances, and the need for outside information.

b. Is the ultimate audit decision based on the tests of accounting records, or is it a cumulative judgment from all of the sources of information? Or would it be proper to argue that all of the other components lead directly or indirectly to evidence on the account balances and the financial statements?

c. Explain how information about the client, i.e., client acceptance/continuance information and previous year's audit work might be considered evidence for this year's audit.

d. Does the auditor have to document how previous audit work and client acceptance/continuation information affects the current year audit? Explain your rationale and how your answer affects current year audit documentation.

Group Activity

7-49   **(Decision Analysis Group Case: Adequacy of Audit Evidence, LO 1, 3, 9)** The *Professional Judgment in Context* scenario at the beginning of the chapter introduced excerpts from the PCAOB inspection of Deloitte & Touche, LLP. The scenario is:

On May 4, 2010, the PCAOB issued its public inspection of Deloitte & Touche, LLP covering their inspection of audits conducted during 2009. In their summary comments regarding the inspection, the PCAOB inspectors stated:

> In some cases, the conclusion that the Firm failed to perform a procedure may be based on the absence of documentation and the absence of persuasive other evidence, even if the Firm claims to have performed the procedure. PCAOB Auditing Standard No. 3, *Audit Documentation* ("AS No. 3") provides that, in various circumstances including PCAOB inspections, a firm that has not adequately documented that it performed a procedure, obtained evidence, or reached an appropriate conclusion must demonstrate with persuasive other evidence that it did so, and that oral assertions and explanations alone do not constitute persuasive other evidence. (p. 3)

The report went on to say:

> In some cases, the deficiencies identified were of such significance that it appeared to the inspection team that the Firm, at the time it issued its audit report, had not obtained sufficient competent evidential matter to support its opinion on the issuer's financial statements or internal control over financial reporting ("ICFR").

It is reasonable to ask, What is the nature of these deficiencies, could this criticism happen to me, and why didn't the firm reviewing partners detect the deficiencies? In order to understand how to answer these questions, the following excerpts describe the nature of deficiencies found on individual audits:

In this audit, the Firm failed in the following respects to obtain sufficient competent evidential matter to support its audit opinion—

- The Firm failed to perform adequate audit procedures to test the valuation of the issuer's inventory and investments in joint ventures (the primary assets of which were inventory). Specifically, the Firm:

  ○ Failed to re-evaluate, in light of a significant downturn in the issuer's industry and the general deterioration in economic conditions, whether the issuer's assumption, which it had also used in prior years, that certain inventory required no review for impairment was still applicable in the year under audit;

  ○ Excluded from its impairment testing a significant portion of the inventory that may have been impaired, because the Firm selected inventory items for testing from those for which the issuer already had recorded impairment charges;

  ○ Failed to evaluate the reasonableness of certain of the significant assumptions that the issuer used in determining the fair value estimates of inventory and investments in joint ventures;

  ○ Failed to obtain support for certain of the significant assumptions that the Firm used when developing an independent estimate of the fair value of one category of inventory; and

      ○ Failed to test items in a significant category of inventory, which consisted of all items with book values per item below a Firm-specified amount that was over 70 percent of the Firm's planning materiality.

- The Firm failed to perform adequate audit procedures to evaluate the issuer's assertion that losses related to the issuer's guarantees of certain joint venture obligations were not probable, because the Firm's procedures were limited to inquiry of management.

Discuss in your small group the following requirements:

a. What is the auditor's responsibility to consider information outside of the client's records and processing to develop sufficient and appropriate audit evidence?

b. Why are the items identified above by the PCAOB considered "critical mistakes" in performing an audit? What is the critical error of omission by the auditing firm and why would the specific problem lead to a deficiency in sufficient appropriate evidence?

c. Why is "inquiry of management" not considered "sufficient information" by itself?

d. Assumptions are assumptions! What is the auditor's responsibility regarding the questioning of the assumptions used by the client? In formulating your response, keep in mind that the client will claim that assumptions are just assumptions and it is difficult to say that one is more correct than another.

e. The chapter talked about the tension between controlling audit costs and managing audit risks at the same time. Explain how the pressures to keep the audit within a time budget might have led to some of the deficiencies noted above by the PCAOB.

f. Presumably Deloitte used a standardized audit program. How could a standardized audit program lead to some of the problems identified above, e.g., failing to test a category of inventory that had book value in excess of 70% of the firm's planning materiality, or limiting the testing of impairment to inventory that had already been assessed as impaired by management?

7-50   **(Accounting Estimates, LO 8)** The SEC took action against Gateway Computer in 2001 because it believed that Gateway systematically understated the allowance for doubtful accounts to meet sales and earnings targets. This is essentially the way the alleged fraud took place:

- Gateway sold most of its computers over the Internet and had a strong credit department that approved sales.

- When sales dropped, management decided to go back to customers who had been rejected because of poor credit approval.

- During the first quarter, it went after the better of the "previously rejected" customers.

- As the need for more revenue and earnings remained, Gateway continued down the list to include everyone.

- However, it did not change any of its estimates for the allowance for uncollectible accounts.

    At the end of the process, the poor credit customers represented about 5% of total income, but the SEC alleged that the allowance account was understated by over $35 million, which amounted to approximately $0.07 per share. In essence, Gateway wanted to show it was doing well when the rest of the industry was doing badly.

Required

a. What is the requirement regarding proper valuation of the allowance for doubtful accounts? Does that requirement differ from account balances that are based on recording transactions as opposed to the allowance being an estimate? In other words, is more preciseness required on account balances that do not contain estimates?

b. What information should the company use in a system to make the estimate of the allowance for uncollectible accounts?

c. What evidence should the auditor gather to determine whether the client's estimate of the allowance for uncollectible accounts is fairly stated?

d. How should the expansion of sales to customers who had previously been rejected for credit affect the estimate of the allowance for doubtful accounts?

e. How important are current economic conditions to the process of making an estimate of the allowance for doubtful accounts? Explain.

7-51   **(Adecco—Audit Evidence for Sales, LO 2, 3, 5)** Adecco SA is the world's largest temporary employment company. It lost several major accounts because customers felt it was not adequately serving their complex staffing needs. It announced that it was not able to deliver its financial statements on schedule. Their auditors had raised questions about accounting and controls as part of an intensive audit of internal controls as mandated by the Sarbanes-Oxley Act. It appears that Adecco recorded revenue for temporary services provided during the first several weeks in January as previous year's income.

The company has a database in which it knows, at any point in time, which temporary employees are assigned to which clients, and the daily billing rates for those employees. The company bills each client at a rotating month end; for some clients, the billing is on the 5th of the month, others are on the 15th of the month, etc. Each client receives only one bill per month and is expected to pay within 30 days after the billing date. The billing is computerized, and the client makes accruals for unbilled revenue at the end of each quarter and year end. Most of the bills are sent electronically, although a few are sent using paper documents.

Required

a. Explain why revenue recognition is always considered "high risk" for each audit engagement.

b. If revenue is overstated, what assertion(s) is (are) the auditor most concerned with?

c. Why might management be motivated to accelerate the recognition of revenue into the current year—even though it makes it difficult to achieve higher revenue in the following year? What factors related to the control environment might have been identified that would have led the auditor to rate the audit as "high risk."

d. One evidence-gathering option was to send out a confirmation to Adecco's clients as to the amount owed to Adecco as of year end. Explain why (or why not) this would be a good audit procedure.

e. What other audit procedures could have been used to determine whether revenue was properly recorded?

7-52 **(MiniScribe—Audit Evidence for Sales, Accounts Receivable, and Inventory, LO 1, 2, 5)** As reported in the *Wall Street Journal* (September 11, 1989), MiniScribe, Inc., inflated its reported profits and inventory through a number of schemes designed to fool the auditors. At that time, MiniScribe was one of the major producers of disk drives for personal computers. The newspaper article reported that MiniScribe used the following techniques to meet its profit objectives:

Fraud

- An extra shipment of $9 million of disks was sent to a customer near year end and booked as a sale. The customer had not ordered the goods and ultimately returned them, but the sale was not reversed in the year recorded.

- Shipments were made from a factory in Singapore, usually by air freight. Toward the end of the year, some of the goods were shipped by cargo ships. The purchase orders were changed to show that the customer took title when the goods were loaded on the ship. However, title did not pass to the customer until the goods were received in the United States.

- Returned goods were recorded as usable inventory. Some were shipped without any repair work performed.

- MiniScribe developed a number of just-in-time warehouses and shipped goods to them from where they were delivered to customers. The shipments were billed as sales as soon as they reached the warehouse.

Required

For each of the items just described, identify the audit evidence that should have been gathered that would have enabled the auditor to uncover the fraud.

7-53 **(Fraud and Investigations, LO 1, 5)** Cendant Corporation was the subject of an intensive fraud investigation. A look at the company's website revealed the following statements contained in a report given to the SEC. The company sold travel and health club memberships. Significant irregularities included the following:

Fraud

Professional Skepticism

- *Irregular charges against merger reserves*—Operating results at the former Cendant business units were artificially boosted by recording fictitious revenues through inappropriately reversing restructuring charges and liabilities to revenues. Many other irregularities were also generated by inappropriate use of these reserves.

- *False coding of services sold to customers*—Significant revenues from members purchasing long-term benefits were intentionally misclassified in accounting records as revenue from shorter-term products. The falsely recorded revenues generated higher levels of immediately recognized revenues and profits for Cendant.

- *Delayed recognition of canceled memberships and "charge-backs" (a charge-back is a rejection by a credit-card-issuing bank of a charge to a member's credit card account)*—In addition to overstating revenues, these delayed charges caused Cendant's cash and working capital accounts to be overstated.

- *Quarterly recording of fictitious revenues*—Large numbers of accounts receivable entries made in the first three quarters of the year were fabricated; they had no associated clients or customers and no associated sale of services. This practice also occurred in the prior two years.

Accounting Errors

The company also had other accounting errors were not classified as accounting irregularities. Approximately 6 to 9 cents per share of the total estimated restatement of earnings will result from the elimination of these errors. These accounting errors include inappropriate useful lives for certain intangible assets, delayed recognition of insurance claims, and use of accounting policies that do not conform to the applicable financial reporting financial reporting framework.

Required

a. How could the auditor have used risk analysis to determine the likelihood that a material misstatement might have existed in Cendant's financial statements?

b. Identify audit procedures (and audit evidence gathered) that would have detected the misstatement of revenues and intangible assets. Be specific to each of the four irregularities identified in the case introduction.

c. How would the auditor's assessment of management integrity and management motivation have affected the nature, timing, and extent of audit procedures identified? Explain the role of professional skepticism in this context.

Group Activity

7-54 **(Linking Risk Factors to Account Balances and Management Assertions, LO 2)** In Ford Motor Company's Annual Report, management disclosed the following risk factors that might affect the financial statements going forward.

a. Continued decline in market share, and a market shift (or an increase in or acceleration of market shift) away from sales of trucks or sport utility vehicles, or from sales of other more profitable vehicles in the United States.

b. Continued or increased price competition resulting from industry overcapacity, currency fluctuations, or other factors.

c. Lower-than-anticipated market acceptance of new or existing products.

d. Substantial pension and postretirement health care and life insurance liabilities impairing our liquidity or financial condition.

e. Worse-than-assumed economic and demographic experience for our postretirement benefit plans (e.g., discount rates, investment returns, and health care cost trends).

f. The discovery of defects in vehicles resulting in delays in new model launches, recall campaigns, or increased warranty costs.

g. Unusual or significant litigation or governmental investigations arising out of alleged defects in our products or otherwise.

Required

a. In a small group, work together to identify a related account balance that might be affected by the risk for each risk factor.

b. For each account balance identified, indicate how the risk will affect the audit evidence that will be gathered. Include what specific assertion is being addressed.

Ethics

7-55 **(Ethics Group Case: Ghost Tickmarking, LO 7, 9)** The purpose of this case is to provide you with an example of a decision setting in which we will explore the ethical issues involved in conducting audit procedures. This case is based on an actual situation that occurred in audit practice. However, names have been changed to achieve confidentiality concerning audit firm personnel issues.

In auditing, entry-level staff members conduct examinations of client records and accounting transactions in order to gain evidence about the appropriate application of the applicable financial reporting financial reporting framework. One task that entry-level staff often complete is comparing original client records of transactions to client reports that summarize those transactions. In this way, auditors gain assurance that the transactions used to construct the financial statements are complete and accurate.

Elizabeth Jenkins was a staff auditor assigned to a large insurance client engagement. She was working on the portion of the audit concerning the client's claims loss reserves (reserves for future claims submitted by those insured by the insurance company). This reserve is analogous to the allowance for doubtful accounts of a company in the manufacturing or service sector. Essentially, the audit firm wants to provide assurance that the client's estimate of the amount of claims that will ultimately be filed is correctly stated on the balance sheet, with the appropriate write-off appearing on the income statement. Elizabeth was asked by the senior accountant on the engagement (Brett Stein) to tie out (i.e., compare) the client's claim loss reserve estimate (which was summarized on a large Excel worksheet) with the client's system-generated reports that provided the underlying data for the reserve estimate. The calculation is complex and involves inputs from several sources. Therefore, the tie-out process was very detail oriented and rather repetitive, involving a significant amount of time and patience to complete accurately.

To demonstrate that she had compared the amount on the claims loss reserve Excel spreadsheet with that on the system-generated reports, Elizabeth was instructed to put a "tick mark" in both documents that would enable her senior to review her work. Along with each tick mark, Elizabeth was instructed to write a short note that described whether the two amounts did or did not agree. Elizabeth proceeded through the task, inserting tick marks where appropriate and noting agreement in all cases between the spreadsheet and the system-generated report. Because Elizabeth was feeling pressed for time and was exceedingly bored with her task, she skipped many of the comparisons and simply inserted tick marks indicating agreement even though she had not compared the numbers. She rationalized her actions by telling herself that this client had good internal controls and she had never found disagreements between source documents in other areas of the audit in which she was involved. In the audit profession, this action is known as "ghost tickmarking."

After Elizabeth had completed the task, she moved on to other parts of the audit as instructed by Brett. Subsequently, Brett reviewed Elizabeth's work. During that review, he recomputed amounts on both the Excel spreadsheet and the system-generated reports. To his surprise, there were instances in which Elizabeth had noted agreement between the two documents when in fact the numbers were not the same.

Brett met with Elizabeth and asked her about what had happened. She readily confessed to her actions. Brett counseled her that this behavior was unacceptable because it implies that audit work is being done when in fact the work is not being done. This puts the audit firm at risk because it provides inappropriate assurance that the client's records are accurate, when in fact they are not accurate. Elizabeth was embarrassed and remorseful and promised not to engage in ghost tick marking in the future. Brett noted the situation in Elizabeth's personnel records and notified the manager and partner on the engagement, along with relevant human resource personnel. The matter was fully documented in Elizabeth's personnel file.

During the course of the year, the supervisory audit firm personnel on all of Elizabeth's engagements were notified of her actions, and her work was subjected to more thorough review as a result. The firm noted no problems with the quality of Elizabeth's work during that time. During her annual review, she was again coached on the severity of her mistake. However, during the annual review process of all staff accountants, the firm did consider firing her based upon the mistake but ultimately decided that her confession, remorseful attitude, and subsequent high-quality work merited that she retain her employment.

Required

a. Try to put yourself in Elizabeth's position for a moment. Have you ever been tempted to do a low-quality job on some task that you considered mundane? Have you ever thought that your low-quality work would remain undiscovered?

b. Why is Elizabeth's misrepresentation of her work so important to the firm?

c. What did Elizabeth ultimately do right in this situation, once her misrepresentation was discovered?

d. Do you agree with the outcome? Do you think the firm was too lenient? Too harsh? What would you recommend the firm do in this situation? Use the ethical decision-making framework from Chapter 3 to help you arrive at a conclusion.

Academic Research Case (LO 3)

SEARCH HINT

It is easy to locate these academic research articles! Simply use a search engine (e.g., Google Scholar) or an electronic research platform (e.g., ABI Inform) and search using the author names and part of the article title.

Academic research addresses the conceptual issues outlined in this chapter. To help you consider the linkage between academic research and the practice of auditing, read the following research article and answer the questions below.

Kaplan, S., O'Donnell, E., & Arel, B. (2008). The influence of auditor experience on the persuasiveness of information provided by management. *Auditing: A Journal of Practice and Theory* 27(1): 67-83.

i. What is the evidence issue that is addressed in the article?

ii. Why is the issue important to the practicing auditor? How does the auditor go about evaluating the source of audit evidence?

iii. What are the major findings of the paper?

iv. What are the implications of these research findings for audit quality, the conduct of audit practice, and overall for the audit profession?

Go to www.cengage.com/accounting/rittenberg for the Ford and Toyota materials.

Source and Reference	Question
Ford 10-K or Annual Report	1. Consider Ford's inventory account on the balance sheet, along with the accompanying footnote. What are the most relevant assertions that management is making with regard to its inventory?
	2. Ford, in particular, is working to change models from SUVs to more fuel-efficient, smaller cars. How might that change affect the valuation of its bigger pickups and SUVs?
	3. What assertions are implied in the Property, Plant, and Equipment account? How would valuation be affected if the company decided to downsize and eliminate a line of pickup trucks?
	4. Examine the assets on the balance sheet of Ford. Identify the assets that are subject to (a) fair value adjustments, (b) impairment tests, (c) estimates to either net realizable value or lower of cost or market value. What are the implications for audit evidence that will be gathered for these accounts?
	5. Consider Ford's debt account on the balance sheet, along with the accompanying footnote. What are the most relevant assertions that management is making with regard to its debt?

Tools Used in Gathering Audit Evidence

LEARNING OBJECTIVES

The overriding objective of this textbook is to build a foundation with which to analyze current professional issues and adapt audit approaches to business and economic complexities. Through studying this chapter, you will be able to:

1 List and describe the tools used by auditors to gather sufficient appropriate audit evidence.

2 Explain the risks associated with sampling procedures and the nature of inferences required of all audit procedures.

3 Discuss the differences between nonstatistical and statistical sampling as a basis for determining the appropriate sampling methodology and apply these sample approaches in appropriate contexts.

4 Describe attribute sampling and use it to test controls.

5 Describe monetary unit sampling (MUS) and use it to test account balances.

6 Analyze MUS sampling results and choose effective follow-up procedures.

7 Describe how to use general audit software (GAS) to analyze data, including sampling data.

8 Discuss the use of, and apply, analytical procedures as a substantive test of account balances and describe how analytical procedures complement and affect other approaches to gathering audit evidence.

9 Apply the ethical decision-making framework to a sampling situation.

CHAPTER OVERVIEW

In prior chapters, we have discussed procedures that auditors might use to test financial statements and internal control assertions. Tests of internal controls provide the auditor with evidence to use in issuing an opinion on internal controls as well as evidence on the reliability of the information system that produces the financial statements. In testing the financial statement assertions, the auditor can take one of three approaches: (1) assess the reasonableness of the assertions by performing substantive analytic procedures, (2) directly test the account balances through tests of details, or (3) use a combination of information about controls and tests of account balances. The primary question not yet addressed can be stated simply as, What is the most efficient method to gather sufficient appropriate audit evidence?" This chapter describes three tools related to gathering audit evidence, including (1) sampling that can be used for both tests of controls and direct tests of account balances, (2) generalized audit software that can be used for analyzing underlying data and for supporting tests of controls and direct tests of account balances, and (3) substantive analytical procedures that provide evidence on the reasonableness

The Audit Opinion Formulation Process

I. Assessing Client Acceptance and Retention Decisions	II. Understanding the Client	III. Obtaining Evidence about Controls and Determining the Impact on the Financial Statement Audit	IV. Obtaining Substantive Evidence about Account Assertions	V. Wrapping Up the Audit and Making Reporting Decisions
CHAPTER 4	CHAPTERS 2, 4–6, and 9	CHAPTERS 5–14 and 18	CHAPTERS 7–14 and 18	CHAPTERS 15 and 16

The Auditing Profession, Regulation, and Corporate Governance	Decision-Making, Professional Conduct, and Ethics	Professional Liability
CHAPTERS 1 and 2	CHAPTER 3	CHAPTER 17

of the account balance. This chapter includes Phases III and IV of the audit opinion formulation process, i.e., gathering evidence about controls and substantive evidence about account assertions. This chapter provides an overview of the various approaches to gathering evidence, with emphasis on audit sampling, generalized audit software, and substantive analytical procedures.

PROFESSIONAL JUDGMENT IN CONTEXT

In 2008, the PCAOB issued its report on its 2004, 2005, 2006, and 2007 inspections of domestic annually-inspected firms. The report provides a summary discussion of certain common issues identified during those inspections. Two of the highlighted issues were audit sampling and substantive analytical procedures.

Regarding audit sampling, the report notes that:

The inspection teams identified deficiencies in firms' performance of audit sampling, including (a) using sample sizes that were too small to obtain enough evidence to form a conclusion about the account balance or class of transactions being tested, (b) failing to appropriately project the effect of errors identified when testing the items selected to the entire population, (c) failing to select the sample in such a way that it could be expected to be representative of the underlying population, and (d) not appropriately testing all the items in the sample.

With respect to substantive analytical procedures, the report states that:

Inspection teams have identified deficiencies in firms' performance of analytical procedures that the firms intended to be substantive tests, including the failure to (a) develop appropriate expectations, including in some instances the failure to appropriately disaggregate data in order to obtain the necessary level of precision for the expectation, (b) establish a threshold for differences that the firm could accept without further investigation, (c) establish a threshold for differences that was low enough to provide the level of assurance that the firm planned to achieve from the test, (d) test the data that the firm used in the analytical

procedures, (e) investigate significant unexpected differences from the firm's expectations, and (f) examine other evidence to obtain corroboration of management's explanations regarding significant unexpected differences.

Auditors who are gathering audit evidence about internal controls and account balances and assertions need to address the following questions related to audit sampling and substantive analytical procedures.

- In testing controls and account balances, what type of sampling should be used?

- In testing controls and account balances, how many individual account items should be selected, and which ones should be selected?

- If a sample contains an error, how is that information used to come to a conclusion regarding errors in the overall population?

- When should substantive analytical procedures be used for gathering audit evidence about account balances?

- What is the appropriate approach for performing and documenting substantive analytical procedures?

- What is the importance of developing an expectation when performing substantive analytical procedures?

- How do the results of substantive analytical procedures affect other testing decisions?

Information from the PCAOB Report can be found in PCAOB Release No. 2008–008, December 5, 2008; available at www.pcaobus.org.

Overview of Tools to Gather Audit Evidence

LO 1

List and describe the tools used by auditors to gather sufficient appropriate audit evidence.

This chapter describes three tools used to gather audit evidence, including (1) sampling that can be used for both tests of controls and direct tests of account balances, (2) generalized audit software that can be used for analyzing underlying data and for supporting tests of controls and direct tests of account balances, and (3) substantive analytical procedures that provide evidence on the reasonableness of the account balance.

Sampling is used in testing both controls and account balances and involves looking at less than 100% of the transactions that occurred during the period under audit. Sampling techniques would be appropriate when an auditor wants to perform procedures such as examining documents, reperforming calculations, or sending confirmations. However, the auditor should recognize that other types of audit procedures such as inquiry, observation, and most analytical procedures would not involve sampling. Exhibit 8.1 outlines alternative approaches to gathering evidence regarding financial statement assertions and includes examples of specific types of evidence that might be gathered and an indication as to when sampling, generalized audit software, or substantive analytical procedures would be appropriate.

Generalized audit software (GAS) are software programs designed specifically for auditors. GAS can be used to facilitate and automate the testing of 100% of a population when appropriate and to help focus the auditor's attention on

Exhibit 8.1	**Audit Evidence Gathering Procedures and Audit Assertions**
Financial Statement Assertion	**Approaches to Gathering Evidence Regarding Financial Statement Assertions**
Existence	• Sampling—take a sample and examine underlying evidence or send out confirmations. • Analytical procedures—comparison of the client's recorded balance with the auditor's expectation, which might be based on previous year's data and other economic indicators. • Examination—100% review of transactions or data on a computer system to determine proper classification. • Computerized audit software—sorting the file to identify the largest items, the smallest items, or the most frequent items within it; also useful for identifying unusual transactions. • Block transactions reviewed for proper classification, e.g., cutoff tests at year end.
Completeness	• Sampling—take a sample to search for underrecorded liabilities. • Analytical procedures—comparison of the client's recorded balance with the auditor's expectation, which might be based on previous year's data and other economic indicators. • Block transactions reviewed for proper classification, e.g., cutoff tests at year end.
Rights	• Sampling—often done in conjunction with existence testing, examining source documents. • Analytical procedures—look for unusual relationships (cash higher or lower than expected or similar anomalies in the underlying data). GAS can assist the auditor in this procedure.
Valuation or Allocation	• Sampling—selecting items and tracing back to source documents, e.g., purchase agreements or invoices. • Analytical procedures—develop models used to predict estimated amounts such as allowance for uncollectible accounts and comparison of model estimates with auditor's expectations. • Computerized audit software—footing the file and testing computations. • Analytical procedures—identify anomalies in underlying data.
Presentation and Disclosure	• Sampling—verify estimates or other items for proper disclosure. • 100% review, such as reading the notes in the financial statements.

specific risk areas or transactions. GAS is software designed to read, process, and write data. Auditors can use GAS to import a client's computerized data; then the software can be applied to the data in a variety of ways, e.g., the data can be scanned, sorted, summarized, stratified, analyzed, and used to obtain samples. Other GAS functions of interest to auditors include identification of duplicate items such as duplicate invoices, gaps in data such as a gap in a check sequence, and outliers in a population such as all invoices that exceed two times the average for a particular customer.

Substantive analytical procedures can be used by auditors to provide evidence on the reasonableness of the account balances. Rigorous analytical procedures that start with the auditor's development of a precise and independent expectation and suggest that the client's account balance is materially correct can then reduce the need for the auditor to perform extensive tests of details.

The choice of the tools used to gather evidence depends on the nature of the client's transactions and the specific assertions being tested. While it is important to understand sampling techniques, it is equally important to know that there are very few accounts where the auditor's conclusions about account balances will be based solely on sampled data. For many accounts and assertions, the auditor will also use generalized audit software and substantive analytical procedures. For example, the auditor testing inventory likely uses a variety of evidence to reach an overall conclusion, such as:

- Computerized footing of the account balance
- Sampling to test valuation
- Analytical procedures to determine potential obsolescence
- Tests of a block of transactions to perform cutoff tests

The evidence obtained through using these various tools are combined in a final review to reach a decision about the correctness of an account balance. That said, the auditor needs to know how each of these tools works in gathering evidence. We start with audit sampling.

Overview of Sampling

All audits involve sampling because the auditor cannot examine 100% of the transactions during a period. Yet the auditor must reach conclusions about the accuracy of the underlying populations that make up an account balance. Every audit will contain some form of audit sampling to test the operation of controls and/or directly test account balances. Why sample? The answer is that an auditor needs an efficient and effective way to reach a judgment about a population that is too large to examine completely.

The auditor constantly faces the challenge of gathering sufficient appropriate evidence as efficiently as possible. Samples should be representative of the population if the auditor is going to minimize the risk of reaching a wrong conclusion about the population. To increase the likelihood that the sample will be representative, samples must be of sufficient size and they must be selected from the appropriate underlying population. There are a few fundamental concepts that, if understood, will assist you in reaching correct conclusions from sampling.

Here is an example to help understand some sampling concepts. When buying a basket of apples, you want to be sure that the number of rotten apples does not exceed some tolerable limit. You may know that the produce manager at the store has good controls: he checks the apples before putting them on the fruit counter (throwing away any that are rotten), places the new apples at the back of the counter so that the older ones are sold first, and checks the old stock to be sure that any that have rotted while on the counter are thrown away. Therefore, you feel safe in buying a basket of apples without spending much time checking for rotten apples because the controls are good. If you are unfamiliar with the store or are aware that the produce manager is careless or does not bother to check the apples, you will want to obtain more assurance that there are not too many rotten apples in the basket. If it is a small basket, you may look at all of the apples. If it is a large basket, you may not have time to check all of them, so you can look at only a few apples to determine whether to buy the basket. However, when you look, you don't want to examine only the apples at the top of the basket, you want a sample that is indicative of all the apples in the basket. Sampling is designed to reduce your risk, that is, the likelihood that you will conclude that most of the apples are good when in fact many are not.

Audit sampling follows these same concepts. The objective of sampling when testing account balances is to estimate the amount of misstatement in an account balance. If there are a large number of errors, the auditor wants to know about them so that the account balance can be corrected. The objective of sampling when testing controls is to determine whether the controls are working effectively. If they are not working effectively, the auditor will need to consider this when deciding on the opinion for internal control and when designing the substantive procedures. However, sampling always contains some risk; that is, the auditor might not look at enough items (e.g., only three apples out of a basket), or the sample might not be representative (e.g., looking at only the apples on the top of the basket). Thus, we must consider how to take samples that minimize the likelihood we will reach an incorrect conclusion about what we are testing. Statistically based sampling allows us to control the risk that we might reach an incorrect conclusion about the population being tested.

There are many types of sampling methods available for use in audits, ranging from pure judgmental samples (the auditor judgmentally chooses which items to look at as well as how many to look at) to various types of statistical sampling techniques that have been formulated explicitly for audit objectives. There is not "one best" sampling method for every situation. However, there is usually "one best" sampling procedure for a specific audit objective. This chapter identifies alternative sampling methods and the situations in which each might be most appropriate.

LO 2

Explain the risks associated with sampling procedures and the nature of inferences required of all audit procedures.

Statistical sampling has become more important in light of recent audit failures. Auditors are increasingly recognizing the need to perform detailed tests of account balances in lieu of overrelying on substantive analytical procedures. Similarly, the auditor must test the operation of controls in order to attest to the effectiveness of a company's internal controls and to plan the appropriate substantive procedures. It is difficult to design a judgmental sample that could be considered more effective or more efficient than a well-designed statistical sample. It is important that auditors understand the power and the judgments required to use statistical sampling procedures effectively.

Audit sampling is defined as applying audit procedures to less than 100% of a population in order to estimate some characteristic about that population. Said another way, it is learning a lot by doing a little. Auditors use sampling to gather evidence to:

- Test controls for the purpose of expressing an opinion on the client's internal controls
- Test controls for the purpose of assessing control risk
- Test for compliance with company policies, governmental regulations, or other criteria
- Test individual items in account balances as a basis for determining whether material misstatements exist in the account balance

When assessing the effectiveness of control procedures, the challenge is to gather sufficient appropriate evidence on the degree to which the client's internal controls are effective in preventing misstatements. Sampling terminology refers to the individual items to be tested as **sampling units**. The sampling units make up the **population**. An example of sampling units might be the

AUDITING *in Practice*

AUDIT SAMPLING GUIDANCE

U.S. and international auditing standards (see SAS 39 and ISA 530) provide extensive guidance on the auditor's use of statistical and nonstatistical sampling when designing and selecting samples, performing tests of controls and tests of details, and evaluating sample results.

sales orders processed during the year that relate to the recognition of revenue. The auditor needs to make four important decisions to increase the likelihood that the sample will be representative of the population:

1. Which population should be tested and for what characteristics (*population*)?
2. How many items should be selected for audit testing (*sample size*)?
3. Which items should be included in the sample (*selection*)?
4. What inferences can be made about the overall population from the sample (*evaluation*)?

Nonsampling and Sampling Risk

The auditor could make an error about the characteristics of the underlying population because either (a) the auditor did not appropriately carry out the audit procedures or inappropriately diagnosed problems (non-sampling risk) or (b) the auditor made an incorrect inference from a sample that was not representative of the population (sampling risk). Fortunately, audit firms can control for both of these risks.

Nonsampling Risk   It is assumed that auditors *carefully* examine all items in the sample and choose the correct procedures in gathering evidence to evaluate the correctness of a transaction. However, there may be cases when the auditor is not careful. Errors in judgments about the correctness of a population that are due to carelessness in the performance of the audit are referred to as **nonsampling risks**. Nonsampling risk could also be due to a lack of knowledge by the auditor performing the audit procedure. The audit firm controls the possibility of such errors through proper training, adequate supervision, and carefully designed audit programs.

Sampling Risk   There is always a risk that any inferences made from a sample might not be correct, unless auditors examine 100% of a population (referred to as a census, i.e., no sampling). There is uncertainty about the projected results because the sampling results are based on only a small part of the population: the smaller the sample, the more the uncertainty; the larger the sample, the less the uncertainty. **Sampling risk** is defined as the risk that an inference drawn from a sample will be incorrect because the sample is too small or otherwise not representative of the characteristics that exist in the underlying population. By using statistical sampling, the auditor can control—and measure—how much risk there will be that the sample might not be representative of the population. Sampling risk can be measured for statistical samples, but not for other sampling approaches.

The auditor must make a number of judgments to determine the size of the sample to be taken and therefore the amount of audit work to be performed. Sample size is determined by two major factors: (1) the size of a misstatement that would make a difference to the auditor's assessment of a material misstatement (**tolerable misstatement**), and (2) the confidence level desired when making inferences about the correctness of the population sampled.

Sampling Risk Related to Tests of Control Procedures   The auditor often uses sampling to gather evidence to assess the effectiveness of controls —most often over transactions—as part of an integrated audit. The auditor wants an accurate estimate of the percentage of time that a control fails; for example, if a control does not work 4% of the time, the auditor will use this information to reach a conclusion about the effectiveness of the control and the extent of substantive testing that should be performed. Because sampling always carries some uncertainty, though, the auditor will usually want to control the worst possible scenario; for example, the auditor may want to be 95% confident that the control does not fail more than 8% of the time. The auditor is always challenged to manage the risks of making incorrect inferences from small sample sizes. These sampling risks are presented in Exhibit 8.2.

Sampling Risk Related to Substantive Testing   Sampling can also be used to estimate the amount of misstatement in an account balance. The auditor can, for example, select a sample of inventory items and perform a price test. If the sample contains pricing errors, the auditor projects these errors to the population to determine whether the population may be materially misstated because inventory is priced incorrectly. Whenever sampling is used, there is always a risk that the sample may not accurately reflect the population. The auditor must consider two potential risks (see Exhibit 8.3): (1) concluding that the book value is correct when it actually is materially misstated (**risk of incorrect acceptance**) and (2) concluding that the book value is materially misstated when it is not (**risk of incorrect rejection**).

The auditor's main concern when performing substantive testing is controlling the risk of incorrect acceptance. With incorrect acceptance, the account balance contains a material misstatement, but the sample results lead the auditor to believe the account does not contain a material misstatement. No additional audit work would be performed and the financial statements will be issued with a material misstatement. On the other hand, if the auditor were to incorrectly reject a population that does not contain a material misstatement, the client will usually object and encourage the auditor to perform additional work. The

Exhibit 8.2	Sampling Risks for Tests of Control Procedures	
	Actual State of Controls	
Auditor's Assessment of Control Risk	**Effective**	**Not Effective**
Low	Correct conclusion	**Incorrect Acceptance of Internal Control Reliability** Control failures in the population are higher than the sample indicates (referred to as the risk of assessing control risk too low). Increases the likelihood that misstatements occur and will not be detected during the audit.
High	**Incorrect Rejection of Control Reliability** Control failures in the population are lower than the sample indicates. Results in more audit testing taking place.	Correct conclusion

Exhibit 8.3	Sampling Risks for Direct Tests of Account Balances

	Condition of the Book Value	
Auditor's Conclusion Based on Sample Evidence	**Does Not Contain a Material Misstatement**	**Contains a Material Misstatement**
Book value **does not contain** a material misstatement	Correct conclusion	**Risk of incorrect acceptance** (leads to audit ineffectiveness)
Book value **likely contains** a material misstatement	**Risk of incorrect rejection** (leads to audit inefficiency)	Correct conclusion

additional audit work should lead to a correction of the inappropriate inference. The risk of incorrect rejection thus affects the *efficiency* of the audit, but it should not affect the auditor's overall conclusion about the fairness of the financial statements.

Selecting a Sampling Approach

Auditors use both nonstatistical and statistical sampling. When properly used, either sampling approach can be effective in providing sufficient audit evidence. Nonstatistical sampling, however, does not allow the auditor to statistically control for the risk of incorrect decision-making. **Statistical sampling** combines the theory of probability and statistical inference with audit judgment and experience. Both statistical and non-statistical sampling require significant audit judgment. The following is a comparison of nonstatistical and statistical sampling:

LO 3

Discuss the differences between nonstatistical and statistical sampling as a basis for determining the appropriate sampling methodology and apply these sample approaches in appropriate contexts.

	Nonstatistical Sampling	**Statistical Sampling**
Sample size	Determined by auditor judgment	Auditor judgment is quantified and sample size determined by probability theory.
Sample selection	Any method that the auditor believes is representative of the population.	The sample must be randomly selected to give each item in the population an equal chance to be included in the sample.
	Judgment sampling can also be directed at a portion of the population, e.g., all transactions during the last 5 days of the year.	The population of interest can also be directed, e.g., the transactions during the last 10 days of the year can be statistically selected.
Evaluation	Based on auditor judgment and projections based on sample results.	Statistical inference is used to assist auditor judgment.

The choice of whether to use statistical or nonstatistical sampling should consider the cost/benefit of making a particular choice as outlined below:

	Cost	**Benefit**
Nonstatistical sampling	• Lower selection cost because only requires audit judgment to determine an appropriate sample size and evaluate the results • Does not provide an objective way to control and measure sampling risk	• Can be based on auditor's prior expectations about errors in the account • May take less time to plan, select, and evaluate the sample

(continues)

PRACTICAL POINT

Samples should be planned to be representative of the population because the sample results will be projected to the population as a whole to draw a conclusion about the population.

	Cost	Benefit
Statistical sampling	• Requires knowledge of statistical sampling methods and/or special computer sampling software is required and often involves training costs • Requires auditor to define acceptable risk and sample objectives to be made in advance	Helps the auditor: • Design an efficient sample • Measure the sufficiency of the evidence • Evaluate the results by providing an objective measure of sampling risk • Gain efficiencies through computerized selection and statistical evaluation • Defend sample inferences because they are based on statistical theory

PRACTICAL POINT

An auditor who applies statistical sampling uses tables or formulas to compute sample size, while an auditor who applies nonstatistical sampling uses only professional judgment. Ordinarily, the nonstatistical sample size should not be smaller than the sample size resulting from an efficient and effectively designed statistical sample.

PRACTICAL POINT

Both statistical and nonstatistical sampling, when properly used, can provide sufficient evidence for auditor conclusions. Statistical sampling allows the auditor to precisely control the risk of making an incorrect inference about the population from which the sample is taken, whereas nonstatistical sampling does not allow such control.

PRACTICAL POINT

The auditor must consider the nature of control failures or misstatements detected in the sample, project the sample findings to the population, and conclude on the overall population. Even if nonstatistical sampling is used, the auditor is required to project sample results to the overall population as an aid in determining if material misstatements exist.

Statistical sampling techniques are especially *efficient* for testing large populations because the validity of the sample is influenced mostly by the diversity of the population examined and the size of the sample—rather than the percentage of the population being examined. National samples predicting election results, for example, are quite accurate using samples of 600 to 3,000 out of 80 million voters. This same kind of efficiency is applicable to auditing. Because both statistical and nonstatistical sample sizes are based on audit judgment, an auditor's decision not to use statistical sampling because the sample size is too large is difficult to justify.

Statistical sampling helps the auditor evaluate the sample by providing a quantitative measure of:

- The most likely and maximum failure rate of a control procedure that is being evaluated for effectiveness
- The most likely and maximum amount of misstatement in the recorded account balance or class of transactions
- The risk that the auditor may make an incorrect judgment about the state of controls or correctness of account balances

In addition to evaluating the results of a sample quantitatively, the auditor should consider the qualitative aspects of control failures and misstatements. Are the sample results caused by errors, or do they indicate the possibility of fraud, and how do the control failures affect other phases of the audit? Combining statistical sampling with audit judgment generally produces a higher-quality audit conclusion than using audit judgment alone.

Gathering Sample Evidence about Control Effectiveness

LO 4

Describe attribute sampling and use it to test controls.

The auditor gathers evidence on the effectiveness of the client's internal control system by examining the significant controls over the financial reporting process. The auditor tests the controls only after determining that their design is such that it would be effective in minimizing the likelihood of material misstatements in the account balances. The assessment of control effectiveness may be based on:

- A sample to test the effectiveness of controls in operation
- The auditor's observation of the controls within significant business processes
- Tests of controls built into the client's computer system
- Inquiry and a review of monitoring reports

AS 5 requires the external auditors to test the effectiveness of internal controls. That testing may include submitting data through the computer system, examining documentation related to the operation of significant controls, performing a "walkthrough" of processes noting the effectiveness of controls in the process, and/or selecting a sample of transactions, and testing for evidence of the effectiveness of control procedures. Sampling concepts do not apply to all tests of controls. Tests of automated application controls are generally done only once or a few times when effective (IT) general controls are present. Sampling generally is not applicable for determining the appropriate segregation of duties and may not apply to tests of operating effectiveness of the control environment.

When sampling is appropriate, the auditor wants to use a sample to infer whether the control in the population is working or not working. The sampling approach commonly used in making such decisions is referred to as attributes estimation.

Statistical Sampling Approach to Testing Controls: Attribute Sampling

The most commonly used statistical method to test controls is **attribute sampling**. An **attribute** is a characteristic of the population of interest to the auditor. Typically, the attribute the auditor wishes to examine is the effective operation of a control; for example, evidence that the client has matched vendor invoice details with the purchase order and receiving report before payment approval, and noting that they match before authorizing a payment for the goods received.

In determining the appropriate sample size, the auditor needs to make judgments on the following items:

- *Sampling Risk*—Sampling risk is the risk of concluding that the controls are effective when they are not effective. Sampling risk is often set the same as audit risk because the auditor's assessment of internal controls determines the nature and extent of other testing. The auditor tests only significant controls.
- *Tolerable Failure Rate*—The auditor's **tolerable failure rate** is the level at which the control's failure to operate would change the auditor's planned assessment of control risk in performing tests of account balances, or a rate at which the auditor would conclude the failure of the control to operate effectively would be considered a "significant deficiency." The tolerable failure rate must be set in advance in order to determine sample size.
- *Expected Failure Rate*—Sometimes a control will fail or be bypassed. Failures occur when personnel are in a hurry or careless, are not competent, or are not properly trained. The auditor likely has evidence on the rate at which a particular control fails based on past experience as modified by any changes in the system or personnel. This is the **expected failure rate**.

It is important to understand that a control failure does not automatically mean that a misstatement has occurred. For example, most companies require a credit approval process before issuing credit. When pressed for time, a marketing manager may approve a sale without obtaining proper credit approval. The control requiring credit approval has failed, but we do not know (a) whether the credit would have been granted if the process had been completed or (b) whether the customer is less likely to pay. Finally, the failure of this control does not affect the proper recording of the initial transaction. It may, however, affect the valuation of receivables at year end.

Steps in Attribute Sampling

Control procedures should be in place to assure that recorded transactions occurred, are complete, are accurate, are properly classified, and are recorded in the proper time period. Control procedures can take many different forms,

PRACTICAL POINT

Setting sampling risk at 5% is akin to sampling with a 95% confidence level.

PRACTICAL POINT

Significant controls are those whose failure could lead to a material misstatement in an account balance.

PRACTICAL POINT

Control failures do not automatically lead to account misstatements. The auditor must consider the likely effect of the control failure on an account misstatement and the likelihood that numerous failures could allow material misstatements to occur.

and how they are implemented affects the auditor's approach to gathering evidence on their effectiveness. Consider the credit approval procedure. The auditor may examine documentation to determine whether credit was properly approved before the goods were shipped (authorization) based on a sample of customer orders that should contain initials signifying an authorized credit approval. However, in many computerized systems, credit authorization is embedded in the logic of the client's computer program. For example, the credit department may set a credit limit for each customer, and the computer calculates whether a customer's credit limit is higher than the customer's current balance plus the value of the new order. The organization may also build logic into the computer program to dynamically change credit limits based on such factors as volume of purchases, payment history, and current credit ratings. In such cases, the auditor cannot examine a sales order for credit approval but must consider instead how to audit the computer program.

Attribute estimation sampling is an especially useful technique in situations where the audit question can be answered with a Yes or No. For example, it can be used to gather evidence to answer questions such as "Was credit properly approved?" or "Was the customer's order shipped before it was billed?" or "Were the expenses claimed by the CEO consistent with company policies?"

When determining a sample size, the auditor considers (a) the most likely control failure rate and (b) the possibility that the control failure rate exceeds some maximum rate that would constitute a significant deficiency. The steps to implement an attribute estimation sampling plan are as follows:

1. Define the attributes of interest and what constitutes failure(s).
2. Define the population in terms of the period to be covered by the test, the sampling unit, and the process of assuring the completeness of the population.
3. Determine the sample size, considering tolerable and expected failure rates along with an acceptable sampling risk.
4. Determine an effective and efficient method of selecting the sample.
5. Select and audit the sample items.
6. Evaluate the sample results and reach a conclusion on the audit objectives.
7. Document all phases of the sampling process.

Step 1. Define the Attributes of Interest and Failures A number of attributes could be tested, but the auditor tests only significant controls. Control procedure failures should be precisely defined to make sure that the audit staff clearly understands what to look for, thereby reducing nonsampling risk. For example, a failure to seek credit approval for a new account, although required by company policy, would be considered a control failure.

Step 2. Define the Population In defining the population, the following factors need to be addressed:

- The period to be covered by the test; e.g., the year when evaluating controls
- The sampling unit; e.g., an item that would indicate the operation of a control
- The completeness of the population

Period Covered by the Tests   The period tested depends on the audit objective. In most instances, the *period* is the time period covered by the audited financial statements. As a practical matter, tests of controls are often performed prior to the balance sheet date and may cover the first ten or eleven months of the year. If the control procedures are found to be effective, the auditor should take additional steps to assure that the controls continue to be effective during the remainder of the year. The additional steps may include making inquiries, further testing of the controls, or gathering evidence of control effectiveness from substantive tests performed later in the audit.

In some situations, the audit objective and time period may be more limited. If the audit objective is to determine that the credit approval process is adequate, for example, the auditor might focus on credit approvals for the time period during which the unpaid receivables were billed. The auditor is not normally concerned with credit approval for sales that have already been collected by the balance sheet date.

Sampling Unit   The sampling unit is the item identified in the population as the basis for testing. It could be a document, an authorized signature, an entry in the computer system, or a line item on a document. One company may require supervisory approval with initials to authorize payment of several invoices. The sampling unit would be the document authorizing the invoices. Another company may require written authorization for each invoice; the sampling unit would be the individual invoices processed for payment.

Completeness of Population   The auditor should take steps to help assure that the population used in sampling is a complete representation of the total population of interest. The auditor normally performs some procedures, such as footing the file and reconciling the balance to the general ledger or reviewing the completeness of prenumbered documents, to assure that the population is complete and consistent with the audit objective.

Step 3. Determine the Sample Size An optimal sample size will minimize sampling risk and promote audit efficiency. The following audit judgments affect the determination of sample size: (1) sampling risk, (2) the tolerable failure rate, and (3) the expected failure rate. For most purposes, the population size is not a major factor. A discussion of the finite correction factor for very small populations is included in Appendix 8A. The table in Exhibit 8.4 gives sample sizes for several combinations of these factors and for both 5% and 10% levels of sampling risk.

The integrated audit should start with an assessment of the failure rate that would lead to the conclusion that the control failure would constitute a significant deficiency or material weakness. For example, let's say a key control is a policy that all purchase orders must be approved by the purchasing manager. The auditor should consider the risk to the financial statements if this control is not working correctly. For example, if purchase orders are not approved by the purchasing manager, purchase orders might be issued by either a staff person or someone in the factory who orders the goods but has them delivered to an alternative location. If that is the case, the auditor must consider the risk of (a) fraud and (b) the effect on cost of sales and inventory to determine what amount is material. If, let us say, 5% of the orders had this incorrect attribute, the auditor might conclude that amount is material and may want to set the tolerable failure rate at no more than 5%.

The determination of sample size using the tables is very straightforward. The auditor:

1. Selects the allowable sampling risk (5% or 10%) based on factors such as audit risk, and whether the auditor will be issuing a separate report on internal control.
2. Determines the tolerable rate of error by looking at the relationship between control failure rate and material misstatement.
3. Uses past knowledge to enter the expected control failure rate. This is important because it controls against rejecting controls when only one error is found.
4. Determines sample size by looking at the intersection of the expected rate of failure and the tolerable rate of failure in the appropriate table.

Once you are familiar with the table, you may use it to analyze other situations.

Exhibit 8.4   Attribute Sample Size Tables

TABLE 1: 5% SAMPLING RISK (RISK OF ASSESSING CONTROL RISK TOO LOW)

Expected Population Deviation Rate	Tolerable Rate										
	2%	**3%**	**4%**	**5%**	**6%**	**7%**	**8%**	**9%**	**10%**	**15%**	**20%**
0.00%	149(0)	99(0)	74(0)	59(0)	49(0)	42(0)	36(0)	32(0)	29(0)	19(0)	14(0)
0.25	236(1)	157(1)	117(1)	93(1)	78(1)	66(1)	58(1)	51(1)	46(1)	30(1)	22(1)
0.50	*	157(1)	117(1)	93(1)	78(1)	66(1)	58(1)	51(1)	46(1)	30(1)	22(1)
0.75	*	208(2)	117(1)	93(1)	78(1)	66(1)	58(1)	51(1)	46(1)	30(1)	22(1)
1.00	*	*	156(2)	93(1)	78(1)	66(1)	58(1)	51(1)	46(1)	30(1)	22(1)
1.25	*	*	156(2)	124(2)	78(1)	66(1)	58(1)	51(1)	46(1)	30(1)	22(1)
1.50	*	*	192(3)	124(2)	103(2)	66(1)	58(1)	51(1)	46(1)	30(1)	22(1)
1.75	*	*	227(4)	153(3)	103(2)	88(2)	77(2)	51(1)	46(1)	30(1)	22(1)
2.00	*	*	*	181(4)	127(3)	88(2)	77(2)	68(2)	46(1)	30(1)	22(1)
2.25	*	*	*	208(5)	127(3)	88(2)	77(2)	68(2)	61(2)	30(1)	22(1)
2.50	*	*	*	*	150(4)	109(3)	77(2)	68(2)	61(2)	30(1)	22(1)
2.75	*	*	*	*	173(5)	109(3)	95(3)	68(2)	61(2)	30(1)	22(1)
3.00	*	*	*	*	195(6)	129(4)	95(3)	84(3)	61(2)	30(1)	22(1)
3.25	*	*	*	*	*	148(5)	112(4)	84(3)	61(2)	30(1)	22(1)
3.50	*	*	*	*	*	167(7)	112(5)	84(4)	76(3)	40(2)	22(1)
3.75	*	*	*	*	*	185(7)	129(5)	100(4)	76(3)	40(2)	22(1)
4.00	*	*	*	*	*	*	146(6)	100(4)	89(4)	40(2)	22(1)
5.00	*	*	*	*	*	*	*	158(8)	116(6)	40(2)	30(2)
6.00	*	*	*	*	*	*	*	*	179(11)	50(3)	30(2)
7.00	*	*	*	*	*	*	*	*	*	68(5)	37(3)

TABLE 2: 10% SAMPLING RISK (RISK OF ASSESSING CONTROL RISK TOO LOW)

Expected Population Deviation Rate	2%	3%	4%	5%	6%	7%	8%	9%	10%	15%	20%
0.00%	114(0)	76(0)	57(0)	45(0)	38(0)	32(0)	28(0)	25(0)	22(0)	15(0)	11(0)
0.25	194(1)	129(1)	96(1)	77(1)	64(1)	55(1)	48(1)	42(1)	38(1)	25(1)	18(1)
0.50	194(1)	129(1)	96(1)	77(1)	64(1)	55(1)	48(1)	42(1)	38(1)	25(1)	18(1)
0.75	265(2)	129(1)	96(1)	77(1)	64(1)	55(1)	48(1)	42(1)	38(1)	25(1)	18(1)
1.00	*	176(2)	96(1)	77(1)	64(1)	55(1)	48(1)	42(1)	38(1)	25(1)	18(1)
1.25	*	221(3)	132(2)	77(1)	64(1)	55(1)	48(1)	42(1)	38(1)	25(1)	18(1)
1.50	*	*	132(2)	105(2)	64(1)	55(1)	48(1)	42(1)	38(1)	25(1)	18(1)
1.75	*	*	166(3)	105(2)	88(2)	55(1)	48(1)	42(1)	38(1)	25(1)	18(1)
2.00	*	*	198(4)	132(3)	88(2)	75(2)	48(2)	42(1)	38(1)	25(1)	18(1)
2.25	*	*	*	132(3)	88(2)	75(2)	65(2)	42(1)	38(1)	25(1)	18(1)
2.50	*	*	*	158(4)	110(3)	75(2)	65(2)	58(2)	38(1)	25(1)	18(1)
2.75	*	*	*	209(6)	132(4)	94(3)	65(2)	58(2)	52(2)	25(1)	18(1)
3.00	*	*	*	*	132(4)	94(3)	65(2)	58(2)	52(2)	25(1)	18(1)
3.25	*	*	*	*	153(5)	113(4)	82(3)	58(2)	52(2)	25(1)	18(1)
3.50	*	*	*	*	194(7)	113(4)	82(3)	73(3)	52(2)	25(1)	18(1)
3.75	*	*	*	*	*	131(5)	98(4)	73(3)	52(2)	25(1)	18(1)
4.00	*	*	*	*	*	149(6)	98(4)	73(3)	65(3)	25(1)	18(1)
5.00	*	*	*	*	*	*	160(8)	115(6)	78(4)	34(2)	18(1)
6.00	*	*	*	*	*	*	*	182(11)	116(70)	43(3)	25(2)
7.00	*	*	*	*	*	*	*	*	199(14)	52(4)	25(2)

Note: The number of expected misstatements appears in parentheses. These tables assume a large population.

* = Sample size is too large to be cost-effective for most audit applications.

Source: *Audit Sampling* (New York: AICPA, 1999), 96–97. Reprinted with permission from AICPA; copyright © 1994 and 1999 by American Institute of Certified Public Accountants.

AUDITING *in Practice*

ILLUSTRATION OF ATTRIBUTE SAMPLE SIZE DETERMINATION

Example 1 (Important Control, Integrated Audit): The auditor sets sampling risk at 5% (implying that the auditor is willing to accept a 5% chance that inferences from the sample will be incorrect), sets the tolerable error rate at 5%, and anticipates that the expected error rate is 1%. The auditor examines the top table in Exhibit 8.4 and finds a sample size of 93.

Example 2 (Noncritical Control, Nonintegrated Audit, No Separate Report on Internal Control): The auditor sets sampling risk at 10% (implying that the auditor is willing to accept more risk than in Example 1), sets the tolerable error rate at 10%, and anticipates that the expected error rate is 1%. The auditor uses the bottom table in Exhibit 8.4 and finds a sample size of 38.

Also note that the number in parentheses after each sample size represents the number of errors the auditor can find without concluding that the control is not working correctly (1 in a sample of 93 for the critical control, and 1 in a sample of 38 in the less critical control).

Working Backwards from Sample Size It is not uncommon to see public accounting firms test controls with samples of 30 or possibly 40 as a standard practice. If the firm makes such choices, the auditor can determine the assumptions used by the firm in adopting that standard by working backwards through the tables, as illustrated in the examples below. Although auditors would not regularly do this, we have included these examples to provide an understanding of the assumptions that must be made by an audit firm to justify such a sample size. The point of both examples is that sample sizes of just 30 or 40 require the auditor to tolerate a fairly high rate of error in the sample, a choice that ultimately yields greater audit risk for the audit firm. The following examples help explain the assumptions needed to support a sample size of 30.

Working Backwards from a Predetermined Sample Size
Example 1: Consider an example from Table 1 of Exhibit 8.4, for sampling risk of 5%. The auditor can only get to a sample size of 29 by assuming a tolerable error rate of 10% and an expected error rate of zero. Any errors found in the sample would cause the auditor to either (a) conclude the control is not working properly or (b) expand the sample to get a more precise estimate. The auditor could get similar results using a tolerable error rate of 15% and allowing the expected error to increase. However, it is vital to note that it is difficult to justify a tolerable error of 15% in a critical control!
Example 2: Consider an example from Table 2 of Exhibit 8.4, for sampling risk of 10%. The auditor can get to a sample size of 28 assuming a tolerable error rate of 8% and an expected error rate of zero. Other combinations work similarly by moving the expected error rate up to 15% and allowing the expected error rate to go as high as 4%.

> **PRACTICAL POINT**
>
> We tend to treat internal control testing as if there were no knowledge of controls from previous years or that the systems have changed. However, in many cases, auditors have such knowledge and the systems do not change dramatically. Auditors often consider the accumulation of total knowledge in making assumptions about sample sizes.

An important factor to consider in sampling decisions concerns whether an integrated audit is being performed. Most often, a firm will use a sampling risk of 5% for integrated audits (following an audit risk of 5%) and then work through the logic of how important the control may be. Further, the auditor may have knowledge about the operating effectiveness of the control from either (a) past experience and knowledge that there has been no change in controls or (b) other testing by the company itself, for example, by the internal audit department. In such cases, the auditor's testing of controls may be supplemental to already existing knowledge about internal controls and is meant to corroborate that knowledge. In such a case, the auditor may be justified using the assumptions just demonstrated that lead to sample sizes of 30 or 40.

Multiple Attributes Auditors frequently test several control procedures or attributes using the same set of source documents. When doing so, the auditor should use the same sampling risk for all the tests. However, the tolerable and expected failure rates for these attributes are likely to be different, resulting in different sample sizes. For example, the auditor may want to test whether sales transactions are classified correctly, whether they have been recorded accurately, and whether there was proper review and approval for credit using tolerable failure rates of 5%, 3%, and 3% and expected failure rates of 2%, 1%, and 0%, respectively. If the auditor sets sampling risk at 10%, the sample sizes range from a high of 176 for proper classification to a low of 76 for correct recording:

Attribute	Tolerable Failure Rate	Expected Failure Rate	Sample Size
1. Evidence of independent review of account distribution (classification)	5%	2%	132
2. Evidence of comparison of description, quantity, and price between the customer's order and sales invoice (accuracy)	3%	1%	176
3. Evidence of proper review and approval for credit (valuation)	3%	0%	76

There are three reasonable approaches to selecting the items for these tests:

- The auditor could select 176 sales transactions (the largest sample size) and audit all of them for attribute 2, three of four for attribute 1, and every other one for attribute 3. This process, however, is quite cumbersome.
- The auditor could examine the first 76 randomly selected documents for all three attributes and documents, sample items 77–132 for attributes 1 and 2, and the remainder only for attribute 2. This process is also quite cumbersome.
- Often the most efficient approach is to test the 176 items for all three attributes. Attributes 1 and 3 will be in some sense "overaudited," but the overauditing may take less time than keeping track of which sample items should be tested for which attribute. Testing for attributes 1 and 3 does not take very long once the auditor has selected the documents in the sample. The auditor's evaluation of the control is based on the 176 items examined and improves the effectiveness of the control risk assessment.

Step 4. Determine the Method of Selecting the Sample Once the sample size has been determined, the auditor must decide how to select a representative sample. Random-based methods help assure that each item in the population has an equal chance of being included in the sample. Statistical sampling requires **random-based selection** because it eliminates the possibility of unintentional bias in the selection process and maximizes the chances that the sample is representative. For nonstatistical sampling, the auditor may use judgment to select a sample that will be representative. A flowchart for choosing among several selection methods is illustrated in Exhibit 8.5.

Random Numbers Random number selection is an efficient sample selection method if there is an easy way to relate the random numbers to the population. For example, a random selection of sales invoices could be based on sales invoice numbers. Most CPA firms and internal audit departments have computer programs that generate and sort random numbers and provide the necessary printout to document the random-number selection process.

Exhibit 8.5   Sample Selection Methods

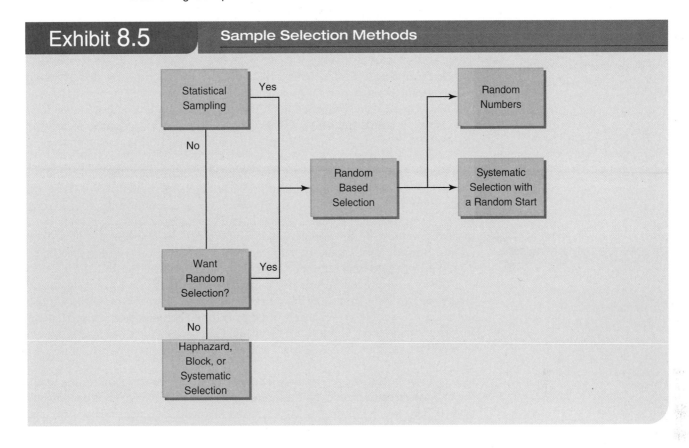

Systematic Selection Several systematic selection methods meet the requirement of randomness and improve audit efficiency when documents are not numbered in a pattern. In order to use systematic selection, the auditor must (a) establish that the population is complete and (b) be sure that there is not a systematic pattern in the population.

Systematic selection involves the determination of an interval (n) and the selection of every nth item to be tested. The sampling interval is determined by dividing the population size by the desired sample size. A random start number between 1 and n is chosen to identify the first sample item. As a result, every item in the population has an equal chance of being tested. Payroll transactions in a payroll journal, for example, may be listed in employee number order. These numbers are not in sequence because of employee turnover. There are 1,300 payroll transactions, and the auditor has determined a sample size of 26. Every 50th transaction ($1{,}300/26=50$) should be selected for testing. To randomize the selection process, a random number from 1 to 50 should be used to identify the first sample item. This could be done, for example, by using the last two digits of a serial number on a dollar bill. If those digits were 87, subtract 50, leaving 37 as the first sample item. Every 50th transaction thereafter would also be included in the sample.

The validity of a systematic sample is based on the assumption that the items in the population are randomly distributed. The auditor must be knowledgeable about the nature of the population to be sure that no repeating or coinciding pattern in the population would cause the sample to not be representative. Many auditors try to increase the chances that the systematically selected samples are representative of the population by the use of multiple random starts.

Haphazard Selection Haphazard selection involves the arbitrary selection of sample items with no conscious bias, but without using a random base. It is

> **PRACTICAL POINT**
>
> Audit software can be used by the auditor to select a random or a systematic sample.

PRACTICAL POINT

Block sampling, in which a block of all transactions that occurred for a period of time both before and after year end, is very useful in performing year-end cutoff tests.

often used in nonstatistical sampling applications. Because it is not random-based, such a sample cannot be statistically evaluated.

Block Sampling   Auditors may want to select transactions by day or week. There are many efficiencies in such an approach, but the danger is that the way the transactions were processed on these days may not be indicative of how they were processed the other 364 days or 51 weeks. This judgmental decision is subject to second-guessing that such a sample could not be representative.

Step 5. Select and Audit the Sample Items When selecting the sample, the auditor should decide how to handle inapplicable, voided, or unused documents. An example of an inapplicable document would be a telephone bill when testing for an error defined as "cash disbursement transactions not supported by a receiving report." If the inapplicable document does not represent a prescribed control procedure, it should be replaced by another randomly selected item.

When a selected item cannot be located, the auditor should assume the worst—that the control procedure was not followed—and assess it as a failure. If many failures of this type are found before finishing the audit of a sample the auditor should conclude that no reliance can be placed on the tested control procedure. In such a situation, the auditor should terminate the test to avoid wasting any more time and discuss it with management and the audit committee.

PRACTICAL POINT

The auditor should consider whether the reasons for missing items have implications in relation to assessing risks of material misstatement due to fraud, the assessed level of control risk, or the degree of reliance on management representations.

Step 6. Evaluate the Sample Results Evaluation of sample results requires the auditor to project those results to the population before drawing an audit conclusion. If the sample failure rate is no greater than the expected failure rate, the auditor can conclude that the control is at least as effective as expected and can assess the control risk according to the original audit plan.

Quantitative Evaluation   If the sample failure rate exceeds the expected failure rate, the auditor should determine whether the projected maximum failure rate is likely to exceed the tolerable failure rate previously set. To make such an assessment, the auditor should use statistical evaluations. Tables such as those in Exhibit 8.6 help the auditor determine the upper limit of the potential failure rate in the population. If the **achieved upper limit** exceeds the tolerable rate, the auditor should (1) test a different control designed to mitigate the same risk, or (2) adjust the nature, timing, and/or extent of the related substantive testing of the accounts affected by the control.

PRACTICAL POINT

Statistically selected samples should be evaluated using statistical evaluation tables or audit software. Judgmentally selected samples can be evaluated by auditor judgment.

In determining what changes to make in substantive audit procedures, the auditor should consider the nature of control procedure failures (pattern of errors) and determine the effect of such failures on potential misstatement in the financial statements. When the achieved upper limit exceeds the tolerable rate, the auditor has to decide whether the control failure, in conjunction with other control failures, leads to a conclusion that there are either significant deficiencies or material weaknesses regarding internal control over financial reporting.

Sample Evaluations—An Illustration   To illustrate the use of the tables, assume that the auditor tested the controls designed to make sure that sales were not billed until shipped using a sampling risk of 5%, a tolerable failure rate of 6%, and an expected failure rate of 1%. Recall what these judgments mean:

- A sampling risk of 5% means the auditor wants to limit the risk to 5% that the actual failure rate in the population will not exceed the tolerable failure rate of 6%. This is equivalent to using a 95% confidence level.
- The maximum acceptable level of control failures is 6%; if there is more than a 5% chance that the actual error rate is greater than 6%, the auditor must conclude that the control is not working at an acceptable level.

| Exhibit 8.6 | Attribute Estimation Sample Evaluation Tables |

TABLE 1: 5% SAMPLING RISK

Sample Size	Actual Number of Control Procedure Deviations Found										
	0	1	2	3	4	5	6	7	8	9	10
25	11.3	17.6	*	*	*	*	*	*	*	*	*
30	9.5	14.9	19.6	*	*	*	*	*	*	*	*
35	8.3	12.9	17.0	*	*	*	*	*	*	*	*
40	7.3	11.4	15.0	18.3	*	*	*	*	*	*	*
45	6.5	10.2	13.4	16.4	19.2	*	*	*	*	*	*
50	5.9	9.2	12.1	14.8	17.4	19.9	*	*	*	*	*
55	5.4	8.4	11.1	13.5	15.9	18.2	*	*	*	*	*
60	4.9	7.7	10.2	12.5	14.7	16.8	18.8	*	*	*	*
65	4.6	7.1	9.4	11.5	13.6	15.5	17.4	19.3	*	*	*
70	4.2	6.6	8.8	10.8	12.6	14.5	16.3	18.0	19.7	*	*
75	4.0	6.2	8.2	10.1	11.8	13.6	15.2	16.9	18.5	20.0	*
80	3.7	5.8	7.7	9.5	11.1	12.7	14.3	15.9	17.4	18.9	*
90	3.3	5.2	6.9	8.4	9.9	11.4	12.8	14.2	15.5	16.8	18.2
100	3.0	4.7	6.2	7.6	9.0	10.3	11.5	12.8	14.0	15.2	16.4
120	2.5	3.9	5.2	6.4	7.5	8.6	9.7	10.7	11.7	12.8	13.8
140	2.2	3.4	4.5	5.5	6.5	7.4	8.3	9.2	10.1	11.0	11.9
160	1.9	3.0	3.9	4.8	5.7	6.5	7.3	8.1	8.9	9.7	10.4
200	1.5	2.4	3.2	3.9	4.6	5.2	5.9	6.5	7.1	7.8	8.4

TABLE 2: 10% SAMPLING RISK

Sample Size	0	1	2	3	4	5	6	7	8	9	10
25	8.8	14.7	19.9	*	*	*	*	*	*	*	*
30	7.4	12.4	16.8	*	*	*	*	*	*	*	*
35	6.4	10.7	14.5	18.1	*	*	*	*	*	*	*
40	5.6	9.4	12.8	16.0	19.0	*	*	*	*	*	*
45	5.0	8.4	11.4	14.3	17.0	19.7	*	*	*	*	*
50	4.6	7.6	10.3	12.9	15.4	17.8	*	*	*	*	*
55	4.1	6.9	9.4	11.8	14.1	16.3	18.4	*	*	*	*
60	3.8	6.4	8.7	10.8	12.9	15.0	16.9	18.9	*	*	*
70	3.3	5.5	7.5	9.3	11.1	12.9	14.6	16.3	17.9	19.6	*
80	2.9	4.8	6.6	8.2	9.8	11.3	12.8	14.3	15.8	17.2	18.6
90	2.6	4.3	5.9	7.3	8.7	10.1	11.5	12.8	14.1	15.4	16.6
100	2.3	3.9	5.3	6.6	7.9	9.1	10.3	11.5	12.7	13.9	15.0
120	2.0	3.3	4.4	5.5	6.6	7.6	8.7	9.7	10.7	11.6	12.6
140	1.7	2.8	3.8	4.8	5.7	6.6	7.4	8.3	9.2	10.0	10.8
160	1.5	2.5	3.3	4.2	5.0	5.8	6.5	7.3	8.0	8.8	9.5
200	1.2	2.0	2.7	3.4	4.0	4.6	5.3	5.9	6.5	7.1	7.6

Note: These tables present upper limits as percentages assuming a large population.
*Over 20%.

Source: *Audit Sampling* (New York: AICPA, 1999), 98–99. Reprinted with permission from AICPA; copyright © 1994 and 1999 by American Institute of Certified Public Accountants.

- The auditor did not expect many errors; the auditor expects the control to not be operating effectively only about 1% of the time; this expectation is based on good past experience with the control and the client's careful monitoring practices.

A sample of 80 was selected from a population of 100,000 sales transactions. From Exhibit 8.5, the auditor knows that if one or fewer control failures are found, the control can be evaluated as effective.

Now assume that 3 control failures were found (a control failure rate of 3.75%). The auditor might conclude that 3.75% is less than 6%, and so the control is working effectively. Remember, the auditor's decision is whether there is more than a 5% risk (95% confidence level) that the control failure rate could be more than 6%. To make this evaluation, the auditor turns to Exhibit 8.5 (Table 1), moves down the first column to find 80 as a sample size, and moves to the right under the column of 3 failures, and finds a figure of 9.5. What does that 9.5 mean? It means that there is a 5% chance that the real error rate exceeds 9.5%. The auditor had set an upper limit of 6%, and this 9.5% clearly exceeds that limit. The control testing does not support a conclusion that the control is working effectively. The auditor needs to assess control risk as higher than was originally set and, further, must perform a qualitative evaluation of the deviations detected.

Qualitative Evaluation   When control failures are found, they should be analyzed *qualitatively* as well as quantitatively. The auditor should try to determine whether the failures (1) were intentional or unintentional, (2) were random or systematic, (3) had a direct dollar effect on the account balance, or (4) were of such magnitude that a material dollar amount of errors could occur and not be detected.

The auditor is much more concerned if the control failures appear to be *intentional*, which might indicate fraud. If the failures are *systematic*, the auditor should be cautious in deciding to isolate the problem and reducing substantive testing. For example, if all of the failures were related to pricing errors—and all were connected to one sales associate—the auditor may expand audit testing to review all of the transactions related to that one sales associate. However, the auditor should not typically reduce substantive testing in other areas because the identified errors appear to be isolated to the one sales associate. The sampling evidence may be signaling that there are other "isolated" failures that did not happen to appear in the sample.

Often, a failure in a control does not lead directly to dollar misstatements in the accounting records. Lack of proper approval for payment of a vendor's invoice, for example, does not necessarily mean that the invoice should not have been paid. While it may have been an appropriate invoice, it might also have been a fictitious invoice.

Linkage of Test of Controls to Substantive Testing   In addition to being the basis of a report on internal controls, the tests of controls are used to determine whether the nature, timing, or extent of the planned substantive testing needs to be modified. For example, if the tests of controls indicate that the client is not careful about assuring that shipment has taken place before billing and recording a sale, the auditor may need to increase sales cut-off testing and/or concentrate on sales recorded just before the balance sheet date. If credit approvals are not working correctly, the auditor will have to take more time to determine whether the allowance for doubtful accounts is reasonable. Additional testing of subsequent collections and follow-up on old, uncollected balances may be needed. Further, if controls are not operating effectively, the auditor will likely choose to rely less on substantive analytical procedures and more on tests of details for those accounts related to identified control failures.

Step 7. Documentation   All of the preceding steps and related decisions regarding the sampling process should be documented to allow for appropriate supervision and provide adequate support for the conclusions reached.

PRACTICAL POINT

If the upper error limit in the appropriate table exceeds the tolerable error rate first set by the auditor, then the auditor's work does not support the original control assessment and control risk must be increased. The remainder of the audit needs to be adjusted accordingly.

Nonstatistical Sampling Approach to Testing Control

If the auditor chooses to use nonstatistical sampling procedures to test the effectiveness of controls, the planning factors are often not quantified. Instead, the auditor addresses significant, tolerable, and expected failure rates through the more global concepts of none, few, and many. Sampling risk is often set as low, moderate, or high. Note, however, if the sampling is done as part of an audit of internal controls, the presumption is that sampling risk must be low. The effect of these factors on sample size follows, assuming that all of the factors are considered in making an overall size determination:

	Condition Leading To	
Factor	Smaller Sample	Larger Sample
Tolerable failure rate	High	Low
Expected failure rate	Low	High
Sampling risk	High	Low
Population size	Small	Large

Even by making these subjective judgments, the auditor cannot quantitatively assess the risk of making an incorrect inference based on the sample results. For this reason, many auditors who use nonstatistical sampling should review the factors and select a sample size consistent with a statistically determined sample.

PRACTICAL POINT

Many accounting firms use a defined sample size, such as 30 or 40, to randomly select sample items. However, if a control failure is found, the auditor concludes the control is not working at a level that would allow the auditor to conclude that a significant deficiency does not exist.

Using Sampling to Gather Evidence about Misstatements in Account Balances and Assertions
Substantive Sampling Considerations

An auditor chooses to perform direct tests of many account balances to gather sufficient evidence by directly examining the composition of account balances. The basic steps involved in sampling for substantive tests of account balances are the same whether nonstatistical or statistical sampling approaches are used:

1. Specify the audit objective of the test.
2. Define a misstatement.
3. Define the population from which the sample is to be taken.
4. Choose an appropriate sampling method.
5. Determine the sample size.
6. Select the sample.
7. Audit the selected items.
8. Evaluate the sample results, including the projection of misstatements to the population.
9. Document the sampling procedure and results obtained.

PRACTICAL POINT

Auditing standards, for example, SAS 111, indicate that the sample size for a nonstatistical sample should be consistent with a statistically determined sample size.

Step 1. Specify the Audit Objective of the Test

A sampling plan for tests of details is typically designed to provide assurance regarding one or more financial statement assertions (e.g., existence of accounts receivable). Specifying the audit objective determines the population to test. For example, if the objective is to determine the existence of customer balances, the sample should be selected from the recorded balances. If the objective is to determine the completeness of accounts payable, the sample should be selected

PRACTICAL POINT

The auditor will likely use a combination of sampling and other audit procedures to test account balances. For example, in testing the valuation assertion regarding inventory, the auditor may take a sample of inventory items to test inventory cost but will use substantive analytical procedures, such as turnover analysis and aging, to help analyze the possibility of obsolete inventory. Sample results are combined with other audit results in making a judgment about the correctness of the account balance.

PRACTICAL POINT

The objective of the audit test always relates to one or more of the assertions about the underlying account balance.

PRACTICAL POINT

The auditor should take care to help ensure that the sampling population is complete and appropriate to the audit objective.

PRACTICAL POINT

Populations involving the testing of the *existence* assertion are generally easy to define because they include all recorded transactions. On the other hand, populations involving the *completeness* assertion are more difficult to define because some of those transactions may not yet be recorded.

from a complementary population, such as cash disbursements made after the balance sheet date. The auditor looks for payments for goods and services received by the balance sheet date that should be payables at year end but were not recorded until after year end.

Sampling is used to audit account balances in two primary ways: (1) to determine the reasonableness of an account balance by performing a detailed analysis of items making up the account balance and (2) to estimate some amount, such as the LIFO index, to estimate the LIFO value of inventory. In this chapter, we focus on using statistical sampling to analyze the correctness of an account balance.

Step 2. Define Misstatements

Misstatements should be defined before beginning the sampling application to (1) preclude the client or auditor from rationalizing away misstatements as isolated events and (2) provide guidance to the audit team. A **misstatement** is usually defined as a difference that affects the correctness of the overall account balance. For example, if a cash payment were posted to the wrong customer's subsidiary account, the overall account balance would still be correct and should not be considered a misstatement. Even so, the auditor should carefully follow up on this finding to be sure it is not evidence of a cover-up of an employee's misappropriation of cash (called *lapping*). If, however, the client inappropriately billed a customer before the end of the period, the premature billing would be considered a misstatement because the overall receivable balance would be overstated at the end of the period.

Step 3. Define the Population

The population is that group of items in an account balance that the auditor wants to test. The population, as defined for sampling purposes, does not include any items that the auditor has decided to examine 100% or items that will be tested separately. Because sample results can be projected to only that group of items from which the sample is selected, it is important to properly define the population. For example, a sample selected from the inventory at one location can be used only to estimate the amount of misstatement at that location, not at other locations.

Define the Sampling Unit   Sampling units are the individual auditable elements and often are made up of individual account balances. However, a sampling unit for confirming accounts receivable could be the individual customer's balance, individual unpaid invoices, or a combination of these two. The choice depends on effectiveness and efficiency of the process and the manner in which the client has recorded the individual items. Some customers are more likely to return a confirmation when asked to confirm one unpaid invoice rather than verify the correctness of an entire account balance. If a customer does not return a positive confirmation, alternative procedures must be performed, including identifying subsequent payments and/or vouching the sales transactions to supporting documents. If customers typically pay by invoice, it will be more efficient to perform alternative procedures on individual invoices than on total balances.

Completeness of the Population   A sample is selected from a physical representation of the population, such as a list of customer balances or a computer file. The auditor needs assurance that the list accurately represents the population. A common procedure is to foot the list and reconcile it with the general ledger.

Identify Individually Significant Items   Many account balances are composed of a few relatively large items and many smaller items. A significant portion of the total value of many accounting populations is concentrated in a relatively few large-dollar items. Because of this, the auditor often will examine all the large-dollar items, in other words, conduct a census. These large-dollar items are often referred to as the **top stratum**. Because the auditor knows the amount of errors in the stratum (all items were evaluated), no estimate of errors is required. The remaining items (*lower stratum*) are then sampled using one of the sampling methods described in this chapter. The audit results reflect the sum of the top-stratum items and the *projected misstatement* derived from the lower-stratum items.

The auditor often uses judgment to determine the cutoff point for top-stratum items. The division of the population into two or more subgroups is referred to as **stratification**. Stratification of the population into several homogeneous subpopulations generally creates audit efficiency. The stratification process can be enhanced with the use of audit software that has the capability of creating a profile of the population of book values.

Step 4. Choose a Sampling Method

Once the auditor has decided to use audit sampling, either nonstatistical or statistical sampling is appropriate for substantive tests of details. The most common statistical approaches for substantive testing are classical variables sampling (beyond the scope of this textbook) and monetary unit sampling (MUS).

MUS, which is discussed below, is based on attributes sampling theory, but is used to express conclusions in monetary terms. MUS is a subset of a broader class of procedures sometimes referred to as **probability proportional to size (PPS) sampling**. The term *PPS* describes a method of sample selection where the probability of an item's selection for the sample is proportional to its recorded amount, while *MUS* is used to describe sample size and evaluation methods (based on monetary units). As is common, we use the terms MUS and PPS interchangeably.

Audit Objective and Selection of Sampling Method   The auditor is usually concerned that asset balances may be overstated. For an account to be *overstated*, the list of items making up the account balance, such as the list of customers' balances, must contain invalid, fraudulent, and/or overstated items. If the sample is selected based on dollars, those items with larger balances are more likely to be included in the sample than those with smaller balances.

> **PRACTICAL POINT**
>
> Variations of MUS sampling are known as dollar-unit sampling, cumulative monetary amounts (CMA) sampling, and combined attributes/variables sampling.

Understatements, on the other hand, are quite a different matter. For an account to be *understated*, either some of the recorded balances are understated or, more likely, material items are not recorded. If the auditor is concerned with understatement, a sampling methodology that emphasizes looking at complementary populations should be considered. No sampling method that samples from items already recorded detects understatements caused by missing items. For example, the auditor could employ a cutoff test to detect missing sales and receivables or examine cash disbursements after year end for evidence of accounts payable that should have been recorded as of year end.

Steps 5, 6, 7, and 8. Determine the Sample Size, Select the Sample, Audit the Selected Items, and Evaluate the Results

Determining the sample size, the method of selecting the sample, and the approach to evaluating the sample results depend on the sampling method used. Whatever the sampling method chosen, consideration must be given to the risk of misstatement in the account, sampling risk, and the auditor's assessment of tolerable and expected misstatement. If a statistical sampling method is employed, the sample must be selected randomly to give each item in the population an equal chance to be included in the sample. The auditor should perform appropriate follow-up work when the audit results indicate a more than expected likelihood of material misstatement.

Tolerable misstatement represents the maximum amount of misstatement the auditor can accept in the population without requiring an audit adjustment or a qualified audit opinion. When planning a sample for a test of details, the auditor should identify the maximum monetary misstatement in the account balance that, when combined with misstatements found in other tests, would cause the financial statements to be materially misstated. Tolerable misstatement is based on planning materiality for the account balance. Different firms have different approaches to determining tolerable misstatement. Some firms arbitrarily set tolerable misstatement at 75% of planning materiality. Other firms have a highly quantified approach.

Expected misstatement is based on projected misstatements in prior-year audits, results of other substantive tests, audit judgment, and knowledge of changes in personnel and the accounting system. It is usually desirable to be conservative and use a slightly larger expected misstatement than is actually anticipated. This conservative approach may marginally increase the sample size, but it minimizes the risk of rejecting book value when book value is not materially misstated. If expected misstatement is greater than tolerable misstatement, sampling is not appropriate unless it is used to estimate the size of the required adjustment to the account balance.

Step 9. Documentation

All of the preceding steps and related decisions regarding the sampling process should be documented to allow for appropriate supervision and provide adequate support for the conclusions reached.

Nonstatistical Sampling to Test Account Balances and Assertions

Nonstatistical samples should be based on the same audit considerations as those used for statistical sampling. There is no way to mathematically control for sampling risk in a nonstatistical sample; the auditor can only project the detected misstatements and make a judgment as to whether the account is likely to be materially misstated, and then decide whether more audit work is needed.

Determine Sample Size

All significant items should be tested. The auditor should select all items over a specific dollar amount, and then, depending on audit objectives, select items with other characteristics, such as items billed in the last week or billed to specific parties. The sample size of the other items to be tested should be based on the same factors used in statistical sampling.

Select the Sample

The auditor should take steps to increase the likelihood that the sample is representative of the population. One way to obtain a representative sample is to use a random-based method, either random dollars or random items, as in statistical sample selection. Another way is to choose items without any conscious bias (**haphazard selection**) other than intentionally selecting more of the large-dollar items.

PRACTICAL POINT

Tolerable misstatement is related to materiality—how much of a misstatement can occur before the auditor gets concerned.

PRACTICAL POINT

When the misstatement from sampling is greater than tolerable misstatement, the results indicate an unacceptably high likelihood that the account is materially misstated.

PRACTICAL POINT

Many firms provide their auditors with automated templates to use in completing and documenting the sampling steps.

PRACTICAL POINT

Random sampling can be used even if the auditor does not plan on using statistical sampling.

Evaluate the Sample Results

Misstatements found in a sample must be projected to the population. For example, the auditor is using nonstatistical sampling to confirm accounts receivable. All 21 customer balances equal to or greater than $50,000 were confirmed. A random sample of 19 balances less than $50,000 was confirmed. The details are presented in the following table:

	Population		Sample		
	Number	Amount	Number	Amount	Misstatement
> = $50,000	21	$2,000,000	21	$2,000,000	$1,500
< $50,000	190	$2,500,000	19	$310,000	$900
Total	211	$4,500,000	40	$2,310,000	$2,400

The misstatement of $1,500 in the top stratum needs no projection to the population because all of these items were tested. However, misstatements in the lower stratum could be projected to the rest of the lower stratum as follows:

$$\$900/\$310,000 \times \$2,500,000 = \$7,258$$

Therefore, the total projected misstatement is $8,758 ($1,500 + $7,258). The $8,758 is the auditor's best estimate, but there is some probability that the actual amount may be higher. Because of the possibility that the population could contain more misstatement than the projected misstatement, research suggests determining an upper limit of three times the projected error (see the *Auditing in Practice—Consideration of Sampling Error in a Nonstatistical Sample* feature). This upper limit should be compared to tolerable misstatement. The auditor may decide that the potential misstatement is not material or that additional work needs to be performed to develop a more precise estimate of the misstatement. Using the preceding illustration and the suggested decision rule, the upper limit would be $26,274 ($8,758 × 3). If the tolerable misstatement is greater than $26,274, the auditor would conclude that there does not appear to be a material misstatement in the population. The auditor would also investigate the nature and cause of the misstatements and whether the misstatements were indicative of additional audit risk or a significant deficiency or material weakness in controls.

AUDITING *in Practice*

CONSIDERATION OF SAMPLING ERROR IN A NONSTATISTICAL SAMPLE

One research study simulated various characteristics of an accounting population, including total book value, the average dollar amount, and the number of items in the population, their variability, and misstatement conditions. A decision rule the researchers considered was if the projected misstatement was less than one-third tolerable misstatement, accept the accounting population; otherwise, reject the accounting population as materially misstated. They found that this decision rule was effective in minimizing the risk of incorrect acceptance.

Source: Lucia E. Peek, John Neter, and Carl Warren, "AICPA, Non-Statistical Audit Sampling Guidelines: A Simulation," *Auditing: A Journal of Practice & Theory* (Fall 1991), 33–48, American Accounting Association.

Statistical Approach to Test Account Balances and Assertions: Monetary Unit Sampling (MUS)

Monetary unit sampling (MUS) is a widely used statistical sampling method because it results in an efficient sample size and concentrates on the dollar value of the account balances. It has been developed especially for use in auditing and has been given various names over time, including dollar-unit sampling, probability proportional to size (PPS), and combined attributes–variables sampling. MUS was designed to be especially effective in testing for overstatements in situations when few or no misstatements are expected. Individual book values must be available for testing.

The population for MUS sampling is defined as the number of dollars in the population being tested. Each dollar in the population has an equal chance of being chosen, but each dollar chosen is associated with a tangible feature such as a customer's balance or an inventory item. Thus, a particular item's chance of being chosen is proportional to its size, hence the term *probability proportional to size sampling* when describing the selection method.

The design of a MUS sample requires the auditor to determine (1) **detection risk**, (2) tolerable misstatement (based on materiality), and (3) expected misstatement in the account balance. The use of detection risk as sampling risk in a MUS sample is based on the view that nonsampling risk has been reduced to a negligible level.

Detection Risk   Detection risk is derived directly from the audit risk model:

$$AR = IR \times CR \times DR$$

MUS sampling is specifically designed to control acceptance risk—inferring an account balance is correct when it is not. The complement of detection risk is the confidence (reliability) level. For example, a 15% *DR* is the same as an 85% confidence level.

Audit Model Illustrated as a Formula   If *AR* is 5%, *IR* is 80%, *CR* is 50%, the resulting detection risk (*DR*) is determined as follows:

$$DR = \frac{0.05}{0.8 \times 0.5} = 12.5\%$$

A lower *DR* leads to a larger sample size and implies that the auditor is relying more on the sampling procedure; a high *DR* implies that the auditor is relying heavily on other sources of audit evidence and is using the sample as a basis for corroborating that evidence.

Sample Size and Selection

The probability of selecting an individual dollar is the same for all dollars in the population. However, when using PPS, each dollar is associated with a sampling unit, for example, an accounts receivable balance composed of many dollars. Thus, the likelihood of any one sampling unit being selected is proportionate to its size. The fixed-interval approach to determining sample size and selecting items to examine requires the calculation of a sampling interval in dollars (*I*):

$$I = \frac{TM - (EM \times EEF)}{RF}$$

where

TM = Tolerable misstatement

EM = Expected misstatement

EEF = Error expansion factor

RF = Reliability factor

The error expansion factor and reliability factor are related to the *DR*; see Exhibit 8.7. The **reliability factor** explicitly controls for the risk of incorrect acceptance of an account balance. It is derived from detection risk.

The **error expansion factor** is derived especially for PPS sampling, and helps control the risk of incorrect rejection by adjusting for additional sampling error introduced by the expected misstatements.

The maximum sample size (*n*) can be derived by dividing the book value of the population by the sampling interval:

$$n = \frac{\text{Population Book Value}}{\text{Sampling Interval}}$$

The sample is often selected using the fixed-interval approach—every *n*th dollar is selected after choosing a random start, which is required to give every dollar in the population an equal chance of being included in the sample. Each selected dollar acts as a "hook" for the entire physical unit in which it occurs, such as a customer's account balance or the extended cost of an inventory item.

Illustration The auditor is planning to confirm accounts receivable to test the existence and valuation assertions. There are 450 customer balances, totaling $807,906. Audit risk has been set as low (5%), and detection risk has been computed to be 15%. Tolerable misstatement is set at $50,000. No misstatements were found in the past year. However, to be safe, the auditor uses an expected misstatement of $5,000. The sampling interval is calculated as follows:

$$I = \frac{\$50,000 - (\$5,000 \times 1.4)}{1.9} = \$22,632$$

Exhibit 8.7 PPS Sample Design and Evaluation Factors

Detection Risk	1%	5%	10%	15%	20%	25%	30%	50%
Reliability factor	4.61	3.00	2.31	1.90	1.61	1.39	1.21	0.70
Error expansion factor	1.90	1.60	1.50	1.40	1.30	1.25	1.20	1.00
Incremental allowance for sampling error:								
Ranked* overstatement errors								
1	1.03	0.75	0.58	0.48	0.39	0.31	0.23	0.00
2	0.77	0.55	0.44	0.34	0.28	0.23	0.18	0.00
3	0.64	0.46	0.36	0.30	0.24	0.18	0.15	0.00
4	0.56	0.40	0.31	0.25	0.21	0.17	0.13	0.00
5	0.50	0.36	0.28	0.23	0.18	0.15	0.11	0.00
6	0.46	0.33	0.26	0.21	0.17	0.13	0.11	0.00
7	0.43	0.30	0.24	0.19	0.16	0.13	0.10	0.00
8	0.41	0.29	0.22	0.18	0.14	0.12	0.09	0.00
9	0.38	0.27	0.21	0.17	0.14	0.11	0.08	0.00
10	0.36	0.26	0.20	0.17	0.14	0.10	0.08	0.00

*Misstatements should be ranked according to their tainting percentages. The largest tainting percentage is multiplied by the largest incremental allowance factor, the second largest tainting percentage is multiplied by the second largest incremental allowance factor, and so forth.

Source: A modification of the tables in the AICPA's *Audit Sampling, Auditing Practice Release*. Reprinted with permission from AICPA; copyright © 1994 and 1999 by American Institute of Certified Public Accountants.

The error expansion factor of 1.4 and reliability factor of 1.9 are obtained from Exhibit 8.7 for a 15% DR. The maximum sample size will be:

$$n = \frac{\$807,906}{\$22,632} = 36$$

If the sample is to be selected manually, it will be easier if a rounded interval is used, such as $22,000. Rounding the interval down assures that the sample size will be adequate. If computer assistance is available for selecting the sample, rounding the interval down is not necessary.

The random start should be between 1 and the sampling interval (1 to 22,000 in the illustration). This number can be obtained from a variety of sources, including the serial number of a dollar bill, a random number table, or a computer-generated random number.

An adding machine or audit software can be used to select the sample. If an adding machine is used, clear the machine, enter the random start, add each book value, and subtotal after each entry, giving a cumulative total for each item. This process is illustrated in Exhibit 8.8 using a random start of $20,000.

The first sample item is the one that first causes the cumulative total to equal or exceed the sampling interval (customer 2 in Exhibit 8.8). Successive sample items are those first causing the cumulative total to equal or exceed multiples of the intervals ($44,000, $66,000, $88,000, and so forth).

The probability of selecting any particular item is proportional to the number of dollars in it, thus the name *probability proportional to size*. For example, if the sampling interval is $22,000, a customer's balance of $220 would have a 1% chance (220/22,000) of being included in the sample. A customer with a book value of $2,200 has a 10% chance of being selected. But there is a 100% chance of including the balance of a customer whose book value is $22,000 or greater.

All items with a book value equal to or greater than the interval will be selected for auditor evaluation. As noted, these items are referred to as *top-stratum items*. The balance for customer 7 has two selection points but it will be examined only once, thus resulting in a sample size that is less than originally calculated.

The population has effectively been divided into two groups: the top-stratum items and the lower-stratum items. The sample selection process uses dollar-based stratification and focuses the auditor on large-dollar coverage with relatively small sample sizes.

Exhibit 8.8 — Fixed Interval Sample Selection

Customer	Book Value	Cumulative Amount	Selection Amount
	Random start	20,000	
1	220	20,220	
2	2,200	22,420	22,000
3	22,000	44,420	44,000
4	880	45,300	
5	6,128	51,428	
6	2,800	54,228	
7	45,023	99,251	66,000 & 88,000
8	10	99,261	
9	8,231	107,492	
10	16,894	124,386	110,000
.	.	.	
.	.	.	
.	.	.	
450	1,900	827,906	

This selection method also tests the mathematical accuracy of the population. Note in Exhibit 8.8 that the last cumulative amount is $827,906. This represents the population total of $807,906 plus the random start of $20,000.

Zero and Negative Balances

Population items with zero balances have no chance of being selected using PPS sampling. If evaluation of sampling units with zero balances is necessary to achieve the audit objective of the test, they should be segregated and audited as a different population. Population items with negative balances require special consideration. For example, credit balances in customer accounts represent liabilities; the client owes money, merchandise, or service. An approach to dealing with negative items is to exclude them from the selection process and test them as a separate population; this should be done when a significant number of such items are included in the population. Another approach is to change the sign of the negative items and add them to the population before selection. This approach is generally used only when there are few negative items and few or no misstatements are expected.

Sample Evaluation

PPS sampling is designed to determine the likelihood that the account balance may exceed the auditor's tolerable misstatement limit. In other words, if the auditor designs the sample with a 15% detection risk and a tolerable misstatement of $50,000, the auditor is testing the hypothesis that there is no more than a 15% probability that misstatements **due to the assertion being tested** can cause the account balance to be overstated by more than $50,000.

When evaluating the sample results, the auditor using MUS projects the misstatement results of the sample to the population and calculates an allowance for sampling risk. The upper misstatement limit is calculated to estimate the potential misstatements in an account balance and to determine whether additional audit work is needed. The **upper misstatement limit (UML)** is defined as the maximum dollar overstatement that might exist in the population given the misstatements detected in the sample, at the specified detection risk level. For example, if the auditor calculated a UML of $41,800 using a 15% detection risk, this would support a conclusion that there is only a 15% chance that the actual amount of overstatement in the population would be greater than $41,800. The UML is derived from the underlying statistical assumptions made about the population being tested. Fortunately, it is easy to calculate. The UML is computed by adding together three components:

- **Basic Precision**—The amount of uncertainty associated with testing only a part of the population (**sampling error**). It is equal to the UML if no errors are found in the sample.
- **Most Likely Misstatement (MLM)**—The best estimate of the actual amount of dollar misstatements that exist in the account balance. This is also called *projected misstatement*.
- **Incremental Allowance for Sampling Error**—An increase in the upper misstatement estimate caused by the statistical properties of misstatements found.

The significance of these three factors depends on whether misstatements are found in the sample:

	No Misstatements	Misstatements
Basic Precision	Interval × R factor	Interval × R factor
+ Most Likely Misstatement	0	Calculate
+ Incremental Allowance for Sampling Error	0	Calculate
= Upper Misstatement Limit	= Basic Precision	Sum of the three

LO 6

Analyze MUS sampling results
and choose effective follow-
up procedures.

No Misstatements in the Sample

If no misstatements are found in the sample, the auditor can generally conclude that the population is not overstated by more than the tolerable misstatement at the specified detection risk level. When no misstatements are found in the sample, the UML is the same as the basic precision, which is calculated as the sampling interval used times the reliability factor ($22,000 × 1.9 = $41,800 in the illustration). Basic precision is an **incremental allowance for sampling error**. Recall that sampling error results from not auditing the entire population. The auditor's best estimate of the total misstatement in the population is zero if no misstatements are discovered in the sample; however, there may be some misstatement in the unaudited items. Basic precision is a measure of the maximum potential misstatement in the unaudited part of the population—at the level of risk specified for the conduct of this audit test. Because the basic precision of $41,800 is less than tolerable misstatement ($50,000), the auditor can conclude that there is less than a 15% probability that the book value is overstated by a material amount. Consequently, no additional audit work would be warranted.

Overstatements in the Sample

When misstatements are detected, the evaluation process is more involved. The auditor's task is to determine whether there is an unacceptable risk that the account balance is misstated in excess of the tolerable misstatement. Thus, it is not just the misstatements found in the sample that are important; it is what they represent about the population. The evaluation is separated into two parts: (1) identified misstatements in the top stratum and (2) projected misstatements found in the lower stratum:

Stratum	Extent Examined	Projection
Top stratum	100%	No projection, because the total misstatement in the top stratum is known.
Lower stratum	All items examined that were chosen in the sample	Misstatements are projected to the lower stratum part of the population.

Recall that every item in the top stratum was examined—there was a complete audit of all items that were over the selection interval. Further, items in the lower stratum were sampled and all items selected in the sample were examined. The amount of misstatement in the top stratum is known with certainty; it does not have to be projected. Any misstatements found in the sample from the lower stratum must be projected to the entire lower stratum and combined with the top-stratum misstatements to estimate the most likely misstatement and the maximum potential misstatement in the account balance.

Misstatement analysis of lower-stratum items consists of identifying the percentage that the book value of each misstated sample item is overstated or understated (referred to as the **tainting percentage**). A tainting percentage is calculated for all sample items with misstatement. The auditor multiplies the tainting percentage by the sampling interval to calculate a projected misstatement. By adding the sum of all projected misstatements to the actual misstatements found in the top stratum, the auditor calculates the most likely misstatement in the population.

Illustration   Using the sample in Exhibit 8.8 with a sampling interval of $22,000 based on a detection risk of 15%, assume the following misstatements were found:

Book Value	Audit Value	Misstatement	Tainting Percent
$45,023	$44,340	$683	NA
2,000	1,940	60	3%
8,300	8,217	83	1%

Exhibit 8.9			Upper Misstatement Limit Calculations					
	UML Factor*		Tainting Percent		Sampling Interval			Dollar Conclusion
Basic precision	1.9	×			22,000	=		41,800
Most likely misstatement:								
Top stratum							683	
Lower stratum								
First largest tainting %			3%					
Second largest tainting %			1%					
			4%	×	22,000	=	880	
Total most likely misstatement								1,563
Incremental allowance for sampling error								
First largest %	0.48	×	3%	=	1.44%			
Second largest %	0.34	×	1%	=	.34%			
				1.78%	×	22,000	=	392
Upper misstatement limit (UML)								43,755

*Upper misstatement limit (UML) factors come from the 15% column in Exhibit 8.7.

There was only one top-stratum misstatement. An item with a book value of $45,023 had an audited value of $44,340—resulting in a $683 top-stratum overstatement. There is no need to project top-stratum misstatements because all of the items in this stratum were audited. However, the amount is used in estimating total misstatement.

The lower stratum contained two misstatements. The tainting percentage is the misstatement divided by the book value. The first lower-stratum misstatement was the result of a book value of $2,000 that had an audited value of $1,940. It was overstated by $60, or 3% (tainting percentage). Because this item was selected from an interval of $22,000, it is assumed that the overstatement is 3%, or $660. Similarly, the second misstatement was $83 (book value of $8,300; audit value of $8,217), resulting in a 1% tainting, or $220 for the interval. The sum of the projected lower-stratum misstatements is therefore $880. This same result can be obtained by multiplying the sampling interval by the sum of the tainting percentages ($22,000 × 4% = $880). The sample evaluation calculations are summarized in Exhibit 8.9.

The most likely misstatement in the population is $1,563 ($683 + $880), the sum of the top-stratum misstatement and the most likely misstatement in the lower stratum. Additional allowance for sampling error is necessary because lower-stratum misstatements were discovered. It is calculated by multiplying the tainting percentages by the incremental allowance for sampling error factors in Exhibit 8.7 and ranking the *tainting percentages* from the largest to the smallest. The largest tainting percentage (3%) is multiplied by the factor in Exhibit 8.7 related to the ranked overstatement misstatement number 1 for a detection risk of 15%:

$$3\% \times 0.48 = 1.44\%$$

The second-largest tainting percentage is multiplied by the factor related to misstatement number 2:

$$1\% \times 0.34 = 0.34\%$$

The products of these calculations are added, and the sum is multiplied by the sampling interval to obtain the incremental allowance for sampling error amount:

$$(1.44\% + 0.34\%) \times \$22,000 = \$392$$

PRACTICAL POINT

The percentage misstatement is always calculated as a percentage of book value. Thus, an account balance of $150 that is overstated by $50 contains a misstatement (tainting) percentage of 33%.

PRACTICAL POINT

Misstatements occurring in top stratum where all the population items are examined have no allowance for sampling risk associated with them. Sampling risk exists only when sampling takes place.

PRACTICAL POINT

The errors are always rank-ordered from highest to lowest in computing the incremental allowance for sampling error.

The UML is:

$$\$43,755 = \$41,800 + \$1,563 + \$392$$

The statistical conclusion is that the auditor is 85% sure that this population is not overstated by more than $43,755. Because the UML is less than the tolerable misstatement ($50,000), the auditor can conclude that, at the desired level of risk, the population does not contain a material amount of overstatement. If the UML had exceeded the tolerable misstatement, additional audit analysis would have been required (see "Unacceptable Sample Results," later in this section). In addition to evaluating the amounts of monetary misstatements, the auditor should consider the qualitative aspects of these misstatements.

Understatements in the Sample   The preceding example assumes that only overstatements were found in the audit sample. However, the auditor may encounter situations in which the account balance may be understated. For example, the auditor might discover that an accounts receivable balance may be understated because the client did not include a freight charge on the invoice. The misstatement is systematic. Assume, for example, that an account balance of $500 had omitted a $50 freight charge. This is a 10% understatement tainting.

When an understatement is encountered, the auditor has two possible courses of action. First, the understatement can be ignored for purposes of this sample evaluation and if there are other audit tests for understatements, this understatement can be included in the other test. Second, the auditor can perform a separate analysis specifically for understatements, following the same format as was used for overstatements in Exhibit 8.9. The auditor would calculate a most likely misstatement of understatement:

$$\$2,200 = 10\% \times \$22,000$$

The basic precision level would remain the same ($41,800); the incremental allowance for sampling error would be:

$$\$1,056 = \$0.48 \times \$0.10 \times \$22,000$$

and the upper misstatement limit for *understatements* would be:

$$\$45,056 = \$41,800 + \$2,200 + \$1,056$$

When misstatements are found in both directions, the auditor considers the directional nature of the misstatements in reaching a conclusion about the **most likely misstatement (MLM)** and net overstatement misstatements. The MLM for the account balance is the net of the over- and understatement misstatements (see the following table). In this case, an MLM of overstatement is $1,563 and the MLM of understatement is $2,200, yielding an MLM (net) in the account of an understatement of $637. The upper misstatement limit in each direction is computed by taking the upper misstatement limit of one direction and subtracting the most likely misstatement in the other direction. In this example, the UML for overstatements would be $43,755 − $2,200, or $41,555. In a similar manner, the UML for understatements would be $45,056 − $1,563, or $43,493. The auditor would be 85% confident that the account balance is not overstated by more than $41,555 or understated by more than $43,493.

PRACTICAL POINT

There is a tendency to focus on most likely error rather than upper misstatement limit (UML). Remember, it is the UML that is important because the auditor wants to control the statistical likelihood that errors of more than that amount could be occurring. When UML is higher than tolerable misstatement, the auditor should do additional audit work.

PRACTICAL POINT

The auditor can always choose to evaluate understatements as a separate audit objective.

	Overstatement	Understatement	Net
Basic Precision	$41,800	$41,800	
Most Likely Misstatement	1,563	2,200	$637
			understatement
Incremental Allowance for Sampling Error	392	1,089	
Total	43,755	45,056	
Most Likely Misstatement—Opposite	−2,200	−1,563	
Direction			
Upper Misstatement Limit	$41,555	$43,493	

Although the auditor may use this evaluation approach when there are both over and understatements, the auditor should use caution in drawing any definitive conclusions regarding the amount of understatement in the account. MUS is not designed to test for the understatement of a population. If the auditor has concerns about the understatement of an account, an alternative approach, such as classical variables approach, may be more appropriate.

Unacceptable Sample Results

When the upper misstatement limit exceeds the tolerable misstatement, the auditor has available several possible courses of action. The auditor can ask the client to correct the known misstatements, analyze the detected misstatements for common problem(s), design an alternative audit strategy, expand the sample, or change the audit objective to estimating the correct value.

Correct the Known Misstatement The client should be asked to correct the known misstatement(s). If this is done, the most likely misstatement, and therefore the UML, can be adjusted for those corrections but not for the projection of misstatements associated with those items. In some cases, simply correcting the known misstatement can bring the UML below the auditor's tolerable misstatement level.

Analyze the Pattern of Misstatements and Design an Alternative Audit Strategy Whenever misstatements are discovered, the auditor should look beyond the quantitative aspects of the misstatements to understand the nature and cause of the misstatements—especially to determine if there is a systematic pattern to the misstatements. If a systematic pattern is found, the client can be asked to investigate and make an estimate of the correction needed. The auditor can review and test this estimate. Further, the auditor can recommend improvements to prevent such errors in the future. For example, assume several confirmation replies indicate that merchandise was returned prior to year end but credit was not recorded until the subsequent year. A careful review of receiving reports related to merchandise returned prior to year end and of credits recorded in the subsequent year will provide evidence regarding the extent of the needed correction. The auditor should also consider the relationship of the misstatements to other phases of the audit—problems in recording receivables may also reveal problems in the accuracy of recorded sales.

Discovering more misstatements than expected in the planning stage of the audit suggests that the planning assumptions may have been in error and internal controls were not as effective as originally assessed. In such cases, the auditor should plan the rest of the audit accordingly. For public companies, significant problems with internal control will cause the auditor to consider whether it is necessary to express an adverse opinion on the effectiveness of the client's internal controls over financial reporting.

Increase the Sample Size The auditor can calculate the additional sample size needed by substituting the most likely misstatement from the sample evaluation for the original expected misstatement in the sample interval formula and

PRACTICAL POINT

There should never be an argument from the client about correcting the known misstatements—from either the top stratum or the lower stratum—because those misstatements are known with certainty.

PRACTICAL POINT

Information on the quality of internal controls is often derived from substantive tests of account balances.

determine a new interval and total sample size based on the new expectations. The number of additional sample items can then be determined by subtracting the original sample size from the new sample size. The new sampling interval can be used for selection of items not already included in the sample.

Change Objective to Estimating the Correct Value   In cases where significant misstatements, are likely, it may be necessary to change from an objective of testing details to an objective of estimating the correct population value. A lower detection risk and a smaller tolerable misstatement should be used because the auditor is no longer testing the balance but estimating the correct population value from the sample. The auditor will expect the client to adjust the book value to the estimated value. A larger sample size will normally be required. Because of the frequency of misstatements underlying the misstated balance, the auditor should use one of the classical statistical sampling methods to evaluate the results.

Summary of MUS Strengths and Weaknesses

As an auditor considers whether to use MUS as the sampling approach for substantive tests of details, it is helpful to review its strengths and weaknesses. Strengths of MUS include:

- MUS is generally easier to apply than other statistical sampling approaches.
- MUS automatically selects a sample in proportion to an item's dollar amount; thus providing automatic stratification of the sample.
- If the auditor expects (and finds) no misstatements, MUS usually results in a highly efficient sample size.

Examples of the circumstances in which MUS might be used include:

- Accounts receivable confirmations (when credit balances are not significant).
- Loans receivable confirmations (e.g., real estate mortgage loans, commercial loans, and installment loans).
- Inventory price tests in which the auditor anticipates relatively few misstatements and the population is not expected to contain a significant number of large understatements.
- Fixed-asset additions tests where existence is the primary risk.

The auditor should also be aware of difficulties in using MUS:

- MUS is not designed to test for the understatement of a population.
- If an auditor identifies understatements in a MUS sample, evaluation of the sample requires special considerations.
- Selection of zero or negative balances requires special design considerations.

Some of the circumstances in which MUS sampling might not be the most appropriate approach include:

- Accounts receivable confirmations in which a large number of credit balances exist.
- Inventory test counts and price tests for which the auditor anticipates a significant number of misstatements that can be both understatements and overstatements.

LO 7

Describe how to use general audit software (GAS) to analyze data, including sampling data.

Using Generalized Audit Software to Obtain Evidence

Much of an auditor's work involves gathering evidence on the correctness of an account balance by examining the details making up the balance. For example, the auditor tests accounts receivable by gathering evidence on existence and accuracy using procedures such as those shown in Exhibit 8.10. Fortunately, the auditor can use computer audit tools to increase the efficiency of many audit procedures.

Visualize an auditor sitting in a chair with a 4-foot-thick printout of the year-end accounts receivable list. Then note the general nature of the procedures performed in Exhibit 8.10:

- Foot the individual accounts making up the total of accounts receivables
- Age the accounts
- Select individual items for further audit tests
- Print confirmations
- Statistically evaluate the results
- Make a judgment on the need for an audit adjustment

Now visualize how long it would take to perform those procedures accurately while working with the paper document (printout) and a calculator. Fortunately, software companies have developed generalized audit software programs to aid in performing direct tests of account balances maintained on computer files. Most of these programs, such as ACL, which is included in your text, can be run on a PC with data that are downloaded from the client's files for testing.

Software packages such as ACL are referred to as **generalized audit software (GAS)**. They are designed to perform common audit tasks on a variety of data files. They have become so powerful and versatile that most firms no longer need mainframe or specialized audit software, which are now usually employed only for very complex data structures or unique processing, such as selecting information about phone calls from automated files during an audit of AT&T.

> **PRACTICAL POINT**
>
> GAS is a specific type of computer-assisted audit tools and techniques, often referred to as CAATTs.

Tasks Performed by GAS

Generalized audit software—such as ACL—can be used to read existing computer files and perform such functions as the following:

- Footing a file
- Selecting a sample—either statistically or judgmentally
- Extracting, sorting, and summarizing data

Exhibit 8.10	Selected Audit Procedures Performed on Detailed Accounts Receivable Records

1. *Obtain* an aged trial balance of individual customer balances from the client.
2. *Foot* the trial balance and check to see if it agrees with the general ledger year-end balance.
3. *Test* the client's aging of the customer balances to determine that individual account balances are correctly classified as current, 1 to 30 days overdue, etc. This test can be done by (1) *selecting* individual account balances and tracing the balances to the subsidiary ledger to determine their appropriate aging or (2) *recomputing* the client's aging process for selected transactions.
4. *Confirm* individual account balances directly with customers by selecting:
   a. All customer balances in excess of $50,000
   b. All customer balances that are overdue and higher than $25,000
   c. A random (MUS) statistical sample of the remaining customer balances
5. *Print* the confirmation requests and send to the customers selected in step 4.
6. *Investigate* all nonresponses to the confirmations and those indicating a disagreement with the client balance by examining underlying supporting documents such as contracts, shipping notices, correspondence with the customer, and by searching for evidence of subsequent payments by the customer.
7. Statistically *evaluate* the sample and make a projection of the potential misstatement in the account balance. Combine the statistical projection with the known misstatements found through other audit procedures.
8. *Analyze* the sample results and make a judgment on whether the account balance needs to be adjusted.

Note: These steps represent only selected procedures that would be performed and should not be viewed as a full audit program.

- Obtaining file statistics (totals, minimum/maximum/average values)
- Evaluating statistical sample results
- Performing analytical review techniques, such as identifying slow-moving inventory and extracting those items for further audit review
- Finding how many transactions or population items meet specified criteria
- Checking for gaps in processing sequences
- Checking for duplicates (e.g., paying the same vendor twice)
- Doing arithmetic calculations
- Preparing custom reports
- Analyzing data for file validity (e.g., missing data and fields with inappropriate values)
- Analyzing data files for unusual patterns of numbers

PRACTICAL POINT

The ability of GAS to search for unusual transactions or anomalies in data, or patterns of data, makes it especially useful in identifying potential fraudulent data.

PRACTICAL POINT

GAS can be useful in testing internal controls that are part of a client's information system.

GAS is the most widely used of all computerized audit techniques, and we have included the most widely used audit software package, ACL, with this text. ACL is user-friendly, fast, and specifically designed for audit work. The audit software is valuable not only when performing year-end audits but also when searching for fraud (e.g., searching for duplicate payments made to vendors). The software is relatively easy to use and follows the graphical interface to operate in many different environments.

GAS is based on auditors' needs to select items from accounts, scan accounts for unusual entries, project errors based on samples, conduct basic mechanical tests such as testing extensions and footings, and perform basic and advanced mathematical functions. GAS can be used to examine files, select records, and create reports specified by the auditor. The approaches to using the capabilities of ACL are described in the ACL appendix posted on the book's website.

Analyze a File Before performing detailed testing, the auditor often wants to gain an understanding of the composition of items making up a population. For example, the auditor might want a graphical analysis of the dollar amounts of individual account balances, such as those that are above or below a certain dollar amount. Alternatively, the auditor might want the audit software to develop a graph of the account balance by deciles. In many cases, the auditor wants to know some combination, such as the number of items past due profiled by dollar amount. GAS is user-oriented and can develop profiles of the data for audit analysis.

Select Transactions Based on Logical Identifiers Auditors often need to review transactions or the details that make up account balances and may be interested in those that meet *specific criteria*. For example, the auditor may want to confirm all customer balances above a specific dollar limit and all those that are past due by a specific period of time. Audit software enables the auditor to select transactions based on the Boolean logic operators: IF, GREATER THAN, LESS THAN, EQUAL TO, NOT EQUAL TO, OR, and AND. This combination of operators gives the auditor great flexibility in selecting transactions. For example, the auditor could extract unpaid invoices greater than $50,000 or greater than 30 days overdue by using the equation:

$$AMOUNT > 50000 \textbf{ OR } INVDATE < \text{‘20101201’}$$

This would result in the selection of all transactions that (a) are over $50,000 in value and (b) were billed before December 1, 2010. On the other hand, the following equation using the logical AND would result in the selection of only items that met both conditions:

$$AMOUNT > 50000 \textbf{ AND } INVDATE < \text{‘20101201’}$$

This would extract only account balances over 30 days old that exceeded $50,000.

Select Statistical Samples   On virtually every audit, the auditor selects samples for further testing. ACL can be used to select PPS samples, attribute samples, simple random samples, and judgmental samples.

Evaluate Samples   ACL saves the selected sample of book values to facilitate statistical evaluation. The auditor needs only to input the exceptions for statistical evaluation and sample projection—including analysis of both top and lower strata. The audited data can be statistically evaluated at the risk levels and tolerable error limits specified by the auditor.

Print Confirmations   ACL is used to select account balances for independent confirmation by outsiders, such as customers, and can print and prepare the confirmations for mailing.

Analyze Overall File Validity   Most computer applications contain edit controls to detect and prevent transactions from being recorded in error. Although the auditor can test the correct functioning of these controls by other means, audit software can assist in evaluating the effectiveness of the controls by reading the computer file and comparing individual items with control parameters to determine whether edit controls were overridden. For example, assume the auditor has tested a control procedure that limits credit to individual customers in accordance with the credit department's rating of the customer. The credit department rates each customer on a 1-to-5 scale, with a 5 representing the least credit risk. A rating of 1 might indicate that shipments can be made only on a prepayment basis, and a rating of 2 might indicate that the total credit cannot exceed $5,000. The auditor uses the software to compare customers' account balances with the maximum specified by the credit policy and generates a printout of each account balance that exceeds the specified credit limit.

Generate Control Totals   The auditor needs assurance that the correct client file is being used. For example, assume that the auditor wishes to query the accounts receivable file containing 13,000 individual records and a balance of $75,482,919. ACL automatically generates control totals such as a record count, the number of debit and credit balances, the largest and smallest balances, and a total of the balance to verify the integrity of the population.

Numerical Analyses   One of the more interesting features of audit software is the ability to perform numerical analyses. A mathematician named Benford studied the nature of numerical patterns and observed that the patterns of numbers across many different applications are about the same. For example, if sales invoices or payroll checks have five-digit numbers, Benford's law would predict the first digit to be the number 1 about 30% of the time. His analysis also predicts the expected frequency of specific numbers occurring as the second number, and so forth, in a 5-digit number. His results are remarkable and the predictive ability of Benford's law is extremely high.

Interestingly, most people committing fraud go to great lengths in perpetrating and covering up the fraud. However, they usually have to assign numbers to documents and, not surprisingly, those numbers often do not follow the patterns of numbers naturally occurring in practice. It is not surprising because the person who is perpetrating the fraud makes up the numbers, and it is extremely difficult to anticipate the occurrence of every digit in a 5-, 8-, or even 10-digit number.

Implementing GAS

The auditor begins the implementation process by meeting with the client's data processing personnel to understand file layout and structure, gain access to the system, obtain copies of the data files at the testing date, or arrange

> **PRACTICAL POINT**
>
> GAS is useful in identifying situations where internal controls have been overridden or may not be functioning properly. The data obtained complements the auditor's testing of controls and formulates part of the evidence used in making a judgment on the adequacy of the client's internal controls over financial reporting.

> **PRACTICAL POINT**
>
> Although it is beyond the scope of this text, virtually all "power users" of GAS utilize Benford's law and supporting GAS modules to analyze accounts where fraud is likely to occur—most prominently in the receivables, payroll, and payables areas.

processing. Once arrangements have been made to facilitate audit software use, the auditor performs the following steps:

1. Identifies the client's computerized files to be read by audit software or to be downloaded to a PC to be read by the audit software and develops a description of the file characteristics to facilitate audit software use, including the following:
    a. File type (e.g., dBase, ASCII, EBCDIC, Access, or Excel)
    b. File description, including specification of each field:
        (i) Length of records and individual data fields
        (ii) Type of field (e.g., alpha, numeric, or date)
2. Determines the computer configuration and operating system on which the file is contained. Develops an understanding of the client's database structure.
3. Determines whether to run the software on the client's computer system or to download the data to a personal computer; as noted earlier, the processing and data storage capabilities of personal computers are such that all but the very largest of a corporate client's data files can be downloaded.
4. Extracts the data from the client's computer system.
5. Runs the software.

GAS as Part of an Audit

Generalized audit software can be used to assist in testing internal control assertions and virtually every assertion related to financial statement account balances—as well as supporting testing of assertions through other means, such as selecting samples to send confirmations on accounts receivable balances. See the *Auditing in Practice* feature that illustrates the breadth of GAS use in testing assertions related to accounts receivable.

Advantages of using GAS as part of the audit include:

- The software is independent of the system being audited and simply needs a read-only copy of the file to avoid any corruption of an organization's data.

AUDITING *in Practice*

Using GAS to Test Financial Account Assertions—Receivables (illustrative examples—not a comprehensive listing)

Assertion	Use of GAS
Existence	1. Statistically select samples for distributing confirmations. 2. Compare sales invoices with shipping documents and/or sales contracts. 3. Select data to perform sales cutoff tests around year end.
Completeness	1. Select data to perform sales cutoff tests around year end. 2. Select a sample of shipping documents and electronically compare with invoices to determine if billed in the proper period.
Rights	1. Statistically select samples for distributing confirmations. 2. Select contracts for notes for audit review.
Valuation	1. Foot the file. 2. Age accounts receivable. 3. Statistically evaluate sample results and make projections of misstatements. 4. Build an estimation on uncollectible accounts based on past collection data. 5. Create a file of current-year write-offs to compare with previous years.
Presentation and Disclosure	Not applicable.

- The software includes many audit-specific routines, such as sampling.
- The software can provide documentation of each test performed in the software that can be used as documentation in the auditor's work papers.
- GAS can help auditors be more efficient in completing their audit responsibilities related to gathering and evaluating audit evidence.

In order for these benefits to be obtained it is important for auditors to have appropriate training and to interact with any information technology auditors that are part of the audit team.

LO 8

Discuss the use of, and apply, analytical procedures as a substantive test of account balances and describe how analytical procedures complement and affect other approaches to gathering audit evidence.

Using Substantive Analytical Procedures to Gather Evidence about Accounts and Assertions

U.S. and international auditing standards allow the auditor the option of performing substantive analytical procedures; they are not required procedures on the audit. However, a primary benefit of performing substantive analytical procedures is that they can reduce the need to perform additional substantive tests of details. In deciding to perform analytical procedures as a substantive audit procedure, the auditor must have concluded positively about the following:

1. *The company has adequate internal controls over the account balance.* The stronger a client's internal controls, the greater reliance an auditor can place on substantive analytical procedures. Importantly, if a company does not have a good control environment the auditor will rely more heavily on tests of details than on substantive analytical procedures.
2. *Detection risk can be relatively high,* thus allowing proper inferences from indirect information to make conclusions about the correctness of an account balance.
3. *The underlying data used in evaluating the correctness of an account balance are both relevant and reliable*—and when using internal data, that data has already been audited. External sources of data that might be used to help develop expectations include analyst reports and industry benchmarking data, while internal sources include budgets and forecasts, operational information for current and prior periods, and information from discussions with management.
4. *Plausible relationships among data may reasonably be expected to exist and continue in the absence of known conditions to the contrary.* The relationships among the data are logical and justified by current economic conditions. For example, a plausible relationship likely exists between store square footage and retail sales by store. Typical examples of other relationships and sources of data that might be used in analytical procedures include the following:

    - Financial information for equivalent prior periods, such as comparing the trend of fourth-quarter sales for the past three years and analyzing dollar and percent changes from the prior year, with prior expectations as to how the current results are expected to compare with these prior periods.
    - Expected or planned results developed from budgets or other forecasts, such as comparing actual division performance with budgeted performance.
    - Comparison of linked account relationships, such as interest expense and interest-bearing debt.
    - Ratios of financial information, such as examining the relationship between sales and cost of goods sold or developing and analyzing common-sized financial statements.
    - Company and industry trends, such as comparing gross margin percentages of product lines or inventory turnover with industry averages, with a prior expectation as to how similar the client is with the industry averages.

PRACTICAL POINT

In higher-risk areas, auditors are less likely to rely on substantive analytical procedures in place of test of details than in lower risk areas.

- Analysis of relevant nonfinancial information, such as analyzing the relationship between the numbers of items shipped and royalty expense or the number of employees and payroll expense.

The Comparison of Worldwide Professional Guidance feature describes U.S. and international standards concerning substantive analytical procedures, revealing relative similarity across these standards setters.

Assumptions Underlying Analytical Procedures

The use of analytical procedures as a basis for performing a preliminary review of potential financial misstatements was covered in Chapter 4. The same principles, including the underlying assumptions and the process for performing the procedures, are still appropriate when using analytical procedures as a substantive test of account balances. Recall that the process of analytical procedures discussed in Chapter 4 includes (1) developing an expectation, (2) defining when the difference between the auditor's expectation and the client's balance would be considered significant, (3) computing the difference between the auditor's expectation and client's balance, and (4) following up on significant differences. However, when using analytical procedures as a substantive test, the auditor will want to develop more precise estimates and use more rigorous approaches to analytical procedures than those used in planning the audit.

The Effectiveness of Substantive Analytical Procedures

The effectiveness of a substantive analytical procedure depends on a number of factors including (a) the nature of the assertion being tested, (b) the plausibility and predictability of the relationships in the data, (c) the availability and reliability of the data used to develop the expectation, (d) the precision of the expectation that the auditor develops, and (e) the rigor of the analytical procedure employed. We discuss the last two factors in greater detail.

Precision of the Expectation

PRACTICAL POINT

Relying primarily on prior year account balances to form expectations considers only a narrow range of information and does not consider changes in the client's business and industry.

The auditor can develop a very general expectation, such as an expectation that interest income will increase over the prior year. This expectation, although it might be sufficient for planning analytical procedures, is likely not precise enough for a substantive analytical procedure. To develop a more precise expectation, the auditor may choose to use disaggregated data. Disaggregation involves breaking data down into their component parts such as different time periods, geographical locations, customer type, or product lines. For example, in the case of interest income, the auditor could disaggregate based on the type of investment, because it is likely that interest rates will vary across investment types. The more you disaggregate the information, the more precise the expectation will be.

AUDITING *in Practice*

PROFESSIONAL JUDGMENT ABOUT ANALYTICAL PROCEDURES

In its inspection of the audit firm KBA Group, the PCAOB noted that in one of KBA Group's audits, the audit team failed to perform and document adequate substantive analytical audit procedures relating to expenses.

While substantive analytical procedures can provide important audit evidence related to income statement accounts, it is important for the audit team to appropriately document and adequately perform these procedures. Otherwise, reviewers of the workpapers, such as the PCAOB, might conclude that the audit team did not obtain sufficient competent evidential matter to support its audit opinion.

See PCAOB Release No. 104-2005-016.

Comparison of Worldwide Professional Guidance

SUBSTANTIVE ANALYTICAL PROCEDURES

AICPA Auditing Standards Board (ASB)	SAS 56 "provides guidance on the use of analytical procedures and requires the use of analytical procedures in the planning and overall review stages of all audits." SAS 56 also permits the use of analytical procedures as substantive tests.
	An important aspect of SAS 56 is the requirement for the auditor to document the process of substantive analytical procedures including the expectation developed by the auditor and follow up on unexpected differences between the auditor's expectation and the client's recorded account.
Public Company Accounting Oversight Board (PCAOB)	AU 329 is the PCAOB's interim standard that addresses substantive analytical procedures. Its source is SAS 56, described above. Thus, the AICPA and PCAOB standard on this topic are identical.
International Auditing and Assurance Standards Board (IAASB)	ISA 520 focuses on substantive analytical procedures and also provides guidance on designing and performing analytical procedures near the end of the audit. ISA 330 also provides guidance on the auditor's response to assessed risks, and includes substantive analytical procedures.
	ISA 520 describes a process similar to that described in SAS 56. However, ISA 520 does not address specific documentation requirements for substantive analytical procedures.
SUMMARY	The three boards' standards regarding analytical procedures are similar to each other, although documentation requirements differ somewhat.

Rigor of the Analytical Procedure

In our discussion of planning analytical procedures in an earlier chapter we discussed two types of analytical procedures: trend analysis (the analysis of changes over time) and ratio analysis (the comparison of relationships between accounts and between an account and non-financial data). While trend analysis is not a particularly rigorous analytical procedure, its rigor can be improved by including more periods in the trend, using disaggregated data, and using appropriate external benchmarks. Similarly, if ratio analysis is going to be used as a substantive analytical procedure, it is important to improve the rigor through the use of disaggregated data and appropriate external benchmarks.

Scanning can also be used as a substantive analytical procedure, although its precision and rigor may not always be sufficient for the level required for substantive analytical procedures. When performing scanning, the auditor will "eyeball" account balances, listings of transactions, journals, and so on in an effort to detect any unusual or unexpected balances or transactions. GAS can be used to sort large amounts of data to make scanning more efficient and effective. As with all analytical procedures, the auditor who is performing scanning has to have an idea of what is usual or expected. The expectation is based on the auditor's knowledge of the client, and of accounting, and just common sense. For example, the auditor would typically not expect to see several entries for round numbers in millions of dollars posted to the revenue journal at the end of each quarter. The auditor would consider such entries unusual and would follow up to investigate this unexpected finding.

Another more commonly used rigorous approach to substantive analytical procedures is a reasonableness test. In a reasonableness test, the auditor will develop an expected value of an account by using data partly or wholly independent of the client's accounting information system. For example, the auditor may develop an expectation of a client's interest income, which is equal to the average amount of investments held by the client for the year multiplied by the average interest rate paid on investments as determined by a source external to the client. While simple models such as this may be sufficient, the rigor of this analytic can be improved by disaggregating the data, possibly by investment type and time period (e.g., separate expectation for each month or quarter). A reasonableness test for revenue may be more detailed. For example, a reasonable test for sales could be based on the number of units sold, the unit price by product line, different pricing structures, and an understanding of industry trends.

One of the most rigorous approaches to analytical procedures is regression analysis. In performing regression analysis, the expected, or predicted, value is determined using a statistical technique whereby one or more factors is used to predict an account balance. For example, the auditor may develop a regression model that predicts revenue for a client that has hundreds of retail stores. The factors used in the model might include store square footage, economic factors such as employment data, and geographical location. Because of the amount of data and level of statistical knowledge required for such a procedure, many firms do not typically perform regression analysis.

Application of Substantive Analytical Procedures

Substantive analytical procedures are not simple techniques, but part of a difficult decision-making process designed to provide evidence about the correctness of an account balance and should be used when the procedures are (a) reliable, and (b) more cost-effective than other substantive procedures.

As an example, consider the audit of natural gas revenue at a utility company. The auditor has tested controls over revenue recognition, including the processes of reading gas meters and the proper pricing of gas sold to customer homes. The auditor has concluded that internal controls are designed and operating effectively. Further, the auditor has concluded that consumers tend to pay their bills and that the consumer does not have independent knowledge of the amount that should have been billed. Given that data, the auditor develops a regression model based on the following:

- Previous year's gas billings,
- Changes in housing developments,
- Changes in pricing of natural gas for the year,
- Changes in efficiency of energy use (index of efficiency considering new furnaces, insulation, and so forth), and
- Economic growth in the area.

Based on these data, the auditor develops a regression model that predicts expected revenue within a tolerable range of error with 95% accuracy. If the auditor finds that the recorded revenue is within that range, there may be no need for further substantive testing of the account balance. Note that this conclusion is based on the assessment that *CR* was low and *DR* could be higher. In areas where significant risks of material misstatement exist, it is unlikely that audit evidence obtained from substantive analytical procedures alone will be sufficient. In those situations, the auditor will likely also need to perform substantive tests of details. However, if substantive analytical procedures provide reliable evidence, the auditor may be able to alter the nature, timing, or extent of detail testing.

AUDITING *in Practice*

GREATER EMPHASIS ON ANALYTICAL PROCEDURES

As globalization affects U.S. auditing practices, there may be an increased reliance on substantive analytical procedures. For example, ISA 330 emphasizes the use of substantive analytical procedures, and as the ASB revises its standards to be more in line with the ISAs there may be an increased emphasis on these procedures in the U.S. standards as well.

If a comparison of the auditor's expectation based on the regression analysis and the client's recorded revenue balance indicated a significant difference, the auditor would want to follow up on this difference. The auditor should consider possible explanations for the difference, and even consider the possibility that the auditor's expectation might be flawed in some way (e.g., the expectation did not incorporate important and recent economic events). Other causes for significant differences could be error or fraud in the client's accounting records. The auditor will also inquire of the client as to possible explanations. However, it is important for the auditor's follow-up to go beyond client inquiry and to include quantification and corroboration. Quantification involves determining whether an explanation for the difference can in fact account for the observed difference. If not, then additional explanations may be needed. Corroboration involves obtaining sufficient evidence that the explanation is accurate. The auditor must not just accept the client's explanation without corroborating that explanation.

> **PRACTICAL POINT**
>
> To improve professional skepticism in evaluating client explanations for significant differences identified as part of substantive analytical procedures, it is helpful for the auditor to develop potential explanations before inquiring of the client. Research has shown that once a client's explanation has been received it may be difficult for the auditor to identify other explanations.

Analytical Procedures Are Not Client Estimates

There is sometimes confusion about the use of analytical procedures because they often look like client estimates. For example, in smaller businesses, the auditor's working papers may have the best data on bad-debt write-offs, percentage of bad debts as a percentage of sales, changes in credit policies, and changes in the volume of sales. The auditor may use the data in testing an estimate of the allowance for uncollectible accounts prepared by the client. However—and this is important—management is responsible for estimating the allowance. The auditor's work is to gather evidence on the veracity of that estimate. The auditor's testing may come from gathering evidence to support the client's underlying assumptions and recomputing the estimate. Alternatively, the auditor's testing may come from a substantive analytical procedure—using accumulated data in the auditor's workpapers, plus additional economic data, to come up with an independent estimate of the proper account balance. That estimate, however, represents audit evidence that the auditor should use in determining whether or not the client's account balance is correct.

> **PRACTICAL POINT**
>
> Substantive analytical procedures are designed to provide independent evidence about account balances—not to replace the client's underlying estimation process.

Summary

Audit evidence for tests of account balances can be gathered in various ways. This chapter describes three tools for gathering audit evidence: (1) sampling that can be used for both tests of controls and direct tests of account balances, (2) generalized audit software that can be used for analyzing underlying data and for supporting both tests of controls and direct tests of account balances, and (3) substantive analytical procedures that provide evidence on the reasonableness of the account balance. The approaches are complementary. Each also requires (a) significant judgments to be made by the auditor and (b) a detailed understanding of the client's processes and risk analysis.

Auditors use both nonstatistical and statistical sampling in testing controls and in performing tests of details. In this chapter, we discussed nonstatistical sampling and emphasized two statistical approaches: (1) MUS sampling for testing account balances and (2) attribute sampling for testing internal controls. Whichever sampling method is used, it is important to design the sample selection in a way that increases the likelihood that a sample is representative of the population. When evaluating a sample, care must be taken to properly identify misstatements and to project them to the whole population before reaching a conclusion about the book value.

GAS will continue to be used extensively to analyze client data, and every auditor should become familiar with software such as ACL, which is included in this text. GAS is an important tool in helping auditors complete their audit procedures efficiently and effectively.

Substantive analytical procedures are also an important audit tool that can enhance both audit efficiency and audit effectiveness. In performing substantive analytical procedures the auditor needs to make sure that the process includes the development of independent and precise expectations, selection of a rigorous analytical approach that uses data at an appropriate level of disaggregation, and follow-up on unexpected differences that includes appropriate quantification and corroboration.

Significant Terms

Achieved upper limit   The maximum likely control procedure failure rate in the population based on an attribute estimation sample.

Attribute   A characteristic of the population of interest to the auditor. Most often it is a control procedure, but it could also be an operational aspect, such as promptly responding to customer inquiries.

Attribute sampling   A statistical sampling method used to estimate the most likely and maximum rate of control procedure failures based on selecting and auditing one sample.

Audit sampling   The application of an audit procedure to less than 100% of the items within an account balance or class of transactions for the purpose of evaluating some characteristic of the balance or class.

Basic precision   The upper misstatement limit when no misstatements are detected in a MUS sample; computed by multiplying the sampling interval by the reliability factor.

Error expansion factor   A factor used in determining the sampling interval/size for MUS sampling to provide for additional sampling error when some misstatement is expected.

Expected failure rate   The auditor's best estimate of the percentage of transactions processed for which the examined control procedure is not operating effectively.

Expected misstatement   The amount of misstatement that the auditor estimates is in the population.

Generalized audit software (GAS)   A computer program that contains general modules for reading existing computer files and manipulating the data contained in the files to accomplish audit tasks; designed to build an easy user interface that translates user instructions into program code to carry out desired audit tests by reading the client's file and performing the necessary program steps.

Haphazard selection   Selection of sample items with no conscious bias; not randomly based and therefore not to be used for statistical sampling.

Incremental allowance for sampling error   Provision for additional sampling error when misstatements are detected in a MUS sample. Factors are determined from tables derived from the underlying sampling distribution.

Misstatement   For substantive sampling purposes, the differences in recorded values and audited values that affect the account total.

Most likely misstatement (MLM)   In MUS sampling, the sum of the top-stratum misstatements and the projection of the lower-stratum misstatements. It is the auditor's best estimate of the total misstatement in the population and should be posted to the summary of possible adjustments.

Monetary Unit Sampling (MUS)   A sampling method based on attribute estimation sampling but involving dollar misstatements rather than failure rates. MUS is most effective when auditing for the overstatement of a population and when no or few misstatements are expected. MUS is often referred to as probability proportional to size (PPS).

Nonsampling risk   The risk of improperly auditing sampled items or misjudging inherent or control risk; includes judgment errors in selecting a sampling method or audit procedure.

Population   The group of transactions or the items that make up an account balance for which the auditor wants to estimate some characteristic, such as the effectiveness of control procedures.

Probability proportional to size (PPS) sampling   A sampling selection method in which each item in the population has a probability of being included in the sample proportionate to the dollar value of the item.

Random-based selection   Sample selection methods in which each item in the population has an equal chance of being selected; only random-based samples can be statistically evaluated.

Reliability factors   Factors related to the detection risk used to determine the sample interval/size for MUS sampling.

Risk of incorrect acceptance   The risk of concluding from a sample that the book value is not materially misstated when in fact it is.

Risk of incorrect rejection   The risk of concluding from a sample that the book value is materially misstated when in fact it is not.

Sampling error   The possibility that the projected misstatement will differ from the actual, but unknown, misstatement in the population.

Sampling risk   The probability that a sample is not representative of the population, which can lead the auditor to the wrong conclusion about the population.

Sampling units   The individual auditable elements, as defined by the auditor, that constitute the population, such as customers' balances or individual unpaid invoices.

Statistical sampling   The application of probability theory and statistical inference in a sample application to assist the auditor in determining an appropriate sample size and in evaluating the sample results.

Stratification   Dividing the population into relatively homogeneous groups called *strata*. Stratification can be performed judgmentally by the auditor but is most often performed with the assistance of generalized audit software to achieve optimum sampling efficiency. It is most often used to identify the largest items in the population for audit testing.

Tainting percentage   In MUS/PPS sampling, the amount of misstatement as a percentage of the sample item's book value. The tainting percentage is calculated individually for each sampled item.

Tolerable failure rate   The auditor's assessment of the maximum rate of control procedure failure that can occur and still allow the auditor to rely on the control.

Tolerable misstatement   The maximum amount of misstatement the auditor can accept in the population.

Top stratum   Population items whose book values exceed the sampling interval and are therefore all included in the test. The top stratum consists of all account balances exceeding a specific dollar amount.

Upper misstatement limit (UML)   The maximum dollar overstatement that might exist in a population, given the sample errors noted, at the specified level of detection risk.

SELECTED REFERENCES TO RELEVANT PROFESSIONAL GUIDANCE	
Topic	**Selected Guidance**
Analytical Procedures	SAS 56 *Analytical Procedures*
	SAS *Analytical Procedures* (Redrafted) (issued but not effective; proposed effective date is December 2012)
	ISA 520 *Analytical Procedures*
	ISA 330 *The Auditor's Responses to Assessed Risks*
Audit Sampling	SAS 39 *Audit Sampling*
	SAS *Audit Sampling* (Redrafted) (issued but not effective; proposed effective date is December 2012)
	SAS 111 *Amendment to Statement on Auditing Standards No. 39, "Audit Sampling"*
	AICPA Audit and Accounting Guides, *Audit Sampling*
	ISA 530 *Audit Sampling*

Note: *Acronyms for Relevant Professional Guidance*

STANDARDS: **AS**—Auditing Standard issued by the PCAOB; **ISA**—International Standard on Auditing issued by the IAASB; **SAS**—Statement on Auditing Standards issued by the Auditing Standards Board of the AICPA; **SSAE**—Statement on Standards for Attestation Engagements issued by the AICPA.

ORGANIZATIONS: **AICPA**—American Institute of Certified Public Accountants; **COSO**—Committee of Sponsoring Organizations; **IAASB**—International Auditing and Assurance Standards Board; **PCAOB**—Public Company Accounting Oversight Board; **SEC**—Securities and Exchange Commission.

Review Questions

8-1   **(LO 1)**   Identify the three main approaches the auditor might use to gather and evaluate audit evidence.

8-2   **(LO 2)**   What are nonsampling and sampling risks? How can each be reduced?

8-3   **(LO 3)**   What factors should be considered when determining whether to use nonstatistical or statistical sampling?

8-4   **(LO 4)** When using sampling to test control procedures, what factors should the auditor consider in setting the:

a. Tolerable deviation rate?

b. Expected failure rate?

c. Allowable risk of assessing control risk too low?

8-5   **(LO 4)** What is the effect of increasing each of the following on an attribute estimation sample size?

a. Sampling risk

b. The tolerable failure rate

c. The expected failure rate

d. Population size

8-6   **(LO 4)** An auditor audited a random sample of 60 cash disbursements and found 1 improperly authorized disbursement (error). The achieved upper limit of control failures is 7.7% at a 5% sampling risk. What does this achieved upper limit mean? How does the auditor decide whether this result indicates the control is working as expected?

8-7   **(LO 2)** Why is it important to specify the audit objective when planning a sample to test an account balance?

8-8   **(LO 5)** When is it most appropriate to use MUS sampling?

8-9   **(LO 6)** A MUS sample results in a number of misstatements, the sum of which is not material. The auditor can project a most likely error and can compute an upper error limit. Which one is the most appropriate in determining whether there might be a material misstatement in the account balance? Explain your rationale.

8-10   **(LO 3)** When using nonstatistical sampling as a test of an account balance, how does the auditor:

a. Determine the sample size?

b. Select the sample?

c. Evaluate the sample results?

8-11   **(LO 5)** What information is needed to design a MUS sample? Where does the auditor gather such information?

8-12   **(LO 5)** What is the relationship between planning materiality and tolerable misstatement in MUS sampling?

8-13   **(LO 5)** When using MUS sampling, explain how the probability of selecting an item is proportional to its size.

8-14   **(LO 5)** All else being equal, what is the effect on a MUS sample size of an increase in:

a. Tolerable misstatement?

b. Expected misstatement?

c. Detection risk?

d. Population size?

8-15   **(LO 5)** What alternatives are available to the auditor when a population contains a few items with negative balances, such as credit balances in accounts receivable, and the auditor wishes to use MUS sampling?

8-16   **(LO 6)** What is basic precision, and how is it determined?

8-17   **(LO 6)** An auditor evaluating a MUS sample of accounts receivable confirmations receives a confirmation response and has to determine whether the difference reported is due to (a) an error on the part of the client, (b) the customer's error, or (c) a timing difference. Explain how each would affect the statistical evaluation.

8-18   **(LO 6)** What alternative courses of actions should an auditor take when the upper misstatement level exceeds the tolerable misstatement in a MUS sample? Are these possible actions any different from those available when using nonstatistical sampling and the sample evaluation indicates a possible material misstatement in the population?

8-19   **(LO 7)** What is generalized audit software (GAS)? What are the major audit tasks for which an auditor would use it? What are its major advantages?

8-20   **(LO 7)** Explain how GAS can test for control effectiveness. For example, describe how an auditor could use GAS to identify whether a company has allowed credit to customers that do not meet its credit policies.

8-21   **(LO 7)** In which ways can GAS assist the auditor in planning and executing statistical sampling?

8-22   **(LO 8)** What are the basic assumptions that must hold for an auditor to justifiably use analytical procedures as a substantive audit procedure?

8-23   **(LO 8)** What is the relationship between the auditor's use of an analytical procedure and a client estimate?

8-24   **(LO 8)** Assume that the auditor concludes that detection risk must be very low. The auditor proposes that sales be audited by examining the relationship of sales and cost of sales to that of the previous two years, as adjusted for an increase in gross domestic product. Explain either why, or why not, this would be a good test of the account balance.

Multiple-Choice Questions

8-25   **(LO 2)** Which of the following is an example of sampling risk?
   a. Improperly assessing the risk of material misstatement.
   b. Testing the wrong population to achieve the audit objective.
   c. Selecting a sample that is not representative of the population.
   d. Inaccurately identifying misstatements in a sample.

*8-26   **(LO 3)** An advantage of using statistical sampling techniques is that such techniques:
   a. Mathematically measure risk.
   b. Eliminate the need for judgmental decisions.

---

*All problems marked with an asterisk are adapted from the Uniform CPA Examination.

c. Define the values of precision and reliability required to provide audit satisfaction.

d. Have been established in the courts to be superior to judgmental sampling.

*8-27   **(LO 4)** Which of the following combinations results in a decrease in an attribute estimation sample size?

	Sampling Risk	Tolerable Rate	Expected Population Failure Rate
a.	Increase	Decrease	Increase
b.	Decrease	Increase	Decrease
c.	Increase	Increase	Decrease
d.	Increase	Increase	Increase

#8-28   **(LO 5)** An auditor selects a statistical sample from a large inventory of replacement parts. Which of the following audit objectives would be most appropriate if the sampling method used is MUS?

a. The auditor plans to estimate the age of individual inventory items.

b. The auditor plans to make a statement concerning the total dollar amount of misstatement in the population from the recorded book value.

c. The auditor wishes to accept or reject the hypothesis that the proportion of defective parts in the population is less than 5%.

d. The auditor wishes to estimate the proportion of defective parts in the population.

#8-29   **(LO 5)** Which of the following best describes an inherent limitation of the Monetary Unit Sampling (MUS) method?

a. The upper error estimate of misstatements tends to be conservative.

b. It is complicated and always requires the use of a computer system to perform the calculations.

c. Errors must be large in order to project most likely misstatements.

d. A great deal of effort is focused on the large-dollar-value items.

8-30   **(LO 7)** Which of the following would not be an appropriate use of GAS?

a. Developing an aging report of accounts receivable.

b. Reading a complete master file for an overall integrity review.

c. Reading a file to select accounts receivable transactions over $5,000 and over 30 days past due for subsequent audit analysis.

d. Submitting transactions to be tagged and traced through the computer system.

8-31   **(LO 7)** Which of the following procedures is *least likely* to be performed by an auditor using GAS?

#All problems marked with a number sign are adopted from the Certified Internal Auditor Examination.

    a. Selection and printing of accounts receivable confirmations from a client's master file.

    b. Evaluation of the audit results based on a statistical sample of inventory.

    c. Calculating an estimate of the allowance for doubtful accounts.

    d. Identification and selection of inventory items with characteristics that the auditor believes indicate obsolete inventory.

8-32   **(LO 1)** The auditor wishes to test the assertion related to the existence of accounts receivable. Which of the following would be the best approach to gathering the audit evidence?

    a. Take an attribute sample of shipping documents and trace to invoices.

    b. Take an attribute sample of invoices and review to see that credit was properly reviewed.

    c. Take a MUS sample and send confirmations to customers.

    d. Use analytical procedures and develop an aging of receivables and compare to the aging analysis from last year to determine whether the differences are material.

8-33   **(LO 2)** Which of the following statements are correct regarding sampling and nonsampling risk?

    I. Nonsampling risk is best addressed through staff training and supervision.

    II. Sampling risk is set in advance by the auditor as a basis for determining sample size.

    III. Nonsampling risk can be minimized by taking larger samples.

       a. I only

       b. I and II only

       c. II and III only

       d. III only

8-34   **(LO 8)** Analytical procedures are best used as a substantive audit procedure in which of the following scenarios?

    a. The auditor's primary objective is to reduce audit costs to a minimum.

    b. Internal control risk is high, and therefore it does not make sense to test controls.

    c. Preliminary analytical review indicates that there are likely to be misstatements in significant account balances.

    d. None of the above.

Discussion and Research Questions

8-35   **(Approaches to Collecting and Analyzing Audit Evidence, LO 1)**
Describe how each of the three approaches to gathering audit evidence discussed in this chapter can be used to test the five financial statement assertions: existence, completeness, rights, valuation, and presentation/disclosure. Provide examples of audit procedures for each of the approaches for each of the assertions.

8-36   **(Attribute Sample Size Determination and Implementation, LO 4)**

Required

a. Sampling risk is 10%. Determine the sample size for each of the following controls:

Control	Tolerable Rate (%)	Expected Rate (%)	Sample Size	Number of Failures	Achieved Upper Limit
1	5	0		0	
2	5	1		3	
3	10	0		1	
4	5	0.5		1	
5	10	3		2	

b. Explain why the sample sizes for controls 2 and 3 are different from those for control 1.

c. What is the general effect on sample size of using a 10% sampling risk vs. a sampling risk of 5%? Explain.

d. Under what conditions would it be better to use the largest sample size for all the controls as opposed to using the individual sample sizes in part (a)?

e. Assume a sample size of 80 is used for all five controls. Determine the achieved upper limit of failures in the population for each control and complete the table in part (a).

f. Based on the answers to part (e), on which of the controls can the auditor place the planned degree of reliance? Why?

8-37   **(Evaluation of Attribute Sample Results, LO 4)**

a. When evaluating an attribute sample, why is the focus on the upper error limit rather than on the mean failure rate in the sample?

b. If the achieved upper limit of control failures exceeds the tolerable rate in an attribute sampling application, what alternative courses of action are open to the auditor?

8-38   **(Evaluation of Attribute Sample Results, LO 4)** The auditor designed an audit procedure to test the following control procedures in the revenue cycle of a company that makes large factory equipment:

1. Credit approval.
2. Sale price taken from authorized sales price list unless specifically approved by the division sales manager.
3. A shipping document exists for each invoice.

A random sample of 100 items was selected from the total population of invoices. The following results were obtained:

Attribute	Failures	Description of Failures
1. Credit approval	3	Approvals were bypassed for sales of equipment to new customers. Each of the new customer sales was the result of efforts by the division sales manager.
2. Sales price	6	Five of the price failures were attributable to a senior salesperson and represented price discounts ranging from 10 to 18%. The other failure was a 5% reduction of a sale by a different salesperson that took place while the division sales manager was on vacation.
3. Shipping	5	No shipping documents could be found. All five sales document exists were recorded in the last week of the year.

In considering your answers to parts (a) and (b) below, note the following information that is available to the auditors from the preliminary assessment of the organization's control environment:

1. The company is experiencing some financial difficulty; earnings have been down. Management is optimistic about this year and hopes to position the company to increase its stock value or to participate in a merger.

2. J. P. Maxwell is in his second year as the division sales manager. A significant portion of his yearly earnings will be based on reported sales and profits.

3. The auditor expected a low failure rate for all three attributes and considers each control to be important.

Required

a. Identify the audit steps the auditor should use to follow up in evaluating the sample findings. Be specific as to each attribute.

b. Assume that the audit follow-up in part (a) reveals the continuance of the same pattern of control procedure failures. Identify the implications for the design of substantive audit procedures and briefly indicate the rationale for your answer.

c. Comment on whether any of the areas noted above would be considered either a significant deficiency or material weakness in internal control.

8-39 **(Attribute Sampling—Public Company, LO 4)** Avation is a large public company and, therefore, the auditor is required to test controls and issue an opinion on the effectiveness of the client's controls as well as the fairness of the financial statements. Avation manufactures specialty clocks used for such things as sales promotions and achievement awards. The auditor is planning to use attribute sampling to test the controls over recording the purchases of raw materials.

The procedures manual describes the following steps that should be taken to order and receive raw material and process invoices for payment:

1. The purchasing department prepares a prenumbered purchase order based on an authorized purchase requisition from the inventory control department and sends a signed copy of the purchase order to the accounts payable department.

2. A receiving clerk prepares and initials a prenumbered receiving report noting the quantity received and forwards a copy to accounts payable.

3. When the vendor's invoice is received by accounts payable, a clerk compares the quantities and prices with the purchase order and receiving report, noting this was done by placing a check mark next to each item.

4. Any invoice with a discrepancy in quantity and/or price is sent to the purchasing department for follow-up where the disposition is noted on the invoice and returned to accounts payable. The clerk also checks the clerical accuracy of the invoice, writes the stock number of each item on the invoice, and initials the invoice, indicating that these steps have been taken.

5. The accounts payable supervisor reviews each invoice and approves it for payment by initialing the invoice. The information, including the payment due date, is then entered into the computer system.

Required

a. Identify the controls to be tested. Your decisions should be based on the controls that, if not working, could lead to a reasonable possibility of material misstatement in the financial statements.

b. Provide examples of audit tests that would allow you to test the controls that you identified in part (a).

c. Provide rough estimates of the appropriate sampling risk and tolerable failure rate for each of the controls identified in part (a) and the appropriate sample size(s). Explain your rationale.

8-40   **(Integrated Audit—Public Company, LO 4)** Assume that you are using attribute sampling to test the controls over revenue recognition of the Packet Corporation, a public company, and will use the results as part of the evidence on which to base your opinion on its internal controls and to determine what additional audit procedures should be performed on revenue and accounts receivable. You have decided to test the following controls and have set sampling risk at 5%, the tolerable failure rate at 5%, and the expected failure rate at 1%. A sample size of 100 is used. The results of your testing are as indicated.

Control	Results
1. All sales over $10,000 must be approved by the sales manager by initialing the customer's order.	1. There were only 25 sales over $10,000 in the sample. All were approved by the sales manager.
2. Credit must be approved by the credit department prior to shipment and noted on the customer's order.	2. Three sales were recorded without evidence of credit approval. The sales manager said she had approved the sales. No customer order could be found for two of the other sampled items.
3. Sales are recorded only when a shipping document is forwarded to the billing department.	3. No shipping document could be found for three of the sampled items.
4. The date of recording the sale must correspond to the date on the shipping document.	4. Four sales were recorded prior to the date of shipment. Your follow-up indicates that a temporary employee worked for the last two months of the fiscal year and was unaware of this requirement.
5. All prices are obtained from the current price list that is periodically updated by the sales manager.	5. All prices agreed with the appropriate price list.
6. The shipping department is not to ship products without first receiving an approved customer's order.	6. No customer order could be found for two sample items as indicated in step (2).
7. The billing department compares the quantity billed with the customer's order.	7. Four billed quantities were for more than the customer order. Three of these took place near year end. In addition, there was no customer order for the two items indicated in step (2).

Required

a. Determine the upper limit of control failures for each of the controls.

b. What impact do these results have on the type of opinion to be given on the client's internal controls?

c. Indicate the potential misstatements that could be the result of the control failures.

d. Determine what substantive audit procedures should be performed in response to each of the control failures identified above.

8-41 **(Sample Misstatements, LO 6)** The auditor uses MUS to select accounts receivables for confirmation. In confirming individual accounts receivable balances, your client's customers reported the exceptions listed below.

Required

Which of these exceptions should be considered misstatements for evaluation purposes, assuming that misstatements are defined as (a) differences that affect the account balance and (b) differences that affect pretax income? Explain your reasoning in each instance.

1. The wrong trade discount was used.
2. The client charged sales tax to a tax-exempt customer.
3. The client failed to record returned merchandise.
4. The invoice contained a clerical error.
5. The payment was posted to the wrong customer's account.
6. The client failed to record a sale.
7. The payment was in transit at the confirmation date.
8. Freight was charged to the customer when the terms were FOB destination.
9. The customer subtracted a cash discount for a payment made after the discount period. The client decided to give credit for the discount taken.

8-42 **(Nonstatistical Sampling, LO 3)** The following information relates to a nonstatistical sample used for a price test of inventory:

	Population		Sample		
	Number	Amount	Number	Amount	Misstatement
≥$30,000	20	$1,600,000	20	$1,600,000	$1,000
<$30,000	200	$1,500,000	20	$185,000	$600
Total	220	$3,100,000	40	$2,785,000	$1,600

Required

a. What is the best estimate of the total misstatement?

b. Are these results acceptable, assuming tolerable misstatement is $25,000? Explain.

c. If the results are not acceptable, what possible courses of action can the auditor take?

8-43 **(Quantifying Judgments, LO 5)** The auditor must quantify the following parameters when using MUS sampling:

1. Tolerable misstatement
2. Expected misstatement
3. Risk of incorrect acceptance

Required

Describe each of these parameters and how they can be determined by the auditor.

8-44   **(Effect of Misstatement Analysis, LO 6)** Your evaluation of a statistical sample indicates that there may be a material misstatement in the population. Upon analyzing the detected misstatements, a common cause was discovered: Most of the misstatements were caused by the failure to record sales returns on a timely basis. That is, sales were returned prior to December 31 but were recorded as January returns because the person who normally records sales returns was on vacation at year end.

Required

How should the auditor proceed to determine whether accounts receivable and sales returns and allowances contain a material misstatement?

8-45   **(Risk Factors and Sample Size—MUS Sampling, LO 5)** The auditor is designing a MUS sample to determine how many accounts receivable confirmations to send. There are 2,000 customer accounts with a total book value of $5,643,200. The estimate of likely misstatement is estimated to be $40,000 and tolerable misstatement is set at $175,000.

Required

a. Complete the following table using the audit risk model:

$$(AR = IR \times CR \times DR)$$

		Risks (%)				
Case	AR	IR	CR	DR	Sampling Interval	Sample Size
1	5	100	50			
2	10	100	50			
3	5	100	25			
4	5	50	20			
5	5	50	10			

b. What is the effect on sample size (increase or decrease) of:

(i) Increasing the audit risk?

(ii) Increasing the detection risk?

(iii) Increasing the tolerable misstatement?

(iv) Increasing the expected misstatement?

8-46   **(MUS Sample Design and Selection, LO 5)** You are planning the confirmation of accounts receivable. There are 2,000 customer accounts with a total book value of $5,643,200. Tolerable misstatement is set at $175,000, expected misstatement is $40,000, and *DR* is 30%.

Required

a. What is the sampling interval?

b. What is the maximum sample size?

c. What is the largest value you can use for a random start?

d. Using the following list of the first 15 items in your population, a random start of $25,000, and a rounded sample interval of $100,000, identify the items to be included in your sample.

Item	Book Value	Cumulative Amount	Sample Item
Random Start			
1	3,900		
2	26,000		
3	5,000		
4	130,000		
5	2,000		
6	260,000		
7	100		
8	25,000		
9	19,000		
10	10,000		
11	9,000		
12	2,500		
13	65,000		
14	110,000		
15	6,992		

e. What is the probability of selecting each of the following population items, assuming a $100,000 sampling interval?

Item	Book Value	Probability of Selection
1	3,900	
2	26,000	
4	130,000	
6	360,000	

f. Why might the final sample size be less than the maximum sample size?

8-47 **(MUS Sample Evaluation, LO 6)** Based on the information in Question 8-46, assume that your sampling interval is $100,000.

Required

a. What is your statistical conclusion if no misstatements are found in the sample? Is the amount acceptable? Explain.

b. Calculate the most likely misstatement and upper misstatement limit and prepare a summary like the one illustrated in the chapter, assuming the following misstatements are found in the sample:

Misstatement Number	Book Value	Audit Value
1	$210,000	$208,000
2	9,000	8,910
3	15,000	14,250

c. Do these results indicate that the account balance, as stated, is acceptable? Explain.

d. If the results are not acceptable, what courses of action are available to the auditor?

8-48 **(MUS Sampling, LO 5, 6)** The auditor is auditing accounts receivable for a long-time client. Because of problems encountered in previous years, the auditor has assessed control risk as moderate and assigns a control risk assessment of 25% and a desired audit risk of 5%. Other factors considered by the auditor:

1. Inherent risk, by firm policy, is assessed at 100%.
2. Client book value is $8,425,000.
3. Tolerable misstatement is set at $200,000.
4. Previous audits have shown an expected error of $40,000 overstatement is reasonable.

Required

a. Calculate detection risk.

b. Calculate (and show the calculation) of the sample selection interval.

c. Assume that the auditor rounds the sampling interval down to the next nearest 10,000. Calculate the largest sample size the auditor would expect.

d. Assume the auditor found the following differences when performing the audit:

Book Value	Audited Value	Nature of Difference
25,000	$15,000	$10,000 was billed to Jason Company, but it should have been billed to Johnson Company. Subsequent follow-up work confirmed that it should be billed to Johnson, and Johnson acknowledged the $10,000 debt.
$40,000	$20,000	Merchandise was returned before year end, but credit was not recorded until the next period.
$325,000	$250,000	Major dispute on cost overrun charges. Subsequent review supports customer position.
$105,000	$100,000	Another dispute on cost overrun. Again customer position is correct.
$122	$0	A credit memo was supposed to have been issued for defective merchandise but was not.

Note: Show all calculations for the items requested below:

(i) Calculate the most likely misstatement and the upper misstatement limit for accounts receivable.

(ii) Discuss the audit implications, that is, whether the audit work supports book value or whether additional audit work should be recommended, and, if so, the nature of the audit work.

8-49   **(MUS Design and Evaluation of Overstatements and Understatements, LO 5, 6)** You are performing a price test of inventory, which has a book value of $2,750,699 and 3,875 items. Tolerable misstatement is $150,000, expected misstatement is $30,000, and the detection risk is 10%.

Required

a. What sampling interval should be used for this sample?

b. Without prejudice to your answer in part (a), assume that the sampling interval was $45,000 and the following misstatements were found. Evaluate these misstatements and determine the most likely upper misstatement limits separately for overstatements and understatements:

Book Value	Audit Value	Misstatement
$ 5,000	$ 4,750	$ 250
10,000	10,300	(300)

8-50   **(MUS Sampling, LO 5, 6)** The auditor is auditing accounts receivable for a long-time client that has good internal controls. The auditor has assessed control risk as low and assigns a control risk assessment of 20% and a desired audit risk of 5%. Other factors considered by the auditor:

1. The auditor will not be performing any other substantive audit procedures.
2. Inherent risk, by firm policy, is assessed at 1.00.
3. Client book value is $9,325,000.
4. Tolerable misstatement is assessed at $215,000.
5. Previous audits have shown an expected error of $45,000 over-statement is reasonable.

Required

a. Calculate the detection risk.

b. Calculate (and show the calculation) of the sample selection interval.

c. Assume the auditor rounds the sampling interval *down* to the next nearest $5,000. Calculate the approximate largest sample size the auditor would expect.

d. The auditor found the following differences when performing the audit work:

Book Value	Audited Value	Audit Difference
$32,500	$15,000	$17,500 was billed to the wrong company due to an error in transcription. Subsequent follow-up work confirmed that it should have been billed to the other company and the other company acknowledged the debt.
$55,000	$20,000	Merchandise was returned before year end, but credit was not recorded until the next period.
$125,000	$???	Major dispute on quality of product delivered. Customer agreed to keep the product and pay the full $125,000, but the client incurred another $60,000.
		$60,000 in costs to keep the customer happy and collect the receivable. The staff is debating whether the audited value should be $125,000 or $65,000. You decide and justify.
$105,000	$85,000	Another dispute on product quality. Customer was satisfied by an issuance of a credit memo shortly after year end, although the item had been in dispute for 6 months.
$500	$400	Credit was supposed to be issued, but was not issued.

Required

a. Calculate the *most likely error* and the *upper error limit* for accounts receivable.

b. Discuss the audit implications, that is, whether the audit work supports book value or whether additional audit work should be recommended, and, if so, the nature of the audit work.

8-51 **(MUS Sampling with ACL, LO 5, 6)** You are auditing the inventory of Husky Manufacturing Company for the year ended December 31, 2009. The book value is $8,124,998.66. Tolerable misstatement is $400,000 and expected misstatement is $10,000. Detection risk is 10% (confidence level of 90%). MUS sampling is to be used for a price test.

Required

a. Calculate the sampling interval and maximum sample size.

b. Calculate the most likely misstatement and the upper misstatement limit assuming the following misstatements were found in the sample:

Book Value	Audit Value
$41,906.45	$36,906.45
335,643.28	333,643.28

c. Use ACL to calculate the sample interval and sample size and evaluate the two misstatements shown in part (b):

　(i) Import the file labeled "Husky Inventory 2009."
　(ii) Choose "Sampling" from the menu, then "Calculate Sample Size," then "Monetary," and fill in the information provided above.
　(iii) Compare the results with part (a).
　(iv) Choose "Sampling," "Evaluate Error," and enter the information using the misstatements in part (b).
　(v) Compare the results with part (b).

8-52 **(Generalized Audit Software, LO 7)** A CPA's client, Boos & Baumkirchner, Inc., is a medium-size manufacturer of products for the leisure-time activities market (camping equipment, scuba gear, bows and arrows, etc.). During the past year, a computer system was installed, and inventory records of finished goods and parts were converted to computer processing. The inventory master file is maintained on a disk. Each record of the file contains the following information:

- Item or part number
- Description
- Location
- Size
- Unit-of-measure code
- Quantity on hand
- Cost per unit
- Total value of inventory on hand at cost
- Date of last sale or use
- Quantity used or sold this year
- Economic order quantity
- Code number of major vendor
- Code number of secondary vendor

In preparation for year-end inventory, the client has two identical sets of preprinted inventory count cards. One set is for the client's inventory counts and the other is for the auditor to use in making audit test counts. The following information has been keyed into the client's system:

- Item or part number
- Description
- Location
- Size
- Unit-of-measure code

When all counts are complete, the counted quantity will be entered into the system. The data will be processed against the disk file and quantity-on-hand figures will be adjusted to reflect the actual count. A computer list will be prepared to show any missing inventory count cards and all quantity adjustments of more than $100 in value. Client personnel will investigate these items and all required adjustments will be made. When adjustments have been completed, the final year-end balances will be computed and posted to the general ledger. The CPA has generalized audit software available that will run on the client's computer and can process the inventory disk files.

Required

a. In general and without regard to the facts in this case, discuss the nature of GAS and list the various types and uses.

b. List and describe at least five ways GAS can be used to assist in the audit of the inventory of Boos & Baumkirchner, Inc. (For example, the software can be used to read the disk inventory master file and list items and parts with a high unit cost or total value. Such items can be included in the test counts to increase the dollar coverage of the audit verification.)

8-53 **(Generalized Audit Software, LO 7)** The auditor wishes to use GAS to assist in the audit of accounts receivable. The auditor's major objectives are to:

- Evaluate existence by sending confirmations to customers.
- Evaluate adequacy of allowance for doubtful accounts by:
  - Examining the file to determine if credit limits had been overridden.
  - Aging A/R.
  - Analyzing composition of credit by credit rating.
  - Sampling receivables to determine if credit rating that is assigned is appropriate.
  - Developing a model that considers economic factors in adjusting the allowance.
- Test valuation through various mechanical tests.
- Test obligations through an examination of credit memos.

Required

a. Identify how GAS can assist the auditor in performing each of these tasks.

b. Indicate which of the tasks require sampling, as opposed to a file validity analysis.

8-54 **(Analytical Procedures, LO 8)**

Group Activity

Required

In your group, use the Internet to locate the financial statements for a company that you are familiar with. Identify specific account balances

Internet

for which analytical procedures would be appropriate for conducting substantive tests of those balances.

8-55   **(Analytical Procedures, LO 8)** The auditor wishes to use analytical procedures as a substantive test.

Required
Indicate how analytical procedures could be used in assisting the auditor in testing the following accounts:

1. Interest expense related to bonds outstanding.
2. Natural gas expense for a public utility company.
3. Supplies expense for a factory.
4. Cost of goods sold for a fast-food franchisor (e.g., a Wendy's or McDonald's).
5. Salary expense for an office (region) of a public accounting firm.

Ethics

Professional Skepticism

8-56   **(Sampling and Substantive Analytical Procedures, LO 3, 8)** Refer to the Professional Judgment in Context at the beginning of the chapter. Identify reasons why these deficiencies may have occurred. Discuss how a lack of ethics or a lack of professional skepticism could have lead to some of these deficiencies.

Professional Skepticism

8-57   **(Evaluating Sampling Results, LO 3, 6)** Assume that you are a senior on an engagement and a member of your team has posed the following questions to you. How would you respond? Also discuss the relevance of professional skepticism.

a. I have tested the first 25 items in the sample of 39. All 25 are free of misstatement. Do I need to test the remaining 14 items?

b. I have identified one misstatement in the sample. Based on discussions with the client, that misstatement is really unique and it is not likely that there would be similar misstatements in the population. Do I need to project that misstatement to the population?

Group Activity

Fraud

8-58   **(Developing expectations in substantive analytical procedures, LO 8)** Assume that you are working on the audit of Vertical Corp. This client is a U.S. communications company that provides wireless and landline local, long distance, and Internet services. You would like to perform substantive analytical procedures for the revenue account.

Required
Part A. In your groups, discuss (a) the pros and cons of using alternative types of analytical procedures and provide an example for each type, (b) approaches to disaggregating the data when developing an expectation, (c) how your decision to use substantive analytical procedures might be influenced if there was a heightened risk of fraud at the client, and (d) the possible benefits of performing substantive analytical procedures.

Part B. Assume that you decide to do a reasonableness test or regression analysis to develop an expectation of Internet Access Revenue. Where would you obtain data to develop your expectation?

8-59   (Substantive Analytical Procedures, LO 8) Assume that you have just finished your substantive analytical procedures in the area of revenue. You used trend analysis and conducted it at a disaggregated level to develop your expectations. You are very pleased that your expectations are almost identical to what is in the client records. Specifically, revenue increased in line with prior period increases and with the industry increases. You let your senior know that you likely don't have any additional work to perform. Your senior asks you reconsider your conclusion. What is likely the primary concern of your senior?

Professional
Skepticism

Fraud

Cases

8-60   (MUS Sampling, LO 2, 3, 5, 6) Mead, CPA, was engaged to audit Jiffy Co.'s financial statements for the year ended August 31, 2011. Mead is applying the following sampling procedures:

For the current year, Mead decided to use MUS sampling in confirming accounts receivable, because MUS sampling uses each account in the population as a separate sampling unit. Mead expected to discover many overstatements but presumed that the MUS sample still would be smaller than the corresponding size for other types of sampling.

Mead reasoned that the MUS sample would automatically result in a stratified sample, because each account would have an equal chance of being selected for confirmation. Additionally, the selection of negative (credit) balances could be facilitated without special considerations.

Mead computed the sample size using the detection risk, the total recorded book amount of the receivables, and the number of misstated accounts allowed. Mead divided the total recorded book amount of the receivables by the sample size to determine the sampling interval. Mead then calculated the standard deviation of the dollar amounts of the accounts selected for evaluation.

Mead's calculated sample size was 60, and the sampling interval was determined to be $10,000. However, only 58 different accounts were selected, because two accounts were so large that the sampling interval caused each of them to be selected twice. Mead proceeded to send confirmation requests to 55 of the 58 customers. Three selected accounts each had insignificant recorded balances under $20. Mead ignored these three small accounts and substituted the three largest accounts that had not been selected in the sample. Each of these accounts had balances in excess of $7,000, so Mead sent confirmation requests to those customers.

The confirmation process revealed two differences. One account with an audited amount of $3,000 had been recorded at $4,000. Mead projected this to be a $1,000 misstatement. Another account with an audited amount of $2,000 had been recorded at $1,900. Mead did not count the $100 difference because the purpose of the test was to detect overstatements.

In evaluating the sample results, Mead determined that the accounts receivable balance was not overstated, because the projected misstatement was less than the allowance for sampling risk.

Required
Describe each incorrect assumption, statement, and inappropriate application of sampling in Mead's procedures.

Ethics

8-61   (Ethical Dilemmas in Audit Sampling, LO 2, 5, 6, 9) This case is to be used in conjunction with the facts in Question 8-50 and can be completed individually or in groups via classroom discussion.

Professional
Skepticism

Part 1. Without regard to the dollar amount of the calculated upper misstatement limit for accounts receivable in Question 8-50, assume you have calculated that the upper misstatement limit is $213,500 and assume the detection risk is 10%. Recall that tolerable misstatement is set at $215,000. What is the implication of the fact that the upper misstatement limit is very close to the materiality threshold? What does the closeness of these dollar amounts imply with regard to whether the accounts receivable amount requires downward adjustment? Using the ethical decision-making framework from Chapter 3, develop an appropriate course of action to take, assuming the following possibilities:

a. You think that the accounts receivable balance is fairly stated because the misstatement is below the tolerable misstatement amount, but you are not entirely convinced of the soundness of your judgment given the nearly material amount of the upper misstatement limit.

b. You collect a larger sample size. You send out ten more accounts receivable confirmations and find two more overstatements, totaling $88,000. Your senior tells you that the client has agreed to write down those two specific accounts receivable. He says that because of this agreement, you should disregard these overstatements for purposes of making a conclusion about the accounts receivable balance in total.

Part 2. Without regard to the dollar amount of the most likely misstatement and the upper misstatement limit for accounts receivable in Question 8-50, assume that the most likely misstatement is $230,000 and assume that the detection risk is 10%. Recall that tolerable misstatement for this engagement is set at $215,000. Your senior tells you he has decided to increase the tolerable misstatement amount to $250,000. His rationale for this change is that the client is in good financial health and has relatively strong internal controls. What is the implication of the change in tolerable misstatement amount with regard to whether the accounts receivable amount requires downward adjustment? Using the ethical decision-making framework (which is based on utilitarian theory and rights theory from Chapter 3), develop an appropriate course of action to address this situation.

Part 3. As noted in Question 8-50, the sample of accounts receivable that you collected revealed five audit differences. For nearly all of those cases, the book value was greater than the audited value. What is management's incentive with regard to potential misreporting associated with accounts receivable (or other assets)? Assume that this pattern of overstatements has become routine on this engagement during the past several years. What does this trend potentially reveal about management? What are the ethical implications of this trend? What should you do?

Following are tables containing financial ratio information commonly used in the automotive industry, for both Ford and Toyota in each of the last five fiscal years. Review this information, along with the underlying financial statements, and then complete the following questions.

Source and Reference	Question

Ford 10-K, pp. FS-1 through FS-8
Toyota 20-F, pp. F4 through F10
	1. Contrast the trends between Ford and Toyota in each of the following categories:
	  1a. Stock valuation
	  1b. Dividends
	  1c. Growth
	  1d. Financial strength
	  1e. Profitability
	  1f. Management effectiveness
	  1g. Efficiency

	2. The ratios that you reviewed above represent the results from the audited financial statements, but assume for a moment that they represent the results from the unaudited financial statements and that you are using the results to complete attention-directing analytical procedures during the planning phase of the audit.
	
	  2a. What account balances warrant the greatest concern/attention in terms of audit planning for Ford? What questions would you ask of Ford management regarding your concerns?
	
	  2b. What account balances warrant the greatest concern/attention in terms of audit planning for Toyota? What questions would you ask of Toyota management regarding your concerns?
	
	  2c. Assume you are performing preliminary audit planning and could specify any statistic that you wanted to review for inventory and receivables, for example, number of days' sales in inventory. Looking at only those two accounts, identify 3 to 5 key financial indicators that you would want to examine in developing an audit program for Ford and/or Toyota. Be prepared to explain to your classmates why you identified that specific statistic. You may assume that you are auditing in a period of either no or slow growth in the economy.

TOYOTA
FIVE YEAR-RATIO COMPARISON

		2009*	2008*	2007*	2006*	2005*
Valuation						
P/E High	highest market price in year (highest price per ADS)/year end earnings per share	(75.17)	23.73	31.8	30.72	25.06
P/E Low	lowest market price in year (lowest price per ADS)/year end earnings per share	(40.62)	17.95	21.78	19.71	19.83
Price to Sales	avg. share price (price per ADS)/per share revenue	1.23	1.35	1.83	1.64	1.41
Price to Book	avg. share price (price per ADS)/(total assets–intangible assets and liabilities) per share	2.39	2.83	3.52	3.09	2.73
Price to Tangible Book	avg. share price (price per ADS)/tangible book value per share	0.87	1.09	1.35	1.2	1.07
Price to Cash Flow	avg. share price (price per ADS)/operating cash flow per share	17.15	11.91	13.55	13.7	11.00
Dividends						
Dividend Yield	annual dividends per share/price per share (price per ADS)	1.24%	1.24%	0.88%	0.85%	0.82%
Payout Ratio	dividends/net income	−100.70%	25.08%	20.63%	17.82%	14.11%
Growth						
Sales Growth	(current year product sales – prior year product sales)/prior year product sales	−21.21%	29.00%	12.46%	3.08%	5.62%
Net Income Growth	(current year NI – prior year NI)/prior year NI	−125.94%	23.11%	19.23%	7.10%	−0.8%
EPS Growth	(current year EPS – prior year EPS)/prior year EPS	−126.30%	24.42%	20.89%	8.46%	2.16%
Capital Spending Growth Rate	capital spending (current year – prior year)/prior year	−14.08%	14.68%	1.83%	31.73%	27.16%
Financial Strength						
Quick Ratio	(current assets – inventory)/current liabilities	1.48	1.55	0.85	0.91	0.99
Current Ratio	current assets/current liabilities	1.70	1.83	1.00	1.07	1.15
LT Debt to Equity	long-term liability/stockholder's equity	0.78	0.67	0.7	0.72	0.73
Total Debt to Equity	total liability/stockholder's equity	1.44	1.23	1.7	1.66	1.63
Interest Coverage	earnings before interest and tax/interest expense	(9.53)	58.05	52.52	93.22	97.23
Book Value Per Share	common stockholder's equity/ average outstanding shares	32.66	37.62	31.35	27.73	25.77
Profitability						
Gross Margin	(revenue – cost of goods sold)/revenue	10.10%	18.14%	19.71%	19.45%	19.84%
EBITD Margin	earnings before interest tax and depreciation/revenue	5.11%	15.85%	16.60%	16.16%	15.34%
Operating Margin	operating income/revenue	−2.25%	8.64%	9.22%	8.93%	9.01%
Pre-Tax Margin	net profit before taxes/revenue	−2.73%	9.27%	9.95%	9.92%	9.46%
Net Profit Margin	net income after tax/revenue	−2.13%	6.53%	6.87%	6.52%	6.31%
Effective Tax Rate	actual income tax paid/net taxable income before taxes	10.08%	37.40%	37.70%	38.10%	37.50%
Management Effectiveness						
Return On Assets	net income/total assets	−1.50%	5.29%	5.05%	4.78%	4.81%
Return On Capital	(net income – dividends)/total capital	−12.18%	18.72%	18.23%	17.26%	17.03%
Efficiency						
Revenue per Employee	Revenue/Employee	$651,464	$830,042	$677,582	$626,214	$650,035
Net Income per Employee	Net Income/Employee	($13,865)	$54,238	$46,517	$40,845	$41,041
Receivable Turnover	sales/average receivable	9.69	11.20	9.74	9.06	9.24
Receivables–Number of Days	365/receivable turnover	37.67	32.59	37.48	40.3	39.49

TOYOTA
FIVE YEAR-RATIO COMPARISON

		2009*	2008*	2007*	2006*	2005*
Inventory Turnover	cost of goods sold/average inventory	10.75	12.19	10.69	10.71	12.05
Inventory–Number of Days	365/inventory turnover	33.95	29.94	34.13	34.08	30.3
Asset Turnover	sales/average total assets	0.67	0.87	0.78	0.76	0.79
Net PPE Turnover	sales/average property plant and equipment (net)	2.73	3.59	3.16	3.14	3.30
Gross PPE Turnover	sales/average property plant and equipment (gross)	1.20	1.63	1.43	1.35	1.34
% of Gross PPE Depreciated	accumulated depreciation/depreciable asset cost	62.48%	60.76%	59.36%	61.71%	65.26%
Depreciation, Depletion, Amortization–Yr to Yr Change	(current year − prior year) / prior year	2.27%	27.07%	13.59%	10.98%	1.24%

*Numbers were taken from the original 20-Fs in that reporting year.

FORD
FIVE YEAR-RATIO COMPARISON

		2009*	2008*	2007*	2006*	2005*
Stock Valuation						
P/E High	highest market price in year/year end earnings per share	11.40	(1.36)	(7.03)	(1.41)	(13.41)
P/E Low	lowest market price in year/year end earnings per share	1.65	(0.16)	(4.82)	(0.9)	6.88
Price to Sales	avg. share price/per share revenue	0.15	0.08	0.09	0.09	0.12
Price to Book	avg. share price/(total assets − intangible assets and liabilities) per share	(2.64)	(0.63)	3.25	(1.58)	2.53
Price to Tangible Book	avg. share price/tangible book value per share	0.09	0.05	0.06	0.05	0.08
Price to Cash Flow	avg. share price/operating cash flow per share	1.11	(62.22)	0.95	1.52	0.95
Dividends						
Dividend Yield	annual dividends per share/price per share	0.00%	0.00%	0.00%	3.22%	3.58%
Payout Ratio	dividends/net income	0.00%	0.00%	0.00%	−3.71%	36.46%
Growth						
Sales Growth	(current year product sales − prior year product sales)/prior year product sales	−18.02%	−16.33%	7.73%	−6.64%	4.33%
Net Income Growth	(current year NI − prior year NI)/ prior year NI	118.52%	−438.82%	−121.59%	−723.17%	−41.96%
EPS Growth	(current year EPS − prior year EPS)/ prior year EPS	114.09%	−368.12%	79.46%	−710.91%	−42.41%
Capital Spending Growth Rate	capital spending (current year − prior year)/prior year	−31.88%	11.19%	−12.06%	−8.9%	11.45%
Financial Strength						
Quick Ratio	(current assets − inventory)/ current liabilities	2.85	2.39	2.63	2.51	2.19
Current Ratio	current assets/current liabilities	2.96	2.52	2.76	2.65	2.31
LT Debt to Equity	long-term liability/stockholder's equity	(19.26)	(9.56)	34.73	(57.9)	12.75

(*continued*)

FORD
FIVE YEAR-RATIO COMPARISON

		2009*	2008*	2007*	2006*	2005*
Total Debt to Equity	total liability/total equity	(25.75)	(13.54)	48.37	(81.06)	19.71
Interest Coverage	earnings before interest and tax/ interest expense	1.41	(0.51)	0.63	(0.74)	1.2
Book Value Per Share	common stockholder's equity/ average outstanding shares	(2.61)	(7.62)	2.84	(1.84)	7.02
Profitability						
Gross Margin	(revenue − cost of goods sold)/revenue	14.59%	11.83%	16.93%	6.88%	17.88%
EBITD Margin	earnings before interest tax and depreciation/revenue	14.90%	5.40%	11.58%	6.23%	13.07%
Operating Margin	operating income/revenue	3.38%	−2.82%	3.27%	25.10%	3.96%
Pre-Tax Margin	net profit before taxes/revenue	2.56%	−9.85%	−2.17%	−9.4%	1.13%
Net Profit Margin	net income after tax/revenue	2.30%	−10.03%	−1.58%	−7.88%	1.14%
Effective Tax Rate	actual income tax paid/net taxable income before taxes	2.30%	−0.40%	31.00%	17.00%	−0.30%
Management Effectiveness						
Return On Assets	net income/total assets	1.39%	−6.72%	20.98%	−4.53%	0.75%
Return On Capital	(net income − dividends)/total capital	1.70%	−8.50%	−1.4%	−6.46%	0.76%
Efficiency						
Revenue per Employee	Revenue/Employee	$597,515.15	$686,746.48	$701,036.59	$565,805.65	$590,296.67
Net Income per Employee	Net Income/Employee	13,722	(68,882)	(11,069)	(44,726)	6,747
Receivable Turnover	sales/average receivable	1.28	1.35	1.49	1.4	1.53
Receivables–Number of Days	365/receivable turnover	285.16	270.37	245.42	261.16	238.28
Inventory Turnover	cost of goods sold/average inventory	14.22	13.57	13.14	13.63	13.78
Inventory–Number of Days	365/inventory turnover	25.67	26.90	27.77	26.78	26.49
Asset Turnover	sales/average total assets	0.57	0.59	0.62	0.58	0.63
Net PPE Turnover	sales/net average property plant and equipment	6.91	6.38	6.49	5.66	5.89
Gross PPE Turnover	sales/average property plant and equipment (gross)	2.27	2.43	2.69	2.51	2.86
% of Gross PPE Depreciated	accumulated depreciation/depreciable asset cost	69.08%	68.05%	61.24%	61.50%	55.74%
Depreciation, Depletion, Amortization–Yr to Yr Change	(current year − prior year) / prior year	−63.19%	64.44%	−39.39%	37.19%	27.12%

*Numbers were taken from the original 10-Ks in that reporting year.

Part A of this exercise focused on using analytical procedures as a planning tool as would typically be done during risk analysis (see Chapter 4). However, analytical procedures may be used as substantive evidence. Look at the line items on the financial statements of Ford Motor Company.

1. Select two account balances that might be most amenable to substantive analytical procedures. Discuss what inputs you would use in order to develop a reasonableness test at a level of precision that would be appropriate for using this as substantive evidence.

2. Under what conditions would it be most appropriate to use substantive analytical procedures? If using substantive analytical procedures for a specific account, is it also necessary for the auditor to perform substantive tests of details?

Academic Research Case (LO 1, 3)

Academic research addresses the conceptual issues outlined in this chapter. To help you consider the linkage between academic research and the practice of auditing, read the following research article and answer the questions below.

Hall, T. W., Hunton, J. E., & Pierce, B. J. (2002). Sampling Practices of Auditors in Public Accounting, Industry and Government. *Accounting Horizons. 16(2):125–136.*

i. What is the issue being addressed in the paper?

ii. Why is this issue important to practicing auditors?

iii. What are the findings of the paper?

iv. What are the implications of these findings for audit quality (or audit practice) on the audit profession?

v. Describe the research methodology used as a basis for the conclusions.

vi. Describe any limitations of the research that the student (and practice) should be aware of.

Effect of Population Size (Finite Adjustment Factor)

Sample size tables assume that the population is very large. A *finite adjustment factor* can be used to determine the appropriate sample size when the sample size from the table is a significant part of the population. Some CPA firms recommend making this adjustment if the sample size is more than 10% of the population. Most sampling computer programs make this adjustment automatically. The formula for determining the sample size for these smaller populations is:

$$n = \frac{n'}{-1 + \frac{n'}{N}}$$

where

n' = the sample size from the table

N = the population size

For example, if the sample size from Exhibit 8.3 is 93 and the population is 800, the adjusted sample size would be 83:

$$83 = \frac{93}{1 + \frac{93}{800}}$$

The effect of the finite correction factor is to reduce sample sizes in smaller populations; it is thus useful in improving audit efficiency and decreasing audit cost. Exhibit 8.11 illustrates the relationship between sample size and population size using a 5% risk of assessing control risk too low, a 5% tolerable rate, and a 1% expected rate. There is a point (C) above which an increase in population size does not affect the sample size. That point is a population of around 20,000 (point C) for this set of parameters. The sample sizes in the sample size table are based on these large populations.

A careful review of Exhibit 8.11 shows why statistical sampling helps achieve substantial economies of scale when auditing large clients. After a certain point, sample size is insensitive to the population size. Thus, a small client with only 800 transactions (point B) requires the auditor to look at about 83 documents (10.375% of the population), whereas a client with 20,000 documents (point C) would require the auditor to look at only 93 documents (0.465% of the population) for the same audit test. For this reason, sampling tends to be used extensively on large clients but not as extensively in audits of small clients.

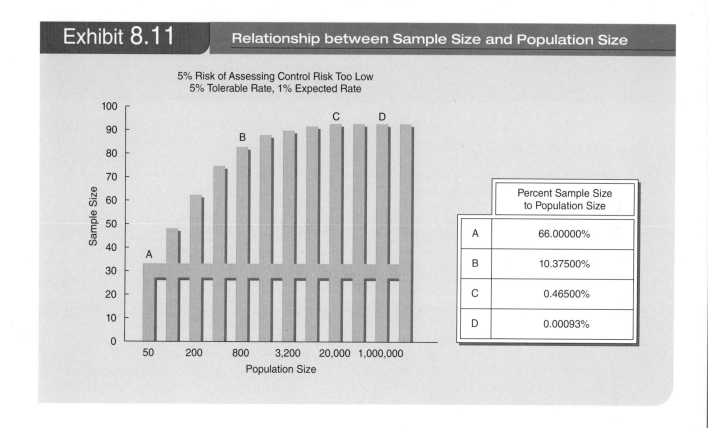

Exhibit 8.11   **Relationship between Sample Size and Population Size**

5% Risk of Assessing Control Risk Too Low
5% Tolerable Rate, 1% Expected Rate

	Percent Sample Size to Population Size
A	66.00000%
B	10.37500%
C	0.46500%
D	0.00093%

9

Auditing for Fraud

LEARNING OBJECTIVES

The overriding objective of this textbook is to build a foundation with which to analyze current professional issues and adapt audit approaches to business and economic complexities. Through studying this chapter, you will be able to:

1 Discuss the prevalence of fraudulent behavior in general and describe users' expectations of auditors' fraud-related responsibilities.

2 Summarize the magnitude of frauds that have occurred in organizations and the effect of the frauds on the economy.

3 Describe the various types of fraud that affect organizations.

4 Describe the auditor's evolving responsibility for fraud detection and high-profile frauds that have affected the design and execution of audits.

5 Describe auditing standards and procedures that reflect a responsibility to detect fraud.

6 Identify and analyze significant fraud risk factors through brainstorming and other planning activities.

7 Use information about identified fraud risk factors to integrate fraud detection procedures into the audit opinion formulation process.

8 Articulate how audit software and other computerized audit tools can assist the auditor in identifying fraud.

9 Describe the auditor's responsibility to report discovered fraud and illegal activities.

10 Distinguish between forensic accounting and auditing.

11 Apply the decision analysis and ethical decision-making frameworks to situations involving possible fraud.

CHAPTER OVERVIEW

Fraud is a major problem. It is estimated that fraud costs American business about 5% of revenue either through the loss of assets or wasteful expenditures. Further, the existence of fraudulent financial reporting not only leads to significant losses by shareholders and other stakeholders, but it jeopardizes the credibility of the auditing profession. Users expect auditors to detect material fraud and determine that appropriate actions, including proper reporting of the fraud, takes place. However, users also expect auditors to detect schemes to commit fraud before they affect the audited financial statements. The auditing profession is conducting research and issuing new standards to detect fraud before it does too much damage to the audited organization. Once the auditor has determined that the risk of fraud is more than inconsequential, that knowledge affects all phases of the audit opinion formulation process, resulting in changes in both how evidence is gathered, how much evidence is gathered, and how the evidence is interpreted and evaluated.

This chapter presents an overview of fraud, describes some of the major frauds that have taken place, identifies fraud risk factors, and identifies audit procedures that are effective in discovering

The Audit Opinion Formulation Process

I. Assessing Client Acceptance and Retention Decisions CHAPTER 4	II. Understanding the Client CHAPTERS 2, 4–6, and 9	III. Obtaining Evidence about Controls and Determining the Impact on the Financial Statement Audit CHAPTERS 5–14 and 18	IV. Obtaining Substantive Evidence about Account Assertions CHAPTERS 7–14 and 18	V. Wrapping Up the Audit and Making Reporting Decisions CHAPTERS 15 and 16
The Auditing Profession, Regulation, and Corporate Governance CHAPTERS 1 and 2		Decision-Making, Professional Conduct, and Ethics CHAPTER 3		Professional Liability CHAPTER 17

most frauds. Audit procedures alone are not the answer. Rather, auditors must approach their relationship with management in a professionally skeptical manner and approach each audit with an attitude that reflects the fact that fraud could be occurring. In terms of the audit opinion formulation process, this chapter focuses on Phase II, understanding the client in terms of evaluating the risk that material fraud exists and deciding what to do about it.

PROFESSIONAL JUDGMENT IN CONTEXT

The Prevalence of Fraud in Organizations

Fraud is a major problem for all organizations, and it includes both outright theft and preparing fraudulent financial statements that inaccurately reflect the organization's true financial status (e.g., in order to boost a company's stock price or to avoid bankruptcy). The magnitude of fraud is surprisingly large and fraud is very common, as illustrated by the following quotes from *The 2010 Report to the Nations on Occupational Fraud and Abuse*:

- "Five percent of annual revenue—that's the estimate of how much money the typical organization loses to fraud."[i]

- "Without question, large financial frauds have been the bane of the auditing profession and get big headlines. But the lion's share of the problem is in small business; 85% of U.S. enterprises gross less than $5 million, and it is those businesses that have the greatest risk of occupational fraud. The "average" CPA (if there is such a thing) doesn't audit multibillion-dollar conglomerates and is much more likely to come across an asset misappropriation scheme in a smaller entity. As data in the report reflect, these schemes are quite common, and most companies have or will experience them."[ii]

- "External audits by themselves detected fewer than 5% of the frauds in our study. In comparison, 8% of the cases were detected by accident. This shows that external auditors are catching relatively few occupational frauds compared to other means of detection."[iii]

In 2010, the Committee of Sponsoring Organizations (COSO) published an update of its continuing studies on financial fraud and shared the following observations related to the magnitude, frequency, and nature of fraud:

- The number of alleged financial frauds increased from 294 to 347 over the period of 1998–2007 as compared to 1988–1997, with a cumulative misstatement of financial statements of over $120 billion.

- The average fraud during the latter period was three times the size of that from the 1988–1997 study.

- The CEO or CFO was named as a perpetrator or co-conspirator in 89% of the cases.

- Revenue misstatements accounted for 60% of the fraud, compared to 50% in the previous study.

In addition to these studies, recent cases in the news provide important insights on frauds that have recently happened. For example, Milwaukee-based Koss Corporation reported an embezzlement of funds orchestrated by its CFO of approximately $31 million over a five-year period of time when the company's reported earnings were only $26 million. The CFO used the funds to buy personal goods, such as expensive coats, jewelry, and other personal items that were mostly kept in storage facilities. Interestingly, the CFO was neither an accountant nor a CPA, the CEO had a college degree in anthropology, most of the board members had served on the board for 20–30 years, and the company made highly technical products that were in very competitive markets.

In still another recent fraud, a senior benefits executive at Hitachi America, Inc. set up a plan to divert approximately $8 million from Hitachi by creating a separate bank account that included the Hitachi name, but that was controlled by him. The funds that were diverted included payments from health providers and insurance companies intended for the Hitachi's employee

(continues)

benefit plans. The executive used the $8 million in the new account to purchase an expensive vacation home, and a new Lexus automobile, among other items.[iv]

These examples above illustrate issues that we will address concerning fraud throughout this chapter, and form the basis for questions that you should consider as you deepen your understanding of the nature of fraud:

1. Why is fraud so prevalent? Can we develop better models to predict when fraud might occur?

2. What are the major types of fraud? What are the major characteristics of fraud that auditors should consider?

3. Do all companies have a risk of fraud?

4. Do controls exist to help mitigate fraud risks?

5. How does the auditor analyze the relationship of fraud risks and fraud-related controls?

6. To what extent should the auditor be responsible for identifying the risk of fraud, and then determining whether material fraud actually exists?

---

[i] Nilsen, Kim, "Keeping Fraud in the Cross Hairs: Report Highlights, common, costly schemes and prevention the target," *Journal of Accountancy* (online version), June 2010.
[ii] Ibid, quote from Joseph Wells commenting on the 2010 National Report to the Nations.
[iii] Ibid.
[iv] Northcountygazette.com, 11/13/08, "$8 million suspect: Dennis M. Dowd victim: Hitachi American Ltd."

An Overview of Fraud and the Auditor's Fraud Related Responsibilities

The Unfortunate Prevalence of Lying and Cheating

LO 1

Discuss the prevalence of fraudulent behavior in general and describe users' expectations of auditors' fraud-related responsibilities.

The prevalence of fraud described in the *Professional Judgment in Context* feature is alarming. However, in many ways, it is not surprising. The Josepheson Institute has studied high school students' attitudes toward cheating for more than a decade, and the results have led the Institute to conclude:

- The hole in the moral ozone seems to be getting bigger; each new generation is more likely to lie and cheat than the preceding one.
- Young people are much more cynical than their elders; they are considerably more likely to believe that it is necessary to lie or cheat in order to succeed. Those who believe dishonesty is necessary are more likely to actually lie and cheat.
- Cheaters in high school are far more likely as adults to lie to their spouses, customers, and employers, and to cheat on expense reports and insurance claims.[1]

These conclusions are not to imply that an increased incidence in fraud is due to young people. Rather, it is important to recognize that a willingness to commit fraud when the individual believes it is justified or necessary has implications for individuals that you will encounter as an auditor. Exhibit 9.1 highlights some of the findings of the Josepheson Institute's survey of high school students in 2009:

---

[1] The Josepheson Institute, "Character Study Reveals Predictors of Lying and Cheating," October 29, 2009, at http://josephsoninstitute.org/surveys/index.html.

Exhibit 9.1 | **High School Student Attitudes about Cheating**

In the real world, successful people do what they have to do to win, even if others consider it cheating.

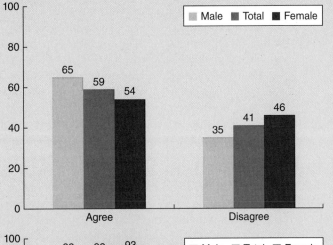

I am satisfied with my own ethics and character.

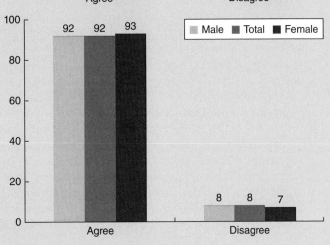

How many times in the past year have you lied to a parent about something significant?

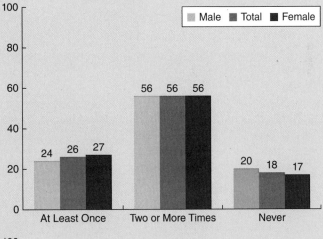

How many times during the past year have you cheated in a test at school?

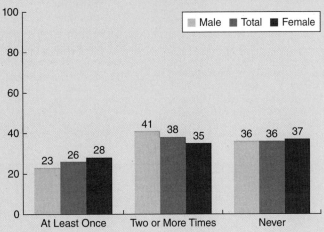

The study is conducted every two years and in every year since its initiation the percentage of students admitting to cheating or lying about something significant has increased. It is interesting to note that 92% of the students are satisfied with their own ethics; yet 82% have lied to their parents about something significant in the past year, and 64% admit to have cheated on a test at school last year (and 82% admit to copying homework). These are all self-reported data so, if anything, they might understate the actual extent of the problems. Cheating or lying happens when there exists an incentive ("I have to get the good grade to get into college"), the person then rationalizes their behavior ("Other people are doing it"), and there has to be some opportunity to accomplish the deception ("I can cheat because my teacher is not watching me closely"). As we proceed through this chapter, you will find that these three factors (hereafter referred to as the fraud triangle) are present in most every financial fraud. Someone may have an economic need that provides an incentive to commit the fraud; the individual rationalizes the behavior (e.g., justifying it by thinking that the actions will not hurt anyone), and there has to be a weakness in the control system that allows the fraud to take place. The bottom line is that the willingness to cheat or lie about something significant is pervasive and auditors should recognize the possibility of fraud taking place in all organizations. Some frauds may be large, some may be small, but more fraud exists than what we normally expect. The audit implication is that we must take care to identify indicators of fraud and then adjust audit procedures to detect fraud if it is occurring.

Given the prevalence of fraud, it is important to consider the auditor's role related to fraud detection. The Center for Audit Quality (CAQ), a group affiliated with the AICPA, is an autonomous policy-making group working to foster high-quality auditor performance and enhance the public's confidence in the audit report. In October, 2010, the CAQ issued a white paper titled *Deterring and Detecting Financial Reporting Fraud—A Platform for Action.*[2] In that paper, the CAQ outlines a framework for future action

AUDITING *in Practice*

USERS' EXPECTATIONS OF AUDITORS' FRAUD-RELATED RESPONSIBILITIES

Auditing standards historically have reflected a belief that it is not reasonable for auditors to detect cleverly implemented frauds. However, it is increasingly clear that the general public, as reflected in the orientation of the PCAOB, expects that auditors have a responsibility to detect and report on material frauds as noted below:

The mission of the PCAOB is to restore the confidence of investors, and society generally, in the independent auditors of companies. There is no doubt that repeated revelations of accounting scandals and audit failures have seriously damaged public confidence.... The detection of material fraud is a reasonable expectation of users of audited

financial statements. Society needs and expects assurance that financial information has not been materially misstated because of fraud. *Unless an independent audit can provide this assurance, it has little if any value to society.* [emphasis added][1]

The financial statement users' message to auditors is clear: Auditors must assume a greater responsibility for detecting fraud and assuring users that the financial statements are free of material fraud.

[1]Douglas R. Carmichael, *The PCAOB and the Social Responsibility of the Independent Auditor,* Chief Auditor, Public Accounting Oversight Board, speech given to Mid-Year Auditing Section meeting of the American Accounting Association, January 16, 2004.

---

[2]Center for Audit Quality, *Deterring and Detecting Financial Reporting Fraud—A Platform for Action,* available at http://www.thecaq.org/Anti-FraudInitiative/CAQAnti-FraudReport.pdf.

including a fraud deterrence and detection plan that recognizes the importance of three fundamental principles:

- A strong, highly ethical *tone at the top* of an organization that permeates the corporate culture, including an effective fraud risk management program, is essential.
- *Skepticism*, a questioning mindset that strengthens professional objectivity, is required of all participants involved in preparing financial statement and related reports.
- Strong *communication* among supply chain participants, including management, the audit committee, internal audit, external audit, and regulatory authorities (where applicable) is key.

The CAQ views fraud as the key element that needs to be addressed in improving the audit's contribution to society and gaining respect for the auditing profession. However, the CAQ also recognizes that preventing and detecting fraud cannot be the job of the external auditor alone; all the parties involved in preparing and opining on audited financial statements need to play a role in preventing and detecting fraud.

Magnitude of Fraud

At one time or another, we have all seen headlines similar to the following:

> "Société Générale Blames Managers; Supervisors Linked to Trader's Fraud, Internal Report Concludes"
>
> "For Subprime Lender [New Century], 'Profit' That Really Wasn't There"
>
> "Parmalat Inquiry Finds Basic Ruses at Heart of the Scandal"
>
> "How Three Unlikely Sleuths Exposed Fraud at WorldCom"
>
> "Did HealthSouth Auditor Miss Key Clues on Fraud Risk"
>
> "Was the Fall of AIG and Lehman Brothers Fraud or Just Greed?"
>
> "Dell Signs Consent Decree with the SEC"

These headlines are just a small sample. Fraud is not confined to large companies, nor is it confined to top executives; it can be perpetrated by any employee within an organization. One study estimated that 85% of the worst frauds were conducted by insiders on the payroll.[3] Further, fraud is not confined to U.S. businesses, where management has been historically motivated to maximize their personal worth through stock options. Frauds at Ahold (The Netherlands), Parmalat (Italy), Sachtiyam (India), and Adecco (Switzerland) reveal that fraud is an international phenomenon.

An estimate from a 2008 study by the Association of Certified Fraud Examiners (ACFE) suggests that companies in the United States have historically lost up to 7% of revenue as a result of fraud, amounting to almost $1 trillion in losses annually. A difficulty occurs in understanding how widespread fraud is occurs because frauds are often not reported. One estimate is that 40% of frauds have been discovered, but not prosecuted, and an additional 40% of frauds have not been discovered.

Fraud Defined

Fraud involves either (a) intentional embezzlements or thefts of funds from a company or (b) the intentional misstatement of financial statements in order to achieve a perception that a company is doing better than it really is doing.

LO 2

Summarize the magnitude of frauds that have occurred in organizations and the effect of the frauds on the economy.

PRACTICAL POINT

The ACFE reports that smaller organizations are the most vulnerable to frauds involving misappropriation of assets (e.g., theft of cash). The average loss caused by a fraud scheme in a small organization is $200,000. In contrast, the average misappropriation scheme in the largest organizations amounts to about half that much. This difference in loss magnitude between small and large organizations can be explained in part by weak internal controls at small organizations.

LO 3

Define the various types of fraud that affect organizations.

---

[3] Ernst & Young, *Fraud: The Unmanaged Risk*; 8th Global Survey, 2002.

Exhibit 9.2   Fraud and Abuse Classification Scheme

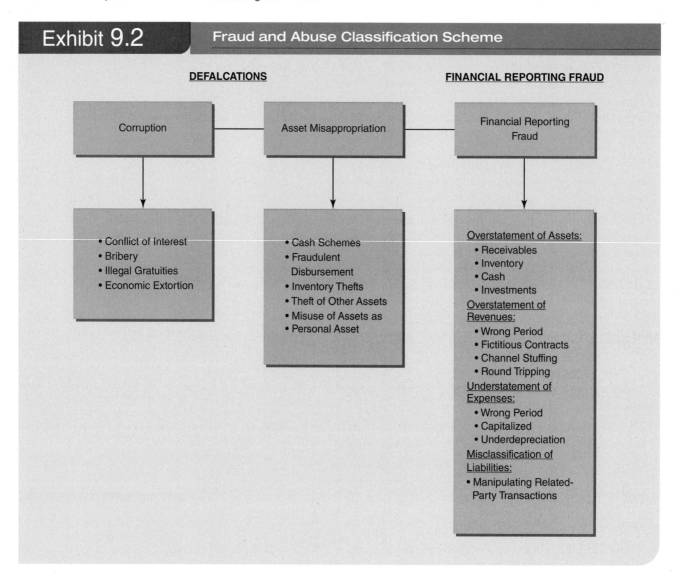

DEFALCATIONS   **FINANCIAL REPORTING FRAUD**

Corruption — Asset Misappropriation   Financial Reporting Fraud

Corruption:
- Conflict of Interest
- Bribery
- Illegal Gratuities
- Economic Extortion

Asset Misappropriation:
- Cash Schemes
- Fraudulent Disbursement
- Inventory Thefts
- Theft of Other Assets
- Misuse of Assets as
- Personal Asset

Financial Reporting Fraud:
Overstatement of Assets:
- Receivables
- Inventory
- Cash
- Investments

Overstatement of Revenues:
- Wrong Period
- Fictitious Contracts
- Channel Stuffing
- Round Tripping

Understatement of Expenses:
- Wrong Period
- Capitalized
- Underdepreciation

Misclassification of Liabilities:
- Manipulating Related-Party Transactions

Thus, a common denominator in all fraud is intentionality. In fact, intent to deceive is what distinguishes fraud from errors. Many auditors routinely find financial errors in their clients' books, but those errors are *not* intentional. Fraud is usually categorized into defalcations or financial reporting fraud. Exhibit 9.2 provides an overview of these two broad categories along with various examples of fraud conducted under each category.

Defalcations

A **defalcation** is a type of fraud in which an employee takes assets from an organization for personal gain. Examples include theft (embezzlement) of assets such as cash and inventory or the manipulation of money transfers. The ACFE categorizes defalcations as (1) corruption and (2) asset misappropriation.

Corruption occurs when fraudsters wrongfully use their influence in a business transaction in order to procure some benefit for themselves or another person, contrary to their duty to their employer or the rights of another. Common examples include accepting kickbacks and engaging in conflicts of interest. For example, Halliburton Corporation reported that in early 2004 two of its

AUDITING *in Practice*

THE FACE OF SMALL BUSINESS FRAUD AND THE IMPORTANCE OF INTERNAL CONTROLS

Diann Cattani was a trusted employee at a small business owned by a husband and wife. As a trusted employee with little oversight from the company's owners, Ms. Cattani was able to use almost $500,000 of company money on personal items over a four-year period. A small business often means a small workforce without sufficient staff to have appropriate segregation of duties and other important controls. In Ms. Cattani's case, she was able to sign checks, oversee the payroll, and communicate with company attorneys and accountants.

Diann grew up in a conservative, religious, family-oriented home. She attended Brigham Young University, where she received an athletic scholarship and worked toward degrees in business management and psychology. She served as a business manager and consultant/facilitator for a successful family-owned consulting firm. From all outward appearances, Diann seemed to have everything going for her; and then one mistake by her travel agent put her on the path of temptation and greed. Her travel agent had mistakenly put a personal family trip by Ms. Cattani on the company credit card. When Ms. Cattani spotted the mistake, she intended to rectify the situation, but growing

personal bills caused her to let the matter slip. Ms. Cattani acknowledges that after that mistake she got greedy and expensed meals, furniture, and other items. She rationalized the initial mistake by telling herself that while she was on vacation she had to answer company e-mails and phone calls, and she continued to rationalize subsequent, but more egregious, behavior. Surprisingly, her bosses never questioned her expenses or required that she provide receipts to prove that her expenses were business related—after all, she was a trusted employee. In this case, trust in employees was treated as an invitation to steal. Opportunities regularly presented themselves. Companies, big and small, need more than trust—they need controls—to help mitigate fraud.

After four years of stealing, Ms. Cattani turned herself in to authorities and left behind a 6-week-old son and two young daughters to serve an 18-month federal prison sentence.

Source: Adapted from "Running the Show: Inside Job," by Arden Dale, *The Wall Street Journal*, April 30, 2007.

---

employees had received kickbacks of $6 million to place orders with a Kuwaiti oil company as part of its efforts in rebuilding the oil infrastructure in Iraq. Corruption occurs because there are:

- Conflicts of interest in certain positions
- Situations where bribery can influence actions
- Situations where illegal gratuities influence action
- Situations where economic extortion can be used

Asset misappropriation occurs when a perpetrator steals or misuses an organization's assets. Asset misappropriations are the dominant fraud scheme perpetrated against small businesses, and the perpetrators are usually employees. Asset misappropriation commonly occurs when employees:

- Gain access to cash and manipulate accounts to cover up cash thefts
- Manipulate cash disbursement through fake companies or employees to gain access to cash
- Steal inventory or other assets and manipulate the financial records to cover up the fraud

In their 2008 Report to the Nation, the ACFE reported that about 85% of the defalcations dealt with the theft of cash. The remaining 15% dealt with thefts of inventory and other miscellaneous assets such as tools. The cash misappropriation schemes can be categorized as:

- *Cash larceny:* stealing cash after it had been recorded
- *Skimming:* intercepting and taking cash before it is recorded on the books
- *Fraudulent disbursements:* funds disbursed fraudulently to an entity that is controlled by the fraud perpetrator

Fraudulent disbursements remain the largest defalcation scheme in accounting. Most of these frauds occur because the company has poor or nonexistent controls over cash disbursements. Examples of methods used to achieve fraudulent disbursements include the following:

- *Billing schemes:* setting up false vendors and paying the vendors for fictitious goods
- *Payroll schemes:* putting fictitious employees on the payroll
- *Expense reimbursement schemes:* overstating expense reimbursement requests
- *Check tampering:* altering checks; e.g., changing the payee or changing the payment amount

Financial Reporting Fraud

The intentional manipulation of reported financial results to misstate the economic picture of the firm is called **financial reporting fraud**. The perpetrator of such a fraud generally seeks gain through the rise in stock price and the commensurate increase in personal wealth. Sometimes the perpetrator does not seek direct personal gain, but instead uses the financial reporting fraud to "help" the organization avoid bankruptcy or to avoid some other negative financial outcome. SAS 99 indicates at least three ways in which financial reporting fraud can take place:

1. Manipulation, falsification, or alteration of accounting records or supporting documents
2. Misrepresentation or omission of events, transactions, or other significant information
3. Intentional misapplication of accounting principles

Common examples of fraudulent financial reporting include overstating revenues or assets, understating expenses, or misclassifying liabilities. Some recent frauds have happened at companies that are probably familiar to you. For example, WorldCom orchestrated its fraud by capitalizing items that should have been recorded as expenses, thereby increasing current-period income. Charter Communications inflated revenue by selling control boxes back to its supplier and then repurchasing them later. Dell, Inc. admitted to manipulating its reported income by not accurately disclosing payments that it received from computer-chip maker Intel for agreeing not to use chips from Intel's rival Advanced Micro Devices. These payments accounted for 76% of Dell's operating income in early 2007. Dell also covered earnings shortages by dipping into reserves and claimed the seemingly strong results were due to strong management and operations.

Financial reporting fraud can also involve financial-related reports that are not a formal part of the financial statements. As an example, publicly traded oil companies are required to report changes in their proved reserves each year. A "proved reserve" is the discovery of an oil field in which the company has determined it is economically feasible to extract the oil from the field at current oil prices. The amount of proved reserves are a best estimate of the millions (billions) of barrels of crude oil that can economically be extracted from the field. During 2004, the SEC successfully brought action against Shell Oil Company, alleging that the company had falsely reported its proved reserves in an effort to make the company look more successful and thus prop up its stock price.

There is a tendency to view financial reporting fraud as involving just large companies in which the executives are concerned about stock options and their stock prices. Exhibit 9.3 provides an example of a small business where the owners were trying to "buy time" for an otherwise failing business to succeed. The company perpetrated fraud by inappropriately grossing up revenue, by capitalizing expenses, and by misclassifying liabilities. The example illustrates red flags indicating fraud that the auditor must be alert to, as well as illustrating how management can conceal a fraud.

Exhibit 9.3	Financial Reporting Fraud—A Small Business Example

COMPANY BACKGROUND

Braggart Apparel Company was acquired by two young entrepreneurs in 1994. The company was primarily in the business of developing products with sporting logos, e.g., major league baseball, NCAA (Notre Dame, University of Michigan, etc.), or NASCAR, that could be sold through department stores. The company had two lines of business: infant wear and adult wear. The company started with about $4 million of sales in 1994 and grew sales to approximately $19 million by the end of 1998. In order to support the growth in sales, the company borrowed approximately $10 million from a local bank and was able to justify the loan because (a) the loan was secured by receivables and inventory and (b) the company had a stable product that was experiencing a high rate of growth.

The company failed in 1999. The bank lost all of the value of its loans. Management did not develop a better model for the business, but was able to use the funds to develop a new Internet business that it subsequently sold to another company for over $100 million. Management had carefully constructed a financial reporting fraud that covered up real business problems.

THE FINANCIAL REPORTING FRAUD SCHEME

The loan covenants of the bank had numerous provisions to protect the bank. Included in these provisions were:

- The company was to maintain a debt/equity ratio that did not exceed 3.5 to 1.
- The company had to maintain tangible net worth of at least $1,500,000.
- The company had to furnish audited financial statements prepared in accordance with GAAP.
- The loan was secured by both accounts receivable and inventory.

The company was in violation of each of these provisions. However, they covered up the fraud in the following way. Braggart had licensed all of its rights for adult wear products to another company that manufactured and sold the product. In turn, the other company would submit 17.5% of their net revenue to Braggart as royalties. Braggart decided to record the gross sales made by the other company as their sales and the difference between that amount and the royalties of 17.5% as cost of goods sold. This allowed the company to show continuing double digit growth in sales when revenue was actually declining. The false increase in sales also masked a problem the company was having with its other products whose return rate had jumped from 3% to over 8%.

Braggart took the position that 75% of its SG&A expenses related to inventory and capitalized the SG&A as part of inventory. The effect was to overstate inventory by about $1.8 million and to overstate income by about the same amount thus showing a profit and meeting the tangible net worth covenant.

Braggart had a $1 million note payable to the original owners of the company for the purchase made in 1994. In 1998 it decided that some of the assets that were recorded in 1994 were incorrect. The company initiated a lawsuit against the original owners claiming it had the right to "offset" the amount of the overstated assets against the note. Although the lawsuit was still pending, the company treated the liability as a "contra liability" thus reducing total liabilities in anticipation of a positive outcome (gain) on the lawsuit. The lawsuit was subsequently decided in favor of the defendants.

LESSONS LEARNED

Financial reporting fraud is based on the motivation of the parties most likely to benefit from the fraud. Eventually, such a fraud always involves manipulation of account balances to present a financial picture that is different than reality. Although company management can often present arguments as to why the financial adjustments met GAAP (right of offset on the note, all expenses relate to getting goods in place to sell, etc.), the auditor must approach the audit with professional skepticism and examine transactions to ensure they comply with the economic substance of the transactions. Further, financial reporting fraud is not confined to large, publicly traded companies.

Evolution of Fraud and Auditor Responsibility

Historically speaking, the initial purpose of an audit was to detect fraud. As early as the 1600s, investors in the ships from England that sailed across the then-known world to engage in trading faced numerous threats—including the potential manipulation of the books that recorded the ship's transactions. Thus, auditors were first employed by the owners of the ships to audit the books to discover fraud perpetrated against the company. This emphasis was on fraud remained the primary focus of the audit through to the early 1900s when the financial markets began to develop in the United States. Then the emphasis shifted to financial reporting to third parties. Fraud investigations concentrated on defalcations or other misappropriations of assets. However, as the

LO 4

Describe the auditor's evolving responsibility for fraud detection and high-profile frauds that have affected the design and execution of audits.

markets developed, publicly traded companies began the initial foray into "cooking the books." Probably the most prominent case of the time was the Great Salad Oil Swindle, as described in Exhibit 9.4. In that fraud, a company secretly moved inventory (liquid oil) through underground pipes to a series of tanks so that the auditor would conclude it owned more inventory than was actually on hand.

Early Focus on Defalcations

Various types of defalcation schemes were devised by fraudsters, but most of them involved gaining access to cash and covering the cash misappropriation through various kinds of accounting entries. One common fraud is known as *lapping,* the taking of cash that was paid on an account (accounts receivable). However, the perpetrator knows that the customer will eventually complain, so the person who took the cash applies an incoming payment from another customer to the first customer's account. Note that this is similar to how a Ponzi scheme works. Perhaps the most famous Ponzi scheme of recent times is the one perpetrated by Bernie Madoff. That Ponzi scheme is described in more detail in Exhibit 9.5.

The Equity Funding Fraud: The Scandal That Changed the Nature of Auditing

In 1973, the Equity Funding fraud was discovered; as a result, the financial world was permanently changed. Equity Funding had an interesting concept: It sold insurance policies that were coupled to mutual fund investments. As the mutual fund increased in value, it would provide sufficient earnings to pay for the insurance policy. Thus, a policy holder would have the lowest-cost insurance policy offered anywhere.

The Equity Funding's growth was remarkable and its stock price had one of the highest multiples on Wall Street. Unfortunately, very little of the growth reflected economic reality. When the fraud was discovered, investigators found that over two-thirds of the policies did not exist. The fraud was not discovered during an audit, however, but only through an informant's tip to a stockbroker. The auditing profession's first reaction was that the scheme was very sophisticated and auditors did not stand a chance in detecting such frauds. However, upon further investigation, the fraud revealed deficiencies in audit approaches

---

Exhibit 9.4   Early Financial Reporting Fraud

THE GREAT SALAD OIL SWINDLE OF 1963

The Great Salad Oil Swindle represented one of the first modern large-scale financial reporting frauds. The concept was simple: the company could overstate its financial position by claiming that it had more inventory than it actually had. Overstated assets provide the company the opportunity to understate expenses and to overstate income. The fraud ultimately cost creditors and suppliers about $150 million (~$1.1 billion in 2008 dollars).

The financial scam was fairly simple: the company stored salad oil in large tanks. It issued numerous receipts all showing a large amount of inventory on hand. The auditor did observe part of the inventory, but did so by checking the various tanks one after another. The company accomplished the fraud by doing the following:

- First, it filled the tanks with a large inside bladder that contained water.
- Second, it created an outer layer with salad oil, so if the auditor checked the oil from an opening on top located near the edge, the auditor would find oil.
- Third, the company pumped the oil underground from one tank to another in anticipation of the auditor's planned inspection route.

While this is a historically relevant fraud, it has practical application today since inventory manipulation continues as a very common means by which to commit fraud.

Exhibit 9.5 | The Bernie Madoff Ponzi Scheme—How It Worked

Ponzi schemes are based on two fundamentals: trust and greed. The trust comes from building a relationship with the potential victims. Usually, in Ponzi schemes, the person perpetrating the fraud has gained trust through (a) direct, observable actions by others, (b) professional or other affiliations, or (c) through references by others. The greed comes from the investors who see an opportunity to obtain higher than usual gains, and because the trust is there, they do not perform their normal due diligence. Both trust and greed were prevalent in the Madoff scheme as described below.

In March 2009, Madoff pleaded guilty to 11 federal crimes and admitted to turning his wealth management business into a massive Ponzi scheme that defrauded thousands of investors of billions of dollars. Madoff said he began the Ponzi scheme in the early 1990s. However, federal investigators believe the fraud began as early as the 1980s, and that the investment operation may never have been legitimate. The amount missing from client accounts, including fabricated gains, was almost $65 billion. On June 29, 2009, he was sentenced to 150 years in prison, the maximum allowed.

A Ponzi scheme, named after the initial perpetrator, Charles Ponzi, who was arrested in the 1920s, is relatively simple: the perpetrator of the Ponzi scheme takes in money from investors and promises them a higher than normal rate of return. Because it is difficult to make such returns, the perpetrator needs to take in more money, and use some of that money to pay returns to the initial investors. Those investors can then "brag" about their returns to others.

Bernie Madoff built a veil of trust by running a legitimate brokerage firm, and at one time was the Chair of NASDAQ. He often appeared on CNBC talking about the securities industry. Madoff took advantage of his unique ties to the investment community to encourage further investment, but he always sold the idea of an investment into his company as one of "special privilege" (only special investors need apply.) He furthered the scheme by engaging some "finders" (other brokers) who were paid commissions to bring in more special investors. Obviously, the scheme can only work as long as the funds brought into the scheme in future years are sufficient to continue to pay all the previous investors. Ponzi schemes *always* become too big and collapse. However, until the collapse, Bernie Madoff led a lifestyle that can be emulated by only a very small group of the world's richest people.

Madoff furthered the scheme by keeping all of the transactions off his formal books. He employed a CPA firm to audit the books, but the firm consisted of only one employee and there is no indication that the CPA firm ever visited Madoff's offices or that any real audit was actually performed. However, note that the investors never asked for such audit reports. This is where the importance of greed plays a part. The investors felt they had a special thing going on (and some of the original investors did). They received significant returns for their investments. They trusted Bernie Madoff, and they let down their guard by not asking for typical due diligence information.

Trust and greed were both prevalent in the Bernie Madoff case. Ponzi schemes, when suspected, are not difficult to find. They require auditors to trace cash flows through the books. None of this took place in the case of Bernie Madoff. Although not verified, the rumor (as reported on a CNBC prime-time special) is that Madoff chose to surrender and plead guilty because one of the investors was the Russian mob and he feared for both his life as well as that of his sons. Madoff is currently serving his life sentence in federal prison, and one of his sons committed suicide two years after the fraud was revealed.

and professional skepticism that the profession had to address. We examine the nature of the Equity Funding fraud in more detail here because of its historical significance in relation to audit standards and user expectations.

How the Fraud Was Perpetrated   The company issued fictitious policies and, through a Ponzi-type scheme, used the cash flow from other policies to cover the fictitious policies. The objective was to grow the stock valuation of the company, and that could be accomplished only by reporting rapidly increasing revenue and profits. How did the company do it all? It engaged in some deceptive practices, including the following.

- Recording all the fictitious policies on the computer system, but omitting the first three digits of the policy number. Any audit sample would show numerous duplicate numbers that could be quickly explained away by a computer logic error.
- Making simple transactions complex. To record a simple transaction to recognize a policy reserve, the company made more than 30 journal entries across the books of four different subsidiaries.
- Employing different audit firms to perform audits of various subsidiaries and another audit firm that audited the parent company; no one audit firm had the "complete picture" of the company's books.

> **PRACTICAL POINT**
>
> The more things change, the more they are the same. Many of the motivations for fraud and the approaches used at Equity Funding were repeated at Enron. Some of the facilitating tools changed, but the nature of the fraud and the motivation of management remained the same. The pattern continues in the recent failures of investment bank and mortgage companies: Assets were recorded that did not exist!

- Leveraging its relationship as the largest client of a local CPA firm which, in turn, became dependent on its relationship with Equity Funding for most of its income.
- Whenever the auditor asked for documentation of insurance policies, the company indicated it would "pull" all the policies from the company files and have them the next day. Then, selected company personnel would have a "policy party," where they would make up bogus policies to be delivered to the auditor the next day.

Lessons Learned from Equity Funding   The auditing profession learned a number of important lessons from the Equity Funding case:

- Auditors take unnecessary risks whenever they do not audit the whole company.[4]
- Auditors need to look at economic assumptions underlying a company's growth. For example, a mutual fund in a declining market will not generate the gains needed to pay the investor's insurance premiums.
- Auditors need to assess risk factors, and when the risk of fraud is high, they must demand stronger audit evidence, including looking for the underlying documents themselves instead of waiting a day for the company to produce them. Auditors should be skeptical of unusual client excuses for failing to produce evidence in a timely manner.
- Computer errors should not be viewed as an excuse, but rather an indication of a systematic problem that requires high levels of auditor skepticism.
- Dominant clients can be a problem. A firm cannot afford to have a client from which it believes it cannot walk away.
- Auditors need to know what motivates management actions. In Equity Funding, much of management's wealth was tied to stock or stock options.
- Auditors should not assume that all people are honest. In Equity Funding, many parties were involved in the fraud (as there were at Enron).
- Most importantly, there were apparent fraud risk factors (discussed in more detail later) that the auditor should have examined.

The profession has reacted in a measured way to the Equity Funding fraud. Most large public accounting firms now require that they audit all of a company—the parent and subsidiaries. Accounting firms have upgraded their computer audit skills. More significantly, firms have recognized that financial reporting frauds will continue and that they should develop risk files for all audit clients—large and small.

Financial Reporting Frauds—The Third COSO Report

The Committee of Sponsoring Organizations (COSO) of the Treadway Commission has conducted three major studies on the incidence of fraud. The most recent study, published in 2010, was of companies that were cited by the SEC during the time period of 1998–2007 for financial reporting fraud. The analysis identified the major characteristics of companies that had perpetrated fraud. The analysis also focused on comparing fraud and non-fraud companies in similar sizes and industries to determine which factors were the best in discriminating between the fraud and the no-fraud companies. Some of the major findings were:

- The amount and incidence of fraud remains high. The total amount of fraud was more than $120 billion spread across just 300 companies.

---

[4] Note that this same problem occurred again in 2003 when the auditor for Parmalat, an Italian Company, let approximately 45% of the company be audited by another audit firm (Grant Thornton).

- The median size of company perpetrating the fraud rose tenfold to $100 million during the 1998–2007 period (as compared to the previous ten years).
- There was heavy involvement in the fraud by the CEO and/or CFO, with at least one of them named in 89% of the cases.
- The most common fraud involved revenue recognition—60% of the cases during the latest period compared to 50% in previous periods.
- One-third of the companies changed auditors during the latter part of the fraud (with the full knowledge of the audit committee) compared to less than half that amount of auditor changes taking place with the non-fraud companies.
- Some fraud risk indicators from prior COSO studies (lack of audit committee expertise, number of meetings per year, etc.) did not distinguish between the fraud and no-fraud companies in the most recent COSO study, likely because these elements of governance were uniformly improved post-SOX.
- Consistent with previous COSO studies, the majority of the frauds took place at companies that were listed on the Over-The-Counter (OTC) market rather than those listed on the NYSE or NASDAQ.

The amount of fraud remained very significant, and included some of the largest frauds in history such as Enron and WorldCom. The SEC's most commonly cited motivations for fraud included the need to meet internal or external earnings expectations, an attempt to conceal the company's deteriorating financial condition, the need to increase the stock price, the need to bolster financial performance for pending equity or debt financing, or the desire to increase management compensation based on financial results.[5]

General Characteristics of Financial Reporting Frauds and Audit Implications

Highlights of selected financial reporting frauds of the past decade are described in Exhibit 9.6. The patterns evident across these frauds imply the following regarding the conduct of the audit:

- The auditor should not be pressured by the client's desire to release annual earnings at an early date.
- If there are potential problems with revenue, the audit cannot be completed until there is sufficient time to examine major year-end transactions.
- The auditor must understand complex transactions to determine their economic substance and the parties that have economic obligations.
- The auditor must clearly understand and analyze weaknesses in an organization's internal controls in order to determine where and how a fraud may take place.
- Audit procedures must be developed to address specific opportunities for fraud to take place, and cannot be addressed by expansion of generalized audit programs.
- The auditor must always exercise professional skepticism when there may be indications of opportunities for fraud to take place.

The implication of these examples is that auditors must exercise professional judgment and professional skepticism in analyzing the possibility of fraud and must be especially alert to trends in performance, or results that are not consistent with other companies, in determining whether extended audit procedures should be performed. Further, those procedures cannot simply be an expansion of normal procedures; for example, the auditor may want to confirm terms of receivables, not just the dollar amounts, or the auditor may need to analyze contracts for special sales. Instead, fraud-specific audit procedures are required.

PRACTICAL POINT

Auditors should always be alert to anomalies in client results, especially in situations in which the client's success is significantly different from that being experienced in the rest of the industry.

PRACTICAL POINT

The 2008 Report to the National by the Association of Certified Fraud Auditors reaffirms that most perpetrators of and circumstances surrounding fraud had common elements that should have alerted both the company and the auditor. These include such things as employees living far beyond their means, lax controls over cash items, and inability to locate documentation, for example, mortgages and evidence of collateral.

---

[5] COSO, Fraudulent Financial Reporting: 1998–2007, An Analysis of U.S. Public Companies, 2010, available at www.coso.org.

Exhibit 9.6	Summary of Major Financial Reporting Frauds

Company	Nature of the Fraud
Enron	Covered up financial problems by: • Shifting debt to off-balance sheet special entities • Recognizing revenue on impaired assets by selling them to special-purpose entities that they controlled • Engaging in round-tripping trades, i.e., trades that eventually found the assets returning to Enron after initially recognizing sales and profits • Numerous other related party transactions
WorldCom	Decreased expenses and increased revenues through the following: • Recorded bartered transactions as sales, e.g., trading the right to use lines in one part of the world to similar rights to another part of the world • Used restructuring reserves established through acquisitions to decrease expenses, i.e., over accrued reserves upon acquiring a company and later "releasing" those reserves to decrease expenses of future periods • Capitalizing line costs (rentals paid to other phone companies)
Lucent	Enhanced quarterly revenues by "channel stuffing"; i.e., increasing sales at the end of the quarter at amounts greater than customers could actually take. Customers were informally given a very large "grace" period in which they could pay for the goods, or return the goods.
Parmalat	Company siphoned cash off of subsidiaries through a complex scheme that: • Overstated cash and included the false recording of cash ostensibly held at major banks • Understated debt by entering into complex transactions with off-shore subsidiaries in tax-haven places such as the Caribbean
HealthSouth	Recorded fictitious revenue across its 250 clinics and hospitals. Some of the billings actually went to the government for Medicare reimbursement. A wide variety of schemes were used including: • Billing group psychiatric sessions as individual sessions, i.e., with ten people in a group the company billed for ten individual sessions instead of one group session • Using adjusting journal entries to both reduce expenses and enhance revenues
Adecco	Overstated revenue by holding the books open for 20–35 days after the end of the year to record sales from the subsequent period as current period sales
Dell	Misstated operating earnings by categorizing a rebate from Intel to Dell if Dell promised not to buy chips from a competitor. Net income was not misstated, but operating earnings were misstated by a material amount.
Koss Corp.	The CFO misappropriated approximately $31 of funds for her personal use during a period of time in which reported earnings was $26 million through a process consisting of: • Intimidation of lower-level employees • Sole approval for large expenditures made through American Express and other corporate credit cards • Lack of supervisory review and approval by CEO • Lack of audit committee oversight • Lack of an effective internal audit function

Auditing Standards That Reflect a Responsibility to Detect Fraud

LO 5

Describe auditing standards and procedures that reflect a responsibility to detect fraud.

Stated simply, the auditor has a responsibility to detect and address material misstatements in an organization's financial statements regardless of whether the misstatements were (a) intentional or just errors, and (b) defalcations or fraudulent financial reporting. That responsibility is generally consistent with the public's expectations of auditors. Fraud, however, has some characteristics that make its detection complex and difficult. For example, fraud:

- is always intentional (and thereby intended to be covered up),
- often involves top management who have the ability to override existing controls,

- often involves complex transactions that may be difficult to understand and account for,
- often starts out small and then increases when it is not detected, thereby making it less susceptible to discovery solely by analytical procedures, and
- is always a response to an incentive or perceived need by those perpetrating the fraud.

The auditor's fraud-related responsibilities are spelled out in ISA 240, "The Auditor's Responsibilities Relating to Fraud in an Audit of Financial Statements" which is very similar to SAS 99, *Fraud in a Financial Statement Audit*." Those responsibilities (among others) are:

- to maintain an attitude of professional skepticism recognizing the possibility that a material misstatement because of fraud could exist, notwithstanding the auditor's past experience with the entity about the honesty and integrity of management and those charged with governance, and
- to have all members of the engagement team discuss the susceptibility of the entity's financial statements to material misstatement because of fraud.

The team discussion on the susceptibility to material fraud, often described as "brainstorming," must be based on a thorough knowledge of the entity, its controls (or lack thereof), the pressures it faces in both its marketplace as well as the stock market, and changes in either the nature of its operations (market, nature of contracts, parties with whom they are doing business). Both SAS 99 and ISA 240 recognize that auditors need to do specific follow-up audit work dealing with the potential of management override of controls including:

- examining non-standard journal entries and other adjustments,
- reviewing accounting estimates for management biases, and
- evaluating the business rationale for significant unusual transactions.

A Standards-Based Proactive Approach to Fraud Detection

ISA 240 and SAS 99 reflect the public's expectation that the auditor will use a proactive approach to fraud detection. That approach must start with planning the engagement with a proper consideration of the likelihood that fraud exists within the company. The planning process alerts auditors to "red flags" or potential fraud factors that must be addressed on every engagement.

Planning the Audit

The proactive approach to fraud detection is consistent with the overall risk-based approach to an audit engagement. In planning the audit, and considering the risk of fraud, the auditor must:

- Understand the business and the risks it faces.
- Understand changes in the economy and how changes in the economy might affect the business.
- Understand potential management motivation to perpetrate a fraud.
- Identify opportunities for other employees to conduct a defalcation.
- Analyze current changes in the company's financial results to determine if the results look reasonable.
- Identify areas that might be indicative of fraud, or of the potential for fraud.

Conducting the Financial Statement Audit—Fraud Awareness

There are ten general steps to an effective audit program that integrate fraud risk assessment and fraud procedures into the audit opinion formulation process.

LO 6

Identify and analyze significant fraud risk factors through brainstorming and other planning activities.

PRACTICAL POINT

When fraud risks are present, the auditor must perform, *at a minimum*, basic tests and cannot assume that accounts such as fixed assets, cash, or payroll expense are not risky.

LO 7

Use information about identified fraud risk factors to integrate fraud detection procedures into the audit opinion formulation process.

These steps, which are based on the exercise of **professional skepticism** throughout the engagement, include:

1. Understand the nature of fraud (types of fraud, motivations to commit fraud, and the manner in which fraud may be perpetrated).
2. Conduct brainstorming session to consider potential opportunities, motivation, and rationalization for fraud and share knowledge with other audit team members.
3. Obtain additional information that may be useful in identifying and assessing fraud risk.
4. Identify the specific fraud risks, including potential magnitude, and areas likely to be affected by a fraud.
5. Evaluate the quality of the company's controls and potential effectiveness in mitigating the risk of fraud.
6. Adjust audit procedures to assure that the audit adequately addresses the risk of fraud and provides evidence specifically related to the possibility of fraud.
7. Gather and evaluate audit evidence.
8. Communicate the possibility that fraud exists to management, and, where applicable, to the audit committee and/or the full board.
9. Determine the appropriate way in which to report any identified fraud.
10. Document the audit approach, starting with Step 1 through the completion of all of the steps identified above.

AUDITING *in Practice*

PROFESSIONAL SKEPTICISM

What is professional skepticism, and how does an auditor maintain proper professional skepticism in an environment in which the auditor's personal experiences might consist only of audits in which no errors or misstatements were ever found? After all, we are all products of our experiences, and many times our audit experience will tell us that we spent extra time investigating something that showed nothing was there—resulting in increased audit time, but no discovery of wrongdoing. How do we approach each situation as something unique, and not the total culmination of our past experiences?

The Center for Audit Quality, in its 2010 report on fraud, describes professional skepticism as follows:

> Skepticism involves the validation of information through probing questions, the critical assessment of evidence, and attention to inconsistencies. Skepticism is not an end in itself and is not meant to encourage a hostile atmosphere or micro-management; it is an essential element of the professional objectivity required of all participants in the financial reporting supply chain. Skepticism throughout the supply chain increases not only the likelihood that fraud will be detected, but also the perception that fraud will be detected, which reduces the risk that fraud will be attempted.

Similar to the CAQ report, ISA 240 describes professional skepticism as follows:

> Professional skepticism is an attitude that includes a questioning mind and a critical assessment of audit evidence. Professional skepticism requires an ongoing questioning of whether the information and audit evidence obtained suggests that a material misstatement due to fraud may exist. (ISA 240, para. 23)

The Standard goes on to state:

> the auditor's previous experience with the entity contributes to an understanding of the entity. However, although the auditor cannot be expected to fully disregard past experience with the entity about the honesty and integrity of management and those charged with governance, the maintenance of an attitude of professional skepticism is important because there may have been changes in circumstances. When making inquiries and performing other audit procedures, the auditor exercises professional skepticism and is not satisfied with less-than-persuasive audit evidence based on a belief that management and those charged with governance are honest and have integrity. With respect to those charged with governance, maintaining an attitude of professional skepticism means that the auditor carefully considers the reasonableness of responses to inquiries of those charged with governance, and other information obtained from them, in light of all other evidence obtained during the audit. (ISA 240, para. 25)

The key elements to successfully exercising professional skepticism include obtaining strong evidence and analyzing that evidence through critical assessment, attention to inconsistencies, and asking probing (often open-ended) questions.

The essence of auditing is to bring professional skepticism to the audit and in order to be alert to all of the possibilities that may cause the auditor to be misled.

An overview of the process to integrate fraud risk assessment and fraud procedures into the audit of financial statements is shown in Exhibit 9.7. Even though ten steps are identified, the auditor makes decisions and takes different pathways throughout the process, depending on the nature of the risks present, the evidence obtained, and whether the evidence indicates a high probability of fraud. The approach outlined in Exhibit 9.7 is an ongoing process throughout the audit.

Exhibit 9.7	Overview of Fraud Risk Assessment and Fraud Risk Response Process

Steps in the Process	Considerations and Actions by the Auditor
	NOTE: *Auditors should exercise appropriate professional skepticism throughout this process.*

1. Understand the nature of fraud (types, motivations to commit fraud, and the manner in which fraud may be perpetrated).	• Recognize that intentional misstatements can arise from:
	  • Defalcations
	  • Fraudulent financial reporting
	• Be aware of factors present when fraud occurs:
	  • Incentive/Pressure
	  • Opportunity
	  • Rationalization

2. Conduct brainstorming session to consider potential opportunities, motivation, and rationalization for fraud and share knowledge with other audit team members.	• Share experienced auditors' insights
	• Analyze evidence that might indicate heightened risk of fraud
	• Discuss known external and internal factors affecting the entity that might:
	  • Create incentive/pressure for fraud
	  • Provide opportunity for fraud
	  • Indicate a culture or other factors that enable management to rationalize committing fraud
	• Discuss whether audit team needs specialists

3. Obtain additional information that may be useful in identifying and assessing fraud risk.	• Inquire of management, audit committee, internal auditors, and others about:
	  • Knowledge of any fraud, suspected fraud, or allegations of fraud
	  • Understanding of the risk of fraud, including specific fraud risk and affected accounts
	  • Controls implemented to mitigate specific fraud risks
	  • Monitoring activities at locations or segments where there is a heightened risk of fraud
	  • Management's communications to relevant stakeholders about its views of business practices and ethical behavior
	• Consider unusual relationships identified in preliminary analytical procedures, especially those related to revenue recognition
	• Review risk factors identified in Steps 1 and 2
	• Consider using GAS to obtain additional fraud related information

4. Identify the specific fraud risks, including potential magnitude, and areas likely to be affected by a fraud.	• Consider the following:
	  • *Type* of fraud that might occur, including the accounts and assertions that may be affected
	  • *Potential significance* of the fraud, both in quantitative and qualitative terms
	  • *Likelihood* of an occurrence of fraud (incentive/pressure, opportunity, rationalization)
	  • *Pervasiveness* of the risk that fraud might occur
	• Presume there is a risk of material misstatement due to fraud relating to revenue recognition

5. Evaluate the quality of the company's controls and potential effectiveness in mitigating the risk of fraud.	• Consider specific controls and broader programs to prevent and detect fraud

6. Adjust audit procedures to assure that the audit adequately addresses the risk of fraud and provides evidence	• Modify nature, timing and/or extent of audit procedures to address fraud risks and to test auditor-generated hypotheses. Modifications could include:
	  • Obtain more reliable evidence
	  • Obtain additional corroborating evidence

(continues)

Exhibit 9.7	Overview of Fraud Risk Assessment and Fraud Risk Response Process (*continued*)

specifically related to the possibility of fraud.	• Increase sample sizes
	• Apply computer-assisted audit techniques to all of the items in an account
	• Perform specific procedures to address risk of management override
	• Consider overall changes to the audit, such as:
	  • Assign more experienced personnel or specialists to the engagement team
	  • Add unpredictability to audit procedures
	  • Increase level of supervision of audit team members
	  • Increase evaluation of the company's selection and application of significant accounting principles

7. Gather and evaluate audit evidence. If evidence signals that a fraud might exist, determine whether or not forensic or specialist auditors are needed to complete the investigation. Reevaluate the need for additional procedures to determine the existence or amount of the fraud.	• Consider the following as part of evidence evaluation:
	  • Discrepancies in accounting records
	  • Conflicting or missing information
	  • Problematic relationships between the auditors and management
	  • Unusual relationships identified in substantive or final analytical procedures
	• Respond to misstatements that may be the result of fraud, as appropriate
	  • Consider the need for forensic or specialist auditors
	  • Reevaluate the need for additional procedures to determine the existence or amount of the fraud
	  • Assess the pervasiveness of the fraud
	  • Consider additional modifications to audit procedures
	  • Consider withdrawing from the engagement if evidence indicates a significant risk of material misstatement due to fraud

8. Communicate the possibility that fraud exists to management, and, where applicable, to the audit committee and/or the full board.	• If fraud is material or involves senior management:
	  • Report fraud directly to the audit committee
	  • Assess whether there is an internal control implication (significant deficiency or material weakness) that should be reported to the management and audit committee
	  • Consider implications to the opinion on internal control, if relevant
	• If fraud is immaterial and does not involve senior management:
	  • Bring fraud to attention of appropriate level of management

9. Determine the appropriate way in which to report any identified fraud.	• Consider communication of fraud to stakeholders external to the client. Reporting may be required to:
	  • Comply with legal and regulatory requirements, including required communications with successor auditors
	  • Respond to a subpoena

10. Document the audit approach, starting with Step 1 through the completion of all of the steps identified above.	• Examples of items to be documented include:
	  • The audit procedures performed to assess the risks of material misstatement due to fraud, including the brainstorming session
	  • Specific fraud risks that were identified, and a description of auditor responses to those risks
	  • The results of the procedures to identify potential management override of controls
	  • Other conditions or analytical relationships that may have led the auditor to believe that additional procedures were necessary, and the auditor's responses in addressing those issues
	  • Any communications regarding fraud made to management, those charged with corporate governance, and/or regulators, and so on

PRACTICAL POINT

The fraud risk assessment and response process described in Exhibit 9.7 applies to all fraud, that is, both defalcations and financial reporting fraud.

The auditor constantly integrates new information into the fraud risk assessment and response process and adjusts audit procedures based on those findings.

Step 1. Understand the Nature of Fraud

Fraud risk is present in every engagement. However, as would be expected, there are specific situations, or combinations of factors, that increase the likelihood that fraud may be occurring within an organization. Fortunately, the

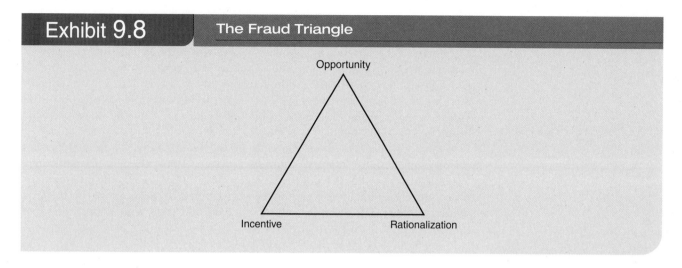

| Exhibit 9.8 | The Fraud Triangle |

We illustrate the fraud triangle with a simple example from a fraud that took place in a construction company.

nature of fraud—both accounting-related and more criminal-related—has been studied for almost five decades and a conceptual model of factors that contribute to an increased likelihood of fraud has been developed. That conceptual model was broadly described earlier by the example of students who were willing to lie or cheat and is more formally described as the "fraud triangle."

The term *fraud triangle* was introduced by career criminologist Don Cressey more than 30 years ago. Cressey started by identifying patterns in fraud cases, and he identified three factors that were consistently present in all frauds. Research over the past two decades has reinforced the validity of the fraud triangle, and no other model has been introduced that is more powerful in predicting fraud.

The three components of the fraud triangle, as shown in Exhibit 9.8 above, include:

- Incentive, or pressure, to commit fraud
- Opportunity to commit and cover up the fraud
- Rationalization—the mindset of the fraudster to justify committing the fraud

We illustrate the fraud triangle with a simple example from a fraud that took place in a construction company. The company did paving as well as sewer and gutter work, and it started small but grew to about $30 million in annual revenue. The construction work was performed at different locations throughout Michigan and Colorado. The company often purchased supplies at the job location, which were signed for by a construction employee and forwarded to the accountant for payment. The company had one accountant, but the president of the company approved all payments and formally signed off on the payments. When the president retired, he was replaced by his son, who spent more time in growing the paving business. He trusted the accountant because of the work the accountant had done for his father, therefore he spent considerably less time in reviewing and signing off on payments (note the lack of skepticism here).

Now let us consider how the fraud triangle becomes relevant in this case. The essence of the fraud was that the accountant prepared bogus invoices for a bogus vendor, set the account up in his name, and prepared receiving slips and purchase orders to gain approval for the payments. First, what were the *incentives/pressures* for the fraud? Like many similar situations, the accountant faced considerable financial problems—mostly associated with taking care of his elderly parents who had high unpaid medical bills. Second, since the new president no longer reviewed items for payment, the *opportunity* (e.g., deficiencies in controls) presented itself. Third, the *rationalization* was a little more complex. Like most frauds, the fraudster thought that it would be a one-time extra payment to get him over the difficult times, and like most frauds, when the fraud was not detected, there was a further opportunity to grow it. The other

PRACTICAL POINT

The key to the fraud risk assessment and response process is for the auditor to use professional skepticism to consider how a fraud might occur, to predict what deficiencies in controls might facilitate the fraudster, and to decide what evidence needs to be gathered to determine if a fraud took place.

part of the rationalization was more subtle: the new president furnished all of the vice-presidents and job supervisors with new pickup trucks. However, the accountant did not receive a similar reward, nor did the accountant receive a very substantial bonus, as compared to the job superintendents. The accountant felt slighted and felt that the amount of money he was taking was no different than what the job superintendents and vice-presidents were getting. In other words, he rationalized his actions to himself by believing that he "deserved" the payments.

If any one of these three elements of the fraud triangle were not present (medical need, poor internal controls, rationalization), then it is significantly less likely that the fraud would have taken place. Thus, when the auditor starts to consider the likelihood of fraud—either through defalcations or through fraudulent financial reporting—the auditor should start with consideration of the three elements of the triangle.

Incentives or Pressures to Commit Fraud   The audit team should consider the incentives or pressures to commit fraud on each engagement, including the most likely areas in which fraud might take place. These incentives include the following:

- Fraudulent Financial Reporting
  - Management compensation schemes
  - Other financial pressures for either improved earnings or an improved balance sheet
  - Debt covenants
  - Pending retirement or stock option expirations
  - Personal wealth tied to either financial results or survival of the company
  - Greed—e.g., the backdating of stock options was performed by individuals who already had millions of dollars of wealth through stock
- Defalcations
  - Personal factors, such as severe financial considerations
  - Pressure to live a more lavish lifestyle than one's personal earnings would allow for
  - Addictions to gambling or drugs

Opportunities to Commit Fraud   One of the most fundamental and consistent findings in fraud research is that there must be an opportunity for fraud to be committed. Although this may sound obvious—that is, "everyone has an opportunity to commit fraud"—it really conveys much more. It means not only that an opportunity exists but either (1) there is a lack of controls or (2) complexities associated with a transaction are such that the perpetrator assesses the risk of being caught as low. For example, a lack of segregation of duties may encourage a perpetrator to think he or she can take cash payments and cover the defalcation through adjustments to accounts receivable. Or the size and complexity of the special-purpose entities at Enron may have led the perpetrators to assess the likelihood of being detected as small. Some of the opportunities to commit fraud that the auditor should consider include the following:

- Significant related-party transactions
- A company's industry position; e.g., the ability to dictate terms or conditions to suppliers or customers that might allow individuals to structure transactions that may be fraudulent
- Management's inconsistency involving subjective judgments regarding assets or accounting estimates
- Simple transactions that are made complex through a disjointed recording process

---

PRACTICAL POINT

One manifestation of management greed was the backdating of stock options that went on for almost a decade before being uncovered in 2006. This scandal led to the resignation of a number of CEOs as well as corporate directors. Management backdated their own stock options to recognize a grant date that corresponded to the lowest price of the company's stock during the grant period. It was a big game played through the motivation to always excel; regular stock options did not satisfy the greed of these people.

- Complex or difficult to understand transactions such as financial derivatives or special-purpose entities
- Ineffective monitoring of management by the board, either because the board of directors is not independent or effective or there is a domineering manager
- Complex or unstable organizational structure
- Weak or nonexistent internal controls

Rationalizing the Fraud Rationalization is a crucial component in most frauds. Rationalization involves a person reconciling his/her behavior, such as stealing, with the commonly accepted notions of decency and trust. This occurs with both defalcations and fraudulent financial reporting. For fraudulent financial reporting, the rationalization normally includes thoughts such as:

- This is a one-time thing to get us through the current crisis and survive until things get better
- Everybody cheats on the financial statements a little; we are just playing the same game
- We will be in violation of all of our debt covenants unless we find a way to get this debt off the financial statements
- We need a higher stock price to acquire company XYZ, or to keep our employees through stock options, and so forth

To some extent, it may be possible that the accounting profession helped push some of the rationalization as many accountants felt that they were adding value to a company if they could find ways to help "dress up the financial statements," even when the financial statements did not accurately portray real economic events. The accounting profession may have unwittingly contributed to the ability of those motivated to commit a financial reporting fraud by:

- Allowing accounting rules to become more permissive; i.e., management would ask auditors to "show them why the accounting was not allowed"
- Thinking they were adding value by using their accounting skills to achieve management's objectives
- Compensating audit partners mostly on sales ability and profitability, rather than true audit quality
- Allowing management to hire and fire the auditors with no significant review by boards
- Letting consulting revenues overpower audit judgments

For defalcations, personal rationalizations often revolve around mistreatment by the company or a sense of entitlement (i.e., the company owes me!) by the individual perpetrating the fraud. For financial statement fraud, it can range from "saving the company" to personal greed. Some common rationalizations for committing fraud involve the fraudster believing that

- fraud is justified to save a family member or loved one
- they will lose everything (family, home, car, etc.) if they don't take the money
- no help is available from outside
- the theft is "borrowing," and fully intends to pay the stolen money back at some point
- something is owed to him or her by the company because others are treated more fairly
- they do not care about the consequence of their actions or of accepted notions of decency and trust

Enron: An Example of the Fraud Triangle The concealment of fraud at Enron was not just the fault of the accounting profession. Many stock analysts did not do detailed analyses of companies and instead substituted "management

> **PRACTICAL POINT**
>
> Updated fraud information and cases can be found at www.aicpa.org/antifraud.

> **PRACTICAL POINT**
>
> Auditing for fraud is not an "add-on" to the financial statement audit. It must be an integral part of every financial statement audit.

guidance" as a basis for predicting future earnings. Management found it could borrow from the future to increase current earnings and did so when incentive contracts were heavily oriented to the current period. Furthermore, management possessed the confidence that it could carry out fraud because they had rationalized that it really was not a fraud, it was just pushing the boundaries of acceptable accounting. As corroborated by the popular book, *The Smartest Men in the Room*, the leaders at Enron carried out the fraud with such bravado because they clearly believed that they were the smartest people in the room. If someone, including the *Wall Street Journal,* chose to disagree, they portrayed it simply as ignorance on the part of those individuals. See Exhibit 9.9 for a description of how these factors all came together to create the Enron fraud—one of the largest frauds in business history. The exhibit shows failures in many different professions that contributed to the corporate downfall.

Exhibit 9.9	Enron: Where Everything Bad Came Together

THE COMPANY

Enron is the fraud of the late 1990s and early 2000s, representing almost everything that was wrong with corporate governance, accounting, financial analysts, banking, and the accounting profession. How did it happen?

Enron was a utility company that developed a new concept and rode the new concept to unbelievable stock market highs. Just prior to its collapse, it had a stock value of $90 per share which eventually became worthless. The concept: it would increase market efficiency by developing the most sophisticated system in the world to trade electricity, natural gas, and related resources. It would divorce the production of energy—a capital intensive process—from the trading and use of the resources. It would improve market efficiency by increasing the scope of energy production and expanding the output of the local utility to the nation—and the world. Energy would flow where the highest market bid for it—a fundamental concept of economics. Enron hired MBA traders who were provided lucrative bonuses for meeting profit objectives. Competition among the traders was encouraged; risks were encouraged; but most of all, reported profits were rewarded.

However, much of the company, at its heart, remained a utility. It needed heavy amounts of cash to support its trading position and it needed to continually report higher profits to sustain stock market valuations. Most of the top executives of the company were compensated primarily through stock.

THE FRAUD

The nature of fraud that took place was widespread. Most of the frauds involved Special Purpose Entities (SPEs) that were partnerships that often involved substantial loans from banks to be secured by assets transferred to the SPE, partners dominated by Enron executives, and a small outside interest (exceeding 3% per the accounting rule). The company transferred devalued assets to the SPEs and recognized gains on the books. It kept borrowing off the books by having the SPEs borrow from banks and purchase Enron assets. It even recognized over $100 million on anticipated sales that it hoped would occur with a joint venture with Blockbuster on rental movies over the Internet. The SPEs were used such that Enron's balance sheet looked healthy because it minimized the debt on the balance sheet; the SPEs also increased reported income by hiding all losses in the SPEs.

FAILURES IN ACCOUNTING AND GOVERNANCE

Why did Enron happen? What were the failures that allowed it to occur? Unfortunately, the answer is that the failures were widespread.

Management Accountability: Management was virtually not accountable to anyone as long as the company showed dramatic stock increases justified by earnings growth. Company management had a "good story" and anyone who questioned them was looked at as being stupid. Compensation was based on stock price. And, apparently stock price was based on a good story and numbers.

Governance: Although the board appeared to be independent, most of the board members had close ties to management of the company through philanthropic organizations. Some board members hardly ever attended a meeting and they certainly did not ask hard questions. Finally, the board waived a "conflict of interest" provision in their code of ethics that allowed Andy Fastow, the treasurer of the company, to profit handsomely from related-party transactions.

(continues)

Exhibit 9.9	Enron: Where Everything Bad Came Together (*continued*)

Accounting: Accounting became more rule-oriented and complex. Accounting allowed practitioners to take obscure pronouncements, such as those dealing with Special Purpose Entities that were designed for leasing transactions and allowed the accounting concept to be applied to other entities for which such accounting was never intended. Accounting was looked at as a tool, not as a mechanism to portray economic reality.

The Financial Analyst Community: The stock market was following the bubble of the dot-com economy and concluded they did not have tools to appropriately value many of the emerging companies. Rather than analyze the underlying fundamentals, the analysts insisted on "earnings guidance" by management. Those that achieved the projected guidance were rewarded; those who did not were severely punished. Analysts came to accept "pro forma accounting statements," more aptly described as what results would have been if nothing bad happened.

Banking and Investment Banking: Many large financial institutions were willing participants in the process because they were rewarded with large underwriting fees for other Enron work. Enron management was smart enough to know that the investment bankers were also rewarded on the amount of fees they brought in the door.

The Accounting Profession: At the time of Enron, none of the largest five public accounting firms referred to themselves as public accounting firms; rather they referred to themselves as professional service firms with diverse lines of business. All of the firms had large consulting practices. Arthur Andersen performed internal audit work for Enron in addition to performing the external audit. The consulting fees of many clients dramatically exceeded the audit fees. Partners were compensated on revenue and profitability. Worse, they were hired by the management teams whom they had to please.

There were plenty of parties at fault.

Step 2. Conduct Brainstorming Session

ISA 315 requires members of the engagement team to discuss the susceptibility of the entity to material misstatement of the financial statements. SAS 109 states that prior to the start of the audit, the engagement team should **brainstorm** about the possibility of material misstatements in general (i.e., because of either error or fraud), and SAS 99 requires brainstorming about the manner in which fraud, specifically, might be committed. This brainstorming exercise should include all members of the audit team and be both thorough and systematic. The audit team should consider factors that might affect management motivation to misstate the financial statements (incentive). The initial analysis is followed up by considering weaknesses in internal control that would allow a fraud to take place (opportunity) and factors that may enable an individual capable of committing a fraud to rationalize perpetrating it (rationalization). When preliminary financial information is available, the audit team should then consider whether any account balances seem to be out of line with expectations. The brainstorming session is designed to develop a list of the most likely places that fraud could occur and how it could occur. SAS 99 includes the following specific brainstorming recommendations:

> **PRACTICAL POINT**
>
> Brainstorming should involve all members of the audit team to cover the wider perspective of experience in auditing various parts of the organization.

- *Consider how fraud can be perpetrated and covered up.* Consider the risk of fraud, including the risk that the fraud could be cleverly covered up in false documents or supporting evidence the auditor normally examines.
- *Presume fraud in revenue recognition.* The auditor should presume that fraud takes place in revenue recognition and overstatement of certain assets that are susceptible to manipulation and cover-up.
- *Consider incentives, opportunities, and rationalization for fraud.* The auditor should specifically consider all the elements that may make fraud more likely, including the nature of executive compensation and pressure to meet earnings targets.
- *Consider industry conditions.* The auditor must understand what is going on in the industry and how it might affect the company. Changing technology is important, as is declining customer demand for the company's products.

AUDITING *in Practice*

BRAINSTORMING: A PERSPECTIVE FROM THE PCAOB

It is especially important that the audit partner participate in the brainstorming session. Further, the brainstorming session should occur at the beginning of the engagement. These points may seem obvious. However, the PCAOB issued a report in January 2007 on observations made during its inspections that related to the auditor's responsibility with respect to fraud. These observations, are based on actual audit engagements and relate to weaknesses in brainstorming and other steps addressing fraud and include:

- Audit team was unable to demonstrate that a brainstorming session had occurred.

- Brainstorming session occurred after planning and after substantive fieldwork had begun.

- Key members of the audit team did not attend the brainstorming session.

- There was no audit documentation that the audit team had made the required inquiries of the audit committee, management, and others about fraud and fraud risks.

- Auditors failed to respond to identified fraud risk factors.

- There was no evidence that the audit team had performed an appropriate examination and evaluation of journal entries.

These observations indicate that there may be times in your work as an auditor that you observe less than ideal brainstorming sessions or responses to fraud risk. If this is the case, you should be aware that these types of behaviors reflect low audit quality and greatly increase achieved audit risk.

- *Consider operating characteristics and financial stability.* The audit team should consider the existence of significant, complex, or convoluted transactions as well as significant changes in financial condition.

PRACTICAL POINT

Brainstorming should identify hypotheses about ways in which fraud might occur, then prioritize the hypotheses in order of likelihood. The prioritization of hypotheses allows auditors to focus on the most likely ways in which fraud may occur.

Brainstorming is not just an audit team exercise. It must be an integral part of the audit approach. An example of how brainstorming would have changed the audit approach and would have discovered a fraud that the auditors did not discover is shown in Exhibit 9.10. In reading the exhibit, it is important to understand that there is a systematic approach to brainstorming. There are implications for each part of the analysis of company operations, that is, its background (e.g., competitors, ownership, and management motivation), the comparison of industry growth with company growth, weaknesses in the client's internal controls, and the process used by the company to make adjustments to sales and accounts receivable. The audit team brainstorms and generates a number of hypotheses as to what might have caused the changes in the client's financial data. The key point is to then challenge each other to determine whether there is one hypothesis that more likely explains the changes

Exhibit 9.10 Using Brainstorming to Change the Audit Approach

COMPANY BACKGROUND

ABC Wholesaling is a wholesaler located in Milwaukee, Wisconsin. It operates in a very competitive industry, selling products such as STP Brand products and Ortho Grow products to retailers such as Walmart, ShopKo, and regional retail discount chains. The company is privately owned and experienced financial difficulty last year. Continued financial difficulty would lead to its major line of credit being called by the bank for immediate repayment. The company is under pressure to show profits this year.

Brainstorming Analysis:

- Industry is very competitive. Wholesalers are being replaced with direct purchases from a fewer number of suppliers.
- Company is privately owned. Management's wealth ego or existence is tied into the success of the company.
- The company must be profitable or its major loan will be called. If it is called, it will most likely put the company out of business.
- Company is relatively small; it is likely that internal controls are not strong.

(continues)

Exhibit 9.10	Using Brainstorming to Change the Audit Approach (*continued*)

Implications:

There is strong motivation to misstate the financial statements. Economic conditions do not favor the client. If there are poor controls, the auditor must consider where the weaknesses will facilitate misstatement. Following SAS 99, it is reasonable to presume that fraud might exist in revenue.

INDUSTRY AND ANALYTICAL ANALYSIS

The auditor has preliminary (unaudited) data for the year as well as a comparison with the previous year:

	Current Year (000) omitted	Previous Year (000) omitted
Sales	$60,000	$59,000
Accounts Receivable	$11,000	$7,200
Percent of Accounts Receivable Current	72%	65%
No. of Days' Sales in Accounts Receivable	64	42
Gross Margin	18.7%	15.9%
Industry Gross Margin	16.3%	16.3%
Increase in Nov.–Dec. Sales over Prior Year	12.0%	3.1%

Brainstorming Analysis:

- Sales have only gone up marginally, but accounts receivable has increased dramatically.
- Number of days in Accounts Receivable has increased, although a greater percentage are classified as current suggesting that sales were recorded at or near the end of the year—possibly to meet profit objectives.
- Gross margin has increased over the past year and is much higher than the industry average.

Implications:

It appears that an unusual amount of revenue was recorded near the end of the year. In a highly competitive industry, it is not reasonable to assume that the company would have dramatically increased gross margin above the industry average. The presumption of misstatement in revenue appears to be proper.

MANAGEMENT INFORMATION AND CONTROLS

Management explains that the change is due to two things: (1) a new computer system that has increased productivity; and (2) a new policy of re-billing items previously sold to customers, thereby extending the due dates from October to April. The re-billing is explained as follows: Many of the client's products are seasonal, for example, lawn-care products. To provide better service to ABC's customers, management instituted a new policy whereby management negotiated with a customer to determine the approximate amount of seasonal goods on hand at the end of the selling season (October). If the customer would continue to purchase from the client, management would re-bill the existing inventory, thereby extending the due date from October until the following April, essentially giving an interest-free loan to the customer. The customer, in turn, agreed to keep the existing purchases and store them on their site for next year's retail sales. Most of the re-billed items occurred with very large customers.

Supplemental Brainstorming Analysis:

- Increased productivity is probably needed to stay even.
- Most sales of this type do not have a return guarantee to a wholesaler.
- The new invoices are all going to companies that normally do not return accounts receivable confirmations (e.g., Walmart).
- The invoice re-billings should not cause sales to increase because the previous sales should have been reversed.

Implications:

The rationale does not explain the large increase in gross margin, nor does it explain the increase in sales.

ADJUSTING THE AUDIT APPROACH

The auditor must consider the possibility that fraud has taken place and has been used to inflate revenue for the amount of the "re-billed invoices." Inflated revenue is one of the few explanations that (a) would explain all the changes in the ratios identified above and (b) be consistent with management motivations and opportunity to keep the company alive. Based on this presumption, the auditor modifies the audit procedures as follows:

1. Develop a list of all re-billed invoices to determine magnitude.
2. For every re-billed invoice, trace billing amounts to credit memos that are issued against the original invoices and to the general ledger.
3. Because many of the clients will not respond to account balance confirmations, consider sending confirmations based on individual invoices, including a high percentage that contain the re-billed amounts.

(continues)

Exhibit 9.10	Using Brainstorming to Change the Audit Approach (*continued*)

4. Examine all customer balances that contain re-billed items and examine cash receipts after year end to see that they are credited to the proper customers.

5. For companies that show a large amount of re-billings, contact the company via phone or some other personal method to verify the existence of the extended credit process.

6. Continue to examine industry information to determine if similar arrangements exist.

POSTSCRIPT

All of the re-billed invoices were fictitious and accounted for the large increase in sales and profitability of the company. The fraud was not found by the auditor, but it would have been easily identified if the auditor followed the six audit procedures described above. Of these, the second procedure, tracing the invoices to credit memos and then to the general ledger, would have definitely led to the discovery of the fraud. The company did generate "fake" credit memos, but they were never recorded in the general ledger. Because the auditor was not skeptical, the auditor never bothered to trace the credit memos to the general ledger (it was viewed as a mundane task).

in account balances than all others. Brainstorming is enhanced when the audit team simultaneously considers all related changes in the financial data.

As a result of the brainstorming analysis, the auditor should adopt audit procedures as shown in Exhibit 9.10 to determine if fraud is present. Further, because there is a possibility of fraud, the auditor needs to apply a higher level of professional skepticism in soliciting and analyzing audit evidence including:

- *Consider the susceptibility of evidence to manipulation.* Management or others will work hard to cover up a fraud. The auditor needs to consider the alternatives management might have to cover up a fraud.
- *Review Unusual or Unexpected Journal entries.* Many frauds are covered up through unsupported journal entries or accounting estimates. A prime example is the fraud at WorldCom, where expenses were reduced through write-downs of reserves as well as by capitalization of expenses.
- *Apply greater skepticism to management responses.* Greater skepticism should be given to management responses coupled with an increase in the amount and persuasiveness of evidence required to corroborate management responses to auditor inquiries.
- *Recognize that technology may facilitate new methods to perpetrate fraud.* New types of organizational structures, new entities, or complex financial instruments provide opportunities to cover up fraud through either unnecessary complexity or even by side agreements among entities. Computerized information systems provide new opportunities to change documentation and new methods of committing fraud.
- *Acknowledge that collusion may be likely.* The collusion may be among entity employees but could also occur between management and third parties.
- *Recognize that there should be less predictability of audit procedures.* The audit team should work to eliminate predictability in audit procedures, such as rotating tests of particular assets over a period of time or conducting surprise audits, to reduce the opportunities for a perpetrator to effectively cover up a fraud.
- *Link analytical procedures to operational or industry data.* The auditor should not look just at relationships within the financial statements. Rather, the auditor should analyze financial data in relationship to other operational data, such as production capacity or purchased supplies, and to industry information.

Auditors need to conduct audits with a mindset that the possibility of material misstatement caused by fraud exists even if all the past experiences with a company have been positive. More to the point, *the auditor should not be satisfied with less-than-persuasive evidence because of a belief that management is honest.* Responses by management to auditor inquiries must be corroborated by factual information and additional analysis.

AUDITING *in Practice*

THE NEED TO REVIEW JOURNAL ENTRIES

In April 2008, the SEC issued an Accounting and Enforcement Release concerning improper professional conduct by an audit partner with the public accounting firm Arthur Andersen LLP in connection with the audit of the financial statements of WorldCom, Inc. An excerpt from that release, which is provided below, emphasizes the importance of reviewing journal entries and maintaining professional skepticism throughout the engagement.

> The fraudulent reduction of WorldCom's line cost expenses was accomplished through the recording of large unsupported journal entries, known as on-top or top-side entries, after the close of each quarter, in even monetary amounts ranging from $38.5 million to $600 million.

> Despite the fact that Respondent's audit team had rated WorldCom as a "Maximum" risk client, despite other risk factors that Respondent either knew or reasonably should have known provided an incentive for fraudulent misstatement of WorldCom's

financial statements, and despite Respondent's awareness that management had the ability to override accounting controls, Respondent did not exercise due professional care in the planning and performance of the audit by failing to design or implement audit procedures to identify and review nonstandard journal entries.

> Respondent placed undue reliance on WorldCom's management's representation that there were no significant top-side journal entries. Respondent failed to exercise due professional care (AU §§ 150.02, 230.01), maintain an attitude of professional skepticism (AU § 230.07), and to obtain sufficient competent evidential matter (AU §§ 150.02, 326.01), by not planning and performing reasonable audit procedures to identify potentially improper or fraudulent top-side journal entries and by relying on management's representation that there were no significant top-side journal entries.

AUDITING *in Practice*

INTRODUCING UNPREDICTABILITY INTO AUDITS

An approach that auditors use to introduce unpredictability into audits is to examine entries or transactions that are below the materiality level and would not typically be examined. Introducing this type of unpredictability into the audit helps uncover fraud by clients who are familiar with the audit firm's approach to determining materiality. Such clients might be tempted to

structure fraudulent transactions at a dollar amount that would not typically appear on the auditor's radar screen. Being unpredictable helps to both uncover existing frauds and to make management concerned enough about being caught that they are less likely to commit fraud in the first place.

Step 3. Obtain Additional Information about Fraud Risk

The auditor's responsibility for planning the audit includes completing specific procedures that could further signal the possibility of fraud. Some of the procedures that may be completed by the auditor include the following:

- Making inquiries of management and others—e.g., audit committee chairs—to obtain their views about risk of fraud and controls set up to address those risks
- Performing preliminary analytical procedures and considering any unusual or unexpected relationships
- Reviewing the risk factors identified earlier (incentive, opportunity, rationalization)
- Reviewing management responses to recommendations for control improvements and internal audit reports

LO 8

Articulate how audit software and other computerized audit tools can assist the auditor in identifying fraud.

Analytical Indicators of Risk   Fraud risk factors are easily identified through analytical comparisons such as trend analysis or ratio analysis. As noted earlier, the auditor cannot be effective by evaluating each ratio or trend by itself; rather, the auditor needs to analyze the effect of all the changes in key financial components to determine interrelationships. Some of the key analytical factors the auditor should consider are shown in Exhibit 9.11.

Using the Computer to Analyze the Possibility of Fraud   Most audit firms use Generalized Audit Software (GAS) to read and analyze a client's data files, especially key files, for possible indications of fraud. The software can be used to provide additional information about fraud risk. Examples include:

Search for duplicates. Many frauds often result in duplicate entries into accounts. However, these entries are often cleverly disguised, for example, with a different name but the same address. Software can be used to identify all duplicates in a file, with the auditor specifying the field on which to test for duplicates (address, name, dollar amount of invoices, etc.).

Analyze unusual patterns in the data. Benford's law has proven very effective in predicting the frequency with which digits appear in numbers of various sizes; for example, the first digit of a five-digit number will be 1 about 30%

Exhibit 9.11   Analytical Indicators of Fraud Risk

Financial Indicator	Potential Fraud Risk
Large revenue increase at end of quarter	Revenue is often manipulated at end of period to meet earnings targets. Fraudulent transactions include • Channel stuffing • Holding books open and recording revenue of subsequent period • Fictitious sales
Sales increase larger than industry that does not seem to be justified by product	The auditor must consider the competitive advantage of the company and its products. If sales are increasing while all of the competitors are experiencing a downturn in sales, the auditor's suspicion of fraudulent or misstated transactions should be heightened.
Unusually large increase in gross margin and net profit	Unusual increases in the gross margin may be due to productivity gains or changes in product lines. However, they are often due to: • Failure to record all costs of goods sold and expenses • Double billing of invoices • Fictitious sales • Decrease in the quality of product
Increase in returns after end of year	Unusual increases in returns after the end of the year usually indicate either (a) quality problems, (b) side agreements on the sale, or (c) channel stuffing.
Increase in number of days sales in receivables	Companies cannot collect cash from fictitious customers, or customers who have side agreements to defer payment or return goods. Significant increases in the number of days sales in receivables, or ratios that are significantly higher than industry averages, should be a signal of high fraud risk.
Increase in number of days sales in inventory	Inventory is often used to hide problems. More frauds have been hidden in fictitious inventory than just about any account other than revenue.
Significant change in debt/equity ratio	Companies that are financially distressed will often be motivated to keep a debt/equity ratio under loan covenant agreements. Financial distress is a strong fraud risk indicator.
Cash flow or liquidity	Companies eventually need cash to pay employees, vendors, debt holders, and owners, so cash flow or liquidity problems provide an incentive to commit fraud.
Financial problems	A company that shows strong sales and profitability, but low or negative cash flow from operations, indicates high fraud risk.

of the time. Most frauds involve the creation of false entries into the accounts. The software can analyze the pattern of digits to determine whether it is unusual and can identify items for more detailed testing.

Identify unusual entries to an account. Most accounts are affected by transactions that are recorded in a subsidiary journal; for example, most credits to accounts receivable should come from a cash receipts journal and most debits should come from a sales journal. Audit software can be used to identify all entries into the account that came from other than these two sources (including unusual journal entries), which the auditor can then investigate. Audit software could also be used to identify other types of unusual entries. For example, an audit team may want to use this software to identify all transactions that were posted at unusual or unexpected times—such as all entries near month end that were posted between midnight and 6 a.m. or were posted on the weekends, because these entries may be unauthorized fraudulent entries.

Identify missing data. Many fraudsters make the mistake of leaving some fields out of files. Audit software can identify all accounts with missing data for further investigation by the auditor.

Step 4. Identify Specific Risks of Fraud

The auditor should recognize that all three components of the fraud triangle need not be present for fraud to occur, but that the likelihood of fraud is much greater when all three are present. The auditor should be aware that certain classes of transactions are highly susceptible to fraud, such as estimates, those that involve judgmental accounting principles, or those that are complex in structure. The auditor must consider the following:

- The *type* of fraud that might occur
- The *potential significance* of the fraud, both in quantitative and qualitative terms
- The *likelihood* of an occurrence of fraud
- The *pervasiveness* of the risk that fraud might occur

Step 5. Evaluate Effectiveness of Internal Control

Internal control weaknesses are a strong indication of fraud risk. The analysis of internal control should be performed in light of the specific fraud risks already identified. Although the traditional emphasis is on the recording of transactions, the analysis must include a consideration of the "tone at the top." An overview of questions that should be addressed in assessing the fraud risk related to "tone at the top" issues is shown in Exhibit 9.12. There are three important points that should always be kept in mind when analyzing controls:

1. A control deficiency, by definition, means that errors or intentional misstatements could occur and not be detected or prevented during the normal processing.
2. The control deficiency, by definition, presents an opportunity for fraud.
3. The auditor needs to consider how such a fraud can take place and adjust the audit procedures to detect the possibility of a fraud.

These points are not debatable; nor is the requirement to expand audit procedures when there are significant control deficiencies. For example, the existence of any of the fraud indicators in Exhibit 9.11 requires the auditor to adjust the audit process to gather additional or different evidence that would uncover a fraud should it be occurring.

Step 6. Adjust Audit Procedures to Respond to Identified Fraud Risks

The "brainstorming process" is designed to identify the likelihood of fraud and how a fraud might happen. Given the audit team's knowledge of the industry,

---

PRACTICAL POINT

The auditor must be able to recognize unusual relationships in accounts, for example, large write-offs or discounts that might signal the likelihood of fraud.

PRACTICAL POINT

Some smaller, privately held businesses will explicitly request the auditor to consider the possibility of defalcations that may be below the auditor's planned materiality level because the audit may also function as a control in these companies.

Exhibit 9.12   Assessing Fraud Risk—The Tone at the Top

Control Area	Questions/Evidence
Corporate Governance	Is the board truly independent and knowledgeable? Does the board meet often enough to understand the company and potential problems? How is the board compensated? Are the directors dominated by management?
Management Control and Influence	Does management have the ability to unduly influence actions by subordinates that seem to instill unusual loyalty to management? For example, using loans to key people who are subsequently forgiven.
Audit Committee	Is the audit committee both independent and financially literate? How active is the audit committee? Does the audit committee follow up to both internal and external audit findings? Does the audit committee understand internal control? Does the audit committee meet with auditors without management present?
Corporate Culture	What is the nature of the organization's corporate culture? How are employees rewarded? How is performance monitored? What pressures are there to make sales or earnings goals? Do employees understand their individual responsibilities for controls? What is the quality of leadership? How is wrongdoing dealt with?
Internal Auditing	Does the company have an internal audit department? Is the internal audit charter consistent with "Best Practices"? How is the budget for the internal audit department developed and approved? How is the scope of internal audit determined? Does internal audit perform primarily control audits or operational audits? Are internal audit recommendations followed up and implemented? How competent is the internal audit activity? Does the internal audit group, or some other group, regularly monitor compliance with the company's Code of Ethics?
Monitoring Controls	Does the organization have effective monitoring controls? Do monitoring controls signal control failures in a timely fashion so that corrective action can be taken?
Whistleblowing	Does the organization have an effective whistleblowing function? Is the whistleblowing function sufficiently independent of management and does the organization have the resources to follow up on problems? Are summaries of items reported to the whistleblowing function summarized and provided to management and the audit committee?
Code of Ethics	Does the company have a code of ethics? Is there evidence that the code of ethics is complied with? Do employees exhibit "buy in" to the code of ethics? Is there evidence encountered during the audit that exhibits non-compliance with the Code? Do employees or managers regularly "pad" their expense accounts? Is there any evidence that corporate assets are misused?
Related Party Transactions	Does the company have a policy regarding related party transactions? Is the policy effective? Does the company regularly engage in related party transactions? Are related party transactions regularly disclosed to the auditor and the board? Are there significant economic motivations for the related party transactions that justify their existence?

management motivations, and the entity's control structure, the team should develop hypotheses about how fraud could be conducted and covered up. These hypotheses should be prioritized based on:

- Analytical procedure results that indicate unusual relationships
- Current economic conditions and their impact on the entity
- Quality of the company's internal controls

The audit team should design specific audit tests based on the ranking of the most likely nature of a fraud and then move down the list. The team should always obtain additional corroboration of management's explanations or representations. For example, in Exhibit 9.10, the most likely explanation is that the client was double-billing customers, but not sending the invoice to the customers and not recording credit memos to the customers. The auditor had traditionally not confirmed accounts receivable because many customers did not respond to the confirmations. However, there is a high risk that accounts receivable is misstated. The auditor must consider alternative ways to gain satisfaction as to the correct balance of receivables.

There are two basic rules the auditor should follow in considering audit procedures:

Rule One: Internal Control Weaknesses. When weaknesses in internal control are found, the auditor should develop audit procedures to explicitly test for the existence of the type of fraud or misstatement that could occur because of the weakness.

Rule Two: Fraud Risk Factors. When the auditor's analysis indicates a high incidence of fraud risk, the auditor must develop specific independent tests to verify management's assertions related to the underlying accounts.

Linking Planned Audit Procedures to Control Deficiencies   A deficiency in internal control means that a misstatement could occur and not be detected or corrected in the ordinary course of processing. Thus, the auditor needs to develop an audit approach that links the weaknesses in internal control to specific audit procedures. Exhibit 9.13 provides such a linkage for internal control deficiencies often associated with defalcations.

Exhibit 9.13 is only a guide. The specific procedures chosen by an auditor will depend on the nature of the deficiencies in the company. For example, a bank teller has access to cash more readily than do other employees, so if there is a control deficiency over the teller process, the auditor has to consider specific ways in which a fraud could be committed.

Linking control deficiencies and audit procedures always involves answering the following questions to identify potential changes to the audit program:

1. What types of misstatements could occur because of the control deficiencies?
2. What account balances would be affected and how would they be affected?
3. What audit procedures would provide evidence on whether the account balance contains misstatements?
4. Do the planned audit procedures emphasize objective evidence that is outside the purview of the parties that have access to the assets?

The auditor has to consider what could go wrong and then decide on the audit evidence that is needed to determine if fraud has occurred. Even if the procedures do not find fraud, it is important that they be performed, because the public expects auditors to look for fraud in conducting a GAAS audit.

Linking Planned Audit Procedures to Fraud Risk Factors   As with control deficiencies, the audit procedures will depend on the nature of the fraud risk indicators and the auditor's preliminary analytical review of the account

PRACTICAL POINT

The audit team should generate its hypotheses about unusual relationships or unexpected account balances before soliciting management's explanations. Management's explanations or bogus excuses might otherwise narrow the auditor's hypotheses.

PRACTICAL POINT

There should be a direct linkage between weaknesses in internal control and the identification of how misstatements, including fraud, could show up in the financial statements and not be prevented or detected in the normal course of operations.

Exhibit 9.13	Linking Internal Deficiencies to Audit Procedures
Internal Control Deficiency	**Suggested Audit Procedures to Detect Possible Defalcations**
Inadequate Segregation of Duties over Disbursements	• Take a statistical sample of all disbursements. Trace those selected to independent receiving reports and other independent evidence of the receipt of goods. Trace to purchase orders issued by someone other than the person disbursing the funds. • Use audit software to identify all disbursements that are sent to P.O. Box numbers rather than street addresses. Examine all of the items selected to: (a) determine the existence of the company by looking into a listing of businesses (Yellow Pages, Better Business Bureau, etc.); and (b) examine underlying support for the disbursement.
Inadequate Segregation of Duties over Cash Receipts	• Confirm accounts receivable with a large statistical sample. • Consider contacting customers directly. • Perform analytical review to determine whether there are (a) an abnormal amount of discounts or (b) unusually large write-offs. • If heightened fraud risk, perform a cash trace by selecting daily receipts and tracing them to cash deposits and account receivable postings.
Inadequate Security over Inventory	• Have the client perform a complete physical inventory, i.e., count the inventory at year end. Observe the inventory counting process, take test counts, and follow up on any differences.
Inadequate Segregation of Duties over Cash	• Perform an independent four-column bank reconciliation that reconciles receipts with deposits, disbursements with withdrawals, and month-end balances. • Obtain an independent bank statement from the bank. • Perform a cash trace by selecting receipts and tracing them to the cash account.

PRACTICAL POINT

For every significant deficiency or material weakness in internal control, the auditor should identify, then investigate, how a fraud could take place and be covered up by an employee or management.

PRACTICAL POINT

The more likely that fraud is prevalent, especially if it involves senior management, the more detailed and secret should be the auditor's procedures.

balances. The audit approach moves from brainstorming to a rank ordering of hypothesized fraudulent activity that might take place. Next, the auditor identifies the type of evidence, such as results of analytical procedures, that could provide insight into the existence of a potential fraud. The auditor then develops and implements audit procedures that are directly responsive to the fraud risks, including altering the nature, timing, and extent of procedures.

The *nature* of audit procedures may be changed to obtain additional corroborative evidence or to obtain more direct evidence. For example, the auditor may extend confirmation procedures to include direct correspondence with customers or may confirm major attributes of a sales contract. Or the auditor may choose to observe the counting of inventory at all locations rather than at selected locations. The *timing* of the gathering of evidence may also change. For an example, more of the substantive testing, such as the observation of inventory or direct tests of accounts receivable, may take place at year end. Cutoff tests for both sales and inventory may be extended and conducted at year end. The *extent* of procedures should be directly related to the audit team's assessment of the likelihood of risk. The team may be encouraged to do more analysis by using generalized audit software to examine a larger percentage or all of a population.

Examples of audit procedures to address fraud risk include the following:

• Performing procedures at locations on a surprise or unannounced basis
• Requiring that inventories be counted and observed at year end
• Reviewing all major sales transactions, particularly those with unusual terms or near the end of the reporting period
• Making oral inquiries of major customers and suppliers
• Performing analytical procedures using disaggregated data that would show more unusual fluctuations
• Examining details of major sales contracts
• Examining financial viability of customers
• Examining in detail all reciprocal transactions or similar transactions between two entities—e.g., sales of similar assets to each other—to determine the

economic viability and the correspondence with similar transactions in the marketplace

- Making a detailed examination of journal entries, particularly those at year end
- Placing more emphasis on independent outside evidence
- Assigning more experienced personnel or specialists to the engagement team
- Paying close attention to accounting areas that are highly subjective or those that are complex
- Decreasing the predictability of audit procedures, for example, surprise visits, observation of assets, and performing more procedures at year end

Exhibit 9.14 provides a brief overview of potential audit responses to various fraud risk factors. Note that in each case, the follow-up responses are specific to the potential problem that was identified in the auditor's fraud risk assessment.

Exhibit 9.15 illustrates the fraud risk assessment and fraud risk response process. The exhibit describes a very successful company, a division of a larger company, headquartered in a small town. Over time, the CFO was able to defraud the company of millions of dollars, which was hidden by overstating assets. The audit firm failed to detect the fraud. The case describes how some of the fraud response procedures discussed in this section would have been effective in detecting the fraud.

> **PRACTICAL POINT**
>
> If evidence signals that a fraud might exist, the auditor will need to determine whether or not forensic or specialist auditors are needed to complete the investigation. The auditor will also want to reevaluate the need for additional procedures to determine the existence or amount of the fraud.

Exhibit 9.14 — Linking Audit Procedures to Fraud Risk Indicators

Fraud Risk Indicator	Audit Procedures to Address Risks
Pressure to meet earnings objectives and an unusual year-end spike in sales to a few large customers	• Use trend analysis to identify unusual fluctuation in sales. • Use audit software (computer analysis) to identify the parties involved in any unusual sales (customers, etc.). • Review all large sales contracts to determine (a) actual shipment of the goods, (b) the existence of unusual terms, and (c) payment date. • Verify that the customers are real business entities. • Confirm, usually orally, the terms of major contracts with the customers. • Examine cash receipts after year end to determine if receipts were collected from the customers.
Financial distress and potential violation of debt covenants	• Perform analytical review of revenue and cost of goods sold and note any unusual changes. • Perform a detailed test of inventory, including observation of inventory and valuation (for manufacturing firms, this is the account most likely to be overstated). • Review debt covenants to determine potential incentive/pressure. • Review all journal entries near the end of the year that are unusual, or could have a significant impact on potentially masking potential violation of the debt covenants. • Review all changes in classification of liabilities. • Review all changes to equity and investigate any unusual entries.
Company is not yet profitable, but under pressure to show sales growth	• Analytically review for unusual sales spikes near the end of the year and investigate all such sales. • Select sales and note: (a) whether actual shipment took place or service was performed, (b) whether there were unusual terms or unusual relationship with customer (bartering, round tripping, etc.), and (c) determine if cash was collected from customer. • Obtain a list of all related parties and search files for any sales made to related parties.
Pressure to meet analysts' projected earnings target	• Review financial statements for unusual ratios, particularly comparison with industry averages. • Test all unusually large capitalization of assets to determine if expenses are being capitalized. Take a sample of debits to capital assets and examine underlying supporting documents. If still suspicious, visit the location and physically examine the asset. • Review all unusual journal entries, including those that involve decreases in previously established "reserve" accounts. • Carefully evaluate the reasonableness of estimates.

Exhibit 9.15	Fraud Detection—The Importance of Common Sense and Business Knowledge

The CFO of Chalmers Outdoors, a manufacturer of all-terrain outdoor vehicles, embezzled $20 million during a period of several years. The auditors never detected the embezzlement. The embezzlements were disguised by inflating inventory and accounts receivable. In fact, about half of the book value of inventory and accounts receivable in the year 2006 was fictitious. A summary of the relevant accounts is contained in the following table ($mil):

	2011	2010	2009	2008
Sales	181	152	110	91
% Growth	19%	38%	21%	
Inventory	22	21	18	13
% Growth	5%	17%	38%	
# Days Sales	44.4	50.4	59.7	35.2
Accounts Receivable	17	18	15	9
% Growth	−6%	20%	67%	
# Days Sales	34.3	43.2	49.8	36.1

Chalmers Outdoors is a subsidiary of Becker Industries, a conglomerate with approximately $1.1 billion in sales each year. The external auditors did not use a risk-based approach to auditing, but instead it relied heavily on the one-person internal audit staff to perform many of the audit procedures.

Chalmers's ATVs are sold to dealers on a floor-plan arrangement with finance companies that typically pay Chalmers within 3 to 5 days of the sale. This is typical for this industry and others like it, such as the automotive industry, watercraft industry, and so forth. The dealer is responsible for handling all the financing for the products.

ANALYTICAL REVIEW

Had the auditors performed an industry comparison, they would have found the following for 2011:

	# Days Sales in Receivables	# Days Sales in Inventory
Chalmers	34.3	44.4
Key Competitor	12.0	26.7
Industry Average	17.0	31.2

Lesson to Be Learned: The analysis clearly shows a large build-up in both receivables and inventory, but the auditor could easily get overwhelmed by both the sales and profit growth of a company. The fraud [a defalcation] was allowed to occur because the company was doing relatively well, had a good product, and was increasing its sales every year. Sales, inventory, and accounts receivable growth are volatile, and inventory and accounts receivable were growing slower than sales. Thus, a superficial review would not indicate a problem. However, analytical review is not just numbers; it also includes application of *industry knowledge*. Even though there is strong growth in sales, accounts receivable should not be growing because of the floor-plan financing, nor should inventory be growing significantly because most sales are "made to order," that is, a dealer must order early in the fall for spring delivery; there is no good reason for inventory to continue to increase in the number of days sales on hand.

Is there a problem that is evident here? Yes, the analytical review, coupled with industry knowledge, indicates the likelihood of problems—either operational or fraudulent. The auditor must now link the risk to specific audit procedures, such as procedures to verify the existence and valuation of inventory and the existence and valuation of valid accounts receivable. At a minimum, the audit should be adjusted to conduct a full count of inventory and to perform more confirmations of receivables and follow-up on cash collected from receivables.

HOW THE FRAUD WAS COVERED UP

The CFO transferred money to his personal account by having a check drawn on the company to another "business" that he controlled. He would override the original journal entry by making such entries as debiting inventory and crediting cash. Why were such journal entries unusual? The answer is that virtually all clients would have computerized processing for the purchase transactions and it would be very unusual to see manual journal entries.

(continues)

Exhibit 9.15	**Fraud Detection—The Importance of Common Sense and Business Knowledge (*continued*)**

THE FRAUD COULD HAVE BEEN DETECTED ANY TIME DURING THE PAST FIVE YEARS

The business risk approach requires that the auditor use the knowledge of the industry to perform various analytical tests to identify items that appear to be abnormal. In this case, $20 million was embezzled from a high-growth profitable company. However, had the auditor paid attention to the company relative to knowledge about floor-plan financing, the rest of the industry, and the quality of internal controls (the CFO was overriding the system), the fraud would have been detected early and saved the company $20 million. The linkage to audit procedures would have included any of the following procedures that were not performed:

- A detailed review and investigation of all manual journal entries, particularly those involving cash, receivables, or inventory
- Testing the existence and valuation of both inventory and accounts receivable by requiring and observing a complete year-end physical count of inventory and confirming accounts receivable with customers
- Adding the amounts in the detailed subsidiary records and agreeing to the control account balances

LESSONS LEARNED

A risk approach to auditing requires thorough understanding of the business, its relationship with suppliers and customers, the ability to link questionable results to specific detailed audit tests, and the professional skepticism to compare client results to industry norms.

Step 7. Gather and Evaluate Audit Evidence

The auditor's skepticism should be heightened whenever the following issues related to evidence are present:

- *There are discrepancies in the accounting records.* These include transactions not recorded in a timely fashion, unsupported transactions, last-minute adjustments, or situations in which the auditor has tips or complaints about alleged fraud.
- *The auditor finds conflicting or missing evidential matter.* Examples include missing documents, altered documents, significant unexplained reconciliations, missing inventory, unavailable or missing electronic evidence, or the inability to produce evidence related to the design and operation of the entity's computerized information system.

When gathering evidence on revenue, the auditor should always be alert to an unusual amount of revenue being recorded near year end or at the end of quarterly reporting timeframes. Similarly, the auditor should gather evidence on all accruals or changes in estimates that occur in a similar timeframe. The audit team should always consider the relationship of reported financial results to underlying economic factors. For example, the auditor should ask whether:

- Reported net income mirrors cash inflows over a period of time.
- There is consistency between operating accounts, most especially those of inventory, accounts receivable, accounts payable, sales, and cost of goods sold.

AUDITING *in Practice*

PROFESSIONAL SKEPTICISM AND RELATIONSHIP WITH MANAGEMENT

When the relationship with management seems strained, the auditor should increase professional skepticism. Examples of such situations might include denial of access to records, undue time pressures, unusual delays in providing requested information, unwillingness to provide electronic data or access to electronic systems, or an unwillingness to revise disclosures in response to an auditor request to make such disclosures more transparent and informative.

- The entity's profitability trends differ significantly from the industry's trends. For example, why would a bank have loan loss rates that are one-half those of the rest of the industry when its loan portfolio mirrors those of the rest of the industry?
- There is a viable relationship between sales and production data.

The bottom line is that auditors need to exercise professional judgment. They need to understand the business and they need to have a strong knowledge base from which to both ask questions and analyze responses they receive. Accomplishing this requires gathering and evaluating sufficient appropriate audit evidence. When discrepancies in evidence exist, the audit team must follow up by gathering further evidence that either corroborates management's view or indicates that there is a real problem requiring financial statement adjustment.

Step 8. Communicate the Existence of Fraud to Those at the Organization

All fraud should be reported to a level of the company at which effective action can be taken to assure that the fraud will be dealt with and the likelihood of similar fraud in the future will be decreased. Whenever fraud involves senior management, or involves misstatements that are material to the financial statements, the existence and nature of the fraud should be reported to the audit committee and, through it, to the board. In some cases, the auditor may be required to ascertain that management has reported the fraud to outside parties—to meet regulatory requirements, for example. Finally, the existence of fraud, by definition, implies that the company has weaknesses in internal control because the fraud was neither prevented nor detected by the internal controls. Depending on the nature and materiality of the fraud, the auditor may need to report on the material weaknesses in internal control.

Step 9. Determine Appropriate Way in which to Report any Identified Fraud

If fraud is found and the financial statements are corrected and the nature of the fraud adequately disclosed, then the financial statements are fairly stated and the auditor need not issue a qualified or an adverse audit opinion. However, the auditor does have a responsibility to communicate the nature of the fraud to key constituents both inside and, in some occasions, outside the organization.

Required Communication Regarding Defalcations   If the financial statements are materially misstated, they obviously must be corrected in order for the auditor to give an unqualified opinion. The question that remains is whether the fraud needs to be specifically identified as a line item in the financial statements in order for the statements to be fairly presented. Consider the following two examples: (1) Wal-Mart and other retailers are susceptible to shoplifting as a normal part of running their businesses; (2) a manufacturing company whose employee steals a material amount of cash receipts does not view the defalcation as a normal part of business.

The profession has responded that GAAP does not require shoplifting loss incurred by a retail firm to be a separate line item on the financial statements, even though many users believe it should be reported as part of management's governance requirements or control reporting. On the other hand, the defalcation in the manufacturing company is not an ordinary business expense; that is, it should not be viewed as a cost of doing business. It is more descriptive of a loss caused by poor or nonexistent internal controls. GAAP would normally require that a material loss caused by defalcations be classified separately from other operating expenses. Because a material defalcation reflects a weakness in internal control it should be reported as such to the audit committee and board of directors. It is the board's and management's responsibility to communicate

LO 9

Describe the auditor's responsibility to report discovered fraud and illegal activities.

with regulatory authorities if the nature of the fraud is such that regulatory authorities require the communication. If the required communication does not take place, the auditor may (a) consider withdrawing from the engagement, (b) consider the potential contingent loss and see that it is disclosed on the financial statements, or (c) modify the audit report to communicate the needed disclosure.

Required Communication Regarding Financial Statement Fraud The auditor must first determine that the financial statements have been corrected. The auditor then must communicate the existence of fraud to management, to the board, and to the audit committee. If the fraud involves top management, the auditor must assess the actions taken by the board to rectify the problem. If sufficient actions are not taken, the auditor must consider the overall control environment and the possible need to resign from the audit engagement. If the financial statements are not corrected, then the auditor should issue a qualified or an adverse opinion. The financial statements should reflect the losses caused by the fraud.

Auditors' Responsibilities for Detecting and Reporting Illegal Acts **Illegal acts** are "violations of laws or governmental regulations … by management or employees acting on behalf of the entity" (AU 317.02). A company that violates tax laws or pays bribes to government officials (foreign or domestic), for example, would be committing an illegal act. Some illegal activities may result in fines against the company as well as the individuals involved; others may not carry fines but still need to be disclosed. Illegal acts often have direct financial statement ramifications. The auditor must therefore design the audit to identify illegal acts that have a direct, material effect on the financial statements.

A number of procedures provide information that could lead to the discovery of such acts if they exist. These procedures include reading corporate minutes, making inquiries of management and legal counsel, and performing various tests of details to support specific transactions or balances. In reviewing such information, the auditor should be especially alert to large payments for unspecified services to consultants or employees, excessively large sales commissions, unexplained governmental payments, and unauthorized or unnecessarily complex transactions.

If such acts are discovered, the auditor is advised to consult the client's legal counsel about the application of relevant laws, because determining whether something is indeed illegal is generally beyond an auditor's professional competence. If illegal acts do affect the financial statements, the auditor should take steps to ensure fair presentation, including both necessary account adjustments and proper disclosure. Finally, the auditor should communicate the nature of these acts to the audit committee of the board of directors or its equivalent and in some cases to the SEC.

Step 10. Document the Audit Approach

The audit team should document the process followed to assess fraud risk and the procedures used to search for fraud, including the rationale for those procedures. The documentation should describe audit planning related to fraud risk assessment (including the results of brainstorming), identified risks, procedures performed and the results of those procedures, the need for corroborating evidence, and any communications to required parties. SAS 99 states that auditor documentation concerning fraud should specifically include:

- The engagement team's planning discussion regarding the entity's susceptibility to material misstatement caused by fraud, including how and when the discussion occurred, the audit team members who participated, and the subject matter discussed

PRACTICAL POINT

The auditor is not required to report directly to the police or the SEC. However, if such reporting is not done in a prompt manner by the company, the auditor should consider resigning. When resigning, the auditor has to identify all significant reasons for the resignation.

PRACTICAL POINT

From a conceptual viewpoint, all significant frauds should be reported as separate line-item losses on a company's financial statements. However, most companies include the costs in other expense items.

PRACTICAL POINT

Nonpublic companies are not required to publicly report on internal control; thus weaknesses that allowed fraud to occur might not get communicated to outside parties.

- The audit procedures performed to assess the risks of material misstatement due to fraud
- Specific fraud risks that were identified and a description of auditor responses to those risks
- The reasons supporting an audit conclusion that risks associated with revenue recognition are *not* a concern on the particular engagement
- The results of the procedures to identify potential management override of controls
- Other conditions or analytical relationships that may have led the auditor to believe that additional procedures were necessary, and the auditor's responses in addressing those issues
- Any communications regarding fraud made to management, those charged with corporate governance, and/or regulators, and so on

Forensic Accounting

LO 10

Distinguish between forensic accounting and auditing.

Forensic accounting is an extension of auditing that focuses on detailed investigation of situations where fraud has already been identified or where fraud is highly suspected. One aspect of forensic accounting focuses on identifying the person who has perpetrated the fraud and having that person confess to the fraud. Forensic accounting builds support for a court case against the person committing the fraud by identifying the fraud, calculating the damages caused by the fraud, and building both factual and testimonial evidence of the fraud. Although forensic accounting builds on evidence concepts in auditing and uses the evidence found during an audit (forged source documents, file details showing duplicate items, etc.), the emphasis is more on interviewing, with a focus on the perpetrator. Forensic accountants will examine 100% of fraud-related documents to accurately measure the cost of the fraud. Auditors, on the other hand, usually rely on sampling to determine whether or not material misstatements or illegal acts might have occurred. It is important to note that conducting a financial statement audit is a separate engagement from conducting a forensic accounting investigation. The audit of financial statements includes serious consideration of the possibility of fraud; the sole purpose of a forensic engagement is to detect, investigate, and document a situation in which fraud almost certainly exists.

Forensic accountants are often asked to provide litigation support, in which they are called on to give expert testimony about financial data and accounting activities. Interestingly, the emphasis in court cases is more on testimonial evidence that is built upon other evidence. Thus, interviewing is one of the most important forensic accounting skills.

Forensic accountants also work on reconstructing account balances; that is, they will go back to source documents and attempt to determine what an account balance should be or determine the amount of fraud directly linked to a perpetrator. Forensic accounting also broadens out into "messy" courtroom subjects, such as hiding assets in divorce cases or determining the exact amount of money lost through a money laundering scheme. Exhibit 9.16 summarizes some of the major differences between forensic accounting and auditing.

Often, a forensic engagement is initiated by management when it suspects a fraud is occurring within the organization. In that case, management may alert the auditor to its concerns and request a separate forensic engagement. Alternatively, the audit of financial statements may uncover hints of fraud. In that case, the external auditor may recommend to management that the audit firm conduct a separate forensic engagement.

Outside of a forensic engagement, SAS 99 indicates that an audit team may want to assign forensic auditing specialists in situations where there are strong indicators of fraud. The rationale for assigning such personnel is that forensic

Exhibit 9.16   Differences Between Forensic Accounting and Accounting

Area	Forensic Accounting	Auditing
Focus	Known frauds or areas where fraud is suspected Getting the perpetrator to confess	Fairness of financial statements Quality of controls
Approach	Interviews Reconstruction of damages 100% examination of targeted files	Sampling, analytical review based on materiality
Scope	Can range from financial reporting frauds in companies to hidden assets for divorce cases to court testimony	Usually audits of financial statements
End Product	Summary of evidence gathered with special emphasis on testimonial evidence Expert witness work in court case	Opinion on audited financial statements and internal control
Underlying Skills	Interviewing—listening Reconstruction of account balances Cyber reconstruction (computer cases) Presentation—expert witnessing work	Objectivity Data gathering and analysis Basic accounting and auditing knowledge Non-confrontational interviewing skills Computer auditing

auditors are accustomed to finding fraud and have developed the necessary skills and professional skepticism to address the fraud risk. Thus, forensic specialists may work on separate forensic engagements, and may also be called upon to assist "regular" auditors in situations of heightened fraud risk.

Summary

Fraud is a widespread international problem. Users of financial statements have a reasonable expectation that auditors will detect and report on fraud, and the auditing profession has recognized that it cannot retain its status and credibility without enhancing its ability to detect fraud. Thus, auditing standards and regulatory expectations have evolved to reflect the presumption that auditors should search for the existence of material fraud on every engagement. There are two major classifications of fraud: financial reporting fraud (involving misstatement of financial statements) and defalcations (corruption and asset misappropriation). The auditor's responsibility is the same for each type of fraud: plan and execute the audit to provide reasonable assurance that material misstatements caused by fraud will be discovered. Financial reporting frauds are less frequent, but the magnitude of dollar loss is more significant compared to defalcations.

There are common patterns in most frauds. The auditor can use these patterns, along with an analysis of control deficiencies and financial trends, to identify fraud risk and the types of audit procedures that would be most effective in detecting fraud.

Significant Terms

Asset misappropriations   A fraud that involves the theft or misuse of an organization's assets. Common examples include skimming cash, stealing inventory, and payroll fraud. It is one type of defalcation.

Brainstorming   A required part of every financial statement audit and conducted at the beginning of the audit. The audit team considers changes in account balances, deficiencies in controls, and motivations to commit fraud to identify areas where fraud is more likely to occur and how it will occur.

Corruption   A fraud in which fraudsters wrongfully use their influence in a business transaction in order to procure some benefit for themselves or another person, contrary to their duty to their employer or the rights of another. It is another type of defalcation.

Debt covenants   An agreement between an entity and its lender that places limitations on the organization (e.g., restrictions on dividend payments or requirements for a specified working capital or debt/equity ratio); failure to satisfy the covenant may result in loans or bonds becoming immediately due and payable or redeemable.

Defalcation (misappropriation of assets)   The theft or embezzlement of funds or other assets from an organization. The theft is usually covered up through fictitious accounting entries.

Expectations gap   The difference between users' expectations that auditors will detect fraud and auditors' willingness to accept responsibility for detecting fraud.

Financial reporting fraud (fraudulent financial reporting)   The intentional misstatement of account balances to portray a misstated economic picture of the firm. The person perpetrating this type of fraud stands to gain from inflated stock prices or bonuses based on reported profits.

Forensic accounting   An investigatory approach to building evidence of a suspected fraud in preparation for a court trial; it often includes reconstructing accounts to determine damages caused by the fraud with an emphasis on testimonial evidence.

Fraud   An intentional embezzlement or theft of funds from a company or the intentional misstatement of account balances in order to create a perception that a company is doing better than it really is doing. The first type of fraud is often referred to as a *defalcation*; the second type is referred to as *fraudulent financial reporting*.

Fraud risk factors   Company or individual characteristics that have most often been associated with the perpetration of fraud.

Fraud Triangle   A conceptual depiction of factors that, when all occurring at the same time, are highly predictive of fraud. The triangle consists of incentive to commit fraud, opportunity to commit the fraud, and the ability to rationalize the fraudulent activities.

Illegal acts   Violations of laws or governmental regulations by management or employees acting on behalf of the entity.

Professional skepticism   An attitude that includes a questioning mind and a critical assessment of audit evidence.

User expectations   The rational expectations of users regarding the auditor's discovery and reporting of fraud, as well as the portrayal of financial statements in a fashion that accurately reflects economic reality within the constraints of GAAP.

SELECTED REFERENCES TO RELEVANT PROFESSIONAL GUIDANCE	
Topic	**Guidance**
Illegal Acts by Clients	SAS 54 *Illegal Acts by Clients*
	ISA 250 *Consideration of Laws and Regulations in an Audit of Financial Statements*
Considering and Responding to the Risk of Fraud	SAS 99 *Consideration of Fraud in a Financial Statement Audit*
	SAS 109 *Understanding the Entity and Its Environment and Assessing the Risks of Material Misstatement*
	SAS *Understanding the Entity and Its Environment and Assessing the Risks of Material Misstatement* (Redrafted) (issued but not effective; proposed effective date is December 2012)
	SAS 110 *Performing Audit Procedures in Response to Assessed Risks and Evaluating the Audit Evidence Obtained*
	SAS *Performing Audit Procedures in Response to Assessed Risks and Evaluating the Audit Evidence Obtained* (Redrafted) (issued but not effective; proposed effective date is December 2012)
	AS No. 12 *Identifying and Assessing Risks of Material Misstatement*
	AS No. 13 *The Auditor's Responses to the Risks of Material Misstatement*
	ISA 240 *The Auditor's Responsibilities Relating to Fraud in an Audit of Financial Statements*
	ISA 315 *Identifying and Assessing the Risks of Material Misstatement Through Understanding the Entity and Its Environment*
	Proposed ISA 315 (Revised) *Identifying and Assessing the Risks of Material Misstatement through Understanding the Entity and Its Environment*
	ISA 330 *The Auditor's Responses to Assessed Risks*

Note: *Acronyms for Relevant Professional Guidance*

STANDARDS: **AS**—Auditing Standard issued by the PCAOB; **ISA**—International Standard on Auditing issued by the IAASB; **SAS**—Statement on Auditing Standards issued by the Auditing Standards Board of the AICPA; **SSAE**—Statement on Standards for Attestation Engagements issued by the AICPA.

ORGANIZATIONS: **AICPA**—American Institute of Certified Public Accountants; **COSO**—Committee of Sponsoring Organizations; **IAASB**—International Auditing and Assurance Standards Board; **PCAOB**—Public Company Accounting Oversight Board; **SEC**—Securities and Exchange Commission.

Review Questions

9-1 **(LO 1, 2)** How prevalent is fraud? What is the effect of fraud on the profitability of businesses globally?

9-2 **(LO 1)** Fraud has always existed, but it seems that the attitude toward fraud may be changing. What are the major changes in the Josephson Institute's survey of high school students' attitudes toward lying or cheating?

9-3 **(LO 1)** The Center for Audit Quality issued a white paper recommending for a broader approach to dealing with fraud. Describe the three major elements of their recommendations and how the parts fit together to better address the occurrence of fraud.

9-4 **(LO 3, 4)** Define the following types of fraud:

- Defalcation
- Asset misappropriation
- Corruption
- Financial reporting fraud

Does the auditor's responsibility for detecting a fraud differ by the type of fraud that is perpetrated? Explain.

9-5 **(LO-3)** Fraud continues to occur at smaller organizations at a rate higher than that of larger organizations. Explain why this is the case.

9-6 **(LO 3)** What are the most common approaches that perpetrators use to commit financial reporting fraud?

9-7 **(LO 3)** You are asked to be interviewed by a student newspaper regarding the nature of accounting fraud. The reporter says, "As I understand it, defalcations are more likely to be found in small organizations, but not in larger organizations. On the other hand, financial reporting fraud is more likely to be found in larger organizations." How would you respond to the reporter's observation?

9-8 **(LO 4)** Define the term *materiality* as it applies to the concept of the auditor's responsibility for detecting material fraud. What are the factors that would cause the materiality threshold in dollars to be lower than it might otherwise have been in a financial statement audit?

9-9 **(LO 5)** What are the major lessons for the accounting profession that have been learned (or should have been learned) from Equity Funding?

9-10 **(LO 5)** What were the major findings of the most recent COSO report on fraudulent financial reporting?

9-11 **(LO 4, 7)** What is the responsibility of the external auditor to detect material fraud? Explain how this responsibility translates to how the audit is planned and conducted.

9-12 **(LO 5)** What is professional skepticism? How is it applied when assessing the fraud risk of an organization, and then auditing that organization for the risk assessed by the auditor?

Professional Skepticism

9-13   **(LO 6)**   Why is it important that the auditor review all major journal entries that arise outside the normal computerized accounting process?

9-14   **(LO 5, 6, 7)**   Does the auditor presume that there is a fraud in some specific accounts? Which accounts? How does this presumption change the nature of audit procedures?

9-15   **(LO 6)**   The fraud triangle identifies motivations/incentives, opportunities, and rationalizations as major factors associated with most frauds. Describe each of these factors and explain how they work together to assist the auditor in assessing fraud risk.

9-16   **(LO 6)**   Identify five factors that would be strong indicators of opportunities to commit fraud. How would the auditor identify the five factors at the beginning of the audit?

9-17   **(LO 6)**   Is the "ability to rationalize" the fraud an important aspect of a fraud profile? What are some of the common rationales used by fraud perpetrators?

9-18   **(LO 5)**   Which major oversight groups failed in their professional responsibilities in the Enron case? How did each group fail? What were the motivations that influenced each group that partially led to the failure? To what extent did Sarbanes-Oxley address many of the factors that caused the failures?

9-19   **(LO 6)**   Explain how "brainstorming" is implemented as part of the audit planning process. What are the advantages of using a "brainstorming" approach to identify the possible existence of fraud?

9-20   **(LO 7)**   What are some procedures the auditor can use to investigate the likelihood that fraud might exist in a company's accounts? The procedures should relate to identifying the potential existence of fraud, not to specifically identifying the fraud.

9-21   **(LO 7)**   Explain the important role preliminary analytical procedures play in identifying fraud risk. Identify three examples of analytical analysis that would increase the auditor's assessment of fraud risk.

9-22   **(LO 7)**   How should the audit be adjusted when the auditor has identified a high risk of fraud occurring?

9-23   **(LO 7)**   Why is it important for the auditor to develop a list of "hypothesized frauds" as opposed to first seeking management's explanations of differences in account balances?

9-24   **(LO 7)**   An auditor may have to perform "extended audit procedures" if the auditor identifies fraud risk as high. Identify five extended audit procedures that might be performed if the auditor suspects there may be fraud in the revenue account.

9-25   **(LO 9)**   What is the auditor's primary responsibility for reporting a fraud that has been detected and corrected? In your answer, be sure to cover the differences in communication when the fraud is considered material as opposed to being not material to the financial statements. To whom should the existence of the fraud be communicated?

9-26   **(LO 9)** Explain the auditor's responsibility for reporting the following:
- A defalcation that the client is willing to correct and portray in the financial statements
- A defalcation that is material, but the client wishes to obscure by recording it in an "other expense" category
- A financial reporting fraud that the client wishes to include in an "other expense" category

9-27   **(LO 9)** In your opinion, should auditors be required to report a material fraud (consider both a defalcation and preparation of fraudulent financial reporting) that was detected during the audit to:
- Users of the company's financial statements?
- Regulatory agencies, such as the SEC?
- Law enforcement officials?
- The audit committee?
- The public press?

9-28   **(LO 5)** Although each fraud is unique, there are commonalities among many of the major financial reporting frauds that have taken place in the past decade. What are the major commonalities and lessons that can be learned through an examination of the frauds at Enron, HealthSouth, WorldCom, Adecco, Lucent, Parmalat, Koss, and Dell Computer?

9-29   **(LO 7)** Explain how an auditor should link control deficiencies to the design of audit tests. Identify the logic process used by the auditor to make the linkage.

9-30   **(LO 7)** Explain what procedures the auditor should employ upon identifying fraud risk factors.

9-31   **(LO 8)** Audit software can be very useful in analyzing data and identifying potential fraud. Identify the major fraud-related procedures that can be performed using audit software.

9-32   **(LO 9)** What are illegal acts? What is the auditor's responsibility for detecting and reporting illegal acts? Does this responsibility differ from the auditor's responsibility for detecting and reporting fraud?

9-33   **(LO 10)** What is forensic accounting? How does it differ from auditing?

Multiple-Choice Questions

9-34   **(LO 1, 2)** Which of the following statements regarding the incidence of fraud is *incorrect*?
   a. Fraud is estimated to cost U.S. businesses between 5 and 7 cents of every dollar of sales.
   b. Fraudulent financial reporting occurs more often than defalcations.
   c. Financial reporting frauds are generally larger in dollar amounts than defalcations.
   d. Research shows that only about one-fifth of all frauds are discovered and prosecuted.

9-35   **(LO 3)** Which of the following best describes the auditor's responsibility for detecting financial reporting fraud versus detecting a defalcation?

   a. There is more responsibility for detecting financial reporting fraud because audits are designed to look for financial misstatements.

   b. The auditor is responsible for detecting financial reporting fraud only if it is material but is responsible for detecting all defalcations caused by a known deficiency in the client's internal control.

   c. The auditor is responsible for detecting material misstatements in the financial statements, thus there is no difference in the responsibility of detecting financial reporting fraud or a defalcation as long as it is material.

   d. The auditor is responsible for detecting financial reporting fraud of any amount if collusion and red flags are present.

9-36   **(LO 3)** Fraudulent financial reporting includes all of the following *except*:

   a. Misappropriation of assets for personal use.

   b. Manipulation, falsification, or alteration of accounting records or supporting documents.

   c. Misrepresentation or omission of events, transactions, or other significant information.

   d. Intentional misapplication of accounting principles.

9-37   **(LO 2, 4)** Frauds are more likely to take place during periods of recession. Should auditors detect more frauds during a recessionary period than a non-recessionary period? Select the best response.

   a. No, because the responsibility for fraud detection does not change.

   b. Yes, because the auditor should adjust audit techniques because of the higher likelihood of fraud.

   c. No, because most of the frauds will be defalcations and the auditor is more focused on financial fraud in the audit of financial statements.

   d. Yes, because the public expects auditors to detect more fraud.

9-38   **(LO 4, 9)** Which of the following statement(s) is/are *correct* regarding the auditor's responsibilities related to fraud?

   a. The auditor is required to report all incidences of material fraud to the audit committee.

   b. The discovery of a material fraud indicates that a company has a material weakness in internal control.

   c. There is no difference in the dollar amount of planning materiality when searching for a defalcation versus searching for financial reporting fraud.

   d. In determining the materiality of fraud, the auditor must consider qualitative factors such as whether or not senior management is involved.

   e. All of the above.

9-39   **(LO 6)** The auditor of a retail organization notes the following changes in ratios during this year-end audit. Your analysis of the industry indicates that most retailers are carrying smaller amounts of inventory this year and sales are starting to recover. As the audit team brainstorms about the likelihood of fraud, which of the items would indicate the highest likelihood of financial fraud?

Ratio	This Year	Last Year
a. Inventory Turnover	6.2	5.4
b. Sales Increase over past year	1.1%	−2.8%
c. Store Operating Cost as % of Revenue	9.4%	9.3%
d. Store Maintenance Costs as % Revenue	3.2%	5.9%

9-40   **(LO 6)** Which of the following is *not* a correct statement regarding the use of brainstorming as part of a financial statement audit?

  a. It is required as a normal part of every engagement.

  b. It should include all members of the audit team.

  c. It should include an analysis of known internal control deficiencies.

  d. It should be performed jointly with the internal audit department.

9-41   **(LO 6)** The auditor notes the following changes in ratios:

	Current	Last Year
Inventory Turnover	7.3	4.2
Accounts Receivable Turnover	2.8	7.3
Revenue Growth	15%	8%
Warranty expense as a % of sales	1.8%	0.5%

From just this information, the auditor should conclude all of the following about fraud risk *except*:

  a. Inventory has declined in quality because of the emphasis on increased sales, leading customers to return items and delay paying accounts receivable.

  b. Accounts receivable growth may be caused by increased sales.

  c. Accounts receivable is older and may be less collectible.

  d. Revenue growth likely includes contracts that have deferred payment terms.

  e. The data would support a hypothesis of fictitious sales near year end.

9-42   **(LO 6)** Which of the following would *not* be considered a motivation to commit fraud?

  a. Personal financial problems

  b. Stock compensation programs

  c. Poor internal controls

  d. Tight debt covenants

9-43   **(LO 3)** The largest form of defalcation (both in dollars and frequency) is:

  a. Theft of cash directly from the company.

  b. Theft of cash through disbursement schemes.

c. Theft of inventory and small tools.

d. Theft of cash by taking customer receipts and writing off accounts receivable.

9-44   **(LO-6)** Which of the following would be considered a "red flag" that should alert the auditor to the increased possibility that financial reporting fraud might be occurring?

a. A privately held company is experiencing a period of financial distress.

b. A publicly held company has experienced a significant increase in earnings in an industry with widely fluctuating earnings.

c. The client needlessly engages in many complex and difficult accounting transactions and is very discretionary in its use of estimates.

d. Managers receive bonuses based on meeting performance goals that have been approved by the board.

e. All would be considered red flags that should be considered by the auditor.

Discussion and Research Questions

9-45   **(Classification of Frauds, LO 3, 4, 6)** The auditing literature has traditionally classified fraud as either "defalcations" or "financial reporting fraud."

Required

a. What is the difference between the two types of fraud?

b. Does the auditor's responsibility for detecting fraud vary with the nature of the fraud committed?

c. Is a defalcation or a financial reporting fraud more difficult to detect? Explain and give an example to support your conclusion.

d. Explain how the personnel committing each type of fraud may differ and how the incentives to commit the fraud might differ. Use the following format in formulating your answer:

	Defalcation	Financial Reporting Fraud
Personnel Most Likely to Commit the Fraud		
Most Likely Incentive to Commit the Fraud		
Rationalization Used to Justify the Fraud		

Professional Skepticism

9-46   **(Audit Responsibility for Fraud Detection, LO 1, 4, 6)** The responsibility of auditors for detecting fraud has increased as users have made it clear that they expect auditors to detect material fraud.

Required

a. In addition to dollar amounts, what other factors should an auditor consider in determining materiality for planning an engagement to detect fraud? How would these other factors affect the planning for the audit?

b. The Center for Audit Quality issued a white paper describing three critical issues that the profession must address to meet the public's expectations for fraud detection and fraud reporting. Identify the three factors and explain how the recommendations, taken as a whole, should assist the profession in meeting user expectations.

c. Explain how the auditor should use preliminary analytical procedures and knowledge of internal control deficiencies to "brainstorm" and plan the audit to detect fraud.

9-47 **(Applying Professional Skepticism, LO-6)** Professional skepticism has been emphasized as an important part of the audit process. However, the need to continually emphasize skepticism implies that auditors have a difficult time remaining skeptical.

Group Activity

Required
In your groups address the following questions.

a. What is professional skepticism? How is professional skepticism used in an audit? Explain how professional skepticism is described in international auditing standards. Are there fundamental differences between U.S. and international auditing standards in terms of professional skepticism?

Professional Skepticism

b. Explain why professional skepticism may be difficult for auditors to fully implement on every audit.

c. Identify the top five things an individual auditor and an audit team should do to help achieve the necessary level of professional skepticism.

International

d. For each of the following cases indicating heightened fraud risk, indicate (a) how a professionally skeptical auditor might interpret the data and (b) how a professionally skeptical auditor might address the possibility of fraud.

- (Case 1) The company is not as profitable as its competitors, but it seems to have good products. However, it has a deficiency in internal control over disbursements that makes it subject to management override.

- (Case 2) The company is doing better than its competitors. Although sales are about the same as competitors, net income is significantly more. Management attributes the greater profitability to better management of expenses.

- (Case 3) The company is financially distressed and is at some risk of defaulting on its debt covenants. The company improves its current ratio and other ratios by making an unusually large payment against its current liabilities, accompanied by highly discounted sales if they customers paid before year end.

- (Case 4) A smaller public company ($165 million in annual sales) has a relatively new CFO who has centralized power under her. Her style is very intimidating even though she is not a CPA and has limited accounting experience. The company has not been able to increase profitability during her time with the company.

9-48 **(Ponzi Scheme, LO 3, 5, 6, 7)** The text describes the Madoff Ponzi scheme, as well as other Ponzi schemes. All of the schemes require elements of both trust and greed. Since Madoff's Ponzi scheme was uncovered, many others have surfaced, including three in Minneapolis; one involving bank loans, another commodities trading, and a third involving investments.

Required

a. What is a Ponzi scheme? Explain how a Ponzi scheme works.

b. How did Madoff carry out his Ponzi scheme?

c. Explain how the elements of the fraud triangle are incorporated into the execution of a Ponzi scheme.

d. Explain how a Ponzi scheme, such as the Madoff scheme, could have been detected by competent auditors.

9-49 **(Equity Funding, LO 3, 5, 7)** The Equity Funding fraud was the first major financial reporting fraud. It was a fraud that people believed would change auditing forever. However, the profession has taken a while to learn the lessons from Equity Funding.

Required

a. The following describes some of the major mechanisms used in conducting the fraud. For each item listed, identify audit procedures or changes in the structure of accounting that would have prevented the failure on the part of the audit firm to detect the Equity Funding Fraud. Organize your answer as follows:

Scheme Used by Equity Funding	Auditing Procedures or Changes Suggested
1. Recording all the fictitious policies on the computer system but omitting the first three digits.	
2. Making simple transactions complex. To record a simple transaction to recognize a policy reserve, the company made more than 30 journal entries across the books of four different subsidiaries.	
3. The company had different auditors for the subsidiaries and for the parent company.	
4. The company was the largest single client of the CPA firm and was the dominant client for the office.	
5. Whenever the auditor would ask for documentation of insurance policies, the company would indicate it would "pull" all the policies from the company files and have them the next day.	

b. Explain why auditors generally prefer to have clients "pull" supporting documents that have been identified for audit testing.

c. What would be the additional cost if the auditor insisted on having the documents produced within the same day?

d. Are there circumstances in which the auditor should insist that the documents be presented during the same day they were selected by the auditor for testing? Explain.

9-50   **(Brainstorming and Fraud, LO 6, 7)** The auditor is to presume that there is fraud in revenue. Consider a company that manufactures high-tech fiber-optic gear. Assume that the Wall Street analysts believe the industry has good growth prospects. The audit client is predicting a 20% increase in sales and a 27% increase in profits for the year under audit. The auditor is planning the audit and knows the following:

Group Activity

- 65% of all sales are made to just five customers.

- There are three companies with very similar products. One has a moderately larger market share and the other has a significantly smaller market share.

- There are indications that the economy is slowing down and it is expected that a slowdown would affect the market for high-tech products that the company sells.

- The company has cut its research and development expenditures in order to maintain the analyst's prediction of earning.

Required

In your groups perform the following:

a. Indicate the types of analytical analysis of the company's preliminary financial results the auditor should perform to facilitate the "brainstorming" and planning of the audit. In your answer, identify key factors that would indicate higher fraud risk. Organize your answer as follows:

Analytical Analysis	Indicators of High Fraud Risk
Example: Analysis of revenue recorded by quarter and increases near the end of the quarter or year end.	

b. What questions should the auditor ask to gain an understanding about the growth prospects and the competitive strength of the industry in which the client operates?

c. Identify four ways in which the client might overstate revenue. For each of these indicate (1) internal control procedures that would have to fail for the fraud to take place; and (2) audit procedures to test for the potential revenue overstatement. Organize your answer as follows:

Fraud	Key Controls That Would Fail	Audit Procedures Needed
1		
2		
3		
4		

9-51   **(Brainstorming and Planning the Audit, LO 6, 7)** The following scenario and analytical information describe a company. Three sets of facts are presented about this company. Perform a brainstorming analysis identifying all the factors that will affect the planning and conduct of the audit. Specifically, discuss in your group the following:

Group Activity

a. Based on the facts presented, what audit questions need to be addressed?

b. Based on the facts presented, what hypotheses can you develop about ways the company could be committing a fraud?

1. **Company Background Facts.** Brandon Apparel group is a manufacturer and wholesaler of apparel. The company was purchased five years ago by two young entrepreneurs and is heavily leveraged. The owners put up $400,000 of their own money and borrowed approximately $6 million to acquire the company from the previous owner. The owners tried to sell the company, but a due diligence review by the potential buyer indicated that some of the assets acquired in previous years did not exist. The company's debt is now over $10 million, equity is about $1.2 million (unaudited), and short-term payables are approximately $1.8 million. The company is relatively small with total sales last year of $13 million. Many of its customers are large, for example, JCPenney, SportMart, MC Sporting Goods, and Kohl's. The industry is competitive. The loan covenants require a debt-to-equity ratio not exceeding 3.5 to 1.0 and maintaining a tangible net worth above $1.5 million. Management fired the previous auditor and has asked you to perform the audit because you are local and know the company better. During the year, the company moved to licensing all of its goods rather than manufacturing them.

2. **Industry and Analytical Analysis Facts.** There is limited industry information available. The following reflects Brandon versus the industry for the current year:

	Brandon	Industry
Revenue increase %	12%	5%
Returns as % of revenue	3.4%	2.8%
Gross margin %	28.5%	43.2%
Inventory—% of assets	58.4%	32.7%
Accounts receivable—% of assets	22.8%	18.2%
Cash—% of assets	0.0%	4.3%
Intangibles—% of assets	9.4%	7.4%

Other financial information: Although the company has shown revenue and profit growth, cash flow from operations has been negative for the past three years.

3. **Management Information and Controls Facts.** Management has determined that it needs to outsource most of the manufacturing to other companies under a licensing agreement. However, for this year, it will continue to record the total amount billed to the retailers as sales even though the licensing agreement provides only a 27.5% payment to Brandon. Next year, they will convert to only recognizing licensing fees as revenue. Most of the large customers do not confirm accounts receivable. The company is implementing an automated bar-coded inventory system at the end of the year that they expect to be more accurate. The company will move the inventory to a new location after the end of the year, where it will be counted on January 8 when it is unloaded and scanned into the new inventory system.

4. **Existence of Contra-liability.** Management has sued the former owners of the company for the $1 million note that is still due to them. The suit alleges that assets originally sold to the owners

five years ago did not exist and according to the contract, the owners have the right to offset the discovery of the nonexistent assets against the notes payable. Accordingly, the company has set up a contra-liability account to show the offset with a corresponding increase in retained earnings.

9-52   **(Fraud Risk Factors and the Decision Analysis Framework, LO 6, 11)** Assume that your client possesses the following characteristics associated with the fraud triangle:

Group Activity

Incentives:

- Need to obtain additional debt or equity financing to stay competitive, including financing of major research and development or capital expenditures
- Significant portions of their compensation (e.g., bonuses, stock options, and earn-out arrangements) being contingent upon achieving aggressive targets for stock price, operating results, financial position, or cash flow

Opportunities:

- Significant related-party transactions
- Audit committee meets the criteria for outsiders, but most members have been involved for many years
- There are no significant monitoring controls, especially those that look for trends in reports
- Control deficiencies dealing with the proper pricing and authorization of transactions by sales personnel identified last year have not yet been rectified

Rationalizations:

- Strong interest by management in maintaining or increasing the entity's stock price or earnings trend
- A practice by management of communicating to analysts, creditors, and other third parties that they will achieve somewhat aggressive earnings and revenue forecasts
- Some attempts by management to justify marginal accounting on the basis that problems noted by the external auditor are immaterial

Required

In your groups address the following:

a. Discuss these client characteristics in your group and then use the seven-step Decision Analysis Framework introduced in Chapter 3 to make an assessment of fraud risk on a scale from 1 (very low fraud risk) to 10 (very high fraud risk).

b. Identify the factors from the preceding description and then discuss which combination of factors will influence the fraud risk assessment.

Note: Once your group has made your fraud risk assessment, you will be asked by your instructor to communicate that assessment to the class as a whole, so be prepared to defend your answer.

Recall that the framework includes the following steps: (1) structure the problem, (2) assess consequences of decision, (3) assess risks and uncertainties of the audit problem, (4) evaluate information/audit evidence-gathering alternatives, (5) conduct sensitivity analyses, (6) gather information/audit evidence, and (7) make decision.

9-53   **(Opportunities to Commit Fraud, LO 3, 6, 7)** An auditor may consider a number of factors when identifying opportunities to commit fraud. The following represent areas that have often been associated with frauds.

Situations Often Associated with Fraud

1. Related-party transactions
2. Industry dominance
3. Numerous subjective accounting judgments
4. Ineffective monitoring mechanisms
5. Complex organizational structure
6. Simple transactions made complex
7. Complex transactions
8. Significant deficiencies in internal control

Required

For each of the situations listed, indicate

a. How the situation presents an opportunity to commit fraud.

b. Whether the fraud is more likely to be a defalcation or financial reporting fraud.

c. The nature of the fraud that is likely to occur.

d. Audit procedures that would detect the fraud if it occurred and was material.

Internet

9-54   **(PCAOB Opinions on Auditors' Fraud Detection Performance, LO 6, 7)** Obtain a copy of the PCAOB's report titled "Observations on Auditors' Implementation of PCAOB Standards Relating to Auditors' Responsibilities with Respect to Fraud," which can be located by visiting Google.com or by linking to the following web address: http://pcaobus.org/Inspections/Documents/2007_01-22_Release_2007-001.pdf.

Required

In the report, the PCAOB summarizes findings from inspections of audit engagements as they relate to the performance of fraud detection audit procedures. The PCAOB report comments on auditor deficiencies in each of the following six areas:

1. Auditors' overall approach to the detection of fraud
2. Brainstorming sessions
3. Auditors' responses to fraud risk factors
4. Financial statement misstatements
5. Risk of management override of controls
6. Other areas to improve fraud detection

Summarize the PCAOB's concerns with respect to problems its inspection teams have noted in auditors' performance in each of the areas listed.

Internet

9-55   **(Auditor Responsibilities for Detecting Fraud, LO 4, 5, 6, 7)** The existence of fraudulent financial reporting has been of great concern to both the accounting profession and regulatory agencies such as the SEC. It has been asserted that companies in trouble frequently go bankrupt shortly after receiving unqualified opinions from auditors. The auditing profession has historically argued that such cases are rare and that the cases appearing in the press give the impression that the profession is doing a poorer job than it actually is.

Required

a. Distinguish between an "audit failure" and a "business failure." Explain why the press may have difficulty in distinguishing between the two.

b. Identify a recent fraud that has been reported in the press or described on the Internet. For the fraud identified:

- Identify the motivations for the fraud.
- Describe how the fraud took place.
- Identify the internal control failures that would have allowed the fraud to take place.
- Identify the audit procedures that should have found the fraud, or if the procedures would not have found the fraud, explain why not.

9-56 **(Audits of Nonpublic Companies, LO 3, 4, 6, 7)** Most recent legislation has dealt with financial reporting fraud that has taken place in publicly traded companies. However, there has not been such legislation for nonpublic companies or for audits of nonpublic companies.

Required

a. Is the auditor's responsibility for detecting fraud any different for audits of nonpublic companies versus audits of public companies? If yes, how does that responsibility differ?

b. Are auditors in smaller companies more likely to find defalcations or financial reporting fraud? Explain.

c. Most small nonpublic companies have inadequate segregation of duties and poor internal control systems. What are the implications of the control deficiencies for the conduct of the audit?

d. Why do smaller nonpublic companies get audits?

e. What are the implications of the fraud standard for the cost of audits of nonpublic companies? Can society evaluate the cost/benefit of the trade-off in costs and the heightened responsibility to detect fraud? How could the trade-off be measured?

f. Who hires the auditor in most nonpublic companies?

*9-57 **(Fraud and Professional Skepticism, LO 3, 4, 6, 7)** Kent, CPA, is the engagement partner on the financial statement audit of Super Computer Services Co. (SCS) for the year ended April 30, 2011. On May 6, 2011, Smith, the senior auditor assigned to the engagement, had the following conversation with Kent concerning the planning phase of the audit:

Professional Skepticism

Kent: Do you have all the audit programs updated yet for the SCS engagement?

Smith: Mostly. I still have work to do on the fraud risk assessment.

Kent: Why? Our "errors and irregularities" program from last year is still OK. It's passed peer review several times. Besides, we don't have specific duties regarding fraud. If we find it, we'll deal with it then.

Smith: I don't think so. That new CEO, Mint, has almost no salary, mostly bonuses and stock options. Doesn't that concern you?

Kent: No. The board of directors approved Mint's employment contract just three months ago. It was passed unanimously.

Smith: I guess so, but Mint told those stock analysts that SCS's earnings would increase 30% next year. Can Mint deliver numbers like that?

Kent: Who knows? We're auditing the 2011 financial statements, not 2012. Mint will probably amend that forecast every month between now and next May.

Smith: Sure, but all this may change our other audit programs.

Kent: No, it won't. The programs are fine as is. If you find fraud in any of your tests, just let me know. Maybe we'll have to extend the tests. Or maybe we'll just report it to the audit committee.

Smith: What would they do? Green is the audit committee's chair, and remember, Green hired Mint. They've been best friends for years. Besides, Mint is calling all the shots now. Brown, the old CEO, is still on the board, but Brown's never around. Brown's even been skipping the board meetings. Nobody in management or on the board would stand up to Mint.

Kent: That's nothing new. Brown was like that years ago. Brown caused frequent disputes with Jones, CPA, the predecessor auditor. Three years ago, Jones told Brown how ineffective the internal audit department was then. Next thing you know, Jones is out and I'm in. Why bother? I'm just as happy that those understaffed internal auditors don't get in our way. Just remember, the bottom line is … are the financial statements fairly presented? And they always have been. We don't provide any assurances about fraud. That's management's job.

Smith: But what about the lack of segregation of duties in the cash disbursements department? That clerk could write a check for anything.

Kent: Sure. That's a reportable internal control deficiency every year and probably will be again this year. But we're talking cost-effectiveness here, not fraud. We just have to do lots of testing on cash disbursements and report it again.

Smith: What about the big layoffs coming up next month? It's more than a rumor. Even the employees know it's going to happen, and they're real uptight about it.

Kent: I know; it's the worst-kept secret at SCS, but we don't have to consider that now. Even if it happens, it will only improve next year's financial results. Brown should have let these people go years ago. Let's face it, how else can Mint even come close to the 30% earnings increase next year?

Required

a. Describe the fraud risk factors that are indicated in the dialogue.

b. Describe Kent's misconceptions regarding the consideration of fraud in the audit of SCS's financial statements that is mentioned in the dialogue. Explain why each is a misconception.

c. If you were performing "brainstorming" as part of the audit plan for SCS, what would be the biggest factors you would identify for audit consideration?

9-58 **(Control Deficiencies and Fraud, LO 6, 7)** The auditor should consider known internal control deficiencies as part of the process of planning the audit.

Required

a. The following is a list of internal control deficiencies that were found at a small manufacturing business. For each deficiency, identify the fraud risk and the extended audit procedures that should be performed.

   1. The individual collecting cash also reconciles the bank account.

   2. The person who approves cash disbursements has access to receiving reports.

   3. There is no locked security or security cameras over inventory held in a warehouse. The warehouse manager assumes responsibility for the items.

   4. Maintenance people use numerous small tools on the job. The company changed its policy from charging the maintenance personnel for the tools to expensing the tools.

   5. Payroll is handled by one person but is reviewed by the CEO when he signs the checks.

   6. Expense reimbursements for the CEO and CFO are only reviewed by themselves for approval.

b. Is the analysis of control deficiencies described a normal part of every financial statement audit or is it only a requirement when fraud is suspected? Explain.

9-59 **(Audit Software, LO 8)** Most CPA firms have responded to SAS 99 by performing detailed file validity analysis using audit software.

Required

a. Explain how audit software can be used in applying Benford's Law to identify inappropriate or unusual patterns in accounts.

b. Would the application of Benford's law be considered a normal part of an audit, or should it be considered only as a response to heightened fraud risk?

c. Explain how audit software might be utilized to identify unusual journal entries and analyze patterns in the journal entries for subsequent audit investigation.

9-60 **(Communicating and Reporting Illegal Acts, LO 9)** An audit client of the Peninsula CPA firm is extensively involved in defense contracting. During the past year, the Defense Department has conducted an ongoing investigation of the client for possible overbillings on governmental contracts. Most of these overbillings would be considered illegal. After an extensive investigation, it is determined that some of the billings were illegal. The client reached an agreement with the Defense Department whereby the client did not admit guilt but agreed to make restitution to the government of $7.2 million, to pay a fine of $600,000, and to establish procedures to assure that the government will not be overbilled in the future.

The client cooperates with the auditor and discloses the details of the investigation and settlement during the course of the audit. The auditor verifies the nature of the act and is convinced that the client's characterization is correct. The auditor discusses the need to disclose the nature of these transactions—the restitution and the fine—either as a line item or in a footnote to the financial statements. Management replies that it has adequately dealt with the situation by classifying the transactions as part of the cost of doing business with the government, that is, as marketing and administrative costs associated with governmental clients. Besides, management states, "The agreement reached with the Defense Department does not require the admission of guilt on our part. Therefore, classifying the costs as losses from illegal acts would be totally improper because there is no allegation or proof of illegality."

Required

a. How should the auditor respond to the client? Indicate explicitly your opinion on the necessary disclosure, if any, in the company's financial statements.

b. Should the situation be discussed with the auditor's attorney or the client's legal counsel (or both) before determining whether an illegal act that should be disclosed has occurred?

c. Should the settlement be discussed with the audit committee before determining the proper treatment on the financial statements? What should your response be if the audit committee believes these transactions do not require separate disclosure because the client did not admit guilt?

d. Would any of your answers change if the client admitted guilt and paid a smaller fine?

Ethics   9-61   **(Ethical Judgments and Fraud Risk Factors, LO 5, 6)** The following set of scenarios is adapted from "Test Your Ethical Judgment" by Kay Zekany, *Strategic Finance* November 1, 2007 and from the Institute of Management Accountants. Each of the scenarios is based on facts in the World Com fraud.

Required

For each scenario, decide which option (a) through (e) is most appropriate and state your rationale.

a. The facts indicate good business practices.

b. The facts indicate a scenario that is perfectly ethical but that does raise a "red flag" in terms of fraud risk.

c. The facts indicate a situation that is improper, but not fraudulent.

d. The facts indicate a situation that is improper and that raises a "red flag" in terms of fraud risk.

e. The facts indicate that fraud is present.

Scenarios

1. There was intense pressure to keep the corporation's stock from declining further. This pressure came from investors, analysts, and the CEO, whose financial well-being was significantly dependent on the corporation's stock price.

2. A group of employees is compensated well in excess of the guidelines of the company's approved salary and bonus

schedules allowable for their positions. However, the overall company pay schedule is appropriate and up-to-date and represents current market conditions.

3. The company closely guards internal financial information, to the extent that even some employees on a "need-to-know basis" are denied full access.

4. Managing specific financial ratios is very important to the company, and both management and analysts are keenly observant of variability in key ratios. Key ratios for the company changed very little even though the ratios for the overall industry were quite volatile during the time period.

5. The internal audit department interacts with the audit committee and board of directors primarily in terms of describing plans for upcoming projects and details on completed projects that emphasize operational effectiveness. However, internal audit primarily interacts throughout the year with the CFO. The CFO directs ongoing activities and is responsible for financial rewards provided to the internal audit department leadership and staff.

6. The CEO gives the internal audit department an operational audit task that has no substantive accounting purpose. The task is extremely time-consuming and diverts departmental resources away from normal activities.

7. In an effort to reduce certain accrued expenses to meet budget targets, the CFO directs the general accounting department to reallocate a division's expenses by a significant amount. The general accounting department refuses to acquiesce to the request, but the journal entry is made through the corporate office.

8. In an attempt to reduce operating expenses, the company capitalizes expenses to an asset account.

9. An accountant in the general accounting department is uncomfortable with the journal entries required to reallocate divisional expenses. He brings his concerns to the CFO, who assures him that everything will be fine and that the entries are necessary. The accountant considers resigning, but he does not have another job lined up and is worried about supporting his family. Still, he never voices his concerns to either the internal or external auditors.

10. The controller of the company was also uncomfortable with the reallocation entries but also does nothing to stop them. In fact, he encourages the questionable accounting entries.

11. Accounting records were either nonexistent or in a state of such disorganization that significant effort was required to locate or compile them.

Cases

9-62   **(Preliminary Analytical Procedures and Fraud Detection, LO 6, 7)** The following facts represent the audited financial statements of a public company for 2011 and 2010, along with management's representation regarding the unaudited amounts (i.e., the UNAUDITED column) and the auditors' projected amounts for 2012 (i.e., the PROJECTED column, which represents their expectations based on industry trends and information that they know about this company's likely financial performance). In addition, financial ratios are presented that summarize the relationships among the various financial statement line items reported in the balance sheet and income statements.

The company is in the telecommunications industry, has been in existence for ten years, and has had unqualified audit opinions throughout that time. The company has generally been successful in maintaining a competitive advantage in the industry, but there is always intense competition and maintaining that advantage (and associated profitability, etc.) continues to be a significant challenge. Assume that you are the audit senior who is considering the planning for this year's audit engagement.

Required

Part 1. Review the financial statements and document the financial trends that seem most important for this company.

Part 2. Describe the patterns in the data that concern you, and explain why those particular patterns cause you concern.

Part 3. Brainstorm to consider possible errors in the financial data that might be consistent with the patterns you identified in Part 2.

Part 4. Considering the results of Part 3, discuss the specific financial statement line items that should receive heightened scrutiny during your audit of this company.

Part 5. Consider the PROJECTED column. Why would it be helpful for auditors to make projections of unaudited data based on industry trends and analysis? How would an auditor actually make such a projection? What could be a downside risk in making such projections?

Balance Sheet (in thousands)

	PROJECTED 12/31/12	UNAUDITED 12/31/12	12/31/11	12/31/10
ASSETS				
Cash	1,046	1,146	1,956	1,339
Receivables	4,200	4,147	3,053	2,154
Less: Allowance	241	240	213	211
Net Receivables	3,959	3,907	2,840	1,943
Inventories	2,787	3,065	2,592	2,657
Other Current Assets	656	635	826	801
Total Current Assets	8,448	8,753	8,214	6,740
PP&E (Net)	27,116	26,869	25,877	23,850
Other Assets	2,400	2,413	2,690	2,556
Total Assets	37,964	38,035	36,781	33,146

**LIABILITIES AND OWNERS'
EQUITY**

Accounts Payable	3,710	3,750	4,093	2,882
Crnt. Portion L.T. Debt	1,637	1,624	1,534	1,355
Income Taxes	277	383	296	300
Tot. Crnt. Liabilities	5,624	5,757	5,923	4,537
Long-Term Debt	17,773	17,773	16,817	15,080
Total Liabilities	23,397	23,530	22,740	19,617
Common Stock	1,624	1,624	1,624	1,624
Retained Earnings	12,943	12,881	12,417	11,905
Total Liabilities and Stockholder's Equity	37,964	38,035	36,781	33,146

Income Statement (in thousands)

	PROJECTED 12/31/12	UNAUDITED 12/31/12	12/31/11	12/31/10
Net Sales	9,643	9,644	9,630	9,649
Cost of Goods Sold	6,875	6,963	6,828	6,851
Gross Profit	2,768	2,681	2,802	2,798
R & D Expenditures	212	163	150	128
S G & A	904	624	882	862
Profit from Operations	1,652	1,894	1,770	1,808
Other Income	6	6	5	5
Interest Expense	925	925	916	913
Other Expenses	9	9	11	8
Income before Inc. Taxes	724	966	848	892
Provision for Inc. Taxes	289	386	382	384
Net Income	435	580	466	508

Selected Financial Ratios

	PROJECTED 12/31/12	UNAUDITED 12/31/12	12/31/11	12/31/10
Current Ratio (Current Assets/ Current Liab.)	1.50	1.52	1.39	1.48
Quick Ratio (Current Assets Less Inventory/Current Liab.)	1.01	.99	.95	.90
Gross Margin %	.287	.278	.291	.290
Income before Taxes as a % of Sales	.075	.100	.088	.092
Net Income as a % of Sales	.045	.060	.048	.052
Inventory Turnover (Cost of Goods Sold/ Ending Inventory)	2.47	2.27	2.63	2.58
Receivable Turnover (Sales/Net Receivables)	2.44	2.47	3.39	4.96

9-63   **(Quality of Accounting, LO 2, 3, 6)** Dot-com companies grew rapidly in the late 1990s. Many opened up "shopping malls" through which they serve as a portal into several different companies. The SEC had expressed concerns about revenue recognition at a variety of dot-com companies. Explicitly, the SEC was concerned that some companies:

- Inflated their total revenue by "including in their revenue figures the total revenues for product sales when they merely are distributing products on behalf of other companies." The SEC felt the companies should recognize only the commission received on distributing the goods as revenue.
- Were booking revenue for "free services" provided to customers.
- Recognized revenue on bartered transactions in which they swapped advertising with other companies.

Required

a. Assuming that some of the items would not increase net income, what is the motivation for the accounting treatments described above? What is the management incentive to inflate revenues?

b. If the auditor believed the accounting treatments met GAAP but did not personally concur that they were the best GAAP alternative, what is the auditor's responsibility to communicate that judgment to other parties?

c. Would preliminary analytical review procedures have been effective in identifying the risks associated with revenue recognition as identified here? Explain.

d. Are the transactions described fraudulent financial reporting? Explain.

9-64   **(Fraud and Defalcations, LO 3, 5, 6, 7)** The following is a list of defalcations that have occurred within various organizations. You may assume that the amounts involved are material.

Required

For each defalcation, briefly indicate:

a. How the auditor would have identified the risk that led to the defalcation; that is, would the auditor have identified the risk primarily through (1) analysis of financial results, (2) review of industry trends, or (3) review of operational procedures?

b. How the defalcation would likely have been detected. Assuming the amounts are material, should most auditors have detected the defalcation? Explain.

c. What types of control procedures would have been effective in preventing or detecting the defalcation?

Defalcations

1. The treasurer of a small city also managed the city's pension fund. Over a period of a few years, the treasurer diverted a substantial amount of the fund's earnings to his personal use. Most of the money was invested in money market funds and certificates of deposit. To cover the diversion, the treasurer systematically under recorded income earned.

2. The purchasing agent of a company set up a fictitious vendor and periodically prepared purchase orders to the fictitious vendor. The agent then created bogus receiving reports and sent the receiving reports, vendor invoices, and purchase orders to accounts payable for processing. The fraud amounted to $125,000 a year for a company with approximately $12,000,000 in annual sales.

3. The social services workers of a state agency set up fictitious files for welfare recipients and paid them monthly support. Because the recipients were fictitious, the social services workers collected the checks and deposited them into a bank account and then transferred the amount to the accounts of the fraud perpetrators. All of the records are kept on computerized files.

4. A purchasing agent systematically paid higher-than-market prices for goods received from an important vendor. In turn, the purchasing agent received various perks from the vendor and kickbacks that amounted to more than half of the purchasing agent's regular annual salary.

5. The supervisor of a small manufacturing company and the payroll clerk colluded to add an extra person to the payroll. Time cards were approved by the supervisor, who split the nonemployee paychecks with the payroll clerk.

6. The branch manager of a bank manipulated the dormant accounts (of inactive depositors) and transferred amounts from those accounts to a fictitious account, from which he eventually withdrew the cash. All of the accounts were computerized. Monthly statements were sent to the customers, but all bank personnel were instructed to refer questions about account balances directly to the manager so he could show personal interest in the customers. He would then correct the accounts of any customers who complained.

7. The accounts receivable bookkeeper opens the mail and makes the cash deposit. Over a period of time, she has diverted significant funds to herself, covering up the diversion either by misstating the accounts receivable totals by improperly footing the accounts, recording fictitious discounts or returns for the amount of money diverted, or writing off as uncollectible the accounts of customers whose payments have been diverted.

ACL Case

9-65   **(ACL Fraud Case)** Do ACL Case 1—Fraud Case in the ACL Appendix.

9-66   **(Benford's Law Case)** Do ACL Case 2—Benford's Law Case in the ACL Appendix.

Academic Research Case (LO 6, 7)

Hoffman, V. B., & Zimbelman, M. F. (2009). Do Strategic Reasoning and Brainstorming Help Auditors Change Their Standard Audit Procedures in Response to Fraud Risk? *The Accounting Review 84(3):811–837.*

i. What is the issue being addressed in the paper?

ii. Why is this issue important to practicing auditors?

iii. What are the findings of the paper?

iv. What are the implications of these findings for audit quality (or audit practice) on the audit profession?

v. Describe the research methodology used as a basis for the conclusions.

vi. Describe any limitations of the research that the student (and practice) should be aware of.

Go to www.cengage.com/accounting/rittenberg for the Ford and Toyota materials.

Source and Reference	Question
	1. Obtain a copy of SAS 99 and read the appendices that list the risk factors associated with fraudulent financial reporting. (*Hint:* a Google search on "SAS No. 99 and fraud risk factor" should help you find the document.) You may want to review Appendix 1 of ISA 240 as it provides a similar list of risk factors.
Ford 10-K, Ford Def 14A. You may also find your analytical procedures results from the Chapter 8 Appendix to be useful.	**2a.** Use the fraud risk factor list as a checklist to review the Ford SEC filings. Which of the risk factors is present for Ford?
	2b. For each risk factor that you identify for Ford, describe an audit procedure or piece of evidence that you could use in your audit testing to determine if this risk factor actually relates to the presence of fraudulent financial reporting. HINT: Appendix 2 of ISA 240 provides examples of possible audit procedures to address risks of material misstatement due to fraud.
	2c. Assume that Ford or Toyota wanted to increase reported earnings this year but wanted to do so by changing accounting estimates. Identify three accounting estimates that could potentially be influenced by management's desire to show increased reported earnings.
	2d. Accounting Estimates. Many accounting estimates are, at least in part, based on a judgment call by the company. The auditor might disagree with the judgment call and will therefore come to a conclusion as to whether the audited financial statements need to be adjusted. If the auditor believes that an accounting estimate is materially misstated, • How does the auditor determine if the misstatement is fraud or if the misstatement is simply a poor internal control system or bad judgment by management? • How should the auditor's finding be reported to the audit committee if the auditor concludes the misstatement was due to: Bad judgment or poor internal controls over financial reporting? Fraud?

10

Auditing Revenue and Related Accounts

LEARNING OBJECTIVES

The overriding objective of this textbook is to build a foundation with which to analyze current professional issues and adapt audit approaches to business and economic complexities. Through studying this chapter, you will be able to:

1 Explain the concept of accounting cycles or processes and their impact on audit approaches and identify the accounts and relevant assertions in the revenue cycle.

2 Describe the approach an auditor would take to perform an integrated audit in the revenue cycle.

3 Identify risks to reliable financial reporting in the revenue cycle, including fraud risks and other risks related to proper revenue recognition.

4 Describe how to use preliminary analytical procedures to identify possible misstatements in the revenue cycle.

5 Describe why it is important for the auditor to develop an understanding of internal controls, identify controls typically present in the revenue cycle, and identify tests of controls used to test the effectiveness of controls in the revenue cycle.

6 Articulate and apply standard substantive audit procedures applicable to testing revenue accounts and assertions and explain how these procedures will be affected by the results of the tests of controls.

7 Articulate and apply standard substantive audit procedures applicable to testing accounts receivable accounts and relevant assertions and explain how these procedures will be affected by the results of the tests of controls.

8 Describe audit procedures for the revenue cycle that address fraud risk.

9 Apply the decision analysis and ethical decision-making frameworks to situations involving the audit of revenue cycle accounts and assertions.

CHAPTER OVERVIEW

This chapter illustrates the audit testing concepts developed earlier in the text by applying those concepts to an integrated audit of the accounts and assertions in the revenue cycle. In terms of the audit opinion formulation process, this chapter primarily involves Phases III and IV, that is, obtaining evidence about controls and obtaining substantive evidence about revenue cycle accounts and assertions. Sales transactions are always material to a company's financial statements because they are subject to manipulation and thus are always considered a fraud risk. Because of this, auditors must pay special attention to the control environment concerning revenue cycle accounts and carefully consider management's motivation to "stretch" accounting principles to achieve desired revenue reporting.

After considering the quality of internal control, as well as fraud risk factors, the auditor should have a good idea of where and what types of misstatements might exist in the account balances. The auditor must decide which substantive audit procedures to perform, how extensively those

The Audit Opinion Formulation Process

| I. Assessing Client Acceptance and Retention Decisions CHAPTER 4 | II. Understanding the Client CHAPTERS 2, 4–6, and 9 | III. Obtaining Evidence about Controls and Determining the Impact on the Financial Statement Audit CHAPTERS 5–14 and 18 | IV. Obtaining Substantive Evidence about Account Assertions CHAPTERS 7–14 and 18 | V. Wrapping Up the Audit and Making Reporting Decisions CHAPTERS 15 and 16 |

| The Auditing Profession, Regulation, and Corporate Governance CHAPTERS 1 and 2 | Decision-Making, Professional Conduct, and Ethics CHAPTER 3 | Professional Liability CHAPTER 17 |

procedures should be performed, and which accounts and account items should be tested. This chapter describes the basic revenue recording process, discusses risks in that process, identifies typical controls in the process that are intended to mitigate those risks, describes the types of revenue-related fraud, discusses an integrated audit of revenue cycle accounts and assertions, and identifies relevant substantive audit procedures.

PROFESSIONAL JUDGMENT IN CONTEXT

Need for Auditors to Be Aware of the Prevalence of Revenue Related Frauds

Studies of fraudulent financial reporting typically highlight the fact that the most common type of financial statement fraud relates to improper revenue recognition. In 2010, the Committee of Sponsoring Organizations (COSO) published a study that provided a comprehensive analysis of occurrences of fraudulent financial reporting that were investigated by the Securities and Exchange Commission (SEC) from 1988 through 2007. Sixty-one percent of the 347 fraud cases profiled in the study related to the improper recording of revenues. The revenue misstatements were primarily the result of fictitiously or prematurely recording revenues. The report describes the various techniques that were used by companies to fraudulently misstate revenues, as follows:

- **Sham sales.** To conceal the fraud, company representatives often falsified inventory records, shipping records, and invoices. In some cases, the company recorded sales for goods merely shipped to another company location. In other cases, the company pretended to ship goods to appear as if a sale occurred and then hid the related inventory, which was never shipped to customers, from company auditors.

- **Conditional sales.** These transactions were recorded as revenues even though the sales involved unresolved contingencies or the terms of the sale were amended subsequently by side letter agreements, which often eliminated the customer's obligation to keep the merchandise.

- **Round-tripping or recording loans as sales.** Some companies recorded sales by shipping goods to alleged customers and then providing funds to the customers to pay back to the company. In other cases, companies recorded loan proceeds as revenues.

- **Bill and hold transactions.** Several companies improperly recorded sales from bill and hold transactions that did not meet the criteria for revenue recognition.

- **Premature revenues before all the terms of the sale were completed.** Generally this involved recording sales after the goods were ordered but before they were shipped to the customer.

- **Improper cutoff of sales.** To increase revenues, the accounting records were held open beyond the balance sheet date to record sales of the subsequent accounting period in the current period.

- **Improper use of the percentage of completion method.** Revenues were overstated by accelerating the estimated percentage of completion for projects in process.

- **Unauthorized shipments.** Revenues were overstated by shipping goods never ordered by the customer or by shipping defective products and recording revenues at full, rather than discounted, prices.

- **Consignment sales.** Revenues were recorded for consignment shipments or shipments of goods for customers to consider on a trial basis.

(continues)

PROFESSIONAL JUDGMENT IN CONTEXT

Need for Auditors to Be Aware of the Prevalence of Revenue Related Frauds (continued)

Of importance to auditors is that the COSO study found that in several instances companies were able to falsify confirmation responses to auditors. In some cases, the falsification was the result of company personnel creating a variety of false documents. In other cases, the falsification was the result of company personnel convincing other parties to alter their confirmation responses. As you read through this chapter, consider the findings of the COSO study and the following questions:

- What fraud risk factors might suggest a heightened risk of the misstatement of revenues?

- What techniques are typically used by companies attempting to fraudulently misstate revenues?

- What controls should companies typically have in place to mitigate the risk of misstatement of revenues?

- How should the audit be adjusted when there is a heightened fraud risk and/or controls are not adequate?

- What substantive procedures should auditors use to test accounts and assertions in the revenue cycle?

- What concerns should auditors have about the value of evidence obtained through confirmations?

Source: The COSO study referred to above can be found at http://www.coso.org/documents/COSOFRAUDSTUDY2010.pdf

Introduction

Revenue and the related receivables account should be presumed to be high risk for most audits because these accounts are highly susceptible to misstatement. The auditor needs to understand the relationships present in the accounts and how to best approach an integrated audit of the related accounts and controls.

The Cycle Approach

LO 1

Explain the concept of accounting cycles or processes and their impact on audit approaches and identify significant accounts and relevant assertions in the revenue cycle.

Financial statements are made up of accounts, such as revenue or accounts receivable, that represent a summary of the company's transactions. Similar transactions that are linked by procedures and controls are often grouped together for analysis and are referred to as a cycle or process. Many accounting transactions follow a defined cycle. For example, transactions related to revenue begin with an initial customer order that flows through to an invoice and recording of a receivable and sale and eventually the collection of cash. The cycle or process concept helps the auditor visualize the income and balance sheet accounts related to most transactions and provides a convenient way to think about audit testing of internal controls and the related account balances. For a particular process, the auditor focuses on the flow of transactions within that process, including how transactions are initiated, authorized, recorded, and reported, and on points in the process where misstatement can occur and on controls that have been designed and implemented to mitigate those risks of misstatement. This understanding of the risks and controls within a process will help the auditor determine the particular audit procedures to use.

We use the terms *cycle* and *process* to refer to the processing of related transactions and their effect on account balances associated with the transactions. **Revenue cycle** transactions include the processes ranging from the initiation of a sales transaction, to shipping a product, billing the customer, and collecting cash for the sale or writing off of uncollectible receivables.

Overview of the Revenue Cycle

In the revenue cycle, the significant and relevant accounts typically include revenue and accounts receivable. The auditor will likely obtain evidence related to each of the financial statement assertions discussed in Chapter 7 for both accounts. However, for specific accounts and specific clients, some assertions are more relevant, and thus require more evidence, than other assertions. For many clients, the existence assertion related to revenue may be one of the more relevant assertions, especially if the client has incentives to overstate revenues. For accounts receivable, the more relevant assertions would likely be existence and valuation. For these relevant assertions, the auditor will need to understand the controls that the client has in place to address the risk of misstatement. The assertions that are determined to be more relevant are the assertions for which the risk of misstatement is higher and for which more audit evidence is needed.

The cycle approach recognizes the interrelationship of material account balances. Audit evidence addressing the existence and valuation of accounts receivable also provides evidence on the existence and valuation of recorded revenue, and vice versa. When examining sales transactions and internal controls over sales processing, the auditor also gathers evidence on credit authorization and valuation of the recorded transactions.

Sales transactions often serve as a basis for computing commissions for sales staff. Sales information is used for strategic long-term decision-making and marketing analysis. Thus, the accuracy of accounting in the revenue cycle is important for management decisions as well as for the preparation of financial statements. The accounts typically affected by sales transactions are shown in Exhibit 10.1.

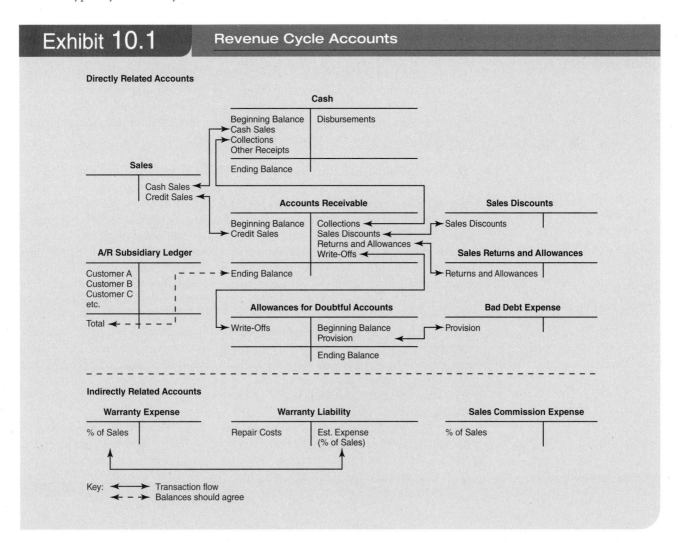

Exhibit 10.1   Revenue Cycle Accounts

The revenue process may differ with each client, and each client may have more than one revenue process. However, the commonalities of the revenue cycle can be used to develop audit programs for most revenue processes for most organizations. For example, a sales transaction for a shirt in a department store differs from a sale of construction equipment, and both of these differ from a book sale on an Internet site. The Internet sale and the retail sale most likely require cash or credit card for payment. The construction equipment sale most likely involves an account receivable, or a loan may be arranged with a third party. Some sales transactions involve long-term contractual arrangements that affect when and how revenue will be recorded. Some organizations generate detailed paper trails for sales documentation; others maintain an audit trail only in computerized form.

The Revenue Accounting System and Related Controls

Most sales transactions include the procedures and related documents shown in Exhibit 10.2, many of which represent controls designed to address the risk of misstatement in the revenue process. We use the term *documents* to apply not only to paper documents but also to electronic documents that provide evidence of the transaction and the responsibilities of each party to the transaction. The auditor should consider the nature of the document (electronic or paper) to determine the specific controls and types of audit procedures needed to verify the effectiveness of the control procedures. For example, a customer's purchase order, the bill of lading (signed by a representative of the common carrier), and a turnaround document (on which the customer writes the amount of payment) are paper-based documents with external validation attributes. On the other hand, a customer may have a contract specifying prices and quantities of goods for a year. Instead of a paper purchase order, the customer might submit a planned production schedule electronically to the company for delivery on a just-in-time basis. Shipments may be delivered and unloaded directly into the production line with no bill of lading, and the customer might pay once a month via electronic funds transfer based on production quantities. The control objectives are the same in both the manual and electronic environment, but the audit approaches and the control procedures differ markedly.

Receive a Customer Purchase Order   Processing begins with the receipt of a purchase order from a customer or the preparation of a sales order by a salesperson. The order might be taken by (1) a clerk at a checkout counter, (2) a salesperson making a call on a client, (3) a customer service agent of a catalog sales company answering a toll-free call, (4) a computer receiving purchase order information electronically from the customer's computer, or (5) the sales department directly receiving the purchase order. The nature and extent of documentation vary considerably across audit clients. For example, among the order takers just identified, it is possible that none of them will generate a paper document.

The sales order document should contain elements that provide a basis for determining that all transactions are properly authorized and completely recorded. These control procedures include requiring the use of prenumbered sales orders, authorization, formal approval for credit, a description of part number, sales price, and shipping terms of the products ordered, and an authorized billing address.

Even if a sales order is not physically generated, the underlying information should be recorded in computerized form. Consider a customer service agent for a catalog merchandiser taking an order over the phone. The information is keyed into a computer file, and each transaction is uniquely identified. The computer file (often referred to as a *log of transactions*) contains all the

Exhibit 10.2 Overview of Sales Process

Documents Generated	Major Processes	Additional Recording Media
1 Customer purchase order or sales order **4** **2** **3** Back order confirmation **5** Packing slip/pick ticket **6** Bill of lading **7** Sales invoice **8** Monthly statement **9** Turnaround document	1. Receipt of customer purchase order or generation of sales order based on customer inquiry. 2. Inquiry of current inventory status. 3. Generation of back order (where applicable and desired by customer). 4. Credit approved for shipment—noted by running credit program. 5. Shipping and packing instructions and documents prepared. 6. Shipping department records goods shipped and sends verification to billing for generation of invoice. 7. Invoice is prepared. 8. Monthly statements sent to customers. 9. Payment is received accompanied with the top of the monthly statement (called a turnaround document).	1. Summary of sales orders listed by salesperson is generated as a control over completeness of sales orders. 2. Acknowledgment of order sent to customer via EDI. 3. Computerized backlog file maintained to generate future shipments and billings. 4. Customer credit file is updated for additional commitment to customer. 5. Packing slips are packed with shipment. 6. Shipping information may be captured by computerized scanner as goods are shipped without the preparation of the documents listed. 7. Computerized recording of sales and accounts receivable and all other related accounts. 8. Report is generated from accounts receivable file. 9. All applicable accounts are updated including accounts receivable, customer credit history, and cash receipts.

information for sales orders taken over a period of time and can be used for control and reconciliation purposes.

Check Inventory Stock Status Many organizations have computer systems capable of informing a customer of current inventory status and likely delivery date. The customer is informed of potential back-ordered items as well as expected delivery date.

Generate Back Order If an item is to be back-ordered for later shipment to the customer, a confirmation of the back order is prepared and sent to the customer. If the back order is not filled within a specified time, the customer is often given the option of canceling the order. An accurate list of back-ordered

> **PRACTICAL POINT**
>
> If paper or electronic documentation is not consistently available to support the client's assertion that a transaction has taken place, the client may be unauditable. Some proof of the validity of client transactions must exist.

items must be maintained to meet current customer demand and future inventory needs. Appending a separate field to the individual inventory records to show back-ordered items usually does this.

Obtain Credit Approval   Formal credit approval policies are implemented by organizations to minimize credit losses. Some companies eliminate credit risk by requiring payment through a credit card. Other companies require that a check accompany the order and generally delay the shipment for the time it takes a check to clear through the banking system to assure that the payment is collectible.

Many industrial companies issue credit to their customers because it is a more convenient way to transact business. However, the company does accept some risk that it ultimately will not receive payment from the customer. There can be many reasons for nonpayment, ranging from (a) dissatisfaction with, or return of, the goods received or (b) inability to make the payments because of financial constraints. Thus, companies need to have a credit approval process that (a) evaluates the creditworthiness of new customers and (b) updates the creditworthiness (including time lines of payments) of existing customers. The credit approval might include a review of sales orders and customer credit information by a computer program that contains current account balance information and credit scoring information to determine whether credit should be extended to the customer. Most companies set credit limits for customers and develop controls to assure that a pending sale will not push the customer over the credit limit.

Prepare Shipping and Packing Documents   Many organizations have computerized the distribution process for shipping items from a warehouse. Picking tickets (documents that tell the warehouse personnel the most efficient sequence in which to pick items for shipment and the location of all items to be shipped) are generated from the sales order or from the customer's purchase order. Separate packing slips are prepared to insert with the shipment and to verify that all items have been shipped. Some companies put a bar code on the shipping container that identifies the contents. The bar code can be scanned by the customer to record receipt of the order.

Ship and Verify Shipment of Goods   Most goods are shipped to customers via common carriers such as independent trucking lines, railroads, or airfreight companies. The shipper prepares a bill of lading that describes the packages to be conveyed by the common carrier to the customer, the shipping terms, and the delivery address. The **bill of lading** is a formal legal document that conveys responsibility to the shipper. A representative of the common carrier signs the bill of lading, acknowledging receipt of the goods.

The shipping department confirms the shipment by (1) completing the packing slip and returning it to the billing department, (2) electronically recording everything shipped and transmitting the shipping information to the billing department, or (3) preparing independent shipping documents, a copy of which is sent to the billing department. The most common approach for verifying the shipment of goods and assuring that they will be billed properly is completing the packing slip and sending a copy to the billing department, but companies are increasingly entering shipping information on a computer screen, which updates a billing database.

Prepare the Invoice   Invoices are normally prepared when notice is received that goods were shipped. Controls should be in place to assure that the invoice corresponds to the sales order as to terms of sale, payment terms, and prices for merchandise shipped.

Send Monthly Statements to Customers   Many companies prepare monthly statements of open items and mail these statements to customers. The *monthly statement* provides a detailed list of the customer's activity for the previous month and a statement of all open items. The volume of transactions in many organizations often dictates that open account statements be prepared on a cycle basis. For example, if you have a MasterCard or VISA account, you may receive a statement around the 5th of the month with a due date of the 16th of the month; one of your classmates may receive her statement around the 20th of the month with a payment due date of the 29th of the month. If the auditor chooses to confirm the correctness of the accounts receivable by direct correspondence with the customer, information about when and how the client prepares monthly statements will be important.

Receive Payments   Control over cash receipts is often addressed separately as part of the cash receipts and cash management cycle. The proper recording of all receipts is crucial to the ultimate valuation of both cash and accounts receivable. Thus, as part of the review of internal control over account receivables, the auditor will normally review these control procedures to assure the completeness and accuracy of cash receipts.

Auditing Internal Controls and Account Balances—The Integrated Audit of Revenue

The auditor of a large public company must report on both internal controls and the financial statements. An integrated audit requires the auditor to test controls to enable the auditor to both (a) render an opinion on the effectiveness of internal controls and (b) determine the level of substantive audit procedures to perform. In audits where the auditor is not required to provide an opinion on internal controls, the auditor may still choose to test controls if such testing would allow for a lower level of control risk and reduced substantive tests of account balances. In both cases, the internal controls need to be evaluated.

Audit Steps for an Integrated Audit

This overview of the steps in an integrated audit builds upon the phases presented in the Audit Opinion Formulation Process diagram at the beginning of the chapter. While the process is discussed as a sequential step-by-step process, it is actually an ongoing iterative process in which the auditor is always assessing whether the evidence obtained from all sources is sufficient and appropriate and adjusting the audit plan to help ensure that sufficient and appropriate audit evidence is obtained. The audit steps associated with an integrated audit for the revenue cycle include the following:

Phases I and II of the Audit Opinion Formulation Process

1.   Continually update information on business risk, including the identification of any fraud risk factors noted during preliminary audit planning. Update audit planning for new risk information.
2.   Analyze potential motivations to misstate sales, as well as the existence of other fraud indicators, and determine the most likely method for sales to be misstated.
3.   Perform preliminary analytical procedures to determine if unexpected relationships exist in the accounts and document how the audit testing should be modified because of the unusual relationships.

> **PRACTICAL POINT**
>
> Gateway Computer was found at fault in an SEC investigation because it changed its credit policies but did not change the way in which it evaluated the allowance for uncollectible accounts.

> **PRACTICAL POINT**
>
> Most companies will have controls that reconcile goods shipped and goods billed on a daily basis. These controls may be manual or automated, and the nature of these controls will influence the nature, timing, and extent of controls testing the auditor will perform.

> **LO 2**
>
> Describe the approach an auditor would take to perform an integrated audit in the revenue cycle.

4. Develop an understanding of the internal controls in the revenue cycle that are designed to address the risks identified in the three previous steps, including the applicability of entity-level controls to the revenue cycle. This understanding will include a review of the client's documentation of internal controls.

Phases III and IV of the Audit Opinion Formulation Process

5. Determine the important controls that need to be tested for the purposes of (a) formulating an opinion on the entity's internal controls and (b) reducing substantive testing for the financial statement audit.

6. Develop a plan for testing internal controls and perform the tests of key controls in the revenue cycle. (For nonpublic companies, the auditor can choose to not test controls, but must determine where material misstatements could occur if controls are not present.)

7. Analyze the results of the tests of controls. If deficiencies are identified, assess those deficiencies to determine whether they are significant deficiencies or material weaknesses. Determine whether the preliminary control risk assessment should be modified (should control risk be assessed at a higher level?) and document the implications for substantive testing. Determine the impact of these deficiencies, and any revision in the control risk assessment, on planned substantive audit procedures by determining the types of misstatements that are most likely to occur.

   If no control deficiencies are identified, assess whether the preliminary control risk assessment is still appropriate, determine the extent that controls can provide evidence on the correctness of account balances, and then determine planned substantive audit procedures. The level of substantive testing in this situation will be less than what is likely required in circumstances where deficiencies in internal control were identified.

8. Perform planned substantive procedures (substantive analytical procedures and direct tests of account balances) based on the potential for misstatement and the information gathered about the effectiveness of internal controls. The substantive procedures will include procedures to address fraud risks. In completing substantive procedures the auditor will continue to assess whether the evidence obtained from all sources is sufficient and appropriate and the auditor may need to adjust the audit plan (either tests of controls or substantive tests) to help ensure that sufficient and appropriate audit evidence is obtained.

Example: An Integrated Audit of Sales and Receivables

The following is an abbreviated example of an audit approach to performing an integrated audit of internal controls and financial account balances in the revenue cycle. Following the example, we present conceptual details concerning each of the steps.

Consider the Risk of Misstatement in the Revenue Cycle (Steps 1 and 2)

As shown in Exhibit 10.3, the auditor continually updates information about the client's industry and its business plans, results from preliminary analytical procedures regarding the company's financial position, and potential deficiencies in internal control to determine the risk of misstatement and to plan the substantive tests of account balances. This exhibit is applicable to the audits of all cycles covered in this text.

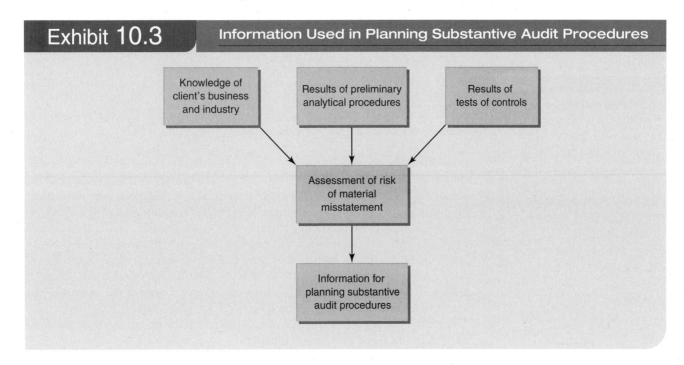

Exhibit 10.3   Information Used in Planning Substantive Audit Procedures

Inherent Risk—Sales

Sales transactions are routine for many organizations and do not pose an abnormally high risk. The sales at retail organizations such as Wal-Mart, for example, are routine and are controlled through computerized cash registers and detailed procedures reconciling sales recorded by the cash registers with deposits at the bank. However, for some organizations, sales may not be routine, or management may override normal processing to achieve a particular sales or profitability goal.

Revenue should be recognized only when it is realized or is realizable and earned. Though these concepts seem simple, they are often difficult to apply in practice. The auditor must understand the following:

- The entity's principal business, that is, what is the entity in the business of selling? For example, if a business sells phone services, but it enters into a one-time agreement to buy equipment from one supplier and then sell the equipment to another supplier, the auditor should question whether this is the client's business.
- The earning process and the nature of the obligations that extend beyond the normal shipment of goods.
- The right of the customer to return a product, as well as the customer's history of returning merchandise.
- Unusual contract returns related to sales transactions, including complex transactions with unusual rights of return.
- Contracts that are combinations of leases and sales.

Complex sales transactions often make it difficult to determine when a sale has actually taken place. For example, a transaction might be structured so that title passes only when some contingent situations are met, or the customer may have an extended period to return the goods. The FASB and IASB have addressed several of these complex issues. Some difficult audit issues include determining:

- The point in time when revenue should be recognized
- The impact of unusual terms, and whether title has passed to the customer

> **PRACTICAL POINT**
>
> The FASB and IASB are developing new guidance that may change the timing in which revenue is recognized.

- Whether all goods recorded as sales have been shipped and were new goods
- The proper treatment of sales transactions made with recourse or that have an abnormal or unpredictable amount of returns

The auditor can identify many of these risks when developing an understanding of business risks and the client's control environment and the types of transactions entered into by the client. The most relevant financial statement assertions for revenues are typically existence and valuation.

Sales with Abnormal Returns Companies that suddenly show an abnormal amount of merchandise returns most likely have problems that should lead the auditor to further evaluate the internal control over revenue and inventory. One example of such a problem was MiniScribe, a manufacturer of disk drives for personal computers. The company had a very aggressive, sales-oriented chairman who communicated specific sales goals to the financial press. Poor quality control led to a high rate of returns by customers. Rather than reworking the returned merchandise to fix defects, MiniScribe shipped the returned disk drives as new products. When the auditors discovered the situation, the company had to write down assets of more than $200 million.

Exhibit 10.4 reports examples of sales transactions that have high inherent risk and have caused problems for auditors.

Inherent Risks: Receivables

The primary risk associated with receivables is that the net amount shown is not collectible, either because the receivables recorded do not represent bona fide claims or there is an insufficient allowance for uncollectible accounts. If a valid sales transaction does not exist, a valid receivable does not exist. Alternatively, if the company has been shipping poor-quality goods, there is a high risk of return. Finally, some companies, in an attempt to increase sales, may have chosen to sell to new customers who have questionable credit-paying ability. The most relevant financial statement assertions for receivables are typically existence and valuation.

Other risks may be directly related to the sales contract. For example, a company may desperately need cash and decide to sell the receivables to a bank, but the bank may have a right to seek assets from the company if the receivables are not collected. Some of the risks affecting receivables include the following:

- Sales of receivables made with recourse and recorded as sales transactions rather than financing transactions.
- Receivables pledged as collateral against specific loans with restricted use. Disclosures of such restrictions are required.
- Receivables incorrectly classified as current when the likelihood of collection during the next year is low.
- Collection of a receivable contingent on specific events that cannot currently be estimated.
- Payment is not required until the purchaser sells the product to its end customers.

After an initial consideration of risk of misstatement, the auditor will use preliminary analytical procedures to identify other areas where there is a heightened risk of misstatement.

Perform Preliminary Analytical Procedures (Step 3)

Continuing with our example, assume the auditor performed a preliminary review of the revenue and accounts receivable accounts and found no unusual activity in either account. The following would be examples of expected relationships:

- No unusual year-end sales activity.
- Accounts receivable growth is consistent with revenue growth.

Exhibit 10.4	Examples of Complex Sales Transactions

DELIVERY

Company A receives purchase orders for products it manufactures. At the end of its fiscal quarters, customers may not yet be ready to take delivery of the products for various reasons. These reasons may include, but are not limited to, a lack of available space for inventory, having more than sufficient inventory in their distribution channel, or delays in customers' production schedules.

Question

May Company A recognize revenue for the sale of its products once it has completed manufacturing if it segregates the inventory of the products in its own warehouse from its own products? What if it ships the products to a third-party warehouse but (1) Company A retains title to the product and (2) payment by the customer is dependent upon ultimate delivery to a customer-specified site?

Answer

Generally, no. The SEC's staff believes that delivery generally is not considered to have occurred unless the customer has taken title and assumed the risks and rewards of ownership. Typically this occurs when a product is delivered to the customer's delivery site (if the terms of the sale are FOB destination) or when a product is shipped to the customer (if the terms are FOB shipping point).

INTERNET SALES

Company B operates an Internet site from which it will sell Company C's products. Customers place their orders for the product by making a product selection directly from the Internet site and providing a credit card number for the payment. Company B receives the order and authorization from the credit card company, and passes the order on to Company C. Company C ships the product directly to the customer. Company B does not take title to the product and has no risk of loss or other responsibility for the product. Company C is responsible for all product returns, defects, and disputed credit card charges. The product is typically sold for $200 of which Company B receives $30. In the event a credit card transaction is rejected, Company B loses its margin on the sale (i.e., the $30).

Question

Should Company B recognize revenue of $200 or $30?

Answer

The SEC's position is that Company B should recognize only $30. "In assessing whether revenue should be reported gross with separate display of cost of sales to arrive at gross profit or on a net basis, the staff considers whether the registrant:

1. Acts as principal in the transaction,
2. Takes title to the products,
3. Has risks and rewards of ownership, and
4. Acts as an agent or broker (including performing services, in substance, as an agent or broker) with compensation on a commission or fee basis."

Source: SEC Staff Accounting Bulletin: No. 101—Revenue Recognition in Financial Statements, December 3, 1999.

- Revenue growth, receivables growth, and gross margin are consistent with the auditor's expectations (based on the current year industry activity or prior year client activity).
- There is no unusual concentration of sales made to customers (in comparison with the prior year).
- The accounts receivable turnover is not significantly different from the auditor's expectations.
- The ratio of the allowance for doubtful accounts to total receivables or to credit sales is similar to the auditor's expectations.

The preliminary analysis does not identify any unexpected relationships and does not identify any additional risks. If there were unusual or unexpected relationships, the audit would be adjusted to address the potential misstatements.

Develop an Understanding of Internal Controls (Step 4)

Once the auditor has obtained an understanding of the risks of misstatement, including inherent risks and fraud risks, for the relevant accounts and assertions in the revenue cycle, the auditor needs to understand the controls that the client has in place to address those risks.

For illustration purposes, we are assuming that the entity-level controls, especially the control environment, have already been tested and any deficiencies have been considered in the design of substantive tests for the revenue cycle. For example, the control environment includes such factors as a commitment to financial accounting competencies and the independence of an audit committee. If either, or both, of these important control components are missing, the auditor must conclude that the risk of material misstatement in the revenue cycle is high and plan to do significantly more substantive testing of the accounts at year end. Further, deficiencies in these controls will likely influence the auditor's opinion on the effectiveness of internal controls.

Once having obtained an understanding of the control environment, the auditor shifts attention to the remaining components of internal control—risk assessment, control activities, information and communication, and monitoring controls. Although all the components of internal controls need to be understood, the auditor will normally find it useful to focus on significant control activities and monitoring controls. Remember, the auditor is required to gain an overall understanding of internal controls for integrated audits and other audits. Such understanding is normally gained by means of a walkthrough of the process, inquiry, observation, and review of the client's systems documentation and the understanding must be documented. In an integrated audit, this understanding will be used to identify important controls that need to be tested.

Identify Important Controls (Step 5)

Continuing our example, assume the auditor has evaluated the entity-level controls and has concluded that there are no significant deficiencies or material weaknesses in the control environment. The financial group is competent, the audit committee is independent and plays an important oversight role, and the company has an effective internal audit activity that periodically looks at internal control over revenue. Further, the client has documented and evaluated internal controls over revenue and receivables and has not found any significant deficiencies. Based on the understanding of the risks in the revenue cycle, the auditor identifies the following key controls for testing:

- Credit authorization and consistency of credit policies
- Updates to, and access of, the computerized price list for goods sold
- Checking of accuracy of quantities and prices for items shipped and billed
- Daily reconciliation of items shipped and items billed

In addition, the auditor is concerned about potential adjusting entries to sales and to receivables (outside of normal adjustments, such as writing off uncollectible accounts). The client has a control that limits the adjustments to authorized personnel, with a separate authorization of all adjusting entries over $25,000 by the CFO. The auditor decides that the controls over the journal entries also require testing.

Design and Perform Tests of Internal Controls and Analyze the Results of the Tests of Controls (Steps 6 and 7)

The auditor designs tests of internal controls and proceeds to test them using the following procedures:

- A sample of shipments is selected and traced to invoices to determine that the goods are billed at the proper price and quantities. The auditor notes shipment approval (control) and daily reconciliation of shipments and invoices. The test of prices verifies that the control over pricing is working properly (no overrides of prices). Each invoice is also examined to determine that credit approval has taken place.
- Access to the price table maintained in the computer is tested through an examination of the computer access logs. The auditor reviews the entries to determine if any accesses were made by unauthorized personnel.
- The invoices are traced into the general ledger, noting that all were properly recorded.
- The auditor also makes inquiries and verifies that there were no changes in the company's credit policies during the year.

No exceptions were found and the auditor concluded that internal controls were working as described. Accordingly, the auditor believes that the preliminary assessment of control risk as "low" is still appropriate. Further, the auditor does not believe it necessary to modify planned substantive procedures.

Perform Substantive Tests (Step 8)

Up to this point the auditor's information indicates that the controls are working effectively and the account balances should be fairly stated. However, the auditor cannot rely solely on control testing to provide evidence on the reliability of the account balances. Substantive procedures (either substantive analytical procedures, tests of details, or both) should be performed for all relevant assertions related to significant accounts. Because revenue is always considered high risk, the auditor performs the following substantive test of details as year-end procedures:

- Examines shipments made during the last 15 days of the year and the first 15 days of the next year to determine that they are (a) appropriate (normal terms, etc.) and (b) are recorded in the correct time period
- Sends a sample of accounts receivable confirmations to customers selected using MUS sampling
- Examines the client's allowance for uncollectible accounts for (a) consistency with past years, (b) subsequent collections, and (c) consistency with industry trends

The nature and amount of direct testing is adjusted for the strength of controls. The auditor could have chosen to perform substantive analytical procedures on the revenue account and, if this did not result in unresolved issues, the extent of the direct testing of account balances could be reduced. It is unlikely that audit evidence obtained from substantive analytical procedures alone will be sufficient evidence for the auditor. When risk of misstatements is higher, the auditor adjusts the direct tests to consider the type of misstatements that might take place.

AUDITING *in Practice*

PERFORMING APPROPRIATE SUBSTANTIVE AUDIT PROCEDURES IN THE REVENUE CYCLE

Numerous PCAOB enforcement cases have highlighted instances in which auditors have not performed sufficient procedures in the area of revenues and receivables. One enforcement action notes that although the client reported accounts receivable of approximately 10% of total assets, the auditors did not confirm accounts receivable despite the fact that auditing standards would generally require them to do so. In this case, the auditors did not perform any procedures to audit accounts receivable aside from obtaining management representations (see PCAOB Release No. 2006-009, PCAOB No. 105-2006-001).

Another enforcement action indicates that the auditors became aware of evidence suggesting that the client's revenue recognition practices may not have complied with GAAP. Specifically, the auditors noted that sales transactions recorded by the client were in fact consignments. Further, for sales that may have been valid, the client did not establish a reserve for estimated future returns even though it had a history of receiving significant product returns. Notwithstanding this information, the auditors issued an audit report stating that the client's financial statements presented fairly, in all material respects, the company's financial position, results of operations, and cash flows in conformity with GAAP (see PCAOB Release No. 105-2007-001).

Finally, PCAOB Release No.105-2007-006 notes a situation in which the audit team had assessed risk at a high level "due to events related to product sales and sales returns." The engagement team had noted that in some instances management's estimates regarding sales returns and reserves had not been sufficient to cover the actual returns. In response to this heightened risk, the audit plan indicated that the engagement team should perform "focused procedures" and increase their professional skepticism. The audit procedures that were performed generated audit evidence suggesting that the client's estimates of future returns were not reasonable; however, the auditor did not adequately analyze or follow up on that evidence.

These enforcement cases highlight the importance of auditors assessing the risk of misstatement in the revenue cycle and then planning, performing, and documenting the audit procedures performed in response to any identified risks. Even more importantly, auditors should not ignore evidence that is obtained and should appropriately follow up on that evidence if it suggests that misstatements in the financial statements are present. While most audits conducted in practice are of high quality, these cases serve to illustrate areas in which problems did arise and you should be alert to the possibility of encountering such situations when you enter the profession.

Performing the Integrated Audit of the Revenue Cycle

Consider the Risks Related to Revenue Recognition (Steps 1 and 2)

LO 3

Identify risks to reliable financial reporting in the revenue cycle, including fraud risks and other risks related to proper revenue recognition.

SAS 99, *Consideration of Fraud in a Financial Statement Audit*, states that the auditor should ordinarily presume there is a risk of material misstatement caused by fraud relating to revenue recognition. As noted in the *Professional Judgment Context* at the beginning of the chapter, a research study of over 300 cases of fraudulent financial statements issued between 1988 and 2007 showed that over sixty percent of the frauds related to the inappropriate recording of revenue. Refer to the *Auditing in Practice—Examples of Improper Revenue Recognition and Receivable Valuation* feature and note the wide range of methods used to inflate revenue and net receivables. Also note that some of the schemes did not affect net income, but the company was motivated to report higher revenues.

In addition, consider the implications for financial statement users of these fraudulent revenue schemes. Imagine that you are a banker who collateralized a loan based on fictitious receivables: If the company defaults on the loan, the collateral that you relied on is worthless. Or imagine that you are a stockholder of a company that reports a $450 million restatement of its income. The stock price will inevitably tumble dramatically, destroying the value of your investment. Consider the fraud that occurred at HBOC, an Atlanta based maker of

AUDITING *in Practice*

EXAMPLES OF IMPROPER REVENUE RECOGNITION AND RECEIVABLE VALUATION

Coca-Cola was charged with coercing its largest distributors to accept delivery of more syrup than they needed at the end of each quarter, thus inflating sales by about $10 million a year.

WorldCom's CEO, Bernard Ebbers, pressured the COO to find and record one-time revenue items that were fictitious and were hidden from the auditors by altering key documents and denying auditor access to the appropriate database.

HealthSouth understated its Allowance for Doubtful Accounts when it was clear certain receivables would not be collected.

Gateway recorded revenue for each free subscription to AOL services that was given with each computer sale, thus overstating pretax income by over $450 million.

Ahold (a Dutch company that is the world's second-biggest operator of grocery stores) booked higher promotional allowances, provided by suppliers to promote their goods, than they received in payment.

Kmart improperly included as revenue a $42.3 million payment from American Greetings Corp. that was subject to repayment under certain circumstances and therefore should not have been fully booked by Kmart in that quarter.

Xerox improperly accelerated $6 billion of revenue from long-term leases of office equipment.

Qwest immediately recognized long-term contract revenue rather than over the 18-month to 2-year period of the contract, inflating revenue by $144 million in 2000–2001. It also inflated revenue by $950 million by swapping network capacity with Global Crossing.

Rite-Aid sold 189 stores to JCPenney. Instead of booking $82.5 million as a one-time gain, it put that amount into an internal reserve account and used it to absorb future operating expenses.

Bristol-Myers inflated 2001 revenues by as much as $1 billion using sales incentives to wholesalers that then packed their warehouses with extra inventory (referred to as *channel stuffing*).

Lucent Technologies improperly booked $679 million in revenue during its 2000 fiscal year. The bulk of this, $452 million, reflected products sent to its distribution partners that were never actually sold to end customers (channel stuffing).

Charter Communications, a cable company, added $17 million to revenue and cash flow in 2000 through a phony ad sales deal with an unnamed set-top decoder maker. They persuaded the set-top maker to tack $20 onto the invoice price of each box. Charter held the cash and recorded it as an ad sale. Net income was not affected but revenue was increased.

Nortel Networks, a telecommunications equipment company, fraudulently manipulated reserve accounts during 2002 and 2003 to initially *decrease* profitability (so as to *not* return to profitability faster than analyst expectations) and to then increase profitability (so as to meet analyst expectations about the timing of a return to profitability and also to enable key executives to receive early "return to profitability" bonuses worth tens of millions of dollars). Nortel's board fired key executives and the company restated its financial statements four times in four years, including remediating a key internal control material weakness associated with the fraud.

Diebold, Inc., an Ohio-based maker of ATMs, bank security systems, and electronic voting machines, agreed to pay $25 million to settle SEC charges related to accounting fraud. The alleged schemes included fraudulent use of bill-and-hold accounting and improper recognition of lease-agreement revenue. When company reports showed that the company was about to miss its analysts' earnings estimate, Diebold finance executives allegedly used these schemes to meet the earnings estimate.

General Electric paid $50 million to settle accounting fraud charges with the SEC for revenue recognition schemes. In the fourth quarters of 2002 and 2003, GE improperly booked revenue of $223 million and $158 million, respectively, for six locomotives reportedly sold to financial institutions, "with the understanding that the financial institutions would resell the locomotives to GE's railroad customers in the first quarters of the subsequent fiscal years." The problem is that the six transactions were not true sales, and therefore did not qualify for revenue recognition under GAAP. It is important to note that GE did not give up ownership of the trains to the financial institutions.

Sources (respectively): Atlanta Business Chronicle, June 2, 2003; *The Wall Street Journal Online,* June 9, 2003; *Accountingweb.com,* July 14, 2003; *Accountingweb.com,* May 19, 2003; *The Wall Street Journal Online,* February 25, 2003; *The Wall Street Journal Online,* February 26, 2003; *The Wall Street Journal Online,* June 28, 2002; *St. Cloud Times,* p. 6A, February 26, 2003; *The Wall Street Journal Online,* February 8, 2001; *The Wall Street Journal Online,* July 11, 2002; *The Wall Street Journal Online,* February 9, 2001; *USA Today,* July 25, 2003; SEC Release 2007-217, September 12, 2007; cfo.com, Ex-Diebold CFOs Charged with Fraud, June 2, 2010; cfo.com, GE Settles Accounting Fraud Charges, August 4, 2009.

software, from 1996 through 1999. In that case the company's financial results reflected the fact that the officers of the company were fraudulently recognizing revenue on transactions that did not comply with GAAP. When the fraud was discovered, the company's share price tumbled from approximately $65 to $34 a share (a loss of about $9 billion in market value). HBOC was not able to sustain operations as an independent company and was soon acquired by another company.

Fraud Schemes in the Revenue Cycle

Fraud investigations undertaken by the SEC and PCAOB have uncovered a wide variety of methods used to misstate accounts in the revenue cycle. Fraud schemes include:

- Recognition of revenue on shipments that never occurred
- Hidden "side letters" giving customers an irrevocable right to return the product
- Recording consignment sales as final sales
- Early recognition of sales that occurred after the end of the fiscal period
- Shipment of unfinished product
- Shipment of product before customers wanted or agreed to delivery
- Creation of fictitious invoices
- Shipment to customers who did not place an order
- Shipment of more product than the customer ordered
- Recording shipments to the company's own warehouse as sales
- Shipping goods that had been returned and recording the reshipment as a sale of new goods before issuing credit for the returned sale
- Accounts receivable are aged incorrectly and potentially uncollectible amounts are not recognized
- Accounts receivable are written off improperly to conceal misappropriation of cash receipts
- Orders are accepted from customers with poor credit, but the allowance for doubtful accounts is not increased accordingly

The frauds listed here could not have taken place had there not been significant internal control failures, including, in many cases, management override of internal controls. The auditor needs to understand the risks of such misstatements and management's incentives for misstatement. The auditor also needs to understand the controls that the client has put in place to address these risks and, in an integrated audit, will test the operating effectiveness of these controls. With an understanding of the risks and the operating effectiveness of the controls designed to address these risks, the auditor can design substantive audit procedures to effectively test for the misstatements. For example, if a large increase in sales near the end of the quarter is noted, the auditor could use audit procedures to examine a large number of those transactions. A sample of sales invoices that show a "ship to" address to the company's own warehouse provides evidence of likely misstatement.

Criteria for Revenue Recognition

When to recognize revenue and how much to recognize are often difficult to determine. Auditors should refer to authoritative guidance, such as that provided by the SEC, the FASB, and the AICPA to determine the appropriateness of their clients' methods of recognizing revenue.[1] The basic concept for

---

[1] Examples of such guidance are *SEC Staff Accounting Bulletin: Codification of Staff Accounting Bulletins,* Topic 13: Revenue Recognition (now referenced as ASC 605); FASB Concepts Statement No. 5; *Audit Issues in Revenue Recognition,* AICPA, 1999; and AICPA Audit Guide, *Auditing Revenue in Certain Industries,* June 1, 2001.

revenue recognition is that revenue should not be recognized until it is realized or realizable and earned.[2] The SEC staff has determined that the following criteria must be met in applying this concept:

- Persuasive evidence of an arrangement exists.
- Delivery has occurred or services have been rendered.
- The seller's price to the buyer is fixed or determinable.
- Collectibility is reasonably assured.[3]

These criteria are not as straightforward as they might seem. For example, the criterion of *delivery* seems simple enough. Consider, however, a situation in which the seller has delivered product to a customer. The customer has the right to return the product and the buyer's obligation to pay is contractually excused until the buyer resells the product. In this case, revenue should not be recognized until the buyer has the obligation to pay, that is, when the product is resold.

The SEC generally does not consider delivery to have occurred until the customer has taken title and assumes the risks and rewards of ownership. Auditors may need to do research to determine when a client should recognize revenue and how to audit revenue. Some revenue recognition areas require special consideration. The following is a sample of some that have emerged in recent years:

- How much should be recognized as revenue when a company sells another company's product but does not take title until it is sold? For example, should Priceline.com (an Internet travel site) record the full sales price of airline tickets it sells or the net amount it earns on the sale (the sales commission)?
- Should shipment of magazines by a magazine distributor to retail stores result in revenue when delivered or await the sale to the ultimate consumers? Assume that the arrangement with convenience stores, e.g. 7-11, is that all magazines not sold can be returned to the distributor when the racks are filled with the next month's magazines.
- Should revenue be recognized in barter advertising in which two websites exchange advertising space?
- At what point in time should revenue be recognized when:
  - The right of return exists.
  - The product is being held awaiting the customer's instructions to ship (bill and hold).
  - A bundled product is sold. As an example, assume that a software company sells software bundled with installation and service for a total of $5,000. Should the total revenue be $5,000 or should the service element be separately estimated and recognized along with an attendant liability to perform the service work? What if the software entitles the user to free updates for a period of three years?

The auditor is expected to know enough about the client's transactions to be able to exercise informed judgment in determining both the timing and extent of revenue to be recognized. Although the judgments may appear to be subjective, the SEC and other authoritative bodies have set forth objective criteria they expect both auditors and managers to use in determining revenue recognition. See the *Auditing in Practice* feature highlighting the importance of professional skepticism when auditing revenue transactions.

> **PRACTICAL POINT**
>
> Revenue should not be recognized unless the company is satisfied that the customer has assumed all of the risks of ownership.

> **PRACTICAL POINT**
>
> Risks to proper revenue recognition are often addressed by the control environment component of the COSO Internal Control Framework. It consists of the tone at the top and the commitment of management to hire competent accounting managers and CFOs with independence and knowledge of accounting treatments. In an integrated audit, the auditor needs to test these aspects of the control environment to opine on the effectiveness of internal control and to design appropriate substantive audit procedures.

---

[2] FASB Concepts Statement 5, *Recognition and Measurement in Financial Statements of Business Enterprises*, paragraph 83.

[3] The *SEC Staff Accounting Bulletin: Codification of Staff Accounting Bulletins*, Topic 13: Revenue Recognition (now referenced as ASC 605) provides several examples of the application of revenue recognition criteria.

AUDITING *in Practice*

CHANNEL STUFFING—THE IMPORTANCE OF PROFESSIONAL SKEPTICISM

The timing of recording a sale is crucial. Criteria for sales recognition include the earnings principle is met, revenue is realized, and the principal revenue-producing activities are met. The SEC investigated Lucent Technologies because it was involved in "channel stuffing." Lucent would load up sales during the last few days of a quarter in order to make preset revenue objectives. The customers would take title to the goods (but not always delivery) because (a) they eventually needed the goods and (b) Lucent provided large incentives (good deals) to take the goods in advance. The SEC said the company was essentially taking normal sales from the next quarter (year) to show sales in the current quarter (year). The SEC argued that the earnings principle was not met and sales should not be recognized. Auditors will need to be professionally skeptical and make judgments on whether unusual amounts of end-of-quarter sales should be recognized as normal revenue.

Fraud Risk Factors—Revenue Recognition

There are many motivations to overstate revenue. For example, bankruptcy may be imminent because of operating losses, technology changes in the industry causing the company's products to become obsolete, or a general decline in the industry. Bonuses or stock options may be dependent on reaching a certain earnings goal. Or, a merger may be pending and management may want to negotiate the highest price possible. In the case of HBOC described earlier, the company had a strong and consistent track record of beating analysts' earnings forecasts. In addition, HBOC's management routinely made optimistic public announcements of the company's revenues, net income, and earnings per share before their auditor's audits or reviews were completed. These earnings expectations put enormous pressure on management not to "disappoint" the market.

These examples are but a few of the risk factors to which auditors should be alert regarding revenue recognition. Identifying and adjusting the audit to address these risk factors involves the following:

- Examining motivation to enhance revenue because of either internal or external pressures.
- Examining the financial statements through preliminary analytical procedures to identify account balances that differ from expectations or general trends in the economy.
- Recognizing that not all of the fraud will be instigated by management; e.g., a CFO or accounting staff person may engage in misappropriating assets for his or her own use (defalcation).

External Risk Factors External factors and other information that the auditor should consider include, but are not limited to, the following:

- Analyst expectations. The auditor needs to be aware of representations made by management to analysts and the potential effect of those expectations on stock prices.
- Industry trends. If the company's performance is significantly different from that of the rest of the industry or the economy, the auditor should be suspicious.
- Investigations. Government regulators such as the SEC conducting investigations of the client's accounting should highlight possible risks for the auditor to consider.

Internal Risk Factors   Internal risk factors should also be examined, including, but not limited to, the following:

- Management compensation schemes, especially those that rely on stock options and therefore current stock prices.
- Expiration of stock options. If stock options are expiring, there may be a tendency to attempt to boost stock price before the option expires.
- Complex transactions. The company engages in many complex sales arrangements when simple transactions would suffice (see the *Auditing in Practice* feature).
- Accounting is not centralized.
- Accounting personnel are not qualified for their positions.
- The CFO does not have an accounting background.
- Internal audit is weak or does not address accounting controls.
- Computerized controls are weak or difficult to understand.
- Aggressive history. The company has a history of aggressive accounting interpretations.
- Growth through stock acquisitions. The company uses stock to grow the company through acquisitions.
- Uninterrupted history of continued growth in earnings per share or revenue.

Unusual Financial Results   If a fraud is taking place, the financial statements usually will contain departures from industry norms and may not differ from the expectations set by management to inflate the price of a company's stock. Thus the auditor must take care to focus on a comparison of both past results and industry trends. Some of the differences the auditor might expect to see include the following:

- Revenue increases in the face of strong competition and competitor's new products
- Revenue increases that are not consistent with industry expectations or the economy
- Higher-than-average gross margins or other significant financial indicators
- Large increase in sales made near the end of the quarter

The auditor usually identifies these risks through a combination of review of industry data coupled with analytical review of the client's preliminary financial data.

PRACTICAL POINT

The first question asked in most court cases is, Why didn't the auditor suspect something when the client's results were so different from those of the rest of the industry? An auditor should be able to answer this question during the course of the audit.

AUDITING *in Practice*

RISKS RELATED TO UNDUE ACCOUNTING COMPLEXITY

WorldCom is a prime example of undue accounting complexity. Transactions were complex, but they were made more difficult to understand and audit by means of several factors. First, many of the accounting personnel were not sufficiently qualified for their positions. Second, the accounting function was spread over three or more places without a good rationale for the decentralization. Third, the decentralization was by function. Many companies have decentralization with a full accounting unit at various places, but WorldCom was not distributed that way; the property accounting function was located in Texas, while the revenue and line cost accounting were in Mississippi, and the equipment control was in Washington, D.C. Consequently, an accounting unit never saw the complete transaction. Only a few people at the very top were aware of the full accounting entries. Auditors should exhibit appropriate professional skepticism when encountering situations such as these.

LO 4

Describe how to use preliminary analytical procedures to identify possible misstatements in the revenue cycle.

Perform Preliminary Analytical Procedures (Step 3)

When planning the audit, the auditor is required to perform preliminary analytical procedures. Procedures such as the following can help auditors identify areas of potential misstatements and design appropriate audit procedures.

Comparison of Revenue Trend with Industry Trends

A client showing revenue growth when the economy or industry is in a downturn should cause the auditor to take a careful look at the client's method of recognizing revenue and consider the possibility of improperly inflated revenue.

Compare Cash Flow from Operations with Net Income

If a client is showing revenue growth and increased net income but is also showing negative cash flow from operations on the cash flow statement, the auditor should be skeptical and look for the possibility that accounts receivable and/or inventory may be inflated.

Other Analytical Procedures

Other analytical procedures can identify unexpected results that should be investigated. Ratio analysis, trend analysis, and reasonableness tests are three standard analytical tools that are routinely used on revenue cycle accounts. When considering the use of analytical procedures, the auditor should independently examine corroborating evidence rather than rely on management explanations of unexpected findings. Typical analytical procedures for the revenue cycle are described next.

Ratio Analysis   Ratio analysis is useful in highlighting account balances that are out of line or different from reasonable expectations. Ratios can be compared across time for a client, as well as compared with the industry ratios. The approach to ratio analysis is similar to what a financial analyst would perform in examining a financial statement. Some ratios focus primarily on revenue accounts, while others focus on receivables and the allowance account. Remember that if there is a fraudulent credit to revenue, there must be a fraudulent debit somewhere else in the financial statements. That debit is most likely to be in the receivables account. Some of the ratios the auditor might want to compute include the following:

- Gross margin analysis, including a comparison with industry averages and previous year's averages for the client
- Turnover of receivables (ratio of credit sales to average net receivables) or the number of days' sales in accounts receivable
- Average balance per customer
- Receivables as a percentage of current assets
- Aging of receivables
- Allowance for uncollectible accounts as a percentage of accounts receivable
- Bad debt expense as a percentage of net credit sales
- Sales in the last month to total sales
- Sales discounts to credit sales
- Returns and allowances as a percentage of sales

The following example taken from a court case demonstrates how ratio analysis may be helpful to the auditor. The company is a wholesaler selling to major retail chains in a competitive industry. The changes in ratios noted by the auditor were as follows:

- The number of days' sales in accounts receivable increased in one year from 44 to 65.

- The gross margin increased from 16.7% to 18.3% (industry average was 16.3%).
- The amount of accounts receivable increased 35% from $9 million to $12 million while sales remained virtually unchanged.

All of these ratios were substantially greater than the industry average. An auditor reviewing these ratios should carefully consider the business reasons for the changes and ask (1) Is there a business reason why these ratios changed? (2) What alternatives could potentially explain these changes? and (3) What corroborating evidence is available for potential explanations? The auditor should develop a potential set of explanations that could account for the change in all three ratios and gather independent corroborating evidence that either supports or contradicts that explanation. The auditor should rank order the potential explanations and then investigate to determine which one is the most appropriate. In this example, the company was engaged in a complicated scheme of recording fictitious sales. A number of other explanations were offered by management—increased efficiency, better computer system, better customer service, and so forth. However, only fictitious sales could account for the change in the gross margin, the increase in the number of days' sales in accounts receivable, and the increase in the total balance of accounts receivable that occurred when sales were not increasing.

Trend Analysis   Trend analysis is based on the assumption that current performance will continue in line with previous performance or industry trends unless something unusual is happening in the company. Unless a company has introduced significant new products or new ways of doing things, it is reasonable to expect a company's performance to parallel industry trends. For example, it might have seemed unusual to some that WorldCom could report continuing increases in earnings when none of its major competitors could do so. Could it be because WorldCom had products the other companies did not have; did they have superior management; or could it be that it was a company that should have merited greater audit skepticism and testing? Some basic trend analysis should include the following:

- Monthly sales analysis compared with past years and budgets
- Identification of spikes in sales at the end of quarters or the end of the year
- Trends in discounts allowed to customers that exceed both past experience and the industry average

The auditor should prepare a graphical illustration of the changes in trends as well as an analysis of the underlying economic data. If an auditor plotted monthly sales and noticed unusual spikes during the last 10 days of June and the last 15 days of December, that would alert the auditor to the need for more investigation of those transactions. The value of the information is enhanced if the analysis is separated by product line, division, geographical area, or some other subclassification.

Reasonableness Tests   Reasonableness tests are based on a simple premise: the auditor can gather a great deal of information about the correctness of an account by examining the relationship of the account to some underlying economic factor or event. For example, revenue from room rental for a motel can be estimated using the number of rooms, the average room rate, and average occupancy rate. Alternatively, the revenue from an electrical utility company should be related to revenue rates approved by a Public Service Commission (where applicable) and demographic information about growth in households and industry in the service area being served. As a final example, interest revenue could be estimated based on the average interest rate and amount of investments held by the client. The value of this analysis could be enhanced by

PRACTICAL POINT

In one audit, a skeptical auditor noted that the number of days in receivables for most clients is around 30. However, the auditor realized that this was an unusually large number for this client and decided to investigate further. The auditor found that the CFO of the client had embezzled several million dollars and had covered it up by recording fictitious accounts receivable. The auditor's knowledge of business procedures and professional skepticism helped uncovered the fraud.

PRACTICAL POINT

An auditor is more effective if he or she has a thorough understanding of the client's business, its industry, the economy, and, more importantly, the services the company must render to generate and sustain a growing customer base.

performing the calculations using monthly data or data based on the various types of investments the client has.

Regression Analysis The auditor can also use more sophisticated analysis for analyzing trends. One of the most powerful tools is regression analysis. Often, regression analysis is performed as a *time-series* analysis by examining trends in relationship with previous results. For example, it might be used to estimate monthly sales by product line based on the historical relationship of sales and independent variables such as cost of sales, selected selling expenses, or growth in total sales for the industry.

Another form of regression analysis is referred to as *cross-sectional analysis*. Rather than comparing relationships over a period of time, cross-sectional analysis is designed to compare results across a number of locations. For example, Home Depot and Lowe's own hundreds of stores—each with one of three basic store layouts and size. Cross-sectional analysis allows the auditor to identify any unusual store performance. For example, the auditor may identify potential problems by comparing sales per square foot of retail space among the stores, looking for those with significantly more sales per square foot than the other stores. More substantive testing should be performed at those suspect stores.

LO 5

Describe why it is important for the auditor to develop an understanding of internal controls, identify controls typically present in the revenue cycle, and identify tests of controls used to test the effectiveness of controls in the revenue cycle.

Linking Internal Controls and Financial Statement Assertions for the Revenue Account (Steps 4 and 5)

The auditor will gain an understanding of the controls that the client has implemented to address the risks associated with misstatements in accounts in the revenue cycle. As part of this understanding, the auditor will focus on the relevant assertions for each account and identify the controls that relate to risks for these assertions. In an integrated audit, this understanding will be used to identify important controls that need to be tested.

Existence/Occurrence

Controls for existence should provide assurance that a sale is recorded only when shipment has occurred and the primary revenue-producing activity has been performed. Sales transactions should be recorded only when title has passed and the company has received cash or a collectible receivable.

A related control is monthly statements to customers. However, the control should be such that the statements are prepared and mailed by someone independent of the department who initially processed the transactions. Further, customer inquiries about their balances should be channeled to a department or individual that is independent of the original recording of the transactions.

Unusual transactions, either because of their size, complexity, or special terms, should require a high level of management review, with the review serving as a control. Upper levels of management—and maybe even the board—should be involved in approving highly complex and large transactions. For normal transactions, authorization should be part of an audit trail and should not be performed by the same person who records the transactions. Credit authorization is often computerized and includes an update of a customer's outside credit rating and a status of the current amounts owed to the client. The credit policies should fit the organization. For example, clients that sell large special-order products should develop credit policies requiring (1) information on past customer payments, (2) current credit rating information from companies such as Dun & Bradstreet, and, in some cases, (3) a customer's audited annual financial statements and/or current interim financial information.

Completeness

Completeness control procedures assure that all valid sales transactions are recorded. Many transactions often go unrecorded because of sloppy procedures. In some cases, companies may choose to omit transactions because they want to minimize taxable income. Thus, the auditor still has to pay attention to completeness controls. Some controls that should be considered by the auditor include the following:

- Use of prenumbered shipping documents and sales invoices and subsequent accounting for all numbers
- Immediate online entry into the computer system and immediate assignment of unique identification by the computer application
- Reconciliation of shipping records with billing records
- Supervisory review, e.g., review of transactions at a fast-food franchise
- Reconciliation of inventory with sales, e.g., the reconciliation of liquor at a bar at the end of the night with recorded sales

Valuation

Implementing controls to assure the proper valuation of routine sales transactions should be relatively easy. Sales should be made from authorized computer price lists—e.g., the price connected to a scanner at Wal-Mart or the price accessed by a salesperson from a laptop. In these situations, the control procedures should assure the correct input of authorized price changes into the computer files and limit access to those files, including the following:

- Limiting access to the files to authorized individuals
- Printing a list of changed prices for review by the department that authorized the changes
- Reconciling input with printed output reports to assure that all changes were made and no unauthorized ones were added
- Limiting authorization privileges to those individuals with the responsibility for pricing

Valuation issues most often arise in connection with unusual or uncertain sales terms. Examples include sales where the customer has recourse to the selling company, franchise sales, bundled sales, cost-plus contracts, or other contracts covering long periods with provisions for partial payments. If these complex transactions are common, the company should have established policies and processes for handling them that should be reviewed by the auditor. Unusual transactions, if material, should be reviewed by the auditor as a part of substantive testing because there is usually not an established process to assure that these transactions are properly valued.

Once a transaction has been initiated and captured, it is essential that the accounting system contain adequate control procedures to verify that the integrity of the transaction is maintained; that is, no transactions are lost, added, or modified during the recording process. Control procedures include periodic reconciliation of input with output and procedures designed to generate prompt follow-up of missing or unusual transactions.

Internal Controls Related to Returns, Allowances, and Warranties

Abnormal returns or allowances may be the first sign that a company has problems. As an example, the problems with MiniScribe described earlier were first evidenced by unusually high rates of returns. In many other cases, companies booked large numbers of sales in the fourth quarter only to be followed by large numbers of returns after the end of the year.

Key controls that the client should implement for identifying and promptly recording returned goods include formal policies and procedures for:

- Requiring that contractual return and warranty provisions be clearly spelled out in the sales contract

PRACTICAL POINT

The auditor should always examine unusual amounts of sales returns after year end to determine the cause of the returns and the appropriateness of previous revenue recognition.

AUDITING *in Practice*

GUIDANCE ON MONITORING CONTROLS

The Committee of Sponsoring Organizations (COSO) published guidance on monitoring controls to help organizations more effectively and efficiently design and implement monitoring controls. Monitoring controls are designed to help assure that internal controls continue to operate effectively and that timely, corrective action is taken when controls are no longer effective in addressing the relevant risks. For revenue transactions, monitoring can be accomplished through separate evaluations that are not part of the daily operations of the organization, but are performed for the primary purpose of testing whether controls continue to be effective. Internal auditors are often the ones who conduct separate evaluations.

Additionally, monitoring can be accomplished through ongoing monitoring procedures that are built into, or are part of, an organization's processes. Ongoing monitoring procedures could involve supervisory reviews, trend analyses, and reconciliations. Consider the example whereby there is a risk related to sales personnel providing incentives to wholesale customers to pack their warehouses at year end with extra inventory that they do not currently need and allowing future credits for unsold goods. A control activity designed to detect whether such action has occurred could involve a policy whereby salesperson compensation is reviewed quarterly by the sales manager and adjusted if returns exceed a certain threshold percentage of sales. Monitoring procedures for this control could include the CFO participating in the review

(an ongoing monitoring procedure) and the audit committee directing periodic testing by internal audit (a separate evaluation).

There are a number of other monitoring controls applicable to revenue transactions, including the following:

- Comparison of sales and cost of sales with budgeted amounts
- Exception reports identifying unusual transactions or dollar amounts (such reports are investigated and corrective action is taken, if needed)
- Reports of transaction volumes that exceed prespecified norms
- Internal audit of the revenue cycle controls and unusual transactions
- Review by division and department management of internal controls and the quality of exception reports for management decision-making
- Computer reports reconciling transactions entered into the system with transactions processed by the system
- Monitoring of accounts receivable for quality, e.g., aging of accounts receivable by customer credit rating
- Reports of transactions that exceed previously stated edit rules
- Independent follow-up of customer complaints

- Approving acceptance of returns
- Granting credit or performing warranty work related to returned merchandise
- Recording goods returned on prenumbered documents that are accounted for to be sure they are all recorded promptly
- Identifying whether credit should be given or whether the goods will be reworked according to warranty provisions and returned to the customer
- Determining the potential obsolescence or defects in the goods
- Assuring proper classification of the goods and determining that the goods are not reshipped as if they were new goods

The company needs a specified methodology to determine whether a reasonable value exists at which the returned items could be recorded in regular or scrap inventory. Returned goods might be scrapped, sold through a company factory outlet store, or reworked and sold as repaired products.

Importance of Credit Policies Authorizing Sales

Formal credit policies are designed to assure the realization of the asset acquired in the sales transaction, that is, realization of the accounts receivable into cash. Control procedures should assure that the organization identifies the acceptable level of credit risks that it should undertake.

The following control procedures should be considered by an organization in controlling its credit risk at the level desired:

- A formal credit policy, which may be automated for most transactions but requires special approval for large and/or unusual transactions
- A periodic review of the credit policy by key executives to determine whether changes are dictated either by current economic events or by deterioration of the receivables
- Continuous monitoring of receivables for evidence of increased risk, such as increases in the number of days past due or an unusually high concentration in a few key customers whose financial prospects are declining
- Adequate segregation of duties in the credit department, with specific authorization to write off receivables segregated from individuals who handle cash transactions with the customer

In some industries, such as financial institutions, statutory rules are intended to minimize the financial credit risk to an organization. For example, banks and savings and loans often have limits on how much they can lend to a specific organization. In such cases, the auditor must be particularly alert to the client's procedures for identifying all borrowers that are related to each other so that the aggregate amount of loans does not exceed statutory regulations.

Documenting Controls

Internal controls can be documented in a flowchart, narrative, and/or questionnaire. Exhibit 10.5 shows an example of an internal control questionnaire for sales and accounts receivable. Each negative answer in the questionnaire represents a potential control procedure deficiency. Given a negative answer, the auditor should consider the impact of the response on potential misstatements in the account. For example, a negative response to the question regarding the existence of a segregation of duties between those receiving cash and those authorizing write-offs or adjustments of accounts indicates that a risk exists

PRACTICAL POINT

Every organization will identify its appetite for risk, including credit risk. Some companies sell primarily to high-risk customers at high rates. Such a strategy is appropriate, but it does mean that the auditor has to closely monitor economic trends that would affect the likelihood that the company's receivables are so risky that the bulk of accounts receivable might be impaired.

PRACTICAL POINT

The auditor can use generalized audit software to list all customers with balances that exceed their credit limit or to identify all accounts past due a certain number of days.

AUDITING *in Practice*

THE IMPORTANCE OF PROFESSIONAL SKEPTICISM IN AUDITING REVENUE

In 2009 the SEC initiated enforcement actions involving executives at a Silicon Valley Company named Tvia. The SEC alleges that Tvia's former vice president of worldwide sales, Benjamin Silva III, made side deals with customers and concealed this information from Tvia's executives and auditors. These side deals resulted in the company's fraudulently reporting millions of dollars in revenue from 2005 to 2007. Importantly, SEC documents note that when Silva joined Tvia in September 2004, he received options on 250,000 shares of Tvia stock, with one quarter of the options vesting after one year and the remainder vesting monthly thereafter for the next three years. In May 2005, Silva received additional options grants. Silva received a 50,000-share options grant, again with one quarter of the options vesting after one year and the

remainder vesting monthly thereafter for the next three years. Silva also received a 70,000-share performance-based options grant, which vested only if the company achieved $5 million in revenue in a fiscal quarter by June 30, 2006.

Auditors need to be alert to instances in which client personnel have significant financial motives to fraudulently overstate revenue. In these situations it is especially important to understand, and if appropriate, test the controls designed and implemented to prevent such behavior. In the event that controls are ineffective, the auditor needs to exercise appropriate professional skepticism and extend substantive testing to obtain sufficient and appropriate evidence.

Exhibit 10.5	Control Risk Assessment Questionnaire: Sales and Receivables

SALES ORDERS

Sales authorized by: (Describe the source and scope of authority, and the documentation or other means of indicating authorizations. Include explicitly the authorization of prices for customers.)

_____

_____

Sales orders prepared by, or entered into the system by:

_____

_____

Individuals authorized to change price tables: (Indicate specific individuals and their authority to change prices on the system and the methods used to verify the correctness of changes.)

_____

_____

Existence of major contracts with customers that might merit special attention during the course of the audit: (Describe any major contracts and their terms.)

_____

_____

Restrictions on access to computer files for entering or changing orders: (Describe access control systems and indicate whether we have tested them in conjunction with our review of data processing general controls.)

_____

_____

	Check (x) one:	
	Yes	**No**
1. Are orders entered by individuals who do not have access to the goods being shipped?	_____	_____
2. Are orders authorized by individuals who do not have access to the goods being shipped?	_____	_____
3. Are batch and edit controls used effectively on this application? If so, describe the controls.	_____	_____
4. Are sales invoices prenumbered? Is the sequence of prenumbered documents independently accounted for?	_____	_____
5. Are control totals and reconciliations used effectively to ensure that all items are recorded and that subsidiary files are updated at the same time invoices are generated? If so, describe.	_____	_____
6. Do procedures exist to ensure that the current credit status of a customer is checked before an order is shipped? If so, describe.	_____	_____
7. Are price lists stored in the computer independently reconciled to authorized prices by the marketing manager or someone in the marketing manager's office?	_____	_____
8. Are duties segregated such that the personnel receiving cash differ from the personnel authorized to make account write-offs or adjustments of accounts?	_____	_____

that an individual could take cash receipts and cover up the theft by writing off a customer's balance. Unless another control compensates for this weakness, the auditor should consider the risk of that specific misstatement in designing the audit program for direct tests of the account balance. Although questionnaires have been used extensively, they are being replaced by control matrices, flowcharts, and documented walkthroughs of processes.

Exhibit 10.6 presents a partially completed control matrix for contract revenue that links the risk of misstatement to the client's control and provides a means for the auditor to document the testing approach and testing results.

Design and Perform Tests of Internal Controls and Analyze the Results of the Tests of Controls (Steps 6 and 7)

Typical tests of controls include inquiry of personnel performing the control, observation of the control being performed, examination of documentation confirming that the control has been performed, and reperformance of the control by the individual testing the control. As an example, in the sales cycle, there may be a control that includes reconciliation between the sales subledger and the general ledger. The approaches to testing the reconciliation control could involve one or more of the following, listed in order of providing least persuasive evidence to most persuasive evidence:

- *Inquiry:* Talk with the personnel who perform the control about the procedures and processes involved in the reconciliation.
- *Observation:* Observe the entity personnel performing the reconciliation.
- *Examination:* Review the documentation supporting completion of the reconciliation.
- *Reperformance:* Perform the reconciliation and agree to the reconciliation completed by the entity personnel.

The auditor uses professional judgment to determine the appropriate types of tests of controls to perform. However, inquiry alone is generally not sufficient evidence and would typically be supplemented with observation, examination, and/or reperformance.

PRACTICAL POINT

Public companies must document their controls to meet the reporting obligations of Sarbanes-Oxley Section 404. The documentation generally consists of matrices, narratives, and flowcharts of the process. The documentation is important for training company personnel and can be used by auditors to understand the design of a client's controls.

Exhibit 10.6	Partially Completed Controls Matrix for Contract Revenue

Control Description	Risk of Misstatement— Relevant F/S Assertion (s)	Testing Approach (Nature of Testing)	Timing of Testing	Extent of Testing	Testing Results (including deficiencies)
A revenue recognition review is performed by the revenue accountant before revenue is recorded.	The risks are that revenue will be recorded before the criteria for recognition of revenue have been met or that revenue will be recorded at the incorrect amount. · Valuation · Existence	· Re-performance of analyses performed by revenue accountant.	Year end		

Note: The matrix is intended as a partial illustration. The matrix would typically be linked to a supporting flowchart that would detail the key controls related to contract review, and all key controls would be included in the matrix.

PRACTICAL POINT

The auditor must test the controls if expressing an opinion on internal controls over financial reporting. The selection of controls to test and the audit procedures are the same as described here for testing the effectiveness of controls in operation.

Examples of testing procedures in the sales cycle include the following:

- *Manually reviewing evidence of control operation*—Take a sample of recorded transactions and determine that the prices agree with authorized prices.
- *Computerized testing of computer controls*—Test controls used to limit access to the computer files, select a number of prices in the system, and reconcile to preauthorized price changes.
- *Testing of monitoring controls*—Management should have controls in place to assist in monitoring proper prices, e.g., gross profit by product line. Management should investigate incidences that deviate from expected results. The auditor will inquire of management personnel who performed these procedures and will examine documentation indicating that management has performed these procedures.

The auditor must decide which approach or combination of approaches provides the best evidence at the least cost. Many auditors use the first approach by taking a sample of transactions and determining that they had been recorded at authorized prices. However, such a procedure is only an indirect test of the control. The auditor will also have to determine that the price used has been properly authorized.

Exhibit 10.7 presents an overview of various controls that might be considered to satisfy specific control objectives, how the controls might be tested, and the audit implication if controls are not working. Note that the tests of controls include selecting samples of transactions to vouch back to supporting documents, reviewing monitoring controls, testing computer access controls, using audit software to match documents and look for gaps or duplicate document numbers, reviewing customer complaints, reviewing documents such as reconciliations and management reports noting timely action taken, and reviewing sales contracts.

Perform Substantive Tests in the Revenue Cycle (Step 8)

Planning for Substantive Testing in the Revenue Cycle

PRACTICAL POINT

For companies attempting to raise capital or expand operations, high sales revenue is useful in convincing lenders and investors to help with these goals. In these situations, the auditor should carefully review and evaluate key sales transactions and should be particularly skeptical of large, unusual, or complex transactions, especially those recorded near year end.

Audit objectives and the related financial statement assertions provide the framework for the development of audit programs in the revenue cycle. Audit evidence addresses the assertions in the context of the general planning factors discussed in Chapter 7 on audit evidence for testing account balances. The audit objectives, related assertions, and typical substantive audit tests for sales and accounts receivable are shown in Exhibit 10.8. The audit objectives are directly derived from the assertions framework. Further, the audit procedures show an integration of tests of transaction processing, substantive analytical procedures, direct tests of the sales and receivables balances, and an integration of evidence derived from related accounts (accounts receivable evidence is applicable to sales assertions, and vice versa). The specific audit procedures to be selected (including the timing and extent of the procedures) depend on evidence the auditor has obtained regarding the risk of material misstatement, including the effectiveness of the internal controls.

Substantive Tests of Revenue

LO 6

Articulate and apply standard substantive audit procedures applicable to testing revenue accounts and assertions and explain how these procedures will be affected by the results of the tests of controls.

The auditor must obtain an understanding of the client's revenue recognition approaches, making sure they are in accordance with GAAP and are properly applied to revenue transactions. Other specific tests follow the assertions developed earlier in the text. The timing and extent of tests depend on the auditor's approach to the integrated audit and the quality of the client's internal control. If the tests of controls suggest that the client's controls related to revenue are effective, the auditor may be able to reduce the extent of substantive testing, perform more testing at an interim date, or use less costly testing procedures. Audit software can assist in many of the tests.

Exhibit 10.7   Control Examples and Tests

Objective	Examples of Controls	How Control Would be Tested	Implications if Control Not Working
1. Recorded transactions are authorized and actually occurred.	a. Sales recorded only with valid customer order and shipping document.	a. Sample recorded sales transactions and vouch back to source documents. Use generalized audit software to match sales with electronic shipping document or customer order.	a. Recorded sales may not have occurred. Extend accounts receivable confirmation work and review of subsequent collections.
	b. Credit is approved before shipment.	b. Use ACL to determine each customer's balance and compare with its credit limit.	b. Receivables may not be collectible. Expand confirmation work and review of subsequent collections.
2. Sales are recorded in the correct accounting period.	a. Computer records sale upon entry of customer order and shipping information. Transactions entered, but not yet processed, are identified for an exception report and followed up.	a. Review monitoring controls (e.g., management's review of transactions entered into the system and not shipped and billed).	a. Company may have unrecorded sales transactions. Discuss with management to determine if it has plans to bill the sales.
	b. Monthly statements are sent to customers. A group independent of those recording the transactions receives and follows up complaints.	b. Review nature of complaints received. Investigate to determine if there is a pattern.	b. Sales may be recorded in the wrong year. Expand sales cutoff testing.
3. All sales are recorded.	a. Prenumbered shipping documents and invoices which are periodically accounted for.	a. Review reconciliations to determine that control is working.	a–c. Expand cutoff tests at year-end to determine that all transactions are recorded in the correct period.
	b. Online input of transactions and independent logging.	b. Use online computer techniques such as ITF to verify transaction trails.	
	c. Monitoring: transactions are reviewed, compared with budgets, and differences are investigated.	c. Review management reports and evidence of actions taken.	
4. Sales are accurately recorded.	a. Sales price comes from authorized sales price list maintained on the computer.	a. Test access controls. Take a sample of recorded sales invoices and trace price back to authorized list.	a. Accounts receivable may be over- or understated due to pricing errors. Expand confirmation and subsequent collection procedures.
5. Sales are correctly classified.	a. Chart of accounts is up to date and used.	a. Take a sample of transactions and trace to general ledger to see if properly classified.	a. Expand test of sales and receivables to determine that all items represent bona fide contracts and not consignment sales or sale of operating assets.
	b. Computer program is tested before implementation.	b. When testing general controls, determine that controls over program changes are working.	b. Expand confirmations to customers.

Exhibit 10.8   Relationships Between Audit Assertions and Substantive Tests—Accounts Receivable and Sales

Audit Objective (Assertion)	Substantive Test
Existence/occurrence: Recorded sales and accounts receivable are valid.	1. Perform substantive analytical procedures. 2. Trace sales invoices to customer orders and bills of lading. 3. Confirm balances or unpaid invoices with customers. 4. Examine subsequent collections as evidence that the sale existed. 5. Scan sales journal for duplicate entries.
Completeness: All sales are recorded.	1. Perform substantive analytical procedures. 2. Trace bills of lading to sales invoice and sales journal. 3. Account for sequence of sales invoices in sales journal.
Rights/obligations: Pledged, discounted, assigned, and related-party accounts receivable are properly accounted for in accordance with GAAP.	1. Inquire of management. 2. Review trial balance of accounts receivable for related parties. 3. Review loan agreements and minutes of board meetings.
Valuation/allocation: Sales and accounts receivable are properly valued and recorded in the correct period. Revenue has been recognized in accordance with GAAP.	1. Verify clerical accuracy of sales invoices and agreement of sales invoices with supporting documents. 2. Trace sales invoices to sales journal and customer's ledger. 3. Confirm balances or unpaid invoices with customers. 4. Foot sales journal and accounts receivable trial balance and reconcile accounts receivable trial balance with control account. 5. Review adequacy of the allowance for doubtful accounts. 6. Perform sales cutoff test.
Presentation/disclosure: Pledged, discounted, assigned, and related-party accounts receivable are properly disclosed. Revenue recognition policies have been properly disclosed.	1. Obtain confirmations from banks and other financial institutions. 2. Inquire of management. 3. Review work performed in other audit areas. 4. Review revenue recognition policies for appropriateness and consistency.

Prior to performing any direct tests of the revenue account, the auditor may choose to perform substantive analytical procedures. If the results of the substantive analytical procedures suggest that the revenue account is reasonably stated, the auditor may be able to reduce the amount of direct testing performed. For example, the auditor may perform a substantive analytic test of interest revenue using a reasonableness test that includes developing an expectation of the client's interest revenue. The expectation would be based on the amount of investments and the interest rate that the client is earning. If the expectation is within an acceptable threshold of the amount recorded by the client, the auditor may be able to reduce the amount of detail testing. However, with most revenue accounts, standard direct tests of the account balances will be performed.

Existence/Occurrence and Valuation   The existence and valuation assertions are usually the most critical for revenue accounts. Vouching a sample of recorded sales transactions back to customer orders and evaluating the quality of evidence of shipment provides support for the assertion that they actually exist. The auditor should compare the quantities billed and shipped with customer orders and verify the clerical accuracy of the sales invoices to provide assurance on valuation. The absence of these supporting documents or evidence of tampering with shipment dates should cause the auditor to consider the possibility of fraud.

Special care should be given to sales recorded just before the end of each fiscal year to be sure that sales have not been inflated by shipping more than the customer ordered. Audit software can be used to identify duplicate recording of sales invoices. Audit software can also select the sample and may be able to compare the detail with the supporting electronic documents. Audit software can also check the clerical accuracy of the invoices and foot the sales journal.

Cutoff Issues   Establishing the proper cutoff for sales transactions is important to assuring the existence and completeness of the revenue transactions in any given period. Procedures applied to sales, sales returns, and cash receipts transactions selected from those recorded during the cutoff period to provide evidence as to whether the transactions have been recorded in the proper period are called **cutoff tests**. The **cutoff period** is usually several days before and after the balance sheet date.

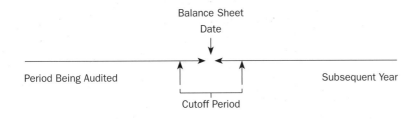

The greatest risk of recording transactions in the wrong period occurs during the cutoff period. The extent of cutoff tests depends on the auditor's assessment of the effectiveness of the client's cutoff controls. If the client has strong controls to assure that transactions are recorded in the correct period, the auditor can minimize such testing. However, it should be emphasized that controls can be overridden and that auditors have historically found a high degree of risk related to recording sales transactions in the correct period.

The following items can be examined to determine whether a proper cutoff has been achieved:

Cutoff Test of	Items to Examine
Sales	Shipping documents and related recorded sales
Sales returns	Receiving reports and related credits to customer accounts
Cash receipts	Deposits per books and per bank, cash on hand at year end

For high-risk clients, the auditor should normally be at the client's location at year end to record the last shipping record, receiving record, and cash and checks ready for deposit for later cutoff testing.

Sales Cutoff   Sales cutoff can be tested in two ways. First, a sample of sales transactions can be selected from the cutoff period to determine the correct time period of recording. The auditor can determine whether the sales were recorded in the correct period by looking at the shipping terms and shipment dates. The auditor may also want to examine the sales contracts to determine the existence of terms that might indicate that the recording of the sale should be postponed; e.g., the customer's right of return (and a high probability of return), the existence of additional performance by the seller, the probability of collection based on some future event (contingency), or the existence of an unusually low probability of collection. Second, if reliable shipping dates are stored electronically, generalized audit software can be used to identify any sales recorded in the wrong period.

PRACTICAL POINT

The extent of cutoff tests may be significantly less in an integrated audit where there is strong evidence that internal controls over shipments are designed and operating effective.

PRACTICAL POINT

Auditors can use generalized audit software to compare billing and shipping dates for recorded transactions and to highlight all items where the shipment date was later on in a different period.

Sales Returns Cutoff   The client should document merchandise returned by customers using receiving reports showing the date, description, condition, and quantity of the merchandise. The auditor can select some of the receiving reports issued during the cutoff period and determine whether the credit was recorded in the correct period.

Completeness   The most important control to assure completeness is pre-numbered shipping and billing documents (even if assigned by the computer). Selecting a sample of shipping documents and tracing them into the sales journal tests for completeness. The auditor can also use audit software to look for gaps in the recorded sales invoice numbers and verify that the missing numbers are appropriate and do not represent unrecorded sales. For example, the gaps may be caused by voided documents or by using different numbers at different locations. In addition, analytical procedures, such as comparing monthly sales by product line with prior periods, may be used. The results may raise the auditor's suspicion that some sales are missing or that sales have been artificially inflated.

Substantive Tests of Accounts Receivable

LO 7

Articulate and apply standard substantive audit procedures applicable to testing accounts receivable accounts and relevant assertions and explain how these procedures will be affected by the results of the tests of controls.

As with planning substantive tests for the revenue accounts, the auditor will consider the results of any tests of controls related to accounts receivable and will then design substantive tests to determine that receivables exist, belong to the client, are complete, are properly valued, and are appropriately presented and disclosed. Although each audit is unique, the auditor most likely perform some standardized audit procedures, such as obtaining and evaluating an aging of accounts receivable, confirming receivables with customers, performing cut-off tests, and reviewing subsequent collections of receivables.

Aging Accounts Receivable   A starting point for the auditor is obtaining a copy of a detailed aged accounts receivable trial balance from the client, manually preparing a trial balance, or using generalized audit software to assist in developing aging information and identifying old outstanding balances (see Exhibit 10.9 for an example of an aged trial balance). A detailed trial balance lists each customer's balance or unpaid invoice with columns to show those that are current, 30 days overdue, 60 days, and so on.

If the client prepared the trial balance, it should be tested for mathematical and aging accuracy to be sure that it is a complete representation of the recorded accounts receivable balance that will appear on the balance sheet. It should be footed and checked for agreement with the general ledger, and the aging should be tested to be sure that the client's personnel or computer program prepared it correctly. Credit balances can also be identified and, if significant, reclassified as a liability.

The aged trial balance can be used to:

- Agree the detail to the balance in the control account
- Select customer balances for confirmation
- Identify amounts due from officers, employees, or other related parties or any nontrade receivables that need to be separately disclosed in the financial statements
- Help determine the reasonableness of the allowance for doubtful accounts by identifying past-due balances

Existence   The timing and nature of audit tests depend directly on the auditor's assessment of the risk of material misstatement for this assertion. The most widely used auditing procedure is to ask the client's customers to confirm the existence and amount of their indebtedness to the client. It is important to realize that though existence is necessary for correct valuation, it does not necessarily assure correct valuation; e.g., a customer might acknowledge the existence of

Exhibit 10.9		Accounts Receivable Aging				
Name	**Balance**	**Current**	**30–60**	**61–90**	**91–120**	**Over 120**
Alvies	154,931	154,931				
Basch	71,812		71,812			
Carlson	115,539	115,539				
Draper	106,682	106,682				
Ernst	60,003			60,003		
Faust	90,907	90,907				
Gerber	241,129	211,643	29,486			
Hal	51,516	51,516				
Harv	237,881	237,881				
Kaas	18,504				18,504	
Kruze	44,765	44,765				
Lere	28,937	28,937				
Misty	210,334	210,334				
Mooney	216,961	216,961				
Otto	273,913	273,913				
Paggen	209,638	209,638				
Quast	88,038					88,038
Rauch	279,937	279,937				
Sundby	97,898	97,898				
Towler	96,408	85,908		10,500		
Zook	31,886	31,886				
	.	.				
	.	.				
	.	.				
Nough	245,927	245,927				
Totals	2,973,546	2,695,203	101,298	70,503	18,504	88,038

the debt but not have sufficient resources to pay it. Confirmation of receivables is required by professional auditing standards under most circumstances. We discuss issues related to confirmations later in this chapter.

Valuation Two valuation questions directly concern the auditor. First, are the sales and receivables transactions initially recorded at their correct value (gross value)? Second, is it likely that the client will collect the outstanding receivables, and do so in a timely fashion (net realizable value)? The first concern is primarily addressed during the auditor's confirmation work and the tests of controls associated with revenue recognition.

The second concern is more difficult and relates to determining the reasonableness of the allowance for doubtful accounts. Accounts receivable should be valued at its net realizable value, that is, the gross amount customers owe less an allowance for doubtful accounts. Estimating the allowance for doubtful accounts is one of the more difficult audit tasks because, at the time of the audit, a single correct answer is not available. In other words, the allowance must be a best estimate. The estimate must reflect the economic status of the client's customers, current economic conditions, and an informed expectation about potential default on payment. The method for developing an estimate of the allowance will be affected by the strength of the client's credit policies and the nature of its business operating environment. In many companies, the determination of the allowance will have a substantial effect on the organization's profitability.

AUDITING *in Practice*

CONFIRMING ACCOUNTS RECEIVABLE

Regulatory enforcement actions provide many examples of auditors not adhering to professional standards related to confirming accounts receivable. Two enforcement actions are summarized below that illustrate this point.

In a PCAOB enforcement action against Moore & Associates, the PCAOB noted that the audit firm's staff often did not do any work to confirm either the existence or the valuation of clients' receivables. At one client, the audit team documented that confirmation procedures were "not applicable" without documenting how they came to that unusual conclusion. Further, for another client, the firm's staff considered confirmation responses from management as acceptable, when in fact the confirmations should have come directly to the auditors from the clients' customers.

An SEC Commission Order describes a situation in which an auditor sent requests for confirmation of accounts receivable balances to 15 of its client's customers. The accounts receivable balance was the most significant asset at this client. In response, the audit firm received only one confirmation, which turned out to be false, representing less than 2% of the total domestic accounts receivable balance; and while the auditor did perform alternative audit procedures to verify the accounts receivable, those procedures were insufficient under professional auditing standards.

Thus, while professional auditing standards are quite clear on the need to confirm accounts receivable, there exist examples in which auditors inexplicably do not adhere to those standards. While most audits are performed properly, these examples serve to illustrate that problems do occur and that you should be aware of such a possibility as you enter the profession.

Estimate of the Allowance for Doubtful Accounts   Recording the allowance for doubtful accounts and determining bad-debt expense for the year is the result of an accounting estimate. The allowance should reflect management's best estimate of accounts receivable that will not be collected at year end. The auditor should understand how management developed the estimate and the controls over management's estimation process and must be aware of any changes in the client's credit policies or changes in the economy that affect the client's customer base. Auditors generally use one or a combination of the following approaches to evaluate the reasonableness of the estimate:

- Review and test the process used by management, as well as the underlying controls, to develop the estimate.
- Develop an independent model to estimate the accounts and update the model each year based on past experience and current economic conditions.
- Review subsequent events or transactions occurring prior to completion of fieldwork, particularly subsequent collections. If the company has actually collected on an accounts receivable subsequent to year end, then it was obviously of value prior to year end.

The auditor can track the history of annual write-offs and provisions for bad debts. If they are approximately equal over a period of years for stable credit sales, or approximately the same percentage of credit sales or receivables from year to year, these estimates would appear to be reasonable. Such estimates are useful but should be modified for changes in economic conditions, customer demographics, credit policies, or products. Blindly following old approaches often results in substantially underestimating a client's collection problems.

The auditor should ask management about the collectibility of customer balances that have not yet been collected in the subsequent period, particularly those that are large and long overdue. The auditor can also review credit reports from outside credit bureaus, such as Dun & Bradstreet (www.dnbisolutions. com), to help determine the likelihood of collection and can check customer correspondence files to gain additional insight into the collectibility of specific accounts. In some cases in which amounts are due from customers whose

PRACTICAL POINT

If the company does not have a process that uses objective data to estimate uncollectible receivables, it has a deficiency in internal control. In a large public company audit, management and the auditor will need to evaluate this deficiency to determine whether it is a significant deficiency or a material weakness.

PRACTICAL POINT

During times of economic uncertainty or sudden downturns, the collectibility of a client's receivables may deteriorate at a fast rate. The auditor needs to consider this external factor when assessing the reasonableness of a given client's estimate of uncollectible accounts.

balances are past due or unusually large, the auditor may want to request a copy of the customer's latest financial statements to perform an independent analysis of collectibility.

Write-Offs   Accounts should be written off as soon as they are determined to be uncollectible. The auditor should inquire about the client's procedures for deciding when to write off an account and determine whether the procedures and related internal controls are reasonable and are being followed. All write-offs should be approved.

Rights and Obligations   Some companies sell their receivables to banks or other financial institutions but may retain responsibility for collecting the receivables and may be liable if the percentage of collection falls below a specified minimum. Receivables that have been sold with recourse, discounted, or pledged as collateral on loans should be disclosed in the notes to the financial statements.

Substantive audit procedures that would reveal these ownership and disclosure issues include the following:

- Reviewing all such arrangements and obtaining confirmations from the client's banks about any contingent liabilities
- Inquiring of management
- Scanning the cash receipts journal for relatively large inflows of cash that are posted from unusual sources
- Obtaining bank confirmations, which includes information on obligations to the bank and loan collateral
- Reviewing the board of directors' minutes, which generally contain approval for these items

Presentation and Disclosure   Financial accounting standards generally require that trade accounts receivable be presented separately from other receivables. For example, material receivables from related parties, including officers, directors, stockholders, and employees, should be shown separately in the financial statements, with appropriate disclosures being provided. Audit procedures directed toward the identification of related-party transactions such as these include the following:

- Reviewing SEC filings
- Reviewing the accounts receivable trial balance
- Inquiring of management and the audit committee
- Communicating the names of identified related parties so that the audit team members can be alert to related-party transactions

Material debit balances in accounts payable for amounts due from vendors should be reclassified as accounts receivable. Receivables that are not due within the normal operating cycle or one year (whichever is longer) should be listed as noncurrent assets. Audit procedures to identify misclassified receivables include making inquiries of management, reviewing the aged trial balance for large or old outstanding balances, reading the board of directors' minutes, and scanning the subsidiary ledger to identify unusually large receivable balances (particularly those that resulted from a single transaction or that were posted from an unusual source).

Substantive procedures to provide evidence related to presentation and disclosure include confirmations from banks and financial institutions, review of loan agreements and the board of directors' minutes, review of the receivables trial balance, and inquiry of management.

Confirming Accounts Receivable

Although each audit is unique, the auditor most likely performs some standardized audit procedures, such as obtaining and evaluating an aging of accounts

---

PRACTICAL POINT

A clever way to cover up embezzlements is to write off the receivables of the company whose funds were taken. Someone independent of those dealing with cash should review documentation and approve all accounts receivable write-offs.

PRACTICAL POINT

When unable to pay an open account when due, a customer may be asked to sign a note receivable requiring payment within a specified period, with interest. The auditor can physically examine or confirm notes receivable. For confirmations, the auditor should ask customers to confirm not only the amount due but also the date of the note, the due date, the interest rate, and, when appropriate, any collateral pledged as security that should be in the client's possession but that should not be included on the balance sheet. The auditor should test the related interest income at the same time as the notes receivable.

PRACTICAL POINT

When a large amount of receivables is sold, the auditor must examine relevant contracts to identify potential recourse to the company.

receivable, confirming receivables with customers, performing cutoff tests, and reviewing subsequent collections of receivables. Confirmation of receivables can provide reliable external evidence for the existence of recorded accounts receivable and should be considered as an audit procedure on every engagement. The requirement for confirming receivables relates to a 1938 landmark case, *McKesson and Robbins,* in which the SEC found a fraud involving very material amounts of fictitious receivables. The misstatements would have been discovered had the auditors simply confirmed the receivables. Current standards generally require the use of confirmations unless one of the following conditions exists:

- Accounts receivable are *not material.*
- The use of confirmations would be *ineffective.* An auditor might determine that confirmations are ineffective if customers have previously refused to confirm balances or customers do not have a good basis on which to respond to the confirmation.
- The auditor's assessment of the risk of material misstatement is low, and that assessment, in conjunction with the evidence provided by other substantive tests, is *sufficient* to reduce audit risk to an acceptably low level.

The PCAOB notes that for the auditor to have appropriate control over the confirmation process, the auditor should be performing the following activities:

- Determining the information and selecting the items to include in confirmation requests
- Selecting the appropriate parties that will receive confirmations
- Designing the confirmation requests, including determining the type of confirmation requests to send and determining that confirmation requests are properly addressed
- Directly sending the confirmation requests, including follow-up requests when applicable, to the confirming parties, and
- Requesting responses directly from the confirming parties.

PRACTICAL POINT

When controls are found to be effective, the number of confirmations can be reduced as long as the number of confirmations is appropriate to provide the auditor sufficient, appropriate evidence.

Information requested in confirmation letters must be *objective and independently verifiable* by the customers from their own records. Recipients may be more likely to reply and identify discrepancies if the confirmation request is sent with their monthly statement. When the verification of an account balance is difficult or complex, the auditor may ask the recipient to confirm supporting information from which the auditor can later compute the ending account balance. For example, instead of asking an individual to confirm an installment loan balance that includes a complex interest calculation, the auditor could request confirmation of the date of the loan, original balance, interest rate, number of installments, and date the last installment was paid. From such information, the auditor could then make the calculation independently.

Types of Confirmations   The two basic types of accounts receivable confirmations are positive confirmations and negative confirmations. **Positive confirmations** are letters sent to selected customers asking them to review the current balance or unpaid invoice(s) due the client and return the letters directly to the auditor indicating whether they agree with the balance. If the customer does not return a signed confirmation, the auditor needs to use follow-up audit procedures to verify the existence of the customer's balance. An example of a positive confirmation is shown in Exhibit 10.10. Notice that it is printed on the client's letterhead, is addressed to the customer, is signed by the client, indicates the balance or unpaid invoice amount as of a particular date—referred to as the

Exhibit 10.10	Positive Confirmation

NSG Manufacturing Company

200 Pine Way, Kirkville, WI 53800

January 10, 2012

A.J. Draper Co.

215 Kilian Avenue

Justice, WI 53622

Our auditors, Rittenberg, Johnstone, & Gramling, CPAs, are making an annual audit of our financial statements. Please confirm the balance due our company as of December 31, 2011, which is shown on our records as $32,012.38.

Please indicate in the space provided below if the amount is in agreement with your records. If there are differences, please provide any information that will assist our auditors in reconciling the difference.

Please mail your reply directly to Rittenberg, Johnstone, & Gramling, CPAs, 5823 Monticello Business Park, Madison, WI 53711, in the enclosed return envelope. PLEASE DO NOT MAIL PAYMENTS ON THIS BALANCE TO OUR AUDITORS.

Very truly yours,

Joleen Soyka

Joleen Soyka

Controller

NSG Manufacturing Company

To: Rittenberg, Johnstone, & Gramling, CPAs

The balance due NSG Manufacturing Company of $32,012.38 as of 12/31/11 is correct with the following exceptions, (if any):

Signature: _____

Title: _____

Date: _____

---

confirmation date—and tells the customer to respond directly to the auditor in an enclosed self-addressed, postage-paid envelope.

A **negative confirmation** is similar in that it asks the customer to review the client's balance but requests the customer to respond directly to the auditor only if the customer disagrees with the indicated balance. Exhibit 10.11 is an example of a negative confirmation. A negative confirmation is less expensive to administer than a positive confirmation because it does not require follow-up procedures when a customer does not return the confirmation. The auditor assumes that a nonresponse has occurred because the customer agrees with the stated balance.

Note that to adequately respond to the positive or negative confirmation request, customers must reconcile any differences between their records and the client's records (e.g., payments already mailed or invoices not yet received). Sometimes this may involve considerable effort on the customers' part, therefore many may not take the time to respond.

Positive confirmations are considered to be more persuasive than negative confirmations because they result in either (1) the receipt of a response from the customer or (2) the use of alternative procedures to verify the existence of

PRACTICAL POINT

When management refuses to allow the auditor to send a confirmation request, the auditor should consider communicating with those charged with governance. Such behavior on the part of management should make the auditor more skeptical about management.

Exhibit 10.11	Negative Confirmation

NSG Manufacturing Company
200 Pine Way, Kirkville, WI 53800
January 10, 2012

B. D. Kruze
8163 Pleasant Way
Lucas, TX 77677

Our auditors are making an annual audit of our financial statements. Our records show an amount of $1,255.78 due from you as of 12/31/11. If the amount is not correct, please report any differences directly to our auditors, Rittenberg, Johnstone, & Gramling, CPAs, using the space below and the enclosed return envelope. NO REPLY IS NECESSARY IF THIS AMOUNT AGREES WITH YOUR RECORDS. PLEASE DO NOT MAIL PAYMENTS ON ACCOUNT TO OUR AUDITORS.

Very truly yours,

Joleen Soyka

Joleen Soyka
Controller
NSG Manufacturing Company

Differences Noted (If Any)

The balance due NSG Manufacturing Company of $1,255.78 at 12/31/11 does not agree with our records because (No reply is necessary if your records agree):

Signature: _____
Title: _____
Date: _____

the receivable. The negative form may be used *only* if all three of the following conditions exist:

1. There are a large number of relatively small customer balances.
2. The assessed level of the risk of material misstatement for receivables and related revenue transactions is low.
3. The auditor has sound reason to believe that the customers are likely to give proper attention to the requests; i.e., the customers have independent records from which to make an evaluation, will take the time to do so, and will return the confirmation to the auditor if there are significant discrepancies.

If the negative form is used, the number of requests sent or the extent of other procedures applied to the accounts receivable balance should normally be increased. Therefore, the auditor has a cost-benefit decision to make in choosing between the two forms. More time per confirmation letter is spent on the positive form; but because it is more reliable, fewer requests need to be sent and/or the extent of other procedures can be reduced. Because positive confirmations provide more reliable evidence, they must be used when the auditor employs statistical sampling in choosing which accounts to confirm. Auditors may choose to use positive confirmations for large receivable balances and negative confirmations for the smaller balances.

PRACTICAL POINT

Because negative confirmations do not provide assurance on each account that is selected, they cannot be used with statistical sampling evaluation techniques.

Auditors should normally confirm the terms of unusual or complex agreements or transactions in conjunction with or separately from the confirmation of account balances. The confirmation may need to be addressed to customer personnel who would be familiar with the details rather than to their accounts payable personnel. Auditors should also specifically inquire about the possibility of bill–and–hold transactions (i.e., transactions in which the seller recognizes the sale and bills the customer but does not actually deliver the goods/services), extended payment terms or nonstandard installment receivables, or an unusual volume of sales to distributors/retailers (possible "channel stuffing") during the confirmation process. Further, the auditor should confirm not only the terms of the transactions but also the potential existence and content of side letters. For example, side letters are often associated with material revenue misstatements, particularly in certain industries.

Confirmations as Audit Evidence   Confirmations may provide evidence for a number of assertions in the revenue cycle. However, the persuasiveness of some forms of confirmations is open to question and the auditor must be aware of potential impairments that jeopardize the integrity of confirmation responses. Confirmations are generally considered to provide *strong* evidence about the *existence* of receivables and the *completeness* of collections, sales discounts, and sales returns and allowances. For example, if a payment had been made, or an invoice was recorded but no shipment occurred, the customer would likely report the discrepancy on the confirmation. A confirmation can be very effective in addressing the existence of fictitious sales. The presumption is that if the fictitious sales are recorded to the account of a *valid* customer, the customer will note that some of the recorded sales are not correct. If the customer is fictitious, the auditor must take care to assure that the confirmation will not be delivered to a location where the client can act as a surrogate and confirm an inappropriate receivable. Confirmations provide only limited evidence about the valuation of the accounts receivable. A customer may respond to a confirmation request by indicating the amount owed, thus providing evidence about the existence of the receivable. However, if the customer is not planning to pay the amount owed, the customer may or may not provide that information when responding to a confirmation request.

Accuracy and Security of Confirmation Process   Confirmations may be prepared manually but are more frequently prepared by using audit software. The auditor should assure that the information in each confirmation is correct and should control the mailing of the confirmation requests so that the client cannot modify them. Customers are requested to return the confirmations directly to the auditor's office in an enclosed self-addressed, postage-paid envelope. Similarly, the mailing should show the auditor's address as the return address in the event that the confirmation is not deliverable. Undeliverable confirmations should raise the auditor's suspicion regarding the validity of the recorded receivable.

Sample Selection   There are several approaches to selecting receivables for confirmation. The auditor can confirm all of the large balances and randomly or haphazardly select some of the smaller balances using either nonstatistical or monetary unit (MUS) sampling. The auditor may decide to include in the sample those accounts that have credit balances, are significant and past due, are related–party accounts, and/or have unusual customer names that are unfamiliar to the auditor.

Sampling Unit   The auditor can choose to identify the sampling unit by confirming a customer's entire balance or selecting one or more of the unpaid invoices that make up that balance. When a balance is composed of several

> **PRACTICAL POINT**
>
> For confirmation procedures to be effective, it is critical that the auditor maintain control of the confirmations from the time they are prepared and mailed until they are returned by the client's customer. The client should never have an opportunity to intercept confirmations when they are mailed or when they are returned from respondents.

Comparison of Worldwide Professional Guidance

CONFIRMATION OF ACCOUNTS RECEIVABLE

AICPA Auditing Standards Board (ASB)	SAS 67 describes confirmations, how they are used in the audit process, and states that "(c)onfirmation is undertaken to obtain evidence from third parties about financial statement assertions made by management." The standard contains a presumptive requirement to perform external confirmation procedures for accounts receivable and if the presumptive requirement is not meet, the auditor is to document the reasons. By *presumptive requirement,* we mean that auditors are assumed to perform confirmations unless the circumstances would clearly warrant that such a procedure is not necessary.
Public Company Accounting Oversight Board (PCAOB)	The PCAOB adopted AU Section 330 as an interim standard in 2003. This is the same standard as SAS 67 which is described above. However, in 2010 the PCAOB issued an Exposure Draft, *Confirmation,* that would supersede AU Section 330 for public company audits. The proposed standard would have guidance similar that found in ISA 505.
	Changes from the current standard (AU Section 330) would limit the internal auditors' involvement in the confirmation process, clarify that the receipt of an oral response to a confirmation request does not meet the definition of an external confirmation, not include exceptions for not confirming receivables, require the auditor to communicate with those charged with governance if the auditor concludes that management's refusal to allow confirmations is unreasonable, limit instances in which negative confirmation requests are the only form of confirmation request to address the assessed risk of material misstatement at the assertion level, and allow auditors to use electronic media to send confirmation requests and receive confirmation responses.
International Auditing and Assurance Standards Board (IAASB)	ISA 505 describes external confirmations. The information contained in ISA 505 is similar to that in SAS 67 (described above). One notable difference is that ISA does not contain a presumptive requirement to perform external confirmation procedures for accounts receivable.
SUMMARY	Confirmations can provide a valuable source of evidence related to the existence of accounts receivable. However, auditors must adhere to professional requirements to send confirmation and be alert to changing standards and guidance in the area.

unpaid invoices, it will help the customer if a list of those invoices is attached to the confirmation. Some customers may use a voucher system and not maintain a detailed accounts payable subsidiary ledger. As an alternative to confirming the whole balance, the auditor can confirm one or more selected unpaid invoices to improve the useful response rate.

AUDITING *in Practice*

THE IMPORTANCE OF PROFESSIONAL SKEPTICISM WHEN RELYING ON EVIDENCE OBTAINED FROM CONFIRMATIONS

Third-party confirmations can provide useful evidence related to accounts receivable balances, but auditors need to be aware of the risks related to this evidence. In late 2009, the International Auditing and Assurance Standards Board (IAASB) issued a practice alert indicating that advances in technology have made confirmations subject to abuse. In 2010, the Public Company Accounting Oversight Board (PCAOB) issued an exposure draft related to confirmations. Both of these publications point out that the usefulness of confirmations as audit evidence can be affected when the third party does not respond, when the communication is provided over a medium such as e-mail that can be manipulated, or when the confirmations have restrictions or disclaimers. It is important for auditors to exercise an appropriate level of professional skepticism when deciding how much assurance they can actually obtain from a confirmation.

Undeliverable Confirmations   The auditor should determine why some confirmations are returned as undeliverable. If the wrong address was used, the correct address should be obtained and another request sent. It is also possible that the customer does not exist. Every effort should be made to determine the customer's existence. For example, the customer's name and address could be located in the telephone directory, in the publication of a credit rating service, or on the Internet. If a valid address cannot be located, the auditor should presume that the account does not exist or might be fictitious.

Follow-Up to Nonresponses: Positive Confirmations   Follow-up procedures are required for positive confirmations that are not returned within a reasonable time after being mailed, such as two weeks. Second, and sometimes third, requests are mailed. If the amount being confirmed is relatively large, the auditor may consider calling the customer to encourage a reply. When customers do not respond to the positive confirmation requests, the auditor should perform other procedures, referred to as **alternative procedures**, to verify the existence and validity of the receivable. Remember that mailed confirmations represent only a sample of the many account balances shown in the client's records. The results of the sample are intended to represent the total population; thus, it is important that the auditor develop sufficient follow-up procedures to gain satisfaction as to the correctness of each of the balances selected for confirmation. Alternative procedures that can be considered include the following:

- *Subsequent collection of the balance after year end*—Care should be taken to assure that these subsequent receipts relate to the balance as of the confirmation date, not to subsequent sales.

Evidence obtained from testing subsequent collections is often believed to be a stronger indicator of the validity of the customer's balance than that obtained from confirmations. If a significant amount of the year-end receivables balance is normally collected before the end of the audit, the auditor may choose to emphasize tests of subsequent collections and minimize or eliminate confirmation work. Testing subsequent collections provides strong evidence about both the existence and collectibility of the related receivables.

- *Examination of supporting documents*—If all, or a portion, of the balance has not been collected, documents supporting the uncollected invoices should be examined. These documents include customer orders, sales orders, bills of lading or internal shipping documents, and sales invoices.

The auditor must consider that evidence obtained from internal copies of customer orders, internal shipping documents, and sales invoices is not as persuasive as that obtained from subsequent cash receipts. Bills of lading are usually external and provide independent verification of shipments.

> **PRACTICAL POINT**
>
> Fraud studies show that fictitious receivables often have P.O. box addresses that can be accessed by management to sign confirmations. The auditor may need to use other methods to verify large accounts when receivables seem unusually high. If subsequent collections are not forthcoming, the auditor should consult business directories and published financial statements to verify the existence of a customer.

Follow-Up to Nonresponses: Negative Confirmations   The basic premise underlying negative confirmations is that if no response is received, the auditor may assume that the customer agrees with the balance and no follow-up procedures are required. This is not always the correct assumption. The customer may not respond even though the balance is wrong because (1) the letter was lost, misplaced, or sent to the wrong address; (2) the customer did not understand the request; or (3) the request was simply ignored and thrown away. The auditor must have some assurance that the reliability of the negative confirmation process is not compromised because of any of the factors just described. The auditor does not expect that a large number of negative confirmations will be returned.

Returned Negative Confirmations   Experience shows that negative confirmations are returned for the following reasons:

- The customer did not understand the request.
- The customer confirms an incorrect amount because there are payments or shipments in transit.
- The amount recorded by the client is in error.

The auditor must perform follow-up work to determine whether the confirmed amount really represents a misstatement. The auditor might look at subsequent cash receipts or vouch back to the customer's order and evidence of shipment to help make this assessment. If errors are detected, the auditor should use expanded procedures to (1) find the underlying cause of the errors and (2) estimate the amount of misstatement in the account balance.

Follow-Up Procedures: Exceptions Noted on Positive Confirmations
Customers are asked to provide details of any known differences between their own records and the amount shown on the confirmation. Differences are referred to as **exceptions**. The auditor should carefully investigate exceptions to determine that the cause of any difference is properly identified as a customer error, a timing difference, an item in dispute, or a client misstatement. Some types of exceptions in returned confirmations that you may encounter are as follows:

- *Payment has already been made*—This exception occurs when the customer has made a payment before the confirmation date, but the client has not received the payment before the confirmation date.
- *Merchandise has not been received*—This exception occurs when the client records the sale at the date of shipment and the customer records the purchase when the goods are received. The time the goods are in transit is typically the cause of this type of exception.
- *The goods have been returned*—This exception might be due to the client's failure to record a credit memo. Such a failure could result from timing differences or from the improper recording of sales returns and allowances.
- *Clerical errors and disputed amounts exist*—Some exceptions occur because the customer states that there is an error in the price charged for the goods, the goods are damaged, the proper quantity of goods was not received, or there is some other type of customer issue. These exceptions should be investigated to determine whether the client's records are in error and, if so, the amount of the error. Such differences might have implications for the valuation of the receivables account.

Some exceptions above are **timing differences** caused by transactions that are in process at the confirmation date, such as in-transit shipments or payments. If the auditor can determine that the timing difference did not result in recording the receivable in the wrong period, the differences do not represent misstatements in the account balance. However, what may initially appear to be a timing difference may actually be the result of **lapping**, which is a way to cover up the embezzlement of cash. Lapping is an irregularity that may be detected by confirmations, as described in the *Auditing in Practice* feature.

Misstatements must be projected to the entire population of receivables to determine whether there is a material misstatement in the account balance. If the projected amount of misstatement appears to have a material effect on the financial statements, the magnitude and cause of such misstatement should be discussed with the client to decide the appropriate follow-up procedures and whether a client investigation should precede further audit work. If subsequent work supports the conclusion of material misstatement, an adjustment will be required, and the client should adjust both the subsidiary and general ledger records to reflect that adjustment.

AUDITING *in Practice*

LAPPING: AN ACCOUNTS RECEIVABLE IRREGULARITY

Lapping is a technique used to cover up the embezzlement of cash. Lapping is most likely to occur when there is an inadequate segregation of duties—an employee has access to cash or incoming checks and to the accounting records. The employee steals a collection from a customer. However, that customer does not receive credit for the payment. If no other action is taken, that customer will detect the absence of the credit for payment on the next monthly statement. To prevent detection, the employee covers the defalcation by posting another customer's payment to the first customer. Then the second customer's account is missing credit, which is covered up later when a subsequent collection from a third customer is posted to the second customer's account (hence the term *lapping*). At no time will any customer's account be very far behind in the posting of the credit. Of course, there will always be at least one customer whose balance is overstated unless the employee repays the stolen cash.

The defalcation can take place even if all incoming receipts are in the form of checks. The employee can either restrictively endorse a check to another company or go to another bank and establish an account with a similar name. If the lapping scheme is sophisticated, very few accounts will be misstated at any one time. Because the auditor selects only a sample for confirmation purposes, it is important that all differences be investigated and the cause for any exceptions determined rather than rationalizing the exception away as an isolated instance. Detailed entries in the cash receipts journal related to credits posted to that customer's account should be traced to the details on the related deposit slips and remittance advices. If the amount the customer paid exceeds the amount of the credit to the account, the detail in the cash receipts journal will not agree with the detail on the deposit slip or with the remittance advice. The pattern of the error should be noted for further investigation.

Procedures When Accounts Are Confirmed at an Interim Date   If the internal controls over receivable transactions are strong, and the auditor has thus chosen to confirm receivables at a date prior to the balance sheet date, additional evidence must be gathered to assure that no material misstatements have occurred during the **roll-forward period** (the period between the confirmation date and the balance sheet date). The procedures used in gathering the additional evidence are often referred to as **roll-forward procedures** and include the following:

- Compare individual customer balances at the interim confirmation date with year-end balances and confirm any that have substantially increased.
- Compare monthly sales, collections, sales discounts, and sales returns and allowances during the roll-forward period with those for prior months and prior years to see whether they appear out of line; if they do, obtain an explanation from management and acquire corroborative evidence to determine whether that explanation is valid.
- Reconcile receivable subsidiary records to the general ledger at both the confirmation date and year end.
- Test the cutoff of sales, cash collections, and credit memos for returns and allowances at year end.
- Scan journals to identify receivables postings from unusual sources and investigate unusual items.
- Compute the number of days' sales in receivables at both the confirmation date and year end, and compare these data with each other and with data from prior periods.
- Compute the gross profit percentage during the roll-forward period, and compare that to the percentage for the year and for prior periods.

The purpose of performing these procedures is to search for evidence concerning the auditor's tentative conclusion that control risk is low and that the accounts do not contain material misstatements.

Summarizing Confirmation Work   The confirmation work should be summarized to show the extent of dollars and items confirmed, the confirmation response rate, the number and dollar amount of exceptions that were not misstatements, and the number and amount of exceptions that were misstatements (cross-referenced to the detailed explanation and disposition thereof). Such a summary helps the reviewers quickly grasp the extent and results of this work. The following is an example of such a summary:

	Items	Amount
Population	3,810	5,643,200.00
Positive confirmations	29	193,038.71
Percent confirmed	0.76%	3.42%
Responses	27	180,100.11
Percent responding	93.1%	93.3%
Exceptions	5	32,061.50
Cleared	4	19,105.82
Misstatements—B-4	1	971.68
Projected to population		30,446.31

Few but Large Sales—Confirmation of Sales   In some businesses, the balance in the sales account is made up of relatively few transactions, but each transaction is for a large dollar amount. In such situations, the auditor should review sales contracts, being careful to review sales recorded just prior to year end or reviewing sales returns posted just after year end. In some situations, the auditor may even choose to confirm recorded sales with major customers. The auditor must be careful, however, to make sure that the customer is legitimate and has a reasonable basis on which to respond to the auditor's inquiry.

Substantive Fraud-Related Procedures in the Revenue Cycle

LO 8

Describe audit procedures for the revenue cycle that address fraud risk.

Substantive tests must be adjusted when specific fraud risk factors are present. This chapter has identified a number of fraud risk factors. Other potential fraud risk factors in the revenue cycle include:

- Excessive credit memos or other credit adjustments to accounts receivable after the end of the fiscal year
- Customer complaints and discrepancies in accounts receivable confirmations (e.g., disputes over terms, prices, or amounts)
- Unusual entries to the accounts receivable subsidiary ledger or sales journal
- Missing or altered source documents or the inability of the client to produce original documents in a reasonable period of time
- A lack of cash flow from operating activities when income from operating activities has been reported
- Unusual reconciling differences between the accounts receivable subsidiary ledger and control account
- Sales to customers in the last month of the fiscal period at terms more favorable than previous months
- Predated or postdated transactions
- Large or unusual adjustments to sales accounts just prior to or just after the fiscal year end

The following fraud-related audit procedures should help address and respond to these fraud risk factors:

- Perform a thorough review of original source documents including invoices, shipping documents, customer purchase orders, cash receipts, and written correspondence between the client and the customer.

PRACTICAL POINT

Information technology provides opportunities for companies to develop fictitious documents to support fictitious balances. The auditor should always insist that the client provide requested documents in a very timely fashion and should be highly skeptical if a client claims that they are unable to locate a document quickly, especially when fraud risk is high.

AUDITING in Practice

LACK OF PROFESSIONAL SKEPTICISM IN REVENUE RECOGNITION FRAUD

Robert A. Putnam, an engagement partner for Arthur Andersen LLP, was in charge of the audit for HBOC, an Atlanta-based maker of software for the healthcare industry, during the period 1996–1999. HBOC had a fantastic earnings track record. In fact, HBOC's management was so confident of the strength of their financial statements that it made public announcements of the company's revenues, net income, and earnings per share before Andersen's audits or reviews were completed, a practice of which Putnam was aware. However, these financial results reflected the fact that senior officers of HBOC were fraudulently recognizing revenue on transactions that failed to comply with GAAP.

Early in 1997, Putnam learned that HBOC's management was inappropriately recognizing revenue on contracts where a sale was contingent on later approval by a customer's board of directors (a "board contingency"). Putnam discussed the issue with Jay Gilbertson, the CFO, who claimed that the board contingencies were perfunctory and contained no real risk of cancellation. Gilbertson agreed to provide documentation supporting his claim, but he never did so. Putnam had additional reason to be skeptical concerning HBOC's accounting practices. During the prior year's audit, the auditors identified an instance where HBOC used side letters in its contract negotiations with customers. A side letter is an agreement containing contract terms that are not a part of the formal contract (often involving rights of return), thereby increasing audit risk because it enables key contract terms affecting revenue recognition to be hidden from the auditor as part of a revenue recognition fraud. Auditors were aware of the risks associated with side letters, and Andersen had warned its audit staff that such side letters often are the cause of material revenue misstatements, especially in the software industry.

Putnam also had reason to be skeptical about the integrity of HBOC's management. During 1997, Gilbertson represented to Andersen that HBOC had complied with the latest draft of SOP 97-2, the new software revenue recognition guidelines prohibiting revenue recognition if any board contingency existed. Despite the new standard, HBOC continued to enter into some contracts with board contingencies.

Despite these issues, Putman failed to expand the scope of the audit to address the increased risk of fraud. In January 1999, McKesson Corporation acquired HBOC. On April 28, 1999, McKesson announced that it "had determined that software sales transactions aggregating $26.2 million in the company's fourth quarter ended March 31, 1999, and $16.0 million in the prior quarters of the fiscal year, were improperly recorded because they were subject to contingencies, and have been reversed. The audit process is ongoing and there is a possibility that additional contingent sales may be identified." After the announcement, the company's share price tumbled from approximately $65 to $34 a share (a loss of about $9 billion in market value).

Ultimately, the SEC determined that Putnam failed to exercise due professional care, failed to adequately plan and supervise the audits, and failed to obtain sufficient competent evidence to afford a reasonable basis for an opinion regarding the financial statements. The SEC issued a cease and desist order against Putnam, and denied him the privilege of appearing or practicing before the commission as an accountant for at least five years. In addition, fraud charges were brought against the management of HBOC.

Source: Adapted from information contained in the following sources: (1) Securities Act of 1933 Release No. 8912, April 28, 2008; (2) Securities Exchange Act of 1934 Release No. 57725, April 28, 2008; (3) Accounting and Auditing Enforcement Release No. 2815, April 28, 2008; and (4) Administrative Proceeding File No. 3-10998.

- Analyze and review credit memos and other accounts receivable adjustments for the period subsequent to the balance sheet date.
- Analyze all large or unusual sales made near year end, and vouch to original source documents.
- Confirm terms of the transaction directly with the customer, such as the absence of side agreements, acceptance criteria, delivery and payment terms, the right to return the product, and refund policies.
- Compare the number of weeks of inventory in distribution channels with prior periods for unusual changes that may indicate channel stuffing.
- Scan the general ledger, accounts receivable subsidiary ledger, and sales journal for unusual activity.
- Perform analytical reviews of credit memo and write-off activity by comparing to prior periods. Look for unusual trends or patterns such as large

numbers of credit memos pertaining to one customer or salesperson, or those processed shortly after the close of the accounting period.

- Analyze recoveries of written-off accounts.
- Inquire of the company's non-accounting personnel (e.g., sales and marketing personnel or even in-house legal counsel) about sales or shipments near year end and whether they are aware of any unusual terms or conditions in connection with these sales.

If any of these procedures were part of the original audit program, the auditor should consider expanding the extent of testing, or in some way modifying the timing or nature of testing, if evidence of potential fraud is discovered.

Summary

Although most businesses have developed highly sophisticated automated processes with appropriate controls for recording transactions in the revenue cycle, misstatements can occur because of (1) the sheer volume of transactions that must be recorded, (2) the complexity of some sales transactions, and/or (3) pressures to record fictitious revenue. Some sales transactions are further complicated by the difficulty of determining the economic substance of the transaction. The auditor must be able to both understand and test the strength of the client's recording process, internal controls, and the business purpose of transactions in order to assess the risk of material misstatement in the revenue cycle. An integrated audit, based on a sound understanding of the client's internal controls, business risk, and fraud indicators, provides for an efficient approach to audit a public company. Audits of smaller companies will usually focus more on direct tests of account balances, with less focus on tests of controls or substantive analytical procedures.

Knowledge of the interrelationships among transactions, account balances, assertions, tolerable misstatements, persuasiveness of alternative procedures, and the various risk factors allows the auditor to develop an effective and efficient audit program. When detection risk is relatively low, the auditor should perform direct tests of the account balances, perform them as of year end, and test relatively large samples. When detection risk is moderate or high, the auditor may use more substantive analytical procedures, perform some procedures at an interim date, and/or use smaller sample sizes.

Significant Terms

Alternative procedures   Procedures used to obtain evidence about the existence and valuation of accounts receivable when a positive confirmation is not returned, including examining cash collected after the confirmation date and vouching unpaid invoices to customers' orders, sales orders, shipping documents, and sales invoices.

Bill of lading   A shipping document that describes items being shipped, the shipping terms, and delivery address; a formal legal document that conveys responsibility for the safety and shipment of items to the shipper.

Cutoff period   The few days just before and just after the balance sheet date; the number of days is chosen by the auditor, depending on the assessment of potential errors made in recording items in the incorrect period (especially sales and receivables).

Cutoff tests   Procedures applied to transactions selected from those recorded during the cutoff period to provide evidence as to whether the transactions have been recorded in the proper period.

Cycle   A group of accounts related to a particular processing task; represents a convenient way to look at the interrelationship of account balances. Normally, but not always, a transaction cycle encompasses all aspects of a transaction from its initiation to final recording in the financial statements. A cycle is sometimes referred to as a process.

Exceptions Differences between a customer's records and the client's records reported on positive or negative confirmations.

Lapping A technique used to cover up the embezzlement of cash whereby a cash collection from one customer is stolen by an employee who takes another customer's payment and credits the first customer. This process continues and at any point in time at least one customer's account is overstated.

Negative confirmation A request to customers asking them to respond directly to the auditor only if they disagree with the indicated balance.

Positive confirmation A request to customers asking them to respond directly to the auditor if they agree or disagree with the indicated balance.

Process See cycle and revenue cycle and process.

Revenue cycle or process The process of receiving a customer's order, approving credit for a sale, determining whether the goods are available for shipment, shipping the goods, billing the customers, collecting cash, and recognizing the effect of this process on other related accounts such as accounts receivable and inventory.

Roll-forward period The period between an interim date, when a substantive procedure or internal control test was performed, and the balance sheet date.

Roll-forward procedures Procedures performed at or after the balance sheet date to update substantive evidence or tests of controls obtained at an interim date.

Side letter An agreement containing contract terms that are not a part of the formal contract (often involving rights of return). Side letters increase audit risk because they enable key contract terms affecting revenue recognition to be hidden from the auditor as part of a revenue recognition fraud.

Timing difference Confirmation exceptions caused by transactions that are in process at the confirmation date, such as in-transit shipments or payments. These are not misstatements.

SELECTED REFERENCES TO RELEVANT PROFESSIONAL GUIDANCE	
Topic	**Selected Guidance**
Auditing of Revenue	AICPA Audit Guide *Auditing Revenue in Certain Industries*
Confirmations	SAS 67 *The Confirmation Process*
	Proposed SAS *External Confirmations* (issued but not effective; proposed effective date is December 2012)
	Proposed AS *Confirmation*
	ISA 505 *External Confirmations*
	AICPA Practice Alert 03-1 *Audit Confirmations*
	IAASB Practice Alert *Emerging Practice Issues Regarding the Use of External Confirmations in an Audit of Financial Statements*

Note: *Acronyms for Relevant Professional Guidance*
STANDARDS: **AS**—Auditing Standard issued by the PCAOB; **ISA**—International Standard on Auditing issued by the IAASB; **SAS**—Statement on Auditing Standards issued by the Auditing Standards Board of the AICPA; **SSAE**—Statement on Standards for Attestation Engagements issued by the AICPA.
ORGANIZATIONS: **AICPA**—American Institute of Certified Public Accountants; **COSO**—Committee of Sponsoring Organizations; **IAASB**—International Auditing and Assurance Standards Board; **PCAOB**—Public Company Accounting Oversight Board; **SEC**—Securities and Exchange Commission.

Review Questions

10-1 **(LO 1)** What is meant by the cycle or process approach to analyzing revenue-related accounts?

10-2 **(LO 1)** Which accounts are typically affected by transactions in the revenue cycle? Identify the relationships among them.

10-3 **(LO 1, 2)** For accounts receivable, what are the more relevant assertions? Why is it important for an auditor to identify which assertions are more relevant?

10-4 **(LO 1)** What are the major activities involved in generating and recording a sales transaction? What are the major documents generated as a part of each activity?

Fraud

10-5 **(LO 3)** Why should auditors ordinarily consider revenue recognition as a fraud risk factor?

10-6 **(LO 3)** In assessing the risks associated with revenue recognition, the auditor will likely consult criteria provided by the SEC. What criteria has the SEC used to help determine if revenue can be recognized? Why might the auditor need to do additional research and consider additional criteria on revenue recognition?

Fraud

10-7 **(LO 3)** Which methods are sometimes used to fraudulently inflate revenue?

10-8 **(LO 3)** What factors sometime motivate management to overstate revenue?

Fraud

10-9 **(LO 4)** Which preliminary analytical procedures can help auditors identify areas of potential misstatements and design appropriate audit procedures?

10-10 **(LO 2)** What steps would the auditor take in performing an integrated audit?

10-11 **(LO 2)** How would the steps outlined in your answer to Review Question 10-10 differ if the auditor were not performing an integrated audit?

10-12 **(LO 3)** What are the basic inherent risks associated with sales and accounts receivable?

10-13 **(LO 2, 5)** Why should auditors develop an understanding of a client's control environment as it affects the accounts in the revenue cycle?

10-14 **(LO 1, 5)** What important control functions are served by mailing monthly statements to customers? Why is it important to separate the duties of responding to customer complaints from the accounts receivable and cash collection functions?

10-15 **(LO 3, 5)** Monitoring controls are effective in alerting management to the potential breakdown of other internal controls. Identify two or three monitoring controls that the auditor might expect to see in a client's revenue cycle. Identify the risks that the controls are intended to address.

10-16 **(LO 5)** In assessing whether the controls are operating effectively, is it necessary for the auditor to reperform the work of the control itself? For example, if someone tests for the correctness of computations and initials the bottom of a document to indicate that such a control procedure has been performed, is it necessary for the auditor to reperform the procedure? Explain the rationale for your response.

10-17 **(LO 5)** Which methods can be used to test the effectiveness of controls in the revenue cycle? Provide examples.

10-18 **(LO 6, 7)** How do auditors use their knowledge about the risk of material misstatement, including their knowledge of the effectiveness of controls, in designing substantive tests?

10-19 **(LO 6, 7)** What is the relationship among audit objectives, account balance assertions, and audit procedures?

10-20 **(LO 6, 7)** Explain how audit evidence gathered about accounts receivable also provides evidence about sales, and vice versa.

10-21 **(LO 6, 7)** Why is it important to directly test sales transactions as well as accounts receivable?

10-22 **(LO 6, 7)** How can the audit of revenue provide a good opportunity to test the completeness assertion for both sales and accounts receivable?

10-23 **(LO 6)** From what population should a sample be selected to test the completeness of recorded sales? Explain your choice.

10-24 **(LO 7)** When might it be advisable to send the confirmation to the customer's personnel who are familiar with the details of sales contracts rather than to the accounts payable department?

10-25 **(LO 6, 7)** Are direct tests of account balances generally more effective in detecting overstatements or understatements? Explain.

10-26 **(LO 7)** What is the effect on the nature, timing, and extent of substantive tests of accounts receivable when the risk of material misstatement is assessed as being low instead of high because of the client's having effective controls?

10-27 **(LO 6, 7)** What are the advantages and disadvantages of performing direct tests of account balances prior to the balance sheet date?

10-28 **(LO 7)** Under what circumstances should an auditor consider confirming individual unpaid invoices as opposed to confirming the customer's total balance?

10-29 **(LO 7)** What is an aged trial balance of accounts receivable? For what purposes does an auditor use it? How does an auditor determine that it is correctly aged?

10-30 **(LO 7)** Distinguish between the positive and negative forms of accounts receivable confirmation.

10-31 **(LO 7)** Which confirmation form, the positive or the negative, is considered the more reliable? Why?

10-32 **(LO 7)** If a confirmation is not returned by a customer, what follow-up work should the auditor perform if it is a

a. Positive confirmation

b. Negative confirmation

10-33 **(LO 7)** Under what circumstances can a customer's confirmation be considered reliable?

10-34 **(LO 7)** When might an auditor consider using negative confirmations? What factors must be present in the client–customer environment to justify the use of the negative confirmation form?

10-35 **(LO 7)** What is a confirmation exception? Why is it important to investigate confirmation exceptions?

10-36 **(LO 7)** What evidence does vouching cash collections after the balance sheet date provide?

10-37 **(LO 6, 7)** What are cutoff tests? What assertion(s) do they test?

Fraud

10-38 **(LO 8)** What are some potential fraud indicators that may be identified by direct tests of revenue cycle accounts? What audit procedures could be used to help determine if fraud actually occurred?

10-39 **(LO 7)** How can the auditor determine whether the allowance for doubtful accounts is reasonable?

Multiple-Choice Questions

10-40 **(LO 5)** A manufacturing client received a substantial amount of goods returned during the last month of the fiscal year and the first month after year end. The client recorded the returns when credit memos were issued (usually six to eight weeks after receipt of the goods). The control procedure that would have led to more timely recording of the goods would include which of the following?

a. Prenumbering receiving reports, which are separately identified for goods returned and serve as a control for issuance of credit memos.

b. Aging schedules of accounts receivable prepared at year end by individuals separate from the billing process.

c. A reconciliation of the detailed accounts receivable with the general ledger accounts receivable account.

d. Prenumbering credit memoranda for which all numbers are periodically accounted.

10-41 **(LO 3)** Which of the following would *not* represent a factor the auditor would consider when assessing the inherent risk associated with a sales transaction?

a. The existence of terms that specify the right of return or the right to modify the purchase agreement.

b. Billing for invoices but agreed-upon shipments of goods at a later date.

    c. Goods billed according to a percentage-of-completion methodology.

    d. The nature of the credit authorization process.

10-42 **(LO 5)** For an audit of a nonpublic company, the auditor generally makes a decision not to test the effectiveness of controls in operation when

    a. The preliminary assessment of control risk is at the maximum.

    b. It is more cost-efficient to directly test ending account balances than to test control procedures.

    c. The auditor believes that controls are designed effectively but are not functioning as described.

    d. All of the above.

10-43 **(LO 5)** A restaurant chain has more than 680 restaurants. All food orders for each restaurant are required to be input into an electronic device, which records all food orders by food servers and transmits the order to the kitchen for preparation. All food servers are responsible for collecting cash for all their orders and must turn in cash at the end of their shift equal to the sales value of food ordered for their I.D. number. The manager then reconciles the cash received for the day with the computerized record of food orders generated. Management investigates all differences immediately.

Corporate headquarters has established monitoring controls to determine when an individual restaurant might not be recording all its revenue and transmitting the applicable cash to the corporate headquarters. Which one of the following would be the best example of a monitoring control?

    a. The restaurant manager reconciles the cash received with the food orders recorded on the computer.

    b. All food orders must be entered on the computer, and there is segregation of duties between the food servers and the cooks.

    c. Management at corporate headquarters prepares a detailed analysis of gross margin per store and investigates any store that shows a significantly lower gross margin.

    d. Cash is transmitted to corporate headquarters on a daily basis.

Use the following information to answer Questions 10-44 and 10-45.

An organization sells products through a catalog and takes orders over the phone. All orders are entered online and the organization's objective is to ship all orders within 24 hours. The audit trail is kept in machine-readable form. The only papers generated are the packing slip and the invoice sent to the customer. Revenue is recorded upon shipment of the goods. The organization maintains a detailed customer database that allows the customer to return goods for credit at any time. The company maintains a product database containing all the authorized prices. Only the marketing manager has authorization to make changes in the price database. The marketing manager either makes the changes or authorizes the changes by signing an authorization form, and his assistant implements the changes.

10-44 **(LO 5)** Which of the following controls would be *least* effective in assuring that the correct product is shipped and billed at the approved price?

   a. Self-checking digits are used on all product numbers, and customers must order from a catalog with product numbers.

   b. The sales order taker verbally verifies both the product description and price with the customer before the order is closed for processing.

   c. The sales order taker prepares batch totals of the number of items ordered and the total dollar amount for all items processed during a specified period of time (e.g., 1 hour).

   d. The product price table is restricted to the director of marketing, who alone can approve changes to the price file.

10-45 **(LO 5)** The auditor wants to determine that only the marketing manager has approved changes to the product price file. Which of the following audit procedures would provide the most persuasive evidence that only those price changes that have been properly authorized by the marketing manager have been made?

   a. Using test data and submitting product orders to be processed and comparing the prices invoiced with the prices in the most recent catalog.

   b. Using Generalized Audit Software to create a listing of all customer orders exceeding a specified dollar limit, and printing out the results for subsequent investigation.

   c. Obtaining a copy of all authorized price changes and manually tracing to the current edition of the organization's catalog.

   d. Obtaining a computerized log of all changes made to the price database and taking a random sample of changes and tracing to a signed list of changes authorized by the marketing manager.

10-46 **(LO 1, 3, 5)** Which of the following should an auditor gain an understanding of during the engagement planning process?

   a. Internal controls related to revenue recognition.

   b. Revenue-related computer applications.

   c. Key revenue-related documents.

   d. All of the above.

†**10-47** **(LO 5)** An auditor performs tests of controls in the sales cycle. First, the auditor makes inquiries of company personnel about credit-granting policies. The auditor then selects a sample of sales transactions and examines documentary evidence of credit approval. This test of controls most likely supports which of management's financial statement assertion(s)?

	Rights and obligations	*Valuation or allocation*
a.	Yes	Yes
b.	No	Yes
c.	Yes	No
d.	No	No

10-48 **(LO 6)** To test the completeness of sales, the auditor would select a sample of transactions from the population represented by which of the following?

a. Customer order file

b. Open invoice file

c. Bill of lading file

d. Sales invoice file

10-49 **(LO 6, 8)** The auditor is concerned that fictitious sales have been recorded. The best audit procedure to identify the existence of the fictitious sales would be to perform which of the following?

Fraud

a. Select a sample of recorded invoices and trace to shipping documents (bills of lading and packing slips) to verify shipment of goods.

b. Select a random sample of shipping documents (bills of lading) and trace to the invoice to determine whether the invoice was properly recorded.

c. Select a sample of customer purchase orders and trace through to the generation of a sales invoice.

d. Select a sample of invoices and trace to a customer purchase order to determine whether a valid customer actually exists.

10-50 **(LO 7)** The confirmation of customers' accounts receivable rarely provides reliable evidence about the completeness assertion because:

a. Many customers merely sign and return the confirmation without verifying its details.

b. Recipients usually respond only if they disagree with the information on the request.

c. Customers may not be inclined to report understatement errors in their accounts.

d. Auditors typically select many accounts with small balances to be confirmed.

*10-51 **(LO 7)** An auditor should perform alternative procedures to substantiate the existence of accounts receivable when:

a. No reply to a positive confirmation request is received.

b. No reply to a negative confirmation request is received.

c. Collectibility of the receivables is in doubt.

d. Pledging of the receivables is probable.

*10-52 **(LO 7)** Negative confirmation of accounts receivable is less effective than positive confirmation of accounts receivable because:

a. Most recipients usually lack the willingness to respond objectively.

b. Some recipients may report incorrect balances that require extensive follow-up.

c. The auditor cannot infer that all nonrespondents have verified their account information.

d. Negative confirmations do not produce evidential matter that is statistically quantifiable.

e. All of the above.

10-53 **(LO 7)** At some clients, the auditor may perform substantive testing procedures at an interim date. In which of the following circumstances is substantive testing of accounts receivable before the balance sheet date most appropriate?

a. The client has a new sales incentive program in place.

b. Internal controls are effective.

c. The client's CFO and V.P. of sales resigned under unusual circumstances.

d. It is a new audit client.

Discussion and Research Questions

10-54 **(Revenue Recognition, LO 3)** Judgments about whether revenue should be recognized are among the most contentious that an auditor faces. The following are situations in which the auditor will be required to either acquire additional information or make decisions about the amount of revenue to be recognized.

Required

a. Identify the primary criteria the auditor should use in determining revenue to be recognized.

b. For each of the following six scenarios:

- Identify the key issues to address in determining whether or not revenue should be recognized.

- Identify additional information the auditor may want to gather in making a decision on revenue recognition.

- Based only on the information presented, develop a rationale for either the recognition or nonrecognition of revenue.

Revenue Recognition Scenarios

1. AOL sells software that is unique as a provider of Internet services. The software contract includes a service fee of $19.95 for up to 500 hours of Internet service each month. The minimum requirement is a one-year contract. The company proposes to immediately recognize 30% of the first-year's contract as revenue from the sale of software and 70% as Internet services on a monthly basis as fees are collected from the customer.

2. Modis Manufacturing builds specialty packaging machinery for other manufacturers. All of the products are high-end and range in sales price from $5 million to $25 million. A major customer is rebuilding one of its factories and has ordered three machines with total revenue for Modis of $45 million. The contracted date to complete the production was November and the company met the contract date. The customer acknowledges the contract and confirms the amount. However, because the factory is not yet complete, it has asked Modis to hold the products in the warehouse as a courtesy until its building is complete.

3. Standish Stoneware has developed a new low-end line of baking products that will be sold directly to consumers and to low-end discount stores (but not Wal-Mart). The company had previously sold high-end silverware products to specialty stores and has a track record of returned items for the high-end stores. The new products tend to have more defects, but the defects are not necessarily recognizable in production. For example, they are more likely to crack when first used in baking. The company does not have a history of returns from these products, but because the products are new it grants each customer the right to return the merchandise for a full refund or replacement within one year of purchase.

4. Omer Technologies is a high-growth company that sells electronic products to the custom copying business. It is an industry with high innovation, but Omer's technology is basic. In order to achieve growth, management has empowered the sales staff to make special deals to increase sales in the fourth quarter of the year. The sales deals include a price break and an increased salesperson commission but not an extension of either the product warranty or the customer's right to return the product.

5. Electric City is a new company in the Chicago area that has the exclusive right to a new technology that saves municipalities a substantial amount of energy for large-scale lighting purposes (e.g., for ball fields, parking lots, and shopping centers). The technology has been shown to be very cost-effective in Europe. In order to get new customers to try the product, the sales force allows customers to try the product for up to six months to prove the amount of energy savings they will realize. The company is so confident that customers will buy the product that it allows this "pilot" period. Revenue is recognized at the time the product is installed at the customer location, with a small provision made for potential returns.

6. Jackson Products decided to quit manufacturing a line of its products and outsourced the production. However, much of the manufacturing equipment it had could be used by other companies. In addition, it had over $5 million of new manufacturing equipment on order in a non-cancelable deal. The company decided to become a sales representative to sell the new equipment ordered and its existing equipment. All of the sales were recorded as revenue.

10-55 **(Preliminary Analytical Procedures, LO 4)** One of your audit clients manufactures fishing boats and sells them all over the country. Boats are sold to dealers who finance their purchases on a floor-plan basis with their banks. The banks usually pay your client within two weeks of shipment. The company's profits have been increasing over the past several years. To perform preliminary analytical procedures you have obtained the following information related to your 2012 audit ($ in millions):

Fraud

**Professional
Skepticism**

	2012**	2011*	2010*	2009*	2008*	Major Competitor (2012)
Accounts Receivable	6.8	3.3	2.3	1.8	1.7	4.2
Inventory	16.0	10.0	7.2	5.5	5.1	13.9
Accounts Payable	3.1	2.6	1.9	1.5	1.4	3.2
Sales	84.7	77.9	56.8	43.6	39.8	110.3
Gross Profit %	19%	17%	18%	17%	18%	21%
Number of Days' Sales in Receivables	29	16	15	16	16	14
Number of Days' Sales in Ending Inventory	69	47	46	46	47	46

*Audited

**Unaudited

Required

a. From the data shown, identify potential risk areas and explain why they represent potential risks.

b. Suggest possible explanations for any unexpected results.

c. What inquiries and follow-up audit procedures might be performed to determine the accuracy of the client's data?

d. How might the CFO use accounts receivable and inventory to conceal the embezzlement of cash?

e. Discuss the importance of professional skepticism when performing preliminary analytical procedures.

10-56 **(Cross-Sectional Analysis of Revenue Using Excel or ACL, LO 4, 6)** You are auditing FloorMart, a retailer with 200 stores around the country. It has two basic sizes of stores—minimarts with 3,000 square feet and maximarts with 7,500 square feet. Both types of stores carry the same types of products. The client has provided an Excel file with the square feet, sales, and inventory at each store. This file must be downloaded from the website www.cengage.com/accounting/rittenberg. Select this text, then select "Student Resources." It is labeled "Floormart Data."

Required

a. Using either Excel or ACL, identify the stores for which sales appear to be out of line with the other stores and will require additional evidence.

b. What substantive procedures would the auditor use to gather the additional evidence?

Fraud

10-57 **(Analytical Procedures, LO 3, 4, 6, 8)** Stainless Steel Specialties (SSS) is a manufacturer of hot water–based heating systems for homes and commercial businesses. The company has grown about 10% in each of the past five years. The company has not made any acquisitions. Following are some of the statistics for the company during the past five years:

OVERVIEW OF OPERATIONAL DATA
STAINLESS STEEL SPECIALTIES (SSS)
(SALES AND NET INCOME REPORTED IN $ MILLIONS)

	2008	2009	2010	2011	2012 (unaudited)
Sales	$800	$880	$950	$1,050	$1,300
Net Income	$28	$38	$42	$52	$68
Stock Price	$17	$24	$19	$28	$47
Economic Growth in Areas Served (Index with 1.00 for 20 × 1)	1.00	1.04	1.09	1.13	1.14
Percent of Heating Market by SSS	8.9%	9.4%	9.6%	10.8%	14.0%
Accounts Receivable	$180	$170	$196	$210	$297
Percent of Sales Made in Last Quarter	38%	36%	40%	38%	43%
Gross Margin	28%	28.3%	28.8%	29.2%	33.6%

Additional information available to the auditor includes the following:

- The company has touted its new and improved technology for both the increase in sales and in gross margin.
- The company claims to have decreased administrative expense thus increasing net profits.
- The company has reorganized its sales process to a more centralized approach and has empowered individual sales managers to negotiate better prices to drive sales as long as the amounts are within corporate guidelines.
- The company has changed its salesperson compensation by increasing the commission on sales to new customers.
- Sales commissions are no longer affected by returned goods if the goods are returned more than 90 days after sale and/or by not collecting the receivables.

SSS has justified the changes in sales commissions on the following grounds:

- The salesperson is not responsible for "quality" issues—the main reason that products are returned.
- The salesperson is not responsible for approving; rather credit approval is under the direction of the global sales manager.

Required

a. What is the importance of the information about sales person compensation to the audit of receivables and revenue? Explain how the information would be used in conducting the audit.

b. Perform analytical review procedures using the data included in the table and the information about the change in performance. What are the important insights that the auditor should gain from performing the analytical review?

c. Why should the auditor be interested in a company's stock price when performing an audit, since stock price is dependent, at least in part, on audited financial reports?

d. What information about SSS might be considered as fraud risk factors?

e. Identify specific substantive audit procedures that should be performed as a result of the analytical procedures performed by the auditor.

10-58 **(Audit Procedures and Objectives, LO 5, 6)** The following is a list of procedures performed in the audit of the revenue cycle:

a. Take a block of shipping orders and account for the invoicing of all items in the block and account for the prenumbering of the documents.

b. Review the general access controls to the computer application and the authorized ability to make changes to computer price files.

c. Recompute the invoice total and individual line items on a sample of sales invoices.

d. Review client documentation to determine policy for credit authorization.

e. Select a sample of shipping notices and trace to invoices.

f. Randomly sample entries into the sales journal and trace back to sales orders and shipping documents.

Required

For each procedure, indicate the control or substantive testing objective that is accomplished. Identify the assertion that most relates to the procedure.

*10-59 **(Linking Risks and Controls, LO 3, 5)** Field, CPA, is auditing the financial statements of Miller Mailorder, Inc. (MMI) for the year ended January 31, 2012. Field has compiled a list of possible risks, including both errors and fraud, that may result in the misstatement of MMI's financial statements and a corresponding list of internal controls that, if properly designed and implemented, could assist MMI in preventing or detecting the errors and fraud.

Required

For each possible risk (possible errors and fraud) numbered 1 through 15, select one internal control procedure from the following answer list that, if properly designed and implemented, most likely could assist MMI in preventing or detecting the errors and irregularities. Each response in the list of controls may be selected once, more than once, or not at all.

Possible Errors and Fraud

1. Invoices for goods sold are posted to incorrect customer accounts.

2. Goods ordered by customers are shipped but are not billed to anyone.

3. Invoices are sent for shipped goods but are not recorded in the sales journal.

4. Invoices are sent for shipped goods and are recorded in the sales journal but are not posted to any customer account.

5. Credit sales are made to individuals with unsatisfactory credit ratings.

6. Goods are removed from inventory for unauthorized orders.

7. Goods shipped to customers do not agree with goods ordered by customers.

8. Invoices are sent to allies in a fraudulent scheme, and sales are recorded for fictitious transactions.

9. Customers' checks are received for less than the customers' full account balances, but the customers' full account balances are credited.

10. Customers' checks are misappropriated before being forwarded to the cashier for deposit.

11. Customers' checks are credited to incorrect customer accounts.

12. Different customer accounts are each credited for the same cash receipt.

13. Customers' checks are properly credited to customer accounts and are properly deposited, but errors are made in recording receipts in the cash receipts journal.

14. Customers' checks are misappropriated after being forwarded to the cashier for deposit.

15. Invalid transactions granting credit for sales returns are recorded.

Internal Control Procedures

a. Shipping clerks compare goods received from the warehouse with the details on the shipping documents.

b. Approved sales orders are required for goods to be released from the warehouse.

c. Monthly statements are mailed to all customers with outstanding balances.

d. Shipping clerks compare goods received from the warehouse with approved sales orders.

e. Customer orders are compared with the inventory master file to determine whether items ordered are in stock.

f. Daily sales summaries are compared with control totals of invoices.

g. Shipping documents are compared with sales invoices when goods are shipped.

h. Sales invoices are compared with the master price file.

i. Customer orders are compared with an approved customer list.

j. Sales orders are prepared for each customer order.

k. Control amounts posted to the accounts receivable ledger are compared with control totals of invoices.

l. Sales invoices are compared with shipping documents and approved customer orders before invoices are mailed.

m. Prenumbered credit memos are used for granting credit for goods returned.

n. Goods returned for credit are approved by the supervisor of the sales department.

o. Remittance advices are separated from the checks in the mailroom and forwarded to the accounting department.

p. Total amounts posted to the accounts receivable ledger from remittance advices are compared with the validated bank deposit slip.

q. The cashier examines each check for proper endorsement.

r. Validated deposit slips are compared with the cashier's daily cash summaries.

s. An employee, other than the bookkeeper, periodically prepares a bank reconciliation.

t. The same employee who issues receiving reports evidencing actual return of goods approves sales returns.

10-60   **(Inherent Risks, LO 3, 6)**   Drea Tech Company has been growing rapidly and has recently engaged your firm as its auditor. It is actively traded over the counter (OTC) and management believes it has outgrown the service capabilities of its previous auditor. However, on contacting the previous auditor, you learn that a dispute led to the firm's dismissal. The client wanted to recognize income on contracts for items produced but not shipped. The client believed the contracts were firm and that all the principal revenue-producing activities were performed. The change in accounting principle would have increased net income by 33% during the last year.

Drea is 32% owned by Anthony Dreason, who has a reputation as a turnaround artist. He bought out the previous owner of Drea Tech (formerly named Johnstone Industries) three years ago. The company's primary products are in the materials handling business, such as automated conveyors for warehouses and production lines. Dreason has increased profits by slashing operating expenses, most notably personnel and research and development. In addition, he has outsourced a significant portion of component part production. Approximately 10% of the company's product is now obtained from Materials Movement, Inc., a privately held company 50% owned by Dreason and his brother.

A brief analysis of previous financial statements shows that sales have been increasing by approximately 20% per year since Dreason assumed control. Profitability has increased even more. However, a tour of the plant gives the impression that it is somewhat old and not kept up to date. Additionally, a large amount of inventory is sitting near the receiving dock awaiting final disposition.

Required

a. Identify the elements of inherent risk associated with the revenue cycle that the auditor should consider.

b. For each element of inherent risk identified, briefly indicate the audit concern and suggest audit procedures to address the risks.

10-61   **(Credit Authorization, LO 5)**   Verona Shoe Company is considering automating its credit approval function. It manufactures a brushed pigskin shoe and acts as a wholesaler by buying closeouts of other brands and selling them to approximately 3,000 retail customers. The company has moved into new lines by recently acquiring the U.S. distribution rights to an important European brand of ski equipment and ski wear. The ski line will be sold to approximately 750 different retail outlets, but three major chains will constitute over 50% of the sales.

Required

a. What factors should the company consider in setting its credit policies? How could data normally contained in the client's computer system assist the company in setting its overall credit policies?

b. Assume that the company chooses to automate much of its credit approval process. Outline the control procedures the company should consider to ensure that credit is granted only in accordance with company credit policies.

c. For each control procedure identified in part (b), briefly indicate how the auditor might go about testing the effectiveness of its operation.

10-62 (Linking Risk and Controls, LO 5) The following table includes a common risk in the revenue cycle that might be present at an audit client. For the risk, identify the relevant financial statement assertion and identify controls, including those related to the control activities and the control environment that the auditor might expect the client to have implemented. Suggest how the auditor might test the controls.

Objective	Risk and Relevant Financial Statement Assertion	Control Environment Controls	Approach to Testing	Control Activities	Approach to Testing
Recognize revenue in accordance with appropriate revenue recognition criteria	RISK: Overstatement— sales agents grant future credits to customer for unsold goods ASSERTION:				

10-63 (Testing Controls, LO 5) Below is a list of controls typically implemented in the processing of sales transactions.

Required

a. For each control identified, briefly indicate the financial misstatement that could occur if the control is not implemented effectively.

b. Identify a test of control that the auditor can do to determine the effectiveness of the control.

Controls Typically Found in Sales Processes

1. All transactions under $10,000 may be approved by the computer authorization program. The credit manager must approve all transactions over $10,000.

2. All invoices are priced according to the authorized price list maintained on the computer. Either the regional or divisional sales manager must approve any exceptions.

3. All shipping documents are prenumbered and periodically accounted for. Shipping document references are noted on all sales invoices.

4. Customer complaints regarding receipt of goods are routed to a customer service representative. Any discrepancies are immediately followed up to determine the cause of the discrepancy.

5. All merchandise returns must be received by the receiving department and recorded on prenumbered documents for receipts. A document is created for each item (or batches of like items). Returns are sent to quality control for testing, and a recommendation for ultimate disposition is made (scrap, rework and sell as a second, or close out as is), noted, and sent to accounting for proper inventorying.

6. The quantity of items invoiced is reconciled with the packing document developed on receipt of the order and the shipping notice by a computer program as the goods are marked for shipment. If discrepancies appear, the shipping document prevails. A discrepancy report is prepared daily and sent to the warehouse manager for follow-up.

7. The company pays all freight charges, but the customer is charged a freight fee based on a minimum amount and a sliding scale as a percentage of the total invoice. The policy is documented and the computer automatically adds the charge.

10-64 **(Credit Card Sales, LO 5)** Jason Co. accepts VISA and MasterCard for any sales transaction exceeding $50. The company has not yet implemented online recording of the credit card transaction, but it does have a toll-free number to call for authorization for all sales over $50. The company has two cash registers, but three clerks work during peak times. The company processes credit card sales as follows.

Blank credit card slips are maintained near the cash register along with two card imprinters. The card imprinter imprints the company's account identification and takes an imprint of the customer's credit card. Normally, credit card sales are rung up on the cash register, as would be done with a cash sale. The credit card receipts are kept in a separate location in the cash register. During peak times, however (such as clearance sales), a special line is set up for credit card customers. The totals are calculated on a regular calculator, and a credit slip is prepared and run through the imprinter. The credit card slips are stored in a convenient location and are recorded on a cash register later in the day. Periodically during the day, the store manager collects all credit card receipts, separates the two copies into one for the store and one for the bank, batches all the slips, and prepares an entry to later record the sales. The batches for the day are collected for deposit. The controller then reconciles the deposits made each day with the credit card sales recorded.

Required

a. Identify the strengths and weaknesses of the controls for credit card sales identified.

b. For each deficiency noted, identify the potential effect on the company's financial statements.

10-65 **(Exception Reports, LO 5)** Computer accounting systems have the ability to generate exception reports that immediately identify control procedure failures or transactions that are out of the norm so that management can determine whether any special action is needed.

Required

a. Identify how the auditor might use each of the following four types of exception reports in assessing the effectiveness of controls.

b. For each type of exception report address the following question. If the exceptions are properly followed up and corrected, would the fact that many exceptions occurred affect the auditor's judgment of the effectiveness of controls and the auditor's assessment of control risk? Explain.

Types of Exception Reports—Sales Processing

1. A list of all invoices over $5,000 for which credit was not preauthorized by the credit manager (the computer program is designed so that if the authorization is not provided within 24 hours of the original notice to the credit manager, the shipment is made as if it were authorized). This exception report goes to the credit manager.

2. A report of any sales volume to one customer exceeding $2 million in a month sent to the sales manager with a copy to the credit manager.

3. A report of exceptions for which shipping documents and packing slips did not reconcile.

4. A report noting that goods ordered were not shipped (or back-ordered) within five days of receipt of the order as is required per company policy.

10-66 **(Control Risk and Misstatements, LO 5, 6, 7)** The audit of the revenue cycle accounts of Acco, Inc. has been planned with a low preliminary assessment of control risk related to each of the relevant assertions. A sample of sales transactions was selected for testing. Each of the following types of control or transaction processing deviations uncovered in the sample was significant enough to cause the auditor to increase control risk assessment from low to moderate.

Required

Discuss the type of financial statement misstatement that may result, the assertion(s) affected, and the effect on the nature, timing, and/or extent of related substantive tests. Each type of failure should be considered independently from the others.

a. No evidence that price and quantity on the invoice were compared with the supporting documents.

b. Failure to approve customer credit before shipping the merchandise on open account.

c. Recording sales before they were shipped.

d. Recording sales several days after they should have been recorded.

e. Recording several sales before and several after they should have been recorded.

f. Lack of customer orders; items were shipped.

g. Lack of shipping documents; customer order was found.

h. Incorrect invoice price.

i. Quantity shipped differed from the quantity billed.

10-67 **(Auditing Revenue and Related Controls, LO 5, 6)** All invoicing for a company is done on a computer system from a price list table incorporated into the system. Only the sales department can change the prices on the approval of the department manager. One copy of the up-to-date price list is printed monthly for verification purposes and is maintained in the sales department. The sales department keeps a list of all changes. The master price printouts are maintained for three months. The quarterly printouts, however, are maintained for one year.

Required

Identify two ways in which the auditor might gain assurance that sales transactions are properly valued.

10-68 **(Directional Testing and Dual-Purpose Tests, LO 5, 6)** During a discussion, one auditor noted that her approach to testing sales transactions was to select a random sample of recorded sales and trace back through the system to supporting documents, noting that all items billed were shipped and were invoiced at correct prices. She stated that she then had good confidence about the correctness of the sales account and, thus, having performed a dual-purpose test, the remaining work on sales (assuming the procedures also evidenced the working of control procedures) could be limited.

A second auditor disagreed. Her approach was to select evidence of shipments, such as prenumbered shipping documents, and then trace forward through the system to the actual invoice, noting the existence of control procedures and the correctness of the invoice processing. If no exceptions were noted, however, she agreed with the first auditor that the remaining audit work on the sales account could be limited.

Required

a. Which auditor is right, or are both right? Explain.

b. What assertion is tested by the second auditor?

c. What is a dual-purpose test? Explain why the tests performed by both of the auditors would or would not be considered dual-purpose tests.

*10-69 **(Audit of Rent Revenue, LO 6)** Bert Finney, CPA, was engaged to conduct an audit of the financial statements of Clayton Realty Corporation for the month ending January 31, 2012. The examination of monthly rent reconciliation is a vital portion of the audit engagement.

The following rent reconciliation was prepared by the controller of Clayton Realty Corporation and was presented to Finney, who subjected it to various audit procedures:

Clayton Realty Corporation

Rent Reconciliation

For the Month Ended January 31, 2012

Gross apartment rents (Schedule A)	$1,600,800†
Less vacancies (Schedule B)	20,500†
Net apartment rentals	1,580,300
Less unpaid January rents (Schedule C)	7,800†
Total	1,572,500
Add prepaid rent collected (Apartment 116)	500†
Total cash collected	$1,573,000†

Schedules A, B, and C are available to Finney but are not presented here. Finney evaluated and tested internal controls and found that they could be relied on to produce reliable accounting information. Cash receipts from rental operations are deposited in a special bank account.

Required

What substantive audit procedures should Finney employ during the audit to substantiate the validity of each of the dollar amounts marked by the dagger (†)?

10-70 **(Performing a Cutoff Test, LO 6, 7)** The following sales were selected for a cutoff test of Genius Monitors, Inc., for the December 31, 2012, financial statements. All sales are credit sales and are FOB shipping point. They are recorded on the billing date.

		Date	
Invoice Number	**Sales Price**	**Shipped**	**Billed**
36590	2,750	12/28/12	12/29/12
36591	25,390	12/29/12	1/2/13
36592	9,200	1/3/13	12/31/12
36593	570	1/2/13	1/3/13

Required

a. What adjusting journal entries, if any, would you recommend that the client make for each of these items? (Do not consider the inventory implications of this cutoff.)

b. What complications do shipping terms of FOB destination create?

c. Under what circumstances might an auditor accept sales that are recorded when shipped, even though they are shipped FOB destination?

10-71 **(Audit of Membership Fees, LO 6)** You are auditing the revenue from membership fees of your local chapter of the Institute of Management Accountants, of which you are not a member. The local chapter receives an allocation of national dues. The remainder of the dues comes from chapter members. The chapter maintains a detailed list of membership.

Required

Describe some substantive analytical procedures you could use to provide some assurance that such revenue is fairly stated.

10-72 **(Cutoff Procedures, LO 6)** Sales cutoff tests are performed to obtain evidence that sales are recorded in the proper period. You are to perform a cutoff test of sales for a manufacturer that uses prenumbered bills of lading and sales invoices. All sales are FOB shipping point.

Required

How would you perform the cutoff test if the primary audit concern is the

a. Existence of sales

b. Completeness of sales

*10-73 **(Accounts Receivable Audit Procedures, LO 7)** As part of the audit of KC Enterprises, the auditor assessed control risk for the existence and valuation assertions related to accounts receivable at the maximum level. Katie, the staff person assigned to the engagement, sent positive confirmation requests to a sample of the company customers based on their balances as of December 31, 2012. For each of the three customers described here, review the relevant confirmation letter and Katie's comments at the bottom of each. Select the procedure that should be followed to clear the exception, if one exists. Choose only one procedure per confirmation. A procedure may be used once, more than once, or not at all.

a.

February 1, 2013

Meehan Marine Sales, Inc.
1284 River Road
Louisville, Kentucky 40059

Re: Balance at December 31, 2012—$267,000

As of December 31, 2012, our records indicate your balance with our company as the amount listed above. Please complete and sign the bottom portion of this letter and return the entire letter to our auditors, GJ LLP, P.O. Box 100, Orlando, Florida 32806.

(continues)

A stamped, self-addressed envelope is enclosed for your convenience.

Sincerely,

_____

KC Enterprises

. . . .

The above balance is   Correct

                            X   Incorrect (show amount) $325,000

If incorrect, please provide information that could help to reconcile your account.

Response: We placed an order for $58,000 on December 26, 2012.

Signature: _____
Title: _____
Date: _____

_____

Katie's note to file:

> Per discussion with the controller and review of relevant documentation, the order for $58,000 was shipped f.o.b. shipping point on December 30, 2012 and was received by the customer on January 3, 2013. Therefore, the client has made no entry to record the sale in 2012.

b.

February 1, 2013

West Coast Ski Center, Inc.
163 Tide Avenue
Monterey, California 93940

Re: Balance at December 31, 2012—$414,000

As of December 31, 2012, our records indicate your balance with our company as the amount listed above. Please complete and sign the bottom portion of this letter and return the entire letter to our auditors, GJ LLP, P.O. Box 100, Orlando, Florida 32806.

A stamped, self-addressed envelope is enclosed for your convenience.

Sincerely,

_____

KC Enterprises

. . . .

The above balance is   Correct

                            X   Incorrect (show amount) $325,000

If incorrect, please provide information that could help to reconcile your account.

Response: We made a payment of $94,000 on December 12, 2012.

(continues)

Signature: _____
Title: _____
Date: _____

_____

Katie's note to file:
> Per discussion with the controller and review of relevant documentation, the company received the payment of $94,000 on December 15, 2012, and posted it to "Other Income."

c.

February 1, 2013

Fish & Ski World, Inc.
5660 Ocean Blvd
Port Arkansas, Texas 78373

Re: Balance at December 31, 2012—$72,000

As of December 31, 2012, our records indicate your balance with our company as the amount listed above. Please complete and sign the bottom portion of this letter and return the entire letter to our auditors, GJ LLP, P.O. Box 100, Orlando, Florida 32806.

A stamped, self-addressed envelope is enclosed for your convenience.

Sincerely,

_____

KC Enterprises

. . . .

The above balance is   Correct

                              X   Incorrect (show amount)   *$325,000*

If incorrect, please provide information that could help to reconcile your account.

Response: Per our records, the following invoices are outstanding:
     Invoice #4212 $72,000
     Invoice #4593 $66,000
     Invoice #4738 $25,000

Signature: _____
Title: _____
Date: _____

_____

Katie's note to file:
> Per review of the A/R aging report, invoices #4593 and 4738 are not on the A/R aging report at December 31, 2012.

Possible procedures:

1. Not an exception, no adjustment necessary. Determine the sufficiency of allowance for doubtful accounts.

2. Exception noted; propose adjustment and request that the controller post it to the accounting records.

3. Verify by examining subsequent cash collections and/or shipping documents.

4. Review appropriate documentation to verify that additional invoices noted on confirmation pertain to the subsequent year.

Fraud

*10-74   **(Accounts Receivable Lapping, LO 7, 8)**   During the year, Strang Corporation began to encounter cash flow difficulties, and a cursory review by management revealed receivable collection problems. Strang's management engaged Elaine Stanley, CPA, to perform a special investigation. Stanley studied the billing and collection cycle and noted the following.

The accounting department employs one bookkeeper who receives and opens all incoming mail. This bookkeeper is also responsible for depositing receipts, filing daily remittance advices, recording receipts in the cash receipts journal, and posting receipts in the individual customer accounts and the general ledger accounts. There are no cash sales. The bookkeeper prepares and controls the mailing of monthly statements to customers.

The concentration of functions and the receivable collection problems caused Stanley to suspect that a systematic defalcation of customers' payments through a delayed posting of remittances (lapping of accounts receivable) is present. Stanley was surprised to find that no customers complained about receiving erroneous monthly statements.

Required

Identify the substantive procedures that Stanley should perform to determine whether lapping exists. Do not discuss deficiencies in the system of internal control.

10-75   **(Existence and Completeness, LO 6, 7)**   The existence and completeness assertions are complementary but require different audit approaches.

Required

a. Why is it more difficult to test for the completeness than the existence/occurrence of an account balance or a class of transactions?

b. What procedures can an auditor use to test the completeness of accounts receivable and sales?

10-76   **(Using Generalized Audit Software, LO 7)**   Your audit client, Daman, Inc., has a computerized accounts receivable system. There are two master files, a customer data file and an unpaid invoice file. The customer data file contains the customer's name, billing address, shipping address, identification number, phone number, purchase and cash payment history, and credit limit. For each unpaid invoice, the second file contains the customer's identification number, invoice number and date, date of shipment, method of shipment, credit terms, and gross invoice amount.

Required

Discuss how generalized audit software could be used to aid in the examination of Daman's accounts receivable.

10-77   **(Audit of Notes Receivable, LO 7)**   You are in charge of your second yearly examination of the financial statements of Clark Equipment Corporation, a distributor of construction equipment. Clark's equipment sales are either outright cash sales or a combination of a substantial cash payment and one or two 60- or 90-day nonrenewable interest-bearing notes for the balance. Title to the equipment passes to the customer when the initial cash payment is made. The notes, some of which are secured by the customer, are dated when the cash payment is made (the day the equipment is delivered). If the customer prefers to purchase the equipment under an installment payment plan, Clark arranges for the customer to obtain such financing from a local bank.

You begin your fieldwork to examine the December 31 financial statements on January 5, knowing that you must leave temporarily for another engagement on January 7 after outlining the audit program for your assistant. Before leaving, you inquire about the assistant's progress in his examination of notes receivable. Among other things, he shows you a working paper listing the makers' names, the due dates, the interest rates, and amounts of 17 outstanding notes receivable totaling $100,000. The working paper contains the following notations:

1. Reviewed internal controls and found them to be satisfactory.
2. Total of $100,000 agrees with general ledger control account.
3. Traced listing of notes to sales journal.

The assistant also informs you that he is preparing to request positive confirmations of the amounts of all outstanding notes receivable and that no other audit work has been performed in the examination of notes receivable and interest arising from equipment sales. There were no outstanding accounts receivable for equipment sales at the end of the year.

Required

a. What information should be confirmed with the customers?

b. State the objectives of auditing the notes receivable and list additional audit procedures that the assistant should apply in his audit of the account for notes receivable arising from equipment sales (Clark has no other notes). No subsidiary ledger is maintained.

c. You ask your assistant to examine all notes receivable on hand before you leave. He returns in 30 minutes from the office safe where the notes are kept and reports that notes on hand that have dates prior to January 1 total only $75,000. List the possible explanations that you would expect from the client for the $25,000 difference. (Eliminate fraud or misappropriation from your consideration.) Indicate beside each explanation the audit procedures you would apply to determine whether it is correct.

10-78 **(ACL Project—Accounts Receivable, LO 7)** You are auditing accounts receivable of HUSKY Corp. as of December 31, 2009. The accounts receivable general ledger balance is $4,263,919.52. The data files must be downloaded from the website www.cengage.com/accounting/rittenberg. The files are labeled "HUSKY Unpaid Invoices 2009" (the 12/31/2009 unpaid invoices), "HUSKY Shipping File 2009" (contains the shipment numbers and shipment dates for those invoices), and "HUSKY Credit Limit 2009" (contains each customer's credit limit). Sales are made FOB shipping point. The auditor has verified the last shipment in 2009 is numbered 62050 and that shipping numbers have been used in proper sequence.

Required

a. Using ACL:

1. Foot the file of unpaid invoices using the menu option **Analyze** then **Statistical** then **Statistics** and agree to the general ledger. Print the statistics for the audit documentation and note the other statistics provided.

2. Identify customers with balances over their credit limit and print out the results. (*Hint:* Before combining files, be sure the matching fields, such as CUSTNUM or INVNUM, have been changed in each table from a number format to ASCII format using the menu item **Edit** then **Table Layout**. Double-click on the field you want to change.

3. Perform a sales cutoff test to identify any unpaid invoices with shipping dates in 2009 and print out the results including the total of those invoices. (*Hint:* In the expression editor, use the **Date** button and find and enter the proper cutoff date.)

4. Age the unpaid invoices, print the aging and graph of the aging, extract (by double-clicking on the over 45 days aging indicator), and print out a list of invoices over 45 days old that also shows the total of those invoices.

5. Summarize your results and describe what procedures should be performed based on those results.

b. Use ACL to stratify the population of customer balances, print the results, and describe how this information could be used to help determine which balances to confirm.

Fraud

Professional Skepticism

10-79 **(Follow-Up Work—Accounts Receivable, LO 7, 8)** You have sent confirmations to 40 customers of Berg-Shovick Express, a long-time audit client experiencing some financial difficulty. The company sells specialized high-technology goods. You have received confirmations from 32 of the 40 positive confirmations sent. A small number of errors were noted on these accounts, but the projected amount of errors on the confirmations returned is just below tolerable error. The following information is available to you:

Book value of receivables	$7,782,292
Book value of items selected for confirmations	$3,100,110
Book value of items confirmed	$1,464,000
Audit value of items confirmed	$1,335,000

Summary of items selected but confirmations not returned:

Name	Outstanding Amount	Management Comments on Account Balance
Yunkel Specialty Mfg.	$432,000	Regular sales, but extended credit terms were given on $200,000 of goods. Yunkel has responded that it does not respond to confirmations.
Hi-Tech Combonitics	$300,000	No response to either confirmation request. Management indicates the sale was a special-term sale, and the goods are being held for the convenience of this company. The company is located in Albuquerque, New Mexico, and recently had a fire in its main production plant but expects to resume production early next month. The goods will be shipped as soon as production begins, but the sale has legally been completed.

Name	Outstanding Amount	Management Comments on Account Balance
Beaver Dam Electronics	$275,000	Account balance represents sales of specialty products made in late December. The president of Berg-Shovick has orally confirmed the receivable because Beaver Dam Electronics is 50% owned by him.
California Hi-Fi	$200,000	Regular sales, but company has renegotiated its account balance due because of defective merchandise. Management has indicated it has issued a credit to the company, but because management had inspected the goods on the customer's property, it did not require the return of the merchandise. It expects the company to pay the $200,000.
Brenner Specialties	$175,000	Regular sales. This is a new company. Most of the sales ($100,000) were made in December.
Sprague Electronics	$100,000	Regular sales. Customer is negotiating a potential return of defective items.
Williams Pipeline	$100,000	Williams is a large company. Prior experience indicates that it does not respond to confirmations.
Long Tom Towers	$54,110	Customer is new this year and is located in Medicine Hat, Saskatchewan.

Required

a. Indicate the audit procedures (and be specific as to what those procedures will accomplish) to complete the work on accounts receivable related to the confirmation process. In other words, identify the specific alternative audit procedures that should be performed. (*Note:* You do not need to specify a particular procedure for each account balance, but you must indicate the necessary procedures that would address all of the open items.)

b. Assuming that all items could not be cleared to the auditor's satisfaction, identify the audit procedures that should be implemented to finish auditing the valuation and existence assertions for accounts receivable.

Cases

10-80 **(Historical Perspective, LO 3, 6, 8)** MiniScribe Case (based on "Cooking the Books," *The Wall Street Journal,* September 11, 1989; and "MiniScribe's Investigators Determine That 'Massive Fraud' Was Perpetrated," *The Wall Street Journal,* September 12, 1989).

Fraud

In October 1988, MiniScribe, a computer disk drive manufacturer, announced its thirteenth consecutive record-breaking quarter, while its competitors were laying off hundreds of employees. MiniScribe's receivables had increased significantly, and inventories had increased to a dangerous level because disk drives can become obsolete from one quarter to the next. The company's stock price had quintupled in just two years. It had apparently risen from the dead under the leadership of Q. T. Wiles, who had resurrected other companies and was known as "Dr. Fix-It." It looked as if he had done it again.

Seven months later, it was announced that MiniScribe's sales gains had been fabricated.

What was supposed to be the crowning achievement of Wiles's career became an epitaph; he resigned and is living in near seclusion. An internal investigation concluded that senior management apparently perpetrated a massive fraud on the company, its directors, its outside auditors, and the investing public. Most of MiniScribe's top management was dismissed, and layoffs shrank its employment by more than 30% in one year. MiniScribe might have to write off as much as $200 million in bad inventory and uncollectible receivables.

Wiles's unrealistic sales targets and abusive management style created a pressure cooker that drove managers to cook the books or perish. And cook they did—booking sales prematurely, manipulating reserves, and simply fabricating figures—to maintain the illusion of unbounded growth even after the industry was hit by a severe slump.

When Wiles arrived at MiniScribe in mid-1985, it had just lost its biggest customer, IBM, which decided to make its own drives. With the personal computer industry then slumping, MiniScribe was drowning in red ink.

Dr. Fix-It's prescription was to cut 20% of the workforce and overhaul the company from top to bottom. As part of the overhaul, several semiautonomous divisions were created. Each division manager set the division's own budget, sales quotas, incentives, and work rules. The company became a chaotic Babel of at least 20 mini-companies that were constantly being changed and reorganized. One employee held 20 different positions in less than seven years.

Wiles turned up the heat under his lieutenants. Four times a year, he would summon as many as 100 employees for several days of intense meetings, at which they were force-fed his idiosyncratic management philosophy. At one of the first such meetings he held, Wiles demanded that two controllers stand, and he fired them on the spot, saying, "That's just to show everyone I'm in control of the company."

At each of these meetings, division managers had to present and defend their business plans. Invariably, Wiles would find such plans deficient and would berate their authors in front of their peers. A former controller says Wiles would throw, kick, and rip the plan books that displeased him, showering his intimidated audience with paper while yelling, "Why don't you understand this? Why can't you understand how to do this?"

Then something changed. Wiles started saying, "I no longer want to be remembered as a turnaround artist. I want to be remembered as the man who made MiniScribe a billion-dollar company." Sales objectives became the company's driving force, and financial results became the sole determinant of whether bonuses were awarded. Wiles said, "This is the number we want to hit first quarter, second quarter, third quarter, and so on," and it was amazing to see how close they could get to the number they wanted to hit.

Hitting the number became a companywide obsession. Although many high-tech manufacturers accelerate shipments at the end of a quarter to boost sales—a practice known as "stuffing the channel"—MiniScribe went several steps beyond that. On one occasion, an analyst relates, the company shipped more than twice as many disk drives to a computer manufacturer as had been ordered; a former sales manager says the excess shipment was worth about $9 million. MiniScribe later said it had shipped the excess drives by mistake. The extras were returned—but by then MiniScribe had posted the sale at the higher number. Wiles denied this practice.

Other accounting maneuvers involved shipments of disk drives from MiniScribe's factory in Singapore. Most shipments went by air freight, but a squeeze on air cargo space toward the end of each quarter would force some shipments onto cargo ships, which required up to two weeks for transit. On several occasions, said a former division manager, MiniScribe executives looking to raise sales changed purchase orders to show that a customer took title to a shipment in Singapore when, in fact, title would not change until the drives were delivered in the United States.

MiniScribe executives tried to persuade an audit team that 1986 year-end results should include as sales the cargo on a freighter that they contended had set sail in late December. The audit team declined to do so. Eventually, the cargo and the freighter, which did not exist, were simply forgotten.

MiniScribe executives also found other ways to inflate sales figures. One was to manipulate reserves for returns of defective merchandise and bad debts. The problem of inadequate reserves grew so great that private analysts began noticing it. MiniScribe was booking less than 1% reserves; the rest of the industry had reserves ranging from 4% to 10%.

To avoid booking losses on returns in excess of its skimpy reserves, defective drives would be tossed onto a "dog pile" and booked as inventory. Eventually, the dog-pile drives would be shipped out again to new customers, continuing the cycle. Returns of defective merchandise ran as high as 15%.

At a time of strong market demand, such ploys enabled MiniScribe to seem to grow almost exponentially, posting sales of $185 million in 1986 and $362 million in 1987. In early 1988, Wiles was confidently forecasting a $660 million year, and he held fast to his rosy forecast even as disk drive sales started slipping industrywide in late spring and nose-dived in the autumn. Meanwhile, Wiles increased the pressure on his managers. Division reports would be doctored as they rose from one bureaucratic level to the next.

Before long, the accounting gimmickry became increasingly brazen. Division managers were told to "force the numbers." Workers whispered that bricks were being shipped just so a division could claim to have met its quota. Others joked that unwanted disk drives were being shipped and returned so often that they had to be repackaged because the boxes wore out.

Employees also joked about shipments to "account BW," an acronym for "big warehouse"—but that wasn't just a joke. MiniScribe established several warehouses around the country and in Canada as "just-in-time" suppliers for distributors. Customers weren't invoiced until they received shipments from the warehouses. MiniScribe, however, was booking shipments to the warehouses as sales. The number of disk drives shipped to the warehouses was at MiniScribe's discretion. It is estimated that between $80 million and $100 million worth of unordered disk drives went to the warehouses.

Wall Street began to smell trouble. Analysts could find no significant customers other than Compaq to support MiniScribe's bullish forecasts. Several major anticipated orders from Apple Computer and Digital Equipment Corp. fell through. MiniScribe reported a fourth-quarter loss and a drop in net income for 1988 despite a 66% increase in sales—on paper, that is. A week later, Wiles abruptly resigned. The stock price tumbled from a high of $15 to less than $3 per share, a decline that upset many stockholders.

An investigative committee of MiniScribe's outside directors reported that senior company officials:

- Apparently broke into locked trunks containing the auditors' working papers during the year-end 1986 audit and changed inventory figures, inflating inventory values by approximately $1 million.

- Packaged bricks and shipped them to distributors as disk drives in 1987, recording $4.3 million in sales; when the shipments were returned, MiniScribe inflated its inventory by the purported cost of the bricks.

- Packaged approximately 6,300 disk drives that had been contaminated to inflate inventory during the fourth quarter of 1988.

Several lawsuits have been filed charging MiniScribe with engineering phony sales artificially to inflate its stock to benefit insiders. The suits also charge that its auditors participated in the conspiracy by falsely certifying the company's financial statements.

Required

Write an analysis of MiniScribe's rise and fall, identifying the following:

a. How MiniScribe inflated its financial statements.

b. The factors that led to the inflated financial statements.

c. The red flags that should have raised the auditor's suspicions about phony sales and other attempts by MiniScribe to inflate income.

d. Substantive audit procedures that could have uncovered the falsified numbers in the financial statements.

Fraud

*10-81 **(Control Risk Assessment—Retail Organization, LO 3, 5)** You are the internal auditor for a company that started over 40 years ago as a local retailer of major home appliances. The company has now grown to include 55 retail stores in 12 metropolitan areas. Because of rapid growth in the number of stores opened in the last three years (46), a professional management team was hired to replace the previous management team, which was composed of members of the owning family. To encourage continued growth, a sales incentive bonus plan was instituted. Under the plan, managers of individual stores receive a bonus based on inventory turnover.

A retail point-of-sale system is used to aid inventory management. Each store is a node with terminals, a local processor, and a storewide database. The nodes communicate with a central systemwide database located at corporate offices. Retail prices for all merchandise are updated once a month to the storewide database, using a master price list provided by corporate offices.

Because the desired margin is achieved for each product sold at the established master price, inventory turnover is viewed as the critical determinant of profitability for each store. Accordingly, sales volume, by product class, is reported weekly to corporate offices. Revenue is also reported weekly, but only in the aggregate. Detailed sales and inventory data, including unit revenue, product class revenue, revenue generated at discount prices, inventory movement, and inventory levels, are produced daily by each store for use by the store manager.

Selling prices are frequently discounted in widely advertised sales. For sale items, sales clerks in each store must override the master price and input the advertised price. Sales at wholesale prices, such as contractor sales, are prohibited by company policy. Damaged goods can be sold at any time at heavily discounted prices at the discretion of the store manager, who assesses damage and sets the sale price.

Over a two-year period, a store manager inflated unit sales by the following acts:

1. Fictitious credit sales were recorded in the last month of the year, with subsequent return of the goods recorded in the first month of the new year. No goods actually changed hands.

2. Undamaged goods were declared to be damaged and sold at prices significantly less than master prices.

3. Sales were completed at wholesale prices.

4. "Sale-priced" merchandise was frequently sold at prices above its advertised sale price.

Acting alone, the store manager also sold selected merchandise for cash with no record made of the sale. Although a register receipt is required for customer pickup, the store manager verbally instructed the warehouse to load the merchandise without a receipt.

Required

a. Identify six internal control deficiencies or management deficiencies that permitted the fraud.

b. Identify four indicators that may have signaled the presence of the fraud.

c. Identify four controls needed to detect the fraud.

d. Describe the responsibilities of the internal auditing department in the situation just described.

10-82 **(Revenue Recognition and Internal Control Deficiencies, LO 2, 3, 4, 5, 6)** UTStarcom is a global leader in the manufacture, integration, and support of networking and telecommunications systems. The company sells broadband wireless products and a line of handset equipment to operators in emerging and established telecommunications markets worldwide. The following excerpt was obtained from the 2004 10-K of UTStarcom, Inc., which reported material weaknesses in the company's internal controls. In describing the company's remediation efforts, the company stated that "planned remediation measures are intended to address material weaknesses related to revenue and deferred revenue accounts and associated cost of sales." These material weaknesses were evidenced by the identification of six separate transactions aggregating approximately $5 million in which revenue was initially included in the Company's fourth-quarter 2004 financial statements before all criteria for revenue recognition were met. In addition, there were other transactions for which there was insufficient initial documentation for revenue recognition purposes, but which did not result in any adjustments to the Company's fourth-quarter 2004 financial statements. If unremediated, these material weaknesses have the potential of misstating revenue in future financial periods. The Company's planned remediation measures include the following:

Group Activity

International

a. The Company plans to design a contract review process in China requiring financial and legal staff to provide input during the contract negotiation process to ensure timely identification and accurate accounting treatment of nonstandard contracts;

b. In March 2005, the Company conducted a training seminar regarding revenue recognition, including identification of non-standard contracts, in the United States and, in April 2005, the Company conducted a similar seminar in China. Starting in May 2005, the Company plans to conduct additional training seminars in various international locations regarding revenue recognition and the identification of nonstandard contracts; and

c. At the end of 2004, the Company began requiring centralized retention of documentation evidencing proof of delivery and final acceptance for revenue recognition purposes."

Required

Address the following issues in small groups or as part of class discussion.

1. Using the disclosures above as a starting point, brainstorm about the challenges regarding internal controls that a company may face in doing business internationally.

2. The company has disclosed its planned remediation efforts for 2004. How might the auditor use that information during the 2005 audit in terms of audit planning?

3. Considering potential analytical procedures relevant to the revenue cycle that were discussed in this chapter, identify what types of analytics might be applied in 2005 to provide evidence that the problems detected in 2004 have been remedied.

4. Considering potential substantive tests of revenue that were discussed in this chapter, identify procedures that might be applied in 2005 to provide evidence that the problems detected in 2004 have been remedied.

Fraud

Ethics

10-83 **(Decision Making Case—Revenue Recognition, LO 6, 7, 8, 9)** Review the *Auditing in Practice* feature focusing on the inappropriate actions of Robert A. Putnam, the engagement partner on the HBOC audit. In this case, we expand on the problems detected in the audit. Summarizing the facts from the SEC's Administrative Proceeding against Putnam dated April 28, 2008, we know the following about the quarterly and year-end audits that led to the problems for Arthur Andersen LLP on the HBOC engagement:

- **Andersen's Review of HBOC's financial statements— First Quarter 1997** HBOC reported $68 million of software revenue during Q1, and the engagement team tested the account balance and found that $14 million was improperly recorded, which overstated pretax income by 9.4%. Most of the improperly recognized revenue related to board contingencies, and the remainder related to revenue recognized on a contract signed *after* quarter end. HBOC management refused to eliminate the improperly recorded revenue, and Putnam did not insist that they do so. Putnam approved an unqualified quarterly review report.

- **Andersen's Review of HBOC's financial statements— Second Quarter 1997** The engagement team learned that HBOC continued to improperly recognize revenue on contracts containing board contingencies, and that the company was improperly recording revenue on sales subject to side letter contingencies that allowed for contract cancellation. Further, the engagement team learned that at least one such contract that had been recorded as revenue in Q1 had been canceled during Q2. The engagement team also learned that HBOC had again recognized revenue on a contract signed after quarter-end. Putnam recommended to HBOC's management that the revenue from these contracts be reversed, but Gilbertson (the CFO) refused to do so. The errors overstated pretax income by 7%. Despite these facts, Putnam approved an unqualified quarterly review report.

- **Andersen's Review of HBOC's financial statements—Third Quarter 1997** The engagement team continued to experience the same difficulties as they had noted in Q2; Putnam continued to do nothing about the problems and continued to approve an unqualified quarterly review report.

- **Andersen's Audit of HBOC's financial statements—1997 Year End** Andersen's year-end audit included testing of HBOC's revenue recognition and accounts receivable. The engagement team used confirmations as their primary substantive evidence on these accounts. The team sent eight confirmation requests (11 *fewer* than they sent during the 1996 audit). The confirmations requested customers to confirm amounts owed to HBOC and to confirm that no revenue contingencies existed on software purchased from HBOC. Only three customers responded, and two of those noted contingencies included in side letters. Putman did not direct the team to send any additional confirmations or to perform any additional audit procedures.

  In addition, the engagement team learned that HBOC was recognizing too much revenue on maintenance contracts and that material amounts should have been deferred to later periods. Putnam asked Gilbertson to increase deferred revenue, but Gilbertson refused, promising to do so in later periods. In addition, HBOC acquired other companies during 1997 and recorded "acquisition reserves" of $95.3 million associated with the expenses of the acquisition. Putnam proposed that HBOC reverse $16 million of the reserves because they were excessive, overstating expenses by 20% (i.e., a cookie jar reserve). Gilbertson refused to make the proposed adjustment. Despite all these problems, Putnam approved an unqualified audit report and disclosed none of the issues to the audit committee.

- **Andersen's Review of HBOC's financial statements—First Quarter 1998** During the review, Putnam discovered that HBOC was misusing the acquisition reserve to offset current period operating expenses, which is in violation of GAAP and had the effect of overstating HBOC's net income. The engagement team also identified another instance of improper revenue recognition associated with a contract involving a side letter. Once again, Putnam proposed an adjusting entry to correct the problems, but Gilbertson refused to make the entry. Putnam again approved an unqualified quarterly review report.

  By April 1998, the engagement manager (Putnam's subordinate) expressed concerns about the earnings management issues occurring at HBOC to Putnam, and Putnam shared the same concerns despite doing nothing to address them. In May 1998, Putnam and the engagement team called a special meeting with Gilbertson and others at HBOC to discuss the issues, and Gilbertson expressed promises to begin properly recording the various transactions.

- **Andersen's Review of HBOC's financial statements—Second Quarter 1998** During the quarterly review, the engagement team again noted a variety of errors. These included inappropriate application of acquisition reserves to reduce current period expenses, recognition of excessive revenue from software maintenance agreements, and an understatement of the allowance for doubtful accounts. Putnam informed Gilbertson that if HBOC did not reverse the application of the acquisition reserves, Andersen would not issue its review report. After a heated discussion, Gilbertson reversed the entry related to acquisition reserves but did not correct any of the other errors. Putnam approved the issuance of the quarterly review report.

- **Andersen's Review of HBOC's financial statements—Third Quarter 1998** The engagement team again discovered the same types of earnings management issues as in prior quarters, but Putnam did not require HBOC to make corrections. Further, Putnam approved an unusual transaction in which HBOC simultaneously sold to and purchased a product from another company. Putnam advised Gilbertson that the accounting for the transaction would only be correct if the sale and purchase were not linked and if there was a defined end user for the HBOC software. Neither of these conditions was true, and Putnam was aware of this fact (and this transaction ultimately led to a restatement of $30 million about a year later). However, Putnam still approved the issuance of the quarterly review report.

- At the November 1998 meeting of HBOC's audit committee, the CEO informed the audit committee that Gilbertson was resigning as CFO, which was an unexpected event. The CEO asked Putnam if he "had a Cendant on his hands," referring to a widely reported financial fraud case at the time. Putnam responded that he knew of no problems or disagreements with Gilbertson.

  In October 1998, McKesson and HBOC announced their merger. Putnam approved the use of Andersen's reports in related filings and made no mention of the associated accounting errors.

- **Andersen's Audit of McKesson's financial statements—1998 Year End** McKesson hired Andersen to complete the audits, and Putnam and the engagement team continued to discover various accounting errors. Still, Putnam did not require the team to expand the scope of audit testing. Putnam again approved the issuance of an unqualified audit report.

  During the spring of 1999, McKesson initially disclosed some of the revenue recognition issues and by the summer of 1999, McKesson reported restatements of the 1997 and 1998 financial statements. Ultimately, six members of upper management of HBOC were charged with securities fraud. The SEC issued a cease and desist order against Putnam and denied him the privilege of appearing or practicing before the commission as an accountant for at least five years.

In many instances of fraudulent financial reporting, the auditor is completely unaware of the fraud until it ultimately unravels. That is certainly NOT the case for the HBOC fraud. Rather, it is very clear that Putnam and his Andersen engagement team were well aware of the fraud and possessed detailed knowledge of precisely how it was accomplished. Yet, they did virtually nothing to address the situation.

Required

1. What was Putnam's critical mistake in the review of Q1 1997? How did that critical mistake affect his willingness to take action to address the problems in the HBOC audit in later periods?

2. What do you think could have motivated Putnam to act as he did? Why do you think that after all the problems that he encountered, he was still willing to acquiesce to the obviously inappropriate sale/purchase transaction in Q3 1998?

3. What other elements of corporate governance failed in the HBOC situation?

4. The confirmation process in the 1997 year-end audit was clearly flawed. What did the engagement team and Putnam do wrong?

5. The McKesson acquisition of HBOC provided an opportunity for Putnam to "come clean" with what he knew. Obviously, McKesson management would have been eager to know about the earnings management issues at HBOC prior to acquiring the company. Instead, Putnam did not reveal the problems he had been encountering, even when asked directly by the CEO and the audit committee. Use the seven-step Decision Analysis Framework introduced in Chapter 3 to make a recommendation about a course of action that would have enabled Putnam to "come clean" during the acquisition process and alert the other parties involved in corporate governance of HBOC and McKesson about the problematic behaviors he had been encountering. Recall that the framework is as follows:

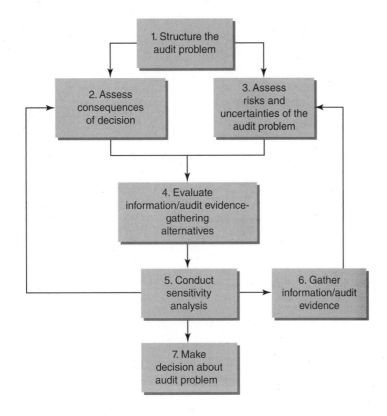

Source: Adapted from "Judgment and Choice," by Robin Hogarth.

Ethics

Fraud

10-84   **(Ethics Case—Revenue Recognition and Professional Conduct, LO 9)** For this case, use the same facts as presented in Problem 10-83. In that case, we focus on the inappropriate actions of Robert A. Putnam, the engagement *partner* on the HBOC audit. In this case, we expand on the problems detected in the audit and ultimately ask that you decide on an appropriate, alternative course of action for the *manager* of the HBOC audit, that is, Putman's subordinate. In the actual case, the audit manager questioned Putnam's actions but never took proactive action (other than talking to Putnam) to correct the known audit deficiencies.

In his book, *The Courageous Follower: Standing Up to and for Our Leaders* (1995), Ira Chaleff describes five characteristics of individuals who stand up to their organizational leaders. These characteristics include the courage to (1) assume responsibility for themselves and their organization, (2) serve the organization in a responsible manner, (3) challenge the behaviors or policies of the leader, (4) participate in transforming an organization or dealing with the difficulties associated with change, and (5) take moral action, including refusing to obey direct orders, appealing to the next level of authority, or resigning.

Required

Individually or in a group, and considering the ideas outlined by Chaleff, use the seven-step ethical decision-making framework from Chapter 3 (given below) to make a recommendation about an alternative, appropriate course of action that the audit manager on the HBOC audit could have taken.

Recall that the seven steps in the ethical decision-making framework are as follows: (1) identify the ethical issue, (2) determine who are the affected parties and identify their rights, (3) determine the most important rights, (4) develop alternative courses of action, (5) determine the likely consequences of each proposed course of action, (6) assess the possible consequences, including an estimation of the greatest good for the greatest number, and (7) decide on the appropriate course of action.

10-85   **(ACL Project, LO 7)** Refer to the ACL Case 3—Accounts Receivable in the ACL appendix posted on the book's website. This case requires the use of ACL to perform certain audit functions on accounts receivable files.

Internet

Professional Skepticism

Ethics

10-86   **(LO 3, 6, 7, 8)** Select one of the following PCAOB Disciplinary Orders (available at www.pcaob.org).

(1) ORDER INSTITUTING DISCIPLINARY PROCEEDINGS, MAKING FINDINGS, AND IMPOSING SANCTIONS

In the Matter of Traci Jo Anderson and Traci Jo Anderson, CPA Respondents

PCAOB Release No. 105-2010-007

(2) ORDER MAKING FINDINGS AND IMPOSING SANCTIONS
In the Matter of Ray O Westergard, CPA, Respondent

PCAOB Release No. 105-2010-003

(3) ORDER INSTITUTING DISCIPLINARY PROCEEDINGS, MAKING FINDINGS, AND IMPOSING SANCTIONS

In the Matter of Williams & Webster, P.S., Kevin J. Williams, CPA, and John G. Webster, CPA, Respondents

PCAOB Release No. 105-2007-001

(4) ORDER INSTITUTING DISCIPLINARY PROCEEDINGS, MAKING FINDINGS, AND IMPOSING SANCTIONS

In the Matter of Armando C. Ibarra, P.C., Armando C. Ibarra, Sr., and Armando C. Ibarra, Jr., Respondents

PCAOB No. 105-2006-001

After reading your selected Disciplinary Order, address the following issues:

a. Identify the key audit deficiencies related to accounts and assertions in the revenue cycle.

b. For each identified deficiency, indicate the appropriate action that should have been taken by the auditor.

c. In assessing the case overall, indicate (1) whether the auditor had an appropriate level of professional skepticism; (2) if applicable, what might have led the auditor to behave in an unethical manner; and (3) whether the sanctions against the auditor/audit firm seems reasonable.

10-87 **(LO 1, 3, 6, 8)** An *Auditing in Practice* feature presented earlier in the chapter discussed the SEC's complaint against Benjamin Silva III, Tvia's vice president of worldwide sales. The complaint alleges a number of actions taken by Silva. For each of the following actions indicate the accounting and/or auditing issue that should be of concern to the auditor and action that might be taken by the auditor.

International

Fraud

**Professional
Skepticism**

a. In an effort to increase revenue, Silva began entering into side agreements with Tvia's customers. Typically, these side agreements promised the customer extended payment terms and obligated Tvia to find a buyer for any product that the customer was unable to sell.

b. On multiple occasions Silva caused Tvia to misapply a payment it received from a new customer in order to pay down delinquent amounts owed by a separate customer. For example, the complaint notes that one "instance concerns Ricom, a Chinese customer which by late 2005 was past due on Tvia invoices totaling more than $740,000. In February 2006, Silva convinced another customer, Protech Perennial Limited ("Protech"), to submit a $100,000 deposit for a then-unavailable line of Tvia chips. On or about February 24, 2006, Tvia received a wire transfer from Protech for $100,000. In order to convince Tvia's finance staff to apply these funds to Ricom's account, Silva falsely claimed that Protech had wired the money on Ricom's behalf, due to purported Chinese Government restrictions on Ricom's wiring money out of that country. By this conduct, Silva mislead [sic] Tvia's CEO, CFO and auditors regarding the collectability of past due amounts owed by Ricom."

Academic Research Case (LO 1, 3)

SEARCH HINT

It is easy to locate these academic research articles! Simply use a search engine (e.g., Google Scholar) or an electronic research platform (e.g., ABI Inform) and search using the author names and part of the article title.

Academic research addresses the conceptual issues outlined in this chapter. To help you consider the linkage between academic research and the practice of auditing, read the following research article and answer the questions below.

Callen, J. L., Robb, S. W. G., & Segal, D. (2008). Revenue Manipulation and Restatements by Loss Firms. *Auditing: A Journal of Practice & Theory 27(2): 1–29.*

i. What is the issue being addressed in the paper?

ii. Why is this issue important to practicing auditors?

iii. What are the findings of the paper?

iv. What are the implications of these findings for audit quality (or audit practice) on the audit profession?

v. Describe the research methodology used as a basis for the conclusions.

vi. Describe any limitations of the research that the student (and practice) should be aware of.

Go to www.cengage.com/accounting/rittenberg for the Ford and Toyota materials.

Source and Reference	Question
Ford 10-K	**1a.** What are the key revenue cycle accounts for Ford? What accounts involve "critical accounting estimates"?
	1b. What does Ford say in Footnote 2 about its use of accounting estimates? What risk do these estimates pose for the auditor?
Ford 10-K and Toyota Annual Report or 20F	**2.** Compare Ford and Toyota's footnotes on finance receivables. What is the audit firm's responsibility regarding the informativeness of the disclosures?
	3. Use the financial ratios provided in the appendix of Chapter 8 for Ford and Toyota. What are the ratios most relevant to the revenue cycle? Why?
Ford 10-K	**4.** Ford lists a variety of risk factors associated with its business. Review those and identify which relate most to the revenue cycle. What evidence might the auditor gather to understand how those risks may affect the financial statement line items associated with the revenue cycle?
Ford 10-K	**5.** Read Ford's "Management Discussion and Analysis" section titled "Key Economic Factors and Trends Affecting the Automotive Industry." What are the main points that Ford management raises regarding its ability to generate revenue and profits in the near term? What does their statements imply about the risks associated with auditing Ford Motor Co.?

Module III: Control Testing— Sales Processing

In this module you will apply attribute sampling to Biltrite's prenumbered sales invoices to evaluate whether sales have been processed properly. Recall from Module II that several deficiencies in the design of the controls suggest an increased likelihood of material misstatement. However, the audit team believes that the use of prenumbered sales invoices and the related requirements (agree invoice to bill of lading and customer invoice, agree prices on invoice to master price list, agree calculations on invoice, and agree that customer balance is within authorized credit limit) is an effectively designed control activity and the audit team would like to rely on that control. Accordingly, the audit team has decided to test sales transactions to see whether this control activity is operating effectively. If the control is operating effectively, the audit team would be able to reduce the assessed level of control risk for the relevant assertions related to sales and accounts receivable, thereby enabling them to decrease the extent of accounts receivable confirmation and other substantive procedures related to the revenue cycle.

Specifically, you want to determine whether the control related to sales invoices is performed effectively. Knowing whether the control is operating effectively will help the audit team determine whether all recorded sales were shipped (existence of sales) and whether all shipments were invoiced and recorded at appropriate amounts (completeness of sales). As discussed previously in the case, invoices are mailed to customers prior to shipment; therefore, customers may have received invoices for goods never shipped. Also, in the absence of prenumbered bills of lading, goods may have been shipped but never billed to the customer. The second possible processing problem is that customers may have exceeded existing credit limits without home office knowledge; you need to test the degree to which this has occurred. Finally, because of lack of input editing, the prices, customer number, and/or product number may be incorrect; you will test for this as well.

Derick has asked you to complete the sampling plan worksheet that he began earlier. He has defined the sampling unit as the prenumbered sales invoice, and the relevant attributes as

1. Bill of lading attached and signed by the carrier;
2. Product prices in agreement with master price list stored in computer;
3. Extensions and footings correct;
4. Quantities and product type in agreement with customer order; and
5. Customer balance within the authorized credit limit.

The population for attribute sampling purposes is the numeric file of sales invoices.

During 2009, 22,400 sales invoices were processed, with document numbers ranging from 10610 to 33009. For each sales invoice number drawn at random and included in the sample, you will request the client to supply the invoice/bill of lading packet and the corresponding customer order. The sales invoice/bill of lading packet can be obtained from the numeric file maintained in CBIS. The customer order, the number of which appears on the face of the invoice, is stored in the computer and can be printed out on demand. You then will examine the documents for the above attributes.

Requirements

1. Based on the deficiencies in the design of controls identified in the sales processing subset of the revenue cycle, does the above sampling plan test address all relevant financial statement assertions related to sales and accounts receivable? If not, which assertion(s) are not considered in the initial plan, and how could the plan be adjusted to address these assertions?

2. Using the spreadsheet program and downloaded data, retrieve the file titled "Attrib." Using the sample size and sample evaluation tables in Chapter 8 and the following data, complete the attribute sampling plan worksheet (in using the "Sample Results Evaluation" table, select the sample size that is closest to your sample size):

   a. A 5% risk of assessing control risk too low has been decided on for all attributes;

   b. Misstatements have been defined, and expected deviation rates set for each attribute as follows:

      1. Bill of lading not attached to packet—1%
      2. Incorrect prices—1%
      3. Extension and/or footing errors—0.5%
      4. Quantities and/or product type not in agreement with customer order—1%
      5. Customer balance exceeds authorized credit limit—1.5%

   c. Tolerable deviation rates of 4% have been set for all attributes; and

   d. The following misstatements were discovered in examining the sample:

Sales Order Number	Misstatement
12511	Bill of lading not signed by carrier
15439	Invoice causing customer to exceed authorized credit limit
18616	Bill of lading missing
23468	Bill of lading missing
27891	Bill of lading missing

3. Print your completed document. (You will need to compress print size or otherwise accommodate a wide document.)

4. What conclusions can you draw based on your completed sampling plan worksheet? What impact might your findings have on the substantive audit programs for Biltrite? Based on the results of your testing, should the aggregate materiality threshold be changed for any part of the revenue cycle?

Module IV: MUS Sampling— Factory Equipment Additions

Module IV may be completed after either Chapter 10 or Chapter 14. Check with your instructor.

Richard Derick has asked you to develop a sampling plan to determine the extent of misstatements in classifying expenditures as repairs and maintenance expense or factory equipment additions. Given the problems noted during control testing (as described in Module II), Derick believes that significant misstatements may have occurred.

The same vendor's invoice frequently contains charges for parts and supplies as well as equipment, and the Biltrite employees preparing the vouchers sometimes fail to distinguish among the charges and simply indicate "factory equipment" as the debit if the invoice amount is large. Inasmuch as this type of misstatement would cause an overstatement in the factory equipment account, Derick instructs you to use MUS sampling to determine the extent to which such misstatements have occurred during 2009.

Of the total debits—$89,860,000 to factory equipment during 2009—major additions in the amount of $77,260,000 have been made to replace worn-out equipment. Derick has decided to audit the major additions in their entirety and sample the remainder.

Requirements

1. What is the objective of performing this test? What is the sampling unit? What is the population?
2. Using the spreadsheet program and downloaded data, retrieve the file labeled "MUS." Locate the following documentation in the file:

   - WP 11.3A—Monetary unit sampling plan;
   - WP 11.3B—Monetary unit sampling plan—projected misstatement; and
   - WP 11.3C—Monetary unit sampling plan—computed precision and upper misstatement limit.

   Scroll to WP 11.3A,"Monetary Unit Sampling Plan." Calculate sample size and sampling interval assuming Derick has set the following parameters:

Risk of incorrect acceptance:	5%
Anticipated misstatement:	$100,000
Tolerable misstatement:	$640,000

3. What factors did he consider in setting these parameters? Print the document.
4. Scroll to WP 11.3B, "Monetary Unit Sampling Plan—Projected Misstatement." This document summarizes all invoices containing posting errors and calculates the projected misstatement. Note the equations that have been incorporated into the document template.
   a. What factor determines whether a "tainting percentage" appears in column 4?
   b. Print the document. (Compress print size or otherwise accommodate a wide document.)
5. Scroll to WP 11.3C, "Monetary Unit Sampling Plan—Computed Precision and Upper Misstatement Limit." Complete the "Incremental Allowance for Sampling Risk" schedule by ranking the projected misstatements as appropriate. (*Hint:* If you forgot how to do this, refer to Chapter 8.)
6. Print the document.
7. Explain the meaning of the following amounts:
   a. Basic precision;
   b. Incremental allowance for sampling error;
   c. Allowance for sampling risk; and
   d. Upper misstatement limit.
8. Evaluate the sampling results. Do they support Derick's concerns regarding possible material misstatement? Note the audit adjustment based on misstatements discovered while examining the sample. Is this adjustment adequate to bring the population into acceptable bounds? If not, what alternate actions might you choose to pursue, based on the sampling results?

Module V: Accounts Receivable Aging Analysis

Richard Derick has asked you to review the accounts receivable aging analysis and the allowance for doubtful accounts and to recommend any audit adjustments or reclassifications you consider necessary. Shelly Ross had prepared the aging analysis and the allowance for doubtful accounts document before being temporarily transferred to the Joplin Mills audit. She should be back early next week, but Derick would like to "wrap up" accounts receivable this week.

Based on the aging analysis prepared by Ross, you have decided to confirm all large accounts and a sampling of the smaller accounts, using positive confirmations.

Requirements

1. Using the spreadsheet program and downloaded data, retrieve the file labeled "AR." Locate the following documentation in this file:
   - WP 3—Accounts and notes receivable—trade
   - WP 3.A—Accounts receivable aging analysis
   - WP 3.C—Allowance for uncollectible accounts

   Scroll to WP 3.A, "Accounts Receivable Aging Analysis."
   a. What proportion of the total dollar amount of accounts receivable have you included in your confirmation requests?
   b. What procedures should you apply in the event of no reply to a request for positive confirmation?
   c. What is the purpose of analyzing subsequent collections?
2. Based on your analysis of subsequent collections and the results of the confirmation process, are you satisfied that you have sufficient evidence to evaluate the existence and valuation assertions?
3. Draft the suggested Reclassification Entry A.
4. Scroll to WP 3.C, "Allowance for Uncollectible Accounts."
   a. What type of correspondence would you examine to satisfy yourself as to the accounts receivable write-offs?
   b. Draft the suggested Audit Adjustment 2. Are you satisfied that the balance in the allowance is adequate after your recommended adjustment?
   c. Scroll to WP 3, "Accounts and Notes Receivable—Trade" (lead schedule). Post Reclassification Entry A and Audit Adjustment 2 to the appropriate locations in the lead schedule.
5. Print the documents 3, 3.A, and 3.C.

11

Audit of Acquisition and Payment Cycle and Inventory

LEARNING OBJECTIVES

The overriding objective of this textbook is to build a foundation with which to analyze current professional issues and adapt audit approaches to business and economic complexities. Through studying this chapter, you will be able to:

1 Describe the activities, accounts, and assertions included in the payment and acquisition cycle.

2 Describe the approach an auditor would take to perform an integrated audit in the acquisition and payment cycle and distinguish that approach from the traditional, nonintegrated audit.

3 Identify risks to reliable financial reporting in the acquisition and payment cycle and discuss relevant fraud considerations in the acquisition and payment cycle.

4 Describe how to use preliminary analytical procedures to identify possible misstatements in the accounts and assertions related to the acquisition and payment cycle.

5 Describe why it is important for the auditor to develop an understanding of internal controls, identify controls typically present in the acquisition and payment cycle, and identify tests of controls used to test the effectiveness of controls in this cycle.

6 Describe the substantive audit procedures that should be used to test accounts payable and related expense accounts and assertions in the acquisition and payment cycle.

7 Explain the complexities inherent in auditing inventory and cost of goods sold.

8 Identify risks to reliable financial reporting associated with inventory and cost of goods sold.

9 Describe typical internal controls over inventory and cost of goods sold.

10 Describe the substantive audit procedures that should be used to test inventory and cost of goods sold.

11 Apply the decision analysis and ethical decision-making frameworks to situations involving the audit of the acquisition and payment cycle, including the inventory and cost of goods sold accounts.

CHAPTER OVERVIEW

In this chapter, we present a general discussion of risks and audit approaches related to the acquisition and payment cycle and the inventory accounts. In terms of the audit opinion formulation process, this chapter involves Phases III and IV, that is, obtaining evidence about controls and substantive evidence about accounts and assertions in the acquisition and payment cycle and for the inventory accounts. Auditors must consider the possibility of fraud when auditing these areas given the many frauds that have taken place through acquisition schemes and in accounting for inventory.

The Audit Opinion Formulation Process

I. Assessing Client Acceptance and Retention Decisions	II. Understanding the Client	III. Obtaining Evidence about Controls and Determining the Impact on the Financial Statement Audit	IV. Obtaining Substantive Evidence about Account Assertions	V. Wrapping Up the Audit and Making Reporting Decisions
CHAPTER 4	CHAPTERS 2, 4–6, and 9	CHAPTERS 5–14 and 18	CHAPTERS 7–14 and 18	CHAPTERS 15 and 16

The Auditing Profession, Regulation, and Corporate Governance	Decision-Making, Professional Conduct, and Ethics	Professional Liability
CHAPTERS 1 and 2	CHAPTER 3	CHAPTER 17

PROFESSIONAL JUDGMENT IN CONTEXT

Inventory Misstatement and Related Internal Control Problems

Ace Hardware is a retailer-owned cooperative, with 4,600 hardware, home center, and building materials stores. In September 2007, Ace Hardware said it discovered a $154 million accounting discrepancy between its general ledger and its actual inventory.

The accounting error was discovered during an internal review of financial reports. The company explained that it had found a difference between the company's 2006 general ledger balance—the company's primary method for recording financial transactions—and its actual inventory records, referred to as its perpetual inventory balance.

Ace hired a law firm and a consulting firm to investigate. The investigation cost about $10 million. As a result of the investigation, in January 2008 Ace Hardware reported that a mid-level employee in the finance department caused a $152 million accounting discrepancy between the general ledger and actual inventory. The former finance worker made journal entries of a "sizeable amount" that masked a difference in numbers between the two ledger books. The ledgers looked as though they were reconciled, but were not. About one-quarter of the error dated to 1995, and the rest took place from 2002 through 2006.

Company officials stressed that the employee did not commit fraud and that no inventory or money was missing. Rather, the company suggested that the finance person was not properly trained or equipped to do the job. The company further suggested that the situation was Ace's fault, in that the finance person was not appropriately trained and that oversight and checks and balances were not in place. Company officials also blamed the error partly on the increasingly complex and competitive retail hardware industry. Specifically, systems in place were not adequate for addressing complications that arose from Ace's recent increase in product imports from Asia.

As you read the following chapter, consider this case and the following questions:

- What types of problems might you detect as you audit your clients' inventory accounts and assertions?

- Do you think the kinds of errors noted here are uncommon?

- What do these control problems imply about the approach the auditor will need to use to audit the inventory-related accounts and assertions?

- What controls can mitigate the risks associated with accounts in the payment and acquisition cycle, including the inventory accounts and relevant assertions?

- Why is it important that companies take periodic test counts of their inventory and reconcile those counts to the general ledger accounts?

- Did the company have a material weakness in internal control over financial reporting related to the improper training of accounting and finance personnel?

Introduction

The acquisition and payment cycle includes processes for identifying products or services to be acquired, purchasing of goods and services, receiving the goods, approving payments, and paying for goods and services received. This chapter presents an integrated framework for auditing the account balances in this cycle.

Significant Accounts and Relevant Assertions in the Acquisition and Payment Cycle

LO 1

Describe the activities, accounts, and assertions included in the payment and acquisition cycle.

The major accounts in the acquisition and payment cycle are inventory, cost of goods sold, accounts payable, and expenses. An overview of the significant and relevant accounts typically included in this cycle is shown in Exhibit 11.1. The auditor will obtain evidence related to each of the five financial statement assertions discussed in Chapter 7 for these accounts. The risk related to each assertion may vary with the account balance tested. The existence and valuation assertions are usually high risk for inventory. On the other hand, completeness and valuation are usually higher risk for expenses and payables. Much of our discussion of the acquisition and payment cycle assumes an audit of a manufacturing client so that we can discuss both inventory and cost of goods sold. For many clients, inventory represents one of the larger and more difficult accounts to audit, so it is therefore often one of the more important and risky parts of an audit. Because of the unique issues associated with auditing inventory (and associated issues with cost of goods sold), we devote an entire section at the end of the chapter to this topic.

The acquisition and payment cycle consists of five distinct activities.

1. Requisition (request) for goods or services
2. Purchase of goods or services according to company policies
3. Receipt of, and accounting for, goods and services
4. Approval of items for payment
5. Cash disbursements

The acquisition process begins with a **requisition** (formal request) for goods and services. An approved requisition will result in a purchase. The receipt of goods or services should cause the recognition of accounts payable with debits to an expense account, an inventory account, or an asset account. Most companies will have specific procedures for approving the payments for these purchases. When the approved payment for goods or services received is made, the payment is reflected as a cash disbursement.

Many companies have an **automated purchasing system** that is a networked software system linking to vendors whose offerings and prices have been preapproved by appropriate management. The technology enables purchasers to negotiate favorable prices with vendors while streamlining the buying process. Best practice for an automated system consolidates all the different functions or

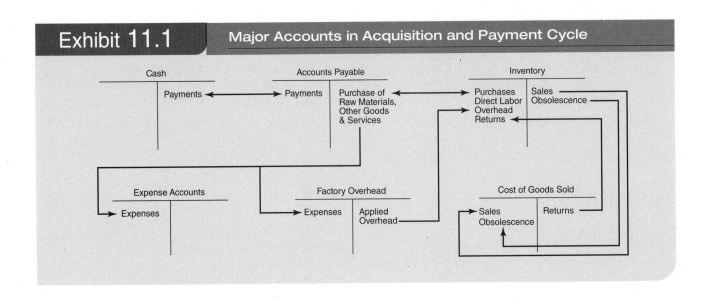

Exhibit 11.1   Major Accounts in Acquisition and Payment Cycle

activities involved, assuring timely and accurate orders. An automated purchasing system will perform the following beneficial tasks:

- Apply preloaded specifications and materials lists to the system to start the process. This will establish a foundation to assure proper checks and balances.
- Automatically flag invoices that do not reconcile with purchase orders.
- Create change orders and analyze variances from purchase orders.

For many clients, the acquisition and payment cycle is a computerized process that is integrated with **supply chain management**. Supply chain management is the management and control of materials in the logistics process from the acquisition of raw materials to the delivery of finished products to the end user (customer). A number of companies have specific contracts with vendors that specify price and delivery terms to meet the client's production or sales needs. Companies such as Wal-Mart and JCPenney have arrangements with some vendors whereby title to the goods does not pass until a consumer purchases them at the checkout counter. The auditor has to understand the contracts and processes to determine when title passes and when the client[1] assumes the risk for the inventory located on the client's premises. Many companies have been successful in reducing inventory levels and associated carrying costs. Thus, if the auditor finds an unusually large amount of inventory on hand, there should be concern about potential obsolescence of the inventory.

> **PRACTICAL POINT**
>
> Most automated purchasing systems are dependent on negotiated contracts with vendors for the quality, pricing, and timeliness of delivery.

Performing the Integrated Audit of the Acquisition and Payment Cycle

Recall the eight general steps to conducting an integrated audit, which we first covered in Chapter 10. We reproduce those steps below and tailor them to the audit of the acquisition and payment cycle:

LO 2

Describe the approach an auditor would take to perform an integrated audit in the acquisition and payment cycle and distinguish that approach from the traditional, nonintegrated audit.

Phases I and II of the Audit Opinion Formulation Process

1. Continually update information on business risk, including the identification of any fraud risk factors noted during preliminary audit planning. Update audit planning for new risk information.
2. Analyze potential motivations to misstate accounts in the acquisition and payment cycle, as well as the existence of other fraud indicators, and determine the most likely method that those accounts might be misstated.
3. Perform preliminary analytical procedures to determine if unexpected relationships exist in the accounts and document how the audit testing should be modified because of the unusual relationships.
4. Develop an understanding of the internal controls in the acquisition and payment cycle that are designed to address the risks identified in the three previous steps, including the applicability of entity-level controls to the acquisition and payment cycle. This understanding will include a review of the client's documentation of internal controls.

Phases III and IV of the Audit Opinion Formulation Process

5. Determine the important controls that need to be tested for the purposes of (a) formulating an opinion on the entity's internal controls and (b) reducing substantive testing for the financial statement audit.
6. Develop a plan for testing internal controls and perform the tests of key controls in the acquisition and payment cycle. (For nonpublic companies,

---

[1] We will refer to the business being audited as the client. However, as noted in Chapter 1, the real client is the audit committee of the public company being audited.

the auditor can choose to not test controls, but must determine where material misstatements could occur if controls are not present.)

7. Analyze the results of the tests of controls.

If deficiencies are identified, assess those deficiencies to determine whether they are significant deficiencies or material weaknesses. Determine whether the preliminary control risk assessment should be modified (should control risk be assessed at a higher level?) and document the implications for substantive testing. Determine the impact of these deficiencies, and any revision in the control risk assessment, on planned substantive audit procedures by determining the types of misstatements that are most likely to occur.

If no control deficiencies are identified, assess whether the preliminary control risk assessment is still appropriate, determine the extent that controls can provide evidence on the correctness of account balances, and then determine planned substantive audit procedures. The level of substantive testing in this situation will be less than what is likely required in circumstances where deficiencies in internal control were identified.

8. Perform planned substantive procedures (substantive analytical procedures and direct tests of account balances) based on the potential for misstatement and the information gathered about the effectiveness of internal controls. The substantive procedures will include procedures to address fraud risks. In completing substantive procedures the auditor will continue to assess whether the evidence obtained from all sources is sufficient and appropriate and the auditor may need to adjust the audit plan (either tests of controls or substantive tests) to help ensure that sufficient and appropriate audit evidence is obtained.

The audit starts with an analysis of risks to reliable financial reporting and includes an analysis of controls to address those risks. The substantive testing of the account balances focuses on material transactions affecting the account balances during the year: purchases, payments, and production.

The relative strengths of the client's internal controls have a significant impact on the audit of the accounts in the acquisition and payment cycle. The *Auditing in Practice* feature highlights the ineffectiveness of controls over inventory at CSK Auto Corp. These control deficiencies were assessed to be material weaknesses in internal control and likely meant that CSK's auditors would have to rely heavily on substantive tests of details to obtain sufficient competent evidence related to inventory.

How does an integrated audit of accounts in the acquisition and payment cycle differ from a more traditional audit? A traditional audit will focus on changes in the accounts during the year and account balances at year end.

AUDITING *in Practice*

INVENTORY CONTROLS AT CSK AUTO CORP.

The following is an excerpt from CSK's Management Report on Internal Controls over Financial Reporting for the year ended February 3, 2008.

The Company did not maintain effective controls over the completeness, accuracy, existence and valuation of its inventory. Specifically, effective controls, including monitoring, were not maintained to ensure that the Company's inventory systems completely and accurately processed and accounted for inventory movements within the Company's distribution network, particularly the disposition of inventory returns from customers. Additionally, the Company did not maintain effective monitoring and review over in-transit inventory, defective product warranty costs, core inventory and related core return liability accounts and shrink expense and shrink accruals. Furthermore, reconciliations of distribution center and warehouse physical inventory counts to the general ledger balances were not performed accurately, resulting in adjustments to year-end inventory balances.

These material weaknesses in inventory-related controls would significantly influence the approach the auditor used to audit the inventory-related accounts.

In contrast, an integrated audit will focus on assessing the controls related to cycle-specific accounts. If the controls are effective, reduced substantive testing related to the account balances is possible.

Our discussion in this section follows the steps of the integrated audit approach introduced in Chapter 10. We have tailored this approach to the audit of the acquisition and payment cycle.

Consider the Risks Related to the Acquisition and Payment Cycle (Steps 1 and 2)

Because of the volume of transactions, as well as the ability to physically move inventory, the acquisition and payment cycle is often the subject of fraud. Most of the frauds involve overstatement of inventory or assets and understatement of expenses. Many disbursement frauds (defalcations) involve fictitious purchases, or in some cases kickbacks to the purchasing agent. Frauds that have taken place include the following:

- Employee theft of inventory
- Employee schemes involving fictitious vendors as means to transfer payments (unnoticed) to themselves
- Executives recording fake inventory or inappropriately recording higher values for existing inventory by creating false records for items that do not exist (e.g., inflated inventory count sheets, and bogus receiving reports or purchase orders)
- Executives misusing travel and entertainment accounts and charging them as company expense
- Schemes to classify expenses as assets (i.e., inappropriately capitalizing items that are truly current-period expenses)
- Manipulation of "restructuring reserves" to manage future income
- Large manual adjustments to inventory accounts

LO 3

Identify risks to reliable financial reporting in the acquisition and payment cycle and discuss relevant fraud considerations in the acquisition and payment cycle.

PRACTICAL POINT

As part of audit planning, auditors must brainstorm about how fraud might occur. In the context of auditing inventory accounts, the team should brainstorm by asking themselves questions such as, If employees worked on the loading dock, how could they steal inventory? In other words, auditors should always be skeptical of the client, the client's employees, and their collective set of motivations and incentives that may not be consistent with accurate financial reporting.

AUDITING *in Practice*

FRAUD IN THE ACQUISITION AND PAYMENT CYCLE AT WORLDCOM AND PHAR-MOR

WorldCom

WorldCom management recorded billions of line rental expenses as fixed assets. In other words, managers inappropriately debited fixed assets rather than debiting expenses, thereby bolstering their current period income. Managers were motivated to engage in the fraud to meet earnings expectations and to show that they were able to manage their "line expenses" better than the rest of the industry. Because the expenses were in line with previous years, their relatively low level did not raise auditor suspicion. In this case, the auditors should have been skeptical that WorldCom was able to achieve what other companies in its industry could not.

Phar-Mor

Phar-Mor, a major discount retailer, had over 300 stores in the 1990s with great operating results and a concept that

captured the imagination of Wall Street. Typical of many frauds, the company was dominated by an officer who viewed the company as his own and diverted more than $10 million to support a now defunct minor-league basketball league. To cover up this misuse of company money, the officers directed the managers of each store to inflate their inventory costs. For example, if a carton of Coca-Cola cost $1.99, they were to value it at $2.99. The overstatements were needed to balance the cash outflow to the creation of an asset. Company management was emboldened to commit the fraud because they knew the auditor would not visit all 300 stores to test inventory valuation.

The auditor should consider a number of potential fraud indicators that affect this cycle, including:

- Inventory that is growing at a rate greater than sales
- Expenses that are either significantly above or below industry norms
- Capital assets that seem to be growing faster than the business and for which there are no strategic plans
- Significant reduction of "reserves," particularly restructuring reserves
- Expense accounts that have significant credit entries
- Travel and entertainment expense accounts, but no documentation or approval of expenditures
- Inadequate follow-up to auditor recommendations on needed controls
- Payments made to senior officers in the form of loans that are subsequently forgiven.

Of course, not all of the risks are associated with fraud. As illustrated in the Ace Hardware situation in the introduction of this chapter, many of the misstatements are caused simply by errors in the accounting systems. Many of the errors will show the same symptoms as identified here as potential fraud risk items and should be investigated accordingly.

Perform Preliminary Analytical Procedures for Possible Misstatements (Step 3)

Several analytical procedures may help the auditor identify potential misstatements of inventory, expense account balances, and accounts payable balances. Calculating and analyzing the dollar and percent change in inventory, cost of goods sold, and expense account balances relative to both past performance and industry performance may identify unexpected results. For example, a number of ratios, often analyzed by product line or location, can provide useful insights. These ratios, including *inventory turnover*, *gross profit margin*, *number of day's sales in inventory* and **shrinkage ratio** can be compared with prior years, industry averages, and auditor expectations. A *common-sized income statement* can help identify cost of goods sold or expense accounts that are out of line with the auditor's expectations, which should be based on prior years, industry information, and the auditor's knowledge of the business.

Cross-sectional analysis of multilocation retail clients can identify locations needing more detailed testing. Inventory per square foot of retail space can be calculated for each location and compared with the average in stores of comparable size and product mix. The auditor can then plan to obtain appropriate evidence for those locations with significantly more or less inventory than expected.

Linking Internal Controls and Financial Statement Assertions for Accounts in the Payment and Acquisition Cycle (Steps 4 and 5)

The acquisition and payment cycle consists of five distinct activities where risks exist and, thus, where the client will likely have implemented internal controls.

1. Requisition (request) for goods or services
2. Purchase of goods or services according to company policies
3. Receipt of, and accounting for, goods and services
4. Approval of items for payment
5. Cash disbursements

Once the auditor has identified the risks in the acquisition and payment cycle, the auditor will gain an understanding of the controls that the client has implemented to address those risks. As part of this understanding, the auditor will focus on the assertions for each account and identify the controls that relate to risks for each assertion. In an integrated audit, or in a nonintegrated audit where the auditor wants to reduce substantive testing, this understanding will be used to identify important controls that need to be tested. The specific controls implemented by the client will vary with the amount of automation of the process. The following discussion highlights typical controls for each of the five activities of the acquisition and payment cycle.

1. Requisition of Goods and Services

The acquisition process begins with the organization's production or sales plan. Some organizations will have long-term production plans. For example, in the automotive industry a manufacturer might schedule production for a month in advance and notify its suppliers of the production plan. In other situations (e.g., Dell Computer), the production process begins when Dell receives an order for the computer. The auditor must thoroughly understand the client's relationships with its suppliers and should examine major contracts that specify delivery, quantity, timing, and quality conditions. The traditional acquisition process begins with recognizing the need for the purchase—either by an individual or a computer program that monitors inventory or production.

Embedded in the requisition process are a number of controls to help assure that all purchases are properly approved. Normally, a requisition form is forwarded to the purchasing department by a supervisor, although some departments may have authority for individual purchases up to a specific dollar limit. Computer-generated purchase orders are often reviewed by the purchasing department, but in some automated systems the purchase order may be electronically communicated to the vendor with no additional review. An overview of a traditional requisition process is shown in Exhibit 11.2.

Exhibit 11.2	Overview of the Requisition Process

INVENTORY

Form of requisition:

- Written requisition for specific products by the production manager or stockroom manager
- Computer-generated requisition based on current inventory levels and production plans

RETAIL ORGANIZATION

- Overall authorization to purchase product lines is delegated to individual buyers by the marketing manager. The authorization is built into the computer as a control. The limits for individual goods can be exceeded only on specific approval by the marketing manager.
- Store managers may be granted authority to purchase a limited number of goods. The store manager's ability to issue a purchase order may be subject to overall corporate limits, usually specified in dollars.
- The supplier may have access to the retailer's inventory database and, by contract, ship replacement merchandise based on sales activity and reorder points.

JUST-IN-TIME MANUFACTURING PROCESS

An agreement is signed with the supplier whereby the supplier agrees to ship merchandise (just in time) according to the production schedule set by the manufacturer. A long-term supply contract is negotiated specifying price, quality of products, estimated quantities, penalties for product shortages or quality problems, and so forth. Specific purchase orders are not issued; rather, the production plan is communicated to the supplier with the specified delivery dates. The production plan serves as the requisition.

SUPPLIES: MANUFACTURING

Requisitions are issued by production departments and sent to the production manager for approval.

SUPPLIES AND MISCELLANEOUS: OTHER DEPARTMENTS

- Formal requisitions are approved by the departmental supervisors.
- Each department may be given a budget for supplies and may have the ability to issue purchase orders directly for the needed items or may be able to purchase a limited number of items without a purchase order.

SERVICE CONTRACTS

Contracts are negotiated directly by the department. For example, the data processing department may negotiate a service contract with a vendor for backup service.

Many companies partner with major suppliers to improve their supply-chain management process. For example, General Motors partnered with Eaton Corporation to furnish already assembled subassemblies that are loaded directly into the production line. This kind of relationship requires close coordination and may never involve a requisition form. It may only involve the development of a long-term contract and the sharing of production schedules with the supplier. Goods are delivered and moved directly into production. There is no formal receiving department, and Eaton Corporation is paid upon the production of an automobile. Since the requisition process is automated, the company will likely implement automated controls in this process.

2. Purchase of Goods and Services

Many organizations centralize the purchasing function in a purchasing department. The rationale for a separate purchasing function is that it:

1. Promotes efficiency and effectiveness
2. Eliminates potential favoritism that could take place if individual department heads were allowed to place orders
3. Reduces the opportunity for fraud by segregating the authorization to purchase from the custody and recording functions
4. Centralizes control in one function

AUDITING *in Practice*

WEAK INTERNAL CONTROLS, UNETHICAL DECISIONS, AND A FICTITIOUS VENDOR

Baird Products manufactures metal parts for the automotive industry. Robert Grant was the manager in charge of the metal casting department, and he reported to Linda Thompson, the facility manager. Thompson trusted Grant and relied on his judgment and honesty. However, Grant developed a fairly lavish lifestyle that included gambling, and he also had three college-age children to support. The purchasing process and controls at Baird are uncomplicated. All purchase requests are to be approved by the department manager and then sent to the accounting department for issuance of the purchase order. The accounting department determines that the purchase is within the budget and that the vendor is on an approved list. Although Accounting requires that approved vendors provide a company name, address, telephone number, and principal contact, there was no actual verification of the vendors, a control weakness that Grant learned about and ultimately exploited.

Grant's fraud began with suppliers for products in his department. He began requiring vendors to provide him with money and gifts in order to maintain their sales volume at Baird, and vendors that refused risked being shut out of business with Baird. Later, the fraud grew larger when he required all the vendors that he dealt with to pay him a "commission" on their sales to Baird. Vendors feared losing sales if they didn't comply, so they did not report this practice to Thompson or other members of management. The fraud grew still larger when Grant set up a fictitious vendor (RGWB Inc.), and embezzled nearly $200,000 over about 18 months. The fraud was finally

discovered when Grant became ill and another employee took over his job during his absence. Baird fired Grant and brought criminal charges against him, but Grant fled and never faced justice. Baird learned the following lessons from this fraud:

- Even though controls are in place, they are sometimes not followed or they are followed incompletely, and if employees understand this control weakness they may exploit it.

- Companies need to have fraud hotlines where employees, vendors, and third parties can report inappropriate activity without fear of intimidation.

- Employees who seem honest and trustworthy sometimes violate that trust. Anyone in a position of trust with control over monetary resources needs to be treated with professional skepticism, both by the company itself and by its external auditors.

- Controls must be strong in the purchasing area, and there should be adequate segregation of duties of individuals who place orders versus individuals who select vendors, compare prices, and make the actual orders. Further, adequate supervision and knowledge of vendors is a vital job for top management.

- For ongoing frauds to be successful it is often necessary for the employee(s) involved to be in a position to continue the fraud on a daily basis. Mandating vacations for all employees can be a useful control in trying to prevent fraud.

Although there are advantages to centralized purchasing, there is a risk that purchasing agents may enter into kickback arrangements with vendors. Controls include requiring competitive bids for large purchases and rotating purchase agents across product lines. Perhaps the most important control is an authorized vendor database. Company employees cannot purchase from vendors other than those in the database, thereby making it difficult to set up fictitious vendors.

In traditional purchasing situations, prenumbered forms are used to establish the uniqueness of each order and the completeness of the purchase order population. The purchase order identifies the quantity and prices of goods ordered, quality specifications, and the delivery date. The receiving department uses the purchase order to determine whether a shipment of goods should be accepted. The accounting department uses the purchase order to determine whether a purchase was authorized and whether the vendor's invoice is correct.

Two variations of the traditional purchase order are becoming more common: the computer-generated purchase order and the supply-chain delivery contract.

Computer-Generated Purchase Order   Good inventory management identifies levels for inventory reorders. When inventory drops below a specified level, or in response to production plans, the company's information system generates a purchase order that is sent directly to a prespecified vendor. Companies may consider additional controls, such as (1) a maximum quantity that can be ordered within a given time period, (2) a minimum amount of previous usage during a specified time period, and (3) a required review by a purchasing agent for some accounts or for high-dollar levels.

Supply-Chain Delivery Contracts with Major Suppliers   A variation of the computer-generated purchase order is the electronic consignment system used by some retailers. As an example, Wal-Mart encourages its partners to monitor store activities, inventory levels, and current trends in sales and authorizes the vendor to ship additional goods to stores when inventory levels decrease. However, the trade-off is that the partner—e.g., Levi Strauss—maintains ownership of its product until a consumer purchases it. When the consumer brings the jeans to the checkout counter, the ownership transfers to Wal-Mart and then to the consumer. The sales information is captured and the accounting system records the sale as well as the cost of goods sold and a payable to Levi Strauss. The contract between the trading partners also specifies controls to assure that Wal-Mart acknowledges receipt of goods and takes steps to assure that the goods are not subject to damage, theft, or loss.

3. Receipt of, and Accounting for, Goods and Services

Receiving departments should make sure that only authorized goods are received, the goods meet order specifications, an accurate count of the goods received is taken, and that accountability is established to assure that all receipts are recorded. Several alternative methods of recording the receipt of goods include the following:

- The receiving department prepares *prenumbered receiving documents* to record all receipts.
- The receiving department *electronically scans bar codes* on the goods received to record quantity and vendor and then visually inspects the goods for quality. The computer prepares a sequentially numbered receiving record for goods scanned in.
- *Departments may receive goods directly*, such as office supplies, and must approve payment for the merchandise.

PRACTICAL POINT

Management implements controls related to the purchase of goods and services to help assure that only authorized purchases are made and that they are made at competitive prices. Some systems can accomplish these objectives without the forms described here. The auditor must make sure that the controls effectively address the risks associated with the purchase of goods and services, regardless of the form of the controls.

PRACTICAL POINT

Controls should be designed to mitigate the risks associated with the arrangements between suppliers and their customers.

PRACTICAL POINT

Companies and vendors are increasingly integrated. If a subcomponent producer fails to deliver quality products, then there is a risk that the product produced will also fail. The auditor will need to consider this risk when assessing the valuation of inventory.

- Goods are received *directly into the production process*. The vendor is paid according to the long-term contract based on the purchaser's actual production, and the vendor is penalized for production delays that are due to failures to deliver the goods.

The traditional receiving process creates a prenumbered receiving document based on a count of the merchandise received. A copy of the purchase order (usually with quantities blanked out to help assure an independent count) is reviewed to determine whether a shipment is authorized. Prenumbered receiving documents establish the completeness of the population and are useful in determining that all goods are recorded in the correct period.

Automated scanning can improve both control and efficiency of the receiving process. Products shipped with bar codes can be directly scanned into the system. Actual receipts can be automatically matched with purchase orders to determine if the shipment contains errors. Goods received into production must match the production process. If they do not, then there is a potential problem of either the production line shutting down or producing the wrong subcomponents. For example, if Eaton fails to deliver the correct subassembly to General Motors, the production line will shut down and General Motors will know the cause. Although this is not a traditional "accounting control," it is very effective because any failure immediately gets the attention of management and the vendor. Thus, there is strong motivation to avoid any mistakes.

As auditors increasingly encounter these integrated order, delivery, and payment supply-chain management systems, they have to consider the types of controls that should be present. Exhibit 11.3 provides an overview of controls that are found in traditional receiving systems and in more automated systems.

Regardless of the approach taken to the receiving function, the auditor must gain assurance that management has sufficient controls to monitor purchases. If errors occur, they are most likely related to the valuation of inventory or expenses.

4. Approval of Items for Payment

Approval typically involves a **three-way match** among the vendor invoice, the purchase order, and the receiving report. This match can occur manually or it can be an automated process.

Traditional Manual Matching   The traditional, document-based acquisition and payment system requires personnel in accounts payable to match the vendor invoice, the purchase order, and the receiving report to determine the validity of the requested payment. If all items on the three documents properly match, the vendor's invoice is set up as an account payable with a scheduled payment date. Discrepancies are reviewed with the purchasing agent. The supporting documentation and authorization are then presented to the treasury department for payment. Internal controls should assure that all items are recorded in a timely manner, that the authorization process includes a review of documents, and that supporting documentation is canceled on payment to avoid duplicate payments.

Automated Matching   The traditional approach to controlling the receipt of, and payment for, purchases is labor-intensive and error-prone. The **automated matching** process represents an efficient alternative. Purchase orders are entered into a purchase order database that is accessed by the receiving department to determine whether an incoming shipment of goods should be accepted. The receiving department electronically records the receipt of goods through scanning of the bar code or other means and cross-references the receipt to the purchase order.

The computerized application matches the three documents (purchase order, receiving document, and vendor invoice), and if the three-way match is within

---

PRACTICAL POINT

Companies need controls to make sure not only the correct quantity of goods is received and is valued at the correct purchase price; they must also have controls to make sure that the goods delivered meet the quality requirements of the company. For example, if Boeing is not sure of the quality of an aircraft engine purchased from General Electric, then it risks failure of its plane. Similarly, if GE is not sure of the quality of the fuel control system it receives from its supplier, it incurs risks of engine failure. The auditor must also understand these risks and controls.

Exhibit 11.3	Comparison of Controls in Traditional and Automated Systems

Traditional Receiving System	Electronic Integrated Receiving System
Purchase orders are prepared and sent to vendors.	Long-term contract is signed with vendor specifying: • Quality • Shipping and delivery requirements • Payment terms • Penalties for performance failures • Reconciliations between trading partners for goods shipped/received
Purchase orders based on: • Projected sales or production • Current inventory levels	Quantities are based on production plans or sales programs. Quantities and delivery times are updated monthly or bi-weekly depending on scheduling and shipping constraints.
Price is either negotiated, or competitively bid among a number of vendors.	Price is locked in with a preferred vendor.
Independent receiving function exists.	Goods are delivered to production line.
Independent, sequentially numbered receiving documents are prepared to provide evidence that the goods are received.	Disruptions of production provide evidence that goods were not delivered.
Accounts payable department matches purchase order, receiving document, and invoice and accrues accounts payable.	Accruals are set up based on contract (production, sales of goods, etc.).
Payments are made via check or by electronic transfer once or twice a month.	Payments are electronically transferred to vendor based on contractual terms.
Differences are identified before payments are made.	Processes are described in the contract to resolve differences between goods received and goods that were shipped by vendor.

a pre-specified tolerance limit, the invoice is approved for payment. A payment date is scheduled, and a check is automatically generated on the scheduled date and is signed using an authorized signature plate. The complete payment process occurs without any apparent human intervention. There is no authorized reviewer, no physical matching, and no individual physically signing the checks. In some systems, the payment may be transferred electronically to the vendor.

The lack of human intervention is compensated for by control procedures and authorization concepts built into the system (referred to as **automated controls**) such as the following:

- *Authorized Vendors*—Purchases can be made only from authorized vendors.
- *Restricted Access*—Access is restricted to databases, in particular to the vendor database and the purchasing database. Anyone with the ability to add a vendor or make unauthorized purchase orders is in a position to set up fictitious vendors and purchases. Therefore, someone outside the purchasing department should maintain the vendor database (a list of approved vendors).
- *Automatic Processes*—Although the receiving department has access to the purchase order (read-only), the use of automatic scanners and other counting devices lessens counting and identification errors.
- *Reconciliations Inherent in the Process*—Most retailers mark retail prices on the goods at the distribution center when they are received. The retail price tickets for an order can be generated from the purchase order. The actual number of tickets used should be reconciled with the goods received, and any leftover tickets should cause an adjustment to be made to the receiving report.

- *Automation of Error-Prone Activities*—Vendor invoices are traditionally entered into the system by accounts payable personnel, thereby segregating this process from the other two functions. An alternative is to receive invoices electronically. It is still important that purchasing and receiving not have the ability to enter vendor invoice data or access the vendor invoice file.
- *Restricted Access to Transferring Funds*—Access to the check signature plate, or authorization of electronic cash transfers, is usually limited to the treasury function.
- *Monitoring*—Activity reports are prepared on a regular basis for management review.

Because most of the control procedures are developed during the system design process, it is important that users and internal auditors actively participate in reviewing the effectiveness of controls designed into the computer application.

5. Cash Disbursements

PRACTICAL POINT

Cash disbursements need proper authorization; supporting documentation (electronic or paper-based) needs to be immediately canceled in order to avoid duplicate payments; and the process must be monitored for unusual activity. In an integrated audit, these controls will be tested and, if working properly, will provide the auditor with evidence on the accuracy of the account balances in the cycle.

PRACTICAL POINT

The computerized process requires authorization for orders, restricted access to the vendor database, automatic reconciliation, and monitoring for unusual activity. In an integrated audit, these controls will be tested and, if working properly, will provide the auditor with significant evidence on the accuracy of the account balances in the cycle.

In a manual system, someone in the organization (the president in some small organizations, the treasurer in others) reviews the completeness of the documentation and signs a check for payment of goods and services. The supporting documents are immediately canceled to avoid duplicate payments. In most automated systems, the checks are generated automatically according to the scheduled payment date and the supporting documents are canceled when the invoice is set up for payment. The most important controls in these systems are (1) review of transactions, by which someone reviews the expenditures and compares them to other key data (e.g., production, budgets, other measures of volume) and (2) the direction of vendor disputes to someone outside the process. Other controls include the periodic review of the system by the internal audit department and periodic reconciliation of inventory on hand with inventory per the books.

Effectiveness of the Design of Controls in the Acquisition and Payment Cycle

If the client's controls in the payment and acquisition cycle are designed effectively and mitigate the relevant risks, the auditor can then test those controls to see if they are operating effectively. Testing of controls is necessary for the completion of the integrated audit. For the traditional nonintegrated audit, the auditor may decide to test the effectiveness of the controls so that substantive testing can possibly be altered or reduced. If the auditor determines that the controls are operating effectively, then the auditor can potentially rely more extensively on substantive analytical procedures to obtain evidence on account balances.

Design and Perform Tests of Controls and Analyze Results of Tests of Controls (Steps 6 and 7)

The internal controls to be tested are those that help to assure that all purchases are authorized and all payments are for goods received, are made at the appropriate amount, in the correct time period, and are paid only once to the authorized vendor. Recall that typical tests of controls include inquiry of relevant personnel, observation of the control being performed, examination of documentation corroborating that the control has been performed, and reperformance of the control by the auditor testing the control. However, all types of tests of controls are not necessarily relevant to every control. Furthermore, many tests of controls involve computerized controls, for example, an automated three-way match.

For manual controls, the auditor may test whether the three-way matching control was operating effectively by taking a sample of payments and tracing them to the documentation corroborating that the control has been performed. Attribute sampling would likely be used to determine and select the sample. In addition, the auditor might take a sample of receiving reports and trace through the system to test controls and the completeness assertion. Significant lags in recording of the liability indicate potential problems that should be addressed during substantive testing of accounts payable at year end.

Evidence of proper authorization should be available for each purchase and payment. Paper-based systems provide evidence of authorization through signatures. To test these types of controls, the auditor will usually look to see if signatures are present, and if not, will follow up with responsible personnel. Computerized systems are controlled through access controls and exception reports that are tested by the auditor using computerized audit techniques, as well as inquiry and examination of documentation.

If the auditor finds that internal controls are effective, then substantive procedures might focus on substantive analytical procedures for the relevant expense accounts and reduced tests of details on the balance sheet accounts. If the controls are found to be ineffective, the auditor will need to perform more direct tests of the account balances rather than relying extensively on substantive analytical procedures.

Perform Substantive Testing of the Accounts in the Acquisition and Payment Cycle (Step 8)

We now focus on the basic substantive audit procedures for accounts in this transaction cycle and how they are affected by the auditor's assessment of the client's internal controls. The scope and extent of testing for these accounts will vary with the complexity of the transactions, the risk of misstatement, and the effectiveness of the controls associated with these accounts.

Substantive Tests of Accounts Payable

The auditor's major concern with accounts payable is that the account will be understated. Therefore, the most relevant assertion is the completeness assertion. The testing to be performed depends on the risk of an understatement of accounts payable. If there is little risk, the testing might be limited to substantive analytical procedures, such as a comparison of underlying expenses with that of the prior year and related tests of the underlying asset or liability account. On the other hand, if there are significant deficiencies or material weaknesses in internal control over acquisitions, the auditor will use one or more of the following testing approaches:

1. Analytical review of related expense accounts and comparisons with other underlying economic data
2. Testing of subsequent disbursements
3. Request for vendor statements (confirmations of payables and reconcile to recorded amounts).

Exhibit 11.4 is an example of a partial audit program for testing accounts payable and purchases. This program is based on an assessment that there are no significant deficiencies or material weaknesses in internal control over these processes.

Analytical Review of Related Expense Accounts This procedure is designed to determine if the accounting data indicate a potential understatement of expenses. If an understatement is likely, the auditor expands accounts payable tests by performing one or both of the two tests of details described next. Analytical review of related expense accounts is used as the primary substantive test on clients for whom control risk has been assessed as low, when no red flags are present to indicate motivation to understate payables, and when the company is not in danger of violating potential debt covenants related to maintenance of working capital.

Testing Subsequent Disbursements The auditor examines a sample of cash disbursements made after the end of the year to determine whether the

		December 31, 2011
		W/P Ref	Done By

Exhibit 11.4 — Typical Manufacturing Company Audit Program—Accounts Payable

AUDIT OBJECTIVES

Assess the control risk over purchase and cash disbursement transactions, and determine the accuracy of relevant assertions (completeness, existence, valuation, presentation, and obligations) related to purchases, operating expenses, and trade accounts payable.

TEST OF CONTROLS AND TRANSACTIONS

1. Review computer matching exception reports to determine number of exceptions and effectiveness of follow-up procedures.
2. Determine whether there have been any changes to the computer programs for processing purchases and disbursements during the year.
3. Test authorization controls by examining effectiveness of access controls to the computer system.
4. Review appropriate account distribution for a selected set of transactions; determine that they are recorded at the correct price and that they are recorded in the correct time period.

PRELIMINARY ANALYTICAL PROCEDURES

Prepare a common-size income statement and compare expenses with the auditor's expectations based on prior periods and knowledge of current environment.
Identify and investigate significant differences.

TESTS OF DETAILS

1. Use generalized audit software to verify mathematical accuracy of accounts payable, and agree to general ledger (valuation).
2. Agree monthly statements and confirmations from major vendors with accounts payable list (existence, completeness, valuation, and obligation).
3. Perform a cutoff test of purchases and cash disbursements.
4. Review long-term purchase commitments, and determine whether a loss needs to be accrued (completeness, presentation, and disclosure).
5. State your conclusion as to the correctness of the account balances.

---

disbursements are for goods and services applicable to the previous year—and, if so, whether a liability was recorded in the previous year. The disbursements review is followed by an examination of unrecorded vendor invoices and receiving reports to determine whether goods or services received in the previous year were properly set up as a payable. If control risk is high or there are fraud-related red flags, the auditor may review 100% of the larger subsequent disbursements.

Reconciling Vendor Statements or Confirmations with Recorded Payables The auditor may choose to request vendors' monthly statements or send confirmations to major vendors requesting a statement of open account items. The auditor reconciles the vendor's statement or confirmation with the client's accounts payable trial balance. The method generates reliable evidence but is costly (in auditor time spent reconciling the amounts) and is used when there is a high risk that the company does not pay vendors on a timely basis.

Other Accounts Payable Substantive Tests: Year-End Cutoff Tests Cutoff (correct time period) errors are common. Some of these difficulties occur because year end is a hectic time, and errors can occur if precautions are not taken to assure timely recording. The subject of cutoff tests is discussed in conjunction with inventory later in this chapter.

PRACTICAL POINT

Requesting vendor confirmations of open items can be a highly effective audit procedure when the auditor suspects material understatement of the accounts payable account. The procedure is audit-labor intensive and is used on clients where control risk is high.

AUDITING *in Practice*

UNDERSTATEMENT OF LIABILITIES AND EXPENSES AT ADVANCED MARKETING SERVICES

Advanced Marketing Services (AMS) is a San Diego-based wholesaler of general-interest books that provides a variety of other services, including promotional and advertising services. A scheme to fraudulently overstate earnings at AMS involved not informing retailers of credits due to them for certain advertising and promotional services that the retailers provided. Instead of contacting the retailers and reconciling amounts, AMS improperly reversed the liability for these credits and thereby decreased expenses and increased its income. An executive at AMS profited from her participation in the fraudulent schemes through her receipt of annual bonuses and sales of AMS stock. An analytical comparison of expenses with the previous years and with sales volumes would have been a good indicator that something was wrong.

Source: SEC AAER No. 2312.

Other Accounts Payable Substantive Tests: Review of Purchase Commitment Contracts   Organizations are increasingly entering into long-term contracts to purchase inventory at fixed prices or at a fixed price plus inflation adjustments. These contracts can extend over a period of years, and there is always some risk that economic circumstances can change and the contracts may no longer be economically viable. The contracts should be examined to determine penalties associated with default, and the auditor should gain sufficient knowledge to assess the client's estimate of the probability of contract default or losses.

Substantive Tests of Expense Accounts

Tests of payables and related cash disbursements provide indirect evidence about the correctness of expense accounts related to acquisitions. However, some additional analysis of selected expense accounts is usually merited, depending on the strength of internal controls tested during the earlier phases of the integrated audit. When evaluating evidence regarding expense accounts, the auditor should consider that management is more likely to (1) understate rather than overstate expenses and (2) classify expense items as assets rather than vice versa.[2] Therefore, the more relevant assertions related to expenses in the acquisition and payment cycle are the completeness assertion and the presentation and disclosure assertion.

The auditor should also perform tests that would identify all significant credits to expense accounts because these credits might indicate inappropriate transfer of costs to asset accounts, or reversals of liabilities. In auditing expense accounts, the auditor is aware that not all expenses are directly related to cash expenditures. For example, interest expense, insurance expense, taxes, pensions, and bonuses are likely to be accrued during the year and the auditor will want to directly test those accruals.

Analytical Procedures on Expense Accounts   When the auditor has concluded that control risk is low for expense accounts, the primary substantive tests may be substantive analytical procedures. In conducting analytical procedures, the auditor should recognize that many account balances are directly

> **PRACTICAL POINT**
>
> It is generally true that companies are more likely to understate expenses. However, many smaller businesses may wish to overstate expenses in order to reduce income taxes. Thus, an auditor's professional skepticism and related audit procedures, should apply equally to the potential for both overstating income and understating income, and the auditor must be alert to the relevant economic incentives of the client.

---

[2] The client may be motivated to minimize income taxes and thus would want to overstate expenses and understate income. In such cases, the auditor should concentrate on items classified as expenses that should be recorded as an asset.

related to the client's volume of activity. Stable relationships are expected between specific accounts (such as cost of goods sold and sales) that can be investigated for unusual discrepancies. Examples of expenses that should vary directly with sales include warranty expense, sales commissions, and supplies expense. The analytical model should be built using either audited data or independently generated data. If the expense account falls within expected ranges, the auditor can be comfortable in concluding that it is not materially misstated. If the account balance is not within the specified ranges, the auditor develops hypotheses as to why it may differ and systematically investigates the situation. The investigation should include inquiries of client personnel and the examination of corroborating evidence (including a detailed examination of the expense accounts, where merited). For example, sales commissions may have averaged 3% of sales over the past five years, and the auditor may expect that trend to continue. If that ratio drops to 1% this year, the auditor should examine the cause of the change. If the auditor obtains sufficient evidence through substantive analytical procedures, the extent of substantive tests of details may be decreased.

Detailed Test of Expense Accounts   Some expense accounts, including some that are not directly related to the acquisition and payment cycle, are of intrinsic interest to the auditor simply because of the nature of the account. These include legal expense, travel and entertainment expense, repairs and maintenance expense, and income tax expense. The legal expense account should be examined as a possible indicator of litigation that may require recording and/or disclosure. Travel and entertainment expense should be examined for questionable or non-business-related items. Repairs and maintenance expense should be examined together with fixed-asset additions to assure a proper distinction has been made between expenditures that should be expensed and those that should be capitalized. Income tax expense and related liability(s) should be examined, often by a colleague who is a tax specialist, to assure that tax laws and regulations have been followed. Underlying documentation should be sampled to determine the nature of the expenditure, its appropriate business use, and the correctness of the recorded item.

The most widely used approach to detailed testing of expenses is to either (a) have the client create a schedule of all larger items making up the expense account (usually done for smaller clients) to be examined, or (b) use audit software to (i) examine randomly selected items from the expense account using sampling and (ii) prepare a list of all credits to the expense items for further review.

AUDITING *in Practice*

EXPENSES AT RITE AID

Executives at Rite Aid conducted a wide-ranging accounting fraud scheme that resulted in the significant inflation of Rite Aid's income. When the fraud was ultimately discovered, Rite Aid was forced to restate its pretax income by $2.3 billion and net income by $1.6 billion, the largest restatement ever recorded at that time. One aspect of the fraud involved **reversals of actual expenses**. Rite Aid's accounting staff reversed amounts that had been recorded for various expenses incurred and already paid (debiting accounts payable and crediting expenses). These reversals were unjustified and, in each instance, were put back on the books in the subsequent quarter. The effect was to overstate Rite Aid's income during the period in which the expenses were incurred. Specifically, entries of this nature caused Rite Aid's pretax income for one quarter to be overstated by $9 million.

This action reiterates another important point: *Sometimes management wants to misstate only a particular quarter to keep their stock price high, with the intent that they can fix problems before the end of the year.*

Source: SEC AAER No. 1581 and No. 2023.

Exhibit 11.5 Partial Audit Program for Travel and Entertainment Expenses

1. Review control testing and assessment of control risk. Consider the potential misstatements that may occur, including any results from fraud brainstorming meetings.

2. Use audit software to read the travel and entertainment expense file and do the following:
   a. Foot the file and agree to the trial balance
   b. Create a sub-file of all reimbursements made to officers or directors; list by each officer
   c. Develop a list of all credits to the account

3. For each item selected, trace back to detailed evidence supporting the expenditure. Examine the supporting documentation to:
   a. Determine completeness of documentation
   b. Determine proper approvals of expenditure
   c. Examine business purpose of the expenditure, and determine that authorized individuals were present and that the expenditure meets with IRS approved guidelines
   d. Determine that expenditure was within company guidelines
   e. Summarize any discrepancies and determine whether or not company should be reimbursed
   f. Discuss potential adjustments with CFO or appropriate personnel, including CEO or audit committee chair for items involving CEO or CFO

4. Develop estimate of potential adjustments and determine if amounts are material.

5. Review list of credits to the account and determine if amounts are material. If amounts are material:
   a. Summarize by type
   b. Investigate source of entry and support for the entry
   c. Make a determination of whether or not the entries were appropriate
   d. Develop an estimate of required changes to the account(s)

6. Record any needed adjustments.

7. If any officer reimbursements exceeded company policy or were not for legitimate purposes, summarize the amounts and discuss with audit committee chair and CEO.

8. Consider whether findings support a conclusion that controls are working effectively. If not, consider impact on Section 404 report on internal control.

9. Summarize findings.

An example of a specific audit program for performing detailed testing of travel and entertainment expense is shown in Exhibit 11.5.

Detailed tests of other expense accounts, such as repair and maintenance expenses, would usually involve taking a sample of debits to the account balance and tracing the items back to supporting documents to determine that (a) adequate support for the payment existed and (b) the classification was appropriate (expense vs. capitalization). The auditor could also use audit software to summarize all credits to the account balance and then investigate any amounts that would be material to determine their source and the appropriateness of the account balances (see the *Auditing in Practice* feature that describes the WorldCom fraud).

Evidence on expense accounts is also gathered through the audits of related asset or liability accounts. For example, if the auditor determines that something is inappropriately capitalized, that determination likely means that an expense is understated. Similarly, if a liability is omitted, it is likely that an expense has been understated.

Review of Unusual Entries to Expense Accounts The vast majority of transactions to expense accounts should be debits that are accompanied by purchases of goods or services that can be validated through independent receipts and by independent vendor invoices. The exceptions to this rule are accounts that represent estimates or accounts that are based on a relationship with specific asset or liability accounts such as fixed assets (depreciation) or bonds (interest expense).

PRACTICAL POINT

A large number of credits to an expense account should always raise the auditor's professional skepticism about the correctness of the account balance, and it requires a separate evaluation of the credits.

PRACTICAL POINT

Credits to expense accounts increase reported net income and are often offset by an increase in fictitious assets.

AUDITING *in Practice*

WORLDCOM

Management at WorldCom wished to keep line expenses at 42% of total costs because (a) line expense was a key ratio followed by Wall Street analysts and (b) it helped to keep reported profits high. One of the processes used was to credit line expense by reducing restructuring reserves. The reserve account would be debited for a round figure, such as:

Restructuring Reserve	$450,000
Line Expense	$450,000

An examination of the credits in the expense account would have provided insight into this highly unusual accounting transaction. It is recommended that repair and maintenance expense be examined at the same time as fixed asset increases. If performed as recommended for the WorldCom audit, the fraud would have been discovered much earlier.

The auditor should examine the following:

- All credits to expense accounts
- All other unusual entries to the accounts

The auditor should search for independent validation of all unusual entries to expense accounts.

Fraud-Related Substantive Procedures

In those audits where there is a heightened risk of fraud related to accounts payable and purchases, the auditor will want to consider performing the following procedures or, if the procedures are already being performed, altering the timing and extent of the procedures.

- Send blank confirmations to vendors that ask them to furnish information about all outstanding invoices, payment terms, payment histories, and so forth. The procedure can be expanded to include new vendors and accounts with small or zero balances.
- Scan journals for unusual or large year-end transactions and adjustments, e.g., transactions not typical, approvals not going through standard processes, or not having the usual supporting documentation.
- Review client's vendor files for unusual items. Unusual items might include non-standard forms, different delivery addresses; or vendors that have multiple addresses.
- Obtain and examine documentation for payments of invoices that are for amounts just under the limit that typically requires some level of approval.

Complexities Related to Inventory and Cost of Goods Sold

LO 7

Explain the complexities inherent in auditing inventory and cost of goods sold.

Accounting for inventories is a major consideration for many clients because of its significance to both the balance sheet and the income statement. **Inventories** are defined as items of tangible personal property that are held for sale in the ordinary course of business, are in the process of production for such sale, or are to be currently consumed in the production of goods or services to be available for sale. Inventory includes such items as steel held for future production of an automobile, electronic goods in a retail store, drugs on shelves in hospitals or pharmaceutical companies, and petroleum products at an oil-refining company.

Inventory is a complex accounting and auditing area because of the following:

- Variety (diversity) of items in inventory
- High volume of activity
- Various accounting valuation methods
- Difficulty in identifying obsolete inventory and applying the lower of cost or market principle to determine valuation

But the accounting issues are only one component of the audit task. Inventory audits take on added complexity because inventory:

- Is often misstated in fraudulent financial statements or defalcations.
- Is easily transportable.
- Exists at multiple locations with some locations being remote from the company's headquarters.
- May become obsolete because of technological advances even though there are no visible signs of wear.
- May be difficult to value.
- Is often returned by customers. Care must be taken to separately identify returned merchandise, check it for quality, and record it at net realizable value.
- Variety of inventoried items increases the knowledge that the auditor must have about the business in order to address obsolescence and valuation questions.
- Valuation methods are complex and can be difficult to apply (e.g., various methods to estimate a LIFO inventory).

Risks and Controls Related to Inventory and Cost of Goods Sold

Inventory and cost of goods sold accounts are prone to errors. Further, inventory frauds are one of the most common frauds used by management to manage earnings and misrepresent the financial position of the company. Exhibit 11.6 identifies some of the possible fraudulent schemes for manipulating inventory and cost of goods sold.

Overview of Internal Controls for Inventory

The auditor usually begins by developing an understanding of the cost components of inventory and how inventory valuation is affected by current market prices. We will concentrate on the inventories of a manufacturing client because that setting is the most complex and normally presents the most difficult audit problems. A well-conceived inventory control system should assure the following:

- All purchases are authorized.
- There is timely, accurate, and complete recording of inventory transactions.
- Receipt of inventory is properly accounted for and independently tested to verify quality in adherence to company standards.
- The cost accounting system is up-to-date; costs are properly identified and assigned to products; and variances are analyzed, investigated, and properly allocated to inventory and cost of goods sold.
- A perpetual inventory system serves as a basis for management reports and to assist in managing inventory.
- All products are systematically reviewed for obsolescence, and appropriate accounting action is taken.

LO 8

Identify risks to reliable financial reporting associated with inventory and cost of goods sold.

LO 9

Describe typical internal controls over inventory and cost of goods sold.

Exhibit 11.6	Approaches for Manipulating Inventory and Cost of Goods Sold	
Event	**Affected Accounts**	**Possible Manipulations**
1. Purchase inventory	Inventory, accounts payable	Under-record purchases Record purchases in a later period Not record purchases
2. Return inventory to supplier	Accounts payable, inventory	Overstate returns Record returns in an earlier period
3. Inventory is sold	Cost of goods sold, inventory	Record at too low an amount Not record cost of goods sold nor reduce inventory
4. Inventory becomes obsolete	Loss on write-down of inventory, inventory	No write off or write down obsolete inventory
5. Periodic count of inventory quantities	Inventory shrinkage, inventory	Overcount inventory (double counting, etc.)

- Management periodically reviews inventory, takes action on excessive inventory, and manages inventory to minimize losses caused by technological obsolescence.
- New products are introduced only after market studies and **quality-control** tests are made.
- Long-term contracts are closely monitored. Excess purchase requirements are monitored and potential losses are recognized.

Accounting System

The accounting system should be capable of individually identifying products and recording transactions in a timely fashion. The control procedures should be designed to address the most relevant assertions, including existence, completeness, valuation, and presentation and disclosure. Many of the controls will be automated within the computer system, and supplemented by the following:

- Self-checking digits incorporated into inventory product identification
- Edit tests on all transactions, especially validity, limit, and reasonableness tests
- Automated updating of inventory records as transactions take place
- Periodic testing of the perpetual inventory system
- Periodic management reports on inventory usage, scrap, defects, and reworks
- Other monitoring activities, such as aging of inventory by product lines, number of customer complaints received, or disputes with major suppliers regarding quality or timely receipt/payment of goods

PRACTICAL POINT

The auditor will test controls over processing that are designed to assure that all goods are recorded, at correct quantities, in the proper time period and that accounts are updated. If these controls are working properly, the extent of substantive testing of account balances can be reduced.

Accounting for Customer Returns

Accounting for customer returns represents a potential problem area. Approved returns should generate a credit memo reducing the customer's accounts receivable balance and debiting the sales returns and allowances account. In many cases, the returned merchandise is defective and has little or no value. The client can choose to (a) not record an entry or (b) record a loss to "defective merchandise" and credit cost of goods sold. If there is value to the returned merchandise, the company should debit inventory for the net realizable value of the inventory and credit cost of goods sold for the same amount. The auditor must determine the procedures the company uses to identify returned merchandise and segregate it from purchased merchandise. Procedures must be in place to determine (a) if the goods can be resold as new or scrapped and (b) whether the

AUDITING *in Practice*

PROFESSIONAL SKEPTICISM ABOUT MANUAL ENTRIES

In 2009, the SEC charged VeriFone Holdings, Inc., a technology company, with falsifying the company's financial statement to improve gross margins and income. VeriFone relied on gross margin as an indicator of its financial results and provided forecasts of its quarterly gross margins to investment analysts. The SEC alleges that a mid-level controller at VeriFone made large manual adjustments to inventory balances quarterly and that there was no reasonable basis for the manual entries. These adjustments allowed the company to meet its internal forecasts and its earnings guidance made to analysts. The adjustments, which were based on incorrect assumptions, allowed the company to improperly inflate its income by over $37 million. The mid-level controller was able to make his unwarranted adjustments, in part, because VeriFone had few internal controls to prevent them. Neither the employee's supervisor nor any other senior manager reviewed the employee's work. Further, proper controls were not in place to prevent the person responsible for forecasting financial results from making adjustments which allowed the company to meet the forecasts.

Auditors should be professionally skeptical about manual entries and require that appropriate documentation supporting the entries be provided to the auditors. Further, in areas where internal controls are not effective, the auditor should implement appropriate substantive procedures due to the heightened risk of misstatement.

Source: SEC AAER No. 3044, September 1, 2009.

goods should be reworked and sold or simply scrapped. Major frauds have involved companies selling returned goods as if they were new.

Quality-Control Process

Effective organizations have quality-control processes that permeate the production and storage functions. The process should identify defective units and either have them reworked on the line or put into scrap. Most companies build quality provisions into supplier contracts, most of which carry severe penalties for noncompliance. The auditor should review quality-control reports and consider the implications for unrecorded liabilities.

Cost-Accounting System

Most manufacturing companies use standard cost systems to assist in controlling costs, streamlining accounting, and costing inventory. Valuation of ending inventory is directly affected by the quality of the client's cost system. The auditor should make inquiries about the following:

- The method for developing standard costs
- How recently the standards have been updated
- The method for identifying components of overhead and of allocating overhead to products
- The methods for identifying variances, following up on their causes, and allocating them to inventory and cost of goods sold

The auditor also tests the procedures for assigning raw material costs to products or cost centers. The auditor should be conversant with activity-based costing systems to determine their appropriateness for allocating costs to products.

An audit program to test the standard cost system is shown in Exhibit 11.7. The program is intended to determine the accuracy and reliability of the standard cost system as a basis for valuing a client's year-end inventory. The audit program assumes a standard cost system, but the concepts implicit in the program could be modified for other systems, such as a job cost system. Note that the program requires the auditor to understand the client's business process as well as its standard cost system (including methods of estimating costs). The program also requires analyses of both variances and individual cost assignments.

PRACTICAL POINT

Manipulating the cost accounting system to inflate the value of ending inventory is often an easy way for management to manipulate reported income. The auditor should always perform an extensive analysis of budget variances.

PRACTICAL POINT

The auditor's knowledge of the business and industry should help identify obsolete inventory and determine the proper accounting for it.

Exhibit 11.7   Audit Program for Standard Cost System

AUDIT OF STANDARD COST SYSTEM

Prepared by _____

Reviewed by _____

	Performed by	W/P Ref

1. Review previous-year audit documentation for a description of the standard cost system. Inquire about any major changes made in the system during the current year.

2. Tour the production facilities and make note of cost centers, general layout of the plant, storage of inventory, functioning of the quality control department, and process for identifying and accounting for scrap or defective items.

3. Examine prior-year audit documentation and current-year variance accounts as a basis for determining the amount of variances identified by the standard cost accounting system. Determine whether the variances imply the need for significant revisions in the standard cost system.

4. Inquire of the process used to update standard costs. Determine the extent to which revisions have been made during the current year.

5. Inquire whether significant changes have been made in the production process during the current year, whether major manufacturing renovations have taken place, and whether new products have been added.

6. Randomly select *X* number of standard cost buildups for products, and for each product buildup selected:
   - Review engineering studies on the cost buildup, noting the items used, amount of product used, and standard cost of the product used.
   - Test the reasonableness of the client's costs by randomly sampling components of product cost and tracing back to purchases or contracts with suppliers.
   - Review payroll records to determine that labor costs are specifically identified by product or cost center and used in calculating variances.
   - Review the reasonableness of the method for allocating overhead to products. Determine whether any significant changes have been made in the method of allocation.

7. Select a representative sample of products requisitioned into work in process, and determine that all entries are properly recorded.

8. Review the method for identifying overhead costs. Select a representative sample of expenditure charged to overhead, and trace to underlying support to determine that the costs are properly classified.

9. Review variance reports. Determine the extent to which the client has investigated and determined the causes of the variances. Determine whether the causes of the variances signal a need to revise the standard cost system.

10. Inquire about the method used by the client to allocate variances to inventory and cost of goods sold at year end. Determine the reasonableness of the method and its consistency with prior years.

11. Document your conclusion on the accuracy and completeness of the standard cost system used by the client. Indicate whether the standard costs can be relied on in assigning costs to year-end inventory.

Testing a Perpetual Inventory System

Most organizations use a **perpetual inventory system** to help manage inventory. If there is a low risk that the perpetual inventory records are inaccurate, the client may save the time and cost associated with a complete year-end count of inventory.

The auditor will normally test perpetual inventory records to determine that (1) authorized receipts and sales of inventory are recorded accurately and promptly and (2) only authorized receipts and sales of inventory have been recorded. The auditor selects transactions from the perpetual records and traces them back to source documents to determine that only authorized transactions have been recorded and that unit costs are accurate. The auditor also selects items from the source documents and traces them to the perpetual records to determine that all receipts and sales are recorded accurately and on a timely basis. Finally, the auditor examines support for any material adjustments made to the perpetual records based on physical counts. These tests are summarized as follows:

Testing Perpetual Records Must Address Accuracy from All Angles

Select Sample from	Trace to	Assertions Tested
Perpetual record	Source documents	Occurrence, valuation, rights
Source document	Perpetual record	Completeness
Perpetual record	Physical count records	Existence, completeness

Systematic Review for Obsolescence

Inventory systems provide a wealth of information for systematically reviewing a company's inventory for potential obsolescence. These procedures are important for the proper valuation of inventory.

Searching for possible obsolescence involves:

- Monitoring turnover or age of products individually or by product lines and comparing the turnover with past performance and expectations for the current period
- Monitoring the impact of competitors' new-product introductions
- Comparing current sales with budgeted sales
- Periodically reviewing, by product line, the number of days of sales currently in inventory
- Adjusting for poor condition of inventory, reported as part of periodic cycle counts
- Monitoring sales for amount of product markdown and periodic comparison of net realizable value with inventoried costs
- Reviewing current inventory in light of planned new-product introductions

Substantive Tests of Inventory and Cost of Goods Sold

Exhibit 11.8 presents the assertions and audit procedures that should be used to gather evidence for a typical manufacturing company, which we will discuss in more detail next.

Existence

Generally accepted auditing standards require auditors to observe the client taking physical inventory in order to ensure existence of inventory. This may be done in its entirety at year end or on a cycle basis throughout the year.

Complete Year-End Physical Inventory Not many years ago, it was standard procedure for most organizations to shut down operations at year end or near year end to take a complete physical count of inventory (often referred to as the "physical"). The client's book inventory was adjusted to this physical inventory (often referred to as the *book to physical adjustment*). These procedures are still followed by many small clients that use a **periodic inventory system**, or where the perpetual records are not sufficiently reliable, or where there are fraud risk indicators.

PRACTICAL POINT

Inventory is susceptible to overstatement because of loss, theft, or decrease in value through obsolescence or defect. It is also susceptible to overstatement because of management manipulation.

PRACTICAL POINT

Valuation problems can occur without obsolescence. For example, in January 2009, Chrysler Corporation reported that its cars were on dealer lots (unsold) for an average of 165 days. Further, it was expected that up to 20% of those dealers might go bankrupt before the end of the year. The implication is that Chrysler dealers may ultimately not be able to sell the cars that they own, and may therefore have to return them to Chrysler itself, leading to backlogs and return issues.

PRACTICAL POINT

Companies with inventory that is immediately marketable or consumable, such as electronic products, are likely to experience employee theft problems if the internal controls are not effective.

LO 10

Describe the substantive audit procedures that should be used to test inventory and cost of goods sold.

Exhibit 11.8	Typical Manufacturing Company Assertions and Audit Procedures for Inventory

Assertions	Audit Procedures
Existence	1. Review the client's proposed physical inventory procedures to determine whether they are likely to result in a complete and correct physical inventory.
	2. Observe the client's count of the annual physical inventory. Perform test counts of the observations and trace to the client's compilation of inventory.
	(Alternative Procedure) Randomly select items from the client's perpetual inventory record and observe (count) the items on hand. Sample should emphasize high-dollar-value items.
Completeness	1. Perform year-end cutoff tests by noting the last shipping and receiving document numbers used before physical inventory is taken. Review the purchase and sales journal for a period of time shortly before and after year end, noting the shipping and receiving document numbers to determine whether the goods are recorded in the proper time period.
	2. Make inquiries of the client regarding the potential existence of goods on consignment or located in outside warehouses. For material items, either visit the locations or send a confirmation to the outside warehouse management.
	3. Make inquiries of the client regarding allowances made for expected returns. Determine client policy for accounting for returned items. Review receipt of transactions for a selected period of time to determine whether significant returns are received and appropriately accounted for.
Rights	1. Review vendor invoices when testing disbursements to determine that proper title is conveyed.
	2. Review sales contracts to determine whether the customer has rights to return merchandise, and whether the rights are such that recognition of a sale might not be appropriate.
Valuation	1. Determine whether the valuation method is appropriate for the client.
	2. Inquire of production and warehouse personnel about the existence of obsolete inventory.
	3. Note potentially obsolete inventory while observing the physical inventory counts. Trace the potentially obsolete items to the client's inventory compilation, and determine whether they are properly labeled as obsolete items.
	4. Test inventory cost by taking a sample of recorded inventory, and trace to source documents including: • Tracing raw material purchases to vendor invoices • Testing standard costs as built up through the standard cost system (see Exhibit 11.6)
	5. Test for the possibility of obsolete inventory that should be written down to market value: • Review trade journals for changes in product technology. • Follow-up potentially obsolete items noted during observation of the client's physical inventory counts. • Use generalized audit software to read the inventory file and age the inventory items and compute inventory turnover. Investigate products with unusually low turnover or items that have not been used or sold for an extended period of time. • Inquire of the client about sales adjustments (markdowns) that have been offered to sell any products. • Verify sales price by reviewing recent invoices to determine whether the sales price is the same as included on the computer file. Use generalized audit software to compute net realizable value for inventory items, and prepare an inventory printout for all items where net realizable value is less than cost. • Analyze sales by product line, noting any significant decreases in product-line sales. • Review purchase commitments for potential loss exposures. Determine whether contingent losses are properly disclosed or recorded. • Use audit software to test extensions and prepare a printout of differences. • Use audit software to foot the inventory compilation. Trace the total to the trial balance.
Disclosure	1. Review client's financial statement disclosure of: • Inventory valuation methods used • FIFO cost figures and LIFO liquidation effects if LIFO is used • The percentage of inventory valued by each different valuation method • The classification of inventory as raw material, work in process, and finished goods • The existence of contingent losses associated with long-term contracts or purchase commitments • Inventory policy regarding returns and allowances, if expected to be material, for merchandise expected to be returned

If a year-end inventory is taken, the auditor should (1) observe the client taking inventory to determine the accuracy of the procedures; (2) make selected test counts that can later be traced into the client's inventory compilation; (3) test the client's inventory compilation by tracing test counts to the compilation, and independently test the client's computation of extended cost; and (4) look for evidence of slow-moving, obsolete, or damaged inventory that may need to be written down to lower of cost or market.

An auditor can use generalized audit software to gather the following types of evidence:

- The mathematical accuracy of inventory records
- Reports of recent shipments to be used for cutoff testing
- Items to be counted during the physical inventory observation
- Evaluations of gross margin amounts by product line
- Analyses of inventory whose cost exceeds the market value
- Comparisons of inventory quantities to budgetary plans
- Lists of inventory items with unusual prices, units, or descriptions

The auditor should review the client's plan to count inventory and plan to observe the client's count. The overall procedures for observing the conduct of the client's physical inventory are shown in Exhibit 11.9. The process assumes that the client systematically arranges the inventory for ease of counting and attaches prenumbered tags (paper or electronic) to each group of products. Supervisory personnel (usually from the accounting department) and the auditors review the counts. The count tags are then used to compile the year-end physical inventory. During the counting process, the client arranges not to ship

> **PRACTICAL POINT**
>
> The audit approach to obsolescence cannot be solely mechanistic (simply calculating ratios, etc.). Rather, the auditor must know the company, its competitors, the market power of the company, industry trends, and the current economic conditions affecting product sales as if it were the auditor's own company. With this knowledge, the auditor has good insight to interpret current analytical information to make reasonable estimates of obsolescence.

Exhibit 11.9	Procedures for Observing a Client's Physical Inventory

1. Meet with the client to discuss the procedures, timing, location, and personnel involved in taking the annual physical inventory.

2. Review the client's plans for counting and tagging inventory items.

3. Review the inventory-taking procedures with all audit personnel. Familiarize them with the nature of the client's inventory, potential problems with the inventory, and any other information that will ensure that the client and audit personnel will properly recognize inventory items, high-dollar-value items, and obsolete items, and understand potential problems that might occur in counting the inventory.

4. Determine whether specialists are needed to identify, test, or assist in correctly identifying inventory items.

5. Upon arriving at each site:
   a. Meet with client personnel, obtain a map of the area, and obtain a schedule of inventory counts to be made for each area.
   b. Obtain a list of sequential tag numbers to be used in each area.
   c. Observe the procedures the client has implemented to shut down receipt or shipment of goods.
   d. Observe that the client has shut down production.
   e. Obtain document numbers for the last shipment and receipt of goods before the physical inventory is taken. Use the information to perform cutoff tests.

6. Observe the counting of inventory and note the following on inventory count working papers:
   a. The first and last tag number used in the section.
   b. Account for all tag numbers and determine the disposition of all tag numbers in the sequence.
   c. Make selected test counts and note the product identification, product description, units of measure, and number of items on a count sheet.
   d. Items that appear to be obsolete or of questionable value.
   e. All high-dollar-value items included in inventory.
   f. Movement of goods into or out of the company during the process of inventory taking. Determine if goods are properly counted or excluded from inventory.

7. Document your conclusion as to the quality of the client's inventory-taking process, noting any problems that could be of audit significance. Determine whether a sufficient inventory count has been taken to properly reflect the goods on hand at year end.

or receive goods or segregates all goods received during the process to be labeled and counted as "after inventory."

The auditor walks through the inventory areas, documenting the first and last tag numbers used as well as tag numbers not used. The auditor also performs the following tasks:

- Makes test counts of selected items and records the test counts for subsequent tracing into the client's inventory compilation
- Takes notations of all items that appear to be obsolete or are in questionable condition; the auditor follows up on these items with inquiries of client personnel and retains the data to determine how they are accounted for in the inventory compilation
- Observes the handling of scrap and other material
- Observes whether there is any physical movement of goods during the counting of the inventory
- Records all high-dollar-value items for subsequent tracing into the client's records

The notation of high-dollar-value items is a check against potential client manipulation of inventory by adding new items or adjusting the cost or quantities of existing items after the physical inventory is completed. Because high-dollar-value items are noted, the auditor can systematically review support for major items included on the final inventory compilation that were not noted during the physical inventory observation.

After the inventory is taken, the auditor's observations and test counts provide an independent source of evidence on the correctness of the client's inventory compilation. Noting the unused tag numbers prohibits the insertion of additional inventory items. The auditor's notation of potentially obsolete items can be used to determine whether the client has properly written the goods down to their net realizable value.

Multiple Locations   Many organizations have multiple locations, thus making it difficult to take an annual inventory. As an example, one major company beset by fraud, Phar-Mor, Inc., had more than 300 stores scattered across the country. The auditors insisted that a year-end physical count be taken but notified the client that they would observe the taking of inventory at only a few

AUDITING *in Practice*

INVENTORY OBSERVATION—THE CASE OF CMH

CMH was an SEC-registered company that went bankrupt after it had materially misstated its financial statements for a number of years. It inflated the reporting of its physical inventory by 50% during two years prior to its bankruptcy. The fraud was perpetrated by "(1) altering the quantities recorded on the pre-numbered, two-part inventory tags used in counting the inventory; (2) altering documents reflected on a computer list prepared to record the physical count of inventory; and (3) creating inventory tags to record quantities of nonexistent inventory."

The SEC asserted that the auditors should have detected the fictitious inventory but did not because the audit firm "left the extent of various observation testing to the discretion of auditors, not all of whom were aware of significant audit planning that should have related directly to the extent of such testing. Observation of inventory

counts at year end was confined to six locations (representing about 40% of the total CMH inventory) as opposed to nine in the preceding year. The field auditors did not adequately control the inventory tags and the auditor did not detect the creation of bogus inventory tags which were inserted in the final inventory computations." The SEC was also critical of the CPA firm for assigning interns to a significant portion of the inventory observation without training them in the nature of the client's inventory or its counting procedures. This is an example of a situation in which lack of auditor professional skepticism led to low audit quality and a subsequent audit failure.

Source: R. W. V. Dickenson, "Why the Fraud Went Undetected," *CA Magazine* April 1977, pp. 67-69.

AUDITING *in Practice*

INVENTORY SHRINK AGE AT RITE AID

One aspect of fraud at Rite Aid involved inventory shrink age. When the physical inventory count was less than the inventory carried on Rite Aid's books, Rite Aid was supposed to write down its book inventory to reflect this "shrink age" (i.e., reduction presumed to be due to physical loss or theft). However, as part of the fraud, Rite Aid failed to record $8.8 million in shrink age. In addition,

in the same year, Rite Aid improperly reduced its accrued shrink age expense (for stores where a physical inventory was not conducted), producing an improper increase to income of $5 million.

Source: SEC AAER No. 1581 and No. 2023.

select locations. To expedite the observation of inventory, the auditor worked with the client to identify the locations that would be observed. Although there was a massive misstatement of inventory by Phar-Mor, Inc., the misstatement was not discovered by the auditors because the company made sure that no material misstatements occurred at the locations visited by the auditors.

When multiple locations contain inventory, the auditor should review a variety of locations to determine that they are comparable and should use analytical procedures to see if the locations not visited seem to have inventory levels that are significantly different from those observed. If there are significant differences, the auditor may need to observe more locations, or at least follow up with other procedures.

Observing Inventory Prior to Year End   Many organizations that take an annual physical inventory find that year end is not the most convenient time to do it. For example, the company may have a natural model changeover and shut down operations during that time, or it may want to take the physical inventory shortly before or after year end to expedite the preparation of year-end financial statements. It is acceptable to have the client take inventory before year end provided that:

- Internal control is effective
- There are no "red flags" that might indicate both opportunity and motivation to misstate inventory
- The auditor can effectively test the year-end balance through a combination of analytical procedures and selective testing of transactions between the physical count and year end
- The auditor reviews the intervening transactions for evidence of any manipulation or unusual activity

Inventory at Customer Locations   As companies move toward innovative partnerships with their suppliers and customers, more agreements will take place where a supplier's goods will be at a retailer such as Wal-Mart, but title will not change until the sale to the customer is made. In these situations, the auditor will need to determine that the client has a sound methodology for determining the amount of inventory that is physically stored at a customer's location. Many times, the client will have monitoring controls with which it examines existing inventory at the customer's locations and compares it to the perpetual records. If such controls do not exist, the auditor will need to consider complementary testing methodologies, which might include (a) confirming inventory amounts with the consignee, (b) examining subsequent payments from customers, or (c) visiting selected consignees to observe inventory.

It is not sufficient for a client to just assert that its inventory is held by another company. The auditor must examine the contract, determine the existence and effectiveness of controls, and examine documentation of reconciliations between

> **PRACTICAL POINT**
>
> An important inventory control is the periodic testing, or **cycle counting**, of the perpetual inventory records by internal audit or other personnel to determine their accuracy, the need for adjustments, and the cause of any major inaccuracies. The auditor should determine that such counts are taken, corrections are made to the records, and major inaccuracies are investigated and action taken to correct the problem.

AUDITING *in Practice*

CONSIDERATION OF FRAUD

AICPA Practice Alert No. 94-2, *Consideration of Fraud in Audit Procedures Related to Inventory Observation*, provides examples of how clients fraudulently manipulate inventory amounts. Auditors should be on the alert for the following:

- Empty boxes or "hollow squares" in stacked goods
- Mislabeled boxes containing scrap, obsolete items, or lower-value materials
- Consigned inventory, inventory that is rented, or traded-in items for which credits have not been issued
- Inventory diluted so it is less valuable (e.g., adding water to liquid substances)
- Altering the inventory counts for those items the auditor did not test count
- Programming the computer to produce fraudulent physical quantity tabulations or priced inventory listings
- Manipulating the inventory counts/compilations for locations not visited by the auditor

- Double-counting inventory in transit between locations
- Physically moving inventory and counting it at two locations
- Including in inventory merchandise recorded as sold but not yet shipped to a customer ("bill and hold sales")
- Arranging for false confirmations of inventory held by others
- Including inventory receipts for which corresponding payables had not been recorded
- Overstating the stage of completion of work-in-process
- Reconciling physical inventory amounts to falsified amounts in the general ledger
- Manipulating the "roll-forward" of an inventory taken before the financial statement date

trading partners, cash remittances, and client accounting records. If red flags are present, the auditor must go beyond these procedures and talk with the trading partner to obtain information on the amount of the client's inventory the trading partner shows on hand. Finally, the auditor needs to develop assurance that the trading partner is a real company.

Comparison of Worldwide Professional Guidance

AUDITING INVENTORY

AICPA Auditing Standards Board (ASB)

SAS 1, Section 331 addresses the auditing of inventory. It states:
"Observation of inventories is a generally accepted auditing procedure. The independent auditor who issues an opinion when he has not employed them must bear in mind that he has the burden of justifying the opinion expressed."

If the auditor is unfamiliar certain inventory (e.g., precious metals, diamonds, coal piles), the auditor needs to obtain the services of specialists to determine whether the inventory actually is as represented by the client.

The standard notes further that if a significant amount of inventory is in a warehouse that is not owned by the client, then the auditor should examine and investigate the warehouse's operations sufficiently enough for the auditor to be satisfied that the warehouse is safeguarding the client's inventory.

Public Company Accounting Oversight Board (PCAOB)

The PCAOB adopted AU Section 331 as an interim standard in 2003. This is the same standard as SAS 1, Section 331 which is described above.

International Auditing and Assurance Standards Board (IAASB)

ISA 501 addresses the auditing of inventory. Like SAS 1, Section 331, ISA 501 advocates the physical observation of inventory by the auditor, so that the auditor can observe the counting of inventory, inspect the condition of the inventory, and perform test counts as necessary.

SUMMARY

Inventory and the valuation thereof is a major component of many clients' audits. Given the importance of this asset, the standard setting bodies basically require that the auditor physically observe the client's inventory to help support the client's assertions related to existence, completeness, and valuation.

Sample Physical Inventory If internal controls are strong, the client may concentrate on testing the accuracy and completeness of the perpetual records by (1) counting all inventory at least once during the year or (2) using statistical sampling to select items to be physically counted. The exact approach and its timing depend on the control environment and sophistication of the client's perpetual inventory system. If the client uses statistical sampling, the auditor should review to make sure the approach is reasonable and statistically valid. The auditor should be present to observe such counts as are deemed necessary and must be satisfied with the effectiveness of the counting procedures used.

Inability of Auditor to Physically Observe Inventory There may be rare cases in which it is difficult or impractical for the auditor to attend the physical inventory counting. For example, the nature and location of the inventory, or where it is held, may pose safety threats for the auditor. In these situations, the auditor must conduct alternative audit procedures. Such procedures could include inspecting documents related to the subsequent sale of specific inventory items to validate their existence and valuation as of the balance sheet date.

If, however, it is simply inconvenient for the auditor to attend the physical inventory counting, then the auditor has an obligation to find a way to be present. If it is truly impossible for the auditor to attend the physical inventory counting, and the auditor is unable to conduct alternative procedures, then the auditor's report would have to be modified as a result of this scope limitation (assuming that inventory is a material amount to the financial statements as a whole). Scope limitations to the standard audit report are discussed in Chapter 16.

Using the Work of a Specialist or Expert

The nature of inventory at some clients may require the auditor to rely on the work of a specialist in determining quantities and valuation of inventory. International auditing standards use the term *expert* rather than specialist; for simplicity we use the term *specialist* but acknowledge that both terms are equally appropriate. For example, a specialist might be needed to determine the physical characteristics relating to inventory on hand or condition of minerals, mineral reserves, or materials stored in stockpiles.

When using the work of a specialist, it is necessary for the auditor to evaluate the professional qualifications of the individual. In making this evaluation, professional auditing standards indicate that the auditor will consider:

- The professional certification, license, or other recognition of the competence of the specialist in his or her field, as appropriate
- The reputation and standing of the specialist in the views of peers and others familiar with the specialist's capability or performance
- The specialist's experience in the type of work under consideration

Further, the auditor needs to understand the nature of the work performed by the specialist. The auditor will want to do the following:

- Obtain an understanding of the methods and assumptions used by the specialist
- Make appropriate tests of data provided to the specialist, taking into account the auditor's assessment of control risk, and
- Evaluate whether the specialist's findings support the related assertions in the financial statements.

Completeness

The auditor normally performs a cutoff test of receipts and shipments of inventory at year end to determine that all items are recorded in the correct time period. The cutoff test is usually accomplished by capturing information on the last items shipped and received at year end and examining samples of transactions recorded in the sales and purchases journals near year end. In addition, audit software can be used to match shipping dates and billing dates if the files containing that information have been tested for accuracy. The auditor should also inquire about any inventory out on consignment or stored in a public warehouse and consider confirming its existence.

> *Cutoff Example*—A sale of $100 is recorded on December 30 for a product costing $80 that is not shipped until the next month. If a physical count of inventory is taken on December 31, this product will be included in the physical count, which will exceed the quantity shown in the perpetual records. The perpetual inventory record is always adjusted to the actual count (in this case by debiting inventory and crediting cost of goods sold). Unless corrected, sales, gross profit, and pretax income are overstated by the full $100. The client can correct this misstatement by reversing the sales entry, including the entry to accounts receivable. Because the perpetual inventory is adjusted to the physical count, that part of the original entry (debiting inventory, crediting cost of goods sold) is already made.

Allowance for Returns   In most situations, the expected amount of returns is not material. However, some companies (e.g., mail-order companies like Lands' End or L.L. Bean) provide return guarantees and expect significant returns—especially after year-end holiday sales. They use previous experience, updated for current economic conditions, to develop estimates of returns. When such returns are material to the overall financial presentation, allowances for returns should be established and the gross profit on the original sale reversed. The allowance is not restricted to mail-order companies; it should be considered when a company is experiencing a large volume of returns.

Rights

Most of the audit work regarding rights to and ownership of inventory is addressed during the auditor's test of the initial recording of purchases. The auditor should also review long-term contracts to determine obligations to take delivery of merchandise, customer rights to return merchandise, or buy-back obligations. Inquiries should be made concerning any inventory held on consignment.

PRACTICAL POINT

If control risk is high and the auditor chooses to observe the inventory counting and recording process, the auditor should not let the client know which locations are going to be observed. Many frauds have been perpetrated by managers who shifted inventory from one location to another in order to double count it—and they succeeded in fooling the auditors because the auditors themselves provided information about which locations they would be visiting on specific dates. A skeptical auditor will not reveal information that could be used by the client to cover up a fraud.

AUDITING *in Practice*

THE IMPORTANCE OF PROFESSIONAL SKEPTICISM IN TESTING THE VALUATION OF INVENTORY

A PCAOB inspection report noted that the auditors under review failed to identify and address a departure from GAAP relating to their client's valuation of inventory. GAAP requires inventory to be valued at the lower of cost or market value. The inspection report notes that the client's consolidated balance sheet reported inventory of $356,973, or approximately 95% of total assets. However, based on cost of goods actually sold during that fiscal year, the client's inventory balance represented approximately 22 years' worth of sales. This fact alone should have increased the auditors' skepticism about the inventory's stated value. Instead, the auditors relied solely on management's representation regarding the valuation of inventory and mechanical tests of inventory costs, and they missed the big picture. Auditing standards require auditors to look at evidence from multiple sources in reaching a conclusion about an account balance.

Source: PCAOB Release No. 2006-009.

Valuation

Valuation is the most complex assertion related to inventory because of the volume of transactions, diversity of products, variety of costing methods, and difficulty in estimating net realizable value of products. A combination of direct tests and analytical procedures is used to estimate inventory valuation. The auditor should verify the correct cost of inventory and then test for lower of cost or market valuation. Usually, the cost part of the valuation assertion is tested by looking at underlying invoices and/or supporting cost records. The auditor usually examines current market data and other information that might indicate a drop in sales price or potential inventory obsolescence.

Direct Tests of Product Costs   Statistical sampling techniques, as discussed in Chapter 8, should be used to select items for testing. Then, the auditor should examine underlying supporting documentation—e.g., invoices—to determine that the cost is recorded correctly. As an example, assume that the auditor selected product YG350 to test the cost of inventory recorded on the FIFO basis as part of a perpetual inventory system:

PRODUCT YG350

| Transaction | TOTAL | | BALANCE | |
	Quantity	Cost	Quantity	Dollars
Beginning balance			100	$1,000
3/1 Purchase	50	550	150	1,550
6/1 Purchase	100	1,200	250	2,750
6/1 Sale	150	1,550	100	1,200
9/1 Purchase	50	500	150	1,700
10/1 Sale	25	275	125	1,425
12/1 Sale	50	600	75	825
12/1 Purchase	75	975	150	1,800

Vendor invoices would be examined for the purchases of the last 150 items (12/1, 9/1, and 6/1) to determine whether $1,800 was the correct cost. (*Note:* You should verify that the recorded cost should have been $1,775.)

Any differences noted between vendor invoices and recorded amounts should be identified as an error and should be projected to the population as a whole using statistical sampling to determine whether they might be material. Similar tests should be performed if the company uses other valuation methods, such as average cost or LIFO. If the company uses a standard cost system, the costs are verified by tests of the cost system and by tracing the selected items to standard costs. Significant variances should be allocated between cost of goods sold and inventory.

Tests for Obsolete Inventory (Net Realizable Value Tests)   Determining the amount that should be written off because of obsolescence is a difficult and challenging audit task because (1) the client will usually state that most of the goods are still salable at current selling prices and (2) net realizable value is only an estimate (i.e., there is no specific, correct price at which inventory should be valued). Thus, the auditor attempts to gather evidence on potential inventory obsolescence from a number of corroborating sources, including the following:

- Noting potential obsolete inventory when observing the client's physical inventory
- Calculating inventory turnover, number of days' sales in inventory, date of last sale or purchase, and other similar analytic techniques to identify potential obsolescence

- Calculating net realizable value for products by referring to current selling prices, cost of disposal, sales commissions, and so on
- Monitoring trade journals and the Internet for information regarding the introduction of competitive products
- Inquiring of management about its approach to identifying and classifying obsolete items

Generalized audit software (GAS) is often used to assist in estimating obsolescence. GAS can be used to:

- Calculate turnover and report items with unusually slow turnover.
- Age inventory and develop a report on inventory that has not been used or sold for an extended period of time.
- Calculate net realizable value by comparing current net selling price with costs and reporting any differences.

Auditors often investigate items that appear to be obsolete by reviewing sales subsequent to year end and discussing future sales prospects with management.

Disclosure

The auditor reviews the client's proposed disclosure for compliance with the guidelines established by the relevant accounting literature. In addition to the normally required inventory disclosures, the auditor must identify any unusual circumstances regarding sales or purchase contracts that would merit additional disclosure. An example of a typical inventory disclosure for Ford Motor Company is shown in Exhibit 11.10.

Cost of Goods Sold

The audit of cost of goods sold can be directly tied to the audit of inventories. If beginning and ending inventory have been verified and acquisitions have been tested, cost of goods sold can be directly calculated. The auditor should apply analytical techniques to cost of goods sold, however, to determine if there are

---

Exhibit 11.10 — **Ford Motor Company Inventory Footnote from the 2009 Annual Report**

All inventories are stated at the lower of cost or market. Cost for a substantial portion of U.S. inventories is determined on a last-in, first-out ("LIFO") basis. LIFO was used for approximately 28% and 24% of inventories at December 31, 2009 and 2008, respectively. Cost of other inventories is determined on a first-in, first-out ("FIFO") basis.

Note 8. Inventories	2009	2008
Inventories at December 31 were as follows (in millions):		
Raw materials, work-in-process and supplies	$ 2,783	$ 2,747
Finished products	3,465	5,091
Total inventories under "FIFO"	6,248	7,838
Less: "LIFO" Adjustment	(798)	(850)
Total Inventories	$5,450	$6,988

At December 31, 2009, inventory quantities were reduced, resulting in a liquidation of LIFO inventory quantities carried at lower costs prevailing in prior years as compared with the cost of 2009 purchases, the effect of which decreased *Automotive cost of sales* by about $33 million.

any significant variations—either overall or by product line—that are unexpected. Significant variations, especially those that cannot be easily explained, might indicate a need for further inventory work. Regression analysis can be used to compare the historical relationships between sales and cost of goods sold by product line by month with the current year. Outliers should then be investigated further.

Fraud-Related Substantive Procedures

In those audits where there is a heightened risk of fraud related to inventory and cost of goods sold, the auditor will want to consider performing the following procedures or, if the procedures are already being performed, altering the timing and extent of the procedures.

- Observe all inventory locations simultaneously.
- Confirm inventories at locations that are outside the entity.
- Compare carrying inventory amounts to recent sales amounts.
- Examine consignment agreements and determine that consignments are properly accounted for.
- Send confirmations to vendors confirming invoices and unusual terms.
- Determine if there are bulk sales at steep discounts as these sales could indicate decreasing values for the company's products.

Summary

Audits of the acquisition and payment cycle include auditing expense accounts, payables, inventory, and cost of goods sold. The inventory and cost of goods sold accounts have been the subject of various manipulation schemes, ranging from outright addition of fictitious inventory, movement of inventory from one location to another, recognition of defective items as good items, capitalization of costs that should be expensed, and the failure to recognize decreases in market value owing to technological changes. Thus, it is critical that auditors exercise appropriate levels of professional skepticism when conducting an audit of the acquisition and payment cycle accounts. The extent of

work the auditor performs in the acquisition and payment cycle depends heavily on the effectiveness of the client's internal control in mitigating the risks to reliable financial reporting. When control risk is assessed as high, the auditor extends the substantive procedures. On the other hand, management of many well-run companies have realized that they must have accurate accounting controls over the acquisition and payment activities if the company is to operate profitably. In such situations, the audit work can concentrate on testing the client's internal controls and corroborating the analysis with substantive analytical procedures and selected detail testing of the appropriate accounts.

Significant Terms

Automated controls   Control procedures and authorization concepts built into the client's computerized system.

Automated matching   A process by which the computer matches a purchase order, receiving information, and a vendor invoice to determine whether the vendor's invoice is correct and should be paid.

Automated purchasing system   A networked software system that links a company's website to

other vendors whose offerings and prices have been preapproved by appropriate management.

Cycle count   Periodic testing of the accuracy of the perpetual inventory record by counting all inventories on a cyclical basis.

Inventories   Items of tangible personal property that are held for sale in the ordinary course of business, are in the process of production for such sale, or are to be currently consumed in the production of goods or services to be available for sale.

Inventory shrink age   Reduction in inventory presumed to be due to physical loss or theft.

Periodic inventory system   A system of inventory recordkeeping in which no continuous record of changes in inventory (receipts and issues of inventory items) is kept. At the end of an accounting period, the ending inventory is determined by an actual physical count of every item, and its cost is computed using a suitable method.

Perpetual inventory system   A system of inventory recordkeeping where book inventory is continuously in agreement with inventory on hand within specified time periods. In some cases, book inventory and stock on hand may be reconciled with each transaction; in other systems, these two numbers may be reconciled less often. This process is useful in keeping track of actual availability of goods and determining what the correct time to reorder from suppliers might be.

Quality control   An approach by an organization to assure that high-quality products are produced and high-quality services are provided. The approach specifies quality requirements for processes and products and integrates those concepts into vendor contracts.

Requisition   A request for the purchase of goods or services by an authorized department or function within the organization; may be documented on paper or in a computer system.

Shrinkage ratio   Ratio of inventory write-down to total inventory.

Supply chain management   The management and control of materials in the logistics process from the acquisition of raw materials to the delivery of finished products to the end user (customer).

Three-way match   A control in which a purchase order, receiving information, and a vendor invoice are matched to determine whether the vendor's invoice is correct and should be paid. This process can be automated or can be performed manually.

SELECTED REFERENCES TO RELEVANT PROFESSIONAL GUIDANCE	
Topic	**Selected Guidance**
Auditing Inventory	SAS 1 Section 331 *Inventories* Proposed SAS *Audit Evidence Specific Considerations For Selected Items* ISA 501 *Audit Evidence—Additional Considerations for Specific Items, Part A, "Attendance at Physical Inventory Counting"*
Auditing Accounting Estimates	SAS 57 *Auditing Accounting Estimates* Proposed SAS *Auditing Accounting Estimates, Including Fair Value Accounting Estimates and Related Disclosures* (Redrafted) (issued but not effective; proposed effective date is December 2012) ISA 540 *Auditing Accounting Estimates, Including Fair Value Accounting Estimates, and Related Disclosures*
Confirmations	SAS 67 *The Confirmation Process* Proposed SAS *External Confirmations* (issued but not effective; proposed effective date is December 2012) Proposed AS *Confirmation* ISA 505 *External Confirmations*
Using Others' Work in the Audit	SAS 73 *Using the Work of a Specialist* Proposed SAS *Using the Work of an Auditor's Specialist* (issued but not effective; proposed effective date is December 2012) ISA 620 *Using the Work of an Auditor's Expert*

Note: *Acronyms for Relevant Professional Guidance*
STANDARDS: **AS**—Auditing Standard issued by the PCAOB; **ISA**—International Standard on Auditing issued by the IAASB; **SAS**—Statement on Auditing Standards issued by the Auditing Standards Board of the AICPA; **SSAE**—Statement on Standards for Attestation Engagements issued by the AICPA.
ORGANIZATIONS: **AICPA**—American Institute of Certified Public Accountants; **COSO**—Committee of Sponsoring Organizations; **IAASB**—International Auditing and Assurance Standards Board; **PCAOB**—Public Company Accounting Oversight Board; **SEC**—Securities and Exchange Commission.

Review Questions

11-1   **(LO 1)** What is supply chain management? What key issues are usually included in agreements between suppliers and their customers to bring efficiencies to the process and assure control?

11-2   **(LO 5)** What significant controls will a company implement in an electronic partnering arrangement with a major supplier to assure that all goods received are (a) properly accounted for, (b) of good quality, (c) within acceptable delivery and quality terms, and (d) paid for properly?

11-3   **(LO 1, 5, 6)** What are the important attributes of good supply chain management, and how do those attributes affect the audit of accounts payable and inventory?

11-4   **(LO 3)** Why might a company understate expenses? Why might a company overstate expenses? How might a company accomplish these inaccuracies? For the auditor, how does professional skepticism play a role in considering these possibilities?

Professional Skepticism

11-5   **(LO 4)** How can cross-sectional analysis performed as a preliminary analytical procedure help the auditor identify potential inventory misstatements for a multilocation retail client?

11-6   **(LO 1, 5)** Identify the major activities of the acquisition and payment cycle and the control objectives that should be addressed in the design of controls for each phase.

11-7   **(LO 1, 5)** Identify the different ways in which the requisition process might be implemented. For each method, indicate how the requisition is authorized and the evidence the auditor would gather to determine authorization.

11-8   **(LO 1, 3, 5)** Why should the function of requisitioning the purchase of goods be segregated from the function of issuing purchase orders?

11-9   **(LO 1, 5)** How does an automated receiving function differ from a traditional manual receiving function? How do the controls differ in the automated function? What controls does the auditor normally find most useful in reviewing the controls over an automated receiving function?

11-10   **(LO 1, 5)** Assume that prenumbered receiving documents are not used in an organization that has attempted to automate much of the purchasing and receiving functions. What management assertion is addressed by having prenumbered receiving documents? What compensating controls should the auditor expect to find when prenumbered receiving documents are not used?

11-11   **(LO 1, 5)** Many organizations use the computer to generate purchase orders. Who is responsible for a purchase when the computer generates the purchase order? How does the responsible individual make sure that computer-generated orders are correct and are generated only for purchases that should be made?

11-12   **(LO 1, 5)**   Explain how an automated matching process works regarding the payment of accounts payable. What controls need to be implemented in the automated matching process to make sure that only authorized payments are made for goods and services actually received and that payments are made at the authorized prices?

11-13   **(LO 6)**   A client with just-in-time inventory does not formally receive goods, but unloads supplies from the railroad car directly into the production line. The client has a long-term contract with the supplier specifying delivery terms, quality requirements, and penalties for noncompliance. The vendor is paid based on production achieved during the month. The auditor is concerned that accounts payable be properly stated at the end of the period. How would the auditor gather evidence to determine that accounts payable are properly recognized for vendors who are part of the just-in-time system?

11-14   **(LO 1, 5)**   What important controls would an auditor expect to find in an accounts payable environment when payments are automatically scheduled and checks or electronic transfers of cash are generated by the computer program?

Group Activity

11-15   **(LO 3, 8)**   Describe some of the common fraud schemes that affect the inventory and cost of goods sold accounts. Discuss in small groups or in the class as a whole instances in which students have experienced or read about fraud schemes in their community or workplaces related to inventory. For example, discuss situations in which students have witnessed or learned about inventory thefts in their workplaces, and how such thefts were accomplished.

Fraud

11-16   **(LO 6)**   What assertions are tested by accounts payable confirmations? What form is used for accounts payable confirmations? Explain why these confirmations are often not used on an audit.

11-17   **(LO 6)**   What assumptions must hold true if the auditor chooses to test the completeness of accounts payable by examining subsequent disbursements and reviewing open accounts payable? What are the options to discover unrecorded accounts payable?

11-18   **(LO 6)**   What information should an auditor gather in reviewing long-term purchase contracts or long-term supply contracts? How might the information affect the audit?

11-19   **(LO 6)**   The auditor often examines some expense accounts, such as legal expenses, in detail even if the account balance is not material. Explain why.

Internet

11-20   **(LO 3, 5, 6)**   Why does the auditor examine travel and entertainment expenses? What would poor controls regarding executive reimbursements say about the "tone at the top" for purposes of evaluating and reporting on internal control? Search the Internet and find a contemporary example to share with the class in which an executive abused travel and entertainment expense accounts to commit fraud.

Group Activity

11-21   **(LO 4)**   How might the auditor effectively use preliminary analytical procedures in the audit of various expense accounts, such as miscellaneous expenses? Give an example of how analytical procedures might be used in the audit of such accounts.

**Professional
Skepticism**

11-22   **(LO 3, 6)**   An auditor has been assigned to audit the accounts payable of a high-risk audit client. Control risk is assessed as high, management integrity is marginal, and the company is near violation of important loan covenants, particularly one that requires the maintenance of a minimum working-capital ratio. Explain how the auditor should approach the year-end audit of accounts payable.

11-23   **(LO 7)**   What factors contribute to the complexity of inventory audits?

11-24   **(LO 3, 8, 9)**   Explain why self-checking digits are an important control procedure found in computerized inventory systems. What potential errors are prevented by the use of self-checking digits?

11-25   **(LO 10)**   What inquiries should the auditor make to understand standard cost systems? How would the auditor test the standard cost system to determine that payroll expenses are appropriately charged to products?

11-26   **(LO 10)**   Compare worldwide professional guidance on auditing inventory accounts. What are the key requirements?

International

11-27   **(LO 3, 8, 9)**   Why is it important that a quality-control function be used for receiving important inventory items? What is the financial statement risk if a manufacturing client does not use such a function?

11-28   **(LO 10)**   During observation of the client's year-end inventory, the auditor notes that shipping document 8702 was the last shipment for the year and that receiving report 10,163 was the last receiving slip for the year. Explain how the information gathered would be used in performing an inventory cutoff test.

11-29   **(LO 10)**   The Northwoods Manufacturing Company has automated its production facilities dramatically during the last five years, to the extent that the number of direct-labor hours has remained steady while production has increased fivefold. Automated equipment, such as robots, has helped increase productivity. Overhead, previously applied at the rate of $7.50 per direct-labor hour, is now being applied at the rate of $23.50 per direct-labor hour. Explain how you would evaluate the reasonableness of the application of factory overhead to year-end inventory and cost of goods sold.

11-30   **(LO 10)**   During the observation of a client's physical inventory count, the auditor noted that the client had changed the numbering system used to identify inventory products. The auditor also discovered several errors in the product numbers recorded on inventory tags and brought the errors to the attention of the supervisor, who corrected each error. The auditor also noted that the count of inventory items was highly accurate. How would these findings affect the year-end audit of inventory?

11-31   **(LO 10)**   The auditor has always received good cooperation from a particular client and has been willing to share information about the audit with the controller on a timely basis. The controller has requested copies of the auditor's observations on the physical inventory because she wants to make sure that a good inventory was taken. Should the auditor comply with this request? State your rationale.

11-32   **(LO 10)**   The auditor has been assigned to the audit of Marathon Oil Company and will observe the testing of inventory at a major storage area in Ohio. The company has approximately 15 different types of fuel oils stored in various tanks. The value of the fuel varies dramatically according to its grade. Explain how the auditor might use a specialist in auditing the inventory.

11-33   **(LO 9)**   Assume that customers are allowed to return merchandise that is defective or that they simply did not like. What is the proper accounting for the returns? What control procedures should be implemented to assure that all returned items are properly recorded?

11-34   **(LO 10)**   The auditor is always concerned that slow-moving or potentially obsolete inventory is included in inventory and that the goods should be reduced to a lower market value. Identify five procedures the auditor might use to determine the existence of obsolete goods or goods whose market value is less than cost.

11-35   **(LO 10)**   During the audit of inventory, you note that the client had generated substantial cost and material variances. The client explains that many of the variances were due to irregular production schedules, heavy overtime for the summer period, and lighter production during other times of the year. The controller has allocated the variances (all negative) to finished goods and work-in-process inventory, based on the relative proportion of each inventory category. Comment on the appropriateness of the allocation method used by the controller.

11-36   **(LO 10)**   Explain the procedures the auditor would use to verify the cost of inventory, assuming the client uses the following valuation approaches:

a.   FIFO valuation on a periodic inventory basis

b.   LIFO based on an index of FIFO cost computed each year and then used to adjust the inventory to LIFO

c.   Average cost on a perpetual inventory basis

11-37   **(LO 10)**   Explain how generalized audit software (GAS) could be used to help identify potentially obsolete inventory.

11-38   **(LO 10)**   Explain the purpose of the test counts and other inventory observations that the auditor notes while a physical inventory is being taken.

11-39   **(LO 10)**   What financial statement disclosures are required for inventory? How does the auditor determine the adequacy of the client's financial statement disclosures?

11-40   **(LO 10)**   Identify two audit approaches that might be used to gain assurance about the correctness of perpetual inventory records.

Multiple-Choice Questions

11-41   **(LO 4)**   Auditors use preliminary analytical procedures to help identify potential misstatements in inventory. Which of the following would not be useful for this purpose?

a. Calculating inventory turnover.

b. Aging inventory.

c. Comparing the percent change in inventory with the percent change in sales.

d. All of the above would be useful.

*11-42 **(LO 4, 6, 10)** The auditor's analytical procedures are facilitated if the client does which of the following?

a. Uses a standard cost system that produces variance reports.

b. Segregates obsolete inventory before the physical inventory count.

c. Corrects reportable conditions in internal control before the beginning of the audit.

d. Reduces inventory balances to the lower of cost or market.

11-43 **(LO 5)** Which of the following controls would be most effective in assuring that recorded purchases are free of material errors?

a. The receiving department compares the quantity ordered on purchase orders with the quantity received, indicated on receiving reports.

b. Vendors' invoices are compared with purchase orders by an employee who is independent of the receiving department.

c. Receiving reports require the signature of the individual who authorized the purchase.

d. Accounts payable personnel match purchase orders, receiving reports, and vendors' invoices before approval for payment.

*11-44 **(LO 5)** Which of the following procedures in the cash disbursements cycle should not be performed by the accounts payable department?

a. Comparing the vendor's invoice with the receiving report.

b. Canceling supporting documentation after payment.

c. Verifying mathematical accuracy of the vendor's invoice.

d. Approving the invoice for payment.

*11-45 **(LO 6)** To determine whether accounts payable are complete, an auditor performs a test to verify that all merchandise received is recorded. The population of documents for this test consists of all:

a. Vendors' invoices

b. Purchase orders

c. Receiving reports

d. Canceled checks

11-46 **(LO 10)** Tracing debits from the inventory account to receiving reports and purchase orders provides evidence that:

a. All receipts of merchandise were properly recorded.

b. Recorded inventory purchases were for goods received and were properly authorized.

c. All vendor invoices have been properly recognized as a purchase and payable.

d. Inventory is not understated.

*All problems marked with an asterisk are adapted from the Certified Internal Auditor Examination.

*11-47   **(LO 10)** After accounting for a sequence of inventory tags, an auditor traces a sample of tags to the physical inventory list and reconciles the sequences counted to the inventory list to obtain evidence that all items:

 a. Included in the list have been counted.

 b. Represented by inventory tags are included in the list.

 c. Included in the list are represented by inventory tags.

 d. Represented by inventory tags that are real.

*11-48   **(LO 10)** Which of the following is *not* one of the independent auditor's objectives regarding the physical observation of inventories?

 a. Verifying that inventory counted is owned by the client.

 b. Verifying that the client has used proper inventory pricing.

 c. Ascertaining the physical quantities of inventory on hand.

 d. Verifying that all inventory owned by the client is on hand at the time of the count.

*11-49   **(LO 10)** The auditor tests the quantity of materials charged to work-in-process by tracing these quantities from the work-in-process accounts to:

 a. Cost ledgers.

 b. Perpetual inventory records.

 c. Receiving reports.

 d. Material requisitions.

*11-50   **(LO 6)** Which of the following audit procedures is best for identifying unrecorded trade accounts payable?

 a. Examining unusual relationships between monthly accounts payable balances and recorded cash payments.

 b. Reconciling vendors' statements to the file of receiving reports to identify items received just before the balance sheet date.

 c. Reviewing cash disbursements recorded subsequent to the balance sheet date to determine whether the related payables apply to the prior period.

 d. Investigating payables recorded just before and just after the balance sheet date to determine whether they are supported by receiving reports.

*11-51   **(LO 10)** When companies use automated inventory systems and information technology (IT) extensively, evidence may be available only in electronic form. What is an auditor's best course of action in such situations?

 a. Assess the control risk as high.

 b. Use audit software to perform analytical procedures.

 c. Use generalized audit software to extract evidence from client databases.

 d. Perform limited tests of controls over electronic data.

*11-52 **(LO 10)** Which of the following would the auditor likely do to obtain assurance that all inventory items in a client's inventory listing are valid?

    a. Trace inventory tags noted during the auditor's observation to items listed in receiving reports and vendors' invoices.

    b. Vouch items listed in receiving reports and vendors' invoices to the inventory listing.

    c. Trace inventory tags noted during the auditor's observation to items in the inventory listing.

    d. Trace items in the inventory listing to inventory tags and the auditor's recorded count sheets.

11-53 **(LO 2, 10)** Consider a nonpublic company where an opinion on internal controls will not be issued. What is the most likely course of action that an auditor would take after determining that performing substantive tests on inventory will take less time than performing tests of controls?

    a. Assess control risk at the minimum level.

    b. Perform both tests of controls and substantive tests on inventory.

    c. Perform only substantive tests on inventory.

    d. Perform only tests of controls on inventory.

11-54 **(LO 10)** The auditor's inventory observation test counts are traced to the client's inventory listing to test for which of the following financial statement assertions?

    a. Completeness

    b. Existence

    c. Valuation

    d. Presentation and disclosure

Discussion and Research Questions

11-55 **(Preliminary Analytical Procedures, LO 4)** One of your audit clients manufactures fishing boats and sells them all over the country. Boats are sold to dealers who finance their purchases on a floor-plan basis with their banks. The dealer's banks usually pay your client within two weeks of shipment. The company's profits have been increasing over the past several years. You expect that trend to continue. You also expect this year's gross margin and inventory turnover to remain consistent with the prior years and to be consistent with the major competitor. You have obtained the following information related to your 2011 audit ($ in millions):

	2011	2010*	2009*	2008*	2007*	Major Competitor (2011)
Inventory	16.0	10.0	7.2	5.5	5.1	13.9
Sales	84.7	77.9	56.8	43.6	39.8	110.3
Cost of Goods Sold	65.9	64.7	46.6	36.2	32.6	92.0

*Audited

Required

a. Calculate the following ratios for each year and the competitor:

(i) Gross margin as a percent of sales
(ii) Inventory turnover.

b. Suggest possible explanations for any unexpected results.

c. What inquiries and follow-up audit procedures might be performed to determine the accuracy of the client's data?

11-56 **(Automated Receiving Function, LO 3, 5, 6)** Hodag Company has automated its receiving function as follows:

1. A receiving supervisor accesses an open purchase order file, listed by vendor, to determine whether a shipment should be accepted. If the shipment is not on the open order list, the supervisor must obtain permission from a purchasing agent before the shipment can be accepted.

2. Most items are accepted, opened, and counted. The counts are entered on paper documents that are copies of the purchase order with the quantity ordered blocked out. The document is batched in the receiving office, and all items are input by a clerk.

3. An automated scanner reads selected items, but the boxes are not opened. The computerized scanning count is automatically recorded on the receiving document. If differences are noted between the scanning from the outside of the carton and the actual contents when opened, an adjusting document is prepared and sent to accounts payable and the purchasing agent.

4. A quality-control department selectively tests goods before they are put into production. Any defective items are noted and a document is sent to accounts payable and the purchasing agent, and the goods are marked for return. The goods are not returned to the vendor, however, unless specifically authorized by the purchasing agent.

5. The receiving document contains information on who should pay freight. If the shipment comes with freight due, the receiving department is authorized to make the payment. Where applicable, the receiving department prepares a charge-back notice for the freight and forwards it to the purchasing agent and accounts payable.

Required

a. What risks are present in the system as described?

b. What additional computerized control procedures would the auditor expect to be implemented in the system described?

c. What audit procedures might the auditor use to assure that goods are accepted and paid for only when the purchase is authorized and that the payments are for the correct quantity and correct price?

Fraud

11-57 **(Potential Fraud in Purchasing Function, LO 3, 5, 6)** Assume the auditor has assessed that the potential is high that some purchase agents are involved in a kickback scheme with vendors who have received preferential treatment. The purchasing agents are receiving gifts or cash payments directly from the vendors for steering new contracts their way or negotiating purchase prices higher than could be obtained elsewhere. The auditor has limited, but as yet unverified, information that some specific purchasing agents have been living a rather lavish lifestyle.

Required

a. What controls would be effective in preventing kickback schemes?

b. What audit procedures might be used to determine whether the purchasing agents might be involved with kickback schemes? Be specific in your procedures. Identify all evidence to be gathered (internal and external), populations from which you will sample, and the specific documentations you will examine.

Professional Skepticism

11-58   **(Expense Fraud, LO 3, 5, 6)** Each year Susan Riley, president of Bargon Construction, Inc., takes a three-week vacation to Hawaii and signs several checks to pay major bills during the period in which she is absent. Riley's vacation often occurs near the end of Bargon's fiscal reporting period because it is a slack time for the construction business. Jack Morgan, head bookkeeper for the company, uses this practice to his advantage. He makes out a check to himself for the amount of a large vendor's invoice and records it as a payment to the vendor for the purchase of supplies. He holds the check for several weeks to make sure the auditors will not examine the canceled check. Shortly after the first of the year, Morgan resubmits the invoice to Riley for payment approval and records the check in the cash disbursements journal. At that point, he marks the invoice as paid and files it with all other paid invoices. Morgan has been following this practice successfully for several years and feels confident that he has developed a foolproof fraud.

Professional Skepticism

Fraud

Required

a. What is the auditor's responsibility for discovering this type of embezzlement?

b. What weaknesses exist in the client's internal controls?

c. What audit procedures are likely to uncover the fraud?

*11-59   **(Organization of Acquisition Function, LO 1, 3, 5, 6)** The organization structure of a manufacturing firm includes the following departments: purchasing, receiving, inspecting, warehousing, and controllership. An auditor is assigned to audit the receiving department. The preliminary survey reveals the following information:

1. A copy of each purchase order is routinely sent to the receiving department by the purchasing department. Intracompany e-mail is used for the notification followed by the physical copy via regular intracompany mail. Each purchase order is filed by purchase order number. In response to a job enrichment program, everyone in the receiving department is authorized to file the purchase orders. Whoever happens to be available when the company mail is received is expected to file any purchase orders it contains.

2. When a shipment of goods is delivered to the receiving dock, the shipper's invoice is signed and forwarded to the controller's office, the vendor's packing slip is filed in receiving by vendor name, and the goods are stored in the warehouse by receiving personnel. In response to a job enrichment program, all persons in the receiving department have been trained to perform all three activities independently. Whoever happens to be available when a shipment arrives is expected to perform all three of the activities associated with that shipment.

Professional Skepticism

Required

a. What are the major deficiencies and inefficiencies in the process as described?

b. How could the process be improved? First, consider the need for strategic production and suppliers. Second, consider how greater computerization could improve the process.

c. Why is it important to have segregation between the purchasing, receiving, and payment functions? How is that segregation maintained when all three functions are automated?

d. Assume the purchasing and receiving functions operate as described. What would your assessment be of control risk? What are the implications for substantive testing of the related account balances? Describe the substantive procedures the auditor should consider for inventory, expenses, payables, and other related accounts.

*11-60 **(Accounts Payable, LO 6)** Paul Mincin, CPA, is the auditor of Raleigh Corporation. Mincin is considering the audit work to be performed in the accounts payable area for the current-year engagement. The prior-year documentation shows that confirmation requests were mailed to 100 of Raleigh's 1,000 suppliers. The selected suppliers were based on Mincin's sample that was designed to select accounts with large dollar balances. Mincin and Raleigh staff spent a substantial number of hours resolving relatively minor differences between the confirmation replies and Raleigh's accounting records. Alternative audit procedures were used for those suppliers who did not respond to the confirmation requests.

Required

a. Identify the accounts payable management assertions that Mincin must consider in determining the audit procedures to be followed.

b. Identify situations in which Mincin should use accounts payable confirmations, and discuss whether he is required to use them.

c. Discuss why the use of large dollar balances as the basis for selecting accounts payable for confirmation might not be the most effective approach and indicate what more effective procedures could be followed when selecting accounts payable for confirmation.

11-61 **(Audit Procedures and Objectives, LO 5, 6)** The following audit procedures are found in audit programs addressing the acquisition and payment cycle.

Required

For each audit procedure described:

a. Identify the objective of the procedure or the audit assertion being tested.

b. Classify the procedure as primarily a substantive test, a test of controls, or both.

Audit Procedures

1. The auditor examines payments to vendors following year end and then reviews any open accounts payable files.

2. The auditor reviews computer-center records on changes to passwords and the client's procedures to monitor unusual amounts of access by password type. The auditor makes inquiries of purchasing agents about how often passwords are changed and whether assistants are allowed to access computer files in their absence in order to efficiently handle inquiries or process standing orders.

3. The auditor reviews a report of all accounts payable items that were not matched by the automated matching system but had been paid upon authorization of the accounts payable department. A sample of selected items is taken and traced to the vendor payment and supporting documentation.

4. The auditor uses software to prepare a report of all debits to accounts payable other than payments to vendors. A sample of the debits is selected and examined for support.

5. The auditor uses software to access all recorded receipts of merchandise that have not been matched to an open purchase order.

6. The client prepares a report from a database showing inventory write-downs by product line and by purchasing agent. The auditor reviews the report and analyzes the data in relation to sales volume by product.

7. The auditor creates a spreadsheet showing the amount of scrap generated monthly, by product line.

8. The auditor downloads client data to create a report showing monthly sales and inventory levels, by product line.

11-62 **(Acquisition Controls—Small Business, LO 5, 6)** Because of the small size of the company and the limited number of accounting personnel, Dry Goods Wholesale Company initially records all acquisitions of goods and services at the time cash disbursements are made. At the end of each quarter, when financial statements for internal purposes are prepared, accounts payable are recorded by adjusting journal entries. The entries are reversed at the beginning of the next period. Except for the lack of an accounts payable or voucher journal, controls over acquisitions are excellent for a small company. (There are adequate prenumbered documents for all acquisitions, proper approvals, and adequate internal verification where appropriate.)

Professional Skepticism

Before the auditor arrives for the year-end audit, the bookkeeper prepares adjusting entries to record accounts payable as of the balance sheet date. He prepares a list of all outstanding balances, by vendor, and gives it to the auditor. All vendors' invoices supporting the list are retained in a separate file for the auditor's use.

During the current year, the accounts payable balance has increased dramatically because of a severe cash shortage. (The cash shortage apparently arose from expansion of inventory and facilities rather than lack of sales.) Many accounts have remained unpaid for several months, and the client is being pressured by several vendors to pay the bills. Because the company had a relatively profitable year, management is anxious to complete the audit as early as possible so that the audited statements can be used to obtain a large bank loan.

Required

a. Explain how the lack of an accounts payable or vouchers journal will affect the auditor's tests of controls and substantive tests for acquisitions and payments.

b. What sampling unit should be used in performing tests of expenses and accounts payable?

c. Assuming no errors are discovered in the auditor's control tests for acquisitions and payments, how will that result affect the verification of accounts payable?

d. Discuss the reasonableness of the client's request for an early completion of the audit and describe the implications of the request from the auditor's point of view.

e. List the audit procedures that should be performed in the year-end audit of accounts payable to meet the cutoff objective.

f. State your opinion about whether it is possible to conduct an adequate audit in these circumstances.

11-63   **(Auditing an Expense Account and Accounts Payable, LO 4, 6)** You have been assigned to audit the factory supplies expense account for a medium-sized manufacturing firm. Here is the relevant data for the past three years:

	2011 (Unaudited)	**2010***	**2009**
Sales	$22,808	$21,900	$20,500
Supplies Expense	784	925	815
Net Income	1,001	985	915
Factory Assets	16,500	14,500	14,800

*Audited

Required

a. Briefly explain how preliminary analytical review techniques might be used to identify potential misstatements in this expense account. Identify potential variables (besides sales) that should be considered in modeling (estimating) the supplies expense account balance.

b. The auditor wishes to test existence, valuation, and classification of the supplies expense account balance. Describe *one* audit procedure (besides analytical review) that would test the three assertions.

*11-64   **(Accounts Payable Procedures, LO 6)** Kane, CPA, is auditing Star Wholesaling Company's financial statements and is about to perform substantive audit procedures on Star's trade accounts payable balances. Star Wholesaling in a privately held company. After obtaining an understanding of Star's internal controls for accounts payable, Kane assessed control risk at the maximum. Kane requested and received from Star a schedule of the trade accounts payable prepared using the trade accounts payable subsidiary ledger (voucher register).

Required

Describe the substantive audit procedures Kane should apply to Star's trade accounts payable balances.

11-65   **(Acquisition and Payment Cycle Audit Procedures, LO 5, 6)** The following are some test procedures frequently performed in the acquisition and payment cycle. Each is to be done on a sample basis.

Required

a. State whether each procedure is primarily a test of controls, a substantive test, or a dual-purpose test.

b. State the purpose(s) of each procedure.

Audit Procedures

1. Trace transactions recorded in the purchase journal to supporting documentation, comparing the vendor's name, total dollar amounts, and authorization for purchase.

2. Account for a sequence of receiving reports and trace selected ones to related vendor's invoices and purchase journal entries.

3. Select a sample of cash disbursements, noting evidence that the details on vendor invoices were clerically checked and compared with the purchase order and receiving report and that the account charged and payment were approved.

4. Same as Procedure 3 but in addition the auditor compares the invoice detail with the supporting documents and assesses the appropriateness of the account charged.

5. Foot the cash disbursements journal, trace postings of the total to the general ledger, and trace postings of individual payments to the accounts payable master file.

6. Account for a numerical sequence of checks in the cash disbursements journal and examine all voided or spoiled checks for proper cancellation.

7. Compare dates on canceled checks with dates on the cash disbursements journal and the bank cancellation date.

11-66 **(Auditing Legal Expenses, LO 6)** You have been assigned the task of auditing legal expenses for the recent year. The client prepares a schedule of all recorded legal expenses and presents the schedule to you for your audit work. You note that the amount on the schedule agrees with the amounts shown in the general ledger.

Required

a. Explain why the auditor should always examine legal expense as a part of the audit.

b. Identify the audit procedures that should be used in examining legal expenses.

11-67 **(Analysis of Errors or Intentional Misstatements, LO 5, 6, 10)** The following errors or omissions or intentional misstatements are included in the accounting records of Westgate Manufacturing Company.

Fraud

Required

a. For each error, identify the management assertion that was not met.

b. For each error, identify a control procedure that should have prevented it from occurring on a continuing basis.

c. For each error, identify a substantive direct test of the account balance that would uncover the error.

Errors or Omissions or Intentional Misstatements Noted

1. Repairs and maintenance expense (account 2121) was charged to equipment (account 1221).

2. Purchases of raw materials are frequently not recorded until several weeks after the goods are received because receiving personnel fail to forward receiving reports to accounting. Upon being pressured by a vendor's credit department, the accounts payable department searches for the receiving report, records the transactions in the accounts payable journal, and pays the bill.

3. The accounts payable clerk prepares a monthly check to Story Supply Company for the amount of an invoice owed and then submits the unsigned check to the treasurer for payment along with related supporting documents. When she receives the signed check from the treasurer, the clerk records it as a debit to accounts payable and deposits the check in a personal bank account for a company named Story Company. A few days later, she records the invoice in the accounts payable journal, resubmits the documents and a new check to the treasurer, and sends the check to the vendor after it has been signed.

4. The amount of a check in the cash disbursements journal is recorded as $4,612.87 instead of the $4,162.87 shown on the face of the check.

5. The accounts payable clerk intentionally excluded from the cash disbursements journal seven large checks written and mailed on December 26 to prevent cash in the bank from having a negative balance on the general ledger. They were recorded on January 2 of the subsequent year.

6. Each month an employee in the receiving department submits a fictitious receiving report to Accounting. A few days later, he sends Westgate an invoice for the quantity of goods ordered from a small company he owns and operates. The invoice is paid when the accounts payable clerk matches the receiving report with the vendor's invoice.

11-68   **(Audit Program for Inventory, LO 10)** You are planning the audit of a company that manufactures outdoor equipment in Chicago and has distribution centers in Chicago, Boston, Tampa, Houston, Denver, and San Francisco. The client has provided a download of its inventory records of finished goods that contains the following information:

- Stock number
- Product line code
- Date of last sale
- Number sold year-to-date
- Number returned year-to-date
- Number of defectives returned year-to-date
- Unit cost
- Quantity on hand
- Extended cost
- Current selling price
- Location code

Required

Write an audit program that identifies the specific procedures for which generalized audit software (GAS) can be used to help you audit this inventory. Your program should focus on the assertions of valuation, existence, and rights (ownership).

11-69   **(Sampling of Perpetual Records, LO 10)** Ace Corporation does not conduct a complete annual physical count of purchased parts in its principal warehouse; instead, it uses statistical sampling to test the accuracy of the perpetual records. Ace believes that statistical sampling is highly effective in testing the records and is sufficiently reliable to make a physical count of each item of inventory unnecessary.

Required

a. List at least five typical audit procedures that should be performed to verify physical quantities when a client conducts a periodic physical count of its entire inventory.

b. Is it acceptable to take a statistical sample to test the perpetual records rather than take a complete physical count of inventory? If it is acceptable, identify the key factors the auditor should consider in determining the acceptability of such a procedure.

c. Identify the audit procedures either different from, or in addition to, normal required audit procedures that should be used in the situation just described (when a client employs statistical sampling to test the perpetual records and does not conduct a 100% annual physical count of inventory items).

d. Assume the client uses FIFO for inventory valuation and has verified the accuracy of the perpetual inventory counts. What procedures should the auditor use to verify the valuation of the inventory?

11-70   **(Inventory Observation, LO 10)** The auditor is required by existing auditing standards, both U.S. and international, to observe the client's physical inventory. That requirement could be met by observing the client's annual physical count of inventory and, in some circumstances, by observing inventory in connection with tests of the accuracy of the client's perpetual inventory.

Required

a. What major purpose is served by requiring the auditor to observe the client's physical inventory count? What are the primary assertions for which the auditor gains evidence during the inventory observation? What is the rationale behind the profession's decision to require the inventory observation?

b. Identify at least five items related to inventory that the auditor should be looking for and should document during observation of the client's inventory.

c. How does the observation process differ when the client takes a complete physical count at or near year end vs. when physical counts are taken throughout the year to test the accuracy of the perpetual records?

11-71   **(Inventory Obsolescence Tests, LO 10)** You have been assigned to the audit of Technotrics, a company specializing in wholesaling a wide variety of electronic products. Its major product lines are stereo and similar electronic equipment, as well as computers and computer add-ons such as hard disks and memory boards. The client has four major warehouses located in Atlanta, Las Vegas, Minneapolis, and Philadelphia. At year end, the client has approximately $250 million in inventory, an increase of $7 million.

Required

a. Indicate how the auditor can gain information about major changes in products handled by the client and about the effect of competition on existing products.

b. Indicate how the auditor might use generalized audit software to search for slow-moving or potentially obsolete goods in the client's year-end inventory.

c. What other procedures might the auditor use in determining whether significant portions of the client's year-end inventory have a market value less than cost?

11-72 **(Inventory Cutoff Problem, LO 10)** The auditor has gathered shipping cutoff information for Johnny M. Golf Company in conjunction with its December 31 year end. The auditor has observed the client's year-end physical inventory and is satisfied with the client's inventory procedures. The client has adjusted the year-end book value to the physical inventory compilation (book to physical adjustment) so that the account balance at year end equals the physical count. For purposes of analysis, you should assume that all items have a gross margin of 30%. The last shipping document and bill of lading used during the current year is 4500 and is the primary evidence regarding whether the goods were shipped before or after inventory. All shipping documents are sequentially numbered, and the auditor has established that the client uses them in order.

The shipping date listed in the journal is the date recorded on the sales invoice. Cost of goods sold is recorded at the same time the invoice is recorded.

DECEMBER SALES JOURNAL

Date	Billed to	Shipping Terms	Ship Date	Ship Number	Amount
12/31	Bartifshoski Electric	FOB shipping point	12/31	4498	$4,500
12/31	Schlagel Electric	FOB shipping point	12/31	4501	$11,000
12/31	Schenk Comptometer	FOB shipping point	12/31	4502	$20,000
12/31	Schoone Const.	FOB shipping point	1/3	4503	$20,000
12/31	Tomahawk Const.	FOB destination	12/31	4496	$10,000

JANUARY SALES JOURNAL

Date	Billed to	Shipping Terms	Ship Date	Ship Number	Amount
1/3	Smith Electric	FOB shipping point	12/31	4504	$10,000
1/3	Lampley Const.	FOB shipping point	1/3	4499	$8,000
1/3	Montana Mt. Const.	FOB shipping point	1/3	4505	$12,000

Required

a. Briefly discuss why the auditor would rely on the shipping document number instead of the recorded shipping date as the primary evidence of whether the goods were shipped before or after inventory.

b. Identify the items that should be adjusted. Prepare a journal entry to record the adjustments to cost of goods sold, inventory, accounts receivable, and sales based on the preceding data. Prepare the journal entries needed only for the December 31 year end.

c. Assume that the client took physical inventory on October 31 and adjusted the books to the physical inventory at that time. Given the information from the December and January sales journals, prepare the necessary year-end adjusting entries. Why are the entries different from those suggested for part (b)?

11-73 **(Inventory Valuation and Adjustments, LO 10)** Inshalla Retail Company keeps its inventory on a perpetual FIFO basis for internal reporting but adjusts the year-end FIFO balance to a LIFO basis using a dollar-value LIFO index. The auditor is satisfied that the FIFO perpetual inventory is accurate. The LIFO adjustment is made by calculating an index for each of the company's four product lines. The index is applied to determine whether there was an increase or decrease in inventory for the year, and the appropriate entry is made.

Required

Explain how the auditor would audit the LIFO adjustment.

11-74 **(Audit of Standard Cost System, LO 10)** Badger Meter of Milwaukee, Wisconsin, designs and manufactures water meters, gasoline meters, and other metering systems to measure and report the flow of liquid through various lines. The company has three manufacturing plants: one in Milwaukee, Wisconsin, one in Lucerne, France, and one in Bustof, Poland. The plant in Milwaukee has been recently modernized and is the most modern of the three. The company uses standard costs to value all work-in-process and finished goods inventory. Because management wants to compare plant productivity across all three of its plants, it uses the standard cost system developed for the Milwaukee plant in all three plants. This allows it to analyze variances at the other plants to determine their relative efficiency. Overhead is applied to products based on the annual depreciation expense charged to each production area. This method is used because factory labor has become less of a factor in the manufacturing process in the United States, although it is not so true for the plant in Poland.

Required

a. Briefly discuss the validity of using standard cost systems as a basis for valuing inventory.

b. How are variances treated in the inventory valuation process?

c. Identify the procedures the auditor would use to audit the standard cost system and the inventory valuation at the Milwaukee plant.

d. Discuss how the information gathered in Milwaukee would be applicable to the audits of the inventory at the other two locations.

11-75 **(Integrated Audit of Acquisition and Inventory, LO 2, 4, 5, 6, 9, 10)**

Required

For each of the following tests related to acquisition and inventory that is performed as part of an integrated audit, indicate the effect of the control deficiency or finding on the planning of substantive tests of the related account balances.

1. The client uses an automated purchasing system. However, in the tests of controls, the auditor finds that access to the system is not restricted as authorized. The auditor finds that purchasing agents routinely override purchase requisitions and also add new vendors without going through the approval process required by company policies.

2. The client does not record returned merchandise.

3. The client does not take cycle counts of the perpetual inventory system. However, other controls over receipt and shipment of inventory are working.

4. The client does not employ a systematic process to evaluate the potential obsolescence in inventory.

5. Many of the travel and expense reimbursements to top management are not accompanied by receipts or a description of the purpose of the expenditure.

6. Preliminary analytical procedures of expense accounts indicate that they are low in comparison with (a) previous years and (b) in relationship to sales.

11-76   **(Persuasive Evidence, LO 2, 4, 5, 6, 9, 10)** How much evidence is needed to be persuasive? Each of the following scenarios describes the auditor's findings related to the effectiveness of internal control in performing an integrated audit.

Required

For each situation, indicate whether additional evidence in the form of substantive tests of account balances is required and, if so, the type and amount of testing that should be performed. Identify the accounts affected.

1. The automated purchasing system for inventory items for direct delivery into production contains appropriate approvals, is accompanied by a long-term contract, and any shortages of delivery automatically generate exception reports that are sent to management.

2. Each department is limited to a $500 per item limit on all purchases other than those that go through regular purchase agents. The auditor took a sample of 30 purchases and found that (a) all were approved by the department and (b) all were under $500. Most of the items were for subscriptions, travel, or miscellaneous expense.

3. The client performs regular cycle counts of perpetual inventory. No major discrepancies have been noted in the last year. The counts are made by inventory specialists, not by internal auditors.

4. Access to adding vendors is working properly.

5. The auditor finds that the same person is in charge of ordering products, reconciling receipt of merchandise with the purchase order and vendor invoice, and then forwarding the approved material to the treasurer for payment.

6. The auditor finds that both the purchasing controls and the shipping controls involving inventory are working properly.

7. The auditor's test of internal controls finds weaknesses in the control environment in the following ways:

    a. Management's compensation is dependent on increased stock valuations.

    b. Management shows little care for basic internal controls.

    c. Management has committed to increased sales and profits for this year.

    d. The audit committee meets four times a year, but the agenda is primarily set by management.

8. In addition to the information contained in situation 7, preliminary analytical procedures indicates that the company's inventory level has risen faster than sales; gross margin has increased over last year. The auditor did not expect these increases.

Cases

11-77 **(CMH Case—SEC Alleged Deficiencies, LO 10)** The SEC alleged that many deficiencies occurred during the audit of CMH, as discussed in the *Auditing in Practice* feature in this chapter. Among the complaints were the following:

Professional Skepticism

1. The audit firm "left the extent of various observation testing to the discretion of auditors, not all of whom were aware of significant audit conclusions which related directly to the extent of such testing. Observations of inventory counts at year end were confined to six locations (representing about 40% of the total CMH inventory) as opposed to nine in the preceding year. The field auditors did not adequately control the inventory tags and Seidman & Seidman [the auditor] did not detect the creation of bogus inventory tags which were inserted in the final inventory computations."

2. The comparison of recorded test counts to the computer lists in the nine warehouse locations in which the inventory count was observed indicated error rates ranging from 0.9% to 38.3% of the test counts, with error rates in excess of 10% in several locations. Management attributed the differences to errors made by a key-punch operator. When the auditors asked to see the inventory tags, the CMH official stated that they had been destroyed.

3. The Seidman auditor who performed the price testing of the CMH inventory determined that, as in previous years, in numerous instances CMH was unable to produce sufficient vendor invoices to support the purchase by CMH of the quantities being tested. This was true even though Seidman & Seidman ultimately accepted vendor invoices reflecting the purchase of the item by any CMH branch, regardless of the location of the inventory actually being price-tested.

4. A schedule of comparative inventory balances reflected significant increases from the prior year. A CMH financial officer wrote on this schedule management's explanations for the increases in inventory accounts.

5. CMH did not use prenumbered purchase orders and shipping documents.

6. There were several differences between the tags reflected on the computer list for the Miami warehouse and the observation of the same tag numbers by Seidman & Seidman auditors. The computer list contained a series of almost 1,000 tags, covering about 20% of the tags purportedly used and more than 50% of the total reported value of the Miami inventory, which were reported as being unused on the tag control document obtained by Seidman & Seidman during its observation work.

7. Because CMH management did not provide sufficient invoices as requested, the auditors relied primarily on vendor catalogs, price lists, and vendor invoices to test the accuracy of the CMH inventory pricing representations.

Required

a. For each of the deficiencies identified, indicate the appropriate action that should have been taken by the auditor.

b. What inventory information should be communicated to an auditor who is not regularly assigned to the audit of a particular client prior to the observation of a physical inventory count?

c. How do questions of management integrity affect the approach that should be taken in planning the observation of a client's inventory-counting procedures?

d. Identify instances in which the auditors in this case did not exercise appropriate professional skepticism. For each of those instances, describe an alternative way that the auditor should have handled this situation.

Ethics

11-78   **(Ethical Decisions in Inventory Valuation, LO 10, 11)** Assume that you are conducting the audit of CollegeWare, a publicly held manufacturer and distributor of printed, embroidered, and embossed specialty clothing and gift items marketed to college students with school-specific logos. The company pays licensing fees and manufactures products in advance of the fall and winter peak sales periods. The stores that sell the company's products have a contractual agreement that they may return a percentage of unsold merchandise. During the current audit year, many stores in the University of Wisconsin and University of Illinois markets canceled orders just before the start of the school year because of changes in school logos. In addition, the percentage of unsold merchandise, and associated returns, was higher than normal for these stores. As a result, CollegeWare has made an adjusting entry to record a loss caused by market decline of inventory (Dr. loss because of market decline of inventory, Cr. allowance to reduce inventory to market value for $40,000). You as the auditor have conducted a physical inventory of the products and, based upon sales data collected from CollegeWare's competitors, you are convinced that the write-down should be for $90,000 (a materially higher amount).

Another issue in the CollegeWare audit is that the company has started implementing plans to change its marketing strategy to include more sales of general-purpose clothes and gift items to mass-merchandising retailers. These retailers are larger, and the initial receivables payments indicate that they present a more reliable pattern of payments, with fewer uncollectible amounts. As such, management has argued that the allowance for doubtful accounts should be reduced and has made the associated adjusting entry (Dr. allowance for doubtful accounts, Cr. other revenue for $40,000).

In the past, you had questioned CollegeWare management about its steady increase in the allowance for doubtful accounts, which had risen by about 3% per year for each of the past five years even though the rate of customer default on receivables had remained steady over that time. However, you had never insisted that management revise its allowance downward because you considered management's estimates to be conservative (i.e., they reduced income rather than increased income). In your opinion, the allowance for doubtful accounts probably *should* be reduced, although it is hard to judge exactly the amount by which the reduction should be recorded because of the relatively recent change in the marketing strategy. In other words, it is difficult for you to dispute whether management's current adjusting entry is recorded at the correct amount.

Required

   a. Comment on why management of CollegeWare may have an incentive to reduce the allowance for doubtful accounts this year.

   b. The overly conservative accounting estimates used by management in its valuation of accounts receivable represent what is commonly referred to as "cookie jar reserves." Using this financial reporting strategy, management sets aside money in allowance accounts that it plans to remove later to cover future losses. In doing so, management allows itself discretion to report income at smoother levels than would otherwise be achieved had the cookie jar reserves not been put in place. Comment on the implications of management's financial reporting strategy.

   c. Use the ethical framework introduced in Chapter 3 to address the dilemmas faced by the auditor regarding what the auditor should require the client to do regarding the client's inventory and accounts receivable balances. Recall that the steps in the framework are as follows:

     • Identify the ethical issue(s).

     • Determine who are the affected parties and identify their rights.

     • Determine the most important rights.

     • Develop alternative courses of action.

     • Determine the likely consequences of each proposed course of action.

     • Assess the possible consequences, including an estimation of the greatest good for the greatest number.

     • Decide on the appropriate course of action.

11-79 **(Decision Analysis Framework Application in Inventory Observations LO 10, 11)** The *Professional Judgment in Context* feature at the beginning of the chapter and the *Auditing in Practice* feature about CMH both describe scenarios whereby people with accounting or auditing responsibilities were lacking the appropriate training or knowledge to conduct their jobs. In a small group in class, assume that you and your classmates were assigned to an audit client and you find yourselves in a similar situation when you arrive to conduct an inventory observation. In particular, you are asked to observe inventory counts of products for which you are unsure of the appropriate measurement technique and are lacking in knowledge of the product itself. The specific setting is a client who uses computerized measurement systems for measuring its oil products that are stored in tanks below the ground. You are uncertain of how the measurement system works and are not able to distinguish between different oil products. The client quickly describes the measurement process and offers to help you identify the different oil products. You are still somewhat unsure of your abilities to conduct this inventory observation.

Group Activity

Required

In your small group, use the seven-step Decision Analysis Framework introduced in Chapter 3 to determine how you should proceed with the inventory observation. Be prepared to discuss your group's answers with the full class following your small group discussion. Recall that the framework is as follows:

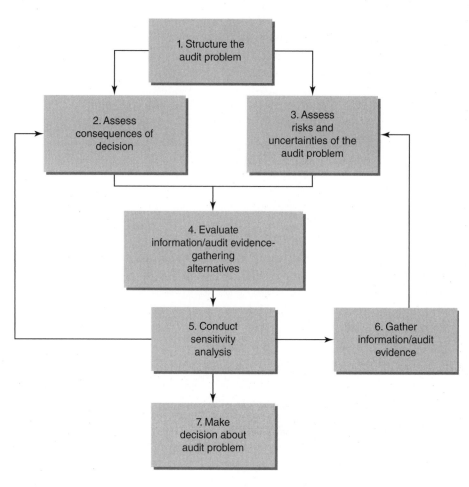

Source: Adapted from "Judgment and Choice," by Robin Hogarth.

Group Activity

11-80 **(Decision Analysis Group Case: Testing of the Inventory Valuation Assertion, LO 10, 11)**

On October 4, 2008, the PCAOB issued its annual inspection report of Grant Thornton LLP (PCAOB RELEASE NO. 104-2008-046). In conducting its inspections, the PCAOB focuses on audit engagements that it considers particularly risky or prone to error on the part of each audit firm. In its inspection report of Grant Thornton LLP, the PCAOB noted the following problems in testing the inventory valuation assertion for a Grant Thornton client.

The firm failed in the following respects to adequately test the valuation assertion regarding inventory:

- There was no evidence in the audit documentation, and no persuasive other evidence, that the firm had performed sufficient substantive procedures to test the raw materials and/or labor and overhead components of inventory at certain of its manufacturing locations. Analytical procedures, consisting of various high-level comparisons, including average cost, inventory balances, gross profit margins, and inventory turnover, were the firm's primary tests, but these procedures failed to meet the requirements for substantive analytical procedures. Specifically, the firm failed to develop expectations that were precise enough to provide the desired level of assurance that differences that may be potential material misstatements, individually or in the aggregate, would be identified, and failed to obtain corroboration of management's explanations of significant unexpected differences.

- The firm failed to evaluate the assumptions that management had used to determine the reserve for obsolete inventory.

Questions for Discussion:

a. The PCAOB report summarized a problem with Grant Thornton's testing of a client's inventory valuation assertion. In a small group, discuss why you believe the PCAOB was dissatisfied with the firm's performance.

b. In your small group, use the decision analysis framework to determine the appropriate steps that the firm could have taken that would have ultimately been acceptable to the PCAOB.

11-81 **(Husky ACL Project—Inventory Obsolescence and Lower-of-Cost-or-Market Testing, LO 10)** You are auditing inventory of HUSKY Corp. as of December 31, 2009. The inventory general ledger balance is $8,124,998.66. HUSKY manufactures lawn and garden tractors, snowmobiles, and supplies. Download the data file labeled "HUSKY 2009 Inventory" from the books' website, www.cengage.com/accounting/rittenberg under Student Resources. This file contains the following information:

SNUMB	Stock number (The first letter is F—finished goods, W—work-in-progress, R—raw material.)
LASTSALE	Date of last sale (finished goods) or use (raw material)
NUMSOLD	Number sold (finished goods) or used (raw materials) year-to-date
UNITCOST	Unit cost
INVQTY	Quantity on hand
EXTCOST	Unit cost × quantity on hand
SELPRICE	Current selling price (finished goods only)
REPLCOST	Current replacement cost (raw material only)

Salespersons receive a 10% commission based on selling price.

Required

Using ACL:

a. Using the menu option **Analyze**, choose **Statistical** then **Statistics** on the amount field, print the statistics, and agree the total inventory to the general ledger.

b. Extract and print out all inventory items that have not been used or sold in six months. Include in the printout the total extended cost of those items.

c. Extract the finished goods into a separate file. (*Hint:* Use the expression **SNUMB = "F"**.)

   (i) Extract those items that have a net realizable value less than cost. Add a column and calculate the amount each of those items should be written down, and print a report that includes those items and the total of the write-down.

   (ii) Add a field and calculate inventory turnover for each item in inventory. Extract and print a report of those items with a turnover less than 2. The report should include the total extended cost of those items.

d. Extract the raw materials into a separate file (see hint in part (c) but replace "F" with "R"):

   (i) Extract those items that have a replacement cost less than cost, add a column and calculate the amount each of those items should be written down, and print a report that includes those items and the total of the write-down.

   (ii) Add a column and calculate inventory turnover for each item. Extract and print a report of those items with a turnover less than 2. The report should include the total extended cost of those items.

e. Prepare a report of the audit implications of your findings, indicating any additional procedures that should be performed.

Academic Research Case (LO 4)

Academic research addresses the conceptual issues outlined in this chapter. To help you consider the linkage between academic research and the practice of auditing, read the following research article and answer the questions below.

Nigrini, M., & Mittermaier, L. (1997). The Use of Benford's Law as an Aid in Analytical Procedures. *Auditing: A Journal of Practice & Theory 16(2):52–67.*

   i. What is the issue being addressed in the paper?

   ii. Why is this issue important to practicing auditors?

   iii. What are the findings of the paper?

   iv. What are the implications of these findings for audit quality (or audit practice) on the audit profession?

   v. Describe the research methodology used as a basis for the conclusions.

   vi. Describe any limitations of the research that the student (and practice) should be aware of.

Go to www.cengage.com/accounting/rittenberg for the Ford and Toyota materials.

Source and Reference	Question
Ford 10-K, Toyota 20-F	**1.** What are the key acquisition and inventory cycle accounts for Ford? What are the critical accounting policies for these accounts?
Ford 10-K, Toyota 20-F	**2.** Compare Ford and Toyota's footnotes on inventory. Calculate the percentage of finished products that each company holds in inventory. What inferences do you draw from this analysis? How could this ratio be used to understand slow-moving inventory, e.g., by geographic region or product line?
Chapter 8 Ford/ Toyota Appendix Materials	**3a.** Use the financial ratios provided in an earlier chapter appendix for Ford and Toyota. What are the ratios most relevant to the acquisition and inventory cycle? **3b.** Think creatively, and develop additional ratios or comparisons that would help you understand this transaction cycle for these automotive companies. In addressing this question, it will be helpful to think about the general ratios that you calculated in Chapter 8, but to then tailor them to this unique industry and business setting.
Ford 10-K	**4.** Ford lists a variety of risk factors associated with its business. Review those and identify which relate most to the acquisition and inventory cycle. What evidence might the auditor gather to understand how those risks may affect the financial statement line items associated with the acquisition and inventory cycle?
	5. As an auditor, what is your obligation regarding the statements that management makes in its management discussion and analysis?

Module VI: Sales and Purchases Cutoff Tests

Along with Richard Derick and the rest of the audit team, you observed Biltrite's December 31, 2009, physical inventory. Derick is satisfied with the inventory-taking procedures and has considerable confidence in the reliability of the ending inventory quantities. He is concerned, however, with the methods used to value the ending inventories (especially the disposition of unfavorable budget variances) and with possible misstatements relating to sales and purchases cutoff. With regard to cutoff, Derick is particularly interested in learning why customers could not confirm details of sales transactions recorded by Biltrite on December 31, 2009. In response to the confirmation and cutoff concerns, he has asked you to examine the appropriate books of original entry and underlying documentation for a few days before and after the balance sheet date. Specifically, you are interested in the following:

1. Were purchases and sales recorded in the proper accounting period?
2. Were purchases recorded at year end included in the physical inventory?
3. Were all materials and purchased parts included in inventory recorded as purchases?
4. Were the finished goods inventory accounts properly relieved for all recorded sales?

You download Biltrite's December voucher register and sales summary. These are partially reproduced in Exhibits BR.7 and BR.8 referred to in Module II. Using these as a focal point, you requested that the client provide you with the documentation supporting certain of the recorded transactions. You now are prepared to record any necessary audit adjustments and reclassifications.

Requirements

1. Using the spreadsheet program and downloaded data, retrieve the file labeled "Cutoff." Study WP 6.4, "Inventory Cutoff," and compare it with the voucher register and sales summary portions reproduced in Exhibits BR.13 and BR.14 in Module II. Comment on any cutoff misstatements that you detect and determine their effect on net income. Do the misstatements appear to be intentional or unintentional? Explain.
2. Draft any audit adjustments suggested by the analysis performed in requirement (1). (Remember that Biltrite maintains perpetual inventory records and adjusts its perpetual inventory to the physical inventory through the appropriate "Cost of Goods Sold" accounts.)

   1. Print the completed document with the proposed cutoff audit adjustments.

Module VII: Search for Unrecorded Liabilities

An important part of every audit is examining vendors' invoices processed after year end. Related to cutoff, as discussed in Module VI, this set of procedures has the purpose of determining that no significant invoices pertaining to the year being audited have been omitted from recorded liabilities. Derick has asked that you examine the document prepared by Cheryl Lucas and entitled "Search for Unrecorded Liabilities," and review it for necessary audit adjustments.

Requirements

1. Using the spreadsheet program and downloaded data, retrieve the file labeled "Liab." Comment on the adequacy of the procedures performed by Lucas.
2. Assuming that you found the following additional unrecorded charges pertaining to 2009, draft Audit Adjustment 6 at the bottom of WP 15.1:
   a. Sales commissions $366,900
   b. Employer's payroll taxes: FICA $94,000, state unemployment $126,000
   c. Printing and copying $27,800
   d. Postage $22,300
   e. Office supplies $18,6002
3. Print the document.

12

Audit of Cash and Other Liquid Assets

LEARNING OBJECTIVES

The overriding objective of this textbook is to build a foundation with which to analyze current professional issues and adapt audit approaches to business and economic complexities. Through studying this chapter, you will be able to:

1 Describe the accounts involved in the audit of cash and other liquid assets and identify the relevant financial statement assertions concerning cash and other liquid assets.

2 Describe the approach an auditor would take to perform an integrated audit of cash.

3 Describe why cash is an inherently risky asset and identify risks related to cash. Consider issues involving materiality, inherent risk, and various cash management techniques.

4 Identify controls typically present in cash accounts and articulate how auditors gain an understanding of internal controls over cash.

5 Identify tests of controls over cash and related accounts.

6 Describe the substantive audit procedures that should be used to test cash.

7 Identify types of marketable securities and other financial instruments, articulate the risks and controls typically associated with these accounts, and outline an audit approach for these accounts.

8 Apply the decision analysis and ethical decision-making frameworks to situations involving the audit of cash and other liquid assets.

CHAPTER OVERVIEW

Cash needs to be controlled for organizations to function effectively. In this chapter, we examine approaches that organizations take to control their cash assets and apply those concepts to the evaluation of control risk over the accounts and to audits of account balances. In terms of the audit opinion formulation process, this chapter involves Phases III and IV, that is, obtaining evidence about controls and substantive evidence about assertions concerning the audit of cash and other liquid assets. Even though a high volume of transactions flows through the cash account, it usually has a relatively small balance. However, because of the vulnerability to error or misappropriation, organizations and auditors usually emphasize the quality of controls over the cash transactions.

We also consider issues concerning the audit of marketable securities and financial instruments. The increase in the variety of financial instruments, particularly derivatives, presents additional risks to organizations. The auditor must understand the nature of the financial instruments used by the organization, the risks inherent in them, and the business purpose of the instruments.

The Audit Opinion Formulation Process

I. Assessing Client Acceptance and Retention Decisions	II. Understanding the Client	III. Obtaining Evidence about Controls and Determining the Impact on the Financial Statement Audit	IV. Obtaining Substantive Evidence about Account Assertions	V. Wrapping Up the Audit and Making Reporting Decisions
CHAPTER 4	*CHAPTERS 2, 4–6, and 9*	*CHAPTERS 5–14 and 18*	*CHAPTERS 7–14 and 18*	*CHAPTERS 15 and 16*

The Auditing Profession, Regulation, and Corporate Governance	Decision-Making, Professional Conduct, and Ethics	Professional Liability
CHAPTERS 1 and 2	*CHAPTER 3*	*CHAPTER 17*

PROFESSIONAL JUDGMENT IN CONTEXT

Fraudulent Petty Cash Transactions at Koss Corporation

Sujata "Sue" Sachdeva, former vice president of finance for Koss Corporation, was involved in a $31 million embezzlement at Koss Corporation. In addition to expenditures at upscale clothing retailers, she used Koss funds on various luxury items such as a personal trainer, limousine rides, vacations, and items for her personal home. Astonishingly, more than 22,000 items—some with price tags still attached—were taken by federal authorities in connection with the investigation. The seized items included fur coats, designer clothing, jewelry, art items, and hundreds of pairs of shoes. As part of the embezzlement scheme, Sachdeva took more than $145,000 from petty cash, in increments ranging from $482 to $9,049. While that is a lot of disbursements coming out of petty cash, it is often true that petty cash doesn't get a lot of attention. Following this embezzlement, Koss took various remediation actions, which included eliminating the petty cash fund so that all reimbursements are processed through standard controlled accounts payable processes.

As you read through this chapter, consider this case and the following questions:

- What controls should be in place to help ensure that cash accounts are not misappropriated?
- What are the audit implications of poor controls over cash accounts?
- What types of audit procedures would auditors employ when auditing cash and other liquid assets?

Introduction to Relevant Accounts

Overview of Cash Accounts

An organization may have many different kinds of bank accounts, each for a special purpose and operating under different internal controls. Major types of bank balances include general checking accounts, cash management accounts, petty cash, and imprest payroll accounts.

General Checking Accounts

A general checking account is used for most cash transactions. The organization's regular cash receipts and disbursements are processed through this account. In some cases, the receipts are received directly by the bank through a lockbox or electronic funds transfers and are directly deposited in the client's account by the bank. Most organizations have cash budgets to assist in planning disbursements, and they have cash management arrangements with the bank to temporarily invest excess funds in interest-bearing securities.

LO 1

Describe the accounts involved in the audit of cash and other liquid assets and identify the relevant financial statement assertions concerning cash and other liquid assets.

Cash Management Accounts

Good cash management requires the organization to earn the greatest possible return on idle cash balances. Most organizations have developed relationships with their financial institutions (not just banks) to move excess cash into and out of short-term savings accounts to generate extra returns. The auditor will need to understand the relationships with these financial institutions, the controls applicable to cash transfers, and the risks to the client occurring from errors or financial problems associated with the financial institution.

Imprest Payroll Accounts

Some organizations disburse their payroll through an **imprest bank account**, into which cash is deposited as needed to cover payroll checks when they are issued. If the employees cash all payroll checks, the bank balance returns to zero. Some state laws require that old, uncashed payroll checks be transferred to the state (escheatment laws). Therefore, most companies do not write off old payroll checks, but instead they search to find the rightful check owner. The need for an imprest payroll account is disappearing as most organizations directly deposit employees' earnings into their bank accounts.

Petty Cash Accounts

Almost all organizations use one or more petty cash funds to disburse funds to employees who are authorized to make various purchases on behalf of the organization. The petty cash fund should have a sufficient amount of money to pay for routine expenses. While most petty cash funds involve only a small amount of money, it is important to recognize that there is a risk of fraud associated with this fund. The auditor should consider the amount of funds that are cumulatively disbursed through the petty cash account throughout the year. The cumulative disbursements made through petty cash funds can become significant.

Overview of Financial Instruments and Marketable Security Accounts

Marketable securities include a wide variety of financial instruments; the auditor must understand the risks associated with these financial instruments. For ease of discussion, most of the instruments can be classified into the following categories:

- Marketable securities (held as temporary investments)
- Short-term cash management securities, such as U.S. Treasury bills, certificates of deposit, and commercial paper (cash equivalents)
- Other short-term hybrid-type securities intended to improve the organization's return on temporary investments (often referred to as financial derivatives)

There are two points about marketable securities and financial instruments that directly affect the proper accounting for those securities. First, there is an obvious implication about whether the security is, indeed, marketable, that is, able to be purchased and/or sold in a functioning market. Second, securities may carry various levels of risk, including the risk that they may not be tradable at all if the market turns sour. The investments in securities might be classified as:

1. Held to maturity
2. Available for trade
3. Held for trade

There are important financial reporting and audit implications for the classification chosen by the company. The held-to-maturity investments are valued at historical cost unless management determines that there is more than a temporary impairment of their value. Both the available-for-trade and the held-for-trade investments are carried at market value. Thus, the auditor has a major judgmental challenge in:

1. Corroborating management's intent in classifying the assets, including gathering information about management's trades in the investments, the importance of market value to management compensation, and
2. Determining market value.

The market value of regularly traded investments (e.g., stocks listed on the NYSE or NASDAQ) is easy to assess because trading data is regularly available. However, for more thinly traded investments (e.g., mortgage-backed securities), the market does not have many participants and a financial crisis can cause the market to dry up. In such cases, the financial institutions that hold many of the investments have been very reluctant to mark the values to market value.

Marketable Securities

Good cash management principles dictate that idle cash be invested. Organizations often develop cash budgets to temporarily invest funds for periods of time ranging from a day to a year. Marketable securities may range from short-term commercial paper to investments in common stock. Because some securities have a duration of more than one year, the auditor must determine management's intent regarding the holding of securities for either a short-term or a longer-term investment.

Other Types of Financial Instruments

During the past decade, there has been a literal explosion of new types of **financial instruments**. The important point is that many of these financial instruments derive their value through the relationship to some other financial instrument. For example, *collateralized debt obligations* (CDOs), a major problem leading to the 2008–2010 financial crisis, derives their value from an underlying set of mortgages that have been marketed to other investors. The CDOs may be backed by either mortgages with high credit ratings, or mortgages with low credit ratings. In some cases, they are based on other derivatives that were based on a set of mortgages that might be once or twice removed from the financial instrument that is being traded. It is beyond the scope of this text to cover all the control and accounting elements other than to state that the basic approach to an audit still applies: that is, know the business purpose for investing in the instrument, understand the risks and controls associated with the instrument, and be familiar with how management determines the value for the instrument.

Relevant Financial Statement Assertions

The five management assertions relevant to cash and other liquid assets are as follows:

1. existence—cash balances exist at the balance sheet date
2. completeness—cash balances include all cash transactions that have taken place during the period
3. rights and obligations—the organization has title to the cash accounts as of the balance sheet date
4. valuation—recorded balances reflect the true underlying economic value of those assets
5. presentation and disclosure—cash and other liquid assets are properly classified on the balance sheet and disclosed in the notes to the financial statements.

For cash and other liquid assets, one of the more important assertions on which the auditor focuses is the existence assertion. For marketable securities, the auditor will be especially concerned with the valuation and presentation and disclosure assertions.

PRACTICAL POINT

The FASB has stated that it should be very rare for a company to change its classification from trading security to intent to hold to maturity. However, the IASB in 2008, under intense political pressure, voted to allow companies to change their classification to intent to hold to maturity and to do it retrospectively to the beginning of the year. This action was designed to avoid showing losses caused by deterioration in market value.

Integrated Audit of Cash

An effective yet efficient audit takes advantage of internal control strengths to minimize direct testing of cash. Most medium- and large-sized organizations have good internal controls over cash. In such cases, the audit will focus on testing the controls and identifying areas where potential misstatements might occur if any significant deficiencies or material weaknesses in internal controls are identified. If there are no significant deficiencies or material weaknesses, minimal substantive testing will be performed. If, however, there are one or more significant deficiencies or material weaknesses in controls, the auditor must determine what types of misstatements could occur and design substantive audit tests to determine if they did occur.

An integrated audit focuses on assessing the controls related to cycle-specific accounts as noted below. Recall the eight general steps to conducting an integrated audit, which we first covered in Chapter 10. We reproduce those steps below and tailor them to the audit of cash.

Phases I and II of the Audit Opinion Formulation Process

1. Continually update information on business risk, including the identification of any fraud risk factors noted during preliminary audit planning. Update audit planning for new risk information.
2. Analyze potential motivations to misstate cash and other liquid asset accounts, as well as the existence of other fraud indicators, and determine the most likely method that those accounts might be misstated.
3. Perform preliminary analytical procedures to determine if unexpected relationships exist in the accounts and document how the audit testing should be modified because of the unusual relationships.
4. Develop an understanding of the internal controls in cash and other liquid asset accounts that are designed to address the risks identified in the three previous steps, including the applicability of entity-level controls over cash and other liquid asset accounts. This understanding will include a review of the client's documentation of internal controls.

Phases III and IV of the Audit Opinion Formulation Process

5. Determine the important controls that need to be tested for the purposes of (a) formulating an opinion on the entity's internal controls and (b) reducing substantive testing for the financial statement audit.
6. Develop a plan for testing internal controls and perform the tests of key controls on cash and other liquid asset accounts. (For nonpublic companies, the auditor can choose to not test controls, but the auditor must determine where material misstatements could occur if controls are not present.)
7. Analyze the results of the tests of controls.

   If deficiencies are identified, they should be assessed to determine whether they are significant deficiencies or material weaknesses. Determine whether the preliminary control risk assessment should be modified (should control risk be assessed at a higher level?) and document the implications for substantive testing. Determine the impact of these deficiencies, and any revision in the control risk assessment, on planned substantive audit procedures by determining the types of misstatements that are most likely to occur.

   If no control deficiencies are identified, assess whether the preliminary control risk assessment is still appropriate, determine the extent that controls can provide evidence on the correctness of account balances, and then determine planned substantive audit procedures. The level of substantive testing in this situation will be less than what is likely required in circumstances where deficiencies in internal control were identified.

8. Perform planned substantive procedures (substantive analytical procedures and direct tests of account balances) based on the potential for misstatement and the information gathered about the effectiveness of internal controls. The substantive procedures will include procedures to address fraud risks. In completing substantive procedures the auditor will continue to assess whether the evidence obtained from all sources is sufficient and appropriate and the auditor may need to adjust the audit plan (either tests of controls or substantive tests) to help ensure that sufficient and appropriate audit evidence is obtained.

We first consider the audit of cash accounts. Specific complexities related to the audit of marketable securities, including derivatives, are discussed later in the chapter.

Consider the Risks Related to Cash (Steps 1 and 2)

Each organization's economic health depends on its ability to successfully manage its cash flow and to temporarily invest its excess funds to maximize the rate of return with a minimum amount of risk. The volume of transactions flowing through these accounts makes them material to the audit—even if the year-end cash balances are immaterial.

Cash management techniques have been developed to (1) speed the collection and deposit of cash while minimizing the possibility of error or fraud in the process, (2) reduce the amount of paperwork, and (3) automate the cash management process. Most cash management is computerized and tied to electronic commerce agreements with vendors and customers. Four of the more important cash management techniques are the use of lockboxes, electronic data interchange (EDI) and automated transfers, cash management agreements with financial institutions, and compensating balances.

Lockboxes   The collection of cash and reduction of the possibility of fraud can be facilitated by the use of **lockboxes**. Customers are instructed to send payments directly to the company at a specific post office box number, which is a depository (lockbox) at the organization's banking institution. The bank receives and opens the remittances, prepares a list of cash receipts by customer, credits the client's general cash account, and notifies the client about details of the transactions. Notification can be either a document listing customer receipts or an electronic list of the same information. This processing by the financial institution is performed for a fee. The client's personnel use the data sent by the bank to update cash and accounts receivable.

LO 3

Describe why cash is an inherently risky asset and identify risks related to cash. Consider issues involving materiality, inherent risk, and various cash management techniques.

AUDITING *in Practice*

LOCKBOX ARRANGEMENTS

Lockbox arrangements have these distinct advantages for the audit client:

- Cash is deposited directly at the bank. There is no delay, and the client immediately earns interest on the deposited funds.

- The manual processing associated with opening remittances, maintaining control of receipts, and developing detail for posting accounts receivable is shifted to the bank.

- The client usually establishes several lockboxes in different geographic locations to minimize the delay between the time the check leaves the customer's premises and when the client receives the cash. This speeds the receipt of cash and allows the organization to use the cash to earn a return.

Electronic Funds Transfers   Many organizations have adopted electronic funds transfers (EFT) as an integral part of their business. Cash transfers are made automatically and instantaneously; checks are not used. Over time, EFT will reduce the use of lockboxes and other cash collection approaches, although they will still be maintained for customers who are unable to make electronic transfers.

Cash Management Agreements with Financial Institutions   Financial institutions provide automated services such as cash management programs for many of their clients. The auditor should determine that (1) adequate procedures are used for monitoring the risk associated with the investments and (2) controls are used to assure that investments are not subject to undue risks.

Compensating Balances   Most companies have short-term loans and lines of credit with their primary financial institution. The line of credit provides the company with a prenegotiated loan, available for use when the company needs it. The financial institutions usually require the company to maintain a specified balance in a non-interest-bearing account. The amount available for the loan is the credit line minus the compensating balance. If the amounts are material, the company is required to disclose the compensating balance arrangement and its effect on the effective rate of interest.

Materiality and Risk Considerations

The auditor's planning for the audit of cash is affected by the business risk, materiality, and risk of material misstatement (inherent risk and control risk) associated with the cash accounts. The auditor generally considers the cash account to be material for the following reasons:

- *Volume of Activity*—The volume of transactions flowing through the account during the year makes the account more susceptible to error than most other accounts.
- *Liquidity*—The cash account is more susceptible to fraud than most other accounts because cash is liquid and easily transferable.
- *Automated Systems*—The electronic transfer of cash and the automated controls over cash are such that if errors are built into computer programs, they will be repeated on a large volume of transactions.

AUDITING *in Practice*

Negative Cash Balances

A negative cash balance does not look good on the financial statements. To avoid showing a negative cash balance, a company may send checks near year end but not record them until after year end. On the other hand, a company wanting to improve its current ratio may record the payment of accounts payable before year end but not mail the checks until after year end. For example, if current assets are $150,000 and current liabilities are $100,000, by recording a $50,000 payment to a vendor, the company improves its current ratio from 1.5:1 to 2:1. The company may hold the checks because it does not have immediate cash coverage.

Auditors must be alert to these and other possible manipulations of cash and short-term investments.

Cash Budgets

Cash and cash budgets are important for a company to sustain its operations over time. For example, many companies have failed in the past several years because they "burned" through their cash too quickly. That is, they used all their cash before they could generate profits and positive cash flow from their entrepreneurial efforts. Thus the analysis of a company's cash flow is a major factor in evaluating overall risk associated with the audit client.

- *Importance in Meeting Debt Covenants*—Many debt covenants may be tied to cash balances or to maintaining minimum levels of working capital. Debt covenants specify restrictions on the organization to protect the lender. Typical covenants restrict cash balances, specify the maintenance of minimum working-capital levels, and may restrict the company's ability to pay dividends. The covenants may affect management's actions in its endeavor to present financial statements that do not violate the debt covenants.
- *Can Be Easily Manipulated*—As the Satyam fraud illustrates, cash can be easily manipulated by either a CEO or CFO with power over the account balances. Satyam partially hid its cash problem when the CEO intermixed some of his personal funds with that of the company.

Inherent Risk

Cash is an inherently risky asset. It can be easily misappropriated because (1) individual transactions vary greatly in size and (2) cash is the most negotiable financial instrument. Cash may be used for unauthorized purposes, posted to the wrong customer's account, or not recorded on a timely basis. Inherent risk for cash is usually assessed as high because of its liquidity and the susceptibility to mishandling.

Perform Preliminary Analytical Procedures to Identify Possible Misstatements in the Cash Accounts (Step 3)

Analytical procedures for cash balances often do not reveal a stable relationship with past cash levels because cash usually has a relatively small ending balance. However, auditors may examine cash in relation to operational data and budgetary forecasts. Further, auditors should be aware of the importance of cash balances to debt covenants. For example, the auditor can read the debt covenants, determine the relevant thresholds for cash or other liquid assets contained in those covenants, and then track how close the company is to violating those covenants over time.

> **PRACTICAL POINT**
>
> Cash is usually well controlled and auditors may fall into a false sense of security regarding cash. When such a false sense of security steps in, a company such as HealthSouth can become more blatant in its fraud. Indeed, HealthSouth overstated its cash balance by $300 million through a series of transactions that masked the real cash balance. The auditor cannot settle for explanations for these activities; real audit testing needs to be performed and persuasive evidence needs to be obtained.

> **PRACTICAL POINT**
>
> The liquidity of cash presents opportunities for fraud that must be considered by the audit team in planning the engagement.

AUDITING *in Practice*

BRAINSTORMING ABOUT FRAUD RISKS CONCERNING CASH AND OTHER LIQUID ASSETS

During planning, auditors will brainstorm about potential fraud risks. Questions to ask in a brainstorming session could include the following:

- Can employees easily convert the company's assets to their own use?
- Are cash and other liquid assets physically available to employees?
- Is there insufficient segregation of duties related to cash and other liquid assets?
- Are the company's records for cash and other liquid assets adequate to provide a transaction trail?
- Have any members of the engagement team received tips about frauds involving cash or other liquid assets from employees, customers, or vendors?
- Is the company in potential violation of its debt covenants?
- Does the company have sufficient cash flow to support continuing operations?

Identify Typical Internal Controls over Cash (Steps 4 and 5)

LO 4

Identify controls typically present in cash accounts and articulate how auditors gain an understanding of internal controls over cash.

The integrated audit of cash involves evaluating the design of internal controls as well as the operation of controls throughout the year. In some smaller organizations, audit efforts will concentrate on substantive testing of these accounts at year end, and therefore testing of the operating effectiveness of the controls will not be part of the audit. Audits of larger organizations more often focus on evaluating and testing internal controls via an integrated audit. In assessing control risk, the auditor is initially concerned with the strength of the control environment and its effects on cash management. For example, does management understand and control the risks inherent in marketable securities? Is the board of directors informed of the organization's investments in risky securities? Does the internal audit department regularly monitor adherence to management's policies? Examples of questions used in assessing the risk and management approaches to mitigate risk related to cash and marketable securities are shown in Exhibit 12.1.

Once the potential risks to the cash accounts have been identified, the auditor will assess the controls the client has in place to minimize those risks. An understanding of the internal controls affecting cash processing is gained through walkthroughs of processing, including interviews, observations, and review of procedures manuals and other client documentation. A questionnaire, such as the one shown in Exhibit 12.2, is often used to guide the auditor in obtaining this understanding. The questionnaire is designed to elicit information about specific controls performed. Usually, the questionnaire identifies the specific individual responsible for performing each procedure, which assists the auditor in evaluating the segregation of duties. As you review Exhibit 12.2,

Exhibit 12.1	Risk Analysis Questionnaire: Cash and Financial Instruments

CASH

1. Does the company have significant cash flow problems in meeting its current obligations on a timely basis? If yes, identify and analyze the steps the company is taking to minimize the problem.

2. Does the client use cash budgeting techniques? How effective are the client's cash management budgeting techniques?

3. Does the company use the cash management services offered by its banker? What is the nature of these arrangements? Have the arrangements been reviewed by management and the board of directors? Are the arrangements monitored on a current basis?

4. Has the client made significant changes in its cash processing during the past year? Have any major changes taken place in the client's computerized cash management applications during the year?

5. Does the client have loan or bond covenants that influence the use of cash or the maintenance of working-capital ratios? Document the restrictions and cross-reference to the audit program. Do the loan covenants change the nature of materiality for the audit?

6. Do management and the board periodically review the cash management process? Does the cash management organization provide for effective segregation of duties, review, and supervision?

7. Are cash transactions, including electronic cash transfers, properly authorized? What authorization is required to make electronic cash transfers?

8. Are bank reconciliations performed on a timely basis by personnel independent of processing? Is follow-up action taken promptly on all reconciling items?

9. Does the internal audit department conduct timely reviews of the cash management and cash handling process? If yes, review recent internal audit reports.

10. Is there any reason to suspect that management may desire to misstate the cash balance? If yes, explain and refer to expanded procedures.

11. Does the company use a lockbox to handle the collection of cash receipts? What is the agreement with the financial institution? What are the organization's controls associated with the lockbox agreement?

12. Who is authorized to make cash transfers, including electronic fund transfers, and what are the procedures by which that authorization is verified before the transfers take place? What procedures does management use to assure that the authorization process is monitored?

13. Are there any restrictions in getting access to cash? For example, does the company have cash in "sweep accounts," or other accounts with financial institutions that may be in trouble, and that may restrict access to cash?

Exhibit 12.1	Risk Analysis Questionnaire: Cash and Financial Instruments (continued)

FINANCIAL INSTRUMENTS, INCLUDING MARKETABLE SECURITIES

1. Does the client regularly invest in financial instruments?

2. Does the client have written policies and guidelines regarding investments in financial instruments? Are the policies approved by the board of directors? What process is used to authorize investments in financial instruments?

3. Does the client have a clear policy as to whether financial instruments are properly classified as "held for trade" versus "held to maturity"? Is there evidence that the client follows the policy?

4. Has management changed the classification of securities during the year from marketable securities to "hold-to-maturity" securities? If yes, what is the reason for the change? If the amounts were significant, were they reviewed by the audit committee and do the audit committee and the board concur with the change?

5. Is there a ready market for the securities classified as financial instruments? If the securities are not traded on a national stock exchange, present evidence on the existence of marketability—including depth and breadth of transactions in the security.

6. If there is not a liquid market for the financial instruments, how does management go about estimating the value of the securities that need to be marked to current market value?

7. To what extent does the client own financial derivatives as part of its security holdings? What are the economic factors that affect the derivatives? Has the client evaluated the market value of the securities?

8. Does the client systematically identify the risks associated with its holdings of financial instruments? Has the board of directors approved the risk associated with the investment in nontraditional securities?

9. Does the company require board approval of significant investments in financial derivatives? If yes, is there evidence that the company both (a) thoroughly understands the risks associated with the investments and (b) can quantify and manage that risk?

10. What is the company's exposure to potential losses on financial instruments? What impact on the client would the potential default of the securities have? Are the securities sensitive to changes in interest rates? If yes, has the client prepared a sensitivity analysis of the securities?

11. Does the company establish limits over the amounts that can be invested in various types of financial instruments with specific counterparties or by individual traders? How are these limits derived and enforced?

12. Does the organization provide for effective segregation of duties among individuals responsible for making investment and credit decisions and those responsible for the custody of the securities?

13. Does the internal audit department conduct regular audits of the organization's controls over marketable securities? If yes, review recent reports.

Exhibit 12.2	Control Activities Questionnaire: Cash Receipts (partial example)

	Yes	No	N/A

Are all payments received deposited intact on a timely basis? Consider:

Procedures for Cash Remittances Received In-House

1. Key Control Activities

   a. A list of incoming receipts is prepared by the person who opens the remittances and who delivers the list to a person independent of the deposit function.

   b. A duplicate deposit slip is prepared by someone other than the person opening the mail.

   c. Deposits are made daily.

   d. An authorized person compares the deposit slip with the listing prepared in step 1(a), noting agreement and completeness of deposit.

2. Documented evidence of performance

   a. The listing prepared in step 1(a) is initialed by its preparer.

   b. The listing is attached to the deposit slip and is initialed by the person in step 1(d).

   c. Bank accounts are independently reconciled.

(continues)

Exhibit 12.2	Control Activities Questionnaire: Cash Receipts (partial example) (*continued*)

	Yes	No	N/A

Procedures for Cash Remittances Received Electronically by Bank on Behalf of Client

1. Key Control Activities

   a. There is an agreement between the bank and client on cash-handling activities, including when the remittances are added to client's account

   b. Procedures and responsibilities for forwarding detailed remittance advices to client on a daily basis

   c. Independent reconciliation of cash received reported by bank, with remittance advices forwarded to company and posted to accounts receivable

   d. Management monitors controls to follow up on discrepancies in accounts receivable postings reported by customers

   e. Access to cash limited through computerized access controls including passwords and biometrics to those individuals with a need to know or to engage in transactions

2. Documented evidence of performance

   a. Reports of daily reconciliations and follow-up by treasury personnel

   b. Periodic review by internal audit or treasury function

   c. Periodic comparison by treasury function with cash budgets and projections

Are payments received completely credited to the correct customer accounts?
Consider:

1. Controls

   a. When the posting process is a function of a computerized application, assurance is gained by:

     (1) Prenumbered batch control tickets include control totals of number of remittances to be processed and total dollars to be applied.

     (2) Edit reports or online edit routines that identify invalid customer numbers, invoice numbers, and invoice amounts.

     (3) Online entry that includes the input of a control total and/or hash total for each payment.

2. Documented evidence of performance

   a. Edit reports and/or processing transmittals, which are saved and signed by the person clearing the exceptions.

   b. The person performing the independent check initials the remittance, noting agreement of the posting operation.

   c. Online entry control totals and/or hash totals are noted on the face of the appropriate documents.

   d. Batch control tickets are agreed to the edit reports and initialed to indicate agreement.

Are all overdue accounts followed up? Consider:

1. Controls

   a. An authorized individual makes regular collection calls on past-due accounts.

   b. The company systematically sends past-due notices to delinquent customers.

   c. Past-due accounts are periodically reviewed by senior collection officials to determine alternative collection procedures.

2. Documented evidence of performance

   a. Review procedures and discuss past-due accounts with the credit manager.

Conclusion

Controls appear adequate to justify a preliminary control risk assessment as:

_____ Low control risk

_____ Moderate control risk

_____ High control risk

note the heavy emphasis on monitoring activities, that is, the development of management reports that signal departure from what is expected and indicate a need for follow-up action.

Types of Controls

To minimize potential misstatements of cash, the auditor recognizes significant risks associated with cash and considers the following types of controls to mitigate those risks:

- Separation of duties
- Restrictive endorsements of customer checks
- Independent bank reconciliations by employees who do not handle cash
- Computerized control totals and edit tests
- Authorization of transactions
- Prenumbered cash receipt documents and turnaround documents
- Periodic internal audits
- Competent, well-trained employees

As highlighted in the *Auditing in Practice* feature on Parmalat, regardless of the effectiveness of individual controls, the auditor should be alert to possible fraudulent acts involving collusion.

Segregation of Duties   The general concept of segregation of duties does not change as processing systems become more automated and integrated. Automation can enhance control, but at the same time there is a risk of errors or irregularities occurring on a larger scale. Companies, have controls to make sure that incoming customer checks and remittance advices are segregated on receipt and processed by different people. Posting to accounts receivable should be based on remittance advices and reconciled to the postings to cash, which are based on checks received. Segregation of duties is further enhanced if inquiries by customers concerning their account balance are referred to an independent group, such as a customer relations department, for investigation. Finally, the individuals who reconcile the bank accounts should not handle cash or record cash transactions.

> **PRACTICAL POINT**
>
> Companies need good cash controls in order to operate effectively. When the company is viewed as high risk, or when controls are poor, the auditor will have to do more detailed testing of the cash account balances.

AUDITING *in Practice*

THE PARMALAT FRAUD AND ITS MANY VICTIMS

Parmalat is an international company based in Italy that produces milk, dairy, and fruit-based beverages. The financial fraud involving Parmalat evolved over a ten-year period and ultimately included the invention of over $11 billion in assets in offshore front companies to offset liabilities at the parent company. The fraud was led by Chairman Calisto Tanzi and his son, Stefano Tanzi, and was orchestrated by the company's Chief Financial Officer, Fausto Tonna. In one of the telling moments of the unraveling of the fraud, representatives of a New York-based private equity firm raised questions about Parmalat's financial statements during meetings regarding a possible leveraged buyout of the company. During the meeting, the representative commented on liquidity problems at Parmalat, which contrasted with Parmalat's issued financial statements showing that the company had a large amount of cash. Stefano Tanzi admitted that the cash was not accounted for and that Parmalat actually had only about 500 million euros in cash.

Approximately 35,000 shareholders lost money in Parmalat's collapse, and shareholders were not the only ones affected by the fraud. Alessandro Bassi, a 32-year-old accountant, who worked in the financial director's office at Parmalat, killed himself by jumping off a bridge near the company's Italian headquarters. Mr. Bassi worked for the company's CFO and had been questioned by a prosecutor in the case earlier on the day of his suicide. Ultimately, Mr. Tanzi admitted to moving over $630 million from the company to family-owned related entities.

One of the most shocking features of the fraud was that it involved a large number of individuals acting collusively in various ways. In the end, 29 former Parmalat executives, along with bankers, auditors, and various financial institutions, were implicated in the fraud.

Restrictive Endorsements Customer checks should be restrictively endorsed for deposit when received. The restrictive endorsement helps prevent modifications and theft of customer remittances.

Independent Bank Reconciliations   Two types of reconciliations should occur:

1. *Reconciliation of Items Received with Items Recorded (Control Totals)*—Reconciliation is made more effective when control procedures exist to establish the initial integrity of the population (e.g., for Kahne, each remittance opened was given a unique identifier before processing). In an electronic environment, the client may have a procedure by which the bank sends details of each remittance directly to the client for posting to cash and accounts receivable. These control totals should be reconciled daily with the amount shown as direct deposits by the bank.
2. *Periodic Reconciliation of the Bank Accounts*—Independent reconciliation of the balance on the bank statement with the balance on the books should identify misstatements and unusual banking activity that may have occurred.

The auditor can test the reconciliation controls by reviewing the client's reconciliations to determine that they were independently performed.

> **PRACTICAL POINT**
>
> Keep in mind that reviewing the client's reconciliations requires the auditor to not only see that work was done, but to discuss the work with open-ended questions, such as, "help me understand the nature of this item" on the reconciliation. The auditor needs to determine not only that the work was initialed by someone, but that the individual performing the reconciliation knew exactly what he or she was doing.

AUDITING *in Practice*

AUTOMATING THE CASH RECEIPTS PROCESS

Kahne Company is a national wholesaler of merchandise ranging from electric motors to electronic surveillance equipment. It has annual sales of more than $2.5 billion, approximately 855,000 customers, 300 branches, and 6,200 employees. Customers may purchase goods at any branch or call the branch to order the merchandise for delivery. The branch's computer is online with the central database.

Some customers pay in cash for merchandise received. All cash receipts are deposited by the branch daily in a local financial institution, and the records are electronically transferred daily to the corporation's Chicago bank account. Most customer purchases are made on authorized accounts with payment due within 30 days.

All payments are directed to the national accounts receivable department. Approximately 16,000 checks totaling about $10 million are received daily; many of the remittances are for small dollar amounts. Most of the processing is automated including the following procedures used when a customer makes a payment by check (for electronic transfers, the objectives are the same, but are automated):

1. An optical scanner that reads the customer's remittance advice to determine the
   a. Customer account number
   b. Customer invoice number
   c. Dollar amount of sale
   d. Invoice date
   e. Freight and tax on the sale

2. A magnetic-ink character recognition (MICR) machine that reads lines from the check and scans for the check amount.

3. An encoder that endorses the back of the check for deposit only and encodes the dollar amount of the check onto the front of it for efficient processing by the company and its financial institution.

Once initial accountability has been established, the receipts are sorted into batches for computer processing. Checks and remittance advices are separated, and differences are reconciled and corrected. Remittance advices are created for cash receipts that do not contain a remittance advice. Most of the processing is handled by computerized equipment with selected manual review and reconciliation to assure that batches of items are not lost and that the credits to accounts receivable do not differ from cash remitted.

Important controls include detailed reconciliation of cash and receivable updates, use of batch control totals for all postings and edit tests that are built into the computer application, segregation of cash receipts and remittance advices for processing and posting, and development of a detailed electronic audit trail for each customer. All inquiries from customers about their account balance are directed to an independent group.

AUDITING *in Practice*

DESKTOP FORGERY—TECHNOLOGY MAKES IT POSSIBLE

The ability to develop fraudulent checks has been enhanced by the widespread availability of quality graphics packages for microcomputers and the lower prices of equipment used to code checks for processing using magnetic-ink character recognition (MICR), which is embedded in the checks and used by the bank to process checks against the customer's account.

To develop fraudulent checks against a company, the following are needed:

- Blank check stock (i.e., the check forms).
- A high-quality graphics program and printer with the capability of duplicating letterheads, different font styles, and signatures.
- A copy of a check from the company whose account the check is to be written against, so that all important aspects of the check (such as MICR coding) can be duplicated.
- A machine to perform MICR coding. The equipment needed to carry out such a scam could be obtained at a cost of somewhere between $10,000 and $30,000.

The equipment is capable of developing a fake check that is virtually indistinguishable from the real check.

Are there any solutions to or safeguards against such frauds? Fortunately, basic controls can be implemented, including the following:

- Develop organization logos that are embedded in the checks, making them difficult to duplicate.
- Use multiple-color checks.
- Restrict the type of paper used in the blank check stock.
- Use separate accounts for low-dollar-value checks.
- Implement edit controls over the use of smaller checks, thus treating the low-dollar accounts as imprest bank accounts.
- Provide timely and thorough independent reconciliations of the account balances.
- Automate more of the cash transactions and install controls over those transactions.

Computerized Control Totals and Edit Tests   Computerized controls should be designed to assure that all items are uniquely identified and that an adequate audit trail exists for transactions. Controls include the following:

- *A Unique Identifier Assigned to Each Item*—The unique identifier establishes the integrity of the total population and provides a basis for assuring that no items are added to or dropped from the population.
- *Control Totals to Assure the Completeness of Processing*—Control totals should be established and reconciled with the computer-generated totals. A control total would also be established to reconcile the debits to cash and the credits to accounts receivable.
- *Edit Tests to Identify Unusual or Incorrect Items*—Standard edit tests such as reasonableness tests, field checks, self-checking digits on account numbers, and alphanumeric tests should be implemented as deemed practical for the particular application.

Authorization of Transactions   Individuals with proper authorization are able to electronically transfer millions of dollars each day. As a result, opportunities for abuse abound. Three authorization and authentication controls should be implemented:

1. Authorization privileges should be assigned to individuals based on unique activities associated with the individual and position. Authorization should follow the principles of "need to know" and "right to know." Authorizations ought to be reviewed periodically by senior management.
2. Authentication procedures should assure that only authorized personnel execute transactions. The authentication process may be implemented through electronic verification by using elements such as passwords, physical characteristics, cards, encryption, or terminals that are hard-wired to the computer. In a manual system, the authorization controls may involve

limiting access to the area where checks are signed and to the prenumbered checks.

3. Monitoring should be established so that a detailed, daily review of transactions occurs and is compared with cash budgets, authorization limits by individuals, and riskiness of transactions.

Prenumbered Documents and Turnaround Documents   Prenumbered documents are important in establishing the completeness of a population. The numbering may occur after the receipt where each remittance is assigned a unique identifier when it is received by the company. Another option is to use **turnaround documents** that customers return with their cash payment. A clerk can quickly review the turnaround document and compare the amount indicated paid with the actual cash remittance. The turnaround document contains other information useful for further processing, such as account number, invoice number, date billed, and date received (entered by clerk).

Periodic Internal Audits   Internal audit departments are effective deterrents when they periodically conduct detailed audits of cash controls and cash management. Internal auditors may also review the development of new systems to determine whether adequate controls have been built into the new systems.

Competent, Well-Trained Employees   Normally, the auditor is aware of the way in which key employees perform their duties. The auditor should document any concerns about employee competence and assess how the audit should be adjusted.

Controls for Petty Cash

Companies should have policies and procedures related to petty cash funds. These controls could include (1) limiting access to petty cash funds by keeping funds in a locked box and restricting the number of employees who have access, (2) requiring receipts for all petty cash disbursements with the date, amount received, purpose or use for the funds, and name of the employee receiving the funds listed on the receipt, (3) reconciling the petty cash fund before replenishing it, and (4) keeping customer receipts separate from petty cash funds.

Controls for Cash Management Techniques

Cash management techniques require controls specific to the risks associated with those techniques.

Lockboxes   Sufficient controls must be established to make sure that all customer remittances received by the bank are posted. For example, all remittance advices should be sent to the client to facilitate follow-up should the customer have any questions about the posting of accounts. The client should also reconcile the total of the remittance advices with the cash deposit recorded by the bank.

Electronic Funds Transfers   The auditor should expect that the EFT agreements with vendors, customers, and banks have adequate controls built into the process. For example, there should be notification of the payment made directly to the client and the bank, there should be automated or manual reconciliation procedures between the client and the bank, and a complete audit trail should be maintained to answer questions about completeness of payments and disputed items.

Cash Management Agreements with Financial Institutions   The auditor is particularly interested in the amount of control given to the financial institution regarding the investment of cash. For example, the auditor would be concerned if most of the cash had been invested in high-risk securities or nonliquid securities if the client did not understand the risks associated with the investments.

Decide Which Controls to Test

Once the auditor understands the various types of controls in place, the decision must be made about which controls to test for formulating an opinion on the entity's internal controls and/or deciding whether or not the control risk warrants reduction of substantive testing. Each audit will be different in this regard because each client will have unique controls in place. The auditor should be aware that it is inappropriate to simply replicate control testing from prior years. Rather, some effort should be made to rotate control testing over time so that different controls are tested on a rotating and somewhat unpredictable basis. Doing so will help prevent frauds in cash and other liquid assets since employees may be deterred from committing a fraud out of fear they will be discovered by the auditor via rotations in control testing.

Design and Perform Tests of Controls and Analyze Results of Tests of Controls (Steps 6 and 7)

Exhibit 12.3 shows an example of an audit program for testing the controls. The first part of the program focuses on gaining an understanding of internal controls; the remaining part identifies tests of controls. The program is designed around the basic control objectives and is cross-referenced to the audit objectives.

    Once the audit program for controls testing is completed, the auditor must analyze the results and document relevant conclusions. If control deficiencies are

LO 5

Identify tests of controls over cash and related accounts.

Exhibit 12.3	Audit Program for Cash Receipt and Cash Management Controls

INTERNAL CONTROL OBJECTIVES

Existence

1. Recorded transactions and events have occurred and pertain to the entity.

Cutoff

2. Transactions are recorded in the correct accounting period.

Completeness

3. All transactions and events that should have been recorded have been recorded.

Accuracy

4. Amounts and other data have been recorded accurately.

Classification

5. Transactions and events have been recorded in the proper accounts.

Procedures	By	Ref.
1. Inquire of management about the existence of lines of credit, special cash management programs, and related fees with the company's primary banking institution. Analyze the arrangements for existence of special risks and for obligations of the client that should be considered in the audit.	————	————
2. Review the company risk analysis and assess the motivation to misstate or manage cash. Consider such items as:		
a. Financial condition of the company		
b. Past problems with cash		
c. Control environment		
d. Financial needs and liquidity problems		
e. Nonexistence of effective monitoring controls		

(continues)

Exhibit 12.3 — Audit Program for Cash Receipt and Cash Management Controls (*continued*)

Procedures	By	Ref.
Based on the risk assessment, determine the risk that material misstatements could be occurring and would not be detected by the control system. Based on the risk assessment, make a preliminary determination as to whether satisfaction regarding controls can be determined by reviewing important monitoring controls, or if it is likely that detailed tests of cash transactions need to be performed.	_____	_____

3. Document internal controls over cash by completing the internal control questionnaire or by flowcharting the process. _____ _____

4. Document the monitoring controls management has developed to determine whether other controls are working effectively. Determine whether:
   a. Monitoring activities are sufficient to alert management to breakdowns in other controls. _____ _____
   b. Monitoring reports are prepared on a timely basis and are reviewed by the proper levels of management. _____ _____
   c. Corrective action is taken on a timely basis, any control breakdowns are identified, and corrective action is taken. _____ _____

   Examples of monitoring controls include:
   - Reconciliations of reported cash receipts with remittances prepared by independent parties
   - Daily review of cash budgets and comparison with actual cash balances
   - Reviews of discrepancies in cash balances
   - Weekly reporting of customer complaints regarding posting of cash balances and prompt investigation to follow up on cause of complaints
   - Reports on all unauthorized attempts to gain access to cash
   - Daily reports on any unusual cash activities by location or personnel

5. Prepare and document a preliminary assessment of control risk. Identify specific controls to be tested if control risk is assessed at less than the maximum. _____ _____

(The following audit steps assume that sufficient controls are present in the system.)

General Tests of Controls

6. Review the frequency of monitoring activities; determine their effectiveness through reviews of the reports, indications of management actions, descriptions of corrective actions taken, and interviews with key personnel. Determine if evidence is persuasive that the monitoring controls are sufficient to attain the broad control objectives. _____ _____

   Note: If monitoring controls are effective, the auditor may determine that control risk is low and there is no need to perform any of the following audit procedures. If some monitoring controls are not effective, then the auditor should test the part of the system that would have been affected by the monitoring controls by selecting relevant techniques as described next.

Testing of Cash Receipts If Monitoring Controls Are Not Effective

7. Perform a walkthrough of the processing of cash collections, starting with their receipt through the preparation of documents for processing. Note how conscientiously and efficiently the work is done, and the procedures used in developing batches and performing reconciliations. Interview supervisory personnel regarding potential problem areas. Identify any concerns regarding employee conscientiousness that would affect the risk assessment. _____ _____

Testing of Specific Controls

8. Select *x* number of cash receipts and determine that the following procedure takes place:
   a. Each remittance is given a unique identifier, which is subsequently entered into the system. (Objective 3) _____ _____
   b. The cash received is the same as the amount applied to the update of accounts receivable. Determine how differences (if any) are handled. Determine that the controls are operating effectively. (Objective 4) _____ _____

Exhibit 12.3	Audit Program for Cash Receipt and Cash Management Controls (*continued*)

Procedures	By	Ref.
c. Cash and remittances are segregated into batches for processing. (Objectives 3 and 4)	_____	_____
d. Documents that are prepared when turnaround documents are not returned with the remittances are accurate. (Objective 4)	_____	_____
e. Batches are prepared according to company standards. Review the reconciliation of batch controls to determine their accuracy and timeliness. (Objectives 2 and 4)	_____	_____
f. Exception reports contain all items rejected by the edit controls. The rejected items are properly followed up and recorded correctly. (Objective 3)	_____	_____
9. Determine who has the authorization to:		
a. Make changes in documents or adjustments when cash amounts differ from invoiced amounts.	_____	_____
b. Make deposits.	_____	_____
c. Make withdrawals.	_____	_____
d. Make transfers among the organization's accounts or between the organization and other entities. (Objective 4)	_____	_____
10. Review reports for unusual cash transactions such as transfer of funds to other accounts, deposits other than through the normal cash receipts process, and disbursements not processed through the regular cash disbursements process. Select a sample of the transactions and review for proper authorization and completeness and correctness of processing. (Objective 1)	_____	_____
11. Review the procedures for authorizing passwords or other access codes for individuals who are authorized to initiate electronic transfers of cash. Select a limited number of transactions and trace back to the authorization. (As part of the general controls review of data processing, determine the procedures for ensuring that passwords are provided only to those properly authorized and that the passwords are kept secure. Determine through testing and observation that such controls continue to exist.) (Objective 1)	_____	_____
12. Review bank reconciliations for completeness, and trace selected items on the reconciliation to the bank statement. Determine that reconciliations are performed by someone independent of the processing. If there is evidence that bank reconciliations are performed regularly and that the auditor has assessed overall risk as low, there may be less need to test the reconciliations or other procedures. (Objectives 1, 2, 3, 4)	_____	_____

Documenting Work Performed

| 13. Document the control risk assessment, including the types of misstatements that might occur because of any deficiencies in controls. Write a brief memo citing implications for the remainder of the audit. | | |

identified, the auditor will determine whether they are significant deficiencies or material weaknesses and will decide whether the preliminary control risk assessment should be increased to a higher level. The deficiencies identified will dictate the nature and extent of substantive audit procedures targeted toward understanding whether the deficiencies manifested in inaccurate financial reporting. If no control deficiencies are identified, the auditor will determine the degree of comfort in relying on the controls and will reduce substantive testing accordingly.

Perform Substantive Testing of Cash Balances (Step 8)

When should the auditor focus on substantive tests of cash balances rather than relying on tests of controls? The auditor should perform substantive tests when control risk is assessed as high, when fraud red flags are present, or (for

LO 6

Describe the substantive audit procedures that should be used to test cash.

nonpublic clients) when the auditor determines it is more efficient to directly test account balances. In determining the specific tests that will be performed, the auditor assimilates information previously gathered regarding control deficiencies, brainstorming about fraud, and the nature of errors found in previous years. Common types of misstatements regarding cash often include the following:

- Transactions recorded in the wrong period
- Embezzlements covered up by omitting outstanding checks or underfooting the outstanding checks on the reconciliation
- Double-counting by manipulating accounts to record the same cash in two checking accounts at the same time (kiting)

Direct tests of cash include tests of year-end bank reconciliations, tests of cash cutoffs and bank transfers, and, in very high-risk situations, tests of deposits.

Independent Bank Reconciliation

The auditor's performance of an independent reconciliation of the client's major bank accounts provides evidence as to the accuracy of the year-end cash balance. The process reconciles the balance per the bank statements with the balance per the books. An independent test of the bank reconciliation is quite effective in detecting major errors, such as those that might be covered up by omitting or underfooting outstanding checks. An example of bank reconciliation documentation is shown in Exhibit 12.4.

When testing the client's bank reconciliation, the auditor should independently verify all material items such as the balance per the bank statement, deposits in transit, outstanding checks, and other adjustments. The auditor should also foot all totals. Fortunately, there are two forms of evidence available from the client's bank to facilitate a test of the reconciliation—a cutoff bank statement and a standard bank confirmation.

The Cutoff Bank Statement   A normal bank statement prepared at an interim agreed-upon date that is sent directly to the auditor is called a **cutoff bank statement**. The auditor asks the client to arrange for the bank to send a cutoff bank statement directly to the auditor for some period after year end, usually two weeks. For example, if the client's year end is December 31, the

AUDITING *in Practice*

SUBSTANTIVE PROCEDURES RELATED TO CASH

Two PCAOB disciplinary proceedings indicate the types of substantive audit procedures related to cash that should be performed and provide examples of when such procedures were not performed. The first example involves Jaspers + Hall PC and its two audit partners. In one audit, they failed to perform sufficient procedures to verify the existence of approximately $155 million of cash, which represented 57 percent of the client's assets. J+H's workpapers included copies of the client's bank statements accounting for approximately two-thirds of the reported cash, but when J+H received no reply to a confirmation request sent to the bank, they failed to perform alternative procedures to verify that the client actually had the cash. They also

failed to perform any procedures or obtain any audit evidence concerning the other one-third of the reported cash. The second example involves Armando C. Ibarra, P.C. and its two audit partners. In one of their audits they failed to audit a client's cash balance of $687,971, which represented approximately 95% of total assets. Basically, they failed to test the cash balance.

The auditor needs to consider the types of substantive procedures for cash that should be performed and then make sure that the engagement team does perform these procedures. This is especially true when the cash balance represents a significant portion of the client's assets.

Exhibit 12.4 — Tests of Client's Bank Reconciliation

ABC Client
December Bank Reconciliation
Year Ended December 31, 2011

Prepared by _BJS_
Reviewed by _____
Date _____

Balance per bank statement		$1,073,852.65*
Add: Deposits in transit:		
12/28 Deposit	$287,000.00†	
12/31 Deposit	300,000.00†	587,000.00 F
Less: Outstanding checks:		
2809	$ 435.56#	
3678	67,892.09#	
3679	75,000.00#	
3899	700.00**	
3901	12,500.00#	
3903	50,000.00#	(206,527.65) F
Adjusted Balance		$1,454,325.00 F
Balance per books		$1,481,350.00 TB
Bank charges not recorded		(25.00)‡
NSF checks:		
Bailey's Main	$ 12,000.00§	
Big Box Inc.	15,000.00!	(27,000.00) F
Adjusted Balance		$1,454,325.00 F

Note: Legend of Audit Work Performed:

* Confirmed per bank. See WP reference C-1.

† Traced to deposits shown on bank statement on 1/3 and 1/4 contained in bank cutoff statement. The 12/31 deposit was traced to bank transfer WP C-12 and was listed as an outstanding check on the subsidiary account.

‡ Traced to bank cutoff statement. Charge was for service fees, which should have been recorded by the client. Amount is not material and no adjustment is proposed.

§ NSF check was returned with 12/31 bank statement. Examined support showing client re-deposited the checks. Traced to deposit in cutoff bank statement and determined that it had not been returned in subsequent statement.

! Examined NSF check returned with 12/31 bank statement. Big Box Inc. is a retail firm that has gone bankrupt. The likelihood of ultimate collection is low. Based on discussion with the client, the amount should be written off. See AJE 35.

Outstanding checks were traced to checks returned on 1/20/10 bank cutoff statements. Checks were examined, and all were dated 12/31 or earlier and were canceled by the bank subsequent to 12/31.

** Check had not cleared as of 1/20/12. Examined supporting document for the check. All appeared proper and no exceptions were noted.

TB Traced to general ledger.

F Footed, no exceptions noted.

client may arrange for the bank to send a cutoff bank statement as of January 14 directly to the auditor. The auditor can examine canceled checks returned with the bank statement to determine that the checks dated prior to year end were included as outstanding checks on the reconciliation and can trace deposits in transit into the statement to determine if they were deposited in a timely fashion. The auditor should be alert for groups of checks that do not clear for an unusually long time after year end. The delay in clearing the bank may indicate the recording of checks but not mailing them until after year end in an effort to improve the appearance of the balance sheet.

The Standard Bank Confirmation   The auditor usually sends a standard **bank confirmation** to each bank with which the company has transacted

AUDITING *in Practice*

CONFIRMATIONS WITH FINANCIAL INSTITUTIONS

Auditors typically send confirmations to financial institutions where their clients have cash accounts or other relationships. However, a PCAOB proposed Auditing Standard (AS) would require the auditor to perform confirmation procedures for cash and other relationships with financial institutions. Specifically, the proposed standard requires the auditor to perform confirmation procedures for cash with financial institutions, such as banks, brokerage firms, trust companies, and other similar entities. The other items that should be confirmed include

(a) other relationships, such as lines of credit, other indebtedness, compensating balance arrangements, and contingent liabilities, including guarantees; and
(b) whether, during the process of completing the confirmation response, any additional information about other deposit or loan accounts has come to the attention of the financial institution. Ultimately, auditors need to stay alert to changes in required procedures and be aware when required procedures may differ between U.S. public companies and other types of organizations.

business during the year. The confirmations have two parts. The first part, shown in Exhibit 12.5, seeks information on the client's deposit balances, on the existence of loans, due dates of the loans, interest rates, dates through which interest has been paid, and **collateral** for all loans outstanding with the bank at year end. The second, shown in Exhibit 12.6, seeks information about any contingent liabilities.

If loans are outstanding, the auditor usually asks for copies of the loan agreements to identify restrictions on the ability of the organization to pay dividends or to determine whether the organization will have to maintain specific working-capital or debt ratios. These requirements are generally referred to as *covenants*, a violation of which will make the loans immediately due and payable unless the financial institution temporarily waives the violation. If covenants are violated and the financial institution will not waive them, the auditor will have to consider whether the client will be able to continue to operate as a going concern and, if it is a long-term debt, reclassify it as a current liability. Additionally, the auditor normally makes inquiries about the existence of cash management or other programs that the client has with the financial institution.

PRACTICAL POINT

Many companies do not issue checks, but pay all of their bills electronically. In such cases, the auditor will need to obtain a list of year-end disbursements per the books to see if they cleared the bank in a timely fashion. The auditor can perform similar tests for on-line deposits.

Obtaining Year-End Cutoff Information In many instances of fraud, management has either held open the cash receipts book to record the next period's sales collections as part of the current period or has mailed checks to vendors but did not record the cash disbursements until the subsequent period. Sometimes these problems occur because a company is in dire financial straits and needs an improved balance sheet to avoid violation of loan covenants.

If the auditor assesses the risk of such irregularities to be high, the following procedures should be considered:

- Obtain information on the last checks issued by the fiscal year end, such as the last check number, and observe that all previous checks had been mailed. The mailing of the checks can be corroborated by observing whether the checks clear the bank in a timely fashion, as evidenced in the bank cutoff statement.
- Obtain information on the last cash receipts. The auditor usually notes the last few receipts as a basis for determining the recording in the correct period. The information is traced to the company's bank reconciliation and bank accounts to determine if items were recorded in the proper period.

These procedures are more likely to be used on smaller businesses that still handle checks manually.

Exhibit 12.5   Standard Bank Confirmation—Account Balances

Financial Institution's Name and Address

[   ]

[   ]

CUSTOMER NAME

We have provided to our accountants the following information as of the close of business on _____, 20___, regarding our deposit and loan balances. Please confirm the accuracy of the information, noting any exceptions to the information provided. If the balances have been left blank, please complete this form by furnishing the balance in the appropriate space below. Although we do not request nor expect you to conduct a comprehensive, detailed search of your records, if during the process of completing this confirmation additional information about other deposit and loan accounts we may have with you comes to your attention, please include such information below. Please use the enclosed envelope to return the form directly to our accountants.

1. At the close of business on the date listed above, our records indicated the following deposit balance(s):

ACCOUNT NAME	ACCOUNT NO.	INTEREST RATE	BALANCE*

2. We were directly liable to the financial institution for loans at the close of business on the date listed above as follows:

ACCOUNT NO./ DESCRIPTION	BALANCE*	DATE DUE	INTEREST RATE	DATE THROUGH WHICH INTEREST IS PAID	DESCRIPTION OF COLLATERAL

_____   _____
(Customer's Authorized Signature)   (Date)

The information presented above by the customer is in agreement with our records. Although we have not conducted a comprehensive, detailed search of our records, no other deposit or loan accounts have come to our attention except as noted below.

_____   _____
(Financial Institution Authorized Signature)   (Date)

_____
(Title)

EXCEPTIONS AND/OR COMMENTS

Please return this form directly to our accountants:

[   ]

*Ordinarily, balances are intentionally left blank if they are not available at the time the form is prepared.

Approved 1990 by American Bankers Association, American Institute of Certified Public Accountants, and Bank Administration Institute. Additional forms available from: AICPA—Order Department, P.O. Box 1003, NY, NY 10108-1003.   D 451 5851

Bank Transfer Schedules

A company with many divisions frequently transfers cash from one division to another. Companies wanting to overstate cash often use a technique called **kiting** to record the same cash twice. They do this by making transfers near year end from one bank account to another bank account, recording the deposit in the second division's account but not recording the disbursement on the first division's account until the next fiscal period. For example, a December 31 transfer would show the receipt on one account but not the disbursement on the other, resulting in the transferred amount being recorded twice. Exhibit 12.7 shows the elements of a simple kiting scheme. A more sophisticated kiting scheme used by the E.F. Hutton Company is illustrated in the *Auditing in Practice* feature.

Exhibit 12.6   Standard Bank Confirmation—Loan Guarantees

(Date)

Financial Institution Official*

First United Bank

Anytown, USA

Dear Financial Institution Official:

In connection with an audit of the financial statements of (name of customer) as of (balance-sheet date) and for the (period) then ended, we have advised our independent auditors of the information listed below, which we believe is a complete and accurate description of our contingent liabilities, including oral and written guarantees, with your financial institution. Although we do not request nor expect you to conduct a comprehensive, detailed search of your records, if during the process of completing this confirmation additional information about other contingent liabilities, including oral and written guarantees, between (name of customer) and your financial institution comes to your attention, please include such information below.

Name of Maker	Date of Note	Due Date	Current Balance	Interest Rate	Date Through Which Interest Is Paid	Description of Collateral	Description of Purpose of Note

Information related to oral and written guarantees is as follows:

_____

_____

_____

_____

Please confirm whether the information about contingent liabilities presented above is correct by signing below and returning this directly to our independent auditors (name and address of CPA firm).

Sincerely,

(Name of Customer)

_____

By: _____

(Authorized Signature)

Dear CPA Firm:

The above information listing contingent liabilities, including oral and written guarantees, agrees with the records of this financial institution.** Although we have not conducted a comprehensive, detailed search of our records, no information about other contingent liabilities, including oral and written guarantees, came to our attention. (Note exceptions below or in an attached letter.)

_____

_____

_____

_____

_____

(Name of Financial Institution)

_____

(Officer and Title)   (Date)

_____

* This letter should be addressed to a financial institution official who is responsible for the financial institution's relationship with the client or is knowledgeable about the transactions or arrangements. Some financial institutions centralize this function by assigning responsibility for responding to confirmation requests to a separate function. Independent auditors should ascertain the appropriate recipient.

** If applicable, comments similar to the following may be added to the confirmation reply by the financial institution. This confirmation does not relate to arrangements, if any, with other branches or affiliates of this financial institution. Information should be sought separately from such branches or affiliates with which any such arrangements might exist.

Exhibit 12.7	Example of Kiting—All Within One Company

Division A
- Transfers $1,000,000 to Division B near the end of the year but records the transaction in the following year.
- Transfer does not clear the bank in the current year.
- Transfer does not decrease the year-end cash balance because it has not been recorded in the current period.

Division B
- Receives $1,000,000 before year end and records the deposit in the current period.
- Deposit may or may not be deposited by year end. If not, the deposit will be shown as a deposit in transit in the division's bank reconciliation.
- Transfer increases the year-end cash balance by the amount of the transfer. The net effect is to overstate cash on the consolidated financial statements by the amount of the transfer.

Result: Cash is recorded in both divisions at year end, resulting in double counting.

The most effective and efficient way to test for the existence of kiting is to prepare a **bank transfer schedule** similar to the one shown in Exhibit 12.8. The bank transfer schedule lists all transfers between the company's bank accounts for a short period of time before and after year end. All transfers are accounted for to determine that they are recorded in the correct period and the client is not overstating the year-end cash account. Note the transfer of check number 8702, recorded as a deposit on December 30—an example of kiting. The check was recorded as a deposit in the Cleveland account on December 31 but was not recorded as a disbursement in the Rockford account until after year end.

Fraud Related Audit Procedures

In those audits where there is a heightened risk of fraud related to cash, the auditor will want to consider performing additional fraud-related procedures, or if the procedures are already being performed, altering the timing and extent of the procedures. These fraud-related procedures could include:

- Scrutinizing disbursements payable to "cash" or unusual sounding vendors.
- Searching for and investigating nonpayroll check disbursements made to employees.

AUDITING *in Practice*

KITING SCHEMES: THE CASE OF E.F. HUTTON

Kiting can occur without fraudulently misstating financial statements. In the 1980s, the SEC accused the brokerage firm of E.F. Hutton of participating in a kiting scheme to earn excess interest at the expense of its customers. Hutton set up an imprest account for disbursements at geographic locations far removed from the customer who would receive one of E.F. Hutton's checks. For example, a bank account might be set up in Billings, Montana, for disbursements to customers located on the East Coast. Hutton's agreement with the bank was that the bank would wire

Hutton with a message indicating the amount of checks cleared each day, and Hutton would wire funds to cover the cleared checks. Meanwhile, Hutton had the use of the cash for the time it took the checks to clear the remotely located bank. The firm eventually settled with the SEC and agreed to refrain from such practices. As the banking system continues to automate, the likelihood of such schemes in the future will lessen because all checks will clear the banks in even shorter periods of time.

Exhibit 12.8	Bank Transfer Schedule—XYZ Company for the Year Ended December 31, 2011					
			DATE DEPOSITED		**DATE WITHDRAWN**	
Transferred from Branch	**Check Number**	**Amount**	**Per Books**	**Per Bank**	**Per Branch Books**	**Per Bank**
Cleveland	15910	$ 45,000	12/26*	12/27†	12/26*	12/30†
Cleveland	15980	100,000	12/28*	12/29†	12/27*	12/31†
Rockford	8702	87,000	12/30*	12/31†	1/2‡	1/3†
Cleveland	16110	25,000	1/3*	1/4†	1/2*	1/5†
Rockford	8725	65,000	1/5*	1/7*	1/4*	1/8†

* Traced to cash receipts/disbursements records.

† Traced to bank statement.

‡ Withdrawal recorded in wrong period. See AJE C-11.

- Investigating voided checks and analyzing voided transactions.
- Comparing bank deposits to cash receipts, noting any time lags in deposit dates.

Complexities Related to the Audit of Marketable Securities and Financial Instruments

Introduction

A company may invest in many types of securities. Some are more marketable than others, some carry promises of greater return (but at much greater risk) than others, and some derive value from either other underlying instruments or future activities. As an extreme example, a financial instrument could be a bet on whether there will be a major drought that would affect farmers' crops in the prairie states during the next near. The value of the instrument is derived from the future activity. More common instruments represent bets on whether someone will fail to pay their mortgage, or there will be changes in currency valuations, or changes in interest rates. Sometimes these are just bets; other times they can be used to hedge underlying transactions to smooth out returns.

Traditional marketable securities are straightforward and include commercial paper, marketable equity securities, and marketable debt securities. These securities are readily traded and management usually intends to hold them for a short period of time. Because they are held for trading, or available for trade, they are valued at market value. In normal market situations, these short-term investments turn over and are not a large problem for the auditor. As an overall guideline, the audit approach to most investments in marketable securities centers on the following major steps:

1. Identify the assets and management's internal controls for safeguarding the investments and maximizing returns within the risk parameters set by the board of directors.
2. Understand the economic purpose of major transactions and/or agreements with financial institutions and the economic impact on the client.

3. Identify the risks associated with the company's financial assets and the parties that hold the risks.

4. Confirm agreements and examine contracts associated with the agreements to determine necessary audit steps and accounting and financial statement disclosure.

5. Review and test transactions and related accounting and disclosure for their economic substance and adherence to appropriate accounting and SEC pronouncements.

6. Determine the existence of a market for the securities and determine the appropriate accounting for year-end account balances.

Audits of Commercial Paper

The term *commercial paper* refers to notes issued by major corporations, especially finance companies, that generally have good credit ratings. An example of an audit program for substantive testing of commercial paper is shown in Exhibit 12.9. Note the specific linkage between assertions and the audit procedures and that the related interest income is tested at the same time.

Audits of Investments in Equity and Debt Securities

Short-term investments include marketable equity securities such as common stocks and corporate bonds. Such investments should be accounted for at market value. An example of an audit workpaper for the testing of marketable equity securities is shown in Exhibit 12.10.

There are several points to be made concerning the audit workpaper in Exhibit 12.10:

1. The client prepares a schedule of all marketable securities it owns at year end. The schedule includes the accrued interest and dividends associated with each security for the period of time held. The auditor is testing both the balance sheet and the related income accounts at the same time.

Exhibit 12.9	Assertions and Audit Procedures: Commercial Paper

Assertion	Audit Procedure
Existence or occurrence	1. Request that the client prepare a schedule of all commercial paper held by the organization at year end. Verify the existence of the securities by either (1) counting and examining selected securities or (2) confirming the existence with trustees holding them. Reconcile the amounts with the general ledger.
Completeness	2. Foot the schedule of commercial paper and examine the securities (step 1). Examine selected transactions and brokers' advices near year end to determine that the transactions are recorded in the correct period.
Rights	3. Examine selected documents to determine if there are any restrictions on the marketability of the documents. Inquire of management as to existence of any restrictions.
Valuation	4. (Note: Commercial paper should be valued at year-end market value.) Determine current market value through reference to a financial reporting service such as or a similar electronic source.
	5. Recompute interest and determine that accrued interest is properly recorded at year end.
Presentation and disclosure	6. Determine management's intent to hold securities as a short-term investment. Document that intention in a management representation letter.
	7. Determine whether the securities are properly classified, and that any restrictions on their use are appropriately disclosed in the notes to the financial statements.

Exhibit 12.10

Nature Sporting Goods Manufacturing Company Marketable Securities for the Year Ended December 31, 2011

Prepared by __AM1__ Date __1/28/12__
Reviewed by _____ Date _____

Marketable Investments	Beginning Balance	PURCHASES Date	PURCHASES Amount	DISPOSALS Date	DISPOSALS Amount	Gain/Loss Disposal	Ending Balance	Market Value (12/31)	INCOME ACCOUNTS Interest	INCOME ACCOUNTS Dividends	Total
Gen. Motors 8% comm. paper	$ 45,000.00	10/31/10		4/30/11	$ 45,000.00*	$ 0.00	$ 0.00	$ 0.00	$ 1,800.00R		$ 1,800.00
Ford Motor 8.25% comm. Paper	100,000.00	12/1/08					100,000.00C	$ 100,000.00†	8,937.50R		8,937.50
1000 Sh Lands' End common stk	22,367.00	10/31/10					22,367.00C	16,375.00†		$ 1,000.00R	1,000.00
1000 Sh AMOCO	48,375.00	12/31/07		7/13/11	62,375.00*	14,000.00R	0.00	0.00		1,000.00R	1,000.00
1000 Sh Consolidated paper	0.00	7/31/09	$ 41,250.00*				41,250.00C	44,500.00†		500.00‡	500.00
2010 Bank America Zero Cpn Bond	1,378.00	6/30/10					1,378.00C	1,587.00†	209.00R		209.00
Totals	$ 217,120.00		$ 41,250.00		$ 107,375.00	$ 14,000.00	$ 164,995.00	$ 162,462.00	$ 10,946.50	$ 2,500.00	$ 13,446.50
	T/B		F		F	F	CF	F	F	F #	F

Market value $162,462.00
Excess cost > Mkt. Value $ 2,533.00§
F

* Correct, per examination of broker's invoice.
C Securities held in broker's account, confirmed with broker.
R Recomputed, no exceptions.
† Per December 31 stock transaction listing in the *Wall Street Journal.*
‡ Amount should be $1,000. Company failed to accrue dividend declared.
T/B Per December 31, 2010 trial balance and 12/31 working papers, schedule M-2.

F Footed.
CF Cross-footed.
§ Loss not recorded. Trace to AJE 31.
|| Traced to year-end trial balance.
Interest and dividend payments verified through examination of Standard & Poor's *Dividend and Interest Digest* for year end December 31, 2011.

2. The document shows three items related to the value of the security:

   - Cost
   - Year-end market value
   - Carrying value for debt instruments

3. Disposals and resulting gains/losses are shown for all accounts during the year.

4. The auditor verifies the cost or sales price of the assets by examining broker's advices evidencing either the purchase or sale of the security. If control risk is low, the verification can be performed on a sample of the transactions.

5. The schedule is an abbreviated worksheet. For most audits, the auditor will have to determine whether securities are properly classified either as intent to hold to maturity or trading. That determination must be corroborated by, and consistent with, management's actions. The appropriate classification determines the accounting valuation.

6. For most investments, the current market value is determined by referring to the year-end closing price in the *Wall Street Journal* or by collecting this data electronically on the auditing firm's own database. For securities that are in illiquid markets, the auditor will have to do substantially more work to determine market value.

7. Income is recomputed on a selected basis for interest, dividends, and realized and unrealized gains and losses.

8. The schedule is footed to determine the mechanical accuracy and the correct valuation of the account.

9. The audit tests address all of the audit assertions except presentation and disclosure. That assertion is verified directly with management and documented separately.

10. Document the conclusion regarding the fairness of presentation of the account balance as adjusted.

If the risk of material misstatement is low, the auditor will test only a small sample of the items. If risk is high, the auditor may verify all the material items on the worksheet.

> **PRACTICAL POINT**
>
> Although it may sound trivial, if a security is to be held to maturity, then there must be an agreed-upon and readily evident date of maturity for the security.

Audits of Derivative Instruments

The use of financial instruments commonly referred to as derivatives has increased greatly. Many of these instruments have been created to take advantage of short-term market anomalies, such as differences in interest rates between short- and long-term securities. Others have been developed for the explicit purpose of removing liabilities from a company's balance sheet. Selected examples of these securities are listed in Exhibit 12.11.

In many cases, financial instruments provide for greater efficiency in the marketplace. As an example, before the 1990s most banks would hold mortgages of their customers for the full term of the mortgage, for example, for 30 years in the case of a 30-year mortgage. This subjected the bank to both (a) default risk and (b) interest rate risk. Banks found they could better manage these risks by selling the mortgages to third parties, such as Freddie Mac. Banks could still make money by originating and servicing loans. The intermediary organizations that purchased the loans then packaged them into risk-rate classes and sold them to various public holders. Some have argued that such an approach spread the risks across a greater number of parties and allowed banks to operate more efficiently in originating and servicing loans. However, someone ultimately is accountable for both default and interest rate risk. If an audit client holds some of these collateralized mortgage obligations as an investment, the auditor must understand the risks to which the client is subjected and whether or not a current market exists for the financial instruments held.

Exhibit 12.11	Examples of Sophisticated Types of Financial Instruments

CALL OPTION

A call option is a financial contract between two parties, the buyer and the seller, in which the buyer has the right (but not the obligation) to buy an agreed quantity of a particular commodity or financial instrument (the underlying asset) from the seller of the option at a certain time (the expiration date) for a certain price (the strike price). The seller (or "writer") is obligated to sell the commodity or financial instrument if the buyer exercises the option. The buyer pays a fee (called a premium) for this right.

PUT OPTION

A put option is a financial contract between two parties, the buyer and the seller, in which the buyer has the right (but not the obligation) to sell an agreed quantity of a particular commodity or financial instrument (the underlying instrument) to the seller of the option at a certain time for a certain price. The seller of the option is obligated to purchase the underlying asset at that strike price, if the buyer exercises the option.

COLLATERALIZED DEBT OBLIGATION (CDO)

A CDO is a financial instrument that is essentially a bet on whether an underlying obligation, most often underlying mortgages on homes, will fail or not fail. The holder can be on either side of the bet. Most financial institutions hold the underlying instrument and sell the bet that the instrument will fail.

EVENT-RISK PROTECTED DEBT

An event-risk debt covenant is associated with bonds and is intended to protect the bondholder in case of a credit downgrading of the bond, such as might happen in the case of a leveraged buyout (LBO). The covenants generally allow the investors to resell the debt to the original issuer at par if a stipulated event (such as a change in ownership) were to occur.

HEDGES

Hedges are an instrument that allows an organization to hedge against a change in some underlying economic event that may affect the company. The three most common have been:

- Foreign currency hedges—to protect against a change of the dollar in relation to some other currency
- Fuel hedge—to protect against future changes in fuel prices, for example, Southwest Airlines hedging against future changes in aviation fuel costs
- Commodity hedge—to protect against (or take advantage of) future changes in commodity prices

FLOATING RATE NOTE

A floating rate note is a debt instrument with a variable interest rate. Interest rate adjustments are made periodically, often every six months, and are tied to a money market index such as the Treasury bill rate or London InterBank Organizational Rate (LIBOR).

JUNK BOND

Junk bonds are high-yielding bonds issued by a borrower with a lower-than-investment-grade credit rating. Many of these bonds were issued in connection with LBOs, while others were issued by companies without long records of sales and earnings.

INTEREST RATE SWAPS

A swap is an instrument that allows an organization to hedge against future changes in interest rates by either swapping financial instruments, usually a fixed-term investment, for a variable-rate investment, or vice versa. Companies usually do not swap the actual instruments, but they make a notational swap with a financial institution that arranges an equal swap in the other direction.

ZERO-COUPON BOND

With no periodic interest payments, these bonds are sold at a deep discount from face value. The holder of the bond receives gradual appreciation in the carrying value of the bond, which is redeemed at face value at maturity. The appreciation in value represents interest income.

SECURITIES SOLD WITH A PUT OPTION

Marketable securities can be sold by an investor (not the original issuer) together with a put option that entitles the purchaser to sell the securities back to the investors who sold the securities at a fixed price in the future. These securities often carry low yields.

Exhibit 12.11	Examples of Sophisticated Types of Financial Instruments (*continued*)

COLLATERALIZED MORTGAGE OBLIGATION (CMO)

These debt obligations are issued as a special-purpose instrument and are collateralized by a pool of mortgages. The financial instrument is handled as a purchase of a group of mortgages using the proceeds of an offering of bonds collateralized by the mortgages. The financial instrument uses the underlying cash flows of the collateral to fund the debt service on the bonds. The bonds are priced based on their own maturity and rate of return rather than that of the underlying mortgages. CMOs have created secondary markets in the mortgage industry and have assisted the industry in attaining greater levels of liquidity. However, they are subject to the default risk of the underlying mortgages.

SECURITIZED RECEIVABLES

Securitized receivables have been converted into a form that can be sold to investors (similar in concept to CMOs). The issuer of the special financial instrument uses the cash flows of the receivables to fund debt service on the securities. In most cases, investors have no recourse to the sponsor or originator of the financial instrument if the underlying loans go into default.

AUDITING *in Practice*

THE FINANCIAL CRISIS OF 2008

The role of Fannie Mae and Freddie Mac was supposed to be to support the housing market by purchasing mortgages from lending institutions and/or by guaranteeing the repayment of those loans in case of homeowner default. Fannie Mae and Freddie Mac bought home mortgage loans from Washington Mutual, IndyMac, Countrywide Financial, and other banks. However, these companies got into serious financial trouble when those home loans began defaulting at an accelerating pace during 2008. As a result, Fannie Mae and Freddie Mac were near collapse and were taken over by the federal government. Some reports claim that the companies' capital positions were worse than initially portrayed and that management had made decisions that ultimately overstated the companies' capital position. In fact, both Fannie Mae and Freddie Mac have had accounting issues in the past, including restatements and adverse opinions on their internal controls. However, critics of the auditing profession have pointed out that neither Fannie Mae nor Freddie Mac received a qualified or going-concern opinion from their auditors to indicate the severity of the underlying accounting issues. This series of events illustrates that complex financial instruments, weak controls, and financial difficulties can result in problems not only for companies but also for their auditors.

In regard to most of the derivative instruments, note the following points:

1. The examples in Exhibit 12.11 are only a few among hundreds of similar instruments existing in the current marketplace.
2. Although there are commonalities among all the instruments, each contains unique features that may shift risks to the investor.
3. Some instruments do not provide recourse to other specific resources in the event of default but try to "sweeten the deal" by providing other terms, such as higher interest rates, to entice users to invest in the securities. For example, most debt securities may be collateralized or provide preference in liquidation. However, many of these securities do not carry such privileges.
4. Although many of the instruments are described as marketable securities, the market is often very thin. Thus, market quotations may not be an accurate assessment of what the marketable value of the specific securities might be at the balance sheet date.
5. Some of the instruments defer the payment of cash to the future, often in the hope that the instrument will be replaced by another one at that time and thus will not constitute a significant cash-flow burden on the issuer.

PRACTICAL POINT

Many financial instruments are designed to help the organization better manage risk. However, they often involve taking on risk, such as betting on an outcome which is uncertain.

PRACTICAL POINT

Market price quotes are useful only if the market is fluid. There must be sufficient trade volumes such that the securities owned by the company, if traded, would not adversely affect current market price.

6. Some of the instruments have specific options, such as the put option that allows the investor to put (sell) the instrument back to the original issuer on the occurrence of a specific event. It would seem that the market value of such instruments would be near par, but remember that the instrument holder's ability to realize par value depends on the original issuer's ability to pay at the time of the triggering event.

Financial institutions often have had significant investments in financial instruments. When there is a ready market for such instruments, and risks can be calculated and controlled, the valuation and disclosure are straightforward. However, there are cases where quoted market values are often illusory and misleading because they are based on quoted sales at volumes significantly lower than the volume of instruments on a company's books. In other words, a security that is regularly traded, or available for trade, is not necessarily readily marketable. The auditor must understand the extent that risks affect the valuation of financial instruments, and those risks must be reflected in the financial reports. Exhibit 12.12 includes a list of risk factors that Statement of Auditing Standard No. 92 indicates as commonly associated with derivative securities.

The risks associated with the new types of financial instruments require the auditor to understand the control procedures that a client has implemented to minimize risks. Guidelines for assessing risks and controls are shown in the *Auditing in Practice* feature.

Audits of Financial Hedges

Most international companies purchase hedges to monitor their exposure to foreign currency fluctuations.

General Audit Approach

This section illustrates a general approach to the audit of sophisticated financial instruments that are part of a currency hedge program.

Understand the Product   Hedges are usually straightforward and have two elements—which may vary by time and by amount:

1. A contract to pay (or receive) payment within a stated period of time; e.g., payments made in dollars within 10 months
2. A contract to purchase (sell) another commodity or currency at the time of payment to offset changes in the pegged transaction value

---

Exhibit 12.12   **Risk Factors Associated with Derivative Securities**

Auditors need to understand the following types of risks that are associated with derivative securities:

- Management's objectives in entering transactions involving derivative securities, and a consideration of how those objectives may relate to the potential for material misstatements in the financial statements
- The proper review by the board and senior management in the decision to initiate the use of derivative securities
- The complexity of features of the derivative securities
- Whether the transaction generating the derivative security involves the exchange of cash, since derivatives not involving an initial cash exchange are subject to heightened risk that they will not be identified for valuation at fair value
- The company's experience (or lack thereof) with derivative securities, along with its ability to appropriately understand and challenge an outside party's valuation of a derivative security
- Whether the derivative is freestanding or an embedded feature of an agreement
- Whether external factors affect the valuation of the securities, e.g., credit risk, market risk, basis risk, or legal risk
- The complex nature of generally accepted accounting principles as they apply to derivative securities

AUDITING *in Practice*

CONTROLLING RISKS ASSOCIATED WITH SOPHISTICATED FINANCIAL INSTRUMENTS

The following management control considerations should exist for all companies that use financial instruments, particularly derivatives:

1. *Identify the Risk Management Objectives*—Investments in financial instruments should follow a well-developed management strategy for controlling risks.

2. *Understand the Product*—Analyzing the economic effect of a transaction on each party is crucial for gaining insight into potential risk. Transactions are becoming more complex, with a single instrument often divided into a dozen or more instruments with differing yields and maturities.

3. *Understand the Accounting and Tax Ramifications*—The FASB has worked on a comprehensive document to clarify the accounting for financial instruments based on risks and obligations. Although the FASB cannot anticipate every kind of instrument that may evolve in the next decade, general concepts in the guide serve to lead the client and management to proper accounting. The potential for tax savings has motivated many of the instruments; thus, potential tax law changes may affect the economics of the instruments.

4. *Develop Corporate Policies and Procedures*—Companies should have explicit policies, preferably in writing, defining the objectives for entering into the new forms of financial transactions. Management should clearly define the nature, risk, and economics of each authorized instrument or type of transaction. The policies should also set limits for investments in specific types of instruments. The board of directors should approve the overall corporate policy.

5. *Monitor and Evaluate Results*—Procedures should be established to monitor the transaction (instrument) on a regular basis to determine whether the expected benefits fall within the assumed risk levels. If the risk was initially hedged or collateral was obtained, the value of the hedge or collateral should be remeasured. Procedures should be in place to react to risk that has grown greater than the entity wishes to bear.

6. *Understand the Credit Risk*—Investors should make sure that proper protection exists against default by counterparties. A mechanism is needed for continued monitoring of the counterparty's economic health. Formal credit-monitoring procedures—similar to credit policies for accounts receivable—need to be considered (even for counterparties with prominent names).

7. *Control Collateral When Risk Is Not Acceptable*—Sometimes credit risk becomes higher than anticipated, but the investor allows the counterparty to keep the collateral. In such cases, investors should implement procedures to assure that they have possession of the collateral.

The product is designed to keep the transaction constant. Currency hedges, for example, are designed such that an organization neither wins nor loses because of shifts in currency value, for example, the change in the exchange rate between the euro and the U.S. dollar. There usually is no collateral with currency hedges, but there may be with other types of hedges.

Identify the Risks and Related Control Objectives   The risks are as follows:

- The instrument categorized as a hedge is not really a hedge; rather, it is a bet that currencies or other referenced data—e.g., commodity prices—will move in a specific direction; if it moves in that direction, the company will gain.
- All the hedging transactions are not identified or disclosed.
- The company is taking on more risk than approved by management or the board.

The auditor would want to make certain that the summary of risks is clearly spelled out to management and the board by the client's financial planning group.

These risks would suggest that the following control objectives are important:

- Hedges should be initiated in accordance with company policies.
- All potentially speculative contracts must be hedges, not speculation.
- All the transactions are fully disclosed and accounted for.

PRACTICAL POINT

If a U.S. company has a German subsidiary and believes that the euro will decline in relationship to the dollar, then the next-year earnings will be less because the euro is less valuable when translated into dollars. The company may pursue natural hedges, such as making some contracts payable to the company in dollars, or the company may place a hedge against the change in security value.

Understand the Accounting   If the transaction is clearly a hedge such that contracts fully offset each other, there are no required entries on the company's books other than the existence of the contracts and the need to disclose the nature of the contracts. On the other hand, if the contracts are not balanced, the entity needs to book the changes in obligations at the end of each accounting period. Therefore, the auditor must undertake procedures to determine that the contracts are balanced and whether obligations may exist.

Determine Existence of Policies and Adherence to the Policies   The auditor should evaluate the specific policies that have been developed and determine whether the monitoring controls and other activities provide evidence of whether these policies are operating effectively.

Monitor the Transactions   The financial accounting system should produce reports that provide the following information on a monthly basis (or more frequently in some instances):

- Settlement of all contracts during the latest reporting period and any gains or losses
- New transactions that are hedged and whether they are fully hedged
- Summary of unhedged transactions that are subject to currency risk
- Planning budget of future transactions that will need hedging
- Summary of issues that should be brought before the financial planning group

The monitoring controls should clearly indicate follow-up actions taken by both the board and management. Unusual gains or losses would be an indication that the controls are not working effectively—planned hedges are not working. Further, there should be periodic testing of the procedures by the internal audit group.

Audit Program

The audit program for currency hedges would include the following steps:

1. Identify the policies and control procedures the company has implemented to assure adherence to the procedures.
2. Review all gains/losses associated with the hedged transactions during the year to determine whether the transactions were hedged.
3. Obtain a summary of all hedges currently in effect. Take a sample of contracts associated with the existing hedges to determine that the contracts insulate the company from the effect of foreign currency fluctuations.
4. Summarize the results of testing to determine if unhedged currency transactions exist. List the unhedged transactions and determine (a) needed disclosure and (b) the appropriate entry to mark the instrument to market.
5. Inquire of management and the financial planning committee about the existence of any other unhedged currency transactions.
6. Inquire of internal audit about any work it has performed regarding hedges. Review the report, especially regarding the existence of controls.
7. Reach a conclusion about the adequacy of the hedges, document the conclusion in the audit documentation, and determine appropriate financial statement presentation.

Summary

Organizations manage cash and liquid assets to maximize their potential return. Companies develop sophisticated agreements with their bankers to invest excess liquid assets in interest-bearing securities. Many audit clients are major investors in financial instruments, some transactions in which are made without a full understanding of the risks associated with the securities. Audits are complex because market values of complex securities are not readily available. A well-informed board of directors is a positive factor in evaluating the potential risk, but an uninformed board may mean that an organization is subject to greater risk than the board or management desires.

The extent of substantive procedures performed on cash accounts depends on the effectiveness of internal controls. For smaller clients, the focus usually will be on verifying the accuracy of the cash balances rather than relying on internal controls. For larger clients with effective internal controls, the extent of substantive testing can be minimized.

The accounting for cash and marketable securities has often been assigned to first-year auditors because it was thought that the auditing procedures were mostly mechanical in nature: reconciling bank accounts, examining canceled checks, and so forth. As this chapter has communicated, the audit of cash and liquid assets is far from mechanical and represents a real challenge at many audit clients.

Significant Terms

Bank confirmation   A standard confirmation sent to all banks with which the client had business during the year to obtain information about the year-end cash balance and additional information about loans outstanding.

Bank transfer schedule   An audit document that lists all transfers between client bank accounts starting a short period before year end and continuing for a short period after year end; its purpose is to assure that cash in transit is not recorded twice.

Collateral   An asset or a claim on an asset usually held by a borrower or an issuer of a debt instrument to serve as a guarantee for the value of a loan or security. If the borrower fails to pay interest or principal, the collateral is available to the lender as a basis to recover the principal amount of the loan or debt instrument.

Commercial paper   Notes issued by major corporations, usually for short periods of time and at rates approximating prime lending rates, usually with high credit rating; their quality may change if the financial strength of the issuer declines.

Cutoff bank statement   A bank statement for a period of time determined by the client and the auditor that is shorter than that of the regular month-end statements; sent directly to the auditor, who uses it to verify reconciling items on the client's year-end bank reconciliation.

Financial instruments   A broad class of instruments—usually debt securities, but also equity or hedges—that represents financial agreements between a party (usually an issuer) and a counterparty (usually an investor) based on either underlying assets or agreements to incur financial obligations or make payments; instruments range in complexity from a simple bond to complicated agreements containing puts or options.

Imprest bank account   A bank account that normally carries a zero balance and is replenished by the company when checks are to be written against the account; provides additional control over cash. The most widely used imprest bank account is the payroll account, to which the company makes a deposit equal to the amount of payroll checks issued.

Kiting   A fraudulent cash scheme to overstate cash assets at year end by showing the same cash in two different bank accounts using an interbank transfer.

Lockbox   A cash management arrangement with a bank whereby an organization's customers send payments directly to a post office box number accessible to the client's bank; the bank opens the cash remittances and directly deposits the money in the client's account.

Marketable security   A security that is readily marketable and held by the company as an investment.

Turnaround document   A document sent to the customer to be returned with the customer's remittance; may be machine-readable and may contain information to improve the efficiency of receipt processing.

SELECTED REFERENCES TO RELEVANT PROFESSIONAL GUIDANCE	
Topic	**Selected Guidance**
Confirmations	SAS 67 *The Confirmation Process* SAS *External Confirmations* (issued but not effective, proposed effective date is December 2012) AICPA Practice Alert 03-01 Audit Confirmations (updated June 2007) Proposed AS *Confirmation* ISA 505 *External Confirmations*
Auditing Securities	SAS 92 *Auditing Derivative Instruments, Hedging Activities, and Investments in Securities* Proposed SAS *Audit Evidence—Specific Considerations for Selected Items (to supersede SAS 92)* AICPA Audit Guide *Auditing Derivative Instruments, Hedging Activities, and Investments in Securities,* with conforming changes as of August 1, 2009.

Note: Acronyms for Relevant Professional Guidance

STANDARDS: **AS**—Auditing Standard issued by the PCAOB; **ISA**—International Standard on Auditing issued by the IAASB; **SAS**—Statement on Auditing Standards issued by the Auditing Standards Board of the AICPA; **SSAE**—Statement on Standards for Attestation Engagements issued by the AICPA.

ORGANIZATIONS: **AICPA**—American Institute of Certified Public Accountants; **COSO**—Committee of Sponsoring Organizations; **IAASB**—International Auditing and Assurance Standards Board; **ISB**—Independence Standards Board; **PCAOB**—Public Company Accounting Oversight Board; **SEC**—Securities and Exchange Commission.

Review Questions

12-1 **(LO 1)** Why is it important to coordinate the testing of cash and other liquid-asset accounts?

12-2 **(LO 1, 3)** Explain the purpose and risks associated with each of the following types of bank accounts:

a. General cash account

b. Imprest payroll account

12-3 **(LO 1, 3)** Evaluate the following statement made by a third-year auditor: "In comparison with other accounts, such as accounts receivable or property, plant, and equipment, it is my assessment that cash and marketable securities contain less inherent risk. There are no significant valuation problems with cash. Marketable securities can be verified by consulting the closing price in the *Wall Street Journal*." Do you agree or disagree with the auditor's assessment of inherent risk? Explain.

Fraud

12-4 **(LO 3, 5)** Why is there a greater emphasis on the possibility of fraud in cash accounts than for other asset accounts of the same size? Identify three types of frauds that would directly affect the cash account and indicate how the frauds might be detected by the auditor.

12-5 **(LO 2, 3, 4, 5, 6)** What factors should be considered when planning the audit of cash and marketable securities?

12-6 **(LO 1, 3, 4)** Describe how a lockbox arrangement with a bank works. What is its advantage to an organization? What risks are associated with it? What controls should an entity develop to mitigate each of the risks identified?

12-7   **(LO 1, 6)** What is a compensating balance? How does the auditor become aware of the existence of compensating balances?

12-8   **(LO 4)** How should duties be segregated in an automated cash receipts processing system? Explain the rationale for the segregation of duties that you recommend.

12-9   **(LO 4, 5)** What are monitoring activities? Identify the major monitoring activities the auditor would expect to find in the cash management system. For each monitoring activity identified, indicate how the auditor would go about testing it to determine its operating effectiveness.

12-10   **(LO 4, 5, 7)** What are the major authorization principles the auditor should investigate regarding both cash management and investments in marketable securities?

12-11   **(LO 4)** Explain how turnaround documents can improve the controls over the cash receipts process. Does the existence of a turnaround document negate the need to assign a unique identification number to each cash receipts transaction? Explain.

12-12   **(LO 2, 4, 5, 6)** What is the impact on the audit if the client does not perform independent periodic reconciliations of its cash accounts? What audit procedures would be dictated by the lack of the client's independent reconciliations?

12-13   **(LO 6)** Explain the purpose of the following audit procedures:
  a. Sending a bank confirmation to all the banks with which the client does business
  b. Obtaining a bank cutoff statement
  c. Preparing a bank transfer statement

12-14   **(LO 6)** What information does an auditor search for in reviewing loan agreements with the client's bank?

12-15   **(LO 5)** How might management use the internal audit function to gain assurance about the effectiveness of its controls over cash and cash management?

12-16   **(LO 3, 4, 6)** Define and illustrate kiting. What procedures should the client institute to prevent it? What audit procedures should the auditor use to detect kiting?

12-17   **(LO 7)** Under what circumstances might it be acceptable to use an audit procedure other than physically examining marketable securities to verify their existence?

12-18   **(LO 7)** How does the auditor determine whether marketable securities are properly classified as short-term securities or long-term investments? What are the accounting implications of the classification as short term or long term? What types of evidence does the auditor gather to substantiate management's classification as a short-term security?

12-19   **(LO 7)** What role should the board of directors have regarding an organization's investment in marketable securities? What documentation would the auditor expect to find regarding the board's oversight role?

12-20   **(LO 7)** What role does collateral play in valuing marketable securities? Would an audit of marketable securities ever require an audit of the underlying collateral? Explain.

12-21   **(LO 4, 7)** How would the absence of each of the following factors affect the auditor's assessment of the control environment? Assume that the company's investment in marketable securities is material to the financial statements.

   a. The board of directors is not actively involved in monitoring the company's policies regarding marketable securities.

   b. The company has an internal audit department, but it does not have any computer audit expertise and has not conducted audits of the cash or marketable securities account during the past three years.

   c. Management does not have written guidelines for investments in marketable securities. The financial executive has been successful in procuring good returns on investments in the past, and management does not want to tamper with success.

12-22   **(LO 7)** In what ways do some of the newer types of financial instruments differ from traditional financial instruments? What additional risks are associated with such securities?

12-23   **(LO 7)** What controls should an organization implement if it wishes to become an investor in more complex financial instruments? Explain the purpose of each control.

Multiple-Choice Questions

12-24   **(LO 6)** XYZ Company concealed a cash shortage by transporting funds from one location to another and by converting negotiable instruments to cash. Which of the following audit procedures would be most effective in discovering the cash cover-up?

   a. Periodic review by internal audit.

   b. Simultaneous verification of cash and liquid assets.

   c. A surprise count of all cash accounts.

   d. A verification of all outstanding checks associated with the year-end bank reconciliation.

12-25   **(LO 7)** An audit client has invested heavily in new equity and debt securities. Which of the following would *not* constitute an appropriate role for the company's board of directors?

   a. Receive and review periodic reports by the internal audit department on compliance with company policies and procedures.

   b. Approve all new investments.

   c. Review and approve written policies and guidelines for investments in marketable securities.

   d. Periodically review the risks inherent in the portfolio of marketable securities to determine whether the risk is within parameters deemed acceptable by the board.

*12-26 **(LO 6)** A cash shortage may be concealed by transporting funds from one location to another or by converting negotiable assets to cash. Because of this, which of the following audit procedures are vital?

a. Simultaneous confirmations.

b. Simultaneous bank reconciliations.

c. Simultaneous verification of all bank accounts and negotiable instruments.

d. Simultaneous surprise cash count.

12-27 **(LO 3)** Which of the following would *not* represent an advantage to using a lockbox arrangement with a bank?

a. It expedites the receipt of cash and provides earlier access to it.

b. It is less costly than processing the cash receipts internally.

c. It provides additional segregation of duties because the bank handles cash.

d. It reduces the organization's susceptibility to fraud caused by diverting cash receipts to personal use.

12-28 **(LO 4)** Internal control over cash receipts is weakened when an employee who receives customer mail receipts also does which of the following?

a. Prepares initial cash receipt records.

b. Prepares bank deposit slips for all mail receipts.

c. Maintains a petty cash fund.

d. Records credits to individual accounts receivable.

12-29 **(LO 5, 6)** The auditor suspects that client personnel may be diverting cash receipts to personal use. The individual who opens the mail also prepares the bank deposit and sends turnaround documents to accounts receivable for posting. Which of the following audit procedures would be the *least* effective in determining whether cash shortages are occurring?

a. Confirmation of accounts receivable.

b. Preparation of a detailed cash trace.

c. Review of all noncash credits to accounts receivable for a selected period.

d. Year-end reconciliation of the bank account.

12-30 **(LO 6)** The auditor obtains a bank cutoff statement for a short period of time subsequent to year end as a basis for testing the client's year-end bank reconciliation. However, during the testing, the auditor notes that very few of the outstanding checks have cleared the bank. The most likely cause for this is that the client

a. Is engaged in a kiting scheme.

b. Prepared checks to pay vendors but did not mail them until well after year end.

c. Was involved in a lapping scheme.

d. Needed to overstate the year-end cash balance to increase the working-capital ratio.

---

*All problems marked with an asterisk are adapted from the Uniform CPA Examination.

12-31 **(LO 6)** The auditor would send a bank confirmation to all banks with which the client had business during the year, because:

a. The confirmation seeks information on indebtedness that may exist even if the bank accounts are closed.

b. Confirmations are essential to detecting kiting schemes.

c. Confirmations provide information about deposits in transit that is useful in proving the client's year-end bank reconciliation.

d. All of the above.

12-32 **(LO 6)** An unrecorded check issued during the last week of the year would most likely be discovered by the auditor when:

a. The check register for the last month is reviewed.

b. The cutoff bank statement is reviewed as part of the year-end bank reconciliation.

c. The bank confirmation is reviewed.

d. The search for unrecorded liabilities is performed.

*Items 12–33 and 12–34 are based on the following:

The following information was taken from the bank transfer schedule prepared during the audit of Fox Co.'s financial statements for the year ended December 31, 2011. Assume all checks are dated and issued on December 30, 2011.

Check No.	BANK ACCOUNTS		DISBURSEMENT DATE		RECEIPT DATE	
	From	To	Per Books	Per Bank	Per Books	Per Bank
101	National	Federal	Dec. 30	Jan. 4	Dec. 30	Jan. 3
202	County	State	Jan. 3	Jan. 2	Dec. 30	Dec. 31
303	Federal	State	Dec. 31	Jan. 3	Jan. 2	Jan. 2
404	State	County	Jan. 2	Jan. 2	Jan. 2	Dec. 31

*12-33 **(LO 6)** Which of the following checks might indicate kiting?

a. 202

b. 303

c. 404

d. 202 and 303

*12-34 **(LO 6)** Which of the following checks illustrate deposits/transfers in transit at December 31, 2011?[7]

a. 101 and 202

b. 101 and 303

c. 202 and 404

d. 303 and 404

12-35 **(LO 6)** An auditor should trace bank transfers for the last part of the audit period and first part of the subsequent period to detect whether:

a. The cash receipts journal was held open for a few days after the year end.

b. The last checks recorded before the year end were actually mailed by the year end.

c. Cash balances were overstated because of kiting.

d. Any unusual payments to or receipts from related parties occurred.

Discussion and Research Questions

12-36 **(Complex Financial Instruments and Ethical Considerations, LO 7, 8)** The advent of sophisticated financial instruments has dramatically changed the nature of investing during the past decade. Many financial instruments offer potentially greater returns for the investor but at higher levels of risk.

Group Activity

Ethics

Required

a. Review the FASB's discussion on financial instruments, or a finance text, to identify various types of financial instruments. Select five instruments that you consider interesting and prepare a report addressing (1) the nature of the instrument, (2) its underlying business purpose, (3) risks associated with the instrument, and (4) special audit procedures that should be applied during the audit of a client with a significant investment in the instrument.

b. Now assume that one of your audit clients has a large investment in a particularly risky financial instrument. This financial instrument exposes the client to significant economic loss in the unlikely event that the marketability of the instrument declines. You do not feel that the client's footnote disclosures adequately reveal the true risk profile of the instrument. What is your ethical obligation to the shareholders of the client with regard to your knowledge of the riskiness of this investment? You should discuss this issue in your assigned group.

Use the ethical decision-making framework outlined in Chapter 3 to formulate your answer. Recall that the steps in that framework are as follows: (1) identify the ethical issue(s); (2) determine who are the affected parties and identify their rights; (3) determine the most important rights; (4) develop alternative courses of action; (5) determine the likely consequences of each proposed course of action; (6) assess the possible consequences, including an estimation of the greatest good for the greatest number and determine whether the rights framework would cause any course of action to be eliminated; (7) decide on the appropriate course of action.

12-37 **(Electronic Funds Transfers, LO 3, 4)** Electronic funds transfer has been identified as a major method of transferring cash for most organizations.

Required

Complete the following:

a. Describe how electronic commerce and electronic transfer of funds work.

b. Identify the major risks that should be addressed by controls regarding electronic transfer of funds.

c. Identify the controls an organization should consider implementing to minimize the risks associated with electronic transfer of cash.

12-38 **(Authorization Concepts, LO 4, 5)** One of the major controls over cash and cash transfers is to make sure that only authorized personnel are handling cash, making cash transfers, or investing excess cash.

Required

a. For each of the following situations, indicate the individual who should be authorized to initiate and implement the transaction:

1. Electronic transfer of excess cash funds to the organization's major account for cash management and investment.

2. Regular disbursement of payment for accounts payable.

3. Transfer of funds to the imprest payroll account.

4. Investment of excess funds in nontraditional financial instruments.

5. Endorsement for daily cash deposits.

b. For each type of authorization identified in part (a), indicate the audit evidence the auditor would gather to determine whether transactions were appropriately authorized.

12-39 **(Audit Approach—Cash, LO 2, 4, 5, 6)** In conversation with another auditor, Fran—an auditor who has been associated primarily with audits of large clients—offers her opinion that "substantive testing of cash accounts is obsolete. The primary emphasis on cash audits ought to be on auditing the controls over the cash process, assessing the risks associated with the control environment, and selectively testing the client's year-end reconciliation." The other auditor, Cheng, replies, "Unfortunately, you have audited in a very sheltered world. Most of the audit clients I see are small and don't have particularly good internal controls. There is little segregation of duties. Most posting of accounts is to computer systems under control of the controller's department. Unless we do a primarily substantive audit, we could not gather enough evidence to render an opinion on cash."

Required

a. What primary elements of internal control must Fran be relying on in reaching her conclusion about the audit approach to cash?

b. For each item identified in part (a), indicate an audit procedure the auditor might utilize to corroborate the initial understanding of the risk or the control.

c. What primary substantive audit procedures would Cheng, the second auditor, most likely use to audit cash accounts at a small business? Describe the audit objectives accomplished with each procedure.

12-40 **(Cash—Audit Evidence, LO 4, 5, 6)** The following items were discovered during the audit of the cash account. For each item identified:

a. Indicate the audit procedure that most likely would have led to the discovery of the error.

b. Identify one or two internal controls that would have prevented or detected the misstatement or irregularity.

Audit Findings

1. The company had overstated cash by transferring funds at year end to another account but failed to record the withdrawal until after year end.

2. On occasion, customers with smaller balances send in checks without specific identification of the customer except the name

printed on the check. The client has an automated cash receipts process, but the employee opening the envelopes pocketed the cash and destroyed other supporting documentation.

3. Same as finding (2), but the employee prepared a turnaround document that showed either an additional discount for the customer or a credit to the customer's account.

4. The controller was temporarily taking cash for personal purposes but intended to repay the company (although the repayment never occurred). The cover-up was executed by understating outstanding checks in the monthly bank reconciliation.

5. The company had temporary investments in six-month certificates of deposit at the bank. The CDs were supposed to yield an annual interest rate of 12% but apparently are yielding only 6%.

6. Cash remittances are not deposited in a timely fashion and are sometimes lost.

7. Substantial bank service charges have not been recorded by the client prior to year end.

8. A loan has been negotiated with the bank to provide funds for a subsidiary company. The loan was made by the controller of the division, who apparently was not authorized to negotiate the loan.

9. A check written to a vendor had been recorded twice in the cash disbursements journal to cover a cash shortage.

*12-41   **(Internal Controls over Cash, LO 3, 4, 6)** Pembrook Company had poor internal control over its cash transactions. The following are facts about its cash position at November 30:

Fraud

- The cash books showed a balance of $18,901.62, which included undeposited receipts.

- A credit of $100 on the bank statement did not appear on the company's books.

- The balance, according to the bank statement, was $15,550.

- Outstanding checks were:
  - no. 62 for $116.25
  - no. 183 for $150.00
  - no. 284 for $253.25
  - no. 8621 for $190.71
  - no. 8623 for $206.80
  - no. 8632 for $145.28

The only deposit was in the amount of $3,794.41 on December 7. The cashier handles all incoming cash and makes the bank deposits personally. He also reconciles the monthly bank statement. His November 30 reconciliation follows:

Balance, per books, November 30		$18,901.62
Add: Outstanding checks:		
8621	$190.71	
8623	206.80	
8632	45.28	442.79
		$19,344.41
Less: Undeposited receipts		3,794.41
Balance per bank, November 30		$15,550.00
Deduct: Unrecorded credit		100.00
True cash, November 30		$15,450.00

Required

a. You suspect that the cashier may have misappropriated some money and are concerned specifically that some of the undeposited receipts of $3,794.41 may have been taken. Prepare a schedule showing your estimate of the loss.

b. How did the cashier attempt to conceal the theft?

c. On the basis of this information only, name two specific features of internal control that were apparently missing.

d. If the cashier's October 31 reconciliation is known to be proper and you start your audit on December 10, what specific auditing procedures could you perform to discover the theft?

*12-42   **(Audit of Cash—Reconciliations, LO 6)** Toyco, a retail toy chain, honors two bank credit cards and makes daily deposits of credit card sales in two credit card bank accounts (Bank A and Bank B). Each day, Toyco batches its credit card sales slips, bank deposit slips, and authorized sales return documents and sends them to data processing for data entry. Each week detailed computer printouts of the general ledger credit card cash accounts are prepared. Credit card banks have been instructed to make an automatic weekly transfer of cash to Toyco's general bank account. The credit card banks charge back deposits that include sales to holders of stolen or expired cards.

The auditor examining the Toyco financial statements has obtained copies of the detailed general ledger cash account printouts, a summary of the bank statements, and the manually prepared bank reconciliations, all for the week ended December 31, as shown here.

Required

Review the December 31 bank reconciliation and the related information contained in the following schedules and describe what actions the auditor should take to obtain satisfaction for each item on the bank reconciliation. Assume that all amounts are material and that all computations are accurate. Organize your answer sheet as follows, using the code contained on the bank reconciliation:

Code Number	Actions to Be Taken by the Auditor to Gain Satisfaction

Toyco

Bank Reconciliation for December 31, 2011

Code No.	BANK A	BANK B
	Add or (Deduct)	
1. Balance per bank statement, December 31	$8,600	$ -0-
2. Deposits in transit, December 31	2,200	6,000
3. Redeposit of invalid deposits (deposited in wrong account)	1,000	1,400
4. Difference in deposits of December 29	(2,000)	(100)
5. Unexplained bank charge	400	
6. Bank cash transfer not yet recorded	-0-	22,600
7. Bank service charges	-0-	500
8. Chargebacks not recorded—stolen cards	100	-0-
9. Sales returns recorded but not reported to the bank	(600)	(1,200)
10. Balance per general ledger, December 31	$9,700	$29,200

Toyco
Detailed General Ledger Credit Card Cash Accounts Printouts
for the Week Ended December 31, 2011

	BANK A	BANK B
	Dr. or (Cr.)	
Beginning balance, December 24	$12,100	$4,200
Deposits: December 27	2,500	5,000
December 28	3,000	7,000
December 29	0	5,400
December 30	1,900	4,000
December 31	2,200	6,000
Cash transfer, December 17	(10,700)	-0-
Chargebacks—expired cards	(300)	(1,600)
Invalid deposits (deposited in wrong account)	(1,400)	(1,000)
Redeposit of invalid deposits	1,000	1,400
Sales returns for week ended December 31	(600)	(1,200)
Ending balance	$9,700	$29,200

Toyco
Summary of the Bank Statements for the Week Ended December 31, 2011

	BANK A	BANK B
	(Charges) or Credits	
Beginning balance, December 24	$10,000	$ -0-
Deposits dated: December 24	2,100	4,200
December 27	2,500	5,000
December 28	3,000	7,000
December 29	2,000	5,500
December 30	1,900	4,000
Cash transfers to general bank account:		
December 27	(10,700)	-0-
December 31	-0-	(22,600)
Chargebacks:		
Stolen cards	(100)	-0-
Expired cards	(300)	(1,600)
Invalid deposits	(1,400)	(1,000)
Bank service charges	-0-	(500)
Bank charge (unexplained)	(400)	(-0-)
Ending balance	$8,600	$ -0-

12-43 **(Bank Confirmations, LO 6)** The AICPA has developed a standard bank confirmation form to assure consistent communication with the banking community.

Required

a. Is the auditor required to send a bank confirmation to banks from which the client receives a bank cutoff statement shortly after year end? Explain.

b. What additional information is gathered through a bank confirmation? Explain how the other information gathered is used on the audit.

Professional Skepticism

c. For each scenario in the following list, recommend an audit procedure or additional audit work that should be performed:

1. The client has one major bank account located in a distant city, and the auditor is not familiar with the bank. The auditor has assessed control risk as high on this engagement. The mailing address of the bank is simply a post office box number, but such a number is not considered unusual.

2. The client has three accounts with its major bank. For two of the three accounts, the confirmation returned by the bank shows different balances from what the client shows. The balance per the client for one of the accounts is the same as the bank shows in the cutoff statement received from the bank shortly after year end. The auditor did not request a cutoff statement on the other account for which the confirmation differs.

3. The returned confirmation shows a loan that the client does not list as a liability.

12-44 **(Electronic Funds Transfers—Monitoring Controls, LO 4, 5, 6)** Assume a major client is involved in transactions with customers such that almost all of the cash receipts are transferred to the client's bank electronically. The bank separates the remittance advices and sends that summary directly to the accounts receivable department of the client. At the end of the day, the bank also sends a complete cash receipts summary to the treasury department. In addition, the client purchases many products through e-commerce relationships with its major suppliers. It has signed contracts whereby a notification of receipt of goods in the client's system will cause an electronic transfer to be made to the major supplier within 10 days (i.e.,10 days of receipts will be paid on the 11th day) according to contracted prices and automated receiving documents.

Required

a. What are the monitoring controls? How might monitoring controls be used to assure that all receipts of cash are handled correctly and on a timely basis?

b. What major monitoring controls would the auditor expect to find over cash receipts? For each monitoring control identified, state how the auditor would test to see whether the control is operating effectively and the implication of effective operation on the conduct of other control tests.

c. What monitoring controls would the auditor expect to find over cash disbursements? For each monitoring control identified, state how the auditor would test to see whether the control is operating effectively and the implication of effective operation on the conduct of other control tests.

d. If effective monitoring controls are not present, and the auditor has identified the client as high risk because of financial liquidity problems, what kind of tests should the auditor perform to see that cash is being recorded correctly and is not overstated?

*12-45 **(Bank Reconciliation, LO 6)** The following client-prepared bank reconciliation is being examined by Kautz, CPA, during an examination of the financial statements of Concrete Products, Inc.:

Concrete Products, Inc.
Bank Reconciliation December 31, 2011

Balance per bank (a)		$18,375.91
Deposits in transit (b):		
December 30	1,471.10	
December 31	2,840.69	4,311.79
Outstanding checks (c):		
837	6,000.00	
1941	671.80	
1966	320.00	
1984	1,855.42	
1985	3,621.22	
1986	2,576.89	
1991	4,420.88	(19,466.21)
Subtotal		3,221.49
NSF check returned Dec. 29 (d)		200.00
Bank charges		5.50
Error check no. 1932		148.10
Customer note collected by the bank		
($2,750 plus $275 interest) (e)		(3,025.00)
Balance per books (f)		$ 550.09

Required

Identify one or more audit procedures that should be performed by Kautz in gathering evidence in support of each of the items (a) through (f) in this bank reconciliation.

12-46 **(Overview and Objectives of Audit Procedures, LO 1, 5, 6)** The following represents a critical review of the documentation of a new auditor for the cash and marketable securities audit areas. Several deficiencies are noted; they resulted in significant errors not being initially identified.

Required

For each of the following items:

a. Identify the audit procedure that would have detected the error.

b. Identify the more relevant financial statement assertion(s) tested by the audit procedure.

Documentation Deficiencies and Financial Statement Misstatements

1. The client was in violation of important loan covenant agreements.

2. The client was engaged in a sophisticated kiting scheme involving transfers through five geographically disbursed branch offices.

3. The December cash register was held open until January 8. All receipts through that date were recorded as December sales and cash receipts. The receipts, however, were deposited daily.

4. Cash disbursements for December were written but the checks were not mailed until January 10 because of a severe cash-flow problem.

5. The client's bank reconciliation included an incorrect amount as balance per the bank.

6. Approximately 25% of the cash receipts for December 26 and December 28 were recorded twice.

7. The client's bank reconciliation covered up a clever fraud by the controller by incorrectly footing the outstanding checks and including fictitious checks as outstanding.

12-47 **(Bank Transfer Problem, LO 6)** Eagle River Plastics Company has a major branch located in Phoenix. The branch deposits cash receipts daily and periodically transfers the receipts to the company's home office in Eagle River. The transfers are accounted for as intercompany entries into the home office and branch office accounts. All accounting, however, is performed at the home office under the direction of the assistant controller. The assistant controller is also responsible for the transfers. The controller, however, independently reconciles the bank account each month or assigns the reconciliation to someone in the department (which, in some cases, could be the assistant controller). The company is relatively small; thus, the controller is also the financial planner and treasurer for the company. As part of the year-end audit, you are assigned the task of conducting an audit of bank transfers. As part of the process, you prepare the following schedule of transfers:

Information from client's records			Information per bank statements	
			Date Cleared	
Date per Branch	Date per Amount	Date Deposited Home Office	per Home Bank	per Branch Bank
12-27	$23,000	12-31	12-31	1-3
12-29	$40,000	12-31	12-31	1-7
12-31	$45,000	1-2	1-3	1-8
1-2	$14,000	12-31	12-31	1-5
1-5	$28,000	1-3	1-7	1-12
1-3	$10,000	1-3	12-31	1-5

Required

a. Identify the audit procedures that would be used to test the correctness of the client's bank transfers.

b. Identify any adjusting journal entries that would be needed on either the home or branch office accounting records as a result of the preceding transactions.

12-48 **(Control Weaknesses, LO 4, 6)** The following are weaknesses in internal controls over cash:

a. The list of authorized check signers is not updated on a timely basis when job assignments are changed or people leave the firm.

b. The person who opens the mail prepares the deposit when the cashier is not available.

c. If a customer does not submit a remittance advice with a payment, the mail clerk sometimes does not prepare one for the accounts receivable department.

d. Occasionally, the treasurer's department does not cancel the supporting documents for cash disbursements.

e. Customer correspondence concerning monthly statements is handled by the person who makes the bank deposits.

f. Bank reconciliations are not prepared on a timely basis. When they are prepared, they are prepared by the person who handles incoming mail.

Required

For each weakness, indicate what audit procedure(s) should be performed to determine whether any material misstatements have occurred. Consider each weakness independently of the others.

12-49 **(Marketable Securities, LO 7)** The client prepared the following worksheet listing all activities in the marketable securities account for the year under audit. For purposes of this question, you may assume that there are no unusual securities except the note from XYNO Corporation (a related party) and a note from Allis-Chalmers Corporation (a customer). Assume also that control risk was assessed as moderate to high and that the auditor decides to concentrate on direct tests of the account balance. The account balances at the beginning and end of the year per the company's trial balance are as follows:

	Beginning Balance	Ending Balance
Investment in marketable securities	$400,000	$675,000
Allowance to reduce securities to market	$ 35,000	$ 35,000
Balance per general ledger	$365,000	$640,000
Interest income		$ 25,000
Dividend income		$ 18,000
Net gain on disposal of securities		$ 32,000

Required

Identify the audit procedures needed to complete the audit of marketable securities for year end. You may assume that the client was audited by the same firm last year. Be sure to cover the steps the auditor would use to determine that the securities are properly classified.

12-50 **(Internal Audit of Investments, LO 4, 7)** The existence of an internal audit department is recognized as a strong element of a company's control environment. Internal auditors can perform financial audits (similar to that of the external audit) or operational audits (audits of the effectiveness of operations and compliance with controls).

Required

Assume that the client has started investing in financial instruments.

a. Develop a comprehensive operational audit program to identify the risk associated with such investments, management controls designed to address those risks, and the effectiveness of the board of directors, management, and the audit committee review of such risks.

b. Assume that management reports that it is using "hedging contracts" to reduce exposure to foreign currency fluctuation as well as future price changes in raw materials. You have read that it is often difficult to determine whether some of these financial instruments are hedges or are speculative investments. In completing this audit:

1. Briefly describe the difference between a hedge and a speculative investment.

2. Briefly describe how the risk should be measured in a speculative investment.

12-51 **(Audit of Collateral, LO 7)** Financial institutions usually require collateral as part of a lending agreement. For example, loans to build shopping centers usually require the property to be put up as collateral in case the borrower cannot repay the loan. The bank then takes title to the collateral. However, as reported by the GAO, many financial institutions, especially savings and loans, did not obtain adequate collateral or were overly optimistic on the value of collateral for many loans.

Required

a. Identify the controls a financial institution might implement to assure that adequate collateral is obtained for loans.

b. During an audit of a financial institution, the auditor becomes concerned about the collateral that exists for some financial instruments in which the company has invested (e.g., collateralized receivables and mortgages). Develop an audit program to address the auditor's concerns regarding adequacy of collateral.

c. How would a deficiency in collateral affect the financial presentation of a company's investment account? Explain.

Cases

12-52 **(Application Controls, LO 2, 4, 5)** Rhinelander Co. is a regional retailer with 45 stores located in the Southeast. The company accepts major credit cards and its own credit card in addition to cash. Approximately 25% of the company's sales are made on the firm's own credit cards. The company has decided to process sales and cash receipts itself. Monthly statements are sent out on a cyclical basis. The customers are requested to return the upper portion of the statement with their remittance as a turnaround document.

The client has attempted to automate the cash collection process. The turnaround documents are machine-readable.

Required

a. Identify the important application controls that this system would include if the auditor had assessed control risk as low.

b. For each control identified, indicate (1) the sources of evidence the auditor would examine to determine whether the control existed and (2) how the auditor would test to determine that the control is functioning as indicated.

12-53 **(Marketable Securities—Control Environment, LO 7)** Justin Company, a medium-size manufacturing client located in the Southwest, produces supplies for the automobile industry. The company is publicly traded on the American Stock Exchange. Joann Sielig took over as chief executive officer three years ago after a successful career working with a New York investment-banking firm. The company had been earning minimal returns, and Sielig is intent on turning the company around. She has analyzed the situation and determined that the company's main manufacturing arm could be treated as a cash cow. In other words, although the operations do not generate a lot of profit, they do generate cash flow that could be used for investment purposes. After analyzing the situations, Sielig has decided that the best opportunities for superior returns lie in investments in high-risk marketable securities. When questioned on this strategy during a board meeting, she cited finance literature that, she asserted, shows greater returns are consistent only with greater risk. However, the risk can be minimized by appropriately diversifying the investment portfolio. Given Sielig's knowledge of the subject and quick grasp of the company's situation, the board gave her complete control over all aspects of management. She personally manages the investment portfolio. Moreover, the board was so impressed with her analysis that she was given an incentive pay contract with an annual bonus based on a percentage of profits in excess of the previous year's profits. In addition, she received stock options.

The company has an internal audit department that reports directly to the CEO (Sielig). Although there is an audit committee, it exists more in form than substance and meets with the director of internal audit only occasionally. The internal audit program for the year is determined by the director of internal audit in conjunction with Sielig and is strongly influenced by two factors: (1) Sielig's perception of areas needing review and (2) areas of potential cost savings.

Sielig has let it be known that all units of the company must justify their existence, and if the internal audit department expected future budget increases it must generate recommended cost savings in excess of the current internal audit budget.

Your CPA firm audits Justin Company. During the preliminary planning for the audit, you note the following:

1. The investment account has grown from approximately 7% of total assets to approximately 30% of total assets.
2. The investment portfolio includes some long-term investments in company stocks; however, many of the stocks held in the portfolio are high-risk stocks (with hopes of greater returns).
3. The remainder of the investment portfolio consists of a wide variety of financial instruments, including junk bonds, collateralized mortgages, and other similar instruments.
4. Broker fees have increased dramatically. There is also a new line item for investment consulting fees. It appears that most of these fees are owed to a company that might be somehow related to Sielig.
5. Most of the securities are held by the brokerage firm, but a few are held by the investment consulting company, and a few others are held directly by the company.
6. The company has shown a 25% increase in reported net income during the past year.
7. The company's stock value has appreciated more than 20% during the past year.

Required

a. Identify the elements of inherent risk and control risk in the preceding scenario that should be considered in planning the audit. For the control environment issues identified, briefly indicate the potential audit implication.

b. Outline an audit program that could be used for auditing the marketable securities account for the current year.

c. Given only the information presented in the scenario, identify the specific factors the auditor would evaluate in formulating an opinion on the required public reporting of internal control over financial reporting.

Professional Skepticism

Internet

12-54 **(Problems with Cash Confirmations, LO 3, 6)** As an example of difficulties that auditors experience in collecting confirmations of cash balances, consider the Parmalat fraud. In that case, the company overstated cash by about $5 billion, which reflected a fictitious amount in a Bank of America account in the Cayman Islands. The Italian segment of the audit firm, Grant Thornton, received a cash confirmation that noted no exceptions to the confirmation the audit firm had sent. Parmalat accomplished the deception, in part, by providing the audit firm with a fictitious bank mailing address. However, it is important to note that SAS 67, "The Confirmation Process," states that "if the combined assessed level of inherent and control risk over the existence of cash is low, the auditor might limit substantive procedures to inspecting client-provided bank statements rather than confirming cash balances" (paragraph 10).

Required

a. SAS 67 allows auditors to use low-cost methods for obtaining substantive evidence regarding the existence and valuation of cash. If those methods are used, what substantive analytical procedures could provide a supplemental low-cost source of evidence?

b. What role does the concept of materiality play in the substantive testing of cash balances?

c. How may the Internet and associated electronic confirmation processes help to avoid fraud associated with cash confirmations?

d. What are two or three key factors the auditor might consider that could have indicated that the cash account was a high-risk account for this client and would require more skeptical audit work?

12-55 **(Decision Analysis related to Cash Confirmations, LO 6, 8)** One of the procedures that you have been assigned to perform on the audit of Reengage Corporation is the sending of bank confirmations. Your audit firm has a policy of sending confirmations to all financial institutions where a banking relationship exists, although the policy acknowledges that there are various instances when it may not be necessary to send confirmations (e.g., accounts with no activity for the period under audit, "petty cash" accounts at branch locations). You note several accounts where the cash balances are relatively small. You believe that it will not be necessary to send confirmations to the financial institutions where Reengage Corporation has an account with a small balance.

Required

a. What type of evidence is obtained through bank confirmations?

b. Use the decision analysis framework from Chapter 3 to determine the appropriate steps to take in deciding on which financial institutions should be sent a confirmation. Recall that the framework is as follows:

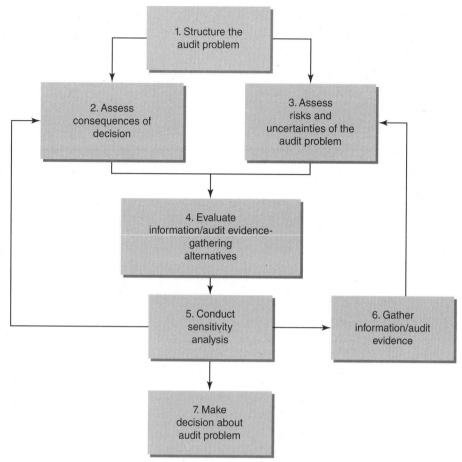

Source: Adapted from "Judgment and Choice," by Robin Hogarth.

12-56   **(Controls over Cash and Tests of Controls, LO 4, 5)** The Canada Border Services Agency (CBSA) receives cash payment for services, fees, and taxes (e.g., customs duties, excise taxes, taxes on goods and services) at various ports of entry around Canada. Cash is defined as payments made in liquid cash, by debit or credit cards, and by checks.

Required

a. What types of controls should the CBSA have over its cash receipts?
b. Given the controls that you identified in part (a), what types of audit procedures should be performed?

Academic Research Case (LO 6)

Aldhizer, G. R. & Cashell, J. D. (2006). Automating the Confirmation Process. *The CPA Journal.76(4):28–32.* Also available at http://www.nysscpa.org/cpa-journal/2006/406/essentials/p28.htm.

i.   What is the issue being addressed in the paper?
ii. Why is this issue important to practicing auditors?
iii. What are the findings of the paper?
iv. What are the implications of these findings for audit quality (or audit practice) on the audit profession?

SEARCH HINT

It is easy to locate these academic research articles! Simply use a search engine (e.g., Google Scholar) or an electronic research platform (e.g., ABI Inform) and search using the author names and part of the article title.

Go to www.cengage.com/accounting/rittenberg for the Ford and Toyota materials.

Source and Reference	Question
Ford 10-K	**1a.** What are the key cash and liquid asset accounts for Ford? What types of marketable securities and financial instruments does Ford possess?
	1b. What are the critical accounting policies for these accounts?
	1c. What risks do these securities and financial instruments pose for Ford? What are the audit implications of those risk disclosures?
Ford 10-K, Toyota 20-F	**2a.** Review the statement of cash flows and management discussion and analysis related to liquidity for Ford. What are the significant trends that you note?
	2b. Review the statement of cash flows for Toyota. How do the trends differ between Ford and Toyota?
	2c. What are the audit implications of the different trends at Ford and Toyota?

As part of the audit of cash and other liquid assets, you may now complete the following exercises contained in the Biltrite audit practice case:

Module VIII: Dallas Dollar Bank—bank reconciliation

Module IX: Analysis of interbank transfers

Module X: Analysis of marketable securities

Module VIII: Dallas Dollar Bank Reconciliation

Biltrite maintains two general demand deposit accounts and a payroll account. One of the general demand deposit accounts and the payroll account are with Dallas Dollar Bank. The second demand deposit account is with Bank Two, the Chicago bank from which Biltrite obtained the $45 million loan referred to previously. As part of the cash audit, Derick has asked you to reperform the reconciliation of all three of the bank accounts for December 2009, and to do an analysis of inter-bank transfers between Dollar Bank and Bank Two.

Recall that Biltrite has reconciled all bank accounts for each of the 12 months. You will begin, therefore, with the company's documentation of its December 2009 reconciliations.

Requirements

1. Using the spreadsheet program and downloaded data, retrieve the file labeled "Bank." Briefly examine the following documentation in this file:

   • WP 1—Cash on hand and in banks;
   • WP 1.B—Bank reconciliation—Dallas Dollar Bank; and
   • WP 1.C—Inter-bank transfer schedule.

   Scroll to WP 1.B, "Bank Reconciliation—Dallas Dollar Bank." Does the Dollar Bank account reconcile for December? What are the possible causes for nonreconciliation?

2. In tracing cash disbursements from the December check register to the bank statement, you learn that check 44264, in the amount of $642,752, was recorded incorrectly as $651,752. Incorporate this misstatement into the appropriate section of the bank reconciliation. Does the account reconcile after you have made this correction? Assuming check 44264 was in payment of accounts payable (refer to Exhibit BR.16), draft the necessary audit adjustment at the bottom of your document.

3. Print the bank reconciliation document.

4. Scroll to WP 1 and record the audit adjustment in the "audit adjustments" column of the lead schedule.

5. The deposit in transit, as well as all but the last two checks outstanding at December 31, cleared with the bank cutoff statement. What specific audit objectives does obtaining a cutoff statement directly from the bank support? If the cutoff bank statement covered the period 1/1/10 through 1/21/10 and the deposit in transit was credited 1/12/10, would you be concerned? If so, why? What additional procedures would you apply to allay your concerns? Note on document WP 1.B that Dollar Bank credited the deposit in transit on 1/3/10.

Module IX: Analysis of Interbank Transfers

Requirements

1. Using the spreadsheet program and downloaded data, retrieve the file labeled "Bank." Scroll to WP 1.C, "Inter-bank Transfer Schedule." Cheryl Lucas, a member of the Denise Vaughan & Co. audit team, prepared this document. As part of your audit training, Derick asks that you examine and review the document and determine the need for possible audit adjustments and reclassifications.

   a. What is the purpose of analyzing inter-bank transfers for a short period before and after the balance sheet date?

   b. Identify possible audit adjustments and reclassifications by examining WP 1.C. Assume that Bank Two check 127332 was dated December 31, 2009, deposited on that date, and also credited by Dollar Bank on December 31, 2009.

   c. As noted previously, Lawton had borrowed $3 million from Biltrite in April 2008, and had planned to repay the loan before December 31, 2009. Did he really repay the loan in December? Do you think the check drawn on Bank Two was reflected as an outstanding check in the 12/31/09 Bank Two reconciliation? Do you think the check was recorded as a December disbursement? If not, why not? (*Hint:* Remember that the loan agreement with Bank Two requires a $10 million compensating balance at all times.)

2. Draft Audit Reclassification B at the bottom of WP 1.C.

3. Print the inter-bank transfer document.

4. Scroll to WP 1. Record Reclassification B from requirement (2) in the reclassification column of the lead schedule. Does the reclassification place Biltrite in default on the loan agreement? If so, what further audit procedures might you elect to apply at this time?

5. Print the lead schedule.

Module X: Analysis of Marketable Securities

Although the addition of the Waistliner Stationary Bike to the product line helped somewhat in increasing Biltrite's fall and winter revenue, business remains quite seasonal, producing large amounts in idle funds to be invested temporarily after the spring and summer bicycle sales seasons have ended. Marlene McAfee, the Biltrite treasurer, usually invests in marketable securities in mid-August and holds them until mid-January. They are sold in late January and February to finance spring inventories of bicycles. McAfee's goals in acquiring short-term investments are to maximize return while minimizing risk of loss from wide temporary price fluctuations. For this reason, the portfolio is limited to debt securities rated AA and above, and common stocks of "blue-chip" companies.

As of December 31, 2009, the portfolio consisted of the following holdings:

Security	12/31/09 Carrying Value	12/31/09 Market Value
Transco, Inc. Preferred	$ 804,024	$ 810,000
Jolly Roger Amusement Parks Common	720,000	660,000
Pets 'R' Us Common	736,000	742,000
General Department Stores Common	660,000	550,000
AT&T 8% Debenture Bonds	930,000	942,000
Daimler/Chrysler 11% Debenture Bonds	1,150,000	1,131,000
Cleveland Electric 9% Debenture Bonds	2,000,000	2,066,000

Requirements

1. Using the spreadsheet program and downloaded data, retrieve the file labeled "Security." Do you think McAfee's securities portfolio is consistent with her stated goals of "maximizing return while minimizing risk of loss from temporary price fluctuations"? Justify your answer.
2. What determines whether marketable securities are to be classified as current or noncurrent on the balance sheet?
3. What are the objectives in the audit of marketable securities? What are the most relevant assertions for the auditor to examine? Examine the audit legends at the bottom of document 2. Have the objectives been satisfied?
4. Enter the market data for each security held at December 31, 2009.
5. Add an audit legend (and explain it at the bottom of the worksheet) regarding how market was determined.
6. Draft Audit Adjustment 8 at the bottom of WP 2 to recognize the understatement of interest revenue. The discrepancy results from failure to recognize accrued interest at 12/31/09 (debit account 1205, "Accrued Interest Receivable").
7. Draft Audit Adjustment 9 to adjust the loss on decline of market value to reflect the corrected amount. The wide disparity in this instance arises because Biltrite, in adjusting to market at 12/31/09, compared market at 12/31/09 with the cost of the 12/31/08 portfolio, rather than comparing 12/31/09 market with 12/31/09 carrying values. For this adjustment, use account 9702, "Loss on Decline of Market Value of Securities," and account 1102, "Allowance for Decline of Market Value of Securities."
8. Print your document.

13

Audit of Long-Lived Assets and Related Expense Accounts

LEARNING OBJECTIVES

The overriding objective of this textbook is to build a foundation with which to analyze current professional issues and adapt audit approaches to business and economic complexities. Through studying this chapter, you will be able to:

1 Identify the accounts and relevant assertions in the long-lived asset cycle.

2 Describe the approach an auditor would take to perform an integrated audit in the long-lived asset cycle.

3 Identify risks to reliable financial reporting in the long-lived asset cycle and explain how management can manage earnings through fixed-asset accounts.

4 Describe how to use preliminary analytical procedures to identify possible misstatements in the accounts associated with long-lived assets.

5 Describe why it is important for the auditor to develop an understanding of internal controls, identify controls typically present in the long-lived asset cycle, and identify tests of controls used to test the effectiveness of controls over fixed assets.

6 Describe the substantive audit procedures that should be used to test long-lived assets and related accounts.

7 Describe the substantive audit procedures that should be used to test for the impairment of long-lived assets.

8 Discuss the risks associated with intangible assets and natural resources and the approach to auditing intangible assets and natural resources.

9 Discuss the risks associated with lease accounting and the audit approach for leases.

10 Apply the decision analysis and ethical decision-making frameworks to situations involving the audit of long-lived asset accounts.

CHAPTER OVERVIEW

In this chapter, we present a general discussion of risks and audit approaches related to long-lived assets and related expenses, intangibles, natural resources, and leases. In terms of the audit opinion formulation process, this chapter involves Phases III and IV, that is, obtaining evidence about controls and substantive evidence about long-lived asset account assertions. Auditors must consider the possibility that management may manage earnings by manipulating fixed-asset or lease accounts. Although types of fixed assets vary widely, there is a commonality in the audit approach to them. Assets are subject to impairment testing each year.

The Audit Opinion Formulation Process

| I. Assessing Client Acceptance and Retention Decisions *CHAPTER 4* | II. Understanding the Client *CHAPTERS 2, 4–6, and 9* | III. Obtaining Evidence about Controls and Determining the Impact on the Financial Statement Audit *CHAPTERS 5–14 and 18* | IV. Obtaining Substantive Evidence about Account Assertions *CHAPTERS 7–14 and 18* | V. Wrapping Up the Audit and Making Reporting Decisions *CHAPTERS 15 and 16* |

| The Auditing Profession, Regulation, and Corporate Governance *CHAPTERS 1 and 2* | Decision-Making, Professional Conduct, and Ethics *CHAPTER 3* | Professional Liability *CHAPTER 17* |

PROFESSIONAL JUDGMENT IN CONTEXT

In 2010, the Committee of Sponsoring Organizations (COSO) published a study that provided a comprehensive analysis of occurrences of fraudulent financial reporting that were investigated by the Securities and Exchange Commission (SEC) from 1988 through 2007. Unfortunately, the results continue to reveal a large number of financial frauds across all sizes of firms and industries. Providing detail on specific types of fraud that were perpetrated, the COSO report states that:

> The two most common techniques used to fraudulently misstate the financial statements involved improper revenue recognition and asset overstatements. The majority of frauds (61 percent) involved revenue recognition, while 51 percent involved overstated assets primarily by overvaluing existing assets or capitalizing expenses. The understatement of expenses and liabilities was much less frequent (18 percent). Misappropriation of assets occurred in 14 percent of the fraud cases, which was similar to the 12 percent reported in COSO's 1999 study.

There are many ways in which fixed assets can be overstated including:

- Fictitious assets on the books (WorldCom)
- Improper and incomplete depreciation (Waste Management)
- Failure to record impairment of assets, especially goodwill (Sun Microsystems)
- Expired or worthless assets left on a company's books (Millacron)
- Assets overvalued upon acquisition, especially in the purchase of a company (WorldCom).

Of course, not all misstatements are due to fraud. Misstatements can also result from (a) insufficient accounting systems and weak controls, (b) improper accounting judgments, and (c) misclassification of expenses as assets. As you read through this chapter, consider the following questions:

- What might motivate management to overstate fixed assets?
- What methods might management use to overstate fixed assets?
- As illustrated by the examples in this feature, overstatement of fixed assets happens frequently. Assume that auditors detect most of the overstatements. What company or economic information, or audit tests/analyses would likely alert the auditor to the possibility of such misstatements and therefore facilitate auditor detection?
- What controls can mitigate the risks associated with misstatements in long-lived asset accounts?
- How can the results of audits be used by clients to improve their control systems over long-lived assets?

Source: The COSO study referred to above can be found at http://www.coso.org/documents/COSOFRAUDSTUDY2010.pdf

Introduction

Long-lived assets (also called **fixed assets**) often represent the largest single category of assets of many organizations. Long-lived assets are those with a useful life extending greater than one year.

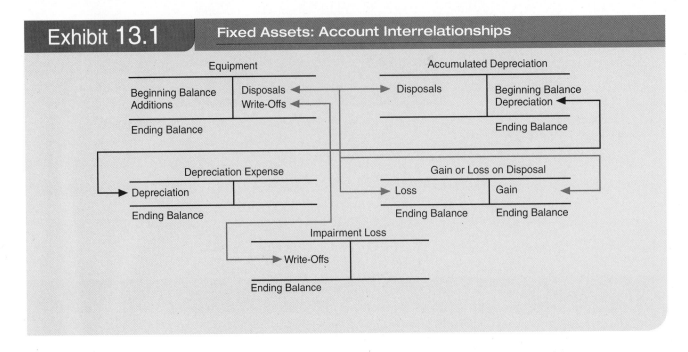

Exhibit 13.1   Fixed Assets: Account Interrelationships

Significant Accounts and Relevant Assertions in the Long-Lived Asset Cycle

LO 1

Identify the accounts and relevant assertions in the long-lived asset cycle.

An overview of the account relationships for long-lived assets is shown in Exhibit 13.1. The asset account (equipment, buildings, or similarly titled assets) represents the culmination of major capital additions and disposals. Unless this is a first-year audit, the beginning balance is established via results of the previous-year audit.

As indicated in Exhibit 13.1, the significant and relevant accounts typically include the long-lived asset, the related depreciation or impairment expense, any related gains caused by disposals, any related losses caused by disposals or impairments, and the accumulated depreciation account. The auditor will likely obtain for these accounts evidence related to each of the five financial statement assertions discussed in Chapter 7. However, for specific accounts and specific clients, some assertions are more relevant, and thus require more evidence, than other assertions. At many clients, the existence and valuation assertions related to the long-lived asset account may be judged the more relevant assertions. Those assertions determined to be more relevant are those for which the risk of misstatement is higher and for which more audit evidence is needed.

Performing the Integrated Audit of Long-Lived Assets and Related Expenses

LO 2

Describe the approach an auditor would take to perform an integrated audit in the long-lived asset cycle.

The audit starts with an analysis of risks to reliable financial reporting and includes an analysis of controls to address those risks. The substantive testing of the account balances focuses on material transactions affecting the account balance during the year: additions, disposals, and write-offs of existing assets and the recognition of periodic depreciation of the assets.

The relative strengths of the client's internal controls have a significant impact on the audit of fixed assets and related expenses. Weak control environments at

WorldCom and Waste Management (see the two *Auditing in Practice* features that follow) resulted in material misstatements in fixed assets and related expenses. The weaknesses in the control environments led to management override of existing controls and ultimately to the ability to commit large frauds.

How does an integrated audit of fixed assets differ from a more traditional audit? A traditional audit will focus on changes in the accounts during the year, including a significant effort directed at recalculating depreciation expense. In contrast, an integrated audit will focus on assessing the controls related to cycle-specific accounts. If the controls are effective, minimal direct testing of changes in account balances is needed.

Our discussion in this section follows the steps of the integrated audit approach introduced in Chapter 6. We have tailored this approach to the audit of long-lived assets as follows:

Phases I and II of the Audit Opinion Formulation Process

1. Continually update information on business risk, including the identification of any fraud risk factors noted during preliminary audit planning. Update audit planning for new risk information.
2. Analyze potential motivations to misstate long-lived asset and related expense accounts, as well as the existence of other fraud indicators, and determine the most likely method by which those accounts might be misstated.
3. Perform preliminary analytical procedures to determine if unexpected relationships exist in the accounts and document how the audit testing should be modified because of the unusual relationships.
4. Develop an understanding of the internal controls over long-lived assets and related expense accounts that are designed to address the risks identified in the three previous steps, including the applicability of entity-level controls to these accounts. This understanding will include a review of the client's documentation of internal controls.

Phases III and IV of the Audit Opinion Formulation Process

5. Determine the important controls that need to be tested for the purposes of (a) formulating an opinion on the entity's internal controls and (b) reducing substantive testing for the financial statement audit.
6. Develop a plan for testing internal controls and perform the tests of key controls in long-lived assets and related expense accounts. (For nonpublic companies, the auditor can choose to not test controls, but must determine where material misstatements could occur if controls are not present.)
7. Analyze the results of the tests of controls.

   If deficiencies are identified, assess those deficiencies to determine whether they are significant deficiencies or material weaknesses. Determine whether the preliminary control risk assessment should be modified (should control risk be assessed at a higher level?) and document the implications for substantive testing. Determine the impact of these deficiencies, and any revision in the control risk assessment, on planned substantive audit procedures by determining the types of misstatements that are most likely to occur.

   If no control deficiencies are identified, assess whether the preliminary control risk assessment is still appropriate, determine the extent that controls can provide evidence on the correctness of account balances, and then determine planned substantive audit procedures. The level of substantive testing in this situation will be less than what is likely required in circumstances where deficiencies in internal control were identified.
8. Perform planned substantive procedures (substantive analytical procedures and direct tests of account balances) based on the potential for misstatement and the information gathered about the effectiveness of internal controls.

The substantive procedures will include procedures to address fraud risks. In completing substantive procedures the auditor will continue to assess whether the evidence obtained from all sources is sufficient and appropriate and the auditor may need to adjust the audit plan (either tests of controls or substantive tests) to help ensure that sufficient and appropriate audit evidence is obtained.

PRACTICAL POINT

Companies very seldom classify operating leases as capital leases because (a) they wish to keep the liability off the books and (b) the recorded expense would be the same over the life of the lease.

LO 3

Identify risks to reliable financial reporting in the long-lived asset cycle and explain how management can manage earnings through fixed-asset accounts.

Consider the Risks Related to Long-Lived Assets (Steps 1 and 2)

Management can manage earnings in a variety of ways related to fixed-asset accounts, including:

- Changing estimated useful lives and residual values without reasonable justification
- Capitalizing costs that should be expensed, such as repairs and maintenance costs
- Improperly accounting for asset restructuring or acquisition
- Failing to properly perform asset impairment adjustments
- Accounting for capital leases as operating leases

The WorldCom fraud case is a classic example illustrating some of the risks relating to long-lived asset accounts (see the *Auditing in Practice* feature). One element of the fraud involved management reducing the accumulated depreciation account by debiting that account and crediting depreciation expense. These entries were performed on a regular basis and, unfortunately, the auditors did not view them as unusual or otherwise worthy of separate investigation. Management also misstated assets by routinely capitalizing a line expense (i.e., cash paid to other carriers when WorldCom used their lines to transmit calls). Finally, upon making new acquisitions, management boosted the value of the assets, but it established reserves for plant closings and related expenses. When the actual expenses were less, management debited the liability and credited the expense, thereby increasing net income in subsequent periods.

Unusual entries, particularly credits to depreciation expense or nonstandard adjusting entries, reflect risk and should attract special attention during the audit. Similarly, debit entries to accumulated depreciation should occur only when assets are retired. Finally, there should be independent valuation analysis of purchases related to acquisitions. Auditors with appropriate levels of professional skepticism will pay attention to high risk areas such as these.

Other risks associated with fixed assets and related expenses include the following:

- Incomplete recording of asset disposals
- Environmental liabilities or claims related to violations of safety and protection regulations, or violation of environmental regulations
- Obsolescence of assets
- Restructuring charges related to changes in the nature of the business
- Incorrect recording of assets, hidden by complex ownership structures designed to keep assets (and related liabilities) off the books
- Incorrect valuation of assets acquired as part of a group purchase, including assets acquired as part of an acquisition of another business
- Amortization schedules or depreciation schedules that do not reflect economic impairment or use of the asset
- Failure to properly recognize impairment in value

The auditor will normally become aware of these risks through review of:

- Industry trends, technological advances, and changes in the location of production facilities

AUDITING *in Practice*

WORLDCOM USES DEPRECIATION RESERVES TO MANAGE EARNINGS

WorldCom was one of the largest bankruptcies in U.S. history. From the first quarter of 1999 through the first quarter of 2002, WorldCom's management improperly released approximately $984 million in "depreciation reserves" to increase pretax earnings by decreasing depreciation expense or increasing miscellaneous income. The "depreciation reserves" were created in a variety of ways, including:

- The cost of equipment returned to vendors for credit after being placed in service was credited to the reserve (accumulated depreciation) rather than the asset itself.

- Following mergers with MCI and other companies, the reserve was used to house differences identified in the course of migrating the capital asset accounting systems of acquired companies onto WorldCom's SAP computer system. These differences were often the result of asset subledgers that were out of balance with related general ledger balances.

- Unsupported additions to an asset account were recorded with a corresponding increase in the reserve.

After the end of each fiscal quarter, management in General Accounting would direct Property Accounting personnel to release large balances from this reserve account (debit to the accumulated depreciation account), usually to reduce depreciation expense. If it was too late in the quarterly closing process to record depreciation expense as a standard adjusting entry, they were directed to prepare a draft journal entry so General Accounting could make the adjustment. WorldCom also inappropriately capitalized line expense (amounts paid to other carriers such as AT&T to use their lines) as fixed assets.

Source: *Report of Investigation* by the Special Investigative Committee of the Board of Directors of WorldCom, Inc., March 31, 2003.

- The business plan for major acquisitions or changes in the way the company conducts its business
- Major contracts regarding capital investments or joint ventures with other companies
- The minutes of board of directors meetings
- Company filings with the SEC describing company actions, risks, and strategies

Many new auditors just returning from an internship believe that the audit of fixed assets is primarily mechanical, for example, recalculating depreciation, tracing amounts to accumulated depreciation, and vouching fixed-asset additions. In some organizations, that may be the case. However, as with all other aspects of the audit, the auditor must understand the client's business strategy, current economic conditions, and potential changes in the economic value of the assets. Auditors can make serious mistakes if they act as if fixed assets are always a low-risk audit area.

Perform Preliminary Analytical Procedures for Possible Misstatements (Step 3)

Analyze Industry Trends and Changes in Product Lines

Even though determining the potential impairment of fixed assets is difficult, the accumulated knowledge of industry product trends, changes in client product lines, and technological changes will assist the auditor in making necessary judgments. An asset may be impaired if it does not generate as much cash flow in future years as it has in the past. A tour of the plant may provide hints that some assets are not fully utilized or are not utilized efficiently. Such observations might indicate a potential impairment in value. At other times, impairments are

LO 4

Describe how to use preliminary analytical procedures to identify possible misstatements in the accounts associated with long-lived assets.

more easily apparent. For example, Ford Motor Company announced plans in 2007 to reduce vehicle production by 20%, to significantly downsize, and to sell off its Jaguar, Aston Martin, Land Rover, and Volvo brands. This restructuring required Ford and its auditors to carefully identify which assets would be discontinued and should receive a write-down to their impaired value.

Analyze Depreciation for Consistency and Economic Activity

We have repeatedly made the point that the auditor must know the business and the economics of the business. Consider a simple example. A local company is in the business of picking up and hauling garbage. Shouldn't the auditors have a fairly good idea of approximately how long the trucks will last? They know the mileage; they know the beating the trucks take every day; they know something about the company's policy for cleaning and repairing the trucks. What if management comes in and makes a decision to extend the depreciable life from five to twelve years when the rest of the industry is at about six years? Does this make sense? See the *Auditing in Practice* discussion of Waste Management, which illustrates the type of fraud that can be committed when auditors are not prepared to review the economics of such decisions. Although the auditor cannot always make a decision as to whether five years is better than six, the auditor needs to be in an position to understand that five years is much closer to economic reality than twelve years.

There are at least four relatively simple techniques that auditors can use to supplement their overall business understanding of the client:

- Review and analyze gains/losses on disposals of equipment (gains indicate depreciation lives are too short, losses indicate the opposite).
- Tour the plant and note the amount of idle equipment.
- Perform an overall estimate of depreciation expense.
- Compare depreciable lives used by the client for various asset categories with that of the industry. Large differences may indicate earnings management.

The auditor can use spreadsheets to develop estimates of depreciation based on costs of assets, estimated lives, and salvage value. Assuming the auditor agrees with the client's estimate of useful life and salvage value, the depreciation estimate can be compared with recorded depreciation as a starting point to determine if additional work is needed.

AUDITING *in Practice*

WASTE MANAGEMENT AND ARTHUR ANDERSEN

Waste Management, Inc., is the nation's largest waste disposal company. The company grew though extensive acquisitions—seemingly all dependent on ever-increasing sales and net income that fueled higher stock prices. Waste Management's previous management recognized the importance of stock prices to pay for more acquisitions, but the company was losing its profitability. Management struck on a new way to increase reported net income—simply increase the estimated lives of all the depreciable assets. The auditors never questioned the change even though the change accounted for virtually all of Waste Management's increase in earnings over a period of years. Finally, the SEC stepped in and said these lives simply are not realistic. Prior to Enron, this was the largest suit that had been filed against Arthur Andersen. Waste Management had misstated earnings by a whopping $3.5 billion. Arthur Andersen paid fines of $220 million and the SEC fined the individual auditors on the engagement. More importantly, Arthur Andersen agreed not to participate in similar actions in the future. This became important as it was at the heart of the government's case against Arthur Andersen in the Enron case, which ultimately led to the firm's downfall.

AUDITING *in Practice*

IN HINDSIGHT, HOW COULD THESE FRAUDS HAVE BEEN DETECTED?

Consider the COSO research findings discussed in the *Professional Judgment in Context* feature whereby fixed assets were often found to be fraudulently overstated. The methods of overstatement included:

- Fictitious assets on the books (WorldCom)
- Improper and incomplete depreciation (Waste Management)
- Failure to record impairment of assets, especially goodwill (Sun Microsystems)
- Expired or worthless assets left on a company's books (Milacron)
- Assets overvalued upon acquisition, especially in the purchase of a company (WorldCom)

How might the auditors have detected these problems? To detect fictitious assets, the auditor should have traced recent acquisitions to the fixed-asset accounts and to original source documents; doing so would have enabled the auditor to realize that such documents did not exist. For improper depreciation, the auditor should have compared depreciation expense over a period of time, adjusted for the volume of business and the number of trucks used. The decrease in depreciation per truck should have led to more detailed investigation, including tests of depreciation on each truck. For the impairment issue, the auditor should have compared current earnings with future expected earnings that were predicted when the goodwill was initially recorded. A dramatic decrease in current earnings signals the need for an impairment adjustment. For the expired assets, the auditor should have noted (a) the relative age of the assets (net book value has decreased), (b) idle equipment during a tour of the factory, and (c) should have traced apparently idle assets to the books. For the assets overvalued at acquisition, the auditor should have determined if the company had used a reputable and certified independent appraiser. If the auditor had doubts, he or she should have hired an appraiser to form an independent opinion.

Linking Internal Controls and Financial Statement Assertions for Long-Lived Assets and Related Expenses (Steps 4 and 5)

The auditor will gain an understanding of the controls that the client has implemented to address the risks associated with misstatements in the long-lived assets, and related accounts. As part of this understanding, the auditor will focus on the relevant assertions for each account and identify the controls that relate to risks for each relevant assertion. In an integrated audit, or in a nonintegrated audit where the auditor wants to reduce substantive testing, this understanding will be used to identify important controls that need to be tested.

Controls for Tangible Assets

To help assure that the existence and valuation assertions for fixed assets are materially correct, controls should be in place to:

- Identify existing assets, inventory them, and reconcile the physical asset inventory with the property ledger on a periodic basis (existence).
- Assure that all purchases, including acquisitions of other companies, are authorized and properly valued (valuation).
- Appropriately classify new equipment according to its expected use and estimates of useful life (valuation).
- Periodically reassess the appropriateness of depreciation categories (valuation).
- Identify obsolete or scrapped equipment and write the equipment down to scrap value (valuation).
- Periodically review management strategy and systematically assess the impairment of assets (valuation).

LO 5

Describe why it is important for the auditor to develop an understanding of internal controls, identify controls typically present in the long-lived asset cycle, and identify tests of controls used to test the effectiveness of controls over fixed assets.

PRACTICAL POINT

Company plans change; economic conditions change. These changes affect the value of the company's assets and should lead to periodic assessments of asset impairments. For example, Ford recognized a pretax impairment charge of $650 million on its investment in Volvo in the first quarter of 2009.

As additional examples, clients should have controls in place to safeguard the assets and to prevent unauthorized journal entries to the account balances.

If the client's controls related to long-lived assets are effective, then the auditor can rely more extensively on substantive analytical procedures to obtain evidence on account balances. For example, substantive analytical procedures can be used to estimate depreciation expense and accumulated depreciation. The auditor can use a property ledger, which should uniquely identify each asset and provide details on cost of the property, acquisition date, depreciation method used for both book and tax, estimated life, estimated scrap value (if any), and accumulated depreciation to date, to develop these estimates.

Controls for Intangible Assets

For intangible assets, controls should be designed to:

- Assure that decisions are appropriately made as to when to capitalize or expense research and development expenditures (presentation and disclosure).
- Develop amortization schedules that reflect the remaining useful life of patents or copyrights associated with the asset (valuation), where applicable.
- Identify and account for intangible-asset impairments (valuation).

Management should have a monitoring process in place to review valuation of intangible assets. For example, a pharmaceutical company should have fairly sophisticated models to predict the success of newly developed drugs and monitor actual performance against expected performance to determine whether a drug is likely to achieve expected revenue and profit goals. Similarly, a software company should have controls in place to determine whether capitalized software development costs will be realized. The auditor should assess both the existence and effectiveness of these controls in determining which substantive tests of account balances need to be performed.

Design and Perform Tests of Controls and Analyze Results of Tests of Controls (Steps 6 and 7)

The auditor of a public company will need to test the controls over fixed assets as part of the integrated audit. Many of the tests can be used to substantiate the changes in account balances during the year, such as by reviewing the controls over purchases to establish that new purchases have been recorded correctly and have been classified properly for depreciation. The auditor may also test the depreciation process and the controls surrounding that process. However, as clearly indicated in the WorldCom and Waste Management cases, the auditor must be alert to negative indications in the control environment and examine all important adjusting entries to the accounts at year end.

Typical tests of controls include inquiry of relevant personnel, observation of the control being performed, examination of documentation corroborating that the control has been performed, and reperformance of the control by the individual testing the control. The following example illustrates a combination of approaches. The Government Accountability Office (GAO) performed an audit at NASA to determine whether NASA had sufficient controls to provide reasonable assurance that assets are protected from loss, theft, and misuse. The GAO found that controls were missing, inconsistently applied, and did not receive the attention needed by qualified personnel. The GAO then recommended that NASA implement a policy requiring the establishment and enforcement of property management training for all personnel involved in the use, stewardship, and management of equipment. Once installed, the

GAO plans to test whether the policy is working. The control (the policy and its implementation) could be tested in a variety of ways, including:

- *Inquiry:* Select a sample of personnel required to complete such training, talk with them about whether they have completed the training and the nature of that training.
- *Observation:* Observe a training session in process, speak to personnel about the training, or observe property management actions in process.
- *Inspection of Training Materials:* Review the training materials and, for a sample of personnel, review documentation showing completion of the training.
- *Inspection of Personnel Actions:* The auditor could select a sample of assets to determine that the protection and use of the assets have improved, i.e., a test to see whether the training resulted in changes in protection of the assets.

The auditor uses professional judgment to determine the appropriate types of tests of controls to perform. However, inquiry alone is generally not sufficient evidence and would typically be supplemented with observation, inspection, and/or reperformance of procedures. If the auditor finds that internal controls are effective, then substantive procedures might be limited to analytical procedures. If the account is such that analytical procedures, by themselves, would not provide evidence to support the accuracy of the account balance, then the auditor will need to perform tests of details. In addition, if the controls are found to be ineffective, the auditor will need to perform more direct tests of the account balances rather than heavily relying on substantive analytical procedures.

> **PRACTICAL POINT**
>
> The choice of substantive procedures depends on (a) the risks associated with the account, (b) materiality of the account, (c) economic and company-specific changes, and (d) control risk. The auditor integrates information from all of the sources to plan the approach to gathering sufficient appropriate audit evidence.

Perform Substantive Testing of the Long-Lived Assets and Related Accounts (Step 8)

We now focus on the basic substantive audit procedures for this transaction cycle and how they are affected by the auditor's assessment of the client's internal controls. Exhibit 13.2 shows a comprehensive audit program for the audit of equipment. In addition to providing evidence concerning the fairness of the account balance, the audit program is designed to gather information that will assist in auditing tax depreciation and the deferred tax liability, because much of the tax difference is due to timing differences associated with depreciation methods.

The scope and extent of testing shown in Exhibit 13.2 will vary with the complexity of assets used, the difficulty in estimating useful life, and the risk associated with the client. In some cases, there will be detailed recomputations. In every instance, the auditor must ask, Do the accounting numbers reflect the economic use of the assets and the business plan being executed by the company?

> **LO 6**
>
> Describe the substantive audit procedures that should be used to test long-lived assets and related accounts.

AUDITING *in Practice*

IMPROVEMENTS IN A CLIENT'S INTERNAL CONTROLS

Consider the NASA example that we began discussing earlier. The GAO concluded that the problems detected at NASA were associated with a lack of specification and implementation of a number of controls to safeguard assets that are part of our national security. NASA did not effectively train staff involved in the equipment inventory process, thereby resulting in various inaccuracies and capitalization misstatements. Responding to these control weaknesses, NASA used the GAO's report to make significant improvements in their operations—leading not only to added security, but to improved operations because of the increased knowledge of equipment on hand.

These control improvements at NASA highlight an important point about the auditor's role: The auditor not only finds errors but also alerts responsive clients to their presence in an effort to help the client improve the overall control environment. Thus, the joint work of the auditor and client leads to both (a) more efficient operations, and (b) improved financial reporting.

Exhibit 13.2   Audit Program: Manufacturing Equipment

Audit Procedures	Done by	W/P Refer.

Overall Concerns

1. Review client accounting manuals to determine the existence of unique accounting issues associated with the client's industry. _____ _____

2. If a first-year audit, make arrangements to review the working papers of the predecessor auditor to verify the beginning account balances. _____ _____

3. Review procedures used by the organization to requisition and approve fixed-asset purchases. Determine whether major capital projects are reviewed by a capital budgeting committee and approved by the board of directors. _____ _____

4. Make inquiries of the client as to major differences between book and tax depreciation. Determine that the client has a system to identify and support timing differences that will become a part of the deferred tax liability. _____ _____

5. Determine if the company has a process in place to, at least annually, examine the potential impairment of assets. _____ _____

Existence

6. Inquire of management about the existence of significant additions or disposals of property, plant, or equipment during the year. _____ _____

7. Request the client to prepare a list of fixed-asset additions and disposals for the year. Foot the schedule and trace selected items to entries in the property ledger. _____ _____

8. Trace the beginning balance per the schedule to prior-year working papers ending balance. _____ _____

9. Inquire of management about the existence of significant new leases or the conversion of leases into purchases during the year. Determine management's approach to capitalizing leases and the appropriateness of the accounting used by management. _____ _____

10. Tour the client's major manufacturing facilities, noting the following:
    - Addition of significant new product lines or equipment
    - Disposal of significant product lines or equipment
    - Equipment that has been discarded, is damaged, or is idle _____ _____

11. Inquire about methods used by the client to identify and assess the impairment of assets. Review the data gathered by management to test for impairment and determine if the data and the approach are reasonable. _____ _____

12. Inquire of management about methods used to physically observe and count equipment on a periodic basis, and reconcile with the PPE ledger. _____ _____

Completeness

13. Select a representative sample of larger acquisitions and examine receiving reports or physically observe the asset. Determine that all items have been recorded in the correct time period (see step 17). _____ _____

14. Review repair and maintenance expense, as well as the Lease Expense account, to determine whether some items should have been capitalized. _____ _____

Rights and Obligations

15. Inquire whether assets have been pledged as collateral, or whether obligations have been assumed in connection with purchases. _____ _____

Valuation

16. For assets identified earlier that no longer have economic value, determine that they have properly been written down to their impaired value. _____ _____

17. Select a sample of additions over $_____ or a MUS sample and examine invoices, construction billings, work orders, etc., to determine that the assets have been valued at cost and are recorded in the proper account. Determine that all trade-ins have been properly valued, and that tax liabilities associated with the trade-in have been properly recognized. _____ _____

18. Select a sample of asset disposals, recompute the gain or loss (and tax obligations) on the disposal, and trace the gain or loss to the appropriate income or expense account. _____ _____

19. Inquire about changes in the estimated useful life of assets. Determine whether changes are recognized in accordance with GAAP. Determine that all new equipment has been properly classified as to its useful life. _____ _____

(Continues)

Exhibit 13.2 Audit Program: Manufacturing Equipment (*continued*)

Audit Procedures	Done by	W/P Refer.

20. Review management's process to measure impaired assets, or to classify property as discontinued operations. Test management's estimate of impaired value through reference to economic plans, evidence of fair market value, estimated cash flow, and so forth. _____ _____

21. Review the accounts for self-constructed assets. Ask the client to develop a schedule of capitalized costs. Determine the methods used to identify the costs, and examine supporting documents for selected entries. _____ _____

22. For new equipment additions, examine the client's determination of economic life and residual value. Evaluate the choices by (a) comparing the choice with previous estimates of economic life and whether those estimates were accurate; (b) developing an understanding of technological changes in the assets and whether the changes will increase or decrease expected life; and (c) comparing the choices with companies in similar industries—either in our audit files or available in public reports. _____ _____

23. Review all non-recurring journal entries (depreciation expense should be the only recurring entry) to both the equipment account and to the accumulated depreciation account. For all material journal entries, trace back to the underlying support for the entry to determine whether the entry is correct. Use generalized audit software to summarize all journal entries affecting the property accounts and associated depreciation. _____ _____

24. If the company has multiple sites for its equipment, or if the company has multiple sites in which the accounting is done, analyze the potential risk and determine whether we should visit additional sites to physically observe the existence of the assets (on high-risk companies). _____ _____

Overall Audit and Economic Review

25. Evaluate the audit analysis of fixed assets to ensure we have gained satisfaction as to the following:
    · The assets reflect the economic life and intended business use for the assets.
    · The depreciation method approximates the actual usage of the assets.
    · The assets deployed are consistent with management's business plan.
    · The assets are used efficiently and there is no further impairment that should be recognized.
    · We fully understand all of the significant accounting entries made to the asset and asset-related accounts during the year. _____ _____

26. Document our understanding of the above factors (number 25) in a memo. _____ _____

Depreciation and Accumulated Depreciation (Valuation)

27. Review the client's depreciation policy and:
    a. Determine whether the approach is consistent with the type of equipment purchased. _____ _____
    b. Determine whether there is a need to revise depreciation policies based on technological changes or the client's experience with similar assets. _____ _____
    c. Determine whether the depreciation approach has been used consistently. _____ _____
    d. Select a few additions and recalculate first-year depreciation according to the proper classification of the property. _____ _____

28. Prepare an estimate of depreciation expense by updating the depreciation worksheet for additions and disposals during the year. _____ _____

29. Develop a schedule of timing differences between tax depreciation and book depreciation. Take the schedule forward to use in determining changes in the deferred tax liability and in tax expense for the year. _____ _____

Presentation and Disclosure

30. Review classification of property accounts and determine that all items are actively used in producing goods or services. _____ _____

31. Review note disclosure to determine that depreciation methods and capitalization methods are adequately disclosed. _____ _____

32. Document management's representations concerning the existence and valuation of the assets in the management representation letter. _____ _____

Tests of Property Additions and Disposals

If the beginning balance is established through previous audit work, the test of property accounts can be limited to selected tests of property additions and disposals during the year.

Additions   The auditor can usually test existence, rights, and valuation by the same procedures. The following procedures are designed to determine that all fixed-asset additions have been properly:

- *Authorized*—by examining purchase agreements, board of directors minutes for major acquisitions, and approval by a capital budgeting committee.
- *Classified Correctly*—based on their function, expected useful life, and established depreciation schedule.
- *Valued Appropriately*—by examining purchase documents such as invoices or construction billings.

This work can easily be performed in conjunction with the internal control work as part of the integrated audit. An efficient approach is to examine a schedule of additions (usually prepared by the client). After the schedule is agreed to the general ledger, the auditor should select a few items in order to test the related controls and vouch the items to vendor invoices and other supporting documentation.

Exhibit 13.3 presents an example of typical audit documentation testing fixed-asset additions. Even though the total fixed-asset account balance may be large, the audit work can be done efficiently by concentrating on the additions and then adjusting the estimates of depreciation expense and accumulated depreciation for changes made during the year.

Inspection of Assets   Normally, the auditor will not visually inspect every addition. However, in the case of large additions—e.g., the construction of a new plant or the acquisition of new facilities—or where there are material weaknesses in the control environment or control activities, the auditor will want to physically verify that the asset exists. The risk of misstatement is often higher in remote locations where the auditor does not normally visit. If those sites show large additions of fixed assets and there are deficiencies in controls, the auditor should adjust the audit program to make sure such sites are visited. If there are other high-risk situations, e.g., assets that are difficult to observe or characteristics of assets are hard to recognize, the auditor may want to verify the existence of contracts with bona fide contractors and, on a selected basis, accompany personnel to sites to observe the processes they have in place to monitor the installation of the assets.

For many manufacturing companies, these tests are supplemented by a tour of the factory to observe the general layout and condition of equipment, as well as the existence of idle equipment. The auditor uses knowledge of the client's strategic plans and industry changes to determine whether additional work should be performed to evaluate whether some assets should be written down to their net realizable value.

Misclassifying Expenses as Assets   WorldCom overstated earnings by capitalizing the costs it paid to other carriers for using their lines on individual calls. The entry was very simple, although WorldCom tried to hide the entry by making many sub-entries across different subsidiaries. The entry was as simple as:

Fixed Assets	$xxx,xxx
Line Expense	$xxx,xxx

The auditor needs to summarize all journal entries to fixed-asset additions from any source other than a purchase of an asset and then gather independent

---

PRACTICAL POINT

Unlike publicly traded companies, nonpublic small businesses may be motivated to *minimize profits* in order to minimize taxes paid. In contrast to the examples given, those companies may wish to expense capital equipment rather than to capitalize the equipment.

Exhibit 13.3   Fixed-Asset Audit Documentation—Equipment, December 31, 2011

PBC
Work Performed by _____ AMt _____
Date _1/28/2012_

Description	Date Purchased	COST				ACCUMULATED DEPRECIATION			
		Beginning Balance	Additions	Disposals	Ending Balance	Beginning Balance	Depreciation Expense	Disposals	Ending Balance
Beginning balance	Various	124,350			124,350	33,429	12,435*		45,864
Additions:									
40′ lathe	10/30/11	–0–	9,852†		9,852	–0–	1,250‡		1,250
1040 press	3/25/11	–0–	18,956†		18,956	–0–	1,895‡		1,895
60′ lathe	5/29/11	–0–	13,903†		13,903	–0–	950‡		950
Disposals:									
Fork lift	6/2/08			7,881§	(7,881)			3,753	(3,753)
Computer	7/2/09			3,300§	(3,300)			2,625	(2,625)
Totals		124,350@	42,711**	11,181**	155,880**††	33,429@	16,530**	6,378**	43,581***††

* Estimated from last year; includes one-half year depreciation for assets disposed of during the year. See Working Paper PPE-4 for calculation of the estimate.
† Examined invoice or other supporting document, noting cost and appropriate categorization for depreciation purposes.
‡ Recalculated, noting that depreciation is in accordance with company policy and asset classification estimated economic life.
§ Traced to asset ledger and verified that equipment had been removed. Examined sales document or scrap disposal document for the disposal of the asset.
@ Traced to December 31, 2010, audit documentation.
** Footed/cross footed.
†† Traced to trial balance.

AUDITING *in Practice*

TESTING ADDITIONS AT WORLDCOM

The SEC issued an Accounting and Auditing Enforcement Release (AAER) concerning improper professional conduct by an audit partner of Arthur Andersen LLP in connection with the audit of the financial statements of WorldCom, Inc. ("WorldCom") for its fiscal year ended December 31, 2001. The AAER lists numerous audit failures in the audit of the plant, property, and equipment (PP&E) accounts at WorldCom. Several of those audit failures related to the testing of additions to the PP&E accounts. For example, the audit team had identified WorldCom as a high-risk client and had classified PP&E as a critical process. The audit team should have been skeptical and adjusted its audit procedures to properly address the heightened risks, but did not do so appropriately.

For example, WorldCom tracked the acquisition, disposition, and transfer of its assets on the PP&E Rollforward Schedule ("Rollforward") each quarter in connection with its quarterly reviews and audit testing. WorldCom's third quarter Rollforward, as of September 30, 2001, was provided to the audit team. The Rollforward showed total additions that included improper entries made by management (part of the fraud). The audit team examined the document, but it did not perform any procedures to verify that property additions on the

sheet were a reflection of assets acquired, were properly valued, or corresponded to the total property additions reflected in WorldCom's balance sheet.

Further, the audit team did not conduct any substantive testing of the PP&E accounts following its testing of an incomplete subset of total PP&E additions as of the end of WorldCom's third quarter. WorldCom subsequently added $841 million in improperly capitalized line costs to its PP&E in the fourth quarter of 2001. The fraudulent additions amounted to nearly half of the total PP&E additions in that quarter. As a result of Andersen's failure to conduct further testing of PP&E balances as of year end, or to examine PP&E activity as of the balance sheet date subsequent to its interim testing, these additional improper and fraudulent additions to PP&E were not subject to auditing. *This is a classic example of a situation in which a lack of professional skepticism on the part of the external auditor contributed to an important audit failure and enabled management to continue to perpetrate their fraud.*

Source: SEC, Accounting and Auditing Enforcement Release No. 2809/ April 14, 2008.

evidence to verify the validity of the entries. Such an approach, coupled with proper skepticism, would have detected one of the major frauds of the 2000 decade.

Companies often have to make judgments as to whether a particular expenditure should be capitalized or expensed as a repair. Most companies have policies, usually based on materiality and the cost of bookkeeping, as to whether expenditures under a certain amount are expenses—even if they appear to be of a capital nature. Usually, the auditor starts by determining if such a policy is reasonable. There are a couple of risks associated with such a policy:

- Some members of management may schedule purchases below the amount to stay under capital budget, such as breaking up a larger purchase into smaller units
- Management might not comply with the policy because they wish to manipulate reported earnings, e.g., decrease reported earnings in a good period, and vice versa in a poor period.

If the auditor perceives that such risks are applicable to a particular client, the auditor will adjust the procedures, usually by requesting that the client prepare a schedule of both fixed-asset additions and repair and maintenance expense transactions. Selected transactions from both schedules can be vouched to vendor invoices, work orders, or other supporting evidence to determine their proper classification.

Disposals and Fully Depreciated Equipment   Many organizations do not have the same level of controls over asset disposals or idle assets as they have for asset acquisitions. For example, the disposal of scrapped equipment might not be

---

PRACTICAL POINT

For clients where the inherent risk is low and internal controls are effective, it may be efficient to perform substantive procedures at an interim date. However, it is critical that the auditor perform appropriate roll-forward procedures for the period from the interim date to the year end.

recorded. Therefore, auditors often use special procedures to determine whether disposals of equipment have been recorded properly. One approach is to use generalized audit software to prepare a printout of fully depreciated (or nearly fully depreciated) equipment and then attempt to locate it. Alternatively, trade-ins noted during the audit of property additions can be traced to the removal of the old equipment from the books. Inquiries can be made of client personnel about any assets that have been removed. Alternatively, the auditor can trace a sample of property to the physical assets to determine their existence.

Decommissioning Costs   Some assets, most notably atomic power plants, must be decommissioned upon completion of their life. The company should be accruing a liability for the decommissioning cost as the asset is being used so that, upon its retirement, the liability represents the present value associated with the decommissioning process. The decommissioning expense should be recognized over the life of the asset.

The following excerpt from Entergy's 2009 Annual Report is an example of the types of disclosures that companies with decommissioning costs make:

> In the fourth quarter 2009, Entergy Gulf States Louisiana recorded a revision to its estimated decommissioning cost liabilities for River Bend as a result of a revised decommissioning cost study. The revised estimate resulted in a $78.7 million increase in its decommissioning liability, along with a corresponding increase in the related asset retirement obligation asset that will be depreciated over the remaining life of the units.

Similar to decommissioning costs, many natural resource companies have an obligation to restore the environment to a condition that existed prior to mining, or other extractive approaches used by the company. Usually, the estimated cost associated with the reclamation of the property is expensed annually and accrued as a liability as the minerals are extracted from the land.

It is important to note that changes in the decommissioning cost liability can dramatically increase or decrease net income and that the estimation of the liability is subject to judgment on the part of management. As such, Entergy's auditors spend a fairly significant amount of time auditing management's estimate of the decommissioning costs liability each period.

Asset Impairment Substantive Procedures

In most cases, long-lived assets are used over their expected physical life; or, if there is significant technological change, the asset lives may be revised to reflect a shorter expected economic life. In some cases, however, management may believe that a whole class of assets is overvalued, but the company does not wish to dispose of the assets. Financial accounting standards require the write-down of fixed assets that are permanently impaired. Further, accounting standards require that goodwill be tested for impairment each year rather than amortizing goodwill over a period of time. Finally, the IASB allows companies to adjust their fixed assets to current replacement cost each year—either up or down, whereas the U.S. standards allow only for downward adjustments in the value of the assets. The nature of making these estimates, as well as the need for valuation specialists or experts, make the audits of impairments difficult. Further, there are certain complexities regarding **asset impairment** that add to the auditor's difficulties:

1. Normally, management is not interested in identifying and writing down assets.
2. Sometimes, management wants to write down every potentially impaired asset to a minimum realizable value (although a one-time hit to current earnings, it will lead to higher reported earnings in the future).
3. Determining asset impairment, especially for intangible assets such as goodwill, requires a good information system, a systematic process, good controls, and professional judgment.

AUDITING *in Practice*

PCAOB OBSERVATIONS

In October 2007, the PCAOB issued a report providing observations identified in the course of its 2004, 2005, and 2006 inspections of registered public accounting firms that audit no more than 100 issuers (i.e., smaller audit firms). The following excerpt from that report highlights audit deficiencies related to the valuation of long-term assets. These are areas that auditors need to pay close attention to when auditing the valuation of long-term assets.

- Inspection teams observed instances where firms' procedures to test and conclude on the valuation of goodwill and other long-lived assets (both tangible and intangible) were inadequate.

- The inspectors observed instances where firms had not challenged managements' assertions that asset values were not impaired, despite evidence of impairment indicators, such as recurring losses and declining revenue prospects.

- Inspection teams also observed instances where firms had not tested the reasonableness of managements' significant assumptions and underlying data used to assess the recoverability of assets.

- In other instances, issuers calculated impairment charges, but the firms failed to test the rationale for the charges and the analyses supporting the values of the assets.

LO 7

Describe the substantive audit procedures that should be used to test for the impairment of long-lived assets.

The auditor must assess management's approach to identifying impaired assets and writing them down to their current economic value. Thus, in order to make estimates of impaired assets, the auditor needs an up-to-date knowledge of changes taking place in the client's industry as well as a thorough understanding of management's strategies and plans. The auditor should look for management controls in this area including:

- A systematic process to identify assets that are not currently in use
- Projections of future cash flows, by reporting unit, that is based on management's strategic plans and economic conditions
- Systematic development of current market values of similar assets prepared by the client,
- Consideration of current market value of the company's stock (often used as part of a goodwill impairment test)

PRACTICAL POINT

Certain events may lead the auditor and management to consider that an asset is impaired. Ford Motor Company notes that the following events trigger them to consider impairments: material adverse changes in projected revenues and expenses, significant underperformance relative to historical and projected future operating results, and significant negative industry or economic trends.

Unfortunately, many companies that have excellent controls over transaction processing do not have the same level of control over periodic assessments of impairment. Thus, a major audit task is to develop a systematic approach to continuously review the overall composition of an entity's asset base in light of current and planned production and technological and competitive developments in the client's industry. The financial reporting objective is to value assets at their economic benefit to the organization and, when that value has been impaired, to write down the assets when there is a permanent decline in economic benefit of the asset.

If there is evidence that an asset has been impaired, the auditor needs to address the valuation issue. The FASB has developed the general concept of valuing impaired assets using two major approaches:

1. Estimate the future economic benefits to be derived from the asset.
2. Obtain an independent assessment of the value of the asset.

The first approach is most often used with assets such as goodwill but could be used for fixed assets such as electric power plants or other assets where the company had developed a capital budget plan to justify the purchase or development of the asset. In this case, a recoverability test determines if the net future cash flows from the asset exceed the carrying value of the asset. If they do, the FASB has determined there is no impairment for accounting purposes. On the other hand, if the undiscounted future cash flows do not exceed the carrying value, the company has an impairment. The expected cash inflows may be less than the carrying value because of competitor actions or a change in the regulatory environment. If there is a change in the estimate of cash flows, the new cash flows should be discounted back to the net present value using the current risk-free interest rate. The value would be compared to the carrying cost of the asset to determine the amount of the impairment to be recognized.

The second approach, often used for equipment, is to look at replacement cost as a measure of asset impairment. In this case, the auditor will do the following:

1. Obtain current market values, where applicable, or if not applicable, obtain an independent appraisal from a reputable, independent, and qualified appraisal firm.
2. Review current transactions to determine if there has been a decrease in purchase price.

If the auditor uses market value for the estimate, it is important that the information comes from a market that is orderly and is liquid.

Risks Associated with Discontinued Operations

Periodically, management decides to discontinue a particular line of operations by shutting down and dismantling production or, more likely, by announcing it will sell the line of business to another company. The accounting treatment for **discontinued operations** continues to evolve, but when a decision is made to discontinue, the company should write down the net assets (including an estimate for liabilities associated with a line of business, if applicable) to a best estimate of net realizable value. In assessing the fair market value, management will normally:

- Request an estimate of value from an investment banker and examine the assumptions and methodology used in making the estimate.
- Examine assumptions made about future net cash flows from the operations and discount them to the current time to develop an independent estimate of value.

The assets will be written down only if the company expects a loss on their disposal. The company will not anticipate and record a gain. Further, the company is not allowed to book an impairment of the assets' expected future operating losses from operating the line of business between the current time and the sale time. The nature of the discontinuance decision and the amount of write-down should be fully disclosed in a note to the financial statements. The auditor needs to determine that management's approach is thorough and the evidence is objective.

Substantive Procedures Related to Depreciation Expense and Accumulated Depreciation

The specific procedures used by the auditor to test depreciation of fixed assets depend on the internal controls and the risk associated with the engagement and the account balances. Recall, risk is increased when a company takes a very convoluted approach to a simple accounting issue, as in the case of WorldCom.

Low Risk: Perform Substantive Analytical Procedures In most situations, the auditor is able to test the controls over depreciation as part of the integrated audit and may determine that the only additional audit procedure to be performed is a substantive analytical analysis to determine that depreciation expense recorded by the client is consistent with the expectations developed by the auditor. Many audit firms use a spreadsheet to estimate changes in depreciation expense. The current estimate of depreciation on assets continuing

PRACTICAL POINT

An auditor must gather corroborating evidence of asset impairment. The first step is a recoverability test. If the asset passes the recoverability test, there is no impairment.

PRACTICAL POINT

Auditors are normally concerned that clients do not write down impaired assets. However, there is evidence that some companies have written off properly valued assets in years of good earnings to help smooth earnings. Accounting should be neutral and based on convincing evidence of asset impairment.

PRACTICAL POINT

The impact of discontinued operations on reported earnings can be significant and should warrant a great deal of auditor attention. As an example, in July 2008, Scholastic Inc. reported earnings per diluted share from continuing operations of $2.82 for the 2008 fiscal year, compared with a $0.57 net loss for the year when it included discontinued operations in its calculation.

in the business is calculated and then modified for assets added or disposed of during the year.

The analytical procedures should incorporate a number of ratios and an overall test of reasonableness to help determine the reasonableness of current charges to the accounts. The ratios might include the following:

- Current depreciation expense as a percentage of the previous-year depreciation expense.
- Fixed assets (by class) as a percentage of previous-year assets—the relative increase in this percentage can be compared with the relative increase in depreciation as a test of overall reasonableness.
- Depreciation expense (by asset class) as a percentage of assets each year—this ratio can indicate changes in the age of equipment or in depreciation policy.
- Accumulated depreciation (by class) as a percentage of gross assets each year—this ratio provides information on the overall reasonableness of the account and may indicate problems of accounting for fully depreciated equipment.
- Average age of assets (by class)—this ratio provides additional insight on the age of assets and may be useful in modifying depreciation estimates.

If the corroborating factors do not support the auditor's estimation, detailed testing should be performed on various fixed-asset classifications.

PRACTICAL POINT

If an error is found in substantive testing, the auditor needs to carefully consider whether the root cause of the problem is indicative of deficiencies in internal control. This consideration may have implications for the audit opinion on internal control effectiveness and for the design of substantive procedures for the financial statement audit.

High Risk: Test the Details   In situations where controls are not sufficient, or when there is high risk associated with the client, the auditor will need to perform detailed tests of depreciation by starting with the fixed-asset ledger, which contains a list of all the assets, their estimated useful life, salvage value, and depreciation method. Because the company is considered high risk, the auditor should use audit software to foot the ledger and agree it to the general ledger and then, taking a sample of items contained in the detailed property ledger, recalculate depreciation for the items chosen. The sampling procedure should be based on the same criteria introduced previously; that is, the auditor considers materiality and risk and takes a sample based on recorded depreciation (rather than asset value). Differences should be projected to the population as a whole. If there are significant differences, the auditor should investigate to determine the "root cause" of the problem and have the client fix the problem. Finally, the auditor should use software to identify all entries into the depreciation and accumulated depreciation accounts that come from other than the normal depreciation entries and asset disposals.

Evaluating Changes   The auditor should make sure that the depreciation methods used are consistent with the prior year unless the client has reasonable justification for changing methods. The notes to the financial statements should be carefully read to be sure all relevant information is disclosed.

Fraud-Related Substantive Procedures for Long-Lived Assets and Related Accounts

In those audits where there is a heightened risk of fraud related to plant, property, and equipment assets, the auditor will want to consider a number of alternative procedures. First, the auditor needs to determine how a fraud might be perpetrated and what accounts might be affected. Second, the auditor needs to understand what controls are not present, or what currently existing controls could be overridden. Finally, the auditor might want to perform analytical procedures to determine (by comparison with previous years, as well as comparison with companies in the industry) if there is an indication of material misstatement. In addition to the above, the auditor should expand planned audit activities and consider:

- Confirming the terms of significant property additions with the selling party.

AUDITING *in Practice*

FIRST-TIME AUDITS

On the first-time audit of a new client, the auditor may not have the advantage of audited opening balances for the fixed-asset accounts. If the client has been audited before, the predecessor auditor should be contacted to determine whether evidence can be gained from the prior audits as to beginning balances. If the auditor cannot use the predecessor auditor's documentation, or if it is the first audit for the client, a statistical sample should be taken to observe existence and to review original invoices to verify cost and ownership. Depreciation expense and accumulated depreciation should also be recalculated. If the client's records are not adequate, the client may have to take a complete fixed-asset physical inventory.

- Accepting only original documents as support of additions (e.g., invoices, purchase orders, receiving reports).
- Examining supporting documentation for significant or unusual reconciling items that are identified in reconciliation of detailed records and the general ledger.
- Determining that the client actually has title to the assets (e.g., review relevant legal documents or public records)
- Employing an appropriate level of professional skepticism by analyzing the client's appraisals that do not seem to be reasonable, and challenging the underlying assumptions.

Of course, the specific procedures selected by the auditor will be based on the types of frauds that the auditor has determined to be most likely to occur at the client.

Special Topics

Intangible Assets and Natural Resources

Intangible Assets

Some organizations have significant amounts of intangible assets. For example, drug companies have patent costs, and franchise licenses make up a significant portion of the total assets of Coca-Cola. Management must determine whether there has been any impairment in these assets, as discussed earlier in this chapter. Goodwill is often a significant intangible asset of many companies. We will defer more in-depth discussion of goodwill impairment to Chapter 14.

Intangible assets should be recorded at cost. However, the determination of cost is not as straightforward as it is for tangible assets, such as equipment. A particularly troublesome area is the cost of a patent. For example, research and development costs related to new products, such as drugs or software, should be expensed as incurred up until the point that there is a viable product and a plan to bring the product to market. Legal costs for obtaining and defending a patent are capital expenditures if the defense is successful. If it is not successful, the patent has no value and any related costs should be expensed. Patents purchased from another company are capital costs. The cost of patents should be amortized over the lesser of their legal life or their estimated useful life. Minor changes to the patented item have been used by drug companies to extend the life of some patented drugs.

As with tangible fixed assets, management must have procedures in place to determine if the book values of patents and other intangible assets have been impaired. Auditors must be sure these procedures are proper and effective

LO 8

Discuss the risks associated with intangible assets and natural resources and the approach to auditing intangible assets and natural resources.

PRACTICAL POINT

Intangible assets related to drug/biomedical development, new software, or patents are significant to many companies, but especially to start-up companies. The auditor must spend time assessing the economic viability of these assets.

AUDITING *in Practice*

SHELL OIL ESTIMATES OF OIL RESERVES

Estimates of proven oil reserves are an important disclosure required by the SEC. The SEC believes the information is important because the future cash flow of the company is dependent on the amount of reserves the company currently owns. Bids to take over other oil companies are often based on the amount of oil reserves a company owns, as some companies find it easier to buy existing reserves than to discover new reserves.

In the late 1990s, the geologist in charge of estimating oil reserves for Shell Oil systematically overestimated the reserves (a known misstatement) in order to enhance the value of the company's stock. Subsequently, the geologist became the CEO of the company. However, when the SEC discovered the systematic overstatement of the reserves by amounts that were material to the company, the company was fined. More importantly, many stockholders and mutual fund investors began questioning the ethics of the CEO and the control environment of the company. The company suffered a large loss of market value, and the pressures from investors led to the resignation of the CEO and a restructuring of the board.

based on knowledge of the industry, competition, expectations of future cash flows, and new-product introductions, as discussed earlier in this chapter.

Natural Resources

Natural resources present unique problems to the auditor. First, it is often difficult to identify the costs associated with discovery of the natural resource. The oil industry debated for years whether all costs incurred in searching for oil (including drilling numerous dry wells) should be capitalized as part of the cost of obtaining a successful well (*the full-cost approach*), or whether only the costs associated with drilling a specific successful well should be capitalized (*the successful-efforts approach*). Second, once the natural resource has been discovered, it is often difficult to estimate the amount of commercially available resources to be used in determining a depletion rate. Third, the company may be responsible for restoring the property to its original condition (reclamation) after the resources are removed. Reclamation costs may be difficult to estimate.

Most established natural resource companies have developed procedures and associated internal controls for identifying costs and use geologists to establish an estimate of the reserves contained in a new discovery. The auditor normally has experience with the quality of the client's estimates but may want to use a specialist to review the geological analysis of new discoveries as a basis for establishing the reserves. Most organizations periodically reassess the amount of reserves as more information becomes available during the course of mining, harvesting, or extracting resources. The auditor should review these estimates and determine their impact on revisions of the depletion rate. The importance of these procedures can be seen in the *Auditing in Practice* feature.

The audit procedures for determining the cost of natural resources are similar to those for other fixed assets. The auditor should test the capitalization of all new natural resources and should verify the costs by examining documents, including the client's own process of documenting all the costs of exploration and drilling.

Depletion expense (the expense associated with the extraction of natural resources) should be based on the items extracted during the year using the units of production method. The company should have production records of daily extractions. In addition, the auditor will be able to substantiate the amount of items sold during the year. Further, the company should have procedures to estimate any changes in reserves in order to update the depletion procedures.

Using the Work of a Specialist   Using the work and relying on the valuation opinions of outside specialists is particularly relevant in auditing natural resources and other long-term assets in which subject-matter expertise is required. Auditing standards on relying on the work of a specialist apply to situations in which the auditor has responsibilities relating to the work of an individual in a field of expertise other than accounting or auditing, and when the auditor uses that work to obtain sufficient appropriate audit evidence. In the area of long-term assets, the auditing standards recognize that the following types of situations often require the auditor to rely on a specialist:

- The valuation of land and buildings, plant and machinery, jewelry, works of art, antiques, and intangible assets
- The estimation of oil and gas reserves
- The interpretation of contracts, laws, and regulations
- The analysis of complex or unusual tax compliance issues

Estimation of Reclamation Expenses   Environmental protection regulations have increased corporate responsibility to restore land used in mining to an agreed-upon natural state. In addition, many state laws require safeguards to protect the environment while the natural resource mining or harvesting takes place. All **reclamation expenses** associated with restoring the property to its original state should be estimated and accrued. The auditor should examine the reasonableness of the procedures used by management to estimate such

> **PRACTICAL POINT**
>
> Changing prices for natural resources result in accounting issues for companies and their auditors. A few years ago, the price of gold was so low that companies shut down many of their mining operations. As prices subsequently rose, companies reopened some of those mines because they could now profitably extract the gold. Was there an impairment a few years ago? Or was it just the result of fluctuating prices? Auditors should be skeptical in evaluating judgments of managers when potential impairments are material.

Comparison of Worldwide Professional Guidance

USING THE WORK OF AN OUTSIDE SPECIALIST/EXPERT

AICPA Auditing Standards Board (ASB)

SAS 73 *Using the Work of a Specialist*
As part of the AICPA's Clarity Project, the ASB has issued a SAS *Using the Work of an Auditor's Specialist* with a proposed effective date of December 2012. The standard is nearly equivalent to ISA 620.

Public Company Accounting Oversight Board (PCAOB)

The PCAOB adopted AU Section 336 as an interim standard in 2003. This is the same standard as SAS 73. Note that once the AICPA's its new standard is effective, there will be divergence in the United States regarding guidance on this topic, as the new AICPA standard will more closely resemble the guidance provided by the IAASB.

International Auditing and Assurance Standards Board (IAASB)

ISA 620 *Using the Work of an Auditor's Expert*
Highlights of this standard include the following:
- The auditor must have sufficient understanding of the subject matter to evaluate the adequacy of the expert's work
- In evaluating the adequacy of the expert's work, the auditor should determine:
  (a) The relevance and reasonableness of the expert's findings or conclusions, and their consistency with other audit evidence;
  (b) If the expert's work involves use of significant assumptions and methods, the relevance and reasonableness of those assumptions and methods in the circumstances;
  (c) If the expert's work involves the use of source data that is significant to that expert's work, the relevance, completeness, and accuracy of that source data.
- If the auditor determines that the expert's work is inadequate, the auditor should:
  (a) Agree with the expert on the nature and extent of further work to be performed by the expert or
  (b) Perform additional audit procedures appropriate to the circumstances.

SUMMARY

The three sets of professional guidance on this topic are similar. One difference is in terminology: the IAASB uses the term *expert,* while the U.S. regulators use the term *specialist.* All of the standards require the auditor to understand the role, knowledge, and objectivity of the specialist and how the specialist's work affects important financial accounts.

LO 9

Discuss the risks associated with lease accounting and the audit approach for leases.

expenses. Reclamation expenses should be amortized against the use of the natural resources as part of the depletion expense.

Leases

Motivation to Lease

Companies engage in leasing transactions for a variety of reasons. Most of the reasons are economic, but in some cases achieving a particular financial statement treatment motivates the lease transaction. Some of the reasons for leases include the following:

- To finance the use of the asset instead of making an outright purchase
- To acquire the use of the asset for relatively short periods of time without having to buy and then sell it
- To acquire the use of the asset for an extended period of time, but keep the asset and related liability off the balance sheet
- To maintain a flexible operating profile, i.e., substitute short-term variable costs for fixed costs

Assume that a company wishes to acquire the services of an automobile for a period of time between three and five years. We will make an additional assumption that the economic life of the car is five years. Alternatives include the following:

- Borrow the necessary funds and purchase the automobile.
- Sign a lease to rent a new automobile for a one-year period. At the beginning of the second year and again at the beginning of the third year, sign lease agreements to rent a new automobile for each of those years.
- Sign a three-year lease.
- Sign a five-year lease.

Clearly, the second option gives the owner more alternatives. It can get another car next year. Most would expect to keep a purchased car for three to five years, or more. The choices also affect accounting. The financial reporting effects of these alternatives, according to current accounting standards, are as follows:

Alternative	Assets	Liabilities	Income Statement
1. Purchase	Automobile	Loans Payable	Depreciation and Interest Expense
2. One-year lease	None	None	Rent Expense
3. Three-year lease	None	None	Lease Expense
4. Five-year lease	Automobile	Lease Obligation	Depreciation and Interest Expense

In most instances, the least costly approach for the company is to purchase the asset; but that may not be economically viable or may not be consistent with the company's business strategy. The choice affects both the economics and the accounting treatment. If the company uses the purchase option (number 1 in the preceding table), the company records both the asset and the loan liability. It depreciates the asset over its economic life, which may be greater than three years, and recognizes interest expense on the liability.

For the leasing options, we have assumed three choices. Under the one-year rental option (number 2 in the preceding table), there is no accounting recognition at the time of signing. The company simply records rent expense each year. The rental payments are usually higher, but the company has a great deal of flexibility. If a company signs a longer-term lease (number 3 in the preceding table), but for less than the economic life of the asset, the company must disclose the lease obligations but does not record the asset or the liability. On the other hand, if the company signs a lease that is nearly equal to the economic life of the asset (number 4 in the preceding table), the company records the present value of the lease as an asset and a liability. It records depreciation and interest expense. This alternative is, in substance, an installment purchase of the automobile.

The risks of ownership (obsolescence, physical deterioration) are usually built into the pricing model by the lessor or the seller. Many companies want to have control of the assets for the economic life but want to structure the purchase contract so that it looks like a lease, thereby keeping the assets and liabilities off the balance sheet. Although there is disclosure of the lease obligations, the company still keeps them off the balance sheet. While accounting has not yet moved to a complete "principles-based" approach, the guidance is that the economic substance of transactions, not its form, should guide accounting. However, as seen next, the form still plays a major part in accounting for leases.

Proper Accounting Treatment

Current accounting principles in the United States (FAS Statement No. 13, FASB ASC 840) require that leases be capitalized if they meet at least one of four conditions:

1. The present value of the minimum lease payments is at least equal to 90% of the asset's fair market value.
2. The lessee can acquire title to the asset at the end of the lease for a bargain purchase price.
3. The lease term covers at least 75% of the useful life of the asset.
4. The lease transfers ownership to the lessee by the end of the lease term.

Capitalized leases are initially recorded at the present value of the future minimum lease payments. The cost of the asset is amortized in the same way as that of purchased assets. Periodic lease payments include interest expense and reduction of principle. If the lease does not meet one of the preceding tests, it is accounted for as an operating lease, in which case only rent expense is recorded.

Audit Approach

The audit approach for leases starts, as it does for all other accounts, with an analysis of controls the company uses to assure proper recording of leases. A general audit approach for leases is as follows:

1. Obtain copies of lease agreements, read the agreements, and develop a schedule of lease expenditures, bargain purchases, and so on.
2. Review the lease expense account, then select entries to the account and determine if there are entries that are not covered by the leases identified in Step 1. Review to determine if the expenses are properly accounted for.
3. Review the four criteria from FASB ASC 840 (formerly SFAS #13) (see the preceding list) and determine if any of the leases meet the requirement of capital leases.
4. For all capital leases, determine that the assets and lease obligations are recorded at their present value. Determine the economic life of the asset. Calculate amortization expense and interest expenses, and determine any adjustments to correct the financial statements. Consider bargain purchase agreements to determine the economic life for depreciation purposes.
5. Develop a schedule of all future lease obligations or test the client's schedule by reference to underlying lease agreements to determine that the schedule is correct.
6. Review the client's disclosure of lease obligations to determine that it is in accordance with GAAP.

PRACTICAL POINT

Auditors must be skeptical and thereby alert to the possibility of management using leases for improper off-balance-sheet financing of asset acquisition.

Summary

The audit of long-lived assets is usually straightforward—test the changes in account balances during the year. However, the auditor should be skeptical and therefore alert to the possibility that management is managing earnings by changing the related estimates without justification or by capitalizing costs that should be expensed.

The major continuing challenge is measuring the impairment of assets and correctly recording depreciation that fits the economic life of the asset. Other special topics involved in the long-lived asset transaction cycle include the audit complexities introduced by intangible assets, natural resources, and leasing transactions.

Significant Terms

Asset impairment   A term used to describe management's recognition that a significant portion of fixed assets is no longer as productive as had originally been expected. When assets are so impaired, the assets should be written down to their expected economic value.

Depletion   Expense associated with the extraction of natural resources. The units of production method is normally used.

Discontinued operations   Elimination of an operational segment by shutting down and

dismantling production or by announcing the sale of a line of business to another company.

Fixed assets   See Long-lived assets.

Long-lived assets   Assets with a useful life extending greater than one year.

Reclamation expenses   Costs associated with restoring land used in mining to an agreed-upon natural state that reflects safeguards to protect the environment.

SELECTED REFERENCES TO RELEVANT PROFESSIONAL GUIDANCE	
Topic	**Selected Guidance**
Using the Work of a Specialist	ISA 620 *Using the Work of an Auditor's Expert*
	SAS 73 *Using the Work of a Specialist*
	SAS *Using the Work of an Auditor's Specialist* (issued but not effective; proposed effective date is December 2012)

Note: *Acronyms for Relevant Professional Guidance*
STANDARDS: **AS**—Auditing Standard issued by the PCAOB; **ISA**—International Standard on Auditing issued by the IAASB; **SAS**—Statement on Auditing Standards issued by the Auditing Standards Board of the AICPA; **SSAE**—Statement on Standards for Attestation Engagements issued by the AICPA.
ORGANIZATIONS: **AICPA**—American Institute of Certified Public Accountants; **COSO**—Committee of Sponsoring Organizations; **IAASB**—International Auditing and Assurance Standards Board; **PCAOB**—Public Company Accounting Oversight Board; **SEC**—Securities and Exchange Commission.

Review Questions

Professional Skepticism

13-1   **(LO 3)** Explain how a skeptical auditor might come to understand management's potential for adjusting earnings through manipulation of fixed-asset accounts.

13-2   **(LO 5)** Considering the risks typically associated with fixed assets, identify the internal controls over fixed assets that you would expect a client to have in place. For specific control procedures identified, indicate their importance to the audit.

13-3   **(LO 2)** How would an integrated audit of fixed assets differ from a traditional balance sheet audit of the fixed assets?

13-4 **(LO 4, 6)** Identify the analytical procedures that may be most effective in performing an audit of depreciation expense. Indicate also how the procedures may provide information on the accuracy of asset accounts. Identify situations in which the performance of the analytic procedures as the major approach to evaluating depreciation would not be appropriate.

13-5 **(LO 1)** One of the significant and relevant accounts for this cycle is long-lived assets. For this account, what would typically be the most relevant assertions for the auditor to consider? Why is it important for the auditor to identify which assertions are more relevant?

13-6 **(LO 6)** What audit procedures might an auditor use to identify fully depreciated equipment? How might the auditor determine that such equipment is properly valued?

13-7 **(LO 3, 6)** Why does an auditor ask the client to prepare a schedule of repair and maintenance expenditures that exceeds some predetermined limit? Why might a company want to expense an item rather than capitalize it?

13-8 **(LO 5, 6)** During the audit of a new client, you uncover an accounting policy stating that all purchases of equipment or other items under $500 will be expensed, regardless of their nature. When you ask the controller about this policy, she says it is a practical way of handling items that are not material. She indicates that the policy saves a tremendous amount of work because the items are not inventoried, capitalized, or depreciated. How would the existence of such a policy affect the audit?

13-9 **(LO 6)** A client has a policy manual that categorizes equipment by type and assigns a depreciation life based on the categorization. All equipment in a category is depreciated using the same depreciation method. How does the auditor determine the reasonableness of the client's approach?

13-10 **(LO 6)** What responsibility does the auditor have to determine the estimated life of a new asset that has been acquired by the company? How might an auditor go about determining whether the estimate of depreciable life by the company is reasonable?

13-11 **(LO 7)** What is meant by *asset impairment*? What are the major audit issues related to asset impairment that must be addressed on an audit?

13-12 **(LO 7)** What is a recoverability test as used in the context of testing for an asset impairment?

13-13 **(LO 7)** What evidence might an auditor gather to determine the proper valuation of an impaired asset?

13-14 **(LO 7)** Assume that a company obtains an appraisal for equipment that may be impaired. Does the auditor need to test the appraisal? What work should the auditor perform to determine that the appraisal should be relied upon as a best estimate of the value of the assets?

13-15 **(LO 8)** What are the major audit difficulties related to patents?

13-16 **(LO 8)** What major audit difficulties are associated with the audit of natural resources?

International

13-17   **(LO 8)** Describe and compare worldwide professional auditing guidance on the use of subject-matter specialists/experts in auditing long-lived assets and related expense accounts.

13-18   **(LO 9)** Explain why a company might choose to lease assets rather than purchase the assets.

13-19   **(LO 9)** Some managers believe there are positive financial reporting benefits to leasing assets for a period of time that is shorter than their economic life. What are those benefits? What key ratios are affected by the decision to purchase versus lease an asset?

13-20   **(LO 9)** What criteria should the auditor examine to help determine whether leases should be capitalized?

13-21   **(LO 9)** Does the auditor have to determine the economic life of a leased asset? Explain.

13-22   **(LO 9)** Describe the basic approach to auditing leases.

Multiple-Choice Questions

13-23   **(LO 3)** Which of the following is *not* a risk related to fixed-asset accounts?

  a. Failing to record asset disposals.

  b. Capitalizing repairs and maintenance expense.

  c. Treating capital leases as if they were operating leases.

  d. Changing depreciation estimates to manage earnings.

  e. All of the above are risks.

*13-24   **(LO 6)** Which of the following errors or questionable practices is most likely to be detected by a tour of the production facility?

  a. Insurance coverage on the facility has lapsed.

  b. Overhead has been improperly applied.

  c. Necessary facility maintenance has not been performed.

  d. Depreciation expense on fully depreciated machinery has not been recognized.

*13-25   **(LO 6)** A company keeps its fixed-asset records on a computer system. A unique, nine-digit, fixed-asset identification number identifies each record in the file. The remaining fields describe the asset, its acquisition date, cost, economic life, depreciation method, and accumulated depreciation. Which of the following audit procedures could *not* be performed using generalized audit software?

  a. Select a sample of assets to be used in verifying existence of the asset.

  b. Recompute accumulated depreciation.

---

*All problems marked with an asterisk are adapted from the Certified Internal Auditor Examination.

c. Verify economic life by determining it is in the proper asset class.

d. Foot the cost and accumulated depreciation fields and trace the totals to the client's general ledger.

†13-26   **(LO 5)** A deficiency in internal control over recording retirements of equipment may cause an auditor to perform which of the following procedures?

a. Inspect certain items of equipment in the plant and trace those items to the accounting records.

b. Foot the subsidiary ledger and agree it to the general ledger.

c. Trace additions to the "other assets" account to search for equipment that is still on hand but is no longer being used.

d. Select certain items of equipment from the accounting records and locate them in the plant.

†13-27   **(LO 6)** In performing auditing procedures, the auditor may note the following circumstances. Which of the circumstances may cause the auditor to conclude that depreciation charges are insufficient?

a. Large amounts of fully depreciated assets.

b. Continuous trade-ins of relatively new assets.

c. Excessive recurring losses on assets retired.

d. Insured values greatly in excess of book values.

13-28   **(LO 7)** Which of the following would *not* indicate possible asset impairment?

a. Unexpected obsolescence.

b. Increased replacement costs.

c. Significant change in planned production.

d. Damage caused by a natural disaster.

13-29   **(LO 8)** In auditing patents, an intangible asset, an auditor most likely would review or recompute amortization and determine whether the amortization period is reasonable. This procedure would support which of management's assertions?

a. Valuation

b. Existence

c. Completeness

d. Rights

13-30   **(LO 9)** Which of the following is true of capitalized leases as compared to operating leases?

a. Only rent expense is reflected in the income statement.

b. The leased asset does not appear on the balance sheet.

c. Liabilities include the lease obligation.

d. Future minimum lease obligations are not required to be disclosed.

---

† All problems marked with a dagger are adapted from the Uniform CPA Examination.

Discussion and Research Questions

13-31 **(Internal Controls and Integrated Audit of Fixed Assets, LO 5, 6)**

Required

The following questions might be addressed in an evaluation of internal controls for fixed assets. For each question:

a. Indicate the purpose of the control.

b. Indicate the impact on the substantive audit procedures if the answer to the question indicates weak controls.

Internal Control Questions

1. Does the client periodically take a physical inventory of property and reconcile to the property ledger?

2. Does the client have a policy manual to classify property and assign an estimated life for depreciation purposes to the class of assets?

3. Does the client have a policy on minimum expenditures before an item is capitalized? If yes, what is the minimum amount?

4. Does the client have a mechanism to identify pieces of equipment that have been designated for scrap? If yes, is it effective?

5. Does the client have an acceptable mechanism to differentiate major renovations from repair and maintenance? If yes, is it effective?

6. Does the client regularly self-construct its own assets? If yes, does the client have an effective procedure to appropriately identify and classify all construction costs?

7. Does the client systematically review major classes of assets for potential impairment?

8. Does management periodically review asset disposal or the scrapping of assets as a basis for reviewing the assignment of estimated life for depreciation purposes?

13-32 **(Generalized Audit Software on Equipment Audit, LO 6)** This is the first-year audit of a company that wants to register with the SEC in the near future. The company has been very successful and uses a database to manage its fixed assets. The auditor had received review reports (but not audits) performed by another auditor in previous years, and that auditor did not note unusual fluctuations in either the depreciation or equipment accounts in previous years. Having implemented the database program only two years ago, the client has recently taken a physical inventory of property and has used the physical inventory to adjust the database. Through planning, the auditor was able to observe the taking of the equipment inventory and was satisfied that it was done properly. The database contains the following information for each asset:

- Property identification number
- Property description
- Date acquired
- Cost
- Class of assets

- Depreciation method
- Salvage value (if applicable)
- Current-year depreciation—book
- Accumulated depreciation—book
- Current-year depreciation—tax
- Accumulated depreciation—tax
- Any adjustments such as write-downs or renovations
- Expected life of asset
- Location of property
- Department or person requesting purchase of item

Required

a. Write an audit program to audit the equipment account for the year. (Ignore tax considerations at this point.)

b. For each step in the audit program, describe how generalized audit software might be used in the audit of property for this client.

c. What audit procedures would have been mandated had the client not taken a physical inventory of property?

13-33 **(Substantive Analytical Procedures—Depreciation, LO 6)** The audit senior has asked you to perform analytical procedures to obtain substantive evidence on the reasonableness of recorded depreciation expense of the delivery vehicles of a client. Changes in the account occurred pretty much evenly during the year. The estimated useful life is six years. Estimated salvage value is 10% of original cost. Straight-line depreciation is used. Additional information:

Delivery Equipment (per General Ledger)

Beginning balance	$380,500
Additions	154,000
Disposals	(95,600)
Ending balance	$438,900

Current year depreciation expense per books—$60,500

Required

Estimate the amount of depreciation expense for the year using analytical procedures. Does the recorded depreciation expense seem acceptable? Explain. What is the impact of the result of this analytical procedure on other substantive procedures that the auditor may perform?

13-34 **(Audit Evidence and Conclusions, LO 6)** The following conclusions were taken from a staff auditor's summary worksheet for fixed assets and the worksheet for prepaid insurance. In small groups, complete the following requirements:

Group Activity

Required

a. For each conclusion or situation listed, identify the type of audit evidence needed to support the auditor's conclusion.

b. Briefly indicate the audit implications if the auditor's conclusion is justified.

Audit Conclusions or Situations

1. The choice of eight years for straight-line depreciation of the company's trucks appears unreasonable. I would suggest that the client change to a six-year life and use DDB depreciation.

2. Insurance coverage appears to be inadequate because the client has chosen to carry only liability insurance on the cement trucks. There is no provision for collision or damage done to the trucks.

3. The client acquired a substantial piece of real estate from the town of Baraboo to build a warehouse in the town's new industrial complex. The land was donated to the company provided it maintains operations for a minimum of ten years and pays real estate taxes on its appraised value. The land is carried on the books at the fair market value at the time of donation of $250,000.

4. Several pieces of idle equipment were noted. It is recommended that the equipment be written down to the scrap value of $50,000 from the current net book value of $185,000.

5. The company has self-constructed the warehouse located in the town of Baraboo. It has capitalized all payroll expenditures directly related to construction of the project. The adjusting entry debited building for $73,000 and credited payroll expense for the same amount.

6. The company completely overhauled ten of its trucks at a significant cost. The overhaul should extend the life of the trucks by at least three years. Because the company performs similar overhauls each year, the cost has been properly charged to repairs and maintenance.

7. The company sold fifteen of its old trucks to Old Sauk Distributors, a new company owned by the brother of the company's chief executive officer. The equipment was old, and a gain of $70,000 on the sale was credited to income.

Fraud

13-35   **(Risks and Property—WorldCom Fraud, LO 1, 6)**   WorldCom engaged in a fraud that involved fixed assets. Assume we know the following about the fixed-asset account called "telecommunications equipment":

Beginning Balance	$3.8 billion
Additions	$2.1 billion
Disposals	$1.6 billion
Ending Balance	$4.3 billion

We also know that the company swapped some of its line capacity—fiber-optic capacity—with other carriers such as Global Crossing and Sprint. The effect of those swaps is included. The swaps include an exchange, but only in physical assets, of the rights to use Sprint's lines for a percentage of their capacity, e.g., lines in the Midwest. In return, WorldCom allowed Sprint (at least ostensibly) to use a portion of its line capacity in the eastern part of the United States.

Required

Identify the specific assertions for the audit of the telecommunications equipment and line capacity account for WorldCom. Identify the substantive audit evidence you would gather and evaluate in addressing each assertion. Use the following format:

Telecommunications and Line Capacity
WorldCom

Detailed Assertions for the Audit of This Account	**Audit Evidence to Be Gathered**

13-36   **(WorldCom Fraud, LO 3, 6)**   The WorldCom bankruptcy is one of the largest in U.S. economic history. Much of the fraud was carried out by capitalizing operating expenses, such as payments to other companies for line rental, as fixed assets. Adjusting journal entries were made at the company's headquarters in Mississippi even though property accounting records were located in Dallas.

Fraud

Required

1. Would it be considered unusual to find debits to fixed-assets coming from a journal entry source rather than a purchase journal? Explain.

2. Would it be considered unusual to find entries to accumulated depreciation and depreciation expense to come from a journal entry source rather than another source?

3. Assume you were auditing WorldCom and in your sample of debits to fixed assets you find an entry for $500,000 with the following notation: "Capitalization of line capacity per CFO, amounts were originally incorrectly recorded as an expense." Explain what you would do to complete the audit of this item. What evidence would you need to see to either corroborate or question the entry?

13-37   **(Analysis of Property Changes, LO 2, 6, 9)**   You are performing the year-end audit of Halvorson Fine Foods, Inc. for December 31, 2011. The client has prepared the following schedule for the fixed assets and related allowance for depreciation accounts. You have compared the opening balances with your prior-year audit working papers. The following information is found during your audit:

1. All equipment is depreciated on a straight-line basis (no salvage value taken into consideration) based on the following estimated lives: buildings, twenty-five years; all other items, ten years. The corporation's policy is to take one-half year's depreciation on all asset acquisitions and disposals occurring during the year.

2. On April 1 of this year, the corporation entered into a ten-year lease contract for a die-casting machine with annual rentals of $5,000, payable in advance every April 1. The lease is cancelable by either party (sixty days' written notice is required), and there is no option to renew the lease or buy the equipment at the end of the lease. The estimated useful life of the machine is ten years with no salvage value. The corporation recorded the die-casting machine in the machinery and equipment account at $40,400, the present value at the date of the lease, and $2,020, applicable to the machine, has been included in depreciation expense for the year.

3. The corporation completed the construction of a wing on the plant building on June 30 of this year. The useful life of the building was not extended by this addition. The lowest construction bid received was $17,500, the amount recorded in the buildings account. Company personnel were used to construct the addition at a cost of $16,000 (materials, $7,500; labor, $5,500; and overhead, $3,000).

4. On August 18, Halvorson paid $5,000 for paving and fencing a portion of land owned by the corporation for use as a parking lot for employees. The expenditure was charged to the land account.

5. The amount shown in the retirements column for the machinery and equipment asset represents cash received on September 5, on disposal of a machine purchased in July 1998 for $48,000. The bookkeeper recorded a depreciation expense of $3,500 on this machine in 2009.

6. Crux City donated land and building appraised at $10,000 and $40,000, respectively, to Halvorson for a plant. On September 1, the corporation began operating the plant. Because no costs were involved, the bookkeeper made no entry for the foregoing transaction.

Halvorson Fine Foods, Inc.
Analysis of Fixed Assets
For the Year Ended December 31, 2011

Description	Final Balance, December 31, 2010	Additions	Retirements	Per Books, December 31, 2011
Assets:				
Land	$22,500	$5,000		$27,500
Buildings	120,000	17,500		137,500
Machinery and equip.	385,000	40,400	$26,000	399,400
	$527,500	$62,900	$26,000	$564,400
Allowance for depreciation:				
Building	$60,000	$5,150		$65,150
Machinery and equip.	173,200	39,220		212,470
	$233,250	$44,370		$277,620

Required

a. In addition to inquiring of the client, explain how you found each of the described items of information during the audit.

b. Prepare the adjusting journal entries with supporting computations that you would suggest at December 31, 2011, to adjust the accounts for the listed transactions. Disregard income tax implications.

13-38   **(Audit of Natural Resources Company, LO 8)**   Red Lake Mining Co. engages in the search for and mining of gold in North America, principally Canada. During the year, it discovered a substantial new source of gold, which it estimates holds 15.5 million troy ounces. At the time of discovery, gold was selling for $400 per ounce, and it is estimated that the cost of mining the gold will approximate $250 an ounce. There is little doubt that all of the gold will be sold at market prices. The company estimates that the cost of discovering the ore was approximately $25 million and that it will cost another $225 million to construct a plant to mine the gold.

Required

a. Because there is a ready market for gold, the controller has proposed that the discovery be valued at the market value, or net market value, of the gold discovered. He says that such a valuation better informs investors as to the real value of the company. Would such a valuation be acceptable?

b. How would the auditor verify the estimate of 15.5 million troy ounces of gold?

c. The controller suggests that a depletion schedule be established based on the $250 million for discovery and plant construction. The audit senior suggests that a depletion allowance be established on the $25 million discovery cost, not the $250 million. Would a depletion allowance based on $250 million be acceptable? Explain.

13-39 **(Leases, LO 3, 9)** While performing analytical procedures on Merrill Traders, Inc., the auditor discovered a substantial increase in lease expense and a corresponding decrease in both the fixed-asset and related depreciation accounts. On further inquiry, the auditor discovered that a substantial amount of equipment and one piece of property were sold to an outside leasing company. The company then leased the property back and leased similar equipment from the lessor. The controller shows the auditor that the lease was contractually constructed so that it would not be considered a sale and leaseback. The proceeds of the sale were used to pay down long-term debt.

Professional Skepticism

The auditor is puzzled. Economically, there appears to be no change in the company's operations, but it may have incurred higher future costs because the lease agreement terms do not appear to be as economically favorable as did the past ownership. For example, the company leases equipment for three years when the expected life is five years, but it is responsible for all maintenance on the equipment.

Required

a. Considering the importance of auditors' professional skepticism, what role do substance vs. form decisions play in the audit of a client and in a situation such as the one described?

b. What substantive audit procedures should be performed to finish the analysis of the lease expense account?

13-40 **(Audit Program for Leases, LO 9)** The Rousch-Fenway Racing Company is in the business of building NASCAR race cars. It also has an engineering department that builds components for other racing teams, as well as for specialty cars built for major manufacturers such as Ford Motor Company. Rousch-Fenway has three lease-related accounts on its books as follows:

	Balance	Last Year
Leasehold Improvement	$4,583,000	$3,600,000
Leased Equipment	1,287,000	832,000
Lease Expense	624,000	515,000

Required

1. Identify the nature of each of these accounts, i.e., asset, liability, and expense.

2. What would cause the accounts to increase during the year?

3. What is the relationship between the first two accounts and the lease expense account?

4. Identify appropriate procedures to audit these lease-related accounts.

Group Activity

13-41 **(Decision Analysis and Asset Impairments, LO 7, 10)** Novelis, Incorporated is the world's leading rolled-aluminum products producer. Following is a description of issues involving asset impairments derived from the company's footnote on fixed assets.

Asset Impairments

1. In connection with the decision to close and sell our plant in Borgofranco, Italy, we recognized an impairment charge of $5 million to reduce the net book value of the plant's fixed assets to zero. We based our estimate on third-party offers and negotiations to sell the business.

2. We recorded an impairment charge of $65 million to reduce the carrying value of the production equipment at two facilities in Italy to their fair value of $56 million. We determined the fair value of the impaired assets based on the discounted future cash flows of these facilities using a 7% discount rate.

3. We announced that we would cease operations in Falkirk, Scotland. We designated certain production equipment with a nominal carrying value for transfer to our Rogerstone facility. We reduced the carrying value of the remaining fixed assets to zero, which resulted in an $8 million impairment charge.

Required

In a small group, complete the first four steps of the seven-step Decision Analysis Framework introduced in Chapter 3 by answering the following questions:

1. What difficulties will the auditor of Novelis face when deciding whether the impairment charges that Novelis incurred are reasonable?

2. What are the consequences of the auditor's decisions in evaluating impairments?

3. What are the risks and uncertainties associated with Novelis's estimation?

4. What types of evidence should the auditor gather to evaluate the reasonableness of management's estimates?

Recall that the framework is as follows:

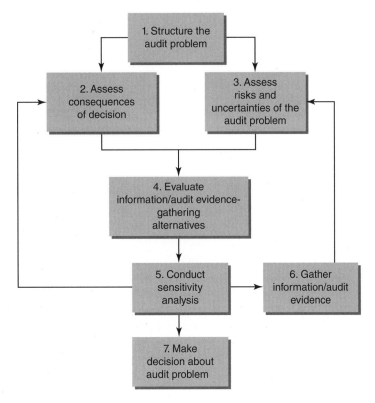

Source: Adapted from "Judgment and Choice," by Robin Hogarth.

13-42   **(Asset Impairments During Recessionary Times, LO 7)**   In Terex Corporation's 2009 Annual Report, the company's CEO, Ronald Defeo, made this statement regarding the recessionary times that his company is facing:

Internet

Group Activity

> I like to say that, "when you are in a hurricane, you have to expect to get wet and blown around!" In 2009, many of our markets declined 70% to 80% almost overnight. Backlogs that looked solid evaporated, and geographies that were growing and demanding more and faster shipments went silent. We were in a capital goods hurricane, and everything about our business changed in the fourth quarter of 2008. So, for most of 2009 we were focused on weathering the storm and preparing for the calm that would inevitably follow. As I write this letter in the early spring of 2010, this is where we find ourselves. Our business has stabilized, but any growth of consequence is going to be hard won.

Difficulties like these are commonplace today, and they can have an important impact on a company's profitability because they are often associated with corporate restructuring, downsizing, and the recognition of asset impairments. A typical example of the disclosures made regarding asset impairments can be found in Starbucks' 2009 Annual Report, which states:

> When facts and circumstances indicate that the carrying values of long-lived assets may be impaired, an evaluation of recoverability is performed by comparing the carrying values of the assets to projected future cash flows, in addition to other quantitative and qualitative analyses. For goodwill and other indefinite-lived

intangible assets, impairment tests are performed annually and more frequently if facts and circumstances indicate carrying values exceed estimated fair values and if indefinite useful lives are no longer appropriate for the Company's trademarks. Upon determination that the carrying values of such assets are in excess of their estimated fair values, the Company recognizes an impairment loss as a charge against current operations. Judgments made by the Company related to the expected useful lives of long-lived assets and the ability of the Company to realize undiscounted cash flows in excess of the carrying amounts of such assets are affected by factors such as the ongoing maintenance and improvements of the assets, changes in economic conditions and changes in operating performance. As the Company assesses the ongoing expected cash flows and carrying amounts of its long-lived assets, these factors could cause the Company to realize material impairment charges.

Required

1. Locate the 2009 Starbucks Annual Report online at its website, www.starbucks.com.

2. What is the dollar magnitude of the impairment charges that Starbucks recorded in 2009 and 2008? Summarize the issues that Starbucks is facing regarding asset impairments, and the relationship between those impairments and the recent recession.

3. What judgments that managers made at Starbucks may affect the ability of the external auditor to assess the reasonableness of the impairment charges?

4. Locate another company online that is also facing economic difficulties. Be prepared to discuss the company that you have chosen with your class or small group, and indicate the following in your report:

   a. Name of your company, and its principal line of business.

   b. Nature of financial difficulties the company is facing.

   c. Nature of the company's long-term fixed assets.

   d. Nature of the impairment charges, and their magnitude as a percentage of total assets, total sales, and net income.

Cases

†13-43   **(Audit of Fixed Assets, LO 2, 5)**   A corporation operates a highly automated flexible manufacturing facility. The capital-intensive nature of the corporation's operations makes internal control over the acquisition and use of fixed assets important management objectives.

A fixed-asset budget that indicates planned capital expenditures by department is established at the beginning of each year. Department managers request capital expenditures by completing a fixed-asset requisition form, which must be approved by senior management. The firm has a written policy that establishes whether a budget request is to be considered a capital expenditure or a routine maintenance expenditure.

A management committee meets each month to review budget reports that compare actual expenditures made by managers to their budgeted amounts and to authorize any additional expenditures that may be necessary. The committee also reviews and approves as necessary any departmental request for sale, retirement, or scrapping of fixed assets. Copies of vouchers used to document department requests for sale, retirement, or scrapping of fixed assets are forwarded to the accounting department to initiate removal of the asset from the fixed-asset ledger.

The accounting department is responsible for maintaining a detailed ledger of fixed assets. When a fixed asset is acquired, it is tagged for identification. The identification number, as well as the cost, location, and other information necessary for depreciation calculations, are entered into the fixed-asset ledger. Depreciation calculations are made each quarter and are posted to the general ledger. Periodic physical inventories of fixed assets are taken for purposes of reconciliation to the fixed-asset ledger as well as appraisal for insurance purposes.

Required

Develop audit objectives and related audit procedures to evaluate internal controls over fixed assets at the corporation. These audit procedures are to test internal controls—not substantive audit procedures.

13-44   **(Asset Impairment and Associated Ethical Considerations, LO 3, 7, 10)**   Your audit firm has been the auditor of Cowan Industries for a number of years. The company manufactures a wide range of lawn care products and typically sells to major retailers. In recent years, the company has expanded into ancillary products, such as recreation equipment, that use some of the same technology. The newer lines of business, while successful, have not been particularly profitable. The company's stock price has languished and management has recently been replaced.

Ethics

The new management team announces that it will close two factories and will phase out one of the newer lines of business. It plans to expand existing products and increase marketing efforts. Even though there is no technological obsolescence of existing products, the new management does not believe the company has a competitive advantage. It wants to take a "one-time hit" to the balance sheet and income statement of $15.3 million (about one-third of total assets) as a reserve for the shutdown of the plants and the disposal of the lines of business. It also plans on severance pay for employees at the two plants.

Required

a. Define the term *impairment of assets* and the proper accounting treatment for asset impairments.

b. Is management typically motivated to understate or overstate the write-down because of asset impairment? Explain.

c. What information should the auditor gather to develop evidence on the proper valuation of the asset impairment? In answering your question, address the following:

- Should the factory assets be treated as individual assets or as a group in determining the realizable value?

- What are the major liabilities the company should consider when shutting down operations and phasing out a line of business? Should those liabilities be considered as part of the "impairment of asset" cost?

- Because the actual disposal of the plants or the costs of shutting them down are estimates, how should the auditor treat material differences in estimates generated by the auditor vs. those generated by management? Should the differences be disclosed or otherwise accounted for?

  d. Assume in this situation that the auditor believes management is overestimating the impairment charge and thus the improvement in future earnings because of reduced depreciation charges in subsequent periods. Further assume that the auditor has gathered and evaluated evidence that convincingly reveals the impairment charge should more reasonably fall in a range from $8 to $10 million, rather than management's estimate of about $15 million. Finally, assume the auditor has discussed the issue with management and it refuses to vary from its original estimate. Management has stated that its assumptions and evidence are just as convincing as the auditor's. Use the seven-step ethical decision-making framework from Chapter 3 to make a recommendation about the course of action the auditor should take.

Recall that the seven steps in the ethical decision-making framework are as follows: (1) identify the ethical issue, (2) determine who are the affected parties and identify their rights, (3) determine the most important rights, (4) develop alternative courses of action, (5) determine the likely consequences of each proposed course of action, (6) assess the possible consequences, including an estimation of the greatest good for the greatest number, and (7) decide on the appropriate course of action.

Fraud

Group Activity

13-45 **(Fraud and the Audit of Long-Lived Assets and Related Expense Accounts, LO 4, 6)** In the *Professional Judgment in Context* case at the beginning of this chapter, we reviewed some of the pertinent findings from the COSO (2010) study on fraudulent financial reporting. The study notes the many ways in which fixed assets can be fraudulently overstated including:

- Fictitious assets on the books (WorldCom)

- Improper and incomplete depreciation (Waste Management)

- Failure to record impairment of assets, especially goodwill (Sun Microsystems)

- Expired or worthless assets left on a company's books (Millacron)

- Assets overvalued upon acquisition, especially in the purchase of a company (WorldCom)

Required

In a small group, and considering the concepts that you learned in this chapter, answer the following questions.

a. What might motivate management to overstate fixed assets?

b. What methods might management use to overstate fixed assets?

c. As illustrated by these examples, overstatement of fixed assets happens frequently. Assume that auditors detect most of the overstatements. What company or economic information, or audit tests/analyses would likely alert the auditor to the possibility of such misstatements and therefore facilitate auditor detection?

d. What controls can mitigate the risks associated with misstatements in long-lived asset accounts?

e. How can the results of audits be used by clients to improve their control systems over long-lived assets?

Academic Research Case (LO 3, 9)

Academic research addresses the conceptual issues outlined in this chapter. To help you consider the linkage between academic research and the practice of auditing, read the following research article and answer the questions below.

Acito, A. A., Burks, J. J., & Johnson, W. B. (2009). Materiality Decisions and the Correction of Accounting Errors. *The Accounting Review 84(3):659–688.*

i. What is the issue being addressed in the paper?

ii. Why is this issue important to practicing auditors?

iii. What are the findings of the paper?

iv. What are the implications of these findings for audit quality (or audit practice) on the audit profession?

v. Describe the research methodology used as a basis for the conclusions.

vi. Describe any limitations of the research that the student (and practice) should be aware of.

FORD MOTOR COMPANY AND TOYOTA MOTOR CORPORATION:
LONG-LIVED ASSETS AND RELATED EXPENSES

Go to www.cengage.com/accounting/rittenberg for the Ford and Toyota materials.

Source and Reference	Question
Ford 10-K, Toyota 20-F	1a. What are the key long-lived asset and related expense accounts for Ford?
	1b. What are the critical accounting policies for these accounts?
	1c. Calculate and compare cycle-specific ratios (e.g., property, plant, and equipment/total assets) that you deem relevant for Ford and Toyota. What are the implications of the differences that you note?
Ford Annual Report Ford 8-K	2a. Read Ford's disclosures about its restructuring plan in the MD&A section of the annual report. What risks does the downsizing reveal about the company? What risks does it pose for the audit firm?
	2b. Read Footnote 24 of Ford's 2009 Annual Report. How does Ford's restructuring plan affect the valuation of its fixed assets?
	2c. Read Ford's 8-K filed March 28, 2010. How does it confirm the disclosures in Ford's 2009 annual report? How is this 8-K filing useful to both Ford's shareholders and audit firm?
Ford Annual Report	3a. Read Ford's description of the impairment of long-lived assets in the MD&A and in Footnote 15 regarding impairment of long-lived assets. What was the monetary value of the impairment? What caused the impairment? What key assumptions and estimates affected Ford's valuation of these assets?
	3b. What are the audit firm's obligations regarding the estimates made in this disclosure? What risks do these estimates pose for the audit firm?

Module XI, substantive testing of plant asset additions and disposals, may be completed at this time.

Module XI: Plant Asset Additions and Disposals

In Module IV, you applied MUS sampling procedures in evaluating the correctness of a subset of debits to the "Factory Equipment" account. You will recall that the debits to account 1530 totaled $89,860,000 for 2009. You will also recall that Derick decided to stratify the population of debits such that $77,260,000 of major additions, representing replacements of worn-out equipment, was to be audited in detail. In Module XI, you will analyze this subset of additions, as well as disposals. You will also complete the "Plant Assets" lead schedule.

Requirements

1. Using the spreadsheet program and downloaded data, retrieve the file labeled "Plant." Locate the following documentation in this file:

   - WP 11—Plant assets and accumulated depreciation—lead schedule (note that AJE 1 from Module IV has already been posted); and

   - WP 11.4—Factory equipment—additions and disposals.

   Scroll to WP 11.4,"Factory Equipment—Additions and Disposals." What is the nature of the "underlying documentation" referred to in the explanation of audit legends E and W?

2. In recording the 2009 disposals, Janel James, Biltrite's plant assets accountant, miscalculated the accumulated depreciation on the assets sold and thereby overstated the gain on disposal by $3,090,000. Draft Audit Adjustment 10 at the bottom of WP 11.4 to correct for this misstatement. In addition, James did not change the standard journal entry for monthly depreciation to reflect additions and disposals during the year. As a result depreciation expense for the year is understated by $800,000. Biltrite depreciates factory equipment on a straight-line basis over a ten-year estimated useful life with zero salvage value. One-half year's depreciation is taken on all additions and disposals. Draft Audit Adjustment 11 at the bottom of WP 11.4 to reflect the depreciation understatement. In recording the under-depreciation, debit account 5300,"Cost of Goods Sold—Pike's Peak Mountain Bike," inasmuch as all overhead accounts have been closed. Any further adjustments, therefore, must be reflected in the cost of sales accounts. Although in Module IV we allocated the adjustment to the five product cost of sales accounts, the present adjustment is less significant in amount, and therefore we will reflect the entire amount in account 5300. (*Note*: Don't forget to enter Audit Adjustments 1, 10, and 11 in the body of the document to arrive at correct adjusted balances.)

3. Scroll to WP 11,"Plant Assets and Accumulated Depreciation—Lead Schedule." Post Audit Adjustments 10 and 11 to the lead schedule.

4. Print documentation 11 and 11.4.

14

Audit of Longer-Term Liabilities, Equity, Acquisitions, and Related-Entity Transactions

LEARNING OBJECTIVES

The overriding objective of this textbook is to build a foundation with which to analyze current professional issues and adapt audit approaches to business and economic complexities. Through studying this chapter, you will be able to:

1 Describe long-term liabilities that require special audit attention because of the subjectivity in determining proper valuation.

2 Discuss the audit approaches to audit debt and owners' equity, including integrated audit considerations.

3 Describe the major valuation issues associated with mergers and acquisitions.

4 Describe the risks related to restructuring charges, the audit procedures related to restructuring

charges, and the approaches for testing potential goodwill impairment.

5 Identify the types of related-entity transactions, describe the proper accounting, and develop an audit approach for related-entity transactions.

6 Apply the decision analysis and ethical decision-making frameworks to situations involving the audit of long-term liabilities, owners' equity, restructuring charges, goodwill, and related-entity transactions.

CHAPTER OVERVIEW

Many accounting areas require a significant amount of informed estimates by management. These include long-term liabilities such as pensions, other postretirement liabilities, and warranty obligations, along with the potential impairment of assets, restructuring charges, and the valuation of assets acquired as part of an acquisition. The auditor must understand the contracts that affect these subjective areas and the information system the client has (or hopefully has) to develop estimates for accounts that may be influenced by management's subjective judgments. The auditor also needs to develop an understanding of the controls the client has implemented in the processes where management's estimates are a critical component. In addition, the auditor must be aware that in some cases, management may use subjectivity to influence the amount of reported earnings. Finally, the auditor should be aware that some of the client's transactions may be with related entities and such transactions require adequate disclosure that clients may prefer not to provide.

I. Assessing Client Acceptance and Retention Decisions
CHAPTER 4

II. Understanding the Client
CHAPTERS 2, 4–6, and 9

III. Obtaining Evidence about Controls and Determining the Impact on the Financial Statement Audit
CHAPTERS 5–14 and 18

IV. Obtaining Substantive Evidence about Account Assertions
CHAPTERS 7–14 and 18

V. Wrapping Up the Audit and Making Reporting Decisions
CHAPTERS 15 and 16

The Auditing Profession, Regulation, and Corporate Governance
CHAPTERS 1 and 2

Decision-Making, Professional Conduct, and Ethics
CHAPTER 3

Professional Liability
CHAPTER 17

This chapter presents an overview of complex accounting issues and develops a framework for the integrated audit of such areas. In terms of the audit opinion formulation process, this chapter involves Phases III and IV, that is, obtaining evidence about controls and substantive evidence about assertions concerning the audit of long-term liabilities, equity, acquisitions, and related-entity transactions.

We emphasize three major themes throughout the chapter: (1) the accounting for many of these areas is still evolving and the auditor should understand the complexities in current accounting standards; (2) companies should have, but often do not have, well-developed information systems with appropriate internal controls to generate data for high-quality accounting estimates; and (3) auditors may consult specialists for objective evidence regarding some of the valuation issues, e.g., assumptions made in computing pension obligations. The auditor must be satisfied that these specialists are independent of the organization, capable, and objective.

PROFESSIONAL JUDGMENT IN CONTEXT

Accounting for Goodwill at Rayovac/Spectrum Brands and the Effects of Excessive Debt

Spectrum Brands (formerly Rayovac Corporation) is a consumer products company that sells batteries (under the Rayovac brand), personal grooming products (under the Remington brand), lawn and garden supplies (under the Spectracide brand), and pet supplies (under the Tetra brand). Starting in the early to mid-2000s, CEO Dave Jones pursued an aggressive growth strategy whereby the former battery producer acquired the other brands using significant debt financing. In this process, the company issued over $2.5 billion in long-term debt. Jones abruptly left the company in May 2007, and new CEO Kent Hussey was left to resolve how to pay off the debt with dwindling profits and amid a significant recession in 2008 and 2009.

When the company reported its third-quarter 2008 results, it showed a $5.58 per share loss. Like other recent filings, the third-quarter results contained the following disclosures regarding components of the company's losses:

- Goodwill and trade names impairment charges of $253.7 million, or $4.76 per share, primarily related to the company's Home & Garden and Global Pet Supply businesses;

- Restructuring and related charges of $14.3 million, or $0.27 per share, primarily associated with the company's strategy to exit Ningbo Baowang, a battery manufacturing facility in China, and company-wide cost-reduction initiatives.

In addition, the company has experienced an interesting reversal in its planned sale of the pet supply unit. The company had initially reported that it would sell the unit for $693 million and use the proceeds to pay down its debt. However, senior lenders refused to approve the deal, and it ultimately was canceled, leaving Spectrum in the difficult position of having to find other sources of cash to pay off its debts.

As of November 2008, analyst forecasts rated the stock as being worth $0 per share, and the NYSE had threatened to delist it. At the same time, executives at the company were being paid handsomely to stay with the company. For example, CEO Hussey would get a $2 million bonus if he remained with the company through December 31, 2009. And the board of directors approved bonuses for four top executives totaling $1.6 million.

(continues)

PROFESSIONAL JUDGMENT IN CONTEXT

Accounting for Goodwill at Rayovac/Spectrum Brands and the Effects of Excessive Debt (continued)

As you read the following chapter, consider this case and the following questions:

- How does the management of long-term debt affect the potential of the company to remain a going concern?

- What are the audit considerations associated with long-term debt? In responding to this question, consider such issues as renegotiating terms, other methods of satisfying the debt holders, and what would constitute audit evidence for revaluation.

- What auditor valuation judgments are necessitated by the presence of goodwill on a client's balance sheet or the existence of restructuring activities?

- What are the audit implications when a company's strategic growth plans go awry?

- What ethical issues do you see for Spectrum Brand's top executives in this situation? Is it fair that they receive handsome pay packages when the company is in such a dire financial condition? The company needs talent to work its way forward to avoid bankruptcy. What are the board responsibilities in such situations?

Introduction: Business Risk and Subjective Judgments

Like the Rayovac/Spectrum Brands feature in the *Professional Judgment in Context* example, a significant number of the mergers and acquisitions in the past twenty years have been economic failures. Companies often overpaid for acquisitions, did not perform due diligence on the acquisitions, and the combined entity seldom achieved the synergies hoped for at the time of the acquisition. One of the largest merger failures was the merger of AOL with Time-Warner, in which the surviving company (Time-Warner) had to take a $94 billion loss on the goodwill associated with the merger (the equivalent of approximately twenty years of earnings). Other valuation issues are also present in acquisitions, such as valuing fixed and intangible assets. Further, there may be some problems in determining whether the acquired company is fully integrated into the company or continues to operate as a separate unit.

Many companies have set up special purpose entities (SPE) to achieve financial reporting goals, while some were set up to achieve operational objectives. Enron was the most egregious user of SPEs, but their use is not limited to Enron, or even the energy field. Many companies are setting up joint ventures or separate research and development entities that may carry risk to the parent that has to be assessed on every audit. The accounting for SPEs has changed and the auditor must make decisions based on the newest guidance—and even more important—make decisions about where U.S. GAAP and IFRS differ on the subject.

Other accounts with high inherent risk associated with longer-term liability valuations include accounts such as warranty liabilities, pension and health benefit obligations, and restructuring-associated obligations. The areas identified in this chapter are some of the riskier areas that an auditor faces.

LO 1

Describe long-term liabilities that require special audit attention because of the subjectivity in determining proper valuation.

Long-Term Liabilities and Owners' Equity

Much of the accounting for long-term liabilities is straightforward. For example, bonds are shown at unamortized issue price and are not adjusted to market unless the company is calling the bonds or is in the process of converting the bonds to equity. However, a number of long-term liabilities require extensive and subjective judgments by the client and the auditor. We turn our attention to a few of these liabilities next.

Long-Term Liabilities with Significant Subjective Judgments

It is difficult to determine the correct balance sheet amount for a number of liability accounts because they require significant judgments and assumptions about future events. These include the following:

- Warranty reserves
- Pension obligations
- Other postretirement benefits—especially health care
- Restructuring costs and obligations

Warranty Reserves

The warranty reserve or liability represents the expected future cost related to the sales of a company's product. The audit program should recognize the past experience of the company but should adjust the estimate of the liability for the following factors:

1. Changes in the product, including manufacturing that either enhances or decreases the quality of the product
2. Changes in the nature of the warranty
3. Changes in sales volume, e.g., if more sales were made during the last quarter this year than in previous years
4. Changes in the average cost of repairing products under warranty

The cost of the future warranty claims is estimated and recorded at the time the product is sold. For example, every time Ford sells a new vehicle, it has to estimate the average cost it expects to incur in meeting its warranty promised at the time of sale. The warranty expense and liability are recorded at the time each sale is made. Costs incurred to satisfy the warranty claims are charged against the liability. The client should continuously monitor warranty claims to determine whether there is an unanticipated change in the number or dollar amounts associated with the claims. If the amounts are significantly different than expected, the client should adjust the warranty liability. The auditor can audit the account by testing the controls that are part of the information system used by the client and/or by performing substantive analytical procedures that involve developing an independent estimate based on the factors identified earlier. For example, the auditor might use regression analysis based on the number of claims, defects causing the claims, dollar amounts to fix each claim, and similar variables to estimate the warranty liability, as well as to generate confidence intervals around the point estimate.

The auditor should inquire as to the veracity of the information system used to track warranty items and to take action to mitigate expenses. A proper control will allow a company to take effective action to prevent a potential problem with its products. For a real-world example involving the automobile industry, see the *Auditing in Practice* feature on Toyota Motor Company.

Pension Obligations

Pensions represent an amalgamation of many items that are difficult to estimate. These include:

- Projected lifetime of pensioners
- Nature of the pension plan, e.g., a defined benefit or a defined contribution plan

> **PRACTICAL POINT**
>
> Accounting principles will continue to evolve and one of the issues that will be addressed in the next few years is whether and how all liabilities should be adjusted to fair market value. If such a change occurs it will present new challenges for management and the auditors.

AUDITING *in Practice*

TOYOTA MOTOR CORPORATION: GROWTH, QUALITY PROBLEMS, AND WARRANTY LIABILITIES

Toyota Motor Corporation has historically been viewed as a high-quality producer of safe and reliable automobiles. So, how did Toyota find itself plagued by recent problems involving accidents, lawsuits, recalls, and high warranty expenses? One prominent theory is that in its attempt to gain market share and exceed the sales of General Motors, the company lost control over the manufacture of some critical vehicle components, including the electrical system and the accelerator. Around 2005, Toyota began a significant shift toward outsourcing important parts of the production process to its key suppliers. However, those suppliers often did not have the same internal controls or reputational incentives associated with product quality as did Toyota. In short, the sales volume goal and related outsourcing led to reduced quality, and the company is now suffering for this strategic misstep. As of March 31,

2010, Toyota had accrued a warranty liability of $2.985 billion related to these problems. During 2010, Toyota responded to its problems by convening an ongoing Special Committee for Global Quality to investigate the causes of quality issues and to determine the best strategies for resolving them.

The audit implication of this story is that it is easy for auditors, much like consumers, to fall into a nonskeptical frame of mind that they are auditing the "best quality automobile company in the world," and therefore the audit of warranty expense and liabilities should be routine. That is why auditors have to be vigilant and alert to changes in processes and data that may indicate that assumptions are no longer applicable.

- Future earnings of employees prior to retiring for defined benefit plans
- Earnings rate on invested pension assets including an assessment of the safety of the invested assets
- Long-term interest rates to discount future costs back to present value
- Changes in pension plans

The client will usually engage an actuarial firm to help make these specialized estimates. These individuals work for management, not the auditor. The auditor must determine that the actuarial firm hired by management is independent, capable, and objective so that the firm's work can be relied upon to provide sufficient reliable information to assist management in developing the liability estimates. The auditor must also evaluate the appropriateness of the actuarial specialist's work as audit evidence. The auditor may also need to hire an actuarial specialist of his or her own to assist the audit team in auditing pension obligations. Such individuals work for the auditor, not management.

There is strong evidence that companies have used pension obligations as a means of smoothing earnings by changing the assumed long-term discount rate or the earnings rate, so this is an important and judgmental area in which the auditor must be careful to exercise appropriate professional skepticism. To give you a sense of the importance and materiality of the amounts that companies pay for pension and related medical costs, consider the following disclosures made in Ford's 2009 Annual Report (Note 18):

> In 2009, we made $900 million of cash contributions to our funded pension plans. During 2010, we expect to contribute $1.1 billion to our worldwide funded pension plans from available automotive cash and cash equivalents. In addition, benefit payments made directly by us for unfunded plans are expected to be about $400 million.

The auditor has an obligation to question significant assumptions. For example, some companies have used assumptions that their pension assets will grow at a rate of 9.5% for the future when historical growth rates have been around 6% (and even less for the past few years). Other assumptions made by actuaries also need to be examined for reasonableness, e.g., average life span; a retired coal miner is not likely to have a retired life expectancy as long as a retired government worker. Professional skepticism and knowledge are required—especially in these difficult areas.

Other Postretirement Benefits

Many companies furnish medical insurance coverage as part of their **postretirement benefits**. The rising cost of medical care has been termed a crisis by many candidates running for public office. To give you a sense of the importance and materiality of the amounts that companies pay for postretirement medical costs, consider the following disclosures made in Ford's 2009 Annual Report (Note 18):

The following table presents estimated future gross benefit payments and subsidy receipts related to the Medicare Prescription Drug Improvement and Modernization Act of 2003 (in millions):

Period	U.S. Gross Benefit Payments ($ millions)	Non-U.S. Benefit Payments ($ millions)
2010	3,820	1,350
2011	3,680	1,330
2012	3,580	1,360
2013	3,470	1,370
2014	3,380	1,390
2015–2019	15,940	7,310

The cost of the medical services is difficult for a company or auditor to estimate. The difficulties of making other postretirement benefit estimates for medical payments can be minimized if the company has a plan that limits the actual medical reimbursements each year. The magnitude of other postretirement benefits, Ford's actions to reduce them, and the judgmental estimates required to calculate this liability are described in the *Auditing in Practice* feature, which includes information taken from Ford's 2009 Annual Report.

The audit of the other postretirement benefits requires estimates of changes in medical expenses, changes in coverage, changes in average life expectancies, and the nature of illnesses to be considered. The client needs an information system to gather and analyze such information in order to make an informed estimate. A failure to have such a system would constitute a material weakness in internal controls over financial reporting.

Bonds and Stockholders' Equity

An organization has an almost infinite number of ways to meet its long-term financing needs. The two most common are issuing bonds (debt) and capital stock (equity). In the remainder of this section, we present a brief overview of audit considerations, including controls implemented by the client, involved with these two financing methods. Many financing instruments are more complex than the ones we describe here and will require extra care when they are encountered. However, the concepts related to risk and valuation of these other financing instruments are based on the fundamental nature of liabilities. Other accounts the auditor may encounter in auditing financing activities include the following:

- Notes payable
- Mortgages payable or contracts payable

PRACTICAL POINT

In 2008, Random House Inc., the world's largest general-interest book publisher, announced that it was freezing its pension plan for current employees and eliminating it for new hires. The action reflects a larger movement that accelerated in the 1980s. Auditors should be alert to changes in their clients' pension plans, and changes in judgmental estimates needed to calculate related liabilities.

LO 2

Discuss the audit approaches to audit debt and owners' equity, including integrated audit considerations.

AUDITING *in Practice*

OTHER POSTRETIREMENT BENEFITS AT FORD: MAGNITUDE, COST-MANAGEMENT, AND ESTIMATION ISSUES

Ford provides significant postretirement benefits to its employees. In 2008, its liability was $10.917 billion, although it fell to $453 million in 2009 after a settlement with the United Auto Workers (UAW) labor union. To accomplish the reduction, Ford transferred its obligation to provide retiree health care to the UAW VEBA Trust, in exchange for an immediate asset transfer of $11.3 billion. The remaining liability for postretirement obligations is calculated based on a judgmental estimation process: "The estimation of our obligations, costs, and liabilities associated with OPEB, primarily retiree health care and life insurance, requires that we make use of estimates of the present value of the projected future payments to all participants, taking into consideration the likelihood of potential future events such as health care cost increases and demographic experience, which may have an effect on the amount and timing of future payments ... The assumptions used in developing the required estimates include the following key factors:

• *Discount rates.* We base the discount rate assumption primarily on the results of a cash flow matching analysis, which matches the future cash outflows for each plan to a yield curve comprised of high quality bonds specific to the country of the plan. Benefit payments are discounted at the rates on the curve and a single discount rate specific to the plan is determined.

• *Health care cost trends.* Our health care cost trend assumptions are developed based on historical cost data, the near-term outlook, and an assessment of likely long-term trends.

• *Salary growth.* The salary growth assumptions reflect our long-term actual experience, outlook and assumed inflation.

• *Retirement rates.* Retirement rates are developed to reflect actual and projected plan experience.

• *Mortality rates.* Mortality rates are developed to reflect actual and projected plan experience.

• Special bonds:
  • Payment-in-kind bonds (pay interest in the form of the issuance of more bonds with a stipulated date on which cash interest must be paid)
  • Convertible bonds, which are convertible into equity
• Mandatory redeemable preferred stock (preferred stock with a mandatory redemption date)
• Stock options and warrants
• Stock options as part of an employee stock compensation program

Bonds

Bonds are issued to finance major expansions or to refinance existing debt. The transactions are few, but each transaction is highly material to the financial statements. Some major considerations in auditing bonds or other long-term debt include the following:

• Proper valuation and amortization of premium or discount
• Correct computation of interest expense
• Proper accounting for gains or losses on refinancing debt
• Proper disclosure of major restrictions contained in the bond indentures

Bond Issuance and Amortization Schedules   Most bonds are marketed through an underwriter with the proceeds going to the issuer after deducting the underwriter's commission. Proceeds from the bond issuance can be traced to a bank deposit. The authorization to issue a bond is usually limited to the board of directors, and the proper authorization should be verified during the year of issuance. A bond premium/discount amortization spreadsheet can be set up that the auditor can use each year to help assure that the bond is appropriately valued and disclosed in the financial statements.

Periodic Payments and Interest Expense   Most companies have agreements with bond trustees to handle the registration of current bondholders and to make the periodic interest payments. The bond issuer makes semiannual interest payments to the trustee, plus a fee for the trustee's service, and the trustee disburses the individual payments to the bondholders. There is usually no need to verify the existence of the liability with the bondholder. Rather, the auditor may verify the current payments with the trustee or vouch the payments to the trustee and update the amortization schedule spreadsheet.

Disclosure: Examination of Bond Indenture   Bond indentures are written to protect bondholders against possible financial decline or against the subordination of the value of the debt by the issuance of other debt. Because violation of the bond indenture agreements makes the bonds currently due and payable, the auditor must clearly understand the important provisions of the agreement to determine whether (1) there is violation of the agreement and (2) the material restrictions are disclosed. Common restrictions include maintenance of a minimum level of retained earnings before dividends can be paid, maintenance of a minimum working-capital ratio, specification of a maximum debt-equity ratio, and specific callable provisions that identify procedures for calling and retiring debt at prespecified prices and dates. Copies of the bond indenture agreement or its highlights are normally maintained in the permanent audit file.

> **PRACTICAL POINT**
>
> Most companies will amortize the bond discount or premium using the effective interest rate method and the auditor should verify that the amortization is computed correctly.

Common Stock and Owners' Equity

The following are the major transactions affecting stockholders' equity that should be addressed during an audit:

- New stock issuances
- Purchase of treasury stock
- Payment of stock dividends or issuance of stock splits
- Sale of treasury stock and proper accounting for the proceeds
- Addition of donated capital through tax incremental financing
- Declaration and payment of cash dividends
- Transfer of net income to retained earnings
- Issuance and eventual redemption of stock options
- Recording of prior-period or comprehensive income adjustments to retained earnings

Although all the assertions apply to the audit of owners' equity, the valuation and disclosure assertions generally receive the most attention.

Valuation   Most stock issuances do not present valuation problems because most stock is issued for cash. However, not all stock is issued for cash. Most states have passed laws to guard against "watered stock," meaning the stock is valued at amounts substantially greater than the value of the assets transferred to the corporation.

Valuation difficulties can occur in determining (1) whether the market value of the stock issued or the market value of the asset acquired is a better representation of value and (2) the proper accounting for an exchange of stock to acquire another business. Further, stock is also issued in the form of stock options and the exercise of those options. The stock option is an expense that is measured at the fair value of the option—usually measured by the Black-Scholes method. Companies then purchase stock on the open market to fulfill the exercise of those options.

Treasury stock transactions should be examined to determine whether they are recorded in accordance with the board of directors' authorization and state corporation laws and are properly valued. Finally, the auditor should verify that the client has made an accurate distinction between stock and capital in excess of par or stated value.

Disclosure   Disclosure includes a proper description of (1) each class of stock outstanding and the number of shares authorized, issued, and outstanding and special rights associated with each class; (2) stock options outstanding; (3) convertible features; and (4) existence of stock warrants. The potential dilutive effect of convertible debt or preferred stock, stock options, and warrants should be disclosed in accordance with relevant accounting guidance in computing primary and fully diluted earnings per share. Any restrictions or appropriations of retained earnings should be disclosed, as well as prior-period adjustments and other comprehensive income adjustments.

Exhibit 14.1 shows an example of a comprehensive audit program for stockholders' equity.

Exhibit 14.1	Audit Program for Stockholders' Equity

OBJECTIVES

A. Determine that all transactions and commitments (options, warrants, rights, etc.) are properly authorized and classified.

B. Determine that all transactions and commitments are recorded at correct amounts in the proper period.

C. Determine that all transactions and balances are presented in the financial statements in conformity with relevant accounting guidance.

Procedure	Done by	W/P
I. Stockholders' Equity		
A. Capital stock and additional paid-in capital—substantive test procedures		
1. For each class of stock, identify the number of authorized shares, par or stated value, privileges, and restrictions.	_____	_____
2. Obtain or prepare an analysis of the activity in the accounts; trace opening balances to the balance sheet as of the close of the year (period) previously audited.	_____	_____
3. Examine minutes, bylaws, and articles of incorporation for provisions relating to capital stock and support for all changes in the accounts including authorization per minutes of board of directors and stockholders' meetings, and correspondence from legal counsel.	_____	_____
4. Account for all proceeds from stock issues (including stock issued under stock option and stock purchase plans):		
a. Recompute sales price and applicable proceeds.	_____	_____
b. Determine that proceeds have been properly distributed between capital stock and additional paid-in capital.	_____	_____
5. If the company does not keep its own stock record books		
a. Obtain confirmation of shares outstanding from the registrar and transfer agent.	_____	_____
b. Reconcile confirmation with general ledger accounts.	_____	_____
6. For stock options and stock option plans, trace the authorization to the minutes of the board of directors' meetings and review the plan and the option contracts. Obtain or prepare and test the analyses of stock options that include the following information:		
a. *For option plans*, the date of the plan, the number and class of shares reserved for option, the method for determining the option price, the period during which options may be granted, and the identity of persons to whom options may be granted.	_____	_____
b. *For options granted*, the identity of persons to whom options are granted, the date of grant, the number of shares under option, the option price, the number of shares as to which options are exercisable, and the market price and value of shares under option as of the date of grant or measurement—first date on which are known both (1) the number of shares the individual is entitled to receive and (2) the option of purchase price, if any.	_____	_____

(continues)

Exhibit 14.1	Audit Program for Stockholders' Equity *(continued)*

Procedure	Done by	W/P
c. *For options outstanding*, the number of shares subject to option at the beginning of the period, the activity during the period (additional shares subjected to option, the number of shares exercised under options, the number of shares associated with options that expired during the period), and the number of shares subject to option at year end (period end).	_____	_____
d. Determine fair market value of options at time of issuance using the Black-Scholes valuation model, or the Lattice model.	_____	_____
7. Identify all stock rights and warrants outstanding as of the balance sheet date, including the number of shares involved, period during which exercisable, and exercise price; determine that the amounts are properly disclosed.	_____	_____
8. Obtain or prepare an analysis of the treasury stock account and		
a. Inspect the paid checks and other documentation in support of the treasury stock acquisitions.	_____	_____
b. Examine the treasury stock certificates; ascertain that the certificates are in the company's name or endorsed to it.	_____	_____
c. Reconcile treasury stock to the general ledger.	_____	_____
9. Determine the amount of dividends in arrears, if any, on cumulative preferred shares.	_____	_____
B. Retained earnings	_____	_____
1. Analyze activity during the period; trace the opening balance to the balance sheet as of the end of the year (period) previously audited; trace net income to financial statement assembly sheets; and trace unrealized loss on noncurrent investments to investment working papers.	_____	_____
2. Determine that dividends paid or declared have been authorized by the board of directors and		
a. Examine paid checks and supporting documents for dividends paid (selected checks to shareholders or to a dividend disbursing agent).	_____	_____
b. Recalculate amounts of dividends paid and/or payable.	_____	_____
3. Investigate any prior-period adjustments and comprehensive income adjustments to determine whether they were made in accordance with GAAP.	_____	_____
4. Inspect supporting documents and authorization for all other transactions in the account, such as treasury stock transactions, considering conformity with GAAP.	_____	_____
5. Determine the amount of restrictions, if any, on retained earnings at end of period that results from loans, other agreements, or state law.	_____	_____

Fraud-Related Substantive Procedures for Equity Accounts   In those audits where there is a heightened risk of fraud related to equity accounts, the auditor will want to consider performing the following procedures or, if the procedures are already being performed, altering the timing and extent of the procedures.

- Confirm terms of equity arrangements and shares held directly with shareholders.
- Confirm with shareholders whether there are any side agreements.
- Employ an appropriate level of professional skepticism and carefully analyze transactions to determine whether the terms and substance of the transactions indicate that the proceeds should be recorded as debt or as equity.
- Confirm with the transfer agent information on issued stock.

Of course, the specific procedures selected by the auditor will be based on the types of frauds that the auditor has determined to be most likely to occur at the client. For example, consider the financial derivatives that were at the heart of the problems that were revealed at Lehman Brothers during 2009 and 2010. In that case, the nature of the derivatives is not necessarily clear, the credit of the counter-party is not clear, and the accounting for the transactions is highly subjective. In that situation, or others like it, specific fraud-related procedures might include the following:

- Confirm contracts and terms with counter parties. Determine who is responsible should losses occur on the contracts.
- Determine if there is a ready market for the security.
- Analyze the risk of failure.
- Determine the total amount of exposure associated with the derivatives.
- Carefully examine whether the company is correctly accounting for the transaction.

Integrated Audit Issues Concerning Bond and Stockholders' Equity Accounts

An effective yet efficient audit takes advantage of internal control strengths to minimize direct testing of long-term debt and shareholders' equity accounts. If the entity has effective internal controls, the audit will focus on testing those controls and identifying areas where potential misstatements might occur if any significant deficiencies or material weaknesses are identified. If there are no significant deficiencies or material weaknesses, reduced substantive testing may be appropriate. If, however, there are one or more significant deficiencies or material weaknesses in controls, the auditor must determine what types of misstatements could occur and design appropriate substantive audit tests to determine if they did occur.

How does an integrated audit of long-term debt and shareholders' equity differ from a more traditional audit? A traditional audit will focus on changes in the accounts during the year and account balances at year end. In contrast, an integrated audit will focus on assessing the controls related to cycle-specific accounts. If the controls are effective, reduced direct testing related to the account balances is possible. Recall the eight steps to conducting an integrated audit. We discuss those steps and their applicability to the audit of long-term debt and shareholders' equity accounts.

Phases I and II of the Audit Opinion Formulation Process

1. Continually update information on business risk, including the identification of any fraud risk factors noted during preliminary audit planning. Update audit planning for new risk information.
2. Analyze potential motivations to misstate long-term debt and shareholders' equity accounts (especially through financial derivatives) and the existence of other fraud indicators, and determine how the accounts might be misstated. For example, the company may want to keep liabilities off the balance sheet through SPEs, or may structure a debt instrument, e.g., mandatorily redeemable preferred stock to look like stock, or the company may issue stock with callable provisions that have more characteristics of debt.
3. Perform preliminary analytical procedures to determine if unexpected relationships exist and document how audit testing should be modified. Examples of analytical procedures that might indicate unexpected relationships would be the joint analysis of liabilities and expenses associated with warranty reserves, medical expenses and associated retirement benefits, and stock option expense.
4. Develop an understanding of the internal controls that are designed to address the risks identified in the three previous steps. In doing so, carefully consider any changes in the control environment that could cause pressure to misstate any of the accounts. Develop an understanding of the information system and associated controls used in developing estimates of warranties, retirement benefits, or in controlling the issuance of stock options.

Phases III and IV of the Audit Opinion Formulation Process

5. Determine the important controls that need to be tested for the purposes of (a) formulating an opinion on the entity's internal controls and (b) reducing substantive testing for the financial statement audit.

6. Develop a plan for testing internal controls and perform the tests of key controls in long-lived assets and related expense accounts. (For nonpublic companies, the auditor can choose to not test controls, but must determine where material misstatements could occur if controls are not present.)

7. Analyze the results of the tests of controls. If deficiencies are identified, assess those deficiencies to determine whether they are significant deficiencies or material weaknesses. Determine whether the preliminary control risk assessment should be modified (should control risk be assessed at a higher level?) and document the implications for substantive testing. Determine the impact of these deficiencies, and any revision in the control risk assessment, on planned substantive audit procedures by determining the types of misstatements that are most likely to occur.

   If no control deficiencies are identified, assess whether the preliminary control risk assessment is still appropriate, determine the extent that controls can provide evidence on the correctness of account balances, and then determine planned substantive audit procedures. The level of substantive testing in this situation will be less than what is likely required in circumstances where deficiencies in internal control were identified.

8. Perform planned substantive procedures (substantive analytical procedures and direct tests of account balances) based on the potential for misstatement and the information gathered about the effectiveness of internal controls. The substantive procedures will include procedures to address fraud risks. In completing substantive procedures the auditor will continue to assess whether the evidence obtained from all sources is sufficient and appropriate and the auditor may need to adjust the audit plan (either tests of controls or substantive tests) to help ensure that sufficient and appropriate audit evidence is obtained. For example, if controls over bonds are well designed and operating effectively, the audit testing may be limited to confirming that the face amount of the loan is still outstanding by corresponding with the bond trustee.

Mergers and Acquisitions

Mergers and acquisitions are a normal part of the business landscape. They present unique accounting and audit challenges, with significant challenges related to the valuation issues. Although the term *mergers* continues to be used, under current accounting all combinations of entities involve an acquisition; that is, one company is determined to be the acquirer.

There are three major valuation issues associated with acquisitions:

1. Valuing the assets and associated liabilities upon acquisition
2. Measuring restructuring charges and recognition of the liability
3. Measuring impairment of assets after operation begins

Acquisition—Asset Valuation Issues

Most acquisitions involve one company acquiring either another company or an operating division of another company. For example, Koch Corporation of Kansas City acquired the consumer products division of DuPont (roughly about 25% of DuPont); Time-Warner Company acquired AOL in a transaction that eventually led to a $94 billion loss for AOL Time-Warner. The complexity of such acquisitions is matched only by the strategic risk of combining the

PRACTICAL POINT

In 2007 and 2008, a number of companies were charged with fraud by the SEC because they had backdated stock options to coincide the lowest price of the stock during the year. Companies should have sufficient controls to prevent such misstatements, and auditors need to ensure that such controls are operating effectively.

LO 3

Describe the major valuation issues associated with mergers and acquisitions.

PRACTICAL POINT

When the auditor is auditing long-term liabilities and transactions related to mergers and acquisitions, the auditor should recognize that the following types of situations often require the auditor to rely on a specialist:

- Assets acquired and liabilities assumed in business combinations and assets that may have been impaired
- The valuation of environmental liabilities, and site clean-up costs
- The actuarial calculation of liabilities associated with insurance contracts or employee benefit plans.

Source: ISA 620

businesses to achieve the synergy of operations contemplated. See the *Auditing in Practice* box for a summary of the "hoped-for" synergies identified in the decision for AOL and Time-Warner to merge.

The major issues associated with valuing an acquisition are as follows:

- Determining the cost of the acquisition
- Valuing the identifiable tangible and intangible assets and liabilities
- Valuing the goodwill

Determining the Cost of the Acquisition

Normally, determining the cost of an acquisition is fairly straightforward—it is the amount paid to acquire the company. There are a number of factors that make the assessment more complicated. These include acquisitions:

- Made via stock rather than cash
- In which the final price is contingent upon the value of the assets received (post-audit)
- In which the final price is contingent on the future performance of the acquired company or division

The first item is usually the easiest but is dependent on the marketability of the stock issued. Some contracts simply specify the number of shares issued, while others require the company to transfer shares equal to a specified market value at a given date.

Most purchase transactions have a "good-faith" clause in which the purchaser has the right to "offset" against the purchase price the value of assets that were represented to exist but do not exist. For example, a company might show $1.3 million in accounts receivable, but after 180 days, the company has collected

AUDITING *in Practice*

THE AOL/TIME-WARNER MERGER

At the time of the merger, AOL was the dominant Internet service provider in the country. The company had recovered from questionable accounting practices and had marketed its brand nationally. Time-Warner had acquired Turner Broadcasting, including the movie studio and a movie library that had begun with Warner Brothers and went back to the start of movie production. The company had anticipated extraordinary synergies: Movies would be offered over the Internet; magazines would primarily be read online; television, especially sporting events, could be offered on an anywhere, anytime basis; and cost savings would occur through staff developing content that could be delivered over multiple media. We have seen the market continue to evolve in this area whereby much of what was anticipated is now happening.

The question: If the synergies looked so good at the front, why did AOL/Time-Warner write off a charge of $94 billion? The answer is that the strategy was seriously flawed:

- Internet delivery of movies, television, or even magazines requires fast downloading and broadband connections; AOL grew by being the premier dial-up provider of services.

- Dial-up services did not support the delivery mechanisms anticipated in the merger.

- The management cultures of the two entities were vastly different (AOL more informal, Time-Warner more analytic and formal).

- There was no strategic plan for integration or management leadership.

- Consumers were slow to move to the Internet to read magazines or download movies; other media such as DVD movies were developed. The business model for making profit on Internet reading of magazines is much different and relies on a new method of placing ads with very little or no subscription services.

In sum, what looked great lacked a fundamental strategy. Without carefully analyzing the strategy, the companies were setting themselves up for failure. The auditor must understand the strategies and the likelihood of their success to evaluate the valuation of assets acquired—and to address the most vexing problem of all: *What do you do if management simply overpays for the purchase?*

only $600,000 and supporting material for the remaining $700,000 cannot be located. In some instances, the contract will allow the offset of the $700,000 against the purchase price, but in other instances it may not. The auditor will have to know the specifics of the contract and the procedures the company will use to resolve disputes on the existence of assets in order to reach a final purchase price.

In many acquisitions, the acquiring company may want the management of the acquired company to stay on and run the business. This occurs many times when a small business is acquired. The managers know the business, they have contacts with the customers, and their cooperation may be crucial to the effective integration of the companies. Often, in these situations, the companies reach an agreed-upon price with significant contingency payments that will be based upon the newly acquired company's reaching pre-specified performance objectives. The auditor and the client must assess the likelihood of the acquired entity's meeting those performance objectives and determine when to recognize the contingency payments as part of the cost of the acquired company. If it is highly likely that the company will meet the objectives, the full cost should be recognized at the time of acquisition.

Valuing Identifiable Tangible and Intangible Assets

The acquiring company needs to bring all the specifically identifiable tangible and intangible assets onto its books at their "fair market value" at the time of acquisition. The fair market value of the assets may differ significantly from the book value of those assets. Usually, the company will hire an independent appraiser to value the tangible assets—e.g., property, machinery, and office equipment. The intangible assets—e.g., patents or copyrights—may be more difficult to value; however, they should normally be valued at the net present value of future (net) cash flows associated with the asset. For example, the copyright to a book might be valued at the net present value of future positive cash flows associated with sales of the book minus the cash outflows to produce and market the book. These estimates may be more difficult to obtain but can often be estimated based on the company's history with similar books.

The use of a specialist to value the tangible assets presents some unique challenges to the auditor. Remember, the auditor cannot simply accept the appraisal and management's assessment of the fair value of the assets. Rather, the auditor must gather independent evidence to determine whether the assessed values are appropriate. In gathering the evidence, the auditor should:

1. Evaluate the qualifications of any specialists, ascertaining whether the individuals are certified, experienced, and reputable.
2. Determine if the specialists hired by management are sufficiently independent of management that they will not be influenced by management's objectives.
3. Review the methodology used by the specialists to determine whether they are sound; e.g., determine if the specialist identifies sales prices for comparable land or property, reconstruction costs for buildings, and so forth.

Valuing Goodwill

In concept, the valuation of **goodwill** is fairly straightforward: it is the excess of purchase cost over the fair market value of identifiable net tangible and intangible assets acquired during the purchase. However, with ASC 350 (formerly SFAS 142), the FASB requires that goodwill be specifically identified with an operating segment or a reporting unit. By definition, these parts of the business must be sufficiently identifiable so that they can be managed as a unit or may be separately identified and sold as a unit. Otherwise, they become a part of the overall company operations. The distinction is important for subsequent valuation because goodwill is tested for impairment on a yearly basis.

The valuation and future testing of goodwill for potential **impairment** are facilitated if the company has used a capital budgeting process to determine the justification for the purchase. The company should have estimated future cash flows, cost savings, and strategic plans to estimate the value of the acquisition. Those future cash flows should have been discounted and compared to the cost of capital in making a decision about the acquisition. If the acquiring company develops such a model, it will (a) likely make better business decisions and (b) serve as a model that can be used for testing goodwill for potential impairment.

Audit Procedures for Restructuring Charges and Goodwill Impairment

Risks and Audit Procedures Related to Restructuring Charges

LO 4

Describe the risks related to restructuring charges, the audit procedures related to restructuring charges, and the approaches for testing potential goodwill impairment.

Whenever an acquisition takes place, the first thing usually heard from management is that it will (a) restructure operations to achieve efficiencies and (b) reduce the workforce by X%. This is usually followed by an estimate of future cost savings. As an example, in October 2008, Merrill Lynch's then CEO, John Thain, predicted that the investment banking firm expected thousands of job cuts after it was acquired by Bank of America. He indicated that the merged organization was committed to saving $7 billion and that the savings would come from those job cuts.

Companies restructure their operations continuously and those costs are reflected in current operating earnings. However, if a company makes a decision to restructure operations and develops a plan for restructuring, which often includes severance pay for employees, disposal of property, and so forth, accounting standards require the one-time employee termination benefits be recognized as a liability on the communication date, i.e., the date on which the restructuring plan is communicated to employees (see ASC 420, formerly SFAS 146). For example, if the company chooses to eliminate the jobs of 1,000 white-collar workers and provide them with an average of $100,000 severance pay to be paid out over the next 18 months, financial accounting standards would require the liability to be recognized at the time when the formal commitment to eliminate the jobs is communicated to employees. The associated expense would be recognized as a separate line item. The estimated costs of the ultimate disposal of property are recognized when the liability is incurred and the fair value of those costs are known with precision.

If not calculated correctly, the restructuring charges can be used to fraudulently manipulate income. See the *Auditing in Practice* feature that describes how restructuring charges and reserves were used by WorldCom to fraudulently inflate reported earnings.

Audit Procedures The auditor should be prepared to audit the estimate of restructuring charges. The auditor cannot rely on conservatism as an excuse to let the client overestimate the reserve for restructuring because the subsequent reversal of the liability will affect future income. The audit procedures should include the following:

1. Review current and proposed financial accounting standards to determine if changes have occurred in accounting for restructuring.
2. Review the detail developed by the company in determining its estimate; this should include the identification of specific assets to be disposed of, number of people to be terminated, union contracts on termination, and planned severance pay.
3. Review specific steps taken to date that would indicate that management has moved beyond a "plan" to terminate to the identification of specific parties or operations that will be affected by the plan. Specific parties or operations must be identified before a liability can be recognized.

AUDITING *in Practice*

THE CASE OF WORLDCOM'S RESTRUCTURING RESERVES

WorldCom grew from a small telephone company that emphasized data transmissions to a company that acquired MCI, then the country's second-largest long-distance telephone carrier—a company that was significantly larger than WorldCom. WorldCom grew through numerous acquisitions that were used to fuel growth and stock market value. In practically every acquisition, WorldCom would set up a restructuring reserve for the expected future costs associated with the integration of the operations into WorldCom and used the offsetting debit to increase goodwill rather than expenses.

As was its common practice, WorldCom always estimated the restructuring costs to be significantly higher than the company expected, thus creating a large amount of "Restructuring Reserves" on the balance sheet. The subsequent expenses associated with the restructuring were significantly less than the reserve that was established.

The Bankruptcy Trustee report on WorldCom indicated that WorldCom would systematically "release" (debit) these reserve (liability) accounts and credit expenses, thereby increasing reported earnings for the period. Clearly, the entries crediting expenses were fraudulent. However, they were enhanced because the auditing firm never questioned the amounts of reserves established in the first place because of an attitude that creating a liability is conservative. It did not consider the effect on future income when the company would choose to take the liability off the balance sheet. It is important to note that conservative accounting in one period creates a base for aggressive accounting in a future period. The audit implication is that conservatism is not necessarily the accounting objective. Rather, the objective is the accurate measurement of the economics and condition of the company.

4. Review and independently test the estimates by reviewing (a) contracts, (b) appraisals for property or estimates from investment bankers, and (c) severance contracts.
5. Mathematically test the estimates.
6. Develop an overall conclusion on the reasonableness of the liability and the appropriateness of the accounting used by the client.

Testing for Goodwill Impairment

Both management and the auditors will perform procedures related to goodwill impairment. Goodwill must be tested by management for impairment every year. However, if not done properly, the testing for impairment may result in too many subjective estimates. The tests for goodwill impairment are greatly facilitated if:

1. The company develops a price for the acquired company that is based on a capital budgeting model; that is, it analyzes the purchase in a systematic fashion that includes an analysis of future cash flows and the company's cost of capital.
2. The company clearly defines a reporting unit for which the goodwill is associated. The company keeps records that show the progress of the reporting unit subsequent to acquisition.

The reporting unit is usually defined as an operating unit that (a) provides separate accounting; (b) is managed as a separate segment; or (c) could be easily separated from the company, such as by a sale of the segment. The concept of the reporting unit usually focuses on the acquired company or segment. On the other hand, the company as a whole may be the reporting unit if the operations are fully integrated. For example, the AOL Time-Warner merger focused on the synergies of the integrated entity, not on the separate value of the Time-Warner business unit. The determination of the operating unit should be made at the time of acquisition, but it may evolve over time. If it changes over time, the client should document the changes and provide a rationale that relates to how the organization is managed.

PRACTICAL POINT

In Spring 2011 the FASB began the process to consider changes to its goodwill impairment guidance. Possible changes are intended to simplify the assessment of goodwill for impairment. The process would begin by first considering qualitative factors to determine whether it is more likely than not that the fair value of a reporting unit is less than its carrying amount before initiating the current two-step process. Auditors should be alert to changing guidance in this area.

Current accounting standards require the company to determine the fair value of the reporting unit and compare it to the reporting unit's carrying value (including goodwill). If the fair value is less than the carrying value, it is inferred that goodwill has been impaired and must be written down. ASC 350 (formerly SFAS 142) requires the impairment of goodwill to be evaluated by the client in a two-step process:

Step 1—The fair value of the reporting unit as a whole is compared to the book value of the reporting unit (including goodwill) and, if a deficiency exists, impairment would need to be calculated.

Step 2—The impairment is measured as the difference between the implied fair value of goodwill and its carrying amount. The implied fair value of goodwill is the difference between the fair value of the reporting unit as a whole less the fair value of the reporting unit's individual assets and liabilities, including any unrecognized intangible assets.

AUDITING *in Practice*

MAXIM PHARMACEUTICALS AND GOODWILL-MAXIM PHARMACEUTICALS

Maxim Pharmaceuticals was a start-up company headquartered in San Diego. It had a number of promising drugs in development and in clinical trials that early analysis indicated would be effective in treating some types of cancer such as melanoma. It also had other promising drugs, including one that had been found to be effective in addressing SARS. The development and approval process for new drugs may take up to ten years before the FDA and other regulatory agencies in Europe will approve a drug to be marketed. For Maxim, virtually all of their drugs were in the development stage.

The early prognoses for Maxim's products were outstanding. Their stock went from $6 per share to approximately $72 per share. Near the market's peak, the company made an important acquisition of another company that had ten drug patents, using the stock to pay for the acquisition. The prognosis for the combined company was excellent. Maxim subsequently sold two of the patents at amounts greater than they paid for the whole acquisition to generate needed cash flow for the company. The company had accounted for goodwill under the previous accounting standards and was amortizing it over fifteen years.

At the end of 2001, the market became impatient with Maxim and its stock price dropped to $4 per share. At $4 per share, the total market value of the company was less than the carrying value (book value) of the company, including approximately $28 million of unamortized goodwill. The market capitalization of the stock showed that the market placed a zero value on goodwill. Consequently, the company took an impairment charge of $28 million during the last quarter of 2001 to recognize the impairment of the goodwill. The market assessment of

Maxim's prospects as reflected in the stock price thus led the company to recognize a loss in the financial statements that would not have been present if the company had continued the old method of accounting for the amortization of goodwill (i.e., not recognizing impairments but instead recognizing the amortization expense straight line over 40 years).

Since 2001, Maxim has obtained approval on some of its drugs. The stock price has more than quintupled from its low, showing that the market places a much higher value on the company and its acquisitions than it did previously. The drugs associated with the previously acquired company appear to have very high promise and the market values those prospects. However, at the end of 2001, the market did not value the prospects nearly as highly. Because impairment is an annual test, the company had to recognize the impairment in 2001.

The subsequent change in market value is not considered; the company is not allowed to write up goodwill to previous levels. The point of this example is that market value can be an elusive and fickle concept. However, it is the best estimate of fair value for the entity as a whole when the company's reporting segment is the whole entity and is required to test impairment on an annual basis. Subsequent events may show that the market was not accurate at a given date; the price may go up or go down. If market price goes down, the company will again test for goodwill impairment the next year. Interestingly, the company could not maintain adequate cash flow and was forced to sell off the patents on its promising drugs and later declared bankruptcy. Although the market may have appeared to have been wrong, the long-term result mirrored the correctness of the impairment.

Exhibit 14.2	Calculating Goodwill Impairment—Maxim Pharmaceuticals

A company has total assets and liabilities as follows (book values in millions):

Assets—excluding goodwill	$125.1
Goodwill	$ 28.0
Total	$153.1
Liabilities	$ 8.0
Stockholder's Equity	$145.1
Total	$153.1

The total market capitalization of the company at fiscal year end is $112 million. Therefore:

Fair Value (FV)	$112.0
Carrying Value (CV) – or Net Book Value	$145.1
Excess CV > FV	$ 33.1
Amount of Goodwill	$ 28.0
Amount of Goodwill Considered to Be Impaired:	$ 28.0

If the excess of CV > FV would have been less than $28 million, the amount of goodwill impairment would have been that amount.

The *Auditing in Practice* example on Maxim Pharmaceuticals illustrates an interesting example of the accounting that takes place when the **reporting entity** is the company as a whole. The exhibit shows a company that the market thought had great prospects. Then the market soured on the company's prospects, forcing a write-down in the value of the company. Subsequently, the market saw great promise in the company and its products.

Impairment Test When Reporting Unit Is the Company   In many instances, such as Maxim and AOL Time-Warner, the reporting unit is the combined company. If the company is a public company, the current fair value can be estimated by examining the current market capitalization of the stock. The company then needs to determine whether fair value is less than or more than the carrying value (book value). If fair value is less than carrying value, an impairment of goodwill is inferred and goodwill is written down to the point where fair value equals carrying value. Exhibit 14.2 shows a computation of the goodwill impairment.

Impairment Test When Reporting Unit Is a Separate Subunit of the Company   When the company as a whole is not the reporting unit, the auditor must gather other evidence to assess potential goodwill impairment. Other sources of information include negotiations to sell the reporting unit, current profitability of the reporting unit, projected cash flows compared with cash-flow projections made at the time of acquisition, and management's strategic plans for using the assets. The client is required to consider the approaches identified to develop an estimate of asset impairment. The auditor must evaluate (a) management's methodology for assessing impairment and (b) whether an objective evaluation of the evidence supports the client's conclusion. Exhibit 14.3 provides an overview of factors the auditor should consider when assessing goodwill impairment.

PRACTICAL POINT

An intangible asset that is not subject to amortization, such as goodwill, needs to be tested for impairment annually, or more frequently if events or changes in circumstances indicate that the asset might be impaired.

Financial Accounting and Audit Considerations for Goodwill Impairment

The impairment tests of goodwill constitute a significant audit problem, and auditor judgment must absolutely be tied to the auditor's knowledge of business

Exhibit 14.3	Overview of Factors Affecting Goodwill Impairment Valuations

Factors to Be Evaluated	Evidence Issues	Potential Audit Problems
Current Fair Market Value of the Entity	Determine Fair Market Value (FMV) of the total entity.	Readily available if publicly traded, but not readily available if not publicly traded.
		Market valuation may be volatile. The FASB addresses this by requiring the impairment test at the same time each year (which might not necessarily be year end).
	Determine FMV of the operating segment.	FMV might not exist. Might require independent appraisals by investment bankers or estimates using cash flow and discounted present value factors.
		Assumptions must be made about competition, economic development, product placement, and so forth. These assumptions will be difficult to verify.
Operating Segment Must Be Clearly Defined	If the acquired company remains intact after the acquisition, it is defined as the operating segment.	No particular problem.
	The purpose of most acquisitions is to integrate the newly acquired business into the operation of the existing business.	The company must set up a systematic methodology to clearly define the operating segment and trace it over time.
	Operating segments may change over time as acquisitions are made. The acquired operating unit may not be distinguishable after a period of time.	Goodwill arising from many acquisitions can be netted into one test at the operating segment level, but not netted at the company level.
Current FMV of Assets and Liabilities of Non-Goodwill Assets	Assets: could be measured by estimated NRV or estimated replacement costs.	Assets are used as a group of assets. It is difficult to estimate FMV of a group because there may be a limited number of buyers for the group.
		Replacement cost data may be difficult and costly to obtain, and the data must be adjusted for usage.
	Liabilities: could be estimated by discounted cash flows using current interest rates properly adjusted for risk.	Interest rates must be adjusted for risk and term.
Goodwill Impairment	The impairment is measured by the difference between market value of the operating segment and the FMV of net assets.	All the difficulties identified previously come into play.
		Estimates are hard to verify because they are based on assumptions. The auditor needs to perform sufficient analysis to determine the reasonableness of assumptions.

AUDITING *in Practice*

EVALUATING IMPAIRMENT OF GOODWILL

XYZ Company was a publicly traded manufacturer of low-cost office furniture. Its board decided to diversify and hired new management to lead the diversification. Prior to diversification, the company had assets of approximately $18 million. New management decided to diversify by buying four separate companies—all in the defense industry—over a period of three years. Although the companies were high-tech, most of the technology was well established, including that of a company that made gyroscopes.

In the first acquisition, XYZ Company assigned most of the excess of purchase price over fair value of net assets to an account called "purchased technology" and amortized the intangible asset over a period of nine years. It reasoned that the company had purchased technology that would allow it to compete for the next few years but that new technology would have to be developed to assure future growth. Only a small amount was allocated to goodwill. In the second acquisition, almost identical in cost and nature, XYZ allocated the excess cost to goodwill rather than to purchased technology. The rationale used by management was that such an allocation was generally acceptable.

The amounts were material in each case, with approximately one-half of the total purchase price allocated to either goodwill or purchased technology. For the two other acquisitions, XYZ allocated about half of the total purchase price to goodwill. The company's assets grew from $18 million to $32 million.

Recall that goodwill is supposed to represent superior earnings power of the acquired company. Thus, profitability of the acquired company is necessary to show the existence of goodwill. Over a period of five years, only one of the newly acquired companies was profitable, and that profit was fairly negligible. Because the prognosis for future profitability was not good, the board of directors instructed management to look into selling the acquired companies and to concentrate on its furniture business. Management solicited outside investment advice. The investment bankers suggested that the newly acquired businesses could be sold for approximately their book value (before considering corporate goodwill). After a two-year period, XYZ Company sold the companies at a loss. The evidence clearly suggested that goodwill had been impaired and should have been recognized much earlier. The fact that it was not recognized earlier led to a court case.

strategy and business risk. The following guidelines have been provided by the FASB to deal with goodwill impairment:

- The impairment tests should be performed at least annually, on the same date, but not necessarily at year end.
- Goodwill within operating segments can be offset (netted); however, goodwill that exists in different operating segments cannot be offset.
- The FMV (fair market value) of assets and liabilities must be independently calculated at the same time that goodwill impairment is tested.
- Clear, objective evidence must be gathered to record the goodwill impairment.

Situations may arise, other than the annual review, in which the impairment of goodwill should also be addressed. These include:

- A significant adverse change in legal factors or the business environment
- An adverse action or assessment by a regulator
- Unanticipated competition that significantly reduces the value of the company or reporting unit's products
- A significant loss of key personnel
- A more-likely-than-not expectation that a reporting unit or a significant portion of a reporting unit will be sold or otherwise disposed of
- A significant decline in operations of a significant asset group within a reporting unit
- A goodwill impairment loss recognized by a subsidiary that issues separate GAAP financial statements and is a component of the reporting (parent) company

> **PRACTICAL POINT**
>
> When all (or most) of the goodwill is related to an individual acquisition and the current market value of the company as a whole is less than its book value, that information requires the auditor to further test goodwill for impairment.

> **PRACTICAL POINT**
>
> An acquisition requires an assessment of the existence of intangibles other than goodwill that may have a finite life. Most appraisal experts assign value to such things as (a) purchased technology, (b) customer account lists and relationships, and (c) patents or copyrights. These items should be conscientiously identified, valued, and amortized over their expected life.

- A significant decline in operations for the industry as a whole, or the economy as a whole—as has happened during the recent recession

An example of how the factors may come together to signal an impairment of goodwill is shown in the *Auditing in Practice* feature on evaluating the impairment of goodwill.

Transactions with Related Entities

LO 5

Identify the types of related-entity transactions, describe the proper accounting, and develop an audit approach for related-entity transactions.

Many companies have transactions with other companies or people that may be related to either the company or to senior management. These are often referred to as "related-party" transactions, but it is better to refer to them as *related-entity* transactions. Related-entity transactions can occur between parents and subsidiaries; between an entity and its owners; between an entity and other organizations in which it has part ownership, such as joint ventures; and between an entity and an assortment of special purpose entities, such as those designed to keep debt off the balance sheet.

The financial frauds of the past decade have led to a realization that related-entity transactions can be used to manipulate financial reporting. In the United States, the FASB and Congress have pushed the profession to improve the financial reporting transparency to fully and fairly portray the economic substance of its transactions—including a full and fair disclosure of all transactions that are not made at "arms length" or are not independent of the organization's management. Users also want to make sure that the corporate governance structure is acting on their behalf. Thus, the auditor should gain assurance that the board of directors is aware of all related-entity transactions and that it has approved (a) the development and operation of any special entities and (b) the transactions with any related entity. As an example of the problems with related entities, read the *Auditing in Practice* feature regarding Enron and Special Purpose Entities (SPEs).

PRACTICAL POINT

Related-entity transactions are common with smaller companies, and they often take place with entities that are mutually controlled by the owner. Their purpose may relate to taxes or to sheltering assets; but whatever the reason, they are high risk if the auditor is not aware of each one.

Accounting for Transactions with Related Entities

The accounting for related-entity transactions is straightforward: Because related-entity transactions are not "arms-length" transactions with outside parties, they need to be either (a) eliminated upon the development of consolidated financial statements, where applicable, or (b) fully disclosed. For the auditor, the relevant risks for these types of transactions typically relate to the presentation and disclosure assertion. Full disclosure requires a description of the:

- Nature of the relationship of the related entities
- Dollar amount and nature of transactions
- Purpose of the transactions
- Future contractual obligations
- Terms of the transactions, manner of settlement, and amounts due to or from related parties

Normally, the company will not make any statements regarding whether the transactions would have been consummated with a nonrelated entity at the same price and terms. The auditor discourages such comments because it is difficult to obtain evidence that transactions are at the same price as would have otherwise been obtained. The SEC requires that all related-entity transactions with senior management be disclosed, including loans or the use of personal assets that might be construed as income. An example of egregious use of corporate assets for personal use is seen in the *Auditing in Practice* feature about Tyco and its CEO, Dennis Kozlowski.

AUDITING *in Practice*

ENRON AND SPES

During the 1980s and 1990s, companies found that they could develop Special Purpose Entities (SPEs) to hide problems. Enron was the master of this strategy. It discovered that it could use a little-known accounting rule on leases to create SPEs to keep debt off the balance sheet. Lenders would make loans to the SPEs as long as the loans were collateralized first by the assets of the SPE and second by Enron stock.

Enron set up SPEs to accomplish three objectives:

1. Keep debt off the balance sheet of Enron

2. Meet cash flow needs

3. Increase earnings

Enron accomplished these three objectives by selling assets it held—e.g., stocks in other companies, receivables, or physical plants—to the SPEs, which were controlled by Andy Fastow, Enron's CFO. Most often, Enron would recognize a gain on the sale of the assets and would record the cash as income from the sale, not as a loan. Over a period of time, Enron used the SPEs to increase cash flow,

recognize millions of dollars in earnings, and keep billions of debt off the balance sheet. Enron thus portrayed a financial picture of health that belied the real problems that the company was experiencing.

Enron had a half-page footnote on related-entity transactions in which it disclosed that the company occasionally had transactions with special entities that were designed to improve the company's borrowing capacity and profitability. None of the details were disclosed.

In one case, Enron had used a SPE to develop a joint venture with Blockbuster to deliver on-demand movies over broadband. Enron then sold all the anticipated profits associated with the future delivery of movies to customers to the SPE and recognized more than $100 million in profits. Enron never sold a single movie because the pilot test never met the feasibility threshold and Blockbuster pulled out of the deal. Nonetheless, Enron recognized $100 million of income on its books based on the anticipation of future profits of SPEs.

Related-Entity Transactions and Small Businesses

Related-entity transactions occur fairly often with smaller, privately held businesses. As an example, a construction company might lease all its equipment from another entity that is owned by the owner of the construction company. The owner may have developed the other company for tax purposes. The auditor must be alert to the nature of these transactions because the small business owner may want to hide them from the banker or other outside users. However, the expectation is that the auditor must gather sufficient information about the company's operations such that reasonable inquiries are made to determine if related-entity transactions are occurring.

Audit Approach for Related-Entity Transactions

The client should have an information system, with effective internal controls, that can identify all related entities and account for all related-entity transactions. The auditor should begin with an understanding of the information system developed by the client to identify such transactions. In some cases, the client may not want to have related-entity transactions discovered. Thus, the approach taken by the auditor will be similar to an approach that might be used to look for the existence of fraud. The audit approach is divided into two complementary sets of procedures:

1. Obtain a list of all related entities and develop a list of all transactions with those entities during the year.
2. Carefully examine all unusual transactions, especially those near the end of the quarter or the end of the year, to determine whether the transactions occurred with related entities.

> **PRACTICAL POINT**
>
> Auditors should be aware that certain transactions may raise the possibility of the involvement of related parties. These transactions include borrowing or lending on an interest-free basis or at interest rates significantly above or below prevailing rates, selling real estate at a price that differs significantly from its appraised value, and making loans with no scheduled terms for repayment.

AUDITING *in Practice*

TYCO, DENNIS KOZLOWSKI, AND WEAK CONTROLS OVER EXECUTIVE POWER

During the 1990s, TYCO was one of the great growth stories on Wall Street. The company grew through expansion and was dominant in a number of niche markets, ranging from fire detectors to plastic hangers. The company was driven to grow by its CEO, Dennis Kozlowski, a person who envisioned himself as the "Jack Welch" of conglomerates. (Welch was a highly successful CEO of General Electric.)

In a court case in 2004, Kozlowski and the CFO were charged with looting the company of millions of dollars, none of which was disclosed. The looting included:

- Spending more than $1 million on his wife's birthday party
- Purchasing works of art for his apartment in New York
- Paying domestic help with Tyco resources
- Charging Tyco for the personal use of company planes and watercraft

Kozlowski also found a way to influence his underlings to develop loyalty to him and his use of corporate assets. He would approve significant loans to high-level managers, ranging anywhere from $100,000 to $3 million. He reserved for himself the right to cancel the loans at any time, thereby providing a gift to the employee. Although the board of directors should have approved such loans, as well as any forgiveness of the loans, Kozlowski chose to treat the corporation's assets as if they were his own. Board approval was never sought for the actions that the CEO reserved to himself. The audit implication of this situation is that the auditor should always examine significant transactions involving senior management. Although there is a concern for fraud, it may also be an indication of more general weaknesses in the organization's ethical culture and control environment.

Once all related entities are identified, the auditor can use generalized audit software to read the client files and list all transactions that occurred with these entities. The auditor then investigates the transactions to determine whether they have been properly recorded. Finally, the auditor determines the appropriateness of management's disclosures.

The other approach focuses on transactions that appear to be unusual. An example might be a large sale of goods near the end of the year at a price that is higher than normal or that has extended terms. The auditor might investigate and find that the transaction has occurred with a brother-in-law or an entity controlled by a related party.

Exhibit 14.4 gives an overview of an audit program for related-entity transactions.

Exhibit 14.5 provides examples of related-entity disclosures that audit clients might include in their financial statements.

> **PRACTICAL POINT**
>
> Procedures to address possible related-entity transactions normally are performed even if the auditor does not suspect that related-entity transactions or control relationships exist.

Variable Interest Entities

The term **variable interest entities** is used to describe a wide variety of ownership relationships a company may have with another entity. As business has become more complex, many businesses develop joint ventures with other entities to produce products utilizing the technologies of both entities in a creative fashion. These types of entities have existed for some time and include companies such as Dow Corning, a 50% joint venture of Dow Chemical and Corning Glass works.

The pharmaceutical industry uses joint ventures to develop and/or distribute new drugs. In some situations, companies will use a variable interest entity to perform research and development, with the sponsoring company maintaining

AUDITING *in Practice*

INSIGHTS FROM THE PCAOB

An excerpt from a PCAOB inspection report issued in October 2007 notes the following issues regarding audit firms' lack of adherence to required auditing standards associated with related-entity transactions. Auditors should be aware of these deficiencies and design their audits to provide reasonable assurance that their clients' disclosures of related-entity transactions are appropriate.

Inspection teams have observed deficiencies related to firms' failures to identify and address the lack of disclosure of related party transactions. They also have identified deficiencies relating to the effectiveness of firms' testing of the nature, economic substance, and business purpose of transactions with related parties. For example, firms have failed to sufficiently test (a) the validity and classification of expenditures made by a controlling shareholder on behalf of an issuer, (b) the collectibility of receivables due

from entities owned or controlled by officers of an issuer, (c) the validity and accuracy of payables owed to related parties, and (d) the appropriateness of the accounting for the extinguishment of a note receivable from an officer of an issuer.

The audit implication of these findings is that related-entity transactions, even if common for a company, should always be considered high risk because they are used when there is something that management wants hidden—whether from the auditor, the banker, or the tax assessor.

Source: "Report on the PCAOB's 2004, 2005, and 2006 Inspections of Domestic Triennially Inspected Firms" (see www.pcaobus.org).

---

a right to purchase any patents or processes developed. The entity may borrow most of the funds for development with collateralization in the form of patents developed and secured by the sponsoring entity's stock or guarantee. The entities may be structured such that the sponsor may have control but may not technically have 50% of the ownership (see Enron example earlier) to avoid the requirement for consolidation. The sponsoring company is thus able to keep debt related to research and development "off the books."

The audit approach for all these variable interest entities is similar to that for related-entity transactions in Exhibit 14.4 and includes the following:

- Develop an understanding of the business purpose of all variable interest ownership relationships.
- Examine all contractual relationships associated with the entity, including those guaranteeing loans and rights to assets.
- Determine the proper accounting for the entity.
- Review the current financial status of the entity to determine whether it creates any contingent liabilities for the organization.
- Summarize findings and review financial statement disclosure.

Disclosure of Other Significant Relationships

Organizations continue to develop close working relationships with suppliers, customers, and, in some cases, competitors. For example, most companies have "approved vendor lists" and a purchasing agent may purchase only from that list. SC Johnson—the maker of Pledge, Windex, Raid, OFF mosquito repellant, and a number of other household products—has a working relationship with Wal-Mart whereby SC Johnson is given the responsibility for managing the inventory in the household cleaner sections of Wal-Mart stores. In exchange for the preferential treatment in deciding where its goods are going to be displayed, as well as managing the inventory levels, SC Johnson agrees that the inventory at the store will be held on consignment by Wal-Mart until the goods are sold. In other words, SC Johnson acquires advantages in displaying its products in the world's largest retailer in exchange for incurring all the carrying costs for the inventory held in the Wal-Mart stores and their distribution

PRACTICAL POINT

A variable interest entity not refer to an interest rate, but rather to percentage of ownership or control by the separate entity by the client. As companies become more integrated with suppliers, customers, or even competitors, the auditor will increasingly encounter variable interest entities on an audit.

PRACTICAL POINT

Accounting for variable interest entities continues to evolve as accounting standard setters deal with the tough issue of determining control for consolidation purposes. Control often occurs with ownership significantly less than 50%.

Exhibit 14.4	Related-Entity Transactions

AUDIT OBJECTIVE: Determine if related-entity transactions occurred during the year and whether they are properly (a) authorized and (b) disclosed in the financial statements.

Audit Procedures

1. Ask the client about processes used to identify related-entity transactions and the client's approach to accounting for related-entity transactions.

2. Ask the client to prepare a list of all related entities. Supplement that list with disclosures that have been made to the SEC of top officers and directors in the company. For smaller businesses, supplement the list with a listing of known relatives who may be active in the business or related businesses.

3. Ask the client for a list of all related-entity transactions, including those with SPEs or variable interest entities, that occurred during the year.

4. Discuss the appropriate accounting for all identified related-entity transactions with the client and develop an understanding of the appropriate disclosure for the financial statements.

5. Inquire of the client and its lawyers as to whether the client is under any investigation by regulatory agencies or law officials regarding related-entity transactions.

6. Review the news media and SEC filings for any investigations of related-entity transactions of the client.

7. Use generalized audit software to read the client's files and prepare a list of all transactions that occurred with related entities per the lists identified above. Compare the list to that developed by the client to help determine the quality of the client's information system.

8. Identify all unusual transactions using information specific to the client including information on (a) unusually large sales occurring near the end of a period, (b) sales transactions with unusual terms, (c) purchase transactions that appear to be coming from customers, and (d) any other criteria the auditor might consider useful.

9. Review the transactions and investigate whether or not the transactions occurred with related entities. If related entities can be identified, determine the purpose of the transactions and consider the appropriate financial statement disclosure.

10. Determine whether any of the transactions were fraudulent, or were prepared primarily to develop fraudulent financial statements. If there is intent to deceive, or if there is misuse of corporate funds, report the fraud or misuse to the Board of Directors. Follow up to determine if appropriate action is taken. If such action is not taken, consult with legal counsel.

11. Determine the appropriate accounting and footnote disclosure. Prepare a memorandum on findings.

Exhibit 14.5	Examples of Footnote Disclosures of Related-Entity Transactions

Note—During 2011, the company sold undeveloped real estate to a major shareholder for $12,250,000, which was the land's appraised value, and recognized a gain of $4,602,000.

Note—The company is a franchisee of XYZ Corp. XYZ owns 10% of the company's outstanding stock and has an option to acquire another 25%. During 2010 and 2011, goods, equipment, and services were purchased from XYZ at the amounts of $4,444,000 and $61,911,000, respectively.

Note—The company occupies, rent free, 5,000 square feet of space in a building owned by its major shareholder.

centers. The prognosis is that many companies will continue to evolve closer relationships—in some cases dependency relationships with other entities that may require footnote disclosure or recognition of contingent liabilities.

The SEC requires disclosure of all customer relationships in which one customer accounts for more than 10% of the sales of a company. The purpose of the disclosure is to inform users of potential economic dependencies that may affect the future of the company. An example of such dependencies is seen in the *Auditing in Practice* feature on Tandy Brands Accessories, a major designer and marketer of fashion accessories, including belts, gifts, small leather goods, eyewear, neckwear, and sporting goods. The auditor must determine that the client has an information system, with appropriate internal controls, that identifies sales by major customers in order to meet this requirement.

AUDITING *in Practice*

TANDY BRANDS ACCESSORIES AND RELIANCE ON SALES TO WAL-MART

Wal-Mart is a major purchaser of Tandy Brands Accessories. In fact, Tandy's June 30, 2009, Form 10-K reports that its two most significant business risks relate to its concentration of sales with several large companies:

> Ten customers accounted for 74% of our fiscal 2009 net sales, including Wal-Mart which accounted for 43% of our net sales. A decision by Wal-Mart or any other major customer, whether motivated by competitive conditions, financial difficulties or otherwise, to significantly change the amount of merchandise purchased from us, or to change the manner of doing business with us, could have a significant effect on our results of operations and financial position. We attempt to mitigate this exposure by selling our products to a variety of retail customers throughout North America.... Like most companies in our industry, we do not enter into long-term contracts with our customers. As a result, we have no contractual leverage over their purchasing decisions. A determination by a major customer to decrease the amount of products it purchases or to discontinue carrying our products could have a material adverse effect on our operations.

Thus, if Wal-Mart stops buying from Tandy, the company would be in serious financial trouble. Disclosure of this vulnerability to investors and other third-party users is at the heart of why such disclosures are required in the company's public filings.

The audit implication of this situation is that the auditor needs to understand whether the company has a sufficient information system and appropriate internal controls to ensure that disclosures required in the 10-K are also accurate. Further, the auditor must understand that a significant change in the relationship with Wal-Mart could have a dramatic effect on the company—including the possibility that the company may not remain a going concern.

Summary

The topics covered in this chapter are complex because (a) they represent significant measurement, valuation, and presentation and disclosure issues; (b) the accounting is often complex; (c) they often require the use of market value that is different from historical cost in estimating values; (d) they often involve the use of specialists—some of whom may not be qualified or do not comply with the same independence standards as the accounting profession; and (e) management is often motivated to use accounting in the areas discussed to portray financial results that differ from economic reality. For that reason, experienced auditors are most often assigned to audits that involve significant estimates or determinations of market value other than historical costs.

Many of the frauds of the past decade have involved estimates of the type covered in this chapter. The audit approach must be objective and challenging and therefore cannot rely simply on management's assessments.

Significant Terms

Goodwill   The excess of the net purchase price for an economic entity over the sum of the fair market values of specifically identifiable tangible and intangible assets; can arise only in connection with the purchase of an organization and identifies superior earning power associated with the entity.

Goodwill impairment   The decrease in the value of goodwill. Measured by comparing the fair value of the reporting entity with the carrying value of entity. If fair value is less than carrying value (including goodwill), the presumption is that goodwill has been impaired. Goodwill should be written down to an amount that would cause fair value to be no more than carrying value.

Postretirement benefits   All postretirement benefits, other than pensions. Must be identified and measured by the company. The accounting treatment is conceptually the same as pensions.

Reporting entity   For accounting purposes, it is the acquired segment or operating segment to which the goodwill from the acquisition is assigned. Tests for goodwill impairment are performed at the operating unit level.

Variable interest entity   A legal business structure that does not have enough capital to support itself because of its lack of equity investors. The financial support for the VIE is provided by an outside source, such as another corporation. A VIE is often created by a corporation to serve as a holding company, which will hold assets or debt.

SELECTED REFERENCES TO RELEVANT PROFESSIONAL GUIDANCE	
TOPIC	**SELECTED GUIDANCE**
Related Parties	SAS 45 *Related Parties section of Omnibus Statement on Auditing Standards—1983*
	SAS *Related Parties* (Redrafted) (issued but not effective; proposed effective date is December 2012)
	ISA 550 *Related Parties*
Auditing Estimates	SAS 57 *Auditing Accounting Estimates*
	SAS 101 *Auditing Fair Value Measurements and Disclosures*
	SAS *Auditing Accounting Estimates, Including Fair Value Accounting Estimates and Related Disclosures* (issued but not effective; proposed effective date is December 2012)
	ISA 540 *Auditing Accounting Estimates, Including Fair Value Accounting Estimates, and Related Disclosures*
Using the Work of a Specialist/Expert	SAS 73 *Using the Work of a Specialist*
	SAS *Using the Work of an Auditor's Specialist* (issued but not effective; proposed effective date is December 2012)
	ISA 620 *Using the Work of An Auditor's Expert*

Note: *Acronyms for Relevant Professional Guidance:*
STANDARDS: **AS**—Auditing Standard issued by the PCAOB; **IAS**—International Standard on Auditing issued by the IAASB; **SAS**—Statement on Auditing Standards issued by the Auditing Standards Board of the AICPA; **SSAE**—Statement on Standards for Attestation Engagements issued by the AICPA.
ORGANIZATIONS: **AICPA**—American Institute of Certified Public Accountants; **COSO**—Committee of Sponsoring Organizations; **IAASB**—International Auditing and Assurance Standards Board; **PCAOB**—Public Company Accounting Oversight Board; **SEC**—Securities and Exchange Commission.

Review Questions

14-1   **(LO 3)** Why do audits of acquisitions and mergers have high levels of inherent risk?

14-2   **(LO 3)** How does a company measure the cost of an acquisition of another company? What factors often complicate the determination of actual cost? Explain how each factor complicates the calculation of cost and the steps the auditor has to take to reach a conclusion about the cost of the acquisition.

14-3   **(LO 3)** How is the amount of goodwill determined at the time of acquisition?

14-4   **(LO 3)** An audit client has acquired another company, and an independent real estate appraiser has been hired to value the assets of the acquired company. What are the audit requirements regarding use of the specialist (appraiser)?

14-5 **(LO 3)** Does the auditor need to engage another independent specialist to test the work of the specialist hired by the company to determine the value of the tangible and intangible assets other than goodwill? Explain, incorporating the idea of the importance of auditor professional skepticism.

Professional Skepticism

14-6 **(LO 4)** How does an auditor test for the impairment of goodwill? What are the significant judgment issues that must be addressed?

14-7 **(LO 4)** What factors might signal the likelihood that goodwill may be impaired? Explain and indicate how the auditor would be aware of each of these factors.

14-8 **(LO 4)** How does an auditor determine the fair value of goodwill if:

- The reporting entity is the total company and the company is publicly traded?

- The reporting entity is the total company and the company is not publicly traded?

- The reporting entity is an operating segment?

14-9 **(LO 4)** Assume the company's stock price goes down in a bear market that occurs at the end of the year. However, the stock price more than doubles in the next year. The company recognized goodwill impairment at the end of the year when the stock price was low. Because the market decline was temporary, should the goodwill be written back up to its original value? What are the problems in using temporary market values?

14-10 **(LO 5)** What is a related entity? What is the proper accounting for transactions with related entities?

14-11 **(LO 5)** The FASB has used the term *variable interest entities* to describe a company's relationship with other entities. Ownership may vary from none, to less than 50%, to a 50–50 joint venture, to majority owned. Explain how the ownership interest in a related entity may vary and the effect of the ownership on the accounting used in preparing financial statements.

14-12 **(LO 5)** What is a special purpose entity (SPE)? Explain how Enron used SPEs to commit financial reporting fraud.

Fraud

14-13 **(LO 5)** What are the broad approaches used to identify and audit related-entity transactions? What are the audit risks associated with related-entity transactions?

14-14 **(LO 5)** Companies may have significant relationships with other entities that do not involve ownership interests but may involve control issues. What is the nature of these relationships? What disclosures are required of these relationships?

14-15 **(LO 5)** What is the required disclosure if management uses company resources for personal purposes—e.g., entertainment, birthday parties, and decorating apartments?

14-16 **(LO 1)** What are the significant estimates that must be made with the following liability accounts?

- Restructuring reserves

- Warranty reserves

- Pension obligations
- Other postretirement liabilities other than pensions

14-17 **(LO 1)** Explain how outside specialists are used in auditing pension obligations.

14-18 **(LO 2)** What information should the auditor note when reading a bond indenture? How is the information used in the audit?

14-19 **(LO 3)** Assume that common stock of a publicly held company is issued to acquire the operating assets of another company (but not the other company). What information should be used to determine the value of the transaction?

14-20 **(LO 2)** A company declared a 5% stock dividend. Identify the evidence the auditor would examine to determine whether the stock dividend was accounted for properly.

14-21 **(LO 2)** Explain how a bond amortization spreadsheet might be used to audit interest expense over the life of a bond.

Multiple-Choice Questions

14-22 **(LO 3)** The audit client has acquired another company by purchase. Which of the following would be the best audit procedure to test the appropriateness of the allocation of cost to tangible assets?
  a. Determine whether assets have been recorded at their book value at the date of purchase.
  b. Evaluate procedures used to estimate and record fair market values for purchased assets.
  c. Evaluate the reasonableness of recorded values using replacement-cost data for similar new assets.
  d. Evaluate the reasonableness of recorded values by discussion with operating personnel.

14-23 **(LO 3)** The auditor must gather independent evidence to determine whether the assessed values provided by a specialist are appropriate. In gathering the evidence, the auditor should:
  a. Evaluate the qualifications of the specialist, ascertaining whether the specialist is certified, experienced, and reputable.
  b. Determine if the specialist is sufficiently independent of management to not be influenced by management's objectives (remember, the specialist is paid by management).
  c. Review the methodology used by the specialist to determine if it is sound; e.g., determine if the specialist identifies sales prices for comparable land or property, and reconstruction costs for buildings.
  d. All of the above.

14-24 **(LO 3)** In accounting for an acquisition, the auditor must determine that there are separate valuations for all of the following *except*:
  a. All the specifically identifiable intangible assets, including an estimate of remaining useful life.
  b. Goodwill associated with the reporting unit.

c. Warranty expense for the previous year.

d. The useful life of physical assets that were acquired.

14-25 **(LO 4)** In determining the potential impairment of goodwill, which of the following would *not* be an appropriate methodology to estimate the fair value of a reporting entity? Assume the reporting entity is not the company as a whole.

a. Determine the fair market value of the entity based on current stock price of the company.

b. Obtain a "fairness" letter from an investment banker as to the value of the reporting entity if it were to be sold to another company.

c. Evaluate current profitability and cash flow in comparison with the capital budgeting model used in acquiring the company.

d. Obtain outside financial analysts' reports of the company's prospects that include a specific discussion of the reporting entity's prospects.

14-26 **(LO 3, 4)** If a company overpays for the purchase of another company, as was the assertion when the merger of AOL and Time-Warner took place, what steps should the client take to be sure the results are fairly portrayed in the financial statements?

a. Review financial analysts' reports; write the excess payment off to owners' equity at the time of acquisition.

b. Increase the value of tangible assets to cover the amount of overpayment because these are amounts that were paid to acquire the assets.

c. Record the excess amount to goodwill, but shorten the estimated life of goodwill for amortization purposes.

d. Record the excess amount as goodwill but test goodwill for impairment annually.

*14-27 **(LO 5)** When auditing related-entity transactions, an auditor places primary emphasis on:

a. Confirming the existence of the related entities.

b. Verifying the valuation of the related-entity transactions.

c. Evaluating the disclosure of the related-entity transactions.

d. Determining the rights and obligations of the related entities.

14-28 **(LO 5)** Which of the following statements is correct regarding transactions between a company and a major customer that accounts for more than 10% of the company's sales?

a. The profit from such transactions should be shown as a separate line item on the financial statements.

b. There is no disclosure required.

c. Disclosure of the nature of the relationship with the related entity and amounts due to and from each entity is required for all companies.

d. Disclosure of the amounts of such transactions must be disclosed for publicly traded companies, but not for privately held companies.

---

*All problems marked with a dagger are adapted from the Uniform CPA Examination.

14-29   **(LO 5)** Which of the following is *not* a procedure that an auditor would use in performing an audit designed to identify and account for related-entity transactions?

a. Send confirmations to all customers inquiring whether they are related entities.

b. Obtain a list of all related entities from the client.

c. Review all large, unusual transactions to determine whether they took place with related entities.

d. Review SEC filings to obtain a list of related entities.

*14-30   **(LO 2)** The auditor's program for the examination of long-term debt should include steps that require which of the following procedures?

a. Verification of the existence of the bondholders.

b. Examination of the bond trust indenture.

c. Inspection of the accounts payable master file.

d. Investigation of credits to the bond interest income account.

*14-31   **(LO 2)** When a client does not maintain its own stock records, the auditor should obtain written confirmation from the transfer agent and registrar concerning which of the following?

a. Restrictions on the payment of dividends.

b. The number of shares issued and outstanding.

c. Guarantees of preferred stock liquidation value.

d. The number of shares subject to agreements to repurchase.

Discussion and Research Questions

Internet

14-32   **(LO 3, 4)** Do an Internet search on the terms *restructuring* and *goodwill impairment*. For each search term, locate one public company that is experiencing this issue. Next, locate each company's most recent 10-K or annual report.

Required

Be prepared to discuss within a small group the following: (a) the company name and its industry, (b) the company's basic business model, and (c) the reasons that the company is going through a restructuring or experiencing a goodwill impairment.

Group Activity

Professional Skepticism

14-33   **(Mergers and Acquisitions, LO 3)** Research has shown that mergers and acquisitions during the past two decades have met with mixed success—with many appropriately labeled as ineffective.

Required

a. What processes should an organization have in place to evaluate the economics of a proposed acquisition?

b. What are the implications to the audit if the processes identified in part (a) are not in place?

c. What are the operational difficulties associated with a merger? More specifically, why is it so difficult to make mergers work the way they were intended to work? What factors should the auditor look at to determine whether a merger is coming together successfully?

d. Why is industry-specific knowledge critical in evaluating the long-term viability of a merger deal? What motivation does management have to convince the auditor that the merger is successful, even when it is really not? In answering this latter question, describe how auditors must exercise professional skepticism in evaluating management's assertions that a merger has been successful.

14-34   **(Purchase Accounting, LO 3)**   Romenesko Conglomerate Co. recently acquired Teasedale Cosmetic Company through a tender offer for all the common stock of Teasedale Cosmetic. Teasedale stock had been trading on the market at $25 per share, but the tender offer was made at $35 per share for all 2 million of the company's shares. Teasedale had a book value of $17 per share at the time of the acquisition. Romenesko gave each shareholder $10 in cash, one-half of a share of Romenesko common stock (trading at $30 per share), and one-tenth of a share of an $8 preferred stock not previously issued for each share owned. Teasedale's condensed balance sheet was as follows before the acquisition (in thousands):

· Cash	$ 300
· Other current assets	3,000
· Property and equipment	22,000
· Intangibles exclusive of goodwill	2,500
· Goodwill	5,000
· Total assets	$32,800

· Current liabilities	$ 4,000
· Pension obligation	3,000
· Long-term debt	8,000
· Deferred taxes	800
· Stockholders' equity	17,000
· Total liabilities and equity	$32,800

Required

a. What are the unique valuation problems the auditor must address in connection with Romenesko's purchase of Teasedale Cosmetics?

b. How should the auditor use a specialist in the valuation of the purchase transaction?

c. What happens to the goodwill that was on Teasedale's books? Explain.

d. What happens to the other intangibles that were on Teasedale's books? Explain.

e. What happens to the deferred income tax liability on Teasedale's books once the purchase is completed?

f. Assume that the client uses a specialist who does not change the value assigned to current assets or liabilities, but reduces the pension obligation to $1.5 million and values the PPE at $30 million and other intangibles at $5 million. Additionally, the current market value of Teasedale's long-term debt is $5 million, but its face value remains at $8 million (also its maturity value). What is the amount of goodwill to be recorded?

14-35   **(Goodwill Impairment, LO 4)**   In 2010, Nelson Communications purchased a controlling interest in Telnetco that resulted in goodwill in the 2010 consolidated financial statements of $4,500,000. There are no other intangible assets. Telnetco continues to be listed on NASDAQ. Near the end of 2011, Nelson estimated that the fair market value of Telnetco was $50,500,000 based on the present value of its future cash flows. Using the assistance of a professional appraisal firm, the fair market value of its net tangible assets was determined to be $46,900,000, resulting in a goodwill write-down of $900,000.

Required

a. Describe the inherent risks to this write-down.

b. Describe the audit evidence needed to evaluate the fairness of this write-down.

c. How might a specialist be of help?

14-36 **(Goodwill Impairment, LO 3, 4)** Merrill Publishing Company has operated primarily as a printer of catalogs, SEC filings, and phone books. During the past few years, it has:

- Expanded into a new product line in magazine publishing through the purchase of Wausau Printing Company

- Developed a professional website that makes all the information in the printed documents available on a subscription basis to the companies that come to it for printing

- Purchased St. Paul Labels, which makes labels for canned products

- Purchased Consumer Custom Design (CCD), which develops designs for cardboard food products; e.g., Wheaties cereal and other food products that are delivered in cardboard containers. The designs are developed on the Internet and are downloaded to companies for printing on their packaging products

The company recorded goodwill of $15 million, $12 million, and $8 million, respectively, for the Wausau, St. Paul Labels, and Consumer Customer Design purchases.

Required

a. Define an operating segment. Identify the criteria that Merrill might use to define an operating segment. Identify when the decision should be made to classify a purchase as part of an operating segment.

b. Assume that Merrill merges the operations of St. Paul Labels and Consumer Custom Design into one operating segment, which it has labeled as food product print design. The segment has been successful, but the operations relating to cardboard design, after three years, continue to fall below expectations. Because the operations are integrated, how would the client and the auditor measure the possible impairment of goodwill in the segment? In other words, it appears that the operations generated from St. Paul Labels are strong while the operations integrated from CCD are weak.

c. What are the problems associated with measuring the impairment of goodwill for the food product print design segment?

d. How would the auditor test for goodwill impairment for the purchase of Wausau Printing Company, assuming that it remains an identifiable segment? Also assume that cash flow and profitability continue to exceed the budget used in determining a purchase price. Does the company still need to obtain an independent assessment of the fair market value of the total company and the operating entity on an annual basis? Discuss the rationale for your answer.

14-37 **(Restructuring Reserves, LO 4)** Many acquisitions require a restructuring of operations to integrate the acquired entity into the acquiring company's business structure.

Fraud

Required

a. What actions does a company typically take in restructuring the organization following an acquisition? What are the advantages of restructuring operations?

b. Assume a company plans to shut down three factories, lay off 5,000 workers, and eliminate one line of business of an acquired company. How does the company compute the cost for disposing of the line of business? What information needs to be gathered to audit the restructuring reserve?

c. Explain how WorldCom used restructuring reserves (liabilities) to fraudulently manipulate reported earnings.

d. Assume that the company had more than a plan; it had specifically identified parties that would be affected by the restructuring. Therefore, the company accrued a restructuring reserve and recognized the expense as an unusual expense below operating income. What should be the proper accounting for future costs associated with the restructuring?

e. How does a company decide that a restructuring plan is complete? What is the proper accounting for a restructuring reserve that remains on the books but for which the restructuring has been completed?

14-38 **(Restructuring and Smoothing Earnings, LO 4)** Maxair Corporation has a history of acquiring a number of companies. It has managed earnings by estimating high reserves for merger-related activity such as terminating employees and closing plants. The actual costs incurred were significantly less than was estimated.

Fraud

Professional
Skepticism

Required

a. What is the proper journal entry that should be made when the company closes a plant and lays off workers and the cost is substantially less than it had estimated? Assume that the layoff is the implementation of a pre-defined plan.

b. In the WorldCom fraud, what did the company do with the reserves when the actual costs of closing plants, terminating employees, and disposing of assets were less than anticipated?

c. Why would management deliberately overestimate (at the time the merger is consummated) the future cost of closing plants and consolidating activities associated with a merger?

d. Identify three pieces of evidence that a skeptical auditor should look at during the merger transaction to determine if the cost of terminating a line of business, closing down a plant, and selling the plant is reasonable. In other words, how would the auditor go about evaluating the original liability estimate?

Fraud

14-39   **(Related-Entity Transactions, LO 5)**   It is common for an entity to have transactions with related entities—some of which are fully owned, some of which share common ownership but are not otherwise related, and others where ownership is small but there is control.

Required

a. What is a related-entity transaction? Provide examples of the parties involved in these types of transactions.

b. There are two basic procedures used in auditing related-entity transactions. Describe these procedures and evaluate the strengths and weaknesses of each approach.

c. Tyco is a conglomerate organization that had $36 billion in revenue. In a court trial, it was alleged that the CEO of the organization fraudulently used corporate funds:

- For a private birthday party (over $1 million)
- To lavishly furnish an apartment in New York City
- To pay domestic help for taking care of the apartment
- To make loans to key executives that were subsequently forgiven by the CEO

   (i)   What audit procedures would have identified these transactions?

   (ii)   Is it reasonable to expect an audit to uncover these types of transactions in a $36 billion company?

   (iii) Should the auditor look for these types of transactions in every audit? Is it reasonable for auditors to look for such transactions?

   (iv)   What controls should an organization like Tyco implement to ensure that such transactions do not take place in the future?

14-40   **(Related-Entity Transactions, LO 5)**   Eisenhower Construction, a privately held company, previously owned all of its construction equipment used for highway work (bulldozers, cranes, graders, and cement trucks). The company recently sold all of the equipment to the owner's son. The son is a 25% stockholder in Eisenhower Construction. The son's new business, Construction Rental, Inc., is 75% owned by the son and 25% owned by the father (75% owner of Eisenhower Construction). Construction Rental has grown dramatically such that less than 20% of its construction rental business is done with Eisenhower Construction. Further, Eisenhower Construction rents about 60% of its equipment from Construction Rental and leases another 40% from FabCo, an independent company. You have been assigned to perform the audit of Eisenhower Construction Company.

Required

a. What is the proper accounting and disclosure of the sale of the equipment during the year on the books and in the financial statements of Eisenhower Construction Company?

b. What is the required disclosure of the rental equipment that was rented from Construction Rental?

c. It turns out that the construction company also does water and sewer work and rents most of the smaller equipment from a daughter of the company's president. However, these rentals were not disclosed to the auditor. What audit procedures would have uncovered the existence of this other related-entity transaction?

Fraud

14-41 **(Related-Entity Transactions, LO 5)**   The relationship between successful organizations is changing. In some cases, competitors even combine efforts to jointly develop new products. In other situations, companies license their products to other companies.

Required

a. What is a related-entity transaction? What distinguishes a licensing transaction from a related-entity transaction? For example, Merck licenses Procter & Gamble to sell all Prilosec OTC drugs because Procter & Gamble has greater knowledge in how to market to the consumer. Is the license a related-entity transaction? If not, why not?

b. How would the auditor normally find out about licensing transactions, joint venture transactions, and SPE transactions?

c. Explain why the SPEs and the transactions that were entered into with those entities during the Enron fraud violated GAAP. What would have been the proper accounting for those transactions?

14-42 **(Warranty Estimates, LO 1, 2)**   You have been assigned to the audit of Oshkosh Truck Corporation. The company is the leading manufacturer of fire trucks and heavy-duty army trucks. All of the basic components are warrantied for 100,000 miles or four years, whatever comes first. There is a different warranty if the trucks are used in desert lands, and that warranty is for 40,000 miles or 18 months, whatever comes first.

Required

a. Identify the components of an information system that Oshkosh Truck should establish to develop an estimate of the warranty liability and warranty expense.

b. Assume the company established an information system to your specifications described in part (a). Write an audit program to audit the accuracy of the process that would provide audit evidence on the reasonableness of the warranty expense and warranty liability account.

c. Assume that last year, 60% of the trucks sold to the army were designated for use in the Middle East and thus carried only the 40,000 miles or 18-month warranty. Explain how this change would affect the recognition of the warranty expense and liability account.

d. Assume that the warranty liability has been growing over the past few years because actual warranty expenditures have been significantly less than estimated. Assume there has been no significant decline in the quality of the vehicles produced.

   (i) What information would the auditor gather to determine whether or not the liability might be materially overstated?

   (ii) If the auditor concludes the liability is materially overstated, what is the proper accounting? The company proposes to reduce the warranty expense this year and in coming years until the warranty liability is not overstated.

14-43 **(Drug Benefits and Postretirement Liabilities, LO 1, 2)**   One of the *Auditing in Practice* features in the chapter discusses Ford Motor Company's reducing a large portion of its other postretirement benefits by transferring its liability to the UAW Union through a one-time payment of $11.3 billion. However, Ford still has a sizeable

**Professional
Skepticism**

liability for postretirement benefits, in large part because of obligations that the company has under the Medicare Prescription Drug Improvement and Modernization Act of 2003.

Required

a. Identify the process that Ford would use to identify the liability for postretirement drug benefits. Identify the data Ford would need to make the estimate.

b. Identify how the auditor might audit the data. What aspects of the data would a professionally skeptical auditor be most concerned about in terms of management judgment on subjective items?

14-44   **(Bond Indentures and Bond Liabilities, LO 1, 2)**   The auditor should review the bond indenture at the time a bond is issued and anytime subsequent changes are made to it.

Required

a. Briefly identify the information the auditor would expect to obtain from a bond indenture. List at least five specific pieces of information that would be relevant to the conduct of the audit.

b. Because auditors are especially concerned with the potential understatement of liabilities, should they confirm the existence of the liability with individual bondholders? State your rationale.

c. A company issued bonds at a discount. Explain how the amount of the discount is computed and how the auditor could determine whether the amount is properly amortized each year.

d. Explain how the auditor could verify that semiannual interest payments are made on the bond each year.

e. The company has a 15-year, $20 million loan that is due on September 30 of next year. It is the company's intent to refinance the bond before it is due, but it is waiting for the best time to issue new debt. Because its intent is to issue the bond next year, the company believes that the existing $20 million bond need not be classified as a current liability. What evidence should the auditor gather to determine the appropriate classification of the bond?

Group Activity

14-45   **(Bond Covenants and Audit Actions, LO 1, 2)**   The following covenants are extracted from a bond indenture. The indenture provides that failure to comply with its terms in any respect automatically advances the due date of the loan to the date of noncompliance (the maturity date is 20 years hence).

Required

In discussions in a small group, work with your classmates to identify the audit steps that should be taken or reporting requirements necessary in connection with each one of the following:

a. The debtor company shall endeavor to maintain a working capital ratio of 2 to 1 at all times, and, in any fiscal year following a failure to maintain said ratio, the company shall restrict compensation of the CEO and executive officers to a total of no more than $500,000. Executive officers for this purpose shall include the chairman of the board of directors, the president, all vice presidents, the secretary, and the treasurer.

b. The debtor company shall insure all property that is security for this debt against loss by fire to the extent of 100% of its actual value. Insurance policies securing this protection shall be filed with the trustee.

c. The debtor company shall pay all taxes legally assessed against the property that serves as security for this debt within the time provided by law for payment without penalty and shall deposit receipted tax bills or equally acceptable evidence of payment of same with the trustee.

d. A sinking fund shall be deposited with the trustee by semiannual payments of $300,000, from which the trustee shall, at her discretion, purchase bonds of this issue.

14-46 **(Audit of Stockholders' Equity, LO 2)** A CPA firm is engaged in the examination of the financial statements of Zeitlow Corporation for the year ended December 31, 2011. Zeitlow Corporation's financial statements and records have never been audited by a CPA. The stockholders' equity section of Zeitlow Corporation's balance sheet at December 31, 2011, follows:

Stockholders' Equity:

Capital stock—10,000 shares of $10 par value authorized:	
5,000 shares issued and outstanding	$ 50,000
Capital contributed in excess of par value of capital stock	58,800
Retained earnings	105,000
Total stockholders' equity	$213,800

Founded in 2003, Zeitlow Corporation has ten stockholders and serves as its own registrar and transfer agent. It has no capital stock subscription contracts in effect.

Required

a. Prepare the detailed audit program for the examination of the three accounts composing the stockholders' equity section of Zeitlow Corporation's balance sheet. (Do not include in the audit program the verification of the results of the current-year operations.)

b. After all other figures on the balance sheet have been audited, it might appear that the retained earnings figure is a balancing figure and requires no further verification. Why would an auditor still choose to verify retained earnings? Discuss.

14-47 **(Audit of Long-Term Debt, LO 2)** The following long-term debt documentation (indexed K-1) was prepared by client personnel and audited by AA, an audit assistant, during the calendar year 2011 audit of American Widgets, Inc., a continuing audit client. The engagement supervisor is thoroughly reviewing the working papers.

Overall Conclusions

Long-term debt, accrued interest payable, and interest expense are correct and complete at 12/31/11.

Required

Identify the deficiencies in the audit documentation (shown next) that the engagement supervisor should discover.

Long-term Debt
December 31, 2011

Prepared by   Initials AA
Approved by   Date 2/10/12

Lender	Interest Rate	Payment Terms	Collateral	Balance December 31, 2010	2011 Borrowings	2011 Reductions	Balance December 31, 2011	Interest Paid to	Accrued Interest Payable December 31, 2011	Comments
First Commercial Bank*	12%	Interest only on 25th of month, principal due in full 1/1/15, no pre-payment penalty	Inventories	$ 50,000†	$300,000‡ 1/31/11	$100,000§ 6/30/11	$ 250,000‖	12/25/11	$2,500**	Dividend of $80,000 paid 9/2/11§ (W/P N-3) violates a provision of the debt agreement, which thereby permits lender to demand immediate payment; lender has refused to waive this violation
Lender's Capital Corp.*	Prime plus 1	Interest only on last day of month, principal due in full 3/5/15	2nd mortgage on Park St. building	100,000†	50,000‡ 2/29/11	—	200,000††	12/31/11		Prime rate was 8% to 9% during the year
Gigantic Building & Loan Assoc.*	12%	$5,000 principal plus interest due on 5th of month, due in full 12/31/12	1st mortgage on Park St. building	720,000†	—	60,000‡‡	660,000††	12/5/11	5,642§§	Reclassification entry for current portion proposed (See RJE-3)
J, Lott, majority stockholder*	0%	Due in full 12/31/12	Unsecured	300,000†	—	100,000‖‖ 12/31/11	200,000††	—	—	Borrowed additional $100,000 from J. Lott on 1/7/10
				$1,170,000† †††	$350,000 †††	$260,000 †††	$ 1,310,000 †††	T/B	$8,142*** †††	

Interest costs from long-term debt

Interest expense for year	$ 281,333***
Average loan balance outstanding	$1,406,667§§

Five-year maturities (for disclosure purposes)

Year-end 12/31/12	$ 60,000
12/31/13	260,000
12/31/14	260,000
12/31/15	310,000
12/31/16	60,000
Thereafter	360,000
	$1,310,000 †††

††† Readded, foots correctly
† Confirmed without exception, W/P K-2
‖ Confirmed with exception, W/P K-3
** Does not reconpute correctly
‡ Agreed to loan agreement, validated bank deposit ticket, and board of directors' authorization, W/P W-7
‡‡ Agreed to canceled checks and lender's monthly statements
‖‖ Agreed to cash disbursements journal and canceled check dated 12/31/09, clearing 1/8/10
*** Traced to working trial balance
† Agreed to 12/31/10 working papers
★ Agreed interest rate, term, and collateral to copy of note and loan agreement
§ Agreed to canceled check and board of directors' authorization, W/P W-7

Cases

14-48 **(Ethical Decisions in Lease Transactions, LO 1, 2, 6)** You are part of an audit team working on the audit for one of the firm's largest clients. This public client is growing and in the past year has increased its use of leases for equipment. In conducting the audit program for the old and new leases, it appears that both the new leases, as well as the previously recorded leases, meet lease capitalization criteria but have been recorded as operating leases. The team has had several meetings to review their analysis to assure that they have the correct answer. The team has concluded that the client will have to capitalize the leases and that prior-years' financial statements likely will have to be restated. The client will not be happy about this.

The team had raised this as a potential issue earlier in the audit with the senior manager overseeing the audit. He is swamped with other parts of the audit as well as with responsibilities for other audits. At that time, he suggested another approach to the issue based on a materiality argument; i.e., simply say that the issue is not material and then it becomes a "non-issue." The team explores this and feels it is not the right way to go. The deadline for completing the audit is fast approaching. To date, no one has apprised the client of the dilemma and the increasingly likely prospect that the company will have to report the leases as liabilities and announce a restatement. At the next team meeting, you raise the issue of whether it is time to let the client know. The team agrees it is time to have that conversation.

You advise your senior manager of the group's recommendation to alert the client to the problem. He is taken aback as he had not adequately gauged the extent of the problem. He knows that the partner who oversees this client account will have serious problems about this outcome—reporting significantly higher liabilities on the balance sheet and a restatement—especially when the audit firm had signed off on the lease accounting in prior audits. It is well known that this is one of the firm's more important audit clients, as well as the most important client for which this partner is responsible. The senior manager says that he is overcommitted with other crucial projects. He again pushes the materiality "solution" to the problem. That is, as in prior years, it can be argued that although the accounting is wrong, the adjustment is not material and can therefore be ignored—especially if one only looks at the income effect each year. You and the team are very uncomfortable with this response and you begin to wonder if the partner shares the senior manager's view.

You are vividly aware of the reputation this partner has for being tough on managers who bring bad news. Thus, you are not at all sure that he will buy the team's recommendation. Yet it is the team's conviction that failing to notify the client of the problem in a timely manner may lead to a serious breach in the client's relationship with the firm and possibly to accusations of negligence.

Required

a. Summarize the ethical difficulty posed in this case scenario.

b. What are the options for approaching the partner in this situation without undermining the engagement team's relationship with the senior manager?

c. What arguments would you make that appeal to the partner's values?

Ethics

14-49 **(Ethical Considerations and Goodwill Impairment, LO 4, 6)** Consider the situation outlined at the beginning of the chapter in the *Professional Judgment in Context* feature. The situation described concerns the aggressive growth strategy pursued by former CEO Dave Jones of Rayovac Corporation, which was renamed Spectrum Brands after the company purchased a variety of other entities and accumulated $2.5 billion in debt. Ultimately, those mergers did not work, Dave Jones left the company, and Spectrum Brands is now nearing bankruptcy and is facing delisting from the NYSE. At the same time, executives at the company are being paid handsomely to stay with the company. For example, the new CEO, Kent Hussey, will get a $2 million bonus if he remains with the company through December 31, 2009, and the board of directors approved bonuses for four top executives totaling $1.6 million.

Required

What ethical issues do you see for Spectrum Brand's board of directors (including its compensation committee)? Is it fair for the top executives to receive handsome pay packages when the company is in such a dire financial condition? Use the ethical decision-making framework outlined in Chapter 3 to formulate your answer.

Recall that the steps in that framework are (1) identify the ethical issue(s); (2) determine who are the affected parties and identify their rights; (3) determine the most important rights; (4) develop alternative courses of action; (5) determine the likely consequences of each proposed course of action; (6) assess the possible consequences, including an estimation of the greatest good for the greatest number, and determine whether the rights framework would cause any course of action to be eliminated; (7) decide on an appropriate course of action.

Group Activity

14-50 **(Decision Analysis related to Goodwill Impairment, LO 4, 6)** In June 2008, the PCAOB issued its report on the 2007 Inspection of PricewaterhouseCoopers LLP (see PCAOB Release No. 104-2008-125). For one of PricewaterhouseCoopers' clients (referred to as "Issuer A" in the PCAOB's inspection report), the PCAOB noted the following:

> In determining the fair value of the reporting units for its goodwill impairment analysis, the issuer added an amount ("award allocation") to the value of certain of the reporting units that was intended to adjust the value of the relevant reporting unit to compensate for certain inter-company purchases. The award allocation was calculated based on certain sales by the relevant reporting unit and, for each reporting unit that received an award allocation, resulted in a higher calculated fair value. The Firm failed to test the underlying data and the calculation of the award allocation. The Firm also failed to assess whether the methodology was applied consistently from year to year and whether the incorporation of the award allocation into the analysis was appropriate. The issuer's impairment analysis indicated that, without this award allocation, the issuer would have been required by GAAP to perform the second step of the goodwill impairment test to determine the amount of impairment, if any, for approximately one quarter of the issuer's reporting units.

In discussions in a small group, work with your classmates to answer the following questions by completing the first four steps of the seven-step "decision analysis framework" introduced in Chapter 3:

1. What difficulties might the auditor have faced when deciding whether Issuer A's approach was reasonable? Why might the audit firm have not appropriately tested Issuer A's analysis?

2. What are the consequences of the auditor's decisions in this case?

3. What are the risks and uncertainties associated with the client's analysis?

4. What types of evidence should the auditor gather to evaluate the reasonableness of management's approach?

Recall that the framework is as follows:

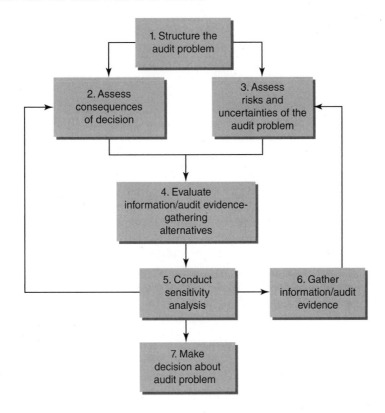

Source: Adapted from "Judgment and Choice," by Robin Hogarth.

Academic Research Case (LO 4)

Moehrle, S. R. (2002). Do Firms Use Restructuring Charge Reversals to Meet Earnings Targets? *The Accounting Review* 77(2):397–413.

i.   What is the issue being addressed in the paper?

ii. Why is this issue important to practicing auditors?

iii. What are the findings of the paper?

iv. What are the implications of these findings for audit quality (or audit practice) on the audit profession?

v.   Describe the research methodology used as a basis for the conclusions.

vi. Describe any limitations of the research that the student (and practice) should be aware of.

SEARCH HINT

It is easy to locate these academic research articles! Simply use a search engine (e.g., Google Scholar) or an electronic research platform (e.g., ABI Inform) and search using the author names and part of the article title.

FORD MOTOR COMPANY AND TOYOTA MOTOR CORPORATION:
PENSION LIABILITIES, GOODWILL IMPAIRMENT, AND WARRANTY LIABILITIES

Go to www.cengage.com/accounting/rittenberg for the Ford and Toyota materials.

Source and Reference	Question
Ford 10-K or Annual Report	**1.** One of Ford's most significant liabilities concerns pensions and other postretirement benefits. What is the nature of estimates required to value these liabilities? What risks do these estimates pose for the audit firm?
	2. Read Ford's MD&A disclosures concerning goodwill impairments. Describe the nature of estimates that management needs to make in order to estimate the impairments. What audit evidence would you want to gather to be assured that management's estimates are reasonable?
Ford 10-K, Toyota 20-F	**3a.** Warranty liabilities are a significant concern for manufacturers like Ford and Toyota. See the footnotes detailing information about warranties for each company. What are the amounts for accrued warranty liabilities and yearly warranty expense for each company?
	3b. What is the nature of estimates required for warranty liabilities?
	3c. What planning analytical procedures can you develop to help you understand the relative size of the warranty accounts for both companies? What inferences do you draw from the comparison of these analytics?

Module IV may be completed after either Chapter 10 or Chapter 14. Check with your instructor.

Module IV: MUS Sampling—Factory Equipment Additions

Richard Derick has asked you to develop a sampling plan to determine the extent of misstatements in classifying expenditures as repairs and maintenance expense or factory equipment additions. Given the problems noted during control testing (as described in Module II), Derick believes that significant misstatements may have occurred.

The same vendor's invoice frequently contains charges for parts and supplies as well as equipment, and the Biltrite employees preparing the vouchers sometimes fail to distinguish among the charges and simply indicate "factory equipment" as the debit if the invoice amount is large. Inasmuch as this type of misstatement would cause an overstatement in the factory equipment account, Derick instructs you to use MUS sampling to determine the extent to which such misstatements have occurred during 2009.

Of the total debits—$89,860,000 to factory equipment during 2009—major additions in the amount of $77,260,000 have been made to replace worn-out equipment. Derick has decided to audit the major additions in their entirety and sample the remainder.

Requirements

1. What is the objective of performing this test? What is the sampling unit? What is the population?

2. Using the spreadsheet program and downloaded data, retrieve the file labeled "MUS." Locate the following documentation in the file:

   - WP 11.3A—Monetary unit sampling plan;
   - WP 11.3B—Monetary unit sampling plan—projected misstatement; and
   - WP 11.3C—Monetary unit sampling plan—computed precision and upper misstatement limit.

   Scroll to WP 11.3A, "Monetary Unit Sampling Plan." Calculate sample size and sampling interval assuming Derick has set the following parameters:

Risk of incorrect acceptance:	*5%*
Anticipated misstatement:	*$100,000*
Tolerable misstatement:	*$640,000*

3. What factors did he consider in setting these parameters? Print the document.

4. Scroll to WP 11.3B, "Monetary Unit Sampling Plan—Projected Misstatement." This document summarizes all invoices containing posting errors and calculates the projected misstatement. Note the equations that have been incorporated into the document template.

   a. What factor determines whether a "tainting percentage" appears in column 4?

   b. Print the document. (Compress print size or otherwise accommodate a wide document.)

5. Scroll to WP 11.3C, "Monetary Unit Sampling Plan—Computed Precision and Upper Misstatement Limit." Complete the "Incremental

Allowance for Sampling Risk" schedule by ranking the projected misstatements as appropriate. (*Hint*: If you forgot how to do this, refer to Chapter 8.)

6. Print the document.

7. Explain the meaning of the following amounts:

   a. Basic precision;

   b. Incremental allowance for sampling error;

   c. Allowance for sampling risk; and

   d. Upper misstatement limit.

8. Evaluate the sampling results. Do they support Derick's concerns regarding possible material misstatement? Note the audit adjustment based on misstatements discovered while examining the sample. Is this adjustment adequate to bring the population into acceptable bounds? If not, what alternate actions might you choose to pursue, based on the sampling results?

Module XII: Estimated Liability for Product Warranty

All Biltrite products are sold under a one-year warranty covering all parts and labor. Repairs are performed locally, either by the dealer who sold the bicycle or by local entities licensed as official Biltrite bicycle repair shops. Biltrite reimburses the dealers and shops for labor and parts. Reimbursement is based on work orders submitted by the repairing agency. The customer signs the work orders, and the serial number of the product repaired also appears on each work order. Defective parts or products replaced must be returned with the accompanying work order. The parts and products are received and logged in on color-coded receiving reports designed for returns.

At the end of each month, the following standard journal entry is posted as an adjustment to estimated product warranty.

8330 Product Warranty Expense

2070 Estimated Product Warranty Liability

For 2009, the company applied 0.5% to cost of goods sold in determining the amount of the monthly adjustment. Debits to account 2070 are for reimbursements and for product and parts replacements. Defective parts and products are "zero valued" and placed in the rework department. Derick has asked you to analyze product warranty and determine the appropriate balance in the liability account. He has already provided you with a partially completed document and a client-prepared analysis of returns over the past four years. You have completed the document and are now ready to evaluate the adequacy of the balance.

Requirements

1. Using the spreadsheet program and downloaded data, retrieve the file labeled "Warranty." Examine the document carefully and comment on its adequacy and completeness. (Note that the 12/31/08 audited balances appear to be unreasonable because you have not yet selected an appropriate provision percentage based on the "data from client-prepared analysis of warranty claims.")

2. Scroll to the bottom of WP 20 and enter audit adjustments already made in previous modules that affect cost of goods sold for 2009. You should identify the following adjustments. (If you weren't assigned the respective modules, ask your instructor for details regarding amounts and accounts.)

   • AJE No. 1 (Module IV correction of repairs expense capitalized as factory equipment); and

   • AJE No. 3 (2009 purchase recorded in 2010, detected in completing Module VI).

3. What comprises the documentation examined by the auditor (audit legend E) supporting the debits to account 2070?

4. How would you audit the client-prepared analysis of warranty claims? (See "Year of Claim/Year of Sale" analysis in the middle of WP 20.)

5. Enter equations in cells C44, D44, and E44 that will calculate the percentage of warranty claims to cost of goods sold for each of the three years 2004–2006.

6. Note the percentage that now appears in cell B46 and the resulting adjustment to product warranty expense.

7. Draft AJE No. 12 on the document.

8. Print the document.

9. Shelly Ross, the other assistant auditor on the engagement, asks why you didn't adjust the prior years under provision through beginning retained earnings. What is your response?

Module XIII: Mortgage Note Payable and Note Payable to Bank Two

In addition to a deferred tax liability relating to temporary book and tax depreciation differences, Biltrite's long-term liabilities consist of the following: 10% mortgage note payable to Dallas Dollar Bank—$60 million; and 12% note payable to Bank Two—$45 million.

In 2004, Biltrite upgraded its manufacturing facilities at a cost of $150 million. The project was financed by issuing 2 million shares of common stock at $25 per share, and by issuing a $100 million 10% mortgage note payable to Dallas Dollar Bank. The mortgage agreement requires repayment in ten annual installments of $10 million each. Interest on the unpaid principal is payable on the first day of each month. The principal installments are due on January 1. The next payment is due on 1/1/10.

The 12% note payable to Bank Two was issued to alleviate the effects of the liquidity problems encountered in 2009. This note is unsecured and requires repayment in ten equal annual installments. Unlike the Dollar Bank mortgage loan, interest on the Bank Two loan is payable annually. The first principal installment, together with interest, is due on 3/1/10. This note contains restrictive covenants, as described earlier, relating to a $10 million compensating balance requirement and restrictions regarding further borrowing and dividend payments.

Derick has asked that you analyze the long-term notes payable, being particularly alert to any violations of the restrictive covenants contained in the Bank Two loan agreement.

Requirements

1. Using the spreadsheet program and downloaded data, retrieve the file labeled "Notes." Locate the following documentation in this file:

   • WP 14—Notes payable and accrued interest—lead schedule; and
   • WP 14.3—Notes payable—long-term.

   Scroll to WP 14.3, "Notes Payable—Long-Term." What are the audit objectives in the examination of long-term notes payable? What would the auditor consider to be the most relevant assertions? Has the evidence provided in the document addressed the audit objectives and the most relevant assertions?

2. Record Reclassification Journal Entry C for the current portion of both notes as of 12/31/07, and enter the amounts in WP 14.3. Now scroll up to WP 14, the lead schedule for notes payable and interest. Post your reclassifications to the lead schedule.

3. Print documentation 14 and 14.3.

4. What is the probable nature of the adjustment to "notes payable—trade" and to "interest payable" appearing in the adjustments column of the lead schedule?

15

Ensuring Audit Quality in Completing the Audit

LEARNING OBJECTIVES

The overriding objective of this textbook is to build a foundation with which to analyze current professional issues and adapt audit approaches to business and economic complexities. Through studying this chapter, you will be able to:

1 Articulate the drivers of audit quality, and relate the concept of audit quality to activities involved in completing the audit.

2 Summarize and resolve detected misstatements.

3 Describe the process by which audit firms make client continuance decisions.

4 Review and assess the appropriateness of the client's accounting for and disclosure of loss contingencies.

5 Review and assess the appropriateness of the client's significant accounting estimates.

6 Review the adequacy of disclosures.

7 Conduct a final analytical review of the financial statements.

8 Identify the purpose of and procedures involved in an engagement quality review (also referred to as a concurring partner review).

9 Review subsequent events that occur after the balance sheet date and assess proper treatment.

10 List and apply the steps involved in assessing the going-concern assumption.

11 Evaluate management representations in certifications required under the Sarbanes-Oxley Act (for public clients) and describe the contents of a management representation letter.

12 Identify issues to communicate to the audit committee.

13 Identify issues to communicate to management via a management letter.

14 Apply the decision analysis and ethical decision-making frameworks to issues involved in completing the audit.

CHAPTER OVERVIEW

In terms of the audit opinion formulation process, this chapter focuses on Phase V, wrapping up the audit. We describe activities that auditors must accomplish prior to completing the audit, each designed to assure that the audit has been conducted in a high-quality manner and that the ultimate audit opinion rendered is appropriate. These activities are varied, ranging from resolving detected misstatements, making client continuance decisions, performing various review-related activities (e.g., reviewing loss contingencies, accounting estimates, and the adequacy of client disclosures, along with conducting analytical reviews of the financial statements, performing engagement quality review, and reviewing for subsequent events), evaluating the client's going-concern status, and communicating with the audit committee and management via a management letter. The common thread among these activities is that while they may be considered at various times throughout the audit, the bulk of the effort or the final conclusions reached associated with these activities occur toward the end of the audit, and they are all focused on helping to achieve high audit quality in various ways. These activities must be completed before an auditor can finally determine the appropriate audit opinion to issue, which is discussed in the following chapter.

The Audit Opinion Formulation Process

I. Assessing Client Acceptance and Retention Decisions	II. Understanding the Client	III. Obtaining Evidence about Controls and Determining the Impact on the Financial Statement Audit	IV. Obtaining Substantive Evidence about Account Assertions	V. Wrapping Up the Audit and Making Reporting Decisions
CHAPTER 4	CHAPTERS 2, 4–6, and 9	CHAPTERS 5–14 and 18	CHAPTERS 7–14 and 18	CHAPTERS 15 and 16

The Auditing Profession, Regulation, and Corporate Governance	Decision-Making, Professional Conduct, and Ethics	Professional Liability
CHAPTERS 1 and 2	CHAPTER 3	CHAPTER 17

Audit Quality and Completing the Audit

Assuring that the audit is conducted in a high-quality manner is paramount to fulfilling users' expectations about the auditor's role in the capital markets. Throughout this textbook, we have discussed various auditing standards that seek to achieve high audit quality. As an auditor reaches the end of any individual audit engagement, he or she will need to undertake various tasks designed to be absolutely sure that the audit report that is issued by the audit firm is accurate, and that the work done on the audit was conducted in a high-quality fashion. Thus, as we near the end of this textbook, it is worthwhile to take a moment to reflect on a very fundamental question: What is audit quality?

A definition published by the GAO (2003) states that a high-quality audit is one performed "in accordance with generally accepted auditing standards (GAAS) to provide reasonable assurance that the audited financial statements and related disclosures are presented in accordance with generally accepted accounting principles (GAAP) and (2) are not materially misstated whether due to errors or fraud."[1] The Financial Reporting Council (FRC) developed "The Audit Quality Framework" to provide guidance on specific drivers of audit quality. The FRC is the United Kingdom's independent regulator responsible for promoting investment in securities through good corporate governance and financial reporting.

The FRC's Audit Quality Framework states that there are five primary drivers of audit quality, including (1) audit firm culture, (2) the skills and personal qualities of audit partners and staff, (3) the effectiveness of the audit process, (4) the reliability and usefulness of audit reporting, and (5) factors outside the control of auditors that affect audit quality. An overview of the FRC framework is shown in Exhibit 15.1. The framework recognizes that effective audit processes, by themselves, are not sufficient to achieve audit quality. Rather, it is a package of factors that includes a culture than influences auditors that in turn influences audit procedures. However, there are other factors—some of which are outside the control of the auditor—that affect audit quality and thereby the overall quality of financial reports. These include such things as the robustness of the accounting framework as well as other factors such as the regulatory and legal environment that are outside the control of the audit firm. This chapter focuses on the crucial tasks that are completed at the end of the audit that relate to this framework and that the audit firm can control. As you examine the factors identified in the FRC's framework, we have highlighted those that are

LO 1

Articulate the drivers of audit quality, and relate the concept of audit quality to activities involved in completing the audit.

---

[1] Government Accountability Office (GAO). 2003. *Public Accounting Firms: Required Study on the Potential Effects of Mandatory Audit Firm Rotation.* GAO Report 04-216 (November).

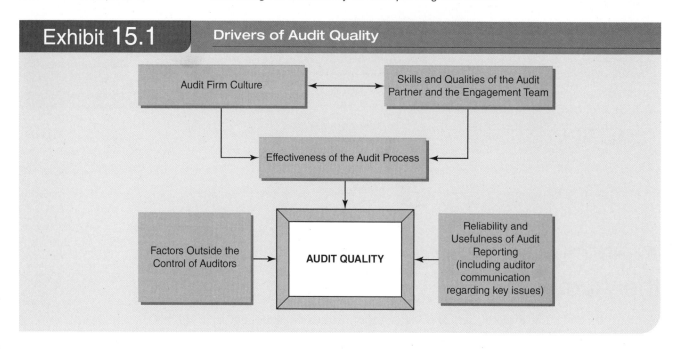

Exhibit 15.1 | **Drivers of Audit Quality**

especially important in completing the audit—even if the items are pervasive throughout the audit engagement.

Audit Firm Culture

According to the FRC, "the culture of an audit firm is likely to provide a positive contribution to audit quality where the leadership of an audit firm:

- Creates an environment where achieving high quality is valued, invested in and rewarded.
- Emphasizes the importance of 'doing the right thing' in the public interest and the effect of doing so on the reputation of both the firm and individual auditors.
- ***Ensures partners and staff have sufficient time and resources to deal with difficult issues as they arise.***
- Ensures financial considerations do not drive actions and decisions having a negative effect on audit quality.
- ***Promotes the merits of consultation on difficult issues and supporting partners in the exercise of their personal judgment.***
- Ensures robust systems for client acceptance and continuation.
- Fosters appraisal and reward systems for partners and staff that promote the personal characteristics essential to quality auditing.
- Ensures audit quality is monitored within firms and across international networks and appropriate consequential action is taken."

Of these ways in which audit quality is improved through audit firm culture, the following specific tasks are completed at the end of each audit, and we discuss them in detail later in the chapter:

1. Summarizing and resolving possible audit adjustments.
2. Client continuance decisions.

Skills and Qualities of the Engagement Team

According to the FRC, "The skills and personal qualities of audit partners and staff are likely to make a positive contribution to audit quality where:

- Partners and staff understand their clients' business and adhere to the principles underlying auditing and ethical standards.
- Partners and staff exhibit professional skepticism in their work and are robust in dealing with issues identified during the audit.
- Staff performing audit work have sufficient experience and are appropriately supervised by partners and managers.
- Partners and managers provide junior staff with appropriate 'mentoring' and 'on the job' training.
- Sufficient training is given to audit personnel in audit, accounting and industry specialist issues."

These audit quality factors are pervasive throughout the conduct of the audit—including the completion of the audit engagement.

Effectiveness of the Audit Process

According to the FRC, "An audit process is likely to provide a positive contribution to audit quality where:

- The audit methodology and tools applied to the audit are well structured and:
    - Encourage partners and managers to be actively involved in audit planning.
    - Provide a framework and procedures to obtain sufficient appropriate audit evidence effectively and efficiently.
    - Require appropriate audit documentation.
    - Provide for compliance with auditing standards without inhibiting the exercise of judgment.
    - *Ensure there is effective review of audit work.*
    - *Audit quality control procedures are effective, understood and applied.*
- High quality technical support is available when the audit team requires it or encounters a situation it is not familiar with.
- The objectives of ethical standards are achieved, providing confidence in the integrity, objectivity and independence of the auditor.
- The collection of sufficient audit evidence is not inappropriately constrained by financial pressures."

Of these ways in which audit quality is improved through the effectiveness of the audit process, the following specific tasks are completed at the end of each audit, and we discuss them in detail later in the chapter:

3. Reviewing the client's accounting for and disclosure of loss contingencies.
4. Reviewing the client's significant accounting estimates.
5. Reviewing the adequacy of other disclosures.
6. Conducting a final analytical review of the financial statements to potentially identify unusual items to make sure such items are explained in the work papers.
7. Completing an engagement quality review (also referred to as a concurring partner review).
8. Reviewing subsequent events that occur after the balance sheet date.

Reliability and Usefulness of Audit Reporting

According to the FRC, "Audit reporting is likely to provide a positive contribution to audit quality where:

- *Audit reports are written in a manner that conveys clearly and unambiguously the auditor's opinion on the financial statements and that addresses the needs of users of financial statements in the context of applicable law and regulations.*

- *Auditors properly conclude as to the truth and fairness of the financial statements.* (Note that under U.S. Standards this is the same as concluding that the financial statements are fairly presented under GAAP).
- *Communications with the audit committee include discussions about:*
  - *The scope of the audit.*
  - *The threats to auditor objectivity.*
  - *The key risks identified and judgments made in reaching the audit opinion.*
  - *The qualitative aspects of the entity's accounting and reporting and potential ways of improving financial reporting.*

Of these ways in which audit quality is improved through the reliability and usefulness of audit reporting, the following specific tasks are completed at the end of each audit, and we discuss them in detail later in the chapter:

9. Evaluating the going-concern assumption.
10. Considering management representations in certifications required under the Sarbanes-Oxley Act (for public clients) and requiring management to sign a representation letter.
11. Communicating with the audit committee.
12. Communicating with management via a management letter.

Factors Outside the Control of Auditors That Affect Audit Quality

The FRC is realistic, and it explicitly recognizes that some factors that affect audit quality are outside of the direct control of the external auditor, e.g., corporate governance and the regulatory environment. The FRC recognizes that good corporate governance goes beyond structure and includes audit committees that are robust in dealing with issues, a greater emphasis on getting things right as opposed to getting done by a particular date, and a regulatory environment that emphasizes audit quality over all else.

LO 2

Summarize and resolve detected misstatements.

PRACTICAL POINT

The client will often make adjustments for misstatements found during the audit, but often does not record (i.e., correct) all of the potential adjustments. Thus, the auditor should keep track of not only misstatements found, but the projected misstatements in the accounts, and the projected amount of misstatements that have not been recorded (i.e., that remain uncorrected in the audited financial statements).

Ensuring Audit Quality: Audit Adjustments and Client Continuance Decisions

Summarizing and Resolving Detected Misstatements

The auditor needs to summarize misstatements found during the audit to determine whether they are material and need to be recorded and corrected. As would be expected, the audit firm's culture, among other things, plays an important role in how such misstatements are evaluated. Further, the auditor of a public company must assess whether the misstatements identified during the audit were the result of significant or material weaknesses in internal control.

Misstatements are likely to be detected that individually are not material, and the auditor may temporarily pass on asking the client to make those adjustments. They should not be forgotten, however. Most public accounting firms use a schedule to accumulate the known and projected misstatements and the carryover effects of prior-year uncorrected misstatements (see Exhibit 15.2). At the end of the audit, management and the auditor must decide which possible

Exhibit 15.2 Summary of Possible Adjustments

W/P Ref	Account/Description	ASSETS Current	ASSETS Noncurrent	LIABILITIES Current	LIABILITIES Noncurrent	Retained Earnings	Net Earnings
Uncorrected Known Errors							
B-4	Sales						972
	Accounts Receivable	(972)					
	Error from A/R confirmations						
	($972 known error and $13,493						
	additional projected error)						
A-1	Accounts Payable			1,500			
	Cash	(1,500)					
	Unrecorded check # 14,389						
Projected Errors							
B-4	Sales						13,493
	Accounts Receivable	(13,493)					
	Projected pricing errors from sample						
Carryover Effect of Prior Year Errors							
U-3	Retained earnings					6,900	
	Salary Exp						(6,900)
	Under accrual of prior year's salaries						
	Subtotal: Income before taxes						7,565
Tax Adjustment							
	Income Taxes Payable (14,465 x 0.34)			4,918			
	Income Tax Expense (7,565 × 0.34)					(2,572)	
	Retained Earnings (6,900 × 0.34)						(2,346)
	Total Likely Error	(15,965)	0	6,418	0	4.554	4,993
	Balance from Trial Balance	19,073,000	1,997,000	(3,346,000)	(13,048,000)	(4,676,000)	1,678,000
	Total Likely Error as % of Balance	0.08%	0.0%	0.19%	0.0%	0.1%	0.3%

DEBIT (CREDIT)

Conclusion: In my opinion, the total likely errors are not material to the financial statements taken as a whole. The projected errors are quantitatively immaterial and do not reflect material weaknesses in internal control. Therefore, no adjustments are required, nor is any additional audit work needed for these account balances.

Marginal tax rate: 34%

PREPARED BY: KMJ   DATE 10-17-12

REVIEWED BY: LER   DATE 10-17-12

adjustments will be "booked," that is, corrected in the financial statements, and which will be "waived," that is, left uncorrected.

In Exhibit 15.2, the first adjustment reflects a pricing error detected by confirming a sample of receivables. The known error is $972, as shown in the first section of the schedule. However, when projected to the population, the projected error for the unknown and unexamined part of the population was

$13,493, as shown in the second section of the schedule. If these were corrected, both sales and accounts receivable would be reduced by $14,465 ($972 + $13,493), resulting in a reduction of pretax earnings and current assets. The second adjustment involves an unrecorded check for $1,500. The third adjustment involves the carryover effects of understating last year's accrued salaries and salary expense ($6,900). Because the carryover effect is to overstate this year's salary expense, the correction is shown as a reduction in the current year's salary expense, thereby resulting in an increase in pretax earnings and a reduction in the beginning balance of retained earnings.

The income-tax effects are then entered into the schedule to show the total effects of correcting these errors. Near the end of the audit, these possible adjustments should be reviewed in the aggregate to determine whether their combined effect is material. The auditor compares the total likely misstatements (the sum of known and projected misstatements) to each significant segment of the financial statements, such as total current assets, total noncurrent assets, total current liabilities, total noncurrent liabilities, owners' equity, and pretax income, to determine if they are, in aggregate, material to the financial statements. In the example in Exhibit 15.2, the total likely error as a percentage of these segments is clearly immaterial, and that conclusion is noted in the work paper.

Management's incentives may affect whether they are willing to book, i.e., correct, these detected misstatements. For example, even though the misstatements in Exhibit 15.2 are immaterial, in some cases detected misstatements are material and management that wishes to show higher net income may put up a fight with the auditor to not correct an income-reducing misstatement. In such a situation, the auditor may feel some pressure to acquiesce to management's demands in order to preserve a harmonious working relationship. It is in these situations in which the audit firm culture is important. It is critical that the engagement partner feels that the audit firm will support him or her in making a decision to insist that management correct a misstatement, even if management does not want to do so. Thus, an audit firm culture that emphasizes "doing the right thing," encourages auditors to take sufficient time to deal with difficult issues. A culture that emphasizes that the audit firm's long-term reputation is more important than the immediate satisfaction of client preferences encourages quality actions by its auditors. A culture that encourages auditors to seek consultation with other members of the audit firm so that the auditor does not feel "alone" in making difficult decisions will be critical in ensuring that the auditor does not acquiesce to inappropriate or aggressive client preferences regarding detected misstatements. In doing so, audit quality is enhanced.

The PCAOB's AS No. 14 provides important insight that auditors must consider as they decide whether management's refusal to correct a detected misstatement is indicative of intentional bias. The PCAOB notes that the following are forms of management bias in this setting:

- "The selective correction of misstatements brought to management's attention during the audit (e.g., correcting misstatements that have the effect of increasing reported earnings but not correcting misstatements that have the effect of decreasing reported earnings).
- The identification by management of additional adjusting entries that offset misstatements accumulated by the auditor. If such adjusting entries are identified, the auditor should perform procedures to determine why the underlying misstatements were not identified previously and evaluate the implications on the integrity of management and the auditor's risk assessments, including fraud risk assessments. The auditor also should perform additional procedures as necessary to address the risk of further undetected misstatement." (AS No. 14, paragraph 25).

If the auditor identifies this type of management bias in the resolution of detected misstatements, the auditor should determine whether the bias, along with its effect of the uncorrected misstatements on the overall financial statements, is material. In addition, this type of management bias should lead auditors to re-evaluate their risk assessments, particularly those related to management integrity and the risk of fraud. We further discuss the resolution of detected misstatements and the "book or waive" decision in Chapter 18.

Client Continuance Decisions

LO 3

Describe the process by which audit firms make client continuance decisions.

Client continuance decisions, which audit firms and individual engagement partners make at the completion of the audit, are just a part of an audit firm's overall portfolio management activities. In essence, one can view an individual audit client like an individual stock in an investment portfolio. That is, some stocks (clients) are more risky, but yield better returns; some stocks (clients) are less risky, but yield weaker returns. Still other stocks (clients) do not present a clear picture of their risk-return profile. In the context of auditing, "better returns" does not just mean higher audit fees, but instead may also include the upside potential of a client that may eventually become publicly traded, the reputational visibility that an audit firm gains when they audit a superior and well-known company, and so forth. In Chapter 4, we introduced you to client acceptance and continuance decisions, and at this point we provide a more theoretical description of how clients come into an audit firm's portfolio, and how they move out of that portfolio. Accomplishing portfolio management, of which client continuance decisions are just one part, is the key to an audit firm's long-run survival and its ability to offer high-quality audit services to its clients. Audit firm culture plays a role in audit firm portfolio management in that some audit firms are willing to provide service to riskier clients than other audit firms.

As depicted in Exhibit 15.3, an audit firm begins each period with a given number of clients in its portfolio. Some clients voluntarily depart from the audit firm, e.g., in the case of a company going bankrupt, merging with another company, or simply changing audit firms because of fee issues, service issues, changes in location, poor working relationships, etc. Other clients are newly accepted into the audit firm's portfolio. These clients are evaluated based upon their relative risk and audit fee profile (as discussed in Chapter 4). The audit firm makes a proposal (and in some cases a formal bid) to the client if the audit firm decides the client is acceptable, and if the client accepts the audit firm adds the client to its portfolio.

Existing clients for which the audit firm provided services in the preceding period are evaluated by the audit firm and individual engagement partner at the completion of the audit to determine whether the audit firm should continue to provide services again in the next period. The process by which this decision is made is called the client continuance decision. In short, the engagement partner and the audit firm must decide, based on what they know about the client, whether it is worthwhile to retain the client in the firm's portfolio. Like the client acceptance decision, the client continuance decision is made based on a consideration of the client's relative risk and audit fee profile. Discontinued clients are those the audit firm eliminates from its portfolio based on the client continuance decision; the clients will be informed that the firm will no longer be associated with them after the current period audit report is issued. Continuing clients are those the audit firm will continue its ongoing relationship with; the firm will continue to be associated with them once the current period audit report is issued.

| Exhibit 15.3 | Client Portfolio Management |

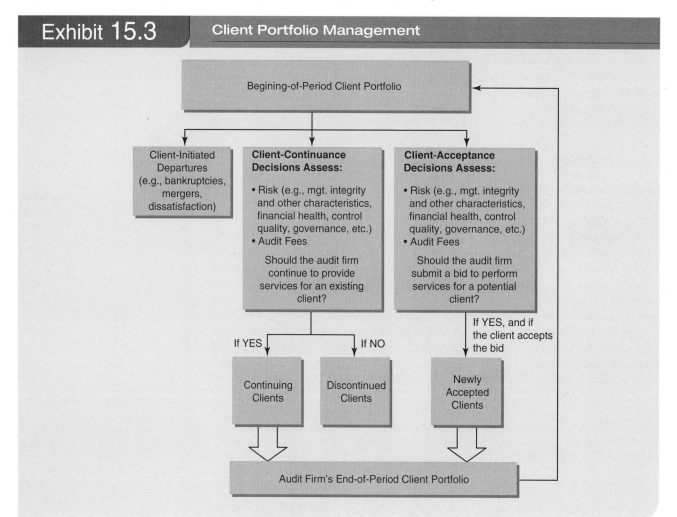

Client Continuance-related Risks

The following are some of the key types of risk that audit firms consider when they make client acceptance and client continuance decisions:

- *Client entity characteristics.* For example, a history of earnings management, a history of making unrealistic promises to analysts, failing to meet market expectations or consistently just meeting those expectations, difficulties in relationships with prior professional service providers such as attorneys, and high-risk business models such as Internet gaming.
- *Independence risk factors.* For example, the engagement partner has a business or family relationship with the client, client management was a former employee of the audit firm, the client purchases consulting services from the audit firm, or the audit firm has some other independence-related conflict with the client.
- *Third party/due diligence risk factors.* For example, the reason for the client to change auditors is unknown or is due to negative relationship factors, the predecessor audit firm is unwilling to discuss the reasons for the client's departure, there have been significant changes in the ownership structure of the entity or evidence that key members of management have prior histories of financial fraud or other types of legal difficulties.
- *Quantitative risk factors.* For example, the client is in significant financial stress, is having difficulty raising capital or paying its existing debts, or is experiencing significant cash flow problems.

- *Qualitative risk factors.* For example, the industry in which the client operates is in either the early development stage or is late in its product life cycle, there are minimal barriers to entry to the client's business model, the business model is weak or untested, there are low profit margins, the client's products have multiple viable substitutes, there are significant supply chain risks, there is significant production or operational complexity, or there are risks related to strong union presence.
- *Entity organizational or governance risks.* For example, the organizational structure is inappropriate for the business operations of the entity, there are weak internal controls, there is weak governance, management is unqualified or lacks integrity, and the internal audit function is weak or non-existent.
- *Financial reporting risks.* For example, the client uses inappropriate estimates in its financial reporting judgments, management has a history of misrepresentations or unwillingness to correct detected misstatements, the financial statement line items involve a significant amount of judgment or complexity, there are large or unusual transactions that management records at quarter or year end, or the prior audit report is other than an unqualified report.

In addition to these risk factors, an important consideration in client continuance decisions involves the audit firm's growth strategy. Audit firms may discontinue serving a client because the client does not fit the profile the firm is hoping to achieve. For example, a Big 4 firm may discontinue serving a smaller client because it is not sufficiently profitable, or the client may not be in an industry the firm wants to emphasize. On the other hand, some smaller audit firms may discontinue serving a larger client because they do not have the size or expertise to serve the client as the client grows larger, becomes more geographically dispersed, or increases in complexity.

Audit firm portfolio management decisions, which include client acceptance and continuance decisions, are critical to achieve audit quality. If an audit firm accepts or continues to provide service to a "bad" client (e.g., a client that is in very weak financial condition, a client that has very poor internal controls, a client that is perpetrating a fraud, or a client with poor management integrity), it may be difficult for the audit firm to provide a high-quality audit. For example, a client in weak financial condition may be unable to pay a reasonable audit fee, and so the audit firm may find itself in a position of not having enough budgeted audit hours to do a high quality job. Or a client with weak internal controls may be difficult to audit because of unreliable financial data. Similarly, a client perpetrating a fraud, or one with weak management integrity, may present financial information that is intentionally unreliable, and so again the audit may be difficult to conduct in a way that results in an accurate audit opinion. Given the importance of client acceptance and continuance decisions to audit quality, audit firms with strong cultures of quality place great emphasis on developing, maintaining, and monitoring systems of internal control that yield good decisions in this regard.

Ensuring Audit Quality: Effectiveness of the Audit Process and Associated Review Activities

As the auditor completes the audit, various types of review activities are conducted to ensure that the client's financial statements are materially correct and to ensure high audit quality. These include:

- Reviewing the client's accounting for and disclosure of loss contingencies
- Reviewing the client's significant accounting estimates

PRACTICAL POINT

For an illustration of how important client continuance decisions can be to the survival of an audit firm, consider the case of Arthur Andersen and its largest client in the Houston office—Enron. Andersen knew that Enron was a high-risk client, but it chose to continue providing services to the company anyway. In this case, a poor client continuance decision for just one client ultimately was a contributing factor in the demise of Andersen.

PRACTICAL POINT

Nearly all the largest audit firms have automated electronic decision support systems that help those firms ensure that their engagement partners are making client acceptance and continuance decisions that will result in client portfolios that are attractive from both an audit fee and a risk management perspective.

LO 4

Review and assess the appropriateness of the client's accounting for and disclosure of loss contingencies.

- Reviewing the adequacy of disclosures
- Conducting a final analytical review of the financial statements
- Completing an engagement quality review (also referred to as a concurring partner review)
- Reviewing subsequent events that occur after the balance sheet date.

Reviewing Contingencies

In ASC 450 (formerly SFAS No. 5, "Accounting for Contingencies"), the FASB provides the standard for accruing and disclosing three categories of potential losses that can be reasonably estimated. Those categories reflect the contingent (not known for sure) nature of those losses and the guiding criteria are organized around probability of outcomes classified as (1) probable, (2) reasonably possible, and (3) remote. It requires the accrual and disclosure of contingent losses that can be both reasonably estimated and that are probable. It also requires the disclosure of a contingent loss if there is at least a reasonable possibility that a loss may have been incurred and either an accrual has not been made or an exposure exists that is greater than the amount accrued. Examples of loss contingencies include the following:

- Threat of expropriation of assets in a foreign country
- Litigation, claims, and assessments
- Guarantees of debts of others
- Obligations of banks under standby letters of credit
- Agreements to repurchase receivables that have been sold
- Purchase and sale commitments

Responsibilities Related to Contingencies

Management is responsible for designing and maintaining policies and procedures to identify, evaluate, and account for contingencies. Auditors are responsible for determining that the client has properly identified, accounted for, and disclosed material contingencies.

AUDITING *in Practice*

POSSIBLE CHANGES IN DISCLOSING LOSS CONTINGENCIES

In 2010 the FASB issued for public comment a proposed standard, *Contingencies (Topic 450): Disclosure of Certain Loss Contingencies* which retains current disclosure requirements while requiring additional disclosures. The proposed standard would require entities to disclose qualitative and quantitative information about loss contingencies so that financial statement users would be to understand (a) the nature of loss contingencies, (b) their potential magnitude, and (c) their potential timing (if known). The proposed standard would require the disclosure of certain remote loss contingencies and provides that the assessment of the materiality of loss contingencies would not consider the possibility of recoveries from insurance or other indemnification arrangements.

The other big practice issue surrounds the need for the auditor and management to make decisions around the concepts contained in the words *probable*, *reasonably possible*, and *remote*. For the most part, practice is coalescing around a working definition of *probable* as "more likely than not," which is the international standard. For now, U.S. GAAP still allows a higher threshold before reaching the "probable" range, which is likely the reason that the FASB is proposing more transparency on the potential nature of contingent losses through the disclosures suggested above.

Sources of Audit Evidence of Contingencies

The *primary source* of information concerning contingencies is the client's management. The auditor should obtain the following from management:

- A description and evaluation of contingencies that existed at the balance sheet date or that arose prior to the end of the fieldwork and which matters were referred to legal counsel
- Assurance in the management representation letter that the accounting and disclosure requirements concerning contingent liabilities have been met
- Major contracts regarding areas where contingencies are often present, e.g., sales of receivables, various financial instruments, and court cases
- Documentation of communication with internal and external legal counsel of the client

The auditor should also examine related documents in the client's possession, such as correspondence and invoices from lawyers. Additional sources of evidence are the corporate minutes, contracts, correspondence from governmental agencies, and bank confirmations. While auditing sales and purchases, the auditor should be alert to any commitments that could result in a loss. For example, consider a situation in which management signed a purchase commitment for raw materials at a fixed price and the materials are to be delivered after year end. If a loss on this commitment exists because of a decline in the market price by year end, the loss should be accrued and the details should be disclosed in the footnotes.

Letter of Audit Inquiry   The primary source of corroborative evidence concerning litigation, claims, and assessments is the client's legal counsel. The auditor should ask the client to send a **letter of audit inquiry** to its legal counsel asking counsel to confirm information about asserted claims and those claims that are probable of assertion. Attorneys are hesitant to provide much information to auditors because their communications with clients are usually privileged. As a result, the American Bar Association and the AICPA have agreed to the following procedures. The letter of audit inquiry should include the following:

- Identification of the company, its subsidiaries, and the date of the audit
- Management's list (or a request by management that the lawyer prepare a list) that describes and evaluates the contingencies to which the lawyer has devoted substantial attention
- A request that the lawyer furnish the auditor with the following:
  1. A comment on the completeness of management's list and evaluations
  2. For each contingency:
     a. A description of the nature of the matter, the progress to date, and the action the company intends to take
     b. An evaluation of the likelihood of an unfavorable outcome and an estimate of the potential loss or range of loss
  3. Any limitations on the lawyer's response, such as not devoting substantial attention to the item or that the amounts are not material

Legal counsel should be instructed by the client to respond directly to the auditors as close to the end of audit fieldwork as possible. The auditor and client should agree on what is material for this purpose. Exhibit 15.4 is an example of a letter of audit inquiry. The lawyer's response should be sent directly to the auditor.

Effect of Contingency on Audit Report

A lawyer's refusal to furnish the requested information either orally or in writing is a scope limitation precluding an unqualified opinion. However, the lawyer may be unable to form a conclusion on the likelihood of an unfavorable

Exhibit 15.4   Letter of Audit Inquiry

Nature Sporting Goods Manufacturing Company
200 Pine Way, Kirkville, WI 53800
(608) 255–7820

January 10, 2012

John Barrington
Barrington, Hunt, & Wibfly
1500 Park Place
Milwaukee, WI 52719

In connection with an audit of our financial statements at December 31, 2011, and for the year then ended, management of the Company has prepared and furnished to our auditors, Rittenberg & Schwieger, CPAs, Madison WI 53711, a description and evaluation of certain contingencies, including that set forth below involving matters with respect to which you have been engaged and to which you have devoted substantive attention on behalf of the Company in the form of legal consultation or representation. Management of the Company regards this contingency as material. Materiality for purposes of this letter includes items involving amounts exceeding $75,000 individually or in the aggregate.

PENDING OR THREATENED LITIGATION

The Company is being sued by General Materials for failure to pay amounts it claims are due it under a purchase agreement dated March 31, 2009. The suit was filed May 23, 2011, claiming we owe it $140,000 for material we purchased January 29, 2011. This material was defective, and we had received written approval from General Materials to destroy it, which we did. General Materials now claims that its management did not properly authorize the approval. The case has gone through the deposition stage and trial is set for April 19, 2012. We believe that General Materials' claim is without merit and that we will prevail in the suit.

Please furnish to our auditors such explanation, if any, that you consider necessary to supplement the foregoing information, including an explanation of those matters as to which your views may differ from those stated and an identification of the omission of any pending or threatened litigation, claims, and assessments, or a statement that the list of such matters is complete.

There are no unasserted claims of which we are currently aware. We understand that should you have formed a professional conclusion that we should disclose or consider disclosure concerning an unasserted possible claim or assessment, as a matter of professional responsibility to us, you will so advise us and will consult with us concerning the question of such disclosure and the applicable requirements of relevant financial accounting standards. Please specifically confirm to our auditors that our understanding is correct.

RESPONSE

Your response should include matters that existed as of December 31, 2011, and during the period from that date to the effective date of your response. Please specifically identify the nature of and reasons for any limitation on your response.

Our auditors expect to have the audit completed on February 28, 2012, and would appreciate receiving your reply by that date with a specified effective date no earlier than February 23, 2012.

OTHER MATTERS

Please also indicate the amount we were indebted to you for services and expenses on December 31, 2011.

Very truly yours,

Joleen Soyka

Controller
Nature Sporting Goods Manufacturing Company

AUDITING *in Practice*

CONTINGENT LIABILITIES

In July 2010 BP released its second-quarter 2010 earnings report. The report discusses the risks associated with the ongoing events and cleanup effort in the Gulf of Mexico due to the oil spill associated with BP. It also includes an income statement with a $32 billion pretax charge and a notation that "second quarter and first half 2010 include a charge of $32,192 million in production and

manufacturing expenses, and a credit of $10,003 million in taxation in relation to the Gulf of Mexico oil spill." In conducting the annual audit, BP's auditors will need to obtain assurance that the reported contingency in connection with the oil spill is accurately reported and disclosed.

outcome or the amount of potential loss because of inherent uncertainties. Such a response is not considered a scope limitation. If the effect of the matter could be material to the financial statements, the auditor may choose to emphasize it by adding an explanatory paragraph to the audit report (covered in Chapter 16).

Reviewing Significant Estimates

Financial statements include a number of estimates and judgments, ranging from those associated with pension liabilities to product warranties, to allowance for doubtful accounts, and to obsolescence of inventory. It is unfortunate that some companies have tried to "manage" or "smooth" earnings by using estimates to create hidden reserves in unusually good years that can be used in years when real profits do not meet expectations. Alternatively, companies may underestimate liabilities or impairment of asset values to achieve reported earning goals. Many of the SEC's criticisms of the accounting profession in the past few years have focused on account balances for which estimates are used extensively. Auditors should be alert to period-end adjusting journal entries that relate to accounts with significant estimates. Ultimately, the auditor is responsible for providing reasonable assurance that:

LO 5

Review and assess the appropriateness of the client's significant accounting estimates.

- Management has an information system to develop all estimates that could be material to the financial statements
- The estimates are reasonable
- The estimates are presented in conformity with GAAP

AUDITING *in Practice*

DISCLOSING CONTINGENT LIABILITIES AT AT&T

In 1998 AT&T changed its defined benefit pension plan to a cash balance plan. A long-running case by current and former AT&T employees was seeking one of the largest potential claims in pension litigation, $2.3 billion. The litigation is based on these plaintiffs' argument that AT&T discriminated against older workers upon implementing this change. In May 2009, the Securities and Exchange Commission questioned AT&T as to why it had not disclosed its potential exposure in the pension case. AT&T responded that it did not believe that the case

met the threshold for disclosure. In June 2010, a judge dismissed the case without trail and an appeal was filed. The relevant question is whether the auditor believed the case did not meet the minimum threshold for disclosure, i.e., reasonably possible and estimable. Such judgments are difficult, but the auditor would have been in a position where the skepticism of his or her judgment would be questioned had AT&T lost the case, or if it loses the case on appeal.

Accounting estimates are based on management's knowledge and experience of past and current events, as well as its assumptions about conditions that it expects to exist and courses of action it expects to take. Estimates are based on subjective as well as objective factors. There is potential for bias in both factors. Examples of accounting estimates include net realizable values of inventory and receivables, property and casualty insurance loss reserves, revenues from contracts accounted for by the percentage-of-completion method, warranty expenses, depreciation and amortization methods, impairment of depreciable assets and goodwill, useful lives and residual values of productive facilities, natural resources and intangibles, valuation and classification of financial instruments, pensions and other postretirement benefits, and compensation in stock option plans. Of course, the auditor will evaluate estimates in these accounts during Phases III and IV of the audit. However, the auditor should also take time at the end of the audit to consider whether, taken together, the estimates made in these accounts are reasonable; that is, they do not result in overly conservative or overly aggressive financial reporting.

In evaluating the reasonableness of an estimate, the auditor normally concentrates on key factors and assumptions that are:

- Significant to the accounting estimate
- Sensitive to variations
- Deviations from historical patterns
- Subjective and susceptible to misstatement and bias
- Inconsistent with current economic trends

The auditor should consider the historical experience of the entity in making past estimates. However, changes in facts, circumstances, or the entity's procedures may cause factors different from those considered in the past to become significant to the estimate. For example, economic changes may occur that increase or decrease the ability of customers to make timely payments; or the company may have changed its credit policies, providing for a longer or shorter time before payment is due or higher or lower sales discount rates. Auditors may be reluctant to challenge management estimates that result in current-period reductions in income (e.g., increases in bad debt expense) and associated increases in reserve accounts (e.g., allowance for doubtful accounts). However, it is important for auditors to remember that management may try to "tap into" these reserves in the future to improve an otherwise weak level of earnings.

Events or transactions occurring after the balance sheet date, but before the audit report date, can be useful in identifying and evaluating the reasonableness of estimates. Examples of these events include collection of receivables, sale of inventory or financial instruments, and the purchase of inventory under a purchase commitment for which an estimated loss was or should have been accrued.

Reviewing the Adequacy of Disclosures

LO 6

Review the adequacy of disclosures.

The auditor's report covers the basic financial statements, which include the balance sheet, income statement, statement of cash flows, a statement of changes in stockholders' equity or retained earnings, and the related notes. If the auditor determines that informative disclosures are not reasonably adequate, the auditor must note that fact in the auditor's report.

Disclosures can be made either on the face of the financial statements in the form of classifications or parenthetical notations and/or in the notes to the statements. Placement of the disclosures should be dictated by the clearest manner of presentation. Ultimately, the auditor must be sure that:

- Disclosed events and transactions have occurred and pertain to the entity
- All disclosures that should have been included are included

Exhibit 15.5	Partial Disclosure Checklist

E. Inventories	Yes	No	N/A
1. Are the major classes of inventory disclosed (e.g., finished goods, work in process, raw materials)?	_____	_____	_____
2. Is the method of determining inventory cost (e.g., LIFO, FIFO) disclosed?	_____	_____	_____
3. If LIFO is used, do the statements adequately disclose FIFO cost?	_____	_____	_____
4. Is the basis for stating inventory disclosed (e.g., lower of cost or market) and, if necessary, the nature of a change in basis for stating inventory and the effect on income of such a change?	_____	_____	_____

- The disclosures are understandable to users
- The information is disclosed accurately and at appropriate amounts

The inventory disclosure checklist in Exhibit 15.5 is an example of a checklist with yes/no responses that helps remind the auditor of matters that should be considered for disclosure. The checklist is also a convenient documentation format for evidence that the auditor adequately evaluated the client's disclosures. Of course, there may be items that should be disclosed but that are not covered by the audit firm's checklist. The auditor, therefore, should not blindly follow a checklist, but use good audit judgment when there are unusual circumstances of which the users should be aware.

AUDITING *in Practice*

FRAUD INVOLVING LACK OF DISCLOSURE AT DELL INC.

In July 2010, the SEC issued a complaint against senior management at Dell Inc., including the company's chairman, CEO, and CFO. The complaint includes allegations that Dell engaged in fraud during the period 2002–2006 by failing to disclose a significant relationship with its major vendor (Intel) that led to Intel's making payments back to Dell. According to the complaint, Intel agreed to make cash payments to Dell in exchange for Dell's promise that it would not purchase microprocessors from Intel's arch-rival, Advanced Micro Devices (AMD). The cash payments were very large, ranging from 10% to 76% of operating income over the period of the fraud. In March 2006, Dell announced that it would begin using AMD as a vendor, and Intel immediately retaliated by ceasing to make its usual cash payments to Dell, thereby resulting in a 36% drop in Dell's quarterly income. In the quarterly earnings conference call, Michael Dell attributed the drop to pricing pressures in the face of slowing demand and to component costs that declined less than expected; of course, these statements were false.

Consider the difficulty that this scheme posed for Dell's auditors, PricewaterhouseCoopers LLP. The most senior members of the management team were actively involved in this deception and had no intention of making full and fair disclosures to investors or the auditors. However, should the auditors have otherwise known of the payments? This question is at the heart of a continuing

debate about auditing vs. forensic accounting (looking for fraud). The auditors, heretofore, had not seen any reason to question management's integrity, but economic situations and motivations change. Further, instituting a standard audit procedure in which audit software is used to search for cash receipts from major vendors (where only cash disbursements are expected) would have likely uncovered the cash received from Intel. Should such procedures—even when fraud is not expected—be performed on every audit because such fraud can occur? Perhaps so, but this would also mean that audit firms would have to systematically think about a host of situations that may occur with all clients and add the standard software analysis to the audits—thereby driving up audit costs (maybe without an increase in audit fees).

This example illustrates the difficulty that auditors sometimes face in their obligation to review the adequacy of disclosures—when faced with fraud, intentional concealment, and collusion among the perpetrators it is very difficult for the auditors to reach an accurate conclusion regarding their audit work. Critics of PricewaterhouseCoopers LLP might say that the audit was conducted in a low-quality manner, thereby resulting in a failure to detect the fraud. What do you think: (a) were the financial statements fraudulently misstated and (b) did PricewaterhouseCoopers have a responsibility to detect the payments from Intel?

AUDITING *in Practice*

EXCERPT OF IFRS DISCLOSURE CHECKLIST

Disclosure checklists help auditors identify items needing disclosure. Below is an excerpt from Deloitte's International Financial Reporting Standards (IFRS) Checklist related to changes in the carrying amount of goodwill. The unique feature of this checklist is that it contains references to relevant standards that the auditor will find useful in evaluating the client's disclosures.

The entity shall disclose information that enables users of its financial statements to evaluate changes in the carrying amount of goodwill during the period. Note: Paragraph 75 of IFRS 3, set out below, specifies the minimum disclosures required to satisfy this requirement. The entity shall disclose a reconciliation of the carrying amount of goodwill at the beginning and end of the period, showing separately:

(a)   the gross amount and accumulated impairment losses at the beginning of the period;

(b)   additional goodwill recognized during the period;

(c)   adjustments resulting from the subsequent recognition of deferred tax assets during the period in accordance with paragraph 65 of IFRS 3;

(d)   goodwill included in a disposal group classified as held for sale in accordance with IFRS 5 and goodwill derecognized during the period without having previously been included in a disposal group classified as held for sale;

(e)   impairment losses recognized during the period in accordance with IAS 36 Impairment of Assets;

(f)   net exchange differences arising during the period in accordance with IAS 21 The Effects of Changes in Foreign Exchange Rates;

(g)   any other changes in the carrying amount during the period; and

(h)   the gross amount and accumulated impairment losses at the end of the period.

The auditor should consider matters for disclosure while gathering evidence during the course of the audit, not just at the end of the audit. For example, during the audit of receivables, the auditor should be aware of the need to separately disclose receivables from officers, employees, or other related parties, and the pledging of receivables as collateral for a loan. One of the key disclosures is a summary of significant accounting policies used by the company. In evaluating this summary, the auditor is guided by the substantive nature of transactions as illustrated in the Dell case above as well as the evolving nature of business as opposed to simply reviewing FASB statements.

Performing Analytical Review of the Audit and Financial Statements

LO 7

Conduct a final analytical review of the financial statements.

Analytical procedures help auditors assess the overall presentation of the financial statements. Auditing standards require the use of analytical procedures in both the planning phase and the final review phase of the audit to assist in identifying account relationships that are unusual. At the conclusion of the audit, the audit team analyzes the data from an overall business perspective. The reviewers are not only looking at the trends and ratios but are asking hard questions about whether the company's results make sense in relationship to industry and economic trends. By performing a final analytical review, the audit firm can help ensure that audit quality was high because any unusual, unexpected, or unexplained relationships can be tracked down and resolved before the issuance of the audit report.

Revenue and Expenses

Analytical procedures performed on the income statement items provide evidence on whether certain relationships make sense in light of the knowledge obtained during the audit. Such procedures may indicate that further audit work needs to be performed before rendering the audit opinion. Ratio analysis, common-size analysis, and analysis of the dollar and percentage changes in each income statement item over the previous year are useful for this purpose. The auditor should have accumulated sufficient competent evidence during the audit to explain any unusual changes, such as changes when none are expected, no changes when they are expected, or changes that are not of the expected size or direction. For example, if the client paid more attention to quality control and order processing during the current year, then sales returns and allowances should have decreased as a percentage of sales. As another example, if a client increased its market share by substantially reducing prices for the last three months of the year and undertaking a massive advertising campaign, a decrease in the gross profit margin should be expected. If these expected changes are not reflected in the accounting records, the audit documentation should contain adequate evidence, supplementing the explanations of management to corroborate those explanations. Otherwise, the auditor should perform more investigation to ascertain the reason for the discrepancies in the data as they could represent account balances that are misstated.

Analytical procedures should include the relationship of income statement changes to pertinent balance sheet accounts. For example, WorldCom decreased line rental cost below the industry norm, but the change was accompanied by a significant increase in fixed assets.

Performing an Engagement Quality Review

In order to assure audit quality, the audit firm should have policies and procedures in place for conducting an internal quality review of each audit before issuing the audit opinion. An experienced reviewer who was not a part of the audit team, but who has appropriate competence, independence, integrity, and objectivity, should perform this independent review, referred to as a **concurring partner review** or **engagement quality review**. The Sarbanes-Oxley Act requires such reviews for audits of public companies. The purpose of these reviews is to help assure that the audit and audit documentation are complete and support the audit opinion on the financial statements and, for larger public companies, on the client's internal controls.

The engagement quality review is a risk-based review where the reviewer evaluates the significant judgments made by the engagement team, as well as the conclusions that the engagement team reached. Some of the procedures the reviewer should perform as part of the review process include:

- Discussing significant matters related to the financial statements and internal controls, including the audit team's identification of material control deficiencies and audit of significant risks
- Evaluating judgments about materiality and the disposition of corrected and uncorrected identified misstatements
- Reviewing the engagement team's evaluation of the firm's independence in relation to the engagement
- Reviewing the related audit documentation to determine its sufficiency
- Reading the financial statements, management's report on internal control, and auditor's report
- Confirming with the lead audit partner that there are no significant unresolved matters
- Determining if appropriate consultations have taken place on difficult or contentious matters
- Evaluating whether the auditor documentation supports the conclusions reached by the engagement team with respect to the matters reviewed
- Assessing whether appropriate matters have been communicated to audit committee members, management, and other appropriate parties

Comparison of the standards for engagement quality/concurring partner review is shown in the *Comparison of Worldwide Professional Auditing Guidance.*

PRACTICAL POINT

The auditor should provide a documented conclusion as to the impact of the final analytical procedures on any additional audit work that may be required.

PRACTICAL POINT

It is important to review the audit for completeness and quality *before* issuing the audit report to the client for distribution to users.

LO 8

Identify the purpose of and procedures involved in an engagement quality review (also referred to as a concurring partner review).

Comparison of Worldwide Professional Auditing Guidance

U.S. AND INTERNATIONAL STANDARDS ON ENGAGEMENT QUALITY REVIEW/CONCURRING PARTNER REVIEW

AICPA Auditing Standards Board (ASB)	The AICPA has no formal requirement for engagement quality/concurring partner review on individual audit engagements. However, the AICPA does require that firms establish specific criteria by which they will decide on a systematic basis the clients that should have such a review. The AICPA still requires the firms to undergo a quality review process at the overall audit firm level on a periodic basis and (a) the absence of specific criteria for engagement quality reviews, or (b) absence of adherence to those criteria would be considered a deficiency when overall audit firm reviews are performed.
	Recall that the AICPA standards concern non-publicly traded entities, and many of the firm's clients may be very small and only have one or two people assigned to the total audit. Thus, in the view of the AICPA (and many smaller firms), it would not make economic sense to have an engagement quality review for clients that are both uncomplicated and small. Some of the criteria that the firms use to decide that an engagement quality review is needed include riskiness of client, size of client, and the extent of outside distribution of audit report (and thus, potentially the legal liability for the auditor).
PCAOB	Section 103 of the Sarbanes-Oxley Act of 2002 requires the PCAOB to ensure that public company audit firms provide an engagement quality review (sometimes known as a concurring partner review or a second partner review) for each audit. The PCAOB's Auditing Standard No. 7, "Engagement Quality Review" requires the engagement quality reviewer to evaluate all significant judgments made by the engagement team and to consider their evaluation of the client's risks. The standard specifically states that the engagement quality reviewer must have competence, independence, integrity, and objectivity, and the standard requires that all phases of the review be carefully documented.
IAASB	The IAASB standard on engagement quality review ("International Standard on Quality Control 1") is similar to AS No. 7, requiring that the engagement quality reviewer evaluate significant risks and the engagement team's responses to those risks, judgments made (particularly relating to addressing risks and materiality), the disposition of misstatements identified during the engagement (whether corrected or not), and matters communicated to management and others charged with governance over the organization.
SUMMARY	The standards setters diverge concerning engagement quality review, with the AICPA not requiring this audit procedure for the non-public entities over which it provides assurance guidance.

In short, such reviews are not required for non-public entities (i.e., privately held entities) in the United States, but they are required for publicly traded entities in the United States and audit engagements internationally.

Documentation of an Engagement Quality Review

The audit documentation should include evidence on the performance of the engagement quality review. This documentation should include the following information:

- Who performed the engagement quality review
- Documents reviewed by the engagement quality reviewer
- Date the engagement quality reviewer provided concurring approval of issuance

Reviewing Subsequent Events

LO 9

Review subsequent events that occur after the balance sheet date and assess proper treatment.

This section presents three situations relating to events occurring after the balance sheet date that require special audit attention:

1. Review of events occurring after the client's balance sheet date but prior to issuance of the audit report, which is a normal part of each audit
2. Subsequent discovery of facts existing at the date of the auditor's report but not discovered during the audit
3. Consideration of omitted audit procedures that come to the auditor's attention after the auditor's report has been issued

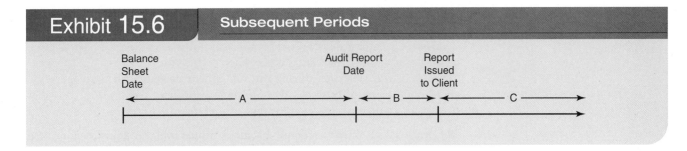

Exhibit 15.6　Subsequent Periods

The timeline in Exhibit 15.6 illustrates these situations. Every audit includes procedures to review events and transactions that occur during the subsequent period, which is the period between the balance sheet date and the audit report date (period A in Exhibit 15.6). The auditor has no responsibilities to continue obtaining audit evidence after the audit report date (periods B and C). The exception to this general rule exists when the client is filing a registration statement with the SEC preparatory to selling new securities. In that case, the auditor must perform a **subsequent events review** up to the effective date of the registration statement. The **effective date** is the date the SEC indicates to the client that it may begin trying to sell the new securities, a date that may be several months after the audit report date.

Normal Review of Subsequent Events

Two types of events have been identified in the professional literature as *subsequent events* that may require dollar adjustments to the financial statements and/or disclosure: Type I subsequent events and Type II subsequent events.

Type I Subsequent Events　Type I subsequent events provide evidence about conditions that existed at the balance sheet date. The financial statement numbers should be adjusted to reflect this information. Footnote disclosure may also be necessary to provide additional information. The following are examples:

- A major customer files for bankruptcy during the subsequent period because of a deteriorating financial condition, which the client and auditor were unaware of until learning about the bankruptcy filing. This information should be considered in establishing an appropriate amount for the allowance for doubtful accounts and in making an adjustment if the allowance is not sufficient to cover this potential loss.
- A lawsuit is settled for a different amount than was accrued.
- A stock dividend or split that takes place during the subsequent period should be disclosed. In addition, earnings-per-share figures should be adjusted to show the retroactive effect of the stock dividend or split.
- A sale of inventory below carrying value provides evidence that the net realizable value was less than cost at year end.

Type II Subsequent Events　Type II subsequent events indicate conditions that did not exist at the balance sheet date, but that may require disclosure. The events that should be considered for disclosure are financial in nature, material, and normally disclosed. The following are examples:

- An uninsured casualty that occurred after the balance sheet date causes a customer's bankruptcy during the subsequent period. Because the customer was able to pay at the balance sheet date, the allowance for doubtful accounts should not be adjusted, but the information should be disclosed.

- A significant lawsuit is initiated relating to an incident that occurred after the balance sheet date.
- Because of a natural disaster such as fire, earthquake, or flood, a firm loses a major facility after the balance sheet date.
- Major decisions are made during the subsequent period, such as to merge, discontinue a line of business, or issue new securities.
- A material change occurs in the value of investment securities.

The financial statement account balances should not be adjusted for these events, but they should be considered for disclosure.

Audit Procedures Concerning the Review of Subsequent Events

PRACTICAL POINT

The audit process ends as of the date of the auditor's report. No subsequent audit work is necessary under ordinary circumstances.

Some of the procedures discussed in previous chapters relate to subsequent events, such as cutoff tests, review of subsequent collections of receivables, and the search for unrecorded liabilities. Additional procedures related to subsequent events include the following:

- Read the minutes of the meetings of the board of directors, stockholders, and other authoritative groups. The auditor should obtain written assurance that minutes of all such meetings through the audit report date have been made available. This can be included in the management representation letter described earlier in this chapter.
- Read interim financial statements and compare them to the audited financial statements, noting and investigating significant changes.
- Inquire of management concerning:

  1. Any significant changes noted in the interim statements;
  2. The existence of significant contingent liabilities or commitments at the balance sheet date or date of inquiry, which should be near the audit report date;
  3. Any significant changes in working capital, long-term debt, or owners' equity;
  4. The status of items for which tentative conclusions were drawn earlier in the audit;
  5. Any unusual adjustments made to the accounting records after the balance sheet date.

Subsequent Discovery of Facts Existing at the Date of the Auditor's Report

PRACTICAL POINT

Many of the PCAOB's inspection reports have identified situations where the review team concludes that the auditor has not gathered sufficient evidence to support the audit opinion. In each of these cases, the auditor goes back to perform additional work to determine whether the financial statements should be changed.

Facts may come to the auditor's attention after the audit report has been issued (period C in Exhibit 15.6) that may have affected the financial statements and auditor's report had the facts been known at the time of issuance. Such facts may come to the auditor's attention through news reports, performing another service for the client, other business contacts, or a subsequent audit. If such facts would have been investigated had they been known at the report date, the auditor should determine the following:

- The reliability of the new information.
- Whether the development or event had occurred by the report date. Issuance of revised financial statements and an audit report is not required when the development or event occurs after the report date.
- Whether users are likely to still be relying on the financial statements. Consideration should be given to the length of time the statements have been outstanding.
- Whether the audit report would have been affected had the facts been known to the auditor at the report date.

If the auditor decides that steps should be taken to prevent further reliance on the financial statements and audit report, the client is advised to make appropriate and timely disclosure of these new facts. The key action is to notify users as soon as possible so they do not continue to rely on information that is now known to be incorrect (see the *Auditing in Practice—Yale Express Case* feature). The appropriate action depends on the circumstances:

- If the revised financial statements and audit report can be quickly prepared and distributed, the reasons for the revision should be described in a footnote and referred to in the auditor's report.
- Revision and explanation can be made in the subsequent-period audited financial statements if their distribution is imminent.
- If it will take an extended amount of time to develop revised financial statements, the client should immediately notify the users that the previously distributed financial statements and auditor's report should no longer be relied on, and that revised statements and report will be issued as soon as possible.

The auditor should make sure the client takes the appropriate action. If the client will not cooperate, the auditor should:

- Notify the client and any regulatory agency having jurisdiction over it, such as the SEC, that the audit report should no longer be associated with the client's financial statements.
- Notify users known to the auditor that the audit report should no longer be relied on. Auditors typically do not know all the users who received the report. Therefore, the appropriate regulatory agency should be requested to take whatever steps are needed to disclose this situation.

Consideration of Omitted Procedures Discovered after the Report Date

After the audit report has been issued, the auditor may discover that an important audit procedure was not performed. Such an omission may be discovered when audit documentation is reviewed as part of an external or internal review program. In this case, the auditor should decide whether the previously issued audit report can still be supported in light of the omitted procedures. If not, the omitted or alternative procedures should be promptly performed and documented.

For example, if the auditor failed to confirm receivables when that should have been done, it may be too late to confirm now. In that case, the auditor could extend the previous work done on subsequent collections to help determine that the receivables were bona fide and properly valued. If the results

PRACTICAL POINT

The auditor has a responsibility to the public for the opinion on the audited financial statements even if information is discovered after the financial statements are issued. The responsibility to the public transcends the responsibility to the client.

AUDITING *in Practice*

YALE EXPRESS CASE

Auditing standard AU 561, "Subsequent Discovery of Facts Existing at the Date of the Auditor's Report," was the result of a lawsuit against the auditors of Yale Express. During 1963, the auditors were performing a management service related to the manner of recognizing revenues and expenses. While performing that service, they discovered that the prior-year audited financial statements contained a material error. An unqualified opinion had been issued on those statements, showing a $1.1 million net income that should have been a $1.9 million net loss. Users were not notified of this until the subsequent year's audited financial statements were issued several months later. The stockholders, upset that they had not been promptly notified, sued the auditors. The court held that auditors could be held liable in such situations. AU 561 was then issued to provide guidance for auditors.

AUDITING *in Practice*

NEED TO WITHDRAW UNQUALIFIED OPINIONS

According to a securities class action fraud court filing in 2010, it was alleged that KPMG failed to withdraw its unqualified audit opinions after learning that its client's (Diebold) prior year financial statements were materially false. The alleged fraudulent practices of Diebold included (1) improper use of "bill-and-hold" accounting, (2) improper recognition of revenue on a lease agreement subject to an undisclosed side buy-back agreement, (3) manipulating reserves and accruals, (4) improperly delaying and capitalizing expenses, and (5) improperly writing up the value of used inventory. The court filing alleges that KPMG issued reports containing unqualified audit opinions that were false and misleading for annual audits conducted for 2003 through 2006. Auditors need to be alert to situations in which the audit opinion should be withdrawn. Failure to do so could result in various consequences, including litigation.

indicate that the previously issued statements and audit report should be modified, the guidance in the previous section of this chapter should be followed. Otherwise, no further action is necessary.

Ensuring Audit Quality: Audit Reporting Decisions Involving Going-Concern Issues, Management Representations, and Communication with the Audit Committee and Management

As the auditor completes the audit, various types of reporting and communication activities are conducted to ensure that the client's financial statements are materially correct, and to ensure high audit quality. These reporting and communication activities include the following:

- Evaluating the going-concern assumption
- Considering management representations in certifications required under the Sarbanes-Oxley Act (for public clients) and requiring management to sign a representation letter
- Communicating with the audit committee
- Communicating with management via a management letter

Evaluating the Going-Concern Assumption

LO 10

List and apply the steps involved in assessing the going-concern assumption.

Business failures result from a variety of causes, such as inadequate financing, cash-flow problems, poor management, product obsolescence, natural disasters, loss of a major customer or supplier, and competition. Investors and creditors become upset when a business fails, particularly when it happens shortly after the auditor has issued an unqualified opinion. However, investors need to realize that an audit opinion is not a guarantee that the business is a going concern. Still, auditors are required to evaluate the likelihood of each client continuing as a going concern for a reasonable period, not to exceed one year from the balance sheet date. As you can see from the *Auditing in Practice* feature on

AUDITING *in Practice*

GOING-CONCERN REPORTING AND BANKRUPTCY FILING AT NORTHWEST AIRLINES

On February 25, 2005, Ernst & Young LLP issued the following opinion about the financial statements of Northwest Airlines:

We also have audited, in accordance with the standards of the Public Company Accounting Oversight Board (United States), the consolidated balance sheets of Northwest Airlines Corporation as of December 31, 2004 and 2003, and the related consolidated statements of operations, stockholders' equity (deficit), and cash flows for each of the three years in the period ended December 31, 2004. Our report dated February 25, 2005 expressed an unqualified opinion thereon.

On September 14, 2005, Northwest Airlines filed for bankruptcy. On March 13, 2006, Ernst & Young LLP issued the following opinion about the financial statements of Northwest Airlines:

We also have audited, in accordance with the standards of the Public Company Accounting Oversight Board (United States) the consolidated balance sheets of Northwest Airlines Corporation (Debtor-in-Possession) as of December 31, 2005 and 2004, and the related consolidated statements of operations, stockholders' equity (deficit), and cash flows for each of the three years in the period ended December 31, 2004. Our report dated March 13, 2006 expressed an unqualified opinion thereon and included explanatory paragraphs related to (i) the Company's reorganization under Chapter 11 of the United States Bankruptcy Code, (ii) the Company's ability

to continue as a going concern, and (iii) the change in method of recognizing certain pension plan administrative expenses associated with the Company's defined benefit pension plans.

Surely, Ernst & Young realized that Northwest was in serious financial difficulty as of early 2005. Given this, consider the following questions as you read this part of the chapter:

- Do you feel that Ernst & Young provided adequate warning to users of Northwest's financial statements as of February 25, 2005?

- Whose responsibility is it to recognize and report on problems regarding the going-concern status of a company?

- What is your reaction to the difference in the information contained in the audit reports dated February 2005 vs. March 2006?

- Auditors cannot predict the future. Given this, what should the auditor's responsibility be to determine whether a company is likely to remain in operation as a "going concern"?

- Why might Ernst & Young have been reluctant to issue an audit report highlighting problems regarding the going-concern status of Northwest Airlines in early 2005?

Northwest Airlines and Ernst & Young LLP, there are instances in which an audit report is issued that does not contain any warning about the impending inability of the company to remain a going concern.

The going-concern evaluation is based on information obtained from normal audit procedures performed to test management's assertions; no separate procedures are required unless the auditor believes that there is substantial doubt about the client's ability to continue as a going concern. However, because the public expects auditors to evaluate the going-concern assumption, many auditing firms regularly use bankruptcy prediction models in analyzing whether a particular client might represent a going-concern problem. If there is substantial doubt about the ability of the client to remain a going concern, the auditor should identify and assess management's plans to overcome the problems and reassess the ability to continue operations.

Comparison of the standards for going-concern considerations is shown in the *Comparison of Worldwide Professional Auditing Guidance.*

Indicators of Potential Going-Concern Problems

Management will often resist a going-concern modification, making the argument that such a qualification will cause investors, lenders, and customers to lose faith in the business and thus cause it to fail. Auditors may be reluctant to issue a going-concern audit opinion because it can be a "self-fulfilling prophecy" that the company will, indeed, go bankrupt. In other words, if an audit

PRACTICAL POINT

The issue of what is a "going concern" may depend on the nature of the bankruptcy filing. A Chapter 11 filing is for reorganization of a business whereby the company is expected to emerge from the bankruptcy. On the other hand, a Chapter 7 filing is to proceed to an orderly liquidation of the business.

Comparison of Worldwide Professional Auditing Guidance

GOING-CONCERN CONSIDERATIONS

AICPA Auditing Standards Board (ASB)

SAS 59 addresses the going-concern issue and discusses how auditors should examine the auditee's ability to continue as a going concern. SAS 59 states that the auditor is responsible for determining if the company being audited can continue in business for the next year. Some of the factors that the auditor should consider include:

- negative trends in the company or industry
- indications of financial difficulties
- internal matters
- external matters, e.g., legal proceedings
- management's plans for the future of the business

If the auditor concludes that the entity cannot continue as a going concern, even after consideration of management's plans, then the audit report should include a going-concern modification.

Public Company Accounting Oversight Board (PCAOB)

The PCAOB has adopted as one of its interim standards AU 341. The description of SAS 59 (above) also applies to AU 341.

International Auditing and Assurance Standards Board (IAASB)

ISA 570 addresses the issue of a company's ability to continue as a going concern. ISA 570 states the following about the going-concern assumption:

"Under the going concern assumption, an entity is viewed as continuing in business for the foreseeable future."

An interesting point that is made in ISA 570 is that in International Accounting Standard 1, the management of the entity is charged with determining if the entity can continue as a going concern. According to ISA 570:

"The auditor's responsibility is to obtain sufficient appropriate audit evidence about the appropriateness of management's use of the going concern assumption in the preparation of the financial statements and to conclude whether there is a material uncertainty about the entity's ability to continue as a going concern."

ISA 570 does state, though, that it is impossible for auditors to predict future events and that "the absence of any reference to going concern uncertainty in an auditor's report cannot be viewed as a guarantee as to the entity's ability to continue as a going concern."

SUMMARY

Users of financial statements have an interest in knowing whether the company will be able to continue in business for the foreseeable future. Auditors use the pronouncements discussed above to help make that determination.

---

firm issues a report stating that the company may not be a going concern, lenders and customers may become so worried that they stop lending money or doing business with the company, thereby hastening its demise. As such, the auditor must carefully analyze all the factors that indicate a going-concern problem and determine if management has a viable plan to address the problems. Potential indicators of going-concern problems include the following:

- Negative trends, such as recurring losses, working-capital deficiencies, negative cash flows from operating activities, and adverse key financial ratios
- Internal matters, such as loss of key personnel, employee strikes, outdated facilities and products, and uneconomic long-term commitments
- External matters, such as new legislation, pending litigation, loss of a key franchise or patent, loss of a principal customer or supplier, and uninsured or underinsured casualty loss
- Other matters, such as default on a loan, inability to pay dividends, restructuring of debt, violation of laws and regulations, and inability to buy from suppliers on credit
- Significant changes in the competitive market and the competitiveness of the client's products

PRACTICAL POINT

The responsibility for assessing going concern is especially important for auditors of smaller or newer public companies with limited operations and limited access to credit or capital. These companies may be especially susceptible to events or conditions that give rise to a going-concern uncertainty.

Exhibit 15.7	Altman Z-Score Models

Z-SCORE FOR PUBLICLY OWNED MANUFACTURING COMPANIES		Z-SCORE FOR PUBLIC AND PRIVATE SERVICE AND MANUFACTURING COMPANIES	
Weight	Ratio	Weight	Ratio
1.2 x	Working capital to total assets	6.56 x	Working capital to total assets
+ 1.4 x	Retained earnings to total assets	+ 3.26 x	Retained earnings to total assets
+ 3.3 x	Return on total assets	+ 6.72 x	Earnings before interest and taxes to total assets
+ 0.99 x	Sales to total assets		
+ 0.6 x	Market value of equity to total debt	+ 1.05 x	Net worth to total liabilities

Interpretation of Z-Score

< 1.81	High potential for bankruptcy	< 1.1	High potential for bankruptcy
> 2.99	Little potential for bankruptcy	> 2.6	Little potential for bankruptcy

A number of studies of bankruptcies have shown that certain combinations of ratios have good predictive power in indicating the likelihood of bankruptcy. Altman developed two combinations of weighted ratios that predict potential bankruptcy (called the **Altman Z-score**): a five-ratio model for publicly owned manufacturing companies and a four-ratio model for public or privately owned manufacturing and service companies.[2] His work has been replicated, and newer models represent variations of his original model.

The Z-scores are calculated as shown in Exhibit 15.7. Z-scores falling below 1.81 in the five-ratio model or below 1.1 in the four-ratio model indicate high potential for bankruptcy. Scores above 2.99 in the five-ratio model or above 2.6 in the four-ratio model indicate very little potential for bankruptcy. For example, using the four-ratio model, a company that has a strong working-capital position, has accumulated significant retained earnings, and is profitable would score above the 2.6 threshold and be unlikely to have a going-concern problem. Although a low Z-score (or a similar score using a different bankruptcy prediction model) does not in itself indicate that the company will fail, it does provide presumptive evidence that there is a going-concern problem. Research has shown that the models are better predictors of problems than are the auditor's qualifications of audit reports.

The auditor must consider all relevant factors in determining whether to modify the audit report. Exhibit 15.8 is a summary of the auditor's decision process regarding going-concern reporting.

Mitigating Factors

If the auditor concludes that there may be a going-concern problem, management's plans to overcome this problem should be identified and assessed. Management may plan to sell nonessential assets, borrow money or restructure existing debt, reduce or delay unnecessary expenditures, and/or increase owner investments. The auditor should identify those factors that are most likely to resolve the problem and gather independent evidence to determine the likely success of such plans. For example, if financial projections are an integral part of the solution, the auditor should ask management to provide that information and the underlying assumptions. The auditor should then consider, and independently test, the adequacy of support for the major assumptions. As another example, if management indicates that their major financial institution is

---

PRACTICAL POINT

In a high-quality audit, the risk of a client not remaining in business needs to be assessed, and any auditor reservations need to be communicated to financial statement users.

PRACTICAL POINT

During the economic recession of 2009, many audit firms issued going-concern opinions for their clients, indicating that they did not have confidence that those companies would survive the downturn. In fact, the recession was so severe that the PCAOB issued Staff Audit Practice Alert No. 3 on December 5, 2008, "Audit Considerations in the Current Economic Environment". The Practice Alert contains advice on how to deal with the audit-related effects of the recession.

---

[2] E. Altman, *Corporate Financial Distress* (New York: John Wiley & Sons, 1983).

Exhibit 15.8   Going-Concern Process

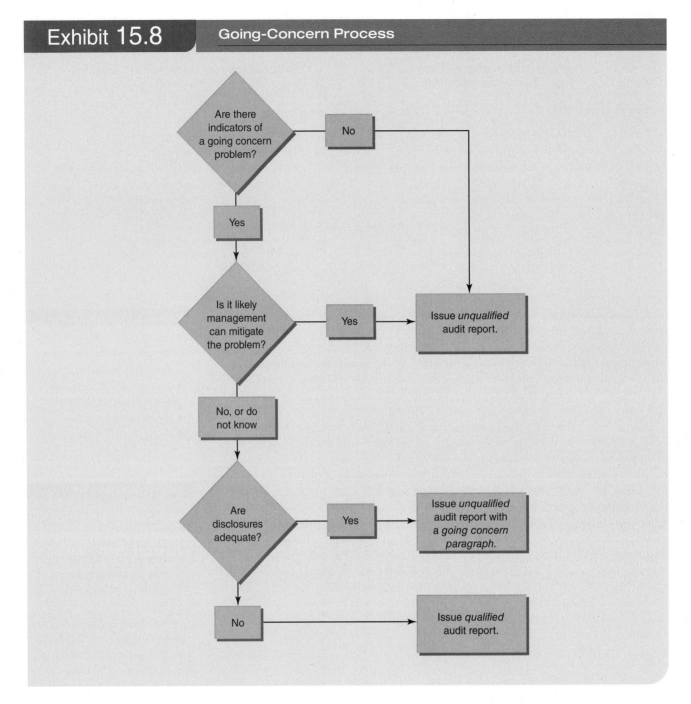

willing to renegotiate the terms of an outstanding loan to provide more favorable terms, the auditor should consider this when evaluating management's recovery plans. Of course, the auditor should confirm the new terms with the bank, likely by speaking directly with the bank rather than relying on management's verbal representations. The auditor should also evaluate the reasonableness of other assumptions made by management, including some of the following:

- Management's assumption about increasing prices or market share should be analyzed in relationship to current industry developments.
- Management's assumptions about cost savings related to a reduction in work force should be recomputed and evaluated to determine if there are hidden costs, e.g., pension obligations that were overlooked by management.

AUDITING *in Practice*

GOING-CONCERN OPINIONS

Approximately 20% of the 2008 audit reports of public companies included a going-concern opinion, with that percentage dropping slightly for the 2009 reports. Of the companies that received a going-concern qualification in 2008, 8.4% were no longer registered with the Securities and Exchange Commission in 2010. More than half of

the going-concern opinions issued in 2008 listed net operating loss as a reason for doubts about the company's future. Other reasons often cited included working capital deficiencies, accumulated retained earnings deficit, and net losses since inception.

- Management's assumptions about selling off assets—either a division or specifically identified assets—should be evaluated in relationship to current market prices.

See the *Auditing in Practice* feature on Eagle Broadband for an example of management's disclosure of its plans to overcome going-concern problems.

Effects on the Financial Statements and Related Disclosures

If the auditor continues to have substantial doubt about the client continuing as a going concern for a reasonable period of time, not to exceed one year beyond the date of the financial statements being audited, the auditor should

AUDITING *in Practice*

GOING-CONCERN REPORTING AT EAGLE BROADBAND INC. FY 2006

Note 22-Financial Condition and Going Concern

The company's financial statements have been presented on the basis that it is a going concern, which contemplates the realization of assets and the satisfaction of liabilities in the normal course of business. The company has negative working capital of $10,613,000, has incurred losses of $26,933,000 and $57,010,000 during 2006 and 2005, and there is substantial doubt as to the company's ability to achieve profitable operations.

There are no assurances that the company will be able to either (1) achieve a level of revenues adequate to generate sufficient cash flow from operations or (2) obtain additional financing through either private placement, public offerings, and/or bank financing necessary to support the company's working-capital requirements. No assurance can be given that additional financing will be available, or if available will be on terms acceptable to the company. If adequate working capital is not available, the company may be required to discontinue its operations. The financial statements do not include any adjustments that might be necessary should the company be unable to continue as a going concern. The company is not currently in default

on any of its payment obligations, and management is addressing the company's current financial condition and obligations by implementing its plans for the upcoming year, including:

- Focusing significant sales efforts on securing large municipal WiFi contracts
- Revising additional operating capital through public and/or private debt and equity offerings
- Reducing debt obligations through the issuance of common stock
- Closely monitoring gross margin performance for all core businesses to assure the company is on track to attain profitability
- Closely monitoring operating expenditures to assure the company remains within its expressed budget

Postscript: As of early 2009, Eagle Broadband no longer was listed on a stock exchange, nor were any annual reports available. Eagle entered into bankruptcy on November 11, 2007, and the remnants of Eagle were purchased by Broadweave, Inc. on July 14, 2008. Management's revelations were highly accurate and effective.

evaluate the adequacy of the client's related disclosures. As of December 2010, FASB has proposed guidance in this area that requires certain disclosures "when management, applying commercially reasonable business judgment, is aware of conditions and events that indicate, based on current facts and circumstances, that it is reasonably foreseeable that an entity may not be able to meet its obligations as they become due without substantial disposition of assets outside the ordinary course of business, restructuring of debt, issuance of equity, externally or internally forced revisions of its operations, or similar actions." The required disclosures include:

- "Pertinent conditions and events giving rise to the assessment, including when such conditions and events are anticipated to occur, if reasonably estimable
- The possible effects of those conditions and events
- Possible discontinuance of operations
- Management's evaluation of the significance of those conditions and events and any mitigating factors
- Management's plans to mitigate the effects of the conditions and events, whether those plans can be effectively implemented, and the likelihood that such plans will mitigate the adverse effects."
- Information about the recoverability or classification of recorded asset amounts or the amounts or classification of liabilities."

Effects on the Audit Report

An explanatory paragraph should be added to the auditor's report when the auditor concludes that substantial doubt remains about the client's ability to continue as a going concern for a reasonable period of time. The paragraph describing the auditor's concern should be added to the standard unqualified audit report. The paragraph should include reference to a footnote in which management describes the financial problem(s) and its plans in more detail. A qualified audit report would normally be issued if the auditor believes the client's disclosure is inadequate. However, the auditor is not precluded from issuing a disclaimer if it is believed to be a better way to communicate the concern.

A concern expressed by observers of the financial markets is that as many as 30% to 40% of companies that ultimately declare bankruptcy have received unqualified audit opinions in the period immediately preceding the bankruptcy declaration, as in the case of Northwest Airlines. Why might auditors be reluctant to issue an audit report highlighting problems regarding the going-concern status of their clients? One explanation is that the auditor's issuance of a going-concern opinion, by itself, might cause the company to go bankrupt (i.e., the self-fulfilling prophecy phenomenon mentioned earlier). Another explanation is that the auditor may be worried that issuing a report when the company might survive will cause it to lose the client and therefore future audit fees. A final explanation is that it is simply very difficult to know beforehand whether or not a financially distressed client will actually cease operations or will somehow pull itself away from that outcome. Auditors do not appear to fare much better than other participants in the financial reporting arena in terms of making that difficult determination.

Evaluating Management Representations

The Certification of Financial Statements

The Sarbanes-Oxley Act requires the CEO and CFO of publicly traded companies to certify that the financial statements are fairly presented in accordance with generally accepted accounting principles. Most CEOs and CFOs have improved internal processes to help them meet their primary responsibility for the reliability of the financial statements. In a high-quality audit, the auditor will review management's processes for certification to ensure that those processes are adequate and that they can be relied upon. Remember, the financial

AUDITING *in Practice*

PCAOB OBSERVATIONS ABOUT GOING-CONCERN ASSESSMENTS

The primary audit standard setter in the United States has been concerned with the failure of registered audit firms to comply with the "going-concern" assessment requirements. In October 2007, the PCAOB issued a report that provided observations identified in the course of its 2004, 2005, and 2006 inspections of registered public accounting firms that audit no more than 100 issuers (i.e., smaller audit firms). The following excerpt from that report highlights audit deficiencies where audit firms failed to demonstrate they had completed requirements related to going-concern assessments.

Some of these firms failed to identify or evaluate the significance of conditions that indicated an entity may not have been able to continue as a going concern, such as cumulative losses since

inception, accumulated capital deficits, and negative working capital.

Other firms identified conditions that could affect the issuer's ability to continue as a going concern, but failed to evaluate management's plans to mitigate the effects of such conditions, or failed to obtain information about the likelihood that such plans could be implemented effectively.

In addition, some firms failed to evaluate the adequacy of an entity's disclosure of the going-concern conditions and managements' plans to mitigate them.

Auditors need to carefully perform and document required going-concern assessments to help ensure the completion of a quality audit.

statements are management's, not the auditor's; but users have an expectation that auditors provide assurance regarding the accuracy of management's assertions. Exhibit 15.9 provides an excerpt of a management certification at Ford Motor Company that illustrates this point.

Management Representation Letter

Auditors should obtain a **management representation letter** (see Exhibit 15.10) at the end of each audit. The letter is a part of audit evidence but is not a substitute for audit procedures that are performed to corroborate the information contained in the letter. The purposes of the letter are to ensure audit quality by doing the following:

- Reminding management of its responsibility for the financial statements.
- Confirming oral responses obtained by the auditor earlier in the audit and the continuing appropriateness of those responses.
- Reducing the possibility of misunderstanding concerning the matters that are the subject of the representations.

The letter is prepared on the client's letterhead, is addressed to the auditor, and should be signed by the chief executive officer and the chief financial officer. The auditor usually prepares the letter for the client to read and sign. The contents depend on the circumstances of the audit and the nature and basis of presentation of the financial statements. It may be limited to matters that are considered material to the financial statements and should include representations about known fraud involving management or employees. If management refuses to sign the representation letter, it means that they are not willing to stand by their verbal representations when asked to do so in writing; in short, it would imply that management was being untruthful in verbal representations. Management's refusal to sign the management representation letter is considered a scope limitation sufficient to preclude the issuance of an unqualified opinion.

The auditor may receive separate representation letters from other corporate officials. The corporate secretary, for example, may be asked to sign a letter representing that all of the corporate minutes (which are usually listed by date) or extracts from recent meetings have been made available to the auditor.

> **PRACTICAL POINT**
>
> Additional representations should be included in audits of public companies related to the audit of internal control. Otherwise, a separate representation letter should be obtained relating to internal controls.

> **PRACTICAL POINT**
>
> The management representation letter does not replace the need to obtain appropriate evidence.

Exhibit 15.9 — Management Certifications at Ford Motor Company

FORD MOTOR COMPANY CERTIFICATION OF CHIEF EXECUTIVE OFFICER

I, Alan Mulally, President and Chief Executive Officer of Ford Motor Company, certify that:

1. I have reviewed this Annual Report on Form 10-K for the year ended December 31, 2009 of Ford Motor Company;

2. Based on my knowledge, this report does not contain any untrue statement of a material fact or omit to state a material fact necessary to make the statements made, in light of the circumstances under which such statements were made, not misleading with respect to the period covered by this report;

3. Based on my knowledge, the financial statements, and other financial information included in this report, fairly present in all material respects the financial condition, results of operations and cash flows of the registrant as of, and for, the periods presented in this report;

4. The registrant's other certifying officer(s) and I are responsible for establishing and maintaining disclosure controls and procedures (as defined in Exchange Act Rules 13a-15(e) and 15d-15(e)) and internal control over financial reporting (as defined in Exchange Act Rules 13a-15(f) and 15d-15(f)) for the registrant and have:

   (a) Designed such disclosure controls and procedures, or caused such disclosure controls and procedures to be designed under our supervision, to ensure that material information relating to the registrant, including its consolidated subsidiaries, is made known to us by others within those entities, particularly during the period in which this report is being prepared;

   (b) Designed such internal control over financial reporting, or caused such internal control over financial reporting to be designed under our supervision, to provide reasonable assurance regarding the reliability of financial reporting and the preparation of financial statements for external purposes in accordance with generally accepted accounting principles;

Dated: February 25, 2010

/s/ Alan Mulally

Alan Mulally

President and Chief Executive Officer

LO 12

Identify issues to communicate to the audit committee.

Communicating with the Audit Committee

There are several items that the auditor should report to the audit committee by the end of the audit to ensure audit quality and help the audit committee fulfill its responsibility to oversee the financial reporting processes of the entity.

Accounting and Audit Issues

PRACTICAL POINT

For public companies, the auditor must reach a conclusion on the most appropriate accounting treatment for a new transaction or an estimate. The auditor's conclusion must be communicated to the audit committee even if the company chose another acceptable accounting treatment and the auditor issued an unqualified opinion on the financial statements.

- *Auditor's Responsibility under Generally Accepted Auditing Standards*—It is important that members of the audit committee understand that audits provide reasonable, but not absolute, assurance about the fairness of the financial statements.
- *Management Judgments and Accounting Estimates*—Accounting estimates are based on judgments. The audit committee needs to be aware of the processes used by management in developing sensitive estimates and how the auditor determined the reasonableness of those estimates.
- *Audit Adjustments*—The auditor should report any audit adjustments that could have a material effect on the financial statements and that may not have been detected except through the audit.
- *Uncorrected Misstatements*—Material misstatements should be corrected by management. Otherwise, the auditor will have to modify the audit opinion. Immaterial misstatements that are not corrected should be reported to the audit committee.
- *Accounting Policies and Alternative Treatments*—Members of the audit committee must be informed about the initial selection of and changes in significant accounting policies during the current period and the reasons therefore. They also need to be informed about the methods used to account for significant unusual transactions and controversial or emerging areas for which there is a lack of authoritative guidance.

Exhibit 15.10 | Management Representation Letter

Nature Sporting Goods Manufacturing Company
200 Pine Way, Kirkville, SI 53800
(608) 255-7820

February 28, 2012 (Audit Report Date)

To Rittenberg, Johnstone, and Gramling, CPAs

We are providing this letter in connection with your audits of the consolidated balance sheets of Nature Sporting Goods Manufacturing Company as of December 31, 2011 and 2010 and the related consolidated statements of income, cash flows, and stockholders' equity for the years then ended for the purpose of expressing an opinion as to whether the consolidated financial statements present fairly, in all material respects, the financial position, results of operations, and cash flows of Nature Sporting Goods Manufacturing Company in conformity with accounting principles generally accepted in the United States of America. We confirm that we are responsible for the fair presentation in the consolidated financial statements of financial position, results of operations, and cash flows in conformity with generally accepted accounting principles.

Certain representations in this letter are described as being limited to matters that are material. Items are considered material, regardless of size, if they involve an omission or misstatement of accounting information that, in the light of surrounding circumstances, makes it probable that the judgment of a reasonable person relying on the information would be changed or influenced by the omission or misstatement.

We confirm, to the best of our knowledge and belief, as of February 28, 2012, the following representations made to you during your audits:

1. The financial statements referred to above are fairly presented in conformity with accounting principles generally accepted in the United States of America.
2. We have made available to you all:
   a. Financial records and related data
   b. Minutes of the meetings of stockholders, directors, and committees of directors, or summaries of actions of recent meetings for which minutes have not yet been prepared
3. There have been no communications from regulatory agencies concerning noncompliance with or deficiencies in financial reporting practices.
4. There are no material transactions that have not been properly recorded in the accounting records underlying the financial statements.
5. We believe that the effects of the uncorrected financial statement misstatements summarized in the accompanying schedule are immaterial, both individually and in the aggregate, to the financial statements taken as a whole.
6. There are no significant deficiencies, including material weaknesses, in the design or operation of internal controls that could adversely affect the entity's ability to record, process, summarize, and report financial data.[1]
7. We acknowledge our responsibility for the design and implementation of programs and controls to prevent and detect fraud.
8. We have no knowledge of fraud or suspected fraud affecting the entity involving:
   a. Management
   b. Employees who have significant roles in internal control
   c. Others where the fraud could have a material effect on the financial statements
9. We have no knowledge of any allegations of fraud or suspected fraud affecting the entity received in communications from employees, former employees, analysts, regulators, short sellers, or others.
10. The entity has no plans or intentions that may materially affect the carrying value or classification of assets and liabilities.
11. The following have been properly recorded or disclosed in the financial statements:
    a. Related-party transactions, including sales, purchases, loans, transfers, leasing arrangements, and guarantees, and amounts receivable from or payable to related parties
    b. Guarantees, whether written or oral, under which the company is contingently liable
    c. Significant estimates and material concentrations known to management that are required to be disclosed in accordance with FASB Accounting Standards Codification (ASC) 275, *Risks and Uncertainties*. (Significant estimates are estimates at the balance sheet date that could change materially within the next year. Concentrations refer to volumes of business, revenues, available sources of supply, or markets or geographic areas for which events could occur that would significantly disrupt normal finances within the next year.)

Exhibit 15.10 Management Representation Letter (*continued*)

12. There are no:
  a. Violations or possible violations of laws or regulations whose effects should be considered for disclosure in the financial statements or as a basis for recording a loss contingency
  b. Unasserted claims or assessments that our lawyer has advised us are probable of assertion and must be disclosed in accordance with ASC 450 (formerly FASB Statement No. 5, *Accounting for Contingencies*)
  c. Other liabilities or gain or loss contingencies that are required to be accrued or disclosed by ASC 450 (formerly FASB Statement No. 5)

13. The entity has satisfactory title to all owned assets, and there are no liens or encumbrances on such assets nor has any asset been pledged as collateral.

14. The entity has complied with all aspects of contractual agreements that would have a material effect on the financial statements in the event of noncompliance.

15. To the best of our knowledge and belief, no events have occurred subsequent to the balance-sheet date and through the date of this letter that would require adjustment to or disclosure in the aforementioned financial statements.

John Edgerton
_____
John Edgerton, CEO

Rene Bollum
_____
Rene Bollum, CFO
_____

[1]Additional representations should be included in audits of public companies related to the audit of internal control. Otherwise, a separate representation letter should be obtained relating to internal controls.

Other Issues Related to the Conduct of the Audit

Other matters to communicate to the audit committee include the following:

PRACTICAL POINT

Auditors of nonpublic companies are required to communicate to management and those charged with governance, significant deficiencies and material weaknesses in internal control.

1. Major accounting and reporting disagreements with management, even if eventually resolved
2. Management's discussion with other public accounting firms regarding the treatment of potentially controversial accounting issues
3. Difficulties encountered in performing the audit
4. Copies of significant written communications between the auditor and management, such as the engagement letter, management representation letter, and reports of significant deficiencies and material weaknesses in internal control over financial reporting

Special Issues for Public Companies

For audits of public companies subject to SEC regulation, the auditor should also report the following to the audit committee:

1. The client's critical accounting policies and practices, why they are considered critical to the financial statements, and the adequacy of their disclosures
2. The acceptable alternative accounting policies and practices and the treatment preferred by the auditor
3. The auditor's judgments about the quality, not just the acceptability, of the client's accounting policies

The auditor should document the reasoning process in judging the quality of the client's accounting policies. The audit documentation should consider the economic substance of significant transactions and contractual agreements, the consistency of application, and the correspondence with FASB concepts.

Further, auditors of public companies are required to communicate with the audit committee all relationships that might reasonably be thought to affect auditor independence (although this communication should begin at the start of the engagement). Finally, when performing an integrated audit, the auditor should communicate to the audit committee all material weaknesses and significant deficiencies in internal control.

Communicating with Management via the Management Letter

LO 13

Identify issues to communicate to management via a management letter.

Auditors often notice things that could help management do a better job. The auditor generally reports these observations in a **management letter** as a constructive part of the audit. Such a letter should not be confused with a management representation letter. The management letter is not required, but it is used to make significant operational or control recommendations to the client. The letter helps to provide management comfort that the auditor has done a high quality job and that the auditor knows and understands the client's business. Staff auditors are encouraged to make notes during the course of the audit on potential improvements. Many of these observations relate directly to control deficiencies or operational matters. Many audit firms consider management's inattention to addressing comments in the letter to be an important risk factor in subsequent-year audits.

> **PRACTICAL POINT**
>
> A management letter shares the auditor's observations on how to improve operations, controls, or the efficiency of financial processing.

Summary

Before issuing an audit opinion, the auditor must determine whether the financial statements are presented fairly in all material respects, whether they contain adequate disclosures, and whether they properly reflect events that have occurred up to the audit report date. In short, various activities must be completed prior to issuing the audit report that, taken together, ensure that the audit was conducted in a high-quality manner. The going-concern issue must be addressed in each audit.

The auditor should be sure that audit risk has been kept at an appropriately low level. An engagement quality review program can help assure that no major audit procedures have been left out and that the documentation supports the audit opinion. Auditors must be sure the audit committee is informed about matters that will help it fulfill its responsibilities for financial reporting. This chapter describes these, and other, actions that auditors must take as they wrap up each audit.

Significant Terms

Altman Z-score A combination of weighted ratios to produce a score of potential bankruptcy developed using a regression model to predict companies that have a high potential for bankruptcy.

Concurring partner review (also referred to as engagement quality review) A review at the end of each audit conducted by an experienced auditor, usually a partner, who was not a part of the audit team, but who has appropriate competence, independence, integrity, and objectivity. The purposes are to help make sure that the audit and audit documentation are complete and support the audit opinion on the financial statements and, for public companies, on the client's internal controls.

Effective date The date the SEC indicates to the client that it may begin trying to sell the new securities described in a registration statement.

Engagement quality review See concurring partner review.

Letter of audit inquiry A letter that the auditor asks the client to send to its legal counsel to gather corroborative evidence concerning litigation, claims, and assessments.

Management letter A letter from the auditor to the client identifying any problems and suggested solutions that may help management improve its effectiveness or efficiency.

Management representation letter A letter to the auditors that the client's chief executive and chief financial officer are required to sign that specifies management's responsibility for the financial statements and confirms oral responses given to the auditor during the audit.

Subsequent events review A review of events occurring in the period between the balance sheet date and the audit report date to determine their possible effect on the financial statements.

SELECTED REFERENCES TO RELEVANT PROFESSIONAL GUIDANCE

Topic	Selected Guidance
Audit Adjustments	SAS 89 *Audit Adjustments* SAS *Evaluation of Misstatements Identified During the Audit* (issued but not effective; proposed effective date is December 2012) AS No. 14 *Evaluating Audit Results* ISA 450 *Evaluation of Misstatements Identified During the Audit*
Loss Contingencies	SAS 12 *Inquiry of a Client's Lawyer Concerning Litigation, Claims, and Assessments* ISA 501 *Audit Evidence—Specific Considerations for Selected Items*
Accounting Estimates	SAS 57 *Auditing Accounting Estimates* SAS *Auditing Accounting Estimates, Including Fair Value Accounting Estimates and Related Disclosures* (Redrafted) (issued but not effective; proposed effective date is December 2012) ISA 540 *Auditing Accounting Estimates, Including Fair Value Accounting Estimates, and Related Disclosures*
Disclosures in the Financial Statements	SAS 32 *Adequacy of Disclosure in Financial Statements*
Omitted Procedures	SAS 46 *Consideration of Omitted Procedures after the Report Date* SAS *Consideration of Omitted Procedures after the Report Release Date* (issued but not effective; proposed effective date is December 2012)
Engagement Quality Review	AS No. 7 *Engagement Quality Review* IAASB *International Standard on Quality Control 1*
Subsequent Events and Subsequent Discovery of Facts	SAS 1 Section 560 *Subsequent Events* SAS 1 Section 561 *Subsequent Discovery of Facts Existing at the Date of the Auditor's Report* SAS *Subsequent Events and Subsequently Discovered Facts* (issued but not effective; proposed effective date is December 2012) ISA 560 *Subsequent Events*
Going-Concern Considerations	SAS 59 *The Auditor's Consideration of an Entity's Ability to Continue as a Going Concern* ISA 570 *Going Concern*
Management Representations	SAS 85 *Management Representations* SAS *Written Representations* (issued but not effective; proposed effective date is December 2012) ISA 580 *Written Representations*
Communications with Client and Management	SAS 60 *Communication of Internal Control Related Matters Noted in an Audit* (Superseded by SAS No. 112) SAS 61 *Communication with Audit Committees* (superseded by SAS 114) SAS 90 *Audit Committee Communications* SAS 114 *The Auditor's Communication with Those Charged with Governance* SAS *The Auditor's Communication with Those Charged with Governance* (issued but not effective; proposed effective date is December 2012) SAS 115 *Communicating Internal Control Related Matters Identified in an Audit* SAS *Communicating Internal Control Related Matters Identified in an Audit* (Redrafted) (issued but not effective; proposed effective date is December 2012) PCAOB Ethics and Independence Rule 3526 *Communication with Audit Committees Concerning Independence* ISA 260 *Communication with Those Charged with Governance* ISA 265 *Communicating Deficiencies in Internal Control to Those Charged with Governance and Management*

Note: *Acronyms for Relevant Professional Guidance*
STANDARDS: **AS**—Auditing Standard issued by the PCAOB; **ISA**—International Standard on Auditing issued by the IAASB; **SAS**—Statement on Auditing Standards issued by the Auditing Standards Board of the AICPA; **SSAE**—Statement on Standards for Attestation Engagements issued by the AICPA.
ORGANIZATIONS: **AICPA**—American Institute of Certified Public Accountants; **COSO**—Committee of Sponsoring Organizations; **IAASB**—International Auditing and Assurance Standards Board; **PCAOB**—Public Company Accounting Oversight Board; **SEC**—Securities and Exchange Commission.

Review Questions

15-1   **(LO 1)** Imagine that you have to explain the concept of "audit quality" to someone unfamiliar with the auditing profession and associated rules. Draft a definition of audit quality that would be understandable to a relatively unsophisticated user of the financial statements. Next, contrast your definition with the one provided by the GAO, which defines a high-quality audit as one performed "in accordance with generally accepted auditing standards (GAAS) to provide reasonable assurance that the audited financial statements and related disclosures are presented in accordance with generally accepted accounting principles (GAAP) and (2) are not materially misstated whether due to errors or fraud."

15-2   **(LO 1)** According to the UK's Financial Reporting Council (FRC), what are the five key drivers of audit quality?

15-3   **(LO 1)** What are some factors outside the control of auditors that are likely to make a positive contribution to audit quality?

15-4   **(LO 2)** What is an "audit adjustment" and why are the resolution of such adjustments important to audit quality? What role should professional skepticism play when management disagrees with the auditor about making an audit adjustment to correct a known misstatement? What types of management bias might be revealed in this type of setting?

Professional Skepticism

15-5   **(LO 2)** How does a summary of possible adjustments help the auditor determine whether the financial statements are fairly presented? What information might it contain? How might an analysis of the summary affect an internal control report on a public company?

15-6   **(LO 2)** Why is audit firm culture important in ensuring that individual audit engagement partners resolve audit adjustments in a high-quality manner?

15-7   **(LO 3)** What are client continuance decisions, and why are these decisions important to the ability of an audit firm to ensure audit quality?

15-8   **(LO 3)** What is audit firm portfolio management? Describe the process by which clients move into and out of an audit firm's · portfolio of clients.

15-9   **(LO 3)** What are some of the risk factors that an audit firm should consider when making the client continuance decision?

15-10   **(LO 4)** What is the primary source of information about litigation, claims, and assessments? What is the primary source of corroborative evidence in this regard?

15-11   **(LO 4)** Why might client lawyers be hesitant to disclose information to auditors?

15-12   **(LO 4)** Who sends the letter of audit inquiry to the client's lawyers? To whom should the lawyer send the response to that letter?

**Professional
Skepticism**

Fraud

15-13 **(LO 4)** What is the effect on the auditor's report of a lawyer's refusal to furnish the information requested in the letter of audit inquiry?

15-14 **(LO 4, 6)** How is a disclosure checklist helpful? What precautions should the auditor take when using such a checklist?

15-15 **(LO 5)** Why should the auditor exercise heightened professional skepticism concerning accounting estimates? What are the major factors that might affect the amounts that are primarily accounting estimates?

15-16 **(LO 6)** Describe the alleged fraud that Dell, Inc. top executives committed that related to inaccurate financial statement disclosures and management representations.

15-17 **(LO 7)** What is the purpose of performing analytical procedures on revenue and expenses at the end of the audit?

15-18 **(LO 8)** What are the purposes of the engagement quality review (concurring partner review)?

15-19 **(LO 9)** What are the types of subsequent events the auditor should identify and evaluate as part of a normal audit? Give an example of each type of subsequent event. How should each type be handled in the financial statements?

15-20 **(LO 9)** With one exception, auditors do not have a responsibility to continue their review of subsequent events beyond the audit report date. What is that exception?

15-21 **(LO 9)** What audit procedures should be performed to search for subsequent events?

15-22 **(LO 9)** List three examples of Type I subsequent events, and list three examples of Type II subsequent events.

15-23 **(LO 9)** Explain the auditor's responsibilities when it is discovered that facts existed at the date of the audit report but were not known to the auditor.

15-24 **(LO 9)** An internal review discovered that the auditors failed to perform a significant audit procedure on an audit completed five months earlier. What steps should the auditors take?

15-25 **(LO 10)** Are auditors required to evaluate the likelihood of a client remaining a going concern as a part of each audit? What types of conditions and factors should auditors look for to help make this evaluation?

15-26 **(LO 10)** An Altman Z-score indicates the possibility that a client will go bankrupt. What effect will this have on the audit report? Explain.

15-27 **(LO 11)** What is a management representation letter? Who prepares it? Who should sign it? When should it be dated? How does it differ from the CEO and CFO certification of financial statements?

15-28 **(LO 12)** What items should the auditor discuss with the audit committee near or at the end of the audit? Why is it important that such items be discussed?

Multiple-Choice Questions

15-29   **(LO 7)** Analytical procedures performed in the overall review stage of an audit suggest that several accounts have unexpected relationships. These results most likely suggest which of the following audit?

a. An adverse report on internal control activities.

b. Fraud exists among the relevant account balances.

c. Additional tests of details are required.

d. The communication with the audit committee should be revised.

*15-30   **(LO 4)** Auditors should request that an audit client send a letter of inquiry to those attorneys who have been consulted concerning litigation, claims, or assessments. The primary reason for this request is to provide which of the following?

a. Information concerning the progress of cases to date.

b. Corroborative evidential matter.

c. An estimate of the dollar amount of the probable loss.

d. An expert opinion regarding whether a loss is possible, probable, or remote.

*15-31   **(LO 4)** In an audit of contingent liabilities, which of the following procedures would be least effective?

a. Reviewing a bank confirmation letter.

b. Examining accounts receivable customer confirmation replies.

c. Examining invoices for professional services.

d. Reading the minutes of the board of directors.

15-32   **(LO 13)** Which of the following matters would an auditor most likely include in a management letter?

a. Communications with the audit committee concerning disagreements with management.

b. Suggestions for improving the client's internal controls.

c. Evaluation of whether the client's financial accounting for pensions is in accordance with GAAP.

d. Management's acknowledgment of its responsibility for the detection of employee fraud.

*15-33   **(LO 11)** Which of the following statements ordinarily is included among the written client representations obtained by the auditor?

a. Management acknowledges that there are no material weaknesses in internal control.

b. Sufficient evidential matter has been made available to permit the issuance of an unqualified opinion.

c. The financial statements are fairly presented in conformity with generally accepted accounting principles.

d. Management acknowledges responsibility for illegal actions committed by employees.

---

*All problems marked with an asterisk are adapted from the Uniform CPA Examination.

15-34   **(LO 1)** A high-quality audit is one performed:

    a. In accordance with the engagement contract signed by both the auditor and the client, and one in which all audit procedures are performed efficiently.

    b. In accordance with generally accepted auditing standards (GAAS) to provide reasonable assurance that the audited financial statements and related disclosures are presented in accordance with generally accepted accounting principles (GAAP) and are not materially misstated whether because of errors or fraud.

    c. In accordance with the engagement contract signed by both the auditor and the audit committee, and one in which all audit procedures are performed to detect both material and immaterial errors in the financial statements.

    d. In accordance with generally accepted auditing standards (GAAS) to provide reasonable assurance that the audited financial statements and related disclosures are presented in accordance with generally accepted accounting principles (GAAP) and are not materially misstated because of weaknesses in internal control.

15-35   **(LO 10)** Cooper, CPA, believes there is substantial doubt about the ability of Zero Corp. to continue as a going concern for a reasonable period of time. In evaluating Zero's plan for dealing with the adverse effects of future conditions and events, Cooper most likely would consider, as a mitigating factor, Zero's plans to:

    a. Make credit terms for sales on account more lenient.

    b. Strengthen internal controls over cash disbursements.

    c. Purchase production facilities currently being leased from a related party.

    d. Postpone expenditures for research and development projects.

*15-36   **(LO 10)** Which of the following audit procedures would most likely help an auditor to identify conditions and events that might make one doubt an entity's ability to continue as a going concern?

    a. Review compliance with the terms of debt agreements.

    b. Confirm accounts receivable from principal customers.

    c. Reconcile interest expense with debt outstanding.

    d. Confirm bank balances.

*15-37   **(LO 9)** Six months after issuing an unqualified opinion on audited financial statements, an auditor discovered that the engagement personnel failed to confirm several of the client's material accounts receivable balances and did not perform alternative procedures that would have replaced the confirmations. Which of the following should the auditor do first?

    a. Request the permission of the client to undertake the confirmation of accounts receivable.

    b. Perform alternative procedures to provide a satisfactory basis for the unqualified opinion.

    c. Assess the importance of the omitted procedures to the auditor's ability to support the previously expressed opinion.

    d. Inquire whether there are persons currently relying, or likely to rely, on the unqualified opinion.

*15-38 **(LO 9)** Which of the following procedures would an auditor most likely perform to obtain evidence about the occurrence of subsequent events?

    a. Confirming a sample of material accounts receivable established after year end.

    b. Comparing the financial statements being reported on with those of the prior period.

    c. Investigating personnel changes in the accounting department occurring after year end.

    d. Inquiring as to whether any unusual adjustments were made after year end.

Discussion and Research Questions

15-39 **(Analytical Review, LO 1, 7)** The audit of GolfDay Company, a manufacturer of bicycle racks and golf carts, is almost finished. Krista Heiss is the most experienced auditor on this audit and is in charge of performing final analytical procedures. The company ships most of its products to a combination of distributors and retailers. The business in totally within the United States at the present time and is seasonal.

Required

    a. Why is it important that final analytical procedures be performed by experienced auditors?

    b. What are some analytical procedures that Heiss might perform?

    c. How can these procedures be useful at this stage of the audit to help ensure audit quality?

15-40 **(Altman Z-Score, LO 10)** Refer to the Biltrite financial statements in the Biltrite Practice Case (Exhibits BR.3 and BR.4 in the introduction to the Biltrite case).

Required

    a. Calculate the Altman Z-score for Biltrite for 2009 using the model for public and private service and manufacturing companies. What does this score tell you about the potential for bankruptcy?

    b. Calculate the Altman Z-score assuming that the total amounts for current assets and current liabilities are reversed as are the total amounts of net worth and total liabilities. What does this score tell you about the potential for bankruptcy?

15-41 **(Contingencies, LO 4)** An audit client is being sued for $500,000 for discriminatory hiring practices.

Required

Indicate the appropriate action the auditor should take for each of the following independent responses to the letter of audit inquiry:

    a. The lawyer stated that the client had a "meritorious defense."

    b. The lawyer stated that there is only a remote chance that the client will lose. The client did not accrue any contingent loss or disclose this situation.

c. The lawyer stated that the client will probably lose, and the amount of loss could be anywhere between $250,000 and $500,000, with no amount within that range being more likely than another. The client disclosed this situation but did not accrue a loss.

d. The lawyer stated that there is a reasonable possibility that the client will lose. The client disclosed this situation but did not accrue a loss.

e. The lawyer stated that the client will probably lose between $250,000 and $500,000, but most likely will lose $400,000. The client accrued a $250,000 contingent loss and disclosed the situation.

15-42   **(Contingencies, LO 4)** Each of the following is an independent situation related to a contingency:

1. The lawyer refused to furnish the requested information.

2. The lawyer was unable to form an opinion on the probability or amount of a pending lawsuit, but the auditor believes that the amount could be material.

3. The client stated that it had not consulted lawyers during the past year.

4. The client refuses to accrue for, or disclose, a pending lawsuit related to the infringement of a patent that is the basis of its major product. It is afraid that it will lose customers. The plaintiff is suing for $2,500,000, which represents 50% of owners' equity. The lawyer believes that the case can be settled for less than the damages claimed.

Required

What should the auditor do in each case?

15-43   **(Summary of Possible Adjustments, LO 2)** During the course of the audit of Nature Sporting Goods for the year ended December 31, 2011, the auditor discovered the following:

- The accounts receivable confirmation work revealed one pricing error. The book value of $12,955.68 should be $11,984.00. The total error based on this difference is $14,465, which includes a $972 known error and an unknown projected error of $13,493.

- Nature Sporting Goods had understated the accrued vacation pay by $13,000. A review of the prior-year documentation indicates the following uncorrected errors:

  Accrued vacation pay was understated by $9,000.
  Sales and accounts receivable were overstated by an estimated $60,000 because of cutoff errors.

Required

Prepare a summary of a possible adjustments schedule and draw your conclusion about whether the aggregate effect of these errors is material. Nature Sporting Goods has made no adjustments to the trial balance numbers shown in Exhibit 15.2. (Note that the retained earnings balance is the beginning balance.) Ignore the errors shown in the exhibit. The income tax rate is 40% for the current and prior year. Note: materiality must be considered in developing your answer.

15-44 **(Going Concern, LO 10)** A staff auditor has just returned from a continuing professional education workshop on current auditing standards. One of her managers has asked her to prepare a training session for the rest of the staff. In particular, he wants her to discuss the standard related to the client's ability to continue as a going concern.

Required

a. Describe the auditor's responsibility for assessing each client's ability to continue as a going concern.

b. Describe the effect on the financial statements and on the auditor's report for each of the following independent situations:

   1. The auditor has substantial doubt as to whether the client is a going concern.

   2. The auditor believes that the note describing the going-concern problem is inadequate.

   3. In the prior-year statements, a going-concern problem had been disclosed and was referred to in the auditor's prior-year report, but the uncertainty has been eliminated this year. Comparative statements will be issued.

   4. The auditor concludes that the client is likely to continue in existence for at least one more year. The same conclusion had been reached in prior years.

   5. The client was forced into bankruptcy by creditors after year end but before the audit was completed.

15-45 **(Going Concern, LO 10)** Read the following scenario, and discuss your answers to the questions below in a small group. This is the third year of an audit of GreenLawns.com. The company has carved out a new market niche for the delivery of lawn and garden supplies, including links with local companies that provide lawn services. The company issued stock two years ago and raised sufficient capital to continue operations through this year. The company is currently trading at five times revenue. The company has shown no profits in its first three years. Revenue growth has been 100%, 65%, and 30%, respectively, over the last three years. The current year revenue is at $220 million. The auditor has examined current cash flow and has serious reservations about the ability of the company to remain a going concern without either some profitability or an infusion of cash. The company has responded with the following management plan:

Group Activity

- Another public offering of stock to raise $200 million in capital, which will be equal to 30% of the existing stock outstanding

- Sign an agreement with at least fifty more local distributors during the year

- Improve warehousing and distribution to cut at least 20% off the distribution costs

- Increase sales by 50% through more advertising, coupons, and better marketing to existing customers

- Improve profit margins by using its purchase power to sign more attractive purchase agreements with vendors, but stay away from major-brand vendors such as Scott's, Ortho products, and so forth.

Required

a. What is the auditor's responsibility to evaluate the effectiveness of management's plan? What action does the auditor take if the auditor does not believe that management's plan will be effective?

b. Assume that the auditor modifies the opinion on the financial statements. What does this action say to the users of the financial statements about confidence in management's ability? Is the auditor engaged to attest to the quality of management?

c. What is the required disclosure regarding management's plans?

d. For each element in management's plan, indicate the auditor's responsibility to assess the element. Indicate audit procedures that should be performed to assess each part of management's plans.

15-46   **(Accounting Estimates, LO 4, 5)** An alfalfa co-op has an agreement with its farmers to purchase alfalfa at a price that is currently 5% above the existing market price. In addition, the co-op has agreed to pay the farmers interest at 2% for each month delivery is delayed beyond December 31, 2011. Management expects that at least 14,500 tons will be delivered sometime after the balance sheet date.

Required

a. What factors should be considered in making an estimate of the loss accrual?

b. Assuming the amount of the purchase commitment is material, what information should management disclose in the footnotes to the financial statements concerning this purchase commitment?

Professional Skepticism

Group Activity

15-47   **(Accounting Estimates, LO 5)** Consider the following areas in which estimates are made in the preparation of financial statements:

- Pension obligation
- Other postretirement benefits
- Warranty liability
- Reserve for uncollectible loans (financial institution)
- Allowance for doubtful accounts (manufacturing company)
- Allowance for returned goods (catalog company like Lands' End or L.L. Bean that have a guaranteed-period warranty on catalog sales)

Required

In a small group, discuss the following for each area:

1. Identify the factors inherent in the account that might significantly affect the dollar estimate of the account balance.

2. For each factor identified, briefly discuss the importance of the item to the overall account estimate. For example, how important is the interest rate assumption to the overall estimate of the pension liability? (*Hint:* You may want to perform a sensitivity analysis to assess the importance of each factor.)

3. For each factor identified, briefly describe audit evidence that should be gathered to determine how the factor should be used in making the accounting estimate. For example, how should the auditor determine the proper interest rate assumption in estimating the account balance?

4. Assuming there are differences between the auditor's estimate and management's estimate, indicate how can a professionally skeptical auditor can determine whether management is attempting to "manage" or "smooth earnings" or whether there is a genuine disagreement on the correct factor to be used in making the estimate.

15-48   **(Audit Communications, LO 4, 11, 13)** Several communications involve the client and auditor.

Required

For each of the following communications, indicate who signs the letter, who receives it, whether it is required or optional, when it should be sent, and its purpose:

a. Lawyer's response to a letter of audit inquiry

b. Management representation letter

c. Management letter

*15-49   **(Subsequent Events, LO 9)** Milton Green, CPA, is auditing the financial statements of Taylor Corporation for the year ended December 31, 2011. Green plans to sign the auditor's report on March 10, 2012. He is concerned about events and transactions occurring after December 31, 2011, that may affect the 2011 financial statements.

Required

a. What are the general types of subsequent events that require Green's consideration and evaluation?

b. What are the auditing procedures Green should consider performing to gather evidence concerning subsequent events?

15-50   **(Subsequent Events, LO 9)** The auditor is auditing financial statements for the year ended December 31, 2011, and is completing the audit in early March 2012. The following situations have come to the auditor's attention:

1. On February 12, 2012, the client agreed to an out-of-court settlement of a property damage suit resulting from an accident caused by one of its delivery trucks. The accident occurred on November 20, 2011. An estimated loss of $30,000 was accrued in the 2011 financial statements. The settlement was for $50,000.

2. Same facts as in part (1), except the accident occurred January 1, 2012, and no loss was accrued.

3. The client is a bank. A major commercial loan customer filed for bankruptcy on February 26, 2012. The bankruptcy was caused by an adverse court decision on February 15, 2012, involving a product liability lawsuit initiated in 2011 arising from products sold in 2009.

4. The client purchased raw materials that were received just before year end. The purchase was recorded based on its estimated value. The invoice was not received until January 31, 2012, and the cost was substantially different than was estimated.

5. On February 2, 2012, the board of directors took the following actions:

    (a) Approved officers' salaries for 2012.

    (b) Approved the sale of a significant bond issue.

    (c) Approved a new union contract containing increased wages and fringe benefits for most of the employees. The employees had been on strike since January 2, 2012.

6. A major customer was killed in a boating accident on January 25, 2012, in Mexico. The customer had pledged his boat as collateral. The boat, which was destroyed in the accident, was not insured. The allowance for doubtful accounts is not adequate to cover the anticipated loss.

Required

For each of the preceding independent subsequent events (which are to be considered material):

a. Indicate and explain whether the financial statements should be adjusted only, adjusted and disclosed, disclosed only, or neither adjusted nor disclosed.

b. Describe how the auditor would have learned about each of these situations.

15-51 **(Subsequent Discovery of Omitted Procedures, LO 9)** During the course of an interoffice quality review, it was discovered that the auditors had failed to consider whether inventory costs of a wholesale client exceeded their market value. The review took place six months after the audit report had been issued. Some prices had apparently been falling near year end. Inventory is a major item in the financial statements, but the auditors do not know whether the market price declines were material.

Required

a. What procedures could the auditors now perform to resolve this audit problem?

b. What should the auditors do if it turns out that inventory was materially overstated?

International

Group Activity

15-52 **(Engagement Quality Review, LO 1, 8)** Consistent quality in the performance of an audit is one of the major concerns of all public accounting firms. However, internal inspections by audit firms themselves, along with external inspections by peer review teams and the PCAOB, point out that although good audit policies and procedures are generally in place, they are sometimes not consistently performed. The result is that audit quality may sometimes be compromised, yet audit firm management is unaware of which particular audits are of inferior quality.

Required

a. How would an engagement quality review partner (concurring partner) help to assure the consistent execution of audit firm policies and procedures?

b. What audit documentation should engagement quality review partners retain to provide evidence that they have properly evaluated the consistent quality of the audit work performed?

c. What implications does the situation above have in terms of providing motivation for documenting the auditor reasoning process in the workpapers? For example, assume that an auditor concludes that all the assumptions regarding warranties are appropriate. What documentation would an engagement quality reviewing partner expect to see to support those conclusions?

d. Describe the different professional requirements for the conduct of engagement quality review, contrasting the standards governing public versus private entities using U.S. auditing standards, and those of entities reporting under international standards.

Cases

15-53   **(Going-Concern Problems and Client Continuance Decisions, LO 1, 3, 10, 14)** Access the following publicly available disclosures made by IRIDEX Corporation on the SEC's website (www.sec.gov):

- 8-K filed 8-29-2007
- 10-K filed 3-30-2007
- 10-K filed 4-10-2008
- Def 14A (proxy) filed 4-28-2008
- Def 14A (proxy) filed 5-4-2009

Required

a. Review the disclosures in the 10-K filed 3-30-2007. Imagine that you are on PwC's engagement team for the 12-31-2006 year-end audit of IRIDEX. Describe the key business that IRIDEX engages in and its three most important strategies for success. What risk characteristics of the company indicate that it may have difficulties remaining a going concern?

b. Review the disclosures in the 8-K filed 8-29-2007. What is the purpose of the 8-K filing? What does it reveal about PwC's ongoing relationship with IRIDEX? Based on the disclosures made in the filing, what risk factors were likely most relevant to PwC in making their client continuance decision about IRIDEX?

c. Review the disclosures in the 10-K filed 4-10-2008. Which audit firm accepted IRIDEX as a new client following PwC's resignation? In what important ways does that audit firm differ from PwC? Considering the concept of audit firm portfolio management, discuss why it is possible for one audit firm to resign from a client like IRIDEX, and another audit firm to accept it as a new client immediately thereafter.

d. Review the audit fee and total fee disclosures in the Def 14A proxy statements filed 4-28-2008 and 5-4-2009. Use that information to compare and contrast the audit fees and total fees that IRIDEX paid to its auditors for the fiscal years ending 12-31-2006, 2007, and 2008. What inferences do you draw from that comparison?

e. Describe the ethical decisions that an auditor must make during portfolio management decisions such as the client acceptance and client continuance decision. What is the relationship between ethics and high audit quality?

*15-54   **(Letter of Audit Inquiry, LO 4)** Cole & Cole, CPAs, are auditing the financial statements of Consolidated Industries Co. for the year ended December 31, 2011. On February 20, 2012, Cole asked the client to draft an inquiry letter to J. J. Young, Consolidated's outside attorney, to corroborate the information furnished to Cole by management concerning pending and threatened litigation, claims, and assessments and unasserted claims and assessments. On March 6, 2012, C. R. Brown, Consolidated's chief financial officer, gave Cole a draft of the inquiry letter for Cole's review before mailing it to Young.

Group Activity

Required

In a small group, work to describe the omissions, ambiguities, and inappropriate statements and terminology in Brown's letter.

J. J. Young, Attorney at Law
123 Main Street
Anytown, USA

March 6, 2012
Dear J. J. Young:

In connection with an audit of our financial statements at December 31, 2011, and for the year then ended, management of the Company has prepared, and furnished to our auditors, Cole & Cole, CPAs, 456 Broadway, Anytown, USA, a description and evaluation of certain contingencies, including those set forth below involving matters with respect to which you have been engaged and to which you have devoted substantive attention on behalf of the company in the form of legal consultation or representation. Your response should include matters that existed at December 31, 2011. Because of the confidentiality of all these matters, your response may be limited.

In November 2011, an action was brought against the company by an outside salesman alleging breach of contract for sales commissions and pleading a second cause of action for an accounting with respect to claims for fees and commissions. The causes of action claim damages of $300,000 but the company believes it has meritorious defenses to the claims. The possible exposure of the company to a successful judgment on behalf of the plaintiff is slight.

In July 2009, an action was brought against the company by Industrial Manufacturing Co. (Industrial) alleging patent infringement and seeking damages of $20,000,000. The action in U.S. District Court resulted in a decision on October 16, 2011, holding that the company infringed seven Industrial patents and awarded damages of $14,000,000. The company vigorously denies these allegations and has filed an appeal with the U.S. Court of Appeals for the Federal Circuit. The appeal process is expected to take approximately two years, but there is some chance that Industrial may ultimately prevail.

Please furnish to our auditors such explanation, if any, that you consider necessary to supplement the foregoing information, including an explanation of those matters as to which your views may differ from those stated and an identification of the omission of any pending or threatened litigation, claims, and assessments or a statement that the list of such matters is completed. Your response may be quoted or referred to in the financial statements without further correspondence with you.

You also consulted on various other matters considered pending or threatened litigation. However, you may not comment on these matters because publicizing them may alert potential plaintiffs to the strengths of their cases. In addition, various other matters probable of assertion that have some chance of an unfavorable outcome, as of December 31, 2011, are unasserted claims and assessments.

C. R. Brown
Chief Financial Officer

Fraud

Ethics

15-55   **(Related-Entity Transactions, Fraud, and Professional Conduct, LO 1, 14)** The facts of this case are drawn from the SEC's Accounting and Auditing Enforcement Release No. 2076 (August 5, 2004).

The Company Perpetrating the Fraud The case involves a fraud perpetrated by MCA Financial Corporation, which was incorporated in 1989 as a holding company for four wholly owned subsidiaries with 45 branch offices in seven states. MCA primarily was involved in the residential mortgage-banking business. MCA's fraudulent scheme was accomplished through related-party transactions and involved the following steps.

MCA purchased distressed rental properties in the city of Detroit, sold them to the Related Limited Partnerships at inflated prices, advanced the Related Limited Partnerships small down payments (usually 10% or 20%), and accepted executed mortgages or land contracts for the remainder of the purchase prices. MCA established the prices at which it sold the rental properties to the Related Limited Partnerships by calculating the value each property would have after substantial rehabilitation, even though rehabilitation work had not been completed or even begun. MCA then recognized the entire gain on each sale as revenue even though MCA knew that the Related Limited Partnerships could not afford to pay for the properties because of the inflated sales prices and the prevailing rental rates. In fact, the Related Limited Partnerships failed to make most of the required loan payments to MCA for the properties.

MCA recorded the money owing from the Related Limited Partnerships as a result of advancing the down payments on the asset side of its balance sheet under the heading of "Accounts Receivable-Related Parties." MCA carried those receivables without any valuation allowance despite the Related Limited Partnerships' inability to repay the receivables. MCA fraudulently sold some related-party mortgages and land contracts to the pools and carried the remainder at cost or with an inadequate allowance for loan losses under the headings of "Mortgages Held for Resale" or "Land Contracts Held for Resale" despite the Related Limited Partnerships' inability to repay and the inadequate collateral. The collateral for these mortgages and land contracts was the real estate that MCA had sold to the Related Limited Partnerships at inflated prices. As a result, MCA knew that foreclosing on the collateral would not result in MCA receiving the full principal amount of the loans. MCA did not disclose in its financial statements that a material amount of its mortgages and land contracts held for resale were related-party mortgages and land contracts.

The Auditors Grant Thornton LLP was one of two firms that jointly provided audit services to MCA and jointly signed reports containing unqualified opinions on MCA's annual financial statements from 1993 through 1998. Doeren Mayhew & Co. P.C., a Michigan accounting firm, was the other firm that jointly provided audit services to MCA and jointly signed reports containing unqualified opinions on MCA's annual financial statements from 1993 through 1998.

Peter Behrens is a CPA who served as an engagement partner for Grant Thornton's joint audits of MCA. Marvin Morris is a CPA who served as an engagement partner for Doeren Mayhew's joint audits of MCA. Benedict Rybicki is a CPA who served as the engagement manager for Doeren Mayhew's joint audits of MCA. Morris obtained personal mortgages through MCA in July 1994 for approximately $344,000 and in July 1995 for approximately $200,000. The 1994 mortgage was discharged when the 1995 mortgage was executed. Morris did not review the auditors' workpapers for several key portions of the 1998 MCA audit, including the workpapers for mortgages and land contracts held for resale and gains on sale of real estate. As late as 2001, Morris stated that he had only ever read the first 13 of the approximately 150 Statements of Financial Accounting Standards. Reading the Statements of Financial Accounting Standards was not "what [Morris did] for a living." Rather, he considered himself a "salesperson."

As the engagement manager, Rybicki signed a workpaper in connection with the 1998 MCA audit (a) confirming that the entire MCA engagement had been performed in accordance with professional standards; (b) confirming that related parties or unusual transactions and relationships were properly disclosed and documented in MCA's financial statements; and (c) agreeing with the issuance of the report containing an unqualified opinion. Rybicki socialized with Alexander Ajemian, MCA's controller, while Doeren Mayhew acted as one of MCA's auditors. Rybicki first met Ajemian in approximately 1987 when both were staff accountants at the Detroit office of Pannell Kerr & Forster. Rybicki and Ajemian both played on Pannell Kerr's softball team. They continued playing on the same team even after each had left Pannell Kerr, including while Ajemian was MCA's controller and Rybicki was the engagement manager for the MCA audits. Rybicki, Ajemian, and the remainder of the softball team often ate and drank together after the games.

Between 1993 and 1998, Rybicki and Ajemian occasionally spent weekends in Petosky, Michigan, where they stayed at a lakefront condominium owned by MCA. During the same time period, Rybicki and Ajemian spoke socially on the telephone, ate together, water-skied, and traveled to the Kentucky Derby. After MCA filed for bankruptcy in 1999 and Ajemian pled guilty in 2001 to federal criminal charges in connection with his conduct at MCA, Rybicki and Ajemian continued socializing. They dined together, attended sporting events, played on the same softball team, and traveled together.

While acting as MCA's auditors, Doeren Mayhew and Grant Thornton personnel, including Behrens, Morris, and Rybicki, sometimes attended a party, known as the "Bean Counters Bash," held by Ajemian annually at his home and paid for by MCA. This party was held to celebrate the completion of the annual audit. MCA executives provided Doeren Mayhew and Grant Thornton auditors with free tickets to Detroit Red Wings hockey games and University of Michigan football games. MCA executives also invited the auditors to tailgate parties paid for by MCA at the football games. Rybicki obtained a personal mortgage through MCA for approximately $59,000 to purchase his house in the early 1990s.

During the 1998 MCA audit, Behrens, Morris, and Rybicki knew that millions of dollars of the mortgages and land contracts held for resale reported in MCA's 1998 annual financial statements consisted of related-party mortgages and land contracts. Behrens, Morris, and Rybicki obtained this knowledge through their preparation of the 1998 MCA audit plan, their review of the 1998 audit workpapers and other materials, their performance of audit procedures during the 1998 audit, their communications with MCA executives, and/or their knowledge of MCA's business from prior audits.

Specifically with respect to the workpapers, Behrens and Rybicki reviewed them as part of the 1998 MCA audit, which showed that MCA sold approximately $10.8 million in real estate to the Related Limited Partnerships in fiscal year 1998. Those workpapers also showed that MCA advanced the Related Limited Partnerships a small down payment for the real estate and accepted an executed mortgage or land contract for the remaining portion of the purchase price. Those workpapers further calculated that approximately $4.9 million of those related-party mortgages and land contracts had not been sold as of MCA's balance sheet date and thus were included in the total mortgages or land contracts held for resale as reported in MCA's 1998 annual financial statements. Rybicki prepared, and Behrens and Morris reviewed, a workpaper in connection with the 1998 MCA audit entitled "Audit Planning." In this workpaper, Rybicki assessed the audit risk on the MCA engagement as "high." Later in the workpaper, Rybicki noted that the reasons for the high-risk assessment were that MCA had "significant and/or frequent difficult-to-audit transactions or balances" and "material, related-party transactions on a recurring basis." Behrens and Rybicki also reviewed workpapers as part of the 1998 MCA audit that contained balance sheets for the Related Limited Partnerships reflecting approximately $57.3 million in liabilities under the heading of "Mortgages and Land Contracts Payable." Behrens and Rybicki additionally reviewed workpapers as part of the 1998 MCA audit that showed approximately $4.0 million of MCA's land contracts held for resale, those that had been pledged as collateral for one of MCA's debenture offerings, were related-party land contracts.

During the 1998 MCA audit, Behrens, Morris, and Rybicki read MCA's 1998 annual financial statements. Those financial statements did not disclose any related-party mortgages or land contracts held for resale or state the total amount of such mortgages and land contracts held for resale. Grant Thornton and Doeren Mayhew issued a report, dated April 28, 1998, containing an unqualified opinion on MCA's 1998 annual financial statements even though Behrens, Morris, and Rybicki knew that MCA had failed to disclose material, related-party mortgages, and land contracts.

Required

a. Summarize the nature of the fraud perpetrated by MCA involving related-entity transactions.

b. Summarize the nature of the inappropriate relationships between MCA and its auditors.

c. Discuss how the concepts of auditor independence and ethics are related, with an emphasis on the facts in this case. Discuss the issue of what personal relationships are or are not acceptable between an audit firm and the client.

d. Recommend changes that these audit firms should make to improve their quality-control procedures.

15-56 **(Ethical Decisions Regarding Summarizing Possible Adjust-ments, LO 2, 14)** One of the fundamental changes brought about by the Sarbanes-Oxley Act of 2002 is that the audit profession is no longer self-regulated for audits of public companies. Now, the Public Company Accounting Oversight Board (PCAOB) has the authority to assess whether audit firms are conducting quality audits. To make that assessment, the PCAOB conducts formal inspections of audits completed by audit firms registered with the PCAOB, and the result of those inspections is made public on the PCAOB's website (www.pcaob.org;

Ethics

follow the links to inspection reports). The inspection teams select certain higher-risk areas for review and inspect the engagement team's workpapers and interview engagement personnel regarding those areas. In addition, the inspection teams analyze potential adjustments to the issuer's financial statements that had been identified during the audit but not recorded in the financial statements.

The reports that have been released to the public contain a variety of examples of audit engagements in which auditors have had difficulty dealing with potential adjustments to client financial statements. One example of such an audit quality problem is evident in the inspection report of Ernst & Young LLP (November 17, 2005), which states:

> The Firm proposed a judgmental audit adjustment (which the issuer recorded) to increase the issuer's reserve for excess and obsolete inventory, even though the Firm's work papers did not include documentation supporting percentages used to estimate this reserve. After the Firm proposed this audit adjustment, the issuer's chief executive officer proposed an adjustment to increase the value of inventory received in a bankruptcy settlement, which was contrary to the issuer's earlier conclusion that the bankruptcy settlement accounting would result in no gain or loss. This adjustment was equal to and offset the excess and obsolete inventory adjustment described above. The Firm failed to assess, or failed to include evidence in the work papers that it assessed, whether the offsetting adjustments described above and another set of offsetting year-end adjustments relating to the accounting for major construction contracts (which in total approximated 24% of the issuer's pre-tax income) indicated a bias in management's estimates that could result in material misstatement of the financial statements, and/or a need for the Firm to reevaluate planned audit procedures.

Required

a. Comment on the PCAOB's inspection process, focusing on (1) why it may be needed to assure audit quality and (2) how it may improve audit quality.

b. Review the issue outlined in the preceding inspection report. Summarize the actions of the client and the corresponding actions of Ernst & Young. Discuss the income statement implications of the journal entries that are at the center of this inspection comment.

c. What were the major concerns of the PCAOB about this issue?

d. Assume that you were the audit manager on the Ernst & Young audit engagement detailed in the inspection report. Assume also that you knew the audit partner had agreed to allow the client to pursue the offsetting series of journal entries that are the subject of this case. Using the ethical decision-making framework from Chapter 3, develop an appropriate course of action to pursue.

15-57   **(Dell, Management Disclosures, and SEC Allegations of Fraud (LO 6, 8)** The text talks about the case of Dell receiving payments from Intel in return for a pledge by Dell that they would not use computer chips from a major Intel competitor (AMD). The payments were large, covering between 10% and 76% of operating income over the 2002–2006 period. The SEC complaint is that the amounts should have been separately disclosed and treated as a reduction of cost of goods sold because the payments could end at any time—and did end when Dell started to use AMD as a supplier. Outside of the financial statements, in management's discussion and analysis, Dell management attributed the decline in earnings to slowing demand and pricing pressures. The SEC case raises important issues that should cause you to think about the scope of the audit. In a small group, discuss the following questions:

Fraud

Professional
Skepticism

Group Activity

Required

a. Why was Dell's recording and disclosure of the payments from Intel materially false and misleading?

b. What changes in the economic environment, or in the management culture of Dell, might have led PwC to become more skeptical of the company and therefore to expand audit procedures?

c. Should using audit software to identify significant cash receipts from vendors be a normal part of every audit engagement? Explain your rationale and consider such things as audit cost and expectations of the audit.

d. Assume that instead of negotiating payments from Intel that Dell would have negotiated a long-term supply contract with Intel that resulted in lower prices for Intel chips as long as Dell agreed not to use a competitor's chips in its products. Should the amount of the price reduction be disclosed as a separate item in the financial statements under GAAP? Why or why not?

e. Assume the company negotiated lower prices with Intel as described in part D. How would the auditor become aware of the lower prices? Consider that, especially in these tougher economic times, almost all companies are negotiating lower prices from their suppliers.

f. Assume the role of the concurring partner. What kinds of review and analysis might have alerted you to the size and nature of the Intel payments?

g. Considering this case and the many ways in which the payments (or price reductions) from Intel could have occurred, how would you decide that the judgments and decisions made by management moves from "aggressive accounting" to "fraud"?

Academic Research Case (LO 8)

Academic research addresses the conceptual issues outlined in this chapter. To help you consider the linkage between academic research and the practice of auditing, read the following research article and answer the questions below.

Epps, K. K. & Messier Jr., W. F. (2007). Engagement Quality Reviews: A Comparison of Audit Firm Practices. *Auditing: A Journal of Practice & Theory 26(2):167–181.*

  i. What is the issue being addressed in the paper?
 ii. Why is this issue important to practicing auditors?
iii. What are the findings of the paper?
 iv. What are the implications of these findings for audit quality (or audit practice) on the audit profession?
  v. Describe the research methodology used as a basis for the conclusions.
 vi. Describe any limitations of the research that the student (and practice) should be aware of.

Go to www.cengage.com/accounting/rittenberg for the Ford and Toyota materials.

Source and Reference	Question
Ford 10-K or Annual Report and Toyota Annual Report	**1.** Calculate the Altman Z-score for Ford and Toyota. What inferences do you draw from these values? What inferences do you draw from comparing the values across the two companies? (You may assume that the market value of equity for Ford and Toyota, respectively as of their 2009 fiscal year ends, is $38 billion and $110 billion.)
	2. What do you predict would happen if Ford's auditors issued a going-concern audit opinion? How would suppliers react? How would debt holders react?
	3. Why might an audit firm be hesitant to issue a going-concern opinion?
	4. What would happen to an audit firm if they do NOT issue a going-concern opinion, and the company goes bankrupt in the following year?

Module XIV: Working Trial Balance

Upon completion of substantive audit testing, the auditor should post all audit adjustments and reclassification entries to the working trial balance and extend the audited balances. The extended balances then form the nucleus for the audited financial statements.

Selected analytical procedures also should be applied at the conclusion of the audit. The results may be compared with those developed during the audit-planning phase. This approach provides added support for audit conclusions contained in the documentation.

Derick has asked you to post the adjustments and reclassifications and to perform the review-phase analytical procedures.

Requirements

1. The instructor's CD contains a file labeled "AJE" (adjusting journal entries). It contains all of the audit adjustments and reclassifications that you developed in prior modules of this practice case. At this time, your instructor will supply you with a printout of this file. Review the adjustments, which will be presented to the client as proposed audit adjustments. Derick has set the following materiality thresholds:

Income statement	$ 435,000
Balance sheet	$1,542,270

   Given these thresholds and referring to the proposed audit adjustments and reclassifications, determine whether the potential adjustments equal or exceed the income statement or balance sheet materiality threshold in the aggregate. Treat income overstatements and income understatements separately. Do not net understatements against overstatements. That is, if aggregate overstatements are $600,000 and aggregate understatements are $500,000, the adjustments should be proposed to Biltrite management, inasmuch as both exceed the income statement materiality threshold.

2. Retrieve the file labeled "WTB." Post the adjustments and reclassifications to the working trial balance. Observe the following rules in making your postings:

   a. Post account increases as positive amounts, and post account decreases as negative amounts;

   b. Postings are in "thousands of dollars," whereas the adjustments and reclassifications are rounded to the nearest dollar. Therefore, in posting the adjustments and reclassifications, round to the nearest $1,000.

   c. Enter AJE numbers as text by typing a single quote before the number "1" so that they do not get included in the final balance.

   d. Do *not* foot the adjustments and reclassifications columns (they will automatically be reflected in the audited column as you post them).

3. Save your file under the title "WTB," then print it.

4. Retrieve the file labeled "AUDBS." Using your printout of the working trial balance, enter the amounts from the audited column in the 2009 balance sheet. Calculate the percentages of individual balance sheet items and components relative to totals for 2009.

5. Calculate the new ratios for 2009 based on the audited financial statements. What is the purpose of applying analytical procedures in the evaluation and review phase of the audit? Is it important to develop expectations as part of performing these final analytical procedures?

6. Print the comparative audited balance sheets together with the related ratios. Compare them with the balance sheets and ratios that you developed and printed in requirement (5b) of Module I. What conclusions can you draw regarding the comparison?

7. Retrieve the file labeled "Budget," which you reviewed as part of your assignment in Module I. You will recall that the purpose for this review was to identify significant budget variances that could be the result of under- or overbudgeting, misstatements in recording data, or intentional misstatement. The auditor, of course, is concerned with the latter two possibilities.

   a. Substitute the audited amounts from your adjusted working trial balance for the unaudited figures in the "Actual 12/31/09" column. Save your file, as revised, under a new file name (e.g., "Biltbudg"), so as not to lose the original Module I file. Print the revised budget/actual comparison.

   b. Do significant variances still exist? If so, are you satisfied that the audit has resolved the causes of the significant variances? (Compare the variances resulting from this analysis with those calculated in Module I.)

   c. If you continue to have concerns about certain variances, what additional evidence-gathering and evaluation procedures do you suggest?

16

Auditors' Reports

LEARNING OBJECTIVES

The overriding objective of this textbook is to build a foundation with which to analyze current professional issues and adapt audit approaches to business and economic complexities. Through studying this chapter, you will be able to:

1 Describe the levels of assurance that an auditor may provide when associated with various auditor services and auditor reports.

2 Describe the information that is included in an audit report, including an audit report for an integrated audit, and articulate differences between U.S. and international standard unqualified audit reports.

3 Identify the types of audit opinions and the circumstances in which each type is appropriate.

4 Explain the differences among audit, review, and compilation engagements in terms of procedures performed, degree of responsibility taken by the accountant, and reports rendered.

5 Explain the procedures and reporting requirements for interim financial information.

6 Discuss the nature of "special reports," when they might be used, and their unique reporting requirements.

7 Describe various attestation engagements and the types of reports that will be issued for these engagements.

8 Apply the decision analysis and ethical decision-making frameworks to various reporting situations.

CHAPTER OVERVIEW

When an auditing firm is associated with financial statements, it must provide a report on those statements. This requirement is designed to prevent any misinterpretation of the nature of the service that was provided or the degree of responsibility the firm assumes. An auditing firm is associated with financial statements whenever it consents to the use of its name in a report, document, or written communication containing the statements, with the exception of tax returns. The requirement also clearly conveys an obligation to report the auditor's findings: An auditor cannot withdraw simply because the auditor's opinion is not what the client wanted. The professional auditing standards provide the rules that the auditors should follow when making reporting decisions, and there exist differences in audit reports internationally. In terms of the audit opinion formulation process, this chapter considers the last phase of the audit process.

In this chapter, we expand on these auditing reporting standards and cover the more common reporting situations. We also discuss various other services that audit firms may provide to their clients and the auditors' reports that are associated with those services.

The Audit Opinion Formulation Process

I. Assessing Client Acceptance and Retention Decisions *CHAPTER 4*	II. Understanding the Client *CHAPTERS 2, 4–6, and 9*	III. Obtaining Evidence about Controls and Determining the Impact on the Financial Statement Audit *CHAPTERS 5–14 and 18*	IV. Obtaining Substantive Evidence about Account Assertions *CHAPTERS 7–14 and 18*	V. Wrapping Up the Audit and Making Reporting Decisions *CHAPTERS 15 and 16*

The Auditing Profession, Regulation, and Corporate Governance *CHAPTERS 1 and 2*	Decision-Making, Professional Conduct, and Ethics *CHAPTER 3*	Professional Liability *CHAPTER 17*

PROFESSIONAL JUDGMENT IN CONTEXT

What Information Do Investors Want to Be Included in an Audit Report?

A report issued in 2010 by the CFA Institute indicated that investment professionals find the audit report to be important in their analysis and use of financial reports in the investment decision-making process. The standard audit report currently contains boilerplate type language related to:

- What was audited and the relative responsibilities of the client and the auditor for the financial statements (introductory paragraph)
- The nature of the audit process (scope paragraph)
- The auditor's opinion on the fairness of the financial statements (opinion paragraph)

While the survey respondents indicated that this information was useful, they also indicated additional information they would like to see in the audit report. One respondent indicated that

> "Because the auditor's report has become rather "boiler-plate" it is not very useful to investors. That being said, the "auditor's report" should be extremely valuable. The auditors possess much information which could be useful to investors."

Specifically, respondents indicate that they would like the report to include more information about:

- Method by which the auditor determines/assesses materiality
- Audit process
- Audited entity
- Circumstances or relationships that might bear on auditor's independence
- Level of assurance actually achieved in the audit

Some specific comments included in the CFA Institute report about additional information that would be useful include:

> "A good example of useful information is the letter that auditors provide to a board of directors where audit findings are discussed."

> "An assessment of issues unique to the audit would be more useful along with comments about accounting judgments and control issues."

> "... audit partner signature"

> "What are the critical matters of judgment where auditors differ from management?"

> "Any areas of weakness found in the audit, and any disagreements with management that were material but did not rise to the level of impacting the clean vs. not clean decision currently disclosed."

> "Experience of lead auditor/manager. Time spent on audit by auditors. Consecutive years of engagement with the company."

> "It would be helpful to understand the types of procedures performed around high risk areas. For example, on companies with significant investment balances, how were valuations tested? 100% confirmation with counterparties? Were independent prices obtained or calculated?"

> "Rather than boiler plate language that remains unchanged from year to year, the level of audit effort required for specific areas of the financial statements needs to be explicitly clarified so that the public can understand where the relative reporting complexity actually comes from."

> "In case of multinationals or holding companies with subsidiaries in different jurisdictions, it may well be the case that more than one company is involved in the audit. I would like to see specific disclosure as to which subsidiaries have been audited by which audit firm."

> "Materiality levels that the auditor uses to drive audit processes need to be quantified."

(continues)

These comments clearly demonstrate that some users believe that additional information in the audit report could be very useful. However, the question arises as to how much information is too much information. As you read through the chapter consider the following questions:

- What information is currently included in the standard audit report?

- How does the standard audit report issued in the United States differ from the standard report issued in other parts of the world?
- What circumstances require a deviation from the standard audit report?
- What types of additional should be included in the audit report?
- How would additional information affect the investor, the audited company, and the audit firm?

Levels of Assurance Provided by Auditors

LO 1

Describe the levels of assurance that an auditor may provide when associated with various auditor services and auditor reports.

Certified Public Accountants have traditionally reported on historical financial statements. These financial statement assurances have ranged from audits to reviews to compilations. Reporting standards based on audits require positive assurance—that is, an explicit statement as to whether the financial statements are presented fairly. Auditors also provide positive assurance when performing other services, such as providing an opinion on prospective financial information or on pro forma financial information. Positive assurance requires auditors to gather sufficient evidence to render an opinion.

For some services, the auditor can provide limited (negative) assurance—that is, a statement that nothing has come to the auditor's attention to indicate that the information is incorrect. Auditors provide negative assurance when performing services such as reviews of annual or interim financial information. Finally, in some situations, the auditor will provide a disclaimer of assurance—that is, a statement providing no assurance, such as when compiling financial information. Even though "no assurance" reports disclaim any assurance, the market sees some value because the CPA looks at the information to see if there are any obvious violations of GAAP. Services for which the auditor is not providing positive assurance, such as when performing reviews and compilations, are not considered audit services, but are considered accounting services.

PRACTICAL POINT

Positive assurance does not necessarily mean that the financial statements are fairly presented. Rather, it refers to whether or not the auditor has gathered sufficient evidence to render an opinion on whether the financial statements are fairly presented.

Audit Reports on Financial Statements and Internal Control over Financial Reporting

LO 2

Describe the information that is included in an audit report, including an audit report for an integrated audit, and articulate differences between U.S. and international standard unqualified audit reports.

In this section, we describe the information that is included in reports that are issued when an auditor performs a financial statement audit. The audit of the financial statements is designed to facilitate an unambiguous opinion by the auditor. With respect to the financial statements, the expectation of both the auditor and the client is that the report will be unqualified; that is, the auditor has no reservations about the fairness of presentation. However, the auditor may have reasons for reservations about the fairness of presentation, or the auditor may have been precluded from gathering sufficient information to render an opinion.

When an integrated audit is performed, the auditor provides an opinion on both the financial statements and on internal control over financial reporting. With respect to internal control, the auditor is expected to provide an unambiguous opinion as to whether those controls are effective as of the client's year end.

Audit reports are designed to promote clear communication between the auditor and the financial statement reader by delineating:

- What was audited and the relative responsibilities of the client and the auditor for the financial statements (introductory paragraph)
- The nature of the audit process (scope paragraph)
- The auditor's opinion on the fairness of the financial statements (opinion paragraph)
- When appropriate, the reason why a standard unqualified opinion cannot be expressed (explanatory paragraph)

Unqualified Audit Reports for U.S.-Domiciled and Foreign-Domiciled Public Companies

For large public companies domiciled in the United States, the auditor's report will also refer to the audit of internal control over financial reporting. The auditor may issue a separate report on internal controls or may issue a combined report on both the financial statements and internal controls. If a separate report is issued, the report on the financial statements will include a paragraph after the scope paragraph (before the opinion paragraph) indicating that an audit of internal controls was performed and providing an opinion. If a combined report on both the financial statements and internal control is issued, it will include two additional paragraphs:

- Definition paragraph (after the scope paragraph) that defines what is meant by internal control over financial reporting
- Inherent limitations paragraph (following the definition paragraph) that discusses why internal control may not prevent or detect misstatements

Exhibit 16.1 Panel A is an example of an unqualified audit opinion on financial statements when the auditor issues a separate report on the effectiveness of internal control. The fifth paragraph in Exhibit 16.1 Panel A summarizes and refers to a separate report on the client's internal controls, which in this case expresses an unqualified opinion on the client's internal control over financial reporting.

Exhibit 16.1 Panel B (audit report for Diageo plc) provides an interesting international contrast to the unqualified audit report shown in Panel A (audit report for Coca-Cola Company). The international audit report for Diageo differs from the U.S. audit report for Coca-Cola in the following ways:

- The auditors in Diageo's report state that they "do not accept or assume responsibility to anyone other than the company and the company's members, as a body, for our audit work," whereas the auditors in Coca-Cola's report state that their "responsibility is to express an opinion on these financial statements based on our audits." Thus, the international report states what the auditors are *not* accepting responsibility for, whereas the U.S. report states what the auditors *are* accepting responsibility for.
- The Diageo report references IFRS as the reporting framework and the IASB as the relevant audit standard setter, whereas the Coca-Cola report references U.S. GAAP as the financial accounting reporting framework, COSO as the internal control reporting framework, and the PCAOB as the relevant audit standard setter.
- The Diageo report directs readers to a website that describes the responsibilities of the auditors, whereas the Coca-Cola report specifically describes each of the various responsibilities that the auditors are assuming.

PRACTICAL POINT

IFRS is generally thought to be a less prescriptive set of accounting standards than U.S. GAAP. Accordingly, IFRS permits company management more judgment than GAAP in applying a particular standard. Auditors need to plan and perform their audit with this in mind.

Exhibit 16.1A — Panel A Unqualified Report on an Integrated Audit for a U.S.-Domiciled Public Company

THE COCA-COLA COMPANY

We have audited the accompanying consolidated balance sheets of The Coca-Cola Company and subsidiaries as of December 31, 2009 and 2008, and the related consolidated statements of income, shareowners' equity, and cash flows for each of the three years in the period ended December 31, 2009. These financial statements are the responsibility of the Company's management. Our responsibility is to express an opinion on these financial statements based on our audits.

We conducted our audits in accordance with the standards of the Public Company Accounting Oversight Board (United States). Those standards require that we plan and perform the audit to obtain reasonable assurance about whether the financial statements are free of material misstatement. An audit includes examining, on a test basis, evidence supporting the amounts and disclosures in the financial statements. An audit also includes assessing the accounting principles used and significant estimates made by management, as well as evaluating the overall financial statement presentation. We believe that our audits provide a reasonable basis for our opinion.

In our opinion, the financial statements referred to above present fairly, in all material respects, the consolidated financial position of The Coca-Cola Company and subsidiaries at December 31, 2009 and 2008, and the consolidated results of their operations and their cash flows for each of the three years in the period ended December 31, 2009, in conformity with U.S. generally accepted accounting principles.

As discussed in Note 1 to the consolidated financial statements, in 2007 the Company changed its method of accounting for uncertainty in income taxes.

We also have audited, in accordance with the standards of the Public Company Accounting Oversight Board (United States), The Coca-Cola Company and subsidiaries' internal control over financial reporting as of December 31, 2009, based on criteria established in *Internal Control—Integrated Framework* issued by the Committee of Sponsoring Organizations of the Treadway Commission and our report dated February 26, 2010 expressed an unqualified opinion thereon.

Ernst & Young LLP
Atlanta, Georgia

Exhibit 16.1B — Panel B Unqualified Report on an Audit for a Foreign-Domiciled Public Company

Independent Auditor's Report to the Members of Diageo plc

We have audited the consolidated financial statements of Diageo plc for the year ended 30 June 2010 which comprise the consolidated income statement, the consolidated statement of comprehensive income, the consolidated balance sheet, the consolidated statement of changes in equity, the consolidated statement of cash flows and the related notes. The financial reporting framework that has been applied in their preparation is applicable law and International Financial Reporting Standards (IFRS) as adopted by the EU.

This report is made solely to the company's members, as a body, in accordance with Chapter 3 of Part 16 of the Companies Act 2006 and in respect of the separate opinion in relation to IFRS as issued by the International Accounting Standards Board (IASB), on terms that have been agreed with the company. Our audit work has been undertaken so that we might state to the company's members those matters we are required to state to them in an auditor's report and for no other purpose. To the fullest extent permitted by law, we do not accept or assume responsibility to anyone other than the company and the company's members, as a body, for our audit work, for this report, or for the opinions we have formed.

Respective responsibilities of directors and auditor

As explained more fully in the directors' responsibilities statement set out in the corporate governance report, the directors are responsible for the preparation of the consolidated financial statements and for being satisfied that they give a true and fair view. Our responsibility is to audit the consolidated financial statements in accordance with applicable law and International Standards on Auditing (UK and Ireland). Those standards require us to comply with the Auditing Practices Board's (APB's) Ethical Standards for Auditors.

Scope of the audit of the financial statements

A description of the scope of an audit of financial statements is provided on the APB's website at www.frc.org.uk/apb/scope/UKP.

(continues)

Exhibit 16.1B — **Panel B Unqualified Report on an Audit for a Foreign-Domiciled Public Company (*continued*)**

Opinion on financial statements

In our opinion the consolidated financial statements:

- give a true and fair view of the state of the group's affairs as at 30 June 2010 and of its profit for the year then ended;
- have been properly prepared in accordance with IFRS as adopted by the EU; and
- have been prepared in accordance with the requirements of the Companies Act 2006 and Article 4 of the IAS Regulation.

Separate opinion in relation to IFRS as issued by the IASB

As explained in the accounting policies set out in the consolidated financial statements, the group, in addition to complying with its legal obligation to apply IFRS as adopted by the EU, has also applied IFRS as issued by the IASB. In our opinion, the consolidated financial statements comply with IFRS as issued by the IASB.

Opinion on other matter prescribed by the Companies Act 2006

In our opinion the information given in the directors' report for the financial year for which the consolidated financial statements are prepared is consistent with the consolidated financial statements.

Matters on which we are required to report by exception

We have nothing to report in respect of the following:

Under the Companies Act 2006 we are required to report to you if, in our opinion:

- certain disclosures of directors' remuneration specified by law are not made; or
- we have not received all the information and explanations we require for our audit.

Under the Listing Rules we are required to review:

- the directors' statement, set out in the corporate governance report, in relation to going concern; and
- the part of the corporate governance report relating to the company's compliance with the nine provisions of the June 2008 Combined Code specified for our review.

Other matter

We have reported separately on the parent company financial statements of Diageo plc for the year ended 30 June 2010 and on the information in the directors' remuneration report that is described as having been audited.

Ian Starkey (Senior Statutory Auditor)
for and on behalf of KPMG Audit Plc, Statutory Auditor Chartered Accountants
KPMG Audit Plc
15 Canada Square
London
E14 5GL

- The wording of the audit opinion in the Diageo report states that the financial statements "give a true and fair view of the state of the group's affairs" and does not mention the term *materiality*, whereas the Coca-Cola report states that the financial statements "present fairly, in all material respects, the consolidated financial position." Thus, the U.S. report integrates the concept of materiality while the international report does not.
- The Diageo report does not include a report on internal controls, whereas the Coca-Cola report does include a report on internal controls.
- The Diageo report contains a paragraph titled "matters on which we are required to report by exception" in which the auditors could describe problems with disclosures or corporate governance, whereas the Coca-Cola report contains no such paragraph.
- The Diageo report is signed by the specific engagement partner of KPMG (Ian Starkey), whereas the Coca-Cola report does not contain the name of the engagement partner of Ernst & Young that is responsible for the audit.

Reporting Outcomes in an Integrated Audit

Recall that in an integrated audit, the auditor expresses opinions on the financial statements and on internal control and must publicly report its assessment of the client's internal control over financial reporting. The auditor could conclude

AUDITING *in Practice*

REPORTING ON FINANCIAL STATEMENTS USING INTERNATIONAL FINANCIAL REPORTING STANDARDS (IFRS)

The SEC's rules allow for some companies known as foreign private issuers to file their financial statements with the SEC using IFRS as issued by the International Accounting Standards Board (the IASB). Further, these companies do not need to reconcile their IFRS financial statement with U.S. GAAP financial statements. However, their auditors must opine on whether the financial statements are in accordance with IFRS as issued by the IASB. In future years, U.S. public companies may also be able to, or be required to, prepare their financial statements using IFRS rather than U.S. GAAP.

As IFRS becomes more prevalent, auditors need to understand these new accounting standards as they will be the criteria on which auditors will assess whether financial statements are fairly presented. The Big 4 audit firms already have experience with conducting audits of financial information prepared in accordance with IFRS as they have issued audit opinions in many other countries that require IFRS reporting. The audit process used by auditors reporting on IFRS-based financial statements will generally be similar to the process described in this text. However, the auditor may be following auditing standards other than those issued by the PCAOB. Following is an excerpt of an audit opinion issued by PricewaterhouseCoopers that highlights an audit where the financial reporting criteria used was IFRS and the generally accepted auditing standards included international, Swiss, and U.S. standards. Therefore, the

scope paragraph refers to multiple auditing standards and the opinion paragraph refers to the fact that the reporting criteria is IFRS.

We conducted our audits in accordance with Swiss Auditing Standards, International Stan-dards on Auditing and the standards of the Public Company Accounting Oversight Board of the United States of America. Those standards require that we plan and perform the audit to obtain reasonable assurance about whether the consolidated financial statements are free of material misstatement. An audit of consolidated financial statements includes examining, on a test basis, evidence supporting the amounts and disclosures in the consolidated financial statements, assessing the accounting principles used and significant estimates made by management, and evaluating the overall consolidated financial statement presentation. We believe that our audits provide a reasonable basis for our opinion.

In our opinion, the consolidated financial statements present fairly, in all material respects, the financial position of the Novartis Group at December 31, 2007 and 2006, and the results of its operations and its cash flows for each of the three years in the period ended December 31, 2007 in accordance with International Financial Reporting Standards as issued by the International Accounting Standards Board.

that there are no material weaknesses, that is, that internal controls are effective. In that case, the auditor would issue an unqualified opinion on internal controls. If the auditor concludes that there are material weaknesses, the auditor would issue an adverse opinion on internal controls.

The existence of a material weakness in internal control does not automatically lead to a material misstatement in the financial statements. It does lead to doing more audit work to assure the fairness of the statements. Therefore, an unqualified opinion on the financial statements may be issued even if there are material weaknesses in the internal controls. For example, the following material weakness was found in the internal controls of Natures Sunshine Products, Inc. as of December 31, 2009:

Accounting for Taxes—The Company's processes, procedures and controls related to the preparation and review of the annual tax provision and the accrual of other non-income tax contingencies were not effective to ensure that amounts related to the tax provision, related current or deferred income tax asset and liability accounts, and non-income tax contingencies were accurate, recorded in the proper period, and determined in accordance with generally accepted accounting principles. Specifically, the Company did not (i) analyze and reconcile certain deferred income and tax payable accounts, (ii) appropriately consider the need to record or disclose contingencies for certain income tax and non income tax positions in accordance with generally

AUDITING *in Practice*

SEC REQUIREMENTS FOR TIMELINESS OF REPORTING

The timeliness of the audit report matters. The SEC wants registrants—and their auditors—to provide timely financial information to investors while at the same time allowing for sufficient time to gather sufficient audit evidence. The

SEC also recognizes that smaller companies may not have the same resources to report on a timely fashion compared to larger companies. Thus, the requirements vary by the size of the filer as shown in the table below:

Size of Filer	Form 10-K (Annual Report)	Form 10-Q (Quarterly Report)
Large Accelerated Filer (Market capitalization greater than $700 million)	60 days after year-end	40 days after end of quarter
Accelerated Filer (Market capitalization greater than $75 million, but less than $700 million)	75 days after year-end	40 days after end of quarter
Nonaccelerated Filer (Market capitalization less than $75 million)	90 days after year-end	45 days after end of quarter

accepted accounting principles, and (iii) file tax returns in certain foreign jurisdictions. Additionally, the Company had insufficient qualifications and training in accounting for taxes.

Deloitte & Touche was able to express an unqualified opinion on the financial statements but expressed the following opinion on internal controls:

> In our opinion, because of the effect of the material weakness identified above on the achievement of the objectives of the control criteria, the Company has not maintained effective internal control over financial reporting as of December 31, 2009, based on the criteria established in Internal Control—Integrated Framework issued by the Committee of Sponsoring Organizations of the Treadway Commission.
>
> Further, Deloitte & Touche's report noted that this material weakness was considered in determining the nature, timing, and extent of audit tests applied in the audit of the financial statements for the year ended December 31, 2009.

PRACTICAL POINT

The profession has developed standardized audit reports to help assure consistent communication to users.

Types of Audit Opinions on Financial Statements

The AICPA's first and seventh principles governing an audit conducted in accordance with generally accepted auditing standards relate to the concepts in this chapter.

Principle 1. The purpose of an audit is to enhance the degree of confidence that users can place in the financial statement. This purpose is achieved when an auditor expresses an opinion on the financial statements.

Principle 7. The auditor expresses an opinion in accordance with the auditor's findings or states that an opinion can not be expressed. The opinion states whether the financial statements are free of material misstatement.

In essence, these principles require auditors to express either an unqualified opinion on the entire set of financial statements and related footnotes, including all years presented for comparative purposes, or to state the reasons that such an opinion cannot be expressed. If the auditor has reservations about the fairness of presentation, the reason(s) must be stated in the auditor's report. Further, if there is a material departure from GAAP, the auditor should explicitly state

LO 3

Identify the types of audit opinions and the circumstances in which each type is appropriate.

The PCAOB is currently considering changes to the auditor reporting model, which may ultimately affect the content of financial statement audit reports. The changes are intended to better inform investors' decisions. New auditor disclosures in audit reports may include information about the risks that the auditor faced in the audit and information about the judgments and estimates management used in the financial statements.

the nature of the departure and the dollar effects (if such amounts are determinable by the auditor) so that a user can appropriately modify the financial statements to determine what the result would be if they had been fairly presented.

There are five basic types of financial statement audit reports:

1. *Standard unqualified report*
2. *Unqualified report with an explanatory paragraph*—the explanatory paragraph may explain the following:
    * A justified departure from GAAP
    * Inconsistent application of GAAP
    * Substantial doubt about the client being a going concern
    * The emphasis of some matter, such as unusually important subsequent events, risks, or uncertainties associated with contingencies or significant estimates
    * Reference to other auditors
3. *Qualified report* because of:
    * A material unjustified departure from GAAP
    * Inadequate disclosure
    * A scope limitation
4. *Adverse report* because of:
    * A pervasive and material unjustified departure from GAAP
    * Lack of important disclosures
5. *Disclaimer of opinion report* because the auditor either lacked independence or was unable to obtain sufficient evidence to form an opinion on the overall fairness of the financial statements, which may occur because of:
    * A scope limitation
    * Substantial doubt about the client being a going concern
    * The CPA firm not being engaged to perform an audit

Standard Unqualified Audit Report

The standard unqualified audit report following the PCAOB's reporting standards is illustrated in Exhibit 16.1 Panel A. Such a report can be issued for public companies only if:

1. There are no material violations of GAAP
2. Disclosures are adequate
3. The auditor was able to perform all of the necessary procedures
4. There was no change in accounting principles that had a material effect on the financial statements
5. The auditor determines that there are no material weaknesses in internal controls over financial reporting
6. The auditor does not have significant doubt about the client remaining a going concern
7. The auditor is independent

For a nonpublic client, the standard unqualified audit report would contain the first three paragraphs and refer to the auditing standards generally accepted in the United States rather than PCAOB's standards. In some cases, the client uses a comprehensive basis of accounting other than GAAP, such as the cash or income tax basis. Audit reports on these non-GAAP-based financial statements are called *special reports* and are discussed later in this chapter.

Unqualified Report with Explanatory Language

There are several situations in which the auditor wishes, or is required, to alter the wording of the standard report. Some of the alterations are informational only and do not affect the auditor's opinion on the financial statements. In the following situations, the auditor changes the wording of the standard report but still issues an unqualified report:

* Justified departure from GAAP
* Inconsistent application of GAAP
* Going-concern doubt

- Emphasis of a matter
- Reference to other auditors

Justified Departure from GAAP

In rare circumstances, the client may have a justified departure from GAAP. Rule 203 of the AICPA Code of Professional Conduct permits the auditor to issue an unqualified opinion when there has been a material departure from GAAP if the client can demonstrate, and the auditor concurs, that *due to unusual circumstances,* the financial statements would have been misleading had GAAP been followed. What constitutes unusual circumstances is a matter of professional judgment. Examples include new legislation or the evolution of a new form of business transaction. An unusual degree of materiality or the existence of a conflicting industry practice does not ordinarily justify a departure from GAAP.

An informational paragraph should be added, either before or after the opinion paragraph, to describe the departure from GAAP, its approximate effects (if they can be practicably determined), and the reasons for which compliance with GAAP would result in misleading statements. An unqualified opinion is appropriate in these circumstances. Exhibit 16.2 shows such a report for Oak Industries.

Inconsistent Application of GAAP

Changes in accounting principles should be fully disclosed so that a reader can make comparisons over time and between companies. A change in accounting principles includes a change from one GAAP to another, such as from FIFO to LIFO, and certain changes in the reporting entity. A change from non-GAAP to GAAP—such as from the cash basis to the accrual basis—is accounted for as a correction of an error but is treated by the auditor as a change in accounting principles. In recent years, the audit reports for many companies contain an explanatory paragraph of accounting changes because of new FASB statements. Changes in accounting estimates and accounting for new transactions are not considered changes in accounting principles.

If the client has changed an accounting principle, has reasonable justification for the change, and has followed GAAP in accounting for and disclosing this

> **PRACTICAL POINT**
>
> PCAOB AS 6 indicates that the audit report should identify the following matters relating to the consistency of the company's financial statements if those matters have a material effect on the financial statements:
>
> a. A change in accounting principle
> b. An adjustment to correct a misstatement in previously issued financial statements.

Exhibit 16.2　　Report Stating a Justified Departure from GAAP

[Standard introductory and scope paragraphs followed by these explanatory and opinion paragraphs.]

As described in Note 3, in May 2001, the company exchanged shares of its common stock for $5,060,000 of its outstanding public debt. The fair value of the common stock issued exceeded the carrying amount of the debt by $466,000, which has been shown as an extraordinary loss in the 2001 statement of operations. Because a portion of the debt exchanged was convertible debt, a literal application of Statement of Financial Accounting Standards No. 84, "Induced Conversions of Convertible Debt," would have resulted in a further reduction in net income of $3,611,000 which would have been offset by a corresponding $3,611,000 credit to additional paid-in capital; accordingly, there would have been no net effect on stockholders' investments. In the opinion of company management, with which we agree, a literal application of accounting literature would have resulted in misleading financial statements that do not properly portray the economic consequences of the exchange.

In our opinion, the consolidated financial statements referred to above present fairly in all material respects the financial position of Oak Industries Inc. and subsidiaries as of December 31, 2002 and 2001, and the results of their operations and their cash flows for each of the three years in the period ended December 31, 2002, in conformity with generally accepted accounting principles.

PricewaterhouseCoopers
San Diego, California
February 10, 2003

change, the explanatory paragraph serves as a flag directing the reader's attention to the relevant footnote disclosure. This flag can be very useful. For example, consider a company that reported a 22% increase in net income and highlighted the increase several times in its annual report to shareholders. But only by noting the additional paragraph in the auditor's report and carefully reading the financial statements and footnotes would the reader have seen that the increase in net income would have been only 6% had there not been a change in an accounting principle.

If the change in accounting principles is not justified or accounted for correctly, or there is inadequate disclosure, the auditor is dealing with a departure from GAAP. As we note later in this section, a GAAP departure will lead to either a qualified audit opinion (see "Qualified Report") or, in some cases, an adverse audit opinion.

Going-Concern Doubt

In every audit, the auditor has a responsibility to evaluate whether there is substantial doubt about the client's ability to continue as a going concern for up to one year following the balance sheet date. If there is substantial doubt about the client's ability to remain a going concern, the auditor should issue an unqualified opinion that contains an explanatory paragraph following the opinion paragraph, as illustrated in Exhibit 16.3 for Lodgian, Inc. The explanatory

---

PRACTICAL POINT

When economic conditions are poor or deteriorating, there likely will be an increase in the number of going-concern opinions that auditors will be issuing. It is generally believed that the issuance of such an opinion is a self-fulfilling prophecy: An entity receiving such an opinion will often be denied access to credit at the same time that investors avoid its stock.

Exhibit 16.3	Unqualified Report with a Going-Concern Paragraph for Lodgian, Inc.

AUDITOR REPORTING ON GOING-CONCERN ISSUE

[The audit report on the 2010 financial statements of Lodgian, Inc. contains the standard introductory, scope, and opinion paragraphs, along with the following going-concern explanatory paragraph.]

The accompanying financial statements have been prepared assuming that the Company will continue as a going concern. As discussed in Note 1 to the consolidated financial statements, the Company has been unable to refinance approximately $101.2 million of its debt on a long-term basis which raises substantial doubt about its ability to continue as a going concern. Management's plans concerning these matters are also discussed in Note 1 to the consolidated financial statements. The financial statements do not include any adjustments that might result from the outcome of this uncertainty.

[The audit report then continues with additional discussion on the company's adoption of the provisions of Financial Accounting Standards Board FASB ASC 810, and an unqualified report on the Company's internal control over financial reporting.]

/s/ Deloitte & Touche LLP
Atlanta, Georgia
March 16, 2010

MANAGEMENT'S EXPLANATION OF THE GOING-CONCERN ISSUE IN THE MD&A SECTION OF THE ANNUAL REPORT

These financial statements have been prepared on a going-concern basis, which contemplates the realization of assets and the satisfaction of liabilities in the normal course of business. However, as discussed in Note 9, as of December 31, 2009, $101.2 million of outstanding mortgage debt has matured, or is scheduled to mature in 2010 without available extension options and the economic recession has negatively impacted the Company's operating results, which affects operating cash flows as well as the Company's ability to refinance the maturing indebtedness. In the absence of an extension, refinancing or repayment of the debt, these factors raise substantial doubt as to the Company's ability to continue as a going concern. The Company surrendered control of the six hotels that secure Pool 3 to a court-appointed receiver in February 2010. Pool 3 had an outstanding balance of $45.5 million at December 31, 2009. The Company is pursuing opportunities to extend or refinance the remaining maturing debt, which totaled $55.7 million at December 31, 2009. However, the Company can provide no assurance that it will be able to refinance or extend the debt. The financial statements do not include any adjustments relating to the recoverability and classifications of recorded asset amounts or the amounts and classifications of liabilities or any other adjustments that may be necessary if the Company is unable to continue as a going concern.

paragraph should be clearly worded to indicate the auditor has *substantial doubt* about the client's continuing as a going concern and refer to management's footnote(s) explaining the problems and plans to overcome the problems. See the example in Exhibit 16.3 for the auditor's explanatory paragraph, along with management's explanation of the going-concern issue.

There may be situations in which the client is experiencing severe financial distress and the auditor does not feel comfortable expressing any opinion. In such cases, the auditor may issue a disclaimer of opinion. Finally, if the auditor is convinced that the company will be liquidated, then the auditor should indicate that liquidation values would be more appropriate.

Emphasis of a Matter

Auditors have the option of attaching a paragraph to an unqualified opinion to emphasize a matter regarding the financial statements. The choice to emphasize a matter is strictly one of auditor judgment. Examples of such matters that have been emphasized by auditing firms in their reports include:

- Significant transactions with related entities
- Important subsequent events, such as a board of director decision to divest a major segment of the business
- Important risks or uncertainties associated with contingencies or significant estimates

Accounting pronouncements, including FASB ASC 275, *Risks and Uncertainties*, (previously referred to as the AICPA's SOP 94-6, *Disclosure of Certain Significant Risks and Uncertainties*) have improved the disclosure of risks and uncertainties in financial statements. **Uncertainties** involve situations that are dependent on the outcome of some future event, such as a court decision on pending litigation. Even if the client properly discloses, accounts for, and makes reasonable estimates concerning risks and uncertainties, the auditor may decide, because of its importance, to bring the financial statement user's attention to the matter by adding a paragraph to the unqualified report. Exhibit 16.4 illustrates an added paragraph for (1) emphasis of an unusually important event and (2) a change in accounting principle for the Cendant Corporation. The previous method of accounting for revenue precipitated the litigation and change in accounting principle.

Reference to Other Auditors—Shared Report

The audit client may have branches, warehouses, factories, or subsidiaries at various locations around the country or overseas, and so another audit firm, hired by the client or by the principal auditor, may perform part of the audit. The

Exhibit 16.4	Unqualified Report with Emphasis of Important Matters for Cendant

UNUSUALLY IMPORTANT MATTER AND CHANGE IN ACCOUNTING PRINCIPLE

[This paragraph followed the opinion paragraph in Deloitte & Touche's unqualified report on Cendant's 1998 financial statements.]

As discussed in Note 18 to the consolidated financial statements, the Company is involved in certain litigation related to the discovery of accounting irregularities in certain former CUC International Inc. business units. Additionally, as discussed in Note 2, effective January 1, 1997, the Company changed its method of recognizing revenue and membership solicitation costs for its individual membership business.

Deloitte & Touche LLP
Parsippany, New Jersey
March 17, 1999

principal auditor needs to decide whether to mention the other auditors in the overall audit report. As described in the *Comparison of Worldwide Auditing Guidance* feature, reporting requirements do differ between U.S. and international auditing standards. Whether another auditor is mentioned in the report, the principal auditor needs to be satisfied with the independence and reputation of the other firm.

Most auditing firms require that they audit the whole entity or will refrain from accepting the client. Care must be taken when relying on other auditor's reports because inadequate audits performed by the other auditors can lead to legal and regulatory action against the principal auditor as well as the other firm. Further, it is very important for the principal auditor to have participated in the audit at a sufficient level, rather than solely relying on the work of the other auditor (see the *Auditing in Practice: Problems When Serving as a Principal Auditor* feature).

If the principal audit firm chooses to mention the other firm in the audit report—often referred to as a **shared report**—the wording of all three paragraphs of the standard report is modified, but no additional paragraph is needed. The resulting opinion is unqualified unless there are other reasons for expressing a different opinion.

The most extensive change appears at the end of the introductory paragraph to indicate the shared responsibility for the overall opinion, including the magnitude of the amounts audited by the other firm. The wording at the end of the scope paragraph and at the beginning of the opinion paragraph is also modified to show the shared responsibility. The name of the other audit firm is mentioned only with its express permission and if its report is also included in the document.

If the other auditor's report is qualified, the principal auditor must consider whether the subject of the qualification is of such nature and significance in relation to the overall financial statements that it would affect the overall opinion. What was material to the segment audited by the other auditor may not be significant to the overall statements.

Qualified Reports, Adverse Reports, and Disclaimers

Occasionally, circumstances are such that the auditor wishes, or is required, to alter the wording of the standard report in a manner that will affect the type of opinion expressed. In these situations the auditor cannot issue an unqualified opinion. There may be an unjustified GAAP violation, or inadequate disclosures, or the auditor may not be able to obtain sufficient competent evidence (a scope limitation). When there is substantial doubt about the client being a going concern, the auditor has an option to issue either an unqualified opinion with an added paragraph as described above or a disclaimer. In addition, the auditor may issue a disclaimer in rare situations in which the auditor is not independent.

The issuance of other than unqualified opinions is unusual. The SEC, with limited exceptions, will not accept financial statements on which the opinion is modified because of client-imposed scope limitations, inadequate disclosures, or GAAP violations. As a result, the auditor has significant clout to encourage the client to correct any material departures from GAAP, to present adequate disclosure, and to not limit the scope.

Unjustified Departure from GAAP

Material departures from GAAP result in either a qualified or adverse opinion:

- *Qualified Opinion*—If the departure from GAAP can be isolated to one item, a qualified opinion can usually be expressed. For example, if a client

Comparison of Worldwide Auditing Guidance

REPORTING REQUIREMENTS WHEN SERVING AS PRINCIPAL AUDITOR

AICPA Auditing Standards Board (ASB)

SAS 1, Section 543, *Part of Audit Performed by Other Independent Auditors* discusses the use of work of other auditors during an audit. The principal auditor has to determine whether his/her involvement in and knowledge of the audit are sufficient to allow him/her to be the principal auditor. The principal auditor then has to decide whether to make reference to the work of any other independent auditors in the audit.

Reference to the other auditor is generally appropriate when the portion of the financial statements audited by the other auditor is material in relation to the whole. The principal auditor's report should clearly indicate the degree of shared responsibility and the portions of the financial statements audited by each. Therefore, modifications should be made to the introductory, scope, and opinion paragraphs.

References to the other audit firm will likely not be made when:
- The other firm is an associated or correspondent firm,
- The other firm is hired by the principal audit firm which directs the work of the other firm,
- The other firm is hired by the client and the principal auditors are able to satisfy themselves the work done by the other firm meets their own requirements, or
- The amounts audited by the other firm are not material to the combined or consolidated financial statements.

If the principal auditor decides to accept responsibility for the other auditor's work, the principal auditor's standard report is issued without modification. In such a case, the principal auditor's report expresses an opinion on the financial statements as if he or she had conducted the entire audit; no reference is made to the other auditor, or the other auditor's work, in the principal auditor's report.

Public Company Accounting Oversight Board (PCAOB)

The PCAOB has adopted the interim standards of the AICPA and thus public company auditors follow the guidance in Section 543 of SAS 1.

International Auditing and Assurance Standards Board (IAASB)

ISA 600 discusses the use of component auditors' work in a principal auditor's work. ISA 600 requires that the report of the principal auditor (called the "group engagement partner") not refer to a component auditor, unless required by law or regulation to include such reference If such reference is required by law or regulation, the auditor's report shall indicate that the reference does not diminish the group engagement partner's or the group engagement partner's firm's responsibility for the group audit opinion.

ISA-600) is significantly broader in scope than the U.S. standard in that it addresses group audits. A *group audit* is an audit of group financial statements. *Group financial statements* are financial statements with more than one component, which is defined as an entity or business activity for which management prepares financial information that should be included in the group financial statements.

SUMMARY

Very often, auditors will have to rely on each other's work during an audit. The three standards boards offer guidance on handling such a situation. An important difference between the U.S. and the international standard is that ISA 600 does not permit the auditor's report to make reference to another independent auditor (component auditor), unless required by law or regulation to include such reference. The AICPA is currently revising its guidance in this area to be better aligned with ISA 600; however, even with the revision this reporting difference will remain between the U.S. and the international standards.

expensed the acquisition cost of some assets that should have been capitalized and depreciated over their useful lives, a qualified opinion would be appropriate (see Exhibit 16.5).

- *Adverse Opinion*—An adverse opinion should be expressed when the auditor believes that the financial statements taken as a whole are *not presented fairly* in

AUDITING *in Practice*

PROBLEMS WHEN SERVING AS A PRINCIPAL AUDITOR

In July 2010, the PCAOB issued Staff Audit Practice Alert No. 6, *Auditor Considerations Regarding Using the Work of Other Auditors and Engaging Assistants from Outside the Firm.* The report notes:

> The PCAOB staff has observed that a number of registered public accounting firms located in the United States ("U.S.") have been issuing audit reports on financial statements filed by issuers that have substantially all of their operations outside of the U.S. Although there is nothing inherently inappropriate about this, observations from the Board's inspection process suggest that some firms may not be conducting those audits in accordance with PCAOB standards. Specifically, some firms may be issuing audit reports based on the work of another firm, or by using the work of assistants engaged from outside of the firm, without complying with relevant PCAOB standards.

The report describes one situation where a U.S. firm was engaged to audit an issuer with substantially all of its operations in China. The U.S. firm retained an accounting firm in China to perform audit procedures. Personnel from the U.S. firm did not travel to China during the audit, and the

audit procedures performed by the other firm represented substantially all of the audit procedures on the issuer's financial statements. The firm in the China region did not issue a report; the U.S. firm issued an audit report stating that it had audited the financial statements and expressed an unqualified opinion on the financial statements. The PCAOB staff, however, concluded that it was inappropriate for the firm to serve as principal auditor and use the work of the other auditor. A firm cannot serve as principal auditor (and, accordingly, may not sign the audit report on the issuer's financial statements) unless the firm's own participation in the audit is sufficient. The Staff Audit Practice Alert notes:

> If an issuer has no significant operations other than those in another country, a registered public accounting firm that plays no significant part in the audit of the foreign operations is highly unlikely to have sufficient participation in the audit to serve as the issuer's principal auditor. A lack of sufficient participation cannot be overcome by using the work of the other auditor, even if the firm assumes responsibility for that work.

---

conformity with GAAP. This can happen when a significant number of items in the financial statements violate GAAP. For example, if the auditor believes the client is no longer a going concern, GAAP may require the financial statements to reflect liquidation values. If the items are presented in accordance with normal going-concern accounting, the statements are not fairly presented (see Exhibit 16.6). Such opinions are very rare.

The choice between a qualified opinion and an adverse opinion is based on the auditor's judgment as to the nature and pervasiveness of the misstatement. This is sometimes a difficult decision.

Exhibit 16.5 | Qualified Opinion Due to a GAAP Violation

[Standard introductory and scope paragraphs followed by these explanatory and opinion paragraphs.]

As more fully described in Note 10 to the financial statements, the Company expenses the acquisition of appliances. In our opinion, generally accepted accounting principles require that appliances be capitalized and depreciated over their estimated useful lives. The effects of this non-GAAP accounting understated pre-tax income by $1.5 million and understated net fixed assets by $1.5 million.

In our opinion, *except for the effect of the recording of appliances as discussed in the preceding paragraph,* the financial statements referred to above present fairly, in all material respects, the financial position of Friendly Village, Inc., as of December 31, 2011 and 2010 and the results of its operations and its cash flows for the years ended December 31, 2011, 2010, and 2009 in conformity with accounting principles generally accepted in the United States of America.

Rittenberg, Johnstone, & Gramling, LLP
February 5, 2012

[Emphasis added.]

Exhibit 16.6 Adverse Opinion for NECO Enterprises

To the Board of Directors
NECO Enterprises Inc.

We have audited the accompanying consolidated balance sheets of NECO Enterprises, Inc. and its subsidiaries as of December 31, 1995 and 1994, and related consolidated statements of loss, deficit and cash flows for the years then ended. These financial statements are the responsibility of the Company's management. Our responsibility is to express an opinion on these financial statements based on our audits.

Except as discussed in the following paragraph, we conducted our audits in accordance with auditing standards generally accepted in the United States of America. Those standards require that we plan and perform the audit to obtain reasonable assurance about whether the financial statements are free of material misstatement. An audit includes examining, on a test basis, evidence supporting the amounts and disclosures in the financial statements. An audit also includes assessing the accounting principles used and significant estimates made by management, as well as evaluating the overall financial statement presentation. We believe that our audits provide a reasonable basis for our opinion.

As discussed in Note 2 to the consolidated financial statements, the Company has presented its consolidated financial statements on the going-concern basis, which states assets and liabilities at historical amounts. Because of the magnitude and complexity of the matters discussed in Note 2 (certain of which are not within the direct control of the Company), including the Company's losses from operations, net stockholders' capital deficiency, defaults or other violations of debt covenants, restrictions on its access to the use of a significant proportion of its remaining liquid assets, its present financial inability to complete development of its land held for resale and land held for rental, and the lack of a significant market for its land held for resale and land held for rental, we believe that the Company can no longer carry out its plans and intentions, which are also discussed in Note 2, and cannot convert or otherwise dispose of its assets in the normal course of its business operations. In these circumstances, it is our opinion that generally accepted accounting principles require the Company's assets and liabilities to be stated at their liquidating values. The effect of this departure from generally accepted accounting principles cannot be reasonably determined; however, amounts ultimately received upon liquidation of the assets and amounts ultimately paid to settle liabilities may be different from the amounts stated in the accompanying consolidated financial statements.

In our opinion, *because of the effects of the matters discussed in the preceding paragraph,* the consolidated financial statements *do not present fairly,* in conformity with accounting principles generally accepted in the United States of America, the financial position of NECO Enterprises, Inc. and its subsidiaries at December 31, 1995 and 1994 or the results of their operations or their cash flows for the years then ended.

Lefkowitz, Garfinkel, Champi & Defrienzo
February 7, 1996

[Emphasis added.]

Inadequate Disclosures

It is presumed that financial statements include all the necessary disclosures to comply with accounting standards and, perhaps more importantly, include disclosures designed to keep the financial statements from potentially being misleading. If the client refuses to make the appropriate disclosures, the auditor should express a qualified or adverse opinion, depending on the significance of the omitted disclosures, and provide the omitted information in the audit report, if practicable. The auditor is not, however, required to prepare and present a basic financial statement, such as an omitted cash-flow statement or segment information.

The introductory and scope paragraphs of the auditor's report are not affected by this situation. The explanatory paragraph should describe the nature of the omitted disclosures, and the opinion paragraph should be modified. Exhibit 16.7 is an example of the qualified opinion for Honda Motor Co., LTD.

PRACTICAL POINT

A Staff Audit Practice Alert issued by the PCAOB focuses on matters that auditors should be sensitive to during economic downturns. In particular, the PCAOB advises auditors to pay particular attention to the adequacy of disclosures and accounting estimates, such as allowance amounts assigned to uncollectible receivables and deferred tax assets. If the auditor determines the client's disclosures are inadequate, the auditor will not be able to issue a standard unqualified opinion.

Exhibit 16.7 Opinion Qualified Because of Inadequate Disclosure

[Standard introductory and scope paragraphs followed by these explanatory and opinion paragraphs.]

The Company's consolidated financial statements do not disclose certain information required by Statement of Financial Accounting Standards No. 131, "Disclosures about Segments of an Enterprise and Related Information." In our opinion, disclosure of this information is required by U.S. generally accepted accounting principles.

In our opinion, *except for the omission of the segment information referred to in the preceding paragraph,* the consolidated financial statements referred to above present fairly, in all material respects, the financial position of Honda Motor Co., Ltd. and subsidiaries as of March 31, 2005 and 2006, and the results of their operations and their cash flows for each of the years in the three-year period ended March 31, 2006 in conformity with U.S. generally accepted accounting principles.

/S/ KPMG AZSA & Co.
Tokyo, Japan
June 23, 2006

[Emphasis added.]

Scope Limitation

An unqualified opinion can be given only when the auditor has been able to conduct the audit in accordance with professional auditing standards. Restrictions on the scope of the audit, whether imposed by the client or by circumstances beyond the auditor's or client's control, may require the auditor to qualify or disclaim an opinion. Examples of circumstances that may limit the audit scope are the timing of the fieldwork, such as being engaged to do the audit after year end; the inability to gather sufficient competent evidence; or an inadequacy in the accounting records. As an example, when a company is audited for the first time, the audit firm is often appointed during the year to be audited. In such a case, the auditor may not be able to obtain sufficient, competent evidence concerning the fairness of the beginning inventory, which affects the current year's income, or of the accounting principles used in the prior year. This may be a scope limitation that is beyond the auditor's control. If the auditor can gather sufficient evidence without being engaged prior to the beginning of the year, then the scope limitation no longer exists and the auditor can render whatever would be the appropriate audit opinion.

- *Qualified Opinion*—Exhibit 16.8 presents an opinion that is qualified because of possible errors that might have been discovered had the scope of the audit not been limited. The scope paragraph refers to the scope limitation, which is then described in an explanatory paragraph. *Note that the exception in the opinion paragraph refers to the possible adjustments rather than to the scope limitation itself.*
- *Disclaimer*—When the client imposes substantial restrictions on the scope of the audit, there is a significant risk that the client is trying to hide important evidence, and the auditor should ordinarily disclaim an opinion. If scope limitations caused by circumstances are such that it is not possible to form an opinion, a disclaimer should also be issued. The wording of the introductory paragraph is modified for a scope limitation, *the scope paragraph is omitted*, an additional paragraph is inserted to describe the scope limitation(s), and the last paragraph clearly states that no opinion can be expressed. Exhibit 16.9 illustrates such a disclaimer.

Disclaimer Due to Going-Concern Doubt

In some reporting situations, doubt about the client continuing as a going concern is such that the auditor is uncomfortable just adding an additional paragraph to an unqualified opinion. In such cases, the auditor may issue a

PRACTICAL POINT

Under most circumstances, the auditor can never accept a limitation on the scope of audit procedures performed. This is true even if the client will not approve an increase in the audit fee to cover the additional work performed.

Exhibit 16.8 — Opinion Qualified Because of a Scope Limitation for Sound Money Investors

To the Board of Directors
Sound Money Investors Inc.

I have audited the accompanying statement of assets, liabilities and stockholder's equity of Sound Money Investors, Inc. as of December 31, 1995 and the related statements of income, changes in stockholder's equity and cash flows for the year then ended. These financial statements are the responsibility of the Company's management. My responsibility is to express an opinion on these financial statements based on my audits.

Except as discussed in the following paragraph, I conducted my audit in accordance with auditing standards generally accepted in the United States of America. Those standards require that I plan and perform the audit to obtain reasonable assurance about whether the financial statements are free of material misstatement. An audit includes examining, on a test basis, evidence supporting the amounts and disclosures in the financial statements. An audit also includes assessing the accounting principles used and significant estimates made by management, as well as evaluating the overall financial statement presentation. I believe that our audit provides a reasonable basis for our opinion.

As discussed in Notes 5 and 6, the Company has purchased certain assets from a corporation wholly owned by two major stockholders and officers of the Company at management's estimate of their values at the date of acquisition. I have been unable to obtain adequate documentation to support the basis and purchase price of such assets.

In my opinion, *except for the effects of such adjustments, if any, as might have been determined to be necessary had I been able to obtain adequate documentation to support the basis of such assets,* the financial statements referred to above present fairly, in all material respects, the financial position of Sound Money Investors, Inc. as of December 31, 1995 and the results of its operations and its cash flows for the year then ended in conformity with accounting principles generally accepted in the United States of America.

Chaslaur, Inc. (CPA)
June 2, 1996

[Emphasis added.]

Exhibit 16.9 — Disclaimer of Opinion Due to Scope Limitation for Alternative Distributors Corporation

We were *engaged to audit* the accompanying consolidated balance sheet of Alternative Distributors Corporation and its Subsidiary as of February 29, 1996 and the related consolidated statements of income, accumulated deficit, cash flows, and statement of stockholders' equity (deficit) for the year then ended. These financial statements are the responsibility of the Company's management.

[Reference to the auditor's responsibility to express an opinion is eliminated because no opinion is expressed.]

[The standard scope paragraph is omitted.]

Detailed accounts receivable records have not been maintained and certain records and supporting data were not available for our audit. Therefore, we were not able to satisfy ourselves about the amounts at which accounts receivable and allowance for doubtful accounts are recorded in the accompanying balance sheet at February 29, 1996 (stated at $1,450,000 and $350,000, respectively), and the amount of net sales and bad debt expense for the year then ended (stated at $7,842,778 and $350,244, respectively).

Because of the significance of the matters discussed in the preceding paragraph, the scope of our work was not sufficient to enable us to express, and *we do not express, an opinion* on the financial statements referred to in the first paragraph.

Gordon, Harrington & Osborn
June 4, 1996, except for Note 2, for which the date is June 12, 1996

[Emphasis added.]

disclaimer of opinion. Such was the case in the auditor's report on the 1995 financial statements of Alloy Computer Products, Inc. that contained the paragraphs shown in Exhibit 16.10.

Exhibit 16.10   Disclaimer for Going-Concern Doubt for Alloy Computer Products

We were engaged to audit the balance sheet of Alloy Computer Products, Inc. as of December 31, 1996 and the related statements of income, cash flows, and retained earnings for the year then ended. These financial statements are the responsibility of the Company's management.

[Reference to the auditor's responsibility to express an opinion is eliminated because no opinion is expressed.]

[The standard scope paragraph was included, except the sentence referring to the audit providing a reasonable basis for the opinion is left out.]

As discussed in Notes 1 and 8 to the financial statements, the Company has suffered recurring losses from operations and negative cash flows and there is significant outstanding litigation against the Company. These issues raise substantial doubt about the ability of the Company to continue as a going concern.

Because of the significance of the uncertainty regarding the Company's ability to continue as a going concern, we are *unable to express, and do not express, an opinion* on these financial statements.

[Emphasis added.]

PRACTICAL POINT

Even though a disclaimer is sometimes used when the auditor has going-concern reservations, the auditor is still responsible for assuring that the items in the financial statements are appropriately valued according to GAAP, including adjustments for impairments and realizability issues.

Disclaimer Due to Auditor Lacking Independence

When auditors lack independence with respect to a client, they, by definition, cannot perform an audit in accordance with professional auditing standards and are precluded from expressing an opinion on the financial statements. In such cases, a one-paragraph disclaimer should be issued stating their lack of independence but omitting the reasons for it. By omitting the reasons for the lack of independence, the auditor is avoiding the possibility of the reader second-guessing the auditor as to independence or lack thereof. The following is an excerpt from an accountant's disclaimer report:

I am not independent with respect to Mineral Mountain Mining and Milling Company, Inc. and the accompanying balance sheets of the Company as of March 31, 2003 and 2002 and the related statements of operations, stockholders' equity and cash flows for the years then ended were not audited by me, and accordingly, I do not express an opinion on them.

Sincerely,

DONALD L. HESS P. A.
Delaine Hess Gruber July 7, 2003

Such a situation should rarely occur. It could happen, for example, when it is discovered late in the audit that one of the auditors on the engagement had a financial interest in the client.

Summary of Audit Report Modifications

Exhibit 16.11 summarizes the major conditions leading to audit report modification. Deciding on the type of opinion is a matter that should not be taken lightly. This is particularly true of the decisions based on the materiality level and pervasiveness of GAAP violations, the significance of scope limitations, and the likelihood of the entity being a going concern. Issuing an inappropriate opinion can lead to legal problems. Because of its importance, the decision is often made after consultation with other professionals.

Exhibit 16.11	Summary of Audit Report Modifications

Condition (Exhibit Number)	OPINION			
	Unqualified	Qualified	Adverse	Disclaimer
Inconsistent application of GAAP	1			
Justified departure from GAAP (16.2)	1 or 2			
Going-concern doubt (16.3,10)*	1			2
Emphasis of a matter (16.4)	1 or 2			
Other auditors—shared report	3			
Unjustified GAAP violation (16.5, 6)**		2	2	
Inadequate Disclosure (16.7)**		2	2	
Scope limitation (16.8, 9)***		2 & 4		2 & 5
Auditor lacks independence				6

1 Explanatory paragraph **after** opinion paragraph
2 Explanatory paragraph **before** opinion paragraph
3 Modify wording of all three paragraphs
4 Modify scope paragraph
5 Modify introductory paragraph and replace scope paragraph with explanatory paragraph
6 One paragraph disclaimer

*The explanatory paragraph in an unqualified report is adequate. However, the auditor is not precluded from issuing a disclaimer.

**The choice depends on materiality and pervasiveness considerations.

***The choice depends on the importance of the omitted procedures to the auditor's ability to form an opinion. If it is a significant scope limitation imposed by the client, a disclaimer should ordinarily be issued.

Other Reports Related to Financial Statement Information

Reviews and Compilations for Nonpublic Companies

Sometimes a client does not need an audit, but wants to engage the auditor to provide a lower level of assurance at a lower cost. Practitioners can perform fewer procedures and report a lower level of assurance on the fairness of the financial statements than would be done in an audit or simply prepare financial statements from the client's records and provide no assurance. The most common of these services are referred to as reviews and compilations. Standards for these services to nonpublic companies were first issued in 1979 (see the *Auditing in Practice: The Evolution of Compilation and Review Standards* feature).

Note that these standards apply only to compilations and reviews of financial statements of *nonpublic companies*. Reporting on reviews of interim financial statements of public companies is covered later in this chapter.

The standards for compilations and reviews of the financial statements of nonpublic entities are called *Statements on Standards for Accounting and Review Services* (SSARSs). The Accounting and Review Services Committee of the AICPA issues these standards, which are separate from those of the Auditing Standards Board (ASB). Exhibit 16.12 is a summary of the basic procedures performed and standard reports issued in audits, reviews, and compilations.

LO 4

Explain the differences among audit, review, and compilation engagements in terms of procedures, the degree of responsibility taken by the accountant, and reports rendered.

PRACTICAL POINT

Reviews and compilations are not as extensive as audits and can only be conducted for private companies. The presumption is that users have access to the company that utilizes a review report or a compilation report. Therefore, such reports are allowed only for nonpublic companies.

AUDITING *in Practice*

THE EVOLUTION OF COMPILATION AND REVIEW STANDARDS

Before the issuance of the compilation and review standards in 1979, there were only two levels of assurance a CPA could provide on a company's financial statements: positive assurance (an audit) or no assurance (a disclaimer). In many situations, small, privately held businesses used the financial reports for internal use and to give to the local banker, who might be quite familiar with the company and its management. The company may have wanted its financial statements to be looked at by a CPA but did not need a full audit. In some cases, the CPA would do extensive work in analyzing the company's financial reports; in other cases, the CPA simply verified that the financial statements agreed with the general ledger and were put together in good form but did not perform any procedures to gain assurance about the numbers in the financial statements. But both levels of service received the same assurance from the CPA, that is, a disclaimer of opinion.

The compilation and review standards were developed to address this particular constituency and to recognize that CPAs often did a considerable amount of work, although less in scope than an audit, on privately held businesses

that received disclaimers of opinions. The work was not sufficient to provide audit assurance, but it was reasoned that the work was sufficient to provide *some assurance* that reflected the limited amount of work performed by the CPA. That negative assurance is now captured in the review report in which a CPA undertakes specific analytic procedures to search for obvious misstatements in a company's financial statements but not enough work to provide assurance that the statements are fairly presented. Thus, the CPA can communicate only that based on the procedures performed, nothing has come to his or her attention that the financial statements are misstated.

Why would a company and its users be interested in such a report? First, it is less costly. Most reviews cost about one-half of what an audit costs. Second, reviews are generally considered higher-margin services by the CPA firms. Third, there is less legal liability associated with the report. Thus, if the company has a bank that will accept a review report as a basis for making a loan, it effectively makes the loan less expensive for the company.

Exhibit 16.12 — Summary of Basic Procedures and Standard Reports for Audits, Reviews, and Compilations

Procedure	Audit	Review*	Compilation*
Assess control risk.	X		
Perform substantive tests of transactions and balances.	X		
Perform analytical procedures.	X	X	
Make inquiries of client personnel to verify or corroborate information supplied by the client.	X	X	
Obtain knowledge of client's organization, assets, liabilities, revenues, expenses, operations, locations, and transactions with related parties.	X	X	
Obtain knowledge of the accounting principles and practices of the industry.	X	X	X
Obtain knowledge of the client's transactions, form of accounting records, qualifications of accounting personnel, the accounting basis to be used for the financial statements, and the form and content of the statements (inquiry & prior experience).	X	X	X
Standard report.	Unqualified opinion	Disclaimer and limited	Disclaimer assurance

*These standards relate to reviews and compilations of **nonpublic** companies only.

Reviews

A **review** is an accounting service that involves performing inquiry and analytical procedures to provide a reasonable basis for expressing *limited assurance* that there are no material modifications that should be made to the financial statements to make them conform with GAAP or, if applicable, with another comprehensive basis of accounting. Reviews may be useful to bankers and vendors who are familiar with the client's business and do not need—or are not willing to demand—an audit, but want some assurance from a CPA.

Review Procedures　A review requires more knowledge and evidence than does a compilation but is significantly less in scope than an audit. In performing this level of service, the CPA should obtain a general understanding of the entity's organization; operating characteristics; types of transactions, assets, and liabilities; compensation methods; types of products and services; operating locations; and related parties. The CPA should also obtain a management representation letter near the end of the engagement, the content of which is very similar to that illustrated in Chapter 15 for an audit.

Standard procedures for conducting a review include the following:

- Inquire concerning actions taken at meetings of the board of directors, stockholders, and other decision-making bodies.
- Inquire whether the financial statements have been consistently prepared in conformity with GAAP or other comprehensive basis of accounting.
- Inquire about any changes in the business activities or accounting principles and practices and events subsequent to the date of the financial statements that would have a material effect on the financial statements.
- Obtain or prepare a trial balance of the general ledger and foot and reconcile it to the general ledger.
- Trace the financial statement amounts to the trial balance.
- Perform basic analytical procedures, such as comparing current financial statement amounts with those of prior period(s) and with anticipated results, such as budgets and forecasts, and studying the relationships of elements of the financial statements that would be expected to conform to a predictable pattern based on the entity's experience, such as interest expense to interest-bearing debt.
- Obtain explanations from management for any unusual or unexpected results and consider the need for further investigation.
- Read the financial statements to determine whether they appear to conform to GAAP.

Inquiries and analytical procedures should be performed for each of the significant line items in the financial statements. To give you an idea of these additional procedures, Exhibit 16.13 lists some of the inquiries and analytical procedures that might be performed for accounts in the revenue cycle. Note that they are significantly less in scope than audit procedures. There is no assessment of the internal control over financial reporting and there are no substantive tests of transactions or balances, such as the confirmation of receivables, review of subsequent cash collections, cutoff tests, or tests of sales transactions processed during the period.

If evidence obtained from such inquiries and analytical procedures does not support the financial statements, the CPA should perform additional procedures and, if the additional evidence indicates material misstatements, have the client correct them. For example, if inquiries concerning proper cutoff of sales leads the CPA to question the client's timing of revenue recognition, the CPA may deem it necessary to perform a cutoff test of sales to determine whether there is a material misstatement. If there is a material misstatement but the client will

Exhibit 16.13 | Inquiries and Analytical Procedures for the Revenue Cycle

INQUIRIES

1. What is the entity's revenue recognition policy? Is the policy proper and consistently applied and disclosed? Have the revenue recognition procedures been updated for changes in accounting principles?
2. Are revenues from sales of products and rendering of services recognized in the appropriate reporting period?
3. Were any sales recorded under a "bill and hold" arrangement? If yes, have the criteria been met to record the transaction as a sale?
4. Has an adequate allowance for doubtful accounts been properly reflected in the financial statements?
5. Have receivables considered uncollectible been written off? Is the amount written off consistent with prior experience, changes in the economy, or trends in the industry?
6. Is the accounts receivable subsidiary ledger reconciled to the general ledger account balance on a regular basis?
7. Are there receivables from employees or other related parties? Have receivables from owners been evaluated to determine if they should be reflected in the equity section of the balance sheet?
8. Have there been significant numbers of sales returns or credit memoranda issued subsequent to the balance sheet date?

ANALYTICAL PROCEDURES

1. Compute number of days' sales in ending receivables and compare with that for prior years.
2. Compute aging percentages of accounts receivable and compare with those for prior years.
3. Compute bad debt expense as a percent of sales for the year and compare with that for prior years.
4. Compare sales growth with information about industry sales growth. Seek an explanation about significant differences between the company's growth rate and that of the industry as a whole.
5. Compare sales results by product line with previous years. Reconcile changes to information available about client strategy.
6. Compute gross margin. If there are significant changes in gross margin, follow up to determine if the changes may be due to revenue recognition or inventory changes.

not correct it, the CPA should modify the review report to bring the misstatement to the reader's attention.

Standard Review Report The standard review report for nonpublic companies is shown in Exhibit 16.14. It has three paragraphs. The first paragraph identifies what was reviewed. It states that the AICPA's review standards (SSARSs) were followed and that the financial statements are the representations of the company's management. The second paragraph describes a review,

Exhibit 16.14 | Standard Review Report

To the Shareholders of Apple Grove Company

We have reviewed the accompanying balance sheet of Apple Grove Company as of December 31, 2011, and the related statements of income, retained earnings, and cash flows for the year then ended, in accordance with Statements on Standards for Accounting and Review Services issued by the American Institute of Certified Public Accountants. All information included in these financial statements is the representation of the management of Apple Grove Company.

A review consists principally of inquiries of company personnel and analytical procedures applied to financial data. It is substantially less in scope than an examination in accordance with generally accepted auditing standards, the objective of which is the expression of an opinion regarding the financial statements taken as a whole. Accordingly, we do not express such an opinion.

Based on our review, *we are not aware of any material modifications that should be made to the accompanying financial statements in order for them to be in conformity with generally accepted accounting principles.*

Rittenberg, Johnstone, & Gramling, LLP
March 1, 2012

[Emphasis added.]

states that it is narrower in scope than an audit, and disclaims an opinion. The third paragraph expresses what is referred to as **limited assurance** (sometimes referred to as **negative assurance**). It tells the reader that the accountant is not aware of any reporting problems based on the review procedures performed. If there is a reporting problem, such as a departure from GAAP, the limited assurance paragraph should be modified to refer to an additional paragraph that explains the departure. If the client will not provide the CPA with a signed management representation letter, or the CPA is unable to obtain the evidence necessary to provide limited assurance, the CPA is precluded from issuing a review report and will ordinarily withdraw from the engagement.

Compilations

Compilations can be performed only for *nonpublic entities* and involve presenting, in the form of financial statements, information that is the representation of management (owners) without the auditor undertaking to express any assurance on the statements. A client may request its CPA to compile financial statements because it does not have the in-house expertise to prepare them or because its banker feels more comfortable with statements prepared by the CPA from the client's records.

Compilation Procedures   The CPA should have a general knowledge of the client's industry, the nature of the client's accounting records, the accounting basis to be used (GAAP or another comprehensive basis of accounting), and the form and content of the financial statements. Such an understanding is obtained through continuing professional education, experience with the client, regular reviews of industry developments, and inquiry of the client's personnel. The CPA is not required to make inquiries or perform procedures to verify, corroborate, or review information provided by the client. However, if the CPA believes that such information may be incorrect, incomplete, or otherwise unsatisfactory, additional or revised information should be obtained. If the client refuses to provide this information, the CPA should withdraw from the engagement. The CPA should read the financial statements, including footnotes, to make sure that they are appropriate in form and free from obvious material misstatement, such as clerical errors or violations of GAAP.

Standard Compilation Report   The standard compilation report is shown in Exhibit 16.15. The standards referred to in the first paragraph are the SSARSs. The second paragraph describes a compilation as taking management's information and putting it into the form of financial statements. The CPA does not take any responsibility for the fairness of the financial statements.

Exhibit 16.15	Standard Compilation Report

To J. R. Race, President
Race Company

We have compiled the accompanying balance sheet of Race Company as of December 31, 2011, and the related statements of income, retained earnings, and cash flow for the year then ended, in accordance with Statements on Standards for Accounting and Review Services issued by the American Institute of Certified Public Accountants.

A compilation is limited to presenting in the form of financial statements information that is the representation of management. We have not audited or reviewed the accompanying financial statements and, accordingly, *do not express an opinion or any other form of assurance on them.*

Rittenberg, Johnstone, & Gramling, LLP
January 29, 2012

[Emphasis added.]

Even though no assurance is provided, many users believe that because the CPA's name is associated with the statements, obvious material misstatements would have been mentioned in the CPA's report. Therefore, it is important that the CPA be careful when preparing the statements to be alert to any obvious misstatement(s). If there is a material misstatement that is not corrected by management, it should be described in the report following the disclaimer paragraph.

Omission of Disclosures for Compilations   The client may request the accountant to compile financial statements that omit substantially all of the required disclosures. This request may be honored if the CPA believes that such omission is not undertaken with the intention of misleading the users. An additional paragraph should be added to the standard compilation report, stating:

> The company has elected to omit substantially all of the disclosures required by GAAP. If the omitted disclosures were included in the financial statements, they might influence the user's conclusions about the company's financial position, results of operations, and cash flows. Accordingly, these financial statements are not designed for those who are not informed about such matters.

CPAs often assist clients by performing computerized record-keeping services to prepare monthly financial statements for the client's use without all of the disclosures. The CPA is not expected to provide the missing disclosures in the compilation report unless a comprehensive basis of accounting other than GAAP is used. In that case, the basis used must be disclosed in a footnote or in the CPA's report.

Compilation Report Not Required   CPAs may prepare the financial statements without a compilation report when these are intended for use by the client only. In such cases, the auditor should include in a written engagement letter a statement that the financial statements are intended solely for the use of specified members of management and should not be used by any other party.

CPA Lacks Independence   If the CPA is not independent of the client, a separate paragraph should be added to the compilation report stating:

> I am [We are] not independent with respect to [client's name].

This does not change the level of assurance provided since none is given. However, if the CPA lacks independence regarding an audit or a review client, the level of assurance is reduced to a disclaimer. Therefore, a CPA lacking independence should ordinarily accept only compilation engagements for nonpublic companies.

Reviews of Interim Financial Information for Public Companies

Interim Financial Information

LO 5

Explain the procedures and reporting requirements for interim financial information.

The SEC requires publicly owned companies to (1) file quarterly financial information with the SEC on Form 10-Q within 40 to 45 days (depending on the company size) after the end of each of the first three quarters of the fiscal year and provide their shareholders with quarterly reports and (2) include certain quarterly information in the annual reports to the SEC (Form 10-K) and in the annual reports to shareholders. Recall that an overview of the reporting time frame for SEC reports is shown in the *Auditing in Practice* feature titled *SEC Requirements for Timeliness of Reporting* earlier in the chapter. The SEC requires publicly owned corporations to have their quarterly financial information reviewed by their independent auditors before it is issued but does *not require* that the auditor's review report be included with the quarterly information, although many companies do include the auditor's report.

Review Procedures for Interim Financial Information   The auditor should perform review procedures (a) on the quarterly information contained in the annual report to shareholders and (b) when engaged to review the quarterly information issued at the end of each of the first three quarters of the fiscal year. These procedures are similar to those required by the SSARSs for reviews of financial statements of nonpublic companies (covered earlier in this chapter):

- Making inquiries
- Performing analytical procedures
- Reading the minutes of board of directors' meetings
- Reading the interim information to consider whether it appears to conform to GAAP

In addition, the auditor should obtain written representations from management concerning such things as their responsibility for the financial information, the completeness of the minutes, and subsequent events. The standards also require auditors to understand the client's accounting and financial reporting practices *and its related internal controls over the preparation of annual and quarterly reports*, normally obtained while auditing the prior-year financial statements and updated as those controls change. With a new client, the auditor must perform the necessary procedures to obtain such an understanding.

Reporting on Interim Statements Presented Separately   The standard report on a review of separately issued interim statements *of public companies* is shown in Exhibit 16.16. It identifies the information reviewed, indicates that the standards of the PCAOB were followed in performing the review, explains the nature of a review, disclaims an opinion, and provides negative assurance that the auditor is not aware of any material departures from GAAP. If the client is a *nonpublic company*, the title would not include the word *Registered* if the CPA firm is

---

Exhibit 16.16   **Review Report on Interim Financial Statements for 3M Company**

REPORT OF INDEPENDENT REGISTERED PUBLIC ACCOUNTING FIRM

We have reviewed the accompanying consolidated balance sheet of 3M Company and its subsidiaries as of September 30, 2010, and the related consolidated statements of income for the three-month and nine-month periods ended September 30, 2010 and 2009 and the consolidated statement of cash flows for the nine-month periods ended September 30, 2010 and 2009. These interim financial statements are the responsibility of the Company's management.

We conducted our review in accordance with the standards of the Public Company Accounting Oversight Board (United States). A review of interim financial information consists principally of applying analytical procedures and making inquiries of persons responsible for financial and accounting matters. It is substantially less in scope than an audit conducted in accordance with the standards of the Public Company Accounting Oversight Board (United States), the objective of which is the expression of an opinion regarding the financial statements taken as a whole. Accordingly, we do not express such an opinion.

Based on our review, we are not aware of any material modifications that should be made to the accompanying consolidated interim financial statements for them to be in conformity with accounting principles generally accepted in the United States of America.

We previously audited, in accordance with the standards of the Public Company Accounting Oversight Board (United States), the consolidated balance sheet as of December 31, 2009, and the related consolidated statements of income, of changes in stockholders' equity and comprehensive income, and of cash flows for the year then ended (not presented herein), and in our report dated February 16, 2010, except with respect to our opinion on the consolidated financial statements insofar as it relates to the effects of the segment realignments discussed in Notes 3 and 17 as to which the date is May 17, 2010, we expressed an unqualified opinion on those consolidated financial statements. In our opinion, the information set forth in the accompanying consolidated balance sheet information as of December 31, 2009, is fairly stated in all material respects in relation to the consolidated balance sheet from which it has been derived.

/s/ PricewaterhouseCoopers LLP
PricewaterhouseCoopers LLP
Minneapolis, Minnesota
November 5, 2010

not registered with PCAOB and the reference would be to the "standards established by the American Institute of Certified Public Accountants."

The disclosure and reporting requirements for interim financial statements differ from those for annual statements. Accruals, such as estimates of bad debt and income tax expenses, are not usually as precise on interim dates as they are at year end. It is assumed that those who receive the interim statements also received the latest annual statements. Information disclosed in the latest annual statements does not have to be repeated in the interim statements except for continuing contingencies and other uncertainties. There should be disclosures of events that occurred since the latest year end, such as changes in accounting principles or estimates and significant changes in financial position.

The negative assurance should be modified when there is a material departure from GAAP or inadequate disclosure. In such situations, a paragraph should be added preceding the negative assurance paragraph describing the problem. The negative assurance paragraph would then read as follows:

> Based on our review, *with the exception of the matter described in the preceding paragraph,* we are not aware of any material modifications that should be made to the accompanying financial statements for them to be in conformity with generally accepted accounting principles.
> [Emphasis added.]

Reporting on Interim Financial Information that Accompanies Audited Annual Financial Statements The SEC requires public companies to present selected quarterly financial information in their annual reports and certain other documents filed with the SEC. Other companies may voluntarily present such information. The auditor's report on the financial statements ordinarily does not need to be modified to refer to the review of the interim information unless:

- The information is required by the SEC but is omitted or has not been reviewed
- The information is presented in the footnotes but is not clearly labeled "unaudited"
- The information does not conform to GAAP
- The information is presented voluntarily, is not reviewed by the auditor, and is not appropriately marked as not reviewed

Special Reports

CPAs issue a wide variety of reports in addition to those described in the preceding sections. The term *special reports* has specific meaning in the auditing standards and refers to the following types of reporting situations:

- Reporting on financial statements prepared in conformity with a comprehensive basis of accounting other than GAAP, often referred to as OCBOA (other comprehensive basis of accounting) statements
- Reporting on specified elements, accounts, or items of a financial statement
- Reporting on compliance with aspects of contractual agreements or regulatory requirements *related to audited financial statements*
- Reporting on special-purpose financial presentations to comply with contractual agreements or regulatory provisions
- Reporting on financial information presented in prescribed forms or schedules

We do not cover all such reports in this section, but provide an overview of the major reports.

Comprehensive Basis of Accounting Other Than GAAP

The SEC requires public companies to follow GAAP. Some non-SEC companies, however, prepare their financial statements on a **comprehensive basis of**

accounting other than GAAP (OCBOA). Some regulatory agencies, such as state insurance commissions, require the preparation of financial statements that conform to prescribed regulatory accounting standards. Auditing standards permit the auditor to issue opinions on such non-GAAP financial statements as long as the accounting basis used is one of the following:

- A cash or modified cash basis
- The basis of accounting used for preparing the income tax return
- The accounting is required for reporting to a governmental regulatory agency
- A basis with a defined set of criteria, substantial support, and applicability to all material items appearing in the financial statements

It is important to recognize that these financial statements are not GAAP statements, and a standard unqualified audit opinion on the fairness of the statements in accordance with GAAP cannot be issued. However, the auditor can give an opinion on whether the statements are fairly presented in accordance with the other comprehensive basis of accounting. To minimize the cost of record keeping, some companies prepare their financial statements using a cash, modified cash, or income tax basis so they do not have to maintain two sets of records, one for tax reporting and the other for financial reporting. Lending institutions sometimes accept audited financial statements prepared on such a basis.

Auditing standards apply to audits of OCBOA financial statements. Thus, an audit of an OCBOA financial statement does not differ in approach or concept from that of an audit of a GAAP-based financial statement. The major difference is that the auditor first must determine whether the client's proposed OCBOA has authoritative support and then determine whether the financial statements are fairly presented according to the criteria associated with the alternative basis.

Recall that auditing involves testing assertions related to prescribed criteria. Thus, auditors may issue opinions on the fairness of the financial statements in accordance with the OCBOA used. It is important that the titles of the financial statements clearly indicate that these are not GAAP-based statements, such as "Statement of Assets, Liabilities, and Capital—Income Tax Basis" and "Statement of Revenue and Expenses—Income Tax Basis." Using such titles as "Balance Sheet" and "Income Statement" without modifiers implies the use of GAAP and should be avoided for these special reports. The reporting requirements are the same as for audit reports on GAAP-based statements except for bringing the reader's attention to the basis of accounting used.

An example of an audit report on financial statements prepared on a modified cash basis is presented in Exhibit 16.17. The titles of the financial statements are different from those for GAAP-based statements. The scope paragraph is the same as for an unqualified audit report on GAAP-based statements. There is, however, an added paragraph referring to a footnote that more fully describes the basis of accounting used and how that basis, in general, departs from GAAP. For the report in Exhibit 16.17, the auditors expressed an unqualified opinion that the financial statements are presented fairly, in all material respects, *on the cash basis of accounting as more fully described in the note.*

In evaluating the adequacy of the disclosures in OCBOA statements, the auditor should apply essentially the same criteria as for GAAP-based statements; the statements, including the accompanying notes, should include appropriate disclosures. The standards require a note summarizing the comprehensive basis of accounting used and a broad indication of how the statements differ from GAAP. In addition to the summary of significant accounting policies, notes typically cover areas such as debt, leases, pensions, related-party transactions, and uncertainties. Distribution of reports on

PRACTICAL POINT

Many smaller businesses often use OCBOAs because they are less costly. However, they do not measure financial results in the same manner as does GAAP.

PRACTICAL POINT

International Standards on Auditing require the auditor to determine whether the criteria for GAAP is established by a body that has the proper authority to set accounting standards and whether the accounting standards are sufficiently encompassing—especially if the body is other than the IASB.

Exhibit 16.17   Report on Modified Cash Basis Financial Statements

REPORT OF INDEPENDENT REGISTERED PUBLIC ACCOUNTING FIRM

UNIT HOLDERS OF SABINE ROYALTY TRUST AND BANK OF AMERICA, N.A., TRUSTEE

We have audited the accompanying statements of assets, liabilities and trust corpus of Sabine Royalty Trust (the "Trust") as of December 31, 2007 and 2006, and the related statements of distributable income and changes in trust corpus for each of the three years in the period ended December 31, 2007. These financial statements are the responsibility of the Trustee. Our responsibility is to express an opinion on these financial statements based on our audits.

[Standard scope paragraph]

As described in Note 2 to the financial statements, these statements were prepared on a modified cash basis of accounting, which is a comprehensive basis of accounting other than accounting principles generally accepted in the United States of America.

In our opinion, such consolidated financial statements present fairly, in all material respects, the assets, liabilities and trust corpus of the Trust at December 31, 2007 and 2006, and the distributable income and changes in trust corpus for each of the three years in the period ended December 31, 2007, on the basis of accounting described in Note 2.

[Last paragraph omitted]

/s/ DELOITTE & TOUCHE LLP
Dallas, Texas
March 11, 2008

Note: The trust is not the same as Bank of America. Rather it is a nonpublic trust that is managed for clients by Bank of America.

statements required for reporting to a regulatory agency should be restricted to the client and that agency.

Specified Elements, Accounts, or Items

Auditors are sometimes asked to express an opinion on one or more specific elements, accounts, or items in financial statements. Such items may be presented in the auditor's report or in a document accompanying the report. The audit may be undertaken as a separate engagement or in conjunction with the audit of financial statements. An audit client may be a retail company, for example, that leases a store. Part of the lease payments are based on the amount of revenues of the store, and the lease agreement may require that an independent auditor provide a report expressing an opinion on whether the revenue is reported to the lessor in accordance with the lease agreement.

The audit report (see Exhibit 16.18) should identify the specific elements, accounts, or items in a financial statement (the subject) and indicate whether the audit was made in conjunction with an audit of the company's financial statements. It should describe the basis on which the item or element is presented and, when applicable, any agreements specifying the basis of presentation if it is not in conformity with GAAP. If considered necessary, the report should include a description of significant interpretations made by the company's management regarding the relevant agreements. If the item or element is prepared to comply with the requirements of a contract or an agreement that results in a presentation that is not in conformity with either GAAP or OCBOA, a paragraph should be added restricting the distribution of the report to those within the entity and the parties to the contract or agreement.

The auditor is not required to do so, but may describe specific auditing procedures in a separate paragraph. The other reporting requirements are the same as for audit reports on GAAP-based financial statements, including the expression of an opinion.

Exhibit 16.18   Report on Specified Elements of a Financial Statement

REPORT OF INDEPENDENT REGISTERED PUBLIC ACCOUNTANT FIRM

To the Trustee on Behalf of Unit Holders of Sabine Royalty Trust:

We have audited the accompanying Statements of Fees and Expenses (as defined in Exhibit C to the Sabine Royalty Trust Agreement) paid by Sabine Royalty Trust to Bank of America, N.A., (the "Trustee"), as trustee and escrow agent, for the years ended December 31, 2007, 2006, and 2005. These statements are the responsibility of the Trustee's management. Our responsibility is to express an opinion on these statements based on our audits.

We conducted our audits in accordance with standards of the Public Company Accounting Oversight Board (United States). Those standards require that we plan and perform the audits to obtain reasonable assurance about whether the Statements of Fees and Expenses are free of material misstatement. An audit includes examining, on a test basis, evidence supporting the amounts and disclosures in the Statements of Fees and Expenses. An audit also includes assessing the accounting principles used and significant estimates made by management, as well as evaluating the overall statement presentation. We believe that our audits provide a reasonable basis for our opinion.

As described in Note 3, the Statements of Fees and Expenses were prepared on a modified cash basis of accounting, which is a comprehensive basis of accounting other than accounting principles generally accepted in the United States of America.

In our opinion, the Statements of Fees and Expenses referred to above present fairly, in all material respects, the fees and expenses paid by Sabine Royalty Trust to Bank of America, N.A., as trustee and escrow agent, for the years ended December 31, 2007, 2006, and 2005, on the basis of accounting described in Note 3.

/s/ PRICEWATERHOUSECOOPERS LLP
PricewaterhouseCoopers LLP
Dallas, Texas
March 12, 2008

Compliance with Contractual Agreements or Regulatory Requirements

Auditors are sometimes requested to furnish a report on the client's compliance with specific contractual agreements or regulations. Auditors may issue such reports as long as the covenants of the agreement or regulatory requirement are *based on information from audited financial statements*. In other words, before a compliance report may be issued, the auditor must have assurance that the financial information subject to the covenants is fairly presented. A bond indenture, for example, may require the bond issuer to maintain a minimum current ratio, to make minimum payments into a sinking fund, or limit dividends to a certain percentage of net income. If such requirements or restrictions are violated, the bonds may become payable on demand of the bondholders rather than at their scheduled maturity date.

A compliance report normally contains *negative assurance* and may be given in a separate report or with the auditor's report accompanying the financial statements. Recall that a negative assurance report simply indicates that the auditor did not find anything that would lead the auditor to conclude that the report is not fairly stated. The report (see Exhibit 16.19) should include a reference to the audited financial statements, specific covenants, and a statement of negative assurance.

PRACTICAL POINT

The description of reports in this section applies to CPAs who are functioning in their external audit role. CPA firms that are providing outsourced internal audit work to clients can issue the reports to their clients with an understanding that such reports are for management's exclusive use.

Circumstances Requiring Explanatory Language in a Special Report

Explanatory language should be added to any of the special reports described in the previous sections when:

- There has been a change in accounting principles that materially affected the subject of the report

Exhibit 16.19	Report on Compliance with a Contractual Agreement

INDEPENDENT AUDITOR'S REPORT

To the Board of Directors and Management of Actup Company and First National Bank of Brace:

We have audited, in accordance with generally accepted auditing standards, the balance sheet of Actup Company as of December 31, 2011, and the related statements of income, retained earnings, and cash flows for the year then ended, and have issued our report thereon dated February 27, 2012.

In connection with our audit, nothing came to our attention that caused us to believe that the company failed to comply with the terms, covenants, provisions, and conditions of sections 25 to 33, inclusive, of the Indenture dated July 23, 2008, with First National Bank of Brace insofar as they relate to accounting matters. However, our audit was not directed primarily toward obtaining knowledge of such noncompliance.

This report is intended solely for the information and use of the boards of directors and management of Actup Company and First National Bank of Brace and should not be used for any other purpose.

/s/ Rittenberg, Johnstone, & Gramling, LLP
Madison, WI
March 3, 2012

PRACTICAL POINT

Many companies provide a variety of information—including annual, quarterly, and even monthly financial information—through their home pages on the Internet. Even if the auditor's report is included with this information, auditors are not yet required to read or consider the consistency of the other information provided by the company on the Internet unless it is included within a formal document such as a 10-K.

LO 7

Describe various attestation engagements and the types of reports that will be issued for these engagements.

- The auditor has substantial doubt about the organization's ability to continue as a going concern
- The auditor makes reference to the report of another auditor as a basis, in part, for his or her opinion
- The auditor expresses an opinion on prior-period information that is different from the opinion previously expressed on that same information

Attesting to Other Information Provided by Management

In addition to providing assurance on the financial information discussed in the preceding sections, the public accounting profession continues to develop criteria and standards to meet the changing needs of the business community. Many of the approaches developed in this textbook for planning, gathering evidence, and reporting on historical financial statements are applicable to this wider scope of services where CPAs can attest to the reliability of a variety of information provided by client management. For example, auditors might attest to some aspect of a company's operations, such as whether the company meets ISO 9000 criteria or whether their XBRL data filed with the SEC agree with their other SEC filings. They may be asked by clients to perform and report on agreed-upon procedures. They may report on prospective financial statements, pro forma financial information, and compliance with laws and regulations.

Attesting to Financial Reporting Using XBRL

Since 2004, the Securities and Exchange Commission (SEC) has taken steps toward requiring XBRL (eXtensible Business Reporting Language) to be used in its filings. The SEC's XBRL Voluntary Filing Program was created to encourage public companies to use interactive data to make it easier for investors to get and use information from SEC filings. The interactive data are basically computer "tags" similar to bar codes used to identify groceries and shipped packages. The interactive data tags uniquely identify individual items in a company's financial statement. The process of tagging financial statement items allows for items to be easily searched on the Internet, downloaded into spreadsheets, reorganized in databases, and used in any number of other comparative and analytical ways by interested users such as analysts, researchers, and investors.

Effective April 13, 2009, the SEC requires domestic and foreign large accelerated filers with over $5 billion in worldwide public common equity float to start submitting XBRL data for periods after June 15, 2009. Requirements are phased in for smaller filers with a requirement to begin for periods either after June 15, 2010, or June 15, 2011, depending on the size of the filing company. The interactive data does not replace the annual financial statements, but must be filed at the same time as the annual financial statements.

Currently, auditor assurance on the tagging process is not required. However, it is likely once XBRL becomes required that there may be a demand for such assurance. Under current standards, an auditor may be engaged to examine and report on whether the XBRL-related documents accurately reflect the information in the corresponding part of the official SEC filings. That engagement is an examination under AT section 101 of the PCAOB's interim attestation standards, *Attest Engagements*. The objectives of this examination are to determine whether:

- the XBRL data agree with the official SEC filings, and
- the XBRL-related documents are in conformity with the applicable XBRL taxonomies and specifications, as well as with the SEC requirements for format and content.

Some of the procedures that the auditor would perform to accomplish these objectives include:

- Comparing the human-readable form of the XBRL-related documents to the information in the official SEC filing
- Determining whether the content in the XBRL-related documents conforms to the SEC requirements
- Evaluating whether the XBRL-related documents comply with the appropriate XBRL and SEC supported XBRL taxonomies
- Testing whether data elements in the XBRL-related documents are matched with appropriate tags in accordance with the applicable taxonomy
- Obtaining a representation letter from management that includes a statement that the XBRL-related documents comply with relevant SEC requirements

The auditor would follow the standards of reporting for attestation engagements that are provided in AT 101. Generally, these standards require the auditor to state the subject matter or the assertion being reported on, provide a conclusion on the subject matter or assertion in relation to relevant criteria, state any reservations about the engagement or the subject matter or assertion, and in some situations, state the restrictions on the use of the report.

Agreed-Upon Procedures

CPAs may be engaged by clients to issue a report of findings based on procedures specified by the client and CPA that are believed to be appropriate to the client's needs. Such an engagement is less in scope than an audit or review.

PRACTICAL POINT

The AICPA provides general standards for attestation engagements for which there is a commonality in reporting and evidence-gathering procedures. Other specific guidance is provided for the following types of services: agreed-upon procedures, financial forecasts and projections, pro forma financial information, internal control in an integrated audit, compliance, management discussion and analysis, and controls at a service organization.

PRACTICAL POINT

A number of countries already require public companies to provide their financial reports using interactive data.

Reports on agreed-upon procedures include a list of the procedures performed, related findings, and a restriction on the use of the report to specified parties. No assurance is provided in these engagements.

Financial Forecasts and Projections

Prospective financial statements are of two types—forecasts and projections. Forecasts are based on management's expected financial position, results of operations, and cash flows. Projections are "what-if" statements: "If we get the loan to expand, this will be the expected financial position, results of operations, and cash flows." CPAs may compile or examine prospective financial statements. *Compilations* involve assembling the prospective statements based on management's assumptions. The compilation report provides *no assurance* about the financial statements or the reasonableness of the assumptions. *Examinations* (the highest level of service) involve evaluating the preparation of the statements, the support underlying the assumptions, and the presentation of the statements. The examination report includes an *opinion* on the statements and underlying assumptions.

Pro Forma Financial Information

Pro forma financial information is historical "what-if" information. For example, stockholders will be provided pro forma information concerning a proposed merger or acquisition of another company or disposition of a significant portion of the existing business. The pro forma information shows what the significant effects might have been had a consummated or proposed transaction (or event) occurred at an earlier date. CPAs may review or examine pro forma information. *Review reports* provide *negative assurance* while *examination reports* provide an *opinion* about management's assumptions, related adjustments, and application of those adjustments to the historical financial statements.

Compliance Attestation

During the course of a normal audit, the auditor tests compliance with laws and regulations that could have a direct, material effect on the financial statements, such as those related to income taxes. As described earlier in this chapter, CPAs may be asked to provide a "special report" on compliance based solely on an audit of financial statements.

There are other situations in which a client engages the CPA to specifically report on either (a) an entity's compliance with requirements of specified laws, regulations, rules, contracts, or grants or (b) the effectiveness of an entity's internal control over compliance with specified requirements. Compliance requirements may be either financial or nonfinancial in nature. Such reports do not provide a legal determination of an entity's compliance, but may be useful to legal counsel or others in making such determinations. CPAs may perform an examination engagement or an agreed-upon procedures engagement on compliance. An *examination report* includes an opinion on compliance with the specified requirements based on specified criteria. An alternative is an *agreed-upon procedures engagement* designed to present specific findings, based on limited procedures, to assist users in evaluating an entity's compliance with specified requirements.

Summary

Auditors provide a variety of services on which they must report. Three basic levels of assurance are contained in those reports: positive assurance (an opinion), negative/limited assurance, and no assurance (disclaimer or compilation). Users of these reports do not have access to the audit documentation of the evidence gathered. Therefore, it is extremely important that auditors be very careful when preparing the reports. Failure to do so can lead to lawsuits and a loss of public confidence in the profession.

Significant Terms

Compilation   A level of service that involves presenting, in the form of financial statements, information that is the representation of management and results in a disclaimer (no assurance about the fairness of the financial statements). Such a service can be provided only to nonpublic companies.

Limited assurance   A statement by the accountant in a report that nothing has been detected to indicate that the information needs to be changed to bring it into conformity with the appropriate criteria, such as GAAP.

Negative assurance   See limited assurance.

Other comprehensive basis of accounting (OCBOA)   Financial statements prepared on a cash or modified cash basis, the basis of accounting used for preparing the income tax return, the basis of accounting required for reporting to a governmental regulatory agency, or some other basis with a definite set of criteria that have substantial support and apply to all material items appearing in the financial statements.

Reissue   To reissue a previously issued audit report on which no audit work has been done after the original report date. A reissued report contains the original report date.

Review   A level of service related to financial statements that involves making inquiries and performing analytical procedures, resulting in limited assurance about the fairness of the financial statements.

Shared report   An audit report that indicates other auditors performed part of the audit.

Special reports   Reports on the following types of situations in which the client engages the auditor to perform specific procedures: to report on financial statements prepared in conformity with a comprehensive basis of accounting other than GAAP; to report on specified elements, accounts, or items of a financial statement; or to report on compliance with aspects of contractual agreements or regulatory requirements related to audited financial statements.

Uncertainties   Situations in which the outcome of some matter cannot be determined as of the end of the audit fieldwork, such as the results of pending litigation.

Update   Regarding the audit report, the process of considering information that comes to the auditor's attention during the current-year audit but is related to prior-year statements presented for comparative purposes. The report date should be the end of the current-year fieldwork.

SELECTED REFERENCES TO RELEVANT PROFESSIONAL GUIDANCE	
Topic	**Selected Guidance**
Attestation Reports	SSAE 10 *Attest Engagements*
	SSAE 10 *Agreed-Upon Procedures Engagements*
	SSAE 10 *Financial Forecasts and Projections*
	SSAE 10 *Reporting on Pro Forma Financial Information*
	SSAE 10 *Compliance Attestation*
	SSAE 10 *Management Discussion and Analysis*
	SSAE 13 *Defining Professional Requirements in Statements on Standards for Attestation Engagements*
	SSAE 15 *An Examination of an Entity's Internal Control Over Financial Reporting That Is Integrated with an Audit of Its Financial Statements*

	SSAE 16 *Reporting on Controls at a Service Organization*
	Proposed SSAE *Reporting on Compiled Prospective Financial Statements When the Practitioner's Independence Is Impaired*
Reports for Accounting and Review Services	SSARS No. 1 *Compilation and Review of Financial Statements*
	AICPA Audit Risk Alert *Compilation and Review Developments—2010/11*
	IAASB International Standard on Review Engagements (ISRE) 2400 *Engagements to Review Financial Statements*
	IAASB International Standard on Review Engagements (ISRE) 2400 *Engagements to Review Financial Statements*
	IAASB International Standard on Review Engagements (ISRE) 2410 *Review of Interim Financial Information Performed by the Independent Auditor of the Entity*
Reports for Financial Statement Audits	SAS 1, Section 543 *Part of Audit Performed by Other Independent Auditors*
	SAS 26 *Association with Financial Statements*
	SAS 58 *Reports on Audited Financial Statements*
	SAS 59 *The Auditor's Consideration of an Entity's Ability to Continue as a Going Concern*
	SAS 62 *Special Reports*
	SAS 87 *Restricting the Use of an Auditor's Report*
	SAS *Overall Objectives of the Independent Auditor and Conduct of an Audit in Accordance with Generally Accepted Auditing Standards* (issued but not effective, proposed effective date is December 2012)
	SAS *Preface to Codification of Statements on Auditing Standards, Principles Underlying an Audit Conducted in Accordance with Generally Accepted Auditing Standards* (issued but not effective, proposed effective date is December 2012)
	Proposed SAS *Audits of Group Financial Statements (Including the Work of Component Auditors)* (issued but not effective; proposed effective date is December 2012)
	Proposed SAS *Forming an Opinion and Reporting on Financial Statements* (issued but not effective; proposed effective date is December 2012)
	Proposed SAS *Modifications to the Opinion in the Independent Auditor's Report* (issued but not effective; proposed effective date is December 2012)
	Proposed SAS *Emphasis of Matter Paragraphs and Other Matter Paragraphs in the Independent Auditor's Report* (issued but not effective; proposed effective date is December 2012)
	Proposed SAS *Reporting on Compliance with Aspects of Contractual Agreements or Regulatory Requirements in Connection with Audited Financial Statements* (Redrafted) (issued but not effective; proposed effective date is December 2012)
	Proposed SAS *Special Considerations—Audits of Financial Statements Prepared in Accordance with Special Purpose Frameworks* (issued but not effective; proposed effective date is December 2012)
	Proposed SAS *Special Considerations—Audits of Single Financial Statements and Specific Elements, Accounts, or Items of a Financial Statement* (issued but not effective; proposed effective date is December 2012)
	AS 5 *An Audit of Internal Control over Financial Reporting That Is Integrated with an Audit of Financial Statements*
	ISA 200 *Overall Objectives of the Independent Auditor and the Conduct of an Audit in Accordance with International Standards on Auditing ISA 570 Going Concern*
	ISA 600 *Using the Work of Another Auditor*
	ISA 700 *The Independent Auditor's Report on a Complete Set of General-Purpose Financial Statements*
	ISA 705 *Modifications to the Opinion in the Independent Auditor's Report*
	ISA 706 *Emphasis of Matter Paragraphs and Other Matter Paragraphs in the Independent Auditor's Report*
	ISA 710 *Comparative Information-Corresponding Figures and Comparative Financial Statements*
	ISA 720 *The Auditor's Responsibilities Relating to Other Information in Documents Containing Audited Financial Statements*
	ISA 800 *Special Considerations-Audits of Financial Statements Prepared in Accordance with Special Purpose Frameworks*
	ISA 805 *Special Considerations-Audits of Single Financial Statements and Specific Elements, Accounts or Items of a Financial Statement*
	ISA 810 *Engagements to Report on Summary Financial Statements*

Note: *Acronyms for Relevant Professional Guidance*

STANDARDS: **AS**—Auditing Standard issued by the PCAOB; **ISA**—International Standard on Auditing issued by the IAASB; **SAS**—Statement on Auditing Standards issued by the Auditing Standards Board of the AICPA; **SSAE**—Statement on Standards for Attestation Engagements issued by the AICPA.

ORGANIZATIONS: **AICPA**—American Institute of Certified Public Accountants; **COSO**—Committee of Sponsoring Organizations; **IAASB**—International Auditing and Assurance Standards Board; **PCAOB**—Public Company Accounting Oversight Board; **SEC**—Securities and Exchange Commission.

Review Questions

16-1 **(LO 3)** Identify the five basic types of financial statement audit reports and explain the circumstances under which each report is appropriate.

16-2 **(LO 3)** What is the difference between a scope limitation and an uncertainty? Give an example of each.

16-3 **(LO 3)** What types of audit opinions are not accepted by the SEC? How do the SEC's requirements affect the conflicts that may arise between the client and the auditor? Discuss potential ethical implications of such conflicts.

Ethics

16-4 **(LO 3)** What factors must the auditor consider when determining whether the financial statements are presented in conformity with generally accepted accounting principles?

16-5 **(LO 3)** Under what circumstances may an auditor express an unqualified opinion when the related financial statements contain a material departure from a FASB or GASB standard?

16-6 **(LO 3)** Under what circumstances must the auditor's report refer to the consistency, or the lack of consistency, in the application of GAAP? What is the purpose of such reporting?

16-7 **(LO 2)** Under what circumstances must the auditor of a public company express an adverse opinion on the client's internal controls over financial reporting?

16-8 **(LO 3)** Why should the auditor ordinarily disclaim an opinion when the client imposes significant limitations on the audit procedures?

16-9 **(LO 3)** Under what circumstances might the auditor choose not to refer to other auditors who worked on a part of the audit? What is a shared report? If the other auditors did not use due professional care and they are mentioned in the audit report, who is ultimately responsible, the principal auditor or the other auditors?

16-10 **(LO 3)** Are comparative financial statements required by GAAP or the SEC? Explain.

16-11 **(LO 3)** GAAS requires that the auditor express an opinion on the financial statements as a whole.

a. Does this mean that the auditor must express the same opinion on all of the financial statements for a particular year? Explain.

b. Does this mean that the auditor must express an opinion on all of the years presented with the current year for comparative purposes if the same public accounting firm audited all years?

c. Explain how the successor's audit report on comparative financial statements should be presented if the predecessor auditor:

(1) Reissues the report on prior years.

(2) Does not reissue the report on prior years.

16-12 **(LO 3)** How would the auditor's opinion differ if the financial statements of a company that was a foreign private issuer were prepared in conformity with IFRS and filed with the SEC rather than prepared in conformity with U.S. GAAP? What other differences exist in the standard audit reports issued in international jurisdictions?

International

16-13   **(LO 4)** What is:

a. A compilation

b. A review

16-14   **(LO 4)** Compare audits, reviews, and compilations in terms of:

a. The types of procedures performed. Consider the following types of procedures in your response:

- Assessing control risk.

- Performing substantive tests of transactions and balances.

- Performing analytical procedures.

- Making inquiries of client personnel to verify or corroborate information supplied by the client.

- Obtaining knowledge of the client's organization, assets, liabilities, revenues, expenses, operations, locations, and transactions with related parties.

- Obtaining knowledge of the accounting principles and practices of the industry.

- Obtaining knowledge of the client's transactions, form of accounting records, qualifications of accounting personnel, the accounting basis to be used for the financial statements and the form and content of the statements.

b. The level of assurance expressed by the accountant.

c. In which situation would an accountant's standard report be least affected by a lack of independence—an audit, review, or compilation? Explain.

16-15   **(LO 6)** What is a special report? When might a special report be issued? What is meant by the phrase *other comprehensive basis of accounting?*

16-16   **(LO 6)** How does an audit report containing an unqualified opinion on financial statements prepared on the cash basis differ from one issued on GAAP-based financial statements?

16-17   **(LO 3)** Why would a client want to issue OCBOA financial statements when it is specifically noted that they are not prepared in accordance with GAAP?

16-18   **(LO 1, 5)** What level of assurance is provided in a CPA's review report of interim financial statements?

16-19   **(LO 5)** Under what circumstances would the auditor's report have to be modified because of the interim information contained in the annual report to shareholders?

16-20   **(LO 7)** Describe the nature of the audit opinion in the auditors' reports on:

a. Prospective financial information

b. Pro forma financial information

c. Compliance engagements

d. Agreed-upon procedures engagements

e. XBRL

16-21   **(LO 3)** Should reports on agreed-upon procedure engagements be widely distributed? Explain.

Multiple-Choice Questions

*16-22 **(LO 3)** In which of the following circumstances would an auditor be most likely to express an adverse opinion on a company's financial statements?

a. Information comes to the auditor's attention that raises substantial doubt about the entity's ability to continue as a going concern.

b. The chief executive officer refuses the auditor access to minutes of board of directors' meetings.

c. Tests of controls show that the entity's internal control structure is so poor that it cannot be relied on.

d. The financial statements are not in conformity with FASB statements regarding the capitalization of leases.

*16-23 **(LO 3)** Tech Company has an uncertainty because of pending litigation. The auditor's decision to issue a qualified opinion rather than an unqualified opinion most likely would be determined by which of the following?

a. Lack of sufficient evidence.

b. Inability to estimate the amount of loss.

c. Entity's lack of experience with such litigation.

d. Adequacy of the disclosures.

*16-24 **(LO 3)** In which of the following situations would an auditor ordinarily issue an unqualified audit opinion without an explanatory paragraph?

a. The auditor wishes to emphasize that the entity had significant related-party transactions.

b. The auditor decides to refer to the report of another auditor as a basis, in part, for the auditor's opinion.

c. The entity issues financial statements that present financial position and results of operations but omits the statement of cash flows.

d. The auditor has substantial doubt about the entity's ability to continue as a going concern, but the circumstances are fully disclosed in the financial statements.

16-25 **(LO 3)** Comparative financial statements include the prior-year statements that were audited by a predecessor auditor whose report is not presented. If the predecessor's report were unqualified, the successor should do which of the following?

a. Express an opinion on the current-year statements alone and make no reference to the prior-year statements.

b. Indicate in the auditor's report that the predecessor auditor expressed an unqualified opinion.

c. Obtain a letter of representation from the predecessor concerning any matters that might affect the successor's opinion.

d. Request that the predecessor auditor reissue the prior-year report.

---

*All problems marked with an asterisk are adapted from the Uniform CPA Examination.

16-26   **(LO 3)** Eagle Company's financial statements contain a departure from GAAP because, due to unusual circumstances, the statements would otherwise be misleading. The auditor should express an opinion that is:

a. Unqualified, but not mention the departure in the auditor's report.

b. Unqualified, and describe the departure in a separate paragraph.

c. Qualified, and describe the departure in a separate paragraph.

d. Qualified or adverse, depending on materiality, and describe the departure in a separate paragraph.

16-27   **(LO 3)** Tread Corp. accounts for the effect of a material accounting change prospectively when the inclusion of the cumulative effect of the change is required in the current year. The auditor would choose which of the following opinions?

a. Qualified opinion or a disclaimer of opinion.

b. Disclaimer of opinion or an unqualified opinion with an explanatory paragraph.

c. Unqualified opinion with an explanatory paragraph or an adverse opinion.

d. Qualified opinion or adverse opinion.

16-28   **(LO 3)** In which of the following circumstances would an auditor usually choose between issuing a qualified opinion or a disclaimer of opinion?

a. Departure from GAAP

b. Inadequate disclosure of accounting policies

c. Inability to obtain sufficient competent evidential matter for a reason other than a management-imposed scope restriction

d. Unreasonable justification for a change in accounting principle

16-29   **(LO 2)** The auditor of a public company believes there is a material weakness in the client's internal controls over financial reporting. Which of the following statements is true?

a. Such a weakness will require an adverse opinion of the financial statements.

b. The auditor should express an adverse opinion on internal controls only if they resulted in a material misstatement in the financial statements.

c. The auditor should express an adverse opinion on the internal controls even though no material misstatements were found in the financial statements.

d. The auditor is not required to express an opinion on internal controls.

16-30   **(LO 5)** An auditor's report would be designated a special report when it is issued in connection with which of the following?

a. Compliance with aspects of regulatory requirements related to audited financial statements.

b. Interim financial information of a publicly held company that is subject to a limited review.

    c. Application of accounting principles to specified transactions.

    d. Appropriate data tagging in XBRL reports.

*16-31   **(LO 4)** During a review of the financial statements of a nonpublic entity, an accountant becomes aware of the lack of adequate disclosure that is material to the financial statements. If management refuses to correct the financial statement presentations, which of the following should the accountant do?

    a. Issue an adverse opinion.

    b. Issue an "except for" qualified opinion.

    c. Disclose this departure from GAAP in a separate paragraph of the report.

    d. Express only limited assurance on the financial statement presentations.

*16-32   **(LO 4)** Before issuing a report on the compilation of financial statements of a nonpublic entity, the accountant should do which of the following?

    a. Apply analytical procedures to selected financial data to discover any material misstatements.

    b. Corroborate at least a sample of the assertions management has embodied in the financial statements.

    c. Inquire of the client's personnel whether the financial statements omit substantially all disclosures.

    d. Read the financial statements to consider whether they are free from obvious material errors.

*16-33   **(LO 4)** Laura Baker, CPA, was engaged to review the financial statements of Hall Company, a nonpublic entity. Evidence came to Baker's attention indicating substantial doubt regarding Hall's ability to continue as a going concern. The principal conditions and events that caused the substantial doubt have been fully disclosed in the notes to Hall's financial statements. Which of the following statements best describes Baker's reporting responsibility concerning this matter?

    a. Baker is not required to modify the accountant's review report.

    b. Baker is not permitted to modify the accountant's review report.

    c. Baker should issue an accountant's compilation report instead of a review report.

    d. Baker should express a qualified opinion in the accountant's review report.

*16-34   **(LO 4)** Which of the following statements should be included in an accountant's standard report based on the compilation of a nonpublic entity's financial statements?

    a. A compilation consists principally of inquiries of company personnel and analytical procedures applied to financial data.

    b. A compilation is limited to presenting in the form of financial statements information that is the representation of management.

    c. A compilation is not designed to detect material modifications that should be made to the financial statements.

    d. A compilation is substantially smaller in scope than an audit in accordance with GAAS.

*16-35 **(LO 4)** When an accountant is engaged to compile a nonpublic entity's financial statements that omit substantially all disclosures required by GAAP, the accountant should indicate in the compilation report that the financial statements are:

a. Not designed for those who are uninformed about the omitted disclosures.

b. Prepared in conformity with a comprehensive basis of accounting other than GAAP.

c. Not compiled in accordance with Statements on Standards for Accounting and Review Services.

d. Special-purpose financial statements that are not comparable to those of prior periods.

*16-36 **(LO 6)** An auditor's report on financial statements prepared on the cash receipts and disbursements basis of accounting should include all of the following *except*:

a. A reference to the note to the financial statements that describes the cash receipts and disbursements basis of accounting.

b. A statement that the cash receipts and disbursements basis of accounting is not a comprehensive basis of accounting.

c. An opinion as to whether the financial statements are presented fairly in conformity with the cash receipts and disbursements basis of accounting.

d. A statement that the audit was conducted in accordance with GAAS.

*16-37 **(LO 5)** The objective of a review of interim financial information of a public entity is to provide an accountant with a basis for reporting whether:

a. Material modifications should be made to conform to GAAP.

b. A reasonable basis exists for expressing an opinion regarding the financial statements that were previously audited.

c. Condensed financial statements or pro forma financial information should be included in a registration statement.

d. The financial statements are presented fairly in accordance with GAAP.

Discussion and Research Questions

International

Internet

16-38 **(Comparison of U.S. and International Audit Reports, LO 2)** Use the Internet to locate the financial statements (and associated audit report) of one company reporting using U.S. accounting standards and another company reporting using international accounting standards.

Required

a. Describe key differences between the two audit reports.

b. Articulate how these differences may affect the relative informativeness of the audit report to users. Which of the reports do you find most useful and why?

c. International audit reports generally are signed by the engagement partner who supervised the audit, whereas such disclosures are not required in the United States. Why is the public disclosure of the engagement partner's name useful? Why might partners in the United States prefer not to sign their names to audit reports? What implications may this difference have for users of the audit reports?

16-39   **(Implications of Risk in Standard Audit Report, LO 2)** What words and phrases in an unqualified audit report imply that there is a risk that the financial statements may contain a material misstatement?

16-40   **(Critique an Audit Report Qualified for a Scope Limitation, LO 3)** You are a senior auditor working for Rittenberg & Schwieger, CPAs. Your staff assistant has drafted the following audit report of a publicly traded U.S. company. You believe the scope limitation is significant enough to qualify the opinion, but not to disclaim an opinion.

To Joseph Halberg, Controller
Billings Container Company, Inc.

We have audited the accompanying balance sheet of Billings Container Company and the related statements of income, retained earnings, and statement of changes in financial position as of December 31, 2012. These financial statements are the responsibility of the Company's management.

Except as discussed in the following paragraph, we conducted our audit in accordance with accounting principles generally accepted in the United States of America. Those standards require that we plan and perform the audit to obtain assurance about whether the financial statements are free of misstatement. An audit includes examining evidence supporting the amounts and disclosures in the financial statements. An audit also includes assessing the accounting principles used as well as evaluating the overall financial statement presentation. We believe that our audit provides a reasonable basis for our opinion.

We were unable to obtain sufficient competent evidence of the fair market value of the Company's investment in a real estate venture due to the unique nature of the venture. The investment is accounted for using the equity method and is stated at $450,000 and $398,000 at December 31, 2012 and 2011, respectively.

In our opinion, except for the above-mentioned limitation on the scope of our audit, the financial statements referred to above present fairly the financial position of Billings Container Company as of December 31, 2012 and 2011, and the results of its operations and its cash flows for the year then ended in conformity with auditing standards generally accepted in the United States of America.

/s/Bradley Schwieger, CPA
St. Cloud, MN
December 31, 2012

Required

Identify the deficiencies in this draft and state how each deficiency should be corrected. Organize your answer around the components of the audit report (introductory paragraph, scope paragraph, and so on).

16-41   **(Choosing the Type of Opinion, LO 3)** Several independent audit situations are presented here. Assume that everything other than what is described would have resulted in an unqualified opinion on the company's financial statements. At your instructor's discretion, complete this problem in small-group format in class.

Required

Indicate the type of opinion you believe should be expressed in each situation and explain your choice. If an explanatory paragraph is needed, indicate whether it should precede or follow the opinion paragraph.

a. The auditor was unable to obtain confirmations from two of the client's major customers that were included in the sample. These customers wrote on the confirmation letters that they were unable to confirm the balances because of their accounting systems. The auditor was able to achieve satisfaction through other audit procedures.

b. The client treated a lease as an operating lease, but the auditor believes it should have been accounted for as a capital lease. The effects are material.

c. The client changed from FIFO to LIFO this year. The effect is material. Address each of the following situations:

(i) The change was properly accounted for, justified, and disclosed.

(ii) The change was properly accounted for and disclosed but was not properly justified.

d. The client restricted the auditor from observing the physical inventory. Inventory is a material item.

e. The client is engaged in a product liability lawsuit that is properly accounted for and adequately described in the footnotes. The lawsuit does not threaten the going-concern assumption, but an adverse decision by the court could create a material obligation for the client.

f. The status of the client as a going concern is extremely doubtful. The problems are properly described in the footnotes.

g. One of your client's subsidiaries was audited by another audit firm, whose opinion was qualified because of a GAAP violation. You do not believe that the GAAP violation is material to the consolidated financial statements on which you are expressing an opinion.

h. You are convinced that your client is violating another company's patent in the process of manufacturing its only product. The client will not disclose this because it does not want to wave a red flag and bring this violation to the other company's attention. A preliminary estimate is that the royalty payments required would be material to the financial statements.

i. The client, with reasonable justification, has changed its method of accounting for depreciation for all factory and office equipment. The effect of this change is not material to the current year financial statements, but is likely to have a material effect in future years. The client's management will not disclose this change because of the immaterial effect on the current-year statements. You have been unable to persuade management to make the disclosure.

16-42 **(Audit Reports, LO 3)** The following are independent audit situations for which you will recommend an appropriate audit report from the types listed. For each situation, identify the appropriate type of audit report from the list below and briefly explain the rationale for selecting the report. At your instructor's discretion, complete this problem in small-group format in class.

Group Activity

Appropriate type of audit report:

a. Unqualified, standard

b. Unqualified, explanatory paragraph

c. Qualified opinion because of departure from GAAP

d. Qualified scope and opinion

e. Disclaimer

f. Adverse

Audit Situations

1. An audit client has a significant amount of loans receivable outstanding (40% of assets) but has an inadequate internal control system over the loans. The auditor cannot locate sufficient information to prepare an aging of the loans or to identify the collateral for about 75% of the loans, even though the client states that all loans are collateralized. The auditor sent out confirmations to verify the existence of the receivables, but only ten of the fifty sent out were returned. The auditor attempts to verify the other loans by looking at subsequent payments, but only eight had remitted payments during the month of January, and the auditor wants to wrap up the audit by February 15. If only ten of the fifty loans were correctly recorded, the auditor estimates that loans would need to be written down by $7.5 million.

2. During the audit of a large manufacturing company, the auditor did not observe all locations of physical inventory. The auditor chose a random number of sites to visit, and the company's internal auditors visited the other sites. The auditor has confidence in the competence and objectivity of the internal auditors. The auditor personally observed only about 20% of the total inventory, but neither the auditor nor the internal auditors noted any exceptions in the inventory process.

3. During the past year Network Computer, Inc. devoted its entire research and development efforts to develop and market an enhanced version of its state-of-the-art telecommunications system. The costs, which were significant, were all capitalized as research and development costs. The company plans to amortize these capitalized costs over the life of the new product. The auditor has concluded that the research to date will likely result in a marketable product. A full description of the research and development, and the costs, is included in a note. The note also describes that basic research costs are expensed as incurred, and the auditor has verified the accuracy of the statement.

4. During the course of the audit of Sail-Away Company, the auditor noted that the current ratio had dropped to 1.75. The company's loan covenant requires the maintenance of a current ratio of 2.0 to 1.0, or the company's debt is all immediately due. The auditor and the company have contacted the bank, which is not willing to

waive the loan covenant because the company has been experiencing operating losses for the past few years and has an inadequate capital structure. The auditor has substantial doubt that the company can find adequate financing elsewhere and may encounter difficulties staying in operation. Management, however, is confident that it can overcome the problem. The company does not deem it necessary to include any additional disclosure because management members are confident that an alternative source of funds will be found by pledging their personal assets.

5. The Wear-Ever Wholesale Company has been very profitable. It recently received notice of a 10% price increase for a significant portion of its inventory. The company believes it is important to manage its products wisely and has a policy of writing all inventory up to current replacement cost. This assures that profits will be recognized on sales sufficient to replace the assets and realize a normal profit. This operating philosophy has been very successful, and all salespeople reference current cost, not historical cost, in making sales. Only inventory has been written up to replacement cost, but inventory is material because the company carries a wide range of products. The company's policy of writing up the inventory and its dollar effects is adequately described in a footnote to the financial statements. For the current year, the net effect of the inventory write-up increased reported income by only 3% and assets by 15% above historical cost.

6. The audit of NewCo was staffed primarily by three new hires and a relatively inexperienced audit senior. The manager found numerous errors during the conduct of the audit and developed very long "to-do" lists for all members of the audit to complete before the audit was concluded. Although the manager originally doubted the staff's understanding of the audit procedures, by the time the audit was finished, he concluded that the new auditors did understand the company and the audit process and that no material errors existed in the financial statements.

16-43   **(Reporting on Accounting Changes, LO 3)** The accounting and auditing literature discusses several different types of accounting changes:

1. Change from one GAAP to another GAAP
2. Change in accounting estimate
3. Change in estimate affected by a change in accounting principle
4. Correction of an error
5. Change from non-GAAP to GAAP (a special case of correction of an error)
6. Change in reporting entity

Required

For which of these types of changes should the auditor add a paragraph to the audit report, assuming that the change had a material effect on the financial statements and was properly justified, accounted for, and disclosed?

16-44 **(Audit Reports and Consistency, LO 3)** Various types of accounting changes can affect the second reporting standard of GAAS. This standard reads: "The auditor must identify in the auditor's report those circumstances in which such principles have not been consistently observed in the current period in relation to the preceding period."

Required

a. Briefly describe the rationale for the standard and the auditor's responsibility in adhering to the standard.

b. For each of the changes listed here, briefly indicate the type of change and its effect on the auditor's report.

   1. A change from the completed-contract method to the percentage-of-completion method of accounting for long-term construction contracts.

   2. A change in the estimated useful life of previously recorded fixed assets. (The change is based on newly acquired information.)

   3. Correction of a mathematical error in inventory pricing made in a prior period.

   4. A change from full absorption costing to direct costing for inventory valuation.

   5. A change from presentation of statements of individual companies to presentation of consolidated companies.

   6. A change from deferring and amortizing preproduction costs to recording such costs as an expense when incurred, because future benefits of the costs have become doubtful. (The new accounting method was adopted in recognition of the change in estimated future benefits.)

   7. A change from amortizing goodwill to testing for impairment each year. (The change was in response to an accounting pronouncement from the FASB.)

   8. A change to include the employer's share of FICA taxes as retirement benefits on the income statement from including it in other taxes.

16-45 **(Other Auditors, LO 3)** You are in charge of the audit of the financial statements of Parat, Inc. and consolidated subsidiaries covering the two years ended December 31, 2012. Another public accounting firm is auditing Nuam, Inc., a major subsidiary that accounts for total assets, revenue, and net income of 30%, 26%, and 39%, respectively, for 2011; and 28%, 20%, and 33% for 2012.

Required

a. What is meant by the term *principal auditor*?

b. What factors should be considered when determining which public accounting firm should serve as the principal auditor?

c. Under what circumstances might the principal auditor decide not to refer to the other audit firm in the audit report on the consolidated statements?

d. If the principal auditor does not refer to the other auditor in the audit report, who is ultimately responsible to third parties if the other auditor was fraudulent or grossly negligent?

e. Write the audit report referring to the other audit firm and expressing an unqualified opinion.

*16-46 **(Critique of Audit Report—Going-Concern Doubt, LO 3)** The following auditor's report was drafted by a staff accountant of Turner & Turner, CPAs, at the completion of the audit of the financial statements of Lyon Computers, Inc. (a nonpublic company) for the year ended March 31, 2012. It was submitted to the engagement partner, who reviewed matters thoroughly and properly concluded that Lyon's disclosures concerning its ability to continue as a going concern for a reasonable period of time were adequate, but there is substantial doubt about Lyon being a going concern.

To the Board of Directors of Lyon Computers, Inc.:

We have audited the accompanying balance sheet of Lyon Computers, Inc. as of March 31, 2012, and the other related financial statements for the year then ended. Our responsibility is to express an opinion on these financial statements based on our audit.

We conducted our audit in accordance with standards that require that we plan and perform the audit to obtain reasonable assurance about whether the financial statements are in conformity with generally accepted accounting principles. An audit includes examining, on a test basis, evidence supporting the amounts and disclosures in the financial statements. An audit also includes assessing the accounting principles used and significant estimates made by management.

The accompanying financial statements have been prepared assuming that the Company will continue as a going concern. As discussed in Note X to the financial statements, the Company has suffered recurring losses from operations and has a net capital deficiency that raises substantial doubt about its ability to continue as a going concern. We believe that management's plans in regard to these matters, which are also described in Note X, will permit the Company to continue as a going concern beyond a reasonable period of time. The financial statements do not include any adjustments that might result from the outcome of this uncertainty.

In our opinion, subject to the effects on the financial statements of such adjustments, if any, as might have been required had the outcome of the uncertainty referred to in the preceding paragraph been known, the financial statements referred to above present fairly, in all material respects, the financial position of Lyon Computers, Inc., and the results of its operations and its cash flows in conformity with generally accepted accounting principles applied on a basis consistent with that of the preceding year.

Turner & Turner, CPAs

April 28, 2012

Required

Identify the deficiencies contained in the auditor's report as drafted by the staff accountant. Group the deficiencies by paragraph. Do not redraft the report.

*16-47   **(Selecting the Proper Audit Opinion and Report Modification, LO 3)**

Group Activity

Required

Audit situations 1 through 8 present various independent factual situations an auditor might encounter in conducting an audit. List A (following) represents the types of opinions the auditor ordinarily would issue, and List B represents the report modifications (if any) that would be necessary. For each situation, select one response from List A and one from List B. Select, as the best answer for each item, the action the auditor normally would take. Items from either list may be selected once, more than once, or not at all. At your instructor's discretion, complete this problem in small-group format in class.

Assume the following:

- The auditor is independent.
- The auditor previously expressed an unqualified opinion on the prior-year financial statements.
- Only single-year (not comparative) statements are presented for the current year.
- The conditions for an unqualified opinion exist unless contradicted in the factual situations.
- The conditions stated in the factual situations are material.
- No report modifications are to be made except in response to the factual situation.

Audit Situations

1. The financial statements present fairly, in all material respects, the financial position, results of operations, and cash flows in conformity with GAAP.

2. In auditing the long-term investments account, an auditor is unable to obtain audited financial statements for an investee located in a foreign country. The auditor concludes that sufficient competent evidential matter regarding this investment cannot be obtained but is not significant enough to disclaim an opinion.

3. Because of recurring operating losses and working-capital deficiencies, an auditor has substantial doubt about an entity's ability to continue as a going concern for a reasonable period of time. However, the financial statement disclosures concerning these matters are adequate.

4. The principal auditor decides to refer to the work of another auditor who audited a wholly owned subsidiary of the entity and issued an unqualified opinion.

5. An entity issues financial statements that present financial position and results of operations but omits the related statement of cash flows. Management discloses in the notes to the financial statements that it does not believe the statement of cash flows to be a useful statement.

6. An entity changes its depreciation method for production equipment from the straight-line to a units-of-production method based on hours of utilization. The auditor concurs with the change, although it has a material effect on the comparability of the entity's financial statements.

7. An entity is a defendant in a lawsuit alleging infringement of certain patent rights. However, management cannot reasonably estimate the ultimate outcome of the litigation. The auditor believes that there is a reasonable possibility of a significant material loss, but the lawsuit is adequately disclosed in the notes to the financial statements.

8. An entity discloses certain lease obligations in the notes to the financial statements. The auditor believes that the failure to capitalize these leases is a departure from GAAP.

List A—Types of Opinions

a. A qualified opinion

b. An unqualified opinion

c. An adverse opinion

d. A disclaimer of opinion

e. Either a qualified opinion or an adverse opinion

f. Either a disclaimer of opinion or a qualified opinion

g. Either an adverse opinion or a disclaimer of opinion

List B—Report Modifications

h. Describe the circumstances in an explanatory paragraph *preceding* the opinion paragraph *without modifying* the three standard paragraphs.

i. Describe the circumstances in an explanatory paragraph *following* the opinion paragraph *without modifying* the three standard paragraphs.

j. Describe the circumstances in an explanatory paragraph *preceding* the opinion paragraph and *modifying the opinion* paragraph.

k. Describe the circumstances in an explanatory paragraph *following* the opinion paragraph and *modifying the opinion* paragraph.

l. Describe the circumstances in an explanatory paragraph *preceding* the opinion paragraph and *modifying the scope and opinion* paragraphs.

m. Describe the circumstances in an explanatory paragraph *following* the opinion paragraph and *modifying the scope and opinion* paragraphs.

n. Describe the circumstances within the *scope* paragraph without adding an explanatory paragraph.

o. Describe the circumstances within the *opinion* paragraph without adding an explanatory paragraph.

p. Describe the circumstances within the *scope and opinion* paragraphs without adding an explanatory paragraph.

q. Describe the circumstances in the *introductory* paragraph without adding an explanatory paragraph and modify the wording of the *scope and opinion* paragraphs.

r. Issue the *standard* auditor's report *without modification*.

16-48   **(Draft an Audit Report, LO 2, 3)** On February 28, 2012, Stu & Dent, LLP completed the audit of Shylo Ranch, Inc. (a nonpublic company) for the year ended December 31, 2011. A recent fire destroyed the accounting records concerning the cost of Shylo's livestock. These were the only records destroyed. The auditors are unable to obtain adequate evidence concerning the cost of the livestock, which represents about 8% of total assets. These are GAAP-based financial statements, and the auditors found no other problems during the audit. The audit report is to cover the 2011 financial statements only. The audit partner has indicated that a qualified opinion is more appropriate than an adverse opinion.

Required

Prepare a draft of the audit report for review by the audit partner.

16-49 **(Comparison of Procedures for an Audit, Review, and Compilation, LO 4)** Compare and contrast the procedures that should be performed on inventory for an audit, review, and compilation. Assume that the auditor has knowledge of the business and industry. Give specific examples of procedures.

16-50 **(Review Report with a GAAP Violation, LO 4)** You have reviewed the financial statements of Classic Company for the year ended June 30, 2012. The only unusual finding is that the company deferred $350,000 of research and development costs rather than expensing them. The costs related to a product that the client believed was certain to be profitable in the future. You believe that the product will be profitable but not that the expenses should have been deferred.

Required

Write the limited assurance and explanatory paragraphs for an appropriate review report.

*16-51 **(Critique of a Compilation Report—Auditor Not Independent and Omission of Substantially All Disclosures, LO 4)** Russ Major, CPA, drafted the following report on October 25, 2011 at the completion of the engagement to compile the financial statements of Ajax Company for the year ended September 30, 2011. Ajax is a nonpublic entity in which Major's child has a material direct financial interest. Ajax decided to omit substantially all of the disclosures required by GAAP because the financial statements will be for management's use only. The statement of cash flows was also omitted because management does not believe it to be a useful financial statement.

To the Board of Directors of Ajax Company:

I have compiled the accompanying financial statements of Ajax Company as of September 30, 2011, and for the year then ended. I planned and performed the compilation to obtain limited assurance about whether the financial statements are free of material misstatements.

A compilation is limited to presenting information in the form of financial statements. It is substantially less in scope than an audit in accordance with generally accepted auditing standards, the objective of which is the expression of an opinion regarding the financial statements taken as a whole. I have not audited the accompanying financial statements and, accordingly, do not express any opinion on them.

Management has elected to omit substantially all of the disclosures required by generally accepted accounting principles. If the omitted disclosures were included in the financial statements, they might influence the user's conclusions about the Company's financial position, results of operations, and changes in financial position.

I am not independent with respect to Ajax Company. This lack of independence is due to my child's ownership of a material direct financial interest in Ajax Company.

This report is intended solely for the information and use of the Board of Directors and management of Ajax Company and should not be used for any other purpose.

Required

Identify the deficiencies contained in Major's report on the compiled financial statements. Group the deficiencies by paragraph when applicable. Do not redraft the report.

Professional Skepticism

16-52 **(Review Procedures for Inventory, LO 4)** You have been assigned to perform a review of a client's inventory containing electric motors, parts for motors, and raw materials used in making the motors.

Required

a. What inquiries and analytical procedures should you perform?

b. What will you do if these procedures do not support the client's inventory values or disclosures?

c. How would your level of professional skepticism differ depending on whether you are performing a review versus an audit engagement?

16-53 **(Effectiveness of Audit, Review, and Compilation Reports, LO 4)** Consider your personal assessment of the persuasiveness of assurances provided by audits, reviews, and compilations, as well as the level of assurance that you believe is given to each type of report by "typical" users. Write a report on your assessment of the assurances provided, as well as your assessment of user interpretations of the assurances received.

16-54 **(Critique of Special Report, LO 6)** A staff auditor of Erwachen & Diamond, CPAs, has prepared the following draft of an audit report on cash-basis financial statements:

Accountant's Report to the Shareholders of Halon Company:

We have audited the accompanying balance sheets and the related statement of income as of December 31, 2012 and 2011. These financial statements are the responsibility of the Company's management. Our responsibility is to express an opinion on these financial statements based on our audits.

We conducted our audits in accordance with auditing standards generally accepted in the United States of America. Those principles require that we plan and perform the audit to obtain reasonable assurance about whether the financial statements are free of material errors. An audit includes examining, on a test basis, evidence supporting the amounts and disclosures in the financial statements. An audit also includes assessing the accounting principles used and estimates made by management, as well as evaluating the overall financial statement presentation. We believe that our audits provide a reasonable basis for our opinion.

As described in Note 13, these financial statements were prepared on the basis of cash receipts and disbursements.

In our opinion, the financial statements referred to above present fairly, in all material respects, the financial position of Halon Company as of December 31, 2012, and the results of operations for the year then ended in accordance with accounting principles generally accepted in the United States of America.

/s/ Donald Diamond, CPA
February 15, 2013

Required

Identify any deficiencies in the report and explain why they are deficiencies.

*16-55   **(Reporting on Specified Elements, Accounts, or Items, LO 6)** Young & Young, CPAs, completed an examination of the financial statements of XYZ Company, Inc., for the year ended June 30, 2012 and issued a standard unqualified auditor's report dated August 15, 2012. At the time of the engagement, the board of directors of XYZ requested a special report attesting to the adequacy of the provision for federal and state income taxes and the related accruals and deferred income taxes as presented in the June 30, 2011 financial statements. Young & Young submitted the appropriate special report on August 22, 2012.

Required

Prepare the special report that Young & Young should have submitted to XYZ Company, Inc.

16-56   **(Compliance Reports, LO 6)** The auditor is auditing the Inguish Company, which has a bond indenture, dated March 26, 2010, with the Last International Bank of Chicago that contains the following covenants in paragraphs E through I:

- Par. E—Maintain at least a 2.5:1 current ratio:
    i. At the end of each quarter
    ii. At fiscal year end
- Par. F—Deposit $250,000 into the bond sinking fund by January 1 of each year until the bonds mature.
- Par. G—Restrict dividend payments to no more than 50% of net income each year.
- Par. H—Make the stated interest payments by the interest dates.
- Par. I—The company shall conform to all pollution standards.

Required

a. Under what circumstances is it appropriate for an auditor to report on the compliance of a client with contractual agreements or regulatory requirements?

b. Which of these covenants would it be appropriate to cover in the compliance report to the bond trustee?

c. Give reasons for excluding any of the covenants from the report.

16-57   **(Compliance Reports, LO 6)**

Required

Answer the following concerning the compliance report for the Inguish Company (refer to Question16-56):

a. Outline the basic elements of a compliance report.

b. Write the paragraph containing negative assurance if

 i. All of the covenants have been met.

 ii. All of the covenants have been met except that the company paid out dividends of $400,000 with net income of only $700,000.

 The indenture states that if there are any violations of the covenants other than timely interest payments, these are to be reported by the management of the company to the trustee within forty-five days of the fiscal year end, such report to include an explanation of the violation, why it happened, and what management plans to do about it. Management has properly reported this violation, which was caused by the declaration of dividends based on preliminary estimates on net income of $850,000. The decrease in audited net income was the result of an unexpected downturn in the stock market during the last two weeks of the year that created an unrealized loss on decline in the market value of the company's current marketable equity securities.

c. What are the audit implications when the client violates one or more of the bond covenants?

Internet

16-58   **(Possible Changes to Information Contained in the Auditor's Standard Report, LO 2)**

Required

Describe the basic information that is included in an auditor's opinion. Also discuss how that report will differ if it also contains a report on the internal controls of the company, that is, reports on an integrated audit. Consider whether the current audit report requirements are sufficient to meet a user's needs. That is, are there changes to the auditor's report that you think would provide more useful information for the investor? Your instructor will let you know whether you are to prepare a written report or a class presentation. In addressing this issue, review the *Professional Judgment in Context* feature at the beginning of the chapter, consider the seven discussion questions raised by the PCAOB in its briefing paper on the auditor's reporting model available at http://pcaobus.org/Rules/Rulemaking/Docket029/2009-07-28_Release_No_2009-005.pdf, and review the PCAOB Concept Release On Requiring The Engagement Partner To Sign The Audit Report, which is available at http://pcaobus.org/Rules/Rulemaking/Docket029/2009-07-28_Release_No_2009-005.pdf.

Cases

16-59   **(Ethical Decisions in Determining the Appropriate Opinion, LO 8)** Assume that you are in a situation where you had doubts about your client's ability to continue as a going concern. Further, assume you have decided that, after performing all the required audit procedures, you can issue an unqualified opinion but need to modify the audit opinion to indicate substantial doubt about the client's ability to continue as a going concern. You have to let the CFO, who is a longtime friend of yours, know of your decision. When you do this, the CFO tries to explain to you that if the company receives a going-concern opinion, it will go under—that the opinion is a self-fulfilling prophecy. The CFO tries to convince you that if your firm does not issue a going-concern opinion, it is very likely the company will be able to weather its financial difficulties and survive. Further, the CFO notes that this is really a matter of professional judgment and believes that many other auditors would not see the need to issue a going-concern opinion.

Ethics

     Use the ethical framework introduced in Chapter 3 to address the dilemma you face regarding what type of opinion to issue. Recall that the steps in the framework are as follows: (1) identify the ethical issue(s), (2) determine who are the affected parties and identify their rights, (3) determine the most important rights, (4) develop alternative courses of action, (5) determine the likely consequences of each proposed course of action, (6) assess the possible consequences, including an estimation of the greatest good for the greatest number, and (7) decide on the appropriate course of action.

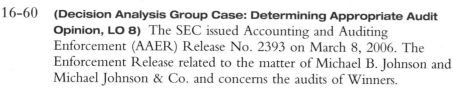

16-60   **(Decision Analysis Group Case: Determining Appropriate Audit Opinion, LO 8)** The SEC issued Accounting and Auditing Enforcement (AAER) Release No. 2393 on March 8, 2006. The Enforcement Release related to the matter of Michael B. Johnson and Michael Johnson & Co. and concerns the audits of Winners.

Group Activity

     The following facts about Johnson and Co.'s audit of Winners are included in the AAER:

- Johnson, age 56, is a resident of Littleton, Colorado. Johnson has been the manager and sole member of Johnson & Co. and a licensed certified public accountant in Colorado since 1975. He also is a licensed certified public accountant in Florida and Mississippi.

- Johnson & Co. is an accounting firm located in Denver, Colorado. Johnson is the only member of, and the only certified public accountant affiliated with, the firm.

- Johnson & Co., through the participation of Johnson, audited the financial statements of Winners Internet Network, Inc. ("Winners"), for the years ended December 31, 1997 and 1998. Johnson supervised the audits and compilations of these financial statements and signed the audit reports for the 1997 and 1998 audits on behalf of Johnson & Co.

- Winners' December 31, 1999 financial statements were prepared and audited by Johnson and Johnson & Co.

- Johnson & Co. issued audit reports accompanying Winners' year-end financial statements for 1997 and 1998 that contained a going-concern modification and an unqualified audit report for 1999. These financial statements contained material misstatements, some of which related to entries made by Johnson or under the direction of Johnson. These reports falsely stated that the financial statements were presented fairly in all material respects in conformity with generally accepted accounting principles (GAAP) and that the audits of these financial statements were conducted in accordance with generally accepted auditing standards (GAAS). These statements were false, since portions of the underlying financial statements were not presented in conformity with GAAP, which, in turn, rendered false the statements that the audits were conducted in accordance with GAAS, since the failure to address a deviation from GAAP in an audit report is a violation of GAAS.

Required

Given the nature of Johnson & Co.'s work on Winners' financial statements for 1997–1999, what type of audit opinion should have been issued?

The decision to be made by Johnson is the type of audit opinion that should be issued for the client. In considering this decision, answer the following questions by completing the first four steps of the seven-step Decision-Analysis Framework introduced in Chapter 3:

1. What difficulties might the Johnson have faced when deciding what type of opinion to issue? Why might Johnson have not issued the appropriate opinions?

2. What are the consequences of Johnson's decisions in this case?

3. What are the risks and uncertainties associated with this decision?

4. In deciding on whether to issue a going-concern modification, what types of evidence should the auditor gather to evaluate the reasonableness of the going-concern assumption?

Recall that the framework is as follows:

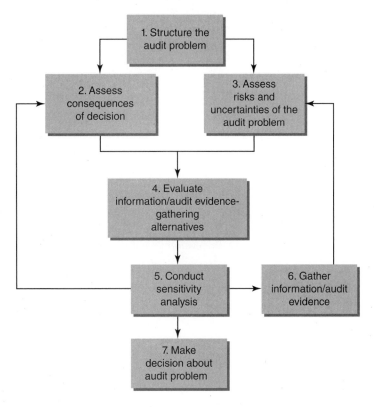

Source: Adapted from "Judgment and Choice," by Robin Hogarth.

Academic Research Case (LO 1, 3)

Academic research addresses the conceptual issues outlined in this chapter. To help you consider the linkage between academic research and the practice of auditing, read the following research article and answer the questions below.

Krishnan, J., Raghunandan, K., & Yang, J. S. (2007). Were Former Andersen Clients Treated More Leniently Than Other Clients? Evidence from Going-Concern Modified Audit Opinions. *Accounting Horizons 21(4):423–435.*

  i. What is the issue being addressed in the paper?

 ii. Why is this issue important to practicing auditors?

iii. What are the findings of the paper?

 iv. What are the implications of these findings for audit quality (or audit practice) on the audit profession?

  v. Describe the research methodology used as a basis for the conclusions.

 vi. Describe any limitations of the research that the student (and practice) should be aware of.

SEARCH HINT

It is easy to locate these academic research articles! Simply use a search engine (e.g., Google Scholar) or an electronic research platform (e.g., ABI Inform) and search using the author names and part of the article title.

FORD MOTOR COMPANY AND TOYOTA MOTOR CORPORATION:
AUDIT REPORTS

Go to www.cengage.com/accounting/rittenberg for the Ford and Toyota materials.

Source and Reference		Question
Ford 10-K or Annual Report	**1.**	What type of audit report did PricewaterhouseCoopers LLP issue for Ford?
Toyota 20-F or Annual Report	**2.**	What type of audit report did PricewaterhouseCoopers LLP issue for Toyota?
	3a.	What are the advantages to Ford and Toyota of using the same audit firm?
	3b.	Why might some companies in the same industry be hesitant to using the same audit firm?

Module XV of the Biltrite audit practice case contains an audit report exercise. This exercise may be completed at this time.

Module XV: Audit Report

The Denise Vaughan audit team completed its audit field work on February 15, 2010. A conference was held on that date involving members of the audit firm and Biltrite management. Participants in the conference were Denise Vaughan, partner in charge of the Biltrite engagement; Carolyn Volmar, audit manager; Richard Derick, in-charge auditor; Trevor Lawton, Biltrite's CEO; Gerald Groth, Biltrite's controller; and Marlene McAfee, Biltrite's treasurer. The Biltrite representatives agreed to all of the audit adjustments and reclassifications proposed by the audit team, and they agreed to reflect them in the December 31, 2009, financial statements. They also agreed to modify and/or add footnote disclosures as recommended by the audit team.

At the conclusion of the conference, the audit team obtained a client representation letter from Biltrite management and presented management with a copy of the "significant deficiencies" letter outlining discovered internal control deficiencies. The original of this letter was sent to Biltrite's audit committee.

The legal action initiated against Biltrite by Rollfast, a competitor, for alleged patent infringement, was not yet settled as of February 15. Because the letter obtained by Derick from Biltrite's outside legal counsel was inconclusive as to the probable outcome of this action, Derick requested an informal conference with the attorney handling Biltrite's case. This conference was convened on February 12, and the participants were Joel Haskins, the attorney, Gerald Groth, Denise Vaughan, and Richard Derick.

Haskins exhibited a degree of pessimism that produced considerable uncertainty as to the probable outcome of the litigation. Inasmuch as the amount of loss could be quite substantial, and the probability of an unfavorable outcome was more than remote but less than likely, Groth agreed to disclose the matter in a footnote to the 2009 financial statements.

Notwithstanding the liquidity problems and loan default, Biltrite has been assured by Bank Two management that the bank plans no foreclosure action, provided Biltrite can restore the minimum required bank balance and continues to earn profits. Moreover, management's expressed plans for dealing with the crisis and continued sales growth during January 2010 have convinced Denise Vaughan that an explanatory paragraph expressing substantial doubt as to continued existence is not necessary.

No scope restrictions were encountered during the audit, either imposed or otherwise. Also assume that Biltrite did not change accounting principles in either 2008 or 2009.

Requirements

1. Using the spreadsheet program and downloaded data, retrieve the file labeled "Report."
2. Modify the report as appropriate to conform to the Biltrite audit results.
3. Print the audit report.
4. Have the audit partner sign the audit report.

17

Professional Liability

LEARNING OBJECTIVES

The overriding objective of this textbook is to build a foundation with which to analyze current professional issues and adopt audit approaches to business and economic complexities. Through studying this chapter, you will be able to:

1 Discuss the liability environment in which auditors operate, the factors that have led to increased litigation against auditors, and the effects of lawsuits on audit firms.

2 Describe laws from which auditor liability is derived, list causes of legal action against auditors, and identify parties that may sue auditors.

3 Explain the impact of key court cases on the public accounting profession.

4 Describe possible causes of action, remedies or sanctions, and auditor defenses under both common law and statutory law.

5 Discuss emerging and unsettled liability issues of concern to auditors.

6 Identify professional requirements that help assure audit quality and minimize auditor exposure to liability suits.

7 Describe defensive actions that audit firms can take to help assure audit quality and minimize the effects of litigation on audit firms and individual auditors.

8 Apply the decision analysis and ethical decision-making frameworks to issues that could result in litigation.

CHAPTER OVERVIEW

Even though most audits are properly performed, a significant percentage of the gross revenues of public accounting firms is spent on professional liability insurance and litigation costs. Litigation costs and settlements have caused some of the world's largest public accounting firms to declare bankruptcy in the past. In today's litigious environment, it is extremely important that auditors use due professional care and provide high-quality audits to minimize such costs. Even with such precautions, the government, investors, and clients may still sue auditors. In this chapter, we discuss the legal environment in which audit firms operate, approaches to minimizing exposure to liability, and several key court cases that have had a significant impact on the profession.

The Audit Opinion Formulation Process

I. Assessing Client Acceptance and Retention Decisions	II. Understanding the Client	III. Obtaining Evidence about Controls and Determining the Impact on the Financial Statement Audit	IV. Obtaining Substantive Evidence about Account Assertions	V. Wrapping Up the Audit and Making Reporting Decisions
CHAPTER 4	CHAPTERS 2, 4–6, and 9	CHAPTERS 5–14 and 18	CHAPTERS 7–14 and 18	CHAPTERS 15 and 16

The Auditing Profession, Regulation, and Corporate Governance	Decision-Making, Professional Conduct, and Ethics	Professional Liability
CHAPTERS 1 and 2	CHAPTER 3	CHAPTER 17

PROFESSIONAL JUDGMENT IN CONTEXT

Should Auditors Be Liable When Clients Commit Accounting Fraud?

A group of investors in American International Group (AIG) sued the company's auditors, PricewaterhouseCoopers, for failing to detect a long-running accounting fraud scheme at AIG. The lawsuit against PwC alleges professional malpractice and negligence over the accounting firm's audits of AIG during a period of accounting manipulations and sham transactions that go back to 1999. Initially, PwC won a dismissal of the suit by indicating that AIG shared the blame since it was AIG employees who committed the fraud. This is a common defense used by audit firms against shareholder claims.

The investor group appealed the dismissal, and the appeal was heard in September 2010. The case is expected to be important in the debate over whether shareholders can pursue a malpractice claim against an audit firm when the company in which the shareholders are invested is at fault for the original offense. The hearing considers the argument not only in the PwC and AIG case, but in other cases where auditors used a defense similar to the one used by PwC.

The American Institute of Certified Public Accountants (AICPA) filed a brief in support of the accounting firms. The brief says that abandoning current legal precedent would "expand auditor liability well beyond the boundaries of established precedent and out of proportion to an auditor's ability to detect and prevent management fraud." In contrast to the AICPA position, a partner with the law firm representing the AIG investors indicated that "auditors are looking for a 'get-out-of-jail free card' that they can play every time their corporate client sues them for failing to detect fraud by a corporate manager."

As you read the following chapter, consider this situation and the following questions:

- Under what conditions, if any, should auditors be held liable if their client's financial statements contain an accounting fraud that the auditors did not detect?
- What defenses are used by auditors in response to litigation?
- What can auditors do to minimize their exposure to litigation?
- What are your reactions to responses of the AICPA and the attorney representing AIG investors?

The Legal Environment

The following headlines from the financial press reflect the litigious nature of the environment in which auditors operate:

"Andersen Surrenders Licenses to Practice Accounting in U.S."

"Subprime Suit Accuses KPMG of Negligence"

"PwC Pays $30M to Settle Claim of Faulty Audit"

"Deloitte, Grant Thornton to Settle Parmalat Suit"

LO 1

Discuss the liability environment in which auditors operate, the factors that have led to increased litigation against auditors, and the effects of lawsuits on audit firms.

"BDO Sued in Madoff Case"

"E&Y Sued over Audits of Failed Hedge Fund"

"Friehling [Madoff Auditor] Pleads Guilty, but Denies Knowing About the Scheme"

"Legal-Liability Awards Are Frightening Smaller CPA Firms Away from Audits"

These headlines represent just a sampling of the coverage the financial press has devoted to legal action against auditors in recent years. Public accounting firms are being sued for the conduct of audits of both large and small clients. Arthur Andersen, one of the world's largest public accounting firms, was forced into bankruptcy and out of business in 2001.

The diverse group of litigants includes class action suits by small investors and suits by the U.S. Department of Justice. Legal liability cases are expensive for audit firms, whether they win or lose. The responsibility of public accountants to safeguard the public's interest has increased as the number of investors has increased, as the relationship between corporate managers and stockholders has become more impersonal, and as stakeholders demand more accountability from organizations. When auditors agree to perform audits, they purport to be experts in assessing the fairness of financial statements on which the public relies. In a substantial majority of audits, auditors use great care, perform professionally, issue appropriate opinions, and serve the interests of the public. Even when an audit is performed at the highest level of quality however, the public accounting firm may be sued and incur substantial legal costs to defend itself. Even if the public accounting firm wins the litigation, its reputation and that of those involved may be unfairly tarnished.

Auditing firms are not unique in being the targets of litigation. Students sue teachers, customers sue manufacturers, patients sue their doctors and hospitals, and clients sue their lawyers and accountants. Factors leading to increased litigation against the auditor that are at work in our society include:

- A liability environment that includes joint and several liability statutes permitting a plaintiff to recover the full amount of a settlement from a public accounting firm, even though that firm is found to be only partially responsible for the loss (often referred to as the **deep-pocket theory**; i.e., sue those who can pay)
- Pressures to reduce audit time and improve audit efficiency in the face of increased competition among public accounting firms
- A misunderstanding by some users that an unqualified audit opinion represents an insurance policy against investment losses
- Contingent-fee-based compensation for law firms, especially in class action suits
- Increased complexity of audits caused by integrated electronic commerce, new types of business transactions and operations, increased international business, and more complicated accounting standards
- Class action suits and associated user awareness of the possibilities and rewards of litigation

Liability Doctrines

Auditors may be subject to either joint and several liability or proportionate liability. Joint and several liability concepts are designed to protect users who suffer major losses because of misplaced reliance on a company and its assertions about financial health. Users suffer real losses, but sometimes those primarily responsible for the losses, such as management, do not have the resources to compensate people for those losses. Society has to determine whether those suffering the losses should be compensated fully for their losses, and by whom. Joint and several liability addresses this problem.

PRACTICAL POINT

Among one the most significant challenges facing auditors is the early detection of fraud, particularly when the client, its management, and others collude specifically to deceive the external auditors. However, when auditors do not discover fraud they often face lawsuits from clients, investors, and other parties for what are perceived to be failed audits.

PRACTICAL POINT

Audit firms depend on consistent execution of audit programs and professional auditors with high levels of competence and skepticism to perform audits. Only by consistent execution - every day by everyone on the engagement team - can audit firms avoid liability. The little things on every audit engagement really do count.

Joint and several liability states that the damages ought to be paid to those suffering losses caused by each party. A party suffering a loss is able to recover full damages from any defendant, including an audit firm, regardless of the level of fault of the party. For example, if a jury decided that management was 80% at fault and the auditor was 20% at fault, the damages would be apportioned 80% to management and 20% to auditors. Unfortunately, in many lawsuits involving auditors, the client is in bankruptcy, management has few assets, and the auditor is the only one left with adequate resources to pay the damages. Joint and several liability then apportions the damages over the remaining defendants in proportion to the relative damages. Under pure joint and several liability, if management has no resources and there are no other defendants, 100% of the damages are then apportioned to the auditing firm. Thus, auditors are often included in lawsuits even if they are only partially responsible for losses incurred by the plaintiffs. The U.S. Congress has limited the extent of joint and several liability damages in federal suits to actual percentage of responsibility if auditors are found liable for less than 50% of damages.

Congress passed the Private Securities Litigation Reform Act (PSLRA) of 1995, which is designed to curb frivolous securities class action lawsuits brought under federal securities laws against companies whose stock performs below expectations. Under this Act, liability is proportional rather than joint and several, unless the violation is willful, that is, the auditor knowingly participated in a fraud. In some situations, a defendant may have to cover some of the obligation of another defendant who is unable to pay his or her share. Under **proportionate liability**, generally a defendant would be required to pay a proportionate share of the damage, depending on the degree of fault determined by the judge or jury.

Because the PSLRA applies only to lawsuits brought in federal courts, many lawyers have taken their cases to state courts. This loophole was closed by the Securities Litigation Uniform Standards Act of 1998, which says, "Any covered class action brought into any state court involving a covered security ... shall be removable to the federal district court for the district in which the action is pending." The 1998 Act forces potential plaintiffs to adhere to the spirit, as well as the letter, of the PLSRA Act of 1995.

Audit Time and Fee Pressures

Clients justifiably view audits as another service that they must purchase, and logically they wish to purchase such services at the most competitive price. However, this places auditors in the difficult situation of facing considerable time and fee pressure in order to provide audit services that are competitively priced and still yield a profit for the audit firm. Auditors should remember that the client exerting the most time and fee pressure might be the client who is attempting to hide something from the auditor and is thus the client whose pressure should be most resisted. Furthermore, if a client exerts too much time and fee pressure, the audit firm should consider whether the client offers the opportunity to make a reasonable profit for the effort required. If not, the audit firm should consider not providing services to the client.

Audits Viewed as an Insurance Policy

Auditors perform a significant role in our free-market economy, but an audit report accompanying a financial statement is not a guarantee that an investment in the audited company is free of risk. Unfortunately, some investors mistakenly view the unqualified audit report as an insurance policy against any and all losses from a risky investment. When they do suffer losses, these investors believe that they should be able to recover their losses from the auditor. This view, coupled

PRACTICAL POINT

Audit firms have reported that "practice protection costs"—i.e., insurance, legal fees, and litigation settlements—are the second-highest costs faced by audit firms, following only employee compensation costs.

PRACTICAL POINT

Although the vast majority of audits do not result in litigation, and most auditors will never be involved in litigation during their professional career, audit firms do face considerable legal costs. Having adequate documentation demonstrating that professional standards were followed may minimize liability if litigation does occur.

PRACTICAL POINT

Audit committees and the board of directors function as the client in public companies. Their direct responsibility to shareholders, as well as the need to protect themselves from litigation, aligns responsibilities to work with auditors to assure adequate audits.

PRACTICAL POINT

During the ten-year period ended in 2009, the annual number of class action litigation claims against the Big Four audit firms ranged from a high of 59 cases in 2003 to a low of 23 cases in 2001. By performing quality audits and taking other appropriate defensive actions, auditors may be able to limit their liability in such cases.

with joint and several liability, encourages large lawsuits against auditors even for cases in which the plaintiffs are aware in advance that the auditor is only partially at fault or is not at fault.

Contingent-Fee Compensation for Lawyers

Contingent fees for lawyers have evolved in our society to allow individuals who cannot afford high-priced lawyers to seek compensation for their damages. Lawyers take **contingent-fee cases** with an understanding that a client who loses a case owes the lawyer nothing; however, if the case is won, the lawyer receives an agreed-upon percentage (usually one-third to one-half) of the damages awarded. This arrangement protects the underprivileged and encourages lawsuits by a wide variety of parties. The plaintiffs have little to lose, and the lawyers have a large incentive to successfully pursue the case.

Class Action Suits

Class action suits are designed to prevent multiple suits that might result in inconsistent judgments and to encourage litigation when no individual plaintiff has a claim large enough to justify the expense of litigation. As an example, from 2007 to mid-2010 there were twenty-four class action cases related to the credit crisis where the auditor was named as a defendant. Often in these cases, the lawyers are working on a contingent fee basis and want to identify every potential member of the class. Newspaper ads and other media sources are sometimes taken out to notify all potential members of the class of their right to join the class action suit and how to do so. Damages in such cases, and thus fees for the lawyers, can be extremely large.

An Overview of Auditor Liability to Clients and Third Parties

The legal environment is extremely complex and diversified, and as a starting point for understanding this environment students should be familiar with:

1. *Laws* from which auditor liability is derived
2. *Causes* of legal action
3. *Parties* who may bring suit against the auditor

These issues are illustrated in Exhibit 17.1 and discussed in the following sections.

PRACTICAL POINT

The development of common and statutory law shows a fine balance between protecting users and avoiding an unreasonable standard of care on the part of the auditors.

LO 2

Describe laws from which auditor liability is derived, list causes of legal action against auditors, and identify parties that may sue auditors.

Laws from Which Auditor Liability Is Derived

Liability that affects public accounting firms is derived from the following laws:

- *Common law*—Liability concepts are developed through court decisions based on negligence, gross negligence, or fraud. Under common law, cases can be based on contract law whereby liability occurs where there is a breach of contract. The contract is usually between the public accounting firm and the client for the performance of a professional service, such as an audit in accordance with professional auditing standards. The contract is typically documented in the audit engagement letter.
- *Statutory law*—Liability is based on federal securities laws or state statutes. The most important of these statutes to the auditing profession are the Securities Act of 1933 (1933 Act) and the Securities Exchange Act of 1934 (1934 Act).

Exhibit 17.1 — Overview of Auditor Liability

(AUDITOR HELD LIABLE? Y = YES, N = NO, NA = NOT APPLICABLE)

Who Can Sue?	Client		3rd Parties		
				Statutory Law	
Under What Law?	Contract Law	Common Law	Common Law	1933 Act	1934 Act
For What?					
Breach of contract	Y	NA	NA	NA	NA
Negligence	Y	Y	?*	Y	N
Gross negligence	Y	Y	Y	Y	Unclear
Fraud	Y	Y	Y	Y	Y

?* Depends on the test used:
- Identified User
- Foreseen User
- Foreseeable User

Causes of Legal Action

Parties that bring suit against auditors usually allege that the auditors did not meet the standard of "due care" in performing the audit or other professional services used by a client. The concept of due care is defined by *Cooley on Torts:*

> Every man who offers his service to another and is employed assumes the duty to exercise in the employment such skill as he possesses with reasonable care and diligence. In all these employments where peculiar skill is prerequisite, if one offers his service, he is understood as holding himself out to the public as possessing the degree of skill commonly possessed by others in the same employment, and, if his pretensions are unfounded, he commits a species of fraud upon every man who employs him in reliance on his public profession. But no man, whether skilled or unskilled, undertakes that the task he assumes shall be performed successfully, and without fault or error. He undertakes for good faith and integrity, but not for infallibility, and he is liable to his employer for negligence, bad faith, or dishonesty, but not for losses consequent upon pure errors of judgment.[1]

Professional auditing standards requiring due professional care reflect this same concept. Auditors are responsible for due care, but that doesn't mean auditors are infallible. The specific responsibility in a particular case depends on whether there is a breach of contract, negligence, gross negligence, or fraud.

Breach of contract occurs when a person fails to perform a contractual duty. As an example, an auditor was hired to find a material fraud. If reasonable procedures would have detected the fraud and the auditor failed to uncover the fraud, the auditor would have breached the contract. As another example, if the auditor agreed to provide the audit report by a certain date, but did not, the auditor would have breached the contract.

Negligence is the failure to exercise reasonable care, thereby causing harm to another or to property. If an auditor, for example, did not detect an embezzlement scheme because of a failure to follow up on evidence that would have brought it to light, but a prudent auditor would have performed such follow-up, the auditor is negligent. The profession's standards require that audits be conducted in accordance with professional auditing standards; thus, a failure to

PRACTICAL POINT

The parties that sue auditors may be either audit clients or third-party users. They may accuse the auditor of breach of contract, or of a tort. A **tort** is a civil wrong, other than breach of contract, based on negligence, constructive fraud, or fraud.

---

[1] D. Haggard, *Cooley on Torts* (4th ed. 1932), 472.

PRACTICAL POINT

It is obviously much more difficult to prove that the auditor was fraudulent in issuing an audit opinion than it is to prove that the auditor was negligent in the conduct of the audit. To prove fraud, the plaintiff must prove intent to deceive.

PRACTICAL POINT

The concept of foreseeability is fundamental to courts in determining whether or not an individual or a class of individuals has "standing" to bring a case forward and whether the plaintiffs have to prove negligence, gross negligence, or fraud.

meet these standards could be construed as negligence on the part of the auditor.

Gross negligence (also referred to as **constructive fraud**) is the failure to use even minimal care or operating with a "reckless disregard for the truth" or "reckless behavior." Expressing an opinion on a set of financial statements with careless disregard of professional auditing standards is an example of gross negligence. Gross negligence is more than failing to comply with professional standards; it is such complete disregard for due care that judges and juries are allowed to infer constructive fraud, or intent to deceive, even though there may be no direct evidence of intent to deceive.

Fraud is an intentional concealment or misrepresentation of a material fact that causes damage to those deceived. In an action for fraud, scienter must generally be proved. **Scienter** means knowledge on the part of the person making the representations, at the time they are made, that they are false. An auditor has perpetrated a fraud on investors, for example, by expressing an unqualified opinion on financial statements that the auditor knows are, in reality, not fairly presented. The purpose of the fraud is to deceive.

Parties That May Bring Suit Against Auditors

In most cases, anyone who can support a claim that damages were incurred based on reliance on misleading financial statements attested to by the auditor is in a position to bring a claim against the auditor. For ease of discussion, these parties are typically labeled as the *client* and *third-party users*. Third-party users can potentially be any of the third-party users identified in Chapter 1.

LO 3

Explain the impact of key court cases on the public accounting profession.

LO 4

Describe possible causes of action, remedies or sanctions, and auditor defenses under both common law and statutory law

Auditor Liability: Common Law and Statutory Law

Common-Law Liability to Clients—Breach of Contract

Auditors are expected to fulfill their responsibilities to clients in accordance with their contracts (usually an engagement letter). Auditors can be held liable to clients under contract law and/or common law for breach of contract; they can be sued under the concepts of negligence, gross negligence, and fraud. In most audit engagements, the client contracts with the auditor to perform specific services, such as to conduct an audit in accordance with professional auditing standards and to complete the audit on a timely basis.

Causes for Action   Breach of contract may occur when there is nonperformance of a contractual duty. Causes for action against the auditor for breach of contract may include, but are not limited to, the following:

- Violating client confidentiality
- Failing to provide the audit report on time
- Failing to discover a material error or employee fraud
- Withdrawing from an audit engagement without justification

Negligence Requirements   A client seeking to recover damages from an auditor in an action based on negligence must prove:

- Duty
- Breach of contracted duty
- A causal relationship existed between the breach and damages
- Actual damages

AUDITING *in Practice*

MISLEADING FINANCIAL STATEMENTS

Although management is responsible for the preparation of financial statements, it is possible that the statements contain material misstatements that should have been discovered by the auditor. If the client was unaware of the misstatements and has suffered losses that are due to the misstatements, the client may attempt to recover the damages from the auditor. For example, the auditor may have failed to discover a fraud that was being perpetrated against the management of the company. The auditor will usually argue that the client was contributorily negligent (the damage was at least in part caused by management's carelessness). Nonetheless, clients have brought successful cases against auditors when financial statements were misleading or frauds were not detected.

The client must show that the auditor had a duty not to be negligent. In determining this duty, courts use as criteria the standards and principles of the profession, including professional auditing standards and financial accounting principles. Liability may be imposed for lack of due care either in performing the audit or in presenting financial information. The auditor must have breached that duty by not exercising due professional care. The client must show there was a causal relationship between the negligence and damage. The client must prove actual damages. The amount of damages must be established with reasonable certainty, and the client must demonstrate that the auditor's acts or omissions were the cause of the loss.

Remedies   Remedies for breach of contract include the following:

- Requiring specific performance of the contract agreement
- Granting an injunction to prohibit the auditor from doing certain acts, such as disclosing confidential information
- Providing for recovery of amounts lost as a result of the breach

When specific performance or an injunction is not appropriate, the client is entitled to recover compensatory damages. In determining the amounts of compensation, courts try to put the client in the position in which it would have been had the contract been performed as promised.

Defenses   The auditor can use the following as defenses against a breach of contract suit:

- The auditor exercised due professional care in accordance with the contract.
- The client was contributorily negligent.
- The client's losses were not caused by the breach.

AUDITING *in Practice*

CLIENTS SUING THEIR INDEPENDENT AUDITORS

In 2006, Fannie Mae sued its auditor KPMG for both negligence and breach of contract. Fannie Mae alleged that the auditor failed to prevent $6.3 billion in accounting errors.

In 2010, *Koss Corp.* filed a lawsuit against its former auditor, Grant Thornton LLP, for failing to find the alleged $31 million fraud perpetrated by the Company's VP of finance. Clients also sue their auditors in jurisdictions outside of the United States. For example, in 2005 Ernst & Young was sued for £700 million by Equitable Life, its former audit client, after the insurance company almost collapsed. The claim was dropped, but could have bankrupted the firm's UK arm if it had succeeded.

Common-Law Liability to Third Parties

In most engagements, the auditor does not know specifically who will be using the financial statements but is aware that third parties will be using them.

Causes for Action   Generally, the courts have held auditors liable to injured third parties when the auditor has been found guilty of gross negligence (constructive fraud) or fraud. Courts differ, however, as to what third parties the auditor should be held liable to for ordinary negligence. To win a claim against the auditor, third parties suing under common law must generally prove that:

- They suffered a loss.
- The loss was due to reliance on misleading financial statements.
- The auditor knew, or should have known, that the financial statements were misleading.

Differing Requirements for Auditor Liability to Third Parties under Common Law

Foreseeability and Negligence: Common Law   The fundamental issue is whether the plaintiff has to prove negligence or whether the plaintiff must prove gross negligence in order to obtain damages from an auditor. Courts in different jurisdictions have taken different approaches to determining a plaintiff's standing to bring a suit for ordinary negligence. The key is the likelihood that an auditor could reasonably foresee that a user might have relied upon the financial statements or other attestation services provided by the auditor. Generally, less foreseeable plaintiffs need to establish a gross negligence claim, whereas foreseeable users, in some jurisdictions, have to establish only a negligence claim.

The Ultramares Case: The Third-Party Beneficiary Test   Common law is based on court decisions. The landmark case of *Ultramares Corporation v. Touche*, decided by the New York Court of Appeals in 1931, set the precedent for an auditor's liability to third parties. The court held that auditors are liable to third parties for fraud and gross negligence, but not for ordinary negligence, unless the plaintiff is in privity of contract (the client or a third-party beneficiary). A **third-party beneficiary** must be specifically identified in the engagement letter as a user for whom the audit is being conducted. If, for example, a bank requires an audit as part of a loan application and is named in the engagement letter, the auditor may be held liable to the bank for ordinary negligence. If the bank had not been named in the engagement letter, however, such liability would not exist. Judge Cardozo, writing the unanimous decision, expressed concern about expansive auditor liability to third parties:

> If liability for negligence exists, a thoughtless slip or blunder, the failure to detect a theft or forgery beneath the cover of deceptive entries, may expose accountants to a liability in an indeterminate amount for an indeterminate time to an indeterminate class.... Our holding does not emancipate accountants from the consequences of fraud. It does not relieve them if their audit has been so negligent as to justify a finding that they had no genuine belief in its adequacy, for this again is fraud. It does no more than say that, if less than this is proved, if there has been neither reckless misstatement nor insincere profession of an opinion, but only honest blunder, the ensuing liability for negligence is one that is bounded by the contract, and is to be enforced between the parties by whom the contract has been made.[2]

This precedent dominated judicial thinking for many years and is still followed in many jurisdictions. For example, in the 1992 case of *Bily v. Arthur Young & Co.* involving the bankruptcy of the Osborne Computer Company, the California

---

[2] *Ultramares v. Touche*, 174 N.E. 441 (N.Y. 1931).

Supreme Court upheld the *Ultramares* precedent. It concluded that extending auditor liability to other third parties "raises the spectre [sic] of multibillion-dollar professional liability that is distinctly out of proportion to: (1) the fault of the auditor (which is necessarily second [to that of management] and may be based on complex differences of professional opinion); and (2) the connection between the auditor's conduct and the third party's injury (which will often be attenuated by unrelated business factors that underlie investment and credit decisions)."[3]

Expansion of Ultramares: The Identified User Test   In the 1985 case of *Credit Alliance Corp. v. Arthur Andersen & Co.*,[4] the New York Court of Appeals extended auditor liability for ordinary negligence to identified users. An **identified user** is a specific third party whom the auditor knows will use the audited financial statements for a particular purpose, even though the identified user is not named in the engagement letter.

Foreseen User Test   The 1965 Restatement (Second) of Torts[5] expanded auditor liability for negligence to identified users and to any individually unknown third parties who are members of a known or intended class of third parties, called **foreseen users**. The client must have informed the auditor that a third party or class of third parties intends to use the financial statements for a particular transaction. The auditor does not have to know the identity of the third party. For example, the client tells the auditor that it plans to include the audited financial statements in an application to some financial institution for a loan. The auditor would be liable to the bank that ultimately makes the loan, even though its identity was not known at the time of the audit. A Rhode Island court in *Rusch Factors, Inc. v. Levin* successfully applied the foreseen users test.[6]

Foreseeable User Test   Some courts have extended auditor liability to **foreseeable users** of audited financial statements. In *Citizens State Bank v. Timm, Schmidt & Co.*, the Wisconsin Supreme Court extended auditor liability to creditors who could foreseeably use the audited financial statements.[7] A similar position was taken in *Rosenblum, Inc. v. Adler*, where the New Jersey Supreme Court noted that the nature of the economy had changed since the *Ultramares* case and that auditors are indeed acting as if a number of potential users rely on their audit opinion. This court made it clear that foreseeable users must have obtained the financial statements from the client for proper business purposes,[8] but this is not true in all jurisdictions.

Summary of Tests of Auditor Negligence in Common-Law Court Decisions

Exhibit 17.2 summarizes the historical evolution of auditor common-law liability to third parties for negligence. Exhibit 17.3 provides a graphical illustration of foreseeability concepts under common law. The current liability status depends on the state and court involved and the precedent the court chooses to use.[9]

> **PRACTICAL POINT**
>
> There are various legal precedence and statutes that may be used as a standard against which to judge the auditor's performance. Auditors should be—and are—held liable to their clients and third parties who show that they relied on audited financial statements for important decisions and suffered losses because of substandard work by the auditors.

---

[3] *Bily v. Arthur Young & Co.*, 834 P.2d 745 (Cal. 1992).

[4] *Credit Alliance Corp. v. Arthur Andersen & Co.*, 483 N.E. 2d 110 (N.Y. 1985).

[5] The *Restatement (Second) of Torts* is published by the American Law Institute. Courts may refer to this treatise when considering an issue of outdated precedent. It offers a unique perspective on the law because its purpose is to state the law as the majority of courts would decide it today. It does not necessarily reflect the rules of the common law as adopted by the courts. Rather, it represents principles of common law that the American Law Institute believes would be adopted if the courts reexamined their common-law rules.

[6] *Rusch Factors, Inc. v. Levin*, 284 F. Supp. 85 (D.C.R.I. 1968).

[7] *Citizens State Bank v. Timm, Schmidt & Co.*, 335 N.W. 2d 361 (Wis. Sup. Ct. 1983).

[8] *Rosenblum, Inc. v. Adler*, 461 A. 2d 138 (N.J. 1983).

[9] Garrison, M. J., & Hansen, J. D. "Using the engagement letter to limit auditors' professional liability exposure," *The Ohio CPA Journal* 1999 (July–September), pp. 59–62.

| Exhibit 17.2 | Tests Used in Common-Law Court Decisions Concerning Auditor Negligence |

| | | TEST | | |
Source	Date	Identified User	Foreseen User	Foreseeable User
Ultramares (N.Y.)	1931	X		
Restatement (2d) of Torts	1965		X	
Rusch Factors (R.I.)	1968		X	
Citizens State Bank (Wisc.)	1983			X
Rosenblum (N.J.)	1983			X
Credit Alliance (N.Y.)	1985	X		
Bily v. Arthur Young (Calif.)	1992	X		

Statutory Liability to Third Parties

Audited financial statements are required to be included in information provided to current and prospective investors in public companies. The Securities Act of 1933 and the Securities Exchange Act of 1934 are the primary federal statutes affecting auditor liability for public clients. These laws, enacted to assure that investors in public companies are provided full and adequate disclosure of relevant information, have been modified over the years. The most recent modification significantly affecting the audit profession has been the passage of the Sarbanes-Oxley Act of 2002.

Causes for Action   Auditors found to be unqualified, unethical, or in willful violation of any provision of the federal securities laws can be disciplined by the SEC.

PRACTICAL POINT

Investors in public companies may sue auditors for damages under common law, statutory law, or both.

Sanctions   The sanctions available to the SEC under the Sarbanes-Oxley Act include the following:

- Temporarily or permanently revoking the firm's registration with the Public Company Accounting Oversight Board (PCAOB), meaning that the SEC will not accept its audit reports
- Imposing a civil penalty of up to $750,000 for each violation
- Requiring special continuing education of firm personnel

| Exhibit 17.3 | Negligence Tests for Auditor's Common-Law Liability to Third Parties |

FORESEEABLE USER

FORESEEN USER

IDENTIFIED USER

The auditor knows the user's identity and specific transaction involved.	User is a member of a limited class of users for a specific transaction. Identity of the specific user may or may not be known to the auditor.	Those who could foreseeably use the financial statements.
Example: The auditor knows that the First National Bank wants audited financial statements as part of the client's application for a loan.	*Example:* The auditor knows that the client needs audited financial statements because it wants to obtain a loan from one of several possible banks.	*Example:* Current and prospective creditors and stockholders are likely to use the audited statements.

Securities Act of 1933

The Securities Act of 1933 requires companies to file registration statements with the SEC before they may issue new securities to the public. A registration statement contains, among other things, information about the company itself, its officers and major stockholders, and its plans for using the proceeds from the new securities issue. Part of the registration statement, called the **prospectus**, must be provided to prospective investors. The prospectus includes audited financial statements.

The most important liability section of the 1933 Act is Section 11, which imposes penalties for misstatements contained in registration statements. For purposes of Section 11, the accuracy of the registration statement is determined at its effective date, which is the date the company can begin to sell the new securities. Because the effective date may be several months after the end of the normal audit fieldwork, the auditors must perform certain audit procedures covering events between the end of the normal fieldwork and the effective date.

In understanding the liability provisions of the 1933 Act, it is important to know that the intent of the SEC is to assure full and fair disclosure of public financial information. Thus, the standard of care is unusually high. Anyone receiving the prospectus may sue the auditor based on damages due to alleged misleading financial statements or inadequate audits.

Causes for Action   Under the 1933 Act, an auditor may be held liable to purchasers of securities for negligence, as well as fraud and gross negligence. Purchasers need to prove only that they incurred a loss and that the financial statements were materially misleading or not fairly stated. They do not need to prove reliance on the financial statements, that such statements had been read or even seen, or that the auditors were negligent.

Defenses   The burden of proof shifts to the auditors, who must prove that (1) they used due professional care, (2) the statements were not materially misstated, or (3) the purchaser did not incur a loss caused by the misleading financial statements.

Securities Exchange Act of 1934

The 1934 Act regulates the trading of securities after their initial issuance. Regulated companies are required to file periodic reports with the SEC and stockholders. These are the most common periodic reports:

- *Annual reports* to shareholders and *10-Ks,* which are annual reports filed with the SEC, both containing audited financial statements. 10-Ks must be filed within 60 to 90 days of the end of the fiscal year. Smaller companies have up to 90 days to file; larger companies must file within 60 days.
- *Quarterly financial reports* to shareholders and *10-Qs,* which are quarterly reports filed with the SEC. 10-Qs must be filed within 40 to 45 days of the end of each of the first three quarters and must be reviewed by the auditors. Smaller companies have up to 45 days to file; larger companies must file within 40 days.
- *8-Ks,* which are reports filed with the SEC describing the occurrence of specific events including a change in auditors.

Causes for Action   Under the 1934 Act, an auditor may be held liable for fraud when a plaintiff alleges that it was misled by misstatements in financial statements in making decisions on purchasing or selling securities. The liability criteria for standing are similar to those in common law. The Act explicitly makes it unlawful to make any untrue statement of a material fact or to omit to state a material fact that is necessary for understanding the financial statements.

PRACTICAL POINT

The Securities Act of 1933 establishes a strong fiduciary responsibility for auditors. The burden of responsibility falls to the audit firm to convince a jury that it performed the audit with due care, or the financial statements were not misstated, or the plaintiff's loss was caused by other factors.

PRACTICAL POINT

The 1934 Securities Exchange Act covers most reports that are filed with the SEC.

In *Herzfeld v. Laventhol, Krekstein, Horwath & Horwath* (1974), the auditors were found liable under the 1934 Act for failure to fully disclose the facts and circumstances underlying their qualified opinion. Judge Friendly stated that the auditor cannot be content merely to see that the financial statements meet minimum requirements of GAAP, but that the auditor has a duty to inform the public if adherence to GAAP does not fairly portray the economic results of the company being audited. More specifically, the trial court judge stated:

> The policy underlying the securities laws of providing investors with all the facts needed to make intelligent investment decisions can only be accomplished if financial statements fully and fairly portray the actual financial condition of the company. In those cases where application of generally accepted accounting principles fulfills the duty of full and fair disclosure, the accountant need go no further. But if application of accounting principles alone will not adequately inform investors, accountants, as well as insiders, the auditor must take pains to lay bare all the facts needed by investors to interpret the financial statements accurately.[10]

Federal courts have struggled with the negligence standard implied by the 1934 Act. The standard of holding auditors responsible for gross negligence or constructive fraud had essentially eroded to a standard of negligence. In 1976, the U.S. Supreme Court provided greater guidance in its review of *Ernst & Ernst v. Hochfelder*. The Court held that Congress had intended the plaintiff to prove that an auditor acted with scienter in order to hold the auditor liable under the 1934 Act. The Court reserved judgment as to whether reckless disregard for the truth (gross negligence) would be sufficient to impose liability.

Although it would appear that the *Hochfelder* ruling ought to provide a great deal of comfort for the auditor, several cases that have followed *Hochfelder* indicate that it is not difficult for a judge or jury to infer "reckless conduct" by the auditor and hold the auditor to that standard. As noted earlier, a plaintiff also has the option to bring the case under common law, under which scienter does not have to be proven by the plaintiff.

Defenses   Generally, showing compliance with GAAP is an acceptable defense by the auditor. However, as shown in the statement of Judge Friendly in 1974, the auditor must take care to make sure that GAAP are not being manipulated to achieve a specific financial presentation result that is not in accord with the substance of the transaction.

Sanctions   Both the 1933 and 1934 Acts provide for criminal actions against auditors who willfully violate provisions of either act and related rules or regulations or who know that financial statements are false and misleading and who issue inappropriate opinions on such statements. Guilty persons can be fined or imprisoned. John Burton, a former chief accountant of the SEC, stated the SEC's position on criminal action against auditors:

> While virtually all Commission cases are civil in character, on rare occasions it is concluded that a case is sufficiently serious that it should be referred to the Department of Justice for consideration of criminal prosecution. Referrals in regard to accountants have only been made when the Commission and the staff believed that the evidence indicated that a professional accountant certified financial statements that he knew to be false when he reported on them. The commission does not make criminal references in cases that it believes are simply matters of professional judgment even if the judgments appear to be bad ones.[11]

PRACTICAL POINT

It is generally believed that the ruling by Judge Friendly in 1974 led to the detailed nature of accounting rules in the United States. The auditors and their clients wanted greater specificity as to whether an accounting treatment fairly portrayed financial results.

---

[10] *Herzfeld v. Laventhol, Krekstein, Horwath & Horwath* [1973–1974] Transfer Binder CCH FED. Sec. Law Reporter #94,574, at 95,999 (S.D.N.Y. May 29, 1974).

[11] John C. Burton, "SEC enforcement and professional accountants: philosophy, objectives and approach," *Vanderbilt Law Review* 1975 (January), p. 28.

AUDITING *in Practice*

CRIMINAL CONVICTIONS OF AUDITORS

Two well known criminal actions against auditors are *United States v. Simon* (*Continental Vending*) and *Equity Funding*.

Continental Vending

In the *United States v. Simon (Continental Vending)* action, the jury found two partners and a senior associate of the public accounting firm of Lybrand, Ross Bros. & Montgomery (a predecessor to PricewaterhouseCoopers, LLP) guilty of a conspiracy involving preparing, and giving an unqualified opinion on, misleading financial statements of Continental Vending Machine Corporation. The case represented the first criminal action against auditors who were found guilty even though they did not personally gain from this conspiracy.[12] Additionally, the judge charged the jury to determine whether the financial statements were fairly presented; it was noted that following GAAP does not automatically lead to fairness.

Equity Funding

In the Equity Funding fraud, approximately two-thirds of the life insurance policies reported to be in force—as well as certain investments—were fictitious, and the audit failed to discover any of the bogus transactions. The senior partner of Wolfson Weiner, Equity's auditors, and the in-charge auditor were convicted of criminal violations of the federal securities laws, and their right to practice before the SEC was automatically suspended. The SEC found that the auditors engaged in acts and practices in flagrant violation of its rules and standards of the accounting profession relating to independence.

Summary of Auditor Liability to Third Parties

Refer to Exhibit 17.1. Auditors are clearly liable to injured third parties for fraud under both common law and statutory law. Because third parties are likely to sue under both common law and statutory law in a specific lawsuit, auditors are essentially liable for constructive fraud as well. Auditors are liable for negligence under the Securities Act of 1933 and possibly under common law, depending on the precedent used by the court.

Third parties must prove the auditor's guilt under common law and the Securities Exchange Act of 1934. Under the Securities Act of 1933 however, auditors must prove their innocence. Auditor defenses include the following:

- Due diligence; that is, the auditor did what a prudent auditor would have done.
- The financial statements were not materially misstated.
- The audit was not the cause of the plaintiff's loss.
- The auditor does not have a duty to the plaintiff.

Exhibit 17.4 illustrates the factors plaintiffs must prove in a lawsuit brought against auditors under the 1934 Act or under common law and possible defenses the auditors might use.

Emerging Liability Issues

Liability Issues of Multinational CPA Firms

Most large U.S. CPA firms are affiliates of international organizations; for example, Deloitte is the U.S. member of Deloitte Touche Tohmatsu (DTT). Such organizational structures have important implications for legal liability, although the legal liability outcomes are not always predictable. For example, compare the differential outcomes in the *Auditing in Practice* feature focused on the

LO 5

Discuss emerging and unsettled liability issues of concern to auditors.

---

[12]*United States v. Simon*, 425 F. 2d 796 (2d Cir. 1969).

Exhibit 17.4 — Litigation Overview: Causes of Action and Possible Defenses

SITUATION

Plaintiffs purchased stock in the stock market. The market price subsequently went up and plaintiffs purchased more stock. Company profits, the economy, and general stock market prices then declined. Plaintiffs sold the stock at a loss. Plaintiffs sued the company's management and auditors under the Securities Exchange Act of 1934 and common law for damages measured by the difference between the highest market price and the sales price. Defendants other than the auditors do not carry professional liability insurance and do not have significant personal wealth. Proofs required of the plaintiffs and possible defenses the auditors might use are summarized in the following table.

Proof	Auditor Defenses
Damage is the difference between the highest market price and the sales price	Damage should be the difference between cost and actual sales price.
Statements were false and misleading.	Statements were in accordance with GAAP or not materially misstated.
Reliance on financial statements when making investment decisions	Plaintiffs relied on a personal guarantee of the president and/or on separate inquiry before buying the stock.
Damage was due to false/misleading financial statements.	Damage was due to the decline in general stock market prices, the downturn in the economy, and reduced company profitability after the plaintiff purchased the stock.
Auditor knowledge of false/misleading financial statements: 1. Knew—fraud/scienter 2. Should have known—negligence, lack of due professional care	Auditor rebuttal: 1. Did not know 2. Used due professional care and followed GAAS, was misled by management
Judgment—joint and several liability. Auditors are 30% responsible for the losses. However, they are required to pay 100% of the damages because the other defendants cannot pay.	Under the 1934 Act and under common law in states that have enacted proportionate liability, this was not a willful act by the auditor and, therefore, the auditor is liable for only 30% of the damages. In other states, work to change state law to proportionate liability.

international accounting network firm BDO with those in the audits of Parmalat discussed below.

Parmalat, a large Italian dairy company, filed for bankruptcy in 2003 after a $17 billion misstatement was discovered in the books that was allegedly devised by former executives and hidden for ten years. In its audits of Parmalat, Deloitte & Touche SpA, the Italian member firm of DTT, failed to discover this massive fraud. Even though DTT organized itself as a network of legally separate and independent partnerships in various countries, class action lawsuits were brought against the United States and international arms of DTT, arguing that the firm acted as one entity. Deloitte argued that DTT's global affiliates cannot be responsible for the actions of other arms. In 2005, Deloitte lost its bid for dismissal of these lawsuits, apparently leaving each affiliate responsible for the quality of audits of the other affiliates.[13] In January 2009 a U.S. federal judge said that plaintiffs can sue Deloitte, its former CEO, and its affiliates for the role of the firm's Italian affiliate in the collapse of Parmalat. Then in November 2009, Deloitte Touche Tohmatsu and its U.S.-based firm Deloitte Touche agreed to pay $8.5 million to settle allegations of fraud by Italian auditors connected to Parmalat's 2003 bankruptcy. This might be considered a noteworthy settlement because the settlement involves the worldwide organization, Deloitte Touche Tohmatsu, who was not sued directly for anything it did, but for audits completed by the affiliate firm in Italy.

---

[13] "Judge Refuses to Dismiss Deloitte's Parmalat Lawsuit," www.Accountingweb.com (July 9, 2005).

AUDITING *in Practice*

INTERNATIONAL ACCOUNTING NETWORK FIRM BDO NOT RESPONSIBLE FOR LIABILITY OF THE U.S. MEMBER FIRM

In 2004 Banco Espirito Santo SA sued BDO Seidman (a U.S. member of BDO International B.V) over faulty audits of E. S. Bankest, a compay in which Banco Espirito invested. In June 2007, a jury awarded Banco Espirito Santo SA $521 million. BDO Seidman was responsible for $170 million in losses, plus $351 million in punitive damages (the largest jury verdict in history against a U.S. accounting firm). BDO Seidman is an accounting firm with annual revenue of about $620 million. The plaintiff, worried about BDO Seidman's ability to pay, also sued the BDO International firm on the grounds that BDO

International is one firm with various units operating around the world. However, in June 2009 the jury in the BDO International trial rejected the bank's argument that BDO International controlled BDO Seidman and thus bears responsibility for the audits. BDO International had insisted its member firms are independent, and thus were separately liable for any losses it incurs.

Postscript: In June 2010 a Florida appeals court reversed the 2007 jury award of $521 million and ordered a new trial.

Liability Impact of Internet Dissemination of Audited Financial Information

An unsettled issue of liability concerns audited financial information disseminated on the Internet.[14] Everyone who owns a computer with access to the Internet has access to such information. The liability implications, if not carefully delineated, are staggering. Perhaps one of the most important cases related to this issue was settled before computers were invented. In *Jaillet v. Cashman*, the court dismissed a case against Dow Jones & Co. in 1920 for misreporting information over its newly developed ticker service. The court ruled that to permit a negligence claim would establish a precedent whereby "there is a liability by the defendant to every member of the community who was misled by the incorrect report." "Practical expediency" made dismissal of such a complaint "absolutely necessary."[15]

Internet reporting is here. Audited financial statements are now being provided using XBRL (extended business reporting language). In 2009, the SEC issued rules requiring companies to provide financial information in a form that can be easily downloaded directly into interactive spreadsheets to make it easier for investors to analyze and to assist in automating regulatory filings. The SEC mandate indicates that all public companies have to report their financials using the interactive data format by 2011, and this interactive data will have to be posted to a company's website.

Under the SEC rules, auditors are currently not required to provide assurance on XBRL data in the context of the financial statement audit. However, the IAASB recognizes that there are some XBRL-related services auditors may choose to perform including:

- Agreed-upon procedures engagements on XBRL-tagged data, to assist management in its evaluation of the XBRL-tagged data and the audit committee in its oversight role.

> **PRACTICAL POINT**
>
> Under the current SEC rules and professional auditing standards, auditors are not required to perform procedures or provide assurance on XBRL-tagged data in the context of audited financial statements. Accordingly, the auditor's report on the financial statements does not cover the process by which XBRL data is tagged, the XBRL-tagged data that results from this process, or any representation of XBRL-tagged data.

---

[14] Much of this information is reported in Miller & Young, "Financial reporting and risk management in the 21st century," *Fordham Law Review* 1997 (April).

[15] *Jaillet v. Cashman,* 189 N.Y.S. 743 (Sup. Ct. 1921) *aff'd,* 194 N.Y.S. 947 (App. Div. 1922) *aff'd,* 139 N.E. 714 (N.Y. 1923).

- Assurance engagements, for example, assurance on the controls related to the XBRL-tagging process and examinations of the accuracy of the XBRL-tagged data itself.
- Assurance engagements on financial information as presented in particular pre-defined instance documents.
- Advice on the XBRL implementation process, where not prohibited by relevant independence requirements.
- Preparation of the XBRL-tagged data, where not prohibited by relevant independence requirements.

Enhancing Audit Quality and Minimizing Liability Exposure

LO 6

Identify professional requirements that help assure audit quality and minimize auditor exposure to liability suits.

Various professional requirements help to assure audit quality, and thus potentially minimize the exposure of public accounting firms and partners to lawsuits. These requirements include (1) auditor independence requirements, (2) quality-control programs, and (3) review programs. Further, there are other actions that firms can take. Each of these approaches is discussed in the following sections.

Auditor Independence Requirements

The AICPA, the PCAOB, and the SEC all have requirements to help assure auditor independence. Examples of these requirements include:

- Partner rotation
- Prohibition of nonaudit services
- Restrictions on permitted nonaudit services
- Auditor independence programs

Partner Rotation

Periodic rotation of partners helps bring a fresh approach to audits and minimize bias that may result from long-term contacts with client management. The Sarbanes-Oxley Act requires that the partner in charge of the audit of a public company and the engagement quality review partner be rotated every five years.

PRACTICAL POINT

There are many ways to mitigate liability throughout the audit opinion formulation process, but most boil down to four main points:

1. Remember that the needs of end users are paramount.
2. Do quality work.
3. Be professionally skeptical in performing audit work.
4. Document the work done and the audit reasoning process.

Prohibited Services

To help assure auditor independence, the Sarbanes-Oxley Act prohibits registered public accounting firms from performing certain services for *public company* audit clients, as described in Chapter 3. The major question that each audit firm should ask before providing services in addition to auditing is the following: "If something goes wrong, would either the nature of the services or the amount of revenue generated from the provision of the service lead a neutral observer to believe that our independence in conducting the audit might have been compromised or impaired?" Addressing that simple question on a regular basis would help the profession avoid many of the losses that it has encountered during litigation.

Restrictions on Permitted Nonaudit Services for Audit Clients

The Sarbanes-Oxley Act requires that the audit committee of a public company be responsible for assessing an audit firm's independence. In addition, it requires that any permitted nonaudit services to be performed by its audit firm must be preapproved by the audit committee unless such services, in the aggregate, amount to less than 5% of the total amount paid to its audit firm during the year. The PCAOB has also implemented rules requiring audit committee preapproval of certain tax services and nonaudit services related to internal control over financial reporting.

The AICPA's Code of Professional Conduct (Code) allows public accounting firms to perform services not specifically prohibited for nonpublic audit clients if the firm determines that independence will not be compromised. The firm should also establish an understanding with the client that the client is responsible to:

- Designate a management-level individual(s) to be responsible for overseeing the services being provided
- Evaluate the adequacy of the services performed and any resulting findings
- Make management decisions related to the service

Quality Control Programs

The most important ingredient in mitigating liability exposure is for firms to implement sound quality-control policies and procedures. The AICPA has developed a set of quality-control elements to assist firms in developing such programs. The quality-control standards apply not only to audit services but to accounting and review services performed by the audit firm. The elements of quality control also serve as criteria for external quality/peer reviews. Firms should consider each of the following broad elements of quality control in establishing quality-control policies and procedures:

- Independence, integrity, and objectivity
- Personnel management
- Acceptance and continuance of clients and engagements
- Engagement performance
- Monitoring

Auditor Independence Programs

One of the elements of a public accounting firm's quality-control program is establishing policies and procedures to provide reasonable assurance that personnel maintain independence in fact and in appearance when performing audits. These policies and procedures include both preventive components (e.g., firmwide training program about auditor independence) and detective components, whereby the firm is able to detect any independence violations that were not prevented by the quality-control system (e.g., inspection and testing program to monitor adherence to independence requirements). Such a program may include the following:

- Firm training programs that emphasize factors that can impede independence
- Firm review of all relationships that may affect auditor independence and individual reporting of all potential relationships that might impair independence
- On-the-job review of performance emphasizing the need for skepticism, objectivity, and the need to corroborate management's explanations

Review Programs

Who audits the auditors? A triad of quality reviews exists to help assure the quality of audits: external inspections/peer reviews, engagement quality reviews, and interoffice reviews.

External Inspections/Peer Reviews

The Sarbanes-Oxley Act requires that the PCAOB perform inspections of registered public accounting firms every year for registered firms that have over 100 *public company* audits and every three years for the other registered firms. Inspection reports are available on PCAOB's website (www.pcaobus.org). Many of these reports identify audit performance deficiencies found by the inspectors.

The AICPA has a Peer Review Program that reviews and evaluates those portions of a firm's accounting and auditing practice that are not inspected by the PCAOB; therefore, for public company auditors the focus of the peer reviews would be on the nonpublic clients of the audit firm. Firms and individuals enrolled in the AICPA Peer Review Program are required to have an **external peer review**, applicable to non-SEC issuers, once every three years covering a one-year period. The goal of the peer review program is to promote quality in the accounting and auditing services provided by AICPA members and their CPA firms.

The reviews are conducted by professionals from another public accounting firm and provide an objective assessment of the appropriateness of the firm's quality-control policies and procedures as well as of the degree of compliance with them. For example, the reviewers determine whether the firm has policies and procedures that encourage personnel to seek assistance from persons having the knowledge, competence, judgment, and authority to help resolve a problem (engagement performance element). The monitoring element requires the firm to have policies and procedures to help assure that the other elements are being effectively applied. Quality improvement is sought primarily through education and remedial or corrective actions. Peer review reports are issued to the firm and most are available from the AICPA to be used by prospective clients, employees, and other interested parties.

Internal Review

There are two kinds of internal peer review programs—concurring partner reviews and interoffice reviews. A partner not otherwise involved in the audit performs an **engagement quality review** (also referred to as **concurring partner review**) near the end of each audit to make sure that documented evidence supports the audit opinion. Such reviews are required for audits of public companies, and it is desirable for firms to conduct these reviews on all audits. The concurring partner should be familiar with the nature of the business being audited. Analytical procedures at this stage of the audit help identify unexpected relationships and trends for which sufficient evidence should be documented. Inadequate evidence indicates a need for more audit work. Some single-partner public accounting firms arrange with other small firms to perform concurring reviews for each other before issuing audit reports.

An **interoffice review** is a review of one office of the firm by professionals from another office to assure that the policies and procedures established by the firm are being followed. Like external inspections/peer reviews, interoffice reviews include selecting and reviewing a sample of audits and other jobs to help assure that quality work was performed.

Other Actions to Assure Audit Quality and Minimize Liability Exposure

The actions just discussed are designed to help assure audit quality, thereby potentially minimizing liability exposure. These actions help assure that the quality of the audit opinion formulation process is of a high level. There are, however, other actions firms can take, including (1) issuing engagement letters, (2) making appropriate client acceptance/continuance decisions, (3) evaluating the audit firm's limitations, and (4) maintaining high-quality audit documentation. Auditors can also take steps to help limit the effects of litigation and to alter the litigation environment. These actions include (1) maintaining appropriate

---

PRACTICAL POINT

An important review performed on any audit is by the partner and manager to determine that the audit team has consistently executed a high-quality audit in accordance with professional auditing standards and that all important accounting and audit issues are documented along with the auditor's reasoning process.

PRACTICAL POINT

To enhance the quality of job performance and help assure quality audits, the AICPA requires that its members in public practice earn at least 120 hours of continuing education credit every three years. State boards have similar continuing education requirements. It is important that professionals seek the education to continue to improve their abilities, not just to meet the reporting requirements. Some state boards require that a minimum number of credits be related to professional ethics.

LO 7

Describe defensive actions that audit firms can take to help assure audit quality and minimize the effects of litigation on audit firms and individual auditors.

insurance coverage, (2) organizing as limited liability partnerships, and (3) evaluating potential litigation reform. The actions taken to avoid or minimize liability exposure are sometimes referred to as **defensive auditing**.

Issuing Engagement Letters

The cornerstone of any defensive practice program is the engagement letter. The engagement letter should clearly state the scope of the work to be done so that there can be no doubt in the mind of the client, public accountant, or courts. Care should be taken, however, when describing the degree of responsibility the auditor takes with respect to discovering fraud and misstatements. If the client wants its auditors to go beyond the requirements of the auditing standards, the auditors should have their attorneys review the wording to make sure that it says not only what is intended but also what is possible.

Client Acceptance/Continuance Decisions

Another element of quality-control deals with accepting and retaining clients. This decision should involve more than just a consideration of management's integrity. Strict client acceptance/continuance guidelines should be established to screen out the following:

- *Clients that are in financial and/or organizational difficulty*—For example, clients that could go bankrupt or clients with poor internal accounting controls and sloppy records.
- *Clients that constitute a disproportionate percentage of the firm's total practice*—Clients may attempt to influence the auditor into allowing unacceptable accounting practices or issuing inappropriate opinions.
- *Disreputable clients*—Most public accounting firms cannot afford to have their good reputation tarnished by serving a disreputable client or by associating with a client that has disreputable management.
- *Clients that offer an unreasonably low fee for the auditor's services*—The auditor may attempt to cut corners imprudently or lose money on the engagement. Conversely, auditors may bid for audits at unreasonably low prices.
- *Clients that refuse to sign engagement or management representation letters*—Allowing clients to waive this requirement increases the probability that the scope of services will be expanded by the court.

PRACTICAL POINT

Some audit firms have policies about not accepting clients participating in certain industries that could be seen as potentially detrimental to the reputation of the audit firm.

Evaluating the Audit Firm's Limitations

An audit firm should not undertake an engagement that it is not qualified to handle. This prohibition is especially important for the smaller, growing firms. Statistics show that firms covered by an AICPA professional liability insurance plan that are most susceptible to litigation are those with staffs of eleven to twenty-five accountants. They appear to become overzealous, undertaking engagements they are not qualified to perform.

Maintaining Accurate and Complete Audit Documentation

The audit team should document everything done on the audit. It is difficult to persuade a jury that anything was done that is not documented. Audit documentation should clearly show evidence of supervisory review, particularly in those areas with the greatest potential for improprieties, such as inventories, revenue recognition, and accounting estimates. The documentation should clearly reflect the identification and investigation of related-party transactions, which are ripe for abuse. The investigation of unusual transactions, such as debt swaps or unusual year-end journal entries, should be carefully documented. These types of transactions often lend themselves to inflation of income and avoidance of loss recognition.

Maintaining Appropriate Insurance Coverage

Many public accounting firms carry professional liability insurance to protect themselves from the full financial impact of lawsuit damages. Such insurance has deductibles that can exceed $25 million for a first loss and places a ceiling on how much will be paid for each case. In addition to the deductible, damages exceeding the ceiling have to be paid from the assets of the public accounting firm. Audit firms set aside funds each year to accumulate assets that may subsequently be used to pay for litigation damages; in this sense audit firms are "self-insured."

Organizing as Limited-Liability Partnerships

Most of the large public accounting firms are limited-liability partnerships (LLPs). The partners of LLPs are taxed like partnerships (i.e., no double taxation). If an LLP goes bankrupt, the partners' personal assets are not at risk for paying the firm's debts, except for the assets of any partners who caused the bankruptcy.

Evaluating Potential Litigation Reform

CPAs, business leaders, and others have often been involved in urging changes in federal and state laws. The need for litigation reform is often based on a line of reasoning indicating that it would take only one or two cases where large settlements could threaten a firm's existence. Those advocating litigation reform are quick to caution that reforms are not to be used to give audit firms a "free pass" for substandard audits.

One change that has been pursued is a change from joint and several liability to proportionate liability at the federal level. There is also extensive effort to get tort reform introduced and passed at the state level, which has been successful in several states and is making progress in many others. For example, in Minnesota prior to 2002, if the public accounting firm was found to be as little as 16% responsible, it could be held liable for 100% of the damages. In 2002, the legislature raised the 16% threshold to 50%. Another change desired by CPAs and others is a reduction in nuisance suits by requiring plaintiffs to pay defendant's court costs if the court determines the case is without merit. There are also efforts directed at limiting liability risk through allowing a contract between the audit client and the auditor, which creates a cap on liabilities.

Summary

The idea that "it can't happen to me" is dangerous for auditors to believe. Professional liability is one of the most significant concerns facing public accounting firms and individual auditors. Although audits should not necessarily be conducted with a paranoid focus on potential litigation, the concepts included in this chapter should be instilled in the minds of every auditor as they "defensively audit" their clients. Performing audit engagements with due professional care significantly reduces the possibility of being held liable, but it does not guarantee avoidance of lawsuits and the costs associated with those lawsuits.

Significant Terms

Breach of contract   Failure to perform a contractual duty that has not been excused; for public accounting firms, the parties to a contract normally include clients and designated "third-party beneficiaries."

Class action suits   Brought on behalf of a large group of plaintiffs to consolidate suits and to encourage consistent judgments and minimize litigation costs; plaintiff shareholders may bring suit for themselves and all others in a similar situation, that is, all other shareholders of record at a specific date.

Common law   Developed through court decisions, custom, and usage without written legislation and operating on court precedence; may differ from state to state or by jurisdiction.

Concurring partner review   See engagement quality review.

Constructive fraud   See gross negligence.

Contingent-fee cases   Lawsuits brought by plaintiffs with compensation for their attorneys contingent on the outcome of the litigation, usually one-third of the damages awarded (including punitive damages), but could be for any amount negotiated between the plaintiff and the lawyer.

Contract law   Stems from case law, the *Uniform Commercial Code,* and other state statutes and establishes the rights and responsibilities of parties to consensual, private agreements.

Deep-pocket theory   The practice of suing another party not based on the level of their true fault in a legal action, but instead suing another party based on the perceived ability of that party to pay damages.

Defensive auditing   Taking actions to avoid lawsuits.

Engagement quality review   An independent review of an audit report and accompanying documentation by a partner or review function independent of the engagement personnel before an audit report is issued (also known as concurring partner review).

External peer review   An independent review of the quality of a public accounting firm; performed by professionals who are not a part of the firm or organization.

Foreseeable user   Those not known specifically by the auditor to be using the financial statements, but recognized by general knowledge as current and potential creditors and investors who will use them.

Foreseen user   Individually unknown third parties who are members of a known or intended class of third-party users who the auditor, through knowledge gained from interactions with the client, can foresee will use the statements. Although foreseen users are not identified in the engagement letter, the auditor may have firsthand knowledge, for example, that the financial statements will be used to obtain a loan from some bank.

Fraud   Intentional concealment or misrepresentation of a material fact with the intent to deceive another person, causing damage to the deceived person.

Gross negligence (also known as constructive fraud)   Failure to use even minimal care or evidence of activities that show a "recklessness or careless disregard for the truth"; evidence may not be present, but may be inferred by a judge or jury because of the carelessness of the defendant's conduct.

Identified user   Third-party beneficiaries and other users when the auditor has specific knowledge that known users will be utilizing the financial statements in making specific economic decisions. They do not have to be named in an engagement letter.

Interoffice review   A review of one office of a firm by professionals from another office of the same firm to help assure that the firm's policies and procedures are being followed.

Joint and several liability   Individual responsibility for an entire judgment against all when one defendant cannot pay the damages awarded to a plaintiff. Apportions losses among all defendants who have an ability to pay for the damages, regardless of the level of fault.

Negligence   Failure to exercise reasonable care, thereby causing harm to another or to property.

Proportionate liability   Payment by an individual defendant based on the degree of fault of the individual.

Prospectus   The first part of a registration statement filed with the SEC, issued as part of a public offering of debt or equity and used to solicit prospective investors in a new security issue containing, among other items, audited financial statements. The Securities Act of 1933 imposes liability for misstatements in a prospectus.

Scienter   An intent to deceive (fraud).

Statutory law   Developed through legislation, such as the Securities Act of 1933 and the Securities Exchange Act of 1934.

Third-party beneficiary   A person who was not a party to a contract but is named in the contract as one to whom the contracting parties intended that benefits be given.

Tort   A civil wrong, other than breach of contract, based on negligence, constructive fraud, or fraud.

SELECTED REFERENCES TO RELEVANT PROFESSIONAL GUIDANCE	
TOPIC	**SELECTED GUIDANCE**
Quality Control and Engagement Review	AICPA Statement on Quality Control Standards 7 *A Firm's System of Quality Control*
	AICPA Statement on Quality Control Standards 8 *A Firm's System of Quality Control* (Redrafted) (effective January 2012)
	SAS No. 25 *The Relationship of Generally Accepted Auditing Standards to Quality Control Standards*
	SAS *Quality Control for an Engagement Conducted in Accordance With Generally Accepted Auditing Standards* (issued but not effective; proposed effective date is December 2012)
	AS No. 7 *Engagement Quality Review*
	IAASB International Standard on Quality Control 1 *Quality Control for Firms That Perform Audits and Reviews of Historical Financial Information, and Other Assurance and Related Services Engagements*
	ISA 220 *Quality Control for Audits of Historical Financial Information*
Independence	SAS *Overall Objectives of the Independent Auditor and Conduct of an Audit in Accordance with Generally Accepted Auditing Standards* (issued but not effective; proposed effective date is December 2012)
	SAS 1 *Codification of Auditing Standards and Procedures*
	PCAOB Rule 3520 *Auditor Independence*
	PCAOB Rule 3523 *Tax Services for Persons in Financial Reporting Oversight Role*
	PCAOB Rule 3526 *Communication with Audit Committees Concerning Independence*
	PCAOB Rule 3525 *Audit Committee Pre-Approval of Nonaudit Services Related to Internal Control over Financial Reporting*
	PCAOB Rule 3524 *Audit Committee Pre-Approval of Certain Tax Services*
	SEC Regulation SX Rule 2-01 *Qualifications of Accountants*
	ISA 200 *Overall Objectives of the Independent Auditor and the Conduct of an Audit in Accordance with International Standards on Auditing*

Note: *Acronyms for Relevant Professional Guidance*

STANDARDS: **AS**—Auditing Standard issued by the PCAOB; **ISA**—International Standard on Auditing issued by the IAASB; **SAS**—Statement on Auditing Standards issued by the Auditing Standards Board of the AICPA; **SSAE**—Statement on Standards for Attestation Engagements issued by the AICPA.

ORGANIZATIONS: **AICPA**—American Institute of Certified Public Accountants; **COSO**—Committee of Sponsoring Organizations; **IAASB**—International Auditing and Assurance Standards Board; **PCAOB**—Public Company Accounting Oversight Board; **SEC**—Securities and Exchange Commission.

Review Questions

17-1   **(LO 1)**   The chapter describes societal and judicial factors that affect lawsuits against auditors. Identify these factors and briefly describe their impact.

17-2   **(LO 2, 4)**   Distinguish between common law and statutory law.

17-3   **(LO 2, 4)**   What are the potential causes of action against an auditor under a breach of contract lawsuit?

17-4   **(LO 4)**   In what significant ways might settlements brought against an auditor under a breach of contract suit differ from those occurring when a client brings a lawsuit under other common-law violations?

17-5   **(LO 4)**   When a client sues the auditor under common law, is the client or the auditor required to furnish the burden of proof? What must be proven in order for the client to receive damages?

17-6   **(LO 4)** What defenses might an auditor use in successfully defending a:

   a. Suit brought about because of breach of contract?

   b. Suit brought under tort law?

17-7   **(LO 4)** What is meant by the *due diligence standard*? What factors might an auditor cite in using due diligence as a defense in a court case?

17-8   **(LO 3)** What precedent was set by the *Ultramares* case? What was the primary argument used by Judge Cardozo in setting the precedent?

17-9   **(LO 4)** Three tests have been used by various courts in common-law decisions to determine which third-party users can successfully bring a suit against the auditor for negligence. Identify each of these tests and describe the parties that are defined in each of these tests.

17-10   **(LO 4)** What are the administrative sanctions the SEC can bring against auditors who have violated statutory law?

17-11   **(LO 4)** Briefly explain the primary purpose of the:

   a. Securities Act of 1933

   b. Securities Exchange Act of 1934

Fraud

17-12   **(LO 4)** What are common causes of action for breach of contract against auditors?

17-13   **(LO 3, 4)** How does the auditor's liability to third parties differ under the 1933 Act and the 1934 Exchange Act? What is the importance of the *Hochfelder* case as it relates to the 1934 Act?

Fraud

17-14   **(LO 7)** What are some of the defensive approaches used by auditors that might cause concern to investors about audit quality? Why would investors be concerned?

17-15   **(LO 1)** What are the negative effects on a public accounting firm of:

   a. Losing a lawsuit?

   b. Winning a lawsuit?

17-16   **(LO 2, 4)** Is there a conceptual difference between an "error" on the part of the auditor and "ordinary negligence"? Explain.

17-17   **(LO 3)** What precedent was set in the *Hochfelder* case described in the chapter? What actions would be necessary to change the precedent?

17-18   **(LO 3)** Why is the *Rosenblum* case a particularly important case in auditor liability?

17-19   **(LO 6)** How do continuing-education requirements for CPAs respond to the need to reduce liability?

17-20   **(LO 6, 7)** What is meant by *defensive auditing*? What are some of the actions a public accounting firm can take to minimize the likelihood of lawsuits?

17-21   **(LO 6)** What is the purpose of the AICPA's Peer Review Program

17-22   **(LO 6)** What are the main elements of any audit firm's programs to assure auditor independence?

17-23   **(LO 1, 7)** Explain the advantage to a public accounting firm of proportionate liability as opposed to joint and several liability.

17-24   **(LO 6)** Explain the difference between the purposes of an engagement quality review (sometimes referred as concurring partner review) and an interoffice review.

17-25   **(LO 6)** How often are registered public accounting firms required to undergo a PCAOB inspection?

17-26   **(LO 6)** Are nonregistered public accounting firms required to have external peer reviews? Explain.

17-27   **(LO 5)** Describe the liability issues and uncertainties for large U.S. CPA firms that are affiliates of international organizations.

17-28   **(LO 4)** Comment on the accuracy of the following statements.

(a) The Securities Act of 1933 broadened the auditor's liability from what had existed under common law and the Securities Act of 1934 narrowed the auditor's liability.

(b) The auditor has a greater burden of defense under the Securities Act of 1933 than under the Securities Act of 1934.

Multiple-Choice Questions

17-29   **(LO 1, 4)** In a common-law suit for damages, the jury awards the plaintiffs $1 million. The jury also determines that management is 80% at fault, the auditors are 15% at fault, and management's counsel is 5% at fault. Assume that management is unable to pay any damages. Under joint and several liability, the auditor would be responsible for damages of what amount?

a. $1 million
b. $750,000
c. $270,000
d. $150,000

17-30   **(LO 1, 4)** Use the same facts as in Question 17-29. Under proportionate liability, the auditor would be responsible for damages of what amount?

a. $1 million
b. $750,000
c. $270,000
d. $150,000

*17-31   **(LO 4)** Nast Corp. orally engaged Baker & Co., CPAs, to audit its financial statements. Nast management informed Baker that it suspected the accounts receivable were materially overstated. Although the financial statements audited by Baker did, in fact, include a materially overstated accounts receivable balance, Baker issued an unqualified opinion. Nast relied on the financial statements in deciding to obtain a loan from Century Bank to expand its operations. Nast has defaulted on the loan and has incurred a substantial loss.

---

*All question marked with an asterisk are adopted from the Uniform CPA Examination.

If Nast sues Baker for negligence in failing to discover the overstatement, Baker's best defense would be which of the following?

a. Baker did not perform the audit recklessly or with intent to deceive.

b. Baker was not in privity of contract with Nast.

c. Baker performed the audit in accordance with generally accepted auditing standards.

d. Baker had not signed an engagement letter.

*17-32   **(LO 4)** If a stockholder sues a CPA for common-law fraud based on false statements contained in the financial statements audited by the CPA, which of the following, if present, would be the CPA's best defense?

Fraud

a. The stockholder lacks privity to sue.

b. The false statements were immaterial.

c. The CPA did not financially benefit from the alleged fraud.

d. The client was guilty of contributory negligence.

17-33   **(LO 4)** In a common-law action against an accountant, lack of privity is a viable defense if the plaintiff:

a. Is the client's creditor who sues the accountant for negligence.

b. Can prove the presence of gross negligence that amounts to a reckless disregard for the truth.

c. Is the accountant's client.

d. Bases the action upon fraud.

17-34   **(LO 4)** Under common law, which of the following statements most accurately reflects the liability of a CPA who fraudulently gives an opinion on an audit of a client's financial statements?

Fraud

a. The CPA is liable only to third parties in privity of contract with the CPA.

b. The CPA is liable only to known users of the financial statements.

c. The CPA probably is liable to any person who suffered a loss as a result of the fraud.

d. The CPA is clearly liable to the client, even if the client was aware of the fraud and did not rely on the opinion.

*17-35   **(LO 4)** Which one of the elements is necessary to hold a CPA liable to a client for negligently conducting an audit?

a. Acted with scienter.

b. Was a fiduciary of the client.

c. Failed to exercise due care.

d. Executed an engagement letter.

*17-36   **(LO 4)** Which of the following, if present, would support a finding of constructive fraud on the part of a CPA?

a. Privity of contract

b. Intent to deceive

c. Reckless disregard

d. Ordinary negligence

*17-37   **(LO 4)** Which of the following penalties is usually imposed against an auditor who breaches contract duties owed to a client in the performance of audit services?

a. Money damages

b. Punitive damages

c. Specific performance

d. Both (a) and (c)

e. All of the above

*17-38   **(LO 4)** Under Section 11 of the Securities Act of 1933, a CPA usually will not be liable to the purchaser:

a. If the purchaser is contributorily negligent.

b. If the CPA can prove due diligence.

c. Unless the purchaser can prove privity with the CPA.

d. Unless the purchaser can prove scienter on the part of the CPA.

Fraud

*17-39   **(LO 4)** Under Section 11 of the Securities Act of 1933, which of the following must be proven by a purchaser of the security?

	Reliance on the Financial Statements	Fraud by the CPA
a.	Yes	Yes
b.	Yes	No
c.	No	Yes
d.	No	No

*17-40   **(LO 6)** Which of the following professional requirements help to assure auditor independence?

a. Partner rotation

b. Prohibition of nonaudit services

c. Restrictions on permitted nonaudit services

d. Auditor independence programs

e. All of the above

Discussion and Research Questions

17-41   **(Liability for Negligence, LO 4)** An auditor was sued for and found guilty of ordinary negligence.

Required

For each of the following situations, indicate the likelihood the plaintiff would win if the plaintiff is:

a. A financial institution that was known to the auditor as the primary beneficiary of the audit, suing under common law.

b. A stockholder suing under common law.

c. A financial institution that was unknown to the auditor loaned money to the client based on the audit financial statements, but the auditor knew only that the client would use the statements to obtain a loan from some financial institution. The plaintiff is suing under common law.

d. An investor suing under the 1934 Exchange Act.

e. An investor suing under the 1933 Act.

17-42   **(Responsibility for Negligence, LO 3, 4)**

a. Compare an auditor's liability to third parties for negligence under *Ultramares, Credit Alliance, 1965 Restatement (Second) of Torts,* and *Rosenblum.* Which approach do you think auditors prefer? Why?

b. Which approach do you think is best for society? Why?

17-43   **(Recoverability of Damages, LO 4)** An auditor issued an unqualified opinion on financial statements that failed to disclose that a significant portion of the accounts receivable was uncollectible. The auditor also failed to follow professional audit standards with respect to inventory. The auditor knew that the financial statements would be used to obtain a loan. The client subsequently declared bankruptcy.

Required

Under what concepts might a creditor who loaned money to the client on the basis of the financial statements recover from the auditor?

17-44   **(Defense Against an Investor, LO 4)** An investor is suing an auditor for issuing an unqualified opinion on the financial statements of Duluth Industries, which contained a material error. The auditor was negligent in performing the audit. The investor had reason to believe the statements were wrong prior to purchasing stock in the company.

   In the subsequent period, Duluth Industries sustained operating losses, the stock price went down by 40%, and the investor sold the stock at a loss. During the period that the investor held this stock, the Dow Jones Industrial Average declined 10%.

Required

What defenses might the auditor use?

17-45   **(Identified User Test, LO 2, 4)** A client applied for a bank loan from First Bank. In connection with the loan application, the client engaged an auditor to audit its financial statements, and the auditor issued an unqualified opinion. On the basis of those statements, First Bank loaned money to the client. Shortly thereafter, the client filed for bankruptcy and First Bank sued the auditor for damages. The audit documentation showed negligence and possible other misconduct in performing the audit.

Fraud

Required

a. Under what circumstances is First Bank an identified user?

b. What exceptions to the identified user test might First Bank argue?

17-46   **(Interpreting the Negligence Standard, LO 2, 4)** It is often difficult for courts to interpret the negligence standard in deciding whether an act or omission by the auditor constitutes a simple error, negligence, or gross negligence. Often the courts look to the standards of prudent professionals in the conduct of auditing to provide guidance.

Required

For each situation listed, briefly describe whether you think the act or omission constitutes negligence, gross negligence, or neither. Support your answer with a brief rationale. Assume that each of the situations led to material errors in the financial statement and to a lawsuit against the auditors.

a. The auditor failed to note that a confirmation signature was a forgery.

b. The auditor had the client mail out the accounts receivable confirmations in order to expedite completion of the audit and to save audit fees. The client and auditor had agreed, in advance, to this procedure as a way to reduce audit fees.

c. The auditor failed to recognize that the client's warranty accrual was understated. The understatement was due to a new-product introduction with which the client had no experience.

d. The client's loan loss reserve (allowance for uncollectible loans) was materially understated. Many of the client's loans were not documented and were not properly collateralized.

e. The auditor failed to discover a material misstatement of sales and accounts receivable. The auditor had noted a large increase in year-end sales and receivables but did not plan any special procedures because previous audits had not indicated any errors. Most of the year-end sales were fictitious.

f. The client had inappropriately charged a material amount of new capital equipment to repairs and maintenance expense. The client did so in order to minimize its tax liability. The auditor did not perform a detailed review of repairs and maintenance, but did note that the account had risen only 15% above the previous year and that sales had increased 5%.

g. Same situation as in part (f), except that the auditor assigned an inexperienced auditor to the audit of maintenance. It was the auditor's first time on the job, and she failed to recognize that items should have been capitalized because she was not familiar with the industry or the client's capitalization policy.

Fraud

17-47   **(1933 Securities Act, LO 4)** The Monicker Co. engaged the accounting firm of Gasner & Gasner to audit the financial statements to be used in connection with a public offering of securities. Monicker's stock is regularly traded on the NASDAQ. The audit was completed and an unqualified opinion was expressed on the financial statements, which were submitted to the SEC along with the registration statement.

Three hundred thousand shares of Monicker common stock were sold to the public at $13.50 per share. Eight months later, the stock fell to $2 per share when it was disclosed that several large loans to two "paper" companies owned by one of the directors were worthless. The loans were secured by the stock of the borrowing corporation and by stock of Monicker that was owned by the director. These facts were not disclosed in the financial statements. The director and the two corporations are insolvent.

Required

Indicate whether each of the following statements is true or false and briefly explain the rationale for your choice.

a. The Securities Act of 1933 applies to the preceding public offering of securities.

b. The accounting firm has potential liability to any person who acquired the stock described in connection with the public offering.

c. An investor who bought shares in Monicker would make a prima facie case if he or she alleged that the failure to explain the nature of the loans in question constituted a false statement or misleading omission in the financial statements.

 d. The auditors could avoid liability if they could show that they were not fraudulent in the conduct of the audit.

 e. The auditors could avoid, or reduce, the damages asserted against them if they could establish that the drop in price was due in whole or in part to other causes.

 f. The SEC would establish contributory negligence as a partial defense for the auditor because the SEC approved the registration statement.

 g. The auditor could reduce the liability if the auditor could prove that the loans were a fraud perpetrated by management to inflate the stock price.

17-48 **(Auditor Defenses, LO 4)** Plaintiffs purchased stock of Shiloh, Inc. in the over-the-counter market. The market price subsequently went up and the plaintiffs purchased more stock. Shiloh's profits, the economy, and general stock market prices then declined. Plaintiffs sold the stock at a loss and sued the company's management and auditors for damages.

Required

What possible defenses might the auditors use against each of the following potential allegations the plaintiffs could make?

 a. The auditors knew the statements were misleading.

 b. The auditors were negligent and should have known the statements were misleading.

 c. The statements were materially false and misleading.

 d. Plaintiffs sustained a loss because of the false/misleading financial statements.

 e. The plaintiffs are a foreseeable user; therefore, the auditors have a duty to the plaintiffs.

17-49 **(Recent Common-Law Cases, LO 2, 3, 4)** Using the Internet resources (general resources or those available through your library, such as LEXIS/NEXIS, *the Wall Street Journal Index*, the *Accountants Index, ABI Inform*, and the *Business Periodicals Index*) prepare briefs of recent common-law cases brought against auditors, including the tests used by the courts to decide the cases. For example, you might consider investigating suits brought against the auditors in connection with the failures of Fannie Mae, Freddie Mac, Bear Stearns, Lehman Brothers, or New Century. In your briefs, discuss (a) the alleged audit deficiency, (b) the damages asserted by the plaintiffs and the linkage of those damages to the auditor, (c) the negligence standard used by the court, (d) the court's findings, and (e) the implications for the broader auditing profession.

Internet

17-50 **(Ethical Decision Making, LO 4, 8)** In 2005, Deloitte & Touche agreed to pay a $50 million settlement concerning its failed audit of Adelphia Communications. The settlement was the largest ever to that date, and included a record penalty of $25 million. Individual auditors found to be unqualified, unethical, or in willful violation of any provision of the federal securities laws can be disciplined by the SEC. Actions taken by the SEC in these types of situations are described in *Accounting and Auditing Enforcement Releases (AAER), Litigation Releases*, and *Administrative Proceedings* available at www.sec.gov.

Internet

Ethics

Required

a. Read AAER 2326 (September 30, 2005; Administrative Proceeding File No. 3-12065) and AAER No. 2842 (June 25, 2008; Administrative Proceeding File No. 3-12065), available at www.sec.gov. These releases relate to the actions of William E. Caswell, CPA, who served as a director and held the most senior, nonpartner position on the Adelphia engagement. What type of improper professional conduct was William E. Caswell, CPA, engaged in? In 2005, what was the SEC's response to this behavior? What was the SEC's response in 2008?

b. Consider Caswell's failure to make sure that Adelphia's disclosure of its liabilities related to the co-borrowing credit facilities was sufficient. Use the seven-step ethical decision-making framework from Chapter 3 to assess Caswell's actions related to this disclosure.

Recall that the seven steps in the ethical decision-making framework are as follows: (1) identify the ethical issue, (2) determine who are the affected parties and identify their rights, (3) determine the most important rights, (4) develop alternative courses of action, (5) determine the likely consequences of each proposed course of action, (6) assess the possible consequences, including an estimation of the greatest good for the greatest number, and (7) decide on the appropriate course of action.

17-51   **(Independence Requirements—Mitigating Exposure to Liability, LO 6)**

Required

a. Explain the advantages and disadvantages of requiring rotation of the partner-in-charge of an audit at least every five years.

b. Providing financial information system consulting services to an audit client is a prohibited service under the Sarbanes-Oxley Act. Under what conditions could providing such services impair an auditor's independence? How might providing such services help improve the quality of an audit?

17-52   **(Inspections/Peer Reviews—Mitigating Exposure to Liability, LO 6)** There are several types of inspections/peer reviews: (1) engagement quality (concurring partner) review, (2) an interoffice review, (3) an inspection of registered CPA firms by PCAOB, and (4) an external peer review of CPA firms.

Required

a. What are the objectives of each type of review?

b. Under what circumstances are each of the types required?

c. To whom are external inspection/peer review reports issued? For what purposes might the reports be used?

17-53   **(Court Influence on Auditing Standards, LO 2, 3, 4)** It has been generally asserted that a standard of "due care" was sufficient to meet the negligence standard. Yet the court system has been an influence on the development of auditing standards in such areas as related-party transactions, discovery of events subsequent to the balance sheet date, and development of specific procedures required on all audits.

Required

a. If adherence to professional auditing standards such as GAAS is generally considered a sufficient defense, why might the courts decide that the auditors were negligent in the court cases cited in the chapter? What standard of negligence might the courts be using?

b. The chapter also talks about the *Herzfeld v. Laventhol et al.* case, in which the judge decided that adherence to a literal interpretation of GAAP was not sufficient for fair presentation. What was the court's rationale? What are the specific implications of the *Herzfeld* case for auditors?

c. What do these court cases imply regarding a literal interpretation of GAAP and GAAS vs. a "substance" interpretation of the accounting and auditing standards?

Cases

*17-54   **(SEC Statutes, LO 2, 4)** To expand its operations, Dark Corp. raised $4 million by making a private interstate offering of $2 million in common stock and negotiating a $2 million loan from Safe Bank. The common stock was properly offered pursuant to Rule 505 of Regulation D, which exempts the offering from the 1933 Act but not the antifraud provisions of the Federal Securities Acts.

In connection with this financing, Dark engaged Crea & Co., CPAs, to audit Dark's financial statements. Crea knew that the sole purpose for the audit was so that Dark would have audited financial statements to provide to Safe and the purchasers of the common stock. Although Crea conducted the audit in conformity with its audit program, Crea failed to detect material acts of embezzlement committed by Dark's president. Crea did not detect the embezzlement because of its inadvertent failure to exercise due care in designing its audit program for this engagement.

After completing the audit, Crea rendered an unqualified opinion on Dark's financial statements. The financial statements were relied on by the purchasers of the common stock in deciding to purchase the shares. In addition, Safe approved the loan to Dark based on the audited financial statements. Within 60 days after selling the common stock and obtaining the loan from Safe, Dark was involuntarily petitioned into bankruptcy. Because of the president's embezzlement, Dark became insolvent and defaulted on its loan to Safe. Its common stock became virtually worthless. Actions have been commenced against Crea by:

- The purchasers of the common stock, who have asserted that Crea is liable for damages under the Securities Exchange Act of 1934.

- Safe, based on Crea's negligence.

Required

a. In separate paragraphs, discuss the merits of the actions commenced against Crea by the purchasers of the common stock and by Safe, indicating the likely outcomes and the reasoning behind each outcome.

b. How would your answer be different if the client filed a registration statement and the purchasers of the common stock were able to bring suit under the 1933 Act?

c. If Dark (the client) sued Crea under common law, indicate the likely outcome and the rationale.

*17-55   **(Federal Securities Laws, LO 2, 4)**

Part A

The common stock of Wilson, Inc. is owned by twenty stockholders who live in several states. Wilson's financial statements as of December 31, 2012 were audited by Doe & Co., CPAs, who rendered an unqualified opinion on the financial statements.

In reliance on Wilson's financial statements, which showed net income for 2012 of $1,500,000, Peters purchased 10,000 shares of Wilson stock for $200,000 on April 10, 2013. The purchase was from a shareholder who lived in another state. Wilson's financial statements contained material misstatements. Because Doe did not carefully follow GAAS, it did not discover that the statements failed to reflect unrecorded expenses, which reduced Wilson's actual net income to $800,000. After disclosure of the corrected financial statements, Peters sold his shares for $100,000, which was the highest price he could obtain.

Peters has brought an action against Doe under federal securities law and state common law.

Required

Answer the following, setting forth reasons for any conclusions stated:

a. Will Peters prevail on his federal securities-law claims?

b. Will Peters prevail on his state common-law claims?

Part B

Able Corporation decided to make a public offering of bonds to raise needed capital. On June 30, 2012, it publicly sold $2,500,000 of 12% debentures in accordance with the registration requirements of the Securities Act of 1933.

The financial statements filed with the registration statement contained the unqualified opinion of Baker & Co., CPAs. The statements overstated Able's net income and net worth. Through negligence, Baker did not detect the overstatements. As a result, the bonds, which originally sold for $1,000 per bond, have dropped in value to $700.

Ira is an investor who purchased $10,000 of the bonds. He promptly brought an action against Baker under the Securities Act of 1933.

Required

Answer the following, setting forth reasons for any conclusions stated:

a. Will Ira likely prevail on his claim under the Securities Act of 1933?

b. Identify the primary issues that will determine the likelihood of Ira's prevailing on the claim.

Ethics   17-56   **(Ethical Decisions and Time Pressure, LO 1, 8)** You have worked as a staff auditor for two and one-half years and have mastered your job. You will likely be promoted to a senior position after this busy season. Your current senior was promoted about a year ago. He appreciates your competence and rarely interferes with you. As long

Group Activity

as he can report good performance to his manager on things she wants, he is satisfied. The manager has been in her position for three years. She is focused on making sure audits run smoothly and is good at this. She is not as strong on the softer skills. Although she is approachable, her attention span can be short if what you are saying does not interest her. You are aware that she expects her teams to perform excellently during this busy season and she hopes to be promoted to senior manager as a result, bringing her closer to her goal of making partner early.

The audit engagement on which you are working has become increasingly difficult since last year's engagement because of some complicated accounting transactions that the client made. There has also been unexpected turnover in accounting personnel at the client. This has made interacting with the client and getting the information you need in a timely manner problematic. However, the engagement time budget and the audit fee remain the same as last year's. Further, four staff auditors are assigned to the engagement, and there are no additional staff available to transfer in to ease the workload. Your senior now tells you that the manager has requested that you, he, and the other staff auditors do an additional analysis of a potential misstatement in one of the client's accounts. Even with your team's current workload there is significant danger that the engagement will run "over budget." You know that if you do the analysis thoroughly, it will further endanger meeting the time budget the manager had planned. The more time you spend on the engagement, the less profitable it will be for the audit firm, which will clearly displease the manager and her superiors.

As a group, the staff auditors discuss the situation and express their concerns regarding the perceptions that running over budget will create and the reputational issues that short-circuiting the analysis could create. When your senior stops by to discuss the new plan, the group raises its concerns. He talks to the group and implies that he would be satisfied if the team did either of the following: complete the analysis and simply not record the hours (doing so would prevent the reported audit hours from going too far over budget) or do a minimal job on the analysis, which would save time and avoid having to question the client too much. You and a few other staff members express discomfort with either of these strategies. It is suggested that the ramifications of the new order be made clear to the manager. The senior wants nothing to do with this. He says, "She doesn't want to hear these details so just use one of the ideas I have already given you."

When he leaves, several staff members start griping about what they are being asked to do. A couple say they are going to leave the firm after this busy season, so they don't really care about this issue. Another says, "We've been told what to do. Let's just get on with it."

Required

a. In a small group, discuss this situation and use the seven-step ethical decision-making framework from Chapter 3 (reproduced below) to make a recommendation about the course of action the staff auditors should take.

Recall that the seven steps in the ethical decision-making framework are as follows: (1) identify the ethical issue, (2) determine who are the affected parties and identify their rights, (3) determine the most important rights, (4) develop alternative courses of action,

(5) determine the likely consequences of each proposed course of action, (6) assess the possible consequences, including an estimation of the greatest good for the greatest number, and (7) decide on the appropriate course of action.

b. How can you do what you feel is the right thing without undermining your senior or undermining the manager's confidence in your ability to get a job done?

Internet

Fraud

17-57 **(Madoff Auditor, LO 2, 4)** One of the headlines provided at the beginning of the chapter refers to David Friehling, the auditor for the Bernard L. Madoff Investment Securities, LLC. Perform research using Internet resources on the actions of Mr. Friehling in connection with these audits and his guilty plea. Based on your research, write a brief memo indicating whether you believe it is evident from the results of the Madoff fraud case that the auditor must have been guilty of some audit failure. In your answer, be sure to comment on an auditor's responsibility to detect fraud and on the likelihood of detecting fraud in cases of collusion.

Internet

Fraud

Professional Skepticism

17-58 **(Recent Litigation, LO 1, 2, 3, 4)** In June 2009 Deloitte agreed to pay almost $1 million to settle a class action lawsuit related to its audits of Beazer, a homebuilding company. The lawsuit claims that Deloitte should have noticed the homebuilder was issuing inaccurate financial statements as the housing market began to decline. A spokesperson for Deloitte indicated that the firm denies all liability and settled to avoid the expense and uncertainty of continued litigation.

Required

a. Using Internet sources, research this case and identify red flags that the auditor should have been aware of in these audits. One source that can get you started on your Internet search is: http://www.cfo.com/article.cfm/13612963?f=search.

b. If these red flags were indeed present during Deloitte's audit, what were the auditors' responsibilities in conducting the audit?

c. Comment on Deloitte's willingness to settle the case while at the same time denying liability.

Internet

Fraud

17-59 **(Recent Litigation, LO 2, 3, 4)** Review the *Professional Judgment in Context* feature on AIG at the beginning of the chapter. Use Internet resources to research this case and determine the outcome of the September 2010 appeals case.

Based on your research, answer the following question. (Your professor will advise you whether you are to prepare a formal written response or you are to be prepared to present your position in class.)

Do you agree with the outcome of the appeals case? Your response should include an indication as to whether you agree with the position of the AICPA or of the attorney representing AIG investors.

Academic Research Case (LO 6)

Brandon, D. M. & Mueller, J. M. (2006). The Influence of Client Importance on Juror Evaluations of Auditor Liability. *Behavioral Research in Accounting* 18:1–18.

i. What is the issue being addressed in the paper?

ii. Why is this issue important to practicing auditors?

iii. What are the findings of the paper?

iv. What are the implications of these findings for audit quality (or audit practice) on the audit profession?

v. Describe the research methodology used as a basis for the conclusions.

vi. Describe any limitations of the research that the student (and practice) should be aware of.

SEARCH HINT

It is easy to locate these academic research articles! Simply use a search engine (e.g., Google Scholar) or an electronic research platform (e.g., ABI Inform) and search using the author names and part of the article title.

18

Advanced Topics Concerning Complex Auditing Judgments

LEARNING OBJECTIVES

The overriding objective of this textbook is to build a foundation with which to analyze current professional issues and adapt audit approaches to business and economic complexities. In this chapter, we build on that foundation by introducing several more complex, judgmental decisions that auditors make. Through studying this chapter, you will be able to:

1 Discuss the nature and types of complex judgments that permeate audit engagements.

2 Review a company's financial statements as a basis for identifying complex audit judgments.

3 Describe and apply a process for making judgments about materiality.

4 Assess whether misstatements, including prior-period misstatements, are material.

5 Distinguish between material weaknesses and significant deficiencies in internal control over financial reporting.

6 Judge the quality of the client's internal audit function and determine the effect of the client's

internal audit function on the performance of the audit.

7 Identify and describe the concepts of fair value and impairment as they apply to auditing.

8 Determine appropriate evidence to gather when testing adjustments to fair market value and impairments.

9 Describe sustainability reporting and articulate the auditors' role in providing assurance on management sustainability reports.

10 Apply the decision analysis and ethical decision-making frameworks to issues involved in making complex audit judgments.

CHAPTER OVERVIEW

In this chapter, we discuss several complex auditing judgments that require an understanding of the basic auditing concepts introduced in earlier chapters. These complex auditing judgments involve assessing materiality, determining whether identified misstatements are material, evaluating internal control deficiencies, evaluating the quality of a client's internal audit function, developing an approach for auditing fair value estimates, and providing assurance related to clients' sustainability reports. These judgments relate to various evidence collection activities (i.e., Phases III and IV), and activities related to wrapping up the audit (i.e., Phase V). The discussion of these complex audit judgments focuses on articulating relevant professional standards and procedures common in audit practice for making these complex judgments.

The Audit Opinion Formulation Process

I. Assessing Client Acceptance and Retention Decisions CHAPTER 4	II. Understanding the Client CHAPTERS 2, 4–6, and 9	III. Obtaining Evidence about Controls and Determining the Impact on the Financial Statement Audit CHAPTERS 5–14 and 18	IV. Obtaining Substantive Evidence about Account Assertions CHAPTERS 7–14 and 18	V. Wrapping Up the Audit and Making Reporting Decisions CHAPTERS 15 and 16

The Auditing Profession, Regulation, and Corporate Governance CHAPTERS 1 and 2	Decision-Making, Professional Conduct, and Ethics CHAPTER 3	Professional Liability CHAPTER 17

PROFESSIONAL JUDGMENT IN CONTEXT

Complexity Tied to Accounting Principles

Beginning in 2008, the FASB debated the need to update its guidance on contingencies, calling for enhanced disclosures based on judgments related to the likelihood that a loss would occur and the potential severity of the loss. An important consideration for auditors in judging the potential materiality of contingencies is the needs of investors and other users of the financial statements and audit report. The two following quotes from letters written to the FASB by investor groups provide insight into these needs:

The exposure draft only requires disclosure of severe financial threats that a company deems remotely probable if the issue is expected to be resolved within a year (FAS 5 Exposure Draft para. 6). There is a long history of companies underestimating the likelihood of severe financial threats—Enron, the subprime lending crisis, and asbestos liabilities are three examples. Typically, these large issues developed for many years, with eventual catastrophic consequences for investors. Therefore, FAS 5 should require companies to disclose all severe threats, regardless of whether they are resolved within a year. (emphasis added) (Calvert Investment Funds, letter to FASB, August 7, 2008)

While reporting entities often choose to characterize the probability of a severe impact risk as "remote," such judgments— later proving erroneous—have been at the core of the poor disclosure records preceding the breaking news of many of the key corporate scandals of the last ten years. Thus, creating an accounting standard that requires disclosure of severe impact threats, even in the face of ostensible "remoteness,"

promises to provide disclosures that are far more protective of investor interests. (Investor Environmental Health Network, letter to FASB, April 8, 2008)

As you read through the rest of the chapter, consider the following challenging questions that you will soon face as an auditor:

- To what extent are auditors equipped with the skills to make judgments regarding the potential severity of a contingency?

- Are the expectations of the users cited above reasonable? If yes, what skills must be developed by the accounting profession and auditors to improve the accuracy of such estimates?

- Can the auditor reasonably judge subjective estimates made by the client, or alternatively, does the auditor need to conclude that most estimates made by a client are acceptable?

- What kind of evidence should auditors be gathering on a systematic basis to evaluate client estimates?

- What do the two quotes imply about materiality of items in a company's financial statement? Is materiality best judged by management? If auditors make materiality decisions, do they need to think more like an investor than an auditor who may have a decision rule that 5% of net income is material?

- When the FASB or IASB develop new accounting standards, how do those standards affect auditor judgment—and the complexity of those judgments?

Complex Audit Judgments

This *Professional Judgment in Context* feature illustrates just a small glimpse of the complex judgments that an auditor will be making on virtually every audit. The auditor has to deal with the past in evaluating accounts that are valued at historical cost; and the auditor must consider the future to determine whether subsequent cash flows justify the continuance of assets at their historical cost. The auditor may

LO 1

Discuss the nature and types of complex judgments that permeate audit engagements.

LO 1

Discuss the nature and types of complex judgments that permeate audit engagements.

also be required to make a judgment as to what the fair value of a security might be at year end. Or, the auditor must make judgments regarding contingencies—including their probability and potential dollar amount. As seen in the preceding quotes, some investors want auditors to assess whether areas could have a severe impact on the organization and assure that they are disclosed adequately. This puts the auditor in a position where users expect the auditor to judge the potential severity of something that may just be emerging and—equally important—to know whether the item might be material to an informed user.

The auditor is going to be faced with the difficult task of making complex and difficult decisions on every audit engagement. These range from making judgments about whether or not a misstatement is sufficiently material to merit a qualified audit report or, more fundamentally, whether the client's accounting position can be justified. Throughout most engagements, the auditor is constantly challenged to evaluate the quality of a client's estimates, including areas such as obsolescence of inventory, allowance for doubtful accounts, pension obligations, warranty obligations, and tax provisions, among others. Seasoned auditors often refer to these issues under the broad term *professional judgment* and infer that the judgments are developed with professional experience. However, recent history shows us that many auditors lack skills in making these "professional judgments." The good news is that there is a systematic process for making most of these judgments and that staff auditors are now involved in making these judgments more than ever before. The rest of this chapter examines the systematic process for making such judgments.

LO 2

Review a company's financial statements as a basis for identifying complex audit judgments.

Complex Judgments in the Financial Statements

PRACTICAL POINT

Areas where subjective judgments are made are almost always high-risk and require significant auditor attention and appropriate professional skepticism.

To quickly get a sense of areas where subjective judgments will be made in an audit organization, we review various accounts on the balance sheet of Ford Motor Company as of December 31, 2009, in Exhibit 18.1. Recall, as of 2009, Ford had formally announced that it had developed a strategic plan to become a much smaller company as it anticipated that annual car production in the United States would be decreasing to about 12 million vehicles per year. Further, Ford had already sold off parts of its "luxury line" of vehicles, including Jaguar and Land Rover, along with pending plans to sell Volvo.

Exhibit 18.1	Ford Motor Company, Balance Sheet Accounts—December 31, 2009 and 2008	
	December 31, 2009	December 31, 2008
ASSETS		
Cash and cash equivalents	$ 21,441	$ 22,049
Marketable securities	21,387	17,411
Finance receivables	76,996	93,484
Other receivables	7,587	5,674
Net investment in operating leases	17,270	25,250
Inventories	5,450	6,988
Equity in net assets of affiliated companies	1,550	1,599
Net property	24,778	24,143
Deferred income taxes	3,440	3,108
Goodwill and other net intangible assets	209	246
Assets of held-for-sale operations	7,923	8,612
Other assets	6,819	9,734
Total assets	$ 194,850	$ 218,298

(continues)

Exhibit 18.1	Ford Motor Company, Balance Sheet Accounts— December 31, 2009 and 2008 (*continued*)

LIABILITIES

Payables	$ 14,594	$ 13,145
Accrued liabilities and deferred revenue	46,599	59,526
Debt	132,441	152,577
Deferred income taxes.	2,375	2,035
Liabilities of held-for-sale operations	5,356	5,542
Total liabilities	201,365	232,825

EQUITY

Capital stock, par value $0.01 per share (3,266 million shares issued of 6 billion authorized)	33	23
Class B Stock, par value $0.01 per share (71 million shares issued of 530 million authorized)	1	1
Capital in excess of par value of stock.	16,786	10,875
Accumulated other comprehensive income (loss).	(10,864)	(10,124)
Treasury stock	(177)	(181)
Retained earnings/(Accumulated deficit)	(13,599)	(16,316)
Total equity/ (deficit) attributable to Ford Motor Company.	(7,820)	(15,722)
Equity (Deficit) attributable to noncontrolling interests	1,305	1,195
Total equity (deficit)	(6,515)	(14,527)
Total liabilities and equity.	$ 194,850	$ 218,298

As you analyze the balance sheet, notice that almost every asset and liability account requires significant judgments, most notably the following:

Assets	Nature of Judgment
Marketable securities	• Subject to fair value estimates; auditor must determine if security is marketable and, for most securities, its fair value.
Finance receivables—net	• Subject to allowance for noncollectibility.
Other receivables	• Subject to allowance for noncollectibility.
Net investment in operating leases	• Subject to impairment testing if plants are closing or equipment is not used.
Inventories	• Subject to lower of cost or market impairments, including an allowance for obsolescence.
Net property	• Subject to impairment testing, especially for plants and distribution centers that are closing; subject to estimates made as to (a) expected life of the assets, and (b) appropriateness of depreciation method.
Deferred income taxes	• Subject to estimates of future profitable operations against which the deferred asset might be utilized.
Goodwill and other intangible assets	• Subject to impairment testing based on (a) current market values, (b) projected cash flows related to the assets and/or (c) current market value of the segment to which the goodwill applies.
Assets of held-for-sale operations	• Subject to impairment testing based on most likely sale or disposal price.

Liabilities	Nature of Judgment
Accrued liabilities and deferred revenue	• Subject to estimates regarding amount of revenue that is properly deferred, as well as the basis for the liability accrual—e.g., pensions, warranty liabilities, and accrued vacation.
Deferred income taxes	• Subject to estimates and assumptions made in preparation of the estimate of income tax expense for the year.
Debt	• Depending on the applicable financial reporting financial reporting framework, the auditor may need to estimate the fair value of the debt, or the rate at which the debt may be settled in the event of default.

In addition, there are complex judgments applicable to the income statement and a number of other significant estimates that must be disclosed in the notes to the financial statements. For example, Ford Motor Company is regularly involved in litigation and the auditor has to make a decision as to when the amounts to be settled in litigation should be estimated. The auditor needs to assess disclosures about whether the company has changed plans on which plants they are going to close, or what lines of business the company may discontinue. All of these changes will require a judgmental estimate of the dollar effect that needs to be recognized or disclosed in the financial statements.

Materiality Judgments

LO 3

Describe and apply a process for making judgments about materiality.

In an earlier chapter, we introduced the concept of **materiality**. In this chapter, we expand on that topic by focusing on the judgmental aspects of making materiality judgments in practice and cover professional guidance that clarifies the auditor's responsibility for materiality judgments. To understand the nature of materiality judgments, consider the AICPA's description of materiality judgment factors in Statement on Auditing Standards No. 107:

> The auditor's consideration of materiality is a matter of professional judgment and is influenced by the auditor's perception of the needs of users of financial statements. The perceived needs of users are recognized in the discussion of materiality in Financial Accounting Standards Board (FASB) Statement of Financial Accounting Concepts No. 2, Qualitative Characteristics of Accounting Information, which defines materiality as "the magnitude of an omission or misstatement of accounting information that, in the light of surrounding circumstances, makes it probable that the judgment of a reasonable person relying on the information would have been changed or influenced by the omission or misstatement."

The PCAOB has moved toward the Supreme Court's definition of materiality, which states that "a fact is material if there is a **substantial likelihood** that the … fact would have been viewed by the reasonable investor as having significantly altered the 'total mix' of information made available" (see AS No. 11, *Consideration of Materiality in Planning and Performing an Audit*).

Both of these definitions recognize that materiality judgments are made in light of surrounding circumstances and necessarily involve both quantitative and qualitative considerations.

Thus, decisions about materiality (1) are a matter of professional judgment, (2) depend on the needs of a reasonable person relying on the information (an investor, potential investor, or other stakeholder), and (3) involve both quantitative and qualitative considerations. Further, we know from audit practice that

PROFESSIONAL JUDGMENT IN CONTEXT

2005 PCAOB Inspection Report of KPMG LLP Regarding Materiality Judgment

The PCAOB reported on an audit in which their inspectors identified a variety of problems, one of which involved the auditors' materiality judgments. In the audit under inspection, the engagement team did not follow the usual practice of basing audit planning materiality on a percentage of pretax income. Instead, they used a percentage of total assets, which resulted in a higher planning materiality than if the maximum percentage of pretax income allowed for by KPMG policy had been used. In addition, the engagement team used 10% of planning materiality (a relatively high percentage) as the threshold (the *"posting threshold"*) below which errors would be treated as inconsequential and would not be considered by the audit team, either individually or when aggregated with other items, to determine whether they were material. Further, for errors in the balance sheet that originated in prior years, the engagement team used a different posting threshold that was based on equity rather than pretax income or total assets. This resulting posting threshold was approximately 18 times higher than the one used in the prior-year's audit.

As a result of applying these thresholds, the engagement team failed to include on the SUAD (**summary of unadjusted audit differences**) several uncorrected accounting errors. The SUAD is a summary of uncorrected errors that is communicated to the audit committee and is described in the management representation letter. The errors on the SUAD are evaluated individually and in the aggregate for materiality. As a result, these errors remained uncorrected on the client's financial statements; the audit committee was never informed of their existence; the errors were not described in the management representation letter and they were not subject to further evaluation by the auditors.

We note that the PCAOB inspection team had the benefit of hindsight in scrutinizing the auditors' materiality judgments. In fact, SAS No. 107 allows for considerable leeway in materiality judgments. Yet, the auditors in this case were criticized for judgments that were subsequently deemed inappropriate. Thus, while professional standards allow for considerable judgment, auditors need to realize that those judgments may fall under the close scrutiny of others. Therefore, while auditors have leeway and are encouraged to apply their professional judgment, they must also be sure that those judgments are defensible and reasonable.

As you read through this section, consider this case and the following questions:

- What would justify a change in the approach used for making the planning materiality decision and the movement away from using pretax income as the materiality base?

- What would justify a change by the engagement team to using the 10% posting threshold rather than a more conservative amount?

- Why might the engagement team believe it was appropriate to use a posting threshold that was eighteen times higher than the one used in the prior year?

- Would the auditor's decisions have been more defensible had the KPMG audit team documented the rationale for the change in planning materiality and materiality thresholds?

- Are the computerized aids developed by firms that base materiality on some measure—e.g., pretax income—both a help and a hindrance to good auditing?

materiality decisions differ from one audit client to another; that is, what is material for one client may not be material for another client, and may change for the same client from one period to another. These points illustrate why auditors find it difficult to make materiality judgments. To add further complexity to the situation, regulators are keenly aware of, and pay particular attention to, the judgmental aspects of auditors' materiality decisions and how those decisions can affect client financial results.

Purpose of Materiality Judgments and Common Benchmarks and Thresholds

The purpose of making materiality judgments is to make sure that the auditor gathers sufficient evidential matter to obtain reasonable assurance about whether

PRACTICAL POINT

Auditors should pay attention to investor comment letters sent to the FASB, SEC, PCAOB, or other regulators to better understand materiality issues from an investor viewpoint. Investors are interested in long-term developing issues, not just short-term trends.

PRACTICAL POINT

In AS No. 14, *Evaluating Audit Results*, the PCAOB makes an important point about the difference between the terms *not material* and *clearly trivial*. An issue that is "clearly trivial" is an item that is of smaller magnitude than would be considered material based on the guidance in AS No. 11, *Consideration of Materiality in Planning and Performing an Audit*. A clearly trivial item will be inconsequential, whether evaluated individually or aggregated with other items. Importantly, the PCAOB notes that "when there is any uncertainty about whether one or more items is clearly trivial the matter is not considered trivial."

PRACTICAL POINT

Audit firms realize that materiality judgments are difficult to make; therefore they spend a great deal of time training staff on how to make these judgments appropriately. Further, they have policies and computer decision aids that assist auditors in making the judgments appropriately.

PRACTICAL POINT

Auditors may rely too heavily on quantitative measures of materiality because such measures do not require as much professional judgment. The SEC has been very critical of auditors' exclusive use of quantitative measures and encourages auditors to document their thought process regarding materiality choices.

the financial statements are free of material misstatement. Statement on Auditing Standards No. 107 provides the AICPA's basic guidance on materiality judgments, and it is very consistent with the PCAOB's AS No. 11, and the IAASB's ISA 320. Overall, existing professional guidance notes that auditors must make materiality assessments for (1) audit planning and (2) evidence evaluation after audit tests are completed.

The auditor considers materiality for the financial statements as a whole (overall materiality) and for particular accounts and disclosures (planning materiality). For purposes of planning the audit, auditors should consider overall materiality in terms of the smallest aggregate level of misstatements that could be material to any one of the financial statements. For example, if the auditor believes that misstatements aggregating approximately $100,000 would be material to the income statement, but misstatements aggregating approximately $200,000 would be material to the balance sheet, the auditor typically assesses overall materiality at $100,000 or less (not $200,000 or less).

Auditors often use variations of several benchmarks and common numeric thresholds as a starting point for making judgments about materiality at the overall financial statement level. The most common benchmarks include net income, assets, or net sales. The following benchmarks, percentage thresholds, and associated materiality judgments are typical:

| | TYPICAL MATERIALITY THRESHOLDS AND JUDGMENTS | | |
Common Benchmarks	Not Material	Likely Material	Always Material
Net income	< 5%	5% to 10%	> 10%
Total assets	< 1%	1% to 1.5%	> 1.5%
Net sales	< 1%	1% to 1.5%	> 1.5%

Audit firms have policies that specify which benchmarks are appropriate, and, as the *Professional Judgment in Context* feature from KPMG's inspection illustrates, consistency in the application of benchmarks and thresholds is important in demonstrating the reasonableness of materiality judgments. Professional judgment is very important in selecting benchmarks appropriate for the client setting. The auditor should consider the following items when identifying benchmarks:

- Financial statement items on which users will focus their attention,
- Nature of the client and industry,
- Size of the client,
- Manner in which the client is financed, and
- Volatility of the benchmark.

Moreover, it is important to recognize that the benchmarks and thresholds represent starting points for the materiality judgment; they should not be used rotely and without applying other judgmental factors. Once the auditor has determined the overall materiality amount based on the quantitative assessment, the auditor also needs to consider qualitative factors to assess whether the materiality amount makes sense for the particular audit client.

After establishing overall materiality at the financial statement level, auditors may decide to set a planning level of materiality that is relevant for particular accounts or disclosures. **Planning materiality** is typically less than overall materiality and helps the auditor determine the extent of audit evidence needed. For example, in performing substantive analytical procedures, the threshold for determining whether differences between the client's account balance and the auditor's expectation should be based on planning materiality. Planning materiality should also be used in determining sample sizes for substantive procedures, as it is used in determining tolerable misstatement. Planning materiality allows for the possibility that some misstatements that are less than overall materiality could, when aggregated with other misstatements, result in a material misstatement of the financial statements overall.

Although different audit firms take different approaches, planning materiality could be the same as overall materiality, or it could be a percentage of overall materiality, generally ranging from 50% to 75% of overall materiality. Professional judgment and assessment of client-specific factors will influence where planning materiality is set. Relevant factors might include whether:

- The client has a history of audit adjustments.
- The audit is a first-year engagement.
- Significant deficiencies or material weaknesses exist in internal controls.

Auditors need to aggregate all potential misstatements in a place where the audit team can assess the materiality of misstatements. The accumulation of such information is often based on **posting materiality**—a materiality level where the auditor believes errors below that level would not, even when aggregated with all other misstatements, be material to the financial statements. There are two approaches used by auditors to set posting materiality. The first is a judgmental approach whereby the auditor sets the posting threshold based on past experience that accumulates into an auditor judgment. This approach is usually not very defensible to third-party users or regulators *unless* the auditor can clearly articulate the reasoning process and show insight into what might be material to users. The auditor will always consider such things as potential default on loan covenants, changes in segment earnings or trends in earnings, or whatever would affect the market's perception of future growth and cash flow for the company.

The second approach to setting posting materiality is a percentage approach, whereby the auditor sets the posting threshold at a range that depends on the auditor's assessment of the likelihood of unfound misstatements (often based on previous experience or on other issues such as the quality of the client's control environment). The range may vary from 10% (for low likelihood of unfound misstatements) to 5% (for high likelihood of unfound misstatements) of materiality at the overall financial statement level. For example, if analytical procedures suggest that a certain account balance may have errors, the auditor will often assign a lower posting threshold—e.g., 5%—because of the higher likelihood of unfound misstatements. If there were proposed adjusting entries to a particular account in prior years, the auditor may also assign a lower posting threshold. Finally, if the consequences of a potential misstatement in an account balance are very high, the auditor may also assign a lower posting threshold. Further, some firms require that all items be posted for analysis by supervisors and to form a record of audit findings.

Common Difficulties in Making Materiality Judgments

Information That Changes the Auditor's Assessment of Materiality

One difficulty that commonly arises in making materiality judgments is that the auditor's materiality judgments at the planning stage may not be the same as those at the evidence evaluation stage, because the auditor may learn certain facts during the audit that cause a change in judgment. For example, if the auditor learns that some audit adjustments may cause the company to default on a loan covenant, or that the trend in earnings in an important segment may

---

PRACTICAL POINT

If a client has significant and nonrecurring charges to nonoperating expenses, then income from continuing operations may be a more appropriate materiality benchmark than net income.

PRACTICAL POINT

For companies with a net loss, auditors sometimes use net *loss* as the benchmark. If a company's net income varies significantly from year to year, the auditor might consider using an average of net income from the prior three to five years as the materiality benchmark.

PRACTICAL POINT

For nonprofit entities, appropriate benchmarks would include total expenses, total revenues, or total assets.

PRACTICAL POINT

If planning materiality is set too high, the auditor may not perform sufficient procedures to detect material misstatements in the financial statements. If planning materiality is set too low, more substantive procedures may be performed than necessary.

PRACTICAL POINT

Posting materiality is a data accumulation and judgment aid that assists the auditor in aggregating information about the potential materiality of misstatements.

change, then the auditor will want to use a materiality level for the rest of the audit that is lower than the original planning materiality. If the auditor discovers one of the following while performing audit procedures, the auditor may need to revise the materiality level and document the new materiality amount, as well as the rationale for changing the amount:

- A change in circumstances (e.g., changes in laws, regulations, or the applicable financial reporting framework that affect investors' expectations about the measurement or disclosure of financial statement items)
- New information (e.g., a change in the auditor's assessment of the client's fundamental riskiness)
- Changes in understanding of the client and its operations (e.g., significant new contractual agreements that highlight a particular aspect of an organization's business that is separately disclosed in the financial statements)
- The materiality levels were initially established based on the client's preliminary financial statements, which differed from the client's final financial statements

Considering Qualitative Factors

Another difficulty that auditors face in making materiality judgments is that they must consider both quantitative effects (i.e., the dollar magnitude of a misstatement) and qualitative effects (i.e., the reason for the misstatement). In Staff Accounting Bulletin (SAB) No. 99, the SEC states that:

> The use of a percentage as a numerical threshold, such as 5%, may provide the basis for a preliminary assumption that—without considering all relevant circumstances—a deviation of less than the specified percentage with respect to a particular item on the registrant's financial statements is unlikely to be material. The staff has no objection to such a "rule of thumb" as an initial step in assessing materiality. But quantifying, in percentage terms, the magnitude of a misstatement is only the beginning of an analysis of materiality; it cannot appropriately be used as a substitute for a full analysis of all relevant considerations.

Some of the considerations that may cause a quantitatively small misstatement to be considered material include whether the potential misstatement:

- Arises from an item capable of precise measurement or arises from an estimate and, if so, the degree of imprecision inherent in the estimate;
- Masks a change in earnings or other trends;
- Hides a failure to meet analysts' consensus expectations for the enterprise;
- Changes a loss into income or vice versa;
- Is in a segment that has been identified as having a significant effect on the company's stock valuation;
- Affects compliance with regulatory requirements;
- Affects loan covenants or other contractual requirements;
- Has the effect of increasing management's compensation—e.g., by satisfying requirements for the award of bonuses or other forms of incentive compensation;
- Involves concealment of an unlawful transaction.

Auditing Multiple Locations

A third common problem is determining how to allocate materiality where:

- There are many client locations.
- Some locations require separate reporting (regulatory reports) in addition to consolidated financial reports.

- There are significant segments and the importance of segments may vary as they are currently assessed by the marketplace.

In some cases, the auditor may be able to aggregate the populations of various locations and perform testing, including the selection of audit samples, from the combined population, in the same manner as when there is one population. For example, if the underlying information system is centralized and separate reporting by location is not necessary, the auditor can treat multiple locations as one population and use planning materiality for testing (and sampling) a particular account balance across multiple locations. This may be the case for inventory observations conducted at multiple locations.

On the other hand, if the information systems across multiple locations are decentralized, or if separate reporting is required, or if certain locations or segments are especially important, the auditor will face additional testing considerations beyond those encountered when testing a single population. These considerations may be applicable for tests of controls or substantive tests of details. Common audit situations where such considerations may apply include inventories, fixed assets, or receivables that are in different locations. The auditor's concern is the materiality level that should be used in testing a particular account at a particular location. In planning tests of account balances (or internal controls) at specific locations, the auditor will likely want to use a materiality amount that is smaller than planning materiality. Different materiality levels may be established for different locations, and the aggregate of the location materiality levels could equal or exceed overall planning materiality.

Consider the auditor whose client has fifteen locations of equal size and the auditor has set planning materiality at $1,500,000. The auditor might allocate $100,000 to each location for a total of $1,500,000. This approach would generally result in overauditing because the achieved audit risk across all locations would be extremely low. An alternative approach would be to allocate $1,500,000 to each location; however, this approach would result in substantial underauditing and an unacceptable risk of audit failure. These are obviously extreme approaches to allocating planning materiality across multiple locations. The auditor will want to apply professional judgment, and, if statistical sampling is used, utilize sampling methodology (often included in ACL) to determine the proper allocation.

Assessing Whether Misstatements Are Material

Aggregating and Netting Misstatements

Professional judgment is particularly important in evaluating whether unadjusted misstatements are material. Even if there are misstatements that are of a lower level than overall or planning materiality, the circumstances surrounding the misstatement may result in a conclusion that the misstatement is material, either individually or when considered with other misstatements.

For most audits there will be multiple misstatements detected during the course of the audit. Should each misstatement be considered individually in terms of judging its materiality? Or should the misstatements be aggregated in judging their overall materiality? The answer is that the auditor should evaluate each misstatement individually, *and* the auditor should consider the aggregate effect of all misstatements. Further, if an individual misstatement causes

PRACTICAL POINT

Tolerable misstatement at an individual location should be less than the materiality level of the financial statements as a whole.

PRACTICAL POINT

Multilocation auditing issues are not completely resolved with the current professional guidance. Audit firms have differing approaches to deal with this complex issue.

PRACTICAL POINT

The audit team should make sure that conclusions reached regarding materiality determinations and considerations are accurately and fully documented in the workpapers.

LO 4

Assess whether misstatements, including prior-period misstatements, are material.

PRACTICAL POINT

The auditor should not assume that an occurrence of error or fraud is an isolated occurrence. In other words, if an auditor finds evidence of one error, he or she should assume that more exist in the financial statements; if an auditor finds evidence of fraud, he or she should assume that more widespread fraud exists in the organization.

PROFESSIONAL JUDGMENT IN CONTEXT

Arthur Andersen's Audits of Sunbeam and Potential Audit Adjustments

During the 1996 and 1997 audits of Sunbeam, Phillip Harlow, the engagement partner on the Sunbeam audits, proposed a number of audit adjustments that management rejected. In fact, about 16% of Sunbeam's reported 1997 income came from the aggregation of misstated items that Harlow had proposed as audit adjustments in 1996 and 1997. For each of the following situations, Harlow decided to pass on the proposed adjustments after incorrectly applying a quantitative materiality analysis:

- Sunbeam recorded total restructuring charges of $337.6 million at year-end 1996. Harlow identified that approximately $18.7 million of this reserve represented restructuring reserves that were not in compliance with GAAP.

- At year-end 1997, Sunbeam recorded $11 million in revenue and $5 million in income from a purported sale of spare parts inventory to its warranty and spare parts fulfillment house. This "sale" did not comply with GAAP requirements for revenue recognition. Harlow proposed a $3 million adjustment to reverse the accounting entries reflecting the revenue and income recognition for this transaction.

- In connection with Andersen's audit of Sunbeam's year-end 1997 financial statements, Harlow proposed adjustments to reverse $2.9 million related to inventory overvaluation in Mexico and $563,000 related to various miscellaneous items.

As you read through this section, consider this case and the following questions:

- What might be the rationale that the proposed adjustments were deemed immaterial?

- What quantitative and qualitative factors should be considered when assessing whether a misstatement is material?

- What factors should an auditor assess when there are uncorrected misstatements from a prior period?

- Should the auditor communicate information about proposed adjustments to the audit committee? Should the same information also be communicated to financial statement users?

Source: SEC AAER No. 1706.

---

the financial statements as a whole to be materially misstated, that effect cannot be eliminated by other misstatements that have a different directional effect on the financial statements. For example, if a company's revenues are materially *over*stated, the auditor is not allowed to conclude that the effect is immaterial if there is an equal and offsetting *over*statement of expenses. Rather, the auditor would conclude in this case that the financial statements *taken as a whole* are materially misstated. The rationale is that the trend in revenue growth may be just as important to a user as the effect on net income.

Evaluating Uncorrected Misstatements

The auditor needs to evaluate whether uncorrected misstatements are material—either individually or in combination with other misstatements. In making this assessment one important issue that auditors must face is the fact that misstatements from prior periods may have been left uncorrected because they were judged immaterial at the time. However, those misstatements may affect the current period's financial results, rendering the current period's results materially misstated. To illustrate, assume that $100,000 is material for a warranty liability account with a balance of $3.075 million and that the warranty liability misstatement is the only issue under consideration. In the first year, the auditor's evidence supports a conclusion that the client's estimate is overstated by $75,000. In the second year, the auditor's evidence supports a conclusion that the client's book value understates the liability by $85,000. Both years' misstatements are under the $100,000 materiality threshold. The effect on two years is as follows:

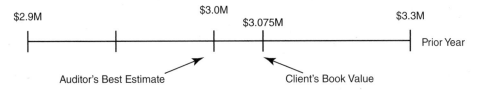

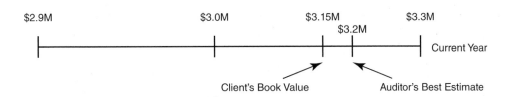

In each year illustrated, the client's estimate of the warranty liability does not differ from the auditor's estimate by a material amount. What is the effect of *not* booking the immaterial misstatements? It is correct that the balance sheet is not materially misstated. However, note that the client's book value is higher than the auditor's best estimate in the prior year and lower than the auditor's best estimate in the current year, resulting in a "swing" of $160,000. Looking at the income statement effect only, not booking the "immaterial amount" in the prior year and not booking the immaterial amount in the current year has caused income to be overstated by a total of $160,000 in the current year—an amount that is above the materiality threshold for the client. Clearly, the direction of the misstatement makes a difference when the effect on the income statement is considered. What has happened is that the client was using the warranty liability account to build a "cookie jar reserve" in the previous year (overestimating the account balance) and was using the account balance to smooth reported earnings in the subsequent year.

> **PRACTICAL POINT**
>
> Most auditors request the client to book all known misstatements (unless recording cost is very high) so there are not carry-overs from year to year. If the client does not want to book the misstatement, the auditor should assume that the client considers the amount to be material.

Subjective Differences between the Auditor and Client

In the example dealing with the warranty estimate, the client may conclude that the estimate is subjective and, that there is no way to determine the "correct" balance until a time in the future when all claims are made. Therefore, the client will maintain that its estimate is as good as the auditor's estimate. Similarly, a client may claim that its subjective estimate of the allowance for uncollectible accounts is as good as the auditor's estimate—and therefore, there is not misstatement in the account balance.

What should the auditor's response be to the client's claim that its estimate is as good as the auditor's estimate? The answer should be fairly simple: The auditor should have gathered systematic evidence that incorporates relevant information about the correctness of the account balance and should be able to defend the veracity of that estimate. Remember, the auditor usually reaches a conclusion about accounting estimates by (a) testing the client's methodology for reaching the estimate (when the auditor believes the client's process is strong and incorporates all relevant variables) or (b) developing his or her own model to come up with the estimate and then comparing that estimate to the amount recorded by the client (when the client does not have a robust estimation methodology). In either case, the auditor should not fall victim to an argument that "no one can determine the right amount, so the client's estimate is as good as mine."

There may be instances when the auditor determines that the client's accounting estimate conforms to the relevant requirements of the applicable financial reporting framework and is reasonable, yet it differs from the amount best supported by the audit evidence. Ordinarily, this difference would not be considered to be a misstatement. However, the auditor should be alert to possible bias by client management.

Considerations Regarding Selective Correction of Misstatements

In some cases, the auditor may become suspicious that management is using subjective differences as a rationale for selectively correcting known misstatements. In AS No. 14, *Evaluating Audit Results*, the PCAOB addresses this issue and labels the selective correction of misstatements as a form of management bias. As such, it is critical that the auditor understand, and truly believe, management's rationale for correcting versus not correcting a known misstatement; it gets to the heart of being a professionally skeptical auditor.

One common ploy that management may use when the auditor proposes to make an adjustment to correct a known misstatement is to identify an additional adjusting entry that offsets the auditor's proposed entry. If this event occurs, professional standards require the auditor to perform procedures to determine why the "new" misstatement was not identified previously. The auditor should also consider implications regarding management integrity, and the auditor should adjust risk assessments, including fraud risk assessments, accordingly.

Regulatory Guidance Concerning Materiality Judgments

The Securities and Exchange Commission (SEC) has expressed concern over the practice of "waiving," that is, not correcting, immaterial adjustments. Companies will sometimes resist correcting an immaterial misstatement, arguing that the effort associated with adjusting the financial statements is not worth the additional precision associated with the immaterial correction. However, the SEC's position is that if management resists making the adjustment, then, by definition, it is material. Auditors have to use their judgment to understand the qualitative reasons for management's refusal to make a correcting entry, but the SEC's position is generally that if management refuses to correct a material misstatement, then the auditor is obligated to issue a qualified or an adverse opinion on the financial statements.

In 2006, the SEC issued SAB 108 to address variation in audit practice concerning quantitative materiality judgments related to the disposition of both current year and prior-year misstatements. Up until that time, auditors used one of two methods to assess materiality: the **rollover method** or the **iron curtain method**. Essentially, the rollover method focuses on the materiality of current year misstatements and the reversing effect of prior-year misstatements on the income statement. This method may allow misstatements to accumulate on the balance sheet. The iron curtain method focuses on assuring that the year-end balance sheet is correct and does not consider the impact of prior-year uncorrected misstatements reversing in later years.

The SEC objected to the variation in financial reporting outcomes that these alternative methods allowed. SAB 108 now mandates what is termed a **dual approach** to uncorrected misstatements. The dual approach requires the simultaneous application of *both* the rollover and iron curtain methods. If a misstatement is material under *either* method, it must be corrected in the current period.

Intentional Misstatements

Sometimes an auditor may uncover an intentional misstatement of a client's financial statements. Even if immaterial, an intentional misstatement may cause serious difficulties in the audit, and for the client. The intentional misstatement may be fraudulent or may be a violation of applicable laws. If the client is publicly traded, Section 10A(b) of the Exchange Act requires auditors to take action upon discovery of an illegal act even if it does not have a material effect on the financial statements, including alerting management and the audit committee. When auditors detect an intentional misstatement, they should (1) reconsider the level of audit risk for the client; (2) consider revising the nature, timing, and extent of audit procedures; and (3) evaluate whether to resign from the audit engagement. Further, the detection of an intentional misstatement likely signals the existence of an internal control material weakness and certainly speaks to control environment issues, such as the "tone at the top" of the organization.

Misstatements in the Statement of Cash Flows

Because of the importance of cash flows to investment decisions, the statement of cash flows has gained in visibility, use, and scrutiny. When the auditor identifies a misstatement in cash-flow classification, the auditor should assess the materiality of the misstatement to determine whether a reclassification is necessary to assure that the statement of cash flows is materially correct. The assessment as to whether the misstatement in classification is material should go beyond the income statement perspective. The auditor should look to factors that are unique to cash flows. For example, cash flow associated with operating activities is often an important measure for investors.

Known vs. Projected Misstatements

Remember that the auditor generally does not examine 100% of all transactions making up an account balance. Usually, the auditor has taken a sample or performed analytical procedures to analyze an account balance. During audit testing the auditor will normally find a combination of:

Misstatements that were found (known misstatements)	$xxx,xxx
Projected misstatements	$yyy,yyy
Most likely misstatements	$ZZZ,ZZZ

In determining materiality, the question often arises as to whether the auditor uses the misstatements that were found or the most likely misstatements to determine materiality. The answer is that the auditor should always use the most likely misstatement. If the auditor does not have complete confidence in the estimated amount for most likely misstatement, then the auditor has not gathered sufficient reliable information on which to base an opinion on the financial statements. In that case, the auditor must collect additional audit evidence.

Conclusions about Internal Control Deficiencies

Nature of Material Weaknesses in Internal Control

In an earlier chapter we noted that an auditor performing an integrated audit will need to provide an opinion on the effectiveness of the client's internal control over financial reporting. If the client has one or more material weaknesses, the auditor will conclude that the client's internal control is not effective. Recall the definitions of significant deficiencies and material weaknesses in internal controls:

- *Significant deficiency in internal control*—A **significant deficiency** is a deficiency, or a combination of deficiencies, in internal control over financial reporting that is less severe than a material weakness, yet important enough to merit attention by those responsible for oversight of the company's financial reporting.
- *Material weakness in internal control*—A **material weakness** is a deficiency, or a combination of deficiencies, in internal control over financial reporting such

PRACTICAL POINT

The discovery of an intentional misstatement, even if immaterial, could affect the auditor's opinion on the effectiveness of the client's internal controls.

PRACTICAL POINT

Auditors need to consider the risk and take appropriate action relating to material misstatements of fact contained in the client's MD&A section of the 10-K filed with the SEC.

PRACTICAL POINT

Auditors should consider whether the statement of cash flows is materially correct, with a focus on assuring appropriate presentation and classification.

PRACTICAL POINT

The auditor should have performed sufficient work to have confidence in the most likely estimate of misstatements in an account balance—and that estimate should be used for making materiality judgments.

LO 5

Distinguish between material weaknesses and significant deficiencies in internal control over financial reporting.

PROFESSIONAL JUDGMENT IN CONTEXT

Assessing Weaknesses in Internal Control

The following statement was taken from the Pall, Inc. Annual Statement and 10-K for 2007 (p. 44). It represents management's assessment of the quality of internal control over financial reporting.

A material weakness is a deficiency, or a combination of deficiencies, in internal control over financial reporting, such that there is a reasonable possibility that a material misstatement of the Company's annual or interim financial statements will not be prevented or detected on a timely basis. The following material weakness was identified as of July 31, 2007: the Company lacked a periodic review to ensure that the income tax impact of certain intercompany transactions were properly considered in the Company's provision for income taxes. The Company has restated its previously issued consolidated financial statements for each of the eight fiscal years in the period ended July 31, 2006 and for each of the fiscal quarters ended October 31, 2006, January 31, 2007, and April 30, 2007 to correct reported provision for income taxes, interest expense, net income taxes

payable, and deferred income taxes in such consolidated financial statements.

As you consider this quote and read the following discussion, ask yourself the following questions:

- What criteria should an auditor (and management) use to determine whether an internal control deficiency is either a significant deficiency or a material weakness?
- Does a restatement of the financial statements imply that there was a material weakness in internal controls?
- Does materiality apply to interim financial reports, or just the annual financial statements? If it applies to interim financial reports, how does the auditor adjust planning materiality—e.g., should it be one quarter of annual materiality?
- Does it make a difference where the deficiency exists; i.e., does it matter whether the deficiency relates to transactions processing, accounting estimates, or the control environment?

that there is a reasonable possibility that a material misstatement of the company's annual or interim financial statements will not be prevented or detected on a timely basis.

There are some important elements in those definitions that should be considered by auditors:

- Severity of internal control deficiencies is directly connected to the possibility of material misstatements occurring in the financial statements.
- A material misstatement in the financial statements—including those requiring restatements—strongly implies a material weakness in internal control.
- Materiality applies to both interim financial statements and annual financial statements.
- A material misstatement does not have to occur to have a material weakness in internal controls. The material weakness means only that a material misstatement *could occur* and would not be prevented or detected by the control system in a timely basis.

In determining the amount of control testing to be performed, particularly in determining parameters for attribute testing, the auditor needs to gather sufficient evidence to persuade the auditor that the control is effective (i.e., there are no material weaknesses in internal control). Thus, the auditor needs to be familiar with these elements in designing control testing.

In the following *Comparison of Worldwide Professional Guidance*, we articulate relevant standards concerning internal control deficiencies.

Assessing Likelihood and Magnitude of Potential Misstatements

When the auditor is evaluating a control deficiency, the auditor needs to assess both the *likelihood* (whether there is a reasonable possibility) of misstatement and the *magnitude* of potential misstatement. AS No. 5 notes that various risk factors

Comparison of Worldwide Professional Guidance

ASSESSING INTERNAL CONTROL DEFICIENCIES IN AN INTEGRATED AUDIT

AICPA Auditing Standards Board (ASB)

SSAE 15, effective in 2008, generally provides the same definitions of control deficiencies, and the same guidance to use in evaluating control deficiencies as is included in the PCAOB's AS 5, which is described below.

Public Company Accounting Oversight Board (PCAOB)

AS 5 provides the definition of control deficiencies, including the definitions of significant deficiencies and material weaknesses which we present in this chapter. AS 5 notes that "The auditor must evaluate the severity of each control deficiency that comes to his or her attention to determine whether the deficiencies, individually or in combination, are material weaknesses as of the date of management's assessment." In assessing the severity of the deficiency the auditor is to consider the likelihood that a misstatement could occur and whether the misstatement could be material. The standard cautions that "The severity of a deficiency does not depend on whether a misstatement actually has occurred but rather on whether there is a reasonable possibility that the company's controls will fail to prevent or detect a misstatement."

International Auditing and Assurance Standards Board (IAASB)

The IAASB does not have auditing guidance in this area.

SUMMARY

The evaluation of control deficiencies is required in an integrated audit where an opinion on internal control effectiveness is being issued. Integrated audits can be performed for both U.S. public and nonpublic entities and the guidance on control evaluation is virtually the same for the audits of both types of organizations.

affect the *likelihood* (whether there is a reasonable possibility) that a deficiency, or a combination of deficiencies, will result in a misstatement. These factors include:

- The nature of the financial statement accounts, disclosures, and assertions involved,
- The susceptibility of the related asset or liability to loss or fraud,
- The subjectivity, complexity, or extent of judgment required to determine the amount involved,
- The interaction or relationship of the control with other controls, including whether they are interdependent or redundant,
- The interaction of the deficiencies, and
- The possible future consequences of the deficiency.

AS No. 5 also identifies factors that affect the *magnitude* of the misstatement that might result from a deficiency. Such factors include:

- The financial statement amounts or total of transactions exposed to the deficiency, and
- The volume of activity in the account balance or class of transactions exposed to the deficiency that has occurred in the current period or that is expected in future periods.

There are a number of other considerations that the auditor should make when assessing a control deficiency.

1. *Control Environment.* Weaknesses in specific components of the control environment have pervasive effects on the financial reporting process. More particularly, deficiencies in the competence of accounting personnel who deal with material account balances are normally considered a material weakness. A good example is the deficiency in personnel with the skills to review the income tax accrual and related expenses in the preceding *Professional Judgment in Context* feature.

> **PRACTICAL POINT**
>
> Internal control over complex and judgmental account balances is particularly important. The auditor should always be alert to changes in client's controls. For example, Gateway Computer, Inc. significantly changed its credit policies for new computer sales, but it used historical data to estimate the allowance for uncollectible accounts. The amount was material to the financial statements and the failure to update the policy is a material weakness in internal control over financial reporting.

AUDITING *in Practice*

CONTROL ENVIRONMENT: SMALL BUSINESS

Assume that a business is not large enough to hire sufficient staff to evaluate complex accounting issues, which could constitute a material weakness. However, the company engages a professional accounting firm (not the client's auditor) to assist it in researching the literature and providing guidance on the appropriateness of accounting choices. If the professional firm is well qualified and its reasoning process documented and supported by the professional literature, there is no material weakness. On the other hand, if the company engaged in complex accounting and did not have the personnel, or did not contract for the appropriate personnel, there is a material weakness in internal control over financial reporting. Auditors should recognize that controls in small businesses may differ from controls typically founded in larger organizations.

PRACTICAL POINT

The auditor is required to evaluate the effectiveness of the audit committee on every engagement. If the audit committee is not providing sufficient oversight, there is a material weakness in internal control over financial reporting.

2. *Repeatability of a Process.* If a deficiency is repeatable, such as in a computerized process, the more likely it is to be material. For example, a process that fails to update prices on inventory or sales could easily result in a material misstatement.

3. *Volume of Transactions Affected.* The auditor needs to assess the percentage of control failures multiplied by the average size of a transaction to determine whether the amounts that could be misstated are material.

4. *Complexity and Subjectivity of the Account Balance.* The more complex and subjective a material account balance is, the more likely that a deficiency will be material. For example, a lack of controls over the computation of pension liability and related expenses would likely be material.

5. *Effectiveness of Oversight and Governance.* One of the key elements of good internal control is that there should be strong oversight coming from the board of directors, and especially the audit committee. A lack of sufficient oversight would be considered a material weakness regardless of whether misstatements are actually detected in the financial statements.

Each of the preceding factors describes a situation in which the auditor is more likely to judge a weakness in internal controls as material. The next two factors highlight the fact that certain situations can mitigate the concerns that the auditor might otherwise have about a potential material weakness in internal controls. Exhibit 18.2 depicts the effect that mitigating factors can have on the assessment of whether an internal control deficiency is a material weakness.

AUDITING *in Practice*

CONTROL TESTING, FAILURE RATES, AND IMPLICATIONS FOR JUDGMENTS ABOUT INTERNAL CONTROL MATERIAL WEAKNESSES

Consider an example in which the auditor takes a sample of forty transactions to test control activities and finds that there is a failure rate that exceeds the tolerable error limit. What should the auditor do? The auditor may want to expand the control testing to get a more precise estimate of the likelihood of errors. Next, the auditor needs to estimate whether a failure of the control is likely (i.e., there is a reasonable possibility) to result in a misstatement in the account balance. Then, that data needs to be projected to the financial statements as a whole to determine whether the failure rate—as predicted—could lead to a material misstatement. If it does, then the weakness is material. If not, the auditor will most likely bring the problem to the attention of the audit committee.

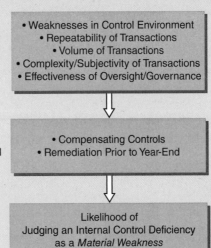

Exhibit 18.2   Factors Affecting the Materiality of Control Deficiencies

Factors that Increase Likelihood of Material Weakness in Internal Control

- Weaknesses in Control Environment
- Repeatability of Transactions
- Volume of Transactions
- Complexity/Subjectivity of Transactions
- Effectiveness of Oversight/Governance

Factors that Mitigate a Potential Material Weakness in Internal Control

- Compensating Controls
- Remediation Prior to Year-End

Likelihood of Judging an Internal Control Deficiency as a *Material Weakness*

6. *Existence of Compensating Controls.* Often there are other controls in place that might compensate for a deficiency in a particular control and that make the original weakness less likely to be judged material. For example, a supervisory reconciliation process may be in place that detects failures in the recording of cash; or periodic inventory counts by internal auditors may compensate for weaknesses in identifying inventory shrinkages or other errors in recording.

7. *Remediation of a Control Deficiency.* The auditor's report addresses whether there are material weaknesses in internal control as of the company's year-end. It is possible that a control deficiency is identified and remediated by the company prior to the company's year-end. Thus, a deficiency that may have been considered a material weakness at an interim date would no longer be considered a material weakness at year end. However, the remediation needs to have occurred early enough in the year so that the auditor has the time to sufficiently test the remediated control.

Indicators of Material Weaknesses   A number of situations would suggest to the auditor that there is a material weakness in internal control. These include:

- Identification of fraud, whether or not material, on the part of senior management,

> **PRACTICAL POINT**
>
> Multiple control deficiencies that affect the same financial statement account increase the likelihood of misstatement, and may, in combination, constitute a material weakness, even though such deficiencies may individually not be material weaknesses.

AUDITING *in Practice*

PCAOB INSPECTIONS NOTE PROBLEMS IN EVALUATION OF CONTROL DEFICIENCIES

In 2009, the PCAOB issued a report identifying noteworthy observations that were derived from inspections conducted during 2008. Inspectors observed instances where auditors inappropriately based their conclusions about the severity of control deficiencies solely on the materiality of the identified errors in the financial statements. Also, some auditors failed to consider relevant risk factors when evaluating the severity of identified control deficiencies. In addition, there were

instances where the auditors did not consider whether certain control deficiencies, in combination with other identified control deficiencies, constituted a material weakness in controls.

When evaluating identified control deficiencies auditors need to take care to understand and follow the relevant professional guidance.

AUDITING *in Practice*

EFFECTIVENESS OF AUDIT COMMITTEE OVERSIGHT

The audit committee is one of the most important elements of effective oversight in any organization. The auditor must evaluate the audit committee's effectiveness—primarily revealed through:

- The quality of accounting and control discussion when the external auditor is present,
- The committee's demonstrated knowledge of accounting issues,
- The committee's receptiveness to fixing problems that are reported to it,

- The independence of the committee—as judged by its actions (not just its relationship to the company),
- Its oversight of the internal audit function, and
- Where applicable, its oversight of the risk management process.

Deficiencies in oversight on any, or a combination, of the above activities would likely constitute a material weakness in internal control over financial reporting.

- Restatement of previously issued financial statements to reflect the correction of a material misstatement, or
- Identification by the auditor of a material misstatement of financial statements in the current period in circumstances that indicate that the misstatement would not have been detected by the company's internal control over financial reporting.

Aggregating Control Deficiencies

When conducting an audit, the auditor keeps a list of the identified misstatements in the financial statements for further evaluation. Similarly, the auditor should keep a list of the identified control deficiencies for further evaluation. Such a list of deficiencies will help the auditor identify whether multiple deficiencies, which individually would not be considered material weaknesses, would affect the same location, or process, or financial statement account such that when considered together, the deficiencies would represent a material weakness. The auditor wants to aggregate deficiencies with similar themes (accounts, locations, etc.) to see if when they are aggregated, if they rise to the level of a significant deficiency or material weaknesses. The summary of deficiencies provides the auditor with the basis for answering the following question: *On an overall basis, do the identified deficiencies represent a significant deficiency or a material weakness?*

Evaluating a Client's Internal Audit Function

LO 6

Judge the quality of the client's internal audit function and determine the effect of the client's internal audit function on the performance of the audit.

When the external auditor obtains the required understanding of a client's internal control, the auditor often will also learn about the client's internal audit function. In many organizations, internal auditors perform a significant amount of work that is relevant to internal controls and the financial reporting processes. Professional external auditing standards provide guidance on the role that internal auditors can play in the financial statement and internal control audits. From an audit risk model perspective, a high-quality internal audit function can reduce overall control risk, and the work of the internal audit function can be relied upon to reduce detection risk. However, these effects will only occur to the extent that the internal auditors have performed relevant activities and are of a sufficient level of quality. When determining the role of the internal auditors in the performance of the external audit, and in assessing the quality of the

PRACTICAL POINT

If the auditor reports a significant deficiency to the audit committee, management, and the board, and then returns next year to find that the control deficiency has not been remediated, then the auditor has to conclude there is a problem with the effectiveness of corporate oversight. Such a lack of corporate oversight would likely constitute a material weakness in internal control over financial reporting.

PROFESSIONAL JUDGMENT IN CONTEXT

PCAOB's Findings Related to Evaluation of a Client's Internal Audit Function

PCAOB inspections are designed to identify and address weaknesses and deficiencies related to how a firm conducts audits. To achieve that goal, the inspections include reviews of certain aspects of selected audits performed by the firm and reviews of other matters related to the firm's quality-control system.

Inspection reports of the following two audit firms included deficiencies related to assessing and relying on the work of a client's internal audit function. The inspection report on Vitale, Caturano & Company, Ltd., dated February 2, 2006, noted that when relying on the company's internal audit function, the auditors failed to perform and document required assessments regarding the client's internal audit department and to consider the impact that control exceptions identified by internal audit would have on the execution of the planned audit approach.

The inspection of Stovall, Grandey & Whatley, LLP, dated August 29, 2005, noted that the audit team failed to evaluate

the quality and effectiveness of an internal auditor's work sufficiently to support the use of that internal auditor's work.

As you read through this section, consider these PCAOB findings and the following questions:

- What responsibilities do external auditors have to evaluate a client's internal audit function?

- What are the key factors that the external auditor should examine in evaluating the work of the internal audit function and in determining whether or not it can rely on the work performed by the internal audit function?

- How can the external audit team make use of work performed by a client's internal audit function?

- Why would an external audit team want to make use of work performed by a client's internal audit function?

internal audit function, it is important for external auditors to have an understanding of the profession of internal auditing.

An Overview of Internal Auditing

The activities of an internal audit function vary widely across organizations. Internal auditors may perform, among other activities, the following assurance and consulting activities: providing assurance on financial statement related items, evaluating the effectiveness of operations and related controls, investigating concerns of fraud, evaluating the effectiveness of internal control processes, performing **operational audits**, evaluating the organization's compliance with laws, regulations, and company policies, and performing information systems and security audits. The Institute of Internal Auditors (IIA) recognizes the breadth of internal audit activities in its definition of internal auditing:

> Internal auditing is *an independent, objective assurance and consulting activity* designed to add value and improve an organization's operations. It helps an organization accomplish its objectives by bringing a *systematic, disciplined approach* to evaluate and improve the effectiveness of *risk management, control, and governance* processes.

The definition recognizes the uniqueness of internal auditing, which provides assurances to top management and the board and at the same time must not be reluctant to recommend improvements to operating managers. The focus is on adding value by bringing a systematic process for objectively obtaining and evaluating evidence to evaluate risk, controls, and operations.

Independent and Objective   Independence and objectivity are related, but they are not the same concept. Objectivity is a personal trait, while independence is primarily a departmental or activity concept. Objectivity implies a detached analytical approach that is conducted without bias to diverse parties who may have a vested interest in the audit findings. Objectivity requires competence in the area being audited, i.e., without sufficient knowledge, the auditor would be relying on someone else to help interpret information gathered as part of the

PRACTICAL POINT

There are two approaches to using the work of a client's internal audit function: (1) use internal auditors as assistants during the audit (not popular with internal auditors), and (2) rely on internal audit work already performed. The first approach works best when the two audit groups coordinate the planning and execution of specific audit tests with the internal audit function.

audit. Objectivity also requires impartiality in gathering and evaluating evidence and reporting the results. Objectivity is necessary if an auditor is to provide both assurance and consulting activities to management and to outsiders.

The concept of independence relates to "scope of services" and freedom to act objectively on audit examinations. Independence is formulated at the department level and provides for freedom of access and reporting without fear of retribution or motivation by intrinsic reward. The requirement for independence is usually found in an **internal audit charter** approved by the board of directors and audit committee. The charter clearly describes the nature and the scope of the internal audit activity, including its reporting responsibilities. When a strong charter and a strong audit committee exist, the internal audit department often has significant independence. Independence is enhanced when the internal audit director reports to the audit committee rather than directly to top management.

Assurance and Consulting Activity   The Institute of Internal Auditors (IIA) defines **assurance services** as:

> An objective examination of evidence for the purpose of providing an independent assessment on governance, risk management, and control processes for the organization. Examples may include financial, performance, compliance, system security, and due diligence engagements.

Various levels of the organization need assurances on organizational performance:

- Management is interested in the efficiency and effectiveness of operational activities, controls, and compliance with company policies, contracts, and governmental laws and regulations.
- The audit committee wants assurances that risks are appropriately addressed, controls are working effectively, and processes are in place to achieve financial reporting objectives.
- Operational management needs objective analyses of risks and controls related to its activities.

Consulting services are defined as:

> Advisory and related [customer] service activities, the nature and scope of which are agreed with the [customer], are intended to add value and improve an organization's governance, risk management, and control processes without the internal auditor assuming management responsibility. Examples include counsel, advice, facilitation, and training.

There are a number of important points in the definition:

- Consulting can occur only when the audit function and the party receiving the services agree upon the nature and the scope of services.
- Consulting covers a broad range of activities that can include (a) facilitating the organization in conducting an assessment of its controls, (b) sharing insights gained during audits that might improve business processes and the efficiency of operations, and (c) serving as a member of a task force to analyze company problems.

It is equally important to recognize that consulting activities are advisory. They do not include decision-making, such as which system to implement; nor do they include implementation, or assuming responsibility for operating a process. Those tasks are reserved for management.

A Systematic and Disciplined Approach   The practice of internal auditing has a defined set of standards to ensure that objective, relevant, and sufficient evidence is gathered and evaluated to address whatever activity is being investigated. The evidence-gathering concept is similar to that of financial auditing, i.e., the auditor is not an advocate of any particular position, and evidence gathering must be unbiased and objective. Internal auditing, like external auditing, starts with a broad understanding of the organization, its objectives, and its risks. The task of the internal auditor is to assimilate the information in a systematic and disciplined fashion that results in an audit program to identify risks, gather evidence, evaluate findings, and suggest improvements.

Risk Management, Control, and Corporate Governance Many of the internal auditor's activities are targeted toward improving risk management, control, and corporate governance within their organization. Understanding the organization's objectives is the fundamental starting point for providing these services. Without understanding objectives, it is not possible to understand what the risks are to achieving those objectives. Sometimes the objectives are explicit, e.g., growing market share; other times they are implied, e.g., achieving reliable financial reporting. Risk management follows from the understanding of the organization's objectives, while controls exist to help manage risks and are therefore integrally related to risks and risk management. Governance is the process by which the organization and its stakeholders gain assurance that activities are conducted in accordance with broad organizational policies, and that accountability is established.

Serving Management and the Audit Committee

One of the unique features of the internal audit function is that it serves the needs of both the audit committee and management. Internal auditors serve the audit committee in at least three major ways:

- Assisting the organization in reviewing the quality of internal controls over financial reporting as part of the Sarbanes-Oxley requirements
- Providing an independent viewpoint on major accounting issues
- Providing feedback on the efficiency of operations and compliance with company and regulatory policies

Internal auditors assist management in its oversight responsibilities as well. Thus, an internal audit department will assist management by evaluating risk management, internal controls, and effectiveness and efficiency of operations. Internal auditors often take the lead in evaluating the effectiveness of management's documentation of controls needed in order for management to provide assurances on the quality of internal controls.

Now that the Sarbanes-Oxley Act requires the CEO and CFO to certify the company's financial statements, they are asking for the help of internal auditors in assuring the reliability of the financial reporting processes.

Staffing an Internal Audit Function

Clients have a number of different alternatives available for staffing their internal audit function. These alternatives range from an internal audit function fully housed within the organization, to partial outsourcing for specific projects, to outsourcing the entire function to an outside provider—including to a public accounting firm (but not the client's auditor). Outsourcing engagements may be ongoing or for specific time periods or specific projects where special capabilities are needed (e.g., special-need IT audits, environmental audits, derivative reviews, contract audits, and enterprise-wide risk management services). Many internal functions need to outsource or co-source some of their work to assure all of their responsibilities are completed in a timely and competent manner. Internal audit activities that are outsourced typically go to public accounting firms or to other specialized firms that perform primarily risk, control, and audit activities. Internal audit outsourcing has represented the fastest growth area in public accounting practice over the past few years, with annual growth rates reaching as high as 60–70%.

The outsourcing providers have assisted many organizations in meeting the reporting requirements of Sarbanes-Oxley. The Big 4 public accounting firms

> **PRACTICAL POINT**
>
> When the external auditor assesses the quality of a client's internal audit function, the external auditor should consider whether the internal audit function adheres to professional internal auditing standards.

> **PRACTICAL POINT**
>
> The SEC's independence rules prohibit a CPA firm from providing both internal and external audit services for the same client.

are often used to supplement existing internal audit departments in specialized areas, such as information technology audits or in performing specialized tasks. These firms and others such as Protiviti and Jefferson-Wells have locations around the globe and are therefore able to provide extended audit services to clients without additional travel costs and without language and cultural problems.

Internal Auditing Standards

The Institute of Internal Auditors (IIA) is the international body that sets standards for the practice of internal auditing across the world. Professional guidance is provided in the IIA's International Professional Practices Framework (IPPF). The IPPF consists of mandatory guidance which includes the Definition of Internal Auditing, the Code of Ethics, and the *International Standards.* The IPPF also consists of strongly recommended guidance which describes practices for the implementation of the mandatory guidance and includes position papers, practice advisories, and practice guides.

The IIA's Code of Ethics, part of the mandatory guidance, is designed to promote an ethical culture in the internal audit profession. The Code of Ethics consists of the following four principles:

- Integrity
- Objectivity
- Confidentiality
- Competency

and rules of conduct that describe twelve norms that internal auditors should follow to put the principles into practice.

The *International Standards for the Professional Practice of Internal Auditing,* another component of the mandatory guidance, outline the basic principles of the practice of internal auditing, provide a framework for performing value added internal auditing, establish the basis for the evaluation of internal audit performance, and foster improved processes and operations. The *Standards* are principles-based, mandatory requirements for the practice of internal auditing.

Internal Auditing Contrasted with External Auditing

External auditors have a defined role: they provide independent assurance to third parties. In contrast, internal auditors provide a wide array of assurance and consulting services to those within the organization. Some of the work performed by the internal auditors can be used by the external auditors completing the audit of internal controls and the financial statement audit. The differences between the two professions are outlined in Exhibit 18.3.

Evaluating the Quality of the Client's Internal Audit Function

With an understanding of the internal audit profession, the external auditor assesses the quality of the client's internal audit function and determines whether the internal auditors' work is both (a) relevant to the external audit and (b) of sufficient quantity and quality.

The external auditor considers three primary characteristics in assessing the quality of the internal audit function: competence, objectivity, and quality of work performance. Exhibit 18.4 presents a list of the factors that the external auditor should consider in evaluating the competence, objectivity, and quality of work.

Exhibit 18.3	Contrast of Internal and External Auditing	

	External Auditing (CPA)	**Internal Auditing (CIA)**
Primary Client	Audit committee of the board of directors (management of nonpublic companies)	Management and the audit committee of the board
Parties Receiving Assurance	Outside stakeholders, regulatory agencies, and stockholders	Audit committee, upper management, and operational management
Scope of Services Performed—Primary	Audits of financial statements, Audits of internal control	Risk analysis Control analysis Operations analysis
Scope of Services— Extended	Attestation services as demanded by market place	Information security and reliability Operational efficiency Compliance reviews Special investigations Fraud investigations
Primary Nature of Services	Audit and assurance	Assurance Consulting
Certification	CPA—required	CIA—Certified Internal Auditor—required by many companies, but not all
Relationship to Organization	Must be independent	Part of the organization, but should report to audit committee to maintain independence; however, much of the internal audit work can be outsourced to outside providers such as public accounting firms
Consulting	Cannot perform consulting for public audit clients, but can be performed for non-audit and non-public clients	Consulting performed when agreed to by management and audit committee
Audit Processes	Gather sufficient, appropriate evidence to render an opinion	Gather sufficient, appropriate evidence to render an opinion, or recommend improvements to a process; includes data analysis, outside confirmations, as well as other procedures normally performed by external auditors
Major Focus	Financial statements, internal controls over financial reporting, and financial reporting processes	Processes, including risks, controls, and effectiveness and efficiency of processes

Exhibit 18.4	Factors to Consider in Assessing the Quality of Internal Audit

Area of Assessment	**Factors to Consider in Assessment**
Competence	• Educational level and professional experience. • Professional certification and continuing education. • Review of quality of audit policies, programs, and procedures. • Demonstrated supervision and review of internal auditors' activities. • Quality of working-paper documentation, reports, and recommendations. • Periodic evaluation of internal auditors' performance—both self-assessment and feedback from auditees and audit committee. • Periodic quality-control assessments performed in accordance with the *International Standards for the Professional Practice of Internal Auditing*.

(continues)

Exhibit 18.4	Factors to Consider in Assessing the Quality of Internal Audit (*continued*)

Area of Assessment	Factors to Consider in Assessment
Objectivity	• Organizational reporting status is sufficient to assure audit coverage of major organizational risks as well as consideration of, and action on, the findings and recommendations of the internal auditors. • Internal auditor has direct access and reports regularly to the board of directors, the audit committee, or the owner-manager. • Board of directors, the audit committee, or the owner-manager oversees employment decisions related to the director of the internal audit function. • Policies that prohibit internal auditors from auditing areas where relatives are employed in important or audit-sensitive positions. • Policies that minimize other potential conflicts of interest, such as auditing an area where they were employed before entering internal audit, or where they will be placed after spending time in internal audit.
Quality of internal audit work	• Scope of work is appropriate to meet the objectives. • Audit programs are adequate. • Working papers adequately document work performed, including evidence of supervision and review. • Conclusions are appropriate in the circumstances. • Reports are consistent with the results of the work performed.

PRACTICAL POINT

When internal audit is of sufficiently high quality and performs work related to that of the external auditor, the external auditor can use the internal auditor's work to reduce the external auditor's work and thereby reduce overall external audit fees. However, the external auditor must perform enough work so the external auditor can assume responsibility for its audit opinions.

PRACTICAL POINT

A best practice is to have oversight of the internal audit function as a responsibility of the audit committee.

PRACTICAL POINT

Audit committees will often ask the external auditors for their evaluation of the chief audit executive (CAE, or director of internal audit).

In assessing the factors in Exhibit 18.4, the external auditor will need to review relevant evidence. For example, in assessing the quality of work, the auditor will want to corroborate the internal auditor's assessments and conclusions by taking a sample of the some of the items examined by the internal auditor or a sample of similar transactions. Although the factors in Exhibit 18.4 could lead one to set up a checklist and tick off each item (e.g., education or certification), the intent is to guide the external auditor in a systematic evaluation of the internal audit function. Most likely, the external audit team has had interaction with various levels of internal audit and has good knowledge of the scope of their work and the competence with which they carry out their work.

The factors listed in Exhibit 18.4 provide a systematic approach to the evaluation of internal audit work. For example, the auditor could see that all of the factors to ensure audit objectivity and independence are present. However, the real test is whether the audit reports reflect the findings of the audits or if there is pressure by an executive (CEO, CFO, etc.) to lessen the impact of the findings. Finally, if the auditor is going to rely extensively on internal audit work, tests of the same transactions, or similar transactions, must be performed to gain assurance that the work and findings are consistent with the expectation based on the documentation found in the internal audit workpapers.

Effect of Internal Audit's Work on the External Audit

Even though the internal auditors' work may affect the external auditor's procedures, the external auditor still needs to perform enough procedures to obtain sufficient, appropriate, evidential matter to support the auditor's report. The responsibility for the external audit rests solely with the external auditor, and this responsibility cannot be shared with the internal auditors.

Comparison of Worldwide Professional Guidance

RELIANCE ON THE INTERNAL AUDIT FUNCTION

AICPA Auditing Standards Board (ASB)

SAS 65 allows the auditor to rely on work already performed by the internal auditor or to use the internal auditors as direct assistants during the auditor. SAS 65 cautions that the internal auditors must be sufficiently competent and objective. Further, the external auditors need to consider the materiality, risk, and evidence subjectivity of an audit area before determining the extent of reliance to place on the work of the internal auditors. Finally, SAS 65 indicates that when internal auditors' work is relied on, the external auditor should evaluate and perform audit procedures on that work.

Public Company Accounting Oversight Board (PCAOB)

AS 5 encourages the external auditor to use the work of the internal auditor as a means to improve audit efficiency, and reminds the auditor to consult the requirements and guidance in the PCAOB's AU section 322 (interim standard), the source of which is SAS 65.

International Auditing and Assurance Standards Board (IAASB)

ISA 610 provides guidance that is quite similar to the ASB's SAS 65. However, ISA 610 does not address circumstances when internal auditors are used to provide direct assistance to the external auditor to carry out audit procedures.

SUMMARY

The standard setting bodies all recognize the impact that a client's internal audit function can have on the performance of the financial statement audit if the internal auditors are competent and objective. Further, the standards highlight that the external auditor "has sole responsibility for the audit opinion expressed, and that responsibility is not reduced by the external auditor's use of the work of the internal auditors." One topic that none of these standards address is the nature and extent of the external auditor's responsibilities in circumstance where the entity has outsourced its internal audit function; the IAASB has indicated that this topic could be addressed in its next revision to ISA 610.

In the *Comparison of Worldwide Professional Guidance*, we articulate relevant standards concerning internal auditing.

In making judgments about the effect of the internal auditors' work on the external auditor's procedures in specific audit areas, the external auditor considers three issues related to the audit areas:

1. Materiality of the financial statement amounts
2. Risk of material misstatement of the assertions related to these financial statement amounts
3. Degree of subjectivity involved in the evaluation of the audit evidence gathered in support of the assertions

For some assertions, such as existence and occurrence, the evidence gathered is objective. For other assertions, such as the valuation and disclosure assertions, more audit judgment is required and the evaluation is more subjective. As the materiality of account balances or detection risk increases, or the subjectivity of evidence evaluation increases, more of the work needs to be performed directly by the external auditor. Examples of areas that meet these criteria include:

- Valuation of assets and liabilities involving significant accounting estimates, and
- The existence and disclosure of related-party transactions, contingencies, uncertainties, and subsequent events.

In contrast, areas that are usually less material or where evidence evaluation is more objective include:

- Cash
- Prepaid assets
- Fixed-asset additions

PRACTICAL POINT

Audit Standard No. 5 by the PCAOB encourages the external auditor to use the work of internal auditors (as well as other objective parties within the organization) when performing the assessment of internal control over financial reporting. In placing such reliance on internal parties, the auditor needs to have a high confidence level that the audit work was completed correctly. That high level of confidence can only be obtained through testing the same or similar transactions.

For some assertions, the external auditor may decide that because of work performed by internal auditors the audit risk has been reduced to an acceptable level and that testing of the assertions directly by the auditor may not be necessary.

Because the auditor has the ultimate responsibility to express an opinion on the financial statements, many of the audit judgments must be made by the external auditor and should not be delegated to the internal auditors. Some of these judgments include assessments of:

- Inherent and control risks
- The materiality of misstatements
- The sufficiency of tests performed
- The evaluation of significant accounting estimates

Auditing Fair Value Estimates

LO 7

Identify and describe the concepts of fair value and impairment as they apply to auditing.

The measurement and communication of accounting information continues to change, with increased emphasis on the *quality* of assets and liabilities. That change requires that almost every account on a company's balance sheet will need to be assessed at fair value (including adjustments to net realizable value), and disclosures will need to reflect information about the nature of the fair value estimation. Auditing fair value amounts requires a different audit approach—the auditor is not auditing transactions that have taken place within the organization, but is instead evaluating outside market values, industry data on sales and

PROFESSIONAL JUDGMENT IN CONTEXT

Evidence and Concerns about Fair Value Estimates

Consider the following statements as you contemplate the challenges associated with auditing fair values—and the potential second-guessing that takes place when the client and auditor estimates do not turn out to be correct. First, consider a quote from the *Journal of Accounting Research* in an article[1] that examined management's approaches in providing assessments of the fair value of an asset:

> We examine management discretion to decide when and how much to write down an asset.... We find that, despite market evidence that Inco Ltd.'s financial statements substantially overvalued the Voisey's Bay nickel mine [one of their operating mines] throughout 1997 to 2000, management chose not to write down the mine until 2002. Inco management used an independent fairness opinion to justify its December 2000 redemption of the tracking stock at 25% of its initial value, indicating almost surely that Inco management was aware of the generally accepted accounting principles (GAAP) impairment. This case illustrates that GAAP's reliance on undiscounted cash flows for impairment decisions allows huge unrecorded disparities between book and market value. The management discretion exercised in this case provides a concrete example of the subjectivity inherent in fair valuation.

Second, consider several quotes from Smartpros.com regarding the potential impairment of goodwill in late 2008[2]:

- *Sun Microsystems issued a preliminary report on its first quarter fiscal 2009 results on Oct. 20. While it expects quarterly revenues in the neighborhood of $3 billion, it foresees a quarterly loss. Management writes, "Based on a combination of factors, including the current economic environment ... the Company has concluded that it is likely that the fair value of one or more of its reporting units has been reduced below its carrying value." Total goodwill is $3.2 billion, but $1.8 billion relates to reporting units in which the goodwill may be impaired.*

- *This earnings season will be filled with billions of dollars of goodwill write-downs. Investors need to be ready for them.*

- *The banking sector may be the hardest hit industry for impairment charges. But, managers in this industry might resist telling the truth. I hypothesize this possibility because these same managers have been unwilling to face the music conducted by fair value accounting. If they don't wish to tell the truth about their toxic investments, they might try to conceal these truths as well. I hope the auditing industry is prepared to hold their collective feet to the fire that the banking industry started. (emphasis added)*

(continues)

PROFESSIONAL JUDGMENT IN CONTEXT

Evidence and Concerns about Fair Value Estimates (continued)

As you read through the remainder of this section, consider the following questions that auditors have to deal with on a regular basis:

- What is fair value and where does it need to be applied?
- What is the best evidence to determine fair value or measuring the impairment of goodwill?
- What are the accounting requirements concerning fair value estimates?
- What does it mean to "mark to model"?

- How does the auditor determine the future cash flows associated with potentially impaired assets such as goodwill, intangible assets, or even property, plant, and equipment?
- Given that it is impossible to predict the future, why do investors and the public expect auditors to predict future cash flows to value existing assets?

[1] Hilton, A. S., and P. C. O'Brien, "Inco Ltd.: Market value, fair value, and management discretion," *Journal of Accounting Research* 2009 (Vol. 47, No. 1), pp. 179–211.

[2] Ketz, E. 2008. Smartpros.com (November).

trends, and models of future cash flows. This new audit approach is fraught with increased risk but may be rewarding for auditors who understand the broad parameters of the marketplace and how they affect particular clients' financial statement accounts.

The Accounting Model for Fair Value Estimates

U.S. guidance for measuring fair values comes from FASB ASC 350 *Intangibles—Goodwill and Other* (previously SFAS 157, *Fair Value Measurements* which was first issued in 2006 and updated in 2008 and again in 2009). ASC 350 provides guidance on developing measures of fair values in situations where fair values are required. Fair value is defined in International Accounting Standard (IAS) 32, *Financial Instruments: Presentation* as the amount for which an asset could be exchanged, or a liability settled, between knowledgeable, willing parties in an arm's length transaction.

Thus, the concept implies an orderly market and may not be applicable to certain distressed assets where no market exists. In such situations, the asset may be required to be valued at the lower of cost or market. To guide management and auditors, FASB recognizes that the persuasiveness of information in making an estimate may differ—and there may be many different sources of relevant information. Therefore, FASB has set a hierarchy of inputs to consider in assessing fair value:

- *Level 1* is quoted prices for identical items in active, liquid, and visible markets such as stock exchanges. An example would be a recent trade on the NYSE of a stock or a bond.
- *Level 2* is observable information for similar items in active or inactive markets, such as two similarly situated buildings in a downtown real estate market.
- *Level 3* is unobservable inputs to be used in situations where markets do not exist or are illiquid, such as during the credit crisis of 2009. This is often referred to as "mark to model" because it is dependent on management's estimates of future cash flows associated with the asset or liability to be valued. Level 3 valuations are generally viewed as highly subjective.

Recall from your intermediate accounting that most asset accounts are subject to realizability, or lower of cost or market tests. We have covered these in previous chapters where we discussed the need to value inventory at the lower of cost

> **PRACTICAL POINT**
>
> Level 3 inputs and the underlying valuation models should be developed in a systematic and rigorous fashion such that the process and underlying model assumptions can be objectively evaluated by the auditor.

LO 8

Determine appropriate evidence to gather when testing adjustments to fair market value and impairments.

or market or to estimate the allowance for either uncollectible loans or uncollectible receivables. As illustrated with the Ford financial statement accounts earlier in the chapter, almost all assets—and a number of liabilities as well—will be subject to some type of realizability or market adjustment.

Goodwill represents a special case that was referred to in the *Professional Judgment in Context* feature. FASB has issued guidance in ASC 350 *Intangibles—Goodwill and Other* stating that the goodwill impairment test is performed annually, as well as on an interim basis at the time events and circumstances warrant. The guidance continues by noting that impairment is the condition that exists when the carrying amount of goodwill exceeds its implied fair value.

Recall, there are two steps to determining the impairment of goodwill:

Step 1: Compare the fair value of the reporting unit with the carrying value of the reporting unit.

Step 2: Measure the impairment by comparing the fair value of the goodwill (on a reporting unit basis) with the carrying value of goodwill.

In Step 1, the presumption is that the fair value determination of goodwill should be determined on the same basis as was the original determination of goodwill and for the same reporting unit. For example, when Time-Warner merged with AOL, the reporting unit was AOL. The difficulty in valuation comes when the organization integrates AOL into the fabric of other operations. Therefore, management's determination of relevant segments and reporting units for goodwill impairment becomes an important judgmental consideration. In Step 2, the judgments become even more difficult as the auditor—and the client—must assess future cash flows from the investment that originally led to the establishment of the goodwill.

Issues in Auditing Adjustments to Fair Market and Impairments

There are a number of account balances that commonly require fair value estimates. Most often, we think about marketable securities because of the financial crisis; but fair value adjustments are also common for property, plant, and equipment that will be sold, for receivables or inventory, and for considering goodwill impairments. We begin by providing an overview of auditing fair value estimates and then explicitly discuss auditing implications of impairments.

Fair Value Estimates

An overview of audit considerations concerning **fair value estimates** is shown in Exhibit 18.5. In analyzing the exhibit, note that there are specific audit challenges relevant to each level of fair value estimation and that the client should have (a) a systematic process to identify each asset that is subject to fair value estimation, (b) a process to identify relevant market values, (c) an analysis of whether the organization has the ability to hold the asset to maturity and whether the decline in value is other than temporary, and (d) a realistic process to estimate future cash flows to discount back to a present value.

Level 1 does not represent unusual challenges for the auditor. However, Levels 2 and 3 represent significant challenges—including determining whether or not an active market exists. Level 2 is broad and applies to financial instruments, property, or lower of cost or market considerations for inventory, loans, or receivables. The audit approach for Level 2 requires the auditor to review and assess:

- The correspondence of the client's assets to similar assets in an active market
- Whether an active market exists for similar assets
- The client's systematic process for estimating fair value

Exhibit 18.5 — Overview of Fair Value Audit Considerations

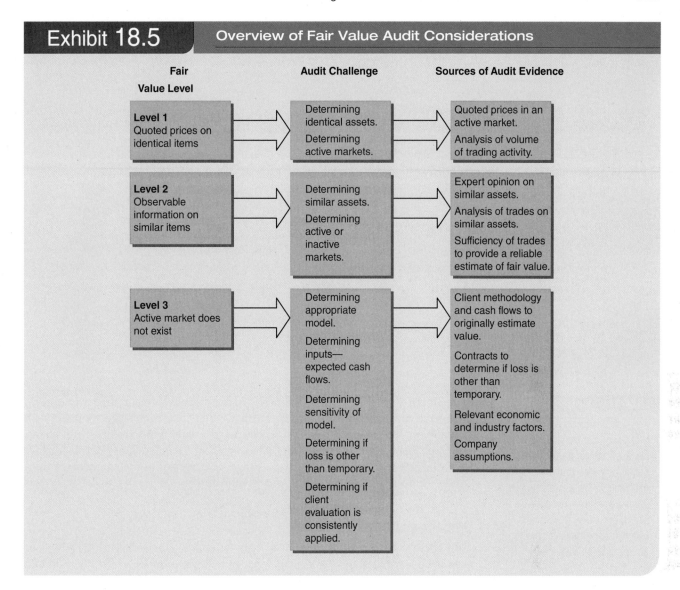

Fair Value Level	Audit Challenge	Sources of Audit Evidence
Level 1 Quoted prices on identical items	Determining identical assets. Determining active markets.	Quoted prices in an active market. Analysis of volume of trading activity.
Level 2 Observable information on similar items	Determining similar assets. Determining active or inactive markets.	Expert opinion on similar assets. Analysis of trades on similar assets. Sufficiency of trades to provide a reliable estimate of fair value.
Level 3 Active market does not exist	Determining appropriate model. Determining inputs—expected cash flows. Determining sensitivity of model. Determining if loss is other than temporary. Determining if client evaluation is consistently applied.	Client methodology and cash flows to originally estimate value. Contracts to determine if loss is other than temporary. Relevant economic and industry factors. Company assumptions.

- Characteristics of any outside appraisers, including whether the appraiser is independent, objective, competent, and has used comparable items in estimating value
- The data used by the company in estimating future cash flows, including whether the data considers economic conditions and changes in the marketplace and uses an appropriate discount rate to determine net present value

The *Auditing in Practice* feature identifies a number of factors that an auditor and client should consider in determining whether a decline in market value is other than temporary. Note that the factors require the auditor to develop an in-depth understanding of the industry, economic trends, and financial health of the parties that are responsible for fulfilling existing contracts. Fundamentally, these requirements are not much different than the understanding that an auditor must have to properly evaluate accounts such as the allowance for doubtful accounts, loan loss reserves, or the market value of distressed inventory.

Audits of Level 3 balances present the most difficulty because they do not involve an observable, active market. The approach—often criticized—is referred to as "marking to model" because the client is expected to estimate fair value based on a model of the future cash flows associated with the

PRACTICAL POINT

Using an outside appraiser or other specialist (to help determine fair values) does not necessarily mean that the client (and auditor) is getting an objective and competent appraisal of fair value. The auditor needs to analyze the credentials of the appraiser and the methodology used by the appraiser before accepting the appraised values as audit evidence.

AUDITING *in Practice*

DETERMINING IF A DECLINE IN VALUE IS OTHER THAN TEMPORARY

SAB 59 and SAS No. 92 describe factors that indicate an other-than-temporary impairment of a security's value has occurred. These factors include:

- The length of time and extent to which the market value has been less than cost.
- The financial condition and near-term prospects of the issuer, including specific events which may affect the issuer's operations or future earnings. Examples include changes in technology or the discontinuance of a segment of the business.
- The intent and ability of the holder to retain its investment in the issuer for a period sufficient to allow for any anticipated recovery in market value.

- Whether a decline in fair value is attributable to adverse conditions specifically related to the security or specific conditions in an industry or geographic area.
- The investee's credit rating and whether the security has been downgraded by a rating agency.
- Whether dividends have been reduced or eliminated, or scheduled interest payments have not been made.
- The cash position of the investee.

Source: Rees, T., & Fick, K. 2009. "Weathering the other than temporary impairment storm," *Journal of Accountancy* (February online edition).

PRACTICAL POINT

Although there was a great deal of criticism that the sale of Merrill Lynch securities at 29 cents on the dollar was a distressed sale that could not be applied to other securities, further trading in similar securities proved the estimate to be representative of future trades in similar assets.

PRACTICAL POINT

Goodwill has to be evaluated for impairment once a year—and not necessarily at the balance sheet date. However, the date for evaluation has to be consistently applied.

PRACTICAL POINT

The auditor's analysis of goodwill and potential impairment is facilitated if the client had documented (and the auditor reviewed) the initial assumptions made by the company in making the acquisition that ultimately resulted in the recording of the goodwill.

instrument or the asset. As an example, many distressed financial instruments do not have a current market value. Further, there is a reluctance to trade such instruments because the value is difficult to ascertain. Thus, auditors and clients use comparisons of distressed sales in the market place, such as Merrill Lynch's sale of distressed assets at $.29 on the dollar, as evidence of market values. Obviously, there is considerable lack of precision in these estimates, and that creates audit risk.

Impairments

We focus our discussion of impairments on those associated with goodwill. It has been estimated that goodwill represented approximately 36% of all assets of major U.S. corporations as of December 31, 2008. Goodwill, which was previously amortized, is now subject to impairment testing on a yearly basis. The first step in judging whether an impairment has occurred is to determine if the market value of the reporting unit is less than the carrying value of the assets of the reporting unit. If so, and assuming other assets have been properly valued, the presumption is that goodwill has been impaired. Then the auditor must estimate the fair value (or impaired value) of the goodwill.

When the company as a whole is not the reporting unit, the auditor must gather other evidence to assess potential goodwill impairment. Other sources of information include negotiations to sell the reporting unit, current profitability of the reporting unit, projected cash flows compared with cash-flow projections made at the time of acquisition, and management's strategic plans for using the assets. The client is required to consider the approaches identified to develop an estimate of asset impairment. The auditor must evaluate (a) management's methodology for assessing impairment and (b) whether an objective evaluation of the evidence supports the client's conclusion.

Exhibit 18.6 provides an overview of factors the auditor should consider when assessing goodwill impairment, and Exhibit 18.7 provides an audit program for goodwill impairment testing.

The audit approach taken for goodwill impairment, as well as fair value estimates, reiterates a fundamental premise stated in the title of this book: The best way to perform an audit is to thoroughly understand the client, its business, its

AUDITING *in Practice*

GOODWILL IMPAIRMENT AT AOL TIME-WARNER

The magnitude of adjustments for impairments of goodwill can be quite substantial. The saga of AOL Time-Warner provides a striking example. As early as 2002, *Business Week* wrote that there was a credibility gap in the company's financial reporting because AOL Time-Warner was not able to integrate the Internet capabilities from AOL to capture synergies with the Time-Warner publishing segments. AOL had taken a $54 billion write-off of goodwill in 2002, only to take another $25 billion write-off in 2008.

Exhibit 18.6	Overview of Factors Affecting Goodwill Impairment Valuations	
Factors to Be Evaluated	**Evidence Issues**	**Potential Audit Problems**
Current Fair Market Value of the Entity	Determine Fair Market Value (FMV) of the total entity.	Readily available if publicly traded, but not readily available if not publicly traded. Market valuation may be volatile. A temporary decline in market value may not be a good indicator of FMV.
	Determine FMV of the operating segment.	FMV might not exist. Might require independent appraisals by investment bankers or estimates using cash flow and discounted present value factors. Assumptions must be made about competition, economic development, product placement, and so forth. These assumptions will be difficult to verify.
Operating Segment Must Be Clearly Defined	If the acquired company remains intact after the acquisition, it is defined as the operating segment.	No particular problem.
	The purpose of most acquisitions is to integrate the newly acquired business into the operation of the existing business.	The company must set up a systematic methodology to clearly define the operating segment and trace it over time.
	Operating segments may change over time as acquisitions are made. The acquired operating unit may not be distinguishable after a period of time.	Goodwill arising from many acquisitions can be netted into one test at the operating segment level, but not netted at the company level.
Current FMV of Assets and Liabilities of Non-Goodwill Assets	Assets: could be measured by estimated NRV or estimated replacement costs.	Assets are used as a group of assets. It is difficult to estimate FMV of a group because there may be a limited number of buyers for the group. Replacement cost data may be difficult and costly to obtain, and the data must be adjusted for usage.
	Liabilities: could be estimated by discounted cash flows using current interest rates properly adjusted for risk.	Interest rates must be adjusted for risk and term.
Goodwill Impairment	The impairment is measured by the difference between market value of the operating segment and the FMV of net assets.	All the difficulties identified previously come into play.
		Estimates are hard to verify because they are based on assumptions.
		Can be subject to manipulation by management.

Exhibit 18.7	Audit Program for Goodwill Impairment Testing

1. Review the methodology that the client initially used in determining the amount it used to purchase the reporting unit. Examine the initial client documents to determine:
   a. Assumptions about economic growth and synergies expected with the acquisition.
   b. Expected cash flow, discounted to present terms.
   c. Cost savings expected from integrated operations.
   d. Assumptions about the general economy, industry growth, and new-product innovation.

2. Compare actual results with those expected since the time of the acquisition.
   a. Determine significant changes in assumptions and projected results.
   b. Estimate the company's acquisition model with new assumptions that reflect current market conditions, actual results, and current information about cost of capital to get an estimate of reporting unit fair value.
   c. Compare fair value with carrying value and determine amount of goodwill impairment.

3. If the client does not have the original data, perform an independent analysis of the industry and develop:
   a. A set of assumptions about future performance based on industry expectations and company products.
   b. An estimated of future discounted cash flows.
   c. A sensitivity analysis of changes in value based on industry and cash-flow assumptions.
   d. A range of estimates and compare to carrying value of the reporting unit and goodwill carrying cost.

4. If the original reporting unit no longer exists because operations have been fully integrated into operations of the parent company:
   a. Compare book value with market value. A market value less than book value is presumptive evidence that goodwill has been impaired.
   b. Determine whether all other assets have been adjusted to fair value, where applicable.
   c. Compute difference between market value and book value to determine the amount of goodwill impairment.
   d. Review assumptions about future operations, industry position, expected future cash flows, and strategic plans for the business to determine if the write-off is part (c) is sufficient.

PRACTICAL POINT

It is better to have all significant reasons and processes documented and challenged by an objective party *within* the audit firm rather than leaving them undocumented and challenged by someone *outside* the audit firm, for example, in a court of law.

LO 9

Describe sustainability reporting and articulate the auditors' role in providing assurance on management sustainability reports.

business opportunities, and its risks. It is only by taking this approach that the audit profession will be able to deal with the challenges of complex judgments that will have to be made on many audits. Going forward, the flexibility in international accounting standards will demand even more audit judgment.

Sustainability Reporting and Assurance

What Is Sustainability?

Sustainability has become an increasingly important topic to organizations and societies around the globe in recent years, and this trend is likely going to intensify. However, what exactly do companies mean by sustainability? A few examples will help to illustrate the concept. MTN Group, a South African mobile phone company, defines sustainability as involving the following:

- "Promoting sound corporate governance practices and ethical responsibility.
- Providing a safe working environment in which the health of our people is protected and their opportunities for self development are enhanced.
- Promoting cultural diversity and equity in the workplace.
- Minimising adverse environmental impacts.
- Providing opportunities for social and economic development in the communities in which we operate" (see www.MTN.com/sustainability/).

Ford Motor Company defines sustainability as "a business model that creates value consistent with the long-term preservation and enhancement of environmental, social and financial capital" (see www.ford.com/go/sustainability), and Ford classifies its sustainability efforts in terms of activities involving climate change, freedom of mobility for people globally, human rights, vehicle safety,

PROFESSIONAL JUDGMENT IN CONTEXT

IFAC and A4S Sustainability Project

On May 4, 2010, the International Federation of Accountants (IFAC) and The Prince's Accounting for Sustainability (A4S) Project entered into a memorandum of understanding to support the global accountancy profession's role in developing sustainable organizations. As the press release states, "Organizations are increasingly seeking new ways to maintain their economic performance and contributions to society in the face of challenge and crisis. Perhaps the most critical challenge facing business and society generally is to live within our ecological limits, while continuing to enjoy economic prosperity. IFAC and A4S believe that an essential part of the answer lies in going beyond traditional ways of thinking about performance and embedding sustainability into strategy, governance, performance management, and reporting processes. Key priorities to support the work of professional accountants in embedding sustainable practices include:

- Raising awareness and facilitating sharing and collaboration across the global accountancy community, for example, through the development of a community website for professional accountancy organizations, business leaders, academics, and other experts to exchange ideas and share good sustainability practice;

- Establishing an international integrated reporting committee to develop a new reporting model that will better reflect the interconnected impact of financial, environmental, social, and governance factors on the long-term performance and condition of an organization; and

- Incorporating accounting for sustainability within professional training and education.

Professional accountants in organizations support the sustainability efforts of the organizations they work for in leadership roles in strategy, governance, performance management, and reporting processes. They also oversee, measure, control, and communicate the long-term sustainable value creation of their organizations."
As you read through the rest of the chapter, consider the following questions:

- What is sustainability?

- What information do organizations provide to external users about their sustainability efforts?

- How do organizations provide assurance that the sustainability disclosures they make are deemed credible and reliable by external users?

and sustaining the long-term viability of Ford Motor Company itself. As another example, Coca-Cola expresses its views about sustainability like this: "Imagine a better world. A world where all people have access to safe water, where packaging has a life beyond its original use, and where communities are healthy and prosperous. This is our vision. The Coca-Cola Company and our bottling partners are committed to making a lasting, positive difference in the world. We are constantly innovating to keep our products affordable and make our business more environmentally and economically beneficial to the communities we serve. And we believe that investing in the economic, environmental and social development of communities will help our business grow" (see www.thecoca-colacompany.com/citizenship/pdf/2008-2009_sustainability_review.pdf).

As these examples illustrate, there are many views on what constitutes sustainability and sustainability reporting, along with many terms that are used to describe these concepts. A report by Ernst & Young Australia summarizes three common sustainability-related terms:

- **Non-financial reporting** is the "practice of measuring, disclosing and being accountable to internal and external stakeholders for organisational performance towards the goal of sustainable development"
- **Corporate social responsibility reporting** is the "continuing commitment by business to behave ethically and contribute to economic development while improving the quality of life of the workforce, their families, the local community and society at large"
- **Triple bottom line reporting** is the "reporting on financial, environmental and social performance"

The term *triple bottom line reporting* best captures the essence of sustainability reporting, and we use this as our definition of the concept. Specifically, we

> **PRACTICAL POINT**
>
> According to KPMG's 2008 International Survey of Corporate Responsibility Reporting, about 80% of the largest 250 companies in the world now issue reports detailing their sustainability efforts and associated outcomes. In 2005, only about 50% of such companies issued sustainability reports.

define **sustainability** as actions taken at the corporate level to ensure economic, environmental, and social responsibility, and we define **sustainability reporting** as voluntary corporate disclosures about sustainability initiatives, plans, and associated outcomes.

PRACTICAL POINT

The Dow Jones Sustainability Indexes (DJSI) are global indexes that track the financial performance of sustainability-driven companies around the world. The DJSI World Index includes more than 300 companies representing the top 10% of the leading sustainability companies out of the biggest 2,500 companies in the Dow Jones Global Total Stock Market Index. The oil company, British Petroleum (BP), was eliminated from the DJSI World Index effective May 31, 2010, because of the massive oil spill in the Gulf of Mexico.

Reporting on Sustainability Activities and Outcomes

What has driven the demand for sustainability reporting? In other words, why do companies bother to make sustainability disclosures? Investor interest, socially responsible investment funds, and the Dow Jones Sustainability Index have demanded these kinds of disclosures, and their voices have been heard by companies. Most corporate websites now include sustainability reports, and the placement on those websites is usually quite prominent.

Companies determine what to report and how to report it by using various available guidelines, the most prominent of which is the Global Reporting Initiative (GRI) G3 Reporting Framework. The overall goals of that framework are to enable sustainability report users to "assess sustainability performance with respect to laws, norms, codes, performance standards, and voluntary initiatives; create a continuous platform for dialogue about expectations for responsibility and performance; understand the impacts (positive and negative) that organizations can have on sustainable development; and compare performance within an organization and between different organizations over time to inform decisions."

The G3 Framework Principles emphasize:

- Sustainability Report Content, including materiality, stakeholder inclusiveness, sustainability context, and completeness.
- Sustainability Report Quality, including balance, comparability, accuracy, timeliness, reliability, and clarity.
- Sustainability Report Boundaries, including careful consideration of the range of entities that should be included in the report.

The G3 Framework Standard Disclosures include the following elements:

PRACTICAL POINT

Over 1,000 companies across 60 countries are now registered with the Global Reporting Initiative (GRI) and issue sustainability reports that comply with its principles and recommended disclosures.

- Strategic Approach, including disclosures that set the context for understanding performance, e.g., strategy and governance.
- Management Approach, including disclosures that explain managers' goals and targets.
- Performance Indicators, including disclosures that provide information about economic, environmental, and social performance.

While the G3 guidance provides criteria that preparers can use in developing their sustainability reporting, the specific disclosures that companies make regarding sustainability differ markedly from company to company. Companies' sustainability reporting is strategic in that it is intended to emphasize a message that is consistent with overall financial reporting goals and marketing initiatives. Exhibit 18.8 provides examples of the widely varying types of information that companies provide in their sustainability reports.

The important point to note from an auditing perspective on the sustainability disclosures in Exhibit 18.8 is that some are "numeric" and could be relatively easy to validate. For example, Siemens' disclosure of the percentage of female employees would be a relatively straightforward number to audit. Other disclosures will require subject-matter expertise. For example, both Ford and Siemens provide information about greenhouse gas emissions, and changes in that metric over time, which would require the assurance provider to understand measurement issues in this scientific area. Other disclosures are more subjective by nature and are more difficult to interpret in terms of how they achieve

Comparison of Worldwide Professional Guidance

INTERNATIONAL STANDARDS FOR SUSTAINABILIITY REPORTING

GRI G3	Global Reporting Initiative Sustainability Reporting Guideline (see *Global Reporting Initiative Sustainability Reporting Guidelines*, 2007, http://www.globalreporting.org/Home). This framework and guidance assist companies in determining how and what to report in terms of their sustainability planning and performance. This framework allows for a great deal of variability in the nature and extent of reporting across organizations.
ISAE 3000	The International Standard on Assurance Engagements provides guidance for the provision of assurance over engagements other than audits or reviews of historical financial information (see *International Standard on Assurance Engagements*, 2005, 2 Jul. 2009, http://www.accountability21.net/uploadedFiles/Issues/ISAE_3000.pdf).
AA1000	The Accountability Assurance Standard provides guidance for the provision of assurance in evaluating whether an organization adheres to the principles of inclusivity, materiality and responsiveness, along with the reliability of associated performance information (see *AccountAbility AA1000 Assurance Standard (AA1000AS 2008).* http://www.accountability21.net/uploadedFiles/publications/AA1000AS%202008.pdf.
General Assurance Standards (ASB, IAASB)	Of course, IAASB and AICPA general standards for providing assurance and attestation services can be adapted to the context of sustainability reporting, but such standards do not address sustainability specifically.

Exhibit 18.8 — Examples of Sustainability Reporting Disclosures

PANEL A: GAP, INC.

Gap, Inc. focuses their sustainability reporting on providing assurance that their manufacturing processes are humane and that their factories worldwide do not violate consumers' preferences to avoid child labor and other "politically incorrect" manufacturing practices. Given this focus, one element of Gap's sustainability reporting describes their process for approving their manufacturing facilities worldwide, and the company also discloses metrics on the number of factories that they monitor as follows:

Region	Number of Garment Facilities	Percent of Garment Facilities Visited
Greater China	252	100
North Asia	100	100
Southeast Asia	425	99
Indian Sub-continent	370	96
Persian Gulf	22	91
North Africa	41	83
Sub-Saharan Africa	59	95
Europe	130	78
United States & Canada	104	80
Mexico/Central America/the Caribbean	143	94
South America	44	91
Total	1690	94%

(continues)

| Exhibit 18.8 | Examples of Sustainability Reporting Disclosures (*continued*) |

In addition, Gap provides detailed disclosures about the working conditions at factories worldwide, including information about:

Child Labor:

Workers are not 14 years old or do not meet minimum legal age requirement

Not in full compliance with child labor laws

Failure to allow eligible workers to attend nightclasses and/or participate in educational programs

Poor age documentation

Wages and Hours:

Pay is below minimum wage

Overtime pay rates are below legal minimum

Work week in excess of 60 hours

Workers cannot refuse overtime without threat of penalty or punishment

Workers do not have at least 1 day off in 7

Violation of local laws on annual leave and/or holidays

Unclear wage statements

Working Conditions:

Physical punishment or coercion

Psychological coercion and/or verbal abuse

Violation of local laws on working conditions

Insufficient lighting

Poor ventilation

Insufficient or poorly marked exits

Obstructed aisles, exits or stairwells

Locked or inaccessible doors and exits

Insufficient number of and/or inadequately maintained fire extinguishers

Insufficient number of fire alarms and/or emergency lights

Not enough evacuation drills

Machinery lacks some operational safety devices

Inadequate personal protective equipment

Insufficient access to potable water

Inadequate first-aid kits

Unsanitary toilets and/or restricted access

Inadequate storage of hazardous and combustible materials

PANEL B: FORD MOTOR COMPANY

Ford Motor Company discloses metrics that relate directly to its definition of sustainability, which emphasizes financial, environmental, and social responsibility as follows:

	2006	2007	2008
Financial			
GQRS customer satisfaction (3 months in service), percent satisfied	74	76	77
Sales satisfaction with dealer/retailer, Ford brand, U.S., percent completely satisfied	81	82	84
Sales satisfaction with dealer/retailer, Ford brand, Europe, percent completely satisfied	81	80	81
Service satisfaction with dealer/retailer, Ford brand, U.S., percent completely satisfied	70	72	74
Service satisfaction with dealer/retailer, Ford brand, Europe, percent completely satisfied	67	68	70
Net income/loss, $ billion	−12.6	−2.7	−14.7
Sales and revenue, $ billion	160.1	172.5	146.3
Environment			
Ford U.S. fleet fuel economy, combined car and truck, miles per gallon (higher mpg reflects improvement)	23.8	25.3	26.0
Ford U.S. fleet CO_2 emissions, combined car and truck, grams per mile (lower grams per mile reflects improvement)	371	352	340
European CO_2 performance, percent of 1995 base (1995 base = 100 percent) (lower percentage reflects improvement)	Ford: 78 Volvo: 86	78 84	77 81
Worldwide facility energy consumption, trillion BTUs	73.8	65.6	61.0
Worldwide facility energy consumption per vehicle, million BTUs	12.2	10.8	12.2
Worldwide facility CO_2 emissions, million metric tonnes	6.7	6.1	5.4
Worldwide facility CO_2 emissions per vehicle, metric tones	1.11	1.01	1.09
North American Energy Efficiency Index, percent (2000 base = 100 percent), (lower percentage reflects improvement)	78.4	74.4	69.9

(continues)

Exhibit 18.8 — Examples of Sustainability Reporting Disclosures (*continued*)

	2006	2007	2008
Society			
Employee satisfaction, Pulse survey, overall, percent satisfied	62	64	66
Overall dealer attitude, Ford, relative ranking on a scale of 1 – 100 percent (summer/winter score)	64/64	69/64	68/69
Overall dealer attitude, Lincoln Mercury, relative ranking on a scale of 1 – 100 percent (summer/winter score)	62/64	66/64	64/66
Ford Motor Company Fund contributions, $ million	58	37	33
Corporate contributions, $ million	25	17	16
Volunteer corps, thousand volunteer hours	80	86	100
Lost-time case rate (per 100 employees), Ford Motor Company	1.1	0.9	0.7
Severity rate (per 100 employees), days lost per 200,000 hours worked	14.5	12.6	13.5
U.S. safety recalls, number per calendar year (including legacy vehicles on the road for 10+ years)	11	15	10
U.S. units recalled, number of million units (including legacy vehicles on the road for 10+ years)	1.7	5.5	1.6
IIHS Top Safety Picks, number of vehicles	6	8	14

PANEL C: SIEMENS

Siemens reports summary data in a similar summary style as Ford, but you will note that the contents of these disclosures differ considerably between the two companies. Neither company's disclosure should be considered "better" or "worse" than the other. Rather, sustainability reporting tends to be very company-specific and industry-specific with companies disclosing metrics that make the most sense given their unique circumstances. That is, the reporting criteria being used across companies is not consistent and even the measures being reported are not consistent.

Siemens' disclosures are as follows:

	2008	2009
Financial		
New orders (in millions of euros)	93,495	78,991
Revenue (in millions of euros)	77,327	76,651
Profit (in millions of euros)	1,859	2,457
Investments in research and development (in millions of euros)	3,784	3,900
Compliance employees worldwide	621	598
Total participants in online and face-to-face training courses (in thousands)	175	219
Environment		
Revenue from the Siemens Environmental Portfolio (in billions of euros)	21	23
Percentage of total revenue generated by the Siemens Environmental Portfolio	27	30
Annual reduction of greenhouse gas emissions at customers' locations attributable to products and solutions from the Siemens Environmental Portfolio (in millions of tons)	158	210
Improvement in resource efficiency:		
Primary energy and district heating (in percent)	21	25
Electrical energy (in percent)	7	13
CO_2 emissions, energy (in percent)	9	17
Water (in percent)	21	29
Waste (in percent)	4	12
Society		
Employees (in thousands)	427	405
Female employees (as percentage of total workforce)	26	25
Women in management (as percentage of total managerial workforce)	13.4	13.6
Female new hires (as percentage of total new hires)	31	34
Expenditures for continuing education per employee (in euros)	582	562
Employee fluctuation rate	13.6	17.4
Donations (in millions of euros)	30.2	30.6

sustainability goals. For example, Gap provides information on the number of manufacturing facilities that they inspect each year, and the percentage of inspections is very high. What does this mean? How is a user of this information assured that the inspections were conducted competently, and that the results of those inspections are meaningfully related to sustainability? Further, while there is a great deal of interest in such reports by external users, unless the reports are consistent in what they measure, and unless what they measure is important, they may not be very meaningful. Finally, the usefulness of the disclosure of these sustainability metrics depends on whether or not users can believe that the disclosures are true and faithfully represent the companies' sustainability efforts. In the next section, we discuss assurance on sustainability reporting, which addresses this latter concern.

Providing Assurance on Sustainability Reporting

Just as users of financial statements demand audits, users of sustainability reports are increasingly demanding assurance that they can rely on these disclosures. Independent assurance on sustainability reporting enhances its credibility. External assurance (e.g., professional assurance providers such as audit firms, stakeholder panels, or statements by subject-matter experts) is preferable to internal assurance (e.g., internal audit) because it is seen as more objective and independent from management. The GRI Reporting Framework states that external assurance over sustainability reports should be:

- Conducted by those with competence in the subject matter and assurance practices,
- Performed in a systematic manner that is evidence-based and includes adequate documentation,
- Assesses whether the sustainability report is reasonable, balanced, and appropriately inclusive,
- Issued by individuals or organizations that are independent of the company issuing the sustainability report,
- Assesses the extent to which the report preparer has applied the GRI Reporting Framework in reaching its conclusions, and
- Results in a report that is publicly available, written in form, and that states the relationship between the preparer of the report and the issuer of the report.

There are two general types of assurance that can be provided:

(1) *Reasonable assurance* (or sometimes called high assurance): the assurance provider's opinion is stated in the positive form, indicating that the information subject to audit is materially correct and that a high level of assurance has been achieved.

(2) *Limited assurance* (or sometimes called moderate assurance): the assurance provider's opinion is stated in the negative form, indicating that the information subject to review has not been found to be materially incorrect, and that "nothing has come to their attention" based on the limited scope procedures and that a moderate level of assurance has been achieved.

In Exhibit 18.9 we provide examples of various reports that provide assurance on sustainability reports. Panel A is an example of reasonable assurance provided by Moss Adams, a third-party provider of assurance services, for Starbucks' sustainability report. Important points to note about this report are that:

- It notes that management is responsible for providing the data, and Moss Adams' responsibility is to express an opinion on the data based on its examination; this wording is similar to a standard audit report.
- It notes that Moss Adams conducted its examination in accordance with the AICPA's attestation standards.

- It describes the procedures used to test management's sustainability assertions, including interviews, confirmations, sampling to validate data, and tests of controls.
- It notes that Moss Adams believes that the disclosures are fairly presented in all *material* respects. (emphasis added)

Panel B provides an example of limited assurance for Coca-Cola's sustainability report provided by BECO Group, a third-party provider of assurance services. In contrast to Moss Adams' report, this report:

- Does not describe the procedures used to test management's sustainability assertions.
- Does not make a positive statement about fair presentation or materiality, but does state that the company's representations are reliable.
- Does provide specific feedback on how Coca-Cola has improved its sustainability reporting from the prior period, and discusses suggestions for further improvements in the future.

> **PRACTICAL POINT**
>
> The SEC has the authority to issue guidance on sustainability disclosures and in 2010 issued interpretive guidance regarding public companies' disclosure requirements for climate change matters.

Exhibit 18.9 — **Panel A: Reasonable Assurance from a Third-Party Provider for Starbucks Coffee Company**

INDEPENDENT ASSURANCE REPORT

To the Stakeholders of Starbucks Coffee Company: We have examined the data identified below (the Data) contained within the Starbucks Coffee Company's Global Responsibility Annual Report (the Report) for the year ended September 27, 2009. Starbucks Coffee Company's management is responsible for the Data. Our responsibility is to express an opinion on the Data listed below based on our examination.

- C.A.F.E. Practices coffee purchases and purchases as a percentage of total coffee purchased as contained in the Coffee Purchasing section
- Fair Trade green coffee purchases as contained in the Coffee Purchasing section
- Certified Organic coffee purchases as contained in the Coffee Purchasing section
- Amount of commitment to investment in farmer loans as contained in the Farmer Loan section

The Criteria used to evaluate the Data are contained in the sections of the Report indicated above. Our examination was conducted in accordance with attestation standards established by the American Institute of Certified Public Accountants, and accordingly, included examining, on a test basis, evidence supporting the Data and performing such other procedures as we considered necessary in the circumstances. Those procedures are described in more detail in the paragraph below.

We believe that our examination provides a reasonable basis for our opinion. Our evidence-gathering procedures included, among other activities, the following:

- Testing the effectiveness of the internal reporting system used to collect and compile information on the Data which is included in the Report;
- Performing specific procedures, on a sample basis, to validate the Data, on site at Starbucks Coffee Trading Company buying operations in Lausanne, Switzerland and Corporate headquarters in Seattle, Washington;
- Interviewing partners (employees) responsible for data collection and reporting;
- Reviewing relevant documentation, including corporate policies, management and reporting structures;
- Performing tests, on a sample basis, of documentation and systems used to collect, analyze and compile the Data that is included in the Report, and
- Confirming certain of the Data to third party confirmations and reports.

In our opinion, the Data for the fiscal year ended September 27, 2009 is fairly presented, in all material respects, based on the Criteria indicated above.

Seattle, Washington
April 2, 2010
www.mossadams.com

Exhibit 18.9	Panel B: Limited Assurance from a Third-Party Provider for Coca-Cola Company

"BECO Group was commissioned by The Coca-Cola Company to provide moderate assurance on the environment and occupational health and safety (EOHS) data, collection process and selected claims in this report. We conclude that the claims related to EOHS performance metrics provide a reliable representation of the Company's efforts and performance. We observed that the data collection process has improved compared to previous years by adding internal control loops focused on completeness and enhancing traceability of the data. We also observed that the Company further developed its sustainability approach by adopting specific targets, established in dialogue with significant stakeholders, as communicated in this report. The Company should further improve the established internal control system by formalizing responsibilities and gaining commitment from the Coca-Cola system on requirements to increase the data accuracy level; seek alignment on the established internal control processes of the different departments to favor an integrated approach and to accomplish better site-level results; and develop a consistent process of publishing statements of a scientific nature in subsequent stages of the scientific research to minimize the risk of misinterpretation of this information by the public."

Source: Coca-Cola 2008/2009 Sustainability Review.

Exhibit 18.9	Panel C: No Assurance from a Stakeholder Committee for Ford Motor Company

"In recent years, Ford has used various external assurance models to improve the report's thoroughness, transparency and utility to stakeholders. For our 2004/5 report, we worked with Ceres and SustainAbility to create a Report Review Committee made up of 13 external stakeholders who advised us on the development of the report. Their feedback on our process and on the content of the report itself was included in the report.

CERES STAKEHOLDER COMMITTEE

For this report and our previous two reports, Ceres convened Stakeholder Committees to advise us. Ceres is a network of investors, environmentalists and other public interest groups that works with companies and investors to address sustainability challenges. Ford agreed to work with a stakeholder team that was selected for it by Ceres. The Ceres Stakeholder Committee that was selected is an independent group of individuals drawn primarily from the Ceres coalition and representing a range of constituencies that have expertise in environmental, social and governance issues.

In reviewing this report, the Committee considered whether the Company adequately reported on its sustainability performance and key impacts, including goals, targets, systems, data and initiatives. The Committee met twice: once to review and comment on the report plan, and once to review and comment on a nearly final draft of the material issues sections of the report.

In this report, we have responded to several suggestions the Committee made during reviews of previous reports, notably the publication of our CO_2 reduction target and a detailed roadmap for achieving it. In addition, the Committee raised a number of questions and made suggestions for improvements to the report, including:

· Questions about the alignment of Ford's product CO_2 goal with U.S. policy alternatives
· Interest in Ford's goals and targets across a range of issues and the suggestion that the Company expand its targets, including setting a target to reduce operational CO_2 emissions
· A suggestion to expand reporting on Ford's political contributions, including contributions to membership organizations that take public policy positions
· Comments on the materiality matrix

Some suggestions were addressed in this report, including:

· Expanded reporting on climate change public policy, emphasizing our support for a comprehensive U.S. policy framework
· Inclusion of a summary of goals, commitments and progress against them
· Revisions to the materiality matrix to respond to stakeholder committee suggestions

Other recommendations will be considered for future reporting. For example, we are exploring providing a list of organizations that we support, including some that lobby on behalf of their members."

Source: 2008/9 Blueprint for Sustainability at Ford Motor Company.

Panel C provides an example of limited assurance from a stakeholder committee convened by Ford Motor Company to evaluate its sustainability reporting initiatives. This report differs from the other two examples in that it:

- Describes the development and makeup of the stakeholder committee.
- Describes the workings of the committee, including the fact that it met just twice.
- Provides no external assurances about the contents of Ford's sustainability report.

At this time, sustainability reporting and the provision of assurance on sustainability reports are constantly evolving. Currently, there is general agreement about what sustainability means, and there exist various frameworks and standards to assist companies in producing relevant and reliable sustainability data for external users. Further, there exists substantial variety in companies' decisions about the level of assurance to provide on sustainability disclosures. Sustainability reporting will likely continue to be a growth area into which auditors can apply their assurance skills to expand services outside of traditional audit assurance services, so be alert for further developments in this emerging area.

> **PRACTICAL POINT**
>
> Internal auditors can provide internal assurance to their boards and management on sustainability measures and can evaluate governance, risks, and controls associated with an organization's sustainability strategies.

Summary

Auditors are increasingly faced with complex audit judgments that permeate virtually every account balance. Auditors need to understand the concept of materiality from a user's perspective and to apply that concept to the integrated audit of both internal control and financial statements. Evaluating internal control deficiencies is an important part of integrated audits. Fair value is becoming an increasing part of audit engagements and will continue to evolve as the FASB and IASB move toward implementation of conceptual frameworks that emphasize fair value and changes in assets and liabilities as the primary focus of financial reporting. As auditors continue to look for opportunities to improve the efficiency of their audits, they will assess whether, and how, they can rely on the client's internal audit function in the conduct of that audit. Finally, as users' demands for sustainability reporting increase, both internal and external auditors will be increasingly called upon to provide assurance on these reports.

This chapter has presented an overview of complex issues that auditors will continue to face and reiterates four fundamental concepts that have been emphasized throughout the text. First, the auditor has to know the client's business, its prospects, its competitive position, and its strategies, almost as well as management does. Second, it is important that the auditor not only deal with complex judgment issues, but do so in a systematic fashion that emphasizes ethical professional judgment. Subjective judgments are not pulled out of the air—they are based on rigorous data gathering and analysis. Third, auditors (and clients) increasingly need to document their decisions regarding complex judgments, including the data used in making the judgments and the reasoning process justifying the conclusions reached. Finally, it is important that as auditors perform their work they employ an appropriate level of professional skepticism.

Significant Terms

Assurance activities Objective professional services that improve the quality of information about processes; effectiveness of controls; reliability of information; or compliance with company, regulatory, or governmental procedures; and the effectiveness and efficiency with which the organization carries out its operations.

Clearly trivial A term presented in AS No. 14 indicating that matters that are clearly trivial will be of a smaller order of magnitude than the level of materiality assessed by the auditor and are considered inconsequential, whether individually or in aggregate, and whether based on any criteria of size, nature, or circumstances.

Consulting services Advisory or partnering activities that add value and improve an organization's operations, in which the nature and scope of services are agreed upon with the client. Examples include counsel, advice, facilitation, process design, and training.

Corporate social responsibility reporting The continuing commitment by business to behave ethically and contribute to economic development while improving the quality of life of the workforce, their families, the local community, and society at large.

Dual approach A method of misstatement correction that requires use of both the iron curtain and rollover methods to determine whether a misstatement is material.

Fair value estimate The price that would be received to sell an asset or paid to transfer a liability in an orderly transaction between market participants at the measurement date.

Iron curtain method A method of misstatement correction that focuses on assuring that the year-end balance sheet is correct; this method does not consider the impact of prior-year uncorrected misstatements reversing in later years.

Material weakness in internal control A deficiency, or a combination of deficiencies, in internal control over financial reporting such that there is a reasonable possibility that a material misstatement of the company's annual or interim financial statements will not be prevented or detected on a timely basis.

Materiality The magnitude of an omission or misstatement of accounting information that, in the light of surrounding circumstances, makes it probable that the judgment of a reasonable person relying on the information would have been changed or influenced by the omission or misstatement.

Non-financial reporting The practice of measuring, disclosing, and being accountable to internal and external stakeholders for organisational performance toward the goal of sustainable development.

Operational audits The evaluation of activities, systems, and controls within an enterprise for efficiency, effectiveness, and economy.

Planning materiality The materiality level that is relevant at the transaction or account balance level, which is typically be less than overall materiality.

Posting materiality The amount below which errors are treated as inconsequential.

Rollover method A method of misstatement correction that focuses on the materiality of the current-year misstatements and the reversing effect of prior-year misstatements on the income statement, thereby allowing misstatements to accumulate on the balance sheet.

Significant deficiency A deficiency, or a combination of deficiencies, in internal control over financial reporting that is less severe than a material weakness, yet important enough to merit attention by those responsible for oversight of the company's financial reporting.

Summary of unadjusted audit differences A summary of uncorrected errors that is communicated to the audit committee, is described in the management representation letter, and that is evaluated individually and in the aggregate for materiality.

Sustainability Actions taken at the corporate level to ensure economic, environmental, and social responsibility.

Sustainability reporting Voluntary corporate disclosures about sustainability initiatives, plans, and associated outcomes.

Triple bottom line reporting Reporting on financial, environmental, and social performance.

SELECTED REFERENCES TO RELEVANT PROFESSIONAL GUIDANCE	
Topic	**Selected Guidance**
Materiality	SAS 89 *Audit Adjustments*
	SAS 107 *Audit Risk and Materiality in Conducting an Audit*
	SAS *Materiality in Planning and Performing an Audit* (issued but not effective; proposed effective date is December 2012)
	SAS *Evaluation of Misstatements Identified during the Audit* (issued but not effective; proposed effective date is December 2012)
	AS No. 11 *Consideration of Materiality in Planning and Performing an Audit*
	AS No. 14 *Evaluating Audit Results*
	SEC Staff Accounting Bulletin 99 *Materiality*

	SEC Staff Accounting Bulletin 108 *Considering the Effects of Prior Year Misstatements When Quantifying Misstatements in Current Year Financial Statements* ISA 320 *Materiality in Planning and Performing an Audit* ISA 450 *Evaluation of Misstatements Identified During the Audit*
Assessing Internal Control Deficiencies in an Integrated Audit	AS No. 5 *An Audit of Internal Control over Financial Reporting That Is Integrated with an Audit of Financial Statements* PCAOB Staff Views *An Audit of Internal Control over Financial Reporting That Is Integrated with an Audit of Financial Statements: Guidance for Auditors of Smaller Public Companies* (January 23, 2009) SSAE 15 *An Examination of an Entity's Internal Control over Financial Reporting That Is Integrated with an Audit of Its Financial Statements*
Relying on the Client's Internal Audit Function	SAS 65 *The Auditor's Consideration of the Internal Audit Function in an Audit of Financial Statements* AS No. 5 *An Audit of Internal Control over Financial Reporting That Is Integrated with an Audit of Financial Statements* ISA 610 *Considering the Work of Internal Auditing* Proposed ISA 610 (Revised) *Using the Work of Internal Auditors*
Fair Value and Impairment Issues	SAS 57 *Auditing Accounting Estimates* SAS *Auditing Accounting Estimates, Including Fair Value Accounting Estimates and Related Disclosures* (Redrafted) (issued but not effective; proposed effective date is December 2012) SAS 92 *Auditing Derivative Instruments, Hedging Activities, and Investments in Securities* SAS 101 *Auditing Fair Value Measurements and Disclosures* SEC Staff Accounting Bulletin 59 *Other-Than-Temporary Impairment of Certain Investments in Debt and Equity Securities* PCAOB Staff Audit Practice Alert No. 4 *Auditor Considerations Regarding Fair Value Measurements, Disclosures, and Other-Than-Temporary Impairments* ISA 540 *Auditing Accounting Estimates, Including Fair Value Accounting Estimates, and Related Disclosures*
Sustainability Reporting (see *Comparison of Worldwide Professional Guidance* in this chapter for more detail on this guidance)	GRI G3 Global Reporting Initiative Sustainability Reporting Guideline International Standard on Assurance Engagements (ISAE 3000) Accountability Assurance Standard (AA) 1000

Note: *Acronyms for Relevant Professional Guidance*

STANDARDS: **AS**—Auditing Standard issued by the PCAOB; **ISA**—International Standard on Auditing issued by the IAASB; **SAS**—Statement on Auditing Standards issued by the Auditing Standards Board of the AICPA; **SSAE**—Statement on Standards for Attestation Engagements issued by the AICPA.

ORGANIZATIONS: **AICPA**—American Institute of Certified Public Accountants; **COSO**—Committee of Sponsoring Organizations; **IAASB**—International Auditing and Assurance Standards Board; **PCAOB**—Public Company Accounting Oversight Board; **SEC**—Securities and Exchange Commission.

Review Questions

18-1 **(LO 1)** Is it reasonable for the auditor to make judgments about the acceptability of subjective estimates made by the client? If yes, explain the process by which an auditor should make such judgments.

18-2 **(LO 1, 3)** What do the two investor letters in the opening *Professional Judgment in Context* feature say about materiality and what auditors should know about what investors need?

18-3 **(LO 2)** Are inventory, accounts receivable, and property, plant, and equipment subject to fair value estimates? Explain and state how the fair value concept is applicable to these accounts.

18-4 **(LO 2)** Operating leases are not normally shown on a balance sheet. However, Ford Motor Co. has an account entitled net investment in operating leases. Explain what this account represents and whether it is subject to fair value estimates.

18-5 **(LO 3)** What makes materiality decisions complex and judgmental?

18-6 **(LO 4)** What are the differences between the rollover method and the iron curtain method in terms of evaluating uncorrected misstatements?

18-7 **(LO 3)** What is the purpose of making materiality judgments?

18-8 **(LO 3)** Auditors need to determine appropriate benchmarks in setting overall materiality. What would be an appropriate benchmark for a profit-oriented entity or an entity whose debt or equity securities are publicly traded? What about a not-for-profit entity? What about an asset-based entity such as a mutual fund?

18-9 **(LO 4)** Should the materiality of misstatements be considered individually or combined to be considered in aggregate with other misstatements when considering whether the financial statements are misstated? When is a misstatement considered clearly trivial?

18-10 **(LO 4)** When might a quantitatively small misstatement be considered material?

18-11 **(LO 3, 4)** Why is it important to assess whether potential misclassifications in the statement of cash flows are material?

18-12 **(LO 4)** The auditor performs a statistical test of inventory and has done enough work such that the upper misstatement limit and most likely misstatement are determined. When determining whether or not the account has material misstatements, does the auditor consider (a) the known errors or (b) the most likely errors—even though the amount is not precisely known?

18-13 **(LO 5)** What are the major factors the auditor should consider when evaluating an internal control deficiency to determine if it is (a) a material weakness, (b) a significant deficiency, or (c) just a deficiency? Explain why each factor is important.

18-14 **(LO 6)** What is objectivity as it relates to the internal audit function? What factors does an external auditor consider when assessing the objectivity of a client's internal audit function?

18-15 **(LO 6)** For what types of assertions and accounts can the external auditor rely on work performed by a client's internal audit function? Are there accounts and assertions where the external auditor would likely not rely on the work performed by a client's internal audit function? Explain.

18-16 **(LO 6)** What factors does an external auditor consider when assessing the competence and quality of work performance of a client's internal audit function?

18-17 **(LO 7)** What is fair value? When are fair value concepts applied?

18-18 **(LO 7)** Fair value guidance suggests that there may be three levels of evidence available to assess fair value. Explain the nature of Level 1, Level 2, and Level 3 fair value estimates and the type of information needed to evaluate each type.

18-19   **(LO 8)** When is an asset impaired? Explain and give an example of an asset that requires frequent impairment testing.

18-20   **(LO 9)** What is sustainability? What is the difference between sustainability reporting and sustainability assurance?

18-21   **(LO 9)** What frameworks exist to assist companies in producing sustainability reports? What frameworks exist to assist third parties in providing reliable assurance over sustainability disclosures?

18-22   **(LO 9)** Is it unethical for a company to provide a sustainability report, but provide no assurance on the reliability of the information contained therein?

Ethics

Multiple-Choice Questions

*18-23   **(LO 3)** Which of the following would an auditor most likely use in making preliminary judgments about materiality?

   a. The anticipated sample size of the planned substantive tests.

   b. The entity's unaudited annual financial statements.

   c. The results of the internal control questionnaire.

   d. The contents of the management representation letter.

*18-24   **(LO 3)** Which of the following statements is correct concerning materiality in a financial statement audit?

   a. Analytical procedures performed during an audit's review stage usually increase planning materiality levels.

   b. The auditor's materiality judgments generally involve qualitative, but not quantitative, factors.

   c. The auditor's materiality judgments generally involve quantitative, but not qualitative, considerations.

   d. Materiality levels are generally considered in terms of the smallest aggregate level of misstatement that could be considered material to any one of the financial statements.

*18-25   **(LO 3, 4)** Which of the following matters is an auditor required to communicate to an entity's audit committee?

   a. Adjustments that were suggested by the auditor and recorded by management that have a significant effect on the entity's financial reporting process.

   b. The auditor's level of detection risk for the audit engagement.

   c. The results of the auditor's analytical procedures performed in the review stage of the engagement that indicate significant variances from expected amounts.

   d. Changes in the auditor's preliminary judgment about materiality that were caused by projecting the results of statistical sampling for tests of transactions.

*All problems marked with an asterisk are adapted from the Uniform CPA Examination.

18-26   **(LO 3)**   Decisions about materiality are

a. A matter of professional judgment.

b. Dependent on the needs of a reasonable person.

c. Involve both quantitative and qualitative considerations.

d. All of the above.

18-27   **(LO 7)**   Which of the following best describes a Level 3 fair value estimate? An estimate based on

a. The value of similar assets traded on a foreign exchange.

b. The value of the same asset, but traded on a foreign exchange.

c. The value is not readily observable in any marketplace and thus requires an estimate using a model.

d. The value is not readily observable, but there are market trades of similar assets that can serve as a surrogate for value of the asset in question.

18-28   **(LO 4)**   A summary of unadjusted audit differences:

a. Is a summary of corrected errors.

b. Should be communicated to the audit committee.

c. Should be communicated in a management letter.

d. Should be evaluated by the audit committee as to whether an adjustment is required.

18-29   **(LO 5)**   Which of the following statements are correct regarding material weaknesses in internal control?

I. The severity of a control deficiency is based on the amount of misstatement in a financial statement that an informed user would consider to be material.

II. The discovery of a material misstatement in the financial statements is prima facie evidence that the company had a material weakness in internal control over financial reporting.

III. A computer program error that could have led to a material misstatement was discovered by management and remediated several months before year end, so it does not constitute a material weakness.

   a. I only

   b. I and II only

   c. I, II, and III

   d. II only

18-30   **(LO 6)**   When assessing an internal auditor's competence, an external auditor would typically obtain information about all of the following except:

a. Quality of work as evidenced in the internal auditor's working paper documentation

b. Educational level and professional experience

c. Professional certifications

d. References from auditees

*18-31   **(LO 6)**   For which of the following audit areas would the external auditor be least likely to rely on work performed by a client's internal audit function?

a. Valuation of a client's restructuring charge

b. Existence of inventory

   c. Cutoff tests of revenue

   d. Existence of cash

*18-32 **(LO 6)** An internal auditor's work would most likely affect the nature, timing, and extent of an independent CPA's auditing procedures when the internal auditor's work relates to which of the following assertions?

   a. Existence of contingencies

   b. Valuation of intangible assets

   c. Existence of fixed asset additions

   d. Valuation of related-party transactions

*18-33 **(LO 6)** Which of the following should the external auditor do when assessing an internal auditor's objectivity?

   a. Evaluate whether the internal auditor's audit programs are consistent with management requests.

   b. Inquire about the internal auditor's educational background.

   c. Consider the organizational level to which the internal auditor reports.

   d. Review the internal auditor's resume.

*18-34 **(LO 6)** In assessing the competence and objectivity of an entity's internal auditor, which of the following would an external auditor be *least* concerned with?

   a. The extent to which the internal audit function complied with professional internal auditing standards.

   b. External quality reviews of the internal auditor's activities.

   c. Previous experience with the internal auditor.

   d. The extent to which the internal audit programs are approved by the external audit function.

18-35 **(LO 8)** Which of the following pieces of evidence would most likely *not* be considered by the auditor in evaluating the potential impairment of goodwill?

   a. The acquisition made by a competitor of a company that is not a direct competitor of the client.

   b. The current market capitalization of the company in comparison with its net book value.

   c. The cash flows and operating data of the reporting unit since acquisition compared with estimates made at the time of acquisition.

   d. The growth or decline in market share of the reporting unit since acquisition.

Discussion and Research Questions

18-36 **(Materiality and Account Balances, LO 1, 3)** The opening *Professional Judgment in Context* feature deals with investor points of view regarding contingencies that are based on a future that is unknown.

Required

   a. What do the quotes from the investment letters tell us about materiality and the nature of accounting disclosures that may be material to users?

b. Auditors "must obtain sufficient appropriate evidence by performing audit procedures to afford a reasonable basis for an opinion regarding the financial statements under audit." With this in mind, and thinking about the comments in the letters:

(1) Because a contingency is something that might happen in the future, is there "appropriate evidence" the auditor might gather to satisfy the investor's disclosure requirements? If so, what is that evidence?

(2) To what extent does the adequacy of note disclosure affect the materiality decision and the auditor's opinion on the fairness of the financial statement presentations?

c. Knowing that we cannot predict the future, comment on whether you think the requests of the investors represent a reasonable expectation that you should be held to when you enter the audit profession. Cite the rationale for your position.

18-37   **(Fair Value Items in the Financial Statements, LO 2)** It was noted that virtually all items in a company's financial statement are subject to some "fair value" comparison and that a company ought to have a systematic process by which to gather information regarding accounting estimates, impairments, and lower of cost or market adjustments.

Required

a. One of Ford's assets is "Net Investment in Operating Leases." What is the nature of such an account, that is, what would the amount represent?

b. What type of information should Ford be collecting regularly to use in determining whether the asset is subject to impairment?

c. If Ford is not collecting the information on a regular basis, does Ford have a material weakness in internal control over financial reporting?

d. Noting that any estimate is subjective, does the standard application of materiality apply to the auditor's estimate of an impairment of this particular asset?

e. Do the same concepts of audit risk apply to the estimate of an impairment for this asset as applies to other assets; i.e., what confidence level should the auditor have that the estimate of the fair value of this asset is correct within a materiality limit for the account? Explain your rationale.

18-38   **(Evaluating Uncorrected Misstatements, LO 4)** Staff Accounting Bulletin No. 108 articulates guidance on applying the dual approach to evaluating uncorrected misstatements. Under the dual approach, a misstatement must be corrected if it is material (using guidelines established in Staff Accounting Bulletin No. 99) under either the rollover method or the iron curtain method. Assume that a liability is overstated by $100 because a $20 misstatement occurred in each year of a five-year period ending in the current period. Also assume that materiality for the income statement is $50 and materiality for the balance sheet is $75.

Required

a. What is the current-year effect of the error under (a) the rollover method and (b) the iron curtain method?

b. What adjustment do you recommend for this year? Explain the rationale for your proposed adjustment.

18-39 **(Evaluating Whether Misstatements are Material, LO 4)** Assume that a client has a recurring late cutoff error. Prior year sales included $10 million of current year sales, and current year sales include $12 million of next year sales.

Required

a. What is the misstatement under the (a) rollover method and (b) the iron curtain method?

b. Now assume that the client had an early cutoff error in the prior year such that $10 million of prior year sales are included in current year sales and a late cutoff error in the current year such that $12 million of next year sales are included in the current year. What is the misstatement under the (a) rollover method and (b) the iron curtain method?

18-40 **(Responsibilities Upon Detecting an Intentional Misstatement, LO 3, 4, 5)** Assume that an auditor finds a material misstatement regarding the financial statements while performing substantive tests of the account balance. More importantly, the auditor concludes that the misstatement involved the misapplication of an accounting principle to achieve a desired financial result and that the misstatement was intentional.

Fraud

Required

a. What actions should the auditor take upon detecting an intentional misstatement in the financial statements? To whom must the misstatement be reported?

b. If the company agrees to correct the misstatement, is there a need to communicate the nature of the misstatement to important stakeholders of the company? If yes, explain the avenues the auditor has available to report the misstatement.

c. What are the implications of detecting an intentional misstatement in terms of evaluating the control environment and the strength of internal controls in general?

18-41 **(Evaluating Whether Misstatements Are Material, LO 4)** During the course of auditing year-end financial statements, the auditor becomes aware of misstatements in a company's financial statements. When combined, the misstatements result in a 4% overstatement of net income and a $0.02 (4%) overstatement of earnings per share. Because no item in the financial statements is misstated by more than 5%, the auditor concludes that the deviation from the applicable financial reporting framework is immaterial and that the accounting is permissible. The auditor notes that the FASB Codification states "The provisions of the Codification need not be applied to immaterial items."

Required

a. Based on the scenario above, may the auditor of these financial statements assume that the identified misstatements are immaterial? Why or why not?

b. What additional information might the auditor choose to analyze to determine whether or not the financial statements are misstated by a material amount?

18-42 **(Applying Materiality, LO 3, 4)** An often contentious area of discussion between the auditor and the client is the preciseness with which an estimate is to be made, for example, an estimate of the warranty liability of an automotive manufacturer.

Required

a. Scenario: Your client argues that because an estimate is subjective the range for materiality ought to be larger than it would be for a less subjective account. Do you agree or disagree?

b. Regarding the preciseness of the estimate, respond to the following quote from an ex-audit partner: "The preciseness of the estimate is dependent on the soundness of the underlying prediction model. If the auditor determines that the inputs are correct and agrees on the model, there is no need for audit judgment."

- Indicate the extent to which you agree or disagree with the statement.

- How might an auditor verify that the model is sound?

- If there is a precise answer, should the auditor overrule the answer with a judgment that contains subjectivity? If you believe the answer is yes, identify the factors that should lead the auditor to override the judgment. If you believe the answer is no, state your rationale.

Internet

Professional Skepticism

Ethics

18-43 **(Changing Assessed Materiality, LO 3, 4, 10)** Read the PCAOB enforcement case against Christopher E. Anderson (PCAOB Release No. 105-2008-003, available at www.pcaob.org). Among the PCAOB's findings is that the audit partner, Anderson, changed materiality during the engagement.

In part, the enforcement case notes that Anderson was a Deloitte audit partner on the NFC audit engagement. Another Deloitte audit team was responsible for auditing NFC's parent company, NIC. In planning the audit of NFC, Anderson had set, at $4.1 million, the quantitative threshold used by the engagement team to, among other things, determine whether to treat a misstatement in NFC's financial statements as material. However, shortly after misstatements were discovered, Anderson accepted a decision, made at Deloitte's NIC engagement team level, that the materiality threshold for the NFC audit should be increased to $6.1 million. Anderson accepted that decision even though he had final responsibility for the NFC audit, believed that the original materiality threshold remained appropriate, and understood that the increased threshold would make it easier to treat known misstatements as immaterial. As a result of applying the 50% higher threshold, Anderson was able to treat a $4.5 million overstatement as immaterial on a quantitative basis.

Required

a. When is it appropriate to change materiality amounts during an engagement and why would the PCAOB have been concerned about Anderson's actions related to changing the materiality amount? Identify instances in which Anderson did not employ an appropriate level of professional skepticism.

b. Using the framework for ethical decision making presented in Chapter 3, assess the actions of Anderson. Recall that the steps in the framework are:

- Identify the ethical issue(s).
- Determine who are the affected parties and identify their rights.
- Determine the most important rights.
- Develop alternative courses of action.
- Determine the likely consequences of each proposed course of action.
- Assess the possible consequences, including an estimation of the greatest good for the greatest number. Determine whether the rights framework would cause any course of action to be eliminated.
- Decide on the appropriate course of action.

18-44   **(Assessing Internal Control Deficiencies, LO 5)** An important judgment made on an integrated audit is determining whether deficiencies in internal control are material weaknesses, significant deficiencies, or are "just" deficiencies.

Required

a. How do the reporting requirements differ if a failure of a control is classified as:

- A nonmaterial, nonsignificant deficiency?
- A significant deficiency?
- A material weakness?

b. Explain the way in which the following factors influence how a control deficiency is classified:

- Weakness in the control environment.
- Repeatability of the process.
- Volume of transactions affected by the control deficiency.
- Complexity and subjectivity of the area in which the control was supposed to be working.
- Existence of complementary controls.
- Remediation of control deficiency before year end.
- Weaknesses in the oversight function of the board.

18-45   **(Internal Control Weaknesses and the Audit Committee, LO 5)** The auditor must interact with the audit committee on a regular basis and is hired or fired by the audit committee. Yet, the auditor is supposed to evaluate the audit committee and determine whether it is carrying out its functions properly.

Required

a. What are the primary factors the auditor should consider in evaluating the effectiveness of the audit committee?

b. Given the factors identified in part (a), outline an audit program to evaluate the effectiveness of the audit committee.

c. Assume the auditor concludes the following regarding the audit committee: (1) only one member is independent, (2) the audit committee does meet quarterly and is efficient in getting its work done in an hour or less, and (3) the committee has decided to cut out executive sessions with the internal and external auditors because they receive enough input during the regular audit meetings. Do these three items constitute a significant deficiency, a material weakness, or neither? Explain your rationale.

Professional Skepticism

Ethics

18-46 **(Internal Control Weaknesses and Financial Statement Restatements, LO 4, 5)** During the audit of Pall Corp., KPMG found a material misstatement related to the client's estimate of income tax expense and the accrued liability. The misstatement had accumulated over a number of years and was found during the auditor's preliminary work. The client was notably upset and terminated a number of staff personnel who were associated with the income tax accrual and hired new personnel who were more competent. There was not enough evidence available for the auditor to determine whether or not the misstatement was intentional—even though it helped the company meet analysts' earnings expectations. As a result, the client had to restate its past financial statements.

Required

a. Does a restatement of financial statements always imply that there was a material weakness in internal controls? Explain.

b. Given the findings in the Pall case as described above:

- Is there sufficient evidence that the client has remediated the weakness in sufficient time to avoid an adverse report on internal control?

- What evidence would the auditor attempt to gather to determine if the misstatement was intentional? What role does professional skepticism play in this setting?

- What would be the audit requirements if the misstatement were intentional?

c. Assume the following scenario. The auditor normally finds numerous errors in the income tax accrual, so the auditor plans to spend more time on the accrual and the client has agreed this makes sense. The auditor then adjusts the accrual to the correct amount.

- Does this approach violate the auditor's code of ethics or the standard on audit independence? Explain your answer.

- Does the client have a significant deficiency or a material weakness given that the client and the auditor have agreed to the approach? Explain.

Professional Skepticism

Group Activity

18-47 **(Assessing Potential Material Weaknesses, LO 5, 6)** With your group members, assess each deficiency described below and determine whether it should be classified as a control deficiency, significant deficiency, or material weakness. Consider each deficiency separately. Be able to support your answer. For scenario (c) specifically discuss the importance of professional skepticism.

a. The client's management was not diligent in systematically communicating company-wide policies and procedures and consistently emphasizing the importance of controls. Based on testing, the internal audit team felt that management did not promote the most appropriate level of control awareness.

b. While the internal audit function at your client, G-Tech, has a formal reporting relationship with the Audit Committee, top management (CEO and CFO) has been the one during the current year that has been calling the shots regarding the internal audit function. For example, top management is able to influence the internal audit plan; has a great deal of say with respect to hiring, firing, and compensating the internal audit director; and has primary responsibility for approving the internal audit budget. In actuality, the Audit Committee has only limited influence in these areas.

c. Your client, SEA, introduced a new product line this year. The total annual revenue for this product line is large enough that a misstatement in the account could be material. For this product line, the revenue is based on contracts that have complex multi-element arrangements. SEA initiates a significant number of new contracts for this product line each week across multiple regions. When preparing these new contracts, a standard contract is used, and modifications to the standard contract are made based on the specific characteristics of the transaction. When a new contract is entered into your client's computerized billing system, client accounting personnel at the regional office are to verify that revenue recognition conforms to the applicable financial reporting framework. As part of the control procedure, a revenue checklist is to be completed and signed off by the client accounting personnel who perform the verification.

Your audit team is satisfied that this primary control is effectively designed. However, a walkthrough and tests of the operating effectiveness of this control by your audit team revealed that these control procedures have not been consistently documented or performed for the new product line. The control has not been operating effectively. The deficiency only relates to this new product line and was not limited to a particular region. In performing internal control testing of this primary control, neither the audit team nor the client has identified a known dollar error related to the deficiency in this primary control.

The audit team, based on appropriate consultation within the firm, agrees that this deficiency in operating effectiveness of this primary control represents a material weakness. However, the client wants to classify the deficiency as less than a material weakness because of a compensating control.

The compensating control is designed as follows. Specifically, a Revenue Accounting Manager at the company headquarters verifies the revenue recognition provisions of a random sample of new contracts on a weekly basis. This manager examines documents that indicate regional accounting personnel have verified the revenue recognition provisions. The manager also re-performs the verification procedure to ensure that revenue recognition provisions have been properly entered into the billing system. The client believes that these weekly verifications by a Revenue Accounting Manager constitute a compensating control that is likely to detect and prevent material misstatements in revenue recognition.

The audit team has indicated the following about the design of the compensating control:

- The compensating control is performed by headquarters personnel who the audit team believes to be appropriate, competent, and qualified to evaluate revenue recognition.

- The random sample examined by headquarters personnel is designed to verify 70% of the total revenue generated from these new product contracts with complex multi-element arrangements.

- Your audit team believes that the design of the compensating control is effective.

The audit team has tested a sample of contracts verified by a Revenue Accounting Manager at the company headquarters who performed the compensating control. The audit team's testing consisted of examining documentation that the control was performed and re-performing revenue recognition verification. The sample size of contracts examined by the audit team was based on your audit firm's guidelines given the risk, the nature of the control, and the frequency with which it was performed. During their tests, the audit team found one contract in the sample for which the compensating control was not properly performed. The audit team reported that there was not a dollar error associated with this control deficiency.

18-48   **(Evaluating the Quality of an Internal Audit Function, LO 6)** Audit Standard No. 5 encourages the external auditor to consider the work of the internal audit in accumulating audit evidence when performing an integrated audit of internal control and financial statements.

Required

a. What information does the external auditor use to assess the internal auditor's objectivity?

b. Can the internal auditor attain the same level of objectivity in an audit as the external auditor? Explain.

c. An external auditor is considering whether to rely on the work performed by a client's internal audit function. The following is known about the internal audit function:

   (1) The internal audit function undergoes periodic external quality reviews to address the quality of its audits and the compliance of the audits with the *International Standards for the Professional Practice of Internal Auditing.* The quality reviews also examine the quality-control procedures used by the function. The internal audit function has always received high marks in these reviews.

   (2) The internal audit function has a history of hiring high-quality staff and subsequently placing that staff in management positions.

   (3) The company has a reputation for hiring technologically competent auditors.

Based what is known about the internal audit function, present arguments for and against relying on the internal audit function's work. What additional information should the external auditor consider before determining the quality of the internal audit function?

18-49   **(Applying Fair Value to Audits, LO 7)** ASC 820 *Fair Value Measurements and Disclosures* (previously SFAS 157) provides guidance for auditors and managers to make judgments regarding fair value.

Required

a. Identify the three levels of fair value evidence and the nature of audit evidence to be gathered for each level.

b. Ford Motor Company announced in 2008 that it was closing its assembly plant in St. Paul, Minnesota. The one-story plant covered approximately three acres of commercially zoned property close to regular transportation lines.

   • What fair value classification is applicable to the plant?

   • What is management's responsibility to determine the fair value of the plant?

   • If management cannot come up with a good estimate of the fair value of the plant, does Ford have a weakness in its internal controls? Explain.

- Assuming management has an estimate of the fair value of the plant, should the auditor (a) primarily test the methodology used by management to come up with the estimate, or (b) hire outside appraisers to provide a fair value estimate of the plant, or (c) both?

18-50 **(Testing Goodwill for Impairments, LO 8)** The scenario regarding goodwill described in the text noted that Sun, Inc. had identified a potential write-down of at least $1.8 billion related to a reporting unit.

Required

a. What is a reporting entity? How does Sun go about determining what constitutes a reporting unit for the purpose of determining a goodwill impairment?

b. Explain how the market value of the firm as a whole influences the need to recognize a goodwill impairment.

c. Assume that the reporting unit was the storage solutions unit. While the past year's results have been poor, management maintains that it has developed significant new products that repositions the company to take a leadership role in storage solutions and that it expects significant improvement in results starting in early to mid-year 2010. Outline the major elements of an audit program to determine whether there is a goodwill impairment, and if there is, the extent of the goodwill impairment.

18-51 **(Fair Values, Materiality, and the Auditor Reasoning Process, LO 4, 7, 8)** A common theme throughout this text is that the auditor should carefully document the reasoning process regarding the assessment of an account balance or an internal control deficiency.

Required

An auditor has documented the reasoning process and it is going to be reviewed by a partner who is not associated with the audit. Identify the expectations of what the review partner will be looking for in each of the following areas.

a. Materiality. What are the key elements of your reasoning process that should be documented regarding:

- Planning materiality.
- Misstatements that were found and not adjusted.

b. The adequacy of the client's estimate of warranty reserves.

c. The adequacy of the allowance for uncollectible accounts.

18-52 **(Sustainability Reporting in the Contemporary Era, LO 9)** Go to the websites of the following organizations and review their agendas and recent activities concerning assurance over sustainability disclosures:

Internet

- AICPA
- IFAC
- IAASB
- PCAOB

International

a. How do the activities of these organizations differ? And how are they similar?

b. If there is an organization that does not address sustainability, comment on the implications of that decision.

c. What are the implications of differences in sustainability assurance provisions internationally?

Group Activity

Internet

18-53 **(Sustainability Reporting Comparisons, LO 9)** In a small group with your fellow students, access the websites of two major manufacturing organizations of your choice. Locate the sustainability reports of these organizations, and find the assurance reports (if provided). Discuss the following questions in your group.

a. How prominent was the link to the sustainability report on each organization's website?

b. Compare the length and detail of both reports, and comment on the differences.

c. Consider the corporate strategy of each organization, and discuss how that strategy relates to the sustainability disclosures made by each organization.

d. Discuss how your perception of each organization differs now that you understand the respective sustainability efforts. Did your perception of the organization improve? Decline? Or change in some other way? Why?

e. Compare the level of assurance provided by each organization. If there are differences in the level of assurance provided, discuss implications for particular elements of the sustainability report.

Cases

18-54 **(Materiality Judgments—Alternative Benchmarks and Qualitative Considerations, Decision Analysis Framework, LO 3, 4, 10)** Panzero Bread is a major retailer of specialty sandwich items and baked goods. The following information represents the company's financial position as of 12/31/10 and 12/31/09.

	12/31/10 (unaudited)	12/31/09 (audited)
Total assets	$698,752,000	$542,609,000
Accounts receivable	$25,152,000	$19,041,000
Total sales	$1,066,691,000	$828,971,000
Cost of goods sold	$842,255,000	$628,534,000
Net income	$57,456,000	$58,849,000
Earnings per share	$1.81	$1.88

The auditor of Panzero Bread identifies the company as possessing high audit risk and has set the posting thresholds for individual accounts at 10% of overall financial statement materiality levels. The auditors have detected an overstatement of accounts receivable of $345,000. The misstatement is not a surprise to the auditors, as they have detected misstatements in this account in the past.

On a per share basis, the misstatement represents $0.01 of earnings per share. The auditor believes that the misstatement should be corrected. Management argues strongly that they prefer not to make the correction because they do not believe it is material; that is, the misstatement represents just over 1% of the account balance. Although left unsaid, the auditor knows that management is under considerable pressure from Wall Street to meet analyst expectations for earnings per share. Reducing earnings per share by even $0.01

would cause the trend in earnings to become even more negative than the unaudited financial numbers already reveal, and it would cause the company to just miss analyst forecasts for earnings per share.

Required

a. Use the three common benchmarks for making materiality judgments (i.e., net income, total assets, and net sales) to establish materiality for the financial statements overall.

b. What difficulties does the auditor face when the alternative benchmarks yield differing conclusions about materiality? What qualitative factors should the auditor consider in making its materiality judgment in that case?

c. Articulate a reason for choosing one particular benchmark among the three calculated in part (a), and use that to calculate the posting threshold for the inventory account.

d. What effect will the qualitative factors in this case have on the auditor's posting threshold for the inventory account?

e. Use the decision framework from Chapter 3 to make a recommendation about how the auditor should resolve the dispute with management regarding whether or not to correct the misstatement. Recall that the framework is as follows:

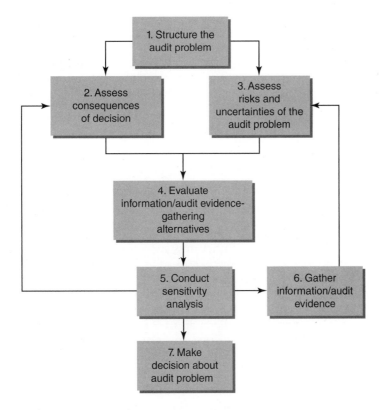

Source: Adapted from "Judgment and Choice," by Robin Hogarth.

18-55 **(Evidence Needed to Support an Evaluation of Whether Misstatement Is Material, LO 3, 4)** SEC Accounting and Auditing Enforcement Release No. 904 describes KPMG's 1993 audit of Structural Dynamics Research Corporation (SDRC). The AAER describes SDRC as a client that inflated revenues and earnings by

Professional Skepticism

Fraud

recognizing both premature and fictitious revenue. The following excerpt from the AAER describes the audit team's work in the area of accounts receivable:

> During the 1993 audit, the engagement team spent considerable time auditing accounts receivable, a critical area of the audit. Particular emphasis was placed on auditing accounts receivable in SDRC's Far East Operations ("FEO") which represented approximately 50% of consolidated accounts receivable at year-end 1993. FEO also accounted for approximately 35% of the revenue recorded by SDRC in 1993. The audit team incorrectly concluded that certain revenue relating to these accounts receivable had been properly recognized and focused their attention on evaluating collectibility.
>
> Based in large part on the percentage of year-end 1992 receivables that were written off in 1993, the audit staff calculated a $5.8 million proposed audit adjustment to increase the allowance for doubtful accounts for FEO receivables. In the aggregate, the audit differences considered by the auditors totaled approximately $3.1 million, which represented approximately 22% of the net income originally reported by SDRC.

Notwithstanding the analysis made by the audit team, both the engagement partner and the concurring partner concluded that the $3.1 million net audit difference was not material to SDRC's financial statements. In reaching that conclusion, they relied in substantial part on management's representations that the rate of write-offs and reversals in 1993 were based on factors that management did not expect to recur in 1994 and that the $5.8 million audit difference calculated by the staff was, therefore, excessive. The auditors "passed" on the audit difference and did not require SDRC to adjust its financial statements.

Required

a. What factors should the audit partners have considered when deciding whether it was appropriate to "pass" on the audit adjustment? What is the role of professional skepticism in this context?

b. What evidence should the auditors have gathered to support their assessment?

c. Is it appropriate to net misstatements when making a materiality decision on whether an adjustment is necessary?

18-56   **(Judging the Quality of a Client's Internal Audit Function and Determining the Effects of Internal Audit's Work, LO 6)** TLD CPAs is performing the audit of REDTOP Sports. You are on the external audit team for that engagement. Following is some information about the client and its internal audit function. After reviewing this information, you will be asked to assess the quality of the internal audit function and whether the external auditor should rely on work performed by the internal auditors.

General Background Information about REDTOP Sports

REDTOP Sports Company is a publicly held manufacturing company. The primary activities of REDTOP Sports Company include the design and manufacture of sporting and athletic goods. The major product lines are bicycle helmets for infants, youths, and adults and other bicycle accessories, including child bicycle seats, car bicycle carriers, and water-bottle cages. In the United States, a number of jurisdictions have passed mandatory helmet regulations and

REDTOP Sports is currently a market leader in this growing market. Sales are made primarily on credit to independent bicycle dealers and sporting goods stores. The sales terms require that balances be paid within sixty days. This practice is consistent with the industry.

Company Objectives and Related Risks

For this company, there is a specific risk associated with potential errors in the valuation of receivables, the existence of receivables, and the cutoff of sales. This risk results from REDTOP Sports' interest in expanding to a global market. Helmet sales in Europe are expected to increase significantly in the near future and REDTOP would like to be in a position to obtain a significant market share in Europe. REDTOP Sports would like to finance this growth through an additional stock offering during the next year. To assure that the stock offering is successful, some pressure has been exerted on management to meet slightly optimistic growth levels over the past two years. Bonuses for top management have been partially based on the achievement of these growth goals.

Summary Financial Information

Sales of REDTOP Sports continue to grow. Over the last five years, sales have climbed at an average annual rate of 27%. When compared to other firms in this industry, the growth in earnings per share (EPS) over the past two years has been at the same level as the growth for the industry: 39%. In comparing this firm to the S&P 500, the firm's EPS has increased at 39% while the EPS of the S&P 500 has increased at 14% (about 2.8 times more).

The growth in accounts receivable has been primarily due to the increased sales demand. Current year recorded sales total $99,133,000. The accounts receivable balance for the current year consists of approximately 500 accounts, primarily from retail and sporting goods stores. The individual accounts range from approximately $300 to $65,000. The year-end balance in the accounts receivable account is $18,248,000 (net of the allowance of $796,000).

Internal Controls and the Internal Audit Function

The company has implemented a system of internal controls in the sales and accounts receivable area that is completely computerized and considered to be moderately complex.

The only significant recent change to the company's internal controls in the sales, billing, and collection area is related to the internal audit function. The internal audit function is performed in-house at REDTOP Sports and is made up of four staff auditors, one manager, and a director. Each staff auditor had two to three years of public accounting experience prior to joining REDTOP's internal audit function. The manager and director of the internal audit function each had at least five years of public accounting experience prior to joining REDTOP five years ago. Both the manager and director have professional certifications.

In previous years, the work of the internal audit function had been primarily operational. For the last 18 months, however, the focus has become much more financial in nature. Audits currently performed by in-house internal audit include operational audits (i.e., employee benefits plan review), compliance audits (i.e., compliance with laws and regulations), and audits of financial controls and financial statement accounts.

The current-year work of the internal auditors was such that some of their activities are related to the accounts receivable account. They have obtained two types of evidence for accounts receivable: (1) evidence about the adequacy of and adherence to internal control policies and (2) evidence related to the accounts receivable balance.

Information about REDTOP's Internal Audit Function

Organizational Status and Communications with the Audit Committee and Management

The authority of the internal audit function has been granted to it by the CEO and the audit committee. In terms of organizational status, the director of internal audit reports directly to the CEO and has direct access to the audit committee. The appointment and termination of the internal audit director are the responsibilities of the CEO. The audit committee is advised of such decisions.

Procedures and Work Processes

Standardized audit programs are not typically used. Rather, the staff auditor responsible for an audit is to develop the audit program during the planning of the audit. Each audit program, therefore, is tailored to the specific objectives of the audit engagement. Modifications to the program are made as necessary during the course of the audit. The internal auditors rarely use computer-assisted auditing techniques. The computers are primarily used for spreadsheet programs and word processing packages. The internal audit function currently does not use any type of generalized audit software.

Workpaper review is the responsibility of the internal audit manager, and staff work is reviewed by the manager periodically throughout each audit. Review notes are prepared and must be cleared before an internal audit report is issued. Supervisory review of workpapers is performed to determine that the workpapers adequately support findings, conclusions, and reports. The director of internal audit has decided not to be directly responsible for any workpaper review; however, the director reviews enough of the work to be comfortable with the conclusions reached in the internal audit report.

Quality Assurance

The internal audit director has established a quality assurance program that requires periodic internal quality reviews. The purpose of the quality assurance review is to provide senior management and the audit committee with an assessment of the internal audit function. These reviews are performed by members of the internal audit staff, but they do not review any of their own work. The results of the current year's review indicated a number of areas where minor improvements could be made. The internal audit director is currently determining how to respond to the need for these improvements. No written action plan has yet been developed.

Accounts Receivable Work Performed by the Internal Audit Function

In testing the controls in the sales, billing, and collection cycle during the year, the internal auditors documented the system of internal controls and performed inquiries and observations of appropriate personnel once during the year. Tests of controls were also performed although the sample sizes for these detailed tests were much smaller than the sample sizes their external auditors would have used. Only minor exceptions in the operating effectiveness were noted.

In testing the existence assertion of accounts receivable during the course of the audit year, the internal auditors had sent out confirmations to customers with accounts receivable balances and accounts written off to justify their conclusions in the area. The number of confirmations sent was about the same as the number that the external auditors normally send out. The accounts receivables for confirmation were selected and evaluated using appropriate methods. The response rate was lower than that experienced on typical external audit engagements. Follow-up work for these no-replies was performed; however, on two of the five exceptions it appeared to be inadequate. While these two exceptions were explained as timing differences in the workpapers, the workpapers contained no documentation to support that explanation.

In testing the valuation of accounts receivable during the year, once each quarter, the internal audit function selected a sample of sales invoices to test the pricing by comparing the invoices with price lists and contracts. Sample sizes were more than adequate. Several pricing errors were noted in the workpapers. These differences were explained as resulting from the use of an outdated price list at the time of the sale. This explanation was documented in the workpapers. At year end, the internal audit function reviewed the analysis of the doubtful accounts and related documents and concluded that the allowance account was mathematically correct and that the method used to compute the allowance was the same as in the prior year.

In determining whether the accounts receivable balances are owned by the company (rights and obligations assertion), the internal audit function reviewed company minutes to determine if the board of directors had approved factoring of any receivables. Inquiry of the credit manager was also made. These activities were performed on a quarterly basis. Based on these procedures, the internal audit function concluded that all of the recorded receivables are owned by REDTOP Sports.

The internal audit function had not performed any tests of cutoff for sales or accounts receivable for either the current or previous audit year.

A review of a sample of the internal audit function's workpaper files for audits of accounts receivable for the current audit year indicated the following. An audit program was included in all but one of these files. For the other file, the staff auditor had prepared a memo at the end of the audit indicating the various steps that were performed. This memo served as the audit program. Of the files reviewed, one file did not adequately document the audit objectives. Although the workpapers were all indexed, the differences across workpapers made it difficult to follow the indexing in some cases. In general, workpaper documentation, while acceptable, could be improved.

Of the files reviewed, it was noted that for two internal audits the workpapers were not reviewed until after the internal audit report was issued. Upon inquiry, the internal audit manager indicated that the primary purpose of workpaper review was to assure that the papers support the information included in the audit report. Given that this responsibility primarily rested with the internal auditor performing the engagement, the internal audit manager indicated that a review of workpapers after the issuance of the audit report was acceptable.

Conclusions are reasonably well documented in the corresponding workpapers. In fact, the documented conclusions appeared appropriate except for one set of workpapers related to the valuation assertion in which the conclusions did not appear to reflect the degree of negative evidence obtained during the audit. Specifically, the number of pricing errors documented seemed rather excessive. The conclusions in the workpapers, however, indicated that pricing errors did not represent a significant problem.

Required

a. Assess the quality of REDTOP'S internal audit function. In doing so, provide assessments of objectivity, competence, quality of work performance, and overall quality. Provide support for your assessments. Assume that your firm uses a scale of 1 = very low, 2 = low, 3 = moderate, 4 = high. Support your assessment with a brief rationale for each of the ratings.

b. Would your assessments in part (a) change if you were told that the internal audit function was outsourced rather than being staffed in-house? Explain.

c. Notwithstanding your assessments in part (a), assume your audit engagement team determined that the quality of the internal audit function was of an acceptable level. Would you be willing to rely on any of the work related to accounts receivable that REDTOP's internal audit function performed during the year? Explain.

d. Could your engagement team use REDTOP's internal audit function in a way other than relying on work they had already performed? Explain.

Academic Research Case 1 (LO 3, 4)

SEARCH HINT

It is easy to locate these academic research articles! Simply use a search engine (e.g., Google Scholar) or an electronic research platform (e.g., ABI Inform) and search using the author names and part of the article title.

Academic research addresses the conceptual issues outlined in this chapter. To help you consider the linkage between academic research and the practice of auditing, read the following research article and answer the questions below.

Seong-Yeon, C., R. C. Hagerman, N. Sandeep, and E. R. Patterson. (2003). Measuring Stockholder Materiality. *Accounting Horizons* 17:63–76.

 i. What is the issue being addressed in the paper?

 ii. Why is this issue important to practicing auditors?

 iii. What are the findings of the paper?

 iv. What are the implications of these findings for audit quality (or audit practice) on the audit profession?

 v. Describe the research methodology used as a basis for the conclusions.

 vi. Describe any limitations of the research that the student (and practice) should be aware of.

Academic Research Case 2

Group Activity

Your group is to select an academic (peer reviewed) research article related to one of the topics covered in this chapter. Please get approval of the article from your instructor prior to making a final decision. The article should have a publication date no earlier than 2005. The article should be one that you and other students would enjoy reading. Your instructor will let you know whether you are to prepare a written report or a class presentation that provides an overview of your selected article. Your overview should address the following questions:

 i. What is the issue being addressed in the paper?

 ii. Why is this issue important to practicing auditors?

 iii. What are the findings of the paper?

 iv. What are the implications of these findings for audit quality (or audit practice) on the audit profession?

 v. Describe the research methodology used as a basis for the conclusions.

 vi. Describe any limitations of the research that the student (and practice) should be aware of.

Hint: You may find the most relevant articles in the following journals: *Auditing: A Journal of Practice and Theory*; *Accounting Horizons*; *Behavioral Research in Accounting*; *The Accounting Review*; and *International Journal of Auditing*. Please note that you are not restricted to these journals.

Go to www.cengage.com/accounting/rittenberg for the Ford and Toyota materials.

Source and Reference	Question
Part A: Materiality	**1a.** Some common numerical thresholds and benchmarks for overall materiality judgments are 5% of net income and 1% of assets. Posting materiality is generally 5% to 10% of overall materiality.
	1b. Calculate these numerical thresholds for Ford and Toyota, assuming 5% for posting materiality.
	1c. Assume for a moment that you discover a $10,000,000 error in inventory. What difficulties would you encounter in deciding whether or not that amount was material?
	1d. The numerical thresholds differ across the two companies. Why does that present a problem for the auditor? For third-party users?
	1e. What is the SEC's position on the use of numerical thresholds?
	1f. What other characteristics of potential misstatements should auditors consider when evaluating their materiality?
	2a. What does the term *netting* mean in the context of misstatement judgments?
	2b. What is the SEC's guidance concerning netting?
	3c. Why is it helpful to financial statement users to have companies avoid netting?
Part B: Sustainability	Locate and review the contents of the most recent sustainability reports for Ford and Toyota.
	1a. What are similarities between the two reports?
	1b. What are differences between the two reports?
	1c. Which of the two reports do you find most informative? Why?
	1d. What level of assurance is provided by independent parties regarding these sustainability reports?

Case Index